HUMAN DEVELOPMENT

HUMAN DEVELOPMENT

Fifth Edition

James W. Vander Zanden

The Ohio State University

McGraw-Hill, Inc.

New York   St. Louis   San Francisco   Auckland   Bogotá   Caracas   Lisbon   London
Madrid   Mexico   Milan   Montreal   New Delhi   Paris   San Juan
Singapore   Sydney   Tokyo   Toronto

Copyright

This book was set in Walbaum by Better Graphics, Inc.
The editors were Jane Vaicunas and James R. Belser;
the designer was Jerry Wilke; the cover designer was Armen Kojoyian;
the production supervisor was Richard A. Ausburn.
The photo editor was Barbara Salz;
the photo manager was Kathy Bendo.
R. R. Donnelley & Sons Company was printer and binder.

Part and Chapter Opening Photos

Part One   Frederick Ayer/Photo Researchers; Chapter 1   James Marshall/Brooklyn Image Group; Chapter 2   Elizabeth Crews; Chapter 3   Frank Siteman/Stock, Boston; Part Two   Howard Sochurek/ Woodfin Camp & Associates; Chapter 4   Alexander Tsiaras/Stock, Boston; Chapter 5   Paul Fusco/ Magnum; Part Three   Frank Staub/The Picture Cube; Chapter 6   Elizabeth Crews/The Image Works; Chapter 7   Michael Nichols/Magnum; Chapter 8   Elizabeth Crews/The Image Works; Part Four   Julie O'Neil/The Picture Cube; Chapter 9   John Eastcott/Yva Momatiuk/The Image Works; Chapter 10   Curtis Willocks/Brooklyn Image Group; Park Five   Lawrence Migdale/Photo Researchers; Chapter 11   Elizabeth Crews; Chapter 12   Elizabeth Crews; Part Six   Bob Daemmrich/ Stock, Boston; Chapter 13   Bob Daemmrich/Stock, Boston; Chapter 14   Arlene Gottfried/Brooklyn Image Group; Part Seven   Costa Manos/Magnum; Chapter 15   Gene Dekovic/Jeroboam; Chapter 16   Ben Blankenburg/Stock, Boston; Part Eight   Joel Gordon; Chapter 17   Bob Daemmrich/Stock, Boston; Chapter 18   Bob Daemmrich/Stock, Boston; Part Nine   John Running/Stock, Boston; Chapter 19   Susan Lapides/Design Conceptions; Chapter 20; Farrell Grehan/Photo Researchers; and Chapter 21   Frank Siteman/The Picture Cube.

Library of Congress Cataloging-in-Publication Data

Vander Zanden, James Wilfrid.
    Human development / James W. Vander Zanden. — 5th ed.
      p.   cm.
    Includes bibliographical references and indexes.
    ISBN 0-07-066997-X
    1. Developmental psychology.   I. Title.
  BF713.V36   1993
  155—dc20   92–15364

Contents in Brief

v

Contents

Preface

I write this preface with a twinge of guilt. It is not uncommon for authors to recount the considerable anguish and burden they experienced while writing their books. Usually, the authors also relate the sacrifices made by their loved ones—typically the spouse and children—while "the author" absorbed himself or herself in the tedious labor. Yet, in all candor, researching and writing this and the earlier editions of *Human Development* has not caused me personal anguish, nor has it imposed hardships on my family. I enjoy the work immensely, and both my family and I have benefited from the insights we have gained from the project across the years.

As noted in the prefaces to previous editions, I had an important personal reason for my deep concern with many of the matters discussed in the text. Several years prior to beginning the first edition, my wife became ill and subsequently died. Our younger son was then an infant and his older brother a toddler. Consequently, except for teaching part-time at Ohio State University, I dropped out of academic life for about five years and functioned more or less as a full-time parent. I found that researching and writing *Human Development* (and subsequently seeing it through later editions) offered profound help in the rearing of my sons. In the early editions, the boys were frequently about, playing in the yard or the living room while I worked on the book in the adjoining den. As is characteristic of youngsters, they were periodically in and out of the den on one matter or another. From time to time, I would take breaks and visit or play with them and their friends. Time has marched on. My sons are now young adults, have received their Ph.D. degrees

in computer science (one from Cornell University at age 24 and the other from the University of Illinois at age 25), and are living happy, productive, and rewarding lives. Even though they are no longer home, we continue to share a warm, caring, and rich relationship.

As a male who reared his youngsters in a single-parent home, I find truth in the argument that equal opportunity for women in public spheres is severely impaired by a gender-role differentiation in which women are assigned primary responsibility for raising children. The childrearing years are also the years that are typically most critical in the development of a career. During this period of the life span, professors secure tenure at good universities; lawyers and accountants become partners in top firms; business managers make it onto the fast track; and blue-collar workers find positions that generate high earnings and seniority. Rearing youngsters is time consuming and disruptive of the activities that commonly make for an orderly and successful career. It is a tragic commentary on our society that those individuals most immediately charged with caring for and raising children are penalized for doing so in countless social and economic ways, particularly in the workplace. I, too, encountered these difficulties. Yet, in hindsight, I would not exchange the rewards and satisfactions I found in parenthood for all the laurels offered by the academic community.

Seeing this textbook through its various editions has been a highly personal and satisfying experience for another reason. As a youngster, I experienced considerable abuse. Indeed, at two-and-a-half years of age I underwent surgery to repair severe internal damage and bleeding inflicted by my father. Due to this and continuing abuse, it is hardly surprising that I had a troubled childhood and adolescence. Nor is it accidental that, in adulthood, I became intrigued by the study of human behavior and made it my career. *Human Development* is testimony to my own search for answers and my dedication to the betterment of the human condition.

I hope that students who read this textbook find answers to questions they have about their own lives, much as I have done in researching and writing it. It is my earnest desire that, through courses in human development and developmental psychology, people may move toward Abraham Maslow's ideal and become self-actualized men and women. From such courses, they should acquire a new vision of the human experience and a sharpening of their observational and analytical skills. In doing so, perhaps they may come to lead fuller, richer, and more fruitful lives.

Most of us share the belief that education is not the sum of eight, twelve, sixteen, or even twenty years of schooling. Instead, it is a lifelong habit, a striving for growth and wise living. Education is something we retain when we have lost our texts, burnt our lecture notes, and forgotten the minutiae we have learned for an exam. Therefore, textbooks that are bereft of controversy and unanswered questions leave students believing that facts are the stuff of education. From these textbooks students derive a false sense of security borne of cramming their heads with information rather than refining their minds with analysis. Consequently, many of the boxes in this edition of *Human Development* offer students an opportunity to think critically about social issues and how these issues relate to their personal lives and world. In sum, the stuff of human development is ultimately real people living their lives in a real world.

Happily, I have seen the field of human development grow and mature over the five editions of this text. I find this fact extremely gratifying and rewarding. In preparing the first edition—published in 1978—I found abundant literature on infancy, early childhood, and old age. But the intervening years of the life span (early and middle adulthood) were only sparsely represented by authoritative studies. Fortunately, this state of affairs has changed. A rich core of material on adulthood now exists, and we can draw upon it for a deeper understanding of this section of the

life span. The growth of this field has increased the satisfaction I have felt in preparing this fifth edition.

Readers of earlier editions will find other evidence of change. In the initial editions, for instance, I highlighted the work of Harry F. Harlow and his associates that dealt with deprivation in infant monkeys. Due to advances in current research and theory, I no longer include this information. We now possess studies that directly examine deprivation and abuse in human infants, research that is not subject to species-specific concerns. Although a number of professors have urged me to reintroduce the material on Harlow, I am committed to utilizing research that is both current and timely. At points, this task has not been an easy one, especially when certain research studies evoke such fond memories. I vividly remember Harlow recounting his excitement and enthusiasm about the infant monkeys during a course I took with him at the University of Wisconsin!

Organization and Focus

As in its previous editions, the fifth edition of *Human Development* features a chronological approach to studying the life span. The twenty-one chapters are organized, by age periods, into nine parts. Within each of these parts, the first chapter addresses physical and cognitive development, and the second chapter discusses issues in psychosocial development. The revised Part One introduces the student to central methods and theories utilized in the study of human development, such as Chapter 1's detailed discussion of how we literally change ourselves in the course of our behavior through the interaction of heredity and environment. Part Two, which discusses prenatal and neonatal periods, commences the study of the individual throughout the life span.

In terms of the text's approach to the study of the life span, this edition of *Human Development* emphasizes development in context. This approach focuses on the development of people within families and the larger ecological context implied by this theme. By examining the groundbreaking work of developmentalists Urie Bronfenbrenner and Paul Baltes, students will fully understand the complex network of "developmental tasks" that shape us as we move through the life span.

Multidisciplinary Approach

Human Development provides students with a vast wealth of information, both in terms of theory and application. This information, however, is not limited only to psychological research and theory. Prepared with a multidisciplinary approach, this edition of *Human Development* draws upon recent contributions made to the disciplines of medicine, sociology, anthropology, biology, history, and women's studies. This approach allows students to see that the study of human development is contingent upon a diverse body of knowledge which incorporates a variety of world views and theoretical approaches.

Thinking Critically

As stated above, a course on human development should do more than provide students with a body of scientific findings. Rote memorization of definitions and facts does not "do justice" to the dynamic nature of this subject matter. We must encourage students to think critically and creatively about their own development and how it is shaped by the world around them. This text will provide students with a deeper understanding of the human experience and the factors that mold our life course.

In addition, *Human Development* will aid students in honing their analytical and observational skills. These new abilities, however, will not be limited only to the classroom. Students will emerge from this course with skills and strategies for overcoming the numerous obstacles that face them throughout the life span. Examples of this kind of material include a detailed discussion of in vitro fertilization (Chapter 3), substance abuse and its effects during pregnancy (Chapter 4), alternative birthing methods (Chapter 4), sexual abuse (Chapter 10), divorce and its correlation to aggressive behavior in children (Chapter 10), teenage parents (Chapter 14), role conflicts and depression in women (Chapter 15), homosexuality (Chapter 16), mid-life changes (Chapter 17), battered women (Chapter 18), and caring for aging parents (Chapter 20).

Commitment to Diversity

In the past, *Human Development* was lauded for its sensitivity to issues of race, class, gender, and ethnicity. The fifth edition continues this legacy by integrating information on cross-cultural, minority, and gender differences wherever possible. Many texts relegate this material to one section, thus perpetuating the marginalization that is so prevalent in our society. The fifth edition of *Human Development* utilizes an integrative approach to demonstrate our commitment to diversity. As teachers and students, constant attention to these issues is an imperative component of our task.

Specific examples of extensive cross-cultural coverage are an examination of the plight of children throughout the world (Chapter 6), cross-cultural communication patterns and research on deaf babies (Chapter 7), a discussion of cross-cultural intelligence findings (Chapter 9), minority students and school performance (Chapter 12), prejudice in later childhood (Chapter 12), cross-cultural issues at work in adolescence (Chapter 14), cross-cultural pregnancy statistics (Chapter 14), and cross-cultural differences in aging (Chapter 20).

New to the Fifth Edition

Expanded Section Coverage on Crucial Issues in Life Span Development. The fifth edition of *Human Development* is unrivaled in its detailed coverage of numerous critical issues. Each chapter features new sections that seek to expand coverage of important new findings. This unique feature manifests our commitment to students' learning and overall breadth of knowledge. Included are detailed discussions of AIDS in children and adults (Chapters 4, 14, and 21), comprehensive coverage of Carol Gilligan's groundbreaking research on self-esteem in addolescent girls (Chapter 13), an updated discussion of genetic screening and counseling (Chapter 3), an important section on Sudden Infant Death Syndrome and drug babies (Chapter 5), a thoroughly revised and much applauded section on language acquisition (Chapter 7), an updated section on learning disabilities and their relationship to the locus of control and learning theory (Chapter 12), new material on maternal employment (Chapter 16), and a searching look at the right-to-die movement (Chapter 21).

Practical and Informative Boxed Material. In an effort to highlight the most current issues in a comprehensive and accessible manner, new boxes are included in almost every chapter of the text. These boxes reinforce important points in the text's coverage and allow students to understand the real-life applications implicit in the study of human development. New boxes cover the sharp rise in cesarean sections (Chapter 4), the crisis in foster care and its implications for the potential resurgence of orphanages (Chapter 8), the mother-blaming epidemic in our culture (Chapter 8), Robert Coles's work on the spiritual life of children (Chapter 11), hyperactivity (Chapter 12), new findings on academic achievement in Japanese, Taiwanese, and U.S. children (Chapter 12), rape and sexual assault (Chapter 15), sociological approaches to poverty (Chapter 16), and the controversy surrounding the "living will" issue (Chapter 21).

Positive Approach to Adulthood and Aging. The text features an extensive, honest discussion of the aging process. Topics discussed include the latest research and theory on biological aging, Alzheimer's disease, memory and cognitive functioning, elderly satisfaction, theories of adjustment, institutional care, psychosocial aging, and bereavement windows.

The Most Current Research and Theory. *Human Development's* fifth edition includes comprehensive discussions of the ground broken by inspirational researchers and theorists such as Bruner, Maccoby, Elkind, Gilligan, Ainsworth, Sroufe, Kübler-Ross, Kagan, Belsky, Baumrind, and Izard. By featuring the most current findings in research and theory, we may truly see evidence of our increased understanding of the life span.

New Photo Program. In thumbing through this new edition, one will undoubtedly note the beauty and creativity of our new photo program. The photos and illustrations utilized in *Human Development* display our continued commitment to diversity. Sensitivity to race, class, gender, ethnicity, and ability (or disability) is of tantamount importance, and this is reflected in the photos we have chosen for this edition.

New References. The fifth edition is not only a useful teaching tool but a thoroughly updated resource for students and instructors as well. Hundreds of new references have been added to the fifth edition of *Human Development*. These new elements are integrated throughout the entire text.

Supplements

Human Development is accompanied by a complete ancillary package of the highest caliber, conceptualized and crafted by Corinne Crandell and Thomas Crandell. The *Student Study Guide* features chapter outlines, summaries, key terms, learning objectives, and self-tests to aid the student in preparing for exams. The *Instructor's Manual* is an excellent resource and reference for the professor, providing learning objectives, alternative ideas for teaching the material that are both creative and rigorous, discussion questions, lecture outlines, student projects, and class exercises. The *Test Bank* includes a balanced mix of factual and conceptual multiple-choice questions that are indexed to the text. Computerized versions of the test bank are available for IBM compatible PCs (5¼″ and 3½″ disk sizes) and Macintosh PCs.

Acknowledgments

In truth, authors have but a small part in the production of textbooks. Consider the thousands upon thousands of researchers who have dedicated themselves to the scholarly investigation of human behavior and life-span development. Consider the labors of countless journal editors and reviewers who assist them in fashioning intelligible reports of their research findings. And, consider the enormous effort expended by the personnel of research-grant agencies and reviewers who seek to funnel scarce resources to the most promising studies. Indeed, a vast number of scholars across the generations have contributed to our contemporary reservoir of knowledge regarding human development. Textbook authors simply seek to assemble the research in a coherent and meaningful manner.

More specifically, a number of reviewers helped me shape and guide the manuscript into its final form. They appraised the clarity of expression, technical accuracy, and completeness of coverage. Their help was invaluable, and I am deeply indebted to them. They include: Dana H. Davidson, University of Hawaii; Timothy Lehmann, Valencia Community College; Bonnie R. Seegmiller, Hunter College; Paul A. Susen, Mount Wachusett Community College; Dennis Thompson, Georgia State University; Joseph M. Tinnin, Richland College; and Alvin Y. Wang, University of Central Florida. Also, many thanks to Linda Mittiga for helping me organize the many pages of unwieldly manuscript.

I thank everyone at McGraw-Hill who helped to produce this attractive, stylish book: James R. Belser, senior editing supervisor; Armen Kojoyian, designer; Richard Ausburn, production supervisor; Kathy Bendo, photo manager; and Barbara Salz, photo editor. It has been a team undertaking at all times.

My special thanks go to Jane Vaicunas and Beth Kaufman, psychology editors, for the kindness they have shown me, for the enthusiasm they brought to the undertaking, and for the professional competence they exhibited in bringing this new edition to fruition.

James W. Vander Zanden

HUMAN
DEVELOPMENT

Part One

The Study of Human Development

Chapter 1

INTRODUCTION

The Major Concerns of Science

A Framework for Studying Development

Major Domains of Development ◆ Processes of Development ◆

The Context of Development ◆ The Timing of Developmental Events

Partitioning the Life Span: Cultural and Historical Perspectives

Cultural Variability ◆ Historical Conceptions of the Life Span

The Nature of Developmental Research

The Longitudinal Method ◆ The Cross-Sectional Method ◆

The Case-Study Method ◆ The Experimental Method ◆ The Social Survey Method ◆

The Naturalistic Observation Method ◆ The Cross-Cultural Method

Ethical Standards for Human Development Research

———————— ◆ ————————

A sign posted in a Western cowboy bar says: "I ain't what I ought to be, I ain't what I'm going to be, but I ain't what I was." This thought captures the sentiment that lies behind much contemporary interest in the study of human development. It is hoped that with knowledge, we will be able to lead fuller, richer, and more fruitful lives. Knowledge offers us the opportunity to improve the human condition by helping us to achieve self-identity, freedom, and self-fulfillment.

The motto in the bar directs our attention to still another fact—that to live is to *change*. Indeed, life is never static but always in flux. Nature has no fixed entities, only transition and transformation. According to modern physics, the objects you normally see and feel consist of nothing more than patterns of energy that are forever moving and altering. From electrons to galaxies, from amoebas to humans, from families to societies, every phenomenon exists in a state of continual "becoming" (Perinbanayagam, 1986). Hence, when you were conceived, you were smaller than the period at the end of this sentence. Over the span of sixty, seventy, eighty, or even ninety years, all of us undergo dramatic changes as we pass from the embryonic and fetal stages through infancy, childhood, adolescence, adulthood, and old age. We start small, grow up, and grow old, just as countless generations of our forebears have done. Change occurs across many dimensions—the biological, the psychological, and social. Life-span perspectives of human development focus upon long-term sequences and patterns of change in human behavior.

Contradictory as it may seem, life also entails *continuity*. At age 70 we are in many ways the same persons that we were at 5 or 25. Many aspects of our biological organism, our gender roles, and our thought processes carry across different life periods. Indeed, features of life that are relatively lasting and uninterrupted give us a sense of identity and stability over time. As a consequence of such continuities, most of us do not experience ourselves as just so many disjointed bits and pieces but rather as wholes—larger, independent entities that possess a basic oneness. Accordingly, much of the change in our lives is not accidental or haphazard.

Scientists refer to the elements of change and constancy over the life span as *development*. **Development** is defined as the orderly and sequential changes that occur with the passage of time as an organism moves from conception to death. Development includes those processes

Continuity Across The Life Span
Development is a continual process beginning with conception and ending with death. Although physical changes may be the most obvious, we also change socially, intellectually, and personally. Yet despite change, we remain in some respects the same, which gives our lives a measure of continuity.
(Viviane Moos/The Stock Market)

that are biologically programmed within the organism and those processes by which the organism is changed or transformed through interaction with the environment.

What we have been saying adds up to the following statement: *Human development over the life span is a process of becoming something different while remaining in some respects the same.* Perhaps what is uniquely human is that we remain in an unending state of development. Life is always an unfinished business, and death is its only cessation (Baltes, 1987; Montagu, 1981).

The Major Concerns of Science
The most incomprehensible thing about the world is that it is comprehensible.—ALBERT EINSTEIN

Life-span development has traditionally been the primary province of psychologists. Most commonly the field is called *developmental phychology* or, if focused primarily on children, *child development* or *child psychology*. Psychology itself is often defined as the scientific study of behavior and mental processes. Thus, developmental psychology is that branch of psychology that deals with how individuals change with time while remaining in some respects the same. Child psychology is that branch of psychology that studies the development of children.

Yet over the past twenty-five years the field of life-span development has become multidisciplinary (Baltes, 1987; Clausen, 1991; Dowd, 1990; Goodnow, 1990; Gottlieb, 1991). The field now encompasses not only psychology but biology, sociology, and anthropology. Indeed, we should avoid the tendency to view the various academic disciplines as somehow separated into "watertight" compartments. At best, academic disciplines are only loosely defined. The borderlines are so vague that researchers give little thought to whether they are "invading" another discipline's field of study. Such overlap encourages a freshness of approach and functions as a stimulus in advancing the frontiers of knowledge. Researchers increasingly welcome aid and collaboration from any qualified person, whether or not that person is in the same discipline.

Social and behavioral scientists who study human development focus on four major issues. First, they undertake to *describe* the changes that typically occur across the human life span. When, for instance, does the child generally begin to speak? What is the nature of this speech? Does speech alter with time? In what sequence does the average child link sounds to form words or sentences?

Second, scientists seek to *explain* these changes—to specify the determinants of developmental change. What behaviors, for instance, underlie the child's first use of words? What part does biological "pretuning" or "prewiring" play in the process? What is the role of learning in language acquisition? Can the process be accelerated? What factors produce language and learning difficulties?

Third, scientists are interested in the *prediction* of developmental changes. What are the language capabilities of a 6-month-old infant likely to be at 14 months of age? Or what are the expected consequences for language development if a child suffers from phenylketonuria (PKU)? In this inherited disorder, which occurs in about 1 out of every 12,000 live births, the child lacks an enzyme needed to metabolize phenylalanine (an amino acid found in protein foods). The result is the buildup of substances that are toxic to the central nervous system. PKU commonly produces mental retardation. In severe cases children are

impaired in the development of language and may never learn to speak at all. Thus, scientists today can predict the likely course of these babies' development.

Fourth, by gaining knowledge, scientists can often intervene in the course of events so as to *control* them. For example, in one form of PKU researchers have found that if infants are put on a low-phenylalanine diet after birth, intellectual impairment can often be minimized (Welsh, Pennington, Ozonoff, Rouse & McCabe, 1990). During the past decade PKU specialists recommended that PKU children stay on their special diets until they were 8 years of age. But recently, PKU clinics in the United States and Europe have reported cases of preteen children who discontinued the diet and are showing a pronounced drop in intelligence. Consequently, many specialists are urging that PKU children stay on their diets until they reach adulthood, when the mature central nervous system becomes capable of resisting the toxic effects of phenylalanine (Holtzman, 1986). As a result of other scientific findings, chemical tests that detect the presence of phenylpyruvic acid in urine are now routinely administered in most states to newborns. In other areas as well, scientists are increasingly looking for ways in which knowledge about human development can assist with real-life problems and real-life institutions.

But even as scientists strive for knowledge and control, they must continually remind themselves of the dangers described by the eminent physicist J. Robert Oppenheimer (1955): "The acquisition of knowledge opens up the terrifying prospects of controlling what people do and how they feel." Chapter 1 returns to this matter later in connection with ethical standards in scientific research.

A Framework for Studying Development

Life is never a material, a substance to be molded. If you want to know, life is the principle of self-renewal, it is constantly renewing and remaking and changing and transfiguring itself.—BORIS PASTERNAK

Doctor Zhivago

If we are to organize information about human development from a variety of perspectives, we need some sort of framework that will allow us to make development meaningful and manageable. Human development involves just too many matters for us to consider simultaneously each and every detail. A framework provides us with *categories* for bringing together bits of information that we believe are related to one another. Categories let us simplify and generalize large quantities of information by "chunking" or "clustering" certain components. A framework, then, assists us in finding our way in an enormously complex and diverse field. One way to organize information about development is in terms of four basic concerns: the major domains of development, the processes of development, the context of development, and the timing of developmental events.

Major Domains of Development

Developmental change takes place in three fundamental domains: the physical, the cognitive, and the psychosocial. **Physical development** entails those changes that occur in a person's body, including changes in weight and height; in the brain, heart, and other organ structures and processes; and in skeletal, muscular, and neurological features that affect motor skills. Consider, for instance, the physical changes that take place at adolescence, which together are called *puberty.* At puberty young people undergo changes in growth and development that are revolutionary. After a lifetime of inferiority, they suddently catch up with adults in size and strength. Accompanying these changes is the rapid development of the reproductive system and the attainment of reproductive capability—the ability to conceive children.

Cognitive development involves those changes that occur in mental activity, including sensation, perception, memory, thought, reasoning, and language. Again consider adolescence. Young people gradually acquire several substantial intellectual capacities. Compared with children, for instance, adolescents are much better able to think about abstract concepts such as democracy, justice, and morality. Moreover, young people become capable of dealing with hypothetical situations (mentally generating a variety of possible outcomes of an event), and they achieve the ability to monitor their own mental experience and control and manipulate their thought processes.

The realm of **psychosocial development** includes those changes that concern a person's personality, emotions, and relationships with others. All societies distinguish between individuals viewed as children and individuals viewed as adults. For example, adolescence is a period of social redefinition, one in which young people undergo changes in their social roles and status. Our society distinguishes between people who are "underage," or minors, and those who have reached the age of majority, or adults. Adults are permitted to drive cars and vote. As we will see in Chapter 13, some societies recognize adolescence through a special initiation ceremony—a *rite of passage* (Steinberg, 1987a).

Although differentiating these domains of development, we will not want to lose sight of the unitary nature of the individual human. Physical, cognitive, and psychosocial factors are intertwined in every aspect of development. Indeed, scientists are increasingly aware that what happens in any one domain depends largely on what happens in the others (Lerner, 1983).

Processes of Development

Development meets us at every turn. Infants are born. The jacket that fitted 2-year-old Mike in the spring is outgrown by winter. At puberty, youth exhibit a marked spurt in size and acquire various secondary sexual characteristics. Individuals commonly leave their parents' homes and set out on careers, establish families of their own, see their own children leave home, retire, and so on. The concepts of *growth, maturation,* and *learning* are important to our understanding of these events.

One of the most noticeable features of early development is the *increase in size* that occurs with changing age, which is commonly termed **growth.** Growth takes place through metabolic processes from within. The organism takes in a variety of substances, breaks them down into their chemical components, and then reassembles them into new materials. Most organisms get larger as they become older. For some, including human beings, growth levels off as they approach sexual maturity. Others—many plant and fish forms—continue the growth process until they die.

Maturation is another aspect of development. It concerns the more or less automatic unfolding of biological potential in a set, irreversible sequence. Both growth and maturation entail biological change. But whereas growth refers to the increase in an individual's cells and tissue, maturation concerns the development of his or her organs and limbs to the point where they become functional. In other words, maturation reflects the unfolding of genetically prescribed, or "preprogrammed," patterns of behavior. Such changes are relatively independent of environmental events, as long as environmental conditions remain normal. As we will see in Chapter 6, an infant's motor development after birth—grasping, sitting, crawling, standing, and walking—follows a regular sequence. Similarly, at about 10 to 14 years of age puberty brings many changes, including ovulation in women and the production of live sperm in men, providing the potential for reproduction.

Learning is still another component of development. It is the more or less permanent modification in behavior that results from the individual's experience in the environment. Learning occurs across the entire life span—in the family, among peers, at school, on the job, and in many other spheres as well. Learning differs from maturation in that maturation typically occurs without any specific experience or practice. Learning, however, depends on both growth and maturation, which underlie an organism's *readiness* for certain kinds of activity, physical and mental. Learning is clearly a critical capability, for it allows an organism to adapt to changing environmental conditions. Hence, learning provides the important element of flexibility in behavior.

As we will emphasize in Chapter 3, the biological forces of growth and maturation should not be counterposed to the environmental forces of learning. Too often the *nature-nurture controversy* is presented as a dichotomy—nature *or* nurture. Clearly, such a view is unacceptable. Carried to its logical conclusion, this dichotomy would define biologically inborn behavior as that which appears in the absence of environment and learned behavior as that which does not require an organism.

Rather, it is the *interaction* between heredity and environment that gives an organism its unique characteristics (Cairns, 1991; Gottlieb, 1991; Lerner, 1991; Turkheimer & Gottesman, 1991). We find that as we interact with the world about us—as we act upon, transform, and modify the world—we in turn are shaped and altered by the consequences of our own actions (Piaget, 1963; Vygotsky, 1978; Werner, 1948; Wolff, 1987). *We literally change ourselves through acting.* For instance, as we pass through life, our biological organism is altered by dietary practices, alcoholic and drug intake, smoking habits, illness, exposure to x-rays and radiation, and so on. Furthermore, as many of us enter school, finish school, seek a job, marry, settle on a career, have children, become grandparents, and retire, we arrive at new self-conceptions and identities. In

Rites of Passage: Puberty Rituals
Some societies induct their youth into adult status by means of initiation ceremonies. The tasks are often unpleasant but young people know that if they accomplish the goals set for them, they will acquire adult status. Here boys in Eastern New Guinea undergo an ordeal in a puberty rite. In the photo to the left, a boy is having his head shaved in preparation for the final event. In the photo to the right, the boys are standing behind their spears, clutching spear throwers in both hands; they are expected to remain in the position without moving for 60 hours. The ceremonies also include beating the boys with sticks in a series of 12 daily fights to teach them to withstand pain without whimpering. *(both, Jen and Des Bartlett/Photo Researchers)*

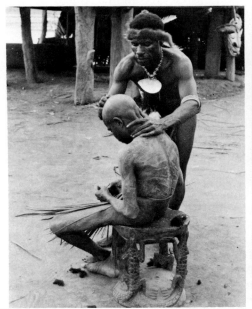

Shakespeare's Seven Stages of Life

The infant mewling and puking . . .
the whining schoolboy . . .
the lover, sighing like a furnace . . .
a soldier, full of strange oaths . . .
the justice, in fair round belly . . .
the sixth age shifts . . .
with spectacles on nose . . .
his shrunk shank . . .

voice turning again toward childish treble . . .
second childishness . . .
sans teeth, sans eyes, sans taste, sans everything.
　　　　　—WILLIAM SHAKESPEARE
　　　　As You Like It, Act 2, Scene 7

these and many other ways we are engaged in a lifetime process in which we are forged and shaped as we interact with our environment. In brief, development occurs at all periods—the embryonic, infancy, childhood, adolescence, adulthood, and old age (see the boxed insert above).

The Context of Development

If we are to understand human development, we must consider the environmental context in which it occurs. In an **ecological approach** to development Urie Bronfenbrenner (1979, 1986*a*; Bronfenbrenner & Crouter, 1983) proposes that the study of developmental influences must include the person's interaction with the environment, the person's changing physical and social settings, the relationship among those settings, and how the entire process is affected by the society in which the settings are embedded. He examines the mutual accommodations between the developing person and these changing contexts in terms of four levels of environmental influence: the microsystem, the mesosystem, the exosystem, and the macrosystem.

The *microsystem* consists of the network of social relationships and the physical settings in which a person is involved each day. Consider, for instance, Charles and Philip. Both are seventh-graders who live in a middle-class suburb of a large U.S. city. In many ways their lives and surroundings seem similar. Yet in truth, they live in rather different worlds. See if you can spot important differences (Bronfenbrenner, 1986*b*):

Charles　Charles is the oldest of three children. Both of his parents work outside the home at full-time jobs, but they are usually able to arrange their schedules so that one parent is home when the children return from school. Should the parents be delayed, they have arranged for an elderly neighbor—a grand-

motherly figure—to be available. Charles often helps his mother or father prepare dinner; the family members who do not cook on a given evening are the ones who later clean up. Homework is taken seriously by Charles and his parents. The children are allowed to watch television one hour each night, but only after they have completed their homework. Charles is enthusiastic about his butterfly collection, and family members help him hunt butterflies on family outings. He is somewhat of a loner, but has one very close friend.

Philip　Philip is 12 and lives with his parents and a younger brother. Both of his parents have full-time jobs that require them to commute more than an hour each way. Pandemonium occurs on weekday mornings as the family members prepare to leave for school and work. Philip is on his own until his parents return home in the evening after they first pick up his brother at a day-care home. Philip's parents experience demanding work schedules and so spend their weekends relaxing. His mother assumes responsibility for the evening meal, which typically consists of pizza, TV dinners, or fast foods. Philip's father remains aloof from housekeeping activities. Although Philip realizes that getting a good education is important, he has difficulty concentrating in school. He spends a good deal of time with his friends, all of whom enjoy riding the bus downtown and going to a movie. On these occasions they "cut up" and occasionally smoke a little marijuana. His parents disapprove of his friends, so Philip keeps his friends and his parents apart.

The *mesosystem* consists of the interrelationships among the various settings in which the developing person is immersed. Consider again the cases of Charles and Philip. Both Charles and Philip come from two-parent, middle-class families in which both parents work. Yet the events in their home environments are having a substantially different effect on their schooling. Charles finds himself in a family setting that is supportive of academic achievement. Without necessarily being aware of it, Charles's parents are employing a principle of the Russsian educator A. S. Makarenko (1967), who was quite successful in working with wayward adolescents in the 1920s: "The maximum support with the maximum of challenge." Although Philip's parents also stress to him the importance of his doing well at school, he is not experiencing the same gentle but firm shove that encourages Charles to move on and develop into a capable young adult. Philip's family has dispensed with the amenities of family self-discipline in favor of whatever is easiest. Moreover, Philip has become heavily dependent on peers, one of the strongest predictors of problem behavior in adolescence (Pulkkinen, 1982).

An environment that is "external" to the developing person is called an *exosystem*. The exosystem consists of social structures that directly or indirectly affect a person's life: the school, the world of work, the mass media, agencies of government, and various social networks. The development of children like Charles and Philip is influenced not only by what happens in the environments in which they themselves spend time but also by what occurs in the settings in which their parents live. Stress in the workplace carries over to the home, where it has consequences for the marital relationship of the parents. Children who feel rootless or caught in conflict at home find it difficult to pay attention in school. Like Philip, they often look to a group of peers with similar histories, who, having no welcoming place to go and little to do that challenges them, seek excitement on the streets. Despite encountering somewhat similar job stresses as those of Philip's parents, Charles's parents have made a deliberate effort to create arrangements that work against his alienation.

The *macrosystem* consists of the overarching cultural patterns of a society that find expression in family, educational, economic, political, and religious institutions. We have seen how the world of work contributes to alienation in Philip's family. When we look to the broader societal context, we note that the United States lags far behind other industrialized nations in providing child-care services and other benefits designed to promote the well-being of families (see Chapters 8 and 10). American parents do not enjoy such benefits as maternity and paternity leaves, flex-time, job-sharing arrangements, and personal leaves for parents when children are ill. In 1987 some 5 million U.S. children under the age of 10 had no one to look after them when they came home from school; an additional 500,000 pre-

schoolers were in the same predicament. Along with most U.S. families today, the families of Charles and Philip are experiencing the unraveling of extended family, neighborhood, and other institutional support systems that in the past were central to the health and well-being of children and their parents.

Differing Social Worlds

Youngsters can live in the same city and nation, yet experience substantially different social worlds. The attitudes and skills they acquire in childhood influence the opportunities that will or will not be available to them as they move into adolescence and adulthood. Social, cultural, and historical forces provide the environmental foundations for who and what we are and what we can become. *(top, Camilla Smith/ Rainbow; bottom, Richard Kalvar/Magnum)*

The ecological approach allows us to view the developing person's environment as a nested arrangement of structures, each contained within the next (Gibson, 1979; Gibson, 1982; Tan, Ray & Cate, 1991; Thelen, 1989; Von Hofsten, 1989). The most immediate structure is the setting in which the person presently carries out his or her daily activities; each ensuing structure is progressively more encompassing, until we reach the most inclusive or societal level. We see people not in some contrived experimental vacuum but actively immersed in a real world of everyday life. However, this advantage is also the ecological approach's major disadvantage: We usually have enormous difficulty studying people in contexts where a great many factors are operating simultaneously. Because so many factors bear on a person, we find it impractical, indeed impossible, to take them all into account. Only as we control a large array of factors can we secure a "fix" on any one of them. We will have more to say on these matters later in the chapter when we consider the nature of developmental research.

The Timing of Developmental Events

Time plays an important role in development. Traditionally, the passage of time has been treated as synonymous with chronological age. The emphasis has fallen on the changes that occur within individuals as they grow older. But more recently, social and behavioral scientists have broadened their focus. They take into ac-count those changes that occur over time not only within the person but also in the environment. Even more critical, scientists examine the dynamic relation between these two processes (Bronfenbrenner, 1986a; Sroufe, Egeland & Kreutzer, 1990). Paul B. Baltes (1979, 1987; Baltes, Featherman & Lerner, 1988; Baltes & Nesselroade, 1984) has contributed to our understanding of these changes by identifying three sets of influences that, mediated through the individual, act and interact to produce development.

1. *Normative Age-graded Influences*   The first set of influences has a strong relation to chronological age. Among youth in early adolescence, like Charles and Philip, these influences include the physical, cognitive, and psychosocial changes that we discussed earlier. Charles and Philip are entering puberty, a condition associated with biological maturation. But they have also encountered age-graded social influences such as the abrupt transition from a highly structured elementary school setting to a less structured and more complex middle school or junior high environment (Swearingen & Cohen, 1985).

2. *Normative History-graded Influence*   The second set of influences concerns historical factors. Although there is considerable cultural similarity among the members of a society, each *age cohort* is unique because it is exposed to a unique segment of history (Elder, 1974; Mannheim, 1952; Riley, 1987, 1988a, 1988b). An **age cohort** (also called a *birth cohort*) is

Cohort Effects: The Great Depression of the 1930s
The stock-market collapse in 1929 heralded an economic depression that was the most prolonged and devastating in American experience. By 1933, one-quarter of the work force was unemployed and the nation's farmers saw their fortunes crumble as agricultural prices fell 63 percent. Countless Americans searched fruitlessly for work and suffered the effects of poverty and malnutrition. These events shaped the lives of the nation's young people and had a profound impact on them in later years. At times their financial prudence has proved a source of contention with generations who grew up during the more prosperous 1950s and 1960s. *(Chicago Historical Society)*

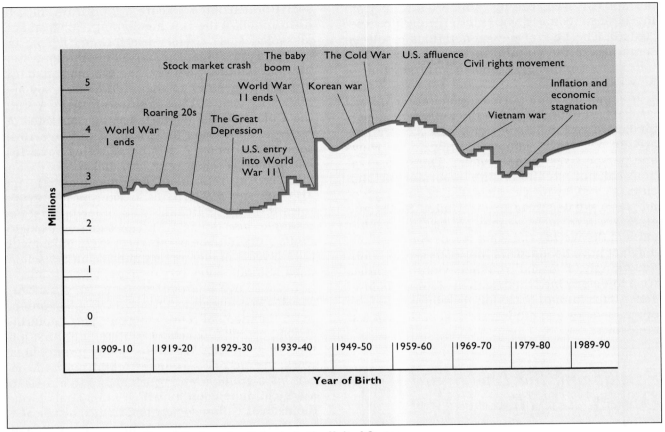

Figure 1-1   The Relative Size of Various Age Cohorts in the United States
Source: Census Bureau.

a group of persons born in the same time interval (see Figure 1-1). Since society changes, the members of different cohorts age in different ways. Each new generation enters and leaves childhood, adolescence, adulthood, and old age at a similar point in time, and so each generation's members experience certain decisive economic, social, political, and military events at similar junctures in life. As a consequence of the unique events of the era in which they live out their lives—for instance, the Great Depression of the 1930s, World War II, the Korean war, the prosperity of the 1950s, and the Vietnam war—each generation tends to fashion a somewhat unique style of thought and life. Not surprisingly, each cohort of U.S. youth over the past sixty years has acquired a somewhat different popular image: the youth of the roaring twenties, the political radicals of the 1930s, the wild kids of the war years, the silent generation of the 1950s, the involved generation of the 1960s, the "Me" generation of the 1970s, and the materialistic generation of the 1980s. Each new generation, then, confronts an environment different from that faced by earlier generations (see the discussion of generations in Chapter 13).

3. *Nonnormative Life Events*   The third set of influences involves unique turning points at which people change some direction in their lives (Brim, 1980; Hultsch & Plemmons, 1979). People may suffer severe injury in an accident, win a lottery, undergo a religious conversion, secure a divorce, or set out on a new career. Nonnormative influences do not impinge on everyone, nor do they necessarily occur in easily discernible sequences or patterns. Although these determinants have significance for individual life histories, the determinants are not closely associated with either age or history.

These influences do not operate only in one direction. Consider age cohorts. They are not simply acted on by social and historical forces. Because people of different cohorts age in distinct ways, they contribute to changes in society and alter the course of history (Riley, 1987, 1988*a*, 1988*b*). As society moves through time, statuses and roles are altered. Older occupants of social positions are replaced by younger entrants from more recent cohorts, with more recent life experiences. The flow of new generations results in some loss to the cultural inventory, a reevaluation of its components, and the introduction of new elements.

In sum, although parental generations play a crucial part in predisposing their offspring to particular values and behaviors, new generations are not necessarily bound to replicate the views and perspectives of their elders. These observations call our attention to the important part that cultural and historical factors play in development. So what is true in the United States and other Western societies may not be true in other parts of the world. And what is true for the 1990s may not have been true in the 1930s or the 1770s. Accordingly, if social and behavioral scientists wish to determine whether their findings hold in general for human behavior, they have to look to other societies and other historical periods to test their ideas.

Partitioning the Life Span: Cultural and Historical Perspectives

Since nature confronts everyone with a biological cycle beginning with conception and continuing through old age and death, all societies must deal with the life cycle. Age is a major dimension of social organization (Figure 1-2 portrays the age distribution of the U.S. population). For instance, all societies use age for **ascription:** People are assigned roles independently of their unique abilities or qualities. Like sex, age is a master status. Age governs entry to many other statuses and makes its own distinct imprint on them. Within the United States, for instance, age operates *directly* as a criterion for driving a car (age 16 in some states and 17 in others) voting (age 18), becoming president (age 35), and receiving Social Security retirement benefits (age 62). Age also operates *indirectly* as a criterion for certain roles through its linkage with other factors. For example, age linked with reproductive capacity limits entry into the parental role; age linked with twelve years of elementary and secondary school usually limits entry into college.

Because age is a master status, most changes in role over a person's life span are accompanied by a change in chronological age—entering school, completing school, getting one's first job, marrying, having children, being promoted at work, seeing one's youngest child married, becoming a grandparent, retiring, and so on. Age is a critical dimension by which individuals locate themselves within society and in turn are located by others. Consider, for example, a young woman who sits down on a bus and glances at the person in the next seat. One of the first things to cross her mind is likely to be "That's an old woman," or "That's a young woman like me." And she automatically adjusts her behavior accordingly—her

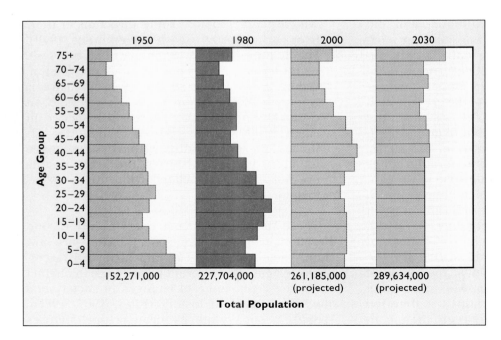

Figure 1-2　U.S. Population by Age
The figure portrays population as a pyramid, the "tree of ages." Age groups are placed on a vertical scale, with the youngest at the bottom and the oldest at the top. On the horizontal axis are plotted the number of people in each age group. By 2030 the traditional pyramid will resemble a rectangle, with about the same number of people in each age group from birth through age 70. Source: Bureau of the Census and the World Bank. Reprinted with permission from *Psychology Today* Magazine. Copyright © 1987 Sussex Publishers, Inc.

language, manners, and conversation (Neugarten & Neugarten, 1987). Age functions as a reference point that allows people to orient themselves in terms of *what* or *where* they are within various social networks—the family, the school, the church, and the world of work. It is one ingredient that provides people with the answer to the question "Who am I?" In brief, it helps people establish their identities.

Cultural Variability

The part that social definitions play in dividing the life cycle is highlighted when one compares the cultural practices of different societies. **Culture** refers to the social heritage of a people—those learned patterns for thinking, feeling, and acting that are transmitted from one generation to the next. Upon the organic age grid, societies weave varying social arrangements. A 14-year-old girl may be expected to be a junior high school student in one culture, a mother of two children in another; a 45-year-old man might be at the peak of a business career, still moving up in a political career, or retired from a career in major league baseball—or dead and worshiped as an ancestor in some other society. All societies divide biological time into socially relevant units: "Lifetime becomes translated into social time, and chronological age into social age" (Neugarten & Hagestad, 1976, p. 35). Although birth, puberty, and death are biological facts of life, it is society that gives each its distinctive meaning and assigns each its social consequences.

Some people even extend their notions of the age grid to include two additional periods: the unborn and the deceased. The Australian aborigines think of the unborn as the spirits of departed ancestors. These spirits restlessly seek to enter the womb of a passing woman and be reborn as a human child (Murdock, 1934). Similarly, the Hindus regard the unborn as the spirits of persons or animals who lived in former incarnations (Davis, 1949).

Among some societies the dead are considered continuing members of the community. The anthropologist Ralph Linton (1936, pp. 121–122) found that when a Tanala of Madagascar died, the person was viewed as merely surrendering one set of rights and duties for another.

Thus a Tanala clan has two sections which are equally real to its members, the living and the dead. In spite of rather half-hearted attempts by the living to explain to the dead that they are dead and to discourage their return, they remain an integral part

Varying Cultural Education
Societies differ culturally in a good many ways. Consequently, youngsters grow up with different social definitions of the behavior that is and is not appropriate for them as members of particular age groups. Pictured above are young Fulanis nomads of the Niger engaged in grooming behaviors. *(Victor Englebert/Photo Researchers)*

of the clan. They must be informed of all important events, invited to all clan ceremonies, and remembered at every meal. In return they allow themselves to be consulted, take an active and helpful interest in the affairs of the community, and act as highly efficient guardians of the group's mores [rules].

Viewed this way, all societies are divided into **age strata**—social layers that are based on time periods in life. Age strata organize people in society in much the same way that the earth's crust is organized by stratified geological layers. Grouping by age strata has certain similarities to class stratification. Both involve the differentiation and ranking of people as superior or inferior, higher or lower. But unlike movement up or down the class ladder the mobility of individuals through the age strata is not dependent on motivational and recruitment factors. In large measure, mobility from one age stratum to the next is biologically determined and, accordingly, irreversible.

Societies show considerable differences in the prestige they accord various age positions. Take old age (Amoss & Harrell, 1981; Simmons, 1945). In many rural societies, such as imperial China, the elders have enjoyed a prominent and authoritative position (Lang, 1946). Among the agricultural Palaung of North Burma, long life was considered a great privilege that befell those who had lived virtuously in a previous incarnation. People showed their respect by taking great care not to step on the shadow of an older person. And young women sought to appear older than their actual age, since women acquired honor and privilege in proportion to their years (Milne, 1924).

In sharp contrast, the elderly in our society today have a more restricted functional position and considerably less prestige. Our favored age stratum is youth. Americans commonly define adulthood as a period of responsibility. In contrast, the youth subculture is portrayed as irresponsible and carefree, dominated by the theme of "having a good time." In short, each culture shapes the processes of development in its own image, defining the stages it recognizes as significant.

People's behavior within various age strata is regulated by social norms or expectations that specify what constitutes appropriate and inappropriate behavior for individuals at various periods in the life span. In some cases, an informal consensus provides the standards by which people judge one another's behavior. Hence, the notion that you ought to "act your age" pervades many spheres of life. Within the United States, for instance, it is thought that a child of 6 is "too young" to baby-sit for other youngsters. By the same token, a man of 60 is thought to be "too old" to do the latest steps in a dance club. In other cases, laws set floors and ceilings in various institutional spheres: For instance, there are laws regarding marriage without parental consent, entry into the labor force, and eligibility for Social Security and Medicare benefits (Neugarten, 1982a, 1982b). We need only think of such terms as "childish," "juvenile," "youth culture," "adolescence," "senior citizen," and "the generation gap" to be aware of the potency of age in determining expectations about behavior in our own society. Indeed, we even find apartment buildings exclusively for a particular age group, such as young singles, and cities designed for a particular age group, such as retired people.

Historical Conceptions of the Life Span

In the United States we commonly think of the life span in terms of infancy, childhood, adolescence, adulthood, and old age. Yet the French historian Philippe Ariès (1962) says that in the Middle Ages the concept of childhood as we know it today was unheard off. Children were regarded as small adults. Child rearing meant little more than allowing children to participate in adult affairs.

The world we think proper for children—the world of fairy tales, games, toys, and books—is of comparatively recent origin. J. H. Plumb (1972) observes that our words for young males—"boy," "garçon," "Knabe"—were, until the seventeenth century, used to mean a male in an independent position: a man of 30, 40, or 50. No special word existed for a young male between the ages of 7 and 16. The word "child" expressed kinship, not an age stage. The arts and documents of the medieval world portray adults and children mingling, wearing the same clothes, and engaging in many of the same activities. Only around the year 1600 did a new concept of childhood emerge (see the boxed insert on page 16). The notion of adolescence is even more recent, dating from the nineteenth and early twentieth centuries in the United States (Bakan, 1972; Demos, 1986). Compulsory school legislation, child labor laws, and special legal procedures for "juveniles" made a social fact of adolescence. Now our society appears to be evolving an additional new stage between adolescence and adulthood: youth—men and women of college age. Recent developments—rising prosperity, the increase in educational level, and the enormously high educational demands of a postindustrial society—have prolonged the transition to adulthood (Keniston, 1970; Modell, 1989). The notion of "old age" has also undergone change in the Western world. Literary evidence indicates that during the Renaissance men were already considered "old" in their forties. Currently, another division is emerging, one between "young-old" and "old-old." Young-old signifies a postretirement period in which

"It's a shame you missed the eighties."

(Drawing by W. Miller; © 1990. The New Yorker Magazine, Inc.)

Child Labor in the United States

Children were widely employed in the textile mills and coal mines of the United States in the nineteenth century. In the intervening years our notions of childhood have shifted so that we now see children as requiring protection from the dictates of the adult world. *(left, AFL-CIO Photo Library/ Photo Researchers; right, Historical Pictures Service)*

there is physical vigor, new leisure time, and new opportunities for community service and self-fulfillment. Old-old characterizes a minority of eldery persons who are in need of special care and support (Neugarten, 1982a, 1982b).

These emerging distinctions have tended to blur many of our assumptions regarding the rights and responsibilities of people with respect to social age. All across adulthood, age has increasingly become a poor predictor of the timing of major life events: health, work status, family status, interests, and needs. As Bernice L. Neugarten and Dail A. Neugarten observe (1987, pp. 30–32): "We have conflicting images rather than stereotypes of age: the 70-year-old in a wheelchair, but also the 70-year-old on the tennis court; the 18-year-old who is married and supporting a family, but also the 18-year-old college student who brings his laundry home to his mother each week." However, even though some timetables are losing their significance, others are becoming more compelling. Young people may feel they are a failure if they have not "made it" in corporate life by the time they are 35. And a young woman who has delayed marriage because of her career may feel under enormous pressure to marry and bear a child upon approaching her mid-thirties. Historical definitions of social age, then, influence the standards a person uses in giving meaning to the life course, in accommodating to others, and in contemplating the time that is past and the time that remains.

The Nature of Developmental Research

To him who devotes his life to science, nothing can give more happiness than increasing the number of his discoveries, but his cup of joy is full when the results of his studies immediately find practical application.—LOUIS PASTEUR

The task of science is to make the world intelligible to us. Albert Einstein once observed that "the whole of science is nothing more than a refinement of everyday thinking." In brief, people do scientific research in much the same way that they do everything else. They make guesses and mistakes; they argue with one another; they try out their ideas to see what works and discard what does not. However, science differs from ordinary inquiry in that it relies on a systematic and formal process for gathering facts and searching for a logical explanation of them, what is called the *scientific method*. The scientific method finds expression in a series of steps that seek to ensure maximum objectivity: (1) selecting a researchable problem; (2) formulating a *hypothesis*—a tentative guess, hunch, or proposition that can be tested to determine its validity; (3) testing the hypothesis; (4) drawing conclusions about the hypothesis; and (5) making the findings of the study available to the scientific community. The scientific method allows researchers to fathom and depict—to detect and establish—objective reality, or the *what is*. This, then, brings us to a con-

Childhood: Innocence Lost?

Nowadays, we often hear that childhood has changed and that the change is for the worse. For instance, in a popular book on children, *Children Without Childhood*, Marie Winn (1983) argues that today's children lack the innocence that once was associated with childhood. Winn says that school-age youngsters are more aware not just of sex and violence but also of injustice, cruelty, corruption, war, and human frailty. Whereas once parents struggled to keep their children innocent—in a "carefree" golden age—they now expose them early to adult experience. Although parents may be well intentioned, Winn worries that "new-era child rearing"—in which parents enlist the child as an equal partner—is turning out to be a disaster. She insists that children do not prosper when they are treated as adults. Rather, children require an appreciable shielding from life if they are to accomplish the important tasks of learning and exploration that have traditionally been associated with childhood.

In a similar vein, Neil Postman (1982) complains that the very notion of childhood is based on secrets from which children are excluded but that society no longer withholds any secrets. Television opens all of life—sex, violence, death, illness, money, and disillusionment—to children. Such practices, he contends, deprive children of childhood, at least as it was understood in past generations.

Observers of the U.S. scene find other sources of concern. Some express alarm that middle-class parents are pushing their children to learn at ever earlier ages. Pressure for high achievement often begins in infancy. On the basis of findings of developmental psychologists, parents are coming to recognize that babies are hardly the lumps of protoplasm that they were once held to be but brainy little creatures with an immense capacity for learning. The new danger is that parents then come to stress performance rather than feeling. At times, working parents attempt to overcompensate for the hours that they are not at home by scheduling a good many high-pressure, "quality-time" activities (for instance, flashing reading and math cards, providing educational toys, and teaching gymnastic and swimming skills). The intrusion of this rat-race mentality into early childhood may not be a good thing (Elkind, 1981, 1986; Flavell, 1985; Langway, 1983). Yet contemporary debates regarding parenting typically overlook the fact that in years gone by childhood was anything but a golden age (Ariès, 1962; McCoy, 1988; Stone, 1977). For hundreds of years children were treated primarily as property (Hart, 1991). Lloyd deMause (1974, p. 1), an authority on psychohistory, writes:

> The history of childhood is a nightmare from which we have only recently begun to awaken. The further back in history one goes, the lower the level of child care, and the more likely children are to be killed, abandoned, beaten, terrorized, and sexually abused.

Many historians depict the child's life as uniformly bleak prior to modern times. Until the eighteenth century, a very large proportion of all children were what we would today call "battered children." In the seventeenth century the wife of John Milton, the author of *Paradise Lost*, complained that she hated to hear the cries of his nephews as he beat them. Beethoven whipped his pupils with a knitting needle and at times bit them. Even royal children were not exempt from the rod. During his childhood Louis XIII (a seventeenth-century French monarch) was regularly beaten. When he was only 17-months-old the young dauphin knew enough not to cry when his father threatened him with a whip (deMause, 1974).

Not until the nineteenth century, according to deMause, did the notion develop that children need continuous guidance and training in order to become civilized. Severe beating and other forms of abuse gave way to more indirect methods of manipulation and guilt arousal—what deMause

sideration of the research designs scientists use for depicting and analyzing human development.

The Longitudinal Method

The **longitudinal method** is a research approach in which scientists study the same individuals at different points in their lives. These people can thus be compared with themselves at regular intervals between birth and death, and the changes that occur over time in their behavior and characteristics can be noted. The method allows researchers to plot individual growth curves in such areas as language, motor, and cognitive development. Longitudinal research provides a means for discovering which childhood behaviors are marked for future use and which

"Two months with this and they blow their preschool entrance exams right out of the water."

(Drawing by Wm. Hamilton; © 1989. The New Yorker Magazine, Inc.)

terms the "socializing mode." More recently, he suggests, a "helping mode" has begun to gain support. This approach involves the proposition that children know what they need better than parents do. It defines the role of parents primarily as one of empathizing with children and helping them fulfill their expanding needs.

Although most historians agree that there has been a progressive improvement in the treatment of children, one of their number—Linda A. Pollock (1984)—cites evidence that the starkness of childhood in earlier times has been exaggerated. Nor should we overlook a mounting body of evidence that family violence, child abuse, and incest are much more common than most Americans have suspected. Indeed, historian John Demos (1986) contends that the battered child is more a product of our time—of our isolated households, atomized relationships, and ambivalence toward children—than of some benighted and brutal time past.

will be lost along the way. And the method offers insight into the routes by which people turn out similarly or differently in adulthood.

A classic longitudinal study was begun by psychologist Lewis Terman in 1921. He followed 1,528 gifted children from California public schools—who later became known as "Termites"—and a control group of children of average intelligence from an early age to adulthood.

The gifted children were selected on the basis of their intelligence quotients, or IQs (between 135 and 200 on the Stanford-Benet Scale), which were said to represent the top 1 percent of the population. He found that the gifted ones were generally taller, heavier, and stronger than youngsters with average IQs. Moreover, they tended to be more active socially and to mature faster than average children (Terman & Merrill, 1937). (So much for the stereotype of the skinny, unpopular book-worm.) One of the effects of the study has been to dispel the belief that the acceleration of bright children in school is harmful. After Terman's death other psychologists continued the project (Holahan, 1988; Rafferty, 1984; Sears, 1977; Sears & Barbee, 1977; Shneidman, 1989). The research has yielded data on subjects ranging from religion and politics through illness, marriage, and emotional development to family history and careers.

When Terman launched his study in the years following World War I, a widely held assumption was that if you were bright as a child, your later life would be marred by physical or mental illness, eccentricity, or social maladjustment. Terman's research dispelled these notions. Now in the seventh decade, the research has revealed that in later life the exceptionally bright youngsters had become better educated, more successful, better satisfied, and more effective and productive members of society than the average American. The Termites included a highly successful motion picture director, an atomic scientist, two dozen top-level research scientists, eight appellate court judges, and a nationally known science fiction writer. However, two members of the study had at some time in their lives received welfare payments, and none had won a Nobel Prize. There were also as many divorces, suicides, and alcohol problems among the Termites as among average Americans.

Although the longitudinal method allows us to study development over time, the approach does have a number of disadvantages. One major problem is sample shrinkage. Subjects drop out because they become ill or die, because they move away, or simply because they become "fed up." Those who remain tend to come from the most cooperative and stable families, which biases the sample. Moreover, it is impossible to test every child at every scheduled testing on every test item. Children get sick or go on vacation. They become upset, so that part of the test must be omitted. They refuse to comply on some items. And they and their parents occasionally forget appointments (Bayley, 1965a; Schaie, Campbell & Rawlings, 1988).

Another problem is that the span of years covered by longitudinal research inevitably includes unusual social or economic events. These factors often distort growth curves and analyses (Bayley, 1965a, p. 189):

War, depression, changing cultures, and technological advances all make considerable impacts. What are the differential effects on two-year-olds of depression-caused worries and insecurities, of TV or no TV, of the shifting climate of the baby-experts' advice from strict-diet, let-him-cry, no-pampering schedules to permissive, cuddling, "enriching" loving care?

Longitudinal studies also require a great deal of money and time. And on long-term studies the

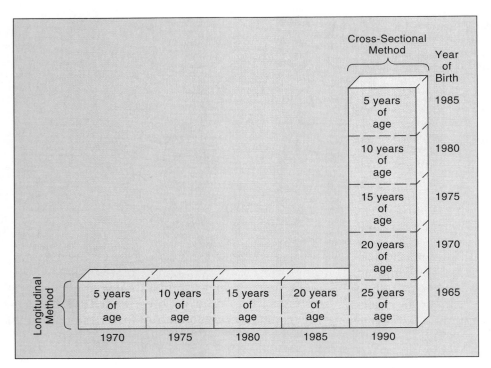

Figure 1-3 Longitudinal and Cross-Sectional Methods
Longitudinal studies are like case histories—they retest the same individuals over a period of years. Cross-sectional studies use the "snapshot" approach—they test different individuals of different ages and compare their performance.

Table 1-1

Longitudinal versus Cross-Sectional Methods

Longitudinal Method	Cross-Sectional Method
Advantages	Advantages
Assesses continuity between early childhood and adult behaviors.	Saves a great deal of time.
Avoids problems associated with sample non-equivalence.	Costs less money than longitudinal studies.
Can portray growth increments and patterns.	Demands no continuity or long-term cooperation among research workers.
Permits the formulation of cause-and-effect statements with more certainty than other research designs.	Does not require that data be "frozen" over long periods until subjects reach the desired age for retesting.
Disadvantages	Disadvantages
Takes considerable time and money.	Does not indicate the direction of change taking place within the sample groups.
Jeopardizes previous expenditures of time and money if research funds give out.	Lumps together children of the same chronological age but different maturational age. Such averaging may conceal changes like those associated with the growth spurt at puberty.
Requires periodic readjustments associated with staff turnover.	Comparability of the groups being studied is always uncertain.
Sample becomes progressively biased because of subject dropouts.	Neglects the continuity of development as it occurs in a single individual.
Researchers must continually relocate the same subjects for retesting.	
Cannot control the environment of the subjects between testing periods.	
Locks researchers into an earlier research design and theory.	

inevitable turnover in staff impairs research continuity. Finally, there is the problem of finding out tomorrow what relevant factors one should have taken into account yesterday. Once set in motion the project is difficult to alter in the light of newer techniques and theories. When innovations are introduced, it is impossible to recapture data using the new or revised methods with the subjects at their earlier ages.

The Cross-Sectional Method

The hallmark of the longitudinal method is its undertaking successive measurements of the *same* individuals. In contrast, the **cross-section method** investigates development by simultaneously comparing *different* groups of persons varying in age (see Figure 1-3). For instance, a researcher might investigate language development by selecting sixty children at each of a number of age levels—8 months, 12 months, 18 months, 24 months, 3 years, 4 years, and 5 years. Such a technique has the advantage of saving a good deal of time. The researcher need not wait many years until all the subjects reach a particular age for retesting. And the researcher does not have to relocate the same subjects. Table 1-1

summarizes the advantages and disadvantages of the longitudinal and cross-sectional approaches.

Cross-sectional research requires careful sampling procedures to make the successive age levels of different subjects reasonably comparable. In fact, uncertainty regarding comparability is the main weakness of cross-sectional studies. We can never be sure that the reported age-related differences between subjects are not the product of other differences between the groups. For instance, the groups may differ in social environment, intelligence, or diet. So the comparability of the groups can only be assumed—an assumption that is often invalid.

To use a metaphor, the aging process is like riding an escalator (Riley, Johnson & Foner, 1972, p. 524):

> Imagine an escalator rising through the several floors (which bound the age strata) of a building. All entrants to the building move directly onto the bottom of this escalator (are born), ride steadily upward (grow older), and exit from the building once they reach the top (die). On the way up, the riders can view the scenes on each of the several floors.

Proponents of the cross-sectional method assume that at successive points in time the riders on the escalator are always *alike* and view essentially the *same* scenes. Critics of the cross-sectional method dispute this assumption. They say that the riders entering the escalator *vary* from one time to the next and view *different* scenes (for instance, women's clothing may have replaced the linen department on the third floor). According to the critics, individuals are not truly comparable from one time period to another.

These problems are highlighted by cross-sectional studies of intelligence. Such studies rather consistently show that average scores on intelligence tests begin to decline around 20 years of age and continue to drop throughout adulthood. But as we will see in Chapter 19, cross-sectional studies do not make allowance for *generational*

Limitations of Cross-Sectional Research: Generational Effects

A major difficulty with cross-sectional research is that individuals who constitute a generation or cohort share many common experiences by virtue of coming of age at a particular time. Consequently, certain unique economic, social, political, or military events take on critical importance in shaping a generation's attitudes and values and its members may not be truly comparable with the subjects of another generation by virtue of their substantially different experiences. A case in point are those youth who passed through the nation's high schools and colleges during the 1960s, a period in which the civil rights movement flowered. "Sit-ins" at segregated lunch counters became a new note on the American scene, gathering momentum in the early 1960s (photo A). In Birmingham, Alabama, police used snarling attack dogs to turn back unarmed civil rights demonstrators during the spring of 1963 (photo B). And in 1968 in Mexico City, site of the Olympic games, American medalists Tommie Smith and John Carlos raised the black power salute during the playing of the national anthem (photo C). (A, *Bruce Roberts—Rapho Photo Researchers; B, Charles Moore/Black Starr; C, UPI/Bettmann Newsphotos*)

A

C

B

(also termed *cohort*) *differences* in performance on intelligence tests.

Each successive generation of Americans has received more schooling than the preceding generation. Consequently, the overall performance of each generation of Americans on intelligence tests improves. Improvement caused by increasing education creates the illusion that intelligence declines with chronological age (see Chapter 19).

Robert Kastenbaum shows how comparisons among people of different age groups can lead to faulty conclusions:

> Occasionally I have the opportunity to chat with elderly people who live in the communities nearby Cushing Hospital. I cannot help but observe that many of these people speak with an Italian accent. I also chat with young adults who live in these same communities. They do *not* speak with an Italian accent. As a student of human behavior and development I am interested in this discrepancy. I indulge in some deep thinking and come up with the following conclusion: as people grow older they develop Italian accents. This must surely be one of the prime manifestations of aging on the psychological level. (Quoted by Botwinick, 1978, p. 364)

A number of researchers have proposed research designs that link a cross-sectional approach with a modified form of the longitudinal method (Bell, 1953, 1954; Schaie, 1965; Schaie, Campbell & Rawlings, 1988). Richard Q. Bell, for instance, outlines a "convergence approach." He undertakes a series of shorter-term longitudinal studies that employ overlapping age ranges. One group is tested at ages 3, 4, and 5; another group at 5, 6, and 7; and still another group at 7, 8, and 9. The method provides "checkpoints" to compare different subjects at the same age. This procedure overcomes some of the difficulties with the cross-sectional method.

The Case-Study Method

A special type of longitudinal study focuses on a single individual rather than a group of subjects. It is called the **case-study method.** Its aim is the same as that of other longitudinal approaches—the accumulation of developmental information. An early form of the case study method was the "baby biography." Over the past two centuries a small number of parents have kept detailed observational diaries of their children's behavior. Charles Darwin, for example, wrote a biographical account of his infant son.

A good deal of the early work of Jean Piaget, an influential Swiss developmental psychologist, was based on the case-study approach (Gratch & Schatz, 1988). Piaget (1952*a*) carefully observed the behavior of his own three children: Lucienne, Laurent, and Jacqueline. He would sit by the crib and record his observations of the child's behavior. Or Piaget would watch the child's eye movements and attempt to determine the direction of the child's gaze.

Case studies have also had a prominent place in the clinical treatment of maladjusted and emotionally disturbed individuals. Sigmund Freud and his followers have stressed the part that early experience plays in mental illness. According to this view, the task of the therapist is to help patients reconstruct their own histories. In the process patients are thought to resolve their inner conflicts. More recently, the clinical approach has been extended to the study of healthy individuals. The humanistic psychologists Abraham Maslow (1967, 1970) and Carl Rogers (1970) take this approach (see Chapter 2).

However, the case-study method has a number of drawbacks. Data secured from only one individual are of questionable value. We hear, for instance, that delinquent Freddie came from a "broken home." But a good many children from single-parent homes never become delinquent. And a considerable share of delinquent children in the United States come from intact homes. In brief, the case-study approach affords little basis for *systematically* comparing people. Furthermore, the observations are frequently biased. In baby biographies the parents' emotional involvement with the child often colors their presentation.

The Experimental Method

I have made a ceaseless effort not to ridicule, not to bewail, nor to scorn human actions, but to understand them.—SPINOZA

The **experimental method** is one of the most rigorously objective techniques available to science. An *experiment* is a study in which the investigator manipulates one or more variables and measures the resulting changes in the other variables. Experiments are "questions put to nature." They offer the most effective technique for establishing a cause-and-effect relationship. This is a relationship in which a particular characteristic or occurrence (X) is one of the factors that determines another characteristic or occurrence (Y). Scientists design an experimental study so that it

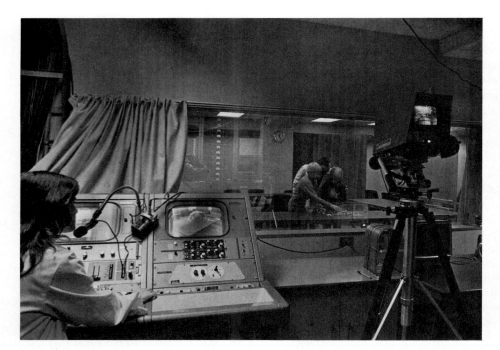

A Small-Group Laboratory
Many college campuses provide researchers with special facilities for observing subjects. For example, this small-group laboratory at Ohio State Univeristy consists of two rooms that are separated by a one-way mirror. Researchers in the control room can observe subjects in the experimental room without themselves being observed (and thus interfering with the spontaneous behavior of the subjects). In the top photograph an observer is watching from the control room. Viewed from the experimental room shown in the bottom photograph, the observer's window is a mirror. The Ohio State small-group laboratory also contains television-like equipment so that in neighboring rooms, individual subjects can view on a television screen the behavior which takes place in the experimental room. This allows subjects to observe and interpret behavior without influencing one another's perceptions and interpretations of it. Moreover, the equipment at Ohio State permits researchers to videotape behavior, so that they can replay the tapes later and study the behavior more closely. *(Patrick Reddy)*

is possible to infer whether X does or does not enter into the determination of Y. To say that X "causes" Y is simply to indicate that whenever X occurs, Y is likely to follow at some later time.

In an experiment reseachers try to find out whether a relationship exists between two variables (X and Y). First, they systematically vary the first variable (X). Second, they observe the effects of such variation upon the second variable (Y). Factor X, the factor that is manipulated in an experiment, is the **independent variable.** It is

independent of what the subject or subjects do. The independent variable is assumed to be the causal factor in the relationship being studied. We call the factor that is affected—that occurs or changes as a result of such manipulation—the **dependent variable.** The dependent variable is usually some measure of the subjects' behavior. For instance, students may talk noisily when the teacher is out of the room but become quiet when the teacher enters. The change in the level of classroom noise—the dependent variable—is then said to be caused by the teacher's presence—the independent variable.

Let us examine these variables in an actual experiment. Richard H. Walters, Marion Leat, and Louis Mezei (1963) wanted to know whether children who see another child being punished for breaking a rule will themselves become less likely to break that rule. In the experiment nursery school boys were individually brought to a room containing a number of attractive toys and told not to play with them.

The independent variable was a movie shown to each boy in which another child (a *model*) violated a similar rule. One group of boys saw a version of the movie in which the child was *punished* by his mother for playing with the forbidden toys. A second group of boys saw another version of the movie in which the child was *rewarded* by his mother for the same behavior. Finally, a third group of boys was *not* shown a movie. Such a group is called a **control group.** The control group is identical to the other groups (called **experimental groups**) except for the fact that the researcher does not introduce change into it. The control group provides a neutral standard against which the changes in the experimental groups can be measured.

In the control group the experimenter brought the child to a specially equipped room. Here the child's behavior could be observed, without the child's knowing it, through a one-way mirror from the adjoining room. The experimenter gave these instructions to the child (Walters, Leat & Mezei, 1963, p. 237):

> In a little while I am going to play a game with you, but I have forgotten something and must go and get

it. You can sit on this chair while you wait for me. Now these toys belong to some other children and have been especially arranged for them. So you better not touch them. But you can look at the book (i.e., the dictionary) while you're waiting for me, if you like.

The child was then left alone for 15 minutes. When the experimenter returned, she played briefly with the child. She then took him back to his classroom.

The children in the experimental groups were told while being taken to the room that they were going to see a movie. In the room a male assistant was introduced to the child. He also ran the movie projector. Each child was given the same instructions by the experimenter as the children in the control group. After showing the movie, the male assistant said (p. 238):

> You remember that Miss Leat had to go and get something. She will be back to see you later. You'd better wait for her here. I'm going to shut the door to make sure nobody will bother you while you are here.

In the study the dependent variable was the speed and frequency with which the boys broke the rule against playing with the toys after the adult left the room. The experiment revealed that boys who had watched the child being rewarded for breaking the rule broke it themselves more quickly and more often than did the boys in the other two groups. In contrast, the group that had seen the model being punished was more unwilling than any of the other groups to break the rule. The performance of the control group fell between the other two groups (see Figure 1-4). The rsearchers concluded that children who watch

Figure 1-4   The Influence of Filmed Social Models on Young Boys' Resistance to Temptation

In the experiment undertaken by Richard H. Walters and his associates, groups 1 and 2 were experimental groups, and group 3 was the control group. The independent variable was introduced in the first two groups but not in the third group.
Source: Adapted from data in R. H. Walters, M. Leat, and L. Mezei, "Inhibition and Disinhibition of Responses Through Empathetic Learning," *Canadian Journal of Psychology,* Vol. 17 (1963), pp. 235–243.

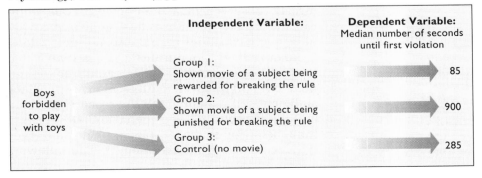

the behavior of another person tend to behave in the same way. This evidence supports the social learning theory of the psychologist Albert Bandura (see Chapter 2).

The Social Survey Method

Researchers are often interested in studying the incidence of behavior in a large population: say, to discover the prevalence of certain child-rearing practices, the extent of premarital sexual relations, the frequency of drug use among teenagers, the impact of a mental health advertising campaign, and so on. In this approach data are collected in numerical form by using various quantitative methods—procedures that entail enumeration and measurement.

Prominent among quantitative methods is the **survey**. Survey data are gathered in two basic ways. In the first, people are interviewed by a researcher who reads them questions from a prepared questionnaire. In the second, individuals

"Next question: I believe that life is a constant striving for balance, requiring frequent tradeoffs between morality and necessity, within a cyclic pattern of joy and sadness, forging a trail of bittersweet memories until one slips, inevitably, into the jaws of death. Agree or disagree?"

(Drawing by Geo. Price; © 1989. The New Yorker Magazine, Inc.)

receive a questionnaire in the mail, fill it out, and return it by mail.

Both mass interviewing and the mass mailing of questionnaires are exceedingly expensive. Furthermore, questioning millions of people is simply impractical. Accordingly, scientists have evolved various techniques for using small samples of people to arrive at broad generalizations about the larger population. Public opinion organizations (including Gallup, CBS, NBC, and Louis Harris) employ small samples of approximately 1,500 representative people to tap the opinions of 200 million Americans with only a small margin of error.

The principle behind polling is simple. Consider a jar filled with 100,000 green and yellow marbles. You do not need to count all the marbles to find out what proportion are green, what yellow. A sample of 1,000 will allow you to estimate the ratio with great confidence, within a small margin of error, as long as each marble has an equal chance of being counted. Doctors proceed on the same assumption when they test our blood. Rather than removing all of it for testing, they take a small sample.

The social survey method has its limitations (Schuman & Scott, 1987). It cannot be used with infants, and it has only limited use with preschool children. Furthermore, individuals are often deeply involved with the data they are reporting. Hence, they may withhold or distort information if they feel that their self-esteem is threatened. Or they may simply be unable to provide certain types of information because of lack of insight.

The Naturalistic Observation Method

In **naturalistic observation** researchers intensively watch and record behavior as it occurs. However, they are careful not to disturb or affect the events under investigation. By this method they can secure more detail and greater depth of insight than by the social survey (Cahill, 1990; Willems & Alexander, 1982). But for the same amount of time and money, fewer people can be directly observed than interviewed. Thus, naturalistic observation affords less range in the types of people it can study than the social survey does.

An advantage of naturalistic observation is that it is independent of the subject's ability or willingness to report on given matters. Many people lack sufficient self-insight to tell the researcher about certain aspects of their behavior. Or because their behavior is illegal, taboo, or deviant, they may be reluctant to talk about it. The following

Tips for Observing Children

One of the best ways to learn about children is to observe them. To provide access to the full drama, color, and richness of the world of children, many instructors have their students watch children in the laboratory or in the field. Here are a number of tips that may prove helpful for the observation of children:

❑ The minimal aids you will need for observation generally include paper, pen, a timepiece, and a writing board.

❑ Record the date, the time interval, the location, the situation, and the age and sex of the subject or subjects.

❑ Most observations take place in nursery school settings. Add diversity to your report by observing children in parks, streets, stores, vacant lots, homes, and swimming pools.

❑ Have the purpose of your research firmly in mind. You should explicitly define and limit in advance the range of situations and behaviors you will observe. Will you watch the entire playground, giving a running account of events? Will you concentrate upon one or two individuals? Will you record the activities of an entire group? Or will you focus only on certain types of behavior, such as aggression?

❑ Describe both the behavior and the social context in which it occurs. Include not only what a child says and does but also what others say and do to the child. Report spoken words, cries, screams, startle responses, jumping, running away, and related behaviors.

❑ Describe the relevant *body language*—the nonverbal communication of meaning through physical movements and gestures. Body language includes smiles, frowns, scowls, menacing gestures, twisting, and other acts that illuminate the intensity and effect of behavior.

❑ Do not substitute interpretations that generalize *about* behavior for descriptions *of* behavior.

❑ Make notes in improvised shorthand. *Immediately after* an observation session, transcribe and enlarge the report in full. The longer the interval between the full recording of observations and the events themselves, the less accurate, the less detailed, and the more biased your report will be.

❑ Make inferences regarding the motivations and feelings of the children as their behavior occurs.

❑ Limit your periods of observation to half an hour, which is about as long as a researcher can remain alert enough to perceive and remember the multitude of simultaneous and sequential occurrences.

❑ At times, children will notice you observing them. If they ask what you are doing, be truthful. Explain it openly and frankly. According to Wright and Barker (1950), children under the age of 9 generally display little self-consciousness when being observed. Furthermore most people—children and adults alike—usually adjust to an observer's presence.

❑ Keep in mind that one of the greatest sources of unreliability in observation is the researcher's selective perceptions influenced by his or her own needs and values. For example, observers who sharply disapprove of aggressive behaviors tend to overrecord these behaviors. Remember at all times that objectivity is your goal.

❑ Use time sampling for some observations. Time your field notes at intervals of one minute or even thirty seconds. You may wish to tally the children's behavior in terms of helping, resistance, submission, giving, and other responses.

❑ Use event sampling—behavioral sequences or episodes—for some observations. Helen Dawe's 1934 study of the quarrels of preschool children provides a good model. Dawe made "running notes" on prepared forms that gave space for recording (a) the name, age, and sex of every subject, (b) the duration of the quarrel, (c) what the children were doing at the onset of the quarrel, (d) the reason for the quarrel, (e) the role of each subject, (f) specific motor and verbal behavior, (g) the outcome, and (h) the aftereffects. The advantage of event sampling is that it allows you to structure the field of observation into natural units of behavior.

account of an interview with a mother about her child-rearing practices is a good example (Maccoby & Maccoby, 1954, p. 484):

> During the interview she held her small son on her lap. The child began to play with his genitals. The mother, without looking directly at the child, moved his hand away and held it securely for a while. . . . [Later] in the interview the mother was asked what she ordinarily did when the child played with himself. She replied that he never did this—he is a very "good" boy. She was evidently unconscious of what had transpired in the very presence of the interviewer.

Naturalistic observation can provide a rich source of ideas for future study. But it is not a particularly strong technique for testing hypotheses. The researcher lacks control over the behavior of the subjects being observed. Furthermore, no independent variable is "manipulated." Consequently, the theorizing associated with naturalistic observation tends to be highly speculative. Still another problem with this method is that the observer's presence may alter the behavior he or she is observing. The knowledge that we are being observed tends to distort our behavior—the so-called *guinea pig effect* (also termed the *Hawthorne effect*). To minimize this problem, some researchers conceal their identity as observers. But this strategy poses ethical problems.

In spite of these shortcomings, there is a decided advantage to observing behavior as it takes place spontaneously within its natural context. Indeed, some researchers argue that artificially planned situations do not do justice to the rich, genuine, and dynamic quality of human life. They insist that rigid interviews, questionnaires, tests, and experiments distort and destroy the natural stream of people's behavior. Rather than compelling the subject to enter the experimenter's world, as other methods do, naturalistic observation requires the experimenter to enter the subject's world.

Through the years researchers have introduced modifications in observational techniques in order to provide greater scientific rigor. One modification involves **time sampling.** The researcher counts the number of times an individual exhibits quarreling, aggression, cooperation, or some other behavior over a systematically spaced interval of time. When studying children, some researchers record the action every five seconds. Other researchers do not want to lose the sequential flow of events. Consequently, they focus on a class of behaviors, such as fighting on a playground, and record the time that is consumed by each episode. This approach is termed **event sampling.** Still other researchers use precoded behavior categories. They determine beforehand what behaviors they will observe. They then record a behavior by code symbols (see boxed insert on page 25).

The Cross-Cultural Method

No animal lives under more diverse conditions than man, and no species exhibits more behavioral variation from one population to another.—ROBERT A. LEVINE

Scientists are interested in establishing which theories hold for all societies, which for only certain types of societies, and which for only one particular society. The **cross-cultural method** is well suited to this purpose. Researchers compare data from two or more societies. Cultures, rather than individuals, are the unit of analysis. The largest number of societies studied in this manner is about one thousand. However, most researchers limit themselves to a smaller sample, generally several adjacent societies in a similar cultural area. They may focus upon a single aspect, such as toilet training or puberty rites, or a wide variety of behaviors and customs. (Triandis & Brislin, 1984; Whiting & Edwards, 1988.)

A considerable number of cross-cultural studies have employed data from the Human Relations Area Files at Yale University (Murdock et al., 1971). These files, which are now available on microfilm to other universities, contain verbatim reports from anthropologists, colonial officials, missionaries, explorers, travelers, and others. Information on some four hundred societies is filed by code numbers and indexed by nearly eight hundred subject categories.

For example, if we were interested in infant care, we would look in the Human Relations Area Files under category 854 (Murdock et al., 1971, p. 136):

> 854   INFANT CARE—care of routine bodily needs, cleaning; dealing with excreta; clothing and swaddling; provisions for sleep (e.g., cradles, cribs); playing with infants (e.g., fondling, dandling, rocking, crooning); emotional care (e.g., distracting techniques, methods of soothing, guarding against emotional upsets); watching and tending; special dangers ascribed to period of infancy; protection from real and supernatural dangers; hygienic and therapeutic measures; methods of holding and carrying infants (e.g., on back, astride hip); distribution of care among members of the family; institutionalized care (e.g., nurseries); etc.

Or if we wished to study adulthood, we would look under category 885 (Murdock et al., 1971, p. 143):

> 885   ADULTHOOD—conception of the prime of life; cultural definition of adult status; differential status and activities of adult males and females prior to and subsequent to marriage; concepts of the ideal man and the ideal woman; etc.

Studies dealing with grandparenthood provide a good example of cross-cultural research. According to the anthropologist A. R. Radcliffe-Brown (1940), tensions between parents and children tend to draw grandparent and grandchild together. To test this hypothesis, a number of researchers have examined cross-cultural data (Apple, 1956; Nadel, 1951). They have found close and warm relationships between children and their grandparents *only* in cultures where grandparents do not serve as disciplinarians. Where grandparents have a disciplinary role, easy,

Cross-Cultural Research
By comparing data from two or more societies, scientists are able to generalize about human development under varying cultural circumstances. One aspect of development that has interested scientists recently is the part the father plays in rearing children. Here a Balinese father of Indonesia relaxes with his family. *(Ken Heyman)*

friendly, playful relations between grandparents and grandchildren are absent.

Like other research approaches, the cross-cultural method has limitations. First, the quality of the data varies from casual, unprofessional accounts by explorers and missionaries to the most sophisticated field work by trained anthropologists. Second, data for some research problems are lacking for many cultures. Third, the data tend to focus on the typical behaviors and practices of a people but seldom provide information on individual differences among them. Nonetheless, as George Peter Murdock (1957, p. 251), a distinguished anthropologist, has written, cross-cultural research demonstrated that it is "unsafe" for the scientist "to generalize his knowledge of Euro-American societies, however profound, to mankind in general."

Ethical Standards for Human Development Research

Hurt not others in ways that you yourself would find hurtful.
A Buddhist Scripture

Research on humans is essential for medical and scientific progress. Human development research can help parents, teachers, social workers, government officials, and many others to make more informed decisions regarding various practices and policies. However, most scientists and lay people recognize that before any new drug or procedure can be approved for use in human beings, it must be tested first on individuals under appropriate experimental controls. Clearly, such experimenting must be undertaken with proper safeguards. More than four decades ago the horrors of medical experiments carried out by German physicians working in Nazi concentration camps dramatized the need for a code of ethics in research.

In the past twenty years or so a number of studies have sparked controversy within U.S. scientific circles. In an experiment under the auspices of the U.S. Public Health Service, a group of southern blacks went forty years without treatment for syphilis. A family-planning clinic in San Antonio randomly gave placebos (fake pills) to applicants for birth-control pills, and this practice resulted in several unwanted pregnancies. Investigators seeking a cure for hepatitis intentionally injected the disease virus into hundreds of mentally retarded children at Willowbrook State School in New York (Frankel, 1978). And in an experiment by Stanley Milgram (1974), subjects were ordered to give other people electric shocks that the subjects believed were strong enough to injure or kill.

The issues posed by such research have led the American Psychological Association to formulate a series of research guidelines. The preamble states (1982, p. 5):

The decision to undertake research should rest upon a considered judgment by the individual psychologist and how best to contribute to psychological science and to human welfare. Having made the decision to conduct research, the psychologist considers alternative directions in which research energies and resources might be invested. On the basis of this consideration, the psychologist carries out the investigation with respect and concern for the dignity and welfare of the people who participate and with cognizance of federal and state regulations and professional standards governing the conduct of research with human participants.

The Society for Research in Child Development has also issued a set of guidelines.

Both sets of guidelines stipulate that subjects should not be compelled to participate in an experiment, and that they should have the freedom to discontinue participation if they wish. Research on children raises particularly complex and sensitive issues, since the legal and moral legitimacy of experimentation on human beings evolves fundamentally from the consent of the subject (Cooke, 1982). However, the capacity of children to give informed consent is limited and at very early ages is impossible. Even so, research suggests that in many cases children over 9 years of age are able to make sensible decisions about whether to take part in research (Fields, 1981; Thompson, 1990). While parents and legal guardians are empowered to decide whether minors under their control will be used as research subjects, children should not be viewed simply as pawns that can be manipulated at will by their elders. Finally, both organizations state that the experiment must assume responsibility for detecting and correcting any undesirable results that may follow from an individual's participation in the research.

In sum, individuals who undertake research assume major responsibilities. Scientists must, of course, proceed in a rigorous and disciplined way, approaching their data from as objective a perspective as is humanly possible. They must not turn their backs on facts or distort facts simply because they find that the facts are leading them to conclusions they may find distasteful. But over and above this traditional obligation, they have a responsibility for the welfare of their subjects.

SUMMARY

1. Human life involves both change and continuity.
2. The field of human development has four major concerns: (a) to identify and describe the changes that occur across the human life span, (b) to explain these changes, (c) to predict occurrences in human development, and (d) to intervene in the course of events in order to control them.
3. Developmental change takes place in three fundamental domains: the physical, the cognitive, and the psychosocial.
4. The concepts of growth, maturation, and learning are important to our understanding of human development. We must not counterpose the biological forces of growth and maturation to the environmental forces of learning. It is the interaction between heredity and environment that gives an organism its unique characteristics.
5. Urie Bronfenbrenner has proposed an ecological approach to development in which he examines the mutual accommodations between the developing person and four levels of environmental influence: the microsystem, the mesosystem, the exosystem, and the macrosystem.
6. Time plays an important role in development. Traditionally, the passage of time has been treated as synonymous with chronological age. But more recently, social and behavioral scientists have broadened their focus to take into account the changes that occur over time in the environment—and the dynamic relation between change in the person and change in the environment. One way of looking at these changes is to consider normative age-graded influences, normative history-graded influences, and nonnormative life events.
7. All societies must deal in one fashion or another with the life cycle. They divide this cycle into strata that reflect social definitions. Such definitions often vary from one culture to another and from one historical period to another.
8. The longitudinal method for studying human development allows the researcher to study the same individuals at regular intervals between birth and death. It provides a means for discovering which childhood behaviors are long lasting and which will be dropped along the way.
9. Whereas the longitudinal method undertakes successive measurements on the *same* individuals, the cross-sectional method compares different groups of people of different ages at the same time.

10. The case-study method is used in baby biographies and in clinical approaches involving maladjusted children and adults.
11. The experimental method is one of the most rigorously objective techniques available to science. It offers the most effective technique for establishing cause-and-effect relationships.
12. The social survey method employs questionnaires and interviews for determining the prevalence of given attitudes and behaviors within a population.
13. Naturalistic observation enables a researcher to study people independently of their ability or willingness to report on themselves. The techniques of naturalistic observation range from reports on the most casual uncontrolled experiences to videotape records taken in a laboratory setting.
14. The cross-cultural method allows scientists to specify which theories in human development hold true for all societies, which for only certain types of societies, and which for only a particular society.
15. Having made the decision to conduct research, a scientist must carry out an investigation with respect for the people who participate and with concern for their dignity and welfare.

KEY TERMS

Age Cohort A group of persons born in the same time period (also referred to as *birth cohort*).

Age Strata Social layers that are based upon time periods in life. Age strata order people in society in much the same fashion that the earth's crust is ordered by stratified geological layers.

Ascription The assignment of roles to individuals independently of their unique abilities or qualities.

Case-Study Method A special type of longitudinal study that focuses on a single individual rather than a group of subjects.

Cognitive Development Those changes that occur in mental activity, including sensation, perception, memory, thought, reasoning, and language.

Control Group That group in an experiment that is identical to the other groups except for the fact that the researcher does not introduce change into it. The control group provides a neutral standard against which the changes in the experimental group can be measured.

Cross-Cultural Method A technique that involves the comparison of data from two or more societies, so that cultures, rather than individuals, are the unit of analysis.

Cross-Sectional Method A research approach that investigates development by comparing different groups of individuals varying in age.

Culture The social heritage of a people; those learned patterns for thinking, feeling, and acting that are transmitted from one generation to the next.

Dependent Variable The factor that is affected in an experimental setting; that which occurs or changes as a result of manipulation.

Development The orderly and sequential changes that occur with the passage of time as an organism moves from conception to death. Development includes hereditary and environmental forces and the interaction between them.

Ecological Approach An approach that emphasizes the environmental context in which development occurs. An ecological approach focuses upon the person's interaction with the environment, the person's changing physical and social settings, the relationship among these settings, and how the entire process is affected by the society in which the settings are embedded.

Event Sampling An observational technique in which the researcher focuses upon a class of behaviors and records the time that is consumed by a given episode.

Experimental Group The group in an experiment in which the independent variable is introduced.

Experimental Method A study in which the investigator manipulates one or more variables and measures the resulting changes in the other variables.

Growth The increase in size that occurs with changing age.

Independent Variable The factor that is manipulated in an experimental setting; the causal factor or determining condition in the relationship being studied.

Learning The more or less permanent modification of behavior that results from the individual's experience in the environment.

Longitudinal Method A research approach that investigates development by studying the same individuals at different points in their lives.

Maturation The more or less automatic unfolding of biological potential in a set, irreversible sequence.

Naturalistic Observation A research approach

that entails intensive watching and recording of behavior as it occurs. The researcher does not disturb or affect the events under investigation.

Physical Development   Those changes that take place in a person's body, including changes in weight and height; in the brain, heart, and other organ structures and processes; and in skeletal, muscular, and neurological features that affect motor skills.

Psychosocial Development   Those changes that concern an individual's personality, emotions, and relationships with others.

Survey   A procedure for gathering data in which people are interviewed through questions read from a prepared questionnaire or people receive a questionnaire in the mail, fill it out, and return it.

Time Sampling   An observational technique in which the researcher counts the number of times that a given behavior is exhibited by a subject in a constant, systematically spaced interval of time.

DEVELOPMENTAL THEORIES

Chapter 2

DEVELOPMENTAL THEORIES

Psychoanalytic Theories

Sigmund Freud: Psychosexual Stages of Development ◆

Erik Erikson: Psychosocial Stages of Development

Behavioral Theory

Humanistic Theory

Cognitive Theory

Jean Piaget: Cognitive Stages in Development ◆ Cognitive Learning and Information Processing

Evolutionary Adaptation Theory

Ethology ◆ Sociobiology

Theoretical Controversy

Mechanistic and Organismic Models ◆ Continuity and Discontinuity in Development

◆

Nothing is so practical as a good theory.—KURT LEWIN

A good many Americans hold theory in low regard, some even in contempt. The word excites an image of detached, ivory tower irrelevance. Given the prevalence of these notions, college students often complain: "Why do we have to bother with all these theories? Why not just let the facts speak for themselves!" Unfortunately, facts do not "speak for themselves." Facts are silent. Before facts can speak, we have to find relationships among them. For example, you may baby-sit, care for younger brothers or sisters, have children of your own, or anticipate having children. What do you do when they misbehave? Do you scold them, threaten them, spank them, forbid them from engaging in a favorite activity, reason with them, or ignore them? What you do is based on a theory—whether explicit or not—about how children learn. Perhaps the theory is embedded in a proverb or maxim: "Spare the rod and spoil the child," "You got to toughen kids up for life," "Just give them loads of love," or "Spanking children causes emotional problems."

Theory is an attempt to make sense of our experiences. We must somehow "catch" fleeting events and find a way to describe and explain them. Only then can we predict and influence the world around us. Theory is the "net" we weave to accomplish these ends. **Theory** is a set of interrelated statements that provides an explanation for a class of events. It is "a way of binding together a multitude of facts so that one may comprehend them all at once" (G.A. Kelly, 1955, p. 18). The value of the knowledge yielded by the application of theory lies in the control it provides us over our experience. Theory serves as a guide to action.

More specifically, a theory performs a number of functions. First, it allows us to organize our observations and to deal meaningfully with information that would otherwise be chaotic and useless. As the French mathematician Jules-Henri Poincaré (1854–1912) observed: "Science is built up with facts, as a house is with stones, but a collection of facts is no more a science than a heap of stones is a house." Second, theory allows us to see relationships among facts and uncover implications that would not otherwise be evident in isolated bits of data. Third, it stimulates inquiry as we search for knowledge about many different and often puzzling aspects of behavior. Theory, then, inspires research that can be used to verify, disprove, or modify it. So research continually challenges us to craft new and better theories (see Figure 2-1).

The psychologist Jerome Bruner (1990, p. 344), who has made significant contributions to our understanding of human development, says: "No theory can ever be *the* true theory." Indeed, he believes that there never will be nor can there be "one sole and unitary way of understanding human nature, its variations, its settings, or its growth." A theory, he insists, can "only be more or less right." Moreover, Bruner argues that "there is no single method that is *the* method or the *best* method for understanding human nature and its variations." He explains that no method can get at *the* truth about *native* human nature because there is no such thing as *native* human nature: "Anything we choose to characterize as human nature occurs in a setting and under the thrall of a way of knowing and is a product of that

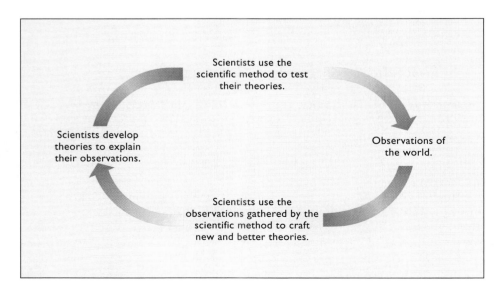

Figure 2-1 *The Relationship Between Theory, the Scientific Method, and Observations of the World.*

Sigmund Freud with His Daughter Anna in 1939
Although Freud reached the pinnacle of his fame in the period between 1919 and his death in 1939, he formulated most of the essentials of his psychoanalytic theory in the decade between 1893 and 1903. Anna Freud, building upon her father's work, pioneered in the psychoanalytic study and treatment of children. *(Keystone/The Image Works)*

setting and that thrall" (p. 344). Bruner offers his thoughts not in a spirit of gloom—to the contrary, he believes they challenge us to pursue an active and vigorous understanding of our world and our encounters with it. His observations provide a context for examining five major types of theory that afford a foundation for the many components of human development.

Psychoanalytic Theories

It is unlikely that the history of psychology—or for that matter, a history of the twentieth century—could be written without discussing the contributions of Sigmund Freud. Both supporters and critics of his theory of personality regard it as a revolutionary milestone in the history of human thought. His notions about how behavior is motivated have been embedded in the work done by a multitude of philosophers, social scientists, and mental health practitioners. And characters in countless plays and novels have been built on Freud's view of people. Central to **psychoan-**

alytic theory is the view that personality is fashioned progressively as the individual passes through various stages: oral, anal, phallic, latency, and genital. Let us turn, then, to a consideration of psychoanalytic theory.

Sigmund Freud: Psychosexual Stages of Development

Freud was born in 1856 in a small town in what is now Czechoslovakia, but he lived most of his life in Vienna. He became a physician and initially distinguished himself through his research on the human nervous system. Early in his career, Freud used hypnosis in treating patients with nervous disorders. But he soon became disenchanted with this method. He began experimenting with the free association of ideas and with dream analysis, work that culminated in his famous psychoanalytic approach. Freud continued to work in Vienna until 1938, when the Nazis invaded Austria. Freud, a Jew, escaped to England. He died in London a year later of cancer, with which he had first been stricken in 1923.

The Role of the Unconscious Freud stressed the role of unconscious motivation—stemming from impulses buried below the level of awareness—in our behavior. According to Freud, human behavior arises out of the struggle that takes place between societal prohibitions and the instinctual drives associated with sex and aggression. As a consequence of being forbidden and punished, many instinctual impulses are driven out of our awareness early in life. Nonetheless, they still affect our behavior. They find new expression in slips of the tongue, dreams, bizarre symptoms of mental disorder, religion, art, literature, and myth. For Freud, the early years of childhood assume critical importance. He believed that what happens to an individual later in life is merely a ripple on the surface of a personality structure that is fashioned during the child's first six years.

Psychosexual Stages Freud said that all human beings pass through a series of **psychosexual stages.** Each stage is dominated by the development of sensitivity in a particular erogenous or pleasure-giving zone of the body. Furthermore, each stage poses for individuals a unique conflict that they must resolve before they pass on to the next stage. Should individuals be unsuc-

cessful in resolving the conflict, the resulting frustration becomes chronic and remains a central feature of their psychological makeup. Alternatively, individuals may become so addicted to the pleasures of a given stage that they are unwilling to move on to later stages. As a result of either frustration or overindulgence, individuals experience fixation at a particular stage of development. **Fixation** is the tendency to stay at a particular stage: The individual is troubled by the conflict characteristic of the stage and seeks to reduce tension by means of the behavior characteristic of that stage.

The characteristics of Freud's three key psychosexual stages of development—the *oral, anal,* and *phallic* stages—are described in detail in Table 2-1. He also identified two later stages, the *latency* period and the *genital* period. He considered these stages less important to the development of the basic personality structure than the stages from birth to age 7. The latency period corresponds to the elementary school years. During this phase, Freud thought children suppress most of their sexual feelings and become interested in games and sports. Boys associate with boys; girls with girls. Sexual reawakening occurs at puberty, launching the genital period. In this

"During the next stage of my development, Dad, I'll be drawing closer to my mother—I'll get back to you in my teens."

(Drawing by Lorenz; © 1991. The New Yorker Magazine, Inc.)

Table 2-1

Freud's Key Psychosexual Stages

Characteristic	Oral	Anal	Phallic
Time period	Birth to approximately 18 months	Approximately 18 months to 3 years	Approximately the third to seventh year
Pleasurable body zones	Mouth, lips, and tongue	Anus, rectum, and bladder	The genitals
Most pleasurable activity	Sucking during the early phase; biting during the later phase	In the early phase, expelling feces and urine; in the later phase, retaining feces and urine	Masturbation
Sources of conflict	Terminating breast feeding	Toilet training	In boys, the Oedipal complex: boys feel sexual love for the mother and hostile rivalry toward the father, leading them to fear punishment through castration by the father. In girls, the Electra complex: girls feel sexual love for the father and hostile rivalry toward the mother, leading them to conclude that they have been castrated (since they lack the penis). Their sense of castration gives girls a feeling of inferiority that finds expression in "penis envy."
Common problems associated with fixation	An immature, dependent personality with overwhelming and insatiable demands for mothering; a verbally abusive and demanding personality; or a personality characterized by excessive "oral" behaviors, such as alcoholism, smoking, compulsive eating, and nail biting.	A hostile, defiant personality that has difficulty relating to people in positions of authority; a superconformist personality characterized by preoccupation with rules, regulations, rigid routines, compulsive neatness, and orderliness; or a stingy, miserly personality.	Sexual problems in adulthood—impotence or frigidity; homosexuality; inability to handle competitive relationships.
Social relationships	Infants cannot differentiate between self and nonself. Consequently, they are self-centered and preoccupied with their own needs.	Since parents interfere with elimination pleasures, the child develops ambivalent attitudes toward the parents. As children resolve the conflict between their needs for parental love and for instinctual gratification, they evolve lifelong attitudes toward cleanliness, orderliness, punctuality, submissiveness, and defiance.	A successful resolution of phallic conflict leads the child to identify with the parent of the same sex. In this fashion the child achieves a sense of masculinity or femininity and gives up the incestuous desire for the parent of the opposite sex.

How Do You Defend Yourself Against Psychic Pain?

According to Freudian theory, *ego defense mechanisms* are activated when an individual confronts serious anxiety and emotional conflicts. These mechanisms are mental devices by which people protect and insulate themselves from psychic pain. Freud believed that all people employ such devices. They become pathological only when they continually serve to distort reality and impair effective functioning. Among the most common defense mechanisms are the following:

❑ *Repression.* In repression an unacceptable or threatening thought or impulse is driven from conscious awareness. When children have been taught that aggression and masturbation are "bad," they may repress knowledge of their own involvement in such practices. By repression they avoid conscious feelings of anxiety and guilt.

❑ *Projection.* People using the mechanism of projection attribute to someone else their own impulses or acts that are too painful to acknowledge. Thus, angry children who have learned that rage is socially unacceptable often project their aggression onto a playmate and justify their own behavior as "self-defense": "He started it."

❑ *Displacement.* When hostilities are removed from the source of frustration and discharged upon another person (a scapegoat), displacement takes place. Children frustrated by a parent or a teacher usually cannot strike back. It would be too dangerous. Instead, they "take out" their pent-up hostility on a weak or defenseless victim—for instance, a pet or a younger child.

❑ *Denial.* At times people protect themselves from unpleasant reality by simply not perceiving it. They refuse to acknowledge its existence. A child with a hostile mother may deny that she is hostile and rejecting. Instead, the child insists that the mother is a kind, loving person. The device of denial spares people the emotional pain that would follow from recognizing the truth.

❑ *Sublimation.* In sublimation unacceptable behavior is repressed and reemerges in a socially acceptable manner. According to some psychoanalytic psychologists, a coin collector is sublimating a desire to retain feces, a boxing fan is sublimating aggression, and an artist is sublimating sexual energies.

❑ *Regression.* Individuals who are under stress may invoke behavior that was characteristic of an earlier stage of development. An illustration is the six-year-old child who regresses to thumb-sucking or bed-wetting when confronted with a new baby in the home.

❑ *Rationalization.* People rationalize by finding a convincing reason for doing something that would otherwise be viewed as unacceptable. Take the teenage girl who wants to break off with her boyfriend but feels guilty about it because "he's been good to me." She can go ahead and make the break, however, if she can justify it through rationalization: "He'd be better off if he could get to know some other girls."

❑ *Reaction Formation.* In reaction formation people protect themselves against recognizing aspects of their personalities that they would find unacceptable by developing the *opposite* behavior. A case in point is the crusader against pornographic movies who watches them in the name of denouncing them. He thus camouflages his own illicit sexual impulses. Shakespeare's oft-quoted line "The lady doth protest too much, methinks" fits the concept of reaction formation.

---

stage the equilibrium of the latency period is upset. Young people begin experiencing romantic infatuations and emotional upheavals.

Appraisal of Freud's Work   For years Freud's ideas dominated much clinical therapy. To many people Freud seemed to open an entirely new psychological world. His identification of key ego defense mechanisms (see the boxed insert above) proved particularly insightful and valuable for psychotherapy, and his emphasis on environment, not biology or heredity, as the primary factor in mental health and illness was particularly hopeful. In fact, people were so fascinated with the novelty of Freud's insights that few questioned their truth. Nonetheless, scientists have come to recognize that Freudian theory is difficult to evaluate. It makes few predictions that can be tested by accepted scientific procedures (Colby & Stoller, 1988; Edelson, 1988; Roazen, 1990). Freudians say that only a personal analysis can reveal the truth of the theory's assertions. Unconscious motivation is, by definition, not in the conscious mind. Consequently, scientists lack the means to observe and study such motivation objectively.

Freud constructed his developmental stages almost entirely on the basis of inferences from adult patients. Recent historical research has depicted Freud as having occasionally claimed cures when there were none and as having suppressed or distorted the facts of cases to prove his theoretical points (Decker, 1990; Goleman, 1990; Raymond, 1991b). In addition, although stressing the importance of the early years, Freud worked with children only rarely (however, child psychoanalysts, such as his daughter Anna, did apply his theories to the treatment of children). Moreover, feminist scholars find psychoanalytic interpretations of the female Electra and "castration" complexes highly problematic and sexist (Bernstein & Warner, 1984; Chehrazi, 1986; Chodorow, 1989; Hunt & Rudden, 1986; Sayers, 1991). Finally, since his patients were suffering from emotional difficulties, critics charge that Freudian theory is a poor guide to healthy personalities.

Over the past 30 years interest in the duration of nursing, severity of weaning, age of toilet training, and other psychoanalytic variables has gradually waned. Moreover, the expected cures from psychoanalysis have proven elusive. By the early 1970s a new generation of U.S. psychiatrists was turning to psychobiology, considering defects of nature, not nurture, to be the primary factor in mental illness. The psychiatrists claimed that neurochemical factors, not childhood traumas, best explained mental illness, and hence they looked to genes, not bad parenting, as the chief means by which mental illness is transmitted from one generation to another.

This recent shift in emphasis away from Freudian thought in no way detracts from the revolutionary significance of Freud's work. Perhaps more than anything else Freud deserves considerable credit for directing attention to the importance of social experience in human development.

Erik Erikson: Psychosocial Stages of Development

Among Freud's major contributions was the stimulus his work gave to other theorists and researchers. One of the most talented and imaginative of these theorists is Erik Erikson (1963, 1968b, 1987). A neo-Freudian psychoanalyst of Danish extraction, Erikson came to the United States in 1933. While acknowledging Freud's genius and monumental contributions, Erikson moved away from the fatalism implicit in Freudian theory, challenging Freud's notion that the personality is primarily established during the first five to six years of life. Erikson said that

Erik H. Erikson

Although Erik H. Erikson did not publish his first book until 1950, when he was forty-eight years old, he then became a leading figure in the psychoanalytic study of human growth and development. His writings over the past four decades have drawn upon field work with the Oglala Sioux of South Dakota and the salmon-fishing Yurok of northern California, and the clinical treatment of disturbed children and adolescents. Erikson has also written biographies of Martin Luther and Mohandas Gandhi. *(Courtesy of W. W. Norton and Company, Inc.)*

the personality continues to develop over the entire life cycle. His is a more optimistic view that emphasizes success, greatness, and the flowering of the human potential.

The Nature of Psychosocial Development Erikson's chief concern is with psychosocial development. In contrast, Freud focused chiefly on psychosexual development. Erikson has formulated eight major stages of development, described in Table 2-2. Each stage poses a unique developmental task and simultaneously confronts individuals with a crisis that they must struggle through. As employed by Erikson (1968a, p. 286), a crisis is not "a threat of catastrophe but a turning point, a crucial period of increased vulnerability and heightened potential." He sees great people of history, such as Martin

Table 2-2

Erikson's Eight Stages of Development

Developmental Stage	Psychosocial Crisis	Predominant Social Setting	Favorable Outcome
1. Infancy	Basic trust vs. mistrust	Family	The child develops trust in self, in parents, and in the world.
2. Early childhood	Autonomy vs. shame, doubt	Family	The child develops a sense of self-control without loss of self-esteem.
3. Fourth to fifth year	Initiative vs. guilt	Family	The child learns to acquire direction and purpose in activities.
4. Sixth year to onset of puberty	Industry vs. inferiority	Neighborhood; school	The child acquires a sense of mastery and competence.
5. Adolescence	Identity vs. role confusion	Peer groups and out-groups	The individual develops an *ego identity*—a coherent sense of self.
6. Young adulthood	Intimacy vs. isolation	Partners in friendship and sex	The individual develops the capacity to work toward a specific career and to involve himself or herself in an extended intimate relationship.
7. Adulthood	Generativity vs. stagnation	New family; work	The individual becomes concerned with others beyond the immediate family, with future generations, and with society.
8. Old age	Integrity vs. despair	Retirement and impending death	The individual acquires a sense of satisfaction in looking back upon his or her life.

Luther and Mohandas Gandhi, as achieving greatness by virtue of the fit between their personal crises and the crises of their times. Their solutions—as expressed in their ideas—become cultural solutions to broader social problems.

According to Erikson (1959, 1980), individuals develop a "healthy personality" by mastering "life's outer and inner dangers." Development follows the **epigenetic principle**—"anything that grows has a ground plan, and . . . out of this ground plan the parts arise, each having its time of special ascendancy, until all parts have arisen to form a functioning whole" (1968*b*, p. 92). Hence, according to Erikson, each part of the personality has a particular time in the life span when it must develop if it is going to develop at all. Should a capacity not be developed on schedule, the rest of development is unfavorably altered. The individual is then hindered in dealing effectively with reality.

Psychosocial Stages   As shown in Table 2-2, the individual is confronted in each of Erikson's eight stages with a major crisis that must be successfully resolved if healthy development is to occur. The interaction that takes place between an individual and society during each stage can change the course of personality in either a positive or a negative direction. Let us briefly consider Erikson's stages of psychosocial development.

❑ *Trust Versus Mistrust (Birth to 1 year)* Basic to Erikson's concept of development is the element of trust. Human life is a social endeavor that involves linkages and interactions among people. Whether children come to trust or mistrust themselves and other people depends on their early experiences. Infants whose needs are met and who are cuddled, fondled, and shown genuine affection evolve a sense of the world as a safe and dependable place. In contrast, when child care is chaotic, unpredictable, and rejecting, children approach the world with fear and suspicion. These basic attitudes are not resolved in a once-and-for-all fashion. They arise again at each successive level of development (Elkind, 1970).

❑ *Autonomy Versus Shame and Doubt (2 to 3 years)* As children begin to crawl, walk, climb, and explore, a new conflict confronts them: whether to assert their wills. When parents are patient, cooperative, and encouraging, children acquire a sense of independence and competence. In contrast, when children are not allowed such freedom and are overprotected, they develop an excessive sense of shame and doubt.

❑ *Initiative Versus Guilt (4 to 5 years)* During this stage the repertoire of motor and mental abilities that are open to children greatly expands. Parents who give their children freedom in running, sliding, bike riding, skating, and roughhousing are allowing them to develop initiative. Parents who curtail this freedom are giving children a sense of themselves as nuisances and inept intruders in an adult world. Rather than actively and confidently shaping their own behaviors, such children become passive recipients of whatever the environment brings.

❑ *Industry Versus Inferiority (6 to 11 years)* During the elementary school years a child becomes concerned with how things work and how they are made (see Kowaz & Marcia, 1991). As children move into the world of school, they gain a sense of industry by winning recognition for their achievements. But they may instead acquire a sense of inadequacy and inferiority. Parents and teachers who support, reward, and praise children are encouraging industry. Those who rebuff, deride, or ignore children's efforts are strengthening feelings of inferiority.

❑ *Identity Versus Role Confusion (12 to 18 years)* As children enter adolescence, they confront a "physiological revolution." Simultaneously, they must answer the question "Who am I?" They try on many new roles as they grope with romantic involvement, vocational choice, and adult statuses. In the process adolescents must develop an integrated and coherent sense of self. When the adolescent

Autonomy Versus Shame and Doubt
Erikson suggests that as children begin to walk and climb, they gain a sense of independence and competence. When children are not permitted the freedom to explore, they become inhibited and develop a sense of shame and doubt. *(Jean-Claude Lejeune)*

"*I still don't have all the answers, but I'm beginning to ask the right questions.*"

fails to develop a "centered" identity, he or she becomes trapped in either role confusion or a "negative identity." The identities and roles of "delinquent" and "hoodlum" are illustrations.

❏ *Intimacy Versus Isolation (Young Adulthood)* As Erikson views intimacy, it is the capacity to reach out and make contact with other people—to fuse one's own identity with that of others. Intimacy finds expression in deep friendships. Central to intimacy is the ability to share with and care about another person without fear of losing oneself in the process (Elkind, 1970). Close involvement, however, may also result in rejection. Consequently, some individuals opt for relationships of a shallow sort. Their lives are characterized by withdrawal and isolation.

❏ *Generativity Versus Stagnation (Middle Adulthood)* By generativity, Erikson means a reaching out beyond one's own immediate concerns to embrace the welfare of society and of future generations. Generativity entails selflessness. In contrast, stagnation is a condition in which individuals are preoccupied with their material possessions or physical well-being. Scrooge in Dickens's *A Christmas Carol*, a self-centered, embittered individual, exemplifies stagnation (Elkind, 1970).

❏ *Integrity Versus Despair (Old Age)* As individuals approach the end of life, they tend to take stock of the years that have gone before. Some feel a sense of satisfaction with their accomplishments. Others experience despair— "the feeling that the time is now short, too short for the attempt to start another life and to try out alternative roads to integrity" (Erikson, 1963, p. 269).

Appraisal of Erikson's Work Erikson's work provides a welcome balance to traditional Freudian theory. Although not neglecting the powerful effects of childhood experience, Erikson draws our attention to the continual process of personality development that takes place *throughout* the life span. He offers a more optimistic view than does Freud. Whereas Freud was primarily concerned with pathological outcomes, Erikson holds open the prospect of healthy and positive resolutions of our identity crises. Erikson's portrait of the life cycle allows "second chances" for opportunities missed and paths not taken. Since U.S. individualism suggests that people can improve themselves and continually refashion their fate by changing their social situation, Erikson's perspective has captured the imagination of the U.S. public. The language Erikson provided—

"identity," "identity crisis," and "the life cycle"—plays a major role in the U.S. way of thinking about adolescence and, beyond this, about the widest range of adult trials and tribulations (Turkle, 1987).

Behavioral Theory

Psychoanalytic theory focuses on those mental and emotional processes that shape the human personality. The data it uses come largely from the self-observations provided by *introspection*. Behavioral theory stands in sharp contrast to this approach. As its name suggests, **behavioral theory** is concerned with the behavior of people—what they actually do and say. Behavioral psychologists believe that if psychology is to be a science, its data must be directly observable and measurable.

Behaviorists are especially interested in how people *learn* to behave in particular ways, and hence the approach is also termed *learning theory*. They deem learning to be a process whereby individuals, as a result of their experience, establish an association or linkage between two events. For example, you very likely have formed an association between a hot stove and a painful, burning sensation, between reading your textbook and passing a course, and between sulking and upsetting your friends. The process by which this occurs is called **conditioning.**

B. F. Skinner

In the 20 years following World War II, B. F. Skinner (left) was the dominant figure in American psychology. His experimental work with pigeons pioneered many facets of behavioral theory. As a strict behaviorist, Skinner did not concern himself with what goes on inside the organism. Instead, he stressed the part that learning processes play in an organism's acquisition of various behaviors. (*Joe McNally/Wheeler Pictures*)

Few psychologists have contributed more to behavioral theory than has B. F. Skinner (1904–1990). During the 1950s and 1960s no U.S. psychologist enjoyed greater prominence or commanded greater influence than did Skinner. Over the past forty years students enrolled in college psychology courses have become familiar with Skinner's famous experimental chamber, which is used for many studies of animal behavior. The apparatus, commonly called a Skinner box, provides a soundproof enclosure that isolates the subject—a pigeon, rat, or mouse—from stray stimuli. When the subject pecks a key or presses a lever in an accidental or exploratory manner, a pellet of food is released. Sooner or later the animal reactivates the food delivery mechanism in the course of random activity. As the process is repeated over time, the animal reaches the point where it pecks the key or presses the lever so as to receive the reward.

Throughout his career Skinner has been especially concerned with the control of behavior. Like other behaviorists, Skinner attempts to divide behavior into units called **responses** and the environment into units called **stimuli.** His experimental work with pigeons illustrates his approach. He carefully watches a hungry pigeon strut about. When the bird makes a slight clockwise turn, Skinner instantly rewards it with a food pellet—a stimulus. Again the bird struts about, and when it makes another clockwise turn, Skinner repeats the procedure. Skinner finds that he can get a pigeon to make a full circle in two to three minutes—the response he was aiming at.

Next, Skinner rewards the bird only when it moves in the opposite direction. Then, he waits until it makes a clockwise circle followed by a counterclockwise circle. In ten to fifteen minutes Skinner is able to condition the pigeon to do a perfect figure eight. Among other things, Skinner has taught pigeons to dance with each other and to play Ping-Pong.

The process whereby one event strengthens the probability of another event's occurring is termed **reinforcement.** Skinner asserts that much of life is structured by arranging reinforcing consequences, or "payoffs." Businesses reward appropriate work behavior by their employees with wages. A doctor must make certain that a patient feels he or she has benefited from an office visit in order to induce the patient to return for further treatment. But reinforcement may also result in maladaptive behavior, including learned helplessness (see the boxed insert on page 44).

Is Helplessness Learned?

Life requires that organisms adjust themselves to their environmental circumstances. Toward this end, they commonly learn various coping mechanisms. Yet research conducted over the past fifteen years by Martin E. P. Seligman and his colleagues (Garber & Seligman, 1980; Nolen-Hoeksema, Seligman & Girgus, 1986; Seligman, 1975, 1978) reveals that some organisms acquire a learned helplessness that impairs their adaptation. **Learned helplessness** refers to a generalized expectancy that events are independent of one's own responses. Consequently, individuals characterized by learned helplessness believe that their coping behaviors are futile.

Seligman stumbled upon learned helplessness while experimenting with dogs that he had traumatically shocked to test a learning theory (Overmier & Seligman, 1967; Seligman & Maier, 1967). In the experiment Seligman and his colleagues had strapped the dogs in a harness and given them electric shocks. Later, they placed the dogs in a two-compartment shuttlebox where the dogs were expected to learn that they could escape shock by jumping across the barrier separating the compartments.

Dogs that had not previously been exposed to shock had little difficulty learning the exercise. But not so with the dogs that had experienced shock under inescapable conditions (the harness). They would initially run about the compartment and howl. Very soon, however, they would settle down and passively endure the shock. Seligman concluded that the experience in the harness had taught the dogs that their responses were of no consequence; hence, they simply gave up. For obvious reasons Seligman's research has been severely criticized as involving cruelty to animals.

Donald Hiroto (1974) undertook a modified version of the experiment with a sample of college students. He assigned the students to one of three groups. The first group heard loud noise that they could terminate by pushing a button four times.

The second group heard the noise but had no way to avoid it. The third group, a control group, did not receive any noise. In the next phase of the experiment all groups were tested with a "noise box." The subjects could turn off the sound merely by moving a lever from one side of the box to the other. Although the first and third groups quickly learned to shut the noise off, the second group typically listened passively to the noise. Apparently they had learned that they were helpless.

Seligman noted that the behaviors that characterize learned helplessness in many ways parallel the symptoms of depressive disorders. Many depressed individuals are characterized by a seeming paralysis of will, a feeling that their responses are inadequate or doomed to failure. Critics have pointed out that there are many varieties of psychological depression, each of which is characterized by somewhat different symptoms (Depue & Monroe, 1978). Seligman (1978, 1990; Burns & Seligman, 1989) has agreed with some of these criticisms and has since limited his interpretation to a smaller subclass of depressive disorders.

Carol S. Dweck and her associates (Diener & Dweck, 1980; Dweck, 1975; Fincham, Hokoda & Sanders, 1989; Goetz & Dweck, 1980) find that many school children who give up when they confront failure in academic settings are also victims of learned helplessness. A belief that their learning outcomes are uncontrollable leads the children to become apathetic. They do tend to ponder the cause of their lack of success, but since they attribute their failure to factors beyond their control, they spend little time searching for ways to overcome failure. In contrast, mastery-oriented pupils confront failure by looking for new solutions to their problems. Furthermore, "helpless" students tend to attribute their failure to inadequate ability rather than to inadequate effort. When these children are taught to attribute their failure to lack of motivation, rather than lack of ability, they show striking improvements in their coping responses.

Many of the principles of learning have found a use in **behavior modification.** The approach applies the result of learning theory and experimental psychology to the problem of altering maladaptive behavior. According to behaviorists, pathological behavior is acquired just as normal behavior is acquired—through the process of learning. They claim that the simplest technique for eliminating an unwanted behavior is usually to stop reinforcing it. But behavior modification may also entail more deliberate intervention in the form of reward or punishment. This procedure is being used effectively for a variety of purposes (Epstein & Wing, 1987; Kalish, 1981; Kipnis, 1987). Behavior modification has aided obese people in reducing and has helped people overcome fear of high places, of taking tests, of sexual inadequacy, of closed-in spaces, and of speaking before an audience.

Our understanding of conditioning has undergone major transformations over the past three decades (Mackintosh, 1983; Rescorla & Holland,

1982; Staddon, 1983). Psychologists no longer view conditioning as a simple, mechanical process involving the association of two events that happen to occur rather closely in time. Organisms do not make pairings between events in a vacuum. The environmental context—the overshadowing of some stimuli, the blocking of others, and the highlighting of still others—assumes critical importance. As seen from a cognitive perspective, organisms learn only when events violate their expectations (Kamin, 1969; Rescorla, 1987, 1988; Rescorla & Wagner, 1972). Over time organisms build an image of the external world and continually compare this image with reality. So by virtue of their previous experiences, they come to expect that certain events will follow the presentation of certain stimuli. When the expected environmental feedback is not forthcoming, their perception changes a bit; they must reevaluate the information that various stimuli provide them. Organisms selectively associate the most informative or predictive stimuli with certain events.

For conditioning to take place, then, a stimulus must tell the organism something useful about events in the world that the organism does not already know. For example, you may retrieve a baseball from a bed of poison ivy. A few hours later, your skin becomes red and itchy, and tiny blisters develop. You are unlikely to link the two events. But should a physician, friend, or coworker point out to you that you are allergic to poison ivy, you grasp the relationship between the blisters and the offending plant. You then take care to avoid contact with poison ivy in the future. You have learned!

Humanistic Theory

To be what we are, and to become what we are capable of becoming, is the only end of life.
—ROBERT LOUIS STEVENSON

In the past thirty years or so a "third-force" psychology has arisen in reaction to the two earlier and established traditions of psychoanalysis and behaviorism. Commonly termed **humanistic psychology,** it stresses the uniqueness of the human conditon. Human beings, it maintains, are different from all other organisms in that they actively intervene in the course of events to control their destinies and shape the world around them. Humanistic psychologists, such as Abraham Maslow (1968, 1970) and Carl R. Rogers (1970), share a common concern with maximizing the human potential for self-direction and freedom of choice. They take a **holistic approach,** one that views the human condition in its totality and each person as more than a collection of physical, social, and psychological components.

Abraham Maslow
Maslow's work helped create a humanistic orientation toward the study of behavior by emphasizing personal growth and the realization of each individual's potential. *(The Granger Collection)*

Third-force psychologists criticize psychoanalytic approaches for portraying people as locked by unconscious instincts and irrational forces into a lifetime that is programmed by childhood events. And they disagree with traditional behaviorist theories that depict people as robots who are mechanically programmed by the conditioning force of external stimuli. Humanistic psychologists argue that both psychoanalysts and behaviorists are mistaken in characterizing people as *passive* beings who are acted upon by forces outside their control. In contrast, Maslow and Rogers portray people as capable of *actively* fashioning their personalities and lives with deliberation and insight.

Psychoanalytic psychologists are primarily concerned with the unconscious, whereas behavioral psychologists label the study of consciousness as "mysticism." Humanistic psychologists, however, place human *consciousness* at the center of the human drama. They insist that it is consciousness—the ability to use symbols and to think in abstract terms—that differentiates human beings from other animals.

One of the key concepts advanced by Maslow is the **hierarchy of needs,** depicted in Figure 2-2. Maslow felt that human beings have certain basic needs that they must meet before they can go on to fulfill other needs. At the bottom of Maslow's pyramid are fundamental requirements to satisfy physiological needs (including food, water, and sex) and safety needs. Next, Maslow identified a set of psychological needs centering on belongingness (love) needs and esteem needs. Finally, at the top of the pyramid, he placed the need to realize one's unique potential to the fullest, what he termed **self-actualization.**

To Maslow, such people as Abraham Lincoln, Albert Einstein, Walt Whitman, Jane Addams, and Eleanor Roosevelt are good examples of self-actualizers. From their lives he constructed what he believed to be a composite picture of self-actualized persons (1970):

❑ They have a firm perception of reality.
❑ They accept themselves, others, and the world for what they are.
❑ They evidence considerable spontaneity in thought and behavior.
❑ They are problem-centered rather than self-centered.
❑ They have an air of detachment and a need for privacy.
❑ They are autonomous and independent.

❑ They resist mechanical and stereotyped social behaviors, although they are not deliberately and flamboyantly unconventional.
❑ They are sympathetic to the condition of other human beings and seek to promote the common welfare.
❑ They establish deep and meaningful relationships with a few people rather than superficial bonds with a great many people.
❑ They have a democratic world perspective.
❑ They transcend their environment rather than merely cope with it.
❑ They have a considerable fund of creativeness.
❑ They are susceptible to **peak experiences** marked by rapturous feelings of excitement, insight, and happiness.

Maslow and other humanistic psychologists believe that scientific inquiry should be directed toward helping people achieve freedom, hope, self-fulfillment, and strong self-identities. Maslow (1955, p. 2) was frank about his goals, for he placed himself in a "tradition that considers the humanistic task of psychology to be that of constructing a scientific system of values to help men live the good life." As such, humanistic psychology is less a research-oriented approach for studying human development than a program of ideals about what psychology should study.

Humanistic psychology has had a substantial impact on educational thinking and practice. A

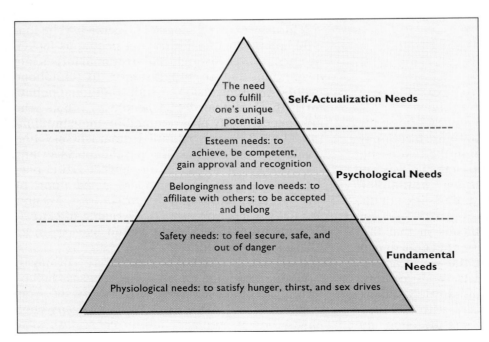

Figure 2-2 Maslow's Hierarchy of Human Needs
According to the humanistic psychologist Abraham Maslow, fundamental needs must be satisfied before an individual is free to progress to psychological needs, which in turn must be met before the person can realize self-actualization needs. Source: From *Motivation and Personality* by Abraham Maslow. Copyright 1954 by Harper & Row, Publishers, Inc. Copyright © 1970 by Abraham H. Maslow. Reprinted by permission of HarperCollins Publishers.

basic humanistic principle of learning is that information will be acquired and used by students only to the degree to which they have discovered the personal meaning of the information. Don E. Hamachek (1977, p. 156) points out:

> Humanistic approaches to teaching and learning keep in mind that students bring their total selves to class. They bring heads that think and feel. They bring values that help them to selectively filter what they see and hear, and they bring attitudinal sets and learning styles that render each student unique and different from all the rest. Humanistic teachers do not only *start out* with the idea that students are different, but they recognize that students may still be different at the *end* of an academic experience.

Humanists favor student-centered education, an approach that found expression in the open-classroom movement of the 1970s. They believe that students should play an active role in making decisions about what is to be learned and when it is to be studied. Viewed from this perspective, students should select their own directions, formulate their own problems, discover their own learning resources, and live with the consequences of their choices. Humanists conceive of teachers chiefly as facilitators. For instance, Carl R. Rogers (1977) questions whether anyone can "teach" anyone else anything worthwhile; he says that *real* learning is self-initiated. Humanist teachers regard themselves as flexible resources to be used by students and as providers of a wide range of learning materials.

Much skepticism prevails among "hard-headed" and "tough-minded" psychologists regarding their humanistic counterparts. Indeed, important differences characterize their intellectual style (Kimble, 1984). The former see their primary task as one of increasing the storehouse of scientific knowledge, whereas the latter take as their primary focus the improvement of the human condition. Moreover, the former view behavior as determined by underlying laws that can be revealed by using the scientific method. In contrast, many humanistic psychologists assert that there is nothing lawful about behavior except perhaps at the level of statistical averages; they investigate behavior by relying on intuition and self-insight. Additionally, critics charge that humanistic psychology turns people inward, encouraging "an intense affair with the self." By emphasizing individual freedom and development rather than the larger social reality, it discourages people from working for social and economic reform. Critics contend that humanistic psychology breeds a narcissistic outlook, one that says that if each of us works on becoming more fully human, then racism, homelessness, hunger, and militarism will vanish (Kohn, 1987).

Cognitive Theory

Like humanistic theory, **cognitive theory** takes issue with a number of behaviorist tenets. In its early formulations behaviorism regarded human life as if it were a "black box": Behaviorism's proponents viewed input or stimuli as entering the "box" at one end and coming out the other end as output or responses. But over the past twenty-five years psychologists have become increasingly interested in what goes on inside the "box." They term these internal factors **cognition**—the act or process of knowing. Cognition involves how we go about representing, organizing, treating, and transforming information as we devise our behavior. It encompasses such phenomena as sensation, perception, imagery, retention, recall, problem solving, reasoning, and thinking. Cognitive psychologists focus on "information processing" and view each person as an "information processor." They are especially interested in the cognitive structures and processes that allow a person to represent mentally events that transpire in the environment. The initial impetus to the study of cognition in the United States came from the work of a Swiss developmental psychologist, Jean Piaget (1896–1980).

Jean Piaget: Cognitive Stages in Development

Intelligence is an adaptation. . . . Life is a continuous creation of increasingly complex forms and a progressive balancing of these forms with the environment.—JEAN PIAGET

The Origins of Intelligence in Children, 1952

Like Freud, Piaget has come to be recognized as a giant of twentieth-century psychology. Anyone who studies Freud and Piaget will never again see children in quite the same way. Whereas Freud was primarily concerned with *personality development*, Piaget concentrated on changes that occur in the child's *mode of thought*. Central to Piaget's work are the **cognitive stages in development**—sequential periods in the growth or maturing of an individual's ability to think—to gain knowledge and awareness of one's self and the environment.

Adjustment as Process When Piaget began to work with children in the early 1920s, little was

Jean Piaget at Work
Piaget spent more than fifty years observing children in informal settings. His work convinced him that a child's mind is not a miniature model of the adult's. We often overlook this fact when attempting to teach children by using adult logic. *(Anderson/Monkmeyer)*

known about the process by which thinking develops. To the extent that they considered the matter at all, most psychologists assumed that children reason in essentially the same way as adults. Piaget soon challenged this view. He insisted that the thought of infants and children is not a miniature version of adult thought. It is qualitatively distinctive and unique. As children "grow up," the form of their thought changes. Consequently, when children say that the sun follows them about when they go for a walk or that dreams come through the window, they are not being illogical. Rather, they are operating from a different mental framework than that of adults.

Piaget depicted children as engaged in a continual interaction with their environment. They act upon, transform, and modify the world in which they live. In turn, they are shaped and altered by the consequences of their own actions. New experiences interact with an existing structure or mode of thought, thereby altering this structure and making it more adequate. This modified structure in turn influences the person's new perceptions. These new peceptions are then incorporated into a more complex structure. In this fashion, experience modifies structure and structure modifies experience. Hence, Piaget viewed the individual and the environment as engaged in continuing interaction. This interaction leads to new perceptions of the world and new organizations of knowledge (Beilin, 1989; Cross, 1976).

Basically, Piaget saw development as adaptation. Beginning with the simple reflexes they have at birth, children gradually modify their repertoire of behaviors to meet environmental demands. By interacting with their environment during play and other activities, children construct a series of schemes—concepts or models—for coping with their world. **Schemes** is the term Piaget used for cognitive structures that people evolve for dealing with specific kinds of situations in their environment. Thus, as portrayed by Piaget, children's thoughts reflect not so much the bits of information that they acquire but the scheme or mental framework by which they interpret information from the environment.

As Piaget viewed adaptation, it involves two processes: assimilation and accommodation. **Assimilation** is the process of taking in new information and interpreting it in such a manner that the information conforms to a currently held model of the world. Piaget said that children typically stretch a scheme as far as possible to fit new observations. But life periodically confronts them with the inescapable fact that some of their observations simply do not fit their current schemes. Then, disequilibrium or imbalance occurs. As a result, children are compelled to reorganize their view of the world in accordance with new experience. In effect, they are required to invent increasingly better schemes or theories about the world as they grow up. **Accommodation** is the process of changing a scheme to make it a better match to the world of reality. Assimilation, then, is the fitting of new experiences to old ones; accommodation is the fitting of old experiences to new ones.

The result of balance between the process of assimilation and accommodation is **equilibrium.** When equilibrium exists, assimilation again occurs in terms of the new model that the child arrived at through accommodation. Thus, as viewed by Piaget, cognitive development is marked by alternating states of equilibrium and disequilibrium. Each stage consists of particular sets of schemes that are in a relative stage of equilibrium at some point in a child's development.

In studying this process, Piaget and other researchers asked children whether or not they ever had a bad dream. One 4-year-old said that she had dreamed about a giant and explained, "Yes, I was scared, my tummy was shaking and I cried and told my mommy about the giant." When asked, "Was it a real giant or was it just pretend?" she responded, "It was really there but it left when I woke up. I saw its foootprint on the floor" (Kohlberg & Gilligan, 1971, p. 1057).

According to Piaget, this child's response is not to be dismissed as the product of wild imagination. Viewed from the perspective of her current scheme, the happenings in dreams are real. As the child matures, she will have new experiences that will cause her to question the scheme. She may observe, for instance, that a "footprint" is not in fact on the floor. This assimilation of new information will result in disequilibrium. Through

accommodation, she will then change her scheme to make it a better fit with reality. She will recognize that dreams are not real events. She will then formulate a new scheme that will establish a new equilibrium. In this new scheme a child her age will typically depict dreams as imaginary happenings. She will still believe, however, that her dreams can be seen by other people.

The process of accommodation continues through additional steps of the same sort. Soon after realizing that dreams are not real, the child comes to recognize that they cannot be seen by others. In the next step the child conceives of dreams as internal, but nevertheless material, events. Finally, somewhere between 6 and 8 years of age, the child becomes aware that dreams are thoughts that take place within her mind.

Characteristics of Piaget's Cognitive Stages
Piaget contended that biological growth combines with children's interaction with their environment to take them through a series of separate, age-related **stages.** The stage concept implies that the course of development is divided into steplike levels. Clear-cut changes in behavior occur as children advance up the developmental staircase, with no skipping of stages allowed. Although teaching and experience can speed up or slow down development, Piaget believed that neither can change the basic order of the stages (Piaget, 1970). Piaget distinguished four stages in the development of cognition or

The Piagetian Processes of Assimilation and Accommodation
In Piaget's view, this baby first tries to obtain the toy by using a familiar grasping scheme (assimilation) and then alters it with new knowledge (accommodation) to get the toy through the bars. *(George S. Zimbel/Monkmeyer)*

intelligence (these stages will be treated in greater detail in later chapters):

- ❑ *Sensorimotor Stage (Birth to 2 years)* During this period infants are busy discovering the relationships between sensations and motor behavior. They learn, for instance, that their hands are part of themselves, whereas a ball is not. They learn how far they need to reach in order to grasp a ball. Perhaps the main feature of this stage is the child's mastery of the *principle of object permanence.* Piaget observed that when a baby of 4 or 5 months is playing with a ball and the ball rolls out of sight behind another toy, the child does not look for it even though it remains within reach. Piaget contended that infants do not realize that objects have an independent existence. This proposition explains a baby's delight in playing peek-a-boo. Around the age of 8 months the child grasps the fact of object constancy and will search for toys that disappear from view (Elkind, 1968*b*). Hence, during the sensorimotor stage infants become able to distinguish between various objects and experiences and to generalize about them. This ability lays the groundwork for later intellectual and emotional development.

- ❑ *Preoperational Stage (2 to 7 years)* A key part of the preoperational stage is the child's developing capacity to employ *symbols,* particularly language. Symbols enable people to deal with things in another time and place. Because of symbols, children are no longer limited to the stimuli that are immediately present. Children use symbols to portray the external world internally—for instance, to talk about a ball and form a mental image of it. They do not have this capacity earlier. In the sensorimotor stage children "know" about a ball in that they can roll it, throw it, or grasp it, but they cannot conceive of a ball as an entity apart from these activities. Now they learn the word "ball" and use it more or less appropriately to refer to round objects (Gardner, 1979).

  Egocentrism is another characteristic of the preoperational stage. By this term Piaget does not mean that the child is self-serving or selfish. Rather, children 4 and 5 years of age consider their own point of view to be the only possible one. They are not yet capable of putting themselves in another's place. They are unaware that the other person has a point of view. A 5-year-old who is asked why it snows will answer by saying, "So children can play in it."

"Look. Mommy! A piece of salad!"

("Family Circus" © 1989 Bill Keane, Inc. Reprinted with special permission of King Features Syndicate.)

- ❑ *Stage of Concrete Operations (7 to 11 years)* This stage is the beginning of rational activity in children. They come to master various logical operations, including arithmetic, class and set relationships, measurement, and conceptions of hierarchical structures. Probably the aspect of this stage that has been most thoroughly investigated is the child's growing ability to "conserve" mass, weight, number, length, area, and volume. Before this stage, for instance, children do not appreciate that a ball of clay can change to a sausage shape and still be the same amount of clay.

  Furthermore, before the stage of concrete operations, children cannot understand that when water is poured out of a full glass into a wider glass that the water fills only halfway, the amount of water remains unchanged. Instead, children "concentrate" on only one aspect of reality at a time. They see that the second glass is half empty and conclude that there is less water in it. In the stage of concrete operations children come to understand that the quantity of water remains the same (see Figure 2-3). Piaget refers to this ability as the *conservation of quantity.* This ability is usually achieved between 6 and 8 years of age.

- ❑ *Stage of Formal Operations (11 Years and Older)* In this stage the child's thought remained fixed upon the visible evidence and concrete properties of objects and events. Now children acquire a greater ability to deal with abstractions. The adolescent can engage in hypothetical reasoning based on logic. When younger children are confronted with the problem, "if coal is white, snow is————," they insist that coal is black. Adolescents, however, respond that snow is black (Elkind, 1968*a*). In other words, the adolescent acquires the capacity for adult thinking.

In the stage of formal operations, young people become capable of abstract thought with respect to a ball. In addition to anticipating what will happen to a ball under various conditions, they now can discuss it in scientific terms and test hypotheses concerning it. They can explain why it is that a billiard ball shot against a surface at one angle will rebound at a particular complementary angle. And they can discuss Newtonian principles about the behavior of spherical objects (Gardner, 1979).

Appraisal of Piaget's Work Piaget's discoveries were largely ignored by U.S. scientists until about 1960. Today, however, the study of cognitive factors in development is of central interest to U.S. psychologists. For the most part, psychologists credit Piaget with drawing their attention to the possibility that an unsuspected order may underlie some aspects of children's intellectual development (Egan, 1980; Gelman & Baillargeon, 1983). Nonetheless, many early American followers of Piaget, such as John H. Flavell, have become disenchanted with the Piagetian model. Flavell (1978, 1982) says that stages imply long periods of stability, followed by abrupt change. But he believes that development does not happen this way. The most important changes happen gradually, over months and even years. In short, human cognitive development is too varied in its mechanisms, routes, and rates to be accurately portrayed by an inflexible stage theory. Growing up, then, is much less predictable than Piaget thought.

A mounting body of evidence also suggests that Piaget underestimated the cognitive capabilities of infants and young children. For instance, the kinds of memory researchers now find in babies at 6 months of age Piaget did not find until babies were 18 months old. Of course, Piaget did not have many of the methods that are now available to scholars, including equipment and procedures to measure the electrical activity of the brain. These methods reveal that by 6 months of age the brain's electrical activity already falls into telltale patterns, showing that babies can distinguish between familiar and unfamiliar pictures and documenting that they have developed mental representations allowing them to compare old and new information (Raymond, 1991*a*). Similarly, the operational thinking capabilities of children from 2 to 7 years of age are considerably greater than Piaget recognized (Brainerd, 1978, 1979). Apparently, children's capabilities depend on the nature or content of the task presented to them, for by altering the components of a cognitive task, one can often elicit from them concrete operational thought and, at times, even formal operational thought. We must therefore conclude that much thinking is specific to the task at hand and that a good many operational capabilities seem to be *available* to 5- and 6-year-old youngsters.

Figure 2-3 The Conservation of Quantity
If a child of 5 or 6 is shown two identical glasses, A and B, which are equally full of liquid, the child will acknowledge that the glasses have the "same to drink." If the liquid from glass A is poured into the taller and narrower glass C, the liquid reaches a higher level. The child is then asked whether there is the same amount to drink in the two differently shaped glasses B and C. Most children younger than 6 respond that C, the tall, narrow glass, has more liquid. Since the preoperational children "center" on height and ignore width, they cannot deal with this transformation. In the next stage, that of concrete operations, the child comes to recognize that the amount of liquid is the same, regardless of differences in the shapes of the containers. Piaget referred to this ability as "the conservation of quantity," an ability that is usually achieved between 6 and 8 years of age.

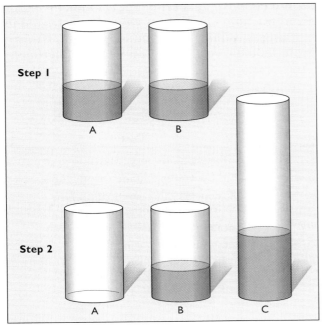

Furthermore, research on other cultures has revealed both striking similarities and marked differences in the performance of children on various cognitive tasks. Certain aspects of cognitive development among children in these cultures seem to conflict with particular assumptions of Piagetian theory (Ashton, 1975; Chapman, 1988; Dasen, 1977; Fischer & Silvern, 1985). We should remember that no theory, particularly one that provides such a comprehensive explanation of development, can be expected to withstand the tests of further investigation without undergoing some criticism (Beilin, 1989, 1990; Daehler & Bukatko, 1985; Halford, 1989, 1990).

It is still relatively soon to determine the ultimate impact that Piaget's theory will have on our understanding of cognitive development. Yet we must recognize that we would not know as much as we do about children's intellectual development without the monumental contributions of Piaget. He noted many ways in which children seem to differ from adults, and he shed light on how adults acquire fundamental concepts such as space, time, morality, and causality (Sugarman, 1987). Contemporary researchers have attempted to integrate aspects of Piaget's theory and cognition learning and information-processing theories (Brown, 1988; Demtrious, 1988; Shulman, Restaino-Baumann & Butler, 1985). However, Piaget's greatest contribution may not have been his theory. His emphasis on the active nature of the child has had a powerful impact on psychological theory and research. And his work directed psychologists to a set of fascinating tasks and questions. Although Piaget's explanations may in some instances be wrong, his work got psychologists interested enough to do the research necessary for better understanding of children's cognitive development.

Table 2-3 summarizes the developmental stages of Freud, Erikson, and Piaget.

Cognitive Learning and Information Processing

Piaget's work gave a major impetus to cognitive psychology. Increasingly, psychologists are directing their attention to the part played by inner, mental activity in human behavior. They are finding, for instance, that mental schemes—variously termed "scripts" or "frames"—function as selective mechanisms that influence the information individuals attend to, how they structure it, how much importance they attach to it, and what they then do with it (Markus, 1977; Vander Zanden, 1987). And as we noted earlier in the chapter, psychologists are also finding that learning consists of much more than merely bringing two events together. People are not simply acted upon by external stimuli. They actively evaluate different stimuli and devise their actions accordingly.

Classic behavioral theory also fails to explain many changes in our behavior that result from interaction with people in a social context. Indeed, if we learned solely by direct experience—by the reward or punishment for our actions—most of us would not survive to adulthood. If, for example, we depended on direct experience to learn how to cross the street, most of us would already be traffic fatalities. Similarly, we probably could not develop skill in playing baseball, driving a car, solving mathematical problems, carrying out chemistry experiments, cooking meals, or even brushing our teeth if we were restricted to learning through direct reinforcement. We can avoid tedious, costly, trial-and-error experimen-

Table 2-3

Developmental Stages of Freud, Erikson, and Piaget			
Age Period	Freud	Erikson	Piaget
Birth to 18 months	Oral stage	Trust vs. mistrust	Sensorimotor stage (birth to 2 years)
18 months to year 3	Anal stage	Autonomy vs. shame and doubt	Preoperational stage (symbolic)
Years 3 to 7	Phallic stage	Initiative vs. guilt	Preoperational stage (intuition, representational)
Years 7 to 12	Latency stage	Industry vs. inferiority	Stage of concrete operations
Years 12 to 18	Genital stage	Identity vs. role confusion	Stage of formal thought
Young adulthood		Intimacy vs. isolation	
Middle adulthood		Generativity vs. stagnation	
Old age		Integrity vs. despair	

Cognitive Learning

Through instruction we can learn a good many behaviors, such as how to cross a street safely. If we had to learn this behavior through trial-and-error procedures, most of us would be traffic fatalities. *(Alan Carey/The Image Works)*

tation by imitating the behavior of socially competent models. By watching other people, we learn new responses without first having had the opportunity to make the responses ourselves. This process is termed **cognitive learning.** (It is also termed *observational learning, social learning,* and *modeling.*) The approach is represented by the work of theorists such as Albert Bandura (1977, 1986, 1989; Bandura & Cervone, 1983), Walter Mischel (1971, 1973), and Ted L. Rosenthal and Barry J. Zimmerman (1978).

Cognitive learning theorists say that our capacity to use symbols affords us a powerful means for comprehending and dealing with our environment. Language and imagery allow us to represent events, to analyze our conscious experience, to communicate with others, to plan, to create, to imagine, and to engage in foresightful action. Symbols are the foundation of reflective thought

and enable us to solve problems without first having to enact all the various solutions (Bandura, 1977). Indeed, stimuli and reinforcements exert little impact on our behavior unless we first represent them mentally (Rosenthal & Zimmerman, 1978).

Evolutionary Adaptation Theory

Historically, psychologists have focused primarily on the environmental influences that come to bear on organisms in fashioning and directing their behavior. But over the past decade they have paid increasing attention to the part that biological patterns play in enhancing an organism's adaptation to a particular environment. The adaptation involves changes in species rather than in individual organisms. Adaptation approaches view human behavior as the unique product of our evolutionary history. We behave as we do because our species has evolved in human ways.

Adaptation theories rest on the theory of evolution advanced in 1859 by the English naturalist Charles Darwin. Darwin proposed a specific mechanism by which adaptation occurs—**natural selection.** The idea behind natural selection is a remarkably simple one. The different organisms produce more offspring than the available resources can support. Since a habitat can support only a limited number of organisms, each one must compete for a "place." Those that are best adapted to the environment survive and pass on their genetic characteristics to their offspring. The others perish, with few or no offspring. So later generations resemble their better-adapted ancestors. The result is evolutionary change. Ethology and sociobiology are major outgrowths of Darwinian theory.

Ethology

Ethology is the study of the behavior patterns of organisms from a biological point of view. Behavior is seen as part of the adaptational package of an organism and as necessary for its survival as its heartbeat or its skeletal structure. Ethologists say that natural selection molds a species' behavior in accordance with environmental costs and benefits. Consequently, organisms are *genetically prepared* for some responses (Eibl-

Eibesfeldt, 1989). For instance, learning in many insects and higher animals is often guided by information inherent in the genetic makeup of the organism. It is preprogrammed to learn particular things and to learn them in particular ways. As we will see in Chapter 7, Noam Chomsky says that the basic structure of human language is biologically channeled by an inborn language-generating mechanism. Such a mechanism helps to explain why the learning of speech proceeds so easily compared with the learning of inherently simpler tasks such as addition and subtraction. Comparable patterns are found in other animals. Early behaviorists thought any behavior an animal is physically capable of performing can be taught by means of conditioning. But this is not the case. Rats readily learn to press a bar for food, but they cannot learn to press a bar in order to avoid an electric shock. Conversely, they can be trained to jump in order to avoid a shock but not to obtain food. In brief, animals are innately prepared to learn some things more readily than others (Gould & Marler, 1987; MacDonald, 1988).

Ethologists also hold that human babies are biologically preadapted with behavior systems like crying, smiles, and coos that elicit caring by adults. Similarly, babies' being "cute"—with large heads, small bodies, and distinctive facial features—induce others to want to pick them up and cuddle them. Ethologists call these behaviors and features **releasing stimuli.** They function as especially potent activators of parenting.

A number of psychologists, among whom John Bowlby (1969) is perhaps the most prominent, compare the development of strong bonds of attachment between human caretakers and their offspring to the process of imprinting encountered among some bird and animal species. **Imprinting** is a process of attachment that occurs only during a relatively short period and is so resistant to change that the behavior appears to be innate. Konrad Lorenz (1935), the Nobel Prize-winning ethologist, has shown that there is a short period of time early in the lives of goslings and ducklings in which they begin slavishly to follow the first moving object that they see—their mother, a human being, a rubber ball, or whatever. Once this imprinting has occurred, it is irreversible. The object becomes "Mother Goose" to the birds, so that thereafter they prefer it to all others and in fact will follow no other. Imprinting (Lorenz uses his native German word *"Prägung,"* which literally means "stamping in") is different from other forms of learning in at least two ways. First, imprinting can take place only during a relatively short period, termed a **critical period.** (For example, the peak period for the imprinting effect among domestic chickens occurs about seventeen hours after hatching and declines rapidly thereafter.) Second, as already mentioned, imprinting is irreversible; it is highly resistant to change, so that the behavior appears to be innate.

Some developmental psychologists have applied ethological notions to human development. However, many prefer the term **sensitive period** to "critical period," for it implies greater flexibility in the time dimension and greater reversibility in the later structure (Oyama, 1979). According to this concept, during certain times of life particular kinds of experience are believed to affect the development of an organism more than they do at other times (Bornstein, 1989; Colombo, 1982). As discussed in the section on Freud, the notion of sensitive periods occupies a central position in psychoanalytic thought. It was Freud's view that infancy is the crucial period in molding an individual's personality. It was the basis of his famous aphorism "No adult neurosis without an infantile neurosis."

Theorists who adhere to the view of sensitive periods generally insist that it is almost impossi-

Programmed to Elicit Parenting?
The noted ethologist Konrad Lorenz believed that human beings are genetically programmed for parenting behavior. It seems that caretaking tendencies are aroused by "cuteness." When Lorenz compared human infants with other young animals, including kittens and puppies, he noticed that they all seem to display a similar set of sign stimuli that arouse parental response. Apparently, short faces, prominent foreheads, round eyes, and plump cheeks all stir up parental feelings. *(Sybil Shackman/Monkmeyer)*

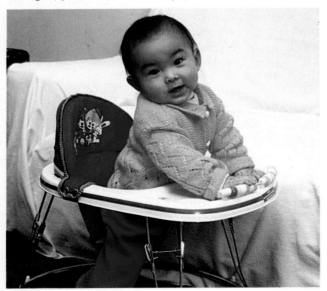

Konrad Lorenz
Here young ducklings follow the eminent Austrian ethologist rather than their mother. Since he was the first moving object that they saw during the critical imprinting period, they came to prefer him to all other objects. *(Thomas McAvoy/Time-Life Picture Agency, © Time, Inc.)*

ble to make up a deficit in a person's development at some later period (Bower, 1974; B. L. White, 1975). However, most life-span developmentalists reject the idea that the first five years of a child's life are all-important. Recent research suggests that the long-term effects of short, traumatic incidents are generally negligible in young children (Douglas, Ross & Simpson, 1968; Thomas & Chess, 1984; Werner & Smith, 1982). And Jerome Kagan comes to a somewhat similar conclusion on the basis of studies that he and his associates conducted in Guatemala (see the boxed insert on page 56). Life apparently offers many individuals a healing capacity, so that they arrive at adulthood without substantial psychological maladjustment. Thus, while all authorities agree that development is influenced by the

child's early experiences, considerable debate rages over just how important these experiences are. Chapter 8 returns to the matter of critical periods in considering attachment, sensory deprivation, and maternal deprivation in early childhood.

Sociobiology

Sociobiology, closely related to ethology (Bell & Bell, 1989; Crawford & Anderson, 1989), is a new and controversial discipline that focuses on the biological foundations of social behavior in species ranging from amoeba colonies to human societies. The novelist Samuel Butler once remarked that "the chick is only an egg's way of making another egg." In the same vein, sociobiology views organisms as only the genes' way of making more genes. It depicts organisms primarily as survival machines for genes. Individual organisms may die, but their genes live on in future generations. The key to the entire process is survival, life's first order of business. To survive—and thus pass on their genes to offspring—organisms must be able to function in their habitat. And if they are to fit better in their environment, organisms must adapt by changing across time.

Sociobiologists apply Darwin's notion of natural selection to social life (Belsky, Steinberg & Draper, 1991; Degler, 1991). They say that natural selection acts on *groups* as well as individuals. The entire group is constantly being tested for its capacity to survive and reproduce in a given environment. Individuals who possess behaviors consistent with group survival have an advantage in their own survival and reproduction. As a consequence, complex group-oriented patterns have evolved, and these patterns are encoded in the genes of each species. Natural selection acts directly not on behavior but on the genes that assemble the organs and structures that make behavior possible.

The sociobiologist Edward O. Wilson (1975, 1984) suggests that a hereditary basis may underlie many kinds of social behavior, including "cannibalism" and "infanticide" among bees, "castes" and "slavery" among ants, "harem formation" in baboon societies, and "homosexuality," "male dominance," "incest avoidance," and "war" among human beings. Consider how he evaluates altruism—self-sacrificing behavior that helps to ensure the survival of other members of one's own species. Wilson notes that a honeybee worker will attack an intruder at the hive with its fishhook-shaped sting. The bee dies, but its sting

Jerome Kagan
on the Early Years

Most Americans—both psychologists and the general public—believe that early experience etches an indelible mark upon the mind. A long intellectual tradition in Western culture has portrayed the adult as locked in a core personality fashioned before the age of 6. It is thus hardly surprising that a good many American parents experience considerable anxiety and guilt over the adequacy of their child rearing.

Jerome Kagan (1984), a Harvard University developmental psychologist, challenges the prevailing belief (also see Bradley, Caldwell & Rock, 1988; Robins & Rutter, 1990; Sroufe, Egeland & Kreutzer, 1990). Since 1971 he and his associates have done research among children in Guatemala. This work has led Kagan to conclude that children are considerably more resilient than we think (Kagan, 1984; Kagan & Klein, 1973).

Among the children Kagan studied is a group in San Marcos, an isolated Indian village on Lake Atitlán. During the first year of life these infants spend most of their time in the small, dark interiors of windowless huts. Their mothers are busy with domestic chores and rarely speak to their babies or play with them. Since the Indians believe that the outside sun, air, and dust are harmful, children are rarely permitted to crawl on the hut floors or to venture beyond the doorway.

Judged by U.S. standards, the infants appear to be severely retarded. They seem undernourished, listless, apathetic, fearful, dour, and extraordinarily quiet. Indeed, to Kagan the children have a ghostlike quality. Both observations and tests suggest that they are 3 to 12 months behind U.S. children in acquiring various psychological and cognitive skills. These skills range from the simple ability to pay attention all the way up to the development of meaningful speech.

Nonetheless, Kagan finds that by age 11 the children show no traces of their early "retardation." On tests of perceptual inference, perceptual analysis, recall, and recognition, they perform in a manner comparable to U.S. middle-class children. According to Kagan, they begin to overcome their early retardation when they become mobile at around 15 months. They leave the dark huts and begin to play with other children, and in the ensuing years they experience challenges that demand and foster intellectual growth and development.

Kagan suggests that a child's experiences can slow down or speed up the emergence of basic abilities by several months or even years. But, he argues, nature will win out in the end. Thus, Kagan reaches the highly controversial conclusion that children are biologically preprogrammed with basic mental competencies—an inherent blueprint that equips them with the essentials for perceptual and intellectual functioning. The content of this functioning changes from culture to culture (Kagan & Klein, 1973, p. 960):

> The San Marcos child knows much less than the American about planes, computers, cars, and the many hundreds of other phenomena that are familiar to the Western youngster, and he is a little slower in developing some of the basic cognitive competencies of our species. But neither appreciation of these events nor the earlier cognitive maturation is necessary for a successful journey to adulthood in San Marcos. The American child knows far less about how to make canoes, rope, tortillas, or how to burn an old milpa in preparation for June planting. Each knows what is necessary, each assimilates the cognitive conflicts that are presented to him, and each seems to have the potential to display more talent than his environment demands of him.

Kagan (1973) also points to the findings of Freda

remains embedded in the flesh of the enemy and continues to leak poison into the wound. The suicide of the individual bee supports the survival of the colony as a whole. Similarly, robins, thrushes, and titmice give warning signals to others of their kind should a hawk appear, thereby drawing the predator's attention to themselves. And during wars human beings are known to throw themselves on top of grenades to shield comrades or aid the rescue of others at the price of certain death to themselves.

Altruistic behavior has long been a puzzle for classical Darwinian theorists. Why should al-truism evolve if it entails surrendering one's own life? Individuals displaying self-sacrificing behavior would die out, while selfish ones would survive and prosper. Wilson provides the answer: In the course of evolution natural selection has been broadened from individual selection to kin selection. **Kin selection** means that evolution favors genes that improve the chances of a *group's* survival. It is irrelevant whether an advantageous gene is passed on to the next generation by a particular individual or by a close relative who has an identical gene. Because all the members of the family or group *share* the gene for self-sacri-

Guatemalan Indian Children
By American standards Guatemalan Indian children's early experiences are devoid of surroundings that stimulate their psychological and intellectual development. Even so, youngsters like the eleven-year-olds shown here appear normally adjusted and healthy. *(C.S. Perkins/Magnum)*

Rebelsky, a developmental psychologist who spent several years in eastern Holland, where a stable, middle-class, nuclear family arrangement prevails. She reported that in one region it is a local custom to isolate a child for the first 10 months. Children are placed in a room outside the house and tightly bound with no mobiles or toys and minimal human interaction. Like the Guatemalan children, these Dutch children emerge at 1 year "retarded," but at 5 years of age they are fully recovered.

Kagan says that his research has implications for the United States' educational problems. He suggests that the poor test performance of economically impoverished and minority-group children should not be taken as evidence of permanent or irreversible defects in intellectual ability. Although various competencies may lag behind those of middle-class children, Kagan concludes that those competencies eventually appear in lower-class children by age 10 or 11. To class children arbitrarily at age 7 as competent or incompetent makes as much sense, Kagan insists, as classifying children as reproductively fertile or sterile depending on whether they have reached physiological puberty by age 13. His conclusions also constitute a mixed blessing for parents. On the one hand, they suggest that unfortunate facts of early childhood do not dictate a blighted adulthood. On the other hand, they also suggest that the effects of good parenting, above a certain threshold, probably do not make a great difference.

ficing behavior, the larger social unit survives even though a few individual members may not. These survivors in turn multiply and transmit altruistic genes to later generations. So a mother who dies in rescuing her three children from a fire sacrifices one copy of her genetic message, but she saves three copies—the three offspring, each carrying all her genes.

Critics raise a number of objections to attempts by sociobiologists to explain human social behavior in biological terms (Kitcher, 1987). For one thing, since human beings share a common genetic heritage, how are we to explain the vast cultural differences among societies? And how are we to explain the rapid changes that occur in the behavior of the members of the same society across time? The answers to these questions, say critics, rest largely with *learning*. When a spider spins a web to catch flies, it acts primarily on instinct. When we weave nets to catch fish, we are acting primarily on learned skills transmitted culturally from one generation to another. Human evolution is unique in that our species gradually evolved biological capacities that have allowed us to create culture and society. Once cultural and social forces were set in motion, we were freed from many of the constraints posed by a fixed biological heritage. Put in psychological terms, our mind has increasingly become an all-purpose reasoning machine.

Critics also raise another point. They see sociobiology as a naive social philosophy fraught with political danger (Lewontin, Rose & Kamin, 1984). To them, sociobiology sounds suspiciously like Social Darwinism, a nineteen-century evolutionary theory that confused social privilege with genetic superiority. Throughout history, people have used related notions of biological determinism as a justification for slavery, for the "final solution" of the "Jewish problem," and for the racism and sexism that persist today. In the 1920s the eugenics movement promised to improve the human species through selective breeding but ended up in the horrible concentration camp "medical experiments" of Josef Mengele in Hitler's Germany. Critics of sociobiology hear an ominous echo in recent advances in genetic engineering that can select and enhance certain genetic characteristics. Already in Singapore the government rewards people who have anything less than a university education for agreeing to be sterilized after the birth of their first or second child, while parents with degrees are given incentives to have large families. Prime Minister Lee Kuan Yew promotes the policy, saying that gradual genetic deterioration will cause Singapore's national "levels of competence" to drop. "Our economy will falter, the administration will suffer, and the society will decline," argues Lee (Wellborn, 1987).

Theoretical Controversy

A clash of doctrines is not a disaster— it is an opportunity.—ALFRED NORTH WHITEHEAD

We have considered five major types of theory dealing with human development. Psychoanalytic theories draw our attention to the importance of early experience in the fashioning of personality and to the role of unconscious motivation. Behavioral theories emphasize the part that learning plays in prompting people to act in the ways that they do. Humanistic theories remind us that individuals are capable of intervening in the course of life's events to influence and shape their own beings. Cognitive theories highlight the importance of various mental capabilities and problem-solving skills that arm human beings with a powerful adaptive and coping potential. And evolutionary adaptation theories allow us to bring into focus various biological patterns that predispose and prepare human beings for particular kinds of behavior.

Each theory has its proponents and its critics. Yet the theories are not mutually exclusive. We need not accept one and reject the others. As we pointed out at the beginning of the chapter, theories are simply tools—mental constructs that allow us to visualize (that is, to describe and analyze) something. Any theory limits the viewer's experience, presenting a tunnel perspective. But a good theory also extends the horizon of what is seen, functioning like a pair of binoculars. It provides rules of inference through which new relationships can be discovered and suggestions as to how the scope of a theory can be expanded.

Furthermore, different tasks call for different theories. For instance, behavioral theory helps us to understand why U.S. children typically learn English and Russian children learn Russian. At the same time, ethological theory directs our attention to ways in which the human organism is neurally prewired for certain activities. Hence, in interaction with an appropriate environment, young children typically find that their acquisition of language comes rather "naturally"—a type of *easy learning*. Simultaneously, psychoanalytic theory alerts us to personality differences and to differing child-rearing practices that influence a child's learning to talk. Cognitive theory encourages us to consider the stages of development and the mental processes that are involved in the acquisition of language. Finally, humanistic theory reminds us that individuals are not passive beings mechanically buffeted about by environmental and biological forces but are themselves creative beings who actively pursue language competence. The distinction between mechanistic and organismic models helps to clarify some of these distinctions.

Mechanistic and Organismic Models

Some psychologists attempt to classify developmental theories in terms of two basic categories: a mechanistic world view and an organismic world view (see Table 2-4). The **mechanistic model** represents the universe as a machine composed of elementary particles in motion. All phenomena, no matter how complex, are viewed as ultimately reducible to these fundamental units and their relationships. Each human being is regarded as a physical object, a kind of elaborate machine. Like other parts of the universal machine, the organism is inherently at rest. It is

Table 2-4

Mechanistic and Organismic Paradigms		
Characteristic	Mechanistic Paradigm	Organismic Paradigm
Metaphor	The machine	The organism
Focus	The parts	The whole
Source of motivation	Intrinsically passive	Intrinsically active
Nature of development	Gradual, uninterrupted adding, subtracting, or altering of parts (continuity)	discrete, steplike levels or states (discontinuity)

inherently passive and only responds when an external power source is applied. This view is *the reactive organism model.* In keeping with this world view, human development is portrayed as a gradual, uninterrupted, chainlike sequence of events. Indeed, one can question whether a machine can be said to "develop." It only changes by some external agent adding, subtracting, or altering the machine's parts (Sameroff & Cavanagh, 1979). Change, then, cannot occur without influence from the environment. Individual differences are the central focus of mechanistic approaches. Behavioral learning theories fall within this tradition.

The **organismic model** focuses not on elementary particles but on the whole. It is the distinctive interrelation between the lower-level components that is seen as imparting to the whole characteristics not found in the components alone. Hence, the whole differs in kind from its parts. The human being is seen as an organized configuration. The organism is inherently active. It is the source of its own acts rather than being activated by external forces. This view is *the active organism model.* Viewed from this perspective, human development is characterized by discrete, steplike levels or states. Human beings are portrayed as developing by constantly restructuring themselves. The new structures that will be formed are determined by the interaction between the environment and the organism (Gandour, 1989; Gottlieb, 1991). The stage theories of Freud, Erikson, and Piaget fall within the organismic tradition.

Proponents of mechanistic and of organismic models practice their trades in somewhat different worlds. Even so, in recognition of the many strands associated with development, most psychologists prefer an **eclectic approach.** This perspective allows them to select and choose from the various theories and models those aspects that provide the best fit for the descriptive and analytical task at hand. Perhaps we can gain a better understanding and appreciation of these controversies by considering an illustration, continuity and discontinuity in development.

Continuity and Discontinuity in Development

Most psychologists agree that development entails orderly sequences of change that depend on growth and maturation as individuals interact with their environment. But in examining developmental sequences, some psychologists focus on their continuity, whereas others emphasize their discontinuity. Those who stress continuity typically fall within the mechanistic camp; those who accentuate discontinuity usually fall within the organismic camp. The former view development as producing smooth, gradual, and incremental change. The latter depict development as a series of steps with clear-cut, even abrupt, changes occurring from one phase to the next.

The two different models of development can be clarified by considering two analogies. The continuous model of development is analogous to the growth of a leaf. After a leaf sprouts from a seed, it grows by simply becoming larger. The change is gradual and uninterrupted. Psychologists who emphasize the part that learning plays in behavior tend to take this point of view. They see the learning process as lacking sharp developmental states between infancy and adulthood. Learning is cumulative, building on itself.

The discontinuous model of development is analogous to the developmental changes that occur in a butterfly. Once a caterpillar hatches from an egg, it feeds on vegetation. After a time it fastens itself to a twig and spins a cocoon within which the pupa develops. One day the pupal covering splits open and the butterfly emerges. Psychologists who adopt the discontinuous model see human development as similar to the process of insect metamorphosis. Each individual is seen

"There's a butterfly all squished up inside that caterpillar just waitin' to get out."

("Family Circus" © 1991 Bill Keane, Inc. Reprinted with special permission of King Features Syndicate.)

mental changes that occur within the cocoon, we have a different impression. We see that butterflylike characteristics are gradually acquired, and consequently, we are more likely to describe the process as continuous (Lewis & Starr, 1979). However, if we look at a seed and then a tree, we are impressed by the magnitude of the change that has occurred.

Increasingly, psychologists are less inclined to divide themselves into sharply opposed camps on the issue of continuity and discontinuity in development. They too recognize that much depends on one's vantage point and hence see both continuities and discontinuities across the life span. Indeed, many studies have shown that development demonstrates some stagelike properties and some consistency across domains (Baumrind, 1989; Fischer & Silvern, 1985; Sternberg & Okagaski, 1989). Thus, "either-or" debates are misconceived. Several psychologists have combined the search for a common sequential order from conception to death with a concern for differences in the way that individuals negotiate and experience the various stages (Neugarten & Neugarten, 1987; Radke-Yarrow, 1989; Rosenfeld & Stark, 1987; Sroufe & Jacobvitz, 1989). The approach to adult development taken by Daniel J. Levinson and his associates at Yale University reflects this latter orientation (see Chapters 15–20). In sum, then, social and behavioral scientists increasingly have come to see development as residing in a relation between organism and environment—in a transaction or collaboration: People work with and affect their environment; and in turn, it works with and affects them (Fischer & Silvern, 1985). We continue our consideration of the interplay between nature and nurture in the next chapter.

as passing through a set sequence of stages in which change constitutes a difference of kind rather than merely of degree. Each stage is characterized by a distinct and unique state in ego formation, identity, or thought. The theories of Sigmund Freud, Erik Erikson, and Jean Piaget are of this sort.

How we view development depends in part on our vantage point. To return to our analogies, when we first observe a caterpillar and then a butterfly, we are struck by the dramatic qualitative change. But when we observe the develop-

SUMMARY

1. Theory is a tool that allows us to organize a large array of facts so that we can understand them. To understand how nature works is to gain the prospect of securing some control over our destiny.

2. Sigmund Freud postulated that all human beings pass through a series of psychosexual stages: oral, anal, phallic, latency, and genital. Each stage poses a unique conflict that the individual must resolve before passing on to the next stage.

3. Critics complain that Freudian theory is difficult to evaluate because it makes few predictions that can be tested by accepted scientific procedures. Nonetheless, Freud's work is generally regarded as a revolutionary milestone in the history of human thought.

4. Erik Erikson, a theorist in the psychoanalytic tradition, identifies eight psychosocial stages, each of which confronts the individual with a major conflict that must be successfully resolved if healthy development is to occur. Erikson's theory draws our attention to the continual process of personality development that takes place throughout a person's life span.

5. Behavioral theory stands in sharp contrast to psychoanalytic theory. Its proponents believe that if psychology is to be a science, it must not rely on introspection but must look to data that are directly observable and measurable.

6. Behaviorists are especially interested in how people learn to behave in particular ways. They deem learning to be a process whereby individuals, as a result of their experience, establish an association or linkage between two events, a process called "conditioning." Behaviorists such as B. F. Skinner divide the environment into units termed "stimuli" and the behavior elicited by stimuli into units termed "responses."

7. Humanistic psychology—also called "third-force" psychology—has arisen in reaction to psychoanalysis and behaviorism. It maintains that human beings are different from all other organisms in that they actively intervene in the course of events to control their destinies and to shape the world around them. Its proponents seek to maximize the human potential for self-direction and freedom of choice.

8. Jean Piaget has come to be recognized as a giant of twentieth-century psychology. For Piaget the critical question in the study of growing children is how they adjust to the world they live in. Scheme, assimilation, accommodation, and equilibrium are key concepts in Paigetian theory. They find expression in four stages of cognitive development: the sensorimotor stage, the preoperational stage, the stage of concrete operations, and the stage of formal operations.

9. Cognitive learning theorists say that our capacity to use symbols affords us a powerful means for comprehending and dealing with our environment. Verbal and imagined symbols allow us to represent events; to analyze our conscious experience; to communicate with others; to plan, to create, to imagine; and to engage in foresightful action.

10. Evolutionary adaptation theory studies the behavior patterns of organisms from a biological point of view. Its proponents rely heavily on the evolutionary theory of Charles Darwin. Ethologists say that evolution applies not only to anatomy and physiology but also to predispositions for certain types of behavior. Organisms are said to be genetically prepared for some responses. Closely related to ethology is sociobiology, whose proponents focus on the biological foundations of social behavior.

11. Each of the five major types of theory we considered has its proponents and critics. Yet the theories are not mutually exclusive; we need not accept one and reject the others. Different tasks simply call for different theories. Thus, most psychologists prefer an eclectic approach to development.

KEY TERMS

Accommodation A central concept in Piagetian theory; the process, in cognitive development, of changing a scheme (mental model) to achieve a better match to the world of reality.

Assimilation A central concept in Piagetian theory; the process, in cognitive development, of taking in new information and interpreting it in such a manner that the information conforms to a currently held scheme (mental model) of the world.

Behavior Modification An approach that applies the results of learning theory and experimental psychology to the problem of altering maladaptive behavior.

Behavioral Theory An approach that is concerned with the behavior of people—what they say and do. Proponents say that if psychology is to be a science, its data must be directly observable and measurable.

Cognition The process or act of knowing; our reception of raw sensory information and our transformation, elaboration, storage, recovery, and use of this information.

Cognitive Learning Our learning of new responses without first having had the opportunity to make the responses ourselves. Cognitive learning is accomplished by watching other people.

Cognitive Stages in Development Sequential periods in the growth or maturing of an individual's ability to engage in thinking (to gain knowledge and awareness of oneself and one's environment).

Cognitive Theory The approach to mental activity that stresses the part that sensation, perception, imagery, retention, recall, problem solving, reasoning, and thinking play in behavior.

Conditioning The process whereby individuals, as a result of their experience, establish an association or linkage between two events.

Critical Period A certain time in life when specific

experiences affect the development of an organism more than they do at other times.

Eclectic Approach A perspective that allows scientists to select and choose from various theories those aspects that provide the best fit for the descriptive and analytical task at hand.

Epigenetic Principle The notion that each aspect of development must develop at a particular time in the life span if it is going to develop at all. Should the capacity not be developed on schedule, the rest of development is unfavorably altered.

Equilibrium A central concept in Piagetian theory; a state of balance between the processes of assimilation and accommodation.

Ethology The study of the behavior patterns of organisms from a biological point of view.

Fixation A central concept in Freudian theory; the tendency to experience, throughout life, tension and its reduction by means of behavior that had great significance during an earlier period of one's life.

Hierarchy of Needs Maslow's concept that human beings have certain basic needs that must be met before they can go on to fulfill other needs. The result is a "pyramid of needs."

Holistic Approach A perspective that views the human condition in its totality and each person as more than a collection of physical, social, and psychological components.

Humanistic Psychology A psychological school of thought that stresses the uniqueness of the human condition, maintaining that human beings, unlike other organisms, actively intervene in the course of events to control their destinies and shape the world around them.

Imprinting A process of attachment that occurs only during a relatively short period and is so resistant to change that the behavior appears to be innate.

Kin Selection The process of evolution put forth by Edward O. Wilson. Evolution favors genes that improve the chances of a group's survival.

Learned Helplessness A generalized expectancy that events are independent of one's own responses.

Mechanistic Model The world view that represents the universe as a machine composed of elementary particles in motion. It portrays human development as a gradual, uninterrupted, chainlike sequence of events and the organism as a reactive being.

Natural Selection The process of evolution described by Charles Darwin. Individuals who are best adapted to their environment stand a better chance of surviving and reproducing than do individuals without these characteristics.

Organismic Model The world view that represents the universe as a whole made up of interactive parts. It is the distinctive interrelation between the lower-level components that is seen as imparting to the whole characteristics not found in the components alone. This model portrays the organism as an active being.

Peak Experience A rapturous feeling of excitement, insight, and happiness experienced by self-actualized individuals; a notion advanced by Abraham Maslow.

Psychoanalytic Theory The view advanced by Sigmund Freud that personality is fashioned in progressive steps, or stages, as an individual passes through the oral, anal, phallic, latency, and genital periods. Unconscious motivation—stemming from impulses buried below the level of awareness—is believed to play a powerful part in such development.

Psychosexual Stages A series of steps or periods, postulated by Sigmund Freud, through which all individuals pass and that are dominated by the development of sensitivity in a particular erogenous zone of the body. The stages are the oral, anal, phallic, latency, and genital periods.

Reinforcement The process whereby one event strengthens the probability of another event's occurring.

Releasing Stimulus An environmental event that functions to activate innately preprogrammed behavior.

Response A unit into which behavior is divided; a concept employed by behaviorists.

Scheme A central concept of Piagetian theory; a cognitive structure that people evolve for dealing with specific kinds of situations in their environment.

Self-Actualization A notion advanced by Abraham Maslow that each individual has a basic need to develop his or her potential to the fullest.

Sensitive Period A certain time in life when particular kinds of experience affect the development of an organism somewhat more than they do at other times.

Sociobiology A new and controversial discipline that focuses on the biological foundations of social behavior in species ranging from amoeba colonies to human societies.

Stages A series of age-related phases or steplike levels, with clear-cut changes in behavior associated with each phase or level.

Stimulus A unit into which the environment is divided; a concept employed by behaviorists.

Theory A set of interrelated statements that provides an explanation for a class of events.

BIOLOGICAL
FOUNDATIONS

Chapter 3

BIOLOGICAL FOUNDATIONS

Reproduction

Reproductive Systems ♦ Fertilization ♦ Infertility and Its Treatment ♦

Genetic Counseling and Testing

Heredity-Environment Interactions

The "Which" Question ♦ The "How Much" Question ♦ The "How" Question

Appendix A: Genetics and Heredity

♦

Today, scientists and engineers are building computerized robots that promise to surpass humans in some capabilities. Such machines can assimilate and retrieve vast quantities of information. And they can perform a good many tasks more efficiently and precisely than can human hands. Some can move about and even mimic the human voice. Yet robots do not "know" anything, nor do they appreciate the significance of anything. They do what they are told and no more. Nor do robots display emotions, feel love, or experience loneliness. In sum, human beings have unique and distinctive properties. To understand these properties, we must begin with a consideration of our biological foundations.

Reproduction

Life goes on and on. Like all other living things, human beings are capable of producing new individuals and thus ensuring the survival of the species. **Reproduction** is the term that biologists use for the process by which organisms create more organisms of their own kind. Biologists depict reproduction as the most important result of all life processes.

Reproductive Systems

Two kinds of sex cells, or *gametes*, are involved in human reproduction: the male gamete, or

sperm, and the female gamete, which is called the *ovum* (egg). A male sperm fuses with a female ovum to form a *zygote* (fertilized egg). A sperm cell is minute. It consists of an oval head, a whip-like tail, and a connecting middle piece, or collar. A sperm cell moves by lashing its tail. A normal

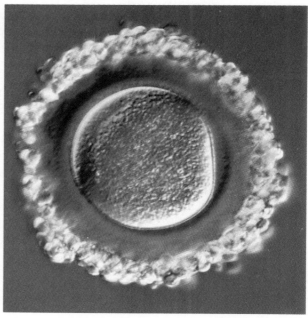

The Ovum
The egg cell is the largest human cell. Other cells are only one-tenth the size of the ovum, which is between 0.1 and 0.2 millimeter in diameter. A protective membrane surrounds the egg cell. A number of yolk granules can be seen in the cytoplasm. *(Lennart Nilsson, from* Behold Man, Little, Brown, *1974)*

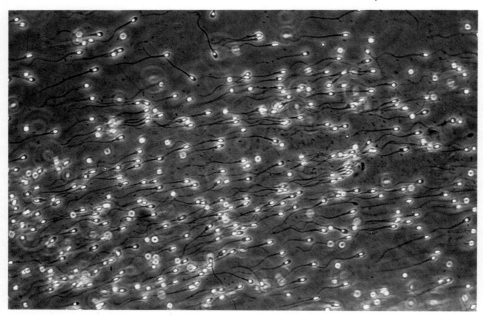

Sperm
Sperm are unusually small cells with very little cytoplasm. Once sperm are ejaculated with semen into the female reproductive tract, they make their way through the cervical canal and than ascend the uterus and oviducts. Of the millions of sperm entering the vagina, only a few thousand complete the journey, and only one succeeds in penetrating the ovum. *(Lennart Nilsson, from* Behold Man, Little, Brown, *1974)*

adult man's testes may produce as many as 300 million or more mature sperm each day.

Ova, on the other hand, are not self-propelled. They contain yolk, the stored food substance that sustains the fetus early in its development. During the embryonic period the developing ovaries of females produce more than 400,000 immature ova. During a woman's fertile years between puberty and menopause, one ovum matures and is released each month. Hence, only some 400 to 500 of the immature ova ultimately reach maturity. The rest degenerate and are absorbed by the body.

The primary male reproductive organs are a pair of testes lying in a pouchlike structure, the *scrotum.* The scrotum is an outpocket of the abdominal cavity (see Figure 3-1). The testes produce sperm and the male sex hormones, called *androgens.* (The principal hormones are testosterone and androsterone.) The androgens are responsible for producing masculine secondary sexual characteristics, including facial and body hair.

Sperm are produced in winding tubules, within each testis. They are then emptied into the *epididymis,* a long, slender, twisted tube, where they are stored. During ejaculation the sperm pass from the epididymis along muscular ducts into the *urethra.* On the way they are mixed with secretions from the *seminal vesicles* and the *prostate gland.* The mixture of the sperm and secretions is termed *semen.* The urethra—a tube that also connects with the bladder—is surrounded by the external reproductive organ, the *penis.*

The primary female reproductive organs are a pair of ovaries—almond-shaped structures that lie in the pelvis (see Figure 3-2). The ovaries produce mature ova and the female sex hormones, *estrogen* and *progesterone.* These hormones are responsible for the development of female secondary characteristics, including the breasts (mammary glands).

Figure 3-1   The Male Reproductive System
This cross section of the male pelvic region shows the organs of reproduction.

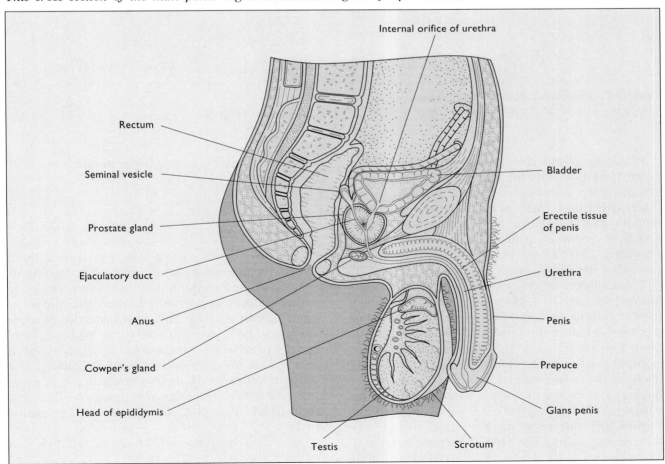

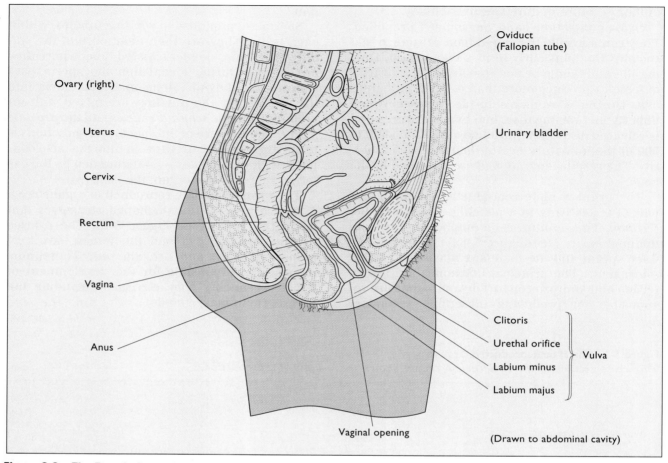

Figure 3-2   The Female Reproductive System
This cross section of the female pelvic region shows the organs of reproduction.

When an ovum is expelled from one of the ovaries, it passes into the abdominal cavity where it is drawn in a siphonlike action into an *oviduct* (Fallopian tube). Each ovary is paired with one oviduct, and it is in the oviduct that fertilization occurs if sperm are present. The oviduct is lined with tiny, hairlike projections, *cilia*, that propel the ovum along its course.

The oviducts are connected with the *uterus*, a hollow, thick-walled, muscular organ that houses the developing embryo. The narrow lower end of the uterus, called the *cervix*, projects into the vagina. The *vagina* is a muscular passageway that is capable of considerable dilation. The penis is inserted into the vagina during sexual intercourse, and the infant passes through the vagina at birth. Surrounding the external opening of the vagina are the external genitalia, collectively termed the *vulva*. The vulva contains the fleshy folds, known as the *labia*, and the *clitoris* (a small

erectile structure comparable in some ways to the penis).

Fertilization

A mature ovum, or egg cell, is produced about every twenty-eight days. (However, variations among women in the length of the ovarian cycle are common and normal.) Toward the middle of each monthly cycle, one ovum usually reaches maturity and passes into one of the oviducts. During the previous fourteen days the ovum matured in a *follicle* (also termed a *Graafian follicle*). Initially, a follicle consists of a single layer of cells; but as it grows, the cells proliferate, producing a fluid-filled sac that surrounds the primitive ovum.

An ovary is composed of many follicles, but normally only one undergoes full development in each twenty-eight-day ovarian cycle. Most women seem to alternate between ovaries from one month to another. Through the influence of hormones secreted by the pituitary gland, the follicle ruptures and the ovum is discharged. This discharge of the ovum is called *ovulation*. If more than one ovum matures and is released, the woman may conceive multiple, nonidentical siblings (fraternal twins). The life span of a mature ovum is short. If unfertilized, the ovum begins to degenerate after twenty-four hours.

Fertilization—the union of a sperm and an ovum—usually takes place in the upper end of the oviduct. At the time of sexual intercourse a man customarily introduces 100 to 500 million sperm into the woman's vagina. Sperm ascend the cervical canal and enter the uterus and oviducts. The process of sperm locomotion is assisted by the female system. Sperm have a high mortality rate within the female tract. The obstetrician Alan F. Guttmacher (1973, p. 35) writes:

> The one sperm that achieves its destiny has won against gigantic odds, several hundred million to

Conception

The photo shows a sperm, its tail thrashing, burrowing into an ovum. *(Lennart Nilsson,* A Child Is Born, Dell, *1990)*

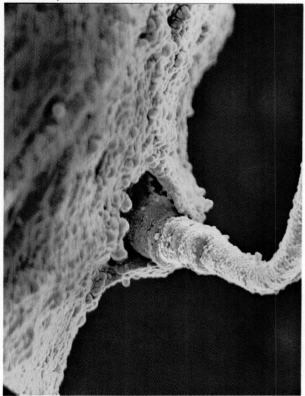

one. The baby it engenders has a far greater mathematical chance of becoming president than the sperm had of fathering a baby.

Even then, however, the newly fertilized egg is extremely vulnerable. For one reason or another, about one-third of all zygotes die shortly after fertilization.

When the follicle ruptures, releasing its ovum, it undergoes rapid change. Still a part of the ovary, the follicle transforms itself into the *corpus luteum*, a small growth recognizable by its golden pigment. The corpus luteum secretes progesterone (a female hormone), which enters the bloodstream and causes the mucous lining along the inner wall of the uterus to prepare itself for the implantation of the zygote. If conception and implantation do not occur, the corpus luteum degenerates and eventually disappears. If pregnancy occurs, the corpus luteum continues to develop and produces progesterone until the placenta takes over the same function. The corpus luteum then becomes superfluous and disappears.

If pregnancy fails to take place, the decreasing levels of ovarian hormones (estrogen and progesterone) lead to *menstruation* about fourteen days after ovulation. Since the thickened outer layers of tissue lining the uterus are not needed for the support of the zygote, they deteriorate. The body sheds them over a three- to seven-day period, when the debris from the wall of the uterus, a small amount of blood, and other fluids are discharged from the vagina. Before the end of a menstrual flow, the pituitary gland secretes hormones into the bloodstream that direct one of the ovarian follicles to begin rapid growth. As a consequence, the cycle starts anew. Should pregnancy occur, a different process is initiated; it will be described in Chapter 4.

Many species are seasonal breeders. For example, songbirds mate in spring, and their nestlings hatch a month later; sheep conceive in the fall, carry their young for six months, and give birth in early spring. Although human beings can and do reproduce at any time of the year, human reproduction nonetheless rises and falls in distinct patterns throughout the year in accordance with latitude and climate. One peak occurs around the spring equinox, in March, and the second in autumn, around October or November. In some regions of the world, people mating during the optimal fertility season have twice the chance of conceiving they have at other times. The optimal period for conception seems to be when the sun shines for about 12 hours a day and the temperature hovers between 50 and 70 degrees Farenheit. For reasons not yet entirely understood, such conditions seem to stimulate a burst of sperm production in men or ovulation in women, or perhaps a combination of the two (Angier, 1990). It is known, for instance, that men living in temperate climates produce on average 32 percent fewer sperm in summer than in winter. Although high temperatures are known to interfere with sperm production, heat alone is not the explanation, because researchers find no difference between men who work outside and men who work in air-conditioned settings. Most likely, an internal biological clock, fine-tuned by the length of daylight, contributes to the seasonal differences (Sperling, 1990). Of interest, fertility peaks are currently less notable in Western nations than they were prior to the era of industrialization, which is associated with indoor lighting and temperature control.

A more detailed discussion of genetics and heredity can be found in Appendix A on page 611.

Infertility and Its Treatment

Although in recent years the media spotlight has focused on the birth-control and abortion controversies, many couples are confronted with an opposite problem, namely, how to conceive the children they desire. **Infertility** is the term employed by the medical profession to refer to a condition in which a couple fails to achieve pregnancy after one year of having engaged in sexual relations with normal frequency (about three or four times a week) and without contraception. As more and more Americans are marrying at later ages and postponing their childbearing years until their thirties, they are increasing the chances that they will experience fertility problems. From 1975 to 1988, the number of first-time mothers in the United States over 30 nearly quintupled, growing from 69,348 to 322,086 (also see Table 3-1). The National Survey of Family Growth, compiled by the National Center for Health Statistics, estimates that "impaired fecundity" (defined as a condition in which women without natural children of their own have difficulty conceiving or carrying a pregnancy to term) occurs at a 4 percent rate for women ages 15 to 24, 15 percent for women from 25 to 34, and 26 percent for 35- to 44-year-old women. Put another way, 74 out of 100 women age 35 or older still have good odds for motherhood (Solimini, 1991).

Table 3-1

The Over-40 Parent Boom			
First births *Women age 40 to 44*		All births *Men age 40 to 44*	
1947	6,600	1945	218,247
1970	2,442	1970	138,012
1975	1,671	1975	84,710
1988	6,745	1988	144,706
All births *Women age 40 to 44*		All births *Men age 45 to 49*	
1947	77,470	1945	89,785
1970	49,952	1970	50,478
1975	26,319	1975	32,351
1988	39,349	1988	40,728

Source: National Center for Health Statistics

A Problem Causing Considerable Anguish Infertility is a problem that causes a good many couples profound anguish. They view parenthood as an integral part of their development as adults. Indeed, they see parenthood as a credential of adulthood. Consequently, the prospect that they may be sterile confronts them with a sense of helplessness at losing control over their life plans. And many feel that their bodies are damaged or otherwise defective. Women speak of feeling "hollow" or "empty"; men speak of feeling like castrates or say that they only "shoot blanks." And some are troubled by their place in the flow of generations. Associated feelings of rage, depression, self-doubt, guilt, and blame can have devastating consequences for the marital relationship (Bouton, 1982; Brozan, 1982a; Higgins, 1990; McEwan, Costello & Taylor, 1987).

Incidence of Infertility Some 3.5 million U.S. couples of childbearing age, one of six couples, are defined as infertile (Blakeslee, 1987; Higgins, 1990). In 1990, more than a million new patients sought treatment for fertility problems, six times as many people as were treated for lung cancer and ten times the number of reported cases of AIDS (Blackman, 1991). In 40 percent of infertility cases the problem can be traced primarily to the man; in another 40 percent, chiefly to the woman; and in the remaining 20 percent, both partners are "subfertile"—or no explanation is found. More than half of all couples with fertility problems can now be helped to achieve pregnancy. Significantly, however, more than half of all couples diagnosed as infertile conceive either after receiving no treatment or after terminating all treatment (Collins, Wrixon, Janes & Wilson, 1983).

Sources of Infertility Medical authorities have differed on how many sperm are required for fertility. The American Fertility Society places the number at over 20 million per milliliter of semen (a normal ejaculation consists of three to five milliliters of semen). However, a number of cases of fertility have occurred below 10 million sperm per milliliter (Bronson, 1977*b*). Male infertility may also be related to the quality of the sperm, which may be characterized by poor motility (rate of spontaneous movement) or unsatisfactory morphology (for instance, a large proportion of the sperm may be abnormally shaped, have egg penetration problems, or contain defective chromosomes). Exposure to environmental toxins and to industrial chemicals such as lead, cadmium, and some pesticides in the workplace can contribute to these conditions; so can the regular use of marijuana, heavy cigarette smoking, and alcohol abuse. Another problem can be traced to tubal blockage, which in some cases can be corrected by microsurgery (surgery performed by using a microscope that magnifies the surgical field four to twenty-five times). Still another rather common cause of infertility is *varicocele*, enlarged or varicose veins in the scrotum (a condition often correctable by surgically tying off the affected veins). Occasionally, some simple factor may be responsible—for example, infrequent intercourse (which is often associated with excessive use of alcohol or some other drug) may be the cause.

About 20 percent of female fertility problems are associated with "hormonal failure." As a result, the ovaries do not produce and release ova. A variety of drugs and synthetic hormones are now available for the treatment of this condition. A premature surging of the luteinizing hormone (LH) prior to ovulation (rather then in mid-cycle when ovulation occurs) has also been linked to infertility and miscarriage (Altman, 1990). Probably the most common cause of female infertility involves congenital or infectious problems (such as gonorrhea and chlamydia) that account for malformation or malfunction of the oviducts. In some cases these conditions have been corrected by microsurgery (or, occasionally, by the methods employed to diagnose tubal problems, such as passing carbon dioxide into the tubes or inserting dye for x-rays). More recently, physicians have begun unclogging the Fallopian tubes with a tiny balloon catheter similar to that used to clear blocked arteries (see Figure 3-3). The poorest candidates for successful microsurgery or balloon catheter procedures are women who have incurred severe tubal damage from gonorrhea. Many infertile women have *endometriosis*, a condition in which the growth of uterine tissue in the abdominal cavity impairs the reproductive tract (mild conditions are treatable by drug therapy, but more severe cases usually require surgery). Finally, some problems may be traced to the environment of the vagina and the cervix, where sperm are deposited by the penis. These problems may involve anatomic difficulties (such as retroversion of the uterus) or the production of sperm antibodies by the female.

In Vitro Fertilization and Related Techniques The 1978 birth in England of Louise Brown, the first "test-tube baby," opened another form of fertility treatment for problems associated with tubal blockage in the female. By 1991, there were more than 470 clinics in twenty-four countries offering the technique. In truth, the procedure is mislabeled, since the growth and development of the fetus do not occur in a test tube but in the uterus. The technique is a method of combining laboratory conception with subsequent natural

Infertility Treatment
These twins were conceived by means of in vitro fertilization. The husband's sperm were brought together with a number of the wife's ova in a laboratory and the developing embryos were later inserted into the wife's uterus. *(Karen Kasmauski/Wheeler Pictures)*

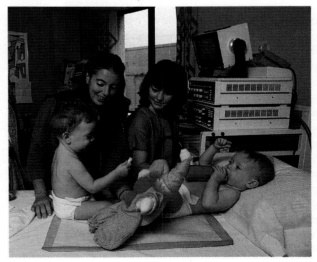

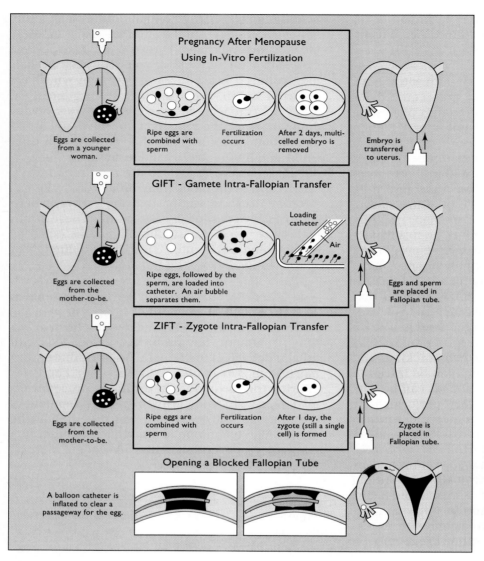

Figure 3-3   Techniques for Helping Childless Couples
The figure shows a number of medical procedures used to facilitate pregnancy. Source: *Time,* November 5, 1990, p. 76.

embryonic and fetal development. In the procedure, termed **in vitro** (meaning "in glass") **fertilization,** the woman is typically treated with a drug that stimulates development of several ova, as opposed to only one. Another hormone stimulates the maturation of the ova. A laparoscope, a tubular device, is inserted through a small incision in the abdomen to find and extract the ova. The woman's husband donates a sperm sample. The sperm and ova are then placed in a medium that facilitates their union. About twelve hours later an embryo is transferred to a different solution, one that supports embryonic development (the medium most suited to fertilization is not, as a rule, good for the developmental stage). Between two and four days later the developing embryo is inserted in the woman's uterus, where,

if all goes well, the embryo implants itself. Unhappily, even in well-run clinics, the procedure is successful only 12 percent of the time. The biggest difficulty is that the embryos often fail to implant. Recently, physicians have successfully employed in vitro fertilization procedures to impregnate a number of postmenopausal women, ages 40 to 44, using ova taken from younger women and fertilized with sperm from the older women's husbands (prior to implantation of the mature eggs, the older women underwent hormone treatment to simulate the womb's environment prior to menopause).

In an effort to increase the chances of implantation, physicians have developed another procedure, *gamete intra-Fallopian transfer,* or GIFT. The technique is similar to in vitro fertilization except that after being briefly cultured in the laboratory one or more ova are mixed with about a hundred thousand sperm from the husband and inserted directly into the Fallopian tube (as would normally occur naturally), and the resulting embryo then drifts into the uterus, where it is much more likely to secure itself than with earlier in vitro procedures. In another variation, called *zygote intra-Fallopian transfer*, or ZIFT, the sperm fertilize the eggs before transfer to the Fallopian tube (rather than the uterus, as with the original in vitro procedure). Figure 3-3 illustrates these procedures.

Controversy Considerable controversy has surrounded in vitro fertilization and GIFT procedures. In 1987, after three years of close study, the Vatican condemned the procedures, even when the sperm and ovum are supplied by husband and wife. The Roman Catholic Church's position stemmed from its long-standing belief that the only morally acceptable way to conceive children is the "natural" way and that to separate love from procreation is a sin (Woodward, 1987). Even more controversial has been childbearing by proxy, which goes far beyond the use of in vitro fertilization in the treatment of oviduct infertility. In cases where the husband is infertile, some couples have turned to artificial insemination by an anonymous donor. Where the wife cannot conceive, some couples have resorted to surrogate mothers, a matter discussed in the boxed insert on page 74.

Genetic Counseling and Testing

Within recent years techniques have been developed to identify many genetic and chromosomal problems before an infant's birth. A variety of tests are now available to parents with strong histories of genetic disease and to couples who, for whatever reason, wish to determine whether the fetus is normal. **Amniocentesis** is one commonly used procedure. In amniocentesis a physician inserts a long, hollow needle through a woman's abdomen into the uterus, drawing out a small amount of the amniotic fluid that surrounds the fetus (see Figure 3-4). The amniotic fluid contains cells of the unborn child, which are then grown in a laboratory culture and analyzed for the presence of various genetic abnormalities.

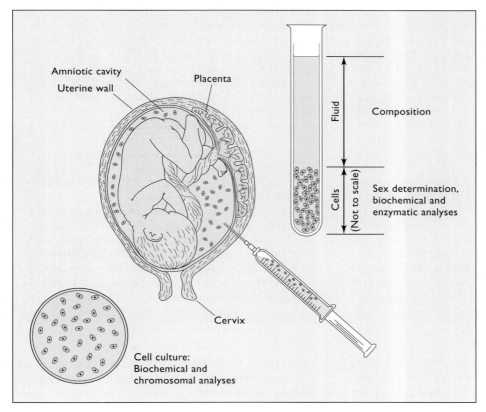

Figure 3-4 Amniocentesis
Amniocentesis is a procedure for detecting hereditary defects in the fetus. A sterile needle is inserted into the amniotic cavity, and a small amount of fluid is withdrawn. This sample is centrifuged to separate fetal cells from the fluid. The cells are then grown in a laboratory culture and analyzed for chromosomal and genetic abnormalities. Source: Eric T. Pengelley, *Sex and Human Life* (Reading, Mass.: Addison-Wesley Publishing Company, 1978). Figure 10.6, p. 176. © 1978; by Addison-Wesley. Reprinted with permission.

Surrogate Parenthood: Who Is a Mother? Whose Baby Will It Be?

Where do babies come from? Nowadays they come from more exotic places than the stork or cabbage patch that evasive parents often offer their children as explanations. Is a mother the woman who nurtures a child in her womb for nine months and gives it birth? Or is she the woman who provides the ovum, arranges for it to be fertilized with a man's sperm (usually her husband's), and contracts with a surrogate to carry the fetus to birth? Such questions arise as advances in reproductive technology make traditional biological definitions of motherhood obsolete (Ames, 1991; Edwards, 1991). More and more infertile couples, in a final, desperate attempt to have a family, have turned to surrogate motherhood. The practice has given rise to countless disputes, such as the landmark Baby M case in 1987 and 1988. The surrogate, Mary Beth Whitehead, was artificially inseminated with sperm from William Stern, whose wife Elizabeth contended that she could not bear a child without significant risk to her health. Whitehead changed her mind after she gave birth to the child. A New Jersey judge, Harvey Sorkow, awarded custody of Baby M to Stern, although Whitehead received visitation rights.

In the Baby M case Whitehead was the genetic mother. Since then events have moved so rapidly that cases like that of Baby M are now deemed "traditional surrogacies." A new wave of "gestational surrogacy" cases have arisen where a surrogate has no genetic link to the child. The issue was highlighted in 1990 by a case in which a surrogate mother, Anna L. Johnson, gave birth to the genetic offspring of Chrispina and Mark Calvert, a boy conceived by in vitro fertilization. A California judge, Richard N. Parslow, denied parental rights to the surrogate mother. Comparing her with a foster parent, he ruled that the woman's womb was little more than a home in which she had sheltered and fed the legal offspring of the genetic parents. Other cases are bound to arise that challenge this argument, for it is precisely the gestational role that afford post-menopausal woman their claim to motherhood. In this latter situation, the donor of a fertilized egg is asked to relinquish her claim to motherhood, while the post-menopausal woman elevates her claim on the basis of having nurtured the child in her womb and giving it birth (Mydans, 1990).

In the absence of clear guidelines provided by legislation, judges have frequently attempted to base their decisions on "the best interests of the child." For instance, Judge Sorkow in the Baby M case questioned Whitehead's fitness as a mother, calling her "manipulative, impulsive and exploitive" as well as "untruthful" and charging that she was too possessive of her children. Sorkow's ruling raises the question about what motives lead a woman to be a surrogate mother. As yet, the number of surrogate mothers who have been studied by psychologists are too few to provide definitive answers to the question. However, no single motive seems to explain why a woman would seek to bear a child for another couple. The money—usually about $10,000, plus all expenses—is a significant factor for 90 percent of the women. Yet a woman who is interested only in money is likely to be a poor candidate. Apparently, the best candidates are women who enjoy being pregnant, feel healthiest when they are pregnant, and give birth easily and with few complications. Compassion for the childless couple—a sense of altruism—also is important, because the woman can then more easily separate from the child when it is born. Deep-rooted psychological factors may also operate, including guilt over a past abortion, gratitude over being adopted oneself, and the need to reenact one's own childhood abandonment. Some of these characteristics may make it difficult for a woman to handle separation and loss well. Among the signs cited by experts that a woman may encounter difficulty in the surrogate mother role are compulsive promiscuity; a long series of unstable relationships; or a history of childhood abandonment, abuse, or incest (Goleman, 1987d).

Surrogate motherhood has raised many issues. There are those who argue that babies are not products to be bought and sold. Opponents say that by receiving a fee, a surrogate is engaging in baby selling. Supporters respond that a surrogate should be compensated for her time and trouble. And how should the matter be resolved if a woman changes

Genetic and chromosomal defects, including those associated with Down's syndrome and about seventy other inherited biochemical disorders, can be detected in this manner. The test can be carried out as early as fourteen weeks after conception, but most physicians prefer to wait until the fetus is 18 to 20 weeks old. The procedure is not without risk, since amniocentesis poses about a 1 percent risk of causing miscarriage. In addition, preliminary evidence suggests

The Ethical Cutting Edge of Biology

Mark and Crispine Calvert, a California couple in their mid-30s, very much wanted to have a baby. But Cris had had a hysterectomy because of uterine tumors. They paid Anna Johnson, 29, a licensed practical nurse, to bear their baby for $10,000. Ova surgically removed from Crispina were fertilized in a laboratory dish with Mark's sperm and three developing eggs were placed in Anna's uterus. One implanted and resulted in the birth of a boy. Anna filed suit for custody of the child but a California court awarded custody to the Calverts, primarily on grounds that Anna had no blood ties to the child. (AP/Wide World Photos)

her mind? One surrogate mother who once was a strong advocate of the arrangement now contends: "All you're doing is transferring the pain from one woman to another, from a woman who is in pain from her infertility to a woman who has to give up her baby" (Kantrowitz, 1987c). Some believe that legislation is needed to regulate surrogate contracts, the legal obligations of the parties, and the legality of payment to surrogates (a number of states have enacted legislation forbidding paid surrogacy arrangements, and a number of others have deemed surrogacy contracts legally unenforceable). But others think that legislation is unnecessary and would infringe on a couple's procreative autonomy under the right of privacy.

Other questions also abound. For instance, if Baby M had been born handicapped and none of the parties wanted her, who would be responsible for the infant? Do donors have a right to know "their" children, and do children have a right to know their donor parents? Is it ethically acceptable for surrogate motherhood to be used for women who do not want to interrupt their careers for childbearing or who are concerned about ruining their figures? Will surrogate motherhood create a class of "breeder women," probably poor women, who rent their wombs to wealthy people? Clearly, the ethical issues raised by surrogate motherhood are exceedingly difficult to resolve.

that children whose mothers had amniocentesis have more frequent ear infections than those whose mothers did not (Lewin, 1990).

Some doctors now utilize amniocentesis as a routine procedure for women who become preg-

nant after the age of 35. Although women over 35 have only 10 percent of the babies born in the United States, they have half of those born with Down's syndrome. Amniocentesis is also often used in cases where a parent is known to carry abnormal chromosomes or where a previous pregnancy was associated with a chromosome abnormality.

More recently, researchers have devised a means of ultrasound scanning, termed **ultrasonography,** that allows physicians to trace the size and shape of a fetus and determine malformations. The procedure, which uses the principles of sonar devised by the navy, bounces sound waves off the fetus. The result is a picture that is safer than that afforded by x-rays. A number of physicians have found that parental viewing of the fetus by means of ultrasonography affords the additional advantage of accelerating parental bonding with the child (Fletcher & Evans, 1983). Still another procedure, *fetoscopy,* allows a physician to examine the fetus directly through a lens after inserting a very narrow tube into the uterus (a blood sample or skin biopsy can also be taken from the fetus). However, this procedure carries a higher risk than amniocentesis does.

Another method is **chorionic villus biopsy.** The chorionic villi are hairlike projections of the membrane that surround the embryo during early pregnancy (see Chapter 4). The physician, guided by ultrasound, inserts a thin catheter through the vagina and cervix and, employing suction, removes a small plug of villous tissue. Although the chorion is not an anatomical part of the embryo itself, it is embryonic rather than maternal in origin. The cells can then be tested and the results known within days, even hours. By contrast, amniocentesis cannot be performed until later in a pregnancy, and its results are not known for about two weeks. Chorionic villus biopsy allows for an early test that then can be checked later in the pregnancy by amniocentesis. In 1991 a large randomized European sample found that patients who used chorionic villus sampling experienced almost 5 percent more fetal and neonatal deaths than women who chose amniocentesis (Rosenthal, 1991). The results have raised concern about the procedure, although many U.S. physicians believe the findings to be a fluke that will not be confirmed by additional research.

The University of California Medical Center in San Francisco recently reported on the results of 3,000 prenatal diagnoses done by amniocentesis at its facilities. More than 2,400 of the women were tested because they were over 35-years-old. The other women were tested because the genetic history of one or both of the partners raised the possibility of a defective fetus. The tests uncovered 113 abnormal fetuses, all but 7 of which were aborted at the parents' request. Of the 3,000

women tested, the amniocentesis was in error in 14 cases, but only 6 of these errors were such as to constitute incorrect guidance in the decision whether to abort or continue pregnancy: 4 of the errors entailed failure to detect a defective fetus; 2 of them, abortion of unaffected fetuses.

In practice, the test results are negative in more than 96 percent of amniocentesis cases. Since most of the women who undergo amniocentesis are in categories of high risk for producing defective children, the procedure has afforded these families many months of relief from anxiety. Some medical authorities point out that prenatal diagnosis also makes childbearing more feasible for people who might otherwise be afraid to have children. It has also been employed to detect life-threatening conditions and to treat the fetus while still in the uterus (Henig, 1982). Many investigators expect that the field of fetal medicine will burgeon in the years ahead. Furthermore, the earlier a genetic problem is identified, the greater the possibility that it might someday be corrected by some sort of treatment while the infant is still in the uterus. For instance, medical scientists hope in the future to transplant a healthy gene directly into the afflicted fetus, thus altering the infant's genetic blueprint. The aim is to treat by editing a "sick gene" out of the infant's hereditary code. In 1990, scientists performed the first federally approved gene therapy when they introduced a grayish liquid containing foreign genes into the blood of a 4-year-old girl who suffers from ADA deficiency, a rare and incurable immune-system disease (by inserting the genes, physicians hope her body will produce ADA, the enzyme she requires, and that her immune system will recover).

In addition, surgery can now be performed on a fetus without undue risk to the mother's health or her chances of having later successful pregnancies. Of the 17 open fetal surgeries undertaken between 1981 and 1989 at the University of California, San Francisco, 14 were "technically successful" and improved the condition of the youngsters at birth. Three did not survive. All the babies had been diagnosed as having life-threatening, congenital defects such as a hole in the diaphragm or blocked bladder. The physicians surgically removed the fetus from the uterus, performed corrective surgery upon it, and put the fetus back in the uterus to complete the pregnancy (Snider, 1991).

But procedures like amniocentesis and chorionic villus biopsy have also produced anguish and sorrow. Parents who learn that they are carriers of genetic diseases often feel ashamed and guilty, mortified to be stigmatized as genetic defectives (Chedd, 1981; Restak, 1975). They are also faced with the difficult decision of whether they should proceed with an abortion if the test results indicate the presence of a defective fetus. No wonder that lasting psychological problems can develop in parents who learn that the child they are expecting is abnormal. Among the problems are severe guilt reactions, depression, termination of sexual relations, marital discord, and divorce. Clearly, parents need psychological counseling in conjunction with genetic counseling.

In time, more and more of us will have to grapple with the uncomfortable issues posed by genetic testing (Blakeslee, 1987; Carey, 1990; Schmeck, 1986*a*). Soon doctors will be able to screen everybody to detect evidence of harmful genes. And in the near future it is likely that a person's entire genome could be mapped at birth. Such information could be useful in adjusting one's lifestyle to minimize the risk of disease. For instance, the link between cigarette smoking and lung cancer is well known, yet many people live their entire lives free of the disease. Currently, the less fortunate ones learn of their susceptibility too late. A genetic map might allow parents to know early, sometimes even before the child is born, that their offspring will have to be particularly careful to avoid smoking. So far the emphasis has been on combating serious hereditary disorders. However, evidence indicates that some couples are using prenatal tests to identify and abort fetuses on the basis of sex. A good many people worry lest we are headed for an age of "made-to-order babies" in which having a child is morally analogous to buying an automobile (Cowley, 1990).

Genetic screening also affords new ways for people to discriminate (Brownlee, 1990; Stipp, 1990). Your genetic profile could be used to determine who you could marry, what jobs you could apply for, and whether insurance companies would consider you a good risk. Complicating matters, geneticists say that every healthy person carries four to eight harmful genes. In this sense, we are all "polluted." Another question is whether you would want to know if you had inherited a harmful gene such as that for Huntington's chorea. Nearly two-thirds of young adults at risk for inheriting the gene say they would like to know if they have it. But others do not want to know lest they spend their lives in constant worry, waiting for the disease to appear. In fact, some people have commited suicide after learning they had the Huntington's gene.

Heredity-Environment Interactions

The way a question is asked limits and disposes the ways in which any answer to it—right or wrong—may be given.—SUSANNE K. LANGER
Philosophy in a New Key

To what extent is human behavior the product of biology, based on the unfolding of genetic characteristics that are present at birth? To what extent is human behavior determined by events in the external environment? And to what extent is it shaped by the interaction of hereditary and environmental components? These issues have concerned thinkers through the ages. Time and again the nature-nurture controversy has been officially pronounced dead because it seems to have been answered for all time. Yet in one fashion or another, each generation resurrects it, threshes it out once more, and then presumes to set it to permanent rest.

Some of the difficulties in the nature-nurture controversy stem from the fact that investigators often operate from different assumptions. Various schools ask different questions and hence come up with different answers. How we phrase our questions structures the alternatives by which the questions are answered.

Scientists began by asking *which* factor, heredity or environment, is responsible for a given trait, such as a mental disorder or a person's level of intelligence. Later, they sought to establish *how much* of the observed differences among people are due to differences in heredity and *how much* to differences in environment. And recently, some scientists have insisted that a more fruitful question is *how* specific hereditary and environmental factors *interact* to influence various characteristics (Anastasi, 1958; Weisfeld, 1982) (see Figure 3-5). Each of these questions leads to its own theories, interpretations, and methods of inquiry.

The "Which" Question

Most students can recall debating in a class or a bull session the question "Which is more important, heredity or environment?" Yet most scientists today reject this formulation. They believe that phrasing the issue in terms of heredity *versus* environment has caused the scientific community, and society at large, untold difficulties. The either-or statement creates a hopeless dichotomy. Counterposing heredity to environment is similar in some respects to debating

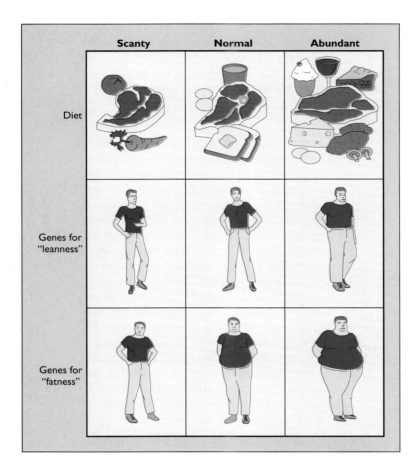

Figure 3-5   Gene-Environment Interaction
A person who has a gene for "fatness" may actually weigh less than one with a gene for "leanness," if the former lives on a scanty and the latter on an overabundant diet. Source: T. Dobzhansky, *Mankind Evolving* (New Haven: Yale University Press, 1962), Figure 2, p. 45. © 1962 by Yale University Press. Reprinted with permission.

whether sodium or chlorine is more important in ordinary table salt. The point is that we would not have salt without both sodium and chlorine.

Every person is a product of heredity and environment. Broadly defined, **heredity** involves the biological transmission of traits from parents to their offspring through genes. *Genes* contain the molecular materials that store the inherited information which serves as a "recipe" or "blueprint" telling cells how to manufacture vital protein substances (including enzymes, hormones, antibodies, and structural proteins). **Environment** entails all the external factors that affect the organism. None of the characteristics that a human being displays could occur in the absence of either an appropriate heredity or an appropriate environment.

The "How Much" Question

As scientists came to recognize the inappropriateness of the "which" question, some of them reformulated the issue. Granted that both heredity and environment are essential for the emergence of any characteristic, they asked, "*How much* of each is required to produce a given trait?" For example, they asked, "Does a person's level of intelligence depend on 80 percent heredity and 20 percent environment, 30 percent heredity and 70 percent environment, or some other ratio?" And they asked, "What are the respective contributions made by heredity and environment to the occurrence of a given mental disorder?"

Family Resemblance Studies   Scientists have traditionally sought answers to the "how much" question by measuring the resemblance among family members with respect to a particular trait. Botanists use similar procedures to discover the separate contributions that heredity and environment make in the plant world. They approach the problem by taking cuttings from a single plant and then replanting the parts in different environments: one at sea level, another at an intermediate elevation, and still another in the alpine zone of a mountain range. Each part develops into a new plant under different environmental conditions. Since the parts of each plant have identical heredities, any observed *differences* in vigor, size, leaves, stems, and roots are directly traceable to differences in environment (Dobzhansky, 1962). This is not to say that environment is more important than heredity. Even when genetic factors are held constant, they still contribute to the plant's characteristics.

Such deliberate experimentation is not possible with humans. Nonetheless, nature occasionally provides us with the makings of a natural experiment. From time to time a fertilized egg, by some accident, gets split into two parts early in development. Each part grows into separate and complete individuals, termed **identical** or **monozygotic twins.** Genetically, each is essentially a carbon copy of the other.

Identical twins are usually reared together by their natural parents. But in some rare cases they are separated at an early age and adopted by different families. The study of identical twins reared under different environmental conditions is the closest approach possible to the experiments with plant cuttings.

In contrast with identical twins, **fraternal** or **dizygotic twins** come from two eggs fertilized by two different spermatozoa. They are simply siblings who happen to be born at the same time. Important evidence can be obtained from comparing the average differences in the characteristics of identical and fraternal twins—for instance, their performance on intelligence tests. Moreover, comparisons can be made between identical twins reared *apart* and fraternal twins reared *together.* Many scientists believe that such comparisons reveal valuable information about the relative contributions that heredity and environment make to a particular trait or behavior (Loehlin, 1989).

Another means for assessing family resemblances is by studying children who were adopted at birth and reared by foster parents. One can compare some characteristic of the adopted children, such as IQ score or the presence of a particular mental disorder, with that of their biological parents and their foster parents. In this fashion researchers attempt to weigh the relative influences of the genetic factor and the home environment.

Behavior Genetics Over the past thirty-five years or so the scientific community has been taking a more tolerant attitude toward heredity's contribution to the variation we observe in people's behavior (Plomin, 1990; Plomin, Lichtenstein, Pedersen, McClearn & Nesselroade, 1990; Plomin & Rende, 1991). Interest in the hereditary aspects of behavior had been subdued for nearly half a century by both behaviorism and psychoanalytic theory. The renewed interest in biological factors is due partly to exciting new discoveries in microbiology and genetics and partly to the failure of social scientists to document a consistently strong relationship between measures of environmental experience and behavioral outcome. Indeed, the pendulum seems to be swinging away from the environmentalists toward the side of the biologists.

Kagan: Timidity Studies One area of recent investigation has been extreme timidity. Jerome Kagan and his associates (Kagan, 1989; Kagan, Reznick, Clarke, Snidman & Garcia-Coll, 1984; Kagan, Reznick & Gibbons, 1989; Kagan, Reznick, Snidman, Gibbons & Johnson, 1988; Reznick et al., 1986) followed forty-one children for eight years, studying "behavioral inhibition." The researchers found that 10 to 15 percent of those studied seem to be born with a biological pre-

Adoption Research
Research has found that the IQ gap between blacks and whites is closed among black children who are adopted as infants by white middle-class parents. *(Erika Stone)*

"Because my genetic programming prevents me from stopping to ask directions—that's why!"

(Drawing by D. Reilly; © 1991. The New Yorker Magazine, Inc.)

disposition that makes them unusually fearful of unfamiliar people, events, or even objects like toys. These youngsters have intense physical responses to mental stress: Their dilated pupils, faster and more stable heart rates, and higher levels of salivary cortisol (a hormone found in saliva) indicate that their nervous system is accelerated by even mildly stressful conditions.

Other researchers have found that shy biological parents tend to have shy children—even when the youngsters are adopted by socially outgoing parents (Daniels & Plomin, 1985). In addition, shy boys are more likely than their peers to delay entry into marriage, parenthood, and stable careers; to attain less occupational achievement and stability; and—when late in establishing stable careers—to experience marital instability. Shy girls are more likely than their peers to follow a conventional pattern of marriage, childbearing, and homemaking (Caspi, Elder & Bem, 1988). Although some children are inherently inhibited and "uptight," they can be helped, by good parenting, to cope with their shyness. In other words, predispositions like that for timidity can be en-

hanced or reduced, but not eliminated, by child-rearing and other nurturing experiences. Kagan offers this additional bit of advice: "Look at whether the child is happy. Some shy kids are. And they often end up doing well in school . . . they become computer scientists, historians. We need these people, too" (quoted by Elias, 1989, p. 1D).

The Minnesota Twin Project. The results of a project at the University of Minnesota similarly suggest that genetic makeup has a marked impact on personality (Bouchard, Lykken, McGue, Segal & Tellegen, 1990; Goleman, 1986c; Leo, 1987; Tellegen et al., 1988). Researchers put 348 pairs of identical twins, including 44 pairs who were reared apart, through six days of extensive testing that included analysis of their blood, brain waves, intelligence, and allergies. All the twins took several personality tests, answering more than 15,000 questions on subjects ranging from personal interests and values to aggressiveness, aesthetic judgment, and television and reading habits. Of eleven key personality traits or clusters of traits analyzed in the study, seven revealed a stronger influence for hereditary factors than for child-rearing factors (see Figure 3-6). The Minnesota researchers found the highest inherited cluster was "social potency" (a tendency toward leadership or dominance), at 61 percent; "social closeness" (the need for intimacy, comfort, and help) was lowest, at 33 percent. Although they had not expected traditionalism (obedience to authority and strict discipline) to be more an inherited than an acquired trait, it is one of the traits with a strong genetic influence (60 percent). Note that the estimates deal with how much genes influence particular behaviors in the general population—but what the percentages will be in a specific person is impossible to say.

The Minnesota researchers do not believe that a single gene is responsible for any one of the traits. Instead, each trait seems to be determined by a large number of genes in combination, so that the pattern of inheritance is complex—what is called **polygenic inheritance**. Such findings do not mean that environmental factors are unimportant. It is not full-blown personality traits that are inherited, but rather tendencies or predilections. In cases of extreme deprivation, in-cest, or abuse, family factors would have a larger impact—though a negative one—than the Minnesota research reveals.

The message for parents is not that it matters little how they care for and rear their children but that it is a mistake to treat all children the same. Children can—and often do—experience the same events differently, and this uniqueness nudges their personalities down different roads. In studies of thousands of children in Colorado, Sweden, and England, researchers found that siblings often respond to the same event (a parent's absence, a burglarized home) and interpret the same behavior (a mother's social preening) in quite different ways (Bergeman, Plomin, McClearn, Pedersen & Friberg, 1988; Dunn & Plomin, 1990; Plomin, DeFries & Fulker, 1988). Birth order, school experiences, friends, and chance events often add up to very different childhoods for siblings (Baker & Daniels, 1990; Plomin, McClearn, Pedersen, Nesselroade & Bergeman, 1988; Plomin, 1989). Youngsters perceive events through a unique filter, each of which is skewed by how earlier experiences affected them. Because each child carries about his

Identical Twins: Jack Yufe and Oskar Stöhr
These identical twins were separated at six months of age, when their parents divorced. They were brought together by the Minnesota researchers at the age of 47. Yufe (left) was raised as a Jew, joined an Israeli Kibbutz in his youth, and served in the Israeli navy. Stöhr (right) was brought up as a Catholic and later became involved in the Hitler youth movement. Despite the differences in their backgrounds, they share many characteristics. When they first met at the airport, both sported mustaches and two-pocket shirts with epaulets, and each carried a pair of wire-rimmed glasses. Both read magazines from back to front, and both dip buttered toast in their coffee. Both excel at sports and have difficulty with math. And both have similar personality profiles as measured by the Minnesota Multiphasic Personality Inventory. (Courtesy Thomas J. Bourchard, Jr., Department of Psychology, University of Minnesota)

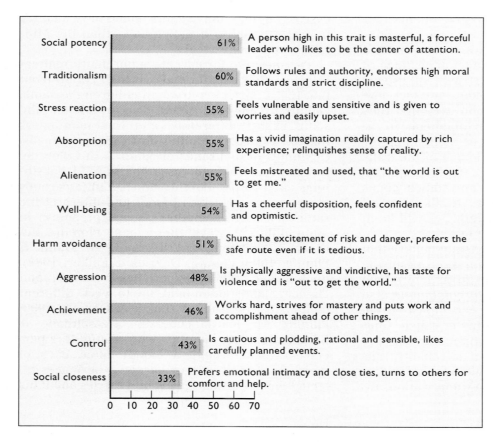

Trait	%	Description
Social potency	61%	A person high in this trait is masterful, a forceful leader who likes to be the center of attention.
Traditionalism	60%	Follows rules and authority, endorses high moral standards and strict discipline.
Stress reaction	55%	Feels vulnerable and sensitive and is given to worries and easily upset.
Absorption	55%	Has a vivid imagination readily captured by rich experience; relinquishes sense of reality.
Alienation	55%	Feels mistreated and used, that "the world is out to get me."
Well-being	54%	Has a cheerful disposition, feels confident and optimistic.
Harm avoidance	51%	Shuns the excitement of risk and danger, prefers the safe route even if it is tedious.
Aggression	48%	Is physically aggressive and vindictive, has taste for violence and is "out to get the world."
Achievement	46%	Works hard, strives for mastery and puts work and accomplishment ahead of other things.
Control	43%	Is cautious and plodding, rational and sensible, likes carefully planned events.
Social closeness	33%	Prefers emotional intimacy and close ties, turns to others for comfort and help.

Figure 3-6   The Roots of Personality
The figure shows the extent to which eleven key traits of personality are estimated to be inherited, as gauged by tests with twins. The traits were measured by the Multidimensional Personality Questionnaire, developed by Auke Tellegen at the University of Minnesota. Source: *New York Times*, December 2, 1986, p. 17. Copyright © 1986 by The New York Times Company. Reprinted by permission.

or her own little customized version of the environment, it seems that growing up in the same family actually works to make siblings different. Even youngsters as young as 14 months of age are acutely aware of the minute-by-minute differences in parental attention and affection doled out to their brothers and sisters, as evidenced by the skill they display in yanking back the spotlight. Parents who try to be evenhanded are foiled by their own consistency because they cannot control the way children perceive these efforts. For instance, a mother may be very affectionate with her youngsters when they are a year of age but emphasize independence with her three-year-olds. However, the three-year-old seems to pay more attention to his sister's being smothered with kisses than to the memory of his having been cuddled when he was a year of age. Such perceived differences, whether real or imagined, can have a powerful influence on personality. So in guiding and shaping children, parents should respect their individuality, adapt to it, and cultivate those qualities that will help them in coping with life. If one child is timid, good parenting would entail helping the child become less so by providing experiences in which success will encourage greater risk taking. If another child is

fearless, parents need to cultivate qualities that temper risk taking with intelligent caution.

Some scholars fear that the results of the Minnesota research will be used to blame the poor and downtrodden for their misfortunes. Political liberals have long believed that crime and poverty are primarily the by-products of unhealthy social environments. So they are distrustful of biological or genetic explanations of behavior. The research findings thus raise a serious concern—that genetic determinism could be misused to "prove" that some races are inferior, that male dominance over women is natural, and that social progress is impossible because of the relentless pull of genes (Angoff, 1988; Leo, 1987; Wellborn, 1987).

Other scholars point out that the research holds promise for preventive medicine. If researchers can find a genetic predisposition for various disorders, we can then work on changing the environment with diet, medication, or other interventions. For example, if offspring of alcoholics are found to have genes that render them susceptible to alcoholism, they could be taught from childhood to avoid alcohol. Scientists can also develop new treatments. For instance, if they find a gene that increases a person's risk for schizophrenia or manic-depressive illness, researchers can find the protein that the gene codes for and better understand the basic mechanism of the disease. Once they understand the basic mechanism, they can search for new ways to treat the disease (Bishop, 1986). In sum, the potential dangers of genetic research are large, but so are its potential benefits.

The "How" Question

A number of scientists, such as the psychologist Anne Anastasi (1958), believe that the task of science is to discover *how* hereditary and environmental factors work together to produce behavior. They argue that the "how much" question, like the "which" question, is unproductive. The "how much" question assumes that nature and nurture are related to each other in such a way that the contribution of the one is *added* to the contribution of the other to produce a particular behavior.

Anastasi, among others (Lerner, 1976, 1978; Weisfeld, 1982; Wohlwill, 1973), disputes this view. She argues that, as applied to human life, neither heredity nor environment exists separately. They are always intertwined, continually interacting. Consequently, Anastasi says, it is a hopeless task to identify "which" of the two factors produces a particular behavior or to determine "how much" each contributes. However, Anastasi recognizes that the role played by hereditary factors is more central in some aspects of development than in others. She thus sets forth the notion of the **continuum of indirectness.** At one end of the continuum are the contributions of heredity that are most direct, such as physical characteristics like eye color and chromosomal disorders like Down's syndrome. At the other end of the continuum are the contributions of heredity that are quite indirect, such as the social stereotypes that the members of a given society attach to various categories of skin color and hair texture.

An analogy may prove helpful in understanding the notion of "interaction" that is so central to Anastasi's position. Consider ordinary table salt. At room temperature sodium is a soft, solid substance that reacts violently with water and hence would produce devastating effects if we were to place it in our mouths. Likewise, chlorine is a toxic greenish-yellow gas that, if inhaled, would irritate our lungs and make us choke. But when sodium and chlorine are brought together, they combine to form sodium chloride, a white crystalline substance that is an essential human nutrient.

Sodium chloride differs *qualitatively* in its characteristics from either sodium or chlorine. It is the molecular *interaction* between the two elements that gives the compound its unique character. Hence, sodium chloride is not a mechanical mixture of sodium and chlorine that we can place in some sort of sieve in order to separate one from the other physically. And by the same token, it is a fruitless task to undertake an assessment of "how much" each element "adds" to the compound. "Which" and "how much" questions, therefore, are relatively meaningless when examining the relationship between the compound sodium chloride and the two elements sodium and chlorine.

Medawar (1977, p. 14) notes another reason that we may not be able to attach exact percentages to the contributions of heredity and environment. Since heredity and environment interact in a relationship of varying dependence, what appears to be a hereditary contribution in one context can be seen as an environmental contribution in another. An example is provided by phenylketonuria (PKU), a severe form of mental retardation that was discussed in Chapter 1. PKU results from the inability of the body to metabolize phenylalanine, a common ingredient of our diet. The disorder is transmitted genetically according to straightforward Mendelian rules. But if a child who has inherited a susceptibility to the disease is given a diet free of phenylalanine, there is no buildup of toxic materials, and the child's development is essentially normal. Hence, under the circumstances of a phenylalanine-free diet, PKU can be viewed as entirely environmental in origin, since PKU shows up in the presence of phenylalanine but not in its absence.

Despite such evidence, both parties to the nature-nurture debate seem generally willing to accept the assumption that inherited traits are not subject to change, at least not readily. Yet examples abound that challenges the assumption that there necessarily is a fixed and permanent blueprint for the development of inherited traits in the gene pattern. As we will see in Chapter 6, a secular increase in size has resulted in Americans today being more than 4 inches taller on average than their predecessors of a century ago. The Ministry of Health and Welfare in Japan reports that between 1946 and 1982 the average height of young adult males increased by about 4 inches. And until recently, American-born children of Japanese parents have been taller, heavier, more advanced skeletally, and during the prepubertal period distinctly longer-legged than their counteparts in Japan. Conversely, some environmentally acquired behaviors are extremely resistant to change, including not only such physically addictive habits as smoking, drinking, and drug addiction but also national, racial, and religious prejudices, attitudes toward crime, money, and marriage, and voting preferences (Angoff, 1988).

Ethical and practical considerations do not allow scientists to manipulate genetic and environmental variables in experiments with humans. But research with animals has furnished many insights into the process by which hereditary and environmental factors dynamically interact to shape the course of development. For example, neurobiologists have investigated how nerve cells interact with visual stimulation to produce vision in rabbits, cats, and monkeys. In one type of study researchers sew one eye of a kitten shut shortly after it is born. Several months later they reopen the eye and find that the cat cannot see with it. The cat cannot use the eye because the absence of stimulation affects the way visual stimuli are processed in the kitten's brain. Only a small fraction of the nerve cells in the kitten's visual cortex within the brain respond with electrical signs when researchers shine light on the deprived eye. In contrast, nearly all these cells respond when light is shone on the normal eye. Thus, early visual experience interacts with genetic endowment to produce sight (Kolata, 1975;

Smith, Bennett, Harwerth & Crawford, 1978). Similarly, researchers in a number of laboratories have demonstrated that giving rodents either enriched experience in a complex environment or formal training leads to measurable changes in their brains (Diamond, 1988; Rosenzweig, 1984).

Heredity and environment interact in complex ways (see the boxed insert on page 85, which deals with resiliency and superchildren). Genes influence the kinds of environment we seek, what we attend to, and how much we learn (Plomin & Daniels, 1987). For instance, psychologists Sandra Scarr and Kathleen McCartney (1983) contend that each stage in a child's psychological development is ushered in by an increment in the child's biological maturation. Only after the child is genetically receptive is the environment able to have any significant effect on his or her behavioral development. Scarr and McCartney believe that children tailor their environment in "passive," "evocative," and "active" ways that conform with their individual genetic predispositions. In the *passive relationship* parents give their children both genes and an environment that are favorable (or unfavorable) to the development of a particular capability. For example, parents who are gifted in social skills are also likely to provide their children with an enriched social environment. In the *evocative relationship* a child evokes particular responses from others because of the child's genetically influenced be-

Promoting Learning
Parents who spend time with their children, interact with them, show interest in their experiences, and cultivate their knowledge and skills foster competent and creative youngsters. Parents are not only biological but also social and cultural links between the hundreds of generations that have gone before and the hundreds yet to come. Thus hereditary and environmental factors interact to fashion the generations of humanity. *(Patrick Reddy)*

Resiliency: Thriving Against Incredible Odds

Clinical psychologists and psychiatrists have traditionally focused on the maladjusted and mentally ill. Now a few of them have begun to study the opposite end of the spectrum—children who thrive despite enormous difficulties (Dugan & Coles, 1989; Garmezy, 1985; Rutter, 1990; Werner, 1990). Termed by some "superchildren" or "invulnerables," they are the offspring of schizophrenics or are children who are abused, extremely poor, or otherwise at risk. E. James Anthony, a psychiatrist who works with the children of psychotic parents, observes:

> They deal with life with an excellence and an adaptive capacity that don't seem to come from anywhere, as if they had carved out these qualities by themselves. We think, here's this awful home; here are these awful parents; here's this awful upbringing, and, we expect, here is the awful result. But, instead, here's a really remarkable child. (Quoted by Pines, 1979a, p. 53)

A disease ecologist, Jacques May, provides us with an analogy regarding vulnerability and risk (Solnit & Provence, 1979). Imagine that we have three dolls, one made of glass, one of plastic, and one of steel. We hit each doll with a hammer. The first doll shatters into hundreds of pieces, the plastic doll is dented, while the steel doll gives off a fine metallic sound. The steel doll represents the superchildren. In the middle range between the two extremes, the plastic doll resembles children who suffer some damage from their adverse circumstances but who manage to function for the most part adequately. The glass doll represents those children who are severely disturbed or subject to recurrent psychotic episodes.

Superchildren tend to share a number of characteristics that serve as buffers—protective factors—against the risks (Pines, 1979a). First, superchildren are quite at ease with people while making others feel comfortable with them. Second, these children are adept at extracting support and encouragement from teachers, relatives, baby-sitters, and other adults who compensate for their parents' inadequacies. Third, superchildren ac-

tively tackle their environment and have a sense of their own power and competence. Fourth, they minimize their emotional involvement with a sick parent and acquire a high degree of independence early in life. And fifth, they are an achieving group who generally show a good deal of creativity and originality.

One thing above all stands out. Superchildren need challenges to become invulnerables. Low-risk conditions do not compel children to mobilize their resources and do not provide the real-life circumstances by which children test, hone, and refine their adaptive capabilities.

Superchildren remind us of Greek mythology. When Achilles' mother, Thetis, learned of the fatal destiny awaiting her son, she tried to immunize him against his fate by plunging him into the protective waters of the river Styx. In so doing, Thetis rendered all of Achilles, except for the heel by which she held him, invulnerable to harm. Later, when Achilles was nine, a seer prophesied that he would conquer Troy but that he would die in the process. His resourceful mother disguised Achilles as a girl, but Odysseus discovered the deception, and Achilles was inducted into military service. Achilles died at Troy when his vulnerable heel was pierced by an arrow. By contrast, Hercules triumphed over nearly impossible dangers by virtue of his own efforts, while his mother looked on, always confident that he would succeed.

Like Hercules, superchildren have not been overprotected from risk. They seem to gain both in confidence and in competence from their encounters with difficulty. Immunity that is self-generated is apparently more complete and long-lasting. In real life, however, there does appear to be a limit to the number and severity of concurrent stresses that even the most resilient children can handle and master. All these examples suggest that we still have a good deal to learn about vulnerability and risk in childhood and at what developmental periods and with what outside resources intervention might be most effective.

havior. For instance, socially engaging children typically elicit from other people more social interaction than do passive, sober children. In the *active relationship* children seek out environments that they find compatible with their temperament and genetic propensities. For example, sociable children search for playmates and even

create imaginary playmates if real ones are not at hand. In short, what children experience in any given environment is a function of genetic individuality and developmental status (Scarr, 1985b). Scientists, then, are increasingly able to apply rigorous measurements to some aspects of the old nature-nurture controversy.

SUMMARY

1. Like all other living things, human beings are capable of producing new individuals of their own kind and thus ensuring the survival of the species. This process is termed "reproduction." Two kinds of cells are involved in human reproduction: the male gamete, or sperm, and the female gamete, or ovum. A male sperm fuses with a female ovum to form a zygote (fertilized egg).

2. A mature ovum is produced about every twenty-eight days. Toward the middle of each monthly ovarian cycle, an ovum usually reaches maturity and passes into one of the oviducts. If sperm are present, fertilization takes place in the upper end of the oviduct. Secretions of progesterone from the corpus luteum prepare the uterus for implantation of the zygote. If pregnancy does not occur, the thickened outer layers of uterine tissue are shed. This process, called "menstruation," generally occurs fourteen days after ovulation.

3. As more and more Americans are marrying at later ages and postponing their childbearing years until their thirties, they are increasing their chances that they will experience fertility problems. Infertility causes a good many couples profound anguish. In vitro fertilization and related techniques have been developed by medical researchers to enhance the chances of pregnancy. But considerable ethical controversy surrounds the procedures.

4. Some infertile couples have turned to surrogate motherhood. Surrogate motherhood has rendered traditional biological definitions of motherhood obsolete and raised countless ethical and legal questions.

5. Some of the difficulties that surround the nature-nurture controversy stem from the fact that investigators often operate from different models or basic assumptions. The manner in which we phrase our questions structures the alternatives by which the questions are answered.

6. Scientists began by asking *which* factor, heredity or environment, is responsible for the fashioning of a given trait. Most scientists have come to recognize that a great many problems arise from inserting the word "versus" between the words "heredity" and "environment." It serves to separate and oppose two components that, in the context in which they are generally discussed, are neither separable nor opposable.

7. When scientists came to recognize the inappropriateness of the "which" question, some of them took a somewhat different approach. They sought to establish *how much* of the observed differences among people are due to heredity and *how much* to differences in environment. Scientists have traditionally sought answers to the "how much" question through studies that measure resemblances among family members with respect to given traits.

8. Recently, a number of scientists have argued that the "how much" question, like the "which" question, leads to no productive end. They have insisted that a more fruitful approach is to be found in the question of *how* specific hereditary and environmental factors work together to influence various characteristics.

KEY TERMS

Amniocentesis   A medical procedure that allows a physician to test for fetal defects by analyzing cells contained in the amniotic fluid.

Chorionic Villus Biopsy   A medical procedure that allows a physician to test for embryonic defects by analyzing cells contained in the chorionic villus.

Continuum of Indirectness   The view that heredity plays a more central role in some aspects of development than in others. At one end of the continuum the contributions of heredity are quite direct; at the other end, quite indirect.

Environment   All the external factors that affect an organism.

Fertilization   The union of a sperm and an ovum.

Fraternal (Dizygotic) Twins   Siblings who are born at the same time and who come from two separate eggs.

Heredity   The biological transmission of traits from parents to offspring through genes.

Identical (Monozygotic) Twins   Siblings who come from a single fertilized egg which splits into two parts early in development. Both parts grow into separate and complete individuals who in most respects are genetically carbon copies of each other.

Infertility A condition in which a couple fails to achieve pregnancy after one year of having engaged in sexual relations with normal frequency and without contraception.

In Vitro Fertilization A procedure that combines laboratory conception with subsequent natural embryonic and fetal development.

Polygenic Inheritance Traits that derive from the interaction of several genes.

Reproduction The process by which organisms produce more organisms of their own kind.

Ultrasonography A procedure employing ultrasounds that allows physicians to trace the size and shape of a fetus and determine malformations.

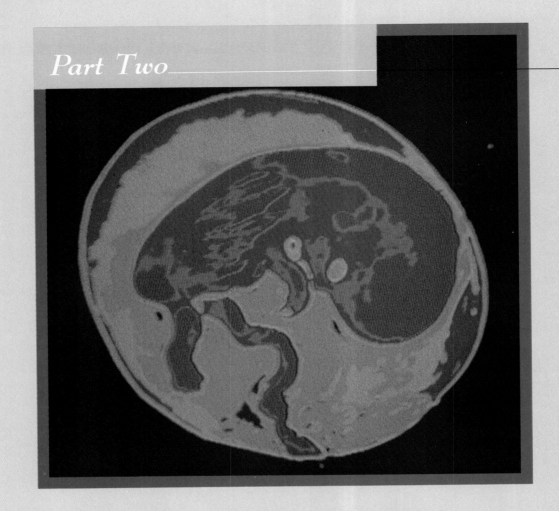

Part Two

The Prenatal and Neonatal Periods

Chapter 4

PRENATAL DEVELOPMENT AND BIRTH

Stages of Prenatal Development

The Germinal Period ◆ The Embryonic Period ◆ The Fetal Period

Prenatal Environmental Influences

Drugs and Other Chemical Agents ◆ Maternal Infectious and Noninfectious Diseases

Maternal Sensitization: The Rh Factor ◆ Maternal Nutrition and Prenatal Care

Maternal Stress ◆ Maternal Age

Birth

The Birth Process ◆ Natural Childbirth ◆ Parent-Infant Bonding

Birthing Rooms and Family-Centered Hospital Care ◆ The Baby's Birth Experience

Complications of Pregnancy and Birth

Toxemia ◆ Caesarean Sections ◆ Prematurity

————————◆————————

One hundred and sixty years ago, the English critic and poet Samuel Taylor Coleridge wrote: "The history of man for the nine months preceding his birth would, probably, be far more interesting, and contain events of greater moment, than all the three score and ten years that follow it." Only in recent years have scientists developed the skill to study these nine crucial months, and they have found that Coleridge was quite right.

Between conception and birth the human being grows from a single cell, barely visible to the naked eye, to a mass of about 7 pounds containing some 200 billion cells. Of this period the physical anthropologist Ashley Montagu writes (1964, pp. 20–21):

> Never again in his life, in so brief a period will this human being grow so rapidly or so much, or develop in so many directions, as he does between conception and birth. . . . During this critical period, the development of the human body exhibits the most perfect timing and the most elaborate correlations that we ever display in our entire lives. The building and launching of a satellite, involving thousands of people and hundreds of electronic devices, is not nearly so complex an operation as the building and launching of a human being.

This chapter will describe the remarkable and important period of prenatal development and the process of birth.

Stages of Prenatal Development

The **prenatal period** is the time elapsing between conception and birth. It normally averages about 266 days, or 280 days from the last menstrual period. Embryologists divide prenatal development into three stages. The first, the **germinal period,** extends from conception to the end of the second week; the second, the **embryonic period,** from the end of the second week to the end of the eighth week; and the third, the **fetal period,** from the end of the eighth week until birth.

The Germinal Period

The germinal period is characterized by (1) the growth of the zygote and (2) the establishment of a linkage between the zygote and the support system of the mother. After fertilization the zygote begins a four-day journey down the oviduct (see Figure 4-1). It is moved along by the action of the cilia and the active contraction of the muscular walls of the oviduct. Within a few hours of fertilization, growth begins with the initiation of mitosis. In **mitosis** the zygote divides, forming two cells identical in makeup to the first cell. In turn, each of these cells divides, making four

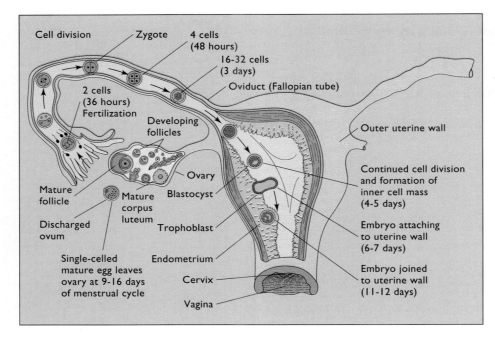

Figure 4-1 Early Human Development: The Course of the Ovum and Embryo
The drawing depicts the female reproductive system, the fertilization of the ovum, and the early growth of the embryo.

cells. The four cells then divide into eight, eight into sixteen, sixteen into thirty-two, and so on.

The early cell divisions in development are called *cleavage.* Cleavage occurs very slowly. It takes about twenty-four hours for the first cleavage and ten to twelve hours for each subsequent cleavage. These cell divisions soon convert the zygote into a hollow ball of cells termed a **blastocyst.**

For two or three days the blastocyst is free within the uterine cavity. When it is about 6 to 7 days old and composed of some 100 cells, the blastocyst makes contact with the *endometrium,* the wall of the uterus. The endometrium in turn becomes vascular, glandular, and thick. The blastocyst "digests" its way into the endometrium through the action of enzymes and gradually becomes completely buried in it. As a result, the embryo develops within the wall of the uterus and not in its cavity. This invasion of the uterus by the blastocyst creates a small pool of maternal blood. During the germinal period the organism derives its nourishment from the eroded tissue and maternal blood that flow through spaces in the outer layer of cells of the blastocyst.

By the eleventh day the blastocyst has completely buried itself in the wall of the uterus. At this stage in development the organism is about the size of a pinhead. As of yet, the mother is seldom aware of any symptoms of pregnancy.

At about the time that the blastocyst starts the implantation process, it begins separating into two layers (see Figure 4-2). The outer layer of cells, called the *trophoblast,* is responsible for embedding the embryo in the uterine wall. The inner surface of the trophoblast becomes the nonmaternal portions of the placenta, the *amnion* and *chorion.* The amnion forms a closed sac around the embryo and is filled with a watery amniotic fluid to keep the embryo moist and protect it against shock or adhesions. The chorion is a membrane that surrounds the amnion and links the embryo to the placenta. The internal disc or cluster of cells that compose the blastocyst, termed the *inner cell mass,* produces the embryo. The amnion, chorion, embryo, and related tissues are depicted in Figure 4-3 as they appear in increasingly differentiated and advanced stages of development. The entire process is controlled by genes: Some genes turn on rapidly as the embryo develops; others turn off slowly; and still others operate throughout the prenatal period and beyond. The patterns of gene activity are complex and involve many different genes (Marx, 1984).

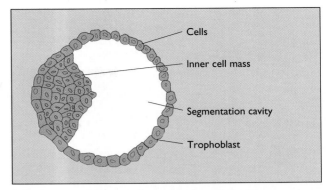

Figure 4-2   Schematic Cross Section of the Blastocyst at About Seven Days
Cleavage of the zygote produces a small ball of cells within which appears a fluid-filled cavity: the segmentation cavity. *The blastocyst differentiates into two layers. The outer layer, the* trophoblast, *gives rise to the non-maternal portion of the placenta; the internal cluster of cells, the* inner cell mass, *becomes the embryo. When the blastocyst is about 6 or 7 days old, it begins implanting itself in the uterine wall.*

Toward the end of the second week the embryonic portion of the inner cell mass begins to separate into three layers: the *ectoderm* (the outer layer), which is the source of future cells forming the nervous system, the sensory organs, the skin, and the lower part of the rectum; the *mesoderm* (the middle layer), which gives rise to the skeletal, muscular, and circulatory systems and the kidneys; and the *endoderm* (the inner layer), which develops into the digestive tract (including the liver, the pancreas, and the gall bladder), the respiratory system, the bladder, and portions of the reproductive organs.

The Embryonic Period

The embryonic period lasts from the end of the second week to the eighth week. It spans that period of pregnancy from the time the blastocyst completely implants itself in the uterine wall to the time the developing organism becomes a recognizable human fetus. This period is characterized by (1) rapid growth, (2) the establishment of a placental relationship with the mother, (3) the early structural appearance of all the chief organs, and (4) the development, in form at least, of a recognizable human body.

The embryo becomes attached to the wall of the uterus by means of the *placenta* (Beaconsfield, Birdwood & Beaconsfield, 1980). The pla-

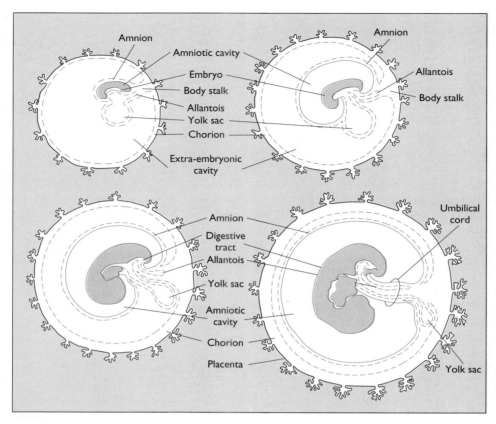

Figure 4-3 Human Embryonic Development: The Early Stages

The figure shown the successive stages in the early development of the human embryo. The primary embryonic membranes are the amnion and the chorion. The amniotic cavity provides a fluid environment that cushions the embryo. The chorion is the embryonic part of the placenta. From the chorion develop villi, small capillaries that extend into the maternal portion of the placenta. The embryo is joined to the placenta by the umbilical cord. The solid lines represent layers of ectoderm; the dashed lines, mesoderm; and the dotted lines, endoderm. SOURCE: From *Biology* by Claude E. Villee and Eldra Pearl Solomon, copyright © 1985 by Holt, Rinehart and Winston, Inc. Reprinted by permission of the publisher.

centa forms from uterine tissue and the trophoblast of the blastocyst. The placenta functions as an exchange terminal that permits the entry of food materials, oxygen, and hormones and the exit of carbon dioxide and metabolic wastes. It is a partially permeable membrane that does not permit the passage of blood cells between the two organisms. This feature provides a safeguard against the mingling of the blood of the mother with that of the embryo. Were the mother's and embryo's blood to intermix, the mother's body would reject the embryo as foreign material.

The transfer between the placenta and the embryo occurs across a web of fingerlike projections—*villi*—that extend into blood spaces in the maternal uterus. The villi begin developing during the second week, growing outward from the chorion. When the placenta is fully developed at about the seventh month of pregnancy, it is shaped like a pancake or disc that is 1 inch thick and 7 inches in diameter. From the beginning, the embryo is linked to the placenta by the *umbilical cord*, a conduit carrying two arteries and one vein. This connecting structure, or lifeline, is attached to the middle of the fetal abdomen.

Development commences with the brain and head areas and then works its way down the body—termed **cephalocaudal development** (see Figure 4-4). In this manner, nature ensures an adequate nervous system for the proper functioning of other systems. During the early part of the third week the developing embryo begins to take the shape of a pear, the broad, knobby end of which becomes the head. The cells in the central portion of the embryo also thicken and form a slight ridge that is referred to as the *primitive streak*. The primitive streak divides the developing embryo into right and left halves and eventually becomes the spinal cord. The tissues grow in opposite directions away from the axis of the primitive streak, a process termed **proximodistal development.**

By the twenty-eighth day the head region takes up roughly one-third of the embryo's length. Also about this time, a brain and a primitive spinal cord become evident. As development progresses during the second month, the head elevates, the neck emerges, and rudiments of the nose, eyes, mouth, and tongue appear. Another critical system—the circulatory system—also develops early. By the end of the third week the heart tube has already begun to beat in a halting manner.

Within four weeks of conception the embryo is about ⅕ inch long—nearly 10,000 times larger than the fertilized egg. About this time the mother usually becomes suspicious that she is pregnant. Her menstrual period is generally two weeks overdue. She may feel a heaviness, fullness, and tingling in her breasts; simultaneously, the nipples and surrounding areolas may enlarge and darken. Also at this time, about one-half to two-thirds of all pregnant women experience a morning queasiness or nauseous feeling. The condition, popularly called "morning sickness," persists for several weeks or months.

The Fetal Period

The final stage in prenatal life—the fetal period—begins with the ninth week and ends with birth. During this time the major organ systems continue to develop and the organs assume their specialized functions. By the end of the eighth week the organism definitely resembles a human being. It is complete with face, arms, legs, fingers, toes, basic trunk and head muscles, and internal organs. The fetus now builds on this basic form (see the boxed insert on page 98).

Development during the fetal period is less dramatic than that during the embryonic period. Even so, significant changes occur. By the tenth week the fetal face acquires a truly human appearance (see Figure 4-5). During the third month the fetus develops skeletal and neurological structures that lay the foundation for spontaneous movements of the arms, legs, and fingers. By the fourth month stimulation of the infant's body surfaces activates a variety of reflex responses. About the beginning of the fifth month the mother generally begins to feel the spontaneous movements of the fetus (called *quickening*, a sensation like a moving butterfly in the abdominal region). Also during the fifth month, a fine, downy, woolly fuzz (*lanugo hair*) comes to cover the fetal body.

At six months the eyebrows and lashes are well defined; the body is lean but strikingly human in proportions; the skin is wrinkled. At seven months the fetus (now weighing about 2½ pounds and measuring about 15 inches in length) gives the appearance of a dried-up, aged person, with red, wrinkled skin covered by a waxy coating (*vernix*); the fetus is now a viable organism and can cry weakly. At eight months fat is being deposited around the body, the fetus gains an additional 2 pounds, and the infant increases neuromuscular activity.

At nine months the dull redness of the skin fades to pink, the limbs become rounded, and the fingernails and toenails are well formed. At full term (thirty-eight weeks) the body is plump; the skin has lost most of its lanugo hair, although the body is still covered with vernix; and all the organs necessary to carry on independent life are functioning. The fetus is now ready for birth.

Figure 4-4   Changes in the Form and Proportion of the Human Body
The drawing depicts the growth of a male's body during the embryonic, fetal, and postnatal stages. Note the developmental changes in the size of the head and limbs in relation to the size of the body. SOURCE: From *From Conception to Birth: The Drama of Life's Beginnings* by Roberts Rugh and Landrum B. Shettles. Copyright © 1971 by Roberts Rugh and Landrum B. Shettles. Reprinted by permission of Harper & Row Publishers, Inc. From *Growth* by W. J. Robbins et al., Yale University Press, 1928. Reprinted by permission.

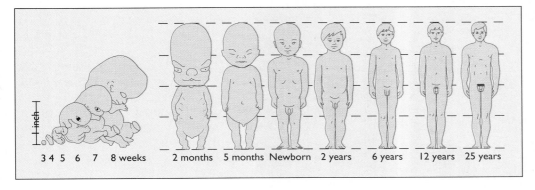

3 4 5 6 7 8 weeks   2 months   5 months   Newborn   2 years   6 years   12 years   25 years

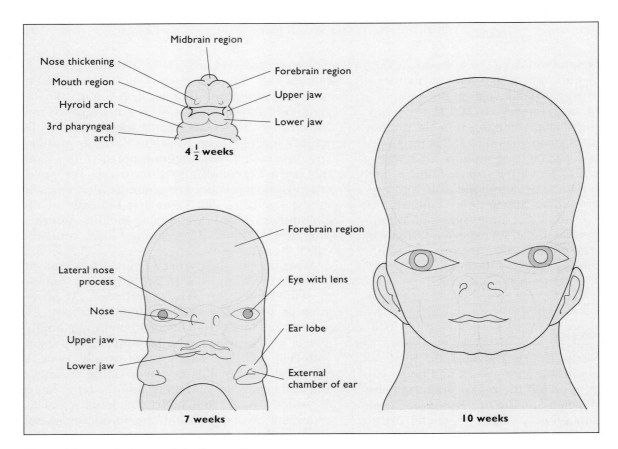

Figure 4-5 Development of the Human Face

Between four and a half and ten weeks the fetal face acquires a truly human appearance. However, even by the tenth week the eyes are still far apart, the ears are not fully elevated, the nostrils are only somewhat closer together, and the mouth is open. SOURCE: Roberts Rugh and Landrum B. Shettles, *From Conception to Birth: The Drama of Life's Beginnings* (New York: Harper & Row, 1971), pp. 48–49. Copyright © 1971 by Roberts Rugh and Landrum B. Shettles. Reprinted by permission of Harper & Row, Publishers, Inc.

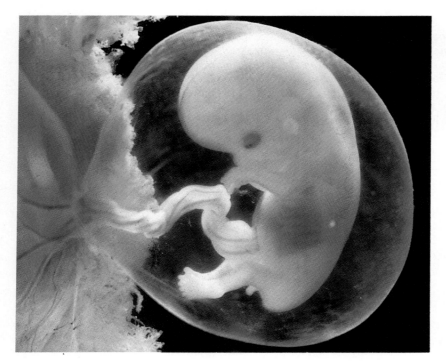

The Fetus at the Ninth Week

At the beginning of the fetal period—about the ninth week—the developing child has already acquired recognizable human features. The face, hands, and feet are forming in a distinctly human fashion. *(Lennart Nilsson, from* A Child Is Born, *Dell, 1966)*

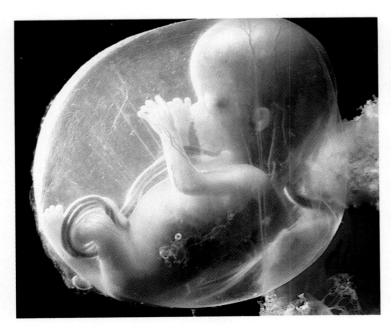

The Fetus at Three Months

At three months the fetus is a little more than three inches long and weighs nearly an ounce. Its head is disproportionally large and appears increasingly like that of a human. By now the external ears and eyelids have formed. The umbilical cord increases in size to accommodate the growing organism. The fetus is developing the skeletal and neurological structures that provide the foundation for moving in its capsule, where it floats weightlessly much in the manner of an astronaut in space. *(Lennart Nilsson, from* Behold Man, *Little, Brown, 1974)*

The Fetus at Four Months

At four months the fetus is more than six inches long and weighs about seven ounces. All the organs have formed. The fetus now increases in size, readying itself for birth in five more months. In about a month the mother will begin to feel the fetus's spontaneous movements. *(Lennart Nilsson, from* Behold Man, *Little, Brown, 1974)*

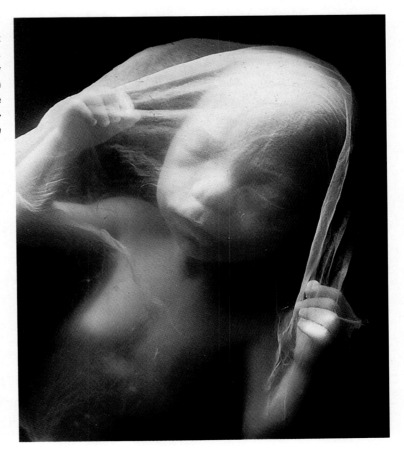

Highlights of Prenatal Development

First Month

❏ Fertilization occurs.
❏ Blastocyst implants itself in the lining of the uterus.
❏ The blastocyst differentiates into the trophoblast and the inner cell mass.
❏ The inner cell mass differentiates into three layers: the ectoderm, the mesoderm, and the endoderm.
❏ Nervous and circulatory systems begin to develop.

Second Month

❏ The head develops rapidly, at first accounting for about half of the embryo's size.
❏ The face and neck begin to form.
❏ The eyes rapidly begin converging toward the center of the face.
❏ Mouth and jaws form and become well differentiated.
❏ Major organs of the digestive system become differentiated.
❏ Buds for the limbs form and grow.
❏ The circulatory system between the embryo and the placenta is completed, and heartbeats begin.

Third Month

❏ The digestive organs begin functioning.
❏ Centers of ossification (bone formation) appear.
❏ Buds for all temporary teeth form.
❏ Sex organs develop rapidly, especially in males.
❏ Arms, legs, and fingers make spontaneous movements.

Fourth Month

❏ The face acquires a human appearance.
❏ The lower parts of the body show rapid growth, with the body outgrowing the head.
❏ Reflex movement becomes brisker.
❏ Most bones are distinctly indicated throughout the body.

❏ In males the testes are in position for later descent into the scrotum; in females the uterus and vagina are recognizable.

Fifth Month

❏ Lanugo hair (a fine, woolly fuzz) covers the whole body.
❏ Vernix (a waxy coating) collects.
❏ The nose and ears begin ossification.
❏ Fingernails and toenails begin to appear.

Sixth Month

❏ Eyebrows and lashes are well defined.
❏ The body is lean but strikingly human in its head and body proportions.
❏ The cerebral cortex becomes layered.
❏ The eyes are completely formed.

Seventh Month

❏ If born, the fetus is capable of living outside the uterus.
❏ The fetus looks like a dried-up, aged person with red, wrinkled skin.
❏ The cerebral fissures and convolutions develop rapidly.

Eighth and Ninth Months

❏ Subcutaneous fat is deposited for later use.
❏ The fingernails reach beyond the fingertips.
❏ A good deal of the lanugo hair is shed.
❏ Initial myelination of the brain takes place. (Myelin is a fatty substance that forms a sheath around the axons of nerve cells.)
❏ The activity of the chief organs is stepped up.
❏ Vernix is present over the entire body.

Recent research with sheep suggests that hormones released by the fetal pituitary and adrenal glands are involved in terminating pregnancy. In sheep, immediately prior to birth, the production of adrenocorticotropic hormone (ACTH) by the pituitary increases and is then followed by a rise in cortisol from the adrenal gland. The increased cortisol alters the enzymatic balance in the mother's uterus, and this development seems to trigger the beginning of labor. Scientists are now carrying out research to discover whether this model for sheep also works in human beings (Palca, 1991).

Prenatal Environmental Influences

To most of us, the concept of environment refers to a human being's surroundings *after* birth. In truth, of course, environmental influences are operating from the moment of conception. The fertilized ovum undertakes a hazardous week-long journey down the Fallopian tube and around the uterus, encountering throughout a highly variable and chemically active medium. We generally think of the uterus as providing a sheltered, warm, and protected environment for prenatal development. But even after implanting itself in the uterus, the embryo is vulnerable to maternal disease, malnutrition, and biochemical malfunctioning.

Most pregnancies end with the birth of normal, healthy babies. Nonetheless, an estimated 10 to 15 percent of all conceptions result in spontaneous abortions or stillbirths (the boxed insert on page 100 considers the mourning associated with the loss of an unborn child). About a quarter of these are the product of chromosomal and gene abnormalities (Mueller, 1983). The remainder result from problems associated with prenatal environment. Another 6 to 7 percent—totaling 250,000 babies each year in the United States—are born with birth defects. Some of these defects arise from environmental factors (Elkington, 1985; Stechler & Halton, 1982). Scientists term any agent that contributes to birth defects a **teratogen** (derived from the Greek word "tera," meaning monster). The field of study concerned with birth defects is called **teratology.**

Drugs and Other Chemical Agents

The thalidomide tragedy in the early 1960s awakened the medical profession and the public alike to the potential dangers of drugs for pregnant women. Thousands of German, English, and Canadian women who had taken thalidomide (a tranquilizer) during the embryonic stage of pregnancy gave birth to infants with malformed limbs. We now know that many drugs and chemical agents cross the placental barrier and affect the embryonic and fetal systems (Elkington, 1985; Hutchings, 1989). Quinine (used in the treatment of malaria) can cause congenital deafness. Barbiturates (sedating drugs) may affect the oxygen supply to the fetus and result in brain damage. Antihistamines may increase the mother's susceptibility to spontaneous abortion. And even aspirin and a number of antibiotics have been tentatively linked in several cases to heart, hearing, and other problems (Barr, Streissguth, Darby & Sampson, 1990; Bowes, Brackbill, Conway & Steinschneider, 1970; Findlay, 1985b; Stuart, Gross, Elrad & Graeber, 1982).

According to current medical opinion, pregnant women should not take drugs except when they have conditions that seriously threaten their health—and then *only* under the supervision of a physician. Some authorities advise against extra vitamins (particularly vitamin A) unless they are prescribed by a physician. Likewise, miscellaneous reports of increased rates of spontaneous abortion and birth defects among coffee drinkers prompted the Federal Food and Drug Administration (FDA) to recommend in 1980 that women stop or reduce their consumption of coffee, tea, and cola drinks during pregnancy (Hronsky & Emory, 1987).

Smoking The nicotine found in tobacco is a drug. When an expectant mother smokes, her bloodstream absorbs nicotine. The drug is then transmitted through the placenta to the embryo (Jacobson, Fein, Jacobson, Schwartz & Dowler, 1984; Mactutus & Fechter, 1984). Chronic smokers are twice as likely to give birth to premature infants as nonsmokers are. This statistic poses a serious hazard, because the mortality rate for premature infants is higher than that for full-term infants. Furthermore, major congenital abnormalities are more prevalent among the infants of women who smoke (Barr, Streissguth, Darby & Sampson, 1990; Everson, 1986). Recent research also suggests that the risk of miscarriage and infant death varies with how much and how long a woman smoked *before* pregnancy. Indeed, even children exposed only to their fathers' smoking before birth have increased risk of developing leukemia, lymphoma, and brain cancer than have those youngsters whose father did not smoke (suggesting that smoking may have damaged the fathers' sperm) (*New York Times,* 1991).

Marijuana An accumulating body of evidence suggests that marijuana use by expectant mothers has detrimental effects on fetal development and neonatal behavior, including infants' neurological development (Fried, Watkinson & Dillon, 1987; Lester & Dreher, 1989; Lind et al., 1983). In addition, a report on marijuana issued by the Institute of Medicine of the National Academy of Science (Relman, 1982) concludes that marijuana suppresses the production of male hormones, decreases the size and weight of the prostate and the testes, and inhibits sperm production. It may also interfere with ovulation in women. THC (the primary psychoactive ingredient of marijuana) crosses the placental barrier, and hence, there is the potential for harm to the

What Might Have Been:
Mourning the Unborn

Miriam Lieberman lost a daughter in her seventh month of pregnancy. One day the child stopped its periodic kicking. At the hospital, she says, the staff "wouldn't look me in the eye; they acted as if it was just another medical procedure." Labor was induced and the baby was stillborn. Mrs. Lieberman returned home, but for weeks thereafter she experienced a good deal of sadness and bouts of crying. She distrusted her feelings because she did not believe she should miss so deeply a child she had never known. Five years later she had a miscarriage, this time in her third month. In the interval she and her husband, Thomas, had had two healthy children. But her living children were not the sole reason that her second loss was less devastating than her first. Rather than "holding it in," as she had done the first time, Mrs. Lieberman talked about her feelings "even with those doctors and nurses who didn't want to hear." She insisted upon tests to determine the cause of the miscarriage because she found the usual answer, "It's nature's way," unsatisfactory. And she joined a support group, meeting with trained counselors and peers who had experienced similar misfortunes (Belkin, 1985).

Parents like Mrs. Lieberman are now finding new ways for confronting a loss that is one of the most devastating crises a family can face. An estimated 525,000 miscarriages and 33,000 stillbirths (fetuses older than twenty weeks) occur annually in the United States. The medical profession is coming to recognize that an attachment between a parent and the child in the womb begins quite early. Research studies and the experience of self-help groups suggest that a loss even in the early weeks of pregnancy can be a cause for mourning and that family members require time and opportunities to work through their grief (Carey, 1984).

A common assumption is that the timing of the loss affects the reactions to it, so that the longer the pregnancy continues, the more severe the loss is. But this assumption is not necessarily true. Much depends on whether the child was wanted or planned, whether there had been prior miscarriages, and how long the parents had tried to conceive.

In addition to experiencing normal grief, many women blame themselves for miscarrying. They tell themselves, "If only I hadn't done this or done that, then maybe this wouldn't have happened." Such a reaction can be especially difficult if a woman concludes that her loss is a kind of punishment for something that happened in her past. Men, too, can experience a miscarriage as devastating. Yet physicians, family, and friends concentrate on how the woman is faring, leaving the man often feeling that his sense of loss does not count. There are also repercussions for a couple in subsequent pregnancies, when unresolved feelings and anxieties from an earlier loss are channeled into the next pregnancy. Many couples experience a sense of vulnerability; they cannot wait to get past "D day"—the day the previous miscarriage occurred (Cole, 1987). Even years later, when the pain has eased, parents may still have thoughts about the child: "If the baby had lived she would be in kindergarten by now" (Belkin, 1985).

What can family members and friends do to help a couple deal with their feelings of sadness? First, parents should be given an opportunity to acknowledge their loss and come to terms with it in their own unique ways. Mourning is different for each person, so do not expect someone to show the same responses you encountered in another neighbor, relative, or friend. Second, and of equal importance, help the parent to grieve openly: Be prepared to listen and reassure the person that his or her sad or angry feelings and seemingly irrational fantasies (kidnapping someone else's child, for instance) are common. Do not give advice on how to avoid future miscarriages, since the woman may interpret your words as implying that she was to blame. And medical personnel should be prepared to answer questions concerning the causes of the miscarriage and what the outlook is for future pregnancies. Finally, support organizations like SHARE, Resolve, the Compassionate Friends, and Resolve Through Sharing can be a source of counseling and support. Rituals, including naming the child and holding a memorial service, can also be appropriate, allowing parents a concrete action for coming to terms with their loss (Cole, 1987).

fetus. However, contrary to some earlier studies, the report concludes that neither marijuana nor THC causes chromosome breaks.

Hard Drugs   Heroin, methadone, and cocaine are capable of producing a wide range of birth deformities (Kalter & Warkany, 1983*b*). Moreover, infants whose mothers are addicted to hard drugs show withdrawal syndromes consisting of hyperactivity, trembling, shrill crying, and vomiting. The infants also display greater irritability and restlessness and have more sleep and feeding disburbances than do their nonaddicted counterparts. Of considerable concern is that the behavioral and psychological difficulties seem to persist throughout early and middle childhood (Chasnoff, 1985; Chira, 1990; Householder, Hatcher, Burns & Chasnoff, 1982; Kantrowitz, 1990; Lester et al., 1991). We will have more to say on these matters in Chapter 5. Researchers also find that cocaine binds tightly to sperm in test tubes, raising the possibility that men who use cocaine may increase the risk of birth defects in their offspring (Friend, 1991).

Alcohol In the Old Testament Samson's mother is admonished by an angel: "Thou shalt conceive, and bear a son. Now therefore beware, I pray thee, and drink not wine nor strong drink." However, not until the past two decades have medical scientists confirmed what many people seem to have known for thousands of years: Alcohol consumed by a pregnant woman can damage her unborn child. At first researchers thought that only the offspring of heavy-drinking alcoholic mothers were at risk for *fetal alcohol syndrome*— a cluster of severe physical and mental defects caused by alcohol damage to the developing child. Now findings suggest that even as little as two drinks a week may do damage. And 4-year-olds whose mothers have three drinks a day when pregnant suffer an average IQ decline of almost 5 IQ points (Streissguth, Barr, Sampson, Derby & Martin, 1989). Fetal alcohol damage appears to be irreversible. No amount of good nutrition and postnatal care erase the growth retardation and brain damage (Brody, 1986*b*; M. W. Miller, 1986; Streissguth, 1984). Consequently, in 1980 the Food and Drug Administration warned pregnant women and women considering pregnancy not to drink any alcoholic beverages, because to do so may endanger the health of their unborn children.

Oral Contraceptives Exposure to female sex hormones has also been linked to birth defects. An estimated 10 percent of pregnant women in the United States use oral contraceptives early in their pregnancies. The birth defects involve the heart, limbs, anus, esophagus, vertebral column, or central nervous system (Nora & Nora, 1973, 1975). One research group examined data on 50,282 pregnancies within the United States (Heinonen, Slone & Shapiro, 1977). Of the children born to 49,240 women who did not receive hormones, 385 had congenital heart defects—a rate of 7.8 per 1,000. In contrast, 19 children born to 1,042 women who took hormones had serious heart abnormalities—a rate of 18.2 per 1,000.

Toxins in the Environment Expectant women often encounter potentially toxic agents in their everyday lives, including hair spray, cosmetics, insecticides, cleaning solutions, food preservatives, and polluted air and water. The specific risk associated with these agents remains to be determined. It is known, however, that contact with chemical defoliants should be avoided. The National Cancer Institute has linked chemical sprays used to destroy jungle and forest areas in Vietnam with a substantial increase in the number of malformed Vietnamese infants. In 1979 the federal Environmental Protection Agency ordered an emergency ban on herbicides containing dioxin (including 2,4,5-T and Silvex). The federal agency took action because of "significant evidence" linking the spraying of dioxin herbicides with an "alarming" rate of miscarriages among women in Oregon. Miscarriages and birth defects also occur at two to three times average rates in areas of California where water is contaminated by chemicals used in high-tech electronics manufacturing (Miller, 1985). And researchers have found that the infants of mothers who ate Lake Michigan fish contaminated with PCBs (a chemical widely used in electrical equipment and other industrial applications before it was banned in 1976) show "worrisome" behavioral and developmental deficits at age 4 (Jacobson, Jacobson, Fein, Schwartz & Dowler, 1984).

Toxins in the Workplace In recent years medical authorities have become increasingly concerned over the hazards to the reproductive process that are found in the places where people work (Elkington, 1985; Kalter & Warkany, 1983*a*). Studies reveal, for instance, that continuous exposure to a variety of gaseous anesthetic agents used in hospital settings is associated with an increased number of spontaneous abortions among women workers *and* among the wives of exposed male workers. The children of these people also have a higher incidence of congenital malformations. A California study disclosed that 29.7 percent of pregnant nurses working in operating rooms had spontaneous miscarriages. The

"I'm glad I'm already borned so I don't hafta go every place with Mommy."

("Family Circus" © 1991 Bill Keane, Inc. Reprinted with special permission of King Features Syndicate.)

figure was only 8.8 percent among pregnant general-duty nurses (Bronson, 1977a). And the University of Massachusetts School of Public Health has found that women working in so-called clean rooms of semiconductor makers—where computer chips are etched with acids and gases—have a miscarriage rate nearly twice the national average (Meier, 1987). As a result of these findings, the American Telephone and Telegraph Company has banned all pregnant women from its semiconductor production lines (Sanger, 1987). Studies are also under way to determine the risks posed by video display terminals, or VDTs, following reports of high miscarriage rates among some VDT users in several industries. VDTs emit unique wavelengths of ionizing radiation.

Sperm are no less susceptible to damage from environmental causes than are ova. This fact has often been overlooked since the reproductive systems of women—not men—are most often studied. Nonetheless, a number of studies suggest a link between male exposure to chemical agents and reproduction. A survey of oral surgeons and dentists who were exposed to anesthetic gas for three hours or more per week revealed that their wives had a 78 percent higher incidence of spontaneous abortions than did the wives of other such practitioners (Bronson, 1977a). Welders

who breathe toxic metal fumes develop abnormal sperm, even after exposure ceases for three weeks. Firefighters who are exposed to toxic smoke have an increased risk of fathering children with heart defects (Blakeslee, 1991). Children of men working at the Sellafield nuclear power plant in England are up to eight times as likely to be stricken by leukemia as children whose fathers do not work at the facility (researchers theorize that cumulative low-level doses of radiation may trigger the damage) (Purvis, 1990). The National Institute for Occupational Safety and Health (NIOSH) has found that male workers exposed to glycol ethers, a class of solvents widely used in the paint and electronics industries, have sperm counts sharply below the national average. Other tests suggest that exposure to arsenic, mercury, some solvents, and various pesticides may also contribute to male infertility, spontaneous abortions, and birth defects. In sum, it makes sense to clean up the workplace not only for mothers but for fathers as well (Blakeslee, 1991).

Maternal Infectious and Noninfectious Diseases

Under some circumstances infections that cause illness in the mother can harm the fetus (Kalter & Warkany, 1983a) When the mother is directly infected, viruses, bacteria, or malarial parasites may cross the placenta and infect the child. In other cases the fetus may be indirectly affected by a high fever in the mother or by toxins produced by bacteria in the mother's body. The exact time during the fetus's development at which an infection occurs in the mother has an important bearing. As described earlier, the infant's organs and structures emerge according to a fixed sequence and timetable. Each organ and structure has a critical period during which it is most vulnerable to damaging influences.

Rubella and Other Infectious Agents If the mother contracts rubella (German measles) in the first three months of pregnancy, there is a substantial risk of blindness, deafness, brain damage, and heart disease in the offspring. In 10 to 20 percent of the pregnancies complicated by rubella, spontaneous abortion or stillbirth ensues. However, should the mother contract the disease in the last three months of pregnancy, there is usually no major damage. Fortunately, a preventive vaccine is now available for rubella. However, a woman must be inoculated at least three months before the beginning of pregnancy. Various other viral, bacterial, and protozoan agents are suspected either of being transmitted to the fetus or of otherwise interfering with normal development. These agents include hepatitis, influenza, poliomyelitis, malaria, typhoid, typhus, mumps, smallpox, scarlet fever, gonorrhea, and cytomegalovirus infection.

Syphilis Syphilis also poses a serious health problem. Should syphilitic mothers not receive treatment with antibiotics, about 25 percent of the fetuses will be aborted or stillborn; many will arrive prematurely; 30 percent will die shortly after birth (Rugh & Shettles, 1971). In some cases the effects of the syphilis spirochete are not immediately apparent at birth. Instead, the disease takes a gradual toll in a deterioration of thought, speech, and motor abilities before the child finally dies. More than three-fourths of known syphilitic pregnant women do not show clinical evidence of the disease. Consequently, the Wasserman test for syphilis should be administered to all pregnant women.

Genital Herpes Of growing concern is the increasing incidence of genital herpes infection. Infants delivered through an infected birth canal stand a risk of contracting the disease, although medical authorities now consider the risk to be somewhat less than earlier research suggested (Prober 1987). Infants whose mothers have had recurrent episodes of herpes infection apparently acquire neutralizing antibodies that lower their risk of contracting the disease. But since 33 percent of infected babies will die and another 25 percent will suffer permanent brain damage, some obstetricians advise delivery by Caesarean section to minimize the chances of infection. Pregnant women with genital herpes also have a considerably higher risk of miscarriage than women without herpes.

AIDS There is substantial risk that women who have been exposed to the AIDS virus (HIV) will give birth to children with the disease. The disease weakens the immune systems of its victims, leaving them prey to unusual infections and forms of cancer. Fighting the spread of the disease is especially difficult because most infants with HIV are born to mothers with no outward signs of disease. Many of the mothers are intravenous drug users and so are at high risk of contracting AIDS from sharing needles. Half to three-quarters of infants infected with HIV have distinct head and face abnormalities, including small head circumference; a prominent, boxlike appearance of the forehead; "scooped out" profile; slanting eyes; blue in the whites of the eyes; and a short, flattened nose. Since craniofacial structures are typically developed during the first trimester of pregnancy, the abnormal features suggest that the virus attacks the fetus early in development. Most prenatally infected youngsters develop symptoms of the disease within the first 12 months of life, including recurrent bacterial infections, swollen lymph glands, failure to thrive, neurological impairments, and delayed development. Often the family is from a lower socioeconomic environment. Consequently, the overwhelming majority of families lack medical insurance and require financial assistance and social services (Task Force on Pediatric AIDS, 1989).

Diabetes Maternal diabetes is another common cause of defects and survival problems for the prenatal infant (Freinkel, 1985; Miller, 1981). Diabetes is a metabolic disease characterized by a deficiency in insulin and an excess of sugar in the blood and urine. If medical measures are not taken to control the mother's diet and to administer insulin artificially, there is a 50 percent probability that the fetus will be aborted or stillborn. Deformities, such as unformed spines, misplaced hearts, and extra ear skin, run as high as one in four. When pregnant women have diabetes, the fetal pancreas is required to adjust to the higher-than-normal sugar level of the diabetic mother by producing increased amounts of insulin itself. This adjustment contributes to abnormal growth of the fetus's pancreas, which in some cases becomes twenty times its normal size. At birth such babies look fat and puffy, and they are about 20 percent overweight. Babies of diabetic mothers often have respiratory problems for a day or so after birth.

Maternal Sensitization: The Rh Factor

The Rh factor is a condition that under some circumstances produces a serious and often fatal form of anemia and jaundice in the fetus or newborn—a disorder termed *erythroblastosis fetalis*. About 85 percent of all whites have the Rh factor; they are called Rh-positive. About 15 percent do not have it; they are Rh-negative. Among blacks only about 7 percent are Rh-negative, and among Asians the figure is less than 1 percent. Rh-positive blood and Rh-negative blood are incompatible. Each blood factor is transmitted genetically in accordance with Mendelian rules (Rh-positive is dominant).

For the most part, the maternal and fetal blood supplies are separated by the placenta. On occasion, however, a capillary in the placenta ruptures, which results in the mixing of a small amount of maternal and fetal blood. Likewise, some admixture usually occurs during the "after-birth," when the placenta separates from the uterine wall.

An incompatibility results between the mother's and the infant's blood when an Rh-negative mother has a baby with Rh-positive blood. Under these conditions, which occur in about 1 of every 200 pregnancies among whites, the mother's body produces antibodies that cross the placenta and attack the baby's blood cells. This condition does not usually cause a problem in a woman's first pregnancy. As yet she lacks sufficient contact with her baby's Rh-positive blood to develop a high level of sensitivity. But successive pregnancies with Rh-positive fetuses may raise the antibodies in the mother's blood to a critical level, creating difficulties for the baby.

Erythroblastosis fetalis can now be prevented if an Rh-negative mother is given anti-Rh antibodies (termed *Rhogam*) shortly after the birth of her first child. They neutralize any Rh-positive blood cells that may enter her circulatory system. As a result, the woman does not produce Rh-positive antibodies, and permanent immunity does not result.

If an Rh-negative mother has already been sensitized to Rh-positive blood by several pregnancies in the absence of Rhogam therapy, her infant can be given an interuterine transfusion. The procedure involves guiding an amniocentesis needle by means of a fluoroscope through the uterus to the lower abdominal region of the fetus. The fetal abdominal cavity is punctured, and the baby is given the transfusion of Rh-negative, nonimmunized blood of the group O blood type. The procedure frequently needs to be repeated at fourteen-day intervals.

Maternal Nutrition and Prenatal Care

The unborn infant's nourishment comes from the maternal bloodstream through the placenta. Consequently, nutritional deficiencies in the mother, particularly severe ones, are reflected in fetal development. Considerable evidence suggests that there is more risk of miscarriage or premature birth for the infants of poorly nourished mothers than for infants of well-nourished mothers. Babies of poorly nourished mothers are also more likely to be underweight at birth; to die in infancy; or to suffer rickets, physical and neural defects, low vitality, and certain forms of mental retardation. These afflictions occur most frequently in native American, black, Chicano, and Puerto Rican children, whose mothers are more likely to be undernourished than the mothers of American whites.

Poor maternal nutrition—associated with war, famine, poverty, and poor dietary practice—has long-term insidious effects on brain growth and intelligence. A seriously deprived fetus may have 15 to 20 percent fewer brain cells than a normal fetus (Brown, 1966; Parekh, Pherwani, Udani & Mukherjie, 1970; Winick, Brasel & Valasco, 1973). Several studies carried out in the United States correlate birth weight and later measured intelligence (Broman, Nichols & Kennedy, 1975; Caputo & Mandell, 1970; Harper & Wiener, 1965). Significantly, of all the factors modifying birth weight, maternal nutrition is generally acknowledged to be the most important (Platt & Stewart, 1971). The effects of fetal malnutrition are often compounded by how the infants deal with others and make use of their environment (Greenberg, 1981a; Zeskind & Ramey, 1981). Their lack of energy, reduced responsiveness, and greater social withdrawal seem to stunt their emotional and intellectual growth. In contrast, more active and involved youngsters tend to elicit greater interest, attention, and interaction over time from their mothers and other caretakers.

One of the major studies revealing a link between birth weight and later intelligence is the extensive follow-up from birth to adolescence of a large sample of premature and normal births in Baltimore (Wiener, 1968; Wiener, Rider, Oppel, Fischer & Harper, 1965). At regular intervals researchers administered intelligence tests to the children and examined their school achievement records. At 3 to 5 years of age, the low-weight babies had a mean IQ of 94.4, compared with 100.6 for the normal-weight babies. The intellectual deficit of the low-birth-weight children persisted at 12 to 13 years of age, the point at which the study was terminated.

Proper prenatal care is also important. Yet in the United States many women either wait until after their fourth month of pregnancy to secure care, or they make fewer than half the number of prenatal visits to physicians recommended by the American College of Obstetricians and Gynecologists. One-third of single mothers receive inadequate care, a rate three times higher than that for married women. Minority women and their children are most affected: 30 percent of Hispanic mothers, 27 percent of blacks, and 16 percent of whites do not secure adequate prenatal care (Singh, Forrest, & Torres, 1990). Overall research suggests that good prenatal care pays off. For instance, a study of newborns in New Hampshire found that each $1.00 spent on prenatal care saves an average of $2.57 in later infant medical costs (Schwartz & Crispell, 1991).

Maternal Stress

The effect of maternal emotions on the unborn infant has long been a subject of folklore. Most of us are well aware that being frightened by a snake, a mouse, a bat, or some other creature will not cause a pregnant woman to give birth to a child with a distinctive personality or birthmark. Likewise, most of us view the claims of some primal therapists that their patients are able to recall experiences in the uterus as far-fetched. Medical science does suggest, however, that severe, prolonged anxiety in an expectant mother can have an effect on her child (Spezzano, 1981; Stott & Latchford, 1976). Of course, no direct neural linkage exists between the mother and the fetus. Rather, Lester W. Sontag (1944), long an important figure in the field of child development at the Fels Research Institute, describes the effects of maternal stress on the fetus as "blood-borne" anxieties. When the mother is anxious or under stress, various hormones such as epinephrine (adrenaline) and acetylcholine are released into her bloodstream. These hormones can pass through the placenta and enter the blood of the fetus. Should a pregnant woman feel that she is experiencing prolonged and unusual stress, she would be well advised to consult a physician, a trained therapist, or someone in the clergy.

Sontag (1966) has studied pregnant women undergoing stress. During periods when mothers are disturbed, fetal body movements increase several hundred percent. The increased activity normally persists for several hours, even when the maternal disturbance is of short duration. When the stress continues for several weeks, the fetal activity is greatly increased for the entire period. Sontag, Reynolds, and Torbet (1944) have also found that prolonged emotional stress is associated with low birth weight, infant hyperactivity, and postnatal adjustment difficulties (feeding problems, irritability, and digestive disturbances). Moreover, mothers who are under considerable emotional stress are more likely than other mothers to experience complications during both pregnancy and labor (Davids, Holden & Gray, 1963; Ferreira, 1969; McDonald, 1968; Stott, 1973.)

However, we must qualify any conclusions about blood-borne anxieties. For instance, long hours and hard, stressful work do not necessarily have an adverse affect on the outcome of a pregnancy. Researchers at the National Institute of Health have found no statistical differences in miscarriages, stillbirths, tubal pregnancies, early deliveries, or low-birth-weight babies between 1,293 physicians who became pregnant during their residencies and 1,494 pregnant wives of medical residents who were not themselves physicians, although the pregnant residents worked almost twice the number of hours as did the pregnant wives of residents (Angier, 1990). There is an additional caveat: Mothers who are under

Pregnancy

Environmental influences come to bear upon the developing fetus in many ways. Even the mother's attitude toward her pregnancy, and the emotional joy or stress that she experiences, can affect the fetal environment. *(Patrick Reddy)*

stress during pregnancy may also continue to be anxious and disturbed after they have given birth. Infant distress may partly reflect a tense mother-child relationship following birth (Stechler & Halton, 1982). In some cases other factors may be responsible. For instance, genetic factors cannot be excluded.

Pregnancy inevitably brings changes in some of a woman's social roles. She may welcome certain roles as a source of ego satisfaction. In some cultures pregnancy enables a woman to prove her biological adequacy, to avoid the reproach of sterility, and to achieve equality with other women. Nonetheless, even for the woman who anticipates motherhood with enthusiasm, pregnancy does produce some tensions and stress. (See Chapter 16.) Indeed, some stress and anxiety are an inescapable feature of expectant motherhood. In moderate amounts such stress probably has no harmful effect on the fetus (Istvan, 1986).

Maternal Age

On the whole, younger women have fewer difficulties in pregnancy and labor than do older women. Until relatively recently, medical practitioners believed that teenage pregnancy is more risky to both mother and baby than pregnancy for women in their twenties. More recent studies suggest that this belief is not valid (Culp, Appelbaum, Osofsky & Levy, 1988; Rebenkoff, 1979; Roosa, 1984). Indeed, the younger women may actually have an easier time during pregnancy and delivery, provided they receive adequate prenatal care. However, adolescent mothers seem to provide parenting of lower quality than do adult mothers. Pregnancy and motherhood are stressful to the adolescent, who is dealing with the demands of parenting concurrent with establishing her own identity and confronting the developmental tasks of adolescence. And adolescent mothers are more likely to experience educational and economic limitations and complicating family problems (Furstenberg, Brooks-Gunn & Chase-Lansdale, 1989; Klein & Cordell, 1987; Miller & Moore, 1990).

Women over 35 run progressively greater risks of complications during pregnancy and delivery, risks involving maternal mortality, miscarriage, twinning, and developmental irregularities in their offspring. Also, as noted in Chapter 3, the incidence of Down's syndrome increases drastically with advancing maternal age. However,

many of the problems of older mothers appear to result less from their age than from the presence of medical conditions that are more common at later ages, among them, diabetes, obesity, and high blood pressure. Many of the general statistics do not apply to the older mother who is otherwise healthy. The current consensus tends to be that a healthy woman in her thirties or forties enjoys a good prospect of giving birth to a healthy infant and remaining well herself. This conclusion is especially good news for women who are postponing childbirth, often to allow for completing education or establishing a career (Angier, 1991; *Harvard Medical School Health Letter*, October 1985; Winslow, 1990).

Birth

Birth is the transition between dependent existence in the uterus and life as a separate organism. In less than a day a radical change occurs. The fetus is catapulted from its warm, fluid, sheltered environment into the larger world. The infant is compelled to depend exclusively on its own biological systems. Birth, then, is a bridge between two stages of life.

The Birth Process

A few weeks before birth, the head of the infant generally turns downward, which ensures that it will be born head first. The uterus simultaneously sinks downward and forward. These changes are termed *lightening*. They "lighten" the mother's discomfort, and she now breathes more easily, since the pressure on her diaphragm and lungs is reduced (see Figure 4-6). About the same time the mother may begin experiencing mild "tuning up" contractions (*Braxton-Hicks contractions*), which are a prelude to the more vigorous contractions of labor.

The birth process consists of three stages: labor, delivery, and afterbirth. During **labor** the strong muscle fibers of the uterus rhythmically contract, pushing the infant downward toward the birth canal (the *vagina*). Simultaneously, the muscular tissue that forms the thick lower opening of the uterus (the *cervix*) relaxes, becoming both shortened and widened, thus permitting the infant's passage (see Figure 4-7).

Labor averages about 14 hours for women having their first babies. Women who have already had at least one baby average about 8 hours. Ini-

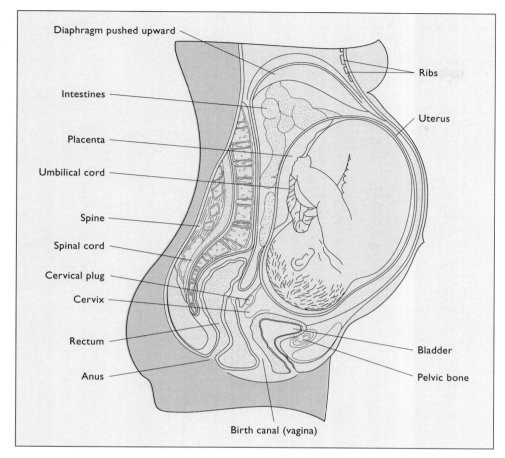

Diaphragm pushed upward

Intestines

Placenta

Umbilical cord

Spine

Spinal cord

Cervical plug

Cervix

Rectum

Anus

Ribs

Uterus

Bladder

Pelvic bone

Birth canal (vagina)

Figure 4-6   The Position of the Fetus About One Month Before Birth
In the month before birth the head of the fetus usually turns downward and the fetus drops slightly (called lightening). SOURCE: Roberts Rugh and Landrum B. Shettles, *From Conception to Birth: The Drama of Life's Beginnings* (New York: Harper & Row, 1971), p. 81. Copyright © 1971 by Roberts Rugh and Landrum B. Shettles. Reprinted by permission of Harper & Row, Publishers, Inc.

tially, the uterine contractions are spaced about 15 to 20 minutes apart and last for about 25 seconds. As the intervals shorten to 3 to 5 minutes, the contractions become stronger and last for about 45 seconds. Either at the beginning of labor or sometime during it, the amniotic sac that surrounds and cushions the fetus ruptures (commonly termed the "bursting of the water bag"). The rupture releases the amniotic fluid, which then flows as a clear liquid from the vagina.

Delivery begins once the infant's head passes through the cervix (the neck of the uterus) and ends when the baby has completed its passage through the birth canal. The stage generally requires 20 to 80 minutes. During delivery, contractions last for 60 to 65 seconds and come at 2- and 3-minute intervals. The mother aids each contraction by "bearing down" (pushing) with her abdominal muscles. *Crowning* occurs when the widest diameter of the baby's head is at the mother's *vulva* (the outer entrance to the vagina). Once the head has passed through the birth canal, the rest of the body quickly follows (see Figure 4-7).

After the baby's birth the uterus commonly stops its contractions for about 5 minutes. The contractions then resume and the placenta separates from the uterus. The placenta is forced into the vagina and is finally totally expelled. This process, termed the **afterbirth,** lasts for about 20 minutes.

The normalcy of the baby's condition at birth is usually appraised in terms of the **Apgar scoring system,** a method developed by Virginia Apgar (1953). The infant is assessed 1 minute and again 5 minutes after birth on the basis of five condi-

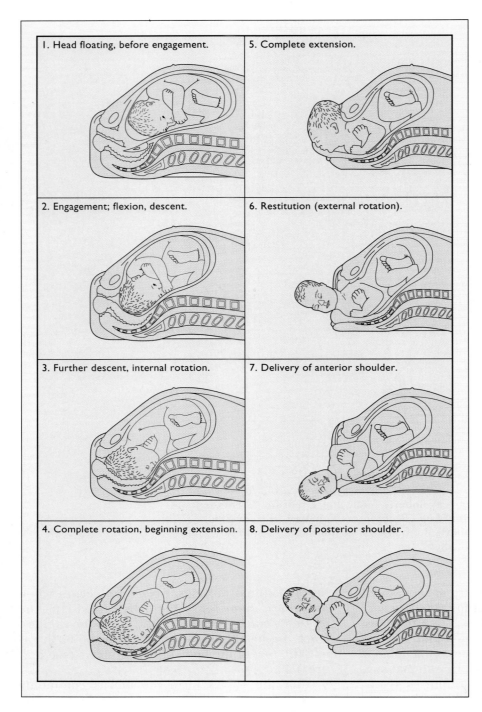

1. Head floating, before engagement.

2. Engagement; flexion, descent.

3. Further descent, internal rotation.

4. Complete rotation, beginning extension.

5. Complete extension.

6. Restitution (external rotation).

7. Delivery of anterior shoulder.

8. Delivery of posterior shoulder.

Figure 4-7   Normal Birth
The principal movements in the mechanism of labor and delivery. SOURCE: Jack A. Pritchard and Paul C. MacDonald, *Williams Obstetrics,* 15th ed. (New York: Appleton-Century-Crofts, 1976), Figure 6, p. 320. Reprinted by permission.

tions: heart rate, respiratory effort, muscle tone, reflex irritability (the infant's response to a catheter placed in its nostril), and body color. Each of the conditions is rated 0, 1, or 2 (see Table 4-1). The ratings of the five conditions are then summed (the highest possible score is 10). At 60 seconds after birth about 6 percent of all infants receive scores of 0 to 2, 24 percent scores of 3 to 7, and 70 percent scores of 8 to 10. A score of less than 5 indicates the need for prompt diagnosis and treatment. Infants with the lowest Apgar scores have the highest mortality rate.

Natural Childbirth

Natural childbirth refers to a variety of approaches that stress the preparation of the

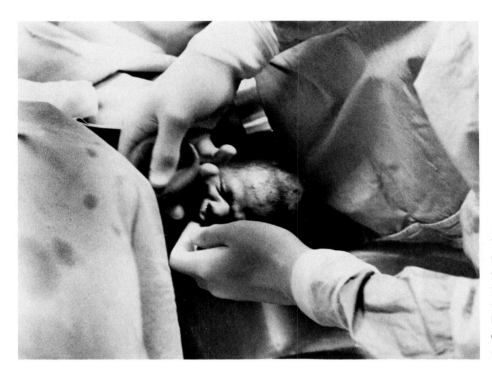

Birth
The baby's head has emerged from the birth canal, although the remainder of the body has yet to appear. The doctor is suctioning mucus from the baby's throat with a hand-operated suctioning device. *(Patrick Reddy)*

A Newborn
Moments after birth, the infant has been placed on the mother's abdomen. The umbilical cord has been cut and tied. Note the umbilical cord to the right of the baby's left leg. It is still attached to the placenta, which has yet to be expelled in the afterbirth. Also note the "molding" of the infant's head from passing through the birth canal. Molding is possible because of the softness of the bones and the loose connection they have with one another at the sutures of the skull. Accordingly, the head offers a narrow cylinder to the birth canal instead of a round ball. In a matter of days the head will again assume a normal shape. *(Patrick Reddy)*

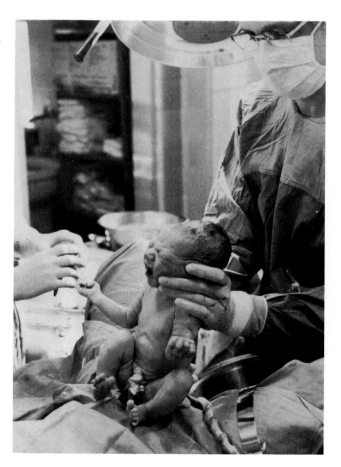

Table 4-1

The Apgar Scoring System					
Rating	Heart Rate	Respiratory Effort	Muscle Tone	Reflex Irritability	Body Color
0	Absent	Absent	Limp	Absent	Pale or blue
1	Below 100	Slow, irregular	Fair flexion	Grimace	Body pink, blue extremities
2	100–140	Good respiration accompanied by crying	Active motion	Cough or sneeze	Pink all over

SOURCE: Adapted from Virginia Apgar, "A Proposal for a New Method of Evaluation of the Newborn Infant." *Anesthesia and Analgesia, Vol. 32* (1953), pp. 260–267.

mother and the father for childbirth and their active involvement in the process. Overall, the term has come to mean an awake, aware, and undrugged mother-to-be. In the 1940s the English obstetrician Grantly Dick-Read (1944) began popularizing the view that pain in childbirth could be greatly reduced if women understood the birth process and learned to relax properly. Childbirth, Dick-Read argued, is essentially a normal and natural process. Anxiety and tension, however, prevent the rhythmic cooperation of the muscles in contraction and interfere with relaxation. All this contributes to the tearing of tissue and the intensifying of pain. Unfortunately, the cultural attitudes and practices of Western societies instill fear and anxiety in the mother. Legends and old wives' tales depict childbirth as a barbaric occurence that produces agonizing pain.

Dick-Read undertook to train prospective mothers to relax, to breathe correctly, to understand their anatomy and the process of labor, and to develop muscular control of their labor through special exercises. He emphasized the role of calm and supportive attendants who act as sources of confidence and security throughout labor. He believed that anesthesia should be available to women. However, he said it should not be imposed on them or routinely administered. In Dick-Read's view childbirth needed to be presented as an emotionally satisfying experience. And he undertook to train the father as an active participant in both prenatal preparation and delivery. Medical authorities are increasingly coming to the conclusion that no mother should ever labor and deliver alone. Evidence suggests that women who have a friendly companion with them during childbirth experience faster, simpler deliveries; have fewer complications; and are more affectionate toward their babies. Having a friend or relative stay with a woman during delivery may be a simple way to reduce delivery

problems, especially for low-income, single, and teenage mothers.

During the 1930s and 1940s Soviet doctors also began the search for more humane approaches to childbirth. They undertook to apply Pavlov's theories of the conditioned reflex to delivery practices. Like Dick-Read, they concluded that society conditioned women to be tense and fearful during labor. They reasoned that if pain was a response conditioned by society, it could be replaced by a different, more positive response. Accordingly, they evolved the *psychoprophylactic method.* Women were encouraged to relax and concentrate on the manner in which they breathed when a contraction occurred.

In 1951 Fernand Lamaze (1958), a French obstetrician, visited maternity clinics in the Soviet Union. When he returned to France, he introduced the fundamentals of the psychoprophylactic method to the maternity hospital he directed. Even more than Dick-Read, Lamaze emphasized the active participation of the mother in every phase of labor. He developed a precise and controlled breathing drill in which women in labor respond to a series of verbal cues by panting, pushing, and blowing. A woman proceeding through a Lamaze delivery may also use a number of cognitive techniques that distract her from the activities of the labor room and provide an additional source of support. These techniques include using visual focus and sucking on hard candies, lemon ices, or ice chips (Wideman & Singer, 1984). The Lamaze method has proved popular among those U.S. physicians and prospective parents who prefer natural childbirth.

Natural childbirth offers a number of advantages. First, childbirth education classes can do much to relieve the mother's anxiety and fear. Second, many wives and husbands find their joint participation in labor and delivery a joyous, rewarding occasion—indeed, what many couples describe as a "peak" experience. Third, the mother takes no medication or is given it only sparingly in the final phase of delivery. Some studies show that infants whose mothers received medication tend to perform less well on standard behavioral tests at 1 month to 1 year of age than do infants whose mothers were not medicated during labor (Brackbill, 1979; Goldstein, Caputo & Taub, 1976; Hollenbeck, Gewirtz, Sebris & Scanlon, 1984; Lester, Als & Brazelton, 1982; Murray, Dolby, Nation & Thomas, 1981; Sanders-Phillips, Strauss & Gutberlet, 1988). Other studies show no discernible long-term effects of drugs administered to the mother during the birth process (Horowitz et al., 1977; Kolata, 1979; Mueller et al., 1971; Yang, Zweig, Douthitt & Federman, 1976). Since considerable controversy exists about the possible harmful effects that analgesic and sedative medication may have upon the infant, safe obstetric practice seems to suggest caution in the administration of these drugs.

Although natural childbirth clearly offers advantages for many couples, it is more suitable for some couples and some births than others. In some cases the pain becomes so severe that wise and humane practice calls for medication. And both proponents and critics of natural childbirth agree that women who are psychologically or physically unprepared for it (and considerable preparation is required) should not consider themselves inadequate or irresponsible if they resort to conventional practice.

Parent-Infant Bonding

One of the advantages claimed for natural childbirth is that it facilitates an emotional bonding between parents and their child. Marshall H. Klaus and John H. Kennell (1976), pediatricians at the School of Medicine, Case Western Reserve University, say that closeness between parent and child in the first minutes of life may have a lasting effect. They term this process **parent-infant bonding.** While recognizing that most parents sooner or later become attached to their children, Klaus and Kennell say that some women have difficulty forming this attachment. Attachment is particularly difficult for mothers whose infants are premature, malformed, or initially unwanted. Moreover, follow-up studies by Klaus and Kennell undertaken one month after birth reveal that women who had early contact with their babies are more affectionate mothers than are women lacking early contact. They fondle their children more, try to soothe them more often, and engage in more eye-to-eye contact. Even at 2 years of age noticeable differences still exist. The mothers are more likely to speak to their children with a greater number of words and questions and with

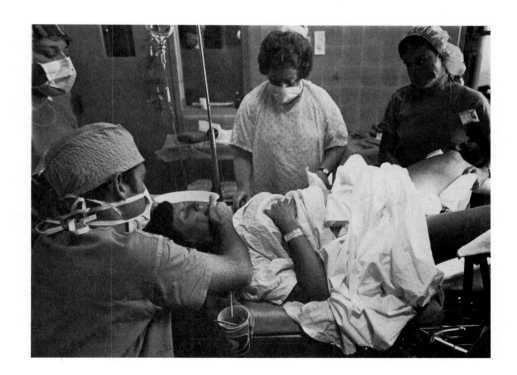

Natural Childbirth
This woman is undergoing an unmedicated delivery employing the Lamaze procedure. The husband is cupping his hand over his wife's mouth to assist her breathing during a contraction and to prevent hyperventilation. The cup at the husband's elbow contains ice chips. The ice chips provide moisture for the woman's mouth, which tends to dry out as a result of the controlled breathing. (*Patrick Reddy*)

fewer commands than do other mothers. These dimensions of the mothers' speech seem to be related to their children's superior verbal performance and competence at age 5. But other scholars find the "bonding doctrine" without scientific merit and believe it fosters unwarranted social stereotypes that portray motherhood as the "font of emotional support" (Sluckin, Herbert & Sluckin, 1983).

Klaus and Kennell and a number of researchers also find that increased contact between fathers and their newborn infants creates a bond, making them better fathers (Keller, Hildebrandt & Richards, 1985). But other research does not support the contention (Lamb, 1982; Palkovitz, 1985). This latter research does not mean that increased involvement by fathers does not have positive effect. Some evidence suggests that birth attendance and increased contact with the newborn can enhance the marital relationship and the father's feeling of inclusion in the expanding family. (For a discussion of father involvement in some other cultures, see the boxed insert on page 114.) However, on the whole, research on early parent-child physical contact finds only weak evidence for its temporary effects and little evidence for its lasting effects. Consequently, fathers need not feel guilt over missing their child's birth. And mothers who have Caesarean deliveries or parents who adopt children should not conclude that they have missed out on something fundamental for a healthy child-parent relationship. A growing body of research suggests that parents who do not have contact with their infant immediately after delivery typically develop as strong an attachment to the youngster as do parents who do have such contact (Grossmann, Thane & Grossmann, 1981; Svejda, Campos & Emde, 1980).

Birthing Rooms and Family-Centered Hospital Care

As a former farmer, if I had separated animal babies from their mothers as soon as they were born, put the babies in a box with a glass window and let the mother only look through the window at them for two or three days, I would have been arrested for cruelty to animals. Yet this is what hospital "routines" do to humans.—ROBERT A. BRADLEY, M.D.

With smaller families and more childbirth classes, many young couples are seeking out a doctor and a hospital that view uncomplicated pregnancies as a normal process rather than as an illness. And they are rebelling against regimented and impersonal hospital routines. They dislike the sterile steel equipment, harsh lighting, uncomfortable stirrups and table, shaving, anesthesia, and the practice of separating mother and child immediately after birth. They do not want the delivery of their babies to be a surgical procedure. And they note that infections can be spread in hospitals—sometimes by physicians and staff. Consequently, more couples are choosing to have babies at home. The medical establishment has reacted with alarm to this trend, insisting that home births pose risks to both the mother and the child (Findlay, 1985*a*; Ryan, 1982).

Dissatisfaction with the maternity care options provided by physicians has contributed to the revival of midwifery. All fifty states have legalized the provision of prenatal care and delivery by midwives so long as the practitioners are registered nurses. But midwives who are not nurses are also seeking legal status. Midwives were fairly common in the United States until the late 1930s. By then, medical groups succeeded in suppressing midwifery by portraying it as dangerous and dirty. The demand for midwives is now being fueled by middle-class and affluent professional women who shun more impersonal, high-tech hospital care and by poor and rural women who lack access to obstetrical and gynecological care (Nazario, 1990; Sullivan & Weitz, 1988).

In response to the home-birth movement, many hospitals have introduced *birthing rooms.* Such rooms have a homelike atmosphere complete with wallpapered walls, window drapes, potted plants, color television, a queen-sized bed, and other comforts. Medical equipment is normally out of view. The woman can give birth assisted by a nurse-midwife or obstetrician and her husband. Other relatives, friends, or even the baby's brothers and sisters may be present. Should complications arise, the woman can be quickly moved to a regular delivery room. This arrangement allows for a homelike birth with proximity to hospital life-saving equipment. The mother and child then return home about six to twenty-four hours after an uncomplicated delivery.

Other hospitals, while retaining more traditional childbirth procedures, have introduced family-centered hospital care, in which birth is made a family experience. The father is an active member of the delivery room team. And in some hospitals children are allowed to see the new baby in the family soon after birth. The plan is usually coupled with *rooming in*, an arrangement in which the infant spends a large portion of time in a bassinet beside the mother's bed. This practice runs counter to the long U.S. hospital tradition of segregating infants in a common nursery.

Rooming in offers the advantages of allowing the mother to get acquainted with her child and of integrating the father early into the child care process. Under the supervision of the nursing staff, parents gain skill in feeding, bathing, di-

apering, and otherwise caring for their infant. Anxieties caused by old wives' tales, misconceptions, and sheer ignorance can be put to rest. Women who desire to breast-feed their babies can initiate the process with the sympathetic help and support of the hospital staff.

The Baby's Birth Experience

In 1975 Frederick Leboyer, a French obstetrician, captured popular attention with his best-selling book *Birth Without Violence* (1975). Whereas Dick-Read and Lamaze focused on the

Birth: A Peak Experience
Many couples report that their joint participation in labor and delivery provides an emotionally satisfying and meaningful experience. The tube attached to the mother's wrist is a precaution taken by many obstetricians in the event that she requires an emergency injection of medication or blood transfusion. Some couples object to such procedures and to the surgical masks, charging that they interfere with the "human" qualities of the birth experience. It is considerations of this sort that have given impetus to the childbirth-at-home and midwife movement. *(Patrick Reddy)*

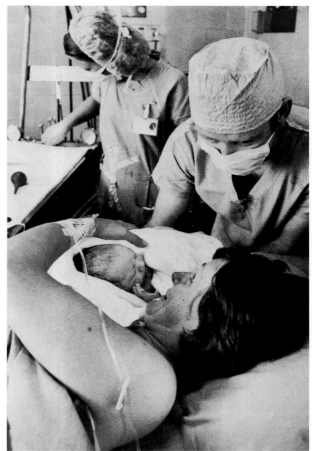

Fatherhood in Cross-Cultural Perspective

The weak link in the family group is the bond between the child and the father. No necessary tie and no easy means of identification exist between the two. Margaret Mead (1949), a leading anthropologist, asserted that human societies have invented the concept of fatherhood as a response to this fact. Bronislaw Malinowski (1964), also a distinguished anthropologist, made the same point. He observed that societies everywhere provide for fatherhood, if only by social definition—the *principle of legitimacy*. The principle of legitimacy is the rule that "no child should be brought into the world without a man—and one man at that—assuming the role of sociological father, that is, guardian and protector, the male link between the child and the rest of the community" (Malinowski, 1964, p. 13).

The Tallensi, a people of the African Sudan, furnish a good example of the principle of legitimacy (Fortes, 1949). If a Tallensi woman is married, any child she bears is the property of, and a member of, her husband's family (descent group). Should the woman be impregnated by a man other than her husband, it causes no problem. The child is easily absorbed into a legal relationship. The genitor (the agent of conception) does not experience fatherly feelings toward the child. The pater (the woman's husband) does feel all the emotions associated with fatherhood, even though he knows he is not the genitor. And the pater receives all the credit customarily given a father among the Tallensi. The child suffers no stigma, nor is it deprived of any legal rights. However, everything is different for a child born of an unwed mother. In this case the principle of legitimacy is violated, so that the child is stigmatized as an inferior and enjoys fewer legal rights.

Since the tie between the father and the child is less immediately visible than that between the mother and the child, some societies have evolved birth rituals that serve to emphasize and highlight the relationship (Paige & Paige, 1973). The *couvade* is the most widespread birth custom involving men. It usually consists of various dietary and occupational observances, as well as the seclusion of the husband during and for a period after childbirth.

The Kurtachi of the Solomon Islands provide a good illustration of the couvade (Blackwood, 1935, p. 159). During pregnancy neither the husband nor the wife is permitted to eat certain foods—a taboo that persists for a period following the child's birth. When the wife begins her labor pains,

> . . . her husband must stop working, and remain indoors, not in the hut where his wife is confined, but in

that of another of his wives, or a neighbor. He must spend his time in sitting idle or dozing, and must on no account carry, or even lift, anything heavy, or touch a knife, axe, or any sharp or pointed instrument. To do the former would injure the child, the latter would cause it to die. This continues for three days. On the fourth day he may go into the hut and see his child. After this he is allowed to walk about the village. . . . He must still refrain from working. On the fifth day he goes, with his wife, and washes in the sea. . . . and he may now resume his usual activities.

Among some peoples, including the Arapesh of New Guinea (Mead, 1935) and the Inuit (Jenness, 1922), the father simulates birth, taking to his bed and going through actions suggestive of labor. Within the United States and other Western nations, some men experience what mental health professionals term the "couvade syndrome" (Greenberg, 1986; Kutner, 1990; Ruben, 1991; Shapiro, 1987). A study of 147 expectant fathers in the Milwaukee area found that about 90 percent of them experienced "pregnancy" symptoms similar to those of their wives. For instance, the men encountered nausea in the first trimester and backaches in the last trimester. The majority of the men reported weight gains ranging from 2 to 15 pounds. And they all lost weight in the four weeks after the babies were born. Couvade may be one way fathers express a bond of sympathy with the expectant mother and a change in social roles (Lewis, 1985). In addition, expectant fathers commonly experience a heightened concern regarding their ability to protect an expanding family. Typically they view this protection in financial terms. However, some men purchase weapons during pregnancy, only to sell them shortly after the baby is born. Wives who see their husbands taking on extra work may incorrectly interpret the behavior as a form of desertion rather than as an expression of the men's worry lest they have enough money to support the mother and child (Kutner, 1990).

In middle-class U.S. culture, emphasis tends to fall upon the wedding ceremony rather than upon specific birth observances (Mead & Newton, 1967). An elaborate wedding emphasizes the man's assumption of economic and social responsibility for a woman and her future children. American men are also permitted to call attention to their new fatherhood by giving cigars to other men or going on a "good drunk." More recently, natural childbirth and family-centered hospital programs have undertaken to make the father an active participant in the childbirth process.

mother, Leboyer focused on the baby. Birth, says Leboyer, is an exceedingly traumatic experience. When expelled from the uterus, the infant is immediately confronted with blinding arc lights and the bustle and noise of the hospital delivery room—a terrifying "tidal wave of sensation surpassing anything we can imagine." So savage is the shock, argues Leboyer, that the infant's nervous system may be permanently damaged. Leboyer calls for a more gentle entry into the world via lowered sound and light levels in the delivery room, the immediate soothing of the infant through massaging and stroking, and a mild, sensuous bath for the newborn.

However, claims like Leboyer's are exceedingly controversial. Canadian researchers have found that Leboyer's method offers no special clinical or behavioral advantage to the infant or mother not offered by a gentle, conventional delivery (Nelson et al., 1980). Other researchers report that despite surface appearances the stresses of a normal delivery are usually not harmful. The fetus produces unusually high levels of the "stress hormones," adrenaline and noradrenaline, which equip it to withstand the stress of birth. This surge in hormones protects the infant from asphyxia during delivery and prepares the infant to survive outside the womb. It clears the lungs and changes physiological properties to promote normal breathing while simultaneously ensuring that a rich supply of blood goes to the heart and brain (Lagercrantz & Slotkin, 1986). Parents can take comfort knowing that from the baby's standpoint the stress of labor during normal birth is likely to be less unhappy and more beneficial than common sense would suggest. By the same token, however, Leboyer has fostered a more humane view of childbirth management that compares favorably with many of the practices prevalent only twenty or thirty years ago.

Complications of Pregnancy and Birth

Although most pregnancies and births proceed without complications, there are exceptions. In a relatively small minority of cases complications may arise during pregnancy or in the birth process. The purpose of good prenatal care under medical supervision is to minimize complications. But if complications should develop, much can be done through medical intervention to help the mother and the child.

Toxemia

Toxemia is a disorder of pregnancy characterized by high blood pressure (*hypertension*), waterlogging of tissues (*edema*), the presence of protein in the urine (*proteinuria*), and occasionally convulsions and coma. Toxemia occurs in 5 to 10 percent of pregnant women, usually during the last three months of pregnancy. In reports of maternal mortality, toxemia ranks as the second or third leading cause of death. Toxemia also poses a problem to the fetus, because toxemia creates a chemical environment in the mother's body that interferes with the proper functioning of the placenta. In severe cases infant mortality approaches 50 percent.

Although scientists have suggested many possible causes of toxemia, no hypothesis has gained wide medical acceptance, and most are not supported by sufficient evidence (Niswander, 1976). Some research indicates that toxemia tends to be more common among lower socioeconomic groups and unwed pregnant teenagers without adequate prenatal care. Here, too, the evidence is not conclusive. But women with high blood pressure, diabetes, and multiple fetuses do pose a higher risk factor.

The treatment of toxemia has changed in recent years. Traditionally, many physicians administered diuretic drugs, which decrease the retention of water in body tissues by increasing the excretion of urine. But some doctors today have discontinued the practice, since diuretics have occasionally been associated with maternal death and damage to the fetus. Many physicians also traditionally placed restrictions on the sodium intake in a patient's diet, but the effectiveness of this practice has recently been seriously questioned. At the present time the most common treatment for toxemia is the administration of medication to control convulsions and enforced bed rest to reduce the woman's blood pressure.

Caesarean Sections

A common delivery procedure is the **Caesarean section,** a surgical technique by which the physician enters the uterus through an abdominal incision and removes the infant. The Caesarean section is employed when the mother's pelvis is too small to allow passage of the infant and when the baby is positioned abnormally, as in some *breech* presentations (a buttocks rather than a head positioning) and *transverse* presentations (a sideways or vertical position). (Nonetheless, fewer than 12 percent of fetuses in breech presentation were delivered by Caesarean section in 1970, whereas today the figure stands at more than 60 percent). The box on page 117 discusses the substantial increase in the number of Caesarean deliveries and the controversy surrounding the practice.

A Caesarean is major surgery and entails some risks, especially to the mother. One recent study shows that major complications occur in about 6 percent of the cases. Complications include hemorrhage, infections, blood clots, and injuries to other organs. Maternal mortality in Caesarean birth is also two to four times higher than it is for vaginal delivery. Caesarean deliveries also require longer hospital stays and higher costs.

Caesarean delivery can be a devastating experience for couples not prepared for it. Fathers may feel left out and helpless. Mothers may experience remorse, depression, and guilt. They may also be taken aback by the pain and temporary incapacitation that accompany surgery. Couples often complain that they miss not having "given birth." Some harbor hostility toward the physicians who "cheated" them out of a natural-birth experience. As a response to these problems, childbirth classes now usually include units on Caesarean birth. Some hospitals allow husbands to be with their wives during a Caesarean delivery. And media materials promote the theme that "Having a Section is Having a Baby."

Prematurity

A **premature infant** is commonly defined as a baby weighing less than 5½ pounds at birth or having a gestational age of less than thirty-seven weeks. Some 6 to 8 percent of all live births in the United States occur before full term. Significantly, the United States ranks twenty-sixth in the world, behind economically impoverished nations such as Bulgaria, in the percentage of low-birth-weight babies (Chira, 1991). Although the National Centers for Disease Control consistently reported a decline in the rate of babies born at less than 5½ pounds between 1975 and 1985, they now find the trend of babies born with low birth weight is on the rise, particularly among blacks. Low-birth-weight babies are born to blacks at twice the rate they are to whites at virtually every income and educational level. Some researchers speculate that the persistently high rate of low-birth-weight infants among blacks reflects gener-

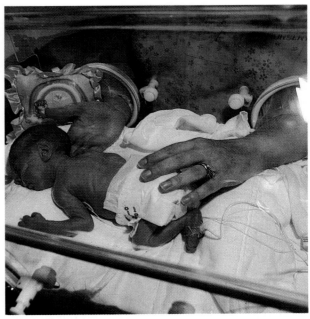

Premature Infants

Medical advances have made possible the survival of a great many premature infants who only two decades ago would have succumbed to death. Like other youngsters, premature infants require skin contact and other human stimulation. Indeed, they seem to require extra handling, cuddling, and personal attention. *(Charles Gupton/Stock, Boston)*

ations of poverty (*Columbus Dispatch*, 1990*a*, 1990*b*).

The survival rate of premature infants correlates closely with their birth weight, with better survival for the larger and more mature infants. Nonetheless, in a number of the nation's better hospitals physicians are saving 80 to 85 percent of the infants weighing 2.2 to 3.2 pounds and, even more remarkably, 50 to 60 percent of those weighing 1.6 to 2.2 pounds (Brody, 1991; Davis, 1986). However, treating premature babies is hardly routine and frequently costs more than $2,000 a day (Rosenthal, 1991).

Intensive-care nurseries for preterm babies are often frightening to parents who are unprepared to encounter their infant in a see-through incubator (Kolata, 1991). The child may be receiving oxygen through plastic tubes inserted in the nose or windpipe. Banks of blipping lights, blinking numbers, and beeping alarms associated with electronic equipment and computerized devices monitor the baby's vital signs.

A leading cause of death in premature infants is a condition called *respiratory distress syndrome (RDS)*. Some 8,000 to 10,000 infant deaths each

The Sharp Rise in Caesareans: Grounds for Concern?

Between 1970 and 1989, the number of Caesarean deliveries in the United States quintupled (from 5.5 percent of all deliveries to nearly 25 percent). Some regard this trend with alarm. They insist that many of the operations are unnecessary. Others regard the trend as medical progress in bringing forth healthy babies in circumstances that might otherwise be tragic. One explanation for the rising incidence of Caesareans is the introduction of new equipment that allows physicians to monitor the effect of birth on the child. When a monitor shows that a fetus is "in distress," Caesarean intervention can be quickly arranged. The threat of malpractice suits has also prompted some physicians to operate when they have the slightest doubt that a healthy baby will result from a vaginal delivery.

Profit also seems to be a motive (a typical 1990 vaginal birth cost on average $4,334 and was associated with a two- or three-day hospital stay compared with $7,186 and four or five days in the hospital for a Caesarean). A study undertaken in Los Angeles County, California, shows that women living in areas with a median family income of more than $30,000 have a first Caesarean birth rate of 22.9 percent as compared with 13.2 percent among women residing in areas with a median family income under $11,000. The rates were highest among non-Hispanic whites (20.6 percent), intermediate among Asian Americans (19.2 percent) and blacks (18.9 percent), and lowest among Mexican-Americans (13.9 percent). The association between socioeconomic status and rates of first Caesarean delivery did not result from differences in maternal age, birth weight, or complications of pregnancy (Gould, Davey & Stafford, 1989).

Repeat Caesareans account for 36 percent of Caesarean deliveries. Since early in this century, physicians have followed the dictum "Once a Caesarean, always a Caesarean." The doctrine was based on a fear that the scars from a Caesarean would rupture if subjected to the forces of labor in a subsequent delivery. However, in recent decades new surgical procedures and lower and horizontal uterine incisions have minimized this risk so that some three in four women can now have a vaginal delivery following a Caesarean.

Despite medical consensus that most women who have had a Caesarean can safely have a vaginal birth, a recent California study suggests that the greater profitability of the surgery is keeping the repeat rate of Caesareans high. Women at private, for-profit hospitals and those with private health insurance have the highest rate of repeat Caesarean sections (*Columbus Dispatch*, 1991). The rate of repeat Caesareans also appears to be tied to the age of the physician. Ninety-eight percent of physicians under 40 say they encourage their Caesarean patients to have vaginal deliveries for subsequent births, compared with 84 percent of physicians over age 55. Fifty-eight percent of women offered vaginal births agreed to try (64 percent with physicians under age 35 versus 57 percent with physicians over age 55). Of those women trying vaginal birth, 63 percent succeeded (68 percent with doctors under age 35 versus 57 percent with doctors over 55). Still, some 42 percent of women offered the option of vaginal delivery chose a Caesarean, often because they previously had had a long and painful labor culminating in a Caesarean and were reluctant to try vaginal birth again (Friend, 1990). Of interest, researchers have found that when a trained woman companion, known as a *doula*, provides constant support during labor and delivery for U.S. inner-city women, the need for Caesarean sections, forceps delivery, and other measures is significantly reduced (Winslow, 1991).

year are linked with RDS; another 40,000 newborns suffer from it. One difficulty is that premature infants lack a substance known as *surfactant*, a lubricant found in the amniotic fluid surrounding a fetus in the womb. It helps inflate the air sacs in the lungs after birth and prevents the lungs from collapsing or sticking together after each breath. The fetus normally does not develop surfactant until about the thirty-fifth week. Recently, investigators have found that by providing premature infants with the substance, many otherwise fatal complications can be avoided and the babies saved. Pediatricians are also finding that many premature, underweight babies can be released from the hospital at 6 weeks of age rather than waiting for two or more months. One study found that such infants later are as healthy as those kept in hospitals for a longer time. And the in-home care was associated with lower medical costs even though each family in the study was assigned a nurse who visited the babies at home regularly to monitor their progress (Brotten, 1986).

The smaller the preterm infant, the greater is the risk of lung disorders, intracranial bleeding, and intestinal complications. Premature infants can also die from too little oxygen and suffer eye and lung disorders from too much. So technicians use special skin sensors that measure blood oxygenation. Among surviving premature infants, there is a somewhat higher incidence of abnormality (Caputo & Mandell, 1970; Keller, 1980; Wilson, 1985). Low-birth-weight individuals are overrepresented in the population of mental retardates and among persons institutionalized for various disabilities. Prematurity is similarly associated with difficulties in language development, problems in various areas of academic achievement, hyperkinesis, autism, and involvement in childhood accidents.

Prematurity affects development in a variety of ways (Duffy, Als & McAnulty, 1990; Goldstein, Caputo & Taub, 1976; Holmes, Nagy & Slaymaker, 1982; Smart & Smart, 1973). First, the relative immaturity of the premature infant makes it a less viable organism in coping with the stresses of birth and postnatal life and more susceptible to infections. Second, the developmental difficulties shown by the premature infant may be associated with the same prenatal disorders that caused the baby to be born early (maternal malnutrition, smoking, poverty, and maternal diabetes). Third, once delivered, the premature infant is treated differently from the full-term child. It is often kept in an incubator and deprived of normal skin contacts and other stimulation. In order to combat this adverse effect, a number of researchers suggest that premature infants be given extra human stimulation in the form of handling, cuddling, talking, singing, and rocking (Gottfried, Wallace-Lande, Sherman-Brown, King & Coen, 1981; Scafidi, 1986; Scafidi et al., 1990; Zeskind & Iacino, 1984).

Finally, although premature infants constitute fewer than 10 percent of all babies, they are represented among battered children at the rate of between 23 and 40 percent, depending on the study quoted. Some researchers attribute this result to the greater likelihood that premature infants have experienced prolonged separation from their parents, impairing the parent-child bonding process (Kennell, Voos & Klaus, 1979). In addition, the characteristics of premature infants—their high-pitched cry, their fragility and

smallness, their greater irritability, their lower levels of visual alertness, and their shriveled appearance—make them less cute and responsive, even somewhat aversive beings, in the eyes of their parents and caretakers (Frodi et al., 1978; Landry, Chapieski, Richardson, Palmer & Hall, 1990; Zarling, Hirsch & Landry, 1988).

The author of this book hastens to add (since he himself was a premature baby) that most premature infants show no abnormalities or mental retardation. Winston Churchill, who was born prematurely, lived to be 91 and led an active, productive life. In contemporary industrialized nations only 5 to 15 percent of low-birth-weight babies experience moderate to severe intellectual impairment. Furthermore, recent advances in the monitoring of premature babies have allowed physicians to anticipate and, in many cases, prevent or minimize some problems through therapeutic interventions. The result has been a reduction in the overall complications and mortality associated with premature birth. However, about 16 to 18 percent of babies weighing less than 1,500 grams (3 pounds, 4 ounces) have lasting neurological impairment; for babies under 750 grams (1 pound, 10 ounces), 25 to 35 percent are so affected; and for those weighing from 500 to 600 grams at birth, 40 to 50 percent will be neurologically impaired (Brody, 1991).

Overall, medical science continues to make important and exciting strides in helping underweight babies (Achenbach, Phares, Howell, Rauh & Nurcombe, 1990). Although smaller-scale studies have shown that child-development programs can help low-birth-weight babies to function better intellectually, a recent large-scale study carried out in sites across the United States, many involving inner-city children, has confirmed the benefits to be realized through developmental interventions. In the four-year study, 985 premature babies were divided into two groups. One group received the special intervention: Parents were counseled in group sessions every two weeks; researchers visited the babies' homes each week, providing the parents with health and developmental information and activities to improve their children's language, cognitive, and social skills; and, at 1 year of age, the children were enrolled in a high-quality educational daycare program. The second group of babies served as a control or comparison group and did not receive special help. By the time the youngsters were 3 years old, those who had received the developmental interventions achieved substantially higher scores on intelligence tests and tests of social functioning. The IQs of the babies weighing from 4.4 to 5.5 pounds at birth were 13.2 pounds higher than those of comparable weight in the control group. The IQs of babies weighing less than 4.4 pounds at birth were 6.6 points higher than those of control-group youngsters. Moreover, control-group babies were nearly three times more likely to be mentally retarded. Developmental psychologist Marc Bornstein,

head of family and child research at the National Institute of Child Health and Human Development, observes: "We were schooled in the 1980's that there are certain problems that you can't throw money at to solve. This is an example of a problem that if we throw money at it in a certain way, we can make healthier children, and presumably, in the long run, have better citizens and a better society" (quoted by Kolata, 1990, p. A10).

SUMMARY

1. The prenatal period normally lasts an average of 266 days. Embryologists divide it into three stages: the germinal period, the embryonic period, and the fetal period.

2. The germinal period is characterized by the growth of the zygote (the fertilized egg) and the establishment of an initial linkage between the zygote and the support system of the mother. The fertilized egg divides in a process termed "mitosis." In about six or seven days the blastocyst begins the process of differentiation into the trophoblast and the inner cell mass. Toward the end of the second week the embryonic portion of the inner cell mass begins to differentiate into three layers: the ectoderm, the mesoderm, and the endoderm.

3. The embryonic period lasts from the end of the second week to the end of the eighth week. It is a period characterized by rapid growth, the establishment of a placental relationship with the mother, the differentiation in early structural form of the chief organs, and the appearance of recognizable features of a human body.

4. The fetal period begins with the ninth week and ends with birth. During this period the differentiation of the major organ systems continues, and the organs themselves become competent to assume their specialized functions.

5. Environmental influences affect the developing organism from the moment of conception and continue throughout the prenatal period.

6. Many drugs and chemical agents are capable of crossing the placental barrier and affecting the embryonic and fetal systems. Current medical opinion suggests that pregnant women should take no drugs except in situations that seriously threaten their health and then only under the supervision of a physician.

7. Maternal infections can damage the fetus in two ways: (a) by direct infection or (b) by indirect toxic effect.

8. Nutritional deficiencies in the mother, particularly severe ones, are reflected in fetal development.

9. When pregnant women are anxious or under stress, they release various hormones into their bloodstream. These hormones can pass through the placenta and enter the bloodstream of the fetus. Women who are under prolonged stress during their pregnancies are more likely to experience complications during both pregnancy and labor. Prolonged maternal emotional stress is also associated with low birth weight, infant hyperactivity, and postnatal adjustment difficulties.

10. On the whole, women between the ages of 17 and 30 have fewer difficulties in pregnancy and delivery, and produce fewer abnormal children, than women above or below these ages.

11. The birth process consists of three stages: labor, delivery, and afterbirth.

12. A growing number of U.S. hospitals are introducing family-centered hospital care in which childbirth is made a family experience. Natural chilbirth and rooming in are common features of this program.

13. Frederick Leboyer has captured popular attention with his opinion that traditional childbirth practices traumatize the child. Most authorities believe, however, that the stresses ordinarily associated with birth do not exceed the infant's physical or neurological capacity.

14. In a small minority of cases complications

may arise during pregnancy or during the birth process. The purpose of good prenatal care under medical supervision is to minimize complications. But if complications should develop, much can be done through medical intervention to help the mother and the child. Among the possible complications are toxemia, births that require Caesarean section, and premature birth.

KEY TERMS

Afterbirth The last stage in the birth process, characterized by the expulsion of the placenta.

Apgar Scoring System A method for appraising the normalcy of a baby's condition at birth.

Birth The transition between dependent existence in the uterus and life as a separate organism; the process of being born.

Blastocyst A hollow ball of cells that develops from a fertilized ovum.

Caesarean Section A surgical technique by which the physician enters the uterus through an abdominal incision and removes the infant.

Cephalocaudal Development Development starting with the brain and head areas and then working its way down the body.

Delivery A stage in the birth process that begins once the infant's head passes through the cervix (the neck of the uterus) and ends when the infant has completed its passage through the birth canal (the vagina).

Embryonic Period The phase in prenatal development that extends from about the end of the second week following conception to the end of the eighth week.

Fetal Period The phase in prenatal development that extends from the end of the eighth week until birth.

Germinal Period The phase in prenatal development that extends from conception to the end of the second week.

Labor A stage in the birth process in which the strong muscle fibers of the uterus rhythmically contract, pushing the baby down toward the birth canal.

Mitosis A process occurring within a few hours of fertilization, when growth of the zygote begins by division, forming two cells identical in makeup to the first cell.

Natural Childbirth A variety of approaches that stress the preparation of the mother and the father for labor and delivery and their active involvement in the childbirth process.

Parent-Infant Bonding The notion that closeness between parent and child in the first minutes of life produces a lasting effect, particularly in cementing attachment ties.

Premature Infant A baby weighing less than 5½ pounds at birth or having a gestational age of less than thirty-seven weeks.

Prenatal Period The time elapsing between conception and birth.

Proximodistal Development Development away from the central axis of the organism.

Teratogen Any agent that contributes to birth defects.

Teratology The field of study concerned with birth defects.

Toxemia A disorder of pregnancy characterized by high blood pressure (hypertension), waterlogging of tissues (edema), the presence of protein in the urine (proteinuria), and occasionally convulsions and coma.

The Newborn

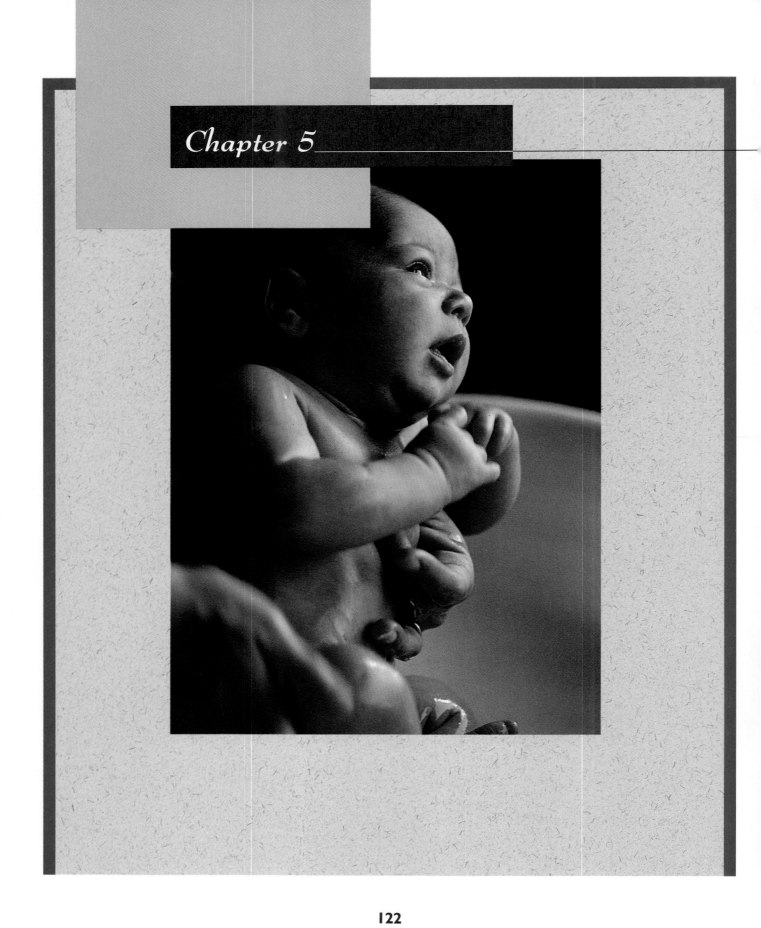

Chapter 5

The Newborn

◆

ntil three decades ago, the human new-born was thought to be little more than an unresponsive vegetable who did nothing except eat, sleep, breathe, and cry. A century ago William James (1842–1910), a distinguished U.S. philosopher and psychologist, described the world of the newborn as "one great blooming, buzzing confusion"—a world in which the infant is "assailed by eyes, ears, nose, skin, and entrails [all] at once." And around the same time G. Stanley Hall (1891), the father of U.S. child psychology, depicted the baby as arriving with "its monotonous and dismal cry, with its red, shriveled, parboiled skin . . . , squinting, cross-eyed, pot bellied, and bow legged." Even so keen and sensitive an observer as Jean Piaget (1952a, p. 23) dismissed the first few months of life as involving merely the exercise of "reflexes."

In light of recent research, however, psychologists are increasingly coming to view what they had previously considered the incompetent neonate as "the amazing newborn" (Acredolo & Hake, 1982). The infant arrives with all sensory systems functioning. To the watchful observer, babies communicate at least some of their perceptions and abilities. Newborns tell us what they hear, see, and feel in the same manner that any other organisms do—through systematic responses to stimulating events. T. G. R. Bower (1977, p. 28), an authority on infant capabilities, observes:

> I suspect that the newborn's social abilities are something parents could have told us about, had we ever bothered to ask them. Many parents have assumed that their babies are, from the beginning, social and make social responses. Nonetheless, there is a whole literature devoted to discussing how the baby comes to be socialized, how he comes to realize that he is a human being, how he comes to have special sets of responses to people that are not elicited by anything else in the environment. A great deal of this effort, although not all of it, has, I feel, been wasted, because right from the moment of birth the baby realizes he is a human being and has specific responses elicited only by other human beings.

In sum, newborns are active human beings who are eager to understand and engage their social world.

The abilities and behavior of neonates will be the focus of this chapter. The term **neonate** refers to a newborn, and the **neonate period** refers to the newborn during the first two weeks following birth.

Newborn Behaviors

A newborn is no beauty. At the moment when infants slip into the world, they are covered with *vernix*, the thick, white, waxy substance mentioned in Chapter 4. And some babies retain their *lanugo*, the fetus's fine, woolly facial and body hair, which disappears by the neonate's fourth month. The matting of their hair with vernix gives newborns an odd, pastelike look.

On the average, a full-term newborn is between 19 and 22 inches long and weighs 5½ to 9½ pounds. Many newborns give the appearance of a defeated prizefighter—a puffy bluish-red face, a broad, flat nose, swollen eyelids, and ears skewed at odd angles. Their heads are often misshapen and elongated, a product of *molding*. (In molding, the soft skull "bones" become temporarily distorted to accommodate passage through the birth canal.) Most infants have chins that recede and lower jaws that are underdeveloped. Bowlegs are the rule, and the feet may be cocked in a pigeon-toed manner. Of even greater interest than its appearance is the neonate's behavior. Neonate behavior can be considered in terms of three broad categories: sleeping, crying, and feeding.

Sleeping

The major "activity" of newborns is sleeping. They spend sixteen or more hours per day in sleep, packaged into seven or eight naps. Sleep and wakefulness alternate roughly in four-hour cycles—three hours in sleep and one hour awake. By six weeks the naps become longer, with infants taking only two to four naps during the day. Beginning about this age, many sleep through most of the night.

Interest in neonate sleeping patterns has been closely linked with interest in newborn states. **State,** as viewed by Peter H. Wolff (1966), refers to a continuum of alertness ranging from regular sleep to vigorous activity. Babies' responses to the environment differ depending on their state (Ashton, 1976). In sleep, for instance, infants are insensitive to touch and most other stimuli. In contrast, infants follow moving objects with their eyes and turn toward sounds when they are alert but relatively inactive (Bower, 1974). Crying and spontaneous smiling are also state-related responses.

The noted pediatrician T. Berry Brazelton (1978) says that state is the infant's first line of

Sudden Infant Death Syndrome

Each year some 7,500 to 10,000 U.S. families experience a devastating tragedy. They put their seemingly healthy baby down in the crib and return to find that the infant has died. Typically, there is no warning. The disorder, termed *Sudden Infant Death Syndrome (SIDS)*, is the second most common cause of death among infants after accidents. Infants who die unexpectedly of causes that cannot be conclusively documented by postmortem examination are commonly classed as SIDS deaths. SIDS frequently results in acute agony for parents, who blame themselves and each other for permitting the baby to smother in bed. However, suffocation from bedding is usually not the cause of the baby's death, although a few deaths do result from suffocation, overbundling, and other accidents caused by parents' poor judgment (Bass, Kravath & Glass, 1986). So some pediatricians say that the safest position in which to put newborns down to sleep is on their side rather than facedown on their abdomens (Gorman, 1991). Complicating matters, SIDS is sometimes used by caretakers to cover up child-abuse deaths (Sharpe & Lundstrom, 1990). It is this image that SIDS babies die of parental neglect or abuse that has speeded the establishment of self-help groups of grieving parents (mothers of SIDS and stillborn babies take an average of 3.9 years to recover; fathers, 4.2 years) (Peterson, 1991). Yet most researchers agree that quality prenatal and postnatal care are not good predictors of crib death, nor does SIDS generally run in families (Blakeslee, 1989; Culbertson, Krous & Bendell, 1988).

Through the years there has been an endless proliferation of theories as to what goes wrong (Mackintosh, 1982). In the broadest sense, the difficulty appears to be a respiratory problem. The babies simply stop breathing while asleep.

According to one view, the infants suffer from *apnea*—spells in which interruptions or pauses occur in breathing during sleep (Naeye, 1980). Some adults experience a similar disorder, but adults have better reflexes to survive and can go longer without suffering severe oxygen deprivation. During the 1980s pediatricians advocated the use of home monitors that sound an alarm if a baby stops breathing for more than 20 seconds. Despite the fitting of untold numbers of babies with home monitors and heightened parental vigilance, SIDS has not diminished, and the apnea hypothesis has fallen into disrepute.

In some cases bacterial or viral infection may trigger sudden death. Babies who have had a cold or runny nose appear to be more susceptible to the disorder (the syndrome peaks in December, January, and February with the seasonal rise in infectious winter diseases). Yet because they lack strong clues that would identify SIDS babies before death, researchers have now turned to theories of brain development. According to this view, some centers of the brain may mature more rapidly than others, resulting in a temporary "misprogramming" of respiration. Neuroscientists are looking at evidence that crib death is caused by a subtle defect in brain stem circuits that control breathing and heart rates during sleep. Other areas of research include inborn metabolic disorders, immune system disorders, brain-cell degeneration, and abnormal pineal glands that control circadian rhythms (Blakeslee, 1989; Culbertson, Krous & Bendell, 1988; Giulian, Gilbert & Moss, 1987). Unhappily, progress in understanding SIDS remains heartbreakingly slow (Willinger, 1989).

defense. By means of state, infants shut out certain stimuli and thereby inhibit their responses. State is also the way infants set the stage for actively responding (Colombo, Moss & Horowitz, 1989). Consequently, the newborn's use of various states reflects a high order of nervous system control (Korner et al., 1988). The Brazelton Neonatal Behavioral Assessment Scale evaluates a neonate's early behavior by how the baby moves from sleep states to alert states of consciousness (Brazelton, 1990).

Wolf (1966) identifies the following states in the neonate:

Regular Sleep Infants are at full rest; little or no motor activity occurs; facial muscles are relaxed; spontaneous eye movement is absent; respirations are regular and even.

Irregular Sleep Infants engage in spurts of gentle limb movement and more general stirring, squirming, and twisting; eye movement is occasional and rapid; facial grimaces (smiling,

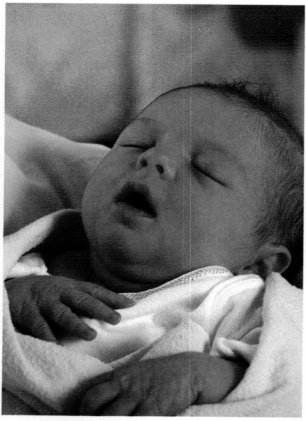

The Sleeping Newborn

In the course of sleep, newborns stir, squirm, and twist their bodies. Their faces display a variety of expressions, including smiling, sneering, frowning, and puckering. (Dan McCoy/Rainbow)

sneering, frowning, puckering, and pouting) are frequent; the rhythm of respiration is irregular and faster than in regular sleep.

Drowsiness Infants are relatively inactive; on occasion, they squirm and twist their bodies; they open and close their eyes intermittently; respiratory patterns are regular but faster than in regular sleep.

Alert Inactivity Although infants are inactive, their eyes are open and have a bright, shining quality; respirations are regular but faster than during regular sleep.

Waking Activity Infants may be silent or may moan, grunt, or whimper; spurts of diffuse motor activity are frequent; their faces may be relaxed or pinched, as when crying; their rate of respiration is irregular.

Crying Vocalizations are strong and intense; motor activity is vigorous; the babies' faces are contorted; their bodies are flushed bright red.

In some infants tears can be observed as early as twenty-four hours after birth.

Crying

Crying in the newborn is an unlearned, involuntary response. At the same time, it is a highly adaptive response that serves to incite the parent to caretaking activities. Humans find few sounds more disconcerting and unnerving than the infant's cry (see the boxed insert on page 127). Physiological studies reveal that the sound of a baby's cry triggers an increase in the blood pressure and heart rate of parents (Bleichfeld & Moely, 1984; Donate-Bartfield & Passman, 1985). If they cannot get the baby to stop crying, parents sometimes wind up feeling distraught, helpless, angry at the baby, and guilty for experiencing the anger. Some parents feel rejected and reject the child in turn. In extreme cases child abuse may result. But simply because caretakers have difficulty getting babies to stop crying does not mean they are doing a bad job. Crying is the chief way that babies communicate. Different cries—each with distinctive pitch, rhythm, and duration—convey different messages.

Crying

Crying is an unlearned, involuntary, but highly adaptive response that encourages caretaking activities by others. Most babies can be soothed by picking them up, holding them, and carrying them about. (Russ Kinne/Comstock)

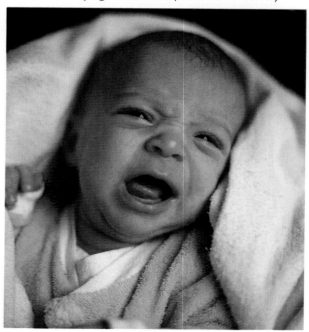

Soothing the Newborn

Since time immemorial, harried parents the world over have been concerned with soothing their babies. One New Hampshire mother recalls, "I never knew when he'd wake up, how many times, and for how long. I was crazy with battle fatigue. . . . After a while, I would have done anything he wanted. I was so desperate for sleep. . . . He called the shots in our household. I felt I was out of control" (quoted by Leonard, 1991, p. 42). Yet the study of infant states tells us that sleep, drowsiness, alert inactivity, and crying are all normal and expected behaviors in a healthy infant. Indeed, crying is functional. During the first week of life crying helps to fill and aerate the infant's lungs. Even so, few of us can escape the psychological discomfort and frayed nerves that are associated with a wailing baby—the piercing cry, flushed red face, jerking body, quivering chin, and trembling arms and legs.

Through the centuries parents have evolved a variety of techniques that both experience and research have shown to be helpful in soothing infants. These techniques include gentle rocking, a pacifier, a pacifier sweetened with a sugar solution, a monotonous, humming sound, and a warm bath (Byrne & Horowitz, 1981; Campos, 1989; Woodson, Drinkwin & Hamilton, 1985). Few techniques are more soothing, however, than simply picking the infant up and putting it to the shoulder, its head supported and just above shoulder level (Korner & Thoman, 1972; Thoman, Korner, & Beason-Williams, 1977). This action affords contact between the adult and child. And the stimulation provided by picking the child up and moving it through space increases its visual alertness. If a pacifier is given to the infant at the same time, its visual attentiveness is further enhanced. Such stimulation serves to interrupt the crying and to shift the infant into another state. Sucrose infused through a pacifier also seems to have a calming effect in human newborns (Smith, Fillion & Blass, 1990). Even so, babies differ greatly in their soothability and in the activities that they find soothing (Birns, Blank & Bridger, 1966; Korner & Thoman, 1972). In sum, parents should not expect a "textbook" baby.

Recently, researchers have found that they can make babies fall asleep more quickly by increasing the amount of sugar and tryptophan (an amino acid) in their evening bottles (Yogman & Zeisel, 1983). They suggest that nursing mothers may obtain the same effect if they eat candy before the infant's bedtime feeding. Tryptophan is employed in the brain to manufacture a message transmitter that is required for sleep. It is commonly found in milk.

Between 1920 and 1940 the U.S. Children's Bureau *Infant Care* pamphlets warned mothers not to "give in" to a crying baby, for to do so would create "a spoiled, fussy baby, and a household tyrant whose continual demands make a slave of the mother" (1924, p. 44). Some contemporary pediatricians take the same view, saying that many parental remedies merely exacerbate the problem because the infants come to depend upon the parents as a "sleep adjunct" (Elias, 1991; Leonard, 1991).

Many psychologists believe that parental advice "not to give in to a crying baby" is ill-founded (Ainsworth & Bell, 1977; Crockenberg & McCluskey, 1986; Crockenberg & Smith, 1982). An infant's crying is not simply a distress signal but a powerful communicative act. How people respond to this act—whether they consistently answer or ignore the cries—teaches the child something about the environment. For instance, a study by Silvia M. Bell and Mary D. Salter Ainsworth (1972) reveals that a responsive mother provides not only the conditions that terminate crying but also a setting that prevents the crying from occurring in the first place. Even more interesting, Bell and Ainsworth found that ignoring babies' cries actually *increases* the likelihood that they will cry more as the first year progresses. Babies who cry little and whose crying *decreases* during the year generally have mothers who respond to them when they cry. Furthermore, infants of responsive mothers are more likely than their opposites to develop channels other than crying to communicate with their mothers. Other researchers have found that parents can reduce their baby's crying by simply spending more time carrying the infant about during the day. A sample of fifty babies held and carried an average of 4.4 hours a day cried 43 percent less overall and 51 percent less during evening hours than babies whose mothers held and carried them about an average of 2.7 hours (H. Hall, 1987).

One must also remember that babies possess a variety of self-soothing mechanisms. They can shift from one state to another independently of outside stimulation. As a result, crying tends to be a self-limiting state, one that is commonly replaced by sleep. Sucking is another built-in device that serves to reduce an infant's stress.

The Desperate Legacy
of Drug Babies

The number of drug-damaged children being born in the United States is growing at epidemic rates. The federal government estimates that between 325,000 and 375,000 drug-exposed babies are born each year (a 1988 survey of 36 urban and suburban hospitals found that 11 percent of newborns had been exposed to drugs in the womb), with a third of those exposed to crack. Children born to mothers who abused drugs during their pregnancies often exhibit a wide range of problems, whether the drug be cocaine, heroin, amphetamines, marijuana, or alcohol. During pregnancy, drugs cross the placenta and enter the fetus's system.

Many youngsters begin their lives with serious handicaps. Some are born prematurely. However, compared with other premature babies, drug-damaged babies are more likely to have suffered an infarct of the brain (a stroke), brain damage, and kidney problems. They are also more likely to be difficult to care for from the moment of birth. Some are sluggish and depressed, others are excitable and jittery, and still others exhibit both types of behavior (Kantrowitz, 1990).

Barry M. Lester, a professor of psychiatry and pediatrics at Brown University, studied the crying patterns of eighty newborns exposed to cocaine and eighty infants not exposed to the drug (Lester et al., 1991). He recorded the youngsters' cries when their heels were pricked in routine blood tests. Newborns who were not exposed prenatally to drugs tended to respond with mild crying that soon subsides. Drug-exposed newborns of normal weight typically reacted promptly with longer cries of higher frequency. Some drug-exposed babies of low birthweight responded slowly to the prick and cried less frequently and with lower amplitude; others initially appeared lethargic and slow to respond but once provoked were nearly impossible to calm. However, since many drug-abusing mothers receive little or no prenatal care and suffer from poor maternal nutrition, disentangling the effects of cocaine exposure from the effects of poverty and disadvantage is often impossible (*New York Times*, 1991).

The drug-related difficulties and defects of crack babies give rise to many developmental problems. As babies, they are frequently irritable and scream inconsolably. They tend to be at the mercy of their impulses, and consequently they behave chaotically. The babies have difficulty finding comfort in cuddling, rocking, or soothing humming sounds. Indeed, they may react with piercing wails and jerky motions. Few people find the behaviors lovable, and so the youngsters' problems may be compounded by abuse (Brazelton, 1990). Further complicating matters, crack often overwhelms parenting impulses, leading some mothers to neglect or abandon their youngsters. Drugs chemically impair functioning so parents have trouble making decisions, taking responsibility for paying the rent, and seeing that there is food on the table for their children (DeCourcy Hinds, 1990).

At eighteen months the facial expressions of children born to drug-abusing mothers tend to be flat and joyless, and their body language displays a lack of enthusiasm for activities that typically entice normal youngsters. The most seriously afflicted youngsters suffer from seizures, cerebral palsy, or mental retardation. Many are overwhelmed by stimuli such as noise or toys; many have difficulty interpreting nonverbal signals; many are easily frustrated, engage in violent and self-destructive behaviors, have trouble concentrating, and learn something only to quickly forget it. Behavior extremes are common, from passivity to hyperactivity, apathy to aggression, and indiscriminate trust to extreme suspicion. Psychologists label such behaviors "disorganized" because the children have trouble focusing on one activity and learning from it. For instance, in nursery school a girl may demand to be left alone, bump into walls, and stare blankly into space; a boy may scream and throw himself on the floor

Most parents typically learn the "language" of crying rather quickly (Bisping, Steingrueber, Oltman & Wenk, 1990; Green, Jones & Gustafson, 1987; Gustafson & Green, 1989; Zeskind & Marshall, 1988). Babies have one cry that means hunger, one that means discomfort, one that means boredom, one that means frustration, and others for such problems as pain or illness. Moreover, most parents can distinguish their baby's cries from those of other youngsters (Lester & Boukydis, 1985; Roberts, 1987b). Children's cries become more complex across time. Around the second month, the irregular or fussy cry appears (Fogel & Thelen, 1987). And about the age of

because he wants to be picked up but cannot articulate his needs. Fine-motor skills may also be hampered, and language acquisition may be slow or impaired (Chira, 1990; Kantrowitz, 1990; Trost, 1989).

Caring for drug-damaged youngsters requires an extraordinary commitment from parents, caretakers, caseworkers, and teachers. Our society is poorly prepared to deal with the crack-damaged children now entering our schools. The youngsters bring with them an alarming array of neurological, emotional, developmental, and learning problems. Many school systems, especially in major cities, already find themselves overwhelmed in educating the children normally entrusted to them. Judy Howard, a leading researcher on cocaine-exposed babies and a UCLA professor of clinical pediatrics, predicts that in some inner-city schools these children will constitute 40 to 60 percent of the students within a few years. The March of Dimes says the number of crack-exposed children could range from 500,000 to 4 million by the year 2000. If we are to help these children learn, we will have to rethink the way our schools are organized. Additional money will be required to hire and train more teachers and expand special education classes staffed with speech and physical therapists. Currently, most schools are not set up to provide the kind of atmosphere and nurturing the youngsters need (Chira, 1990). And special care is costly, running up to five times the cost for an average child in a regular classroom (Trost, 1989).

Drug use during pregnancy has brought new issues before the nation's courts. Prosecutors say they are upset by the serious harm being done to babies by drug-using mothers-to-be and insist they must find legal remedies to prevent it. But health, feminist, and civil liberties groups argue that it is counterproductive to treat the problem as a legal issue and that it is unconstitutional to hold pregnant women to a higher standard than other Americans. Both sides agree that the best solution is prevention and early treatment, not punishment, but resources designated for prevention and treatment are frequently inadequate. Many court cases against pregnant women contend that the fetus has separate interests from the mother and that a woman has a legal obligation to guard the fetus. But this argument invokes the "slippery slope" notion and creates a fine line: Do women become criminals if they take one drink, or is it four? Do they endanger a child by taking aspirin? Is there a legal obligation for pregnant woman not to gain excessive weight or to seek prenatal care?

Since most states do not deem a fetus to be a child, child abuse statutes do not apply to fetal abuse. So recent cases have charged the mother with delivering a drug to the child through the umbilical cord during the 90 seconds or so after the child has left the birth canal but before the umbilical cord is severed. Critics of this approach say that harm to the child does not make a woman's addiction more criminal than a man's addiction but merely highlights the severity of her addiction. Moreover, they note that penalties tend to fall more heavily on poor minority women (for instance, in Florida's Pinellas County, pregnant black users are nearly 10 times more likely to be reported for substance abuse than are pregnant white drug users). Prosecutors tend to respond with the argument that children have a constitutional right to be born drug-free (Hoffman, 1990; Lewin, 1990).

Clearly, societal problems revolving about drug use by pregnant women are complex and difficult to solve. It seems necessary to salvage addicted mothers if only because there are not enough foster homes for their youngsters. If these problems are not addressed, and addressed promptly, our nation will throw away two generations—the infants and their mothers (Brazelton, 1990).

---

9 months, the child's cry becomes less persistent and more punctuated by pauses while the youngster checks how the cry is affecting a caregiver (Bruner, 1983).

The neonate's cry is also proving to be an important aid in the early detection of certain abnormalities and diseases. There are times when unusual crying provides the first indication that something may be wrong with an infant (Frodi & Senchak, 1990; Porter, Porges & Marshall, 1988; Zeskind & Lester, 1978, 1981). Brain-damaged and Down's syndrome babies, for instance, produce a less sustained cry with less rhythmic flow in the crying than do normal infants (Fisichelli & Karelitz, 1963). Similarly, the cry of the malnourished infant has an initial longer sound, higher pitch, and lower amplitude than the cry of the well-nourished baby. Babies exposed prenatally to cocaine by their mothers present special problems (see the box on page 128).

Feeding

Neonates spend a good deal of the time that they are awake feeding. Indeed, their hunger and sleep patterns are closely linked. Newborns may feed eight to fourteen times during the day: Some infants prefer intervals as short as one and one-half hours; others, intervals of three to four hours; and still others, two- or three-hour intervals during the day and four- or five-hour intervals at night. Fortunately, infants come to require fewer daily feedings as they grow older. Most put themselves on three to five meals by the time they are twelve months old.

Self-Demand Feeding During the 1920s and 1930s many medical authorities recommended placing infants on a regular four-hour feeding schedule. Mothers were encouraged to hold fast to a strict schedule. According to the behaviorist John B. Watson, a leading authority of the period, a child's character would be improved if its immediate needs were ignored. Today, Watson's advice is rejected by most doctors. Pediatricians have come to recognize that babies differ markedly. They encourage parents to feed a baby when it is hungry. Thus, the infant picks its own part of the twenty-four-hour cycle in which to feed and sleep—termed *self-demand feeding*.

Breast Feeding/Bottle Feeding Whatever schedule parents follow, they have to decide whether the baby will be breast-fed or bottle-fed. Before 1900 the vast majority of mothers breast-fed their babies. But in the ensuing years bottle feeding became increasingly popular, so that by 1946 only 38 out of every 100 women left the hospital with a nursing baby. This figure dropped to 21 percent in 1956. Since then, breast feeding has gained in popularity, especially among middle- and upper-class parents. However, in recent years the trend seems to be reversing, particularly among low-income, young, and minority women (breast feeding dropped from about 60 percent of all women surveyed in 1984 to 52 percent in 1989) (Hilts, 1991).

Breast feeding offers a number of advantages. It provides emotional and psychological rewards that are not available to women who bottle-feed their infants. Indeed, many women report that the physical act of nursing is a sensually pleasurable experience. And there are some, especially those influenced by the psychoanalytic tradition, who believe that the intimate contact afforded by breast feeding creates a sense of security and well-being in the infant that leaves a permanent, favorable impact upon its later personality.

Breast feeding is also practical. The milk is always ready and at the proper temperature. And the traveling mother is free of the paraphernalia required of the nonnursing mother—the tote bag, bottles, and sterile water. Even more important, researchers have found that mother's milk harbors an arsenal of immunological weapons that protect the infant against infections until its own defenses are built up. Simultaneously, the substances in breast milk seem to stimulate the infant's own antibody machinery and the maturation of the intestinal tract. The chief disadvantage of breast feeding is that it limits the physical freedom of the mother. In addition, some research suggests that breast-fed infants are more irritable and more difficult to console than are bottle-fed youngsters, although breast-fed neonates have a more optimal physiological organization as evi-

Breast Feeding

In many areas of the world, including parts of Indonesia, breast feeding may be prolonged until another youngster is born. Nursing affords both nutritional and emotional benefits to the child and serves as a bonding mechanism between mother and infant. *(Paul Fusco/Magnum)*

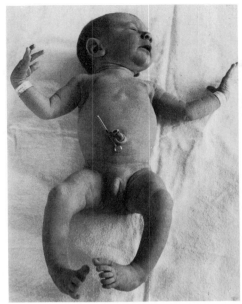 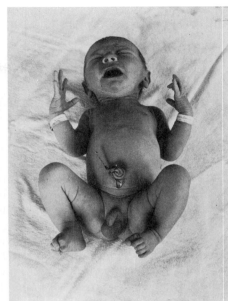

The Two Stages of The Moro Reflex
The Moro reflex occurs when a baby suddenly loses support for the head and neck. The infant extends the arms and legs (a) and then contracts them as if in an embrace (b). *(Patrick Reddy)*   (a)   (b)

denced by various measures of heart rate and response tone (DiPietro, Larson & Porges, 1987).

The advantage of bottle feeding is that it gives mothers the physical freedom that breast feeding denies them. Morever, fathers can get involved in feeding their infants. And commercial milk preparations tend to fill babies up more, so that they can go longer between feedings. There is also no reason that bottle feeding cannot be—indeed, it should be—accompanied by nurturing, physical contact with the baby. The decline of breast feeding in developing countries, however, has led to malnutrition and intestinal diseases for increasing numbers of infants (Hinds, 1982; Popkin, Bilsborrow & Akin, 1982). Since many of the mothers live in poverty, they have only contaminated water to mix with the formula powder. Furthermore, they frequently overdilute the expensive formula, making what should be a four-day supply last for three or more weeks.

One final word of caution. Infants of breast-feeding mothers should be regularly monitored by a pediatrician if the mother is taking medication or other drugs. In some cases these agents can be transmitted to the child in the mother's milk and constitute a health hazard. Also, the Committee on Nutrition of the American Academy of Pediatrics recommends that breast-fed infants be provided certain supplements, including vitamin D, iron, and fluoride (available in combined preparations). Finally, pediatricians have recently encountered evidence that cow anti-

bodies are a likely factor in infant colic (it seems that the immature systems of many babies are unable to process the antibodies). Levels of cow antibodies are high in milk-based formulas and in the breast milk of mothers who consume dairy products.

Reflexes

The newborn infant is hardly a blank tablet (*tabula rasa*), as the English philosopher John Locke believed. On the contrary, the baby comes equipped with a number of behavioral systems ready to be activated. These systems are termed "reflexes." A **reflex** is a relatively simple, involuntary, and unlearned response to a stimulus. In other words, it is a response that is triggered automatically through built-in circuits. Reflexes are the evolutionary remains of actions seen in animals lower in the phylogenic scale (Cratty, 1970). Although reflexes generally are no longer necessary for human survival, they are good indicators of neurological development in infants. Researchers estimate that the human is born with at least twenty-seven reflexes. Let us consider some of them.

Moro and Startle Reflexes   The *Moro reflex* is elicited when infants suddenly lose support for their necks and heads. Babies throw out their arms and then bring them together, as in an embrace. Simultaneously, they throw out their legs and return them to a flexed position against the body. You can obtain the Moro reflex by holding an infant with one hand under the small of the back and supporting the head with your other hand. Then, suddenly, lower the hand under the baby's head about an inch. The baby itself often triggers the reflex when it coughs or sneezes.

The Moro reflex is different from the *startle reflex*. The startle reflex is activated when the neonate hears a loud noise or is suddenly touched. The startle reflex resembles the Moro reflex except that the initial extension of the Moro reflex is absent—the infant flexes but does not extend the arms. Furthermore, in the startle reflex the infant's fingers remain closed, whereas in the Moro reflex the hands curl slightly as if preparing to grasp something. In fact, if you place your finger in the baby's hand when someone provides the stimulus for the Moro reflex, you will be able to feel the infant's grip tighten on your finger.

Both the Moro and the startle reflexes may set off a cycle of crying and reflexing. Steady pressure on babies at some point on their bodies usually serves to break the cycle and calm them.

The Moro reflex appears during the ninth week after conception and disappears in six or seven months after birth. A weak Moro reflex provides an early clue that the infant's central nervous system may be malfunctioning. If the reflex is present beyond the ninth month, it may indicate mental retardation.

Rooting Reflex When infants are gently touched near the corner of the mouth, they "root," or turn their heads toward the stroking object. Then, they open their mouths and try to suck. A mother who is unfamiliar with the reflex often attempts to push the infant's head toward her breast. Since babies respond by moving toward, rather than away from, the source of stimulation—in this case the mother's hand—they give the appearance of rejecting the breast. This response may inaugurate a vicious circle of frustration for both the mother and the infant: the mother repeatedly "forcing" the baby's head toward her breast and the baby persistently "rejecting" the breast.

Sucking Reflex If the soft palates of their mouths are touched, infants begin sucking with a rapid burst of five to twenty-four sucks. They then take a brief rest. Mothers tend to jiggle the infant, breast, or bottle when the infant pauses. Feeding appears to be an exchange of turns, in which the infant's pause is answered by the mother's jiggling and the end of jiggling is answered by the next burst (Kaye & Wells, 1980). Babies put both the nipple and the areola, the dark area around the nipple, into their mouths. Sucking also seems to promote grasping activity in newborns, with grasping becoming more intense when youngsters are sucking than when they are pausing (Buka & Lipsitt, 1991). In addition, sucking appears to be more than just a way to get sustenance, for infants appear to suck simply for the sake of sucking (Blass, 1990; Brake, Fifer, Alfasi & Fleischman, 1988; Koepke & Barnes, 1982). Thumbs, by virtue of their convenience, seem to offer special appeal. Most children, however, outgrow thumb-sucking by the age of three.

Babinski Reflex The *Babinski reflex* is triggered by gently stroking the outer edge of the sole of the foot. This action causes an extension in the infant's big toe and a fanning out of the other toes. The Babinski reflex disappears within a year. Thereafter, the toes curl downward when the sole is stroked.

Palmar and Plantar Grasp Reflexes Touching the palm of the infant's hand results in a grasping action that is often strong enough to support the infant's weight—the *palmar grasp reflex*. If pressure is applied against the ball of the foot, the toes flex, assuming a grasping position—the *plantar grasp reflex*. Some researchers believe that these two reflexes are the rudimentary remains of the grasping activity needed by primate ancestors. The palmar grasp reflex reaches its greatest strength toward the end of the first month. It is gradually replaced by voluntary grasp between the fourth and seventh months. The plantar grasp reflex disappears by the end of the first year.

Stepping Reflex Around the end of the second week of life, 58 percent of all infants will "walk" if held in an upright position, tilted slightly to one side, and permitted to touch a level horizontal surface. This action is the *stepping reflex*. The walking pattern involves a lifting and flexing of the knee but does not entail any arm swing. The neonate can be made to "climb" stairs while supported in this fashion. The reflex disappears by about the third month.

Swimming Reflex If neonates are submerged in water with their stomachs down, they make rhythmic swimming movements that are capable of propelling them a short distance. This response is the *swimming reflex*. The babies gener-

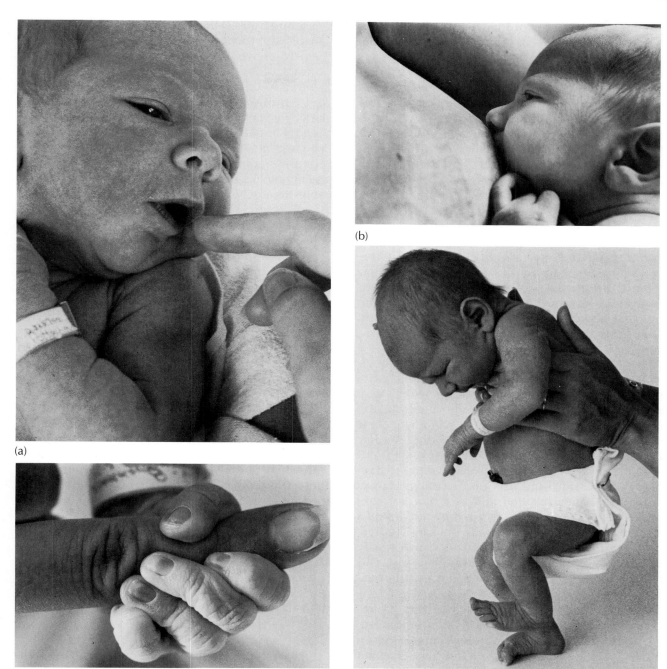

Reflexes

Newborns are equipped with a number of behavioral systems that are ready to be activated. These systems are called reflexes. The photos depict the rooting reflex (a), the sucking reflex (b), the palmar grasp reflex (c), and the stepping reflex (d). *(Patrick Reddy)*

ally hold their breath and do not ingest water. Obviously, caution must be employed with newborns, since they are unable to keep their heads above the water level and thus may suffocate. The swimming reflex usually disappears in about five months.

Memory: Habituation

If we present the same stimulus to an infant several times in a row, the infant will soon stop responding to it. If we then withhold the stimulus for a short period, the infant recovers the reflex response, perking up and paying attention to the stimulus (Kisilevsky & Muir, 1991; Tarquinio, Zelazo, Gryspeerdt & Allen, 1991). This process is termed **habituation.** In habituation studies, the infant is exposed to a stimulus—for instance, a sound, an odor, or a light—at regular but short intervals. When the baby no longer responds to the stimulus, a slightly different stimulus is introduced. If the infant then responds, in proves that the baby can distinguish the latter stimulus from the preceding one. It also proves that the infant is habituated to the initial stimulus and not simply fatigued. Habituation is considered a good indication that a child's brain and nervous system are functioning properly. Indeed, relatively greater amounts of looking at novel stimuli, or reciprocally lesser amounts of looking at familiar stimuli, is a good indication of efficient information processing in infancy and seems related to intellectual performance in childhood (Bornstein, 1989; Lecuyer, 1989; Tamis-LeMonda & Bornstein, 1989).

Habituation represents an early *adaptive* response to the environment. If infants attended to every stimulus that came along, they would soon be exhausted. It would serve no purpose, for example, if they rooted continually whenever their cheeks accidently touched their bedding. Rather than anticipating the nipple after a few such encounters, infants simply stop this fruitless exercise. But if a new and different stimulus comes along, the babies respond to it.

Habituation gives us insight into an infant's early memory processes. If babies respond differently to a stimulus the tenth time they experience it from the way they responded the first time, this pattern suggests that they have "remembered" the stimulus. Using this reasoning, E.N. Sokolov (1958/1963, 1969), a Russian psychologist, has formulated a memory theory of habituation. According to Sokolov, a mental representation or an internal model of a repeated stimulus is formed in the nervous system. If a new stimulus input matches this model, the associated reflex is inhibited (it loses its novelty value for the infant). If the stimulus fails to match the model, the reflex is activated as usual.

Learning

Can newborns learn? The answer to this question depends on the type of behavior involved. Most developmental psychologists agree that habituation is a very simple and elementary form of learning. Since repeated stimulation produces a lessening of response and, equally important, novel stimulation reestablishes the response, clearly newborns can "learn" to distinguish among stimuli.

But, we may ask, can neonates learn in the more traditional sense—can they adjust their behavior according to whether it succeeds or fails? Arnold J. Sameroff (1968) conducted a study involving neonate sucking techniques and tentatively suggests the answer is yes. Generally recognized is that two nursing methods are available to newborns. One approach—*expression*—involves pressing the nipple against the roof of the mouth with the tongue and squeezing milk out of it. A second method—*suction*—entails creating a partial vacuum by reducing the pressure inside the mouth and thus pulling the milk from the nipple. Sameroff devised an experimental nipple and nutrient delivery apparatus that permitted him to regulate the supply of milk that an infant received. He provided one group of babies with milk only when they used the expressive method (squeezing the nipple); he gave the second group milk only when they used the suction method.

Sameroff found that the infants adapted their responses according to which technique was reinforced. For instance, the group that was given milk when they used the expressive method diminished their suction responses—indeed, in many cases they abandoned the suction method during the training period. In a second experiment Sameroff (1968) was able to induce the babies, again through reinforcement, to express milk at one of two different pressure levels. These results suggest that learning can occur among two- to five-day-old, full-term infants. Various other researchers have likewise demonstrated learning in newborns (Cantor, Fischel & Kaye, 1983; DeCasper & Carstens, 1981; Siqueland, 1968).

Psychologist Anthony DeCasper and his colleagues have also investigated whether learning can occur among babies still in the womb. They believe they have found evidence that some kind of learning is occurring, although its exact mechanism is not known. The researchers devised a nipple apparatus that activates a tape recorder. By sucking in one pattern, newborns would hear their own mothers' voices; by sucking in another pattern, they would hear another woman's voice. The babies (some just hours old) tended to suck in a way that would allow them to hear their mothers' voices. In sum, the children's preferences were affected by their auditory experiences before birth (DeCasper & Fifer, 1980).

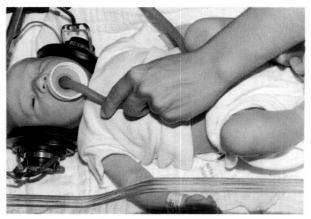

Can a Fetus Learn?
This baby is participating in Anthony DeCasper's research on learning in fetuses and newborns. The infant sucks to hear a tape recording of his mother reading a story that she read aloud, on a regular basis, while pregnant. The rate of sucking is much higher for the familiar story than for another one.
(Walter Salinger, courtesy Professor Anthony DeCasper)

In another DeCasper experiment women seven and a half months pregnant read a story out loud to the fetus three times daily for four weeks. At the end of the period, recordings of that story and a different one were played, and the fetal heart rates were monitored for signs of change (when scientists place a tiny microphone in the uterus, they find that bass sounds penetrate better than treble, with the result likened to Lauren Bacall talking from behind a heavy curtain) (Begley, 1991). The familiar story caused a decrease in the heart rates, whereas unfamiliar ones caused a slight increase. In other tests sixteen pregnant women read Dr. Seuss's *The Cat in the Hat* to their unborn children twice a day for the last six weeks of gestation—a total of about five hours. After they were born, the infants sucked in order to hear a tape recording of their mothers' reading Dr. Seuss's poem more often than their mothers' reading stories by other authors having a different meter. Some parents have interpreted these findings as saying that they can give their infants a developmental head start by teaching them things before they are born. For instance, they might try to create a musical prodigy by playing classical music to the fetus. But not everyone thinks this sort of thing is a good idea. Although twenty years ago we gave fetuses and newborns little credit for having cognitive and learning capabilities, today the pendulum may be swinging optimistically too far in the opposite direction. We need to remind ourselves that much of the work in this area remains

conjecture (Cohen, Hoffman, Kelley & Anday, 1988; Kolata, 1984; Roberts, 1987*a*; Weiss, Zelazo & Swain, 1988). Many of the responses that babies show are adaptations to specific stimuli for which newborns are biologically prepared (Sameroff & Cavanagh, 1979).

The Senses

What is the world like to the newborn? Possessed of "no language but a cry," as the English poet Alfred, Lord Tennyson, once suggested, babies are not able to satisfy our curiosity by giving us an account of their experiences. Even so, it is becoming increasingly clear that infants do not perceive their environment as the "great blooming, buzzing confusion" that William James called it in 1890. The infant is hardly incompetent. Indeed, as André-Thomas observes, "the neonate is not a neophyte" (quoted by Kessen, 1963). Today, sophisticated monitoring equipment is permitting us to pinpoint what the infant sees, hears, smells, tastes, and feels. Psychologists now recognize that infants are capable of doing much more and doing it much earlier than was believed possible even ten to fifteen years ago. Indeed, these new techniques and the insights they have afforded have been hailed by some psychologists as "a scientific revolution" (Goode, 1990).

Let us consider the processes of sensation and perception. **Sensation** refers to the reception of information by our sense organs. **Perception** concerns the *interpretation* or *meaning* that we assign to sensation.

Vision

The Eye altering alters all.—WILLIAM BLAKE
The Mental Traveller, 1800–1810

A full-term newborn is equipped at birth with a functional and intact visual apparatus. However, the eye contains a number of immaturities. The retina and the optic nerve, for instance, are not fully developed (Abramov et al., 1982). Nonetheless, both the central retina and the peripheral retina function at birth (Lewis, Maurer & Kay, 1978). Neonates also seem to lack visual accommodation. The muscles that control the lenses are not fully developed. As a result, the lenses are fixed in focus for about a month. Thus, only objects that are about 7 to 9 inches from the neonate's eye are in focus (Haynes, White & Held, 1965). In part this fixed focus may be a blessing. It limits the stimulus input with which infants must cope. As a rule, the eyes do not focus normally, adjusting to different distances, until infants reach about four months of age. Although some of the structures within the visual system are not completely formed, the eye is prepared at birth to distinguish among most aspects of its visual field (Bronson, 1974; Hershenson, 1967; Reese & Lipsitt, 1970).

The neonate pays more attention to some things than to others (Fantz, Fagan & Miranda, 1975; Haith, 1980; Morton, Johnson & Maurer, 1990). Research by Robert L. Fantz confirms that neonates are able to distinguish among various

Baby-Testing Apparatus

The photo shows the "looking chamber" employed by Fantz in his studies of perceptual development in children. The infant is placed on her back looking up at two panels. Contrasting visual stimuli—a face and a patch of newsprint, a red circle and a bull's-eye, a bull's-eye and newsprint—are placed on the panels. The baby's eye movements are then observed to determine which of the two panels she looks at more frequently and for longer periods. (Courtesy Dr. Robert L. Fantz)

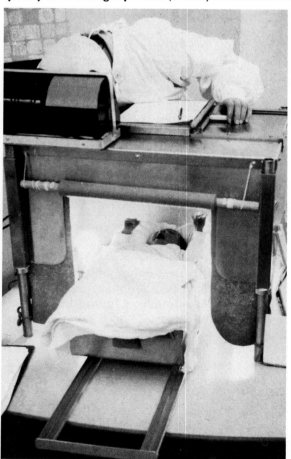

visual patterns. In one experiment Fantz (1963) found that infants from ten hours to five days old look longer at a schematic black-and-white face than at a patch of newsprint; longer at newsprint than at a black-and-white bull's-eye; and longer at a bull's-eye than at a plain red, white, or yellow circle. Fantz has also demonstrated that neonates are more attracted to pattern than to color differences, to "complex" than to "simple" figures, to oval than to plain shapes, and to curved than to straight contours (Fantz, 1966; Fantz & Miranda, 1975). Other researchers find that neonates can follow slowly moving objects with their eyes (Haith & Goodman, 1982; McGurk, Turnure & Creighton, 1977). And Maurice Hershenson (1964, 1967) has shown that neonates can discriminate among degrees of brightness. All this research points to an important conclusion: The world of the neonate is not an undifferentiated, chaotic mass of stimuli. Infants perceive a more organized and coherent world than previously suspected—one in which objects and events are related to one another (Antell, Caron & Myers, 1985).

T. G. R. Bower (1971, 1974, 1977) suggests that some of the infant's perceptual responses revolve around built-in abilities. In an experiment with infants between one and two weeks of age, Bower used special experimental equipment to project a *virtual image* of a solid object in front of the babies. A virtual image is an optical illusion. It looks three-dimensional in space, although it is empty air to the sense of touch. Bower found that the neonates responded with unmistakable surprise whenever their hands reached the location where the "object" seemed to be: They would emit a howl, accompanied by a change in facial expression. In contrast, none of the infants showed surprise when they reached out and touched an actual object that had been placed before them. Bower interprets this study as revealing that at least one aspect of eye-hand interaction is biologically prewired in the infant's nervous system. Other researchers confirm that some aspects of infant eye-hand coordination appear to be preprogrammed (Bruner & Koslowski, 1972; Cruikshank, 1941). However, the pattern observed in newborns of placing the hand in the mouth also seems to be a built-in ability and not necessarily related to hand-eye coordination (Blass, Fillion, Rochat, Hoffmeyer & Metzger, 1989; Rochat, Blass & Hoffmeyer, 1988).

Psychologists Andrew N. Meltzoff and M. Keith Moore (1977, 1979, 1983) also report that neonates can imitate other people's facial and man-

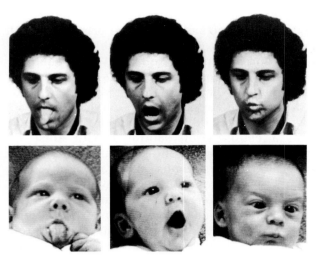

Figure 5-1   The Neonates's Ability to Imitate
Andrew N. Meltzoff and M. Keith Moore have found that
infants younger than 3 days old can imitate certain
gestures, such as sticking out the tongue and opening
and closing the mouth. SOURCE: A. N. Meltzoff and M. K.
Moore, "Imitation of Facial and Manual Gestures by
Human Neonates," *Science*, Vol. 198 (1977), pp. 75–78.
Copyright 1977 by the American Association for the
Advancement of Science.

ual gestures. The researchers first have an adult
look at a neonate and display a passive and ex-
pressionless face. Then, in random order the
adult performs four actions: He purses his lips, he
sticks out his tongue, he opens his mouth wide,
and he opens and closes his hand. The adult
pauses with a neutral expression in between each
demonstration. Later, observers view each infant
on videotape and pick the variation they believe
the baby is imitating. When Meltzoff and Moore
compared these choices with the adult's actions,
they found that the babies had consistently varied
their expressions and hand movements to match
those of the adult (see Figure 5-1).

The Meltzoff and Moore research suggests that
babies may be born with the ability to imitate
facial gestures. The babies can see another person's facial expressions but not their own. Imitation without having seen their own reflection in a
mirror or having other learning experiences
shows that newborns have some inherent degree
of coordination among their senses. They successfully match the gesture they observe with a
gesture they can only *feel* themselves perform.
Findings such as these suggest that we may need
to rethink some of our notions regarding the cognitive capabilities of newborns. Additionally, the
ability to respond to and imitate a human face

means that neonates play an active role in structuring their social experiences right from birth:
They have the ability to influence the behavior of
their caretakers.

Not all psychologists, however, accept the research done by Meltzoff and Moore (Anisfeld,
1979; Kaitz, Meschulach-Sarfaty, Auerbach &
Eidelman, 1988; Koepke, Hamm, Legerstee &
Russell, 1983; McKenzie & Over, 1983). They al-
lege that behaviors like tongue protrusion are
merely an inborn prepackaged motor program
that is "tripped" or "released" by the adult's behavior. For example, Sandra W. Jacobson (1979)
finds that neonates will stick out their tongues at
a pen or some other object moving toward their
mouth. Since babies will open their mouth to a
wide variety of stimuli, Jacobson says we cannot
call it imitation. Nonetheless, other researchers
such as Field, Woodson, Greenberg, and Cohen
(1982) have experimentally monitored the faces
of seventy-four babies as they looked at adult
models who made happy, sad, or surprised expressions and found that 2-day-old newborns imitated the expressions. Unhappily, the issue of
newborn cognitive ability is still unresolved, and
the question remains: How much do infants know
and when do they know it (Abravanel & Sigafoos,
1984; Bjorklund, 1987; Moss, Colombo, Mitchell &
Horowitz, 1988; Reissland, 1988)?

Hearing

At the time of birth the hearing apparatus of
the neonate is remarkably well developed. Indeed, the human fetus can hear noises three
months before birth (Birnholz & Benacerraf,
1983). However, for several hours or even days
after delivery, the neonate's hearing may be
somewhat impaired. Vernix and amniotic fluid
frequently stop up the external ear passage, while
mucus clogs the middle ear. However, these mechanical blockages disappear rapidly after birth.

Educators have long recognized that hearing
plays an important part in the process by which
children acquire language. But research by
William S. Condon and Louis W. Sander (1974*a*,
1974*b*) purporting to show that newborns are attuned to the fine elements of adult speech took
the scientific community by surprise. The researchers made videotapes of neonate-adult interaction and minutely analyzed them frame by
frame. To ordinary viewers, the hands, feet, and
head of an infant appear uncoordinated, clumsily
flexing, twitching, and moving about in all direc-

tions. But Condon and Sander say closer examination reveals that the infant's movements are synchronized with the sound patterns of the adult's speech. For example, if an infant is squirming about when an adult begins to talk, the infant coordinates the movements of brows, eyes, limbs, elbows, hips, and mouth to start, stop, and change with the boundaries of the adult's speech segments (phonemes, syllables, or words). The newborns, who were from 12 hours to 2 days old, were equally capable of synchronizing their movements with Chinese or English.

Condon and Sander conclude that if infants, from birth, move in precise, shared rhythm with the speech patterns of their culture, then they participate in millions of repetitions of linguistic forms long before they employ them in communication. By the time children begin to speak, they have already laid down within themselves the form and structure of their people's language system. So Condon and Sander say that this complex, ongoing "dance" of the neonate in the presence of human speech has functional significance for later language development. Unhappily, other researchers have not been able to replicate the Condon-Sander findings. Indeed, John M. Dowd and Edward Z. Tronick (1986) conclude that speech-movement synchrony requires reaction times inconsistent with an infant's limited motor abilities and that the methodology used by Condon and Sander is flawed in many ways. So, again, we find that considerable controversy surrounds the question "How much do infants know, and when do they know it?"

Taste and Smell

Both taste—*gustation*—and smell—*olfaction*—are present at birth. Neonate taste preferences can be determined by measuring sucking behavior. Newborns relax and suck contentedly when provided with sweet solutions, although they reveal a preference for sucrose over glucose (Engen, Lipsitt & Peck, 1974). Infants react to sour and bitter solutions by grimacing and breathing irregularly (Crook, 1978; Jensen, 1932; Rosenstein & Oster, 1988). The findings for salt perception is less clear; some researchers find that newborns do not discriminate a salty solution from water, whereas other investigators find that salt is a negative experience for newborns (Bernstein, 1990; Rosenstein & Oster, 1988). Charles K. Crook and Lewis P. Lipsitt (1976) found that newborns decrease their sucking speed when receiving sweet fluid, which suggests that they savor

the liquid for the pleasurable taste. Hence, the hedonistic aspects of tasting are present at birth (Acredolo & Hake, 1982) (see Table 5-1).

Newborns respond to different odors, and the vigor of the response corresponds to the intensity and quality of the stimulant. Trygg Engen, Lewis P. Lipsitt, and Herbert Kaye (1963) tested olfaction in 2-day-old infants. At regular intervals they held a cotton swab saturated with anise oil (which has a licorice smell) or asafetida (which smells like boiling onions) under an infant's nose. A polygraph recorded the babies' bodily movements, respiration, and heart rate. When they first detected an odor, infants moved their limbs, their breathing quickened, and their heart rate increased. With repeated exposure, however, habituation occurred (infants gradually came to disregard the stimulant). The olfactory thresholds decreased drastically over the first few days of life, meaning that the neonates became increasingly sensitive to nasal stimulants (Lipsitt, Engen & Kaye, 1963). Other researchers have confirmed that neonates possess well-developed olfactory abilities (Rieser, Yonas & Wikner, 1976; Self, Horowitz & Paden, 1972).

More recently, researchers have demonstrated that breast-fed neonates prefer their mother's underarm pads to those of other nursing mothers. But the infants did not show a preference for their father's underarm pads over those of strangers. Nor did bottle-fed babies display a preference for their own mothers' pads, presumably because of insufficient skin contact. These findings suggest that olfactory cues play a crucial part in a breast-feeding newborn's recognition of its mother (Cernoch & Porter, 1985; Makin & Porter, 1989).

Cutaneous Senses

Heat, cold, pressure, and pain—the four major cutaneous sensations—are present in neonates (Humphrey, 1978). Kai Jensen (1932) found that a bottle of hot or cold milk (above 124°F or below 72°F) caused an irregular sucking rhythm in neonates. On the whole, however, neonates are relatively insensitive to small differences in thermal stimuli. Neonates also respond to body pressure. Touching activates many of the reflexes discussed earlier in the chapter, including the rooting, sucking, Babinski, palmar, and plantar reflexes.

We infer from neonates' responses that they experience pain sensations. So far, research has not detailed just what these experiences are. A study by Lewis P. Lipsitt and N. Levy (1959) indi-

Table 5-1

Neonate Responses to Strong Tastes

Response	Percentage Responding	
	Less than Twenty Hours Old (N = 75)	Three to Seven Days Old (N = 100)
Sweet		
Retraction of mouth angle	81%	87%
Satisfied smile	77	73
Eager sucking and licking of upper lip	99	97
Sour		
Pursed lips	100	98
Wrinkled nose	77	73
Repeated blinking	89	70
Increased salivation	81	65
Flushing	76	64
Bitter		
"Archlike" lips with depressed mouth angles	97	96
Protruding tongue	79	81
Salivation and spitting	76	87
Expression of "anger" and dislike	79	86
Vomiting	45	52

SOURCE: *Adapted from J. E. Steiner, "Facial Expressions of the Neonate Infant Indicating the Hedonics of Food-Related Chemical Stimuli," in J. M. Weiffenbach (ed.),* The Genesis of Sweet Preference *(Washington, D.C.: U.S. Department of Health, Education and Welfare, 1977).*

cated that babies have an increasing sensitivity to mild electric shock during the first five days of life. Furthermore, these researchers found a sex difference in responses to shock, with girls showing more sensitivity than boys. Observation of neonate and infant behavior also suggests that gastrointestinal upsets are a major source of discomfort. And male infants increase their crying and fussing during circumcision, providing additional evidence that neonates are sensitive to pain (see the boxed insert on page 140 on circumcision).

Individual Differences Among Newborns

Training a baby by the book is a good idea, only you need a different book for each baby.—DAN BENNETT

According to popular wisdom, "A baby is a baby—if you've seen one, you've seen them all." Parents of large families know that this maxim simply is not true. Infants differ—indeed, differ radically—from one another. Babies are individualists from the moment they draw breath. One baby may react to a loud noise or close physical contact in a manner opposite to that of another. Overall, the breadth and scope of individual differences in the behavior of babies is impressive.

Cuddlers and Noncuddlers

One particularly striking difference among newborns is their reaction to cuddling. H. R. Schaffer and Peggy E. Emerson (1964) studied the reactions of thirty-seven neonates to physical contact and found that the babies could be classed as *cuddlers* or *noncuddlers*. Mothers of cuddlers describe their infants in these terms: "He snuggles into you"; "She cuddles you back"; and "He'd let me cuddle him for hours." In contrast, mothers of noncuddlers give different reports of what happens when they hold their babies on their laps, press them against their shoulders, or kiss them. These mothers say, "He

Circumcision: The Unkindest Cut of All?

Each year more than 1 million U.S. male newborns undergo an operation that most medical professionals now believe is unnecessary. The operation is *circumcision*, the removal of the foreskin (prepuce) that covers the tip (glans) of the penis. Through the years the procedure has been a religious rite for Jews and Muslims. Among some African and South Pacific peoples circumcision is performed at puberty to mark the passage of a youth to manhood. In contrast, circumcision has never been common in Europe (which perhaps explains why Michaelangelo's famous statue depicts Jewish King David as uncircumcised).

Until about fifteen or so years ago, U.S. physicians promoted circumcision as a health measure and a protection against cancer of the penis (and, in sexual partners, cancer of the cervix). The procedure was also viewed as a means to prevent venereal disease and urinary tract infections. And people long believed that unhealthy secretions were harbored beneath the foreskin. Additionally, supporters of circumcision have contended that about 5 percent of all uncircumcised infants will require the operation later in life at a time when surgery is more complex and risky.

But in recent years the purported benefits of circumcision have come under increasing scrutiny and have been found wanting. Although cancer of the penis may be more prevalent in uncircumcised men, it is a relatively rare disease that occurs primarily among the elderly. Moreover, the self-cleansing role of the foreskin is now better appreciated, and parents are being warned not to clean beneath it lest the tissue tear and form constricting scars that could necessitate circumcision later in a boy's life. The surgery also has attendant risks: 1 in 500 cases results in significant health problems, including serious bleeding and infection.

Because physicians now maintain that there are few valid medical indications for routine circumcision of the newborn, the practice has been on the decline. In 1985, 59.5 percent of U.S. newborn boys were circumcised, down from about 68 percent in 1979. In the past many parents had their sons circumcised so that they would resemble their father and other boys. Now the like-father-like-son tradition seems to be crumbling.

won't allow it—he fights to get away"; "try and snuggle him against you and he'll kick and thrash, and if you persist he'll begin to cry"; and "She struggles, squirms, and whimpers when you try to hold her close."

Although noncuddlers object to *close* physical contact, they do not resist other forms of handling. They actively enjoy being swung, bounced, and romped with in a manner that involves contact but not restraint. They like being kissed or tickled and playing other "skin games," provided they are not held. Furthermore, noncuddlers tolerate being held as long as they are kept in motion, as when a parent carries them about. Schaffer and Emerson found other differences between cuddlers and noncuddlers during the first two years of life. In motor development, for instance, noncuddlers are typically ahead of cuddlers; they develop the ability to sit unsupported, to stand with support, and to crawl sooner than cuddlers do.

Differences in Temperament

Research in infant temperament has become quite active in recent years (Goldsmith & Campos, 1990). **Temperament** refers to the relatively consistent, basic dispositions inherent in people that underlie and modulate much of their behavior (McCall, 1987). For example, as we noted in Chapter 3, Jerome Kagan and his associates (Kagan, 1989; Kagan, Reznick, Clarke, Snidman & Garcia-Coll, 1984; Kagan, Reznick & Gibbons, 1989; Kagan, Reznick, Snidman, Gibbons & Johnson, 1988; Reznick et al., 1986) find that some children are born with a tendency, or "vulnerability," toward extreme timidity when faced with an unfamiliar person or situation. These differences persist as they grow up and have profound social consequences. Thus, when the youngsters attend their first day at school, the timid ones tend to remain quietly watchful at the outskirts of activity, whereas their uninhibited counterparts are all smiles and eager to approach other children. Given our society's cultural bias, uninhibited people are more popular than inhibited ones, and so timid youngsters are placed under pressure by parents and others to be more outgoing. Kagan believes this bias is regretable. Instead, he emphasizes that we should provide our children with an environment that is, within reason, respectful of individual differences. Although uninhibited children may grow up to be popular adults, inhibited children may invest more energy in schoolwork and become intellectuals if they are afforded settings that value academic achievement. Kagan notes that although we push our inhibited children toward the uninhibited end of the scale, in other cultures, such as China, uninhibited behavior is likely to be viewed as disrespectful and unseemly (Guillen, 1984).

Alexander Thomas and his associates (Thomas & Chess, 1987; Thomas, Chess & Birch, 1970; Thomas, Chess, Birch, Hertzig & Korn, 1963) have come to conclusions quite similar to those of Kagan from their studies of more than two hundred children. They found that babies show a distinct individuality in temperament during the first weeks of life that is independent of their parents' handling or personality styles. Thomas views temperament as the stylistic component of behavior—the *how* of behavior as opposed to the *why* of behavior (motivation) and the *what* of behavior (its content). Some babies Thomas terms *difficult babies*—they wail and cry a great deal, have violent tantrums, spit out new foods, scream and twist when their faces are washed, eat and sleep in irregular patterns, and are not easy to pacify. Other infants are characterized as *slow-to-warm-up babies*—infants who have low activity levels, adapt very slowly, tend to be withdrawn, seem somewhat negative in mood, and show wariness in new situations. And still others are termed *easy babies*—infants with generally sunny, cheerful dispositions, who adapt quickly to new routines, foods, and people. Roughly 10 percent of all infants are difficult babies, 15 perent are slow-to-warm-up babies, and 40 percent are easy babies. The remaining 35 percent show a mixture of traits that do not readily fit into these categories.

Thomas (1986) has introduced the notion of "goodness of fit" to refer to the match between

Cuddlers and Noncuddlers
Some youngsters are cuddlers who enjoy close physical contact (left). Others are noncuddlers who resist contact that is physically constraining (right). Even so, noncuddlers typically like being swung, bounced, and romped with, and they enjoy tickling games so long as they are not held tightly. *(Suzanne Szasz/Photo Researchers; Jeffrey W. Myers/Stock, Boston)*

the characteristics of infants and their families. A good match is one in which the opportunities, expectations, and demands of the environment are in accord with the child's temperament. When the match is good, optimal development is fostered. Conversely, a poor fit makes for a stormy household and contributes to distorted development and maladaptive functioning. He emphasizes that parents need to take the unique temperament of their baby into account. Children do not react in the same ways to the same developmental influences. Whereas domineering, highly authoritarian parental behavior makes one child anxious and submissive, it leads another to be defiant and antagonistic. As a consequence, Thomas and his colleagues (1963, p. 85) conclude, "There can be no universally valid set of rules that will work equally well for all children everywhere."

Parents with difficult babies often feel considerable anxiety and guilt. "What are we doing wrong?" they ask. Thomas (1963, p. 94) has a reassuring answer for such parents:

The knowledge that certain characteristics of their child's development are not primarily due to parental malfunctioning has proven helpful to many parents. Mothers of problem children often develop guilt feelings because they assume that they are solely responsible for their children's emotional difficulties. This feeling of guilt may be accompanied by anxiety, defensiveness, increased pressures on the children, and even hostility toward them for 'exposing' the mother's inadequacy by their disturbed behavior. When parents learn that their role in the shaping of their child is not an omnipotent one, guilt feelings may lessen, hostility and pressures may tend to disappear, and positive restructuring of the parent-child interaction can become possible.

All this research highlights the importance of adjusting child-rearing practices to the individual infant. A given environment does not have identical functional consequences for all children. Much depends on the temperamental makeup of the child. Other researchers have found merit in this position (Kutner, 1989; Peters-Martin & Wachs, 1984; Sprunger, Boyce & Gaines, 1985). In sum, both factors—environment and temperament—interact to shape the child's personality.

Parent-Child Interaction: A Two-Way Street

Psychologists and psychiatrists have traditionally emphasized that parents have a profound influence on their children's personalities. Indeed, the notion has long been popular in some educational circles that children are blank tablets on which the finger of experience writes. According to this view, children are essentially passive beings, acted on by environmental forces that condition and reinforce them in one fashion or another.

But increasingly, social and behavioral scientists have recognized that this view is misleading. Infants are much more complicated than many people give them credit for, and they have a considerable effect on everyone around them. In some respects this realization was a kind of reaction against prevailing notions that blamed the parents for everything. Clearly, children are active agents in the socialization process; they are not only influenced by, but themselves influence, their caretakers. For instance, even very young infants seek to control their mothers' actions. The infant and the mother may be looking at one another. Should the baby look away and upon turning back find mother's gaze turned away, the baby will start fussing and whimpering. When the mother again gazes at the infant, he or she stops the commotion. Infants quickly learn elaborate means for securing and maintaining their caretaker's attention (Heimann, 1989; Lewis, 1977). Indeed, as Harriet L. Rheingold (1968, p. 283) observes; "Of men and women he [the infant]

"Are there any hugs left in your arms for me?"

("Family Circus" © *1989 Bill Keane, Inc. Reprinted with special permission of King Features Syndicate.)*

Parent-Child Interaction

Parents do not merely socialize their children in the ways of their society. Children also influence them. A dynamic interchange occurs between parent and child whereby each party reciprocally shapes the behavior of the other. *(Joel Gordon)*

makes fathers and mothers." Thus, to a surprising degree, parents are the product of the children born to them. They themselves are molded by the very children they are trying to rear.

The characteristics of the infant—the intensity of its responses, its cuddliness, its physical attractiveness, and its temperament—elicit various types of behaviors from adults. Indeed, we need not be around infants for long to become aware of the fact that different feelings are evoked in us by babies who wail no matter what we do to calm them and babies who quickly and cheerfully respond to our soothing efforts. Parenting is easier for predictable and cheery babies—the "easy babies" described by Thomas. But it is often otherwise for "difficult" babies. Any number of researchers have found that difficult and unsoothable babies are overrepresented among abused children (Korner, 1979). Constant fussing, colicky fretfulness, highly irritating crying, and other exasperating behaviors seem to provoke violence in some parents. Furthermore, some battered children continue to be abused in a succession of foster homes where no other child previously had been abused. Sadly, some children appear to convert seemingly "normal" parents into "abnormal" ones. The behavior of these children simply exceeds their parents' coping capabilities. Many such parents develop feelings of intense guilt, inadequacy, helplessness, and rage that, in individuals with low flash points, may

erupt in violent outbursts. Consequently, the burden, stress, and disappointment of rearing a difficult youngster can serve to tip the balance in a precarious parent-child relationship. Clearly, parent and child are caught up in an interacting spiral.

Yet, as some researchers emphasize, many "difficult" babies are difficult in part because of the parenting they receive. Caretakers' attitudes toward a child and their beliefs regarding parenting outcomes act as selective filters or sensitizers that influence their reaction to the child's behavior (Bugental & Shennum, 1984; Lerner & Galambos, 1985). T. Berry Brazelton (1962) cites the case of a newborn who essentially was capable of only two states. In the one state the child would appear to be in a deep stupor, during which time he would be difficult to rouse. In the other state he was hyperactive, exceedingly sensitive to stimulation of any sort, and given to frequent and long episodes of screaming. Neurological examination failed to detect any abnormalities. From the start the mother viewed herself as "rejected" by the child. She felt overwhelmed and incapable of reaching the child in his state of withdrawal and unable to comfort him in his state of agitation. The net result was an unsatisfactory parent-child relationship. Psychiatrists working in a number of experimental settings are developing tactics for dealing with such problems. The therapy can entail adding or subtracting sensory stimuli, exercising overly tense muscles, providing affection that is absent at home, and counseling parents (Okie, 1981).

Moreover, what a person sees as "difficult" in a child is relatively subjective and does not necessarily coincide with the conclusions that would be reached by an objective observer or a developmental psychologist. And what is difficult in one situation may not be difficult in another, such as persistence in play when children are expected to amuse themselves versus persistence in play when being called to dinner. Additionally, what is difficult at one age (distractibility for a child getting ready to go off to school) may not be difficult at another age (distractibility as a mechanism to sooth a fussing infant) (Rothbart, 1987). Meaning, then, does not inhere in a child's behavior; people impute meaning to it. And they carry their attributions regarding children's behavior over into their later encounters with them. So the consequences of their attributions at any given time partially determine their attributions at a subsequent time (Klein, 1984).

Researchers have noted a variety of additional factors that play a part in influencing parental behavior (Tronick & Cohen, 1989). Josephine V. Brown and her associates (1975) found in a sample of urban black mothers that the mothers rubbed, patted, touched, kissed, rocked, and talked more to male than to female newborns. Mothers of first-born infants spend more time feeding their infants than do mothers of later-born infants (Bakeman & Brown, 1977). And both mothers' and fathers' behaviors are affected during parent-child interaction by the presence of the other (Lamb, 1976; Lytton, 1980). All these studies suggest that the socialization process is a two-way street, a reciprocal, interactive, and transactive relationship involving parent and child.

SUMMARY

1. Sleeping, crying, and feeding are the chief behaviors of the neonate.
2. An infant's responses at any given time are related to its state. The following states have been identified in the neonate: regular sleep, irregular sleep, drowsiness, alert inactivity, waking activity, and crying.
3. Crying in the newborn is an unlearned, involuntary, and adaptive response that serves to incite the parent to caretaking activities.
4. The infant's hunger and sleep patterns are closely linked. Newborns spend much of their waking time in feeding. Both breast feeding and bottle feeding offer advantages and disadvantages.
5. The newborn is equipped at birth with a number of reflexes—behavioral systems that are readily activated. These responses include the Moro reflex, the startle reflex, the rooting reflex, the sucking reflex, the Babinski reflex, the palmar grasping reflex, the plantar grasping reflex, the stepping reflex, and the swimming reflex.
6. Habituation represents an early adaptive response to the environment. Habituation is also an early form of memory.
7. Newborns show the effects of learning through conditioning.
8. A full-term newborn is equipped at birth with a functional and intact visual apparatus. The eye is prepared to respond differentially to most aspects of its visual field.
9. At the time of birth the hearing apparatus of the neonate is remarkably well developed. Taste, smell, and cutaneous sensations are present in the neonate.
10. In the first days of life infants can be distinguished in terms of their reactions to external stimuli. Some babies are cuddlers, others noncuddlers.
11. Babies show distinct individuality in temperament during the first weeks of life. This temperament is independent of their parents' handling and personality styles. Researchers find that the socialization process is a two-way street, a reciprocal, interactive, and transactive relationship involving parents and child.

KEY TERMS

Habituation An adaptive response in which an infant who is repeatedly presented with the same stimulus soon ceases to respond to the stimulus. If the stimulus is then withheld for a short period, the infant recovers the reflex response.

Neonate A newborn.

Neonate Period The first two weeks following birth.

Perception The process by which individuals interpret sensation.

Reflex A relatively simple, involuntary, and unlearned response to a stimulus.

Sensation The process by which individuals receive information through their sense organs.

State A continuum of alertness ranging from regular sleep to vigorous activity.

Temperament The relatively consistent, basic dispositions inherent in people that underlie and modulate much of their behavior.

Part Three

Infancy: The First Two Years

Chapter 6

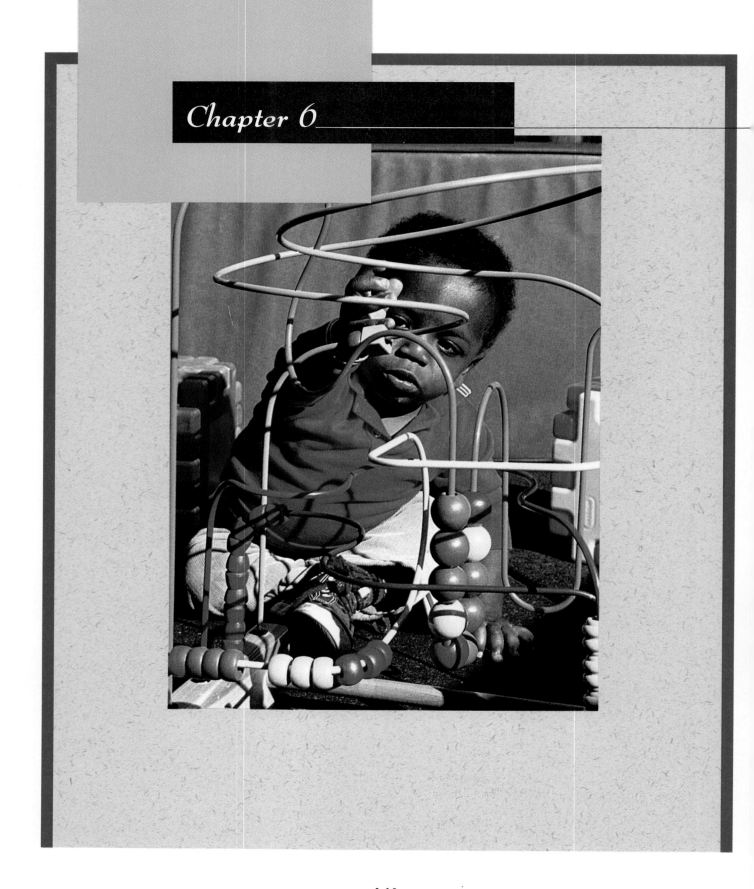

INFANCY: DEVELOPMENT OF BASIC COMPETENCIES

Physical Growth

Rate of Growth ◆ Malnutrition ◆ Secular Increase in Size ◆ Growth of Key Systems and the Brain ◆ Principles of Development

Motor Development

Rhythmical Behaviors ◆ Locomotion ◆ Manual Skills ◆ Handedness

Perceptual Development

Visual Constancy ◆ Depth Perception ◆ Perception of Form ◆ Perception of the Human Face ◆ Interconnections Among the Senses

◆

A hallmark of the first two years of life—the period we term **infancy**—is the enormous amount of energy children expend in exploring, learning about, and mastering their world (MacTurk, McCarthy, Vietze & Yarrow, 1987; Messer et al., 1986; White & Watts, 1973). Few characteristics of infants are more striking than their relentless and persistent pursuit of competence. They continually initiate activities by which they can interact effectively with the environment. Healthy children are active creatures. They seek stimulation from the world around them. In turn, they act on their world, chiefly on caretakers, to achieve the satisfaction of their needs. Significantly, babies begin to show warmth toward significant caretakers between 2 and 4 months of age, whereas their ability to communicate a full range of emotions—including curiosity, pleasure, assertiveness, and anger—gradually flowers between 3 and 8 months.

Recurring through all forms of the child's behavior is the struggle to adapt. In the process the neonate's abilities are perfected and expanded. About the time that children are 11 to 15 months old, they can crawl, walk, and climb. No longer are they passively limited, as at 6 months, to cribs, high chairs, playpens, carriages, and other places where they are put by caretakers. Parents quickly discover that if they are to protect valuables from the assaults of their child, they must place the objects out of reach.

Pursuing Competency

Infants initiate behaviors that bring them into active contact with their environment and allow them to develop and perfect basic skills. *(Pankaj Shah/The Stock Market)*

Children at 1 year of age are poised for fundamental development in language and social skills. The ability to understand and later to use speech opens great new channels by which they acquire information and influence the significant people in their lives. By the age of 1 babies have already formed a variety of social attachments to other people. As they move into the second year of life, they begin to gain an awareness of themselves as distinct individuals. Indeed, as their cognitive capabilities increase, babies gain more and more pleasure from their ability to affect what happens to them and to the world around them (Redding, Morgan & Harmon, 1988). Normal, healthy youngsters contribute a good deal to their own well-being. All the while, greater demands are placed on children by the environment: Parents expect them to develop various controls over their behavior, to master toilet training, and to eat and sleep at scheduled times. Thus, the child is caught up in an expanding web of involvement with the larger human enterprise.

Physical Growth

Growth is the only evidence of life.—**John Henry Cardinal Newman**
Apologia pro Vita Sua, 1864

As children, we became bored very early with relatives who exclaimed, "My, you've grown!" Yet as adults, we keep making the same remark to children, for they do grow at a surprising rate and change in wonderful ways. Their development is especially dramatic during the first two years of life. Indeed, the change from the newborn to the walking, talking, socially functioning child whom we meet hardly 600 days later is awesome.

Rate of Growth

The pituitary gland, in conjunction with the hypothalamus (a structure at the base of the brain composed of a tightly packed cluster of nerve cells), secretes hormones that play a critical part in regulating children's growth (Guillemin, 1982). Too little of the growth hormones creates a dwarf, and too much creates a giant. The physical growth of children generally takes place in an orderly fashion. Predictable changes occur at various age levels. Many investigators (Gesell, 1928; Meredith, 1973; Tanner, 1970, 1973) have analyzed the developmental sequence of various characteristics and skills. From these studies psychologists have evolved standards, called

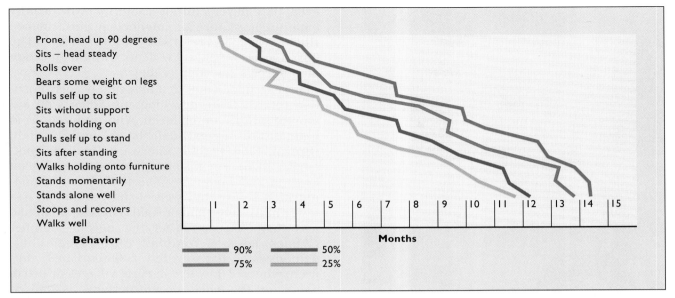

Figure 6-1   Norms for Gross Motor Behavior
The percentage of infants displaying a given behavior at a particular age. Although children differ as individuals in the rate at which they mature, they show broad similarities in the sequence of development. SOURCE: Adapted from W. K. Frankenburg and J. B. Dodds, "The Denver Developmental Screening Test," *Journal of Pediatrics,* Vol. 71 (1967), p. 186.

norms, for evaluating a child's developmental progress relative to the average of the child's age group. Although children differ considerably in their individual *rate* of maturing, they show broad similarities in the *sequence* of developmental change (see Figure 6-1). Among infants, length and weight are the indices most strongly correlated with behavioral development and performance (Lasky et al., 1981).

Growth is unevenly distributed over the first twenty years of life. From birth to age 5 the rate, or velocity, of growth in height declines sharply. And on the whole, about twice as much of this growth occurs between the ages of 1 and 3 as between the ages of 3 and 5. After age 5 the rate of growth in height levels off so that the velocity is practically constant until puberty. At puberty there is again a marked acceleration of growth, called the *adolescent growth spurt* (see Chapter 13).

Boys tend to be slightly taller than girls until the age of 11. But the adolescent growth spurt occurs earlier among girls, and at age 11 girls temporarily shoot ahead. Boys regain their height advantage around the age of 14 (Tanner, 1970, 1973). Furthermore, relative to the growth norms of their age group, broadly built children tend to grow faster than average, and slenderly built children slower than average (Bayley, 1935).

One of the most striking and perhaps most fundamental characteristics of growth is what James M. Tanner (1970, p. 125), a noted authority on the subject, calls its "self-stabilizing" or "target-seeking" quality:

Children, no less than rockets, have their trajectories, governed by the control systems of their genetical constitution and powered by energy absorbed from the natural environment. Deflect the child from its growth trajectory by acute malnutrition or illness, and a restoring force develops so that as soon as the missing food is supplied or the illness terminated the child catches up toward its original curve. When it gets there, it slows down again to adjust its path onto the old trajectory once more.

Thus, children display a compensatory or remedial property of "making up" for arrested growth when normal conditions are restored.

Malnutrition

Although children typically make up for arrested growth, the effects of prolonged malnutrition are longlasting. Where protein and calorie malnutrition are severe, marasmus and kwashiorkor occur. *Marasmus* usually develops in children younger than 1 year of age. It is characterized by severe weight loss and irritability.

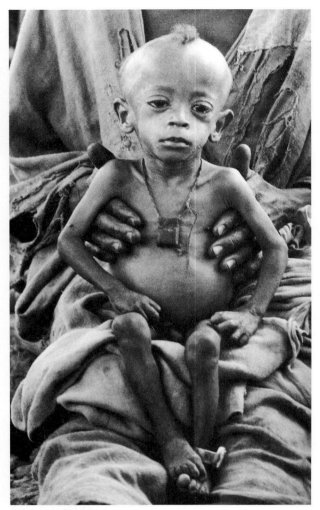

The Heavy Toll of Malnutrition

This Ethiopian child shows the ravages of malnutrition. The tragedy of the sub-Saharan region of Africa has been captured in recent years by press and television portrayals of the massive sufferings of its people. An estimated 35 million people in Africa live on the interfaces of deserts and arable land and are threatened by hunger. The overworking of marginal lands for crops, cattle grazing, and firewood has contributed to "desert creep." *(Chris Steele Perkins/Magnum)*

ever, they never entirely catch up with healthy children in stature or intellectual performance (Eichenwald & Fry, 1969; Lozoff, 1989). (The boxed insert on page 152 deals with the question of children's selection of diets.)

Research indicates that inadequate early nutrition retards brain development. Reports on autopsied brains of children who suffered from malnutrition reveal deficits in brain weight (Brown, 1966; Parekh, Pherwani, Udani & Mukherjie, 1970). For instance, autopsies on sixteen Chilean and Jamaican babies who died of malnutrition before they were 2 showed that all had fewer brain cells than normal. Three of them had less than 40 percent of the normal number (Winick, Rosso & Waterlow, 1970). Studies also demonstrate that severely malnourished children, whether they live in rural villages or urban slums, on the whole do not perform as well on intelligence and cognitive tests as do children with adequate diets (Jelliffe & Jelliffe, 1979; Kaplan, 1972; Levitsky, 1979; Sigman, Newmann, Jansen & Bwibo, 1989). This cognitive gap can be narrowed if appropriate nutritional therapy is instituted, particularly if it takes place at an early age (Barnet et al., 1978; Barrett, Radke-Yarrow & Klein, 1982; McKay, Sinisterra, McKay, Gomez & Lloreda, 1978; Super, Herrera & Mora, 1990).

Almost 23 million children around the world are classified by the World Health Organization and agencies of the United Nations as severely malnourished. Moreover, every day, about 150 million children under age 5 in developing nations go to bed hungry (more than the entire population of Brazil). Even the wealthy United States has pockets of poverty, especially among the Appalachian, black, Spanish-speaking, and native American populations. Of all U.S. age groups, children are the most likely to live under impoverished conditions. The boxed insert on page 154 examines the plight of the world's children.

Kwashiorkor typically occurs in children between 1 and 3 years old. Its chief characteristics are apathy, loss of hair, severe skin disorders, and a protuberant belly resulting from enlargement of the liver and water retention in the abdomen. Children develop kwashiorkor when their diet is deficient in protein, even if it contains enough calories. Follow-up studies of children treated for marasmus and kwashiorkor reveal that during recovery they grow at an accelerated rate. How-

Secular Increase in Size

Decade by decade over the past century the average stature of children has been increasing in the United States, western Europe, and Japan (Roche, 1979). This phenomenon is termed the **secular increase in size.** Today, the average height of U.S. men is slightly more than 5 feet 9 inches, and of women, 5 feet 4 inches. This is a gain of about 4 inches in the past hundred years. Among children 6 to 11 years old, the rate of increase was about 10 percent during the ninety years before 1965. For average 10-year-old boys that increase amounted to a gain of about ½ inch per decade. Ten-year-olds of the 1950s were about ½ inch taller than 10-year-olds of the 1940s (Schmeck, 1976). As you can see from Figure 6-2, this increase in size has important consequences for you if you harbor athletic ambitions.

Two different theories have been advanced to explain the secular increase in size. One attributes it to environmental factors associated with improvement in diet, better health and prenatal care, and immunization against serious childhood diseases. The other theory focuses on genetic factors associated with hybrid vigor resulting from increased interbreeding across local, regional, and national populations.

The trend toward increased size in the United States, however, seems to have ended. The leveling-off appeared several decades ago among population samples representing Americans in the highest socioeconomic classes. It now also holds

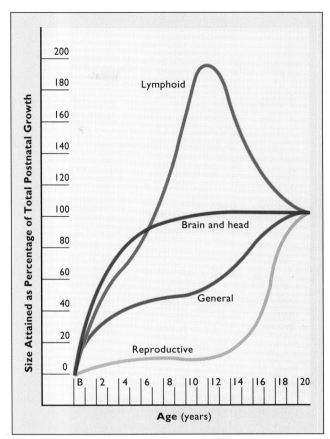

Figure 6-3   The Parts of the Body Grow at Different Rates
These curves are based on the percentage of a person's total growth attained by age 20. Thus, size at age 20 is 100 on the vertical scale. The lymphoid system includes the thymus and lymph nodes. The curve labeled "Brain and head" includes the brain, the skull, and the spinal cord. The curve labeled "General" covers the skeletal system, lungs, kidneys, and digestive organs. The reproductive system covers testes, ovaries, prostate, seminal vesicles, and Fallopian tubes. SOURCE: Richard E. Scammon, "The Measurement of Man (Minneapolis: University of Minnesota Press, 1930), Figure 73, p. 193. Reprinted by permission.

for virtually every segment of the U.S. population. Americans may have reached the limits of their genetic potential for stature (Schmeck, 1976).

Growth of Key Systems and the Brain

Not all parts of the body grow at the same rate. The growth curve for lymphoid tissue—the thymus and lymph nodes—is quite different from that for tissue in the rest of the body (see Figure 6-3). At 12 years of age it is more than double the

Figure 6-2   Secular Increase in Size: Baseball Players
Over the past 110 years the average baseball player has grown an average 5 inches taller and has gained 26 pounds. SOURCE: USA Today, September 7, 1990.

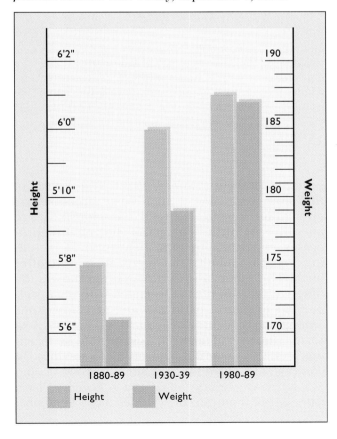

Do Young Children Instinctively Know What to Eat?

In the 1920s and 1930s the pediatrician Clara Davis undertook a series of pioneering studies on the selection of food by infants and young children. Health professionals interpreted the results as meaning that given a wide variety of choices, children will instinctively select and consume a well-balanced diet. Yet Davis never drew this conclusion, nor can it be concluded from her data. The youngsters were provided only with fresh unprocessed foods (oatmeal, wheat, beef, bone marrow, eggs, and vegetables); no food combinations, sugars, syrups, or sweetened foods were included. Davis found that infants select a combination of these foods in quantities sufficient for their growth and health. Even so, individual preferences would appear and disappear, and each child went on "food jags." The infants preferred bone marrow, milk, eggs, bananas, apples, oranges, cornmeal, whole wheat, and oatmeal; they did not particularly care for vegetables. Davis (1938) concluded that young children should be provided only foods that have the highest nutritional values and that their appetites are a reliable guide to the amount of food they should consume. She pointed out that "self-selection" has doubtful value if the diet is selected from nutritionally inferior foods. The provision of an assortment of nutritious foods, rather than a genetic ability to select needed foods, may have been responsible for the dietary adequacy she observed. More recently researchers have confirmed that parents need not force-feed preschoolers. Youngsters who do not eat much at

"I guess I'm always hungary between meals because I spend too much time between meals."

("Dennis The Menace" ® used by permission of Hank Ketcham and © 1991 by North American Syndicate.)

one meal typically make up for it at another meal. Like Davis, the researchers find that toddlers' eating behavior is erratic and unpredictable, but on whole the youngsters take in almost the same number of calories each day (Hellmich, 1991).

---

level it will reach in adulthood; after twelve it declines until maturity. In contrast, the reproductive system grows very slowly until adolescence, at which point it accelerates. The internal organs, including the kidneys, liver, spleen, lungs, and stomach, keep pace with the growth in the skeletal system, and these systems therefore show the same two growth spurts in infancy and adolescence.

The nervous system, which develops more rapidly than other systems, is in some respects largely complete by 4 years of age. At birth the brain is already about 25 percent of its adult weight; at 6 months, nearly 50 percent; at 2½ years, 75 percent; at 5 years, 90 percent; and at 10

years, 95 percent (Tanner, 1970). Those parts of the brain that control such basic processes as circulation, respiration, and consciousness are operative at birth. The parts that control processes less critical to immediate survival, including physical mobility and language, mature after birth. The rapid growth of the brain during the first two years of life is associated with the development of neural pathways and of connections among nerve cells, particularly in the *cerebral cortex* (the part of the brain responsible for learning, thinking, reading, and problem solving). In contrast, most reflexes, like sucking, rooting, and grasping, are organized at the *subcortical level* (the part of the brain that guides basic biological

Obesity, dietary deficiencies and excesses, dental caries, and iron deficiency are among the nutritional problems of U.S. children. Each of these problems is related to the amount and type of food that children consume. Dietary patterns established early in childhood also have consequences for the later developmenet of heart disease, high blood pressure, and cancer. So that healthy dietary patterns are set and a balanced diet is ensured, experts in nutrition recommend that the diet of young children be limited to a variety of fresh or frozen vegetables and legumes; dairy products; fresh and unsweetened fruits and fruit juices; breads, pastas, rice, cereals, and other grain products; and lean meats (Story & Brown, 1987).

The environment in which caretakers provide food is also important. In many cultures, food and eating are a major arena for the enactment of social relationships and moral issues (consider, for example, the food taboos and rules regarding spiritual pollution among the Hindu castes of India). Although food is a primary source of pleasure to human beings, it also is a frequent source of fear and distress in its role as a fattening agent or as a carrier of carcinogens. So we accept or reject many substances because of knowledge regarding what they are, their origins, or their symbolic meanings. Human parents typically provide their children with extensive guidance. And well they do because infants under 2 years of age are inclined to mouth almost any object that they can physically accommodate. It matters little that the items are normal foods, inedible objects (sponges and paper), items adults deem offensive (human hair, a dried whole fish, or imitation dog feces), and dangerous objects (imitation liquid soap). By 3 years of age, many items that adults reject as inedible are also rejected by children. It seems that one of the major things children learn about food during their early years is what is *not* food and hence what needs to be avoided (Rozin, 1990).

Parents should not use food as a bribe, reward, or punishment (for instance, "If you are good, I'll give you some candy!"). In fact, rewarding a child for consuming a food tends to reduce even more the child's preference for it after the rewards cease (Birth, Birch, Marlin & Kramer, 1982). Nor should children be coaxed to eat everything they are served. Sweets need not be excluded from a child's diet, but they should be limited to amounts that do not interfere with the consumption of basic foods at mealtime. The dinner table must not become a battlefield. Feeding problems often begin in the high chair when children are forced to relinquish control over when, what, and how much they eat. But at the same time, children gain the power to manipulate their parents, triggering waves of frustration, anger, and guilt. Allowing children greater leeway "liberates" the family cook and can make mealtime a more relaxed experience (Dullea, 1984).

functioning, including sleeping, heart rate, hunger, and digestion). The rapid development of the cortex during the first twelve months provides the foundation for children's less stereotyped and more flexible behavior (Chugani & Phelps, 1986; Clifton, Morrongiello, Kulig & Dowd, 1981). See Figure 6-4.

The cortex is divided by a deep fissure into two halves, a left and right hemisphere. The two hemispheres are connected by a thick band or cable of nerves—the corpus callosum—which carries messages back and forth between them. Each hemisphere specializes in certain functions (see Figure 6-5). Typically, the left hemisphere is more adept in some types of reasoning operations that involve the step-by-step processing of information. And in most people the left hemisphere also controls speech. The right hemisphere is typically specialized for nonlinguistic, visuospatial functions. In everyday life the lateralization of function between the hemispheres is minimized because information is readily passed between them through the corpus callosum (Best, 1985). Evidence suggests that different regions of the left and right hemispheres develop at different rates and ages, apparently the product of genetically programmed maturation (Hahn, 1987; Thatcher, Walker & Giudice, 1987). Such predetermined patterns in brain development allow new behaviors, which in turn mediate new inter-

The Next Generation:
The Plight of the World's Children

What is the status of the world's future generation? Perhaps the best way to approach this question is to begin with the United States, presumably a wealthy nation. Children are the poorest group in our society, with nearly one of every four children under 6 years of age living below the poverty line (in Canada, West Germany, and Sweden, the rate is less than 10 percent) (Barden, 1990). After nearly three decades of the Great Society's war on poverty and a decade of record economic growth, 43 percent of black children, 36 percent of Hispanic children, and 14 percent of white children were poor in 1989. More than half of youngsters living in a household headed by a single mother are impoverished. Nor does employment of a parent guarantee escape from poverty (Bane & Ellwood, 1989). Forty-four percent of poor two-parent families have at least one full-time worker, and 25 percent of impoverished households have a parent who works part-time. For those families desperate enough to accept the stigma of hopelessness—being unwed, unemployed, and even homeless—our society provides handouts such as Aid to Families with Dependent Children. But to qualify a family must first identify itself as a "failure," with the label often taking on self-fulfilling properties (Brazelton, 1990; DeParle & Applebome, 1991; Popkin, 1990; Sanders, 1990). In blighted inner-city neighborhoods, crack is rapidly intensifying the problems of youngsters; in these neighborhoods mothers may be addicted and the selling of the drug by children is commonplace (Applebome, 1991; Kolata, 1989; Lemann, 1991).

As the United States entered the 1990s, it trailed seventeen other developed nations in its infant mortality rate. The U.S. rate is 9.7 per 1,000 live births, compared with a low of 5 infant deaths per 1,000 in Japan and a high of 25 deaths per 1,000 in the Soviet Union. In the District of Columbia, the rate tops 23 per 1,000, worse than that in Costa Rica or Jamaica (Johnson, Ludtke & Riley, 1990). The infant mortality rate for U.S. blacks is twice that of whites (Altman, 1990). Although the United States does a good job saving ill babies who would have died in less-developed countries, overall the country does a poor job in prenatal care. Ominously, the infant mortality rate could soar during the 1990s, with drugs, AIDS, and syphilis being major culprits (Bacon, 1990; Friend, 1990).

Other statistics are also appalling. Consider a single day's destiny for our nation's children: Every 8 seconds of the school day, a child drops out of school. Every 26 seconds, a youngster runs away from home. Every 47 seconds, a child is abused or neglected. Every 7 minutes, a youngster is arrested for a drug offense. Every 36 minutes, a child is killed or injured by a gun (Johnson, Ludtke & Riley, 1990).

Worldwide, the annual death rate for children under 5 is 14 million. Respiratory infections are the leading cause of death among infants and small children worldwide. They annually account for more than 40 percent of the deaths among infants and children under the age of 5. Of the 6.5 million deaths from respiratory infections, 3 million result from pneumonia, 2 million from measles (although people usually think of measles as causing a rash, most deaths from this viral disease are associated with related respiratory infections), and 1.5 million from pertussis (whooping cough). Diarrheal diseases, despite the benefits of oral rehydration, still acount for about 5 million childhood deaths each year. Tetanus accounts for 1 million deaths, and a wide variety of other causes account for the remaining 2.5 million deaths. The latest threat is AIDS. The World Health Organization estimates that in the course of the 1990s, some 2.5 million African children may die of AIDs and an additional 3 to 5 million may be AIDS orphans (children whose parents died of the disease).

Most infant deaths occur in underdeveloped nations. For instance, the death rate from acute respiratory infections in Paraguay has typically run about thirty times higher than in the United States. Malnutrition plays a major role in deaths from respiratory infections, since malnourished children fare poorly when struck by them. Bacterial pneumonia is a primary killer of children, both in its own right and as a complication of other illnesses. Poor sanitation, crowded living conditions, and possibly air pollution are cited as additional factors underlying the higher death rates in less developed countries. Moreover, the quality of medical care is often poor in urban ghettos and outlying rural areas (many complications associated with respiratory infections respond favorably to antibiotics).

Vaccines are now available to protect children against diphtheria, whooping cough, tetanus, polio, measles, and tuberculosis. Although the World Health Organization (WHO) launched a worldwide campaign in 1974 to vaccinate all the world's children against these six deadly diseases by 1990, it has fallen far short of its goal. Even in the United States, one-fourth of preschoolers and one-third of poor children under 5 are currently

Public Housing: A Dream That Failed?
In 1949 the Truman Administration launched a program to construct 800,000 new units of public housing. The housing projects were designed in the optimistic hope that they would offer a solution to problems of slums and urban poverty. Instead, many of the projects have become havens for gangs, crime, and drugs. The playgrounds at the Robert Taylor Homes in Chicago have deteriorated into concrete wastelands and some apartments in the 28 buildings have become burnt-out shells. Residents like Connie Henry and her family, pictured above, have the goal of leaving the project for safe housing elsewhere. (Eli Reed/Magnum)

not immunized. Although the American Academy of Pediatrics supports vaccinations, the organization points out that some children experience serious side effects. The pertussis part of the vaccine has been linked with convulsions, brain damage, and even death once in every 310,000 vaccinations; one out of about 5 million doses of polio vaccine causes paralysis; and some children run fevers for several days after receiving the measles vaccine, and, in extremely rare instances, encephalitis (inflammation of the brain) occurs. Even so, most pediatricians believe that the benefits of immunizations far outweigh their risks.

The United Nations Children's Fund (Unicef) estimates that most of the 100 million children who are expected to die in the 1990s could be saved for the amount of money U.S. cigarette companies will spend on advertising or Soviet citizens on vodka.

Spending on children is a bargain. Consider prenatal care for pregnant women. Regular monitoring of an expectant mother can cost as little as $500 while greatly increasing the chances she will give birth to a healthy baby. In contrast, the costs of intensive care for an underweight baby is about $3,000, and underweight babies have considerably higher rates of blindness, deafness, and mental retardation (see Chapter 4). Similarly, a year of preschool costs on average $3,000 per child, whereas a year in prison amounts to $17,000. And though a measles shot costs $8, hospitalization for a child with measles costs $5,000 (Johnson, Ludtke & Riley, 1990). Overall, Unicef estimates that most of the world's children could be saved from death and malnutrition at a cost of $2.5 billion a year. And universal primary education could be achieved for an additional $5 billion each year.

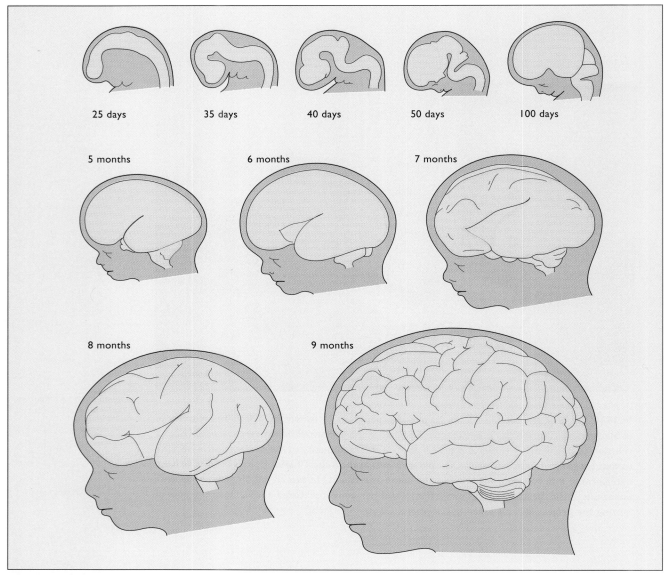

Figure 6-4   The Developing Brain
The development of the human brain. SOURCE: Adapted from W. M. Cowan, "The
Development of the Brain," in *The Brain* (San Francisco: W. H. Freeman, 1979), p. 59.

actions with the environment, which in turn influence brain development.

PET (positron emission tomography) scanners
are providing evidence that the biological or metabolic activity of the brain undergoes substantial
change between birth and adulthood. In the procedure a radioactive form of sugar is injected into
the bloodstream and passes into the brain. More
active neurons, or brain cells, consume more
"fuel." So a PET scan allows scientists to map the
brain's metabolic activity. They have found that
the metabolic rate of the baby's brain is about

two-thirds that of the adult's. By the age of 2 the
rate approximates that of the adult's, with rapid
increases occurring in the activity of the cerebral
cortex. By age 3 or 4 the metabolic rate of the
child's brain is about twice that of the adult's. The
brain stays supercharged until the age of 10 or 11.
Metabolic rate then tapers off, reaching the adult
rate at about age 13 or 14 (Blakeslee, 1986).

Researchers speculate that a highly dynamic
brain during childhood makes a good deal of
sense. The developing brain is a generalized
brain with many connections. This structure per-

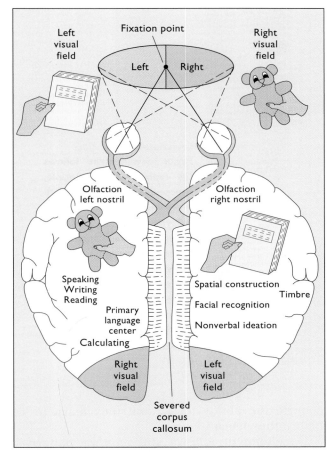

Figure 6-5   The Two Hemispheres of the Brain
This drawing of the brain viewed from above shows the complementary dominance of the cerebral hemispheres for different operations. For most individuals language, mathematics, and analytical thinking are chiefly left-hemisphere activities. Spatial, pattern, and musical recognition appear to be right-hemisphere activities.

Principles of Development

Development follows the **cephalocaudal principle,** proceeding from the head to the feet. Improvements in structure and function come first in the head region, then in the trunk, and finally in the leg region. At birth the head is disproportionately large. In adults the head makes up only about one-tenth to one-twelfth of the body, but in newborns it is about one-fourth of the body. In contrast, the arms and legs of newborns are disproportionately short. From birth to adulthood the head doubles in size, the trunk trebles, the arms and hands quadruple in length, and the legs and feet grow fivefold (Bayley, 1935, 1956) (see Figure 6-6).

Motor development likewise follows the cephalocaudal principle. Infants first learn to control the muscles of the head and neck. Then, they control the arms, the abdomen, and, last, the legs. Thus, when they begin to crawl, they use the upper body to propel themselves, dragging the

A Positron Emission Tomography (PET) Scan
By injecting patients with a radioactive form of glucose, physicians can track the fuel consumption of brain cells. In the scan shown here, the red parts of the brain are the most active. PET scanners are providing information on the brain's internal chemistry. Scientists can ask a person to think about moving a toe without actually moving it, and reveal through the scan the specific area of the brain that is in control of the behavior. *(Dan McCoy/Rainbow)*

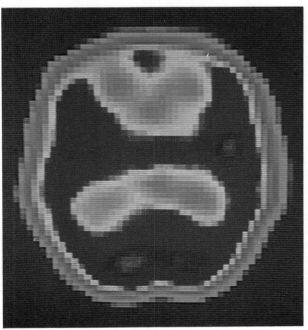

mits the child's experience in the environment to shape the architecture of the brain, strengthening the neural circuits that are used and sacrificing those that are not used. Consequently, the brain has a decade or so to determine which connections the person is going to use. In short, nature resembles a sculptor who first builds a framework and adds more and more plaster to it, producing a rough image. Then, the sculptor chips away at it until the definitive form is assumed (Greenough, Black & Wallace, 1987). These new findings about brain development may help explain why children whose speech areas are destroyed recover their ability to speak, whereas a similar injury in teenagers results in permanent loss of speech.

Cephalocaudal Principle
Motor development follows the cephalocaudal principle, proceeding from the head to the feet. This eight-month-old youngster has mastered crawling on her hands and knees and now has progressed to the more sophisticated "bear crawl." She no longer uses her knees but instead propels herself with her feet. Shortly she will be standing by herself. *(Elizabeth Crews)*

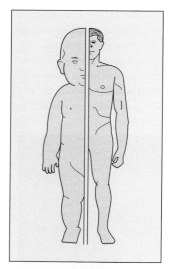

Figure 6-6   Cephalocaudal Development
The cephalocaudal principle, which says that growth progresses from head to foot, is demonstrated by the contrasting body proportions of the newborn and the adult. The head is about one-fourth of the infant's body but only about one-twelfth of the adult's. The trunk is a much larger portion of the infant's body than the adult's, while the leg of the adult is proportionately twice as long as the newborn's.

legs passively behind. Only later do they begin to use the legs as an aid in crawling. Similarly, babies learn to hold their heads up before they

acquire the ability to sit, and they learn to sit before they learn to walk.

Development follows still another pattern—the **proximodistal principle.** According to this principle, development proceeds from near to far—outward from the central axis of the body toward the extremities. Early in infancy, babies have to move head and trunk in order to orient the hands when grasping an object. Only later can they use arms and legs independently, and it is still longer before they can make refined movements with the wrists and fingers. On the whole, control over movement travels down the arm as children become able to perform increasingly precise and sophisticated manual and grasping operations. Another way of expressing the same principle is to say that in general, large-muscle control precedes fine-muscle control. Thus, the child's ability to jump, climb, and run—activities involving the use of large muscles—develops ahead of the ability to draw or write—activities involving smaller muscles.

Motor Development

Reaching, grasping, crawling, and walking—behaviors which infants come to do with considerable proficiency—have proved highly complex and problematic tasks for engineers designing computers and robots. Yet "motor accomplishments" we deem awe-inspiring when performed by a computer or a robot we typically take for granted when performed by human youngsters (Pick, 1989). Not surprisingly, much of the early psychological research devoted to motor development was primarily descriptive in much the manner that we might describe the mechanical activities of a computer or robot (Halverson, 1931; McGraw, 1935).

We are now beginning to appreciate the complexity of children's motor development. Much depends on their overall physical growth. To crawl, walk, climb, and grasp objects with precision, they must have reached certain levels of skeletal and muscular development. As their heads become smaller relative to their bodies, their balance improves (imagine how difficult it must be to move around with a head that is one-fourth of one's total size). As children's legs become stronger and longer, they can master various locomotive activities. As their shoulders widen and their arms lengthen, their manual and mechanical capacities increase. As children become able to reach out and touch people and things and navigate by themselves, their physical and social world expands (Gustafson, 1984). And as they get older, they can more effectively use feedback information (knowledge of results) to improve their motor performance (Barclay & Newell, 1980). Motor development occurs in accordance with maturational processes that are built into the human organism and that find expression through a child's interaction with the environment.

In recent years researchers have focused on action—behaviors driven by the interaction of multiple components or systems (Legerstee, Corter & Kienapple, 1990; Thelen, 1989). For instance, Eugene C. Goldfield (1989) shows that crawling emerges from the convergence of three developing capabilities: kicking, reaching, and orienting the head-eye system to objects and persons in the environment. None of these capabilities is limited to crawling alone, but the confluence of the capabilities and their emerging interactions permit the evolution of crawling behaviors.

Overall, locomotion entails movement resulting from the dynamic interplay among the motives that inspired it, the cognitive information that guided it, and the mechanical body parts (muscles, bones, and joints) that produced it. In isolation none of these elements yields locomotion. Locomotion arises only in the course of interaction within an environmental context that fashions and channels some goal-oriented outcome, such as movement toward a toy, cat, or person. In brief, infants have to develop concepts of how the world can be *used* rather than simply what the world *is*. For instance, much information that infants gain from their sense organs is not ordinarily available to them except when they independently crawl or walk about and "manipulate" the world. The information they derive depends on cognitive processes that develop through real-life experience (Bremner, 1988).

Nor do capacities like locomotion typically emerge in a straight-line or linear manner. They develop through processes of backing and filling and waxing and waning that result in the dissolving of old configurations and the emergence of new ones that in turn afford new modes of exploration and knowledge (Mathew & Cook, 1990; Rochat, 1989; Thelen, 1989; Thelen & Fogel, 1989). In sum, locomotion is not performed in a vacuum but as an ongoing process whereby infants—organisms built to seek and receive information from the environment—tailor and modify their actions to achieve particular ends (Palmer, 1989; Reed, 1982).

Rhythmical Behaviors

Probably the most interesting motor behavior displayed by young infants involves bursts of rapid, repeated movements of the limbs, torso, or head (Thelen, 1981). They kick, rock, bounce, bang, rub, thrust, and twist. Infants seem to fol-

Rhythmical Behaviors
Healthy infants engage in repeated movements in which they kick, rock, bounce, bang, rub, thrust, and twist their limbs, torso, or head. The burst of rapid, repeated body movements occurs during the fifth month, just before infants begin to crawl. (A. Jalandoni/Monkmeyer)

low the dictum "If you can move it at all, move it rhythmically."

Such behaviors are closely related to motor development and provide the foundation for the more skilled behaviors that will come later. Hence, rhythmical patterns that involve the legs, like kicking, begin gradually, increase at about 1 month, peak immediately prior to a child's initiation of crawling at about 6 months, and then taper off. Likewise, rhythmical hand and arm movements appear before complex manual skills. Thus, bouts of rhythmic movement seem to be transitional behaviors between uncoordinated activity and complex voluntary motor control. They represent a stage in motor maturation that is more complex than that found in simple reflexes yet less variable and flexible than that found in later cortically controlled behavior.

Infants most frequently begin their kicking or rocking movements upon the appearance of a caretaker, an interruption in feeding, the presentation of a toy, or the grasping of an object. For the young infant these incidents seem to demand, "Do something!"—greet the caretaker, express frustration, show delight, or manipulate the object (Lester, Hoffman & Brazelton, 1985). However, the immature central nervous system responds in a way that as yet is not goal-directed.

Locomotion

The infant's ability to walk, which typically evolves among U.S. youngsters between 11 and 15 months of age, is the climax of a long series of developments (Thelen, 1986). As shown in Figure 6-7, these developments progress in a sequence that follows the cephalocaudal principle. First, children gain the ability to lift up the head and, later, the chest. Next, they achieve command of the trunk region, which enables them to sit up. Finally, they achieve mastery of their legs as they learn to stand and to walk.

For most infants the seventh month brings a surge in motor development. Usually, children begin by *crawling*—moving with the abdomen in contact with the floor. They maneuver by twisting the body and pulling and tugging with the arms. Next, they may progress to *creeping*—moving on hands and knees while the body is parallel with the floor. Some children also employ *hitching*—sitting and sliding along the floor by "digging in" and pushing themselves backward with the heels. In this form of locomotion they often use the arms to aid in propulsion. Indeed, an occasional infant

varies the procedure by sitting and then, employing each arm as a pendulum, bouncing across the floor on its buttocks.

By 7 or 8 months children resemble a perpetual-motion machine. They relentlessly tackle new tasks. At 8 months they pull themselves to a standing position but usually have difficulty getting down. Often, they fall over backward but, undaunted, keep practicing. The urge to master new motor skills is so powerful in infants this age that bumps, spills, falls, and other obstacles only momentarily discourage them.

The stages and the timing of motor development shown in Figure 6-7 are based largely on studies of infants from Western cultures. But the possibility that there are considerable differences among cultures in the timing of motor development has been raised by a number of studies of African infants (Ainsworth, 1967; Keefer, Tronick, Dixon & Brazelton, 1982; Kilbride, Robbins & Kilbride, 1970). Marcelle Geber and R. F. Dean (1957a, 1957b) and Geber (1958) tested nearly 300 infants living in an urban area of Uganda. They found that these babies were clearly accelerated in motor development relative to Caucasian infants. The African precocity is greatest during the first 6 months of life, after which the gap between the two groups tends to decrease. It closes by the end of the second year.

Geber had advanced somewhat contradictory explanations for the apparent precocity of the Ugandan infants. At first, she appeared to favor a genetic explanation (Geber & Dean, 1957a, p. 1061). Subsequently (1958), she attributed it to environmental factors that are associated with stimulating child-care practices, especially the warmth and solicitude shown the neonate by adults. Ainsworth (1967) also emphasizes the part played by the close infant-mother relationship, including the intimate physical contact, the mother's constant availability, and the postural adjustments required of infants when they are carried about on the mothers' backs.

Researchers have also discovered exceptions to standard Western development patterns among the Balinese of Indonesia (Mead & MacGregor, 1951; p. 81):

> Where the American children go from frogging [a position resembling that of a frog] to creeping on all fours, then to standing and walking, with squatting coming after standing, the Balinese children . . . combine frogging, creeping, and all-fours simultaneously in a flexible, interchangeable state, from which they go from sitting to squatting to standing.

Other differences have also been noted between

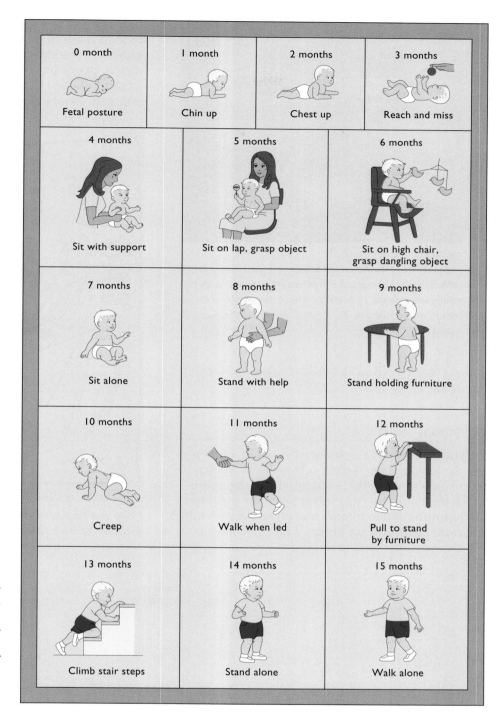

Figure 6-7   The Sequence of Motor Development
The ages at which the average infant achieves a given behavior. SOURCE: M. M. Shirley, *The First Two Years: A Study of Twenty-Five Babies,* Vol. 2 (Minneapolis: University of Minnesota Press, 1933), Figure 1. Reprinted with permission.

infants of Western and non-Western societies. Hopi Indian children of the Southwest, for instance, begin walking about a month or so later than Anglo children do (Dennis & Dennis, 1940). A similar pattern appears to hold for the Zinacantecos, a group of Mayan Indians living in southeastern Mexico (Brazelton, Robey & Collier, 1969). The hunting-and-gathering Ache of east-

ern Paraguay are even more delayed. Motor retardation is apparently adaptive in a nomadic tropical forest environment where exploratory behavior among youngsters is often dangerous. Significantly, Ache children catch up to U.S. children by the time they are 8 to 10 years of age (Kaplan & Dove, 1987). In sum, cross-cultural research reveals that variations occur across popu-

Cross-Cultural Variation
The Hopi Indians of the American Southwest bind their infants to cradle-boards. Although the practice limits motor activity, the youngsters begin to walk at about the same time as children in other cultures do. (Michal Heron/Woodfin Camp & Associates)

lations in the course and timing of motor development (LeVine, 1970).

Manual Skills

The child's development of manual skills proceeds through a series of orderly stages in accordance with the proximodistal principle—from the center of the body toward the periphery. At 2 months of age infants merely make a swiping movement toward an object with the upper body

and arms. They do not attempt to grasp the object. At 3 months of age their reaching consists of clumsy shoulder and elbow movements. Their aim is poor, and their hands are fisted.

After about 16 weeks children approach an object with hands open (see Figure 6-8). At about 20

''Has anything landed in his mouth yet?''

("Grin and Bear It" by Wagner © 1991. Reprinted with special permission of North American Syndicate.)

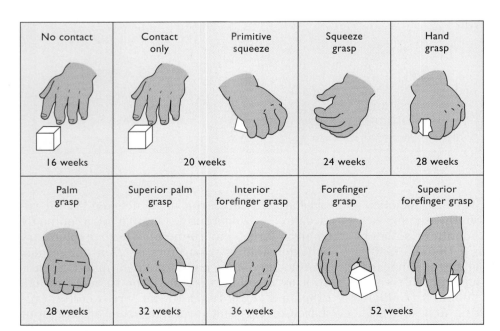

No contact	Contact only	Primitive squeeze	Squeeze grasp	Hand grasp
16 weeks	20 weeks	24 weeks	28 weeks	
Palm grasp	Superior palm grasp	Interior forefinger grasp	Forefinger grasp	Superior forefinger grasp
28 weeks	32 weeks	36 weeks	52 weeks	

Figure 6-8 Development of Manual Skills During the First Year of Life
Children's manual dexterity progresses from a crude squeeze at twenty weeks to fingertip and forefinger grasping at age 1. SOURCE: H. M. Halverson, "An Experimental Study of Prehension in Infants by Means of Systematic Cinema Records," *Genetic Psychology Monographs*, Vol. 10 (1931), pp. 212–215. Reprinted with permission.

Manual Dexterity
This thirteen-month-old child has grasped the relationship between keys and the opening of a door. She is attempting to gain entrance to the apartment through her own independent activity. *(Patrick Reddy)*

weeks children become capable of touching an object in one quick, direct motion of the hand; occasionally, some of them succeed in grasping it in an awkward manner.

Infants of 24 weeks employ a corralling and scooping approach with the palm and fingers. At 28 weeks they begin to oppose the thumb to the palm and other fingers. At 36 weeks they coordinate their grasp with the tips of the thumb and forefinger. Finally, at 52 weeks they master a more sophisticated forefinger grasp (Ausubel & Sullivan, 1970; Halverson, 1931).

Handedness

Some 5 to 10 percent of the U.S. population is left-handed; the rest is primarily right-handed. Handedness is often mistakenly viewed as a specific trait comparable to eye color, but actually it is relative: Individuals prefer their right or left

hands to a greater or lesser degree (Corballis, 1983). Indeed, there are rare cases in which people are bimanual, or ambidextrous, possessing equal skill with both hands for such tasks as writing or drawing. And some people are hand-specific, preferring the left hand for some activities, such as pitching a baseball, and the right for others, such as playing tennis.

Handedness is only one manisfestation of lateral preference. Newborns tend to turn their heads and eyes rightward (Goodwin & Michel, 1981; Liederman & Kinsbourne, 1980). Most adults choose the right foot for crushing an insect or a lighted cigarette. Similarly, most display right-eyedness in sighting a telescope and right-earedness when pressing an ear against a door to hear what is happening on the other side (Coren, Porac & Duncan, 1981). Observations of such one-sided tasks indicate that human beings are decidedly biased toward the right in their lateral preferences (Searleman, Porac & Coren, 1989).

Handedness develops gradually, tending to alternate between right-handedness and ambidex-

Lateral Preference
Most infants turn their heads and eyes to the right in sleeping. *(Frank Siteman/The Picture Cube)*

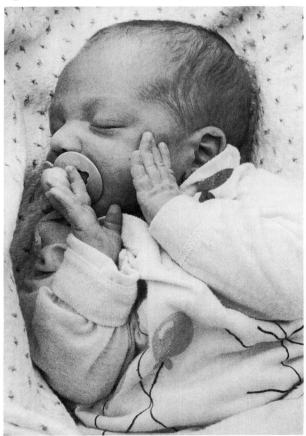

terity (Gesell & Ames, 1947; Ramsay, 1985). Before 2 years of age children generally display considerable versatility in shifting from one hand to the other (McCormick & Maurer, 1988). Much depends on the position of the object for which the child is reaching. By the time they are 2, most children shift toward right-handedness. But between 2½ and 3½, they again shift back toward ambidexterity, using both hands with approximately equal frequency and proficiency. It is not until they are around 4 years of age that most children begin to show a strong preference for use of the right hand. Two years later, when they enter the first grade, shifts from one hand to the other have become relatively infrequent.

A disproportionate number of mathematicians, engineers, musicians, and artists are left-handed. For instance, Michelangelo, Leonardo De Vinci, Pablo Picasso, Paul McCartney, and Benjamin Franklin were southpaws. But whereas the average right-hander dies at age 75, the average southpaw dies nine years earlier at age 66 (Coren & Halpern, 1991). Some of the elevated risk left-handers encounter is due to environmental factors that elevate their accident susceptibility in a right-handed world (7.9 percent of southpaws die from accident-related injuries versus 1.5 percent of right-handers). Moreover, left-handers are twelve times more likely than right-handers to have learning and reading disabilities and are twice as likely to suffer immune disorders in which the body attacks its own tissues. The neurologist Norman Geschwind suggests that the culprit is an excess production of, or sensitivity to, the male hormone testosterone in the fetus (Kolata, 1983; Marx, 1982). One would expect that boys (who are exposed to more testosterone than are girls in prenatal development) would be more likely than girls to be affected, and indeed, almost twice as many males as females are left-handed. Boys are also more prone to learning disorders. And among students in the top category of math performance, boys outscore girls by thirteen to one.

Research reveals that testosterone affects the development of brain structures. Geschwind believes that high levels of testosterone slow growth on the left side of the brain during the prenatal period. In doing so, it may contribute to learning disabilities, for the brain's left hemisphere affects language development. Moreover, testosterone influences the immune system by reducing the size of the thymus gland, which allows the body to distinguish its own tissue from foreign agents (without these "recognizer" cells, the body attacks its own tissue).

Geschwind contends that an increase in testosterone in some pregnancies is nature's way of providing for a greater diversity of brains in the human population. Although increasing the risk of autoimmune disease, the brain organization that promotes left-handedness also leads to superior skills in math and related areas (since mathematical ability is generally believed to be primarily a left-hemisphere function). Of course, if nature "overdoes" it, the result can be serious learning problems. Geschwind suggests that having children with learning problems is the price the population pays for having some of its members gifted in mathematical thought and logic. But whether handedness derives primarily from prenatal, genetic, or learning factors has been the source of considerable controversy. Most likely, however, is that handedness depends on a combination of these factors.

Perceptual Development

During the first six months of life there is a considerable discrepancy between infants' vast sensory capabilities and their relatively sluggish motor development. Their sensory apparatus yields perceptual input far beyond their capacity to use it. As a result of maturation, experience, and practice, they have already acquired the ability to extract information from the environment at a phenomenal rate. When these perceptual abilities become linked with the big spurt in motor development that begins around the seventh month, the child surges ahead in an awesome fashion. Hence, ten to eleven months later, at 18 months of age, the child is an accomplished social being (see Figure 6-9). Let us consider the nature of an infant's developing perceptual capabilities.

Visual Constancy

Perception is oriented toward *things*, not toward their sensory *features*. We can perceive features such as "blueness," "squareness," or "softness," but we generally experience them as qualities of objects. We are aware of a blue car, a square block, or a soft pillow, not of "blueness," "squareness," or "softness" as distinct entities. We fashion and build our world in terms of things—objects that endure and that we encounter again and again. It seems that 3- to 5-month old infants are able to recognize object boundaries and object unity by detecting surface sepa-

1. Walks alone; seldom falls

2. Sits down in small chair

3. Turns pages two or three at a time

4. Builds tower of three blocks

5. Fills cups with cubes

6. Dumps pellet from bottle

7. Imitates stroke

8. Identifies one picture

9. Hurls ball

10. On command, puts ball on chair

11. Walks into ball

12. Pulls toy

Figure 6-9 Aspects of the Behavioral Development of a Child at 18 Months
The skills that have been developed by a child some 540 days following birth are truly awe inspiring. SOURCE: H. Knobloch and B. Pasamanick, *Gesell and Amatruda's Developmental Diagnosis,* 3rd ed. (New York: Harper & Row, 1974), pp. 82–83. Reprinted by permission.

rations or contours (Spelke, 1988; Spelke, Von Hofsten & Kestenbaum, 1989).

One of the most intriguing aspects of perceptual experience is **visual constancy**—the tendency for objects to look the same to us despite fluctuations in sensory input. We perceive the colors, sizes, and shapes of objects as relatively unchanging regardless of changes in the colors, sizes, and shapes that their images project on the retina of our eye. For instance, we see the color of coal as black even though the amount of light reflected from it changes. This phenomenon is called *color constancy.* Likewise, an object does not appear to shrink as we move father away from it, even though the size of the image on our retina becomes smaller. This phenomenon is *size constancy.* Finally, we see a door as a rectangle even though its shape becomes a trapezoid as the door opens, with the edge that is toward us appearing wider than the hinged edge. This phenomenon is *shape constancy.*

Since the earliest days of their discipline, psychologists have been interested in how the visual constancies arise in children. A major problem, however, is that the child's inner perceptual experiences are not directly accessible to us. We must make *inferences* regarding the inner perceptual process from what a child says or does following the presentation of a perceptual stimulus. Among the indicators that investigators have used are changes in the infant's eye orientation, sucking rate, body movements, skin conductance, heart rate, and conditioned responses. Most researchers believe that color, size, and shape constancies become apparent in infants at about 4 to 6 months of age (Catherwood, Crassini & Freiberg, 1989; Cohen, DeLoache & Strauss, 1979; Dannemiller, 1989; Haith & Campos, 1977; McKenzie, Tootell & Day, 1980). However, T. G. R. Bower (1976) claims to find visual constancy among infants at 6 weeks of age, a capability he attributes to an innate genetic mechanism. Perhaps for the present it is best if we keep an open mind about visual constancy and await further research.

Depth Perception

Eleanor Gibson and her husband James Gibson have both had distinguished careers as psychologists (Reed, 1988). When their daughter was about 2 years old, the Gibsons visited the Grand Canyon in Arizona. One day the child ventured close to the rim of the canyon, and the mother became alarmed for her safety. James Gibson, an authority on perception, assured his wife that a child their daughter's age was in little danger. He told her that 2-year-olds can recognize the depth of a drop-off as well as an adult can. Eleanor Gibson was not impressed by this scholarly observation and made the child move well back from the rim.

Some years later, the memory of this episode led Eleanor Gibson to undertake a **visual cliff experiment** with the assistance of one her students, Richard D. Walk (Gibson & Walk, 1960). In this technique an infant is placed on a center board between two glass surfaces upon which the child can crawl (see Figure 6-10). One side—the shallow side—is covered on the underside with a checkered material. The other side—the deep side—provides an illusion of a cliff by the placement of checkered material several feet below the glass. The infant's mother stands alternately at the shallow and deep sides and coaxes the infant to crawl toward her. If infants can perceive

depth, they should be willing to cross the shallow side but not the cliff side, since the cliff side looks like a chasm.

Gibson and Walk tested thirty-six infants between 6½ months and 14 months of age. Twenty-seven of the infants ventured off the center board and crawled across the shallow side toward their mothers. Only three, however, could be enticed to cross the cliff side. A number of infants actually crawled *away* from their mothers when beckoned from the deep side; others cried, presumably because they could not reach their mothers without crossing the chasm. Some patted the glass on the deep side, ascertaining that it was solid, but nonetheless backed away. Apparently, they were more dependent upon the visual evidence than on the evidence provided by their sense of touch. This research suggests that the vast majority of babies can perceive a drop-off and avoid it by the time they become capable of creeping.

Infants' *binocular vision*—the ability to tell the distances of various objects and to experience the world three-dimensionally—undergoes a sudden burst between 3 and 5 months of age (Petrig, Julesz, Kropfl, Baumgartner & Anliker, 1981; Pines, 1982a; Yonas, Granrud & Pettersen, 1985). The fact that the ability arises quite suddenly and rapidly suggests to some psychologists that it represents a change in that portion of the brain (the visual cortex) responsible for vision. During the postnatal period neural connections undergo substantial growth and elaboration. Apparently, these developmental changes result in the two

Figure 6-10 The Visual Cliff Experiment

In the visual cliff experiment the child is placed on a center board that has a sheet of glass extending outward on either side. A checkered material is placed on one side about 40 inches below the glass, thus providing the illusion of depth. Despite its mother's coaxing and the presence of a safe glass surface, a 6-month-old infant generally will not crawl across the "chasm." The infant will, however, venture across the shallow side of the apparatus to reach its mother. SOURCE: Adapted from E. J. Gibson and R. D. Walk, "The 'Visual Cliff,'" *Scientific American,* Vol. 202 (1960), p. 65.

Deep side   Shallow side

Glass over pattern surface

Floor pattern seen through glass

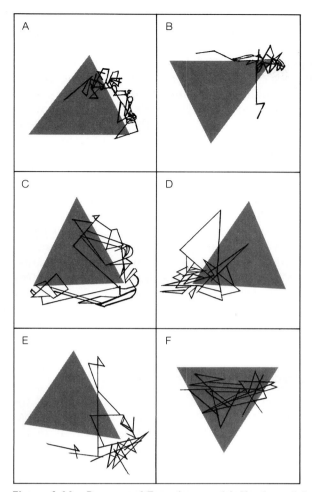

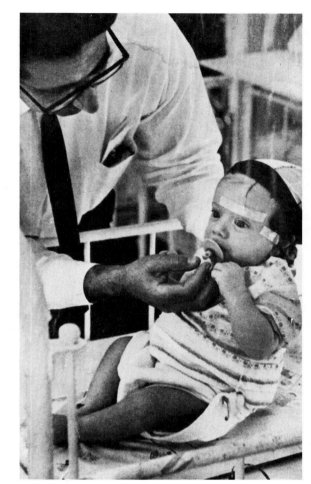

Figure 6-11   Perceptual Experiment with Newborn Infants

In this experiment babies are shown a large black triangle on a white field. Infrared marker lights are placed behind the triangle and reflect in the infant's pupils. This procedure allows researchers to trace and photograph a newborn's eye movements. The tracings (left) reveal that infants tend to look to the corners of the triangle. Even so, the tracings from six different infants show the wide variation in patterns of scanning among babies. SOURCE: Photograph courtesy Dr. William Kessen; data from P. H. Salapatek and W. Kessen, "Visual Scanning of Triangles by the Human Newborn," *Journal of Experimental Child Psychology*, Vol. 3 (1966), pp. 155–167.

eyes' working in concert and allowing the brain to extract reliable three-dimensional information from perceptual processes.

Perception of Form

Over the first two years of life the way infants focus on and organize visual events changes. During the first two months babies attend to stimuli that move and to those that contain a high degree of contrast. Even very young infants actively engage in *visual scanning.* As children get older, their scanning patterns become more exhaustive and less redundant. Consequently, the information they collect is more directly relevant to the task.

Researchers study infants' visual scanning by means of corneal photography. They train a movie camera and lights on an infant's eye and give the baby something to look at. The lights that they beam at the baby's eye are filtered so that the infant does not see them, but the movie film picks up their reflections. Later, the researchers develop the film, project it, and measure where the light reflections fall on the infant's eyeball. This process allows them to make a fairly precise map of the parts of an object that are capturing an infant's interest and the course of the baby's scanning activity (Maurer & Maurer, 1976).

Corneal photography reveals that newborn infants, when viewing an object such as a triangle, tend to focus on a relatively limited portion of the figure. Furthermore, if they are shown a black triangle on a white field, the infants' eyes hover on the corners of the triangle, where the contrast between black and white is strongest. Since infants do not usually scan the sides of the triangle, it is doubtful that they perceive the figure in its entirety (Salapatek, 1975; Salapatek & Kessen, 1966) (see Figure 6-11). Although infants of 2 to 4 months of age perceive the parts of a figure, they do not bring them together in a figure arrangement until they are about 4 to 5 months of age. If they are shown a cross inside a circle, younger infants are more likely to see it as a cross *and* a circle rather than as a cross *within* a circle. But as they mature, they increasingly respond to the whole rather than to the individual parts (Cohen, DeLoache & Strauss, 1979; Fisher, Ferdinandsen & Bornstein, 1981; Linn, Reznick, Kagan & Hans, 1982).

We are uncertain whether very young infants prefer to look at familiar or novel objects (Rose, Gottfried, Melloy-Carminar & Bridger, 1982; Wetherford, 1973). Research does clearly reveal, however, that infants older than 2 or 3 months have a decided preference for moderately novel stimuli (Cohen & Gelber, 1975; Fantz, Fagan & Miranda, 1975). Jerome Kagan (1970, 1972*b*), a developmental psychologist, finds that children between 3 and 12 months old are attracted most of all to stimuli that are sufficiently familiar to be recognized but sufficiently different to provide new information. Stimuli that are either too familiar or too novel receive little attention. Kagan believes that infants evolve a mental model, or scheme, from their accumulating experiences with a particular type of object or event. This mental representation is not a photographic image of the object or event. Instead, it is a stereotyped version or caricature. For example, a child develops a conception of the human face as an oval-shaped object with a hairline, two eyes, a nose, and a mouth.

About 1 year of age, Kagan suggests, children take a new approach to stimuli and form a *hypothesis*. A child now interprets some unusual experience by mentally *transforming* the event into a form that is already familiar. Previously, the child used a scheme to attend to or ignore a stimulus. Now the child actively uses the scheme to find meaning in very unusual stimuli. The child tries to understand why an event is odd and how it can be related to something familiar.

Kagan has experimentally shown infants oval images that resemble a human face. In some cases the features are disarranged—the mouth appears on the forehead, one eye on the cheek, another eye on the chin, and so on. To a child at 4 months of age, such images are sufficiently novel that the baby usually attends to them. But when the infant is 8 months old, the discrepancy is not great enough to hold the baby's attention. However, beginning around age 1 and continuing through age 3, children again show interest in the disarranged images.

Kagan takes these findings as confirming his thesis. Infants under 1 year old look at stimuli that resemble an existing scheme. Around 1 year of age they are challenged by seemingly nonsensical and confusing stimuli and try to make sense out of them. Kagan says that the older children are formulating hypotheses regarding the nature of the incoming information. A scheme functions for them as a standard against which they check their hypotheses.

Perception of the Human Face

One of the infant's visual preferences is the human face. This interest is highly adaptive, since an adult face is a critical element in the infant's natural environment. Robert L. Fantz (1963) found, for instance, that infants from 10 hours to 5 days old looked longer at a facelike stimulus than they did at newsprint, a bull's-eye, or different color disks. There is some question, however, whether the face is interesting to infants during the first 10 weeks of life because it is a face or because it is a complex object (Maurer & Salapatek, 1976).

For infants under 3 months of age the realism of the facial image does not appear to be crucial. They will smile just as frequently at a face with its features distorted or scrambled as they will at a realistic face (Ahrens, 1954; Fantz, 1970; Hershenson, Kessen & Munsinger, 1967). Similarly, the outer outline or contour of the facial image seems more crucial than the realism of its features (Haaf, 1974).

Daphine Maurer and Philip Salapatek (1976) found, in a study employing corneal photography, that 2-month-old infants tend to inspect the *external* contour of the face, usually devoting long periods of time to a particular area, such as the hairline, chin, or ear. One-month-old babies apparently can discriminate the faces of their mothers from the faces of strangers, probably by differences in the hairline or chin.

Person Permanence
This eight-month-old child is showing that he has grasped the concept of person permanence—the notion that an individual exists independently of visual display. This aspect of perception in the infant, which is extremely important in both the cognitive and social development of the child, is discussed further in Chapter 8. *(Alice Kandell/Photo Researchers)*

At about 5 to 7 weeks of age a dramatic change occurs in face looking. Infants invariably inspect one or more *internal* features of the face, especially the eyes. Indeed, talking to a child increases its scanning in the eye area. It is highly likely that this activity carries special social meaning for the infant's caretakers and enhances parent-infant bonding (Haith, Bergman & Moore, 1977).

Current research suggests that infants can detect the horizontally paired eyes in the upper part of the head by the third to fourth month. The mouth becomes differentiated by the fifth month and the broader facial configuration by the fifth or sixth month. And by the sixth to seventh month infants come to recognize individual faces (Caron, Caron, Caldwell & Weiss, 1973; Gibson, 1969). And they prefer faces that we as adults typically define as being "attractive" (Langlois, Ritter, Roggman & Vaughn, 1991). Such findings are consistent with Eleanor Gibson's (1969) view that object perception in infancy begins first with the differentiation of an object's parts and later progresses to the larger structure in which the parts are embedded.

Marie E. Barrera and Daphine Maurer (1981*a*, 1981*b*) have demonstrated that 3-month-olds can recognize the photographed face of the mother and discriminate it from another face. Moreover, they can recognize and discriminate faces of strangers. Apparently, infants do not require experience with pictures to be able to see them as more than a "frozen patchwork of flat colors" (Dirks & Gibson, 1977). Moreover, by 7 months of age they distinguish between happy and fearful facial expressions (Nelson & Dolgin, 1985). Indeed, 3-month-old infants show sensitivity to smiling when their parents encourage the youngsters by their behavior to be responsive to smiling faces (Kuchuk, Vibbert & Bornstein, 1986). In sum, infants have already developed rather sophisticated perceptual capabilities by the time they reach 6 or 7 months of age (Ludemann & Nelson, 1988; Nelson & Collins, 1991).

Interconnections Among the Senses

Our sensory systems commonly operate in concert with one another. We expect to see things we hear, feel things we see, and smell things we taste. We often employ information we gain from one sensory system to "inform" our other systems (Acredolo & Hake, 1982). For instance, even newborns move both their head and their eyes in efforts to locate the source of sounds, especially when the sounds are patterned and sustained.

Scientists have advanced two opposing theories about how the interconnections among systems evolve. Take the development of sensory and motor coordination in infants. One viewpoint holds that infants only gradually achieve an integration of eye-hand activities as they interact with their environment. In the process of adapting to the larger world, infants are seen as pro-

Eye-Hand Coordination

This ten-month-old child displays a high degree of eye-hand coordination in manipulating the sink plunger. (Patrick Reddy)

gressively forging a closer and sharper coordination between their sensory and motor systems. This approach has been most clearly expressed by Jean Piaget, whose position is treated in Chapter 7. According to Piaget, infants initially lack cognitive structures for knowing the external world. Consequently, they must actively construct mental schemes that will allow them to structure their experience.

The opposing theory holds that eye-hand coordination is biologically prewired in the infant's nervous system at birth and emerges according to a maturational schedule. This interpretation is favored by T. G. R. Bower (1971, 1974, 1976). Bower finds that newborn infants engage in visually initiated reaching. Apparently, when neonates look at an object and reach out for it, both the looking and the reaching are part of the same response by which the infants orient themselves toward the object (Von Hofsten, 1982). It is as if infants prepare themselves for an encounter with

an external event by pointing "feelers" toward it. Bower finds that in the average newborn this precocious eye-hand interaction vanishes, although it reappears again between 4 and 5 months of age. Hence, the built-in coordinations have later to be differentiated and reestablished on a new basis.

By 5 to 6 months of age children are adept reachers. But at this age inability to see the hand disrupts a child's behavior. This result confirms that the infant is employing visual feedback to enhance reaching accuracy (Lasky, 1977; Rose, Gottfried & Bridger, 1979). Seemingly, then, the eye-hand coordination of newborns and very young infants is biologically pre-wired. The eye-hand coordination of somewhat older babies, however, is accomplished by monitoring and progressively reducing the "gap" between the seen target and the seen hand. So for this later sort of reaching, the youngster must attend to its hand. In sum, eye-hand coordination changes early in life from using the felt hand to using the seen hand (Bushnell, 1985). These findings suggest that some behavior and intellectual development do not occur in a strictly cumulative and incremental manner. Development is often characterized by patterns of skill acquisition, loss, and reacquisition on new foundations and levels.

One fact stands out in any consideration of infants' sensory abilities: Infants actively search out and respond to their environment. Their natural endowment predisposes them to begin learning how the world about them operates; as they mature, they refine their ability to take information from one sense and transfer it to another. All the senses, including seeing, hearing, and touch, create a system that is a whole. Information gained from multiple systems is often more important than that gained from one sense, precisely because it is interactive (Lamb & Sherrod, 1981; Perris & Clifton, 1988; Rochat, 1989).

Summary

1. Children's physical growth takes place in a generally orderly fashion, with predictable changes occurring at given age levels. Growth, however, is unevenly distributed over the first twenty years of life. One of the most striking and fundamental characteristics of growth is its "self-stabilizing" or "target-seeking" quality.

2. Not all body systems grow at the same rate: (a) The nervous system grows more rapidly than other systems. (b) At 12 years of age, a child's lymphoid tissue is more than double the level it will reach in adulthood; after 12 it declines until maturity. (c) The reproductive system grows very slowly until adolescence, at which point its growth accelerates. (d) The skeletal and internal organ systems show two growth spurts, one in early infancy and the other at adolescence.

3. Development follows two patterns: the cephalocaudal principle and proximodistal principle.

4. The sequence of motor development proceeds in accordance with the cephalocaudal principle. Children gain mastery first over the head muscles, then the trunk muscles, and finally the leg muscles.

5. Young infants display bursts of rapid, repeated movements of the limbs, torso, and head. They seem to follow the dictum "If you can move it at all, move it rhythmically." The behaviors are closely related to motor development and provide the foundation for later, more skilled outputs.

6. The child's development of manual skills proceeds through a series of orderly stages in accordance with the proximodistal principle—from the center of the body toward the periphery. On the whole, large-muscle control precedes fine-muscle control.

7. Right- or left-handedness develops gradually rather than appearing in an immediate all-or-none manner. It does not become well established until a child is between 4 and 6 years of age.

8. Perception is oriented toward things, not toward their sensory features. We fashion and build our world in terms of things. This fact is demonstrated by visual constancies: color constancy, size constancy, and shape constancy.

9. The visual cliff experiment reveals that children possess depth perception at a very early age.

10. Over the first two years of life infants typically undergo a patterned sequence of changes in their method of focusing on and organizing visual events. Jerome Kagan suggests that children under 1 year of age have a decided preference for moderately novel stimuli. About 1 year of age, however, they come to employ a hypothesis for interpreting the nature of incoming information. Whereas children under 1 year old use a scheme, or mental model, to attend to or ignore a stimulus in terms of its degree of novelty, children over 1 year use the scheme to find meaning in very unusual stimuli.

11. The eye-hand coordination of newborns and very young infants apparently is biologically prewired. The eye-hand coordination of somewhat older babies, however, is accomplished by monitoring and progressively reducing the "gap" between the seen target and the seen hand. Eye-hand coordination, then, changes early in life from using the felt hand to using the seen hand.

KEY TERMS

Cephalocaudal Principle The rule that development proceeds from the head to the feet. Improvements in structure and function come first in the head region, then in the trunk, and finally in the leg region.

Infancy The first two years of life following birth.

Norms Standards for evaluating a child's developmental progress relative to the average of the child's age group.

Proximodistal Principle The rule that development proceeds outward, from the central axis of the body toward the extremities.

Secular Increase in Size The name given to the fact that decade by decade over the past century, the average stature of children at any given age has been increasing in the United States, western Europe, and Japan.

Visual Cliff Experiment A technique in which an infant is placed on a center board between two glass surfaces upon which the child can crawl. One side—the shallow side—is covered on the underside with a checkered material. The other side—the deep side—provides an illusion of a cliff by the placement of checkered material several feet below the glass. The infant's mother stands alternately at the shallow and deep sides and entices the infant to crawl toward her. The technique is used to determine depth perception in animals and in human infants.

Visual Constancy The tendency for objects to look the same to us despite fluctuations in sensory input.

INFANCY: COGNITIVE AND LANGUAGE DEVELOPMENT

Chapter 7

INFANCY: COGNITIVE AND LANGUAGE DEVELOPMENT

Cognitive Development

Piaget: The Sensorimotor Period ◆ Neo- and Post-Piagetian Research ◆ Jerome S. Bruner on Modes of Cognitive Representation ◆ Continuity in Cognitive Development from Infancy

Language and Thought

The Functional Importance of Language ◆ Language as the Container of Thought ◆ Language as a Determinant of Thought

Theories of Language Acquisition

Learning and Interactionist Theories ◆ Innateness Theory ◆ A Resolution of Divergent Theories?

Language Development

Communication Processes ◆ The Sequence of Language Development

◆

We do not live to think, but, on the contrary, we think in order that we may succeed in surviving.—JOSÉ ORTEGA Y GASSET

Our cognitive and language abilities are probably our most distinctive features as human beings. Cognitive skills enable us to gain knowledge of our social and physical environment. Language enables us to communicate with one another. Without either, human social organization would be impossible. If we lacked these abilities, we might still have families. The family organization is not peculiar to human beings. It also appears elsewhere in the animal kingdom. But without cognitive and language abilities our families would probably not have the structure we recognize as typically human. We would lack rules about incest, marriage, divorce, inheritance, and adoption. We would have no political, religious, economic, or military organizations; no codes of morality; no science, theology, art, or literature. We would be virtually toolless. In sum, we would be without culture, and we would not be human (White, 1949). This chapter surveys the processes by which cognition and language develop in us during the early years of childhood.

Cognitive Development

Man is obviously made to think. It is his whole dignity and his whole merit.—PASCAL

Pensées

As discussed in Chapter 2, *cognition* refers to the process of knowing. It encompasses such phenomena as sensation, perception, imagery, retention, recall, problem solving, reasoning, and thinking. We receive raw sensory information and transform, elaborate, store, recover, and use this information (Neisser, 1967).

Mental activity allows us to "make something" out of our perceptions. We do so by relating some happening to other events or objects in our experience. We employ information from our environment and our memories to make decisions about what we say and do. Since such decisions are based on information available to us and our ability to process the information intelligently, we view them as rational. It is this capacity that allows us to intervene in the course of events with conscious deliberation. For instance, if we show youngsters aged 13 to 24 months the simple steps involved in "making spaghetti" with clay, a garlic press, and a plastic knife and then allow them to undertake the task for themselves, they are able

to recall the sequence of events and repeat them—sometimes eight months later. Clearly, these youngsters are obtaining knowledge from their senses, imitating the actions of others, and remembering the information, all evidence of higher cognitive functioning. Indeed, a mounting body of evidence suggests that 16- and 20-month-olds are capable of organizing their recall of novel events around causal relations—they know that "what happens" occurs in such a way that one event ordinarily follows another event and that this same sequence of events will again unfold in the same manner in the future (Bauer & Mandler, 1989; Meltzoff, 1988*a*. 1988*b*).

Psychologists are increasingly coming to view infants as very complex creatures who are capable of experiencing, thinking about, and processing enormous amounts of information (Perris, Myers & Clifton, 1990). Building on the developing competencies detailed in the previous chapter, infants begin to form associations between their own behavior and events in the external world in the early months of their lives. As they do so, they progressively gain a conception of the world as an environment that possesses stable, recurrent, and reliable components and patterns. Such conceptions allow them to begin functioning as effective beings who cause events to happen in the world about them and who evoke social responses from others (Lamb & Sherrod, 1981; Bakeman, Adamson, Konner & Barr, 1990).

Piaget: The Sensorimotor Period

Man's mind stretched to a new idea never goes back to its original dimensions.
—OLIVER WENDELL HOLMES

As discussed in Chapter 2, the Swiss developmental psychologist Jean Piaget contributed a great deal to our understanding of how children think, reason, and solve problems. Perhaps more than any other person, Piaget was responsible for the rapid growth of interest in cognitive development over the past three decades. In many respects the breadth, imagination, and originality of his work overshadowed other research in the field.

Piaget charted a developmental sequence of stages during which the child constructs increasingly complex notions of the world. He provided an account of how the child acts at each level and how this activity leads to the next level (covered in Chapter 2). Piaget devoted his most detailed analysis to the first two years of life, which he calls the "sensorimotor period."

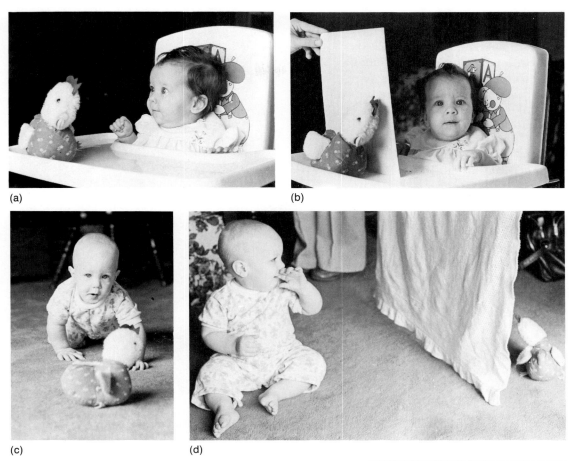

(a)　(b)

(c)　(d)

Evolution of the Notion of Object Permanence

Jean Piaget pointed out that an infant four months old does not recognize that an object has an independent existence that extends beyond the immediate perception of it. If we remove an object from the baby's vision, the four-month-old will not search for it even though the object remains within reach (photographs *a* and *b*). Between six and nine months of age, however, the child will retrieve the object. During this period children grasp the principle that an object continues to exist even though it is out of sight—the notion of object permanence (*c, d,* and *e*). *(Patrick Reddy)*

(e)

In Piaget's terminology, **sensorimotor** indicates that the major tasks of the period revolve around the coordination of motor activities with sensory inputs (perceptions). Thus, babies develop the capacity to look at what they are listening to. Moreover, they learn to guide their grasping and walking by visual, auditory, or tactile cues. In sum, during the sensorimotor period the infant comes to *integrate* the motor and perceptual systems. This integration lays the foundation for the development of new adaptive behaviors.

A second characteristic of the sensorimotor period is that babies develop the capacity to view the external world as a permanent place. Infants fashion a notion of **object permanence:** They come to view a thing as having a reality of its own that extends beyond their immediate perception of it. As adults, we take this notion for granted. However, infants do not necessarily do so during their first six to nine months. Hence, during the sensorimotor period a baby becomes capable of searching for an object that an adult has hidden under a cloth. The child now searches for it on the basis of information about where the object went. In so doing, the infant understands that the object exists even when it cannot be seen. This developing ability provides a fixed point for constructing conceptions of space, time, and cause.

According to Piaget, a third characteristic of the sensorimotor period is the inability of infants to represent the world to themselves internally. They are limited to the immediate here and now. Since they cannot symbolically fashion mental representations of the world, they "know" the world only through their own perceptions and their own actions upon it. Thus, children in the sensorimotor stage know food in that they can eat and manipulate it with their fingers. But they cannot conceive of it apart from these activities. Infants have a mental picture of food only insofar as *actual* sensory input reveals the food's existence. This mental picture disappears when the sensory

Living in the Here and Now
Piaget contended that infants in the sensorimotor period know the world only through their own perceptions and actions upon it. They thus know food only from the point of view that they eat it and play with it—but they cannot form a stable mental picture of it. Many contemporary developmental psychologists dispute this view and believe that infants are capable of internally representing the world about them in imagery. (Elizabeth Crews)

"They put these strings around a banana to hold it together."

("Family Circus" © 1990 Bill Keane, Inc. Reprinted with special permission of King Features Syndicate.)

input ceases. According to Piaget, infants are unable to form a static mental image of food "in their heads" in the absence of the actual visual display.

The sensorimotor period begins with genetically given reflexes. It ends with the appearance of language and other symbolic ways of representing the world.

Neo- and Post-Piagetian Research

Piaget's work has stimulated other psychologists to investigate children's cognitive development. They have been intrigued by the idea that infants do not think about objects and events in the same ways adults do. In particular, they have studied infants' notions regarding object permanence (Benson & Uzgiris, 1985; Haake & Someg-ville, 1985). This ongoing work is revising and refining Piaget's insights. For example, researchers have found that infants possess a set of object search skills more sophisticated than Piaget had imagined. Many of the errors that youngsters make in searching for items do not reflect an absence of basic concepts of objects and space. Even by 5 months of age they may have an understanding that an object continues to exist when the view of it is blocked. However, they appear to be incapable of coordinating their movements in a search for it (Baillargeon & Graber, 1988; Rubin, 1986; Sophian & Yengo, 1985; Yates & Bremner, 1988).

Moreover, developmental psychologists find that children do not develop an interest in objects and object skills in a social vacuum. Rather caretakers set the stage for youngsters by "playing" with them, clueing babies as to *what* they should do and *when* they should do it (Bruner, 1972, 1991). Additionally, by playing with infants, parents provide experiences that youngsters cannot generate by themselves (Vygotsky, 1978). In the course of such activities, infants acquire and refine their capacities for "intersubjectivity," so that by the end of the first year they share attention, emotional feelings, and intentions with others. All the while infants gain the unique "sense" and essential skills of their society's culture. Caregivers—the curators of culture—transmit the knowledge, attitudes, values, and behaviors essential for effective participation in society. Mere biological organisms are gradually transformed into genuine social beings capable of manipulating objects and acting in concert with others. Put another way, parents bring their babies' behavior into the framework of socially generated meanings, providing the content and context of cultural awareness (Stern, 1985; Trevarthen, 1988). In sum, a *sociocultural* link ties variations in what caretakers do when they play with their youngsters with the children's later cognitive and language performance (Bakeman, Adamson, Konner & Barr, 1990; Hunter, McCarthy, MacTurk & Vietze, 1987; Jones & Adamson, 1987).

Jerome S. Bruner on Modes of Cognitive Representation

One of the first U.S. psychologists to appreciate the importance of Piaget's work was Jerome S. Bruner. Bruner is a distinguished psychologist in his own right who has served as president of the American Psychological Association. Many of Bruner's papers show a strong Piagetian influence, especially in the way he treats the stages of cognitive development.

Through the years, however, Bruner and Piaget developed differences of opinion about the roots and nature of intellectual growth. Most particularly, the two men fell out over Bruner's view that "the foundations of any subject may be taught to anybody at any age in some form" (1970, p. 53). Piaget, in contrast, held to a rigorous stage approach, in which knowledge of certain subjects can be gained *only* when all the components of that knowledge are present and properly developed. (The boxed insert on page 181 examines the relationship between children's home environment and their early cognitive and language competence.)

One of Bruner's primary contributions to our understanding of cognitive development concerns the changes that occur in children's *favored* modes for representing the world as they grow older (Bruner, Olver & Greenfield, 1966). At first, during the time that Piaget called the sensorimotor period, the representative process is *enactive:* Children represent the world through their motor acts. In the preschool and kindergarten years *ikonic* representation prevails: Children use mental images or pictures that are closely linked to perception. In the middle school years the emphasis shifts to *symbolic* representation: Children use arbitrary and socially standardized representations of things. Doing so enables them to manipulate internally symbols that are characteristic of abstract and logical thought.

Thus, according to Bruner, we "know" something in three ways: through doing it (enactive), through a picture or image of it (ikonic), and through some symbolic means such as language (symbolic). Take, for instance, our "knowing" a knot. We can know it by the actual physical operations entailed in tying it; we can have a mental image of a knot as an object on the order of a pretzel (or a mental "motion picture" of the knot being formed); and we can represent a knot linguistically by combining four alphabetical letters, k-n-o-t (or by linking utterances in sentences to describe the process of tying string). Through these three means human beings increase their ability to achieve and use knowledge.

Continuity in Cognitive Development from Infancy

The prediction of mental competence and intelligence later in life from cognitive performance in infancy has been a topic of abiding interest among psychologists. Until relatively recently, psychologists believed that there is little continuity between early and later capabilities. But now they are increasingly concluding that individual differences in mental performance in infancy are, to a moderate extent, developmentally continuous across childhood and perhaps beyond (Baumrind, 1989; Bornstein & Sigman, 1986; Sternberg & Okagaki, 1989).

Information-processing models of intelligence have contributed to this reassessment (see Chapter 9). For people to mentally represent and process information concerning the world about them, they first must pay attention to various aspects of their environment. Two components of attention seem most indicative of intelligence in youngsters: (1) *decrement of attention*—the gradual decrease in the attention that infants pay to an object or event that is unchanging; and (2) *recovery of attention*—the renewed interest that infants show when something new happens. Youngsters who tire more quickly when looking at or hearing the same thing are more efficient processors of information. So are those who prefer the novel over the familiar. These infants typically like more complex tasks, show advanced sensorimotor development, explore their environment rapidly, play in relatively sophisticated ways, and solve problems rapidly. Similarly, the rapidness with which adults learn something is associated with measures of their intelligence; given equivalent opportunities, more intelligent people learn more than less intelligent people in the same amount of time. Not surprisingly, then, psychologists are finding that decrement and re-

covery of attention seem to predict childhood cognitive competence more accurately than do more traditional tests of infant development.

The patterns children revel in attending to information reflect their cognitive capabilities and, more particularly, their ability to construct workable schemes of the visual and auditory worlds. As Harriet L. Rheingold (1985) points out, mental development proceeds through transformations of novelty into familiarity. Each thing in the environment begins as something new, and so development progresses as infants turn something new into something known. In turn, what is known provides a context for recognizing what is new, and so the known provides the foundation for further mental development. Both the familiar and the novel, then, compel attraction and are reciprocal processes central to lifetime adaptation.

Language and Thought

Language is the armory of the human mind, and at once contains the trophies of its past and the weapons of its future conquests.—SAMUEL TAYLOR COLERIDGE

Human beings are set apart from other animals by their possession of a highly developed system of language communication (see Figure 7-1). This system allows them to acquire and transmit the knowledge and ideas provided by the culture in which they live. To be sure, a number of scientists claim that skills characteristic of the use of language have been developed in a dozen or so

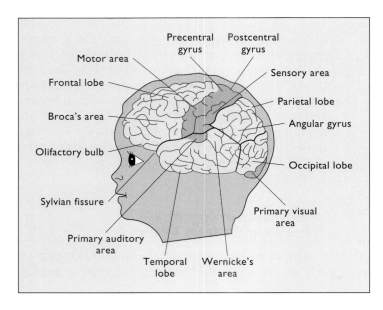

Figure 7-1   Areas of the Brain Associated with Speech
The drawing shows the left hemisphere of the cortex, where for most individuals speech is located in Broca's and Wernicke's areas. (From T. G. R. Bower, *Development in Infancy*, W. H. Freeman and Company, 1974. Reprinted by permission.)

The Home Environment:
Boosting Baby's Brain

Many parents wonder if they can boost their baby's intellectual development. The findings of an accumulating body of research suggest that good parenting can make a difference. The quality of the parent-infant relationship plays a key part in children's early cognitive and language competence. Parental behaviors affect infants' competence in a number of ways (Ainsworth & Bell, 1974; Olson, Bates & Bayles, 1984). First, children's learning is directly enhanced if parents provide them with immediate positive feedback when they say or do novel, creative, or adaptive things. Second, children's developmental competence is encouraged when parents provide a nonrestrictive environment that allows them to engage in exploratory behavior. And third, children who are securely attached to their caretakers are more apt than others to undertake competent exploration of their surroundings.

Effective parents are aware of their children's developmental needs and guide their own behavior to meet these needs. They accept their children while nonetheless encouraging them to capitalize on their strengths and compensate for their weaknesses (Bradley & Caldwell, 1984). Additionally, parents who are responsive to their youngsters at early ages are also the ones most likely to continue to be responsive as their children get older, producing a cumulative trend (Bronfenbrenner, 1986*b*).

These findings have had both positive and negative influences. On the positive side, the research results encourage interventions with infants who are at risk for delayed cognitive development, particularly those from impoverished homes (Seitz, Rosenbaum & Apfel, 1985; Yarrow et al., 1984). The key interventions involve encouraging parents to increase their levels of positive verbal and object-centered communication with their offspring (Olson et al., 1984). When observing a crying or defiant infant, parents can be helped to determine why the behaviors are occurring; infer the needs, motivations, and limitations in the youngster that very likely underlie the behaviors; and select the most appropriate responses (Dix, Ruble, Grusec & Nixon, 1986).

On the negative side, the research findings have caused some parents to indulge in what educational psychologists call "hot-housing," or trying to "jump-start" youngsters toward success. The image of a toddler calling out "Five!" when peering at five red dots on a white flash card or reading aloud from *The Cat in the Hat* brings joy to the hearts of many parents. Yet too many parents are pushing very young children too hard to gain academically oriented skills. Many of these parents are dual earners who feel guilt over not caring full-time for

Pushing Children Too Hard to Gain Academic Skills?
The importance of a good education in achieving success in American life has led some parents to undertake activities that they think will give their youngsters a "head start." But developmental psychologists say that the efforts may be counterproductive if youngsters are pushed through inappropriate methods or beyond their developmental capabilities. *(Ethan Hoffman/Archive Pictures)*

their children. In an effort to compensate and make sure that their children have all possible advantages, parents place them in pressured preschool programs. Some parents fear that if their children are not reading and multiplying by age 4, they will not get into Harvard by age 18. But in this situation they are merely transferring their own overly ambitious goals to their children. Thus far, the only proven beneficiaries of preschool programs have been culturally deprived youngsters. If children are pressured to learn through inappropriate methods, they often begin to dislike learning. Young children learn best from their own experience—from self-directed activity, exploring real objects, talking to people, and solving real-life problems, such as how to balance a stack of blocks. And they seem to benefit from having stories read to them on a regular basis. When caretakers intrude in children's self-directed learning and insist on their own learning priorities, such as mathematics or reading, they interfere with children's own impulses and initiative. Parents and other caretakers, then, must take into consideration the style of learning appropriate for the very young (Elkind, 1981, 1986, 1987).

chimpanzees (Gibbons, 1991). But, although the skills exhibited by the chimps are clearly related to human skills, they are hardly equivalent to our intricate and subtle language capacity. And the methods by which chimps typically must be trained are quite different from the spontaneous ways in which children learn a language. Apes learn to deal with signs sluggishly and often only after being plied with bananas, cola, and M & M's (Gould, 1983; Limber, 1977). **Language** is a structure system of sound patterns (words and sentences) that have socially standardized meanings. Language provides a set of symbols that rather thoroughly catalog the objects, events, and processes in the human environment (De Vito, 1970). Specifically, language is made up of three components: *phonology,* the joining together of units of sound to form words; *semantics,* a system of meanings associated with words; and *syntax,* rules for joining words to form phrases and sentences.

Language and cognition have a number of characteristics in common. Like language, cognition has three principal elements: a system of categories used to organize perceptual input (comparable to phonology); rules for assigning meaning to information by recognizing objects or events and placing them within appropriate categories (similar to semantics); and mechanisms for ascertaining the interrelations among various categories (akin to syntax). Indeed, some psycholinguists such as Noam Chomsky (1975) consider the study of language to be a "branch of cognitive psychology" and claim that a theory of language is necessarily a theory of mind. Yet even though language and cognition share many similarities, language is at least in part acquired and processed by principles that are unique to it (Blakeslee, 1991; Hilts, 1991; Pinker, 1991; Yamada, 1991).

The Functional Importance of Language

Language is by its very nature a communal thing; that is, it expresses never the exact thing but a compromise—that which is common to you, me and everybody.—THOMAS ERNEST HULME

Language makes two vital contributions to the human condition. First, it enables us to communicate with one another (*inter*individual communication). Second, it facilitates thinking (*intra*individual communication). The first contribution, called **communication,** is the process by which people transmit information, ideas, attitudes, and emotions to one another ("tune themselves together"). This feature of language allows human beings to coordinate complex group activities. They fit their developing lines of activity to the developing actions of others on the basis of the "messages" they provide one another. Thus, language provides the foundation for family, and for economic, political, religious, and educational institutions—indeed, for society itself.

Language has enabled human beings, alone of all animals, to transcend biological evolution. Evolutionary processes took millions of years to fashion amphibians—creatures that can live on land or in water. In contrast, a second set of amphibians—astronauts who can live in the earth's atmosphere or in the space outside it—have "evolved" in a comparatively short time (Brown & Herrnstein, 1975).

The difference is that biological evolution works only through genes, whereas cultural evolution takes place through the linguistic transmission of information. Each generation of human beings does not need to go through the entire inventive process associated with science, technology, agriculture, art, and law again. Culture permits each new generation to spring from the shoulders of the preceding one. Thus, human anatomy did not alter so that it could survive in space. Rather, human beings increased their knowledge to the point where they could employ it to complement and supplement their anatomy. In this manner they made themselves spaceworthy.

The second contribution of language is that it facilitates thought and other cognitive processes. Language enables us to encode our experiences by assigning names to them. It provides us with concepts by which we dissect the world around us and categorize informational input. Thus, language helps us to partition the environment into manageable units and into areas that are relevant to our concerns.

Moreover, the association between a verbal symbol and experience allows us to use the symbol in the absence of experience. As a result, we are able to refer to the parts of our experience that are not immediately present. Thus, language allows us to deal with past experiences and to anticipate future experiences. It enlarges the scope of our environment and experience.

It is this second function, the relation of language to thought, that has been the subject of intense debate. According to one view, language is merely the container of thought. The contrary view holds that language is the determinant of thought. Let us examine each of these positions more closely.

Language as the Container of Thought

Language is the dress of thought.—SAMUEL JOHNSON

Those who hold that language is the container of thought say that thought takes place *independently* of language. They believe that words are not necessary for thought but only for conveying it to others. For instance, some types of thought are primarily nonverbal visual images and "feeling." Probably you are most aware of language as a vehicle for conveying thought when someone asks you to describe something—your mother, the view from your room, the main street in your hometown. You seek to translate a mental picture into words. But often, you find that the task of verbally transmitting a visual image is complex and difficult.

Piaget (1952a, 1962) took the view that structured language presupposes the prior development of other kinds of mental representation. On the basis of his studies, Piaget concluded that language has only a limited role in young children's mental activity. According to Piaget, children form mental images of objects (water, food, a ball) and events (drinking, sucking, holding), and these images are based on mental reproduction or imitation, not on word labels. Thus, the children's task in acquiring words is to map language onto their preexisting concepts. Or, put another way, infants adapt sensorimotor schemes for communicative purposes.

In our discussion in the pages ahead we will see that Piaget vastly oversimplifies matters. Abstract cognitive capabilities do not necessarily precede structured language. Indeed, some of our language abilities are independent of our cognitive abilities (Blakeslee, 1991; Hilts, 1991; Yamada, 1991). For now, suffice it to note that there is not a clear nor invariant order across time by which cognitive insights come first followed by linguistic achievements (Bates, O'Connell & Shore, 1987; Bates & Snyder, 1987). Even so, for some domains, representation does precede language. For instance, William Zachry (1978) finds that solid progress in mental representation is necessary for some forms of language production. He suggests, like Piaget, that in stage 6 (the beginning of thought) children gain the ability to represent motor schemes (certain generalized activities) internally as images. Thus, the various actions associated with bottles would come to be represented by such visual images as holding a bottle, sucking a bottle, pouring from a bottle, and so on. Later, the child comes to represent the motor scheme—the activities associated with "bottle"—by the auditory sound—the word "bottle." This auditory image ("bottle") enters the child's implicit "dictionary." It becomes a semantic "marker" that represents the qualities associated with a bottle—holdable, suckable, pourable, and so on. In this matter, Zachry says, words come to function as semantic markers for internal representations.

Researchers also find that children approach the task of "word learning" equipped with preexisting *cognitive biases* that lead them to prefer some possible meanings over others (Behrend, 1990; Markman & Hutchinson, 1984; Waxman & Kosowski, 1990). More specifically, children seem predisposed to "whole object" meanings for nouns: They assume that a new noun refers to an entire object rather than to one of its parts. By way of illustration, consider the noun *dog*. Youngsters must learn that *dog* may refer both to a specific object (for instance, Fido) and other category members (for example, Buck, Spot, and Fang), yet the word is not applicable to individual aspects of the object (for instance, its nose or tail), to relationships between the object and other objects (for example, between a dog and its toy), or to the object's behavior (for instance, the dog's eating, barking, or sleeping). Were children to weigh these and countless other possible meanings before arriving at the correct mapping of the word (the correct mapping being Fido and Fido, Buck, Spot, and Fang), they would be overwhelmed by an unmanageable sea of "dog-related" inputs. Youngsters need not follow the laborious route. They bring a *bias* in thinking

Acquiring Language

Although maturational processes may "ready" children for language use, they do not guarantee that children will acquire the capacity to use language. Youngsters also require social interaction that encourages them to develop and refine their language capabilities. *(Elizabeth Crews/The Image Works)*

with them, one that allows "fast mapping"—the capturing of the basic elements of an experience to the exclusion of other experiences. Put another way, a cognitive bias guides the word-learning process by placing limits on the number of possible meanings youngsters have to entertain for a new noun. Basic terms such as *dog* are learned earlier and used more frequently by youngsters than either superordinate (for instance, *animal*) or subordinate (for example, *collie*) terms. Apparently, basic terms correspond to the level of conceptuation that is most readily available to infants (Rosch, 1978). In addition, children are cognitively biased toward an assumption that words refer to mutually exclusive categories (Markman, 1987; Markman & Wachtel, 1988; Taylor & Gelman, 1989). So we see that *some* aspects of linguistic development are linked to a preexisting level of conceptual development.

It also seems that infants as young as 4 months of age possess the ability to partition the color spectrum into four basic hues—blue, green, yellow, and red. The range of light wavelengths that is visible to adults—the *color spectrum*—extends from 400 to 700 millimicrons. The blues and violets correspond to short wavelengths (near 400 millimicrons), the reds to long wavelengths (near 700 millimicrons). Infants respond to differences in wavelength as though they perceive *categories* of hue—blue, green, yellow, and red. For example, they respond differently to two wavelengths selected from adjacent adult hue categories, such as "blue" at 480 millimicrons and "green" at 510 millimicrons. However, infants do not respond differently to two wavelengths selected from the same adult hue category although separated by a similar physical distance (30 millimicrons), such as "blue" at 450 and "blue" at 480 millimicrons. It seems, then, that the mental representations of infants are organized into blue, green, yellow, and red—rather than as exact wavelength codes (Bornstein, 1976; Bornstein & Marks, 1982). Only later do the children come to apply verbal labels (words) to these categories. Such findings suggest that color organization *precedes* and is not a product of the categories (the verbal labels "blue," "green," "yellow," and "red") provided by language and culture. More recent research confirms that infants spontaneously form categories during the prelinguistic period (Haynes, Rovee-Collier & Perris, 1987; Mervis, 1985; Roberts, 1988; Sherman, 1985; Younger & Gotlieb, 1988). In some respects, then, children's knowledge of language depends on a prior mastery of concepts about the world to which words will refer (Bruner, 1979; Jones, Smith & Landau, 1991).

Language as a Determinant of Thought

The second viewpoint is that language develops parallel with or even prior to thought. Consequently, language is said to shape thought. This theory is set forth in the writings of sociologists who are termed symbolic interactionists and follow in the tradition of Charles Horton Cooley (1902, 1909) and George Herbert Mead (1934). It is also endorsed by anthropologists sympathetic to the approach of Edward Sapir (1949) and Benjamin L. Whorf (1956) and by contemporary Russian developmental psychologists whose work bears the imprint of L. S. Vygotsky (1962; Wertsch, 1985).

This perspective emphasizes the part that concepts play in allowing human beings to partition stimuli into manageable units and into areas that are relevant to their concerns. Through **conceptualization**—grouping perceptions into classes or categories on the basis of certain similarities—children and adults alike can identify and classify informational input. Without the ability to categorize, life would be chaotic. By virtue of categories, objects need not be treated as unique. In using categories, people "tune out" certain stimuli and "tune in" others. Consequently, they are able to view the same object as being the same despite changes in stimulus display (despite the fact that the object varies from perspective to perspective and from moment to moment). And people are able to treat two different but similar objects as equivalent—as being the same kind of thing. Since categories allow human beings to make the mental leap from the specific to the general, they provide the basis for more advanced cognitive thinking. Significantly, researchers find that language increases the time infants look at objects beyond the time that the actual verbal labeling occurs, suggesting that infants are *biased* to look at objects in the *presence* of language (Baldwin & Markman, 1989).

Concepts also perform a second service. They enable individuals to go beyond the immediate information provided to them. People can mentally manipulate concepts and imaginatively link them to fashion new adaptations. This attribute of concepts allows human beings to make additional inferences about the unobserved properties of objects and events (Bruner, Goodnow & Austin, 1956).

The Role of Naming
Naming—verbally labeling—facilitates the process by which children come to put a "handle" on their experiences and render them meaningful. Accordingly, language expedites much mental activity and functioning. *(Michal Heron/Woodfin Camp)*

Human beings have an advantage over other animals in that they can use *words* in the conceptualization process. Some social and behavioral scientists claim that the activity of "naming" or "verbally labelling" (1) facilitates thought by producing linguistic symbols for integrating ideas, (2) expedites memory storage and retrieval via a linguistic code, and (3) influences perception by sensitizing people to some stimuli and desensitizing them to others.

Critics contend, however, that it is easy to oversimplify and overstate the relationship between language and various cognitive processes. Eric H. Lenneberg (1967) and Katherine Nelson (1972) note that children's first words are often names of preexisting cognitive categories. As pointed out in the previous section, color organization in infants *precedes* learned categories provided by language. The suggestion here is that language is not the sole source for the internal representation on which thought depends. Nor is language the sole source for the representation of information in memory (Kimball & Dale, 1972; Perlmutter & Myers, 1975, 1976). And language has at best only a minor impact upon perception.

The language-as-the-container-of-thought and language-as-a-determinant-of-thought perspectives stand in sharp contrast. The one argues that speech shapes thought; the other that thought shapes speech. Yet many linguists and psychologists believe that the two views are not mutually exclusive—that language and thought *interact* in such a fashion that each reciprocally influences

and shapes the other. So language and thought operate not as well-bounded, separated spheres but in tandem (Acredolo & Goodwyn, 1988; Pinker, 1991). Indeed, the interaction between the two is exceedingly complex, because thought (cognition) and language are each composed of many separate, underlying skills and mechanisms (Bates, Thal, Whitesell, Fenson & Oaks, 1989; Fogel & Thelen, 1987; Pinker, 1991; Yamada, 1991). The problem in some respects parallels the learnings and nativist controversy surrounding the acquisition of language, a matter to which we now turn our attention.

Theories of Language Acquisition

But I gotta use words when I talk to you.
But here's what I was going to say.—T. S. ELIOT
Sweeney Agonistes

How are we to explain the development of speech in children? Is language acquired through learning processes? Or is the human organism biologically "preprogrammed" or "prewired" for language usage? These questions expose a nerve in the longstanding nature versus nurture controversy, with environmentalists and nativists (hereditarians) vigorously and heatedly disagreeing on their answers.

Learning and Interactionist Theories

Growing numbers of psychologists are exploring the language environment in which infants and children are reared (Hoff-Ginsberg, 1986; Wexler & Culicover, 1981). Some have followed in the tradition of B. F. Skinner (1957), who argues that language is acquired in the same manner as any other behavior, namely, through learning processes of reinforcement (Whitehurst & Valdez-Menchaca, 1988). (See Chapter 2.) Others have studied the *interaction* between caretakers and youngsters that contributes to the acquisition of language (Jones & Adamson, 1987; Stevenson, Ver Hoeve, Roach & Leavitt, 1986). Indeed, learning to use language may begin quite early. As we noted in Chapter 5, DeCasper's research suggests that babies may have a sensitivity to speech that starts even before birth. While in the uterus they seem to hear "the melody of language." After birth this sensitivity provides them with clues about which sounds belong together.

"Pleasant dreams, Billy, and here's Daddy with one of your favorite bedtime stories."

(Drawing by Bernard Schoenbaum; © 1989. The New Yorker Magazine, Inc.)

The ability of neonates to discriminate between speech samples spoken in their mother's native language and in an unfamiliar language may derive from the unique melodic qualities found in the linguistic signals to which they were exposed prenatally (Fernald, 1990).

Caretaker Speech Much recent research has focused on caretaker speech. In **caretaker speech** mothers and fathers systematically modify the language that they employ with adults when addressing infants and young people. Caretaker speech differs from everyday speech in its simplified vocabulary; higher pitch; exaggerated intonation; short, simple sentences; and high proportion of questions and imperatives. Parents use caretaker speech with preverbal infants in numerous European languages, Japanese, and Mandarin Chinese (Fernald, 1990; Grieser & Kuhl, 1988). For their part, young infants show a listening preference for caretaker speech with its higher overall pitch, wider pitch excursions, more distinctive pitch contours, slower tempo, longer pauses, and increased emphatic focus (Cooper & Aslin, 1990; Fernald, 1985).

Speech characterized by the first two characteristics of caretaker speech—simplified vocabu-

lary and higher pitch—is termed *baby talk*. Baby talk has been documented in numerous languages, from Gilyak and Comanche (languages of small, isolated, preliterate Old World and New World communities) to Arabic and Marathi (languages spoken by people with literary traditions). Furthermore, adults phonologically simplify vocabulary for children—"wa-wa" for "water," "choo-choo" for "train," "tummy" for "stomach," and so on. Baby talk also serves the psychological function of marking speech as affectionate (Moskowitz, 1978).

Motherese When infants are still in their babbling phase, adults often address long, complex sentences to them. But when infants begin responding to adults' speech, especially when they start uttering meaningful, identifiable words (around 12 to 14 months), caretakers invariably speak what is termed **motherese**—a simplified, redundant, and highly grammatical sort of language.

Many of the features of motherese result from the process of carrying on conversations with immature conversational partners (Snow, 1977). Parents tend to restrict their utterances to the present tense, to concrete nouns, and to comments on what the child is doing or experiencing. And they typically focus on what objects are called ("That's a doggie!" or "Johnnie, what's this?"), the color of objects ("Bring me the yellow ball. The *yellow ball.* No, the *yellow* ball. That's it. The yellow ball!"), and where objects are located ("Hey, Lisa! Lisa! Where's the kitty? Where's the kitty? See. On the steps. See over there on the steps!"). The pitch of the caretaker's voice is correlated with the child's age: the younger the child, the higher the pitch of speech. Apparently most parents intuitively adopt vocal rhythms to direct their youngsters' attention and to cue their infants to their own emotions before verbal explanations and requests are of any use (Raymond, 1991; Warren-Leubecker & Bohannon, 1984). In addition, the intonation of infant-directed motherese—the melodies inherent in mother

Motherese
Caretakers typically speak to infants in a simplified, redundant, and highly grammatical sort of language. *(Rameshwar Das/Monkmeyer)*

speech—offers more reliable cues of a speaker's communicative intent than does speech directed by adults to other adults (Fernald, 1990). Motherese seems to derive less from parental concern with providing mini language lessons than from efforts to communicate to their youngsters. And as we will see later in the chapter, infants also use intonation effectively to express desires and intentions before they master conventional phonetic forms (Lewis, 1936/1951).

Interactional Nature of Caretaker Speech The interactional nature of caretaker speech actually begins with birth (Rheingold & Adams, 1980). Hospital staff, both men and women, speak to the newborns in their care. The speech focuses primarily on the baby's behavior and characteristics and on an adult's own caretaking activities. Moreover, the caretakers speak as though the infants understand them. Their words reveal that they view the newborns as persons with feelings, wants, wishes, and preferences. Similarly, a burp, smile, yawn, cough, or sneeze typically elicits a comment to the child from the caretaker (Snow, 1977). Often, the utterances are in the form of questions to which the caretakers answer as they imagine the children might respond. If a baby smiles, a parent may say, "You're happy, aren't you?" Or if the child burps, the caretaker may say, "Excuse me!" Indeed, caretakers impute intention and meaning to infants' earliest behavior, making the babies appear more adept than they in fact are. By building on these imputations, children's language acquisition is facilitated much in the manner of self-fulfilling prophecies. Infants with depressed mothers are handicapped in this respect because their mothers are less likely than nondepressed mothers to use the exaggerated intonation contours of motherese and because their mothers are slower to respond to their early attempts at vocalization (Bettes, 1988).

Innateness Theory

Rather than stressing the part that learning plays in language acquisition, some psychologists—such as Noam Chomsky (1957, 1965, 1968, 1980), Eric H. Lenneberg (1967, 1969), and Peter D. Eimas (1985)—focus on the biological endowments that human beings bring to the environmental context. Such psychologists, called *nativists,* view human beings as having evolved in ways that make some kinds of behavior, like language acquisition, easier and more natural than others. Youngsters are said to begin life with the underpinnings of later speech perception and comprehension, as they begin life with the specialized anatomy of the vocal tract and the speech centers in the brain. Nativists contend that human beings are "prewired" by their brain circuitry for language use. The potential for the behavior has been "built into" human beings by genes and only needs to be elicited by an appropriate environmental setting. At most, nativists say, the environment is no more than a "triggering mechanism" for language, in the same way that nutrition triggers growth.

Nativists point out that although the languages of the world appear on the surface to be extremely diverse, they share certain underlying similarities. Philip S. Dale (1976, p. 3) observes:

> In analyzing a new language a linguist knows that certain aspects of speech-sound production are likely to be important (where the tongue is, whether or not the passage to the nasal cavity is open, and so on); that there will be subjects and predicates; that it will be possible to ask questions, give commands, deny statements, and more. Similarly, the child may already "know" about certain universal aspects of language; this knowledge may be innate or at least present by the time the child approaches the task of language acquisition. Indeed, the assumption of such prior knowledge may offer an explanation for the presence of language universals in adult languages.

Even deaf children manifest a natural inclination to develop a structured means of communication (see the boxed insert on page 189).

Limitations of Learning and Interactionist Theories   In many respects the nativist position has been shaped, sharpened, and clarified as its proponents have done battle against learning and interactionist theories. Let us consider a number of the major inadequacies that the nativists find in the position of these theorists.

First, nativists point out that children acquire language with little difficulty. Even very young children do so, despite the fact that they must master an incredibly complex and abstract set of rules for transforming strings of sounds into meanings. By way of illustration, consider that there are 3,628,800 ways to rearrange the ten words in this sentence. "Try to rearrange any ordinary sentence consisting of ten words." However, only one arrangement of the words is grammatically meaningful and correct. Nativists say that a youngster's ability to distinguish the one correct sentence from the 3,628,799 incorrect

possibilities cannot arise through experience alone (Allman, 1991). Likewise, consider how formidable a foreign language such as Japanese or Arabic seems to you. The Soviet scholar Kornei Ivanovich Chukovsky observes:

> It is frightening to think what an enormous number of grammatical forms are poured over the poor head of the young child. . . . If an adult had to master so many grammatical rules within so short a time, his head would surely burst. (Quoted by Slobin, 1972, p. 82).

Second, nativists note that the child's problem is further complicated by the garbled nature of much adult speech. Nativists argue that from a grammatical point of view the speech children hear about them is "noisy slop." Furthermore, the words we utter in speaking are more like one giant word than neat packages of words. Usually, we do not pause between words. Reflect for a moment on how a conversation carried on in an unfamiliar language sounds to you. Indeed, linguists have experimentally shown that even in our own language we often cannot make out a word correctly if it is taken out of context. From recorded conversations linguists splice out individual words, play them back to people, and ask the people to identify the words. Listeners can generally understand only about half the words, although the same words were perfectly intelligible to them in the original conversation (Cole, 1979).

Third, nativists observe that children's speech is not a mechanical playback of adult speech. Children combine words in unique ways and also make up words. Expressions such as "I buyed," "foots," "gooder," "Jimmy hurt hisself," and the like reveal that children do not imitate adult speech in a strict fashion. Rather, according to nativists, children are *fitting* their speech to underlying language systems with which they are born.

Chomsky's Theory of Language Development   Noam Chomsky (1957, 1965, 1968, 1975), a linguist at the Massachusetts Institute of Technology, has provided a nativist theory of language development that has had a major impact on education and psychology over the past thirty years. Supporters and critics alike acknowledge that Chomsky's theoretical formulations have provided many new directions in the study of linguistics.

Central to Chomsky's position is the observation that mature speakers of a language can un-

Deaf Children Invent Their Own Sign Language

Oral language (speech) is part of most infants' environment. This is not the case, however, for deaf children. Nonetheless, deaf infants manage to create a sign language of their own—stereotyped gestures to refer to objects around them. Susan Goldin-Meadow and Heidi Feldman (1977) studied six deaf children ranging in age from 17 to 49 months. The children's parents had normal hearing. Despite their children's deafness, the parents wanted the children to depend on oral communication. Consequently, they did not expose the children to a manual sign language.

The researchers observed the children in their homes at periodic intervals. At the time they were studied, the children had learned only a few spoken words. In contrast, each child had individually developed a languagelike system of communication that included properties found in the language of hearing children. First, the children would indicate the object to be acted on, next the action itself, and finally the recipient of the action (should there be one). For instance, one child pointed at a shoe and then pointed at a table to request that the shoe (the object) be put (the act) on the table (the recipient). On another occasion the child pointed at a jar (the object) and then produced a twisting motion (the act) to comment on how his mother had opened the jar. Interestingly, even when the children were playing alone, they employed signs to "talk" to themselves, as hearing children would.

Once the researchers had determined that the children had acquired a sign language, the question that confronted them was, Who had first elaborated the signs, the children or their parents? The researchers concluded that most of each child's communication system was original and *not* invented by the parents. Some of the children used complex combinations of words before their parents did. Moreover, although the parents produced as many different characterizing signs as the children, only about a quarter of the signs were common to both parties.

Goldin-Meadow and Feldman (1977, p. 403) were especially impressed by the deaf children's achievements, in view of the ability of Lucy, Washoe, and other chimpanzees to employ sign language, which has aroused considerable interest:

> While chimpanzees seem to learn from manual language training, they have never been shown to spontaneously develop a language-like communication system without such training—even when the chimp is lovingly raised at a human mother's knee. On the other hand, even under difficult circumstances, the human child reveals a natural inclination to develop a structured communication system.

Additional research by Goldin-Meadow with deaf children has confirmed that children have a strong bias to communicate in languagelike ways (Goldin-Meadow & Mylander, 1983, 1984).

Other researchers find that deaf babies of deaf parents babble with their hands in the same rhythmic, repetitive fashion as do hearing babies who babble with their voices (Petitto & Marentette, 1991). Sounds such as "goo-goo" and "da-da-da" that hearing babies make arise as the signs and motions characteristic of American Sign Language among deaf youngsters (most of the hand motions of the deaf infants are actual elements of American Sign Language—gestures that do not in themselves mean anything but that have the potential to indicate something when pieced together with other gestures). Significantly, deaf children also pass through the same stages that are observed in the vocal babbling of hearing children (they string together signs and motions in much the same manner that hearing youngsters string together sounds). It seems that the gestures of deaf babies have the same functional significance as the babble noises of hearing babies, for they are far more systematic and deliberate than are the random finger flutters and fist clenches of hearing youngsters. Such results suggest that language is distinct from speech: Speech is only one of the signals that human beings have available for communicating with one another. In addition, the research suggests that manual and vocal babbling alike are an inherent feature of the maturing brain as it acquires the structure of language.

derstand and produce an *infinite* set of sentences, even sentences they have never before heard or uttered and so could not have learned. Accordingly, he argues that human beings possess an *inborn language-generating mechanism,* which he terms the **language acquisition device (LAD).** As viewed by Chomsky, the basic structure of language is biologically channeled. The human brain is wired to simplify the chaos of the auditory world by sorting through incoming frequencies and shunting speech sounds into forty or so intelligible *phonemes* (the smallest units of language). In the process of language acquisition children merely need to learn the peculiarities of their society's language, not the basic structure of language. Although Chomsky's theory has attracted a good deal of attention as well as controversy, it is difficult to test by established scientific procedures and hence remains neither verified nor disproved.

In support of his view, Chomsky cites data on linguistic universals. He points out that although the world's languages differ in their surface characteristics, which he calls *surface structure,* they have basic similarities in their composition, which he terms *deep structure.* The most universal features of deep structure include grammatical relations between subject (noun) and predicate (verb) and the possibility of posing questions, giving commands, and expressing negatives.

Chomsky says that sentences may have the same surface structure but different deep structures. Consider the sentence "They are eating apples":

1. (They) [(are eating) (apples)].
2. (They) [(are) (eating apples)].

Sentence 1 means that some people are eating apples. Sentence 2 means that the apples are for eating rather than for cooking. The surface structure of the sentence is the actual sound or word sequence. The deep structure refers to the intent of the sentence (the thought behind it).

By the same token, two sentences can have different surface structures but identical deep structures:

1. Hank pushed the bike.
2. The bike was pushed by Hank.

Chomsky suggests that through preverbal, intuitive rules—which he terms *transformational grammar*—individuals turn deep structure into surface structure, and vice versa. Such transformational grammar (rewrite rules) is biologically built into the functioning of the human organism. Chomsky does *not* claim that a child is genetically endowed with a specific language (English, French, or Chinese). He simply maintains that children possess an inborn capacity for generating productive rules (grammar).

Note that Chomsky's theory deals only with syntax (rules for joining words to form phrases and sentences). Critics point out that he does not provide a model for understanding crucial aspects of meaning or semantics.

A Resolution of Divergent Theories?

Most psychologists agree that there is a biological basis for language. But they continue to disagree over how much the input from parents and other caretakers matters. The most satisfactory approach seems to be one that looks to the strengths of each theory and focuses on the complex and many-sided aspects of the development of language capabilities. Indeed, language acquisition cannot be understood by examining learning or genetic factors in isolation. Rather, complex and dynamic *interactions* take place between biochemical processes, maturational factors, learning strategies, and the social environment (Blount, 1975; Hoff-Ginsberg & Shatz, 1982; Nelson, 1977; Pinker, 1991). Complex skills such as communication are multidetermined, incorporating elements of sensation, perception, cognition, affect, and motor control (Fogel & Thelen, 1987). No aspect by itself can produce a language-using human. Instead of asking which factor is most important, we need to study the ongoing process by which the factors dynamically come together. We must understand both learning and genetic components in order to understand either. For instance, psychologist Steven Pinker (1984) accepts Chomsky's central assumption that children have innate capabilities for formally structuring grammar. But he then goes on to explore the stepwise procedures that move the learner toward language mastery as the youngster is involved in complex transactions with the environment.

Although he is commonly identified with the nativist school, Eric H. Lenneberg (1969, p. 641) suggests one approach for viewing the continual interchange that goes on between the organism and the environment:

> Maturation may be characterized as a sequence of states. At each state, the growing organism is capable of accepting some specific input; this it breaks down and resynthesizes in such a way that it makes itself develop into a new state. This new state makes the organism sensitive to new and different types of input, whose acceptance transforms it to yet a further state, which opens the way to still different input, and so on.

In conclusion, infants are biologically adapted to acquire a linguistic tradition. They possess a genetically determined plan that leads them toward language usage. Their attentional and perceptual apparatus seems biologically pretuned to make phonetic distinctions. But simply because human beings possess a biological predisposition for the development of language does not mean that environmental factors play no part in language acquisition. Indeed, language is acquired only in a social context (Huttenlocker, Haight, Bryk, Seltzer & Lyons, 1991; Von Tetzchner, Siegel & Smith, 1989). Youngsters earliest vocalizations, even their cries, are interpreted by caregivers, who in turn use these interpretations to determine how they will respond to the youngsters.

Language Development

What is involved in learning to talk? This question has fascinated people for centuries. The Greek historian Herodotus (1964, pp. 102–103) reports on the research of Psammetichus, ruler of Egypt in the seventh century B.C.—the first attempt at a controlled psychological experiment in recorded history. The king's research was based on the notion that vocabulary is transmitted genetically and that children's babbling sounds are words from the world's first language:

> Psammetichus . . . took at random, from an ordinary family, two newly born infants and gave them to a shepherd to be brought up amongst his flocks, under strict orders that no one should utter a word in their presence. They were to be kept by themselves in a lonely cottage, and the shepherd was to bring in goats from time to time, to see that the babies had enough milk to drink, and to look after them in any other way that was necessary. All these arrangements were made by Psammetichus because he wished to find out what word the children would first utter. . . . The plan succeeded; two years later the shepherd, who during that time had done everything he had been told to do, happened one day to open the door of the cottage . . . [and both children ran up to him and] pronounced the word "becos."

When the king learned that the children had said "becos," he undertook to discover the language to which the word belonged. From the information produced by his inquiries, he concluded that "becos" was the Phrygian word for "bread." As a consequence, the Egyptians reluctantly yielded their claim to being the most ancient people and admitted that the Phrygians surpassed them in antiquity.

Communication Processes

Becoming competent in a language is not simply a matter of employing a system of rules for linking sounds and meaning. Language also involves the ability to use such a system for communication. The essence of language is the ability to transmit messages. Yet language is only one channel or form of message transmission. We also communicate by *body language* (also termed *kinesics*)—the nonverbal communication of meaning through physical movements and gestures. For instance, we wink an eye to demonstrate intimacy; we lift an eyebrow in disbelief; we tap our fingers to show impatience; we rub our noses or scratch our heads in puzzlement. We also communicate by gaze: We look at the eyes and face of another person and make eye contact. One way we use gazing is in the sequencing and coordination of speech. Typically, speakers look away from a listener as they begin to talk, shutting out stimulation and planning what they will say; at the end of the utterance they look at the listener to signal that they have finished and are yielding the floor; and in between they give the listener brief looks to derive feedback information. In infant development caretakers at first let babies vocalize at will and tailor their behavior around them. At around 18 months, however, many youngsters begin approximating the adult use of the gaze in conversations. By the end of the second year most children seem to pattern their looks in exactly the way that adults do: looking up at the ends of their own turns to signal that they are finished and looking up at the end of the other person's turn to confirm that the floor is about to be offered to them. Even so, children show considerable differences in the consistency and frequency of these behaviors (Rutter & Durkin, 1987). Girls reveal a stronger tendency to engage in symbolic gesturing than do boys, and the tendency is particularly strong among firstborn girls (the obvious hypothesis being that parents of firstborns create more opportunities of this sort than do parents of nonfirstborns (Acredolo & Goodwyn, 1988).

Another nonverbal behavior is pointing. Pointing—index-finger extentions—can be observed in infants as young as 2 months old, but as yet the pointing is not the expression of an intentional act (Trevarthen, 1977). In contrast, pointing at the end of the first year is an intentional act (Fogel & Thelen, 1987). The pointing gesture (usually combined with an intense gaze) is a nonverbal precursor of language. Mothers commonly employ pointing when talking to their youngsters. Children use the gesture to mark out features of a book or to call attention to an activity. Mothers typically look at the object and verbally acknowledge the gesture. They supply the infants with the names and properties of the object and with descriptions of their own and the infants' behavior

Pointing

Pointing is typical of one-year-old youngsters. They point as a gesture to call attention to an aspect of their environment. The activity is usually accompanied by an intense gaze. *(Michal Heron/Woodfin Camp)*

(Leung & Rheingold, 1981). Although pointing begins to emerge at about 9 months of age, children do not commonly synchronize their gestures with verbal labeling until they are about 14 months old (Murphy, 1978). Thus, an infant's evolving ability to employ language occurs within the context of a rich repertoire of early action-based symbols and nonverbal behaviors (Acredolo & Goodwyn, 1988). And reciprocally, children in the 12- to 16-month age range use adult language as an aid in the acquisition and manipulation of gestural symbols (Bates, Thal, Whitesell, Fenson & Oakes, 1989).

Another form of communication is *paralanguage*—the stress, pitch, and volume of vocalizations by which we communicate expressive meaning. Paralanguage involves *how* something is said, not *what* is said. Tone of voice, pacing of speech, and extralinguistic sounds (such as sighs) are examples of paralanguage. By the late babbling period infants already control the intonation, or pitch modulation, of their utterances (Moskowitz, 1978).

Most of the research on language development has focused on *language production,* the ability of children to string together sounds so as to communicate a message in a meaningful fashion. Until recently, little research dealt with *language reception,* the quality of receiving or taking in messages. Yet children's receptive capacities tend to outdistance their productive capabilities. For instance, even very young babies are able to make subtle linguistic discriminations—as between the sounds *p* and *b* (Eimas, 1985).

Older children similarly make finer distinctions in comprehension than they reveal in their own language productions (Bates, Bretherton & Snyder, 1988; Bates, O'Connell & Shore, 1987; Nelson, 1985; Oviatt, 1980). Consider the now somewhat classic conversation the linguist Roger Brown had with a young child (Moskowitz, 1978): The child made reference to "fis," and Brown repeated "fis." The child was dissatisfied with Brown's pronunciation of the word. After a number of exchanges between Brown and the child, Brown tried "fish," and the child, finally satisfied, replied, "Yes, fis." Although the child was as yet unable to pronounce the distinction between *s* and *sh,* he knew that such a sound difference did exist.

The Sequence of Language Development

Until a couple of decades ago, linguists assumed that children merely spoke an imperfect version of adult language, one that reflected their handicaps of limited attention, limited memory span, and other cognitive deficits. However, linguists now generally accept that children speak their own language—a language with characteristic patterns that develop through a series of stages.

Children reveal tremendous individual variation in the rate and form of language development (Nelson, 1981, 1985; Whitehurst, 1982). Indeed, some children may not begin to talk until well into their third year, whereas others are producing long sentences at this point. Such variations do not appear to have implications for adult language skill, provided that a child is otherwise normal. Table 7-1 summarizes the typical milestones in language development of the "average" child.

Early Vocalizations Crying is the most noticeable sound uttered by the newborn. As discussed in Chapter 5, variations on the basic rhythm include the "mad" and "pain" cries. Although it serves as the infant's primary means of communication, crying cannot be considered true language. Young infants also produce a number of other sounds, including yawns, sighs, coughs, sneezes, and belches. Between the sixth and eighth week infants diversify their vocalizations and employ new noises when playing alone, including "Bronx cheers," gurgling, and tongue games.

Table 7-1

Milestones in Language Development

Age	Characteristic Sounds
1 month	Cries; makes small throaty noises.
2 months	Begins producing vowellike cooing noises, but the sounds are unlike those of adults.
3 months	Cries less, coos, gurgles at the back of the throat, squeals, and occasionally chuckles.
4 months	Cooing becomes pitch-modulated; vowellike sounds begin to be interspersed with consonantal sounds; smiles and coos when talked to.
6 months	Vowel sounds are interspersed with more consonantal sounds (*f, v, th, s, sh, z, sz,* and *n* are common), which produce babbling (one-syllable utterances); displays pleasure with squeals, gurgles, and giggles, and displeasure with growls and grunts.
8 months	Displays adults intonation in babbling; often uses two-syllable utterances such as "mama" or "baba"; imitates sounds.
10 months	Understands some words and associated gestures (may say "no" and shake head); may pronounce "dada" or "mama" and use holophrases (words with many different meanings).
12 months	Employs more holophrases, such as "baby," "bye-bye," and "hi"; many imitate sounds of objects, such as "bow-wow"; has greater control over intonation patterns; gives signs of understanding some words and simple commands (such as "Show me your nose").
18 months	Possesses a repertoire of 3 to 50 words; may begin using two-word utterances; still babbles, but employs several syllables with intricate intonation pattern.
24 months	Has repertoire of more than 50 words; uses two-word utterances more frequently; displays increasing interest in verbal communication.
30 months	Rapid acceleration in learning new words; speech consists of two or three words and even five words; sentences have characteristic child grammar and rarely are verbatim imitations of adult speech; intelligibility of the speech is poor, although children differ in this regard.
36 months	Has a vocabulary of some 1,000 words; about 80 percent of speech is intelligible, even to strangers; grammatical complexity is roughly comparable to colloquial adult language.
48 months	Language well established; deviations from adult speech are more in style than in grammar.

Source: Adapted from F. Caplan, The First Twelve Months of Life *(New York: Grosset & Dunlap, 1973) and E. H. Lenneberg,* Biological Foundations of Language *(New York: John Wiley & Sons, 1973), pp. 128–130.*

Cooing and Babbling Infants begin making cooing sounds around their third month and babbling sounds by the sixth month (see Table 7-1). In *cooing,* babies make squealing-gurgling noises, which they sustain for 15 to 20 seconds. In *babbling,* they produce sequences of alternating vowels and consonants that resemble one-syllable utterances, for example, "da-da-da." Babies appear to engage in cooing and babbling for their own sake. Indeed, infants seem to play with sounds. They enjoy the process and explore their own capabilities. Among the most frequently babbled sounds are nasals such as *n* and *m,* glides such as *y* and *w,* and single-stop consonants such as *d, t,* or *b,* followed by a vowel formed with the tongue near its "home" position, such as the *eh* sound in "bet." Consonants such as *l, r, f,* and *v* and consonant clusters such as *st* are rare.

Deaf infants also go through the cooing and babbling phase, even though they have never heard any spoken sounds. They babble in much the same fashion as normal infants do, despite the fact that they cannot hear themselves (Lenneberg, 1967). This behavior suggests that a hereditary mechanism underlies the early cooing and babbling process. However, deaf babies later show a somewhat more limited range of babbling sounds than normal children do. Furthermore, unless congenitally deaf children are given special training, their language development is severely retarded (Oller & Eilers, 1988).

These observations suggest that although vocal behavior emerges through maturing mechanisms, it flourishes only in the presence of adequate environmental stimulation. And deaf babies, of course, are incapable of "talking back," the process of vocal contagion and model imitation noted by Piaget.

However, children to not seem to learn language simply by hearing it spoken. A boy with normal hearing but with deaf parents who communicated by the American Sign Language was daily exposed to television so that he might learn English. Because the child suffered from asthma, he was confined to his home. Consequently, he interacted only with people at home who, as family members or visitors, communicated in sign language. By the time he reached 3 years of age, he was fluent in sign language but he neither understood nor spoke English. This observation suggests that in order to learn a language, children must be able to interact with people in that language (Hoff-Ginsberg & Shatz, 1982; Moskowitz, 1978).

Holophrastic Speech Most developmental psychologists agree that children speak their first word at about 10 to 13 months of age. However, the precise time that a child arrives at this milestone is often difficult to determine. The child's first word is so eagerly anticipated by many parents that they read meaning into the infant's babbling—for instance, they note "mama" and "dada" but ignore "tete" and "roro." Hence, one observer may credit a child with a "first word" where another observer would not.

Children's first truly linguistic utterances are termed holophrases. **Holophrases** are single words that convey different meanings depending on the context in which they are used. G. de Laguna (1927, pp. 90–91) first noted the characteristics of holophrases more than sixty years ago:

> It is precisely because the words of the child are so indefinite in meaning, that they can serve such a variety of uses. . . . A child's word does not . . . designate an object *or* a property *or* an act; rather it signifies loosely and vaguely the object together with its interesting properties and the acts with which it is commonly associated in the life of the child. . . . Just because the terms of the child's language are themselves so indefinite, it is left *to the particular setting and context to determine the specific meaning for each occasion.* In order to understand what the baby is saying you must see what the baby is doing.

The utterance "mama," a not uncommon word in the early repertoire of English-language youngsters, provides a good illustration of a holophrase. In one situation it may communicate "I want a cookie"; in another, "Let me out of the playpen"; and in another, "Don't take my toy away from me." A holophrase is most often a noun, an adjective, or a self-invented word. Only

gradually do the factual and emotional components of the infant's early words become clearer and more precise in their discriminatory power.

Nelson, Rescorla, Gruendel and Benedict (1978) found that children typically pass through three phases in their early learning of language. At about 10 to 13 months of age they become capable of matching a number of words used by adults to already existing concepts, or mental images, such as the concept "bottle" discussed earlier in the chapter. One study reveals that the average child of 13 months *understands* about fifty words. In contrast, the *production* of fifty words does not occur until six months later (Benedict, 1976).

In the second phase, usually occurring between 11 and 15 months of age, children themselves begin to produce (utter) a small number of words. These words are closely bonded to a particular context or action.

In the third phase—from 16 to 20 months—children produce a good many words, but they tend to extend or overgeneralize a word beyond its core sense. For instance, one child, Hildegard, first applied the word "tick-tock" to her father's watch, but then she broadened the meaning of the word, first to include all clocks, then all watches, then a gas meter, then a firehose wound on a spool, and then a bathroom scale with a round dial (Moskowitz, 1978). In general, children overextend meanings on the basis of similarities of movement, texture, size, and shape.

Overgeneralization apparently derives from discrepancies between comprehension and production. For example, one child, Rachel, overextended "car" in her own verbal productions to include a wide range of vehicles. But she could pick out a motorcycle, a bicycle, a truck, a plane, and a helicopter in response to their correct names. Once her vocabulary expanded—once she acquired the productive labels for these concepts—the various vehicles began to emerge from the "car" cluster (Rescorla, 1976).

Children first tend to acquire words that relate to their own actions or to events in which they are participants (Bloom, 1978; Edmonds, 1976; Greenfield & Smith, 1976; Shore, 1986). Nelson (1973) noted that children begin by naming objects whose most salient property is change—the objects do things like roll (ball), run (dog, cat, horse), growl (tiger), continually move (clock), go on and off (light), and drive away (car, truck). The most obvious omissions in children's early vocabulary are immobile objects (sofas, tables, chests, sidewalks, trees, grass).

Learning Words By Doing
Children's first words typically relate to their own actions or to events that are important to them. Words relating to eating tend to be among the first words youngsters acquire.
(Robert McElroy/Woodfin Camp)

Children also typically produce a holophrase when they are engaged in activities to which the holophrase is related. Marilyn H. Edmonds (1976, p. 188) observed that her subjects:

> named the objects they were acting on, saying "ball" as they struggled to remove a ball from a shoe; they named where they placed objects, saying "bed" as they put their dolls to bed; they named their own actions, saying "fall" when they fell, they asserted possession, saying "mine" as they recovered objects appropriated by siblings; they denied the actions of their toys, yelling "no" when a toy cow fell over; and so forth.

Very often, a child's single-word utterances are so closely linked with action that the action and speech appear fused. In a Piagetian sense a word becomes "assimilated" to an existing sensorimotor scheme—the word is fitted or incorporated into the child's existing behavioral or conceptual organization (see Chapter 2). It is as if the child *has* to produce the word in concert with the action. Edmonds (1976, p. 188) cites the case of a child at 21 months of age who said "car" forty-one times during thirty minutes as he played with a toy car.

Two-Word Sentences When they are about 18 to 22 months olds, most children begin to use two-word sentences. Examples include "Allgone sticky," said after washing hands; "More page," a request to an adult to continue reading aloud; and "Allgone outside," said after a door is closed behind the child ("allgone" is treated as one word, since "all" and "gone" do not appear separately in children's speech). Most of the two-word sentences are not acceptable adult English sentences. And in most cases they are not imitations of parental speech; typical constructions are "More wet," "No down," "Not fix," "Mama dress," "Allgone lettuce," and "Other fix" (Braine, 1963, Clark, Gelman & Lane, 1985). Two-word sentences represent attempts by children to express themselves in their own way through their own unique linguistic system.

As in the case of holophrases, one often must interpret children's two-word sentences in terms of the context. Lois Bloom (1970), for instance, observed that one of her young subjects, Kathryn, employed the utterance "Mommy sock" in two different contexts with two different meanings. "Mommy sock" could mean that Mommy was in the act of putting a sock on Kathryn, or it could mean that Kathryn had just found a sock that belonged to Mommy.

Children's actual utterances are simpler than the linguistic structures that underlie them (Brown, 1973). Dan I. Slobin (1972, p. 73) observes that even with a two-word horizon, children can convey a host of meanings:

Identification: "See doggie."
Location: "Book there."
Repetition: "More milk."
Nonexistence: "Allgone thing."
Negation: "Not wolf."
Possession: "My candy."
Attribution: "Big car."
Agent-action: "Mama walk."
Agent-object: "Mama book" (meaning, "Mama read book").
Action-location: "Sit chair."
Action-direct object: "Hit you."
Action-indirect object: "Give papa."
Action-instrument: "Cut knife."
Question: "Where ball?"

Children also use intonation to distinguish meanings, as when a child says, "*Baby* chair" to indicate possession and "Baby *chair*" to indicate location.

Three-Word Sentences When children begin to use three words in one phrase, the third word frequently fills in the part that was implied in the two-word statement (Slobin, 1972). "Want that" becomes "Jerry wants that" or "Mommy milk" becomes "Mommy drink milk."

Psycholinguist Roger Brown (1973) characterizes the language of 2-year-old children as *telegraphic speech*. Brown observes that words in a telegram cost money, so that we have good reason to be brief. Take the message, "My car has broken down and I have lost my wallet; send money to me at the American Express in Paris." We would word the telegram, "Car broken down; wallet lost; send money American Express Paris." In this manner we omit eleven words: "my," "has," "and," "I," "have," "my," "to," "me," "at," "the," "in." The omitted words are pronouns, prepositions, articles, conjunctions, and auxiliary verbs. We retain the nouns and verbs (Brown, 1973, pp. 74–75):

> The adult user of English when he writes a telegram operates under a constraint on length and the child when he first begins to make sentences also operates under some kind of constraint that limits length. The curious fact is that the sentences the child makes are like adult telegrams in that they are largely made up of nouns and verbs (with a few adjectives and adverbs) and in that they generally do not use prepositions, conjunctions, articles, or auxiliary verbs.

Apparently, children's mental ability develops more rapidly than their ability to formulate their ideas in linguistic terms. With the passage of time, however, children acquire the ability to construct longer sentences and employ more complex grammatical operations for expressing their ideas (Shore, O'Connell & Bates, 1984). All the while, the childrens' vocabularies surge: Most U.S. children learn to comprehend more than 14,000 words between the ages of 2 and 6; they average six to nine new words per day (Templin, 1957).

SUMMARY

1. Jean Piaget characterized children's cognitive development during the first two years of life as "sensorimotor." The child's major task during this period is to integrate the perceptual and motor systems in order to arrive at progressively more adaptive behavior.

2. Another hallmark of the sensorimotor period is the child's progressive refinement of the notion of object permanence.

3. Piaget's work has stimulated other psychologists to investigate children's cognitive development. This ongoing work is revising and refining Piaget's insights. Researchers find that infants possess a set of object skills more sophisticated than Piaget had imagined. Moreover, psychologists find that children do not develop an interest in objects and object skills in a social vacuum. Parents provides youngsters with experiences that the youngsters cannot generate by themselves.

4. Individual differences in mental performance in infancy are, to a moderate extent, developmentally continuous across childhood and perhaps beyond. The patterns children reveal in attending to information reflect their cognitive capabilities and, more particularly, their ability to construct workable schemes of the visual and auditory worlds.

5. Human beings are set apart from other animals by their highly developed system of language communication. Language enables people to communicate with one another (interindividual communication). Language also facilitates thought (intraindividual communication).

6. Historically, there have been two opposing views in scientific circles regarding the relationship between language and thought. The first view is that thought takes place independently of language and that language is merely the container of already established thought. The second is that language shapes thought by providing the concepts or categories into which individuals mentally sort their perceptual stimuli.

7. Environmentalists and nativists disagree strongly about the determinants of language. Environmentalists argue that language is learned. Nativists insist that human beings possess an inborn language-generating mechanism.

8. Many scientists have concluded that the acquisition of language cannot be understood by examining either learning or genetic factors in isolation from one another. Complex interactions take place between biochemical processes, maturational factors, learning strategies, and the social environment.

9. The essence of language is the ability to transmit messages. Yet language is only one form of message transmission. We also communicate by body language—the nonverbal communication of meaning through physical movements and gestures. Another form of communication is paralanguage—the stress, pitch, and volume of vocalizations by which we communicate expressive meaning.

10. Children speak their own language, one that has its own characteristic patterns. Speech develops through a series of stages: early vocalizations (primarily crying), cooing and babbling, holophrastic speech, two-word sentences, and three-word sentences.

KEY TERMS

Caretaker Speech A systematically modified version of the language used with adults with which parents address infants and young children. Caretaker speech differs from everyday speech in its simplified vocabulary; higher pitch; exaggerated intonation; short, simple sentences; and high proportion of questions and imperatives.

Communication The process by which people transmit information, ideas, attitudes, and emotions to one another.

Conceptualization The grouping of perceptions into classes or categories on the basis of certain similarities.

Holophrase Children's first truly linguistic utterance; a single word that conveys different meanings depending on the context in which it is used.

Language A structured system of sound patterns (words and sentences) that have socially standardized meanings.

Language Acquisition Device (LAD) An inborn language-generating mechanism that, according to Noam Chomsky, all human beings possess. Chomsky believes that the brains of children are prewired with the basic structure of language. As they encounter the words and sentences of their society's particular language, they reinvent the rules of grammar and become able to speak.

Motherese A simplified, redundant, and highly grammatical form of language employed by parents in communicating with their infants.

Object Permanence The notion that an object continues to exist when it is outside the perceptual field.

Sensorimotor A concept in Piaget's terminology that refers to the adaptive integration of the motor and perceptual systems over the first two years of life.

Thought The ability of an individual to represent and act mentally on absent objects and events.

Chapter 8

INFANCY: PSYCHOSOCIAL DEVELOPMENT

The Development of Emotion and Social Bonds

Early Parenting: Myths and Facts

◆

In the orphanage, children become sad and many of them die of sadness.

From the Diary of a Spanish Bishop, 1760

Above all else, people are *social* beings. As Harriet L. Rheingold (1969*b*, p. 781), a developmental psychologist, puts it, "The human infant is born into a social environment; he can remain alive only in a social environment; and from birth he takes his place in that environment." Humanness, then, is a social product.

This fact is starkly reflected in two separate cases involving children who were reared under conditions of extreme isolation. The cases of Anna and Isabelle are similar in a number of respects. Ashamed of their illegitimate birth, the children's mothers had kept them hidden in secluded rooms over a period of years. Anna and Isabelle received only enough care to keep them alive. When they were discovered by local authorities, both were extremely retarded, showing few, if any, human capabilities or responses. In Anna's case (Davis, 1949, pp. 204–205):

> . . . [the child] could not talk, walk, or do anything that showed intelligence. She was in an extremely emaciated and undernourished condition . . . completely apathetic, lying in a limp, supine position and remaining immobile, expressionless, and indifferent to everything.

Anna was placed in an institution for retarded children, where she died of hemorrhagic jaundice at 10 years of age.

In contrast with Anna, Isabelle received special training from members of the staff at Ohio State University. Within a week after training was begun, she attempted her first vocalization. Isabelle rapidly progressed through the stages of social and cultural learning that are considered typical of U.S. children. She finished the sixth grade at age 14 and was judged by her teachers to be a competent and well-adjusted student. Isabelle is reported to have completed high school, married, and had her own normal family.

A report on the two cases by sociologist Kingsley Davis (1949, pp. 207–208) concluded:

> Isolation up to the age of six, with failure to acquire any form of speech and hence missing the whole world of cultural meaning, does not preclude the subsequent acquisition of these. . . . Most of the human behavior we regard as somehow given in the species does not occur apart from training and example by others. Most of the mental traits we think of as constituting the human mind are not present unless put there by communicative contact with others.

More recently, interest has focused on Genie, a girl who was found in 1970 at the age of 13 after having experienced a childhood of severe and unusual deprivation and abuse (Curtiss, 1977; Pines, 1981). From the age of 20 months she had been locked in a small room by her father and rarely saw anyone. Her vocalizations and noises were punished by beatings. Under these conditions, it is not surprising that Genie did not develop language.

From the time of Genie's discovery a program was undertaken to rehabilitate and educate her. Over the course of eight years Genie made considerable progress in the comprehension and production of language. Yet her speech was still far from normal, resembling a somewhat garbled telegram. For instance, it lacked proforms ("what," "which," "this," and the like), movement rules (she produced no passive sentences, such as "John was hit by the ball"), and auxiliary structure (for instance, she consistently omitted "have" and "will" in such sentences as "Tom will go home"). After living for a few years with a foster family, Genie was able to approach strangers and initiate physical contact, and she seemed to expect kindness, not hostility, from adults. Nonetheless, some of her behavior remained strange—a not surprising outcome given the deprivation of her formative years. In 1978 Genie's mother became her legal guardian and removed her from the special program in which she had been participating. Likewise, all research on Genie's language and intellectual development was halted.

For a discussion of other kinds of child abuse and neglect, see the boxed insert on pages 204–206.

The Development of Emotion and Social Bonds

We are molded and remolded by those who have loved us; and though the love may pass, we are nevertheless their work, for good or ill.—FRANÇOIS MAURIAC

The importance of children's early years in shaping their psychological and social being has been emphasized by many child psychologists. As we noted in Chapter 2, Erik Erikson maintains that the essential task of infancy is the development of a basic trust in others. He believes that during infancy children learn whether the world is a good and satisfying place or a source of discomfort, frustration, and misery. If the child's basic needs are met with genuine and sensitive care,

Learning Basic Trust
According to Erik Erikson, an infant's first social achievement is coming to terms with the fact that his mother periodically moves out of sight. As the child develops confidence that she will return, he is less likely to cry and rage when she departs. *(Polly Brown/The Picture Cube)*

the child develops a "basic trust" in people and evolves a foundation of self-trust (a sense of being "all right" and a complete self). In Erikson's view, a baby's first social achievement is the willingness to let its mother move out of sight without undue anxiety or rage, because "she has become an inner certainty as well as an outer predictability" (1963, p. 247).

Many psychologists, especially those influenced by the Freudian tradition, hold that children's early relationships serve as prototypes for their later relationships with people. Viewed from this perspective, the flavor, maturity, and stability of a person's relationships derive from his or her early ties. However, as pointed out in Chapter 2, most contemporary developmental psychologists dispute the view that the first several years of a child's life are all-important. They stress instead that development occurs across the entire life span. Hence, no one period is more critical than another. These psychologists do not deny that development is influenced by early experiences. But they portray human beings as considerably more resilient than Freud and his followers imagined them to be.

Nevertheless, the psychoanalytically oriented psychologists highlighted for us the importance of healthy emotional development. In recent years the study of children's emotional life has again become a central concern of psychologists. The strict behaviorism of B. F. Skinner had essentially eliminated the study of emotions from the curriculum of behavioral science during the 1940s and 1950s. And during the 1960s and 1970s developmental psychologists centered their attention on cognitive growth, a legacy of Jean Piaget. Legions of scientists devoted their attention to how people formed opinions, made decisions, learned skills, and solved problems. They saw emotion as peripheral, of interest mostly when it interfered with rational thought or found deviant expression in the form of mental illness.

"I'm so happy, if I had a tail I'd wag it!"

However, over the past decade or so, a renewed interest in the study of emotions is correcting the predominantly behavioral and cognitive view of human development. In the process, psychologists are rejecting the image of humankind as simply a "stimulus-response black box" or a "thinking machine" (Goode, 1991).

The Role of Emotion

It is terribly amusing how many different climates of feeling one can go through in a day.—ANNE MORROW LINDBERGH
Bring Me a Unicorn

Emotions play a critical part in our daily existence. Indeed, if we lacked the ability to experience love, joy, grief, and rage, we would find it difficult to recognize ourselves as human. Emotions set the tone for much of our lives and even, at times, override our most basic needs. For instance, fear can preempt appetite. Anxiety can drive a man from his lover's bedroom. And despair can lead a person to a fatal flirtation with a pistol (Goode, 1991).

Most of us have a gut-level feeling of what we mean by the term "emotion." Yet we have difficulty putting the feeling into words. Psychologists have similar problems (Dodge, 1989; Malatesta, Culver, Tesman & Shepard, 1989). Indeed, they have characterized emotion in different ways. Some have viewed it as a reflection of physiological changes that occur in our bodies, including rapid heartbeat and breathing, muscle tension, perspiration, and a "sinking feeling" in the stomach. Others have portrayed it as the subjective feelings that we experience—the "label" we assign to a state of arousal. Still others have depicted it in terms of the expressive behavior that we display, including crying, moaning, laughing, smiling, and frowning. Yet emotion is not one thing but many, and it is best characterized as a combination of all these components. Thus, we may view **emotion** as the physiological changes, subjective experiences, and expressive behaviors that are involved in such feelings as love, joy, grief, and rage. Emotions, then, are not simply "feelings" but rather processes by which individuals establish, maintain, and terminate relations between themselves and their environment (Campos, Campos & Barrett, 1989). For instance, joyful people are likely to continue what they are *doing,* while simultaneously their facial expressions and behaviors *signal* other people that they too should keep up

their interaction. In contrast, sad people tend to feel that they cannot successfully attain some goal, and their sadness signals others that they need help.

Charles Darwin was intrigued by the expression of emotions and proposed an evolutionary theory for them. In *The Expression of Emotions in Man and Animals,* published in 1872, Darwin contended that many of the ways in which we express emotions are inherited patterns that have survival value. He observed, for instance, that dogs, tigers, monkeys, and human beings all bare their teeth in the same way during rage. In so doing, they communicate to other members of their own species and to other species important messages regarding their inner dispositions.

Functions of Emotions Contemporary psychologists have recently followed up on Darwin's leads, noting that emotions perform a number of functions (Bretherton, Fritz, Zahn-Walter & Ridgeway, 1986; Campos, Barrett, Lamb, Goldsmith & Stenberg, 1983). First, emotions seem to have evolved as adaptive processes that enhance survival. For instance, fear of the dark, fear of being alone, and fear of sudden happenings are adaptive because there often exists a clear association between these events and potential danger. Second, emotions influence the mental operations we bring to bear in information processing. For example, our emotions influence our categorizing and appraisal of events as dangerous or beneficial and provide the motivation for patterning our subsequent behavior. And third, emotions assist us in fitting our actions to the developing actions of others. For instance, by reading other people's facial, gestural, postural, and vocal cues, we gain indirect access to their emotional states. Knowing that a friend is afraid or sad allows us to more accurately predict the friend's behavior and to respond to it appropriately. Moreover, the "reading" of another person's emotional reactions permits social referencing, a matter to which we now turn our attention.

Social Referencing Social referencing refers to the practice whereby an inexperienced person relies on a more experienced person's interpretation of an event to regulate his or her subsequent behavior. By the time they are 1 year old, most infants engage in social referencing: They typically look at their parents when confronted with new or unusual events. They then base their behavior on the emotional and informational messages that their parents communicate. Social referencing varies with age; it probably begins about 6 months of age and increases thereafter (Walden & Baxter, 1989; Walden & Ogan, 1988). Apparently youngsters care little whether it is their fathers or their mothers who are doing the signaling (Dickstein & Parke, 1988; Hirshberg & Svejda, 1990).

Youngsters of 10 months of age use the emotional expressions of others to appraise events like those encountered in the visual cliff experiment discussed in Chapter 6. When they approach the illusory "drop-off," they look to their mothers' expressions and modify their own behavior accordingly. When their mothers pose an angry or fearful face, most youngsters will not cross the "precipice." But when their mothers pose a joyful face, they will cross it. Infants show similar responses to their mothers' vocalizations that convey fear or joy. This research reveals that infants actively seek out information from others to supplement their own information and that they are capable of using this information to *override* their own perceptions and evaluations of an event (Campos, Barrett, Lamb, Goldsmith & Sternberg, 1983).

Emotional Development in Infants

Psychologists influenced by ethological theory have played a central role in the recent burst of studies on the emotional life of children (see Chapter 2). They have been influenced by Darwin's ideas and the more recent work of Paul Ekman (1972, 1980). Ekman and his colleagues have shown subjects from widely different cultures photographs of faces that people from Western societies would judge to display six basic emotions: happiness, sadness, anger, surprise, disgust, and fear. They find that subjects in the United States, Brazil, Argentina, Chile, Japan, and New Guinea label the same faces with the same emotion. Apparently, among all peoples of the world, regardless of culture, certain constants connect specific emotions and specific facial expressions. Ekman takes these findings as evidence that the central nervous system of human beings is genetically prewired for the facial expression of emotion. The face, then, provides a window by which other people can gain access to our inner emotional life and by which we gain similar access to their inner life. But the window is not entirely open. Early in life we learn to disguise or inhibit our emotions. We smile even

though we are depressed, look calm when we are irate, and put on a confident face in the presence of danger.

Psychologist Carroll E. Izard (1977, 1980; Izard & Malatesta, 1987) has been a central figure in the study of children's emotional development and has introduced his own "differential emotions theory." Like Ekman, Izard contends that each emotion has its own distinctive facial pattern. Izard says that a person's facial expression colors what the thinking brain "feels." For example, the muscular responses associated with smiling make you aware that you are joyful. And when you experience rage, a specific pattern of muscle firings that is physiologically linked with anger "informs" your brain that you feel rage and not anguish or humiliation. In sum, the feedback from sensations generated by your facial and related neuromuscular responses yield the distinctive subjective experiences that you recognize as different types of feeling.

Izard finds that babies have intense feelings from the moment of birth. But at first, their inner feelings are limited to distress, disgust, and interest (see Figure 8-1). In the course of their maturation new emotions—one or two feelings at a time—develop in a lawful, orderly fashion. Izard says that emotions are preprogrammed on a biological clock: Infants gain the social smile (joy) around 4 to 6 weeks of age; anger, surprise, and sadness about 3 to 4 months; fear at 5 to 7 months; shame, shyness, and self-awareness about 6 to 8 months; and contempt and guilt during the second year. But psychologist Joseph Campos (1983) disagrees with Izard. He believes all the basic emotions are in place at birth, depending on a prewired process for which neither experience nor social input is required. Campos says that many of an infant's emotions do not become apparent to observers until later, so the first *experience* of an emotion does not necessarily coincide with its first *expression*. Further complicating matters, the early signs of an emotion may differ from later ones. For instance, when 4-month-olds are frustrated, they direct their anger at the immediate cause (a person's hand), whereas at 7 months they direct their anger at the person (Stenberg, Campos & Emde, 1983). And although infants typically do not show fear until they are 5 to 7 months old, abused infants as young as 3 months show fear when a male stranger approaches them; abused youngsters similarly display sadness much earlier than usual (Gaensbauer & Hiatt, 1984). Whether emotions emerge only in the course of maturation or

Child Abuse and Neglect

If you must beat a child, use a string.
Talmud: Baba Bathra

Officials of the National Center of Child Abuse and Neglect (a federal agency) estimate that around 1 million U.S. children suffer neglect or physical abuse each year. *Neglect* is defined as the absence of adequate social, emotional, and physical care. *Abuse* is defined as nonaccidental physical attack on or injury to children by individuals caring for them. Most cases involve emotional neglect of some kind; about 20,000 children are found to be the victims of physical abuse, and an additional 113,000 of sexual abuse. (We will consider sexual abuse in Chapter 10). A variety of labels have come to be used in considering the "mental injury" children suffer from neglect and abuse, including psychological maladjustment, mental cruelty, emotional abuse and neglect, and emotional maltreatment (Hart & Brassard, 1987). The recent epidemic of cocaine and crack use has contributed to a substantial increase in the incidence of child abuse and neglect, placing growing demands on the child-welfare system (Trost, 1990).

Psychologist Byron Egeland has engaged in a longitudinal study of children who are at risk because of poor quality of care (Egeland & Brunquell, 1979; Egeland & Jacobvitz, 1984; Egeland, Jacobvitz & Sroufe, 1988; Egeland & Sroufe, 1981*a*, 1981*b*). He and his associates find that the psychological unavailability of caretakers affects a child's development as seriously as does physical abuse and neglect. Emotionally unresponsive mothers tend to ignore their youngsters when the children are unhappy, uncomfortable, or hurt, and they do not share their children's pleasures. Consequently, the children find that they cannot look to their mothers for security and comfort. Both physically abused and emotionally deprived children typically have low self-esteem, poor self-control, and negative feelings about the world. However, whereas physically abused youngsters tend to show high levels of rage, frustration, and aggression, those reared by emotionally unavailable mothers tend to be withdrawn and dependent and to exhibit more severe mental and behavioral damage as they become older.

Apparently, many abusive parents misread signs of pain, hunger, and distress in their children. When shown slides of youngsters exhibiting positive or negative emotions, abusive mothers are less likely than other mothers to identify the babies' emotions correctly. Indeed, they often see negative emotions as positive ones. Abusive parents do not necessarily ignore their children's emotional displays. Rather, they misinterpret their meaning, and so they respond inappropriately. For instance, the parent may attempt to feed a child who is experiencing pain. Parents become frustrated when they try to help a child but miss the boat. And as frustration mounts, so does the likelihood of child abuse (Camras et al., 1988; Camras et al., 1990; Kropp & Haynes, 1987; Moss, 1987). Within this kind of environmental setting, abused youngsters acquire biased and deficient patterns for processing social information: They overlook significant cues in other people's behavior; they incorrectly attribute hostile intentions to other people; and they lack competent strategies for solving interpersonal problems. Because they come to view and experience the world in deviant ways, many of them later perpetuate the abusive patterns of their parents and mistreat their own children (Dodge, Bates & Pettit, 1990).

To generalize about parents who abuse children is difficult. Multiple factors are usually involved. Furthermore, the relative importance of the various factors differs for different individuals, times, and social environments (Bybee, 1979; Herrenkohl & Herrenkohl, 1981; Martin and Walters, 1982). Nonetheless, a number of social factors are related to abuse and violence (Gelles, 1980). Research suggests that child abuse is more prevalent among economically disadvantaged families (Garbarino & Crouter, 1978; Gelles & Straus, 1979; Tan, Ray & Cate, 1991; Trickett, Aber, Carlson & Cicchetti, 1991). However, this finding does not mean that child abuse is confined to lower-socioeconomic-status households; it is found across the class spectrum. Child abuse is also related to social stress in families (Conger, Burgess & Barrett, 1979). For instance, high levels of marital conflict, interspousal physical violence, and job loss is associated with a higher incidence of child maltreatment (Dodge, Bates & Pettit, 1990; Steinberg, Catalano & Dooley, 1981). In addition, child abuse is more common among parents suffering from mental illness and substance addiction (Walker, Downey & Bergman, 1989). And families that are socially isolated and outside neighborhood support networks are more likely to abuse children than are families with rich social ties (Garbarino & Sherman, 1980; Trickett & Susman, 1988).

Psychiatrists Brandt G. Steele and Carl B. Pollock (1968) made intensive studies of sixty families in which significant child abuse had occurred. The parents came from *all* segments of the population: from all socioeconomic strata, all levels of intelligence and education, and most religious and ethnic groups. Steele and Pollock found a number of elements common to many child abusers. On the whole, these parents demanded a great deal from their infants, far more than the babies could understand or respond to (1968, p. 110):

> Henry J., in speaking of his sixteen-month-old son, Johnny, said, "He knows what I mean and understands it when I say 'come here.' If he doesn't come immediately, I go and give him a gentle tug on the ear to remind him of what he's supposed to do." In the hospital it was found that Johnny's ear was lacerated and partially torn away from his head.

The parents also felt insecure and unsure of being loved, and they looked to the child as a source of reassurance, comfort, and affection (Steele & Pollock, 1968, p. 110):

> Kathy made this poignant statement: "I have never felt really loved all my life. When the baby was born, I thought he would love me; but when he cried all the time, it meant he didn't love me, so I hit him." Kenny, age three weeks, was hospitalized with bilateral subdural hematomas [multiple bruises].

Steele and Pollock found that child abusers had been raised in the same authoritarian style that they were recreating with their own children. Indeed, abusive parents tend to be less satisfied with their youngsters and to experience child rearing as more difficult and less enjoyable than do nonabusive parents (Bugental, Blue & Cruzcosa, 1989; Trickett & Susman, 1988). Other researchers have confirmed that abusive parents are themselves likely to have been abused when they were children (Simons, Whitbeck, Conger & Chyi-In, 1991; Steinmetz, 1977; Widom, 1989a, 1989b). Indeed, evidence suggests that the pattern is unwittingly transmitted from parent to child, generation after generation—what researchers and professionals have termed a "cycle of violence" and the "intergenerational transmission of violence." Even so, abuse does not always or necessarily lead to abuse: Among adults who experienced abusive childhoods, between one-fifth and one-third abuse their own youngsters (Kaufman & Zigler, 1987; Widom, 1989b). However, the greater the frequency of violence, the greater the chance that the victim will grow up to be a violent parent (Straus, Gelles & Steinmetz, 1980).

Probably no more than 10 percent of abusing parents show severe psychotic tendencies or other signs of serious psychiatric disorders. In this small percentage of cases it may be advisable to remove the child from the home. Psychiatrists estimate that the other 90 percent of abusing parents are treatable if they receive competent counseling (Helfer & Kempe, 1977). Indeed, most parents want to be good parents. Parent education programs—classes that teach parenting skills—often help prevent fathers or mothers who have abused their children from doing so again (Hey, 1986b).

Abusing parents usually do not abuse all their children—one is commonly selected to be the victim. Some children appear to be more "at risk for abuse" than other children. They include children who were premature infants, were born out of wedlock, possess congenital anomalies or other handicaps, or were "difficult" babies. Overall, a child viewed by an abuse-prone parent as being "strange" or "different" is more at risk than are other children in the family (Brenton, 1977; Soeffing, 1975).

Maltreated children show a variety of symptoms. Infants may not thrive, and they may lag in motor, social, and language development. Preschoolers may display a lack of basic trust, "frozen watchfulness," and anxious and compliant behavior among adults. School-aged children may internalize the feeling that they are responsible for family problems and perform poorly on academic tasks. And adolescents may show masked depression, rebelliousness, anger, truancy, and antisocial behavior (Dean, Malik, Richards & Stringer, 1986; Hoffman-Plotkin & Twentyman, 1984; Kaufman & Cicchetti, 1989; Kempe & Kempe, 1978; Klimes-Dougan & Kistner, 1990; Lamb, Gaensbauer, Malkin & Schultz, 1985; Olweus, 1980; Rohrbeck & Twentyman, 1986). In addition, being neglected or abused as a child increases an individual's risk for delinquency, adult criminal behavior, and violent criminal behavior. Even so, the majority of neglected and abused youngsters do not become delinquent, criminal or violent. A good many other events in children's lives—for instance, their natural abilities, their temperaments, their networks of social support, and their participation in therapy—may mediate the adverse consequences of child abuse and neglect (Egeland, Jacobvitz & Sroufe, 1988; Widom, 1989a, 1989b).

Since teachers are the only adults outside the family whom many children see with any consistency, they are often in a position to detect signs of child abuse or neglect and to begin to remedy the situation by reporting it to the proper authorities. In fact, most states require teachers to report cases of child abuse, and the law provides them with legal immunity for erroneous reports made in

(continued)

good faith. The American Human Association has published a list of the signs teachers should look for as possible tip-offs of child abuse or neglect. They include the following:

❑ Does the child have bruises, welts, or contusions?
❑ Does the child complain of beatings or maltreatment?
❑ Does the child frequently arrive early at school or stay late? (The child may be seeking an escape from home.)
❑ Is the child frequently absent or late?
❑ Is the child aggressive, disruptive, destructive, shy, withdrawn, passive, or overly compliant?
❑ Is the child inadequately dressed for the weather, unkempt, dirty, undernourished, tired, in need of medical attention, or frequently injured?

Over the past fifteen years the problem of child abuse and neglect has emerged as one of the most pressing issues of our time. Nonetheless, considerable ambivalence still exists on the subject. At the same time that we condemn abuse and neglect, many Americans condone the physical punishment of children at home and at school. Indeed, in the 1977 case of *Ingraham* v. *Wright*, the U.S. Supreme Court held that physical punishment in school is neither cruel nor unusual punishment.

One difficulty in mapping effective strategies to deal with child abuse has been that most reports of child abuse turn out to be unsubstantiated. Of the 1.9 million reports of child abuse and neglect received nationwide in 1985, social workers confirmed approximately 750,000 cases of child maltreatment. However, more than half of those cases involved instances of neglect, with the most common problem being latchkey children left unsupervised at home. So caseworkers spend more time investigating dead ends than working on real cases.

Because of the recent proliferation in programs and services for troubled children and families, people find that through these agencies they can quickly obtain social services that they otherwise could not get. They often call about child abuse but they really want social services (Hey, 1986*b*). Additionally, although no one doubts that child abuse is a serious problem that warrants widespread vigilance, some families are the victims of unfounded reports of child abuse and neglect emanating from vindictive neighbors or irate former spouses. Moreover, callers on child abuse hot lines constantly press operators to investigate complaints about immoral lifestyles ("The parents drink and smoke pot all day"). Some child safety specialists defend current reporting practices, insisting it is better to err on the side of caution. But others suggest that a better job of screening out inappropriate reports is necessary, because there are insufficient funds to send a social worker to investigate every home where someone thinks there might be a problem with a child (Besharov, 1988; Melton & Limber, 1989; Wald, Carlsmith & Leiderman, 1988; Whitman, 1987).

are present at birth, we know that infants' emotional expressions become more graded, subtle, and complex beyond the first year of life (Demos, 1986; Kopp, 1989). Moreover, infants show an increasing ability to discriminate among vocal clues and facial expressions, particularly happy, sad, and angry ones, in the first five months of life (Caron, Caron & MacLean, 1988; Haviland & Lelwica, 1987; Kuchuk, Vibbert & Bornstein, 1986; Schwartz, Izard & Ansul, 1985). Even more significantly, infants progressively come to modify their displays of emotion and their behaviors on the basis of their appreciation of their mother's displays of emotion and behaviors (Cohn & Tronick, 1987; Lester, Hoffman & Brazelton, 1985).

Izard and others have also turned up evidence of continuity, or stability, of emotional expression in children (Fox, 1989; Trotter, 1987). The amount of sadness a child shows during a brief separation from its mother seems to predict the amount of sadness that the same child shows six months later. And the amount of anger a child shows when receiving a painful inoculation at 2 to 7 months of age predicts the amount of anger the same child displays at 19 months of age (Izard, Hembree, Dougherty & Spizziri, 1983; Izard, Hembree & Huebner, 1987). Additionally, emotional expressions and behaviors in infancy are related to personality characteristics at 5 years of age. Izard and his colleagues measured the fixation time, heart rate, and facial expressions of infants as they looked at a human face, a store mannequin face, and an object with scrambled facial features. They then tested the same youngsters five years later. The infants who had looked longest at the faces were the most sociable; those who looked the least showed the greatest shyness and withdrawal behavior. Izard concludes that emotional expressions have a strong biological component and that behaviors

Joy: Mouth forms smile, cheeks lifted, twinkle in eyes

Anger: Brows drawn together and downward, eyes fixed, mouth squarish

Surprise: Brows raised, eyes widened, mouth rounded in oval shape

Distress: Eyes tightly closed, mouth, as in anger, squared and angular

Interest: Brows raised or knit, mouth may be softly rounded, lips may be pursed

Disgust: Nose wrinkled, upper lip raised, tongue pushed outward

Sadness: Inner corners of brows raised, mouth corners drawn down

Fear: Brows level, drawn in and up, eyelids lifted, mouth retracted

Figure 8-1 Carroll Izard: Infant Facial Archetypes of Emotion
The photos depict the facial expressions that Izard believes are associated with the basic emotions. (SOURCE: Carroll Izard.)

in infancy tell us something about the personality or enduring characteristics of a person. And if infants have distinctive personalities, then caretakers should treat them in ways that recognize their different characteristics and needs. Once again, we see that parenting practices need to be tailored to the individual child's capabilities (Trotter, 1987).

Izard does not deny that in some measure learning conditions and experience modify a child's personality (Hyson & Izard, 1985). For instance, a mother's mood affects how an infant feels and acts (Field et al., 1988; Termine & Izard, 1988). When mothers of 9-month-old youngsters display a sad face, their children often reflect the same facial expression and engage in less vigorous play than when their mothers appear happy. Izard believes that "the interactional model of emotional development is probably correct. Biology provides some thresholds, some limits, but within these limits, the infant is certainly affected by the mother's moods and emotions" (quoted by Trotter, 1987, p. 44). Many other psychologists concur with this assessment. Indeed, much parental socialization is directed toward teaching children how to modulate their feelings and expressive behavior in ways that conform to cultural norms (Malatesta, Grigoryev, Lamb, Albin & Culver, 1986).

Stanley and Nancy Greenspan (1985) have also undertaken a search for "stages" in children's emotional development. They chart the emotional progress of the typical healthy child from birth through age 4, outlining six stages. In the first three months of life infants learn to calm themselves, and they develop a multisensory interest in the world. The second stage, lasting until a youngster is about 7 months of age, is a time for "falling in love"; infants develop a joyful interest in the human world and engage in cooing, smiling, and hugging. In the third stage, continuing through 10 months of age, infants develop intentional communication—a human dialogue—with the imporant people of their lives (for instance, they lift their arms to a caretaker, give and take a block offered to them, gurgle in response to a caretaker's speech, and enjoy peekaboo games). From about 9 to 18 months, the fourth stage, toddlers learn how to integrate their behavior with their emotions, and they begin to acquire an organized sense of self (for example, they will run to greet a parent returning home or lead a caretaker to the refrigerator in order to show hunger, instead of simply crying for dinner). In the fifth stage, from 18 months to 3 years of age, children begin to acquire an ability to create their own mental images of the world and to use ideas to express emotions and regulate their moods. Between 2 and 4 years, the sixth stage, they expand these capacities and develop "representational differentiation," or emotional thinking; they distinguish among different feelings and understand how they are related; and they learn to tell fantasy from reality. According to the Greenspans, the more that negative factors interfere with a child's mastering of emotional milestones, the greater is the probability of compromised intellectual and emotional development later on.

Theoretical Perspectives on Emotional Development

We humans are full of unpredictable emotions that logic cannot solve.—CAPTAIN JAMES KIRK, "STAR TREK"

Changes in the development of emotion have been explained from differing theoretical perspectives. Cognitive developmentalists, following in the tradition of Jean Piaget, look chiefly to shifts that occur in cognitive structures or schemes (Emde, Kligman, Reich & Wade, 1978; Kagan, 1984; Lewis, 1988; Lewis & Michalson, 1983; Piaget, 1963; Sroufe, 1979). These developmentalists say that the emergence of "true" emotions requires the *prior* establishment of elementary forms of cognitive activity (thought processes) that allow for "awareness" and "consciousness." So cognitive developmentalists typically discount Izard's notion that neonates experience emotion and instead label "precursor affects" those responses that "appear to be" emotional behaviors. For instance, the transition from the "emotion" of *distress*—viewed by cognitive developmentalists as simply a neonatal response to visceral discomfort—to *disappointment* occurs about the second or third month and is attributed by cognitive developmentalists to the emergence of primary circular reactions (see Chapters 2 and 7). The shift from mere distress to *anger*, occurring somewhat later in the first year, is said to derive from infants' growing conception of causality and intentionality. And by the end of the first year, *fear* replaces *wariness* due to the acquisition of object permanence (Fogel & Thelen, 1987). In sum, cognitive approaches tend to ignore or deemphasize the evolutionary, preadapted nature of emotions and instead depict emotions as products of developing thought processes (Malatesta, Culver, Tesman & Shepard, 1989).

An alternative theoretical perspective says that emotional development is driven by noncognitive forces (Campos & Stenberg, 1978; Izard &

Haynes, 1986; Steiner, 1979). Nativists point to evidence showing that in many instances emotional expressions operate independently of thought. For instance, animals who have had their cerebral hemispheres removed (the "thinking" portions of the brain), leaving the brain stem intact, nonetheless exhibit emotional displays (Steiner, 1979). Indeed, accumulating research reveals that the emotional system can act *independently* of conscious, cognitive processes, because anatomically emotions and cognitive processes operate from different areas of the brain. In many cases, the amygdala (a part of the brain that registers emotion) triggers an emotional reaction *before* the thinking brain has fully processed nerve signals. For instance, if in the corner of your eye you see an object that looks like a snake, the amygdala sends an alarm signal that makes you jump; you react even before other brain centers have had time to figure out whether the object was actually a snake, a piece of rope, or a section of garden hose (Goleman, 1989). Viewed in this fashion, noncognitive factors play a primary role and cognition only a secondary role in the development of emotion: You do not first appraise a situation cognitively and then decide what to "feel" but the reverse (Bretherton, Fritz, Zahn-Waxler & Ridgeway, 1986; Fogel & Thelen, 1987). In other words, you make a "quick and dirty" assessment that the object is something to fear. This assessment is then elaborated and refined by the thinking regions of your brain, allowing you to conclude, for instance, that the object is a section of garden hose and not a snake.

If indeed the emotional and cognitive systems can operate independently, we may have an explanation of why so much of emotional life is difficult to understand and control with the rational mind. For instance, fear may be learned without the cortex (the higher brain center that enables you, among other things, to think, to read, and to solve problems) being involved. Psychotherapists have long known that emotional memories, including deep fears and resentments, are particularly persistent and resistent to change. If portions of the brain are anatomically and functionally segregated, it is conceivable that some learning occurs during the first two years of life in emotion-centered areas and that this learning is subject to limited recall in later years. Put another way, once your emotional system learns something (like an intense, persistent, irrational fear of spiders, heights, or close spaces—a *phobia*), it may have extreme difficulty letting go of it. This explanation may also help us to understand why the emotional experiences of life's early years, which psychoanalysts point to as key to later emotional life, are so powerful (Goleman, 1989). (See Chapter 2.) And we would have an explanation for Izard's observation that 2-month-old human youngsters show anger in response to pain stimuli before the cognitive schemes believed necessary to handle anger are in place (Izard, Hembree, Dougherty & Spizziri, 1983). However, more research is needed on these matters before we can arrive at definitive conclusions.

In practice neither cognitive developmental nor nativist theorists take an either-or stance. Both recognize that emotions have a biological foundation *and* are affected by cognitive maturation and social interaction. The theorists differ primarily in the degree to which they emphasize biological or cognitive factors and in how they conceptualize the interplay between these components (Malatesta, Culver, Tesman & Shepard, 1989). You will recall, for instance, that Izard's differential emotions theory held that an infant's early emotions are prewired, preadapted, and stereotyped *but* that social experience rapidly exerts influence on infants' subsequent development. Izard emphasizes that the intense and unregulated emotional expressions of early infancy give way in time to emotional expressions that are tempered and modulated in the service of goal-directed behavior and interpersonal harmony (Izard & Malatesta, 1987). And later, typically in the toddler or preschool period, youngsters acquire the ability to uncouple their expressive behavior from their feelings; for example, they smile despite experiencing intense displeasure, they mimic distress that they really do not feel, or they put on a poker face (Cole, 1985; Izard & Malatesta, 1987). Of particular importance in children's emotional development is their ability to establish attachment bonds.

Attachment

Attachment is an affectional bond that one individual forms for another and that endures across time and space (Ainsworth, 1989; Ainsworth & Bell, 1970; Bretherton & Waters, 1985). An attachment is expressed in behaviors that promote proximity and contact. Among infants these behaviors include approaching, following, clinging, and signaling (smiling, crying, and calling). Through these activities a child demonstrates that specific people are important, satisfying, and rewarding. Some writers call this constellation of

socially oriented reactions *dependency* (Gewirtz, 1972; Macoby & Masters, 1970), and lay people refer to it simply as "love."

What Is the Course of Attachment H. Rudolph Schaffer and Peggy E. Emerson (1964) studied the development of attachment in sixty Scottish infants over their first 18 months of life. They identified three stages in the development of infant social responsiveness. During the first two months of life (the first stage), infants are aroused by *all* parts of their environment. They seek arousal equally from human and nonhuman aspects. The second stage is one of *indiscriminate attachment.* During this stage, which occurs around the third month, infants become responsive to human beings as a general class of stimuli. They protest the withdrawal of any person's attention, whether the person is familiar or strange. When they are about 7 months old, babies enter the third stage, that of *specific attachment.* They begin displaying a preference for a particular person and, over the next 3 to 4 months, make progressively more effort to be near this attachment object.

One way children show specific attachment is through *separation distress*—the tendency of children to cry, become upset, and stop their usual activities following the departure of a primary caretaker. Children are less likely to display separation distress when they crawl or walk away from a caretaker than when the caretaker leaves them. Separation distress typically appears in North American children at about 8 months of age, rises to a peak at 13 to 15 months, and decreases thereafter.

Children differ greatly in the age at which specific attachment occurs. Among the sixty babies in the Schaffer and Emerson study, one showed specific attachment at 22 weeks, whereas two did not display it until after their first birthdays. Cross-cultural differences also play a part in this development (Oppenheim, Sagi & Lamb, 1988; Sigman, Neumann, Carter & Cattle, 1988; Van IJzendoorn, 1990). Mary D. Salter Ainsworth (1967) found that infants in Uganda show specific attachment at about 6 months of age—a month or so earlier than the Scottish infants studied by Schaffer and Emerson. Similarly, Lester, Kotelchuck, Spelke, Sellers, and Klein (1974) found that separation protest occurred earlier among infants in Guatemala than among those in the United States.

Both Ainsworth and Lester and his colleagues attribute the precocity of the Ugandan and Guatemalan infants to cultural factors. Ugandan in-

Fostering Secure Infant-Parent Attachments
Developmental psychologists are confirming what people in countless societies have independently discovered for themselves. A solid attachment between child and caretaker affords a great many benefits. Not only does it promote a youngster's emotional and social development; it eases and even forestalls episodes of fussing and crying. Here an Indonesian mother *(left)* and a Niger mother *(right)* facilitate physical and social contact with their children by culturally evolved carrying contrivances. *(Paul Fusco/Magnum; Richard Wood/The Picture Cube)*

fants spend most of their time in close physical contact with their mothers (they are carried about on the mother's back). Accordingly, separation is a rare occurrence. In the United States infants are placed in their own rooms shortly after birth. Such separation is virtually unknown in Guatemala, where most rural families live in a one-room rancho. As a consequence, separation seems to be a more noticeable event to Guatemalan children, and they respond to it earlier than children reared in the United States.

Schaffer (1971) suggests that the onset of separation protest is directly related to a child's level of object permanence. Social attachment depends on the ability of infants to differentiate between their mother and strangers and on their ability to recognize that their mother continues to exist even when she is not visible. (In terms of Piaget's framework, outlined in Chapter 7, these abilities do not appear until the fourth sensorimotor stage.) Indeed, Silvia M. Bell (1970) finds that in some instances the concept of **person permanence**—the notion that an individual exists independently of immediate visibility—may appear in a child before the concept of object permanence. Studies by other researchers also confirm that

protests over parental departures are related to a child's level of cognitive development (Kagan, Kearsley & Zelazo, 1978; Spelke, Zelazo, Kagan & Kotelchuck, 1973).

Who Are the Objects of Attachment?   In their study of Scottish infants Schaffer and Emerson found that the mother was most commonly the first object of specific attachment (in 65 percent of the cases). However, there were some instances in which the first attachment was to the father or a grandparent (5 percent). And in 30 percent of the cases initial attachments occurred simultaneously to the mother and another person. Furthermore, the number of a child's attachments increased rapidly. By 18 months only 13 percent displayed attachment to only one person, and almost one-third of the babies had five or more attachment persons. Indeed, the concept of attachment as originally formulated was too narrow (Weinraub, Brooks & Lewis, 1977). Since infants have ongoing relationships with their fathers, grandparents, and siblings, these psychologists suggest that the focus of theory and research should fall on the *social network*—an encompassing web of ties to significant others. In this regard Michael E. Lamb (1976) finds that U.S. infants 8 months of age show no preference for one parent over the other on his measures related to attachment.

What Are the Functions of Attachment? Ethologically oriented psychologists point out that attachment has adaptive value in keeping infants alive. It promotes proximity between helpless, dependent infants and protective caretakers. But attachment also fosters social and cognitive skills. According to this view, four complementary systems coordinate the behavior of the child and the environment (Lamb & Bornstein, 1987). The first, the *attachment behavioral system,* leads to the development and maintenance of proximity and contact with adults. The second, the *fear-wariness behavioral system,* encourages youngsters to avoid people, objects, or situations that may be a source of danger to them; this system is often called "stranger wariness" and will be discussed later in the chapter. The third, the *affiliative behavioral system,* encourages infants, once the wariness response diminishes, to enter into social relationships with other members of the human species. And the fourth, the *exploratory behavioral system,* provides babies with feelings of security that permit them to explore their environment knowing that they are safe in the company of trusted and reliable adults (Jones, 1985).

How Do Attachments Form? Psychologists have advanced two different explanations of the origins or determinants of attachment, one based on an ethological perspective and the other on a learning perspective. The psychoanalytically oriented ethologist John Bowlby (1907–1990) (1969, 1988) says that attachment behaviors have biological underpinnings that can be best understood from a Darwinian evolutionary perspective. For the human species to survive despite an extended period of infant immaturity and vulnerability, both mothers and infants were endowed with innate tendencies to be close to each other. This reciprocal bonding functioned to protect the infant from predators when humans lived in small nomadic groups.

According to Bowlby, human infants are biologically preadapted with a number of behavioral systems ready to be activated by appropriate "elicitors" or "releasers" within the environment. Thus, close physical contact—especially holding, caressing, and rocking—serves to soothe and quiet a distressed, fussing infant. Indeed, an infant's crying literally compels attention from a

caretaker. And smiles accomplish much the same end. Rheingold (1969a, p. 784) observes:

As aversive as the cry is to hear, just so rewarding is the smile to behold. It has a gentling and relaxing effect on the beholder that causes him to smile in turn. Its effect upon the caretaker cannot be exaggerated. Parents universally report that with the smile the baby now becomes "human." With the smile, too, he begins to count as a person, to take his place as an individual in the family group, and to acquire a personality in their eyes. Furthermore, mothers spontaneously confide that the smile of the baby makes his care worthwhile. In short, the infant learns to use the coin of the social realm. As he grows older and becomes more competent and more discriminating, the smile of recognition appears; reserved for the caretaker, it is a gleeful

The Smile as a Universal Bonding Mechanism
A human face "triggers" an infant's smile, which in turn invites cuddling behaviors from caretakers. According to ethologists, babies are genetically "equipped" with smiling as an "elicitor" of such behaviors. (*Barbara Gundle/Archive*)

response, accompanied by vocalizations and embraces.

Sucking, clinging, calling, approaching, and following are other kinds of behavior that promote both contact and proximity. Hence, viewed from the evolutionary perspective, a child is genetically programmed to a social world and "in this sense is social from the beginning" (Ainsworth, Bell & Stayton, 1974, p. 997). And parents, in turn, are said to be genetically predisposed to respond with behaviors that complement the infant's behaviors (Ainsworth, Blehar, Waters & Wall, 1979). The baby's small size, distinctive body proportions, and infantile head shape apparently elicit parental caregiving (Alley, 1983).

Whereas Bowlby believes that inborn mechanisms account for attachment behaviors, learning theorists attribute attachment to socialization processes. According to psychologists such as Robert R. Sears (1963, 1972), Jacob L. Gewirtz (1972), and Sidney W. Bijou and Donald M. Baer (1965), the mother is initially a *neutral* stimulus for her child. She comes to take on rewarding properties, however, as she feeds, warms, dries, and snuggles her baby and otherwise reduces the infant's pain and discomfort. Since the mother is associated with the satisfaction of the infant's needs, she acquires *secondary reinforcing* properties—her mere physical presence (her talking, smiling, and gestures of affection) becomes valued in its own right. Thus, according to learning theorists, the child comes to acquire a need for the presence of the mother. In brief, attachment develops.

Learning theorists stress that the attachment process is a two-way street. The mother also finds gratification in her ability to terminate the child's piercing cries and with it to allay her own discomfort that is associated with the nerve-wracking sound. Furthermore, infants reward their caretakers with smiles and coos. Thus, as viewed by learning theorists, the socialization process is reciprocal and derives from a mutually satisfying and reinforcing relationship.

Do Early Attachment Patterns Predict Later Relationships? Freud (1940, p. 188) saw the child's relationship to the mother as having life-long consequences, calling it "unique, without parallel, established unalterably for a whole lifetime as the first and strongest love-object and as the prototype of all later love relations—for both sexes." This Freudian premise has underlaid much research on attachment behaviors, drawing attention to the influence a mother has on her developing child. Mary Ainsworth and her colleagues devised a procedure called the **strange situation** to capture the quality of the attachment in the infant-parent relationship (Ainsworth, 1983; Ainsworth & Wittig, 1969). The technique consists of a series of eight episodes in which researchers observe infants in an unfamiliar playroom. The youngsters are given an opportunity to explore toys and interact with an unfamiliar adult both in the presence and in the absence of the mother.

In the course of her research Ainsworth became intrigued by differences in the behavior of children, especially the way they react upon reunion with their mothers. About 60 percent of the infants used the mother as a secure base from which to explore the unfamiliar environment and as a source of comfort following separation. When their mother left the room and then returned, the infants would greet her warmly, show little anger, or indicate they wanted to be picked up and comforted. These children Ainsworth called *securely attached infants* (pattern B attachments). Other infants, about 10 percent, snubbed or avoided the mother on her return. These children were called *avoidant infants* (pattern A attachments). Still others, about 20 percent, were reluctant to explore the new setting and would cling to the mother and hide from the stranger. However, when the mother returned, they would mix active contact seeking with squirming, continued crying, and pushing the mother away. These youngsters were called *resistant infants* (pattern C attachments.) More recently, a number of researchers have added another category, *disorganized/disoriented infants* (pattern D attachments). Whereas infants in the A, B, and C categories possess a coherent strategy for dealing with the stress of separation and reunion, D-pattern youngsters seem to lack coherent coping mechanisms (Carlson, Cicchetti, Barnett & Braunwald, 1989).

Ainsworth contended that the A, B, and C patterns of attachment behavior in the strange situation reflect the quality of maternal caregiving children receive during their first 12 months of life. She traced the origins of the A and C patterns to a disturbed parent-child relationship, one in which a mother was rejecting, interfering, or inconsistent in caring for the child. The mothers would often over- or understimulate their babies, fail to match their behavior to that of their children, be cold, irritable, and insensitive, and afford perfunctory care. In contrast, the securely attached infants (pattern B attachment) seemed to have received consistent, sensitive, and responsive mothering (Ainsworth, Bell & Stayton, 1974). And even though mothers are influenced by the temperaments of their youngsters (for instance, whether they are irritable and difficult), this factor does not seem to be critical in determining a mother's responsiveness to her child's signals and needs (Belsky & Rovine, 1987; Smith & Pederson, 1988; Sroufe, 1985; Vaughn, Lefever, Seifer & Barglow, 1989). On the whole, other researchers have confirmed the Ainsworth findings, although the strength of the relationship may not be as strong as Ainsworth initially suggested (Belsky, 1990; Bretherton & Waters, 1985; Donovan & Leavitt, 1989; Isabella, Belsky & Von Eye, 1989; Lamb, Gaensbauer, Malkin & Schultz, 1985). Moreover, the quality of a relationship, once formed, is not necessarily permanent (Crockenberg & McCluskey, 1986).

Early attachment behaviors are also predictive of children's functioning in other areas. Mastery motivation seems to be associated with secure attachment. And some studies report a relationship between attachment security and cognitive development, although hardly ever a relationship with language acquisition. The effects of early attachments similarly carry over to later social relationships. For instance, classifications derived from the strange situation predict social functioning in the preschool with teachers and peers. Youngsters judged to have secure attachments to their mothers are socially more competent in preschool, sharing more and showing a greater capacity to initiate and sustain interaction. Such children are also more accepting of their mothers' showing attention to their older brothers and sisters, and secure older siblings are more likely to assist and care for their younger brothers and sisters than are insecure older siblings (Teti & Ablard, 1989). And the B-pattern children seem more resilient and robust when placed in stressful or challenging circumstances (Bretherton & Waters, 1985; Lamb, Gaensbauer, Malkin & Schultz, 1985). These findings are consistent with the speculations of attachment theorists that young children who enjoy a secure attachment to their parents develop internal "working models" of their parents as loving and responsive and of themselves as worthy of nurturance, love, and support. By contrast, youngsters with insecure attachments develop "working models" of the caregiver as unresponsive and unloving and of themselves as unworthy of nurturance, love, and support (Ainsworth, 1989; Bowlby, 1969, 1988; Bretherton & Waters, 1985; Cassidy, 1988; Denham, Renwick & Holt, 1991; Ward, Vaughn & Robb, 1988). Not surprisingly,

since child-rearing practices differ from one society to another, attachment patterns also vary from culture to culture. A-patterns are relatively more prevalent in western European nations and C-patterns in Israel and Japan (Van IJzendoorn & Kroonenberg, 1988).

Stranger Wariness and Stranger Anxiety

Wariness of strangers, an expression of the fear-wariness behavior system, usually emerges about a month or so after specific attachment begins. **Stranger anxiety** seems to be rather common among 8-month-old infants, although some infants show fear of strangers at 6 and 7 months of age. When encountering a strange person, particularly when a trusted caretaker is absent, many youngsters frown, whimper, fuss, look away, and even cry (Morgan & Ricciuti, 1969; Waters, Matas & Sroufe, 1975). Even at 3 and 4 months of age some babies stare fixedly at a strange person, and, occasionally, this prolonged inspection leads to crying (Bronson, 1972).

Twenty-five years ago psychologists took for granted that "fear of the stranger" was a developmental milestone that occurred in normal children. But then researchers found that youngsters do not invariably fear unfamiliar people (Rheingold & Eckerman, 1973). In fact, a more common reaction is one of acceptance and friendly overtures. Furthermore, mothers show significantly more "wary" behaviors than their infants do. Clearly, subtle negative behaviors on the approach of an unfamiliar person are not a response unique to infants. Hence, an infant's wariness toward strangers may simply reflect the fact that it is becoming an increasingly sophisticated participant in human interaction (Kaltenbach, Weinraub & Fullard, 1980).

Developmental psychologists find that the setting in which children encounter a stranger plays an important part in their response. Infants are both attracted to and wary of novel actions. So situational factors do much to determine which reaction will be activated. For one thing, babies show the greatest amount of stranger anxiety when their mothers are not present and the least amount when their mothers hold them. They also show fear when an unfamiliar adult comes near them and attempts to pick them up or take them from their mothers' arms (Bronson, 1972; Lamb, Gaensbauer, Malkin & Schultz, 1985; Morgan & Ricciuti, 1969). Friendly responses are more likely if infants are given ample time to "warm up" to a friendly stranger. Additionally, infants are more likely to seek out strangers and maintain contact with them in the absence of their mothers if they are in unfamiliar surroundings. Apparently, the stranger is the most comforting object available in an alien environment (Brookhart & Hock, 1976). And infants are more likely to react positively to a child than to an adult stranger (Greenberg, Hillman & Grice, 1973). In concluding our discussion of these matters, it is worth reminding ourselves that youngsters are not interchangeable or stereotyped beings, and so they display their unique and individual personalities in the ways they respond to strangers and to strange situations (Thompson, Connell & Bridges, 1988).

Early Parenting: Myths and Facts

Attachment plays an important role in children's early development. But what are the consequences for children who lack caring parents? In other words, how important is "mother love"? During the 1930s and 1940s studies by Margaret A. Ribble (1943), René Spitz (1945, 1946), and William Goldfarb (1945) did much to draw both scientific and humanitarian attention to the prob-

lems of homeless and neglected children. This work popularized the concept of **maternal deprivation**—the view that the absence of normal mothering can result in psychological damage and physical deterioration in children. In the intervening decades clinical and behavioral scientists have come to recognize that "maternal deprivation" is actually a catchall term. It encompasses many conditions, including insufficient sensory stimulation, the failure to form attachment bonds, the disruption of attachment bonds, unstable or rejecting mothering, inadequate intellectual stimulation, and even malnutrition. Since the term "maternal deprivation" has become so highly charged and a synonym for all that is destructive in child care, most researchers prefer to avoid it and use terms that refer to specific conditions, such as *social deprivation* and *sensory deprivation*.

Institutionalized Children

Psychologists have long recognized that children raised in orphanages, foundling homes, and other institutionalized settings generally do not flourish compared with children reared by their parents in home surroundings. Records of the Dublin Foundling Home reveal, for instance, that

"Listen to me, John. Tell them this is our final offer. Let 'em know we'll take an option at twenty-five million over five years—not a penny more, not a minute longer! If they balk, stall them for time and get back to me."

(Drawing by Koren; © 1989. The New Yorker Magazine, Inc.)

between 1775 and 1800 only 45 of the 10,272 children admitted survived (Kessen, 1965). And in 1915 James H. M. Knox, Jr., of the Johns Hopkins Hospital noted that in spite of adequate physical care, 90 percent of the infants in Baltimore orphanages and foundling homes died within a year of admission (Gardner, 1972).

The first large-scale study of infants raised in an institutional setting was undertaken by René Spitz (1945, 1946), an Austrian psychoanalytic physician. He compared infants who had been reared in a foundling home during the first year of life with infants reared in a prison nursery. In the foundling home the overworked nursing personnel provided the babies with good physical care but little or no individual contact and attention. By contrast, babies in the prison nursery spent most of their time with their mothers, receiving individual care and love. Spitz found that the infants raised by their own mothers made considerably better progress by all standards of development.

William Goldfarb (1945, 1947, 1949) came to a somewhat similar conclusion. He compared the development of two groups of children when they were between 10 and 14 years of age. One group had lived for a little more than three years in a foundling home before being placed in foster homes. The other group had been reared wholly in foster homes (except for a short period early in their lives). Goldfarb found that compared with the children who had been reared in foster homes, the children who had spent their early years in the foundling institution were socially immature, apprehensive, less able to inhibit deviant behavior, deficient in intellectual and language development, and insatiable in their need for affection (although they were unable to form genuine social bonds). Goldfarb blamed these intellectual and emotional scars on the absence of adequate mothering during the children's first three years.

A third study, by Wayne Dennis (1973), also emphasizes the retarding effects of institutional life on infants. However, Dennis concluded that the source of the difficulty was not the absence of a mother-child tie but the absence of adequate cognitive experiences. For a period in the 1950s and again in the 1960s, Dennis studied children at the Crèche, a foundling home in Beirut, Lebanon. Because of a staff shortage at the home, infants were taken from their cribs only to be bathed or changed. Two- and three-year-old children spent most of their time in cribs and playpens. They had little or no opportunity to walk or creep about on the floor. It is not surprising, therefore, that infants under 1 year of age could not sit alone, crawl, or creep and that children 2 years of age could not walk.

Intelligence tests were administered to the children at the Crèche when they were 2 years old. The children had an average IQ score of 53 (a score that classed them as mentally deficient). However, foundlings who were adopted *within* the first two years of life improved rapidly in their capabilities. By the age of 4 these children had attained an IQ of approximately 100. Although the test scores of those adopted *after* they were 2 years old increased beyond the mean score of 53 that they had registered at adoption, they retained the absolute deficiency in mental age they had shown at that time. (For instance, those adopted at age 6 were already three years retarded, so that at age 15 they had an average mental age of only 12.) Thus, Dennis concluded that after 2 years of age the effects of deprivation caused by inadequate cognitive experience are irreversible. (The boxed insert on page 219 examines the new discipline called developmental psychopathology.)

Recently, researchers have demonstrated that physical contact and sensory stimulation serve to improve the sensorimotor functioning of children in institutionalized settings (Rheingold, 1961; Saltz, 1973; Skeels, 1966; White, 1969). Indeed, even a small amount of extra handling highlights the value of "enrichment," at least over the short term. As as pointed out in Chapter 2, children show greater resilience than child psychologists believed was the case only a few decades ago. But note that, as in most other matters, children differ. Some show greater vulnerability to deprivation experiences than others do (Langmeier & Matějček, 1974; Rutter, 1974; Schaffer, 1966). Overall, the research on institutionalized infants gave encouragement to the trends toward earlier adoption and the use of foster homes rather than institutions. But, as explained in the boxed insert,

Importance of Sensory Stimulation
Children benefit from a rich sensory environment at all ages. Even young infants require stimulating settings for maximum cognitive development. *(George Goodwin/Monkmeyer)*

the orphanage arrangement is again being spawned by the growing number of parentless youngsters in our midst.

How Important Are Early Parenting Practices?

Early in this century Sigmund Freud revolutionized the view of infancy by stressing the part early experience plays in fashioning the adult personality (see Chapter 2). Central to Freud's thinking was the idea that adult neurosis has its roots in childhood conflicts associated with the meeting of instinctual needs (sucking, expelling urine and feces, and masturbation). Over the past seventy years, Freudian thinking has had an important influence on child-rearing practices in the United States. Many pediatricians, clinical psychologists, and family counselors have accepted major tenets of Freudian theory, especially as popularized by Dr. Benjamin Spock. (Spock's all-time, best-selling *Baby and Child Care* first appeared in 1946 and has since gone through multiple paperback revisions and editions.)

According to the Freudians, the systems of infant care that produce emotionally healthy personalities include breast feeding, a prolonged period of nursing, gradual weaning, a self-demand nursing schedule, delayed and patient bowel and bladder training, and freedom from punishment. Research, however, has offered little or no support for these premises. In an extensive study of child-rearing practices, William H. Sewell and Paul H. Mussen (1952) found no tie between the type of feeding school children had received as infants and their oral symptoms such as nail biting, thumb-sucking, and stuttering. Likewise, a longitudinal study carried out by M. I. Heinstein (1963) revealed no significant differences in the later behavior of bottle-fed and breast-fed babies.

Research has also demonstrated that other variables emphasized in psychoanalytic literature, including those associated with bladder and bowel training, are not related to later personality characteristics (Behrens, 1954; Schaffer & Emerson, 1964; Sewell, 1952). Psychologists now generally concede that such practices in themselves have few demonstrable effects on later development. Children are not the psychologically fragile and vulnerable beings depicted by the Freudians. They are considerably more resilient and less

Growing Controversy:
Is It Time to Bring the Orphanage Back?

Psychologists and child-welfare experts agree that children who are unlikely to be reunited with their birth families should be integrated into new families as soon as possible. They see adoption as the preferable arrangement. Foster care, although capable of providing youngsters with adequate physical care, is no match for the psychological and interpersonal benefits that accrue to children who become members of permanent families. Permanent adoption is positive for infant attachment and bonding, childhood happiness, self-esteem, social adjustment, intellectual development, and adult educational and career attainment (Barth & Berry, 1988).

For one reason or another, a good many youngsters do not find families willing to adopt them. Often they are seen as poor candidates because of their age, ethnicity, or emotional and behavioral problems. In recent decades these youngsters have been placed in foster homes. But now the supply of foster homes is no longer keeping up with the demand. In 1990 an estimated 360,000 youngsters were in foster homes, up 28.6 percent from the 280,000 three years earlier. The number is expected to reach 840,000 by 1995. Yet in 1990 there were only 125,000 foster homes.

A number of factors have contributed to the crisis in foster care. First, the crack epidemic among expectant mothers has resulted in youngsters unable to go home to addicted parents or to find people willing to adopt them (see Chapter 5). And for their part, many foster families suffer from burnout because they cannot deal with the emotional and behavioral problems of the children currently coming to them. Complicating matters, payments to foster parents have not kept pace with inflation, making recruitment even more difficult. Whereas the yearly payment for the care of a foster child averages $4,000, it costs about $8,000 to support a foster child and $20,000 or more if the youngster has severe medical or related problems. Then too, more and more women are opting to enter the job market as new employment opportunities open to women (Stone, 1990).

What can be done for youngsters who cannot find either permanent or foster-home placement? Many communities are edging toward solutions that resemble small orphanages. Most orphanages had closed in the 1950s, as the nation's social welfare system turned to programs for keeping families together and for getting people out of institutions. Orphanages became virtually extinct because of their Dickensian reputation as hellholes run by abusive caretakers. But by 1990 there were again more than 1,000 orphanages in the United States, each capable of caring for 8 to 125 children. For the squeamish, orphanages are now called "group homes" or "congregate care" institutions.

Contemporary proponents of orphanages say that foster care falls short because youngsters are frequently shuttled from one crowded home to another. In contrast, orphanages afford a stable environment and allow siblings to remain together. Then too, many children bear such severe physical and mental scars that most foster parents are unable to give them adequate care. Until there is a long-term national program providing for family intervention, drug treatment, day care, adequate housing, and better education, many children are thought to be safer and better off in orphanages (Creighton, 1990; Lundstrom, 1990).

Yet critics see the orphanage movement as spawned by people who want "simple, cheap answers." They depict orphanages as warehouses for unwanted children. And they amass evidence showing that some group facilities are as truly horrible as those of earlier decades when many orphanages were little more than de facto prisons (Creighton, 1990; Lundstrom, 1990).

Clearly, there are a growing number of orphaned youngsters in our midst. No one denies that it would be preferable to place children in permanent adoptive homes or high-quality foster homes. But there are not enough families willing to open their doors to desperate children. Most welfare professionals are reluctant to turn to an orphanage solution, yet it is a solution being forced upon the welfare system in the absence of adequate crisis intervention programs for at-risk families. Residential facilities in which there is a continuity of staff and in which the staff relates to each child on an individual basis may not be as harmful for a child as a parentless family. Unhappily, good facilities are the exception rather than the rule.

Toilet-Training: A Foundation of Adult Neurosis?
Freud believed that adult neurosis has its roots in childhood conflicts, such as those accompanying toilet-training. But research shows that children are not as psychologically fragile and vulnerable as Freud believed and that emotionally healthy personalities do not depend on Freudian child-rearing practices. *(Lew Merrim/Monkmeyer)*

easily damaged by traumatic events and emotional stress than was once thought to be true (see Chapters 2 and 10). Nor can parents expect to inoculate their children with love against future misfortune, misery, and psychopathology. And contrary to Freudian expectation, many people who had nurturant and devoted parents during their early years feel unloved as young adults.

Rather than looking for critical developmental phases in the lives of children, as did Freud and his followers, today's psychologists are increasingly examining children's everyday interactions with their parents. They find that infants learn a good many lessons from the continuities that take place in these early relationships. Parents frequently *scaffold* their interactions with youngsters through their attention and choice of behaviors; they provide a framework around which they and their babies interact. In the game of peekaboo, for example, parents initially cover their babies, then remove the covering, and finally register "surprise" at the reappearance. As infants become more skilled at the game, they remove the covering themselves. Turn-taking experiences of this sort equip children to deal with turn-taking sequences with their siblings and peers (Vandell & Wilson, 1987).

It seems to be the small moments—not the dramatic episodes or traumas—that make up the bulk of the expectations that children evolve and

bring to their later relationships. By way of illustration, consider infants' small acts of assertion that are associated with their development of autonomy. At 4 months of age children assert themselves by averting their eyes from those of a caretaker; by 12 months they can crawl or walk away; and at 18 months they can say "No." Such acts of will allow children to evolve a sense of themselves as independent beings. How parents and other caretakers react to these acts can stymie or skew an infant's normal urge for independence (Goleman, 1986d).

Psychiatrist Daniel Stern has videotaped infants and their mothers during their normal activities. His research shows the role countless small exchanges play in fashioning children's patterns for interacting with others. For instance, Stern videotaped the activity between a 25-year-old mother and her twin sons, Fred and Mark, in periodic three-hour sessions over the first fifteen months of their lives. When the boys were 3½ months old, the mother would firmly attempt to establish eye contact with Fred. When she did so, Fred would look away. However, as soon as the mother turned away, Fred would look back at her. The cycle would repeat itself until Fred was in tears. With the other twin, Mark, the mother seldom tried to force eye contact. Mark was allowed to end the exchange when he wanted. When the infants were 15 months old, Fred seemed considerably more fearful and dependent than Mark. Fred also used the same aversion of his face to end contact with other people. Mark, in contrast, greeted people openly and would look them straight in the eye. Rather than breaking eye contact by turning his face away and down, Mark would turn his head slightly to the side and up, still displaying a smile. Stern believes that a temperamental mismatch between mother and child often leads to problems like those shown by Fred. The mother's hidden beliefs and fantasies also influence the process. In this case the mother thought Fred was more "like his father" and Mark was more like herself.

Like the work of Alexander Thomas centering on the "goodness of fit" between parent and child, Stern says the attunements that evolve between children and their caretakers have long-term consequences (see Chapter 5). Parents attune themselves to their youngsters by letting them know they have a sense of their feelings. For instance, if a baby squeals in delight, the mother may give the baby a gentle shake. In doing so, the mother "matches" the child's level of excitement. Attunements are often quite subtle: The mother may pitch her voice to her baby's

Developmental Psychopathology

Of every 100 human babies, 3 are born with major defects. This figure has not changed substantially since the United States began keeping these data in the late 1960s—or for that matter, since studies dating from the 1890s in Denmark. The defects have a variety of causes. Some, like sickle-cell anemia, Tay-Sachs disease, and Down's syndrome, derive primarily from genetic or chromosomal factors (see Chapter 3). Others, like some cases of blindness, deafness, heart defects, and mental retardation, arise from prenatal teratogens, such as drug use by a pregnant woman or her infection by a disease like measles (see Chapter 4). Still others are due to the interaction among several genes and one or more environmental factors, including neural tube defects such as spina bifida and anencephaly (the absence of all or most of the brain) (Adler, 1987).

The study of these and other defects is multidisciplinary. In recent years a new discipline has been emerging that focuses on one set of problems–abnormal or dysfunctional behavior Kazdin, 1989). The discipline is called **developmental psychopathology.** It considers those "developmental" processes whereby early patterns of individual adaptation evolve to later patterns of adaptation. The aim of developmental psychopathology is to understand the origins and course of disordered behavior. But additionally, studying the links between pathology and behavior also increases our understanding of the processes of continuity and change that underlie developmental patterns (Lerner, Hertzog, Hooker, Hassibi & Thomas, 1988; Spreen, 1988; Sroufe & Rutter, 1984). So developmental psychopathology is concerned with normal processes of change, abnormal processes, and the relationship between the two. In 1990 the National Center for Health Statistics released survey findings showing that one in five youngsters are affected by developmental, learning, and behavioral disorders (some 10.7 million children and adolescents) (Friend, 1990).

One pitfall in the study of psychopathology in youngsters has been *adultomorphism*—the tendency to see in the disorders of infants and children the replicas and predecessors of seemingly similar conditions in adults. To treat children like miniature adults often exaggerates similarities while obscuring important differences between them in disordered behavior. Moreover, the manner in which symptoms are expressed may differ over the course of development. Some disorders originate early in life and tend to persist into adulthood, for example, mental retardation and infantile autism. Other disorders appear almost exclusively during childhood, such as functional enuresis (nighttime bed-wetting). Still others are more prevalent among children and adolescents, for instance, anorexia and bulimia (see Chapter 13). Additionally, some disorders typically encountered among adults may also be found among children, although in somewhat modified form, for example, schizophrenia and bipolar mood disorder (Garber, 1984; Kazdin, 1988a; Kovacs, 1989).

Most children with emotional problems grow up to be substantially normal, although compared with other youngsters, children with emotional problems are twice as likely to have psychiatric difficulties in adulthood (Rutter, 1980). A good many factors influence rates of childhood dysfunction, including age, sex, ethnic background, socioeconomic status, and locale. For example, researchers find a greater prevalence of disturbance among boys than among girls and among youths in urban rather than rural settings (Kazdin, 1989). Some of the early problems experienced by youngsters include poor peer relations, academic difficulties, and antisocial behavior. Even so, behaviors diagnosed as emotional disturbance at one age may fall within the range of normality at another. For example, separation anxiety upon leaving for school takes on quite a different meaning for a teenager than for a 6-year-old. Children's behavior also varies from context to context. A case in point are "six-hour" retarded children who function poorly in an academic environment but who perform quite well in the home or the community. Since all children at some time or another display some behaviors that are more or less abnormal, developmental psychopathologists assess behavior in terms of its intensity (excessive magnitude or extreme form), frequency (rate it is emitted), duration (whether it dissipates over time), and the number and combination of symptoms (one or two problem behaviors are of less significance than a large number of problems). Clearly, developmental psychopathology offers promise of opening new vistas in our understanding of human development (Garber, 1984). And, most significantly, it has contributed to important advances in the diagnosis, assessment, and treatment of childhood disorders (Kazdin, 1988b,). Unfortunately, however, the investigation of child and adolescent mental health problems has lagged greatly behind parallel work with adults. It seems that children do not constitute a strong "pressure group" to lobby on their own behalf in the manner that adult groups do. Yet the benefits realized by children in the course of psychotherapy closely parallel those obtained with adults (Kazdin, 1989; Tuma, 1989).

"Goodness-of-Fit" Between Children and Their Caretakers
It is the "small moments" that comprise the bulk of childhood experience. In the continual interaction that occurs in everyday life, much depends on the temperamental and social match between parent and child. Where each is comfortably attuned to the other, the flow of the childhood experience is smooth and supportive and is likely to carry over into positive and healthy relationships with other people. *(Tom Grill/Comstock)*

The Role of the Father

When men abandon the upbringing of their children to their wives, a loss is suffered by everyone, but perhaps most of all by themselves. For what they lose is the possibility of growth in themselves for being human, which the stimulation of bringing up one's children gives.—ASHLEY MONTAGU

In keeping with the strong influence that the psychoanalytic tradition has had on U.S. life, researchers have focused almost exclusively on the mother-child tie (see the boxed insert on pages 222–223, for example). At the same time, the role of the father has been largely ignored. Over the past fifteen years, however, all this has changed. We have seen something of a revolution in the thinking of child developmentalists about the importance of fathers in the development of young children (Biller, 1982; Grossman, Pollack & Golding, 1988; Lamb, 1981; Pruett, 1987). Moreover, being a father often makes a major contribution to a man's self-concept, personality functioning, and overall satisfaction with life (Levinson, Darrow, Klein, Levinson & McKee, 1978; Levy-Shiff & Israelashvili, 1988). Men are increasingly coming to recognize that a closer relationship with children is beneficial to both child and adult. Significantly, infants make a considerable contribution to the development of fatherliness through eliciting, evoking, provoking, promoting, and nudging fathering from men (Pruett, 1987).

The historic neglect of the father's role in child rearing has been linked with the notion that women are somehow more inclined toward child care and parenting than men are. One speculation is that biological predeterminers contribute to a more nurturant, "maternal" disposition in women and a more instrumental, "paternal" disposition in men (Erikson, 1964*b;* Harlow, 1971; Rossi, 1977). Others suggest that the differences between men and women are products of the distinct, socially defined roles assumed by mothers and fathers (Parsons, 1955).

Evidence supporting the view that child care is more compatible with the "natural" inclinations of one sex rather than the other is, at best, very limited (Berman, 1980; Jackson, 1989). If anything, the physiological responses that human beings display to infant coos, cries, and other signals seem to be *species-specific* (genetically preprogrammed within human organisms) (Frodi & Lamb, 1978). The ability to nurture, then, is not the property of one or the other of the sexes. But many contemporary men find they lack parenting "role models" among the men they have known.

squeal or give a quick shimmy in response to the infant's shaking a rattle. Stern contends that these behaviors give infants a reassuring sense of being emotionally connected to other people. Patterns of life-long social relationships begin with such simple encounters. But contrary to Freudian assertions, the psychological imprints of the early years are not irrevocably set for the entire life span. Relationships throughout life continually shape and reshape our working schemes or models of social relationships. Viewed in this fashion, no single event in childhood is the source of a psychological difficulty in adulthood. Rather, the problems arise from an accretion of small episodes (Goleman, 1986*d*).

What many of them end up asking themselves is not "What would my wife do?" but "What would my mother do?" (Pruett, 1987). In short, our culture prepares females for parenting to a far greater extent than it does males. Simultaneously, women in the Western world have traditionally been expected to be the ones to assume primary responsibility for child care. Nonetheless, societies throughout the world show considerable variation in their definitions of the parenting roles. For instance, in a survey of 141 societies, fathers in 45 societies (32 percent) maintained a "regular, close" or "frequent, close" proximity with the infant. At the other extreme, in 33 societies (23 percent), fathers exhibited no or rare instances of close proximity (Crano & Aronoff, 1978).

Increasingly, researchers are concluding that men have at least the potential to be as good caretakers of children as women are. Ross D. Parke and his colleagues (Parke, 1979; Parke & Sawin, 1977) have observed the behavior of both middle-class and lower-class parents of newborns on hospital maternity wards. Fathers are just as responsive as mothers to their infants' vocalizations and movements. Fathers touch, look at, talk to, rock, and kiss their babies in much the same fashion as mothers do. However, in response to their infants' vocalizations, fathers are more likely than mothers to increase their vocalization rate; mothers, in contrast, are more likely to react with touching. And fathers, when alone with their infants, are as protective, giving, and stimulating as mothers. In fact, fathers are more likely than mothers to hold their babies and to look at them. Mothers exceed fathers in only one kind of stimulation—they smile at their babies more.

Parke and his associates have measured the amount of milk that is left over in a baby's bottle after feeding time. Babies drink virtually the same amount of milk when fathers do the feeding as when mothers do. Furthermore, fathers are equally competent in correctly reading subtle changes in infants' behavior and reacting to them. Fathers respond to such distress signs as sneezing, coughing, or spitting up just as quickly as mothers do. At these times fathers (like mothers) momentarily cease feeding, look more closely to check for any problems, and talk to the baby. However, fathers tend to leave child care to their wives when both parents are present.

All of this is not to say that mothers and fathers are interchangeable. Each makes his or her own unique contribution to the care and development of children. Research suggests that the mother-child and father-child relationships may well be qualitatively different and may have a different influence on a child's development (Biller, 1982; Brachfeld-Child, 1986; Bridges, Connell & Belsky, 1988; Harris & Morgan, 1991; Lamb, 1975, 1977a, 1981; McGovern, 1990; Power, 1985; Stevenson, Leavitt, Thompson & Roach, 1988). Michael E. Lamb (1977a) finds, for instance, that mothers most often hold babies to perform caretaking functions, while fathers most often hold babies to play with them. Indeed, according to some studies, fathers spend four to five times as much time playing with their infants as in caring for them— diapering them, feeding them, washing them, and the like. And Henry B. Biller (1974, 1976) notes that whereas mothers are more likely to inhibit their children's exploration of the environment, fathers encourage curiosity and challenge their children to attempt new cognitive and motor activities.

Researchers similarly find that U.S. mothers play more verbal games with their babies. The games are characterized by "turn-taking" dialogues composed of rapidly alternating bursts of words or cooing and brief pauses. Mothers also play more conventional games, such as

"My mom doesn't bug me about my homework anymore. My father taught me how to look busy."

(Cole © 1990 from the *Wall Street Journal*. Permission, Cartoon Features Syndicate.)

Blaming Mothers

Psychotherapists have traditionally assumed that when youngsters develop problems or get into trouble their mothers must have done something wrong. Just as the flu comes from viruses and strep throat comes from bacteria, so emotional and behavioral problems are seen as coming from inadequate mothers. Indeed, mothers have fared rather poorly in psychological literature. If they veer too far in one direction, they are deemed cold and rejecting; too far in the other, overemotional and overprotective. Even attentive mothering that appears outwardly warm, supportive, and loving comes across in psychological literature as "enmeshed" and "fused"—in brief, as emotionally disturbed. And whereas mothers are depicted according to how they *are* (usually negatively), fathers are described by what they *do* (frequently positively) (Birns & Hay, 1988; Caplan, 1989; Smith, 1990).

Much psychotherapy has had its roots in the work and insights of Sigmund Freud. Significantly, Freud tended to dismiss mothers in his writings with a few quick, judgmental strokes. For instance, he devoted only four sentences to Dora's mother in his famous "Case of Hysteria" although the piece runs 120 pages (Freud, 1940; Decker, 1990; Smith, 1990). He never met the mother, but nonetheless wrote: "From the accounts given me by the girl and her father I was led to imagine her as an uncultivated woman and above all as a foolish one, who had concentrated all her interests upon domestic affairs. . . . She presented the picture, in fact, of what might be called the 'housewife's psychosis.' She had no understanding of her children's more active interests, and was occupied all day long in cleaning the house."

Idealistic myths surrounding the "good mother" have led countless U.S. women to assume much of the blame for their children's subsequent difficulties and problems. These mothers imagine that they caused irreparable psychological damage by having yelled at their youngsters, used television as a baby sitter, stayed late at work, forgotten to serve a vegetable, or left a bad marriage. Not too long ago childhood autism—a severe and debilitating form of mental illness—was attributed to the cold and rejecting behaviors of "refrigerator mothers." And schizophrenia was seen as the product of intrusive, ambivalent, and conflicted mothering. Now these disorders are recognized as having strong biological and genetic determinants. By the same token a generation of psychoanalysts and psychiatrists popularized the notion that the right mother and the right amount of mother love could overcome most, if not all, obstacles (Smith, 1990).

Readers should not interpret these comments as suggesting that children are not harmed by poor parenting nor benefited by good parenting. Some mothers—and fathers as well—are perfectly dreadful. Rather, we need to expand our panorama and see the multiplicity of factors that influence human development. This textbook devotes over 600 pages to the task. Moreover, parenting occurs within a social context. Consider, for instance, those youngsters residing in drug-infested, inner-city housing projects. When these youngsters are

peekaboo. In contrast, fathers play more physical games with their children. They tend to touch their infants in rhythmic tapping patterns. And they also play more rough-and-tumble games, such as tossing the baby in the air (Parke, 1979; Power & Parke, 1983; Russell, 1982). One should not conclude that either type of parental stimulation is superior to the other. They are simply different. Each parent affords the child somewhat different kinds of experiences. However, many of these gender differences in play styles are not found among Swedish fathers and mothers (Lamb, Frodi, Hwang, Frodi & Steinberg, 1982).

Fathers are important in still another respect. Studies show that a mother performs better in the parenting role when the father provides her with emotional support and encouragement (Belsky, 1981, 1990; Dickstein & Parke, 1988; Pedersen, 1980; Zur-Szpiro & Longfellow, 1982). The man who gives warmth, love, and ego gratification to his wife helps her feel good about herself, and she is then more likely to pass on these feelings to their child. Indeed, many of today's fathers are different from those of a decade or so ago. They are much more likely to have been with the wife at the delivery of the baby. And they are less likely to take a traditional view of their role (Crouter, Perry-Jenkins, Huston & Hale, 1987). But by getting involved in the nurturing process, they can create feelings of competition with the wife and marital strain. Some researchers find that when fathers become involved in day-to-day parenting, they feel more involved and competent as parents. But they also tend to be more critical of the wife's parenting. And although the wives of these men praise their husbands' parenting, they them-

evaluated at mental-health centers, they are often judged victims of "neglected and umotivated" mothering. Yet their mothers are also "victims," frequently lacking the power and resources necessary for parenting and for protecting their youngsters from neighborhood perils. The mothers have little money, few ways to earn a livelihood, no physical safety, and limited networks of social support. As Janna Malamud Smith (1990, p. 38) observes: "Primary responsibility for raising children cannot be simply equated with primary responsibility for harming children."

American families and communities have undergone vast changes in recent decades. Yesterday's extended families and involved neighbors (particularly those found in working-class ethnic neighborhoods) have progressively given way to today's television sets, dangerous streets, and impersonal malls. Family rituals, even dinners together, have declined, and more and more children come home to empty homes. Journalist Richard Louv spent three years traversing the nation, interviewing more than 3,000 children, parents, teachers, volunteers, and professionals. He recounts how large numbers of youngsters must care for themselves and spend much of their time on their own. For instance, one child noted that her parents seemed consumed by their jobs and that she and her eight brothers and sisters were left to "do whatever we want." She cooked her own food and handled "everything myself." She said, "I never really knew my parents too well, or my grandparents or any of my relatives. . . . It's kind of like a separate world of mine." This isolation of children from their parents leaves Louv deeply troubled, and he expresses worry that U.S. childhood and family life are unraveling.

Other institutions are unable to compensate for overwhelmed parents because of stingy public finances. Some libraries have been compelled to cut back on their hours. Many inner-city schools have become little more than custodial institutions with the education of children at a bare minimum. Good social workers and day-care workers are becoming increasingly difficult to find and retain at wages below those of trash collectors and building custodians. All the while the U.S. workplace operates largely oblivious of family dictates and pressures.

Louv's interviews reveal that Americans are concerned with these developments and are eager to make our institutions more responsive to children and families. He offers a vision of families more interconnected with one another and with schools, libraries, and community centers, all affording a sense of belonging to young and old alike. And he believes that corporations need to assume greater responsibility for providing part-time employment, parental leaves, and day care for children and the elderly. In sum, the future of the nation's children is not the simple province of mothers but of fathers, relatives, friends, employers, librarians, neighbors, teachers—indeed the entire society and its institutions.

---

selves voice less satisfaction with life and are more self-critical of how they carry out their family responsibilities (Baruch & Barnett, 1986).

Research seems to indicate that boys are more affected by the absence of a father than girls are (Biller, 1982; Levy-Shiff, 1982). In comparison with other boys, boys from fatherless homes exhibit less well-internalized standards of moral judgment. They tend to evaluate the seriousness of misbehavior according to the probability of detection or punishment rather than in terms of interpersonal relations and social responsibility (Hoffmann, 1971). Research data also reveal that the absence of a positive father-son relationship impairs a boy's overall academic achievement and his IQ test performance (Biller, 1971; Carlsmith, 1964; Epstein & Radin, 1975; Nugent, 1991). The extent of the impairment is greater the younger the child when he lost his father and the longer the father has been absent (Blanchard & Biller, 1971; Carlsmith, 1964). Moreover, one of the most consistently reported effects of the father's absence on a boy is a deterioration in school performance (Lamb, 1981). And the mother's remarriage, especially if it occurs early in the child's life, appears to be associated with an improvement in intellectual performance (Lessing, Zagorin & Nelson, 1970; Santrock, 1972).

Note, however, that the presence of the father is no guarantee of adequate fathering (Belsky, Youngblade, Rovine & Volling, 1991). The quality of the father-child relationship seems to be more important than the father's mere physical tenancy (Lamb, 1981). Perhaps in the final analysis, the matter is not so much one of fathering or mothering as one of parenting.

The important complementary role of the father points up the need for modern societies to give wider thought and support to staggered working hours, temporary leave time to deal with family needs, and paternity leaves (Lamb & Sagi, 1983; Pruett, 1987). In the past twenty years Sweden has launched a major effort to involve fathers more actively in the rearing of their children. It has extended to fathers most of the child-care benefits—such as time off at nearly full pay—that it extends to mothers. According to Sweden's Ministry for Social Affairs, about 10 to 12 percent of eligible fathers now take paternity leave. Another aspect of the program allows parents of preschoolers to work shortened weeks at little loss in pay. Parents are also given time off to care for sick children.

Multiple Mothering

In the United States the preferred arrangement for raising children is the nuclear family, which consists of two parents and their children. The view that mothering should be provided by one figure has been celebrated and extolled by most professionals as the key to good mental health (Bowlby 1969). Yet this view is a culture-bound perspective, for children throughout the world are successfully reared in situations of **multiple mothering**—an arrangement in which responsibility for a child's care is dispersed among several people.

In some cases one major mother figure shares mothering with a variety of mother surrogates, including aunts, grandmothers, older cousins, nonkin neighbors, or co-wives. Consider, for example, the diffused nurturance given a child among the Ifaluk of Micronesia (Spiro, 1947, pp. 89–97):

> For the Westerner, the amount of handling the infant receives is almost fantastic. The infant, particularly after it can crawl, is never allowed to remain in the arms of one person. In the course of a half hour conversation, the baby might change hands ten times, being passed from one person to another. . . . The adults, as well as the older children, love to fondle the babies and to play with them, with the result that the infant does not stay with one person very long. . . . Should an infant cry, it is immediately picked up in an adult's arms, cuddled, consoled or fed. . . . There is little distinction between one's own relatives and "strangers." . . . If he needs something anyone will try to satisfy his need. Every house is open to him and he never has to learn that some houses are different from others.

Israeli Kibbutzim

Beginning in 1908, Jews from the ghettos of Eastern Europe undertook the establishment of some 280 rural settlements in what is now the state of Israel. They based the communities on social equality, collective production and education, and direct participatory democracy. All incomes are pooled, members use a communal dining hall, and children are cared for and educated in communal children's homes. *(Louis Goldman/Photo Researchers)*

Another fascinating approach to child care is found in the Israeli agricultural settlements that have a collective form of social and economic life (termed *kibbutzim*). From early infancy children are reared in a nursery with other children by two or three professional caretakers. Their own mothers visit them regularly and are primarily responsible for meeting their children's affectional needs. The burden of discipline and punishment falls primarily upon the professional caretakers (Devereux et al., 1974). Despite this arrangement of "concomitant mothering," systematic observation, testing, and clinical assessment have demonstrated that kibbutz children are within the normal range in intelligence, motor development, mental health, and social adjustment (Kohen-Raz, 1968; Maccoby & Feldman, 1972; Moyles & Wolins, 1971; Regev, Beit-Hallahmi & Sharabany, 1980).

Child Day-Care Centers

More than half of U.S. mothers of preschool children are in the work force (compared with 14 percent in 1950 and 29 percent in 1970). This trend, and the increase in single-parent families, has given considerable impetus to the child day-care movement in the United States. According to a 1990 Census Bureau study, U.S. families spend an estimated $15.5 billion annually on child care. Families in which the employed mother lives in poverty spend about 25 percent of their income for child-care services; better-off families pay about 6 percent of their family income on child care. Of those working mothers who use child care arrangements for their children under age 5, 29.9 percent make provision for care in their own home; another 35.6 percent secure care in someone else's home; 24.4 percent use organized child-care facilities; and 8.9 percent of the mothers care for the child at work (Trost, 1990). Overall, the child-care arrangements of U.S. working parents break down at a surprising rate. Although most parents strive for continuity, about one-half of employed mothers who pay for child care change their arrangements each year (Shellenbarger, 1991).

Sharply divergent views exist among Americans regarding the desirability of day-care facilities. For that matter, experts in child development are themselves in disagreement. Some worry that day care may do serious emotional and psychological damage to children—damage that may not show up until the teen or adult years. Others say that good-quality day care does not help children, but it does not hurt them either. And still others applaud day care as liberating for the mother and enriching for the child. In any event, modern societies are increasingly confronting this question: How are we to manage the successful care and rearing of future generations of children when parents spend a substantial portion of time at work away from home?

Many critics of day care say that children require continuity, stability, and predictability in their care. Followers of the psychoanalytic tradition emphasize that a child's emotional breadth and depth and capacity to love are derived from the experience of love in the early years. But in a center children must share the attention of a day-care worker with other youngsters. Add to this vacations and job turnover, and a child ends up with no one special person to be close to. Complicating matters, problem children are rarely the favorites of overburdened workers, yet they are usually the children who need love the most (Fraiberg, 1977).

Over a decade ago Jerome Kagan, a noted Harvard developmental psychologist, also thought day care for children was a poor idea. But in recent years he has reversed his opposition on the basis of research he undertook with Richard B. Kearsley and Philip R. Zelazo (1978). Kagan and his associates set up a day-care facility for thirty-three children from middle- and working-class homes in the South End of Boston. The children entered the center at around 4 months of age and left it at 29 months. The caretakers were carefully selected on the basis of their nurturing qualities, and the center afforded a ratio of one worker for each three or four children.

Like other investigators of day care, Kagan and his associates compared the infants placed in day-care facilities with home-reared children of the same age, social class, and ethnic background. The researchers found that the day-care children were not much different—intellectually, emotionally, or socially—from their home-raised counterparts. And the day-care children were neither more nor less attached to their mothers than the other children. However, the home-raised youngsters were somewhat more socially advanced at 29 months of age than the day-care children.

Much day-care research has been undertaken in university-based or university-connected centers. Such centers have high staff-child ratios and well-designed programs directed at fostering the children's cognitive, emotional, and social development (many of the child-care workers are highly motivated and dedicated students preparing for careers as teachers). Yet most of the day care currently available to North American parents is not of this type and quality. Unfortunately, where group size is large, the ratio of caretakers to children is low, and the staff is untrained or poorly supervised, a child's well-being is compromised (Belsky, 1990; Vandell, Henderson & Wilson, 1988; Vandell & Powers, 1983).

There is an additional problem associated with low-quality day-care facilities. They commonly function as networks for spreading a variety of diseases, particularly hepatitis A, diarrhea, dysentery, and other intestinal illnesses. Although day-care centers often serve more meals than a restaurant on a given day, their workers typically have little training in handling food and display lapses in sanitary routines. And since children enter and leave many of the centers in an erratic pattern, there is considerable opportunity for the mixing of infected and susceptible children.

Some years ago Jay Belsky and Laurence D. Steinberg (1978) surveyed the research then available on day care. They concluded that the day-care experience neither improves nor impairs most children's intellectual development. For economically disadvantaged children, however, the day-care experience can lessen the decline in IQ scores that typically takes place among children from "high-risk" environments. Furthermore, high-quality day care is not disruptive of children's emotional bonds with their mothers. Finally, day care increases the degree to which children interact, both positively and negatively, with peers.

Research in the intervening years has for the most part confirmed these earlier findings (Burchinal, Lee & Ramey, 1989; Field, 1991; Phillips, McCartney & Scarr, 1987). However, Belsky (1984b, 1988, 1990) has since reversed his position. From his research involving the strange-situation procedure, Belsky now concludes that babies who spend more than twenty hours a week in nonmaternal care during the *first* year of life are at increased risk of forming an "insecure attachment" to their mothers and developing emotional and behavioral problems as they grow older. The children evidence greater aggression, noncompliance, and even social withdrawal in the preschool and elementary school years (Belsky & Rovine, 1987; Belsky & Rovine, 1988). Belsky believes that mothers are typically more sensitive to and attentive of a child's first efforts at communication than are employed babysitters. In addition, working parents often find their work so consuming and stressful that they have little energy left over for their youngsters. But, by the same token, Belsky emphasizes that his findings do not point in any consistent ways to risks to day-care children after the first 12 to 18 months. In fact, Belsky (1990) reiterates his view that high-quality preschool day care for youngsters older than 1 year of age can positively influence child development. And he observes that "even mediocre care is likely to pose little long-term threat to a child's well-being if the family is harmonious and nurturant and the work place is rewarding to parents" (1990, p. 897). Unfortunately, however, many youngsters are doubly penalized because family characteristics and child-care quality tend to be related: Parents who experience more stress in their lives, who engage in less optimal child-rearing practices, and whose youngsters have formed less secure maternal attachments are more likely to place their youngsters in low-quality child care than are less stressed parents, parents employing more optimal child-rearing practices, and parents of youngsters with more secure maternal attachments (Howes, 1990; Howes, Rodning, Galluzzo & Myers, 1988; Howes & Stewart, 1987). And when sources of risk accu-

mulate, child development is more likely to be compromised (Belsky, 1990; Howes, 1990).

Some evidence suggests that children enrolled in day care for extended periods of time show increased aggression toward peers and adults and decreased cooperation with adults. But this result may be a culture-bound outcome. Studies of peer-group socialization in Israel, the USSR, and a number of other contemporary societies reveal quite different outcomes. In brief, the U.S. peer group may simply predispose children toward greater aggressiveness, impulsiveness, and egocentrism.

Unquestionably, we would like solid answers to questions regarding the effects of day care on children. Yet most researchers recognize that we still have much to learn about the impact of day care on children, parents, the family, and social institutions in general (Belsky, 1990; Clarke-Stewart, 1989; Rodman, Pratto & Nelson, 1985; Schindler, Moely & Frank, 1987). For now, perhaps the safest conclusion we can make is this: Most research suggests that high-quality day care is an acceptable alternative child care arrangement. Children display remarkable resilience. Infants around the world are raised under a great variety of conditions; the day-care arrangement is just one of them. The effects of day care depend to some extent on the amount of time a child spends at a center and on the quality of parent-child interaction during the time that the family is together. And as has been pointed out in previous chapters, home care, in and of itself, does not guarantee secure attachments or healthy social and emotional development.

We would be amiss were we to conclude our discussion without pointing out that child day care within this country is in a sorry state. Tales of woe are a common bond among contemporary parents. Public opinion polls show that only 8 percent of parents of preschoolers believe the child-care system is working "very well," 38 percent have little faith in the system, and 53 percent say it is working "only somewhat well." Much dissatisfaction lies with the cost, availability, and quality of the care. And, significantly, financially well-off Americans are just as dissatisfied as those who are poor. Moreover, some 84 percent of parents believe that quality child care should be provided to all youngsters regardless of their parents' income (Harris, 1989).

The United States has simply not come to terms with the requirements and ramifications of rearing a generation of children outside the home while their parents work. Most states are lax in their regulation of day-care centers, and there is an absence of federal policies and guidelines (Wingert & Kantrowitz, 1990). Moreover, parents find that child care is costly and the vast majority cannot afford to buy quality day care at full market prices. Yet, simultaneously, child-care workers are poorly paid: They earn 30 percent to 60 percent less per hour than do those who serve children as kindergarten or elementary school teachers, and they earn 40 percent less than other workers at the same levels of education (Fuchs, 1990). Poorly trained child-care workers, coupled with a high turnover rate, create an unstable environment for children who need consistency and dependability in their lives. In sum, working parents in the United States are faced with a serious problem: Day care is often of poor quality, very costly, and hard to find. In contrast, Western European nations such as Sweden have well-developed and competent national child day-care systems (Cutler, 1989; Lamb et al., 1988).

SUMMARY

1. Humanness is a social product that arises as children interact with the significant people in their environment. Erik Erikson stresses the importance of an infant's early years in fashioning a basic trust in others, an essential foundation for successful social functioning.

2. Emotions perform a number of functions. First, emotions seem to have evolved as adaptive processes that enhance survival. Second, emotions influence the mental operations we use in information processing. And third, by reading other people's facial, gestural, postural, and vocal cues, we gain indirect access to their emotional states.

3. Psychologists influenced by ethological theory have played a central role in the recent burst of studies on the emotional life of children. Carroll E. Izard finds that babies have intense feelings from the moment of birth. But at first, their inner feelings are limited to distress, disgust, and interest. In the course of their maturation new emotions develop in a regular, orderly fashion.

4. Changes in the development of emotion have been explained from differing theoretical perspectives. Cognitive developmentalists look chiefly to shifts that occur in cognitive structures or schemes. In contrast, nativists say that in many instances emotional expressions operate independently of thought.

5. Attachment behaviors promote proximity between helpless, dependent infants and protective caretakers. But attachment also fosters social cognitive skills. Psychologists commonly use the strange-situation procedure to capture the quality of the attachment in the parent-child relationship. The patterns of attachment behavior revealed by the strange-situation procedure reflect the quality of maternal caregiving children receive during their first twelve months of life.

6. A good many children display stranger anxiety during the second six months of life. However, infants are both attracted to and wary of novel objects; hence, the situation does much to determine which reaction will be activated.

7. Children reared in institutional settings generally do not develop well compared with children reared in home surroundings. The impairment experienced by many institutionalized children derives from conditions of social and sensory deprivation.

8. Freudians stress the view that the development of emotionally healthy personalities is associated with breast feeding, a prolonged period of nursing, gradual weaning, a self-demand nursing schedule, delayed and patient bowel and bladder training, and freedom from punishment. However, research has provided little or no support for these psychoanalytic assumptions.

9. The mother-child and father-child relationships are qualitatively different and apparently have a different impact on a child's development.

10. Infants around the world are raised under a great variety of conditions. Among them are multiple mothering and child day care. Children display remarkable resilience. Research suggests that multiple mothering and high-quality day care are acceptable child-care arrangements.

KEY TERMS

Attachment   An affectional bond that one individual forms for another and that endures across time and space.

Developmental Psychopathology   A discipline that studies those "developmental" processes whereby early patterns of individual adaptation evolve to later patterns of adaptation.

Emotion   The physiological changes, subjective experiences, and expressive behaviors that are involved in such feelings as love, joy, grief, and rage.

Maternal Deprivation   The absence of normal mothering resulting in psychological damage and physical deterioration in children. Since the term "maternal deprivation" has become so highly charged and a synonym for all that is destructive in child care, most authorities prefer to avoid it and use terms that refer to specific conditions, such as "social deprivation" and "sensory deprivation."

Multiple Mothering   An arrangement in which responsibility for a child's care is dispersed among several people. In some cases one major mother figure shares mothering with a variety of mother surrogates.

Person Permanence   The notion that an individual exists independently of immediate visibility.

Social Referencing   A process in which an inexperienced person relies on a more experienced person's interpretation of an event.

Stranger Anxiety   Increasing wariness of strangers shown by infants beginning around the eighth month, although some infants show fear of strangers at 6 and 7 months of age.

Strange Situation   A procedure developmental psychologists use to capture the quality of the attachment in the parent-child relationship.

Part Four

Early Childhood: 2 to 6

Chapter 9

EARLY CHILDHOOD: EXPANDING COMPETENCIES

Cognitive Development

Intelligence

◆

Intelligence and the Nature-Nurture Controversy ◆

The Early Development of Intelligence ◆ **Conceptual Foundations for Learning**

Information Processing and Memory

Early Memory ◆ **Information Processing** ◆ **Metacognition and Metamemory** ◆

Categorizing as a Memory Strategy ◆ **Rehearsing as a Memory Strategy**

Cognitive Foundations for Social Interaction

Roles ◆ **The Self**

Gender Identification

Hormonal Influences on Gender Behaviors ◆ **Social Influence**

on Gender Behaviors ◆ **Theories Regarding the Acquisition**

of Gender Identities ◆ **Mothers, Fathers, and Gender Typing**

◆

*Passing hence from infancy, I came
to boyhood or rather it came to me, displacing
infancy. Nor did that depart—(for whither
went it?)—and yet it was no more.*

Confessions of St. Augustine

During the period between age 2 and 6, children enlarge their repertoire of behaviors. They refine their previously learned skills and evolve new ones for relating to other people and to the larger world. By doing so, they become progressively integrated into the broader context of group life. And in this way the child's needs and capacities are fused with the ideas and sentiments of the culture. The process is one of psychic amalgamation, in which a child becomes human and society perpetuates itself from one generation to the next (Davis, 1949).

Simultaneously, children progressively develop as social beings in their own right. Erik Erikson (see Chapter 2) suggests that children acquire a sense of autonomy or independence as they struggle with their own conflicting needs and rebel against parental controls. These upheavals find expression in what are popularly called the "terrible twos," when toddlers display negativism and temper tantrums. Children come to see themselves as individuals who are separate from their parents, although still dependent on them (Crockenberg & Litman, 1990; Erikson, 1963; Kuczynski & Kochenska, 1990).

During this period children become physically better coordinated. Walking, climbing, reaching, grasping, and releasing are no longer simply activities in their own right but, rather, the means for new endeavors. Their developing skills give children new ways to explore the world and to accomplish new things. All the while they be-

come more adept at gathering and processing information (Bartsch & Wellman, 1989; Beal & Belgrad, 1990; Hale, 1990; Moses & Flavell, 1990).

In turn, the expansion of their social and physical worlds confronts children with new developmental requirements. According to Erikson, children between 3 and 5 years old need to acquire a sense of initiative. They actively seek new opportunities for affecting the environment and, in doing so, achieve a sense of their own effectiveness in the world. Early childhood thus lays the cognitive and social foundations for the more complex life of the school years (see Table 9-1).

Cognitive Development

In the preschool period mental development is characterized by the rapid expansion of cognitive abilities. Children become more adept at obtaining information, ordering it, and using it. Gradually, these abilities evolve into the attribute called *intelligence*. Whereas sensorimotor processes largely dominate development during infancy, a significant transition occurs after 18 months toward the more abstract processes of reasoning, inference, and problem solving. By the time children are 7 years old, they have developed a diversified set of cognitive skills that are functionally related to the elements of adult intelligence.

Intelligence

For lay people and psychologists alike the concept of intelligence is a rather fuzzy notion. In some ways intelligence resembles electricity.

Table 9-1

Motor and Skills Development Among Preschoolers

Age 2	Age 3	Age 4	Age 5
Can run	Can stand on one foot	Can do stunts on a tricycle	Can skip
Can kick a large ball	Can hop on both feet	Can descend a ladder, alternating feet	Can hop on one foot for 10 feet
Can jump 12 inches	Can ride a tricycle	Can gallop	Can copy squares
Can navigate stairs alone	Can propel a wagon with one foot	Can cut on a line with a scissors	Can copy letters and numbers
Can construct tower of six to eight blocks	Can copy a circle	Can make crude letters	Can throw a ball well
Can turn pages of a book singly	Can draw a straight line	Can catch a ball with elbows in front of the body	Can fasten buttons that are visible to the eye
Can put on simple clothing	Can pour from a pitcher	Can dress self	Can catch a ball with elbows at the sides
Can hold a glass with one hand	Can catch a ball with arms extended		

Like electricity, intelligence "is measurable, and its effect, but not its properties, can be only imprecisely described" (Bischof, 1976, p. 137). Even so, David Wechsler (1975), a psychologist who devised a number of widely used intelligence tests, has proposed a definition that has won considerable acceptance. He views **intelligence** as a global capacity to understand the world, think rationally, and cope resourcefully with the challenges of life. Seen in this light, intelligence is a capacity for acquiring knowledge and functioning rationally and effectively, rather than the possession of a fund of knowledge. Intelligence has captivated the interest of psychologists for a variety of reasons, including a desire to devise ways of teaching people to better understand and increase their intellectual abilities.

Intelligence as a Composite of Abilities One recurrent issue dividing psychologists is whether intelligence is a single, general intellectual capacity or a composite of many special, independent abilities. Alfred Binet (1857–1911), the French psychologist who devised the first widely used intelligence test in 1905, viewed intelligence as a general capacity for comprehension and reasoning. Although this test used many different types of items, Binet assumed that he was measuring a general ability that found expression in the performance of many kinds of tasks.

In England Charles Spearman (1863–1945) quickly rose to eminence in psychological circles by advancing a somewhat different view. Spearman (1904, 1927) concluded that there is a general intellectual ability, labeled the *g* (for "general") factor, that is employed for abstract reasoning and problem solving. He viewed the *g* factor as a basic intellectual power that pervades all of a person's mental activity. However, since an individual's performance across various tasks is not perfectly consistent, Spearman identified special factors (the *s* factors) that are peculiar to given tasks—for instance, arithmetic or spatial relations. This approach is known as the **two-factor theory of intelligence.** More recently, J. P. Guilford (1967) has carried the tradition further by identifying 120 factors of intellect. Not all psychologists are happy, however, with such minute distinctions. Many prefer to speak of "general ability"—a mixture of abilities that can be more or less arbitrarily measured by a general-purpose intelligence test.

Different Kinds of Intelligence In recent years psychologist Howard Gardner (1983, 1985) has been working with gifted children. On the basis of

Early Intelligence Testing
With the development of IQ tests in the early 1900s, seemingly a scientific instrument was at hand for evaluating the intellectual capabilities of the members of various ethnic groups. Immigrants in the United States from non-English-speaking nations tended to score rather poorly. With a score of about 100 considered "normal," the average score of Jews, Hungarians, Italians, and Poles was about 87. Some psychologists like Henry Goddard concluded that these groups were intellectually inferior—indeed, even "feeble-minded." *(Culver Pictures)*

his experiences, he suggests that there are seven distinctive intelligences: linguistic, logical-mathematical, spatial, musical, bodily-kinesthetic, and two forms of personal intelligence—interpersonal (knowing how to deal with others) and intrapersonal (knowledge of oneself). Consider, for instance, the value of interpersonal or social intelligence. It allows individuals to take maximum advantage of the resources of other people. Gardner observes: "Your intelligence can be in other people, if you know how to get them to help you. In life, that's the best strategy: mobilize other people" (quoted by Goleman, 1990, p. B1). However, Gardner not only carves up the mind into these separate faculties but also contends that the separate intelligences are located in different areas of the brain. So when a person suffers damage to the brain through a stroke or tumor, all abilities do not break down equally. And youngsters who are precocious in one area are often unremarkable in others. In fact, otherwise retarded people occasionally exhibit extraordinary ability in one area, most commonly mathematical calculation. (Retarded people of this type are called "idiots savants.") These observations lead Gardner to say that the much-maligned in-

Creativity

We commonly value creativity as the highest form of mental endeavor and achievement. Whereas intelligence implies quick-wittedness in learning the predictable, creativity implies original and useful responses. We often assume that high intelligence and creativity go hand in hand. Yet psychologists find that high intelligence does not ensure creativity. Research reveals that differences between above-average and very high scores on intelligence tests have at best only a low association with creativity (Hattie & Rogers, 1986; Kershner & Ledger, 1985; Moran, Milgram, Sawyers & Fu, 1983; Wallach & Kogan, 1965). Even so, although high intelligence does not guarantee creative activity, low intelligence seems to work against it. An above-average intelligence—although not necessarily exceptional intelligence—seems essential for creative achievement (Mac Kinnon, 1975).

In some cases too much brainpower can even get in the way of creativity. Psychologist Dean Keith Simonton (1984, 1988a, 1988b) has looked into the lives of many renowned creators and leaders of the past century. He concludes that the optimal IQ for creativity is about nineteen points above the average of people in a given field. Nor is formal education essential. Many famous scientists, philosophers, writers, artists, and composers never complete college. Formal education often instills role methods for doing things that blind people to offbeat but creative solutions. Albert Einstein (1949, p. 17) describes the stifling effects that formal education had on his early scientific creativity: "The hitch in this was the fact that one had to cram all this stuff into one's mind for the examinations, whether one liked it or not. This coercion had such a deterring effect on me that, after I had passed the final examination, I found the consideration of any scientific problem distasteful for an entire year."

Creative people seldom have bland personalities. Psychologists at the Institute of Personality Assessment and Research (located on the Berkeley campus of the University of California) have investigated the characteristics of creative individuals. They provide a unified picture of the productive scientist as an individual who is challenged by the unknown, by contradictions, and by apparent disorder. Such individuals are somewhat distant and detached in their interpersonal relationships, preferring to deal with things and abstractions rather than with people. They are self-confident, self-sufficient, self-directing, and independent; resist pressures toward conformity; and often have strong, forceful personalities (Barron, 1969; Taylor & Barron, 1963).

Psycholinguist Vera John-Steiner (1986) interviewed one hundred men and women active in the humanities, arts, and sciences, and she sifted through the notebooks, diaries, and biographies of creative individuals such as Albert Einstein and Leo Tolstoy. She finds that scientists and artists almost invariably mention their talent and interest was revealed early in life and was often encouraged and nurtured by their parents or teachers. During her childhood British novelist Margaret Drabble and her family wrote plays together and put out their own magazine. And biologist Julian Huxley shared his interest in birds and flowers with his family. Occasionally, a teacher has an inspirational role. Writer James Baldwin was influenced as a child by a teacher who "encouraged his reading, discussed with him the movies he saw, shared with him some of her views on . . . world

telligence quotient (IQ) ought to be replaced with an "intellectual profile."

The relative importance of these seven intelligences differs from one historical period to another and from one culture to another. In a hunting-and-gathering society an ability to add and subtract affords few social benefits compared with those that flow from being quick, agile, and well coordinated. In the Caroline Islands of the South Pacific a Puluwat boy casts off in the dead of night, using his knowledge of waves, winds, and stars to reach any of hundreds of islands merely by fitting his observation to the spatial map in his head. And among the Japanese, interpersonal intelligence—the ability to work well in group settings and to arrive at harmonious decisions—assumes key importance.

But critics such as Sandra Scarr (1985a) dispute Gardner. They say that he is really talking about talents, not intelligences. They have difficulty calling "intelligence" what people typically label "human virtues."

Intelligence as Process   Quite different from an "abilities" approach to intelligence are those perspectives that view intelligence as a *process*—they are not so much interested in *what* we know but in *how* we know. Proponents of this approach are less concerned with the "stuff" that allows people to think intelligently and more concerned

issues . . . and demonstrated to him that even a white person can act with courage in the face of white racism" (quoted in John-Steiner, 1986). Even so, a good many creative individuals do not spend their childhood years basking in parental love and warmth. Instead, rather cool and even detached relationships are commonplace between parents and their creative sons and daughters. Perhaps such parents inadvertently encourage a rebellious attitude in their children that fosters independent thinking and action (Siegelman, 1973).

Most psychologists agree that a natural gift is not sufficient to produce creative effort. What seems to be required is the fortuitous convergence of innate talent and a receptive environment (Greeno, 1989). According to one view, creativity requires that a person reorganize a tie or connection with some situation in the world, so creativity entails much more than a reorganization of the thinking apparatus. Creative accomplishment is exceedingly difficult precisely because it necessitates changing not merely the contents and organization of one's mind but an inclusive system of relationships involving the world, other people, or an established set of cultural concepts (Getzels & Csikszentmihalyi, 1976). For this reason it may be much easier to stifle creativity than to stimulate it (Amabile, 1983; Bales, 1984; Tyler, 1983).

When people are inspired by their own interests and enjoyment, they are more likely to explore unlikely paths, take risks, and in the end produce something unique and useful. Dr. Salvador E. Luria of the Massachusetts Institute of Technology, mentor to several famous scientists and himself a Nobel laureate, says, "The most important thing is to leave a good person alone." Adds Dr. Mahlon B.

Hoagland, scientific director of the Worcester Foundation for Experimental Biology, "I've often said that running a scientific institution is a lot like running an artist colony. The best an administrator can do is leave people alone to do what they want to do" (quoted by Haney, 1985, p. C-1). And although creative people may have innate talent, they have to nurture their creativity with discipline and hard work.

The psychological literature yields a number of tips that parents and teachers can use to encourage creative thinking and originality among children:

❏ Respect children's questions and ideas.
❏ Respect children's right to initiate their own learning efforts.
❏ Respect children's right to reject, after serious consideration, the ideas of caretakers in favor of their own.
❏ Encourage children's awareness and sensitivity regarding environmental stimuli.
❏ Create "thorns in the flesh," confronting youngsters with problems, contradictions, ambiguities, and uncertainties.
❏ Afford children opportunities to make something and then do something with it.
❏ Give youngsters an opportunity to communicate what they have learned and accomplished.
❏ Use provocative and thought-producing questions.
❏ Encourage children's sense of self-esteem, self-worth, and self-respect.

In short, situational, cognitive, motivational, and personality characteristics all play a part in creativity.

with the operations involved in thinking. For instance, as discussed in Chapter 2, Jean Piaget concerned himself with the stages of development during which given modes of thought appear. He focused on the continual and dynamic interplay between children and their environment through which they come to know the world and to modify their understanding of it. Since Piaget did not view intelligence in set or fixed terms, he had little interest in the static assessment of individual differences in ability.

Intelligence as Information Processing More recently, a number of cognitive psychologists have proposed an information-processing view of

intelligence—a detailed, step-by-step analysis of how we manipulate information (Hunt, 1983; Siegler & Jenkins, 1989; Sternberg, 1982, 1984, 1986b, 1988). They are trying to unlock the doors to the mind by getting "inside intelligence," seeking to understand the mental processes whereby people solve problems not only on tests but in everyday life. By way of illustration, try this question: If you have black socks and brown socks in your drawer, mixed in a four to five ratio, how many socks must you take out to ensure getting a pair the same color? To find the answer, you must grasp what is important and ignore irrelevant details—a task that requires insight. The ratio of socks is unimportant. The answer is three: If the

IQ and Race

Since the turn of the century, psychologists have been testing members of various racial and ethnic groups and have found differences in their average IQ scores (Vander Zanden, 1983). Some psychologists have cited these differences as evidence of different innate intellectual capacities among the groups. For instance, Arthur R. Jensen (1969, 1973b) has argued that hereditary factors are "strongly implicated" in the average 15-point difference that he finds in IQ performance between blacks and whites.

Long before Jensen published his research, many psychologists were challenging interpretations of racial differences in IQ test performance. The first major counterattack came in the 1920s, when educators took a second look at the intelligence test scores of a sample of World War I recruits. The results revealed that blacks from the South, where economic and educational handicaps were greatest, scored lower than northern blacks. Even more important, blacks from some northern states had higher average scores than those of whites from some southern states. Evidently, the superior environmental opportunities enjoyed by northern blacks accounted for their superior test performance. More recently, researchers have found that the IQ gap between blacks and whites has closed for black children who are adopted as infants by white middle-class foster parents (Moore, 1986; Scarr & Weinberg, 1976). And data from the National Assessment of Educational Progress and from the College Entrance Examination Board show consistent reductions during recent years in the size of average achievement differences between white and black students (Angoff, 1988; Jones, 1984).

Elsewhere in the world disadvantaged groups also perform more poorly on intelligence tests than do advantaged groups. "Castelike" minorities, such as the Burakumi in Japan, Harijans (untouchables) in India, and the Maoris in New Zealand score on average 10 to 15 points below children of their country's dominant group. Yet these same youngsters do as well as their more privileged peers when they are treated similarly (Goleman, 1988). For example, when the Burakumi (an outcast group) come to the United States, where they are treated much like other Japanese youngsters, their children do as well on IQ tests and in school as do other Japanese (De Vos, 1967). Social status is so highly correlated with IQ that it casts suspicion on IQ scores as reflecting intelligence rather than one's position within society. Indeed, some evidence suggests that the bulk of a person's IQ score is determined by the amount of time an individual spends in school, presumably because schools instill certain skills that contribute to success on IQ tests (Raymond, 1991).

Given findings such as those cited above, many psychologists challenge an underlying assumption of those who say heredity is of primary importance in intellectual performance: the assumption that intelligence and IQ test performance can be equated. A number of psychologists contend that IQ tests are biased in favor of white middle-class Americans. For instance, the items on the Stanford-Binet test are restricted to subjects found in the school curriculum. Although such tests tend to predict academic performance to some degree, they predict performance outside the school only poorly (Anastasi, 1988; McClelland, 1973). Furthermore, items are not taken from machine shop,

first is black and the second is brown, the third must be one or the other.

In studying children in grades 4 through 6, Robert J. Sternberg (1986b) and his colleagues compared how children they had identified as gifted and those not so identified approached this problem. Three findings emerged. First, the gifted children were better able to solve the socks problem because they ignored the irrelevant information regarding ratios. Second, supplying nongifted children with the insights needed to solve this sort of problem increased their performance, whereas it had no effect on the gifted children because they already possessed the insights. And third, insight skills can be developed

by training. In a five-week training program both gifted and nongifted youngsters achieved significant improvement in their scores, relative to the scores of an untrained control group. Moreover, these skills were evident in a follow-up study a year later. In short, even though insight skills differentiate between the more and less intelligent, they are trainable in both groups. Sternberg says that this sort of understanding can be achieved only by studying the cognitive processes underlying intelligence: it is not supplied by global intelligence test scores. Interest in intelligence and information processing has stimulated research in creativity, a matter considered in the boxed insert on pages 234–235.

music class, art class, and other areas; rather, the tests deal only with reading, writing, and arithmetic. Critics say that the tests make "a narrow, biased collection of items the 'real measure' of all persons." Significantly, many black ghetto children and Spanish-speaking children are quite competent problem solvers in nonschool environments. They learn and profit from their experiences in ways that are not revealed by their IQ scores and school-related achievements (Garcia, 1972; Miller-Jones, 1989; Ogbu, 1985, 1986).

Some critics charge that IQ tests have been used by U.S. elites to justify privilege and to define inequality, injustice, and racism as natural, proper, and moral. If intelligence is largely inherited, then little can be done to improve people's abilities through education. And if people's abilities cannot be improved, then differences in power and rewards, being largely inherited, are here to stay. Hence, existing social arrangements and stratification systems are defined as unchangeable and fair (Lewontin, Rose & Kamin, 1984).

Carrying the argument even further, some environmentalists suggest that if IQ tests do not measure intelligence but merely the mastery of white middle-class values and language skills (reflected in the "trivial kinds of items" found on IQ tests), then the tests serve as a device to ensure the continued advantage of existing elites. Although most occupational positions are theoretically open to all Americans on the basis of merit, the use of IQ tests for educational and job placement serves to guarantee that the sons and daughters of the elite—having acquired the "proper" credentials as measured by IQ tests—are thus able to secure the best positions.

Institutional Racism

Institutional racism has historically served to impose more burdens and give fewer benefits to blacks than to whites. Whites control the gates that regulate the flow of people into positions and offices of power, status, and privilege. And white gatekeepers have systematically barred blacks from these positions. (Patrick Reddy)

Clearly, the issue of IQ testing is not simply an academic squabble; it has profound consequences for the course of our society (Matarazzo, 1990; Weinberg, 1989). All of us must become familiar with the various arguments and the evidence so that we can take a stand on the issues involved.

Intelligence and the Nature-Nurture Controversy

Psychologists differ in the relative importance that they attribute to heredity and environment in fashioning an individual's intelligence. As discussed in Chapter 3, some investigators of the nature-nurture issue have asked the "which" question, others the "how much" question, and still others the "how" question. And since they ask different questions, they come up with different answers.

The Hereditarian Position Arthur R. Jensen, an educational psychologist at the University of

California (Berkeley), has been a leading representative of the viewpoint that favors heredity. In 1969 he argued, in the prestigious *Harvard Educational Review*, that hereditary factors have a major influence on "racial" differences in intelligence, touching off an impassioned and bitter exchange in academic circles. In the intervening years Jensen (1973a, 1973b, 1977, 1980, 1984) has not appreciably altered his views. His position on IQ and race is especially controversial (see the boxed insert above).

Like others who phrase the nature-nurture question primarily in terms of "how much," Jensen has sought his answer in family resemblance studies (see Chapter 3) based on intelligence tests. Psychologists have devised tests of intelligence, employing a single number termed the *intelligence quotient*, or *IQ*, to describe various intellectual abilities. Today's intelligence tests provide an IQ score based on the test-taker's performance relative to the average performance of other individuals of the same age. Many psychologists believe that the assessment of intellectual abilities is one of their discipline's most significant contributions to society. But other psychologists say that it is a systematic attempt by elitists to "measure" people so that "desirable" ones can be put in the "proper" slots and the others rejected (see box on pages 236–237).

Table 9-2 summarizes current data on IQ performance from family resemblance studies. Note that the data in the table make reference to the correlation coefficient. A **correlation coefficient** is a numerical expression of the degree of relationship between two variables or conditions. It tells the extent to which two groups of measures tend to covary, or go together.

A correlation coefficient can range from −1.00 to +1.00. If it is +1.00, there is a *perfect positive relationship* between two variables—meaning that as one of the variables increases, the other also increases. If it is −1.00, there is a *perfect negative relationship* between two variables—meaning that as one of the variables increases, the other decreases. If the correlation coefficient is .00, there is no relationship between the variables.

More specifically, if there is no relationship between the IQ scores of pairs of individuals, the correlation coefficient would be .00. Thus, knowing the IQ score of one twin would tell us nothing about the IQ score of the other twin. If the correlation coefficient is +1.00, the correspondence in IQ scores between pairs of individuals would be perfect. Thus, knowing the IQ score of one twin would tell us the IQ score of the other twin. But we seldom find a correlation coefficient of .00 or +1.00. Usually, the figure falls somewhere in between. What we need to remember is this: The nearer the correlation coefficient is to +1.00, the closer the overall correspondence of the IQ scores of one twin is to those of the other twin in the pairs being studied. Note that correlation coefficients do not in themselves imply any causal link between variables.

The data in Table 9-2 reveal that the median IQ correlation coefficient of separated identical twins in three studies is +.72. Data are also shown from twenty-nine studies of fraternal twins of the same sex who were reared together.

The median IQ correlation coefficient of the fraternal twins is +.62. In sum, the identical twins reared in *different* homes are much more alike in IQ than the fraternal twins raised *together* (Jensen, 1972). Also note in Table 9-2 that as the biological kinship between two people increases (gets closer), the correlation between their IQ scores increases. On the basis of this and other evidence, Jensen concludes that from 60 to 80 percent of the variation in IQ scores in the general population is attributable to genetic differences and the remainder to environmental differences.

The Environmentalist Rebuttal A number of scientists dispute the claim by Jensen and like-minded psychologists that differences in intelligence are primarily a function of heredity. Some disagree with the formulation of the nature-nurture question in terms of "how much" and insist that the question should be *how* heredity and environment interact to produce intelligence. And others such as Leon J. Kamin (1974, p. 1) go so far as to assert: "There exist no data which should lead a prudent man to accept the hypothesis that IQ test scores are in any degree heritable." Psychologists of Kamin's view, commonly termed *environmentalists*, argue that mental abilities are learned. They believe that intellect is increased or decreased according to the degree of enrichment or impoverishment provided by a person's social and cultural environment (Feuerstein, 1979, 1980).

Kamin (1974, 1975, 1977, 1981; Lewontin, Rose & Kamin, 1984) has vigorously challenged the adoption and identical-twin research that the advocates of heredity use to support their conclusions. He insists that it is improper to speak of individuals as being reared in differing environments simply because they were brought up in different homes. In some cases identical twins labeled as being "reared apart" were hardly separated at all: They were raised by relatives, or they lived next door to one another, or they went to the same school. Similarly, environmentalists charge that studies of adopted children are biased by the fact that adoption agencies traditionally attempt to place children in a social environment that is religiously, ethnically, and racially similar to the one into which they were born.

Environmentalists cite evidence of their own to bolster their argument that differences in intelligence are primarily a function of social conditions. Psychologist Benjamin S. Bloom (1969) found that Israeli children of European Jewish

Table 9-2

Correlation Coefficients of IQ Scores Compared with the Degree of Family Relationship

Correlations Between	Number of Studies	Median Correlation Coefficients
UNRELATED PERSONS		
Foster parent and child	6	+.19
Children reared together	6	+.34
COLLATERALS		
Cousins	4	+.15
Half siblings	2	+.31
Siblings reared apart	2	+.24
Siblings reared together	69	+.47
Dizygotic twins, different sex	18	+.57
Dizygotic twins, same sex	29	+.62
Monozygotic twins, reared apart	3	+.72
Monozygotic twins, reared together	34	+.86
DIRECT LINE		
Parent and child, different sex	12	+.39
Parent and child, same sex	14	+.40

Source: Adapted from Thomas J. Bouchard, Jr., and Matthew McGue, "Familial Studies of Intelligence: A Review," Science, *Vol. 212 (1981), pp. 1055–1059.*

parents have a mean IQ of 105. In contrast, Israeli children of Middle Eastern Jews have an IQ of only 85. The scores differ, however, for children residing on collective farms (*kibbutzim*), where they spend twenty-two hours of the day in a nursery. Under the intensive learning experiences provided in the nurseries, both European and Middle Eastern Jewish children have an average IQ of 115—a 10-point improvement for the one group and a 30-point improvement for the other. Environmentalists insist that such evidence shows how flexible IQ can be and how it can be altered under different social conditions.

Contemporary Scientific Consensus Most social and behavioral scientists believe that any extreme view in the nature-nurture controversy is unjustified at the present time (Horn, 1983, 1985; Walker & Emory, 1985). Estimates based on twin and adoption studies suggest that hereditary differences account for 45 to 80 percent of the variation found in the intelligence test performance of

Cultural Bias in Intelligence Testing

A "noncultural" or "culture-free" intelligence test is an impossibility. Membership in a particular culture influences what an individual is likely to learn or fail to learn. It would be ridiculous, for instance, to give these Spanish-speaking youngsters in Mexico the Stanford-Binet intelligence test, designed by and for English-speaking Americans. *(Paul Fusco/Magnum)*

a population (Leohlin, Horn & Willerman, 1989; Loehlin, Willerman & Horn, 1988). For instance, Thomas J. Bouchard, Jr., and his team of University of Minnesota twin researchers find that 70 percent of the IQ differences among people is attributable to genetic factors (Bouchard, Lykken, McGue, Segal & Tellegen, 1990). (See Chapter 3 for a more detailed account of the Minnesota twin studies.) But other experts think that a 70 percent heritability estimate is too high (Kolata, 1990). For example, sociologist Christopher Jencks (1972) has employed path analysis—a statistical technique—to partition the amount of variance within a group into an estimate of 45 percent for heredity, 35 percent for environment, and 20 percent for gene-environment covariance.

Jencks has introduced the third element of gene-environment covariance because he feels that dividing IQ into hereditary and environmental components oversimplifies the matter. For example, consider the following circumstances (Loehlin, Lindzey & Spuhler, 1975, pp. 77–78):

> Suppose that intelligent parents tend to provide their children with genes conducive to the development of high intelligence, but also tend to provide them with environments favorable to the development of this trait, such as good schools, intellectual stimulation at home, and so forth. We may need to divide the observed variance among individuals in a population into a component that is associated with genetic endowment, when intellectual stimulation is held constant, a component that is associated with environmental stimulation, with genetic potential constant, and a third component associated with the covariance of heredity and environment, that is, with how the first two components vary relative to each other.

If, as in this example, genes and environment reinforce each other, the added component of variance cannot logically be assigned to either nature or nurture. Rather, it is a result of the association of their separate effects.

The Early Development of Intelligence

Jean Piaget, the Swiss developmental psychologist, pioneered the study of the development of intelligence in infants and children. He called the years between two and seven the **preoperational period.** The principal achievement of that period is the developing capacity of children to represent the external world *internally* through the use of symbols. *Symbols* are things that stand for something else. They free children

"Will you take the roof off this for me, please?"

("Family Circus" © 1990 Bill Keane, Inc. Reprinted with special permission of King Features Syndicate.)

from the rigid boundaries of the here and now. Using symbols, they can represent not only present events but past and future ones. The acquisition of language facilitates children's ability to employ and manipulate symbols.

Difficulties in Solving Conservation Problems
Piaget observed that although children make major strides in cognitive development during the preoperational period, their reasoning and thinking processes have a number of limitations. These limitations can be seen in the difficulties preschool children have when they try to solve conservation problems. **Conservation** refers to the concept that the quantity or amount of something stays the same regardless of changes in its shape or position.

A preoperational child cannot understand that when water is poured out of a full glass into a wider glass, which it fills only halfway, the amount of water remains unchanged. Instead, the child sees that the new glass is half empty and concludes that there is less water than before.

Similarly, if we show a child under 6 two parallel rows of eight evenly spaced pennies and ask which row has more pennies, the child always correctly answers that both rows have the same number. But if, in full view of the child, we move the pennies in one of the rows farther apart and again ask which row has more pennies, the child will reply that the longer row has more. The child fails to recognize that the number of pennies does not change simply because we made a change in another dimension, the length of the row (see Figure 9-1).

Piaget said that the difficulties preschoolers have in solving conservation problems derive from the characteristics of preoperational thought. These characteristics inhibit logical thought by posing obstacles that are associated with centering, transformations, reversibility, and egocentrism.

Centering Preoperational children concentrate on one feature of a situation and neglect other aspects, a process termed **centering**. When water is poured out of a full glass into a wider glass, preschool children focus on only one attribute. They fix their attention on either the height or the width of the water in the glass while ignoring the other dimension. In order to solve the conservation problem correctly, they must *decenter*—that is, they must attend simultaneously to both height and width.

Likewise, in the case of the pennies, children need to recognize that a change in length is compensated for by a change in the other dimension, density. Thus, there is no change in quantity. Here, too, the ability to decenter—to explore more than one aspect of the stimulus—is said by Piaget to be beyond preoperational children.

States and Transformations Another characteristic of preoperational thinking is that children pay attention to *states* rather than *transformations* (see Figure 9-2). In observing water being poured from one glass into another, preschool children focus on the original state and the final state. The intervening process is lost to them. They do not pay attention to the gradual shift in the height or width of the water in the glasses as the experimenter pours the liquid. Preoperational thought fixes on static states. It fails to link successive states into a coherent sequence of events.

The inability of preschool children to follow transformations interferes with logical thinking. Only by appreciating the continuous and sequential nature of various operations can we be cer-

Figure 9-1   Conservation Experiment with Pennies
Children are first shown two rows of pennies arranged as in A. *The experimenter asks if both rows contain the same number of pennies. Then with the children watching, the experimenter spreads out the pennies in the bottom row, as in* B. *Children are once again asked if both rows contain the same number of pennies. Preoperational children will respond that they do not.*

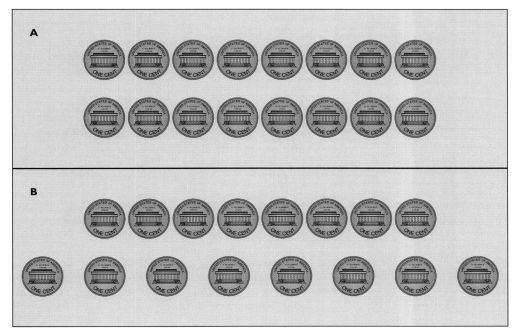

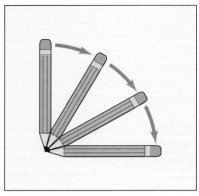

Figure 9-2   An Experiment in Preoperational Thinking
Hold a pencil in an upright position, then slowly lower it to a horizontal position while a child under 7 watches it. Immediately afterward, the child will not be able to draw the sequence of events or arrange in order a series of prepared drawings reconstructing the movement of the pencil. Children in Piaget's preoperational period (ages 2 to 7) pay attention only to initial and final states, not to transformations. They cannot identify the successive movements required for the pencil to shift from the upright to the prone position. Adapted from T. J. Bouchard, Jr., and M. McGue, "Familial Studies of Intelligence: A Review," *Science*, Vol. 212, 1981, pp. 1055–1059. [Copyright © 1981 by The American Association for the Advancement of Science.]

tain that the quantities remain the same. Since preoperational children fail to see the relationship between events, their comparisons between original and final events are incomplete. Thus, they cannot solve conservation problems.

Nonreversibility   According to Piaget, the most important characteristic of preoperational thought is the child's failure to recognize that operations are **reversible**—that they can be turned back to an earlier state. In other words, we can always go back to the starting point in a series of operations. After we pour water from a narrow container into a wider container, we can demonstrate that the amount of water remains the same by pouring it back into the narrow container. But preoperational children do not understand that the operation can be reversed. Once they have carried out an entire operation, they cannot *mentally* regain the original state. Awareness of reversibility is a requirement of logical thought.

Egocentrism   Still another element that interferes with the preschool child's understanding of reality is **egocentrism**—lack of awareness that there are viewpoints other than one's own. According to Piaget, preoperational children are so absorbed in their own impressions that they fail to recognize that their thoughts and findings may

be different from those of other people. Children simply assume that everyone thinks the same thoughts they do at the same time they do.

More recent research suggests, however, that although egocentricity is characteristic of preoperational thinking, preschool children are nonetheless capable of recognizing other people's viewpoints (Brownell, 1986; Gelman & Ebeling, 1989; Hay, Murray, Cecire & Nash, 1985; Ross & Lollis, 1987). While emotionally toddlers can often be quite *self-centered*, they are not necessarily *egocentric* in the sense of not understanding other perspectives (Dunn, 1988). Increasingly researchers are uncovering many *sociocentric* (people-oriented) responses in young children. Indeed, some have questioned the characterization of children as egocentric. Consider the following evidence:

❏ **Talking and communication**   Catherine Garvey and Robert Hogan (1973) found that during the greater part of the time that children 3 to 5 years of age spend in nursery school, they interact with others, largely by talking. Furthermore, most of their speech is mutually responsive and adapted to the speech or nonverbal behavior of a partner (Spilton & Lee, 1977).

❏ **Sharing**   Harriet L. Rheingold, Dale F. Hay and Meredith J. West (1976) have shown that children in their second year of life share with others what they see and find interesting. In laboratory settings, for instance, children commonly share by showing objects to other people, giving them objects, and engaging others as partners in playing with the objects. Rheingold and her associates also found considerable evidence for sharing behavior in field observations. Children usually pointed at objects—a window display, an airplane, an automobile, or a picture on a cereal box—in order to call another person's attention to them. Indeed, the researchers observed pointing behavior in children even before their first birthday. Rheingold and her colleagues (1976, p. 1157) concluded:

In showing an object to another person, the children demonstrate not only that they know that other people can see what they see but also that others will look at what they point to or hold up. We can surmise that they also know that what they see may be remarkable in some way and therefore worthy of another's attention. . . . That children so young share contradicts the egocentricity so often ascribed to them and reveals them instead as already able contributors to social life.

Sociocentric Behavior

Developmental psychologists are discovering that young children are considerably less egocentric and more sociocentric than early studies indicated. *(Patrick Reddy)*

Rheingold, 1981; Taylor, 1988; Yaniv & Shatz, 1990).

❏ **Altruism** Researchers have found evidence of altruistic and prosocial behavior even in very young children (Buckley, Siegel & Ness, 1979; Dunn, 1988; Radke-Yarrow, Zahn-Waxler & Chapman, 1983; Zahn-Waxler, Radke-Yarrow & Brady-Smith, 1977). Not untypical are the following examples: A 2-year-old boy accidentally hits a small girl on the head. He looks aghast. "I hurt your hair. Please don't cry." Another child, a girl of 18 months, sees her grandmother lying down to rest. She goes over to her own crib, takes her own blanket, and covers her grandmother with it (Pines, 1979*b*). Chapter 11 will consider prosocial behavior at greater length.

In conclusion, newly developing lines of research reveal that we have been hampered in our efforts to understand children by adult-centered concepts and by our preoccupation with the adult-child relationship—in other words, by *adult egocentrism.* Moreover, in recent years psychologists have moved increasingly away from Piaget's notion of broad, overarching stages to a more complex view of development. Rather than searching for major overall transformations, they are scrutinizing separate domains such as causality, memory, creativity, problem solving, and social interaction. Each domain has a somewhat unique and flexible schedule that is affected not only by age but also by the quality of the environment (Chance & Fischman, 1987).

Conceptual Foundations for Learning

Piaget's procedures have also tended to underestimate many of the cognitive capabilities of preschool children. Indeed, recent research has raised an important new issue concerning children's conceptual foundations for learning. Toddlers seem to possess a significant *implicit understanding* of certain basic principles. (Greeno, 1989). Here we will consider two spheres of conceptual knowledge for illustrative purposes: causality and number concepts:

Causality Piaget concluded that children younger than 7 or 8 fail to grasp cause-and-effect relationships. When he would ask younger children why the sun and the moon move, they would respond that heavenly bodies "follow us about because they are curious" or "in order to look at

Hence, by the time children are about 1 year of age, they seem to have acquired the ability not only to take the visual perspective of others but also to begin sharing with them their own perspective of the world (Dunn, 1988; Leung &

us." Or if Piaget showed 4-year-olds a bicycle and asked them what makes the wheels turn, they might reply, "The street makes the bicycle go." Such fanciful explanations for events led Piaget to emphasize the shortcomings associated with young children's intellectual operations.

But contemporary developmental psychologists who investigate the thinking of young children find that they already understand a good deal about causality (Shultz, Fisher, Pratt & Ruff, 1986; Shultz & Kestenbaum, 1985; Shultz & Wells, 1985). **Causality** involves our attribution of a cause-and-effect relationship to two paired events that recur in succession. Causality is based on the expectation that when one event occurs, another event, one that ordinarily follows the first, will again follow it. Apparently the rudiments for the causal processing of information are already evident among 3-month-old infants. And by the time youngsters are 3 to 4 years old, they seem to possess rather sophisticated abilities for discerning cause-and-effect relationships (Bauer & Mandler, 1989; Gelman & Kremer, 1991;

Gopnik & Graf, 1988; Gupta & Bryant, 1989; White, 1988).

Young children's grasp of causality is demonstrated in a variety of experiments (Pines, 1983). One such experiment involves a toy rabbit named Fred and a series of upright wooden blocks that topple over like dominos. When the last domino falls over, it trips a small but visible lever that sends Fred flying from a platform. Three- and four-year-olds can correctly predict about 75 percent of the time that as the blocks fall over, they will trigger Fred's release regardless of whether the rod pushing over the first domino is long or short and regardless of whether one of the blocks is hidden from view.

Young children are also capable of distinguishing between animate and inanimate objects. They do so by considering the cause of an object's movement. Living things move because of self-generating forces within them, whereas nonliving things move only when activated by external forces. Thus, children talk a good deal about the inability of a doll to propel itself, apparently a fact

"You want a laser-scanning microscope and you still believe in Santa Claus?"

that is quite significant to them. The difficulty that young children may have in determining what makes the sun or moon move is perhaps one reason they responded as they did to Piaget's inquiry.

The versatility of young children in grasping causality has led some psychologists to conclude that human beings are biologically prewired to understand the existence of cause-and-effect relationships (Pines, 1983). Children appear to operate on an implicit theory of causality. Clearly, the ability to appreciate that a cause must always precede an effect would have enormous survival value in the course of evolution. Hence, as in the case of language, children may be preordained to distinguish between cause and effect.

Number Concepts Piaget also deemphasized children's counting capabilities, terming counting "merely verbal knowledge" and asserting that "there is no connection between the acquired ability to count and the actual operations of which the child is capable" (Piaget, 1941/1965 p. 61). Yet young children seem to have an implicit understanding for some number concepts. Preschool youngsters can perform successfully on tasks requiring modified versions of counting procedures and can judge whether a puppet's performance in counting is correct (Gelman & Gallistel, 1978; Gelman & Meck, 1986). Counting is the first formal computational system children acquire. It allows youngsters to make accurate quantitative assessments of amount, rather than having to rely solely on their perceptual or qualitative judgments.

Some researchers suggest that preschoolers have a preexisting, implicit knowledge of five counting principles; (1) the stable order principle (lists of number names must be generated in a consistent sequence); (2) the one-one principle (there must be a one-to-one correspondence between the names of numbers and objects when counting); (3) the cardinal principle (the last number name in a sequence represents the number of elements in a mathematical set); (4) the abstraction principle (any collection of objects can be counted); and (5) the order irrelevance principle (items can be legitimately counted in any sequence) (Gelman & Meck, 1986; Gelman, Meck & Merkin, 1986; Greeno, Riley & Gelman, 1984). However, not all developmental psychologists agree that counting is an "easy" cognitive accomplishment. They say youngsters must acquire substantially more intellectual input than can be attributed to "implicit knowledge" (Frye, Braisby, Lowe, Maroudes & Nicholls, 1989; Steffe & Cobb, 1988). Even so, infants seem to possess some basic knowledge of "quantity" well before they could have acquired such knowledge from their learning experiences (Resnick, 1986, 1989).

Information Processing and Memory

Memory is a net; one finds it full of fish when he takes it from the brook; but a dozen miles of water have run through it without sticking.—OLIVER WENDELL HOLMES
The Autocrat of the Breakfast Table

Memory is a critical cognitive ability. Indeed, all learning implies memory. In its broadest sense, **memory** refers to the retention of what has been experienced. Without memory we would react to every event as if we had never before experienced it. Furthermore, we would be incapable of thinking and reasoning—of any sort of intelligent behavior—if we could not use remembered facts. Hence, memory is critical to information processing.

Early Memory

During infancy and childhood we learn a prodigious amount about the world (Gottfried & Rose, 1980; Greco & Daehler, 1985; M. W. Sullivan, 1982). Yet by adulthood our memories of our early experiences have faded, a phenomenon termed *childhood amnesia*. We remember as adults only fleeting scenes and isolated moments prior to the time we reached 7 or 8 years of age. Although some individuals have no recollections prior to 8 or 9 years of age, many of us can recall some things that took place between our third and fourth birthdays. Most commonly, first memories involve visual imagery, and most of the imagery is in color. In many cases we visualize ourselves in these memories from afar, as we would look at an actor on a stage (Nelson, 1982).

Just why early memories should wane remains an enigma (Goleman, 1981). Sigmund Freud theorized that we repress or alter childhood memories because of their disturbing sexual and aggressive content. Others, particularly Piagetians and cognitive developmentalists, claim that adults have trouble recalling the events of child-hood because they no longer think as children do (for instance, adults typically employ, as aids to memory, words and abstract concepts that do not mesh with the mental habits they employed as young children). Still others say that the brain and nervous system are not entirely formed in the young and do not allow for the development of adequate memory stores and effective retrieval strategies. Finally, there are those who contend that learning often occurs during the first two years of life in emotion-centered areas of the brain and that this learning is subject to limited recall in later years (see Chapter 8). Nonetheless, our understanding of childhood amnesia continues to be elusive, with theorizing remaining at the speculative level.

Information Processing

Memory includes recall, recognition, and the facilitation of relearning. In *recall* we remember what we learned earlier, such as the definition of a scientific concept or the lines of a play. In *recognition* we experience a feeling of familiarity when we again perceive something that we have previously encountered. In the *facilitation of relearning* we find that we can learn material that is already familiar to us more readily than we can learn totally unfamiliar material.

On the whole, children's recognition memory is superior to their recall memory. In recognition the information is already available, and children can simply check their perceptions of an occurrence against their memory. Recall, in contrast, requires them to retrieve all the information from their own memory. Children ten years of age who are shown sixty pictures and asked to remember them can *recognize* about 90 percent of the pictures the next day, but they can *recall* only about 30 percent of them (Kagan, Klein, Haith & Morrison, 1973).

Memory permits us to store information for different periods of time. Some psychologists distinguish between sensory information storage, short-term memory, and long-term memory (see Figure 9-3). In **sensory information storage**, information from the senses is preserved in the sensory register just long enough to permit the stimuli to be scanned for processing (generally less than 2 seconds). It provides a relatively complete, literal copy of the physical stimulation. For instance, if you tap your finger against your cheek, you note an immediate sensation, which quickly fades away.

Short-term memory refers to the retention of information for a very brief period, usually not more than 30 seconds. For example, you may look up a number in the telephone directory and remember it just long enough to dial it, whereupon you promptly forget it.

Figure 9-3   Simplified Flow Chart of the Three-Store Model of Memory
Information flow is represented by three memory stores: the sensory register, the short-term store, and the long-term store. Inputs from the environment enter the sensory register, where they are selectively passed on to short-term storage. Information in the short-term store may be forgotten or copied by the long-term store. In some cases individuals mentally rehearse information in order to keep it in active awareness in short-term storage. Complicated feedback operations take place among the three storage components.

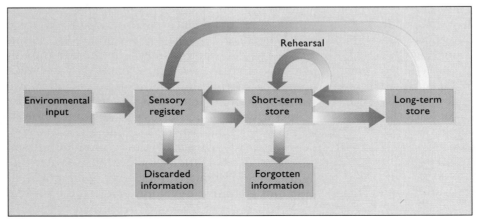

Long-term memory is the retention of information over an extended period of time A memory may be retained because it arose from a very intense single experience or because it is repeatedly rehearsed. Through yearly repetition and constant media reminders, you come to remember that Memorial Day is in late May, Labor Day in early September.

Metacognition and Metamemory

As children develop, they become increasingly active agents in the remembering process (Chechile, Richman, Topinka & Ehrensbeck, 1981; Kail & Nippold, 1984; HcGilly & Siegler, 1990). The development of memory occurs in two ways: through alterations in the biological structuring of the brain (its "hardware") and through changes in types of information processing (the "software" of acquisition and retrieving). Researchers have observed striking changes as a function of age, both in children's performance on memory tasks and in their use of memory strategies. As they grow older, children acquire a complex set of skills that enables them to control just what they will learn and retain. In short, they come to "know how to know," so that they can engage in deliberate remembering (Brown, 1975, 1982; Craik & Lockhart, 1972; Moore, Bryant & Furrow, 1989). Overall, memory ability catapults upward from birth through age 5, and then it advances less rapidly through middle childhood and adolescence (Chance & Fischman, 1987).

Human beings require more than the factual and strategic information that comprises a knowledge base. They must also have access to this knowledge base and apply strategies appropriate to task demands. This flexibility in calibrating solutions to specific problems is the hallmark of intelligence. Flexibility reaches its zenith in the conscious control that adults bring to bear over a broad range of their mental functioning (Brown, 1982; Fabricius, Schwanenflugel, Kyllonen, Barclay & Denton, 1989; Wellman, 1985a, 1985b). Individuals' awareness and understanding of their mental processes is termed **metacognition.** Their awareness and understanding of their memory processes is termed **metamemory.**

Research reveals that even 3-year-olds engage in intentional memory behavior. They appear to understand that when they are told to remember something, they are expected to store and later retrieve it. Indeed, even 2-year-olds can hide, misplace, search for, and find objects on their own (Wellman, 1977). By the time children enter kindergarten, they have developed considerable knowledge of the memory process. They are aware that forgetting occurs (that items get lost in memory), that spending more time in study helps them retain information, that it is more difficult to remember many items than a few, that distraction and interference make tasks harder, and that they can employ records, cues, and other people to help them recall things (Fabricius & Wellman, 1983; Kreutzer, Leonard & Flavell 1975; Wellman, 1977). They also understand such terms as "remember," "forget," and "learn."

Categorizing as a Memory Strategy

One strategy that facilitates remembering is to group information into meaningful categories. Sheila Rossi and M.C. Wittrock (1971) found that a developmental progression occurs in the categories children use to organize words for recall. In this experiment children ranging from 2 to 5 years old were read a list of twelve words ("sun," "hand," "men," "fun," "leg," "work," "hat," "apple," "dogs," "fat," "peach," "bark"). Each child was asked to recall as many words as possible. The responses were scored in pairs in terms of the order in which a child recalled them: rhyming ("sun-fun," "hat-fat"); syntactical ("men-work," "dogs-bark"); clustering ("apple-peach," "hand-leg"); or serial ordering (recalling two words serially from the list). Rossi and Wittrock found that rhyming responses peak at 2 years of age, followed by syntactical responses at 3, clustering responses at 4, and serial-ordering responses at 5. In many respects the progression is consistent with Piaget's theory, which depicts development as proceeding from concrete to abstract functioning and from perceptual to conceptual responding.

Other research also confirms that changes occur in children's spontaneous use of categories during the developmental span from age 2 to adolescence. While children as young as 2 benefit from the presence of categories in recall tasks, older children benefit even more. For one thing, recall increases with age. For another, children of age 4 to 6, in comparison with older children, show less categorical grouping of items in recall tasks, fewer subordinate categories in tasks requesting that similar items be grouped together, and lower consistency in the assignment of items to selected categories (Jablonski, 1974; Levy,

Schlesinger & Braine, 1988; Nelson, 1988; Price & Goodman, 1990; Wellman, Collins & Glieberman, 1981). Adolescents adopt even more sophisticated strategies, grouping items into logical categories such as people, places, and things, or animals, plants, and minerals (Chance & Fischman, 1987).

Rehearsing as a Memory Strategy

Another strategy that facilitates memory is *rehearsing*, a process in which we repeat information to ourselves. Many individuals who are adept at remembering people's names cultivate the talent by mentally rehearsing a new name several times to themselves when they are introduced to a person. Researchers have demonstrated that children as young as 3 are capable of various rehearsal strategies. For instance, if 3-year-olds are instructed to remember where an object is hidden, they often prepare for future memory retrieval by extended looking at, touching, or pointing to the hiding place (Wellman, Ritter & Flavell, 1975).

As children grow, their rehearsal mechanisms become more active and effective (Chance & Fischman, 1987; Cuvo, 1975; McGilly & Siegler, 1989; Naus, Ornstein & Kreshtool, 1977; Ornstein, Naus & Liberty, 1975). Some researchers believe that the process is facilitated through language, as children become increasingly skillful at verbally labeling stimuli. According to these investigators, the organizing and rehearsing process inherent in naming is a powerful aid to memory (Loughlin & Daehler, 1973; Rosinski, Pellegrino & Siegel, 1977). And as children come to process information in more sophisticated ways and learn how and when to remember, they become capable of making more decisions for themselves. As discussed in the boxed insert, parents and teachers can cultivate children's decision-making skills.

Cognitive Foundations for Social Interaction

The information-processing and memory skills acquired during the preschool years have profound implications for children's ability to function as members of society (Dixon & Moore, 1990; Eder, 1989, 1990; Kihlstrom et al., 1988). In order to enter sustained social interaction with others, we must impute meaning to the people around us. All of us, children and adults alike, confront the social world in terms of categories of people—we classify them as adults, doctors, teachers, storekeepers, and so on. Society does not consist merely of so many isolated individuals. It is composed of individuals who are classed as similar because they play similar roles. And just as we impute meaning to others, we must also attribute meaning to ourselves. We have to develop a sense of ourselves as distinct, bounded, identifiable units. In sum, we acquire conceptions of roles and self.

Roles

All the world's a stage,
And all the men and women merely players.
They have their exits and their entrances,
And one man in his time plays many parts.
—WILLIAM SHAKESPEARE
As You Like It, *Act II, Scene 7*

In order to function effectively within social settings, children must develop the mental capacity to "locate" or "place" individuals in a wide variety of social categories: brother, neighbor, dentist, store clerk, playmate, and so on. Social psychologists call such categories **roles.** Roles specify who does what, and when and where they do it. Roles define the expectations that group members hold regarding an individual's behavior in a given setting. As such, roles are key ingredients in group life. Without roles society would be an impossibility.

Roles impinge on us as sets of social norms that define our *obligations* and *expectations*. Obligations are the actions that *others* can legitimately insist that we perform. Expectations are the actions that *we* can legitimately insist that others perform. Every role is tied to one or more other roles and is *reciprocal* to these other roles. Without children there would be no fathers; without wives, no husbands; without patients, no doctors; without teachers, no students. And vice versa: without fathers there would be no children; without husbands, no wives; without doctors, no patients; without students, no teachers.

In sum, roles provide social guidelines that define for us our obligations and our expectations. Roles link us within a social network through the web created by their interconnections. Hence, we are joined in social life through role relationships, the expectations of the one end being the obligations of the other. For example, the obligations of the father role—to provide economic support for his offspring, to furnish moral direction, to communicate a sense of warmth and accep-

Teaching Children to Decide

In the course of their everyday lives children confront situations requiring some measure of problem solving and decision making. What should they do when they are being teased? Should they accept a playmate's dare? How should they respond when they are excluded by a group of friends? Yet many youngsters have not evolved skills for dealing with these situations. They have only a limited ability to reason critically. Given this state of affairs, psychologists Maurice J. Elias and John Clabby (1986) have conducted research with more than three hundred children to identify how parents and schools might foster youngsters' decision-making skills.

They find that children reared in authoritarian families are disadvantaged in making their own decisions because their parents provide few opportunities for them to exercise decision making. The youngsters may seem easier to manage on a day-to-day basis, but when their parents are not around, they have few problem-solving skills they can enlist. Elias and Clabby caution that children require warmth, firmness, and limits. There are some things that parents should decide, such as bedtime. But within a restricted framework children should have opportunities to choose among alternatives. Their research reveals that youngsters who have acquired problem-solving skills have higher self-esteem and seem better adjusted than do peers who have few of these skills.

Elias and Clabby (1986) have evolved a strategy by which parents and teachers can help children master decision-making skills. The youngsters are taught first to look for signs of their own feelings of tenseness or distress so that when they are confronting a problem, they can identify: "I feel upset." They are then asked to encapsulate the problem into a statement: "I feel upset because Jenny won't let me play with her." Next, they are encouraged to formulate a goal: "I want Jenny to play with me." Once the goal is in mind, children are helped to come up with a number of solutions: "I could yell at Jenny," "I could tell Jenny I would like to play with her," "I could suggest that Jenny and I play house," and so on. The youngsters are asked to anticipate the likely consequences of each approach and then to decide on the best solution. Once a course of action is decided on, children are assisted in planning its execution and in anticipating obstacles. Finally, youngsters try out the solution and later evaluate its effectiveness.

Elias and Clabby (1986) believe that teaching children to make decisions and solve problems develops their capacity to think independently. Such an ability sustains them in the face of negative peer pressure concerning the use of drugs or alcohol. The authors point out that if young people believe their own ideas are valuable, they are less likely to make choices simply because of the crowd's influence. If Elias and Clabby's conclusions are valid, then helping children acquire decision-making skills may prove more effective in the long run than school programs that focus only on target problems. For instance, telling children about drugs and their harmful consequences may not have much meaning for children who have not been thinking about drugs. But with a broader foundation in problem solving, youngsters can use the skills in a wide variety of circumstances.

tance—are the expectations of the child role. The expectations of the father role—to be obeyed, to be respected, to be shown affection—are the obligations of the child role. Children must grasp such expectations and obligations in order to function effectively within a group setting.

Both Piaget and the sociologist George Herbert Mead (1934) pointed out that children must overcome an egocentric perspective if they are to participate in mature social interaction. For children to play their role properly, they must know something about other roles. This requirement derives from the reciprocal character of roles discussed above. Hence, in human interaction we *construct* our acts point by point by *fitting* them to those of the other person. We start or stop, abandon or postpone, implement or transform given lines of action on the basis of the feedback we receive from others (Bakeman & Adamson, 1984; Blumer, 1969; Turner, 1962).

During the early preschool years children can recognize that people are independent agents who initiate action, and they begin to understand the nature of social roles (Howes, Unger & Seidner, 1989; Watson & Fischer, 1980). Some categories for classing people apparently emerge quite early. For instance, 6-month-old infants are able to distinguish between an adult and a baby, suggesting that infants use age as one dimension to categorize the social world (Lewis & Brooks-Gunn, 1979). By 18 months most middle-class children can pretend that they are carrying out

Roles and the Self

In order to play our own role successfully, we must know the requirements both of our role and others' roles. According to George Herbert Mead, in the course of translating the requirements of our role into action, we imagine ourselves in the role of the other person. This process of self enables us to take into account the behavior of the other person when we fashion our own reciprocal behavior. *(Charles Harbutt/Archive)*

some action (for instance, pretending to drink from an empty cup). This ability testifies that they view themselves as agents producing behavior. By the time they reach 2 years of age, they can make a doll do something, as if it were acting on its own, thus demonstrating an elementary ability for representing other people as independent agents. Most 3-year-olds can make a doll carry out several role-related activities, revealing knowledge of a social role (for example, they can pretend to be a doctor and examine a doll). Four-year-olds can typically act out a role, relating one social role to a reciprocal role (for instance, they can pretend that a patient doll is sick and that a doctor doll examines it, in the course of which both dolls make appropriate responses). During the late preschool years children become capable of combining roles in more complicated ways (for example, being a doctor and a father at the same time). Hence, most six-year-olds can pretend to carry out several roles simultaneously.

Whereas evidence suggests that 24- to 30-month-old youngsters can manage roles in cooperation with their peers rather quickly and effectively, this capability is as yet infrequent and largely accidental among 18-month-olds (however, adults can generally "scaffold" an infant about 12-months-old into a successful joint activity by taking a very rudimentary skill that the child possesses and linking it cooperatively to their own superior skill). Although 12-month-old

children interact socially with one another, not until 18 to 24 months do peer interactions revolve around "sharing meanings" that have a common theme and turn-taking. It seems that children must develop a concept of the *self* in order to "take the role of the other"—to represent and monitor both their own and a partner's behavior in fashioning their own behavior (Brownell & Carriger, 1990; Pipp, Fischer & Jennings, 1987).

The Self

Man can be defined as the animal that can say "I," that can be aware of himself as a separate entity.—ERICH FROMM

Among the cognitive achievevments of the child's early years is a growing self-awareness—the human sense of "I." At any one time, we are confronted with a greater quantity and variety of stimulation than we can attend to and process. Accordingly, we must select what we will notice, learn, infer, or recall. Selection does not occur in a random manner but depends on our use of internal cognitive structures—mental "scripts" or "frames"—for processing information. Of particular importance to us is the cognitive structure that we employ for selecting and processing information about ourselves. This structure is the **self**—the system of concepts we use in defining ourselves. It is the awareness we have of ourselves as separate entities who are able to think and initiate action. In sum, the self provides us with the capacity to observe, respond to, and direct our own behavior. The sense of self distinguishes each of us as a unique individual—different from others in society. It gives us a feeling of placement in the social and physical world and of continuity across time. And it provides the cognitive basis for our identities.

Sociologists who follow in the tradition of George Herbert Mead view the self as crucial to role playing. The self enables us to imagine ourselves in other people's positions and see what they expect of us in a given role. In imagination, we put ourselves in their shoes—mentally exchange roles—to grasp the requirements for sustained interaction. In so doing, we "get outside ourselves" and view ourselves as objects.

Michael Lewis and Jeanne Brooks-Gunn (1979) studied children's emerging sense of self in a novel way. They observed children's reactions to their reflections in a mirror. Their sample involved young children aged 9, 12, 15, 18, 21, and 24 months. The children were placed individually in front of a mirror, and their actions were recorded on videotape. Then, each child's mother took her child away from the mirror, wiped the child's nose and, in doing so, placed red paint on it, and brought the child back to the mirror. The videotapes of the children's behavior at this point showed a clear developmental pattern. Few children under 12 months of age responded to the paint. But 25 percent of those between 15 and 18 months, and 88 percent of those at 24 months, responded by touching their noses. Such a reaction suggests that they had a sense of self-awareness in that they knew what their own faces looked like.

Lewis and Brooks-Gunn also found that infants as young as from 9 to 12 months of age are capable of making some distinction between pictures of themselves and pictures of others. However, the evidence for this discrimination becomes stronger at about 15 months when they become particularly attuned to physical features associated with their sex and their age (they discern that females have differently shaped faces and different hairstyles from males and that babies have faces and heads that are shaped differently from those of adults). Of particular interest is children's use of *self-referents*—their own proper names and personal pronouns. Such self-referents emerge between the ages of 18 and 30 months (Lewis & Brooks-Gunn, 1979; Lewis, Sullivan, Stanger & Weiss, 1989).

Lewis and Brooks-Gunn suggest that there are four major advances in infants' self-knowledge during the first two years of life. At first, from birth to 3 months, infants are especially fascinated by human faces (see Chapter 6). The second advance takes place between 3 and 8 months of age when infants come to recognize themselves in mirrors and experimental TV screens through contingency cues (when the image of the body moves along with the self, one recognizes the self in that image). The third advance in self-knowledge occurs between 8 and 12 months of age as infants come to construct the self in Piagetian terms as a permanent object with enduring qualities. Finally, the fourth advance occupies the second year. During this phase children gain knowledge of particular physical attributes that distinguish them from other children and adults. They also gain a sense of "mine" with respect to toys and territory (Levine, 1983).

The development of a sense of self as separate and distinct from others is a central issue of children's early years (Neisser, 1988; Stern, 1985). This fundamental cognitive change facilitates numerous other changes in social development. Youngsters come to view themselves as active

agents who produce outcomes. Indeed, they derive pleasure from being "self-originators" of behavior. And so they insist that they be allowed to perform activities independently, behavior sometimes pejoratively labeled "the terrible twos." All the while toddlers increasingly focus on the outcomes of their activities rather than simply on the activities themselves (children younger than a year-and-a-half concentrate more on the flow of activities than on the ends or consequences to which their activities lead).

Toddlers also gain the ability to monitor their ongoing activities with respect to an anticipated outcome and to use external standards for measuring their task performance (first evident at about 26 months of age). By the time they are 32 months old, they recognize when they err in performing certain tasks and they correct their mistakes. For instance, in building a block tower, youngsters are not only better able to avoid errors in stacking blocks but to manipulate and rearrange the blocks when their first efforts fail (Bullock & Lutkenhaus, 1988; Kagan, 1981, 1984; Kopp, 1982).

A concept of the self may also be necessary for self-conscious and self-evaluative emotions, because a notion of self seemingly precedes both self-conscious emotions (for instance, embarrassment) and self-evaluative emotions (for example, pride or shame) (Lewis, Stanger & Sullivan, 1989; Lewis, Sullivan, Stanger & Weiss, 1989; Stipek, Gralinski & Kipp, 1990). Having de-

("Family Circus" © 1991 Bill Keane, Inc. Reprinted with special permission of King Features Syndicate.)

veloped self-conscious and self-evaluative emotions and the ability to evaluate objects and behavior in terms of some standard (particularly negative emotions when engaging in some transgression), youngsters gain the ability to inhibit their behaviors. in the absence of caretakers—in brief, social control becomes *self*-control (Kagan, 1984; Sears, Maccoby & Levin, 1957).

During the preschool years young children conceive of the self strictly in physical terms—body parts (the head), material attributes ("I have blue eyes"), and bodily activities ("I walk to the park") (Broughton, 1978; Johnson, 1990; Keller, Ford & Meacham, 1978; Seiman, 1980). Children view the self and the mind as simply parts of the body (Damon & Hart, 1982). For the most part, children locate the self in the head, although they may also cite other body parts like the chest or the whole body. And they often say that animals, plants, and dead people also have selves and minds.

Between 6 and 8 years of age children begin to distinguish between the mind and the body. The emerging distinction between the mental and the physical allows children to appreciate the subjective nature of the self. They begin to recognize that a person is unique not only because each of us looks different from other people but also because each of us has different feelings and thoughts. Hence, children come to define the self in internal rather than external terms and to grasp the difference between psychological and physical attributes. During adolescence the distinction between mind and body and the qualities of the self become more finely articulated (see Chapter 13).

Gender Identification

One of the early attributes of self is gender. A major developmental task for the child during the first six years of life is to acquire a gender identification. All societies appear to have seized on the anatomical differences between men and women to assign **gender roles**—sets of cultural expectations that define the ways in which the members of each sex should behave.

Societies throughout the world display considerable differences in the types of activities assigned to men and women (Intons-Peterson, 1988; Murdock, 1935). In some societies, for instance, women do most of the manual labor; in others, such as that of the inhabitants of the Marquesas Islands, cooking, housekeeping, and baby tending are male occupations.

Most people evolve gender identities that are reasonably consistent with the gender role standards of their society. **Gender identities** are the conceptions that people have of themselves as being male or female. Over the past thirty years a good deal of research has explored the process by which children come to conceive of themselves in masculine or feminine terms and to adopt the behaviors that are considered culturally appropriate for them as males or females. It has also

Girls as Tomboys

Some parents worry when their daughters display behavior that they interpret as "masculine." Of interest, only a third of the heterosexual women in a study conducted under the auspices of the Kinsey Institute described themselves as "highly feminine" in their childhood. *(Rick Smolan/ Stock, Boston)*

activated debate regarding the psychology of sex differences, a topic considered in the boxed insert on page 254.

Hormonal Influences on Gender Behaviors

What are little boys made of?
What are little boys made of?
Frogs and snails,
And puppy dogs' tails,
That's what little boys are made of.

What are little girls made of?
What are little girls made of?
Sugar and spice
And all that's nice
That's what little girls are made of.
—J. O. HALLIWELL

Nursery Rhymes of England, 1844

Some research suggests that biological differences between men and women contribute to the development of behavioral differences (Hines, 1982; Hines & Shipley, 1984; Mitchell, Baker & Jacklin, 1989). This research, primarily conducted with lower animals, reveals various linkages between hormonal conditions, brain functions, and behavior (Hines, 1982; Money & Ehrhardt, 1972). Endocrine glands secrete hormones—special chemical messengers—that are carried by the bloodstream to every part of the body. Among the most important are *testosterone*, the major male sex hormone, and *progesterone* and *estrogen*, the two principal female sex hormones. Each sex has some male and some female hormones. Differences between the sexes, and also within the two sex groups, result from differences in the *ratio* in which these hormones are present in the individual.

Researchers at the Oregon Regional Primate Research Center have experimented with the prenatal altering of hormone ratios in rhesus monkeys by injecting female rhesus monkey fetuses with male hormones. After birth these masculinized females exhibit genital alterations and behaviors typical of male monkeys. They engage in much of the rough-and-tumble play, the threatening gesturing, and the sexual mounting characteristic of male monkeys. Indeed, sometimes a masculinized female works her way up to the dominant position in her troop by sheer aggressiveness (Phoenix, Goy & Resko, 1969).

Over the past thirty years experimental studies with rats, guinea pigs, and monkeys have revealed that their brains contain sensitive tissues that have a bisexual potential. During the prenatal period these tissues become "imprinted" and subsequently serve to stimulate either masculine or feminine mating behavior at puberty.

Testosterone suppresses the "female" pattern, so that "male" neural tissues become organized in programming later male sexual responses. If the ratio of testosterone is minimal, the sensitive brain areas differentiate as "female." It is as if some inner behavioral dial is set at "male" or "female" during prenatal life (Gerall, 1973; Hines & Shipley, 1984; MacLusky & Naftolin, 1981; Scarf, 1972*a*).

John Money (1987), a psychologist at Johns Hopkins Medical Center, suggests that a somewhat similar bipotential for maleness or femaleness exists prenatally in human beings. He believes that the parts of the brain involved in sexuality are prenatally primed to make people more or less sensitive to certain kinds of environmental experiences. Money's research reveals that if the existing hormone balance is altered prenatally, it will result in altering postnatal behavior patterns. For example, if a female human fetus is given male hormones at a critical period during its development, the child who is born will tend to be more aggressive and more receptive to a variety of stimuli that are considered masculine in our culture than the average female. This phenomenon is most apparent in cases of girls suffering from *adrenogenital syndrome* (Ehrhardt & Meyer-Bahlburg, 1981). The condition is caused by a genetic defect in which the adrenal glands produce an excess of male hormones during the prenatal period. Somewhat similar effects are produced among females whose mothers were administered male hormones to prevent miscarriage during pregnancy.

In one group of twenty-five girls with adrenogenital syndrome who were studied by Money and his associates, twenty claimed to be "tomboys." Compared with a matched group of other girls, the girls with the adrenogenital syndrome showed considerably less interest in dolls and infant care. The tomboys preferred to be outdoors playing athletic games. Many of them had a high level of physical energy and liked playing with boys more than girls. They tended to prefer toy cars, trucks, and guns and showed little interest in cosmetics, perfume, jewelry, or hairstyles. While all the control-group girls were certain that they wanted to be mothers when they grew up, one-third of the girls with adrenogenital syndrome said that they would prefer not to have children. They also lagged behind their age-mates in beginning their dating life and venturing into the beginnings of love play. But despite these signs of tomboyishness, they showed no indication of lesbianism in their erotic interests. Hence, although possibly influencing gender-related be-

What Is the "Essential" Nature of Men and Women?

Intense debate currently surrounds questions regarding the "essential" or "basic" nature of men and women. Western culture has traditionally depicted the concepts "male" and "female" as opposites—as symbols of profound differences. Indeed, for centuries ignorance, superstition, and prejudice have surrounded both the popular and the scientific view of male-female differences. To find out which generalizations are justified and which are not, psychologists Eleanor E. Maccoby and Carol N. Jacklin (1974) spent three years compiling, reviewing, and interpreting over two thousand books and professional papers dealing with some eighty areas of performance and behavior where sex difference had been suspected, including motivation, social behavior, and intellectual ability. They could find only four fairly "well-established" sex differences between boys and girls:

❏ Beginning at about age 11 girls exhibit greater verbal ability than boys.
❏ Boys are superior to girls on visual-spatial tasks in adolescence and adulthood, though not in childhood.
❏ At about 12 or 13 years of age boys move ahead of girls in mathematical ability.
❏ Boys are more aggressive than girls.

Rather than settling the controversy, the Maccoby-Jacklin findings intensified it. Other psychologists promptly launched new surveys of the literature of gender differences and came to quite different conclusions. For instance, Julia Sherman (1978) and Janet Shibley Hyde (1981) reexamined the evidence for the three cognitive gender differences that Maccoby and Jacklin considered to be "well-established" (verbal ability, visual-spatial ability, and mathematical ability). They concluded that the magnitude of the differences is at best quite small. In the years that have intervened since the Maccoby-Jacklin survey, the gap between male and female performance on standardized tests has disappeared on verbal tests and narrowed on mathematics tests; only among highly precocious math students does the disparity between males and females remain large (Feingold, 1988; Holden, 1991; Hyde, Fennema & Lamon, 1990; Hyde & Linn, 1988).

Most psychologists agree that it is premature to look only to biology for explanations of gender differences in aptitude test scores, particularly because the gaps seem to be diminishing. Indeed, some psychologists have concluded that if all we know about a child is the child's sex, we know next to nothing about the child's cognitive abilities (Plomin & Foch, 1981). By way of illustration, consider the matter of self-confidence (Roberts, 1991). Educators find that it is a major factor predicting academic success. One explanation for the narrowing of the gender gap in mathematics is that the sexual revolution has made contemporary girls more confident about their mathematical talents and capabilities than previous generations (Kolata, 1989a). Even so, much bias remains. Research shows that girls are still treated differently in school than are boys and that parents, teachers, and peers hold higher academic expectations for boys than for girls (Eccles et al., 1983; Eccles, Adler

havior, the introduction of excess male hormones during the prenatal period does not appear to affect sexual orientation.

Quadagno, Briscoe and Quadagno (1977) suggest an alternative, nonhormonal hypothesis to that offered by Money. They believe that much of the modification of gender behavior in these girls was due to their having been reared differently by their parents. Furthermore, the girls may have been unsure of their role as mothers owing to certain biological problems (for instance, a number of the girls experienced a delay in the onset of menstruation). Even so, much of the animal literature supports the conclusion that prenatal endocrine factors play a part in influencing later behaviors. That human beings are immune to such influences seems unlikely. A number of

researchers suggest that hormonal factors again assume a major role at puberty, "pushing" individuals in the direction of male or female sex identities and behaviors (Imperato-McGinley, Peterson, Gautier & Sturla, 1981).

Perhaps the safest conclusion we can draw at the present time is that hormones "favor" a person for one kind of gender behavior or another. But even though hormones may predispose a person toward given kinds of behavior, they do not dictate that the behavior be learned. Rather, hormones make it easier for an individual to learn certain gender-related behaviors. And these behaviors are constantly being shaped and modified by the environment.

Some researchers have also looked to physical differences in the structure of the brain among

& Kaczala, 1982; Eccles & Jacobs, 1986). For instance, teachers typically call on boys more often than girls and give them more positive feedback than they do girls (Keegan, 1989). Other disparities also persist. A 1988 survey by the College Board found that 59 percent of college-bound male seniors, contrasted with 52 percent of female seniors, had taken trigonometry. The comparable figures for calculus were 21 percent for boys and 15 percent for girls. And whereas 51 percent of the boys had taken physics, only 35 percent of the girls had done so (Berger, 1989). When they reach college, women face a larger proportion of male than female instructors. A study of high-school valedictorians revealed that roughly equal numbers of boys and girls believed they were brighter than their peers. After two years of college, 22 percent of the boys believed they were intellectually superior to their peers but only 4 percent of the girls did (Kolata, 1989b). In sum, many factors weigh against women in math and science. As a result, young women may develop less confidence in their math abilities, less interest in studying math and physical science, and less interest in pursuing careers in math- and science-related fields (Eagly, 1987; Jacklin, 1989; Wilson & Bouldizer, 1990).

Much debate has also surrounded the matter of aggressiveness (Eagly, 1987). Five years after her earlier study Maccoby (1980, p. 211) again concluded: "The tendency of males to be more aggressive than females is perhaps the most firmly established sex difference and is a characteristic that transcends culture." And in 1990 she again reiterated this view (Maccoby, 1990). But psychologist Todd Tieger (1980) disagrees. On the basis of his survey of the literature, Tieger said that gender differences in aggression become observable in children's spontaneous behavior only at about 5 years of age. During these early years adults encourage boys to display aggression, whereas girls are pressured to inhibit it. Commenting on Tieger's review, Maccoby has acknowledged that aggressiveness is less a trait of individuals than it is behavior that characterizes people in certain situations (Maccoby & Jacklin, 1980). Moreover, when differences in aggression are found between men and women, the differences usually are not large (Hyde, 1984). So women, like men, can be expected to be aggressive when social expectations support aggression and to inhibit it in those domains where it is discouraged (Perry, Perry & Rasmussen, 1986).

Overall, the variations within each sex far exceed the differences between the sexes. Significantly, when asked whether man or woman is more intelligent, the English scholar and poet Samuel Johnson replied: "Which man? Which woman?" Apparently there is little that is inherently either male or female, although a society's definitions often make differences appear so (Condry & Ross, 1985; Deaux & Major, 1987; Fagot, Hagan, Leinbach & Kronsberg, 1985). The only firm differences relate to primary sexual attributes and functions: Women menstruate, gestate, and lactate; men ejaculate.

male and female animals as a possible source of behavioral differences. For instance, a number of investigators report that male and female rats differ in the tissue of several brain regions (for example, in the density of synaptic connections among nerve cells of the hypothalamus) (Hines, 1982; MacLusky & Naftolin, 1981).

Researchers have likewise scrutinized the human brain for sex differences (Gibbons, 1991). The human brain is composed of two hemispheres, each of which is specialized for certain kinds of tasks. For example, the left hemisphere typically excels at verbal processing (see Chapter 6). Some evidence suggests that patterns of cognitive specialization of the hemispheres are stronger, on the average, in males than in females (Hines, 1982). These differences in the lateralization of function may be related to sex differences in the shape and size of the human *corpus callosum* (the thick band or cable of nerves that carries messages back and forth between the two hemispheres) (De LaCoste-Utamsing & Holloway, 1982). However, we do not know whether sex differences in the structuring of particular regions of the brain are the source of differences in gender identity, behavior, sexual orientation, or cognitive processes.

Social Influences on Gender Behaviors

The fact that hormonal factors sometimes contribute to behavioral differences between men and women does not mean that environmental influences are unimportant. The major role played by environment is highlighted by **hermaphrodites**—individuals having the reproductive organs of both sexes. As a consequence of prenatal detours at critical junctures, individuals may develop both male and female internal reproductive organs; or they may possess external reproductive organs that are ambiguous, so that they appear to be one sex at birth only to find at puberty that they are the other.

John Money has conducted research with hermaphrodites that reveals the crucial part that social definitions play in influencing a child's gender identity. One of his most dramatic case histories is that of the identical-twin boy whose penis was accidentally cauterized during circumcision. When the child was 17 months old, his parents decided, in consultation with medical authorities, that he should be reared as a girl. Surgical reconstruction was undertaken to make him a female. Since then, the child has successfully developed a female gender identification. Although the child was the dominant twin in infancy, by the time the twins were 4 years old there was little doubt about which twin was the girl and which the boy. At 5 the girl preferred dresses to pants; enjoyed wearing hair ribbons, bracelets, and frilly blouses; experimented happily with styles for her long hair; headed her Christmas list with dolls and a doll carriage; and, unlike her brother, was neat and dainty (Money & Tucker, 1975).

In another case an individual who appeared "male" at birth learned at puberty, when breasts began to develop, that he possessed female sex organs. He demanded and received medical assistance, which enabled him to marry and, except for his inability to impregnate a woman, live an impeccably male life.

On the basis of his research with hermaphrodites, Money (Money & Tucker, 1975, pp. 86–89) concludes that the most powerful factors in the shaping of gender identity are environmental:

> The chances are that society had nothing to do with the turnings you took in the prenatal sex development road, but the minute you were born, society took over. When the drama of your birth reached its climax, you were promptly greeted with the glad ritual cry, "It's a boy!" or "It's a girl!" depending on whether or not those in attendance observed a penis in your crotch. . . . The label "boy" or "girl," however, has tremendous force as a self-fulfilling prophecy, for it throws the full weight of society to one side or the other as the newborn heads for the gender identity fork [in the road], and the most decisive sex turning point of all. . . . [At birth you were lim-

ited to] something that was ready to become your gender identity. You were wired but not programmed for gender in the same sense that you were wired but not programmed for language.

Clearly, anatomy in itself does not provide us with our gender identity. Because of being labeled a boy or a girl, a highly stylized treatment of the child is inaugurated that is repeated countless times each day. Boys receive more toy vehicles, sports equipment, machines, toy animals, and military toys; girls receive more dolls, doll houses, and domestic toys. Boys' rooms are more often decorated with animal motifs; girls' rooms with floral motifs accompanied by lace, fringes, and ruffles (Rheingold & Cook, 1975). Although the sexual revolution may have reshaped many nooks and crannies of U.S. life, it failed to reach very deeply into the toy box. Indeed, surveys on children's toys reveal that the girls' market has actually regressed to an earlier era, with more toys than ever involving play with hair, cosmetics, and clothing and an acting out of the "future"—going on dates and getting married (popular board games encourage preteen girls to compete for the date of their dreams). Boys' toys still center about competition and conflict—"good guys versus bad guys" motifs (Lawson, 1989). Behind many parents' concerns about the type of toys their children play with are unexpressed fears about homosexuality. Yet there is absolutely no evidence that children's toy preferences have anything to do with their later sexual preferences (Collins, 1984b).

Although women everywhere give birth to children and men do not, there is little evidence to support popular notions that somehow biology makes women kinder and gentler beings or that nature equips them specifically for nurturing roles (Whiting & Edwards, 1988). Psychologist Jerome Kagan, who has spent more than thirty-five years studying children, speculates that any propensity women may have for caretaking can be traced to an early awareness of their role in procreation: "Every girl knows, somewhere between the ages of 5 and 10, that she is different from boys and that she will have a child—something that everyone, including children, understands as quintessentially natural. If, in our society, nature stands for the giving of life, nurturance, help, affection, then the girl will conclude unconsciously that those are the qualities she should strive to attain. And the boy won't. And that's exactly what happens" (quoted by Shapiro, 1990, p. 59). Kagan's observations lead us to inquire as to the psychological processes that are at work in attuning youngsters to their gender roles, a matter to which we now turn our attention.

Theories Regarding the Acquisition of Gender Identities

Social scientists have proposed a number of theories regarding the process by which children psychologically become males or females. Among these theories are the psychoanalytic, cognitive learning, and cognitive-developmental approaches.

Psychoanalytic Theory According to Sigmund Freud, children are psychologically bisexual at birth. They develop their gender identities as they resolve their conflicting feelings of love and jealousy in relation to their parents (see Chapter 2). A boy develops a strong love attraction for his mother but fears that his father will punish him by cutting off his penis. The usual outcome of this Oedipal situation is for a boy to repress his erotic desire for his mother and identify defensively with the potential aggressor, his father. As a consequence of coming to feel identified with their fathers, boys later erotically seek out females.

Meanwhile, Freud said, girls fall in love with their fathers. A girl blames her mother for her lack of a penis. But she soon comes to realize that she cannot replace her mother in her father's affections. So most girls resolve their Electra conflicts by identifying with their mothers and later by finding suitable men to love.

Cognitive Learning Theory Cognitive learning theorists take the view that children are essentially neutral at birth and that the biological differences between boys and girls are insufficient to account for later differences in gender identities. They stress the part that selective reinforcement and imitation play in the process of acquiring a gender identity (see Chapter 2). Viewed from this perspective, children reared in normal

Acquiring Gender Identities

The members of society typically take considerable pains to socialize their children in the roles they deem appropriate for men and women. Children pick up the gender expectations that permeate their environment, and adults also intervene to cue children when they engage in behavior thought to be inappropriate for their gender. (Left, Alan Carey/The Image Works; right, Joel Gordon)

family settings are rewarded for modeling the behavior of the same-sex parent. And the larger society later reinforces this type of imitation through systematic rewards and punishments. Boys and girls are actively rewarded and praised, both by adults and by their peers, for what society perceives to be sex-appropriate behavior, and they are ridiculed and punished for behavior inappropriate to their sex (Eisenberg, Wolchik, Hernandez & Pasternack, 1985; Fagot, 1985; Smetana, 1986; Weitzman, Birns & Friend, 1985). Walter Mischel (1970) claims that children attend to, learn from, and imitate same-sex models more than opposite-sex models largely because they think of same-sex models as more like themselves.

Albert Bandura (1972a, 1973; Bussey & Bandura, 1984) gives an additional dimension to cognitive learning theory. He points out that in addition to imitating the behavior of adults, children engage in observational learning (see Chapter 2). According to Bandura, children mentally encode a model's behavior as they watch it, but they will not imitate behavior they have observed unless they believe that it will have a positive outcome for them. He says that children discern which behaviors are appropriate for each sex by watching the behavior of many male and female models. They notice which kinds of behavior are performed by which sex in which kinds of situations. In turn, they employ these abstractions of sex-appropriate behavior as "models" for their own imitative actions. But not everything learned is performed. Thus, although boys may know how to wear a dress and apply makeup, few boys actually choose to perform these behaviors. Rather, they are most likely to perform those behaviors that they have coded as appropriate to their own gender. Consequently, the responses children select from their behavioral repertoires depend chiefly on the consequences they anticipate will follow from the behaviors (Perry & Bussey, 1979).

Cognitive-Developmental Theory Still another approach, which is identified with Lawrence Kohlberg (1966; Kohlberg & Ullian, 1974), focuses on the part that cognitive development plays in children's acquisition of gender identities. This theory claims that children first learn to label themselves as males or females and then attempt to acquire and master the behaviors that fit their gender category. This process is called *self-socialization*. According to Kohlberg, children form a stereotyped conception of maleness and femaleness—an oversimplified, exaggerated, cartoonlike image. Then, they use this stereo-typed image in organizing their environment. They select and cultivate behaviors that are consistent with their gender concepts.

Kohlberg distinguishes between his approach and cognitive learning theory in these terms. According to the cognitive learning model, the following sequence occurs: "I want rewards; I am rewarded for doing boy things; therefore I want to be a boy." In contrast, Kohlberg (1966, p. 89) believes that the sequence goes like this: "I am a boy; therefore I want to do boy things; therefore the opportunity to do boy things (and to gain approval for doing them) is rewarding."

Genital anatomy plays a relatively minor part in young children's thinking about sex differences. Instead, children notice and stereotype a relatively limited set of highly visible traits—hairstyle, clothes, stature, and occupation. Children use the stereotyped *schemes* or *models* of gender that they evolve to structure their experiences and to make inferences and interpretations regarding gender behaviors (Bem, 1981, 1989; Martin, 1989; Martin & Halverson, 1981; Martin, Wood & Little, 1990; Picariello, Greenberg & Pillemer, 1990; Serbin & Sprafkin, 1986). These schemes or models begin developing rather early in life (Fagot & Leinbach, 1989; Levy & Carter, 1989; Martin & Little, 1990). Thus, Michael Lewis finds that by 12 months of age boys are more likely to look at pictures of boys when they are given a choice of pictures, whereas girls are more likely to look at pictures of girls (Collins, 1984b). Likewise, when given a choice of toys, boys more often play with "boy" toys and girls more often play with "girl" toys (Caldera, Huston & O'Brien, 1989). Apparently, by the time they are 3 years of age, 80 percent of U.S. children are aware of gender differences. By the age of 26 months most children can reliably indicate what sex they are and what sex others are. And by 36 months most youngsters categorize tasks like driving a truck or delivering mail as "masculine" and cooking, cleaning, and sewing as "feminine" tasks (Fagot, Leinbach & Hagan, 1986; O'Brien & Huston, 1985; Weinraub et al., 1984). Significantly, children tend to "forget" or distort information that runs counter to their developing gender schemes (Bigler & Liben, 1990; Carter & Levy, 1988; Weisner & Wilson-Mitchell, 1990).

Evaluation of Theories It is easy to become caught up in the bickering between differing theorists and to overlook the extent to which their theories converge. All three theories that we have considered stress the importance of children's knowledge about gender stereotypes as powerful

Sexist Toys

Children are taught their culture's definitions of appropriate male and female behaviors in a great variety of ways. Notice the gender typing of the occupations on the play board. Lawrence Kohlberg suggested that children use these stereotyped images in selecting and cultivating behaviors that are consistent with their gender concepts. *(Patrick Reddy)*

determinants of sex-typed behavior. And all three emphasize that behavioral differences between the sexes are at least in part perpetuated by the fact that children are more inclined to imitate the behavior of same-sex models than they are to imitate the behavior of opposite-sex models.

Each of the theories has some merit (Hyde & Rosenberg, 1976). Psychoanalytic theory has had historical importance in directing our attention to the part that early experience plays in fashioning an individual's gender identity and behavior. Cognitive learning theory has contributed to our knowledge by highlighting the social and cultural components of gender role development and the importance of imitation in the acquisition of gender behaviors (Fagot, Leinbach & Hagan, 1986). And cognitive-developmental theory has shown how a gender scheme, or mental model, leads youngsters to sort incoming information on the basis of gender categories and then to adopt the gender-linked characteristics (Cann & Newbern, 1984; Serbin & Sprafkin, 1986). So rather than

counterposing the three theories in an either-or fashion, many psychologists prefer to see them as supplementing and complementing one another.

Mothers, Fathers, and Gender Typing

Social psychologists suggest that gender stereotypes arise in response to a society's sexual division of labor and serve to rationalize this division by attributing to males and females basic personality differences (Hoffman & Hurst, 1990). It is hardly surprising, then, that parents have clear stereotypes regarding the behaviors they expect to be associated with male infants and female infants. Daughters are more often described by both their mothers and their fathers as "little," "beautiful," "pretty," and "cute" than sons are. Furthermore, there are marked and relatively consistent differences in paternal and maternal reactions to female and male infants (Parke, 1979). Fathers are more likely than mothers to view their sons as "firm," "large-featured," "well-coordinated," "alert," "strong," and "hard." And they are more likely than mothers to describe their daughters as "soft," "fine-featured," "awkward," "inattentive," "weak," and "delicate" (Rubin, Provenzano & Luria, 1974).

Evidence suggests that in U.S. society the father plays the critical role in encouraging "femininity" in females and "masculinity" in males in traditional terms (Block, 1974; Johnson, 1975; Langlois & Downs, 1980; Lynn, 1974, 1976; Weinraub et al., 1984). Fathers tend to be more concerned than mothers over their children's development of culturally appropriate sex roles, although this difference may be waning (Lynn, 1974, 1976; Fagot & Hagan, 1991). And fathers treat their sons differently from daughters (Siegal, 1987; Lytton & Romney, 1991). For instance, at 12 months of age boys are punished more by their fathers than girls are. Furthermore, whereas fathers give trucks and dolls with equal frequency to their daughters, most fathers withhold dolls from their sons (Snow, Jacklin & Maccoby, 1983).

Both fathers and mothers are more eager to push their sons toward masculinity than their daughters toward femininity. David B. Lynn (1976, p. 406), observes:

> For many [parents], the issue is less a positive concern that the boy may be masculine than a negative concern that he not be feminine. Being a "sissy" means doing anything that little girls do. To a large extent masculinity is defined through negative admonishments: "Don't cry," "Don't dress up in your sister's clothes," "Don't play with dolls."

Parents generally express more negative reactions when boys make choices culturally defined as feminine than when girls make choices commonly defined as masculine. Additionally, fathers' fears of homosexuality, in themselves or their sons, lead many men to inhibit displays of love and tenderness toward their sons (Parke, 1981).

Over the past forty or so years the following theory has dominated psychological inquiry and thinking regarding masculinity: Boys learn to be masculine by identifying with their own fathers. Mentally healthy men have a good, firm sense of themselves as masculine beings. However, since fathers are frequently absent from many U.S. homes during the formative years, large numbers of males grow into manhood lacking a secure sense of their masculinity. Male difficulties are compounded because so many teachers in the early grades are women. The results are very often homosexuality, exaggerated and overcompensating masculine behaviors, negative attitudes toward women, and poor psychological functioning.

These entrenched tenets are now being subjected to scrutiny and challenge (Stevenson & Black, 1988). The psychologist Joseph H. Pleck (1981) has examined the evidence in support of traditional assumptions regarding masculinity and found the evidence wanting. He concludes that a boy's masculinity is not necessarily related to the masculinity of his father, a father's absence does not produce inadequate masculinity, and homosexuals do not invariably lack a sense of masculinity. In fact, Pleck believes that the old assumptions have damaging consequences for both men and women. They reinforce conven-

Sex Typing

Gender roles represent the earliest division of labor among human beings. We all are born into societies with well-established cultural guidelines for the behavior of men and women. Each society attempts to fashion its boys into men and its girls into women in accordance with these expectations. *(Rick Smolan/Stock, Boston)*

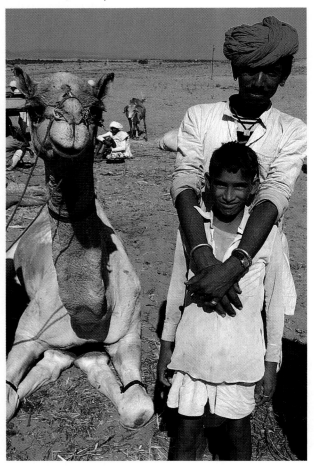

tional expectations of what it means to be a man, feed feelings of inadequacy if these expectations are not achieved, and inhibit the expression of many emotions.

Many people successfully integrate aspects of both the traditional masculine and the traditional feminine gender roles within their own gender role concepts. **Androgyny** is the term commonly used to refer to the capacity of men and women to be both masculine and feminine in their attitudes and behavior—both tough and tender, dominant and submissive, active and passive. At first, psychologists portrayed androgyny as a balance between masculinity and femininity (a scale ranging from high masculinity at one end to high femininity at the other end, with androgyny defined as the middle range). But in re-

cent years they have increasingly come to view as androgynous those persons who score high in masculinity *and* in femininity. So a person can be simultaneously high in masculine and feminine attributes, high in one but low in the other, or low in both. They class a person with high scores on both masculine and feminine attributes as "androgynous," a person scoring high on feminine but low on masculine attributes as "feminine," a person high on masculine but low on feminine attributes as "masculine," and persons with low scores of both masculine and feminine attributes as "undifferentiated" (Vander Zanden, 1987). The advantages or disadvantages of each pattern depend, to a great extent, on the situational context in which people find themselves.

SUMMARY

1. Intelligence refers to a person's general problem-solving abilities. Psychologists have applied differing models to the study of intelligence. Some psychologists view intelligence as a composite of many special, independent abilities. Others depict it as a process deriving from the interplay between children and their environment. Still others portray intelligence as an information-processing activity.

2. Psychologists differ in the relative importance that they attribute to heredity and environment in fashioning an individual's intelligence. However, most social and behavioral scientists believe that any extreme view regarding the nature-nurture controversy is unjustified at the present time.

3. Jean Piaget calls the years between 2 and 7 the "preoperational period." The principal achievement of the preoperational period is the developing capacity of children to represent the external world internally through the use of symbols.

4. During the preoperational period children have difficulty solving conservation problems. Logical thought is inhibited by obstacles associated with centering, transformations, reversibility, and egocentrism.

5. Recent research suggests that toddlers possess a significant implicit understanding of certain basic principles, including causality and number concepts. Such implicit understandings provide an important conceptual foundation for children's learning.

6. Memory is an integral component of cogni-

tion. Without memory we could not think or reason. Memory includes recall, recognition, and the facilitation of relearning.

7. As children develop, they become increasingly active agents in the remembering process. Among the strategies that facilitate remembering are grouping information into meaningful categories and rehearsing information.

8. To function as effective members of society, children need to develop the capacity mentally to "locate" or "place" individuals in their appropriate social categories. Sociologists call these categories "roles."

9. Through the cognitive structure termed the "self," we are able to take the viewpoint of other people and imagine what they anticipate and expect of us in a given role. It allows us imaginatively to exchange roles in order to grasp the requirements for sustained social interaction. A sense of self does not develop all at once, in an all-or-none fashion; it evolves through early, middle, and later childhood and, in fact, changes throughout life.

10. Research by John Money suggests that a bipotential for maleness or femaleness exists before birth. According to Money, prenatal hormones influence the subsequent course of a child's attraction to "masculine" or "feminine" behaviors.

11. On the basis of his research with hermaphrodites, Money concludes that the most powerful factors in the shaping of gender

identity are environmental. Individuals are wired but not programmed for gender identity.

12. Psychoanalytic theory stresses the part that Oedipal conflicts play in shaping children's gender identities. Cognitive learning theory emphasizes the part played by selective reinforcement and imitation. Cognitive-developmental theory claims that children first come to categorize themselves as male or female and then attempt to acquire and master those behaviors that fit their gender category.

13. Evidence suggests that in U.S. society the father plays the critical part in encouraging "femininity" in females and "masculinity" in males.

KEY TERMS

Androgyny   The capacity of men and women to be both masculine and feminine in their attitudes and behavior.

Causality   The attribution of a cause-and-effect relationship to two paired events that recur in succession.

Centering   Concentration on one feature of a situation while neglecting other aspects. The process is characteristic of preoperational children.

Conservation   The concept that the quantity or amount of something stays the same regardless of the changes in its shape or position.

Correlation Coefficient   A numerical expression of the degree of relationship between two variables or conditions.

Egocentrism   Lack of awareness that there are viewpoints other than one's own.

Gender Identity   The conception that people have of themselves as being female or male.

Gender Role   A set of cultural expectations that define the ways in which the members of each sex should behave.

Hermaphrodite   An individual having the reproductive organs of both sexes. As a consequence of prenatal detours at critical junctures, individuals may develop both male and female internal reproductive organs; or they may possess external reproductive organs that are ambiguous, so that they appear to be one sex at birth only to find at puberty that they are the other.

Intelligence   A global capacity to understand the world, think rationally, and cope resourcefully with the challenges of life.

Long-Term Memory   The retention of information over an extended period of time, through repeated rehearsal or because of a very intense single experience.

Memory   The retention of what has been experienced or learned.

Metacognition   Individuals' awareness and understanding of their mental processes.

Metamemory   Individuals' awareness and understanding of their memory processes.

Preoperational Period   According to Piaget, a stage in cognitive development that occurs between 2 and 7 years of age. The principal achievement of the period is the developing capacity of children to represent the external world internally through the use of symbols. The period's primary limitation is the inability of children to solve conservation problems.

Reversible   Operations capable of being turned back in opposite order to an earlier state. Children in the preoperational period fail to recognize that operations are reversible.

Role   A definition that specifies who does what, and when and where they do it; an expectation that group members hold regarding people's behavior in given settings.

Self   The system of concepts we use in defining ourselves; an awareness of oneself as a separate entity who is able to think and initiate action.

Sensory Information Storage   The preservation of information from the senses just long enough to permit the stimuli to be scanned for processing (generally less than 2 seconds).

Short-Term Memory   The retention of information for a very brief period, usually not more than 30 seconds.

Two-Factor Theory of Intelligence   An approach that views intelligence as made up of two components: (1) a general, or g, factor that is employed for abstract reasoning and problem solving, and (2) special, or s, factors that are peculiar to given tasks.

EARLY CHILDHOOD: INTEGRATION INTO THE HUMAN GROUP

Chapter 10

EARLY CHILDHOOD: INTEGRATION INTO THE HUMAN GROUP

◆

What we desire our children to become, we must endeavor to be before them.—ANDREW COMBE
Physiological and Moral Management of Infancy

Children are newcomers to the human group, strangers in an alien land. Genes do not convey *culture*—the socially standardized lifeways of a people. Clyde Kluckhohn (1960, pp. 21–22), a distinguished anthropologist, provides an illustration of this point:

> Some years ago I met in New York City a young man who did not speak a word of English and was obviously bewildered by American ways. By "blood" he was as American as you or I, for his parents had gone from Indiana to China as missionaries. Orphaned in infancy, he was reared by a Chinese family in a remote village. All who met him found him more Chinese than American. The facts of his blue eyes and light hair were less impressive than a Chinese style of gait, Chinese arm and hand movements, Chinese facial expression, and Chinese modes of thought. The biological heritage was American, but the cultural training had been Chinese. He returned to China.

The process of transmitting culture, of transforming children into bona fide, functioning members of society, is called **socialization.** Through socialization children acquire the knowledge, skills, and dispositions that enable them to participate effectively in group life. Since infants enter a society that is already an ongoing concern, they need to be fitted to their people's unique social environment. They must come to guide their behavior by the established standards—the accepted dos and don'ts—of their society.

The magnitude of a child's accomplishment over a relatively short period is truly astonishing. By their fourth birthday most U.S. children have mastered the complicated and abstract structure of the English language. And they can carry on complex social interactions in accordance with U.S. cultural patterns.

The enormity of this achievement strikes us when as adults we find ourselves in a society with a different culture from our own. Edmund Carpenter (1965, p. 55), an anthropologist, describes his feelings when he first began living among the Aivilik, an Eskimo people:

> For months after I first arrived among the Aivilik, I felt empty, clumsy. I never knew what to do, even where to sit or stand. I was awkward in a busy world, as helpless as a child, yet a grown man. I felt like a mental defective.

Only as Carpenter slowly and patiently learned the cultural ways of the Aivilik and became accepted by them did he feel comfortable in the new setting.

By the time a child reaches the age of 2, the socialization process has already begun. Developmental psychologists David P. Ausubel and Edmund V. Sullivan (1970, p. 260) observe:

> At this time parents become less deferential and attentive. They comfort the child less and demand more conformity to their own desires and to cultural norms. During this period [in most societies] the child is frequently weaned, is expected to acquire sphincter control, approved habits of eating and cleanliness, and do more things for himself. Parents are less disposed to gratify his demands for immediate gratification, expect more frustration tolerance and responsible behavior, and may even require performance of some household chores. They also become less tolerant toward displays of childish aggression.

Hence, it is within the family setting that the child is first introduced to the requirements of group life.

Family Influences

A young branch takes on all the bends that one gives it.
Chinese proverb

Early human development takes place largely within the context of the family. Significantly, children born over the past two decades have experienced a family environment quite unlike that of earlier generations. Moreover, many of the children are at risk for a variety of problems. Today, one out of five children is born out of wedlock, compared with one in ten in 1970 and one in twenty in 1960. Some 38 percent of unwed mothers are teenagers. Nearly one in four children is born into poverty. More than 20 percent of children today live with one parent. Nearly two-thirds of children go home from school to an empty house, because their parents (or parent) are at work. What is happening to our children is of concern to us all, whether or not we are parents. Today's children will bear the responsibility for the next generation of children and a growing population of dependent adults (Feistritzer, 1987). This stage of affairs leads us to take a closer look at family influences and parenting.

Determinants of Parenting

Until relatively recently, most socialization research focused on the processes whereby parental child-rearing strategies and behaviors shape and influence children's development. For the most part, psychologists and psychiatrists paid little attention to the parents themselves and the context in which they carried on their parenting. Also neglected was the part children play as active agents in their own socialization and in influencing the behavior of their caretakers. This focus has changed over the past decade, resulting in a more balanced perspective. Jay Belsky (1984a) has provided a framework that differentiates among three major determinants of parental functioning: (1) the personality and psychological well-being of the parent; (2) the characteristics of the child; and (3) the contextual sources of stress and support operating within and upon the family (see Figure 10-1).

The Parent Parenting, like other aspects of human functioning, is influenced by the relatively enduring characteristics, or personality, of a man or woman (Belsky, 1990; Cox, Owen, Lewis & Henderson, 1989). So, as you might expect, troubled parents are more likely to have troubled children. A six-year study of 693 families found that 66 percent of children with emotionally troubled mothers had psychological problems; 47 percent had problems in families where only the

father had symptoms; and 72 percent had problems when both parents were disturbed (double the rate for children with two healthy parents) (Parker, 1987). Other researchers find that constant parental irritability has an adverse effect on children's emotional well-being and on their development of cognitive skills (Goleman, 1986a, 1986d). Mothers suffering from psychological depression tend to be less affectionate, responsive, and spontaneous with their infants and be less patient and more punitive with their older youngsters than nondepressed mothers (Conger, McCarty, Yang, Lahey & Kropp, 1984; Fleming, Flett, Ruble & Shaul, 1988; Kochanska, Kuczynski, Radke-Yarrow & Welsch, 1987). In contrast, toddlers whose parents are happily married have more secure emotional ties to their parents and, as a result, seem to enjoy intellectual and other advantages over children of unhappily married people (Belsky & Isabella, 1988; Bradley & Caldwell, 1984; Bristol, Gallagher & Schopler, 1988; Cummings, Pellegrini, Notarius & Cummings, 1989; Goldberg & Easterbrooks, 1984; Grych & Fincham, 1990; Howes & Markman, 1989).

The Child Children's characteristics influence the parenting they receive (see Chapter 5). These characteristics include such variables as age (Kagan & Moss, 1962; Roberts, Block & Block, 1984), gender (Cowan & Avants, 1988; Egeland & Farber, 1984; Maccoby & Jacklin, 1974; Martin, 1981; Pianta, Sroufe & Egeland, 1989), and tem-

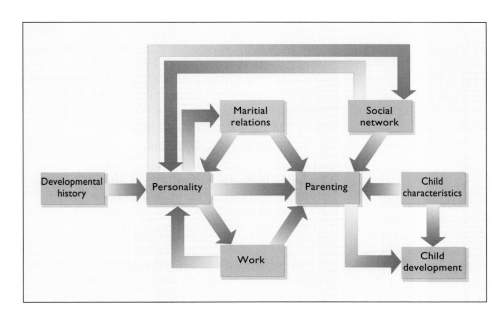

Figure 10-1 Jay Belsky's Process Model of the Determinants of Parenting
Belsky contends that three key interrelated determinants are associated with competent parental functioning: the personal psychological resources of parents, characteristics of the child, and contextual sources of stress and support. SOURCE: Jay Belsky, "The Determinants of Parenting: A Process Model," *Child Development*, Vol. 55 1984, Figure 1, p. 84. [Copyright © Society for Research in Child Development.]

perament (for instance, aggressiveness, passivity, affectionateness, moodiness, and negativity) (Bell, 1968; Crowell & Feldman, 1988; Pettit & Bates, 1989; Rutter, 1987). And some children are simply more difficult to rear than others. Anderson, Lytton, and Romney (1986) observed thirty-two mothers as they talked and played with three different boys, ages 6 to 11. Half the mothers had wayward sons who had been referred to a mental health facility and diagnosed as having serious behavior problems; the other half were mothers of sons with no serious behavior problems. The researchers counted the mothers' positive and negative actions, their verbal requests, and the extent to which the boys complied with the women in the course of the play sessions. The mothers of the difficult and nondifficult youngsters did not differ in their behavior. In addition, the wayward boys were substantially less compliant than were the other boys, regardless of how the women behaved or related to them. Overall, evidence suggests that parents and other adults typically react to disobedient, negative, and highly active youngsters with negative, controlling behavior of their own (Belsky, 1990; Bugental, Blue & Lewis, 1990).

Sources of Stress and Support Parents do not undertake their parenting in a social vacuum. They are immersed in networks of relationships with friends and relatives. And in many cases they are employed. These arenas of social interaction may be sources of both stress or support, or both. For instance, difficulties at work commonly spill over to the home, and so arguments at work are likely to be followed by arguments between a husband and wife in the evening (Menaghan & Parcel, 1990). Yet one strength of the human condition is the propensity we have for giving and receiving support. Social support has a beneficial effect on us irrespective of whether we are under stress (Crnic & Greenberg, 1990; Stevens, 1990). When we are integrated in social networks and groups, we have regular access to positive experiences and a set of stable, socially rewarded roles in the community. Support systems also buffer or protect us from the potentially harmful influence of stressful events (Crockenberg & McCluskey, 1986; Quittner, Glueckauf & Jackson, 1990; Zarling, Hirsch, & Landry, 1988). Not surprisingly, then, research undertaken among Japanese and U.S. mothers shows that the adequacy of a woman's mothering is influenced by the perception she has of her marital relationship. Where a women feels she has the support of her husband, she is more likely to involve herself with her infant (Durrett, Richards, Otaki, Pennebaker & Nyquist, 1986; Grossman, Pollack & Golding, 1988). Likewise, researchers find that parents with little social support do a poorer job of parenting than do parents who are integrated in well-functioning support systems. They are likely to have more household rules and to use more authoritarian punishment techniques (Belsky, 1984a). This latter result raises questions regarding the suitability of differing parenting practices, to which we now turn our attention.

The Search for Key Child-Rearing Practices

Parents wonder why the streams are bitter, when they themselves have poisoned the fountain.—JOHN LOCKE

Most authorities agree that parenting is one of the most difficult tasks any adult faces. Moreover, most parents are well intentioned and desire to succeed at parenting. Since the task is a difficult one that encompasses many years and consumes much energy, parents have often looked to experts in child psychology to provide them with guidelines for rearing mentally and physically healthy youngsters (Goodnow, 1988; Miller, 1988). But when parents turn to "authorities," they encounter immense frustration (Young, 1990). They confront an endless array of child-rearing books, misinformation, gimmickry, and outright quackery.

As we have already noted, until relatively recently, psychologists assumed that socialization effects flow essentially in one direction, namely, from parent to child. So for some fifty years—roughly between 1925 and 1975—they dedicated themselves to the task of uncovering the part that different parenting practices have in shaping a child's personality and behavior. Three dimensions emerged from this research:

❑ The warmth or hostility of the parent-child relationship (acceptance-rejection).
❑ The control or autonomy of the disciplinary approach (restrictiveness-permissiveness).
❑ The consistency or inconsistency that parents show in using discipline.

The Warmth-Hostility Dimension Many psychologists have insisted that one of the most significant aspects of the home environment is the warmth of the relationship between parent and child (Becker, 1964; Franz, McClelland & Weinberger, 1991; Kandel, 1990; McClelland, Con-

Child-Rearing Advice in the 1920s
In 1928, the leading Behaviorist, John B. Watson, advised parents to treat their children as young adults, to be "objective and kindly firm," but to eschew "mawkish, sentimental" displays of affection. *(Culver Pictures)*

stantian, Regalado & Stone, 1978; Sears, Maccoby & Levin, 1957; Symonds, 1939). Parents show warmth toward their children through affectionate, accepting, approving, understanding, and child-centered behaviors. When disciplining their children, parents who are warm tend to employ frequent explanations, use words of encouragement and praise, and only infrequently resort to physical punishment. Hostility, in contrast, is shown through cold, rejecting, disapproving, self-centered, and highly punitive behaviors (Becker, 1964).

Wesley C. Becker (1964), in a review of the research on parenting, found that love-oriented techniques tend to promote children's acceptance of self-responsibility and to foster self-control through inner mechanisms of guilt. In contrast, parental hostility interferes with conscience development and breeds aggressiveness and resistance to authority.

The Control-Autonomy Dimension Psychologists have emphasized that a second dimension also assumes critical importance in shaping the home environment: the restrictions that parents place on a child's behavior in such areas as sex play, modesty, table manners, toilet training, neatness, orderliness, care of household furniture, noise, obedience, and aggression toward others (Becker, 1964, Sears, Maccoby & Levin, 1957). On the whole, psychologists have suggested that highly restrictive parenting fosters de-

pendency and interferes with independence training (Maccoby & Masters, 1970). However, as Becker (1964, p. 197) observes in his review of the research literature, psychologists have had difficulty coming up with a "perfect" all-purpose set of parental guidelines:

> The consensus of the research suggests that both restrictiveness and permissiveness entail certain risks. Restrictiveness, while fostering well-controlled, socialized behavior, tends also to lead to fearful, dependent, and submissive behaviors, a dulling of intellectual striving and inhibited hostility. Permissiveness on the other hand, while fostering outgoing, sociable, assertive behaviors and intellectual striving, tends also to lead to less persistence and increased aggressiveness.

Combinations of Parenting Approaches Rather than examine the warmth-hostility and control-autonomy dimensions in isolation from one another, a number of psychologists (Becker, 1964; Schaefer, 1959) have explored their four combinations: warmth-control, warmth-autonomy, hostility-control, and hostility-autonomy. Figure 10-2 utilizes these descriptive categories to show various parent-child relations and their assumed consequences.

Warm but restrictive parenting is believed to lead to politeness, neatness, obedience, and conformity. It also is thought to be associated with immaturity, dependency, low creativity, blind acceptance of authority, and social withdrawal and ineptness (Becker, 1964; Levy, 1943). Eleanor E. Maccoby (1961) found that 12-year-old boys who had been reared in warm and restrictive homes were strict rule enforcers with their peers. Compared with other children, these boys also displayed less overt aggression, less misbehavior, and greater motivation toward schoolwork.

Psychologists report that children whose homes combine warmth with democratic procedures tend to develop into socially competent, resourceful, friendly, active, and appropriately aggressive individuals (Becker, 1964; Kagan & Moss, 1962; Lavoie & Looft, 1973). Where parents also encourage self-confidence, independence, and mastery in social and academic situations, the children are likely to show self-reliant, creative, goal-oriented, and responsible behavior. Where parents fail to foster independence, permissiveness often produces self-indulgent children with little impulse control and low academic standards.

Hostile (rejecting) and restrictive parenting is believed to interfere with children's developing self-identities and a sense of personal adequacy

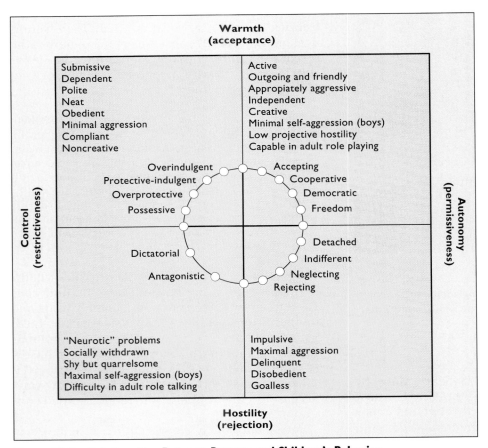

Figure 10-2   Relationships Between Parents and Children's Behavior
This figure represents the four combinations of the warmth-hostility and control-autonomy dimensions of parenting: warmth-control, warmth-autonomy, hostility-control, and hostility-autonomy. The terms around the circle (in black) are types of parental behavior. Listed in each box (in color) are children's personality traits that are associated with each of the four combinations of parenting. Of course, even at best, these descriptions are only general tendencies and not hard-and-fast results. SOURCE: Adapted from E. S. Schaefer, "A Circumplex Model for Maternal Behavior," *Journal of Abnormal and Social Psychology,* Vol. 59 1959, p. 232; and W. C. Becker, "Consequences of Different Kinds of Parental Discipline," in M. L. Hoffman and L. W. Hoffman (eds.), *Review of Child Development Research* New York: Russell Sage Foundation, 1964, pp. 169–208.

and competence. Children come to see the world as dominated by powerful, malignant forces over which they have no control. The combination of hostility and restrictiveness is said to foster resentment and inner rage. Some of the anger is turned against the self or experienced as internalized turmoil and conflict. This situation can result in "neurotic problems," self-punishing and suicidal tendencies, and inadequacy in adult role playing (Becker, 1964).

Parenting that combines hostility with permissiveness is thought to be associated with delinquent and aggressive behavior in children. Rejection breeds resentment and hostility, which,

when combined with inadequate parental control, can be translated into aggressive and antisocial actions. When such parents do employ discipline, it is usually physical, capricious, and severe. It often reflects parental rage and rejection and hence fails as a constructive instrument for developing appropriate standards of conduct (Becker, 1964).

Consistency in Discipline   Consistency in discipline is the third dimension of parenting that many psychologists have stressed is central to a child's home environment. Effective discipline is consistent and unambiguous. It builds a high degree of predictability into the child's environment. Although it is often difficult to punish children on a consistent, regular basis, research by Ross D. Parke and Jan L. Deur reveal that erratic punishment generally fails to inhibit the punished behavior (Deur & Parke, 1970; Park & Deur, 1972). In the case of aggression, researchers have found that the most aggressive children are those whose parents are permissive toward aggression on some occasions but severely punish it on others (Sears, Maccoby & Levin, 1957). Research suggests that parents who use punishment inconsistently actually create in their children a resistance to future attempts to extinguish the undesirable behavior (Deur & Parke, 1970; Parke, 1974).

Inconsistency can occur when the same parent responds differently at different times to the same behavior. It can also occur when one parent ignores or encourages a behavior that the other parent punishes (Gjerde, 1988; Vaughn, Block & Block, 1988). On the basis of his observation of family interaction patterns in the homes of 136 middle-class preschool boys, Hugh Lytton (1979) found that mothers typically initiate more actions designed to control their children's behavior than fathers do. However, the boys were less inclined to obey their mothers than they were their fathers. But when their fathers were present, they were more likely to be responsive to their mothers' commands and prohibitions. By the same token, the father's presence spurred the mother's behavior. She was more likely to reinforce the child's compliance, especially by positive, friendly acts. Lytton says it seemed as if she "knew" what was "expected" of her as a mother. However, she did not always carry it out to the same extent when she was alone with the child.

Parenting Styles

Diana Baumrind (1966, 1971*a*), a developmental psychologist, provides another scheme for examining and analyzing patterns of parental authority. She distinguishes among **authoritarian, authoritative, permissive,** and **harmonious parenting:**

❑ **Authoritarian parenting** The authoritarian parent attempts to shape, control, and evaluate a child's behavior in accordance with traditional and absolute values and standards of conduct. Obedience is stressed, verbal give-and-take discouraged, and punitive, forceful discipline preferred.

❑ **Authoritative parenting** The authoritative parent provides firm direction for a child's overall activities but gives the child considerable freedom within reasonable limits. Parental control is not rigid, punitive, intrusive, or unnecessarily restrictive. The parent provides reasons for given policies and engages in verbal give-and-take with the child, meanwhile responding to the child's wishes and needs.

❑ **Permissive parenting** Permissive parents seek to provide a nonpunitive, accepting, and affirmative environment in which the children regulate their own behavior as much as possible. Children are consulted about family policies and decisions. Parents make few demands on children for household responsibility or orderly behavior.

❑ **Harmonious parenting** Harmonious parents seldom exercise direct control over their children. They attempt to cultivate an egalitarian relationship, one in which the child is not placed at a power disadvantage. They typically emphasize humane values as opposed to the predominantly materialistic and achievement values they view as operating within mainstream society.

In a number of studies of white middle-class nursery-school children, Baumrind (1971*a*) found that different types of parenting tend to be related to quite different behaviors in children. Authoritative parenting was often associated with self-reliant, self-controlled, explorative, and contented children. In contrast, the offspring of authoritarian parents tended to be discontented, withdrawn, and distrustful. (And, as pointed out in the boxed insert, in some cases authoritarian parenting may be associated with child abuse and incest.) The least self-reliant, explorative, and self-controlled children were those with permissive parents.

The harmonious parents identified by Baumrind were only a small group. Of the eight children studied, six were girls and two were boys. The girls were extraordinarily competent, independent, friendly, achievement-oriented, and intelligent. The boys, in contrast, were cooperative but notably submissive, aimless, dependent, and not achievement-oriented. Although the sample was too small to be the basis for definitive conclusions, Baumrind tentatively suggests that these outcomes of harmonious parenting may be sex-related.

Baumrind believes that authoritative parenting gives children a comfortable, supported feeling while they explore the environment and gain interpersonal competence. Such children do not experience the anxiety and fear associated with strict, repressive parenting or the indecision and uncertainty associated with unstructured, permissive parenting. Laurence Steinberg, Julie D. Elmen, and Nina S. Mounts (1989) also find that authoritative parenting facilitates school success, encouraging a healthy sense of autonomy and positive attitudes toward work. Adolescents whose parents treat them warmly, acceptingly, democratically, and firmly are more likely than their peers to develop positive beliefs about their achievement and so are more likely to do better in school. In addition, authoritative fathers and mothers seem more adept at "scaffolding" than other parents. **Scaffolding** supports a child's learning through intervention and tutoring that provide helpful task information attuned to the child's current level of functioning (Pratt, Kerig, Cowan & Cowan, 1988).

On the basis of her research, Baumrind (1972) found a number of parental practices and attitudes that seem to facilitate the development of socially responsible and independent behavior in children:

❏ Parents who are socially responsible and self-assertive people and who serve as daily models of these behaviors foster these characteristics in their children.
❏ Parents should employ firm enforcement policies geared to reward socially responsible and independent behavior and to punish deviant behavior. This technique uses the reinforcement principles of conditioning (see Chapter 2). Parents can be even more effective if their demands are accompanied by explanations and if punishment is accompanied by reasons that are consistent with principles the parents themselves live by.
❏ Parents who are nonrejecting serve as more attractive models and reinforcing agents than rejecting parents do.
❏ Parents should emphasize and encourage individuality, self-expression, initiative, divergent thinking, and socially appropriate aggressiveness. These values are translated into daily realities as parents make demands upon their children and assign them responsibility.
❏ Parents should provide their children with a complex and stimulating environment that offers challenge and excitement. At the same time, children should experience their environment as affording security and opportunities for rest and relaxation.

Much research confirms Baumrind's findings and insights (Baldwin & Skinner, 1989; Booth, Mitchell, Barnard & Spieker, 1989; Freund, 1990; Holden & West, 1989; Kuczynski, Kochanska, Radke-Yarrow & Girnius-Brown, 1987; Lytton, 1980; Pettit & Bates, 1989). The ability to "achieve one's goals without violating the integrity of the goals of the other" is undoubtedly a major component in the development of social competence (Bronson, 1974, p. 280). Clearly, disciplinary encounters between parents and their youngsters provide a crucial context in which children learn strategies for controlling themselves and for controlling others. So parents who model competent strategies are more likely to have children who also are socially competent (Hard, Ladd & Burleson, 1990; Maccoby & Martin, 1983; Putallaz, 1987).

By way of illustration, consider Erik Erikson's (1963) notion that how toddlers resolve the stage of autonomy versus shame and doubt is linked to parental overcontrol (see Chapter 2). One indication that 2-year-olds are coming to terms with autonomy issues is their ability and willingness to say *no* to parents. The acquisition of *no* is a spectacular cognitive achievement because it accompanies youngsters' increasing awareness of the "other" and the "self" (Spitz, 1957) (see Chapter 9). *Self-assertion, defiance,* and *compliance* are distinct dimensions of toddler behavior. For instance, if a mother tells her toddler girl to pick up her toys and place them in a box, and the child says, "No, want to play," the youngster would be *asserting* herself. If instead the toddler takes more toys from the box or heaves a toy across the room, she would be *defying* her mother. But if the child follows her mother's instructions, she would be *complying.*

Susan Crockenberg and Cindy Litman (1990) shows that the way parents handle these autonomy issues have profound consequences for their youngsters' behavior. When parents assert their power in the form of negative control—threats, criticism, physical intervention, and anger—children are more likely to respond with defiance. Youngsters are less likely to become defiant when a parent combines a directive with an additional attempt to guide the child's behavior in a desired direction. This latter approach provides the toddler with information about what the parent wants, while inviting power sharing. For instance, if the parent asks the child to do something—"Would you pick up your toys, please?"—or attempts to persuade the child through reasoning—"You made a mess, so now you'll have to clean it up"—the parent implicitly validates for the child that she is a distinct and separate person with her own individual needs. This approach—consistent with Baumrind's authoritative style of parenting—keeps the negotiation process going and allows the toddler to "decide" to adopt the parent's goal. It seems that children are more willing to accept other people's attempts to influence their behavior if they perceive that they are participating in a reciprocal relationship where their attempts to influence others will also be honored (Maccoby & Martin, 1983; Parpal & Maccoby, 1985).

Guidance alone seems less effective than guidance combined with control. An invitation to comply—"Could you pick up the toys now?"—seems to afford the toddler a choice, and the child may feel free to turn it down in the absence of a clear and firm expression of parental wishes. This approach—guidance without control—is consistent with Baumrind's permissive style of parenting and seems to be linked to less competent child behavior. When toddlers assert themselves and their parents follow with a power directive—"You better do what I say or I'll spank you!"—the children may interpret the behavior as an assertion of parental power and a diminution of their own autonomy, an approach in keeping with Baumrind's authoritarian style of parenting (Crockenberg & Litman, 1990).

Overall, it seems that parents who are most effective in eliciting compliance from their youngsters and deflecting defiance are quite clear about what they want their children to do—yet all the while they are prepared to listen to their children's objections and to make appropriate accommodations in ways that convey respect for their youngsters' individuality and autonomy. At times, the process of achieving compliance may be somewhat extended and complex with the parent explaining, reasoning, persuading, suggesting, accommodating, and compromising. These parental behaviors encourage and elicit competent behavior from the child (Crockenberg & Litman, 1990). Of course much also depends on the situation and the ability of youngsters to comprehend their parents' instructions (Kaler & Kopp, 1990). Mothers tend to offer suggestions more often in playful exchanges, whereas they issue imperatives more frequently in limit-setting contexts (Lytton, 1980).

Gaining Perspective on Parenting

The parenting dimensions and styles that we have considered thus far in the chapter have had as their focus global patterns and practices. But they are much too abstract and gross to capture the subtleties of parent-child interaction. In

"According to this, everything we've done up to now is right."

(Drawing by Koren; © 1990. The New Yorker Magazine, Inc.)

everyday life parents reveal a great variety of parenting behaviors, depending on such factors as the situation; the gender and age of the child; parents' inferences regarding the child's mood, motives, and intentions; the child's understanding of the situation; the social supports available to the parent; and the pressures parents feel from other adults (Dix, Ruble & Zambarano, 1989; Gretarsson & Gelfand, 1988). For instance, parents can be warm or cold, restrictive or permissive, and consistent or inconsistent, depending on the setting and circumstances (Clarke-Stewart & Hevey, 1981; Grusec & Kuczynski, 1981; Passman & Blackwelder, 1981). The child's response to being disciplined also modifies the parent's behavior and the parent's choice of future disciplinary measures. And the way the child *perceives* the actions of the parent may be more decisive than the parent's actions in themselves. Thus, children are not interchangeable, responding in identical fashion to the same type of caretaker input.

The Harvard Child-Rearing Study   A follow-up on a classic study helps us in clarifying some of these matters. In the 1950s three Harvard psychologists carried out one of the most enterprising studies of child rearing ever undertaken in the United States. Robert Sears, Eleanor Maccoby, and Harry Levin (1957) attempted to identify those parenting techniques that make a difference in personality development. They interviewed 379 mothers of kindergartners in the Boston area and rated each mother on about 150 different child-rearing practices. Some twenty-five years later, a number of Harvard psychologists led by David C. McClelland (McClelland, Constantian, Regalado & Stone, 1978) contacted many of these children—then 31 years old, most of them married and with children of their own.

McClelland and his associates interviewed the individuals and administered psychological tests to them. They concluded that not much of what people think and do as adults is determined by the specific techniques of child rearing their parents used during their first five years. Practices associated with breast feeding, toilet training, and spanking are not all that important. It is how parents *feel* about their children that *does* make a difference. What mattered was whether a mother liked her child and enjoyed playing with the child or whether she considered the child a nuisance, with many disagreeable characteristics. Furthermore, children of affectionate fathers were more likely as adults to show tolerance and understanding than were the offspring of other fathers.

The Harvard researchers (McClelland, Constantian, Regalado & Stone, 1978, p. 53) conclude:

> How can parents do right by their children? If they are interested in promoting moral and social maturity in later life, the answer is simple: they should love them, enjoy them, want them around. They should not use their power to maintain a home that is only designed for the self-expression and pleasure of adults. They should not regard their children as disturbances to be controlled at all costs.

The Harvard Preschool Project   Another group of Harvard researchers shed additional light on effective parenting. Burton L. White and his colleagues studied the development of overall competence in children (White & Watts, 1973). The goal of the research, christened the Harvard Preschool Project, was to find ways to optimize human development. The researchers intensively studied the mother-child interactions of thirty-one toddlers with different competence ratings. White (1973, p. 242) concludes that a number of child-rearing practices appear to foster competence:

> [The effective mothers] talk a great deal to their children. . . . They make them feel as though whatever they are doing is usually interesting. They provide access to many objects and diverse situations. They lead the child to believe that he can expect help and encouragement most, but *not all* the time. They demonstrate and explain things to the child, but mostly on the child's instigation rather than their own. . . . They are secure enough to say "no" to the child from time to time without seeming to fear that the child will not love them. They are imaginative, so that they make interesting associations and suggestions to the child when opportunities present themselves. They very skillfully and naturally strengthen the child's intrinsic motivation to learn. They also give him a sense of task orientation, a notion that it is desirable to do things well and completely. They make the child feel secure.

One finding of considerable interest was that the most effective mothers did not devote the bulk of their day to child rearing. They were busy women and in some cases held part-time jobs. Instead of giving the children all their time, these effective mothers tried to create an environment compatible with the burgeoning curiosity of their toddlers. They recognized that a youngster and a spotless, meticulously kept home are incompatible. Their children had access to small, manipulable, visually detailed objects (toys, plastic refrigerator containers, empty milk cartons, old shoes, magazines, and the like) and to materials

Sexual Abuse of Children

Most of us find the idea that parents may be sexually attracted to their children so offensive that we prefer not to think about it. Indeed, only in the past decade or so have professionals come to view the sexual abuse of children as a major mental health problem. Even more recently, as the taboos against talking about incest crumble, a number of prominent individuals have indicated that they were the victims of childhood sexual abuse, including Roseanne Arnold, Oprah Winfrey, La Toya Jackson, and former Miss America Marilyn Van Derbur Atler (Darnton, 1991; Gorman, 1991). Estimates of the prevalence of child sexual abuse range from 6 percent to 62 percent for females and from 3 percent to 31 percent for males (Peters, Wyatt & Finkelhor, 1986). Whatever the number, sexual abuse is a problem affecting large numbers of youngsters. **Sexual abuse of children** is commonly defined as forced, tricked, or coerced sexual behavior between a child and an older person (Gelles & Conte, 1990).

Most research has dealt with the sexual abuse of females. The perpetrator is commonly the father, an uncle, or another male authority figure in the household. In cases of father-daughter incest, the fathers tend to be "family tyrants" who use physical force and intimidation to dominate their families (Finkelhor, 1979; Herman & Hirschman, 1981). However, the daughter chosen as the object of the father's sexual attention may be exempted from physical attack and may tolerate the father's sexual advances so as to preserve her privileged position. Sexual contact usually begins when the child is between 5 and 12 years old, and it typically consists at first of fondling and masturbation. The behavior continues over time and may eventually proceed to intercourse.

Sexually abused children are usually afraid to tell others about their experiences. However, they may show a variety of behavioral problems or bodily complaints (particularly urinary problems or pelvic pain). On occasion the child may exhibit sexual knowledge and preoccupations that are precocious for her age. Not uncommonly, teenage runaways and prostitutes are the victims of incest. Drug abuse, behavior problems, learning difficulties, sexual promiscuity, runaway behavior, gastrointestinal and genitourinary complaints, compulsive rituals, clinical depression, low self-esteem, and suicidal behavior are often associated with the experience (Forward, 1989; Gelles & Conte, 1990; Morrow & Sorell, 1989). And the women tend to show lifetime patterns of psychological shame and stigmatization.

Mothers in incestuous families are usually passive, have a poor self-image, and are overly dependent on their husbands. They frequently suffer from mental illness, physical disability, or repeated pregnancy. Under these circumstances, much of the housework and child care falls on the oldest daughter, who is the one most likely to be sexually victimized by the father. Although incest commonly involves the oldest daughter, the behavior is often repeated with younger daughters, one after another. Moreover, a father's incestuous behavior places his daughters at greater risk of sexual abuse by other male relatives and family intimates.

Unfortunately, there is little known or written about male victims, even though there is an increase in the number of boy victims being identified (Everstine & Everstine, 1989). The available evidence suggests that boys and girls respond differently to sexual victimization. Because boys are socialized to gain control of themselves and their environments, boys may feel their masculine competence has been compromised or destroyed when they are sexually abused. Or they may attempt to "minimize" the importance of the abusive events. Complicating matters, male victims often face the additional problem of stigmatization as homosexual since the large majority of abusers are male (Bolton, Morris & MacEachron, 1989).

Incest victims and their families can find help by consulting a women's center, a rape crisis center, or the child protective services in a community. Sexual abuse should always be reported to the appropriate authorities. Adults should never dismiss a child's complaint of sexual abuse; false complaints are quite rare. Measures need to be taken that strengthen the role of the mother in the family and the relationship between the mother and daughter. All parties—the child, the offender, the mother, and other family victims—should receive professional treatment (Eversteine & Everstine, 1989; Forward, 1989; Haugaard & Reppucci, 1988; Herman & Hirschman, 1981).

Interest in developing programs to help youngsters escape or prevent abuse began in earnest in the early 1980s. By the 1990s, a good many prevention programs had been designed that employed multiple modes of audiovisual technology (film, video, audiotape, and filmstrip) and format (story books, coloring books, songs, plays, and board games). The materials and programs are based on a number of assumptions: Many children do not know what constitutes sexual abuse, children need not tolerate sexual abuse, and children should inform responsible adults upon being sexually touched by an older person. Researchers have attempted to evaluate materials and programs (Gelles & Conte, 1990). Most generally they report positive results, but self-protection against sexual abuse is a complex process for any child, and programs are seldom comprehensive enough to have a long-term, meaningful impact (Reppucci & Haugaard, 1989).

that help to develop motor skills (scooters, tricycles, and so forth). Also, the effective mothers did not necessarily drop what they were doing to respond to their toddlers' requests. If they were busy they said so, giving the child a small but realistic taste of things to come in the larger world. Overall, children whose mothers expected them to learn very little developed more slowly than children whose mothers expected them to begin learning early in life.

Summing Up   Clearly, parenting is not a matter of employing a surefire set of recipes or formulas. Parents differ and children differ. Parents who employ identical "good" child-rearing techniques have children who grow up to be exceedingly different (Martin, 1981). Furthermore, situations differ, so that what may work in one setting may boomerang in another. As highlighted by the Harvard research, the essence of parenting is in the parent-child *relationship.* In interaction with one another parents and children evolve ongoing accommodations that reflect one another's needs and desires. Parent-child relationships differ so much, both within the same family and among families, that in many respects each parent-child relationship is unique (Elkind, 1974).

If we can distill a message from the work of contemporary developmental psychologists regarding parenting it would be this: Enjoy your children and love them. There is no mysterious, secret method you must master. It is the child that matters, not the technique. Be skeptical of the exaggerated claims of the popularizers and commercializers of this or that fad. Trust yourself. On the whole, most parents do very well.

The developmental psychologist Michael Lewis places these matters in sound perspective:

> To my mind, the critical thing a scientist can do is to show parents the process by which they can understand their own children—to show how we work, rather than to behave as experts dispensing information. You can assess your children as a scientist does. . . . Connect your own facts about your children, and act on them. Do what parents have always done—inquire of peers who have children, and of older people who have been through it. (Quoted by Collins, 1981*a*, p. 17)

Finally, note that even the experts do not put all their faith in books. They too find, "You have to be yourself—be genuine. You can't raise your children by someone else's rules and principles" (Fedak, 1981). And most experts say that if they

How Parents Feel About Their Youngsters Makes a Difference
Increasingly psychologists are reaching the conclusion that how parents feel about their children makes a greater difference than the specific child-rearing techniques they employ. Parenting is not a matter of magical formulas but one of enjoying children and loving them. *(Steve McCurry/Magnum)*

ran into difficulty, they would not hesitate to consult another expert about their children. Parents should not think that they must handle their problems all by themselves.

Single-Parent Families and Children of Divorce

About 80 percent of white children, 67 percent of Hispanic children, and 38 percent of black children currently live with both biological parents. Twenty percent of all youngsters live in single-parent households, 9 percent with one biological parent and a stepparent, and 4 percent live with neither parent. The fastest increase in the number of single-parent families came in the 1970s; the numbers continued to rise during the 1980s, but at a slower rate than the previous decade. Some 42 percent of contemporary white children and 86 percent of contemporary black children will live in a single-parent household sometime in their youth. Eighty-five percent of single-parent white children and 94 percent of black children live with their mothers (Lewin, 1990).

Until recently, many psychologists and sociologists viewed the single-parent family as a lamentable, defective, and even pathological arrangement in need of fixing. Many professionals referred to it as "broken," "disorganized," or "disintegrated" (for example, see Cavan, 1964). But over the past twenty years professionals have increasingly come to recognize that the single-parent home is a different but viable family form (Bilgé & Kaufman, 1983; Brandwein, Brown & Fox, 1974; Marotz-Baden, Adams, Bueche, Munro & Munro, 1979). Nonetheless, the nation's schools in large measure continue to stigmatize the children and their situations as abnormal, both in school practices and in the attitudes of school personnel.

Many single-parent families do have serious financial problems, although this is hardly evidence of pathology (Hoffman & Duncan, 1988; McLanahan & Booth, 1989; Seltzer, 1991). Of the 12 million U.S. youngsters—nearly 25 percent of the national total—who live below the federally defined poverty level, the vast majority are found in single-mother households. One major difference between husband-wife families and one-parent families is that many of the former have two incomes and the latter have at most one income. In addition, women's employment tends to pay less well and is more sporadic than that of men. Census Bureau figures reveal that more

than 9.4 million women in the United States are raising children without the children's father. About 59 percent of these women have been awarded child support, but only 51.3 percent of these mothers receive full payment (24.9 percent receive partial payments, and 23.9 percent do not receive any payments) (Dunn, 1990). (The boxed insert examines the impact that changes in the divorce laws have had on women and children.) Among never-married mothers only 6 percent get any financial help from their children's fathers (Fletcher, 1989; Jencks, 1982). Significantly, 74 percent of never-married mothers aged 15 to 24 live in poverty. And children who live with divorced single-parent mothers are likely to experience a dramatic decline in their standard of living compared with their predivorce, two-parent household (DeParle, 1991; Furstenberg & Cherlin, 1991; Hoffman & Duncan, 1988).

In the United States the major cause of single-parent families is divorce, which typically involves many stressful changes in family relationships. The most frequent family arrangement in the period immediately following a divorce is one in which children are living with their mothers and having only intermittent contact with

"I thought we agreed that the dining room was a buffer zone."

(Drawing by Wm. Hamilton; © 1991. The New Yorker Magazine, Inc.)

their fathers. Divorce is a process that begins well before parents separate and continues long afterward (Cherlin et al., 1991; Furstenberg & Cherlin, 1991). E. Mavis Hetherington, Martha Cox, and Roger Cox (1976, 1977) made a two-year longitudinal study in which they matched a preschool child in a divorced family with a child in an intact family, on the basis of age, sex, birth-order position, and the age and education of the parents. In all, forty-eight divorced couples were paired with forty-eight intact families.

Hetherington, Cox, and Cox (1977, p. 42) found that the first year after the divorce was the most stressful—for both parents:

> The divorced mother complained most often of feeling helpless, physically unattractive, and of having lost the identity associated with her husband's status. Fathers complained of not knowing who they were, of being rootless, of having no structure or home in their lives. The separation induced profound feelings of loss, previously unrecognized dependency needs, guilt, anxiety, and depression in both parents.
>
> Divorce was a blow to both parents' feelings of competence for the first year. They thought they had failed as parents and spouses and doubted their ability to adjust well in any future marriages. They felt that they did not handle themselves well in social situations, and that they were incompetent in sexual relations.

Many of the stresses that parents experience following divorce and the accompanying changes in their lifestyles are reflected in their relationships with their children (Wallerstein & Kelly, 1980; Webster-Stratton, 1989). Indeed, stressful events in the life of the mother are more predictive of adjustment in the children than are stressful events in the life of the child (Guidubaldi & Perry, 1985; Hodges, Tierney & Buchsbaum, 1984). Hetherington, Cox, and Cox (1976, p. 424) found that the interaction patterns between the divorced parents and their children differed significantly from those encountered in the intact families:

> Divorced parents make fewer maturity demands of their children, communicate less well with their children, tend to be less affectionate with their children and show marked inconsistency in discipline and lack of control over their children in comparison to parents in intact families. Poor parenting seems most marked, particularly for divorced mothers, one year after divorce, which seems to be a peak of stress in parent-child relations. [Many of the mothers referred to their relationship with their child one year after divorce as involving "declared war" and a "struggle for survival."] Two years following the divorce, mothers are demanding more . . . [independent and] mature behavior of their children, communicate better and use more explanation and reasoning, are more nurturant and consistent and are better able to control their children than they were the year before. A similar pattern is occurring for divorced fathers in maturity demands, communication and consistency, but they are becoming less nurturant and more detached from their children. . . . Divorced fathers were ignoring their children more and showing less affection [while their extremely permissive and "every day is Christmas" behavior declined].

Hence, many single-parent families had a difficult period of readjustment following the divorce, but the situation generally improved during the second year. Other researchers confirm this finding (Ambert, 1984; Elias, 1987).

Hetherington found that much depends on the ability of the custodial mother to control her children. Homes in which the mother loses control are associated with drops in children's IQ scores, poorer school grades, and a decrease in children's problem-solving skills. Children whose mothers maintain good control show no drop in school performance. Hetherington also found that when single-parent mothers lose control of their sons, a "coercive cycle" typically appears. The sons tend to become more abusive, demanding, and unaffectionate. The mother responds with depression, low self-esteem, and less control, and her parenting becomes worse (Albin, 1979; Baldwin & Skinner, 1989; Hetherington, 1989). In contrast, mothers and daughters in mother-headed families often express considerable satisfaction with their relationships, except for early-maturing girls whose heterosexual and older-peer involvements frequently weaken the mother-child bond (Hetherington, 1989). Moreover, children and adolescents living in single-parent homes, particularly boys, are at substantially greater risk for discipline problems in school, dropping out of school, and engaging in delinquent behavior than are peers living in intact families (Dawson, 1991; Hetherington, 1989; Kline, Johnston & Tschann, 1991; Needle, Su & Doherty, 1990; Steinberg, 1987b; Webster-Stratton, 1989). However, some of the adverse effects of family disruption derive from the economic deprivation and lower socioeconomic status that flow from divorce rather than from single parenthood itself (Acock & Kiecolt, 1989; McLanahan & booth, 1989; Smith, 1990).

Hetherington (1989) undertook a follow-up study six years later, asking, "Which children are the winners, losers, and survivors six years after divorce?" (p. 11.) Children from divorced or re-

Do No-Fault Divorce Laws Victimize Women and Children?

Changing patterns of marriage and divorce have brought about a revolution in U.S. life. Today, a married couple is as likely to be parted by divorce as by death. And more than half of U.S. children are likely to experience the dissolution of their parents' marriage by the time they are 18. Moreover, the legal process of divorce has undergone substantial transformation since the advent of no-fault divorce laws in 1970, changing the meaning of marital partnerships and marital commitments. Sociologist Lenore Weitzman (1985, 1990) had studied the economic and social consequences of the new divorce laws for women and children in the United States. Under the old laws men were required to support a dependent former wife; today, courts expect most women to be responsible for themselves after divorce.

Weitzman (1985) analyzed some 2,500 divorce decrees issued both before and since California's no-fault reforms became law in 1970. Additionally, she interviewed family court judges and prominent divorce lawyers and more than 100 recently divorced couples in the Los Angeles area. She had begun her research assuming that no-fault divorce was a path-breaking improvement for women and families. But she found otherwise. The laws, designed by their framers to treat women and men equally, have in practice created hardship for divorced women and their children. She particularly targets the nonsupport of children by divorced fathers, a record of inadequate awards, rampant default, and insufficient enforcement. Consequently, in the first year after divorce the standard of living of the typical divorced woman with young children plummets 73 percent, while that of her divorced husband goes up 42 percent. Older children suffer, too, since child support ends at age 18 in many states.

Weitzman (1985) sought to understand why divorce has become "a financial catastrophe for most women." She found that most courts do not require husbands to contribute more than one-third of their income to the support of their ex-wives and children. Moreover, judges frequently order the family home be sold, with half the proceeds going to the wife, resulting in the woman having to find a much smaller house with less elbow room for herself and her children. Furthermore, valuable but often intangible assets acquired during the marriage—credit, pensions, insurance, entitlements, professional credentials, and future earning power—usually follow the husband. Finally, a divorced woman is likely to enter a competitive labor market without skills, seniority, or ample opportunity for training (see also Fassinger, 1989; McLanahan & Booth, 1989; Peterson, 1989).

Weitzman (1985) also highlights the plight of older homemakers, because both their husbands and society had promised the women that marriage is a lifetime commitment and homemaking an honorable occupation. But no-fault divorce changed the rules in the middle of the game—after the women had fulfilled their share of the bargain. Now the women find that they are unable to make up for the twenty-five or so years they spent out of the labor force (also see Uhlenberg, Cooney & Boyd, 1990). Weitzman says that the new laws give a clear message to young women in planning their futures: Divorce may send you into poverty if you invest in your family ahead of your career. She urges judges and legislators to rethink current notions about alimony and to recognize it as an acceptable way to compensate long-married women for their marital contributions.

Weitzman (1985, 1990) does not favor a return to the earlier system with its rancorous charges of cruelty and adultery, its use of private detectives for spying on spouses, and the legal wrangling over the assignment of guilt. Most of her recommendations consist primarily of adjustments in the interpretation, enforcement, and administration of current laws: the inclusion of "career assets"—pensions and retirement benefits, education and training, enhanced earning capacity, medical and health insurance, and other entitlements—along with material goods when marital assets are divided; effective child-support enforcement measures such as withholding wages, property liens, and the threat of jail; and assurance of an equal share of the marital property to long-married, older homemakers. She adds that the parent with the major responsibility for minor children should also be allowed continued use of the home—the home being defined as part of the child-support award rather than as an unequal division of property. In sum, Weitzman places the problems that divorced women and their children face in the context of society, tracing the structural forces that generate poverty and hardship. Although no-fault laws in many states differ from those in California, and perhaps bias her research, they do not seem to invalidate her major findings. However, Weitzman chiefly examined the short-term, immediate effects of divorce. Over a longer term, many divorced women adjust by working more hours and by taking jobs with higher pay in order to restore a measure of the standard of living they lost (Peterson, 1989).

married families were overrepresented in three categories. One cluster of youngsters—"aggressive, insecure" children—were prone both to impulsive, irritable outbursts and to sullen brooding periods of withdrawal at home and school. These children were unpopular with their peers, had difficulties in school, had few areas of satisfaction, and experienced low levels of self-esteem—all contributing to their lonely, unhappy, angry, anxious, and insecure childhoods. Two other clusters—"opportunistic-competent" and "caring-competent" children—seemed to adapt quite well. They were high in self-esteem, were popular with their peers and teachers, functioned at average or above-average levels in the classroom, and gave little evidence of behavior problems. Youngsters in both categories exhibited competence, flexibility, and persistence in dealing with demanding and stressful circumstances. However, in their social relationships, opportunistic-competent children were quite manipulative, attempting with considerable success to ingratiate themselves with people in power (parents and teachers and high-status peers). Caring-competent youngsters were much less inclined toward manipulative behaviors and were disposed toward helping and sharing behaviors, often befriending neglected or rejected peers.

In 1971, clinical psychologists Judith S. Wallerstein and Joan Kelly (1980) began a study of sixty middle-class California families undergoing divorce. Included in the families were 131 children and adolescents, all of whom were developmentally normal, doing well in school, and in good mental health. The researchers then reinterviewed the family members eighteen months, five years, and ten years after the divorce (Wallerstein & Blakeslee, 1989; Wallerstein, Corbin & Lewis, 1988). Unfortunately, the lack of a control group of comparable intact families makes it difficult to arrive at definitive conclusions (see Chapter 1). Even so, the study is insightful.

Wallerstein and her associates found that the preschoolers often responded to their parents' divorce with pervasive feelings of sadness, strong wishes for reconciliation, and worries about having to take care of themselves. Many of them also had to deal with deep anger toward one or both parents, feelings of rejection, and guilt for having caused the breakup. In contrast, older children and adolescents were better able to accurately assign responsibility for the divorce (and so not blame themselves), to resolve loyalty conflicts, and to assess and to cope with the transitions accompanying family dissolution. Older children also were more likely to find social support networks outside the family and many "grew up faster"—but often at the expense of their family ties (also see Hetherington, 1989; Weiss, 1979).

The follow-up studies suggested that much depends on the age of children at the time of divorce. The cognitive immaturity of the preschoolers proved beneficial to many of them. Ten years after divorce they had fewer memories of either parental conflict or their own earlier fears and anxieties than did the older children. And many had also evolved a close relationship with the custodial parent. It seems that most young children adapt quite well to divorce if they do not encounter substantial new sources of personal or family stress. Even so, at least one-third of the children showed symptoms of depression and were functioning poorly five or ten years later. In contrast, with their younger counterparts, adolescents—who retained active memories of the conflict and stress that accompanied the divorce—were more consciously troubled. After ten years, half of the children in the study had gone through a parent's second divorce. At the ten-year mark, 35 percent had poor relationships with both parents, and 75 percent felt their fathers had rejected them. Fathers generally had difficulty retaining a strong or particularly meaningful relationship with their youngsters without daily contact. Many of the men wanted to be good fathers, but they lacked the resources to span the emotional and geographical distances (also see Cooney & Uhlenberg, 1990; Dudley, 1991).

Researchers find that the quality of the child's relationship with *both* parents is the best predictor of his or her postdivorce adjustment. Children who maintain stable, loving relationships with both parents appear to experience fewer emotional scars (they exhibit less stress and less aggressive behavior, and their school performance and peer relations are better) than do children lacking such relationships (Clingempeel & Reppucci, 1982; Peterson & Zill, 1986). The importance for the child of maintaining a postdivorce relationship with both parents has led to the concept of joint legal custody (Ferreiro, 1990; Luepnitz, 1982; Seltzer, 1991). Under this arrangement both parents share equally in the making of significant child-rearing decisions, and both parents share in regular child care responsibilities. The child lives with each parent a substantial amount of time (for example, the child may spend part of the week or month in one parent's house and part in the other's). Joint custody also eliminates the "winner-loser" character of custodial disposition and much of the sadness, sense of loss, and loneliness that the noncustodial parent frequently feels.

Single-Parent Families

Although the single-parent family has traditionally suffered a bad reputation, it is increasingly recognized as a viable family form. Most children are resilient and can flourish in a wide variety of family arrangements so long as they are loved and their basic needs are met. *(Camilla Smith/Rainbow)*

But joint custody is not an answer for all children. Critics point out that parents who cannot agree during marriage cannot be expected to reach agreement on rules, discipline, and styles of parenting after marriage. And they say that alternating between homes interferes with a child's need for continuity in his or her life (Goldstein, Freud & Solnit, 1973; Simon, 1991). Furthermore, the geographically mobile nature of contemporary society and the likelihood of parental remarriage render a good many joint-custody arrangements vulnerable to collapse (Benedek & Benedek, 1979; Simon, 1991). So probably it is not surprising that initial evidence suggests that joint-custody arrangements do not differ from sole-custody arrangements in children's adjustment to divorce (Johnston, Kline & Tschann, 1989; Kline, Tschann, Johnston & Wallerstein, 1989; Maccoby, Depner & Mnookin, 1990).

Despite the problems that many parents and children have during the first year or two follow-ing divorce, most authorities believe that divorce is not necessarily disastrous for children. With respect to school achievement, social adjustment, and delinquent behavior, the differences are small or nonexistent between children from one- and two-parent homes of comparable social status (Burchinal, 1964; Guidubaldi & Perry, 1985; Kinard & Reinherz, 1986; Kohn, 1977). Some research suggests that children and adolescents from single-parent homes show less delinquent behavior, less psychosomatic illness, better adjustment to their parents, and better self-concepts than those from unhappy intact homes (Cooper, Holman & Braithwaite, 1983; Nye, 1957; Raschke & Raschke, 1979). Even so, neither an unhappy marriage nor a divorce is especially congenial for children. Each alternative poses its own sets of stresses (Wallerstein & Kelly, 1980).

Many authorities argue that the behavior problems of some children who have divorced parents derive not directly from the disruption of family bonds but from the difficulties in interpersonal relations with which the disruption is associated (Block, Block & Gjerde, 1986; Cherlin et al., 1991; Emery, 1982; Furstenberg & Cherlin, 1991; Rutter, 1974). They point to the part that parental conflict, tension, and discord play in feeding negative self-conceptions and identities, in jeopardizing youngsters' sense of security, in hindering children's development of peer relationships, and in increasing children's susceptibility to illness (Cummings, Pellegrini, Notarius & Cummings, 1989; Gottman & Katz, 1989; Jouriles, Pfiffner & O'Leary, 1988). Psychiatrists and clinical psychologists note that in many cases divorce actually serves to reduce the amount of friction and unhappiness that a child experiences; consequently, divorce leads to better behavioral adjustments (Demo & Acock, 1988; Hess & Camara, 1979; Hetherington, 1979; Mechanic & Hansell, 1989). Indeed, most divorced mothers believe that their children are living better lives in a divorced family than in a family agonized by marital conflict (Goode, 1956). However, high levels of marital conflict before divorce predicts a more difficult parent-child relationship after parental separation, and a poorer parent-child relationship, in turn, is related to impaired emotional and behavioral adjustment in youngsters after separation (Tschann, Johnston, Kline & Wallerstein, 1989). Overall, research strongly suggests that it is the *quality* of children's relationships with their parents that matters much more than the fact of divorce (Emery, 1982; Hess & Camara, 1979; Rutter, 1974). These and other findings suggest that as a nation we may need to change our view of what constitutes a "normal" family.

Sibling Relationships

*Big sisters are the crab grass
in the lawn of life.*—CHARLES M. SCHULZ
Peanuts

Some of the most important relationships that children have within the family are those they have with brothers and sisters. A child's position in the family *(birth order)* and the number and sex of his or her siblings are thought to have major consequences for the child's development and socialization. These factors structure the child's social environment, providing a network of key relationships and roles. An only child, an oldest child, a middle child, and a youngest child all seem to experience a somewhat different world because of the different social webs that encompass their lives. Some psychologists contend that these and other environmental influences operate to make two children in the same family as different from one another as are children in different families (Daniels, 1986; Daniels, Dunn, Furstenberg & Plomin, 1985; Rowe & Plomin, 1981). These psychologists say that there is a unique *microenvironment* in the family for each child. In this view there is not a single family but, rather, as many "different" families as there are children to experience them. These psychologists conclude that the small degree of similarity in personality found among siblings results almost totally from shared genes rather than from shared experience. In short, the unique aspects of each sibling's experiences in the family are more powerful in shaping his or her personality than what the siblings experience in common. Many of the differences in the family environment are more obvious to children than to their parents. And much depends on how children perceive and interpret parental affection and discipline (Goleman, 1987*b*).

Sibling interactions often continue across the life span (Cicirelli, 1989; Goetting, 1986; Gold, 1989; Gold, Woodbury & George, 1990; Suggs, 1989). The "pioneering function" of older brothers and sisters may persist lifelong, providing role models in coping with bereavement, retirement, or widowhood (McGloshen & O'Bryant, 1988; O'Bryant, 1988; Sobel, 1980). And many individuals rely on a living sibling for help and companionship in old age (Chatters, Taylor & Neighbors, 1989; O'Bryant, 1988). Indeed, by virtue of today's frequent divorces and remarriages, some children form stronger bonds with their siblings than they do with their parents or stepparents (Beer, 1989; Cicirelli, 1980; Goetting, 1986). Sibling rela-

tionships typically become more egalitarian but also less intense as youngsters move into later childhood and adolescence (Buhrmester & Furman, 1990).

Through the years research has been focused on firstborn children, for they appear to be fortune's favorites (Cicirelli, 1978). Firstborns are overrepresented among students in graduate and professional schools (Goleman, 1985), at the higher-IQ levels (Zajonc, 1976), among National Merit and Rhodes Scholars, in *Who's Who in America* and *American Men and Women of Science,* among individuals on *Time's* cover, among U.S presidents (52 percent), among the 102 appointments to the Supreme Court (55 percent were either only children or firstborns), among men and women in Congress, and in the astronaut corps (twenty-one of the first twenty-three United States astronauts who flew on space missions were either only children or firstborn sons). However, these birth-order advantages do not hold in a good many families and for individuals from lower socioeconomic backgrounds (Ernst & Angst, 1983; Glass, Neulinger & Brim, 1974). Furthermore, some research suggests that middle children tend to have lower self-esteem than do firstborns and lastborns, perhaps a function of their less well-defined position within the family (Goleman, 1985; Kidwell, 1981, 1982). And some, but not all, researchers find that later-born children possess better social skills than do firstborns (Miller & Maruyama, 1976; Snow, Jacklin & Maccoby, 1981).

Fewer effects related to birth order are found in the United States than in most other societies. A cross-cultural study of thirty-nine societies reveals that firstborns are more likely than later-borns to receive elaborate birth ceremonies, to have authority over siblings, and to receive respect from siblings. In comparison with other sons, firstborn sons generally have more control of property, more power in the society, and higher social positions (Rosenblatt & Skoogberg, 1974). Moreover, older siblings act as caretakers for their younger siblings in a good many cultures (Dunn, 1983).

A number of explanations have been advanced to account for differences between firstborn and later-born children. First, research reveals that parents attach greater importance to their first child (Clausen, 1966; Sears, Maccoby & Levin, 1957). There are more social, affectionate, and caretaking interactions between parents and their firstborns (Cohen & Beckwith, 1977; Jacobs & Moss, 1976). Thus, firstborns have more exposure to adult models and to adult expectations and pressures (Baskett, 1985).

A second explanation of the differences between first- and later-born children derives from **confluence theory,** a model devised by psychologist Robert B. Zajonc (1975, 1983, 1986; Zajonc, Markus, Berbaum, Borgh & Moreland, 1991) and his colleagues. Confluence theory gets its name from the view that the intellectual development of a family is like a river, with the inputs of each family member flowing into it. According to Zajonc, the oldest sibling experiences a richer intellectual environment than younger siblings do. He contends that each additional child "waters down" the intellectual climate by increasing the incidence of interactions with childish minds as opposed to adult minds. So the more older siblings a person has, the lower will be his or her intellectual level because of the decrease within the family intellectual environment. Zajonc says that the same principle helps explain why twins tend to score about five points below the norm on IQ tests. On the other hand, any adult added to the family—grandparent, uncle, or aunt—helps raise the intellectual quality of the environment. Zajonc believes the firstborn is also advantaged for another reason. The eldest child plays a parent-surrogate or teacher role in dealing with later-born siblings. Such a "helper" role appears to be instrumental in the development of verbal and cognitive skills (Cicirelli, 1973; Dunn, 1983). However, critics fault the confluence model, especially the mathematical operations that Zajonc has used in testing it (Brackbill & Nichols, 1982; Galbraith, 1982; Retherford & Sewell, 1991; Rodgers, 1984).

A third explanation—the **resource dilution hypothesis**—extends the confluence model to encompass more resources than simply a rich intellectual environment. This theory says that in large families resources get spread thin, to the detriment of all the offspring. Family resources include such things as parental time and encouragement, economic and material goods, and various cultural and social opportunities (music and dance lessons and travel at home and abroad). Sociologists commonly employ the resource dilution hypothesis to explain the relationship they find between the number of siblings and educational attainment: Increases in the number of siblings are associated with the completion of fewer years of schooling and the attainment of fewer educational milestones (positions in student government, on the school newspaper, in drama groups, and so on). Put another way, families with

"I wish we never had P.J."

("Family Circus" © 1990 Bill Keane, Inc. Reprinted with special permission of King Features Syndicate.)

few children can offer greater educational advantages to their offspring; conversely, families with large numbers of children can offer fewer educational advantages to their children. In this manner, family size is linked to greater or lesser degrees of achievement (Blake, 1989; Steelman & Powell, 1989).

A fourth explanation, which was first advanced by Alfred Adler, stresses the part that sibling power and status rivalry play in a child's personality formation (Ansbacher & Ansbacher, 1956). Adler viewed the "dethroning" of the firstborn as a crucial event in the development of the first child. With the birth of a brother or sister, the firstborn suddenly loses his or her monopoly on parental attention (Kendrick & Dunn, 1980). This loss, Adler said, arouses a strong lifelong need for recognition, attention, and approval that the child, and later the adult, seeks to acquire through high achievement. An equally critical factor in the development of the later-born child is the competitive race for achievement with older and more accomplished siblings. In many cases the rancor disappears when individuals get older and learn to manage their own careers and married lives (Sorel, 1980).

The sex of a child's sibling may also be of significance. Individuals with an older, opposite-sex sibling are especially likely to have rewarding interactions with strangers of the opposite sex (Ickes & Turner, 1983). And Helen Koch (1956) found that the sex of a sibling has consequences for a person's gender role performance. She showed that children imitate their older siblings' behavior and that, as a result, boys who have a slightly older sister tend to develop a less masculine role than do firstborn boys or boys with older brothers. Likewise, girls with older brothers are more disposed toward "tomboy" behavior than girls with older sisters.

However, more recent research by Gerald S. Leventhal (1970) reveals that men with older sisters often display more masculine behavior as traditionally defined in the United States than men with older brothers do. In a family of two male children the younger boy may adopt behavior patterns opposite to those of his older brother to avoid unfavorable comparison with his more accomplished brother. Another study, made by Karen Vroegh (1971), shows that neither the sex of all a child's siblings nor the sex of a child's older siblings has any consistent effect on gender role identity. Hence, the effect of the sex of one sibling upon the gender role identity of another remains unresolved. Very likely, the relationship is considerably more complex than that suggested by Koch's earlier research. This conclusion is supported by other recent studies (Abramovitch, Corter, Pepler & Stanhope, 1986; Grotevant, 1978; Scarr & Grajek, 1982). As discussed in Chapter 3, the relationships between young siblings are particularly affected by the children's relationships with their parents (Dunn, 1983; MacKinnon, 1989; Stocker, Dunn & Plomin, 1989).

In sum, birth order, family size, and the sex of a child's siblings do not stand up well as indicators of how well an individual child will fare in life. Many unique genetic and environmental factors intervene in individual families, producing wide differences among families and among their members (Heer, 1985).

Peer Relationships

Man is a knot, a web, a mesh into which relationships are tied.—ANTOINE DE SAINT–EXUPÉRY

We have seen that children enter a world of people, an encompassing social network. With time, specific relationships change in form, intensity, and function, but the social network itself stretches across the life span. Yet social and behavioral scientists mostly ignored the rich tapes-

try of children's social networks until the past two decades or so. They regarded social intimacy as centering on one relationship, that of the infant and mother. Thus, they treated the ties that young children have with other family members and with age-mates as if they did not exist or had no importance. However, a growing body of research points to the significance of other relationships in the development of interpersonal competencies. This section will discuss children's peer relationships and friendships. **Peers** are individuals who are approximately the same age. Early friendship is a major source of a youngster's emotional strength, and its lack can pose lifelong risks (Flaste, 1991; Selman & Schultz, 1990). (Also see Chapter 12.)

Peer Relationships and Friendships

Friendship is a single soul dwelling in two bodies.—ARISTOTLE

From birth to death we find ourselves immersed in countless relationships. Few are as important to us as those we have with our peers and friends (Berndt & Ladd, 1989; Schneider, Rubin & Ledingham, 1985; Tesch, 1983). Thus, not surprisingly, research reveals that peer relationships and friendships are in their own right a meaningful experience in the lives of young children (Gottman, 1983; Mueller & Cooper, 1986). Carol O. Eckerman, Judith L. Whatley, and Stuart L. Kutz (1975) studied sixty normal, home-reared children under two years of age. Each child was paired with an age-mate in a laboratory setting. Although interactions were infrequent, children from 10 to 12 months old occasionally smiled and "vocalized" to each other, offered and accepted toys, imitated each other, and struggled over or fussed about toys. At each age interval between 10 and 24 months, children paid increasingly more attention to toys and peers and less attention to their mothers. Furthermore, the children increasingly integrated their activities with toys and peers, so that by 2 years of age social play predominated.

In another study Judith Rubenstein and Carollee Howes (1976) observed a number of 18-month-old children who regularly played together in a one-to-one situation in their homes. A greater amount of positive social interaction took place among these long-acquainted peers than among the unacquainted children studied by Eckerman, Whatley, and Kutz. During a peer's visit the acquainted children would spend over

50 percent of their time socially interacting with each other. Other research also shows that acquainted peers have more positive interaction with each other, and engage in less conflict, than unacquainted peers do (Becker, 1976; Doyle, Connolly & Rivest, 1980; Hartup, Laursen, Stewart & Eastenson, 1988).

Children as young as 3 years of age form friendships with other children that are surprisingly similar to those of adults (Rubin, 1980). And just as different relationships meet different needs for adults, so do they for young children. Some relationships are reminiscent of strong adult attachments; others of relationships between adult mentors and protégés; and still others of the camaraderie of adult coworkers. Although young children may lack the reflective understanding that many adults bring to their relationships, they nonetheless often invest their friendships with an intense emotional quality (Selman, 1980). Moreover, some young children bring a considerable measure of social competence to their relationships and a high level of mutuality and give and take (Berndt, 1981*a*, 1981*b;* Brownell, 1990; Hartup, 1983; Krantz, 1982; Masters & Furman, 1981). As we pointed out in Chapter 8, attachment theory predicts that the quality of the mother-child tie has implications for a child's close personal relationships. Researchers confirm that preschoolers with secure maternal attachments enjoy more harmonious, less controlling, more responsive, and happier relationships with their peers than do preschoolers with insecure maternal attachments (Park & Waters, 1989).

A variety of studies reveal that with increasing age, peer relationships are more likely to be formed and more likely to be successful (Furman & Bierman, 1984; Ladd & Emerson, 1984). Four-year-olds, for instance, spend about two-thirds of the time when they are in contact with other people associating with adults and one-third of the time with peers. Eleven-year-olds, in contrast, spend about an equal amount of time with adults and with peers (Wright, 1967).

A number of factors contribute to this shift in interactive patterns. First, as children grow older, their communicative skills improve, facilitating effective interaction (Eckerman & Didow, 1988; Gottman, 1983). Second, children's increasing cognitive competencies enable them to attune themselves more effectively to the roles of others (Bronson, 1985; Fabes, Eisenberg, McCormick & Wilson, 1988; Furman & Bierman, 1983; Hartup, 1989; Miller & Aloise, 1989; Selman, 1980). Third, nursery and elementary school attendance offers increasing opportunities for peer interaction. And fourth, increasing motor competencies expand the child's ability to participate in many joint activities.

Interestingly, children of preschool age assort themselves into same-sex play groups (Jacklin & Maccoby, 1978; LaFreniere, Strayer & Gautheir, 1984; Maccoby, 1988, 1990). In a longitudinal study, Eleanor E. Maccoby and Carol N. Jacklin (1987) found that preschoolers at 4½ years of age spent three times as much time playing with same-sex playmates as they did with opposite-sex playmates. By 6½ years of age, the youngsters were spending eleven times as much time with same-sex as with opposite-sex partners. Moreover, preschool girls tend to interact in small groups, especially two-person groups, whereas boys more often play in larger groups (Eder & Hallinan, 1978; Lever, 1978). One reason for this difference is that boys tend to select games that require a larger number of participants than those selected by girls. (But these differences in the play activities of boys and girls are often fostered by parental and teacher socialization prac-

Same-Sex Play Groups
This 1941 photo depicts recess at a black Veysey school in Greene County, Georgia. A similar pattern of same-sex play groups prevails on contemporary playgrounds. *(Library of Congress)*

tices.) The two sexes have somewhat different play styles. Boys' play has many rough-and-tumble physical qualities to it and strong overtones of competition and dominance. Girls engage in more intimate behavior than boys do, and two-person groups are conducive to intimate behavior. Girls are more likely than boys to disclose intimate information to a friend and to hold hands and display other signs of affection. We will provide a more detailed discussion of same-sex groupings in Chapter 12.

Peer Reinforcement and Modeling

Children play an important part as reinforcing agents and behavioral models for one another—a fact that adults at times overlook. Much learning takes place as a result of children's interaction with other children (Azmitia, 1988; Hall & Cairns, 1984). Here is a typical example (Lewis, Young, Brooks & Michalson, 1975, p. 27):

> Two four-year-olds are busily engaged in playing with "Playdoh." The room echoes with their glee as they roll out long "snakes." Each child is trying to roll a longer snake than the other. The one-year-old sibling of one of the children, hearing the joyful cries, waddles into the room. She reaches for the Playdoh being used by her sibling. The older child hands the one-year-old some Playdoh, and the child tries to roll her own snake. Unable to carry out the task and frustrated, the one-year-old becomes fussy, at which point the older sibling gives the child a knife. The four-year-old then shows the sibling how to cut the snakes the other children have made.

Indeed, the old one-room school functioned, and functioned well, with the teacher teaching the older children and the older children teaching the younger boys and girls.

One way that children influence one another is through actions that encourage or discourage given behaviors. Robert G. Wahler (1967) demonstrated the importance of such reinforcement processes by enlisting five children in a nursery school as his experimenter confederates. These children were instructed to ignore certain classmates when they showed a specific behavior and pay positive attention to them when they showed another behavior. The result was that the classmates performed the ignored activity less often, and the rewarded activity more often, than they had done before. Then, Wahler's child confederates resumed their usual patterns of peer interaction, and the behavior of their classmates returned to what it had been before the experiment. In general, spontaneous peer reinforcement increases with age, occurring more frequently among 4-year-olds than among 3-year-olds (Charlesworth & Hartup, 1967).

Seeing other children behave in certain ways can also affect a child's behavior. Indeed, imitating one another's nonverbal play actions is the predominant strategy that toddlers between 16 and 32 months of age use to coordinate their activities. By means of imitate-in-turn and follow-the-leader games, youngsters gain a sense of connectedness, of other children being like themselves, and of successfully exerting social control over the behavior of others (Eckerman, Davis & Didow, 1989; Eckerman & Stein, 1990). In addition, a study by Robert D. O'Connor (1969) reveals that severely withdrawn nursery school children engage in considerably more peer interaction after they watch a twenty-minute sound film that portrays other children playing together happily. And as noted in the boxed insert "Helping Children Cope with Their Fears" in Chapter 11, modeling has proved to be an important tool for aiding children to overcome various fears.

Play

It is a happy talent to know how to play.—RALPH WALDO EMERSON

Americans tend to view play as an irrational, trivial, and ephemeral activity, one that is not especially important. To the extent that the United States has inherited the Puritan work ethic—where busyness is equated with virtue, and idleness with evil—play has been regarded as a suspect activity. Yet play makes an important contribution to personal and social development over a person's entire life span. Historians and anthropologists find that play can be traced back through antiquity to the earliest peoples. **Play** may be defined as voluntary activities that are not performed for any sake beyond themselves. They are activities that people commonly view as being outside the serious business of life.

There are many forms of play, including pretend play, exploration play, games, social play, and rough-and-tumble play. In recent years pretend play has captivated the interest of many psychologists (Fein, 1981; Pederson, Rock-Green & Elder, 1981) who have viewed make-believe or fantasy behavior as an avenue for exploring the "inner person" of the child and as an indicator of underlying cognitive changes. Thus, during the first two years children's play shifts from the simple, undifferentiated manipulation of objects to an exploration of the objects' unique properties and to make-believe play involving ever more complex and cognitively demanding behaviors

Varied Types of Play
Different patterns of play characterize nursery-school children.
These photos show (a) unoccupied play, (b) associative play,
and (c) cooperative play. (a and c, Elizabeth Crews; b, Jerry
Howard/Stock, Boston)

(Forys & McCune-Nicolich, 1984; O'Connell & Bretherton, 1984). As might be expected, the proportion of children who engage in pretend play with other youngsters increases with age. Some researchers suggest that social pretend play may exceed the cognitive capacities of children under 3 years of age (Rubin, Fein & Vandenberg, 1983). But others document social pretend play among some children at age 2, although more complex forms of social pretend play indeed appear later (Howes, 1985; Howes, Unger & Seidner, 1989). As we saw in Chapter 9 and will discuss in Chapter 11, pretend play is associated with the development of children's role-taking capabilities.

In a classic study Mildred B. Parten (1932) observed the play of children in nursery school set-

tings. She identified six types of play, based on the nature and extent of the children's social involvement:

❏ **Unoccupied play** Children spend their time watching others, idly glancing about, or engaging in aimless activities (standing around, getting on and off a chair, tugging on their clothing, and so on).
❏ **Solitary play** Children play with toys by themselves and make no effort to get close to or speak with other children.
❏ **Onlooker behavior** Children watch other children at play, occasionally talking to them or asking them questions. However, they do not themselves join the play.

❏ **Parallel play** Children play independently beside other children but not with them. Although they play close together and with similar toys, they do not interact.

❏ **Associative play** Children interact with one another, borrowing or lending play material, following one another with carts, cars, or trains, and attempting to influence each other's behavior. Each child does as he or she sees fit; no division of labor or integration of activity takes place.

❏ **Cooperative play** Children integrate their play activities. In this kind of play the members usually take on different role responsibilities, and they often think of themselves as belonging to a group from which other children are excluded.

Once Parten had developed her descriptive categories, she made use of the time-sampling technique (see Chapter 1) to classify children's activities. She discovered that social participation among preschoolers tends to increase with age. Parallel play predominated among two-year-olds and remained an important type of behavior throughout the preschool period. Associative play came to the foreground among 3-year-olds, slightly exceeding parallel play in overall frequency. Cooperative play likewise increased among 3- and 4-year-olds (Parten & Newhall, 1943).

More recent studies suggest, however, that there is considerable variation among preschool children in the relative frequency of the various types of play (Barnes, 1971; Rubin, Fein & Vandenberg, 1983). For instance, one study finds that the incidence of parallel play is greater among lower-class than among middle-class children. The incidence of associative and cooperative play is greater among middle-class children (Rubin, Maioni & Hornung, 1976). This study also reports that girls engage in more parallel play than boys, while boys engage in more associative and cooperative play than girls. Other research shows that while some children go through successive stages of predominantly solitary, then parallel, and then group play, many others do not (Smith, 1978). In fact, some children alternate between periods of predominantly group play and periods of predominantly solitary play.

Edward Mueller and his associates (Mueller & Brenner, 1977; Mueller & Lucas, 1975) find that toddlers within play-group settings often progress in developmental fashion from object-centered contacts to sophisticated interchanges. Object-centered contacts arise when two or more children simultaneously become interested in the same plaything. At first, they engage in an "act-watch" rhythm—they take turns playing with an object that can be manipulated by only one child at a time. Little conscious sharing occurs at the beginning of the process. But as the process continues, children become aware of the responses of other children. They then try to determine what other reactions they can produce in their peers. Once two or more children discover and pay attention to one another's potential for making responses, a fully social peer relationship becomes possible. In similar fashion, parallel play frequently functions as a prelude to group play (Bakeman & Brownlee, 1980).

Psychologists believe that play makes a number of major contributions to children's development (Rubin, Fein & Vandenberg, 1983; Weisler & McCall, 1976):

❏ **Children's exploratory and play behavior is a vehicle of cognitive stimulation** (Piaget, 1952a) Through play children make motor and sensory discoveries concerning sizes and shapes, up and down, hard and soft, smooth and rough, and so on. They handle, manipulate, identify, order, pattern, match, and measure. In building up and tearing down, children learn about the properties of things and gain conceptions of weight, height, volume, and texture (Fenson, Kagan, Kearsley & Zelazo, 1976; Galda & Pellegrini, 1985; McCall, 1974).

❏ **Play prepares children for life, but on their own terms** Children at play can experience themselves as active agents in their environment, not merely as reacting ones. In the family and at school children are usually called on to perform according to set patterns. But in the world of play, they can trim the world down to manageable size and manipulate it to suit their whims (Caplan & Caplan, 1973; Galda & Pellegrini, 1985).

❏ **Play provides opportunities for rehearsing adult roles, a process called "anticipatory socialization" (Merton, 1968)** Children can play house, store, school, or clinic and try on the roles of spouses, merchants, teachers, and medical personnel. Games are particularly effective vehicles by which young children learn to take turns and relate their activities to those of a partner (Howes, Unger & Seidner, 1989; Mead, 1934; Ross, 1982).

❏ **Play helps children build their own sense of identity** Play allows them to get outside themselves and view themselves from other perspectives. In so doing, they come to shape

"You behave back there or we're turning this car around right now!"

("Family Circus" © 1989 Bill Keane, Inc. Reprinted with special permission of King Features Syndicate.)

and mold their self-images and self-conceptions.

❏ **Play allows for both reality and fantasy** Play is a pliable medium that enables children to come to terms with their fears—of villains, witches, ghosts, lions, dogs, robbers, and so on. Through imaginary episodes children can harmlessly confront these creatures and perhaps even triumph over them.

By virtue of these functions, play makes a vital contribution in the development of children.

Peer Aggression

Much human aggression takes place in the context of group activity. **Aggression** is behavior that is socially defined as injurious or destructive. Even young children display aggression. Across time children come to express aggression somewhat differently. With increasing age their aggressive behavior becomes less diffuse and more directed (Feshbach, 1970). The proportion of aggressive acts of an undirected, temper-tantrum type decreases gradually during the first three years of life, then shows a sharp decline after the age of 4. In contrast, the relative frequency of retaliatory responses increases with age, especially after children reach their third

birthdays. Verbal aggression also increases between 2 and 4 years of age.

Children have a considerable influence on one another in the expression of aggressive behavior (Hall & Cairns, 1984). Gerry R. Patterson, Richard A. Littman, and William Bricker (1967) have described how the process frequently operates in nursery school settings. They recorded the aggressive interactions that occurred among thirty-six nursery school children over a twenty-six-week period. They found that when an aggressive response (for instance, a kick or a punch) was followed by crying, withdrawing, or acquiescing, the attacker was likely to aggress against the victim again. These reactions functioned as positive reinforcers for the aggressor. When aggressive behavior was followed by punishment (for instance, retaliatory responses, efforts to recover the seized item, or teacher intervention), aggressors were more likely to pick a different victim for their future aggression or to alter their interactions with the original victim. Hence, the feedback provided for aggressors influences their subsequent behavior.

The researchers also found that while some children entered nursery school with a repertoire of aggressive behaviors, others were passive and unassertive at first. But after the relatively unaggressive children learned to counteraggress and thus end other children's aggressive acts, they themselves began to aggress against new victims.

Even so, some children appear more prone to engage in aggressive behavior than do others (Boldizar, Perry & Perry, 1989; Cumming, Iannotti & Zahn-Waxler, 1989; Deluty, 1985). In some cases aggressiveness derives from a developmental lag in children's acquisition of role-taking skills (Hazen & Black, 1989; Selman, 1980). But this is not the entire story. More aggressive children, particularly boys, report that aggression produces tangible rewards and reduces negative treatment by other children (Perry, Perry & Rasmussen, 1986; Perry, Perry & Weiss, 1989). Additionally, researchers find that youngsters who see and hear angry exchanges among adults become emotionally distressed and respond by aggressing against their peers (Cummings, Iannotti & Zahn-Waxler, 1985). Anthropologist Douglas P. Fry (1988) suggests that this observation may hold cross-culturally. He studied aggressive behaviors among children in two neighboring Zapotec-speaking communities of Mexico. Levels of violence, including homicide rates, were substantially higher in one of the Indian communities than in the other. Not surprisingly, youngsters from the more aggressive

Peer Aggression
Many aggressive children attribute hostile intentions to their peers even under benign circumstances. Consequently, they are more likely than other children to respond with aggression in interpersonal settings. *(Cynthia R. Benjamins/Picture Group)*

community engaged in considerably more actual fighting and rough play than did their counterparts in the other community. Fry's research suggests that community differences in levels of aggression are perpetuated from one generation to the next as youngsters learn their community's patterns for handling and expressing aggression.

Situational factors, especially competition, may also precipitate aggression (Vander Zanden, 1984). Research has shown that the keener the competition for valued but scarce resources, the more aggressively children behave (Rocha & Rogers, 1976; Santrock, Smith & Bourbeau, 1976). Indeed, where children can maximize their payoff by aggressively defeating their opponent, aggressive responses are reinforced. Moreover, competitive situations frequently arouse feelings of rivalry that extend beyond merely winning the competition; children then go out of their way to hurt their opponents (Rocha & Rogers, 1976).

Bullies and Victims

Some youngsters hate to go to school, not because of teachers, schoolwork, and tests but because a bully has turned every hall, stairwell, playground, and classroom into an arena of fear. The phenomenon does not necessarily begin as a teenage problem; it can be observed even among

3-year-olds. Estimates vary on the extent of the problem. In a pioneering study in Sweden Dan Olweus (1978, 1979, 1980) found that about 20 percent of school-age boys were involved, half of whom were bullies and half their victims. But the figure may run higher in U.S. schools. A 1984 study by the National Association of Secondary School Principals revealed that even in the best-administered schools, 25 percent of students said that the possibility of being bullied was one of their most serious concerns (Collins, 1986).

Olweus found in his study of Swedish boys that "bullies" react aggressively in many different situations, possess weak inhibitions against aggressive tendencies, and have positive attitudes toward violence. They tend to be fearless, tough youngsters. In contrast, "whipping boys"—youngsters who are teased, ridiculed, hit, and pushed about—tend to be anxious, insecure, and isolated children, physically weaker and more athletically inept than other boys, and somewhat low in self-esteem. These latter youngsters seem to "attract" aggression and become its recurrent victims. Some researchers report that victimized preschoolers frequently have a history of insecure attachment with their caregivers which causes them to radiate an anxious vulnerability (Troy & Sroufe, 1987). Often victimized youngsters are also "ineffectual aggressors"—they become easily embroiled in conflicts only to end up losing the battles amidst an exaggerated display of misery and frustration (Perry, Williard & Perry, 1990).

Psychologist Nathaniel M. Floyd has studied 230 juvenile bullies and their victims during three years with the Board of Cooperative Educational Services of South Westchester, New York (Floyd & Levin, 1987). He, too, finds that bullies and victims are often drawn to one another and that the resulting interaction—almost a "dance" that goes on between them—cannot be understood by looking at one side or the other. The bully sees in the victim a part of himself that he has had to renounce. A bully at school is frequently a victim of abuse and neglect at home (Dodge, Bates & Pettit, 1990). In the course of growing up most children gain a sense of strength and independence. But if they are humiliated and battered, they may begin to hate the vulnerable side of themselves. When they encounter another youngster who is vulnerable, their own inner feelings of humiliation and shame are activated. And because in their home environments they have learned aggressive responses and come to identify with the aggressor parent, a weaker child provokes hostility rather than compassion. Their dominating veneer masks an underlying sense of inadequacy and fear that they are not in control. Their victims tend to come from one of two family backgrounds. They too may be abused youngsters, but instead of identifying with the aggressor parent, they look to the victim parent for comfort and support. Or they may be boys who are pampered and discouraged from gaining autonomy through physical competence (Floyd & Levin, 1987).

Psychologists L. Rowell Huesmann, L. D. Eron, and P. W. Yarmel (1987) have tracked 870 children from Columbia County, New York, from the time they were 8 until they were 30. Although the research found that bullies do not seem to have lower intelligence than other youngsters, as adults they score lower on tests of intellectual achievement. Their teachers loathed them because they were troublemakers, and, apparently, their school difficulties interfered with their learning. They also had more run-ins with the law and had less desirable jobs than their more peaceable peers. And just as they were more likely to have been abused as children, the grown-up bullies were far more likely to abuse their spouses and punish their children severely. Although boys were more likely to be aggressive than girls, the "meaner" girls also tended to punish their own children more harshly and to raise "meaner" children. Moreover, other re-searchers find that youngsters with poor peer adjustment are at risk for later life difficulties (Parker & Asher, 1987). Researchers also find that the belligerence of bullies may have an additional source. Bullies have a perceptual bias that leads them to see and retaliate against threats where none exist. They tend to attribute hostile intentions to other youngsters who actually mean them no harm (Dodge, Coie, Pettit & Price, 1990; Dodge & Frame, 1982; Dodge & Somberg, 1987; Goleman, 1987a).

Experts favor early intervention to head off bully-victim problems because the longer they persist, the more intractable they become. They recommend that schools inaugurate programs that teach bullies—or those likely to become bullies—peaceable ways of getting along with others. In such programs bullies learn how to better handle situations that get them frustrated and angry. Other techniques involve role playing that gives children practice in cooperative skills and dealing with disagreements. Role playing can also be used to help victims deal with situations in which other youngsters taunt them. Moreover, victims can be taught assertiveness skills through role playing, group discussions, and counseling.

Television and Video Games

Authorities are expressing increasing concern over the effects of media violence on the behavior of the nation's youth (Eron, 1982; Friedrich-Cofer & Huston, 1986; Huesmann, 1986). A report prepared by the National Institute of Mental Health concludes that there is "overwhelming" scientific evidence that "excessive" violence on television leads directly to aggression and violent behavior among children and teenagers (Pearl, 1982). Terming television a "beguiling" instrument that has become "a major socializing agent of American children," the report finds that "television violence is as strongly correlated with aggressive behavior as any other behavioral variable that has been measured." The American Academy of Pediatrics (1990) agrees, saying that heavy television viewing is one cause of violent or aggressive behavior in children and contributes substantially to childhood obesity. The nation's pediatricians ask parents to cut their youngsters' television viewing in half or more.

According to the A. C. Nielsen Company, a firm that specializes in assessing the popularity of television programs, the television set stays on an average of fifty-three hours a week in homes with preschool children. This figure compares with forty-three hours a week in the average U.S. household. Significantly, U.S. youngsters spend more time watching television than any other activity except sleep (Huston, Watkins & Kunkel, 1989). Many of the programs directed toward child audiences are saturated with mayhem, violence, and aggression. Significantly, children watch informative programming such as "Sesame Street" less with age, whereas cartoon and comedy viewing increases (Huston, Wright, Rice, Kerkman & St. Peters, 1990; Pinon, Huston & Wright, 1989).

The "Bugs Bunny–Roadrunner" cartoons are typical of Saturday morning programs, averaging fifty violent acts per hour (Zimmerman, 1983). In one sequence a mean gray coyote barrels down a highway chasing the roadrunner (a birdlike creature). The coyote crashes into a tree. Shortly afterward, he falls off a cliff and a 2-ton boulder lands on top of him. A slab of highway pavement then flips over and buries the coyote. Next, a piano wired with dynamite blows up in his face, and the coyote flies through the air, landing with a mouthful of piano keys.

A variety of studies reveal that viewing media violence fosters aggressive behavior in a number of ways (Bandura, Ross & Ross, 1961, 1963; Geen & Thomas, 1986; Huesmann, 1986; Liebert & Sprafkin, 1988; Rule and Ferguson, 1986; Widom, 1989*a* and 1989*b*). First, media violence provides opportunities for children to learn new aggressive skills. Second, watching violent behavior weakens children's inhibitions against behaving in the same way. And third, television violence affords occasions for *vicarious conditioning,* in which children acquire aggressive behaviors by imaginatively participating in the violent experiences of another person. Research also demonstrates that media violence increases children's toleration of aggression in real life—a "psychic numbing" effect—and reinforces the tendency to view the world as a dangerous place (Drabman & Thomas, 1974; Singer, Singer & Rapaczynski, 1984).

In a study by Lynette K. Friedrich and Aletha H. Stein (1973) children attending a nine-week nursery-school session were shown three types of television programs each day between the fourth and seventh weeks of the term. One group of children watched aggressive *Batman* and *Superman* cartoons. A second group watched the *Mister Rogers' Neighborhood* program, in which socially valued and cooperative activities are highlighted. And a third group watched informational films that contained little or no aggressive or prosocial material. Careful records were kept throughout the nine-week period to assess each child's be-

Is TV Becoming a "Plug-In Drug" for Our Youngsters?
The average youngster in the United States will have watched 5,000 hours of television by the time he or she enters first grade and 19,000 hours by the end of high school. Some researchers report that too much television viewing hurts cognitive development and school performance. Indeed, television has been blamed for virtually everything from trouble in reading to street crime. Whatever the case may be, no institution other than the family and the school has a larger impact upon our nation's children. (*Ted Thai/Time Magazine*)

havior before, during, and after the child had been exposed to the programs.

Friedrich and Stein (1973) found that children who witnessed the aggressive films showed a decline both in their ability to tolerate mild frustrations and in their willingness to accept responsibility. Even more important, children who had shown high levels of aggression before the study became even more aggressive after exposure to the *Batman* and *Superman* cartoons. On the other hand, the aggressive cartoons had no effect on the behavior of children who were initially low in aggression. Other studies have also found that children who are already predisposed to be aggressive are more likely to imitate aggressive models than other children are (Bailyn, 1959; Schramm, Lyle & Parker, 1961; Slife & Rychlak, 1982).

Children who watched the *Mister Rogers' Neighborhood* programs were encouraged to be cooperative and supportive of other people—to show sympathy, affection, friendship, altruism, and self-control. In the concluding weeks of the school session these children became increasingly persistent in completing their tasks, conscientious in obeying rules, and tolerant of frustrating circumstances. As for prosocial interpersonal behavior, it remained largely unchanged among children from families of higher socioeconomic class, but it increased among children from families of low socio-economic class. In sum, an accumulating body of literature suggests that television provides entertainment for children but functions as an important socializer as well (Condry, 1989; Friedrich-Cofer & Huston, 1986; Geen & Thomas, 1986; Pearl, 1982; Rice, Huston, Truglio & Wright, 1990; Rice & Woodsmall, 1988). Significantly, even youngsters only 14 months of age imitate televised models (Meltzoff, 1988).

Many of the educational and psychological findings regarding television viewing extend to video games. In the early 1970s there was Pong, a simple electronic table tennis game. Then came Pac-Man, Roadrunner, Space Invaders, Asteroids, and others. By 1980 video games had developed such a considerable following among youngsters that physicians attributed a hand ailment—"space invaders cramp"—to excessive video game playing. A decade later, by 1990, Nintendo dominated children's play. Nearly one-third of U.S. homes owned a Nintendo set (a survey of the 30 top-selling toys found that 25 were video-game related) (Provenzo, 1991; Winn, 1991).

Many parents harbor concern for the developmental drawbacks that a time-consuming involvement with video games may have for a youngster. And there are ample grounds for concern (Provenzo, 1991; Kinder, 1991). Video games allow youngsters little opportunity to make decisions for themselves, to fashion their own fantasies, and in turn to construct their own problem resolutions. Most games do not reward individual initiative, creativity, or thought. Nor do the games afford sufficient freedom for youngsters to experiment with ideas, develop resourcefulness, and use their imaginations. Critics contend that not only do existing video games constitute an impoverished cultural and sensory environment, but the contents of many Nintendo games are appallingly violent and sexist. In addition, children accustomed to the quick gratifications that video games provide may be unwilling to expend the arduous efforts necessary to play a musical instrument well or to excel at some other endeavor. Yet there is also room for optimism. Video-game technology offers educators abundant opportunities for reaching and assisting children in creative learning, thinking, and acting. Clearly, video games, like television, are phenomena of such tremendous import and significance for our society as to demand our serious

"Naturally, we like to think that all our preschool candidates have anchor potential."

(Drawing by D. Reilly; © 1991. The New Yorker Magazine, Inc.)

Schooling for 4-Year-Olds?

The push for more preschool education is gaining momentum in the United States. The age at which youngsters start formal schooling has been dropping. With kindergarten for 5-year-olds becoming nearly universal, there is a growing demand to make formal instruction available to all 4-year-olds. Significantly, the ground swell for preschool education has paralleled the appearance of reports by various educational commissions expressing concern over the quality of U.S. schools. The reports have emphasized the need for more attention to basics, higher academic standards, greater rigor in teaching, and longer school days and years. Although few of the commission have viewed early schooling as a solution to our educational problems, proponents say preschool education would reduce school failure, lower dropout rates, increase test scores, and produce more competent high-school graduates.

An additional rationale for early schooling is mounting evidence showing that it can make a positive difference in the lives of disadvantaged students. Head Start and related programs have spurred the development and cognitive growth of economically disadvantaged 3- and 4-year-olds. But psychologists such as Edward F. Zigler (1987), who oppose formal schooling for toddlers, contend that to extrapolate these findings to all children is inappropriate. For one thing, the benefits were obtained only by disadvantaged youngsters. For another, the intervention programs were not limited to remedial academic training; they also provided primary health and social services and targeted the family as a whole.

Should the Age for Formal Schooling Be Lowered?
As the number of households in which both parents work increases, pressure has mounted to start public schooling at age four and to have the schools provide supervised settings for latchkey youngsters before and after school. But many educators and psychologists express concern lest children be immersed into a formal educational environment that is ill-suited for most four-year-olds. (Miro Vintoniv/Stock, Boston)

Other developments are also spurring the early-schooling movements. Many ambitious parents harbor high aspirations for their toddlers and believe that formal schooling at an early age will help superparents raise superchildren. Simultaneously, the growing number of working mothers and the

attention. We confront a considerable challenge in channeling television and video games in healthful, positive directions.

Preschools and Head Start Programs

Much of what was said in Chapter 8 about child day-care centers also holds for preschools. Like child day-care programs, the preschool experience has been seen by a number of educators, child psychologists, and political leaders as a possible solution to many of the massive social problems of illiteracy, underachievement, poverty, and racism that confront Western nations. Hopes

such as these led in 1965 to the inception of the Head Start program as an offshoot of the War on Poverty. The program was designed to provide children from low-income families with early intervention education in nursery school settings. Educators believed that appropriate services from outside the family could compensate for the disadvantages these youngsters experienced during their early years. (These hopes also gave impetus to a movement to begin schooling youngsters at four years of age, a matter discussed in the boxed insert.)

Early evaluations of Head Start, particularly a 1969 report by the Westinghouse Learning Corporation, led to the view that early-childhood pro-

proliferation of single-parent homes are fueling pressures for quality day care for young children. Zigler (1987) suggests that much of the demand for early education is really a smoke screen for free day care. Given the high cost of day care, parents naturally would like to shift the burden to the public school system.

Critics of early schooling such as Zigler cite research that questions whether 4-year-old children are ready to take on formal learning. Educators find that older toddlers are more likely to succeed during their school careers, whereas their younger counterparts are more likely to fail. Kindergarten children who turn 5 during the latter half of the year seem to be at a disadvantage when it comes to physical, emotional, social, and intellectual development. Additionally, children who are nearly 6 when they enter kindergarten tend to receive better grades and score higher on achievement tests throughout their schooling experience than do those who begin kindergarten having just turned 5. Being bright and verbally skillful and being ready for school do not seem to be the same thing. It is easy to confuse the superficial poise and sophistication of many of today's children with inner maturity (Mittenthal, 1986). Indeed, evidence suggests that early schooling boomerangs: Youngsters whose parents push them to attain academic success in preschool are less creative, have more anxiety about tests, and, by the end of kindergarten, fail to maintain their initial academic advantage over their less-pressured peers (Raymond, 1989).

Many psychologists and educators remain skeptical of approaches that place 4-year-olds in a formal educational setting. They question whether environmental enrichment can significantly alter the built-in developmental timetable of a child reared in a nondisadvantaged home. They do not deny, however, the value of day-care centers and nursery schools that provide a homelike environment and allow children considerable freedom to play, develop at their own pace, and evolve their social skills. But they point out that many of the things children once did in first grade are now expected of them in kindergarten, and they worry lest more and more will now be asked of 4-year-olds. These psychologists and educators believe we are driving young children too hard and thereby depriving them of their childhood.

Even so, Zigler (1987) notes preschool education has one potential advantage. A weakness of Head Start is that it is for poor children, while more affluent children go elsewhere. In effect, there is a built-in economic segregation of children. Zigler advocates a return to the concept of the community school as a local center that provides social services required by the surrounding neighborhood. Such full-service schools would, in addition to supplying other programs, afford full-day, high-quality child care for toddlers in current school facilities. Although the preschool programs would include developmentally appropriate educational components, they would primarily be places for recreation and socialization. As Zigler (1987, p. 259) notes, "Our four-year-olds have a place in school, but it is not at a school desk."

grams provide negligible benefits. With few exceptions, the report claimed, the gains in IQ that children exhibited while in the program were not maintained when the program was discontinued. In recent years, however, longer-term data have become available that reveal, contrary to the earlier conclusions, that socioeconomically disadvantaged children in such programs do indeed get a head start (Burchinal, Lee & Ramey, 1989; Haskins, 1989; Lazar & Darlington, 1982; Schweinhart & Weikart, 1985; Lee, Brooks-Gunn & Schnur, 1988; Lee, Brooks-Gunn, Schnur & Liaw, 1990). Children who had participated in the preschool programs in the 1960s have performed as well as or better than have their peers in regular school and have had fewer grade retentions and special-class placements. The project has also provided hundreds of thousands of young children with essential health care services.

Although the improvement in children's IQ scores typically dissipates within several years, the children ultimately achieve a higher academic level than do those children lacking preschool instruction. Children who have been in compensatory-education classes score significantly higher on mathematics achievement tests and have a better self-image than do their peers in control groups. The programs have also produced dramatic "sleeper effects" on children later in adolescence and young adulthood. Youth

Selecting a Preschool

There are many different types of preschools and programs. Some, such as Montessori schools and schools following the techniques of psychologists Carl Bereiter and Seigfried Engelmann, emphasize the teaching of a variety of cognitive skills with an academic content. Traditional nursery schools, in contrast, typically seek to expand a child's social environment, provide stimulating material for physical and cognitive development, and foster a sense of individual self-worth. Below are listed a number of tips that parents may wish to employ in picking a school for their youngster:

❏ Inquire of neighbors about their experiences with various preschools.

❏ Visit a school at least twice—once alone and once with your youngster.

❏ Meet the teachers and aides who will be caring for your child.

❏ Determine whether the staff is professionally trained and, particularly, whether the director has a degree in early-childhood education.

❏ Determine the student-teacher ratio: There should be at least one teacher for every eight 3- to 5-year-olds and no more than sixteen youngsters in the entire group.

❏ Determine the goals of the program; for instance, whether it stresses academics or social development.

❏ Determine the approach that the school and the individual teachers take toward discipline.

❏ Pay close attention to the interactions that go on between teachers and children and among the children themselves.

❏ Appraise the physical facilities; for instance, does the school have adequate space for play, accessible toilets and wash basins, ample facilities for children when the weather is inclement, and inviting playthings?

❏ Select a school that offers a program that is consistent with your family's values.

❏ Select a school that is compatible with the family budget, because one that is too expensive may contribute to family stress.

❏ Select a school whose location fits your daily patterns of living and does not entail excessive transportation.

Give yourself enough time to find a preschool that seems right for you and your child. It takes patience, assertiveness, and persistence. The only way to find out about preschools is to get out there and look.

---

who were in a Head Start program engage in less antisocial and delinquent behavior and are more likely to finish high school and get jobs or go to college than are their peers who were not in a program.

Another significant impact of Head Start has been its effects on parents. The program has given parents access to community resources and has provided support for the entire family. It has contributed to an improvement in parenting abilities and in later parent participation in school programs.

In sum, the payoff of Head Start programs has been not only in education but in dollars, for in the long run its participants are less likely to need remedial programs as children and social support systems like welfare as adults. Apparently, children with preschooling learn how to extract a better education from the school system. Moreover, a program's effectiveness is increased by involving the parents, strengthening their ties to

schools and bringing them into partnership with the educational enterprise (many parents are themselves afraid of school or have had bad experiences with it, problems that need be addressed lest the parents pass on their fears to their youngsters) (Wasik, Ramey, Bryant & Sparling, 1990). Nor will just any nursery school do. It must be a quality program (see the boxed insert).

Finally, as disadvantaged youngsters grow older, they continue to need the same comprehensive services and special attention that Head Start programs afford them in their early years. But few schools have the money or staff to provide them. Indeed, persistent disadvantage—the dismal quality of inner city schools and the disintegration of the families and neighborhoods in which Head Start children reside—make it difficult to sustain the intellectual and academic momentum that Head Start affords (Chira, 1990; Lee, Brooks-Gunn, Schnur & Liaw, 1990).

SUMMARY

1. Since infants enter a society that is already an ongoing concern, they need to be fitted to their society's cultural ways, a process termed "socialization."

2. Love-oriented parenting techniques tend to promote a child's conscience formation and self-responsibility. In contrast, parents who show hostility and rejection tend to interfere with conscience development and to breed aggressiveness and resistance to authority.

3. Restrictive parenting tends to be associated with well-controlled as well as fearful, dependent, and submissive behaviors. Permissiveness, while fostering outgoing, sociable, assertive behaviors and intellectual striving, also tends to decrease persistence and increase aggressiveness. Effective discipline is consistent and unambiguous. The most aggressive children are those whose parents are permissive toward aggression on some occasions but severely punish it on other occasions.

4. Many developmental psychologists distinguish among authoritarian, authoritative, permissive, and harmonious parenting. Authoritative parenting tends to be associated with self-reliant, self-controlled, explorative, and contented children. In contrast, the offspring of authoritarian parents tend to be discontented, withdrawn, and distrustful.

5. One indication that 2-year-olds are coming to terms with autonomy issues is their ability and willingness to say *no* to parents. Self-assertion, defiance, and compliance are distinct dimensions of toddler behavior. The way parents handle these autonomy issues have profound consequences for their youngsters' behavior.

6. Divorce is a stressful experience for both children and their parents. The interaction patterns between divorced parents and their children differ from those encountered in intact families. Children often respond to their parents' divorce by pervasive feelings of sadness, strong wishes for reconciliation, and worries about having to take care of themselves.

7. Firstborn children seem to be fortune's favorites. Three explanations have been advanced to account for differences between firstborns and later-borns: (a) First-borns have greater exposure to adult models and to adult expectations and pressures. (b) They function as intermediaries between parents and later-borns, a role that appears to foster the development of verbal and cognitive skills. (c) The "dethroning" of the firstborn by later siblings arouses a strong lifelong need for recognition, attention, and approval.

8. Peer relationships are in their own right a meaningful experience in the lives of young children. Such relationships become more likely to be formed and more successful with increasing age.

9. Children are important to one another as reinforcing agents and behavioral models.

10. Play makes a number of major contributions to children's development. It functions as a vehicle of cognitive stimulation, allows children to handle the world on their own terms, provides for anticipatory socialization, fosters an individual sense of identity, and enables children to come to terms with their fears.

11. With increasing age, children's aggression becomes less diffuse, more directed, more retaliatory, and more verbal.

12. Children who have participated in quality Head Start programs indeed do get a head start. They achieve a higher academic level than do those children lacking preschool instruction. The programs have also had positive "sleeper effects" on children later in adolescence and young adulthood.

KEY TERMS

Aggression Behavior that is socially defined as injurious or destructive.

Authoritarian Parenting Child-rearing practices that are aimed at shaping a child's behavior in accordance with traditional and absolute values and standards of conduct. Obedience is stressed, verbal give-and-take discouraged, and punitive, forceful discipline preferred.

Authoritative Parenting Child-rearing practices that provide firm direction for a child's overall activities but give the child considerable freedom within reasonable limits.

Confluence Theory A model that views intellectual development of a family as resembling a river, with the inputs of each family member flowing into it.

Harmonious Parenting Child-rearing practices in which almost no control is exercised over a child, although the parents appear to have control in that their children seem to sense intuitively what their parents want and try to do it.

Peers Individuals who are approximately the same age.

Permissive Parenting Child-rearing practices in which the parent seeks to provide a nonpunitive, accepting, and affirmative environment in which the children regulate their own behavior as much as possible.

Play Voluntary activities that are not performed for any sake beyond themselves; activities that people commonly view as being outside the serious business of life.

Resource Dilution Hypothesis In large families resources get spread thin, to the detriment of all the offspring.

Scaffolding Strategies by which parents support a child's learning through intervention and tutoring that provide helpful task information attuned to the child's current level of functioning.

Sexual Abuse of Children Forced, tricked, or coerced sexual behavior between a child and an older person.

Socialization The process of transforming children into bona fide, functioning members of society. Socialization is the channel through which children acquire the knowledge, skills, and dispositions that enable them to participate effectively in group life.

Part Five

Later Childhood: 7 to 12

Chapter 11

Later Childhood: Advances in Cognitive and Moral Development

Cognitive Sophistication

Period of Concrete Operations ◆ Cognitive Style ◆ Person Perception

Understanding Emotion and Dealing with Fear

Moral Development

Psychoanalytic Theory ◆ Cognitive Learning Theory ◆ Cognitive-Developmental Theory ◆

Moral Behavior: Consistency or Inconsistency? ◆ Correlates of Moral Conduct

Prosocial Behavior

◆

. . . We went home and when somebody said, "Where were you?" we said, "Out," and when somebody said, "What were you doing until this hour of night?" we said, as always, "Nothing." . . .
But about this doing nothing: we swung on swings. We went for walks. We lay on our backs in backyards and chewed grass. I can't number the afternoons my best friend and I took a book apiece, walked to opposite ends of his front porch, sank down on a glider at his end, a wicker couch at mine, and read. We paid absolutely no attention to each other, we never spoke while we were reading, and when we were done, he walked me home to my house, and when we got there I walked him back to his house, and then he—aria da capo. . . .
We strung beads on strings: we strung spools on strings; we tied each other up with string, and belts and clothesline. We sat in boxes; we sat under porches; we sat on roofs; we sat on limbs of trees. We stood on boards over excavations; we stood on tops of piles of leaves; we stood under rain dripping from the eaves; we stood up to our ears in snow. We looked at things like knives and immies and pig nuts and grasshoppers and clouds and dogs and people. We skipped and hopped and jumped. Not going anywhere— just skipping and hopping and jumping and galloping. We sang and whistled and hummed and screamed. . . .
—ROBERT PAUL SMITH, DESCRIBING HIS ELEMENTARY SCHOOL YEARS*

In this passage the writer Robert Paul Smith portrays the marked development that occurs during the elementary school years in children's ability to receive, create, and use knowledge about their physical and social worlds. Erik Erikson (see Chapter 2) singles out the elementary school years as one of his psychosocial stages. He calls this period the stage of *industry versus inferiority*. During these years, Erikson says, children confront the challenge of developing healthy self-conceptions. They must master the social and learning skills that are essential for the school setting and that lay the foundations for coping with the tasks of adulthood. If children fail to acquire these skills, they may develop feelings of inferiority. From peers, parents, and teachers they receive continual feedback regarding their adequacy. This feedback shapes their self-images and self-esteem.

Cognitive Sophistication

An important feature of the elementary school years is an advance in children's ability to learn about themselves and their environment. During this period they become more adept at processing information in that their reasoning abilities become progressively more rational and logical

* Reprinted from *"Where Did You Go?" "Out." "What Did You Do?" "Nothing."* by Robert Paul Smith, by permission of W. W. Norton & Company, Inc. Copyright © 1957 by Robert Paul Smith. Copyright renewed 1985 by Joseph Smith and Daniel Smith.

(S. A. Miller, 1986). A crucial component of these reasoning abilities is an understanding of fiction, appearance, and reality (Woolley & Wellman, 1990). Consider, for instance, what happens if you take hold of a joke sponge that looks like a nice, solid piece of granite. Although it looks like a rock, upon squeezing it, you realize it is a sponge. However, a 3-year-old youngster is less certain. Children at this age often do not grasp the idea that what you see is not necessarily what you get. But by the time they are 6 or 7 years old, most children appreciate the appearance-reality distinction that confronts us in many forms in everyday life (Flavell, 1986; Flavell, Flavell, Green & Moses, 1990).

Underlying the improvement in children's intellectual capabilities is a growing awareness and understanding of their own mental processes, what psychologists term *metacognition* (Cox, Ornstein, Naus, Maxfield & Zimler, 1989; Lovett & Flavell, 1990) (see Chapter 9). In many respects Jean Piaget's stages constitute sets of so-called **executive strategies,** which are analogous to the tasks performed by a corporate executive. Executives select, sequence, evaluate, revise, and monitor the effectiveness of problem-solving plans and behavior within their corporations. Applied to human mental functioning, executive strategies refer to the ability to integrate and orchestrate lower-level cognitive skills. At higher stages the strategies are more complex and more powerful than at lower stages. Psychomotor skills provide a good illustration of these processes (see the boxed insert).

Period of Concrete Operations

Piaget calls middle childhood the **period of concrete operations.** He refers to it as "concrete" because children are bound by immediate physical reality and cannot transcend the here and now. Consequently, during this period children still have difficulty dealing with remote, future, or hypothetical matters.

Despite the limitations of concrete operational thought, this period witnesses major advances in children's cognitive capabilities. Its hallmark is that various classifying and ordering activities begin to occur internally as mental activities. For example, in the preoperational period before 6 or 7 years of age, children arrange sticks by size in their proper sequence by physically comparing each pair in succession. But in the period of concrete operations children "mentally" survey the sticks, then quickly place them in order, usually

Psychomotor Skills

Psychomotor skills involve "mind-guided" muscular movements and their coordination (Adams, 1987). They are voluntary as opposed to involuntary or reflex activities. These skills entail learned capabilities that find expression in rapid, accurate, forceful, or smooth movements of the body. For example, in driving a car, we link a variety of complex perceptual and cognitive operations to motor behavior in order to apply the brakes, accelerate, and steer left or right. Likewise, children employ psychomotor skills in the course of their activities, including using a pencil, writing on a blackboard, painting pictures, employing measuring instruments, and playing.

Psychomotor behavior has a number of characteristics (Sage, 1971). First, it necessitates an organized sequence of movements (for instance, in the jump shot in basketball both knee bending and elbow flexion precede elbow extension, and wrist flexion takes place with the release of the ball). Second, the behavior requires synchronization (for example, in a tennis serve the movements of the legs, shoulders, arms, and wrist must be brought into play in a synchronized operation). And third, the behavior must be goal-directed (for example, fullbacks are taught to fold their hands close to their stomachs and charge into the line after receiving a fake handoff from the quarterback so as to mislead opponents).

Paul M. Fitts and Michael I. Posner (1967) identify three main phases in the learning of motor skills:

1. **Early or cognitive phase.** At first, the learner seeks to "understand" the task. Accordingly, a helpful strategy for the instructor is to identify the separate parts of the skill, demonstrate each, then give the learner an opportunity to practice each part (for instance, one usually teaches beginning swimmers the kick, arm and hand movements, head positioning, and breathing techniques as separate skills). During this phase learners typically depend on a good many cues that later they can dispense with (for example, the inexperienced automobile driver tends to look for the control pedals, and beginning typists often watch their fingers on the keys).

2. **Associative or intermediate phase.** As learning progresses, learners are able to integrate the new patterns and eliminate inappropriate responses. The individual skills become progressively fitted into a sequential order, so that each aspect of the movement becomes the signal for the next.

3. **Final or autonomous phase.** In the final phase people no longer need to "think about what to do next." The activity requires little conscious attention or cognitive regulation. In fact, at this stage conscious introspection tends to impair smooth performance.

Much motor learning takes place through feedback. Feedback provides information about the performance or about the consequences of the performance. As such, it affords the kind of input that allows individuals to make adjustments in their responses. Feedback also has reinforcing properties, which derive from the rewarding effect of correct performance and the punishing effect of incorrect performance. And finally, feedback provides motivation and increases the interest level (Adams, 1984, 1987; Clark & Watkins, 1984; Sage, 1971).

without any actual measurement. Since the activities of preoperational children are dominated by actual perceptions, the task takes them several minutes to complete. Children in the period of concrete operations finish the same project in a matter of seconds, since their actions are directed by internal cognitive processes.

Conservation Tasks As concrete operational thought evolves, a liberation occurs in children's thought processes. This unfreezing of the rigidity of preoperational thought allows them to solve conservation problems. **Conservation** requires the recognition that the quantity or amount of something stays the same despite changes in shape or position. It implies that children are mentally capable of compensating in their minds for various external changes in objects. Concrete operational thought entails a reorganization of cognitive structure—a progressive amalgamation of experience and mental activity.

Elementary school children come to recognize that pouring liquid from a short, wide container into a long, narrow one does not change the quantity of the liquid—in brief, that the amount of liquid is conserved. Whereas preoperational children fix ("center") their attention on either the width or the height of the container and ignore the other dimension, concrete operational chil-

(a)

(b)

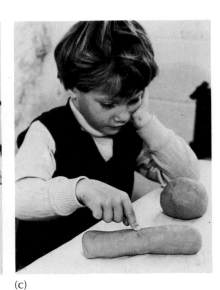
(c)

A Conservation Experiment

(a) Place two balls containing the same amount of clay in front of a four-year-old child and ask if they are the same size. Invariably the child will say yes. (b) As the child watches, roll one of the balls into a long, sausage-like shape and again ask if the clay objects are the same size. (c) The child will now claim that one of the clay objects is larger than the other. In this case, the child said that the sausage-shaped clay is larger than the clay ball. Not until the child is several years older will he come to recognize that the two different shapes contain the same amount of clay—that is, he will come to recognize the principle of the conservation of quantity. *(Patrick Reddy)*

dren *decenter* (focus simultaneously upon both width and height). Furthermore, concrete operational children attend to *transformations*—to the gradual shift in the height or width of the fluid in the container as it is poured by the experimenter. And most important, according to Piaget, they attain *reversibility* of operations. They recognize that the initial state can be regained by pouring the water back into the original container. (Decentering, transformations, and reversibility were discussed in Chapter 9.)

As is true of other cognitive abilities, children acquire some conservation skills earlier, some later (see Figure 11-1). Conservation of discrete quantities (number) occurs somewhat before conservation of substance. Conservation of weight (the heaviness of an object) follows conservation of quantity (length and area) and is in turn followed by conservation of volume (the space that an object occupies). Piaget calls this sequential development, with each skill dependent on the acquisition of earlier skills, *horizontal décalage.*

Horizontal décalage implies that repetition takes place within a single period of development such as the period of concrete operations. Consequently, a child acquires the various conservation skills in steps. The principle of conservation is first applied to one task, such as the quantity of

matter—the notion that the amount of an object remains unchanged despite changes in its position or shape. But the child does not apply the principle to another task, such as the conservation of weight—the notion that the heaviness of an object remains unchanged regardless of the shape that it assumes. It is not until a year or so later that the child extends the same type of conserving operation to weight. The general principle is the same with respect to both quantity and weight: In each case children must perform internal mental operations and no longer rely on actual measurement or weighing to determine whether an object is larger or weighs more. However, children typically achieve the notion of the invariance of quantity a year or so before that of the invariance of weight (Flavell, 1963).

Inducing Conservation Piaget's research was largely ignored by U.S. psychologists until about 1960. No sooner had his work gained attention than U.S. researchers became intrigued with the question of whether the development of conservation could be accelerated through training procedures. To his dismay, Piaget found that Americans are preoccupied with accomplishing things in the least possible time and that children's education is no exception. On his visits to

Conservation Skill	Basic Principle	Test for Conservation Skills	
		Step 1	Step 2
Number (Ages 5 to 7)	The number of units in a collection remains unchanged even though they are rearranged in space.	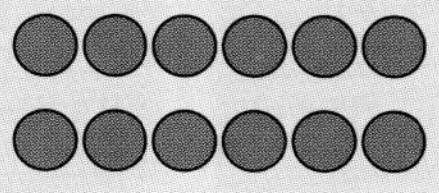 Two rows of pennies arranged in one-to-one correspondence	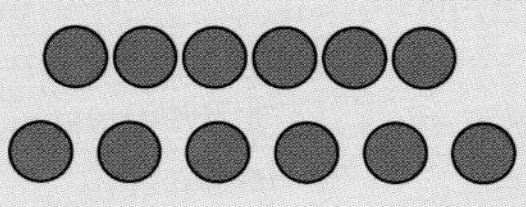 One of the rows elongated or contracted
Substance (Ages 7 to 8)	The amount of a malleable, plastic-like material remains unchanged regardless of the shape it assumes.	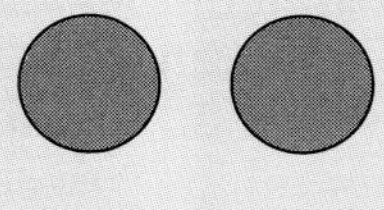 Modeling clay in two balls of the same size	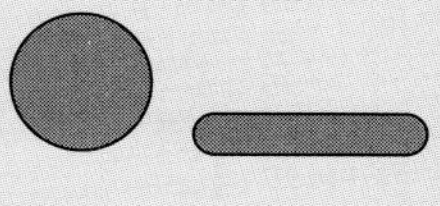 One of the balls rolled into a long, narrow shape
Length (Ages 7 to 8)	The length of a line or object from one end to the other end remains unchanged regardless of how it is rearranged in space or changed in shape.	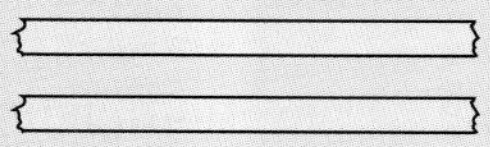 Strips of cloth placed in a straight line	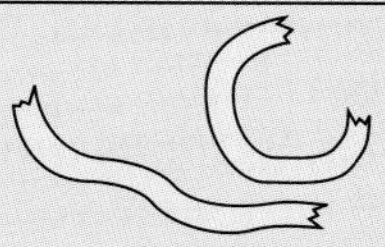 Strips of cloth placed in altered shapes
Area (Ages 8 to 9)	The total amount of surface covered by a set of plane figures remains unchanged regardless of the position of the figures.	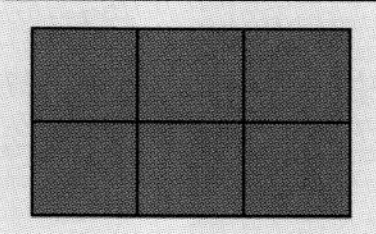 Square units arranged in a rectangle	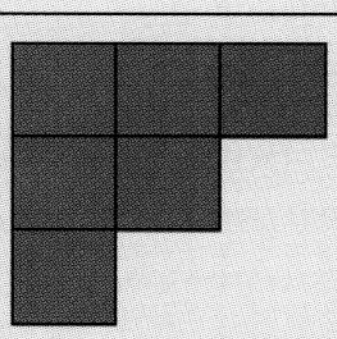 Square units rearranged
Weight (Ages 9 to 10)	The heaviness of an object remains unchanged regardless of the shape that it assumes.	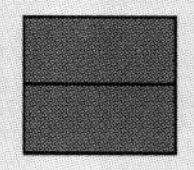 Units placed on top of each other	 Units placed side by side
Volume (Ages 12 to 14)	The space occupied by an object remains unchanged regardless of a change in its shape.	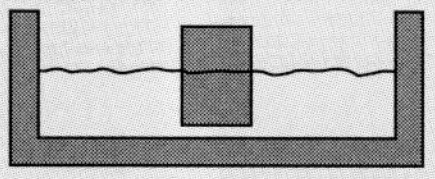 Displacement of water by object placed vertically in the water	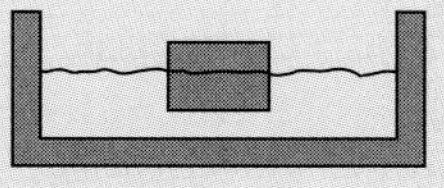 Displacement of water by object placed horizontally in the water

Figure 11-1   Sequential Acquisition of Conservation Skills
During the period of concrete operations, Piaget says, children develop conservation skills in a fixed sequence. For example, they acquire the concept of conservation of number first, then that of substance, and so on.

the United States audiences repeatedly bombarded Piaget with the question "Is it possible to speed up the learning of conservation concepts?"

Piaget (1970; p. 31) responded to what he called "the American question" as follows:

> Acceleration is certainly possible but first we must find out whether it is desirable or harmful. . . . Perhaps a certain slowness is useful in developing the capacity to assimilate new concepts. . . . [B]lindly to accelerate the learning of conservation concepts could be even worse than doing nothing.

A good many U.S. psychologists believe that Piaget's concern was ill founded. Indeed, Jerome S. Bruner (1970; p. 53) states: "The foundations of any subject may be taught to anybody at any age in some form." Learning theorists reject Piaget's stage formulations (see Chapters 2 and 3) and disagree with Piaget's view that children below the age of 6 cannot benefit from experience in learning conservation because of their cognitive immaturity.

In the early 1960s any number of psychologists attempted to teach young children conservation skills. For the most part, they were unsuccessful (Field, 1981; Flavell, 1963; Kuhn, 1974; Smedslund, 1961). However, more recently, a number of researchers have successfully used cognitive learning methods (see Chapter 2) to train for conservation (Botvin & Murray, 1975; Zimmerman, 1978; Zimmerman & Rosenthal, 1974). Furthermore, psychologists are finding that the content of a task decisively influences how a person thinks (Spinillo and Bryant, 1991). By altering the cognitive properties of a task, one often can elicit preoperational, concrete operational, or formal operational thinking from a child (Chapman & Lindenberger, 1988; Sternberg & Downing, 1982).

Cross-Cultural Evidence   Over the past thirty years children throughout the world have served as subjects for a variety of experiments designed to test Piaget's theory. Research has been conducted in over 100 cultures and subcultures, from Switzerland to Senegal and from Alaska to the Amazon (Ashton, 1975; Bardouille-Crema, Black & Feldhusen, 1986; Gaudia, 1972; Greenfield & Bruner, 1971). The results show that regardless of culture, individuals do appear to move through Piaget's hierarchical stages of cognitive development—the sensorimotor, preoperational, concrete operational, and formal operational periods—in the same sequence. (However, some cultural groups do not attain the state of formal operations.)

But cross-cultural research suggests that there is a developmental lag in the acquisition of conservation among children in non-Western, nonindustrialized cultures. Not entirely clear is whether this lag is due to genuine differences between cultures or to flaws in research procedures that use materials and tasks alien to some cultures.

The research also raises a question about whether the acquisition of conservation skills in the period of concrete operations occurs in the invariant sequence (horizontal décalage) postulated by Piaget (see Figure 11-1). Children in Western nations, Iran, and Papua New Guinea exhibit the expected Piagetian pattern (Ashton, 1975; Elkind, 1961; Prince, 1968). Thai children, however, appear to develop conservation of quantity and weight simultaneously (Boonsong, 1968). And some Arab, Indian, Somali, and Australian aborigine subjects conserve weight before quantity (deLemos, 1969; Hyde, 1959).

Other cultural differences are also found. Children of pottery-making families in Mexico perform better on conservation of substance tasks than their peers from non-pottery-making families (Ashton, 1975). And Patricia M. Greenfield (1966) found in her studies involving Wolof children in Senegal, West Africa, that it made a difference whether the experimenter or the children themselves poured the water in the classic Piagetian experiment involving wide and narrow containers. Two-thirds of a group of children under 8 years old who themselves transferred the water achieved the concept of conservation. In contrast, only one-fourth of a group who had watched the experimenter pour the water then realized that the amount of water was the same. The children attributed "magical action" to the experimenter that they did not attribute to their own performance. Clearly, cultural factors need to be taken into account in considering children's performance on cognitive tests.

Cognitive Style

Piaget has shown us that children pass through somewhat similar stages in intellectual functioning between birth and adulthood. But researchers have demonstrated that people differ in their *ways* of processing information. In dealing with various aspects of our environment, each of us employs a particular **cognitive style,** which may be defined as the stable preferences that each of us exhibits in organizing and categorizing our perceptions (Wenckstern, Weizmann & Leenaars, 1984).

One way that people differ in cognitive style is in their approach to problem solving. Some respond to a problem very rapidly without worrying

Cognitive Style
Children differ in the way they approach problem-solving tasks. Some respond very rapidly, giving minimum consideration to accuracy. Others are more deliberate and reflective, taking more time to arrive at an answer. *(Joseph Nettis/Photo Researchers)*

about accuracy. Others of equal intelligence take considerably more time. The former group is termed *impulsive;* the latter, *reflective* (Kagan, 1966). Presumably, reflective people, unlike impulsive ones, pause to consider alternative solutions before suggesting an answer to a problem.

Research has revealed that reflective children tend to perform better than impulsive children on reading tasks (Kagan, 1965), recognition memory tests (Siegel, Kirasic & Kilburg, 1973), tasks involving reasoning (Kagan, Pearson & Welch, 1966), and creative projects (Fuqua, Bartsch & Phye, 1975). In contrast, impulsive children excel at some intellectual tasks requiring broad analysis (Smith & Nelson, 1988; Zelniker & Jeffrey, 1976). Furthermore, whereas reflective children favor a direct and assertive approach on a reasoning task entailing social conflict, impulsive children prefer a more passive and yielding approach (Peters & Bernfeld, 1983).

Another dimension of cognitive style is *field independence* versus *field dependence* (Witkin & Goodenough, 1981). In colloquial terms, some people tend to be "splitters" while others are "lumpers." This characteristic shows up in tests requiring people to find simple figures that are camouflaged by more complex figures. The skill involved is the ability to isolate some characteristic of a scene from a deceiving background. To some extent, individuals move from field dependence toward field independence during development. But even so, at each age individual differences remain.

Field-independent people tend to analyze the elements of a scene; they focus on items as being separate from their backgrounds. In contrast,

field-dependent people tend to categorize a scene as a whole and to overlook the individual items that compose it. Overall, researchers find that field-independent people are more likely to have an impersonal orientation toward others, whereas field-dependent individuals tend toward a more interpersonal orientation. Not surprisingly, people often describe field-independent individuals as cold, manipulating, and distant, whereas they characterize field-dependent individuals as warm, considerate, and accommodating. Also research indicates that field-independent college students tend to be attracted to mathematics, the natural sciences, engineering, and subjects that require a high level of analytical reasoning. Field-dependent students tend to major in the humanities, the social sciences, education, and fields that involve a global and often service-oriented perspective.

Educators are increasingly coming to recognize the importance of differences in cognitive style among students. They used to ask which method (or methods) was best—lecture, recitation, or discussion; a highly structured classroom or a more informal classroom; programmed instruction or a live teacher. And the answer was that for the mythical *average* student it makes little difference which alternative is employed. But when the data were examined student by student, researchers found that some of them improve, others remain unaffected, and still others regress under certain teaching conditions. The process of averaging the pluses, the minuses, and the no-changes masks the fact that different strategies work better with different students (Cronbach & Snow, 1977; Cross, 1976). Hence, considerably more attention needs to be given to breaking lock-step practices in education and making allowance for individual differences.

Person Perception

The elementary school years are a time of rapid growth in children's knowledge of the social world and of the requirements for social interaction. Consider what is involved when we enter the wider world of people (Lee, 1975; Vander Zanden, 1984). We need to assess certain key statuses of the people we encounter, such as their age and sex. We must also consider the behavior in which they are involved (walking, eating, reading), their emotional state (happy, sad, angry), their roles (teacher, clerk, parent), and the social context (church, home, restaurant).

Accordingly, when we enter a social setting, we mentally attempt to "place" or "locate" people within the broad network of possible social relationships. By scrutinizing them for a variety of clues—certain telltale "signs" or "marks"—we place them in social categories. For instance, if they wear wedding rings, we infer that they are married; if they wear business clothes during working hours, that they are employed in white-collar jobs; if they are in a wheelchair, that they are handicapped; and so on. Only in this manner can we decide what to expect of given people and what they expect of us. In sum, we activate *stereotypes*—certain exaggerated cultural understandings—that guide us in identifying the mutual set of expectations that will govern the social exchange.

Research by W. J. Livesley and D. B. Bromley (1973), based on a sample of 320 English children between 7 and 16 years of age, has traced developmental trends in children's perceptions of people. The study reveals that the number of dimensions along which children conceptualize other people grows throughout childhood. The greatest increase in children's ability to distinguish people's characteristics occurs between 7 and 8 years of age. Thereafter, the rate of change is generally much slower. Indeed, the differences between children who are 7 years old and those who are 8 are often greater than the differences between 8-year-olds and 15-year-olds. This observation leads Livesley and Bromley (1973; p. 147) to conclude that "the eighth year is a critical period in the developmental psychology of person perception."

Children under 8 years of age describe people largely in terms of external, readily observable attributes. Their conception of people tends to be inclusive. It embraces not only personality but also an individual's family, possessions, and physical characteristics. At this age children categorize people in a simple, absolute, moralistic manner and employ vague, global descriptive terms such as "good," "bad," "horrible," and "nice." Consider this account by a 7-year-old girl of a woman she likes (Livesley & Bromley, 1973; p. 214):

> She is very nice because she gives my friends and me toffee. She lives by the main road. She has fair hair and she wears glasses. She is forty-seven years old. She has an anniversary today. She has been married since she was twenty-one years old. She sometimes gives us flowers. She has a very nice garden and house. We only go in the weekend and have a talk with her.

When they are about 8 years old, children show rapid growth in their vocabularies for appraising people. Their phrases become more specific and precise. After this age children increasingly come to recognize certain regularities or unchanging qualities in the inner dispositions and overt behaviors of individuals. Here is a description of a boy by a 9-year-old girl (Livesley & Bromley, 1973; p. 130):

> David Calder is a boy I know. He goes to this school but he is not in our class. His behavior is very bad, and he is always saying cheeky [impudent] things to people. He fights people of any age and he likes getting into trouble for it. He is always being told off by his teachers and other people.

Around the same age children also become aware that people display what seem to be incompatible qualities: For instance, sometimes they are "bad" and other times "good"; sometimes they are "mean" and other times "nice." As they move into their teens, children become capable of integrating one quality with another. A 14-year-old girl describes her girlfriend in these terms (Livesley & Bromley, 1973; p. 222): "Sometimes she gets a bit cross but that doesn't last long and soon she is her normal self."

In summary, Livesley and Bromley find the following developmental changes in the ways in which children see and describe people:

❑ Children use an increasing number of descriptive adjectives and categories.
❑ They display greater flexibility and precision in the use of these categories.
❑ They exhibit greater coherence, integration, and complexity in the ideas they form about people.

❏ They become more adept at recognizing and describing the subtle qualities that people reveal in their behavior.

❏ They show greater insight into people and are increasingly capable of analyzing and interpreting their behavior.

❏ They display more care in formulating statements about people in order to provide accurate and convincing descriptions of them.

Hence, a rapid development occurs during middle childhood in children's abilities to make "psychological" inferences about other people—their thoughts, feelings, personality attributes, and general behavioral dispositions (Barenboim, 1977, 1981; Graziano, Moore & Collins, 1988).

Understanding Emotion and Dealing with Fear

Cognitive factors also play an important part in setting the tone for the emotional life of youngsters. You will recall from our discussion in Chapter 8 that emotion entails the physiological changes, subjective experiences, and expressive behaviors that are involved in such feelings as love, joy, grief, and rage. As they interact with their mothers, fathers, siblings, peers, teachers, and others, children acquire a set of guidelines that mentally or cognitively mediate their inner experience of emotion and their outer expression of it (Lewis & Saarni, 1985). For example, our society expects different emotional behavior of women than of men, and so parents, by responding more favorably to a daughter's sadness than to a son's sadness, encourage boys to suppress their sadness (Fuchs & Thelen, 1988).

Moreover, children's knowledge of their emotional experiences changes markedly from ages 6 through 11. Children increasingly attribute emotional arousal to internal causes; they come to know the social rules governing the display of emotion; they learn to 'read' facial expressions with greater precision; they better understand that emotional states can be mentally redirected (for instance, thinking happy thoughts when in a sad state); and they realize that people can simultaneously experience multiple emotions (Harris, 1985; Harter & Buddin, 1987; Masters & Carlson, 1984; Thompson, 1987; Whitesell & Harter, 1989). And as children grow older, they become able to identify and attach labels like "anger," "fear," "sadness," and "happiness" to their inner states (Russell & Ridgeway, 1983). Children also better understand how other people feel and why they

feel as they do (Strayer, 1986). All the while they become more adept at changing, containing, and hiding their feelings (Carroll & Steward, 1984; Coles, 1986). For instance, they realize that the emotions they experience internally need not be automatically translated into overt action (rage need not become aggression) (Saarni, 1979). (The boxed insert examines coping with stress during childhood.)

Fear plays an important part in the lives of young children (Kendall, Howard & Epps, 1988; King, Hamilton & Olldendick, 1988). Psychologists define **fear** as an unpleasant emotion aroused by impending danger, pain, or misfortune. Some psychologists use the terms "fear" and "anxiety" interchangeably. Others define fear as a response to tangible stimuli (for instance, snakes, fast-moving vehicles, or high places) and anxiety as a diffuse, unfocused emotional state. In actual practice, however, distinguishing between fear and anxiety is often difficult. Psychologists also distinguish between fear and phobia. Whereas fear may be viewed as a normal reaction to threatening stimuli, **phobia** is an excessive, persistent, and unadaptive fear response (usually to benign or ill-defined stimuli).

Between 2 and 6 years of age children's fear of certain tangible and immediate situations

"Hey! Don't be scared, Joey! Thunder is just a loud cloud."

("Dennis The Menace" ® used by permission of Hank Ketcham and © 1991 by North American Syndicate.)

Helping Children
Cope with Their Fears

Early and provident fear is the mother of safety.—EDMUND BURKE

Fear is an inescapable and necessary human emotion. It fosters caution and prudence and increases our energy in times of danger. But fear can also outlast its usefulness or become misplaced, so that it interferes with healthy adaptations to life. Instead of aiding us to mobilize our resources, fear may immobilize them.

Many fears that children develop cannot be avoided, nor should they be. Rather, a child can be encouraged to develop constructive mechanisms for coping with fear. Here are some techniques that psychologists have found useful for helping children deal with fear (Formanek, 1983; Jersild & Holmes, 1935b; Jersild, Telford & Sawrey, 1975):

❏ Create an accepting situation in which children feel at ease in sharing their fears with you. Help them to appreciate that adults, including yourself, also have fears.

❏ Encourage a child to acquire skills that will provide specific aid in dealing with the feared situation or object. Children are usually eager to shed their fears, and they are most successful when they themselves develop the competence to do so. Children who are afraid of the dark can be provided with the means to "control darkness": a nightlight with a readily accessible switch can be placed next to their beds.

❏ Lead children by degrees into active contact with and participation in situations that they fear (an approach termed *desensitization*). This technique has been successfully employed in the reduction of fears associated with snakes, spiders, heights, airplanes, and hospitals.

❏ Give children opportunities to encounter a feared stimulus in normal environmental circumstances and to deal with it on their own terms. That is, they should be permitted to inspect, ignore, approach, or avoid the stimulus as they see fit. And pair the feared stimulus with pleasant activities.

❏ Allow the child to observe the fearless actions of other children and adults when they encounter the same stimulus that the child fears. In one study a group of nursery school children who were afraid of dogs watched another child their own age happily playing with a dog. After eight sessions in which they saw the child romp with the dog, two-thirds of the children were willing to play with the experimental dog and with an unfamiliar dog as well (Bandura, Grusec & Menlove, 1967).

In contrast, the following techniques are relatively ineffective and may complicate the child's difficulties:

❏ Coercing the child into contact with the feared situation by physical force, scolding, or ridicule ("Don't be such a baby!" or "Come on, pet the nice doggie. He won't hurt you!").

❏ Making fun of the child's fear.

❏ Shaming the child before others because of the fear.

❏ Ignoring the child's fear.

❏ Goading children into trying things they are not ready for, such as riding a roller coaster or diving off a diving board.

In sum, although caretakers cannot protect children from all fear (and it would be undesirable if they could), they can help children deal with their fears in a constructive manner.

---

decreases (Formanek, 1983; Jersild & Holmes, 1935a; 1935b). For instance, they become less afraid of noises, strange objects and persons, falling, high places, and sudden movements accompanied by changes in light (shadows and flashes). But they become more afraid of imaginary creatures, the dark, and being alone or abandoned. Between 6 and 9 years of age children often fear preternatural figures, such as ghosts, Dracula, and monsters. And as children move into the elementary school years, fears regarding their personal safety (fears of kidnapping, accidents, and storms) tend to decline, while social fears associated with school (worries about grades and teachers) increase. Two-thirds of U.S. elementary

school children are afraid that "somebody bad" might get into their homes, and one-fourth are afraid that when they go outside, somebody might hurt them. Nowadays, children seem more afraid than they were in the past of lung cancer, pollution, and muggings (Brozan, 1983b).

Children's fears are not completely irrational. For example, most of the children who say that they are afraid to go outside also say that in the past someone (child or adult) outside the home hurt them or made them afraid. Another finding is that some children are afraid of their parents; one in ten children name their fathers as the person they are most afraid of (Flaste, 1977). In some circumstances children have legitimate concern that a parent may abuse them or a divorced parent kidnap them. Note, however, that children show marked differences in their susceptibility to fear and in the sources of their fears.

Although fear can sometimes get out of hand and take on incapacitating and destructive qualities, it does serve an essential "self-preservation" function (see the boxed insert). If we did not have a healthy fear of fierce animals, fire, and speeding automobiles, few of us would be alive today. Selma H. Fraiberg (1959; p. 11), a clinical psychologist, observes:

> [The child] learns to *anticipate* "danger" and prepare for it. And he prepares for "danger" by means of *anxiety!* . . . From this we immediately recognize that anxiety is not a pathological condition in itself but a necessary and normal physiological and mental preparation for danger.

Of course, youngsters differ in their willingness to take risks. Some children seem drawn to the excitement of risk much more than their peers do. They seek out stimulation in ways that concern their parents and teachers. Indeed, we tend to categorize children by the frequency and appropriateness of the risks they take, describing a child as cautious or reckless and timid or bold. Risk taking finds different avenues of expression. Children who excel in sports, music, art, or writing routinely take risks that their peers avoid—behaviors we deem "creative" (see Chapter 9). But the pursuit of novelty, variety, and excitement can also lead children to seek out dangerous risks such as running away from home, experimenting with drugs, or playing with fire (Konner, 1990; Kutner, 1990). So our consideration of emotion and fear lead us to inquire how these factors come to bear as children encounter morally relevant situations (Eisenberg, 1986; Hoffman, 1984; Nunner-Winkler & Sodian, 1988).

Moral Development

Morals are an acquirement—like music,
like a foreign language, like piety, poker, paralysis—
no man is born with them.—MARK TWAIN

As human beings, we live our lives in groups. Because we are interdependent, one person's activities can affect the welfare of others. Consequently, if we are to live with one another—if society is to be possible—we must share certain conceptions of what is right and what is wrong. Each of us must pursue our interests, be it for food, shelter, clothing, sex, power, or fame, within the context of a moral order governed by rules. Morality involves how we go about distributing the benefits and burdens of a cooperative group existence.

A functioning society also requires that its standards of morality be passed on to children—that moral development take place in its young. **Moral development** refers to the process by which children adopt principles that lead them to evaluate given behaviors as "right" and others as "wrong" and to govern their own actions in terms of these principles.

Historically, there have been three major philosophical doctrines regarding the moral development of children. One is the doctrine of "original sin," favored by theologians such as Saint Augustine (A.D. 354–430). According to this view, children are naturally sinful beings. As such they require redemption through the deliberate and punitive intervention of adults. Another view, put forward by John Locke (1632–1704), maintains that the child is morally neutral—a *tabula rasa*—and that training and experience determine whether the child becomes righteous or sinful. The third doctrine, represented by the writings of Jean Jacques Rousseau (1712–1778), holds that children are characterized by "innate purity" and that immoral behavior results from the corrupting influence of adults.

Each of these views finds expression in the three major contemporary psychological approaches to moral development. The first approach appears in modified form in the work of Sigmund Freud. The second is represented in cognitive learning theory, which treats moral development as a function of conditioning and modeling experiences. And the third approach is reflected to some degree in the cognitive-developmental theory of moral behavior as formulated by Jean Piaget and Lawrence Kohlberg.

Psychoanalytic Theory

Psychoanalytic theory (see Chapter 2) was the first fully psychological model of moral development. According to Freud, moral development is rooted in the emergence of the *superego,* a concept roughly equivalent to that of "conscience." Freud said that children possess various inborn drives—basic sexual and aggressive instincts—that are called the *id.* Parents frustrate these drives in order to socialize children in accordance with the standards of the wider society. This action generates hostility in the children toward their parents. But since children fear the loss of parental love and anticipate parental re-

Coping with Stress During Childhood

The image of children in pain and anguish stirs our adult sense of vulnerability, concern, and indignation. Many of us are moved to respond, intercede, and attempt to heal (Elfant, 1985). Yet all children must confront distressing situations and circumstances. Indeed, stress is an inevitable component of human life, so coping with stress is a central feature of human development. Psychologists view **stress** as a process involving the recognition of and response to threat or danger (Fleming, Baum & Singer, 1984). When we think and talk about stress, we usually mention its negative consequences—a stomachache, a tension headache, a tight throat, an aching back, a short temper, crying jags, dizzy spells, sleepless nights, asthma attacks, and countless other unpleasant outcomes. Yet without some stress we would find life drab, boring, and purposeless. Stress can be beneficial if it contributes to personal growth and increases our confidence and skills for dealing with future events (Goodhart, 1985). And so it is also with children. As suggested by the Chinese word, stress is composed of two characters—one meaning danger and the other opportunity. Danger and opportunity are not so much opposites as two sides of a single coin.

Coping behaviors are a central aspect of stress. When we confront difficult circumstances, we typically seek ways for dealing with them. **Coping** involves the responses we make in order to master, tolerate, or reduce stress (Fleming, Baum & Singer, 1984; Lazarus & DeLongis, 1983). There are two basic types of coping, *problem-focused coping* and *emotion-focused coping* (Folkman & Lazarus, 1985). Problem-focused coping changes the troubling situation, whereas emotion-focused coping changes one's appraisal of the situation.

Lacking specific information on how children respond to stress, professionals and social workers have often drawn inferences from the adult literature. But as psychologists have come to recognize that children are not miniature adults, they have increasingly turned to the study of stress and coping among children. In the course of this work psychologists are finding that popular notions are not always accurate. For instance, such events as hospitalization, birth of a sibling, divorce, or war are not necessarily or universally stressful. Children's perception of such events greatly influences their stress reactions. Many of the stressors long cited by clinical psychologists as extraordinarily stressful are actually experienced by children as less stressful than such events as being ridiculed, getting lost, or receiving a poor report card (Compas, 1987).

Yet adults and children are alike in one important respect. People who feel in control of a situation experience a sense of empowerment. Individuals with a high sense of mastery believe that they can control most aspects of their lives. But those unable to gain mastery—to exert influence over their circumstances—feel helpless (see the discussion in Chapter 2 on learned helplessness). Both children and adults with a low sense of mastery believe that their attempts at control are futile. Apparently a general sense of mastery moderates the negative effects of stress and encourages problem-focused as opposed to emotion-focused coping (Folkman & Lazarus, 1985).

Researchers find that an important moderator of an individual's experience of stress is **locus of control**—people's perception of who or what is responsible for the outcome of events and behaviors in their lives. When people perceive the out-

taliation, they repress their hostility and incorporate—in Freudian terms, **internalize**—the parental prohibitions.

The process of taking on, or internalizing, parental standards leads children to behave morally in order to avoid self-punishment, anxiety, and guilt. It is as if children become their own parents through the mechanism of the superego; external punishment is transformed into self-punishment and external control into self-control. Thus, by adopting their parents' evaluations of their own behavior, children incorporate within themselves the moral standards of the wider society.

Freud (1930) said that civilization requires people to restrain their instinctual impulses toward aggressive behaviors. Guilt feelings are the mechanism by which this restraint is achieved. Aggressive impulses are turned *inward* on oneself. Freud (1930, p. 134) concluded that "the price we pay for our advance in civilization is a loss of happiness through the heightening of the sense of guilt." And in Freud's view, excessive guilt is the foundation of many mental disorders.

All the details of orthodox psychoanalytic theory are no longer accepted by most behavioral and social scientists. But the assumption that so-come of an action as the result of luck, chance, fate, or powerful others, they believe in *external control*. When individuals interpret an outcome as the consequence of their own abilities or efforts, they believe in *internal control* (Chan, 1978; Fleishman, 1984; Lefcourt, Miller, Ware & Sherk, 1981; Phares, 1976; Rotter, 1966; Weigel, Wertlieb & Feldstein, 1989). Internal control typically increases with the age of a child (Penk, 1969). Scores on psychological measures of internal-external control tend to be relatively external at the third grade, with internality increasing in the eighth and tenth grades (Crandall, Katkovsky & Crandall, 1965).

In evaluating matters of stress, coping, and locus of control, three factors stand out in the emerging body of research as being of particular importance: (1) the characteristics of the child, (2) developmental factors, and (3) situation-specific factors (Altshuler & Ruble, 1989; Band & Weisz, 1988; Compas, 1987). Let us examine each of these factors in turn.

Dispositional and temperamental differences among children play a central role in influencing their coping responses (Kagan, 1983). Children differ in their sensitivity to the environment, with some showing signs of arousal and distress to a much wider array of events than others. So they must cope with a greater number of stressful situations than do more stress-resistant youngsters. Moreover, children differ in the way they react once they are aroused or threatened. For example, whereas some become aggressive and enraged, others become withdrawn and sullen, and still others resort to daydreaming, fantasizing, and escapist behaviors.

Developmental factors also play a part. For instance, 3- to 5-year-olds are distinguished from older youngsters by their difficulty in comprehending the finality of death. Similarly, children's emerging sense of self in middle childhood makes them more vulnerable to events that threaten their self-esteem than they were to these same events in an earlier period. Additionally, cognitive problem-solving skills differ as a function of age; as children get older, their ability to devise strategies for coping with stress expands, and they become more planful (Maccoby, 1983).

And finally, situational factors influence how children experience and deal with stress. Parents mediate many of the effects of stressful crises. A caretaker's irritability, anxiety, self-doubt, and feelings of incompetence are likely to intensify a child's fears of hospitalization. On the other hand, support from the family can have a steeling effect, buffering the influence of stressors (Garmezy, 1983; Rutter, 1981). Children's self-esteem is strengthened when they know that they are accepted by their parents and others despite their difficulties or faults. And resourceful caretakers can help them to define and understand their problems and find ways for dealing with them (Dubow & Tisak, 1989). "How to" books that supply programmatic strategies for assisting children often overlook the special nature of an individual child's experiences. Caretakers need to decipher a highly specific code if they wish to understand and help each child.

cialization occurs at least in part because children *identify* with their parents remains a major tenet of much contemporary research and therapy.

Cognitive Learning Theory

To make your children capable of honesty is the beginning of education.—JOHN RUSKIN
Time and Tide, 1867

In discussing cognitive learning theory, Chapter 2 emphasized the important part that imitation plays in the socialization process. According to psychologists such as Albert Bandura and Walter Mischel, children acquire moral standards in much the same way that they learn any other behavior. In contrast to the psychoanalytic position, social learning theorists deny that moral behavior comes from some single agency like the superego. In addition, they deny that moral behavior represents some unitary trait such as honesty. Rather, they insist that social behavior is variable and dependent on situational contexts. Most actions lead to positive consequences in some situations and not in others. Consequently,

Internalizing Adult Standards
Initially expectations regarding proper and improper behavior are external to children. But as youngsters grow older, an increasing proportion of their behaviors become governed by internal monitors. As they immerse themselves in the life of their society, most children develop self-conceptions that regulate their conduct in accordance with the standards of the group. These expectations pertain not only to prohibited behavior— what people "ought not" do, but they also define what individuals "ought" to do. *(Richard Hutchings/ Photo Researchers)*

individuals develop highly discriminating and specific response patterns that fail to generalize across all life circumstances (Mischel & Mischel, 1976).

Studies carried out by cognitive learning theorists have generally been concerned with the effect that models have on other people's resistance to temptation (Bandura, Ross & Ross, 1961, 1963). In such research children typically observe a model who either yields or does not yield to temptation. Chapter 1 described an experiment of this sort by Richard H. Walters, Marion Leat, and Louis Mezei (1963). One group of boys individually watched a movie in which a child was punished by his mother for playing with some forbidden toys. A second group saw another version of the movie in which the child was rewarded for the same behavior. And a third group, a control group, did not see any movie. The experimenter took each boy to another room and told him not to play with the toys in the room. The experimenter then left the room.

The study revealed that boys who had observed the model being rewarded for disobeying his mother themselves disobeyed the experimenter more quickly and more often than the boys in the other two groups. The boys who had observed the model being punished showed the greatest reluctance of any of the groups to disobey the experimenter. In short, observing the behavior of another person does seem to have a modeling effect on children's obedience or disobedience to social regulations. Of interest, other research reveals that dishonest or deviant models often have a considerably greater impact on children than do honest or nondeviating models (Grusec, Kuczynski, Rushton & Simutis, 1979; Rosenkoetter, 1973; Ross, 1971; Stein, 1967).

"How do you know when the yellow light means slow down and when it means to speed up?"

("Dennis The Menace" ® used by permission of Hank Ketcham and © 1991 by North American Syndicate.)

Cognitive-Developmental Theory

Cognitive learning theorists view moral development as a cumulative process that builds on itself gradually and continuously, without any abrupt changes. In sharp contrast to this idea, cognitive-developmental theorists like Jean Piaget and Lawrence Kohlberg conceive of moral development as taking place in stages. They see the course of moral development as divided into steps, with clear-cut changes between them. Consequently, a child's morality in a particular stage differs substantially from that of earlier and later stages. Although the learning and developmental perspectives are frequently counterposed to one another, they nonetheless provide complementary and interdependent analyses of human social interaction (Gibbs & Schnell, 1985).

Jean Piaget The scientific study of moral development was launched over sixty years ago by Jean Piaget. In his classic study, *The Moral Judgment of the Child* (1932), Piaget said that there is an orderly and logical pattern in the development of children's moral judgments. This development is based on the sequential changes associated with children's intellectual growth, especially the stages that are characterized by the emergence of logical thought.

In keeping with his interactionist perspective (see Chapter 2), Piaget believed that moral development occurs as children act upon, transform, and modify the world they live in. As they do, they in turn are transformed and modified by the consequences of their actions. Hence, Piaget portrayed children as *active* participants in their own moral development. In this respect Piaget differed from the cognitive learning theorists. As depicted in cognitive learning theory, the environment acts on children and modifies them; children are *passive* recipients of environmental forces. Cognitive learning theorists picture children as learning *from* their environment rather than, as Piaget would have insisted, in dynamic interaction *with* their environment.

Piaget provided a two-stage theory of moral development. The first stage, that of **heteronomous morality,** arises from the unequal interaction between children and adults. During the preschool and early elementary school years, children are immersed in an authoritarian environment in which they occupy a position decidedly inferior to that of adults. Piaget said that in this context children develop a conception of moral rules as absolute, unchanging, and rigid.

(Hence, the stage is also termed one of *moral realism* and a *morality of constraint.*)

As children approach and enter adolescence, a new stage emerges in moral development—the stage of **autonomous morality.** Whereas heteronomous morality evolves from the unequal relationships between children and adults, autonomous morality arises from the interaction among status *equals*—relationships among peers. Such relationships, when coupled with general intellectual growth and a weakening in the constraints of adult authority, create a morality characterized by rationality, flexibility, and social consciousness. Through their peer associations young people acquire a sense of justice—a concern for the rights of others, for equality, and for reciprocity in human relations. Piaget described autonomous morality as egalitarian and democratic, a morality based on mutual respect and cooperation. (Hence, the stage is also termed the *morality of cooperation.*)

Lawrence Kohlberg Lawrence Kohlberg (1963, 1969, 1981*a*, 1984; Colby & Kohlberg, 1987) refined, extended, and revised Piaget's basic theory of the development of moral values. Like Piaget, Kohlberg focused on the development of moral *judgments* in children rather than on their actions. He saw the child as a "moral philosopher."

Like Piaget, Kohlberg gathered his data by asking subjects questions about hypothetical stories. One of these stories (1963, pp. 18–19) has become famous as a classic ethical dilemma:

> In Europe, a woman was near death from a special kind of cancer. There was one drug that the doctors thought might save her. It was a form of radium that a druggist in the same town had recently discovered. The drug was expensive to make, but the druggist was charging ten times what the drug cost him to make. He paid $200 for the radium and charged $2,000 for a small dose of the drug. The sick woman's husband, Heinz, went to everyone he knew to borrow the money, but he could only get together about $1,000, which is half of what it cost. He told the druggist that his wife was dying, and asked him to sell it cheaper or let him pay later. But the druggist said, "No, I discovered the drug and I'm going to make money from it." Heinz got desperate and broke into the man's store to steal the drug for his wife. Should the husband have done that?

On the basis of responses to this type of dilemma, Kohlberg identified six stages in the development of moral judgment. He grouped these stages into three major levels: the *preconventional level* (stages 1 and 2); the *conventional level*

Games and Moral Conduct

In games young people learn the importance of rules for ordering human affairs. Piaget believed that autonomous morality arises out of the reciprocal interaction that takes place among peers. Children's moral development is enhanced in different ways by one-on-one games, group competitions, and individual achievements. *(Richard Hutchings/Photo Researchers; Martin Rogers/Woodfin Camp; Jose Carrillo/Stock, Boston)*

(stages 3 and 4); and the *postconventional level* (stages 5 and 6). These levels and stages are summarized in Table 11-1, together with typical responses to the story of Heinz. Study the table carefully for a complete overview of Kohlberg's theory. Note that the stages are based not on whether the moral decision about Heinz is pro or con but on what reasoning is used to reach the decision.

Each of Kohlberg's levels reflects a different type of relationship between the *self* and *society's rules and expectations.* The preconventional level is characteristic of most children under 9 years of age, some adolescents, and many criminal offenders. At this level rules and expectations are *external* to the self. The conventional level is typical of most adolescents and adults. At this level the self has *internalized* the rules and expectations of the wider society. The postconventional level is attained by less than 25 percent of all Americans. At this level individuals *differentiate* between themselves and the rules and expectations of others, preferring instead to define their values in terms of rationally considered, self-chosen principles.

According to Kohlberg, people in all cultures employ the same basic moral concepts, including justice, equality, love, respect, and authority. Furthermore, all individuals, regardless of culture, go through the same stages of reasoning with

Table 11-1

Kohlberg's Stages in the Development of Moral Judgment

Level One	Preconventional	Child's Response to Theft of Drug
Stage 1	*Obedience-and-punishment orientation.* The child obeys rules to avoid punishment. There is as yet no internalization of moral standards.	*Pro:* Theft is justified because the drug did not cost much to produce. *Con:* Theft is condemned because Heinz will be caught and go to jail.
Stage 2	*Naïve hedonistic and instrumental orientation.* The child's behavior is motivated by a selfish desire to obtain rewards and benefits. Although reciprocity occurs, it is self-serving, manipulative, and based on a marketplace outlook: "You can play with my blocks if you let me play with your cars."	*Pro:* Theft is justified because his wife needs the drug and Heinz needs his wife's companionship and help in life. *Con:* Theft is condemned because his wife will probably die before Heinz gets out of jail, so it will not do him much good.

Level Two	Conventional	Child's Response to Theft of Drug
Stage 3	*"Good boy"—"nice girl" morality.* The child is concerned with winning the approval of others and avoiding their disapproval. In judging the goodness or badness of behavior, the child considers a person's intentions. The child has a conception of a morally good person as one who possesses a set of virtues; hence, the child places much emphasis on being "nice."	*Pro:* Theft is justified because Heinz is unselfish in looking after the needs of his wife. *Con:* Theft is condemned because Hienz will feel bad thinking of how he brought dishonor on his family; his family will be ashamed of his act.
Stage 4	*"Law-and-order" orientation.* The individual blindly accepts social conventions and rules. Emphasis is on "doing one's duty," showing respect for authority, and maintaining a given social order for its own sake.	*Pro:* Theft is justified because Heinz would otherwise have been responsible for his wife's death. *Con:* Theft is condemned because Heinz is a lawbreaker.

Level Three	Postconventional	Child's Response to Theft of Drug
Stage 5	*Social contract orientation.* The individual believes that the purpose of the law is to preserve human rights and that unjust laws should be changed. Morality is seen as based on an agreement among individuals to conform to laws that are necessary for the community welfare. But since it is a social contract, it can be modified as long as basic rights like *life* and *liberty* are not impaired.	*Pro:* Theft is justified because the law was not fashioned for situations in which an individual would forfeit life by obeying the rules. *Con:* Theft is condemned because others may also have great need.
Stage 6	*Universal ethical principle orientation.* Conduct is controlled by an internalized set of ideas, which, if violated, results in self-condemnation and guilt. The individual follows self-chosen ethical principles based on abstract concepts (e.g., the equality of human rights, the Golden Rule, respect for the dignity of each human being) rather than concrete rules (e.g., the Ten Commandments). Unjust laws may be broken because they conflict with broad moral principles.	*Pro:* Theft is justified because Heinz would not have lived up to the standards of his conscience if he had allowed his wife to die. *Con:* Theft is condemned because Heinz did not live up to the standards of his conscience when he engaged in stealing.

Sources: Lawrence Kohlberg, "The Development of Children's Orientations toward a Moral Order," *Vita Humana,* Vol. 6 (1963), pp. 11–33; "Stage and Sequence: The Cognitive-Development Approach to Socialization," in D. A. Goslin (ed.), *Handbook of Socialization Theory and Research* (Chicago: Rand McNally, 1969), pp. 347–480; "Moral Stages and Moralization," in T. Lickona (ed.), *Moral Development and Behavior: Theory, Research, and Social Issues* (New York: Holt, Rinehart and Winston, 1976), pp. 31–53.

respect to these concepts and in the same order (Walker, de Vries & Bichard, 1984). Individuals differ only in how quickly they move through the stage sequence and how far they progress along it. Hence, it is Kohlberg's view that what is moral is not a matter of taste or opinion—there is a universal morality.

Kohlberg and his associates have tested individuals in the United States, the Bahamas, Great Britain, Israel, Mexico, Turkey, Taiwan, and Malaysia. He interprets the data from these tests as confirming his view that each child must go through the same, unvarying sequence of stages.

When Taiwanese village boys, for instance, were asked whether a man should steal food for his starving wife, a typical answer from a preadolescent was: "Yes, because otherwise he will have to pay for her funeral, and that costs a lot." A Malaysian of the same age was likely to say: "Yes, because he needs her to cook his food." Although the cultural content of the replies differed (funer-

Do Children of All Cultures Pass Through the Same Stages of Moral Development?

Lawrence Kohlberg answers this question affirmatively. Based on the cross-cultural research he and his associates undertook, Kohlberg concluded that all youngsters pass through the same, unvarying sequence of stages. *(Ken Graves/Jeroboam)*

als are less important in Malaysia than in Taiwan), the stage 2 orientation (the evaluation of behavior in terms of one's own selfish needs) remained constant.

Kohlberg (1978, 1980, 1981a, 1984) revised his thinking about moral development several times. At one point he seemed to drop his sixth stage, which some had criticized as Ivy League elitist and culturally biased. In his sixth stage Kohlberg had tried to capture the ideal of brotherhood and community embodied in the philosophies of such individuals as the late Rev. Martin Luther King, Jr. However, at a symposium in the late 1970s, Kohlberg lamented his difficulty in finding stage 6 persons: "Perhaps all the sixth-stage persons of the 1960s had been wiped out, perhaps they had regressed, or maybe it was all in my imagination in the first place" (quoted by Muson, 1979, p. 57). Even so, prior to his death in 1987, he posited yet another—a seventh—stage of development that is more religious and transcendental in substance (Kohlberg, 1981b). Furthermore, as we will discuss in Chapter 15, research by Carol Gilligan (1982) suggests that Kohlberg's moral dilemmas capture men's but not women's moral development. Her work reveals that men and women have differing conceptions of morality: Men have a morality of justice, the one described by Kohlberg, and women have a morality of care.

Overall, it seems reasonable to conclude that there is considerable merit to Kohlberg's position that the course of moral development tends to follow a regular sequence, particularly in Kohlberg's first four stages (Colby, Kohlberg, Gibbs & Lieberman, 1983; Nisan & Kohlberg, 1982; Snarey, 1985; Walker, 1982, 1989; Walker & Taylor, 1991a). Even so, differences exist among individuals, both in the order and in the rate of attainment of given levels. These differences largely derive from variations in social influences (Holstein, 1976; Miller & Bersoff, 1988; Simpson, 1974, 1976; Smetana, Killen & Turiel, 1991; Wainryb, 1991). However, Kohlberg's higher stages of moral judgment reflect the ways in which Western conceptions of law have evolved. Hence, they do not necessarily hold across different cultural contexts (Boyes & Walker, 1988; Shweder, Mahapatra & Miller, 1987). For instance, members of societies that promote the ideals of collective equality and happiness approach Kohlberg's moral dilemmas somewhat differently (Snarey, 1987). For instance, a village leader in Papua New Guinea placed blame for the Heinz dilemma on the entire community: "If nobody helped him [save his dying wife] and so he [stole to save her], I would say we had caused that problem" (Tietjen & Walker, 1985, p. 989). Some sociologists carry this argument even further and contend that "moral reasoning and behavior are determined largely by social factors—role demands, class interests, national policies, and ethnic antagonisms" (Cortese, 1990, p. 2). Although Kohlberg's work remains stimulating and provocative, interest in it and the orthodox Piagetian model has waned in recent years. Even so, Piaget's and Kohlberg's works have impacted upon educational practice as educators have used these theories to establish new curricula at schools to emphasize moral development (Power, Higgins & Kohlberg, 1989). And many psychologists say parents can use the stage theories to gain insight into their children's development and at each phase help their children to make moral decisions about their behavior (Grusec, 1991; Namuth, 1991; Walker & Taylor, 1991*b*).

Elliot Turiel Psychologist Elliot Turiel (1983, 1989; Helwig, Tisak & Turiel, 1990; Turiel, Killen & Helwig, 1987), like others in the cognitive-developmental tradition, views thought as actively constructed from children's interactions with the environment. And he considers thinking as progressing through a developmental sequence that represents qualitative changes from simpler to more complex levels of cognitive organization. However, he parts company with Kohlberg by distinguishing between two domains of social knowledge: the societal and the moral.

The societal realm involves those social rules and expectations that children must conform to as participants in the unique culture that characterizes their society. For instance, U.S. youngsters must learn that teachers and doctors are to be addressed by titles, that to be naked in public is unacceptable even if it is 90 degrees and sunny outside, and that only girls and women wear dresses. Actions of this sort are social conventions, which, while helpful for maintaining social order, are arbitrary. There is nothing inherently right or wrong about the actions.

In contrast with social conventions, moral concerns derive from factors intrinsic to actions, particularly their consequences—whether or not they bring harm to others, violate the rights of others, or impair the general welfare. Moral issues, then, are neither arbitrary nor determined by cultural standards. The violation of moral standards is viewed as wrong, irrespective of the presence of governing rules, while conventional acts are viewed as wrong only if they violate a cultural rule. Not surprisingly, people view conventional standards as relative and alterable, while they see moral prescriptions as universal and unchangeable (Nucci, 1986; Tisak & Turiel, 1988).

Turiel and his colleagues find that just as children's conceptions of morality undergo development, so also do their notions of social convention (Nucci, 1986; Smetana, 1984). Even though children may come to know what is "expected" of them and conform to these expectations, only with time do they begin to understand why such behaviors are considered reasonable and right. Indeed, to understand social conventions, children must acquire insight into interpersonal relationships and the role of behavioral norms. Turiel claims that children pass through seven developmental levels that reflect underlying concepts of social organization. This development follows an oscillating pattern between periods affirming social conventions and phases negating them. However, not all psychologists are comfortable with the distinction that Turiel makes between the domains of social convention and morality. They point out that the dictates of social organization necessarily intrude within both realms, and that disentangling them is difficult (Gabennesch, 1990; Rest, 1983).

William Damon Kohlberg's dilemmas deal with adult moral issues such as the one encountered by Heinz. William Damon (1977) has taken a somewhat different approach by posing moral dilemmas that are within the realm of children's experience. One area he has investigated is distributive justice—how individuals go about sharing scarce things. For instance, Damon (1977, p. 78) asks children how they would distribute among themselves an uneven number of toys:

James (four years, eight months): Suppose you and Sammy are playing together and you have these [five] toys? Would you give him any? *I would give him these two.* Why these two? *Because I got to keep three. These are the ones I like.* Suppose Sammy said, "I want to have more"? *If he took one then I would take one back from him.* Why is that? *Because I want three.* What will Sammy do then? *He will say that's OK, because he likes these* [the two toys originally given].

By studying children between 4 and 9 years of age, Damon has identified orderly progression in the way they reason about distributive justice:

❏ **Level 1** Children simply assert their choices and do not attempt to justify them: "I should get more ice cream than my sister because I like ice cream and want more."

❏ **Level 2** Children justify their choices on the

basis of external, observable traits such as size, age, or some other characteristic: "I should get more because I am bigger (run faster, am a boy, am older, and so on)."

❑ **Level 3** Children evolve notions in which fairness is equated with strict equality: "Everyone should get the same."

❑ **Level 4** Children begin to develop notions of merit and deserving: "Those who work hardest (are smartest, act best, and so on) should be rewarded because they deserve it."

❑ **Level 5** Children gain a sense of moral relativity. They come to recognize that different people can have different, yet equally valid, justifications for their claims to scarce things (the claims of persons with special needs, such as the poor, are weighed heavily): "She should get the most, but he should get some too" (a benevolent outlook).

❑ **Level 6** Children attempt to balance the conflicting claims deriving from notions of equality (everyone should receive an identical quantity of rewards) and notions of equity (rewards should be distributed proportionally among individuals in accordance with their contributions and their needs). They try to take into account all the potential claims for justice and to choose the claims that appear most relevant to the specific situation.

Damon notes that children rarely employ any one type of reasoning exclusively. But as they get older, they tend to use the more advanced levels of reasoning with greater frequency.

Moral Behavior: Consistency or Inconsistency?

> *There is no well-defined boundary line between honesty and dishonesty. The frontiers of one blend with the outside limits of the other, and he who attempts to tread this dangerous ground may be sometimes in the one domain and sometimes in the other.*—O. HENRY
>
> "Bexar Script No. 2692," Rolling Stones, 1912

The fact that people know what constitutes moral behavior does not guarantee that they will actually behave in a moral manner (Blasi, 1980). The monumental and classic research of Hugh Hartshorne and Mark A. May (1928; Hartshorne, May & Maller, 1929; Hartshorne, May & Shuttleworth, 1930), carried out more than half a century ago, revealed that practically all children cheat some of the time, regardless of how carefully they have been taught to be honest. These researchers investigated the moral behavior of

"I'm sorry I did it, an' I'm really sorry I got caught!"

("Dennis The Menace" ® used by permission of Hank Ketcham and © 1988 by North American Syndicate.)

some 11,000 children in classroom work, home duties, party games, and athletic contests. The children were given opportunities to lie, cheat, or steal under circumstances in which they thought that they were not being observed (although they were).

The inconsistency in the children's behavior was striking. Hartshorne and May found it impossible to predict, for instance, whether a child who cheated on a spelling test would also cheat on an arithmetic test. They concluded (1928, p. 411) that

> neither deceit nor its opposite, "honesty," are unified character traits, but rather specific functions of life situations. Most children will deceive in certain situations and not in others. Lying, cheating, and stealing as measured by the test situations used in these studies are only very loosely related.

The finding that morality was specific to situations, rather than a general character trait, was not limited to the children's actions. The children's scores on tests of moral knowledge and opinion also varied widely depending on whether the test was taken at a children's club, at home, in the classroom, or in Sunday school. The researchers concluded (Hartshorne, May & Shuttleworth, 1930, pp. 107–198): "A child does not have a uniform generalized code of morals but varies his opinions to suit the situation. . . ."

The Hartshorne and May findings did not support the notion of a unified or unitary conscience or superego. Recent research has confirmed the Hartshorne and May conclusion that morality is not primarily a "character trait" but a function of the situation in which individuals find themselves (Kohlberg, 1976; Kurtines, 1986; Mussen, Harris, Rutherford & Keasey, 1970; Rosenhan, Moore & Underwood, 1976; Sears, Rau & Alpert, 1965; Thorkildsen, 1989). In addition, Roger V. Burton (1976) reanalyzed a portion of the Hartshorne and May data. Burton concluded that some of the children studied by Hartshorne and May tended to be more consistently honest and some more consistently dishonest than others. Even so, he too noted that inconsistency rather than consistency was the dominant pattern.

Morality as Situational

The research by Hugh Hartshorne and his associates suggests that morality is not primarily a character trait but a function of the situation in which children find themselves. These children's "little white lies," for example, would be impossible to predict from situation to situation. (Dave Schaefer/The Picture Cube)

"Before I can escort you across the street, you'll have to sign this form releasing me of any liability. . . ."

(Carpenter © 1990 from the Wall Street Journal. Permission, Cartoon Features Syndicate.)

Correlates of Moral Conduct

As discussed in the previous section, moral conduct tends to vary among individuals and within the same individuals in different situational contexts. Research on morality has focused on developmental transitions and universal processes more than on individual differences. Questions regarding individual differences are somewhat discomforting, for they imply that some people are more moral than others. And most of us are loathe to label youngsters as uncaring and unprincipled (Zahn-Waxler, 1990). Even so, a number of researchers have attempted to specify which personal and situational factors are most closely associated with moral behavior.

Intelligence Maturity in several of the aspects of moral reasoning described by Piaget and Kohlberg tends to be positively correlated with IQ (Keasey, 1975; Lickona, 1976). Furthermore, a negative relationship has been found between IQ and dishonest behavior (Hartshorne & May, 1928). But this relationship tends to be limited to

Robert Coles:
Chronicler of Childhood

For three decades, child psychiatrist Robert Coles has studied the effects of poverty, desegregation, and other social forces on children. He has talked with youngsters from Northern Ireland to South Africa and from the Arctic to Nicaragua. In 1973 Coles won the Pulitzer Prize for his series *Children of Crisis.* Rather than studying the psychologically troubled patients customarily seen by psychiatrists, Coles concentrates on normal children. Often they are youngsters confronting horrible stress like the black children who desegregated the schools of the South in the 1960s. He probes what motivates them, what frightens them, and what allows them to persevere. In the course of his writing, he debunks the view that children are fragile creatures ready to wilt under the slightest difficulty. Even under terrible circumstances, youngsters have an amazing capacity to extract from their environment what they require (Sanoff, 1990). In sum, Coles examines both what is vulnerable and what is resilient and strong about children.

Coles's approach is personal, not detached: "I see (children) in the course of their lives, I see them in their homes and in their schools, and in churches or Sunday schools or Hebrew schools or mosques. I basically go out into the world. I don't confine myself to patients that come to a hospital" (quoted by Farley, 1990, p. 4D). His goal is to find out from children what they think about. To help him in his interviews, he often provides children

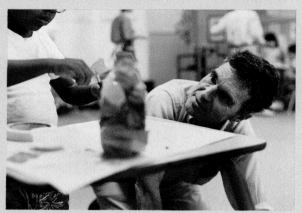

Robert Coles

Coles' primary method for studying youngsters is "to enter their world" and observe the behavior at the children's level. *(Alex Harris)*

with a box of crayons and asks them to draw for him what otherwise they would have difficulty verbalizing. Many academic psychologists criticize his work because they believe it lacks number-crunching depth. Since Coles is cautious of generalizations about human beings and focuses upon individual lives, his critics contend that his research is insufficiently scientific and that he relies on detailing lives as a substitute for careful, tough-minded analysis. But Coles replies that he does not

tests of the academic type. Apparently, the experiences that low-IQ and low-achieving children have with failure in school lead them to try to improve their academic status by cheating. The relationship between IQ and honesty disappears or declines when the context is nonacademic or when the risk of getting caught is low (Burton, 1976). Overall, being smart and being moral are not the same.

Age Research provides little evidence that children become more honest as they grow older. There may be a small correlation between age and honesty, but it seems to be due to other variables that also correlate with increasing age, such

as an awareness of risk and an ability to perform the task without the need to cheat (Burton, 1976).

Sex In the United States girls are commonly stereotyped as being more honest than boys, but research fails to confirm this popular notion. Hartshorne and May (1928) found, for instance, that girls tended to cheat more than boys on most of the tests that the researchers observed. Other studies undertaken during the intervening half century show no reliable sex differences in honesty (Burton, 1976).

Group Norms The Hartshorne and May (1928) research revealed that one of the major

seek to produce hard research data: "I'm not trying to formulate high theory, or come up with statistics or formulations. I'm trying to describe human complexity as it unfolds in a life. This is what I think our best novelists have taught us how to do. . . . Maybe more of us in the social sciences and psychology could learn from novelists" (quoted by Farley, 1990, p. 4D).

With the publication of *The Spiritual Life of Children* (1990), Coles has indicated he has completed his eight-volume project on children and will now study the elderly. In *The Spiritual Life of Children*, Coles looks at God through children's eyes. Coles, his wife, Jane, and their three sons talked with more than 1,000 Christian, Jewish, and Muslim youngsters, as well as those from agnostic and atheistic homes. As with his other works dealing with such matters as the moral and political life of children, Coles approaches the religious life of children by listening to them with the fewest possible theories and presuppositions. He seeks to portray what children think God is like, what they think they themselves are like, and what is important to them about life.

Coles comes up with a wide variety of responses, much—but not all—conditioned by the culture of which the children are a part, be it life on a Hopi Indian reservation, on an Israeli settlement, in a Pakistani neighborhood in London, or in a U.S. community in Massachusetts. A Hopi girl—using the analogy of birds circling over her people and hearing her "grandmother talk about our people"—provides a complex cosmology that integrates nature, her ancestors, and her present life. A 10-year-old Jewish boy sees Moses as the friend of God who soothes Him when He is angry. Muslim youngsters in London portray "the truth" that one's duty is to surrender to Allah. And a black girl in Lawrence, Massachusetts, draws God with raggedy, sharp teeth, a being who is ready to blow drug dealers and gang leaders "away with a hurricane."

Coles sees children as spiritual pilgrims looking for "a little help in knowing what this life is about." At stake in religious thought is "the nature of our predicament as human beings, young or old— *and* the way our minds deal with that predicament. . . ." Even children whose parents were atheists or agnostics could draw God as they thought those who believe in Him would represent Him. They would draw white gods, black gods, big gods, handsome gods, and ugly gods. As with adults, religion frequently provides youngsters with a sense of wholeness and cohesion at times of crisis, such as the death of a loved one. Coles finds that children wonder about space and time and finitude—questions that most of us have. Religion provides them with a mechanism by which to speculate about such matters and get a "handle on life." And as they enter later childhood, many of them become capable of more complex kinds of theological thought.

---

determinants of honest and dishonest behavior was the group code. When classroom groups were studied over time, the cheating scores of the individual members tended to become increasingly similar. This result suggests that group social norms were becoming more firmly established. Other research confirms the view that groups play an important part in providing guideposts for the behavior of their members and in channeling their members' behavior (Asch, 1952; Sherif, 1936).

Motivational Factors Motivational factors are a key influence in determining honest or dishonest behavior. Some children have a high achievement need and a considerable fear of failure, and they are likely to cheat if they believe that they are not doing as well on a test as their peers (Gilligan, 1963; Shelton & Hill, 1969). Risk of detection also plays a part (Hill & Kochendorfer, 1969).

Prosocial Behavior

A man was going from Jerusalem to Jericho, and he fell among robbers, who stripped him and beat him, and departed, leaving him half dead. Now by chance a priest was going down that road; and when he saw him he passed by on the other side. So likewise a Levite, when he came to the place and saw him, passed by on the other side. But a Samaritan, as he journeyed, came to where he was; and when he saw him, he had compassion, and went to him and bound up his wounds, pouring on oil and wine; then he set him on his own beast and brought him next to an inn, and took care of him. And the next day he took out two denarii and gave them to the innkeeper, saying, "Take care of him; and whatever you spend, I will repay you when I come back."

Luke 10:30–35

Moral development is not simply a matter of learning prohibitions against misbehavior (Batson, 1990). It also involves acquiring **prosocial behaviors**—ways of responding to other people through sympathetic, cooperative, helpful, rescuing, comforting, and giving acts. Some psychologists distinguish between helping and altruism. *Helping* entails behavior that benefits or assists another person, regardless of the motivation that underlies the behavior. **Altruism,** in contrast, implies that the behavior is carried out to benefit the other person without the expectation of an external reward. Thus, we label a behavior altruistic only if we are fairly confident that it was not undertaken in anticipation of return benefits.

According to Piaget, a child younger than 6 or 7 is too egocentric to understand another person's point of view. And traditional Freudians believe that altruistic behavior requires a superego, an internalized morality that children do not acquire until they resolve the Oedipal conflict (at about 6 years of age). Nonetheless, psychologists are finding that many infants are capable of comforting others who are crying or in pain. And by about 18 months many children imitate other people's crying and grimaces. For example, a mother bumped her elbow and exclaimed "Ouch!" Her 20-month-old son thereupon screwed up his face, rubbed his own elbow, and said, "Ow." Then he tried to rub *her* elbow. Seemingly, he first tried to understand what type of hurt was involved. This insight then allowed him to engage in the altruistic action (Pines, 1979*b*).

Furthermore, children of 18 months, when permitted to do so, often follow their parents through a round of household chores and undertake activities that we would label as helping behaviors if performed by an adult (Rheingold, 1982). Sweeping, gathering papers, dusting, and putting clothes in a drier are among the tasks that young children are likely to initiate. Although they may be unsuccessful at sweeping bits of dirt onto a dustpan, they nonetheless persist, placing the dirt particles on the pan or in a basket by hand. A few will precede or accompany their acts by a verbal statement such as "Sandy sweep," and a majority will do so by 24 months of age. The frequency and complexity of helping behaviors increase during the second year. By the time they are 2½, many youngsters will empty the contents of one wastebasket into another and bring chairs from one room to another in order to complete the setting of a table.

Although altruistic behaviors appear quite early, not all parents want their children to be Good Samaritans. Parents commonly teach their children not to be too generous and not to give away their toys, clothes, or other possessions. And in public places they may urge their children to ignore and not worry about some nearby person who is suffering or experiencing misfortune.

Research suggests that warm, affectionate parenting is essential for the development of helping and altruistic behaviors in children (Bryant & Crockenberg, 1980; Eisenberg, Lennon & Roth, 1983; Yarrow, Scott & Waxler, 1973). Yet nurturing parenting is not enough (Barnett, 1987; Koestner, Franz & Weinberger, 1990; Radke-Yarrow & Zahn-Waxler, 1976; Zahn-Waxler, Radke-Yarrow & King, 1979). Rather, parents must have the ability to convey a certain intensity about their own concern for other living things. If a cat is hit by a car, what matters in the development of a child's prosocial behavior is whether the parent appears to care about the cat—speaks about the cat's suffering and attempts to do something to alleviate it—or seems callous and unconcerned. Or should the child hurt someone else, the parent needs to describe to the child how the other person feels. Apparently, helping is often associated with *empathy*—feelings of emotional arousal that lead a child to take another perspective and to experience an event as the other person experiences it (Batson et al., 1988; Chapman, Zahn-Waxler, Cooperman & Iannotti, 1987; Eisenberg & Miller, 1987; Fabes, Eisenberg & Miller, 1990; Iannotti, 1985). Yet there is a fine line between encouraging altruism and fostering guilt; parents should not inject too much intensity into such situations lest their youngsters become overanxious. Moreover, parental warmth and nurturing alone can encourage selfishness. So parents need to provide guidelines and set limits on what youngsters can get away with (see the discussion in Chapter 10 dealing with Diana Baumrind's authoritative style of parenting).

In Chapter 10 we reviewed a study undertaken by Robert Sears, Eleanor Maccoby, and Harry Levin (1957) with 379 mothers of kindergartners in the Boston area in an attempt to identify those parenting techniques that make a difference in personality development. Twenty-six years later some 75 of the subjects were relocated and asked to complete a psychological measure of empathy

(Koestner, Franz & Weinberger, 1990). Significantly, the researchers found that children who were well-behaved and got along well with their classmates were no more likely to develop high levels of empathic concern than were youngsters who were active and quarrelsome. The single most powerful predictor of empathy in adulthood was how much time the children's fathers had spent with them. It seems that youngsters who saw their fathers as sensitive, caring beings were themselves more likely to grow up this way. In addition, mothers' tolerance of their children's dependency—reflecting their nurturance, responsiveness, and acceptance of feelings—was related to higher levels of empathic concern among the 31-year-old adults. Other researchers also find that the development of empathy is most likely to occur in a family environment that provides opportunities for youngsters to observe and interact with others who encourage emotional sensitivity and responsiveness (Barnett, 1987).

Many investigators have demonstrated that a child's sharing and helping behavior can be increased when adults (1) model the behavior before the child and (2) reinforce the behavior when the child displays it (Fabes, Fultz, Eisenberg, May-Plumlee & Christopher, 1989; Froming, Allen & Jensen, 1985; Gelfand, Hartmann, Cromer, Smith & Page, 1975; Grusec & Skubiski, 1970; Rushton, 1976; Staub, 1978). Not surprisingly, researchers also find that adults' actions speak louder than their words. Lecturing influences children's verbal comments but has practically no effect on their overt behavior. Indeed, research by Elizabeth Midlarsky, James H. Bryan, and Philip Brickman (1973, p. 323) suggests that adult hypocrisy may boomerang. The study involved a sample of seventy-two sixth-grade girls.

Each of the girls played a game with an adult model in which both received winnings from a "rigged" pinball machine. After the model had completed her games, she told the children:

> Now it is your turn. But before you begin, let me remind you about the poor children [a canister for poor children stood nearby]. Please think about them as you are playing and about how very much they would love to receive the prizes that these chips can buy. It would make them very happy to get toys and candy—because it is so easy for a needy child to feel forgotten. Let us let them know that we remember them.

This research revealed that when the adult modeled selfish behavior (kept her winnings) but preached altruism and praised the child when the child dropped a chip into the canister, the child was less likely to be charitable on subsequent occasions than when the hypocritical adult had not praised the child. In brief, by approving charitable behavior, a selfish-acting, generous-sounding model actually serves to discourage it.

David Rosenbaum (1972) found that young people who were involved in the civil rights movement of the 1960s were more likely to be fully committed—to leave their homes, schools, and jobs so that they could participate full-time—if their parents had also been prosocial activists in an earlier era (such as in the Spanish Civil War, World War II, or religious education). And in another study involving volunteers at telephone crisis-counseling centers, sustained altruism was more common among volunteers reared by nurturant parents who modeled altruism than among volunteers of less nurturant parents who modeled altruism to a lesser degree (Clary & Miller, 1986).

SUMMARY

1. An important feature of the elementary school years is a marked growth in children's cognitive sophistication. During this time, which Piaget calls the *period of concrete operations,* children achieve mastery of conservation problems. They become capable of decentering, attending to transformations, and recognizing the reversibility of operations.
2. Considerable controversy exists about whether the development of conservation can be accelerated through training procedures.

There is also some question about whether the acquisition of conservation skills in the period of concrete operations occurs in the invariant sequence—horizontal décalage—postulated by Piaget.
3. Although all children tend to pass through the same sequence of cognitive stages outlined by Piaget, they differ in cognitive style. Some children are impulsive and respond to problems very rapidly and with minimum consideration for accuracy; others are reflective and take considerably more time in responding.

Children differ in still another dimension of cognitive style, that of field independence and field dependence.

4. The greatest increase in children's ability to distinguish people's characteristics occurs between 7 and 8 years of age. Thereafter, the rate of change is generally much slower.

5. Cognitive factors play an important part in influencing children's understanding of emotion. Children increasingly attribute emotional arousal to internal causes; they come to know the social rules governing the display of emotion; they learn to "read" facial expressions with greater precision; they better understand that emotional states can be mentally redirected; and they realize that people can simultaneously experience multiple emotions.

6. There are three major psychological approaches to moral development: the psychoanalytic, cognitive learning, and cognitive-developmental theories.

7. The psychoanalytic view conceives of the child as a bundle of sexual and aggressive drives that need to be subordinated by adults to societal objectives. As a consequence of internalizing parental standards, children behave morally so as to avoid self-punishment, anxiety, and guilt.

8. Cognitive learning theory views moral development as a cumulative process that builds in a gradual and continous process. Children acquire moral standards primarily through imitating the observable values and behavior of others.

9. Cognitive-developmental theorists such as Jean Piaget and Lawrence Kohlberg conceive of moral development as taking place in stages. The course of moral development is seen as divided into stepped levels, with clear-cut changes distinguishing one phase from the next.

10. Research reveals that morality tends to be specific to situations. Most children will cheat, lie, or steal in certain situations and not in others. Little support exists for the notion of a unitary conscience or superego. Some individuals tend to be more consistently honest than others, some more consistently dishonest. But inconsistency is the more dominant tendency.

11. Intelligence, age, and sex differences play a small part in moral conduct. Group codes and motivational factors have a much larger role.

12. Moral development represents more than simply learning prohibitions against misbehavior. It also involves acquiring prosocial behaviors. Not surprisingly, research reveals that adults' actions speak louder than their words and that adult hypocrisy may boomerang.

KEY TERMS

Altruism Behavior that is carried out to benefit another without expectation of an external reward.

Autonomous Morality The second stage in Jean Piaget's two-stage theory of moral development. Moral judgments derive from an egalitarian and democratic perspective that is based upon mutual respect and cooperation.

Cognitive Style The stable preferences that individuals exhibit in organizing and categorizing their perceptions.

Conservation The concept that the quantity or amount of something stays the same regardless of any changes in its shape or position.

Coping The responses people make in order to master, tolerate, or reduce stress.

Executive Strategy A method for selecting, sequencing, evaluating, revising, and monitoring a problem-solving plan and behavior.

Fear An unpleasant emotion aroused by impending danger, pain, or misfortune.

Heteronomous Morality The first stage in Jean Piaget's two-stage theory of moral development. Judgments are rigid and absolute and derive from moral rules laid down by persons in authority, such as parents.

Internalize The concept from Freudian psychoanalytic theory that children incorporate within their personalities the prohibitions of their parents. Since children fear the loss of parental love and anticipate parental retaliation if they express open hostility and defiance toward their parents, the children repress their hostility and take on their parents' moral standards.

Locus of Control People's perception of who or what is responsible for the outcome of events and behaviors in their lives.

Moral Development The process by which children adopt principles that lead them to evaluate given behaviors as "right" and others as "wrong" and to govern their own actions in terms of these principles.

Period of Concrete Operations One of Piaget's four stages in the development of cognition, or intelligence. The stage marks the beginning of rational activity in children, one in which various classifying and ordering activities begin to occur internally as mental activities.

Phobia An excessive, persistent, and unadaptive fear response (usually to benign or ill-defined stimuli).

Prosocial Behavior (Altruism) Ways of responding to others that include sympathetic, cooperative, helpful, rescuing, comforting, and giving acts.

Psychomotor Skill A mind-guided muscular movement and its coordination.

Stress A process involving the recognition of and response to threat or danger.

Chapter 12

LATER CHILDHOOD: THE BROADENING SOCIAL ENVIRONMENT

The World of Peer Relationships

Developmental Functions of Peer Groups ◆ Same-Sex Groupings ◆ Social Acceptance and Rejection ◆ Self-Esteem ◆ Conformity to the Peer Group ◆ Racial Awareness and Prejudice

The World of School

Developmental Functions of Schools ◆ The Effectiveness of Schools ◆ Motivating Students ◆ School Performance and Social Class

◆

Life is with people.
Jewish Proverb

School is the child's first big step into the larger society. Some U.S. children enter the world of school when they are enrolled in a day-care program, others when they attend preschool, still others when they enter elementary school. When they attend school on a regular basis, children are outside their homes and their immediate neighborhoods for several hours a day. In this new setting teachers become a major source of potential influence. In school children also encounter other children of approximately the same age and grade level who will pass with them through a series of classrooms. Thus, school is a radical departure from a child's previous way of life. The environment it affords has a major influence on the development of a child's personality, intellectual capabilities, interpersonal skills, and social behavior.

The World of Peer Relationships

As children in elementary school develop and refine their cognitive and social skills, they become increasingly self-directed. Consequently, they choose a large portion of their own social contacts. Many of these contacts are with peers with whom they form "chum" relationships (McGuire & Weisz, 1982). From 6 to 14 years of age children's conceptions of friendship show an increasing emphasis on reciprocity, intimacy, and mutual understanding (Brendt & Perry, 1986; Rholes & Ruble, 1986; Sullivan, 1953; Youniss, 1980). The information that they consider important to know about a friend also undergoes developmental change (Selman, 1980). Preschoolers cite nonintimate information that enables friends to get together, such as their living near one another. During middle childhood children begin focusing on a friend's preferences, such as his or her favorite games, activities, and people. As they enter adolescence, young people become increasingly concerned with a friend's internal feelings and personality traits. Hence, there is a progressive shift from concern with the observable and external qualities of a friend to concern with a friend's internal psychological world. Clearly, peer relationships assume a vital role in children's development.

Developmental Functions of Peer Groups

There are many different kinds of peer relationships and groups: a friendship, a school or neighborhood clique, a scout troop, a basketball or baseball team, a gang, and so on. Children may simultaneously be involved in a number of peer relationships. These relationships provide a world of children, in contrast to a world of adults.

Sometimes, peer groups are in open conflict with adults, as in the case of delinquent gangs. A gang's behavior is oriented toward evading and flouting the rules and regulations of school and the larger adult-dominated society. Nondelinquent children also find themselves in conflict with parental expectations, as when they argue, "The other kids can stay out till twelve o'clock; why can't I?" At the other extreme, the expectations of some peer groups may fully accord with those of adults. This agreement is usually true of scout organizations and religious youth groups.

Peer groups serve a variety of functions. First, they provide an arena in which children can exercise independence from adult controls. Because of the support they receive from their peer group, children can gain the courage and confidence that is needed for weakening their emotional bonds to their parents. By creating peer standards for behavior and then appealing to these standards, the peer culture operates as a

"Dinner's ready, Billy. Lead your followers to the bathroom sink."

("Family Circus" © 1991 Bill Keane, Inc. Reprinted with special permission of King Features Syndicate.)

Peer Relationships

In their relationships with other youngsters of approximately the same age, young people acquire interpersonal skills essential for the management of adult life. Peer groups provide them with experiences in equalitarian relationships. In contrast, children are subordinates when dealing with adults. *(Paul Fusco/Magnum)*

pressure group. The peer group becomes an important agency for extracting concessions for its members on such matters as bedtime hours, dress codes, choices of social activities, and amounts of spending money. It affirms children's right to a considerable measure of self-determination (Ausubel & Sullivan, 1970; Siman, 1977). Hence, the peer group furnishes an impetus for young people to seek greater freedom and provides them with support for behavior they would never dare attempt on their own.

Second, peer groups give children experience with relationships in which they are on an equal footing with others. In the adult world, in contrast, children occupy the position of subordinates, with adults directing, guiding, and controlling their activities. Group living calls for relationships characterized by sociability, self-assertion, competition, cooperation, and mutual understanding among equals. By interacting with peers, children learn the functional and reciprocal basis for social rules and regulations. They practice "getting along with others" and subordinating their own interests to group goals. As discussed in Chapter 11, Jean Piaget views these relationships among status equals as the foundation for the stage in moral development that he terms autonomous morality.

Third, the peer group is the only social institution in which the position of children is not marginal. In it children can acquire status and realize an identity in which their own activities and

concerns are supreme. Furthermore the "we" feeling—the solidarity associated with group membership—furnishes security, companionship, acceptance, and a general sense of well-being. And it helps children avoid boredom and loneliness during the unstructured hours when school is not in session.

Fourth, peer groups are agencies for the transmission of informal knowledge, superstitions, folklore, fads, jokes, riddles, games, and secret modes of gratification. In the United States, for instance, only a portion of sexual information is learned through parents or schools. Peer groups transmit the larger part of this information (and misinformation). Even when sex education is not limited to the peer group, some types of sexual behavior (such as "necking") require private experimentation, since instruction would be awkward and embarrassing. Peer groups are especially appropriate for the mastering of self-presentation and impression-management skills, since inadequate displays will often be ignored or corrected without severe loss of face. Upstairs, behind the garage, and in other out-of-the-way places children acquire and develop many skills essential for the management of adult life (Fine, 1981, 1987).

Obviously, peers are as necessary to children's development as adults are. The complexity of social life requires that children be involved in networks both of adults and of peers (Furman, 1987; Furman & Buhrmester, 1985; Hartup, 1989; O'Brien & Bierman, 1988; Zarbatany, Hartmann & Rankin, 1990).

Same-Sex Groupings

A striking feature of peer relationships during the elementary school years is **sex cleavage**—the tendency for boys to associate with boys and girls with girls. For many individuals same-sex friendships are closer and more intense in late childhood and early adolescence than at any other phase of the life span. Although the social distance between the sexes is clearly present at preschool age, it increases greatly from the preschool to the school-age years and remains strong through middle childhood (Hayden-Thomson, Rubin & Hymel, 1987; LaFreniere, Strayer & Gauthier, 1984; Maccoby & Jacklin, 1987). Research reveals, for instance, that when first-grade children are given photographs of everyone in their class and asked to point out their best friend, 95 percent select a child of the same sex as themselves. Moreover, when they are asked to point out their four best friends, 82 percent likewise choose children of the same sex (Haskett, 1971). As we pointed out in Chapter 9, whatever characteristics may differentiate the sexes, the way boys and girls are socialized in Western nations magnifies the differences greatly. And in the early school years peers intensify the pressure for gender separation.

Although first-grade children overwhelmingly name members of their own sex as best friends, both boys and girls can be observed playing together on school playgrounds during recess. By the third grade, however, children have divided themselves into two sexual camps. This separation tends to reach its peak around the fifth grade. Much of the interaction between groups of boys and girls at the fifth-grade level takes the form of bantering, teasing, chasing, name calling, and displays of open hostility. This "them-against-us" view of the opposite sex serves to emphasize the differences between the sexes. As such, this view may function as a protective phase in life during which children can fashion a coherent sex-based identity. Some evidence suggests that gender segregation may be a universal process in human social development (Edwards & Whiting, 1988; Maccoby, 1988).

Development psychologist Eleanor E. Maccoby (1988, 1990) finds that gender segregation asserts itself in cultural settings in which children are in large enough numbers to permit choice. Indeed, children systematically frustrate adult efforts to diffuse their preferences for interacting with same-sex peers. For example, in modern coeducational schools, gender segregation is most marked in lunchrooms and other settings that are not structured by adults. Maccoby finds that boys' avoidance of girls, and girls' avoidance of boys, is not closely linked to participation in gender-typed activities. Preschool youngsters spend considerable time engaged in gender-neutral activities, and gender segregation prevails in these activities as well as when the children are playing with trucks or dolls.

Maccoby believes two factors give rise to gender segregation. First, boys and girls have differing styles for interacting with their peers, and so they segregate themselves into same-sex groups because they find play partners of the same sex more compatible. Boys engage in a good deal of rough-and-tumble play—teasing, hitting, poking, pouncing, sneaking-up on, mock fighting, piling on, chasing, holding, and pushing one another. Moreover, high levels of competitive and dominance-oriented behaviors prevail among boys

(Dodge, Price, Coie & Christopoulos, 1990; Pettit, Bakshi, Dodge & Coie, 1990). Boys and men seem to evolve social structures—well-defined roles in games, dominance hierarchies, and team spirit—that allow them to function effectively in group settings.

Maccoby contends that rough-and-tumble play and competitive and dominance-oriented behaviors make many girls wary and uncomfortable. For instance, boys are more likely than girls to interrupt one another; use commands and threats; heckle a speaker; tell jokes or suspenseful stories; try to top another person's story; and call other youngsters names. In contrast, girls in their own groups are more likely than boys to engage in "collaborative speech acts"—they express agreement, pause to give another girl a chance to speak, acknowledge a point made by a previous speaker, smile, and provide nonverbal signals of attentiveness. In sum, boys' speech serves egoistic functions and is used to "stake out turf," whereas girls' conversation tends to be a socially binding undertaking. It is not that girls are unassertive among themselves; rather, girls pursue their ends by toning down coercive and dominance-type behaviors and using strategies that facilitate and sustain social relationships (Miller, Danaher & Forbes, 1986; Sachs, 1987; Sheldon, 1989).

Maccoby believes a second factor also contributes to gender segregation among youngsters. Girls have a good deal of difficulty influencing boys. As youngsters advance through the preschool years, girls increasingly make polite suggestions to one another whereas boys increasingly use direct demands in their peer relationships (Serbin, Sprafkin, Elman & Doyle, 1984; Fagot, 1985). Maccoby suggests that girls find it aversive to try to interact with boys because boys become increasingly unresponsive to them and so girls go their separate ways. In other words, girls find it exceedingly difficult to establish reciprocity in their relationships with boys.

The prevalence of this childhood sex cleavage provided Sigmund Freud with his concept of *latency* (see Chapter 2). In Freud's view, once children no longer look on the parent of the opposite sex as a love object (thereby resolving their Oedipal or Electra conflict), they reject all members of that sex until they reach adolescence. Hence according to Freud, the elementary school years are a kind of developmental plateau, one in which sexual impulses are repressed.

But more recent research casts doubts on Freud's notion that sexual interests are minimal during the elementary school years. Carlfred B.

("Dennis The Menace" ® *used by permission of Hank Ketcham and* © *1988 by North American Syndicate.)*

Broderick and George P. Rowe (1968) studied a sample of 1,029 Pennsylvania school children between 10 and 12 years of age. They found that preadolescents exhibit the developing roots of adult heterosexual interests and activities (see Figure 12-1). In their sample 84 percent of the girls and 62 percent of the boys indicated that they expect to get married; 71 percent of the girls responded that they had a boyfriend and 56 percent of the boys that they had a girlfriend; and 51 percent of the girls and 47 percent of the boys admitted to having been in love.

Broderick and Rowe suggest that children typically pass through a series of stages in the course of heterosexual social development. First, preschool children acquire an awareness of marriage as involving a relationship between a man and a woman who are attracted to each other. Second, and somewhat later, children come to view marriage as an attractive and desirable prospect in their own imagined future. Third, children single out some member of the opposite sex as being especially attractive to them and then place this person in the special category of "boyfriend" or "girlfriend" (Broderick & Rowe, 1968, p. 100):

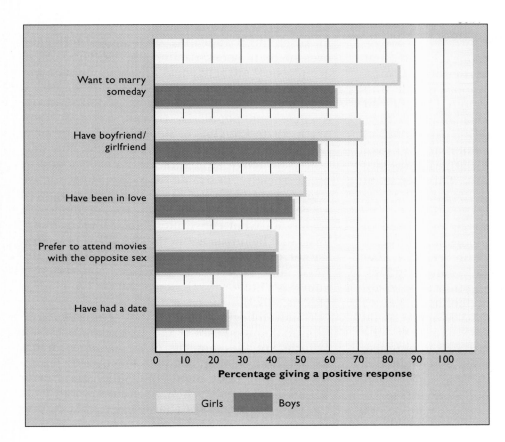

Figure 12-1 Beginnings of Adult Heterosexual Interests in Preadolescents

The figure charts the percentage of girls and boys who responded positively to items on a questionnaire measuring their social heterosexual development. In all, there were 1,029 subjects in the sample (530 boys and 499 girls), consisting of all 10- to 12-year-olds in the fifth, sixth, and seventh grades of ten central Pennsylvania schools. SOURCE: Adapted from Carlfred B. Broderick and George P. Rowe, "A Scale of Preadolescent Heterosexual Development," *Journal of Marriage and the Family,* Vol. 30 (1968), p. 99, Table 2. Copyrighted 1968 by the National Council on Family Relations, 3989 Central Ave., N.E., Suite #550, Minneapolis, MN 55421. Reprinted by permission.

At this [preadolescent] age the boyfriend-girlfriend relationship was quite likely to be nonreciprocal and . . . commonly the object of the affection was unaware of his or her status. Despite the largely imaginary nature of these relationships, however, the children who feel these attachments apparently take them quite seriously. The majority described themselves as having been "in love."

Having been "in love" appears to lay the foundation for the fourth stage, an appreciation of the desirability of engaging in an activity with a member of the opposite sex, such as going to see a movie together. And fifth, appreciating the possibility of companionship with a member of the opposite sex leads to the next major step, actually going out on a date. In sum, the Broderick and Rowe research reveals that even though same-sex friendships predominate among 10- and 11-year-old children, the children show a steady and progressive development of cross-sex interests as they advance toward puberty. Whether these patterns in heterosexual social development are peculiar to children reared in the United States, or whether they can be generalized to children reared in other cultural settings, remains to be determined.

Social Acceptance and Rejection

Peer relationships often take on enduring and stable characteristics: the properties of a **group,** which can be defined as two or more people who share a feeling of unity and are bound together in relatively stable patterns of social interaction. Group members commonly have a psychological sense of oneness—an assumption that their own inner experiences and emotional reactions are shared by the other members. This sense of oneness gives individuals the feeling that they are not merely *in* the group but *of* the group.

A group's awareness of unity is expressed in many ways. One of the most important is through shared **values,** which are the criteria that people use in deciding the relative merit and desirability of things (themselves, other people, objects, events, ideas, acts, and feelings). Values play a critical part in influencing people's social interaction. They function as the standards—the social "yardsticks"—that people use to appraise one another. In short, in fashioning accepting or rejecting relationships, people size up one another according to various group standards of excellence.

Peer groups are no exception. Elementary school children arrange themselves in ranked hierarchies with respect to a variety of qualities. Even first-graders have notions of one another's relative popularity or status. (Boys, for instance, regularly rate one another in terms of such attributes as "toughness.") Consequently, children differ in the extent to which their peers desire to be associated with them.

One common measure used for assessing patterns of attraction, rejection, or indifference is **sociometry** (Asher, Hymel & Renshaw, 1984; Bukowski & Newcomb, 1985). The technique involves a questionnaire or interview in which people are asked to name the three (or sometimes five) individuals in the group whom they would most like to sit next to (eat with, have as a close friend, go on a picnic with, live next to, have on their own team, or whatever). Researchers also use sociometry to establish patterns of rejection, discrimination, antagonism, or whatever by asking people to name the individuals whom they would least like to interact with in a given context. The data derived from a sociometric study can be presented in a *sociogram,* which depicts the patterns of choice existing among members of a group at a given time (see Figure 12-2).

Physical Attractiveness and Body Build Researchers have found a good many qualities that make children appealing or unappealing in the eyes of their peers. Among the most important are physical attractiveness and body build. Studies using many different methods have reported a significant relationship between physical attractiveness and popularity (Byrne, Ervin & Lamberth, 1970; Langlois & Stephan, 1977; Lerner & Lerner, 1977; Stephan & Langlois, 1984). Furthermore, attractive strangers are typically rated as more socially desirable than are unattractive strangers (Adams & Crane, 1980). The marked agreement that is found among the members of a society on what constitutes "good looking" suggests that beauty is not in the eye of the beholder. Rather, physical attractiveness is culturally defined and is differently defined by different cultures (Cavior & Dokecki, 1973; Langlois & Downs, 1979).

Children begin to acquire these cultural definitions at about 6 years of age; by the age of 8 their criteria are the same as older people's. Before age 6 children's conceptions of physical attractiveness tend to be highly individualistic (Cavior & Lombardi, 1973). Then, as children shift from the thought processes characteristic of the pre-

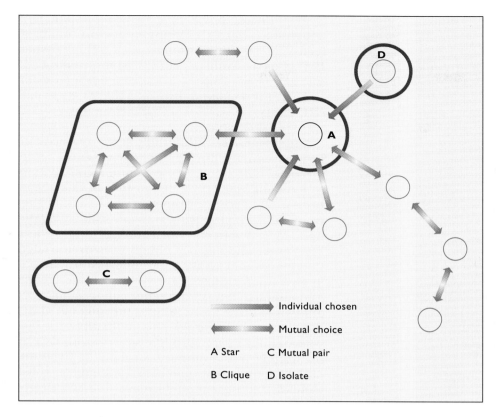

Figure 12-2 A Sociogram
Sociometry is a technique used for identifying the social relations in a group. Each individual is asked to name three (or sometimes five) group members with whom he or she would like to participate in a particular activity. It is a simple method, inexpensive, and easy to administer. The data gathered can be graphically depicted in a sociogram like this one, which portrays the network of relationships and identifies popular individuals (stars), as well as friendship pairs, and social isolates.

operational period to those of the period of concrete operations, they come to judge physical attractiveness in much the same manner as adults.

Stereotypes and appraisals of body configurations are also learned relatively early in life (Kirkpatrick & Sanders, 1978; Staffieri, 1967). "Lean and muscular," "tall and skinny," and "short and fat" are all bodily evaluations that influence the impressions people form of one another. Evidence suggests that negative attitudes toward fatness are already well developed among kindergarten children (Staffieri, 1967). Among boys, a favorable stereotype of the *mesomorph* (the person with an athletic, muscular, and broad-shouldered build) is evident at age 6. However, boys' desire to look like a mesomorph does not appear until age 7 and is not clearly established until age 8 (Staffieri, 1967).

Behavioral Characteristics A variety of behavioral characteristics appear related to children's acceptance by their peers. Popular children tend to be described by their associates as active, outgoing, alert, self-assured, helpful, good-natured, peppy, cheerful, and friendly. They are children who, although interested in others, do not too

obviously or aggressively seek attention; they are active but not hyperactive; and they are confident but not boastful (Dodge, 1983; Hartup, 1970). Children who successfully gain entry into ongoing interaction apparently possess the ability to read the social situation and adapt their behavior to it on an ongoing basis (Putallaz, 1983; Putallaz & Sheppard, 1990; Putallaz & Wasserman, 1989). They take "a process view" in which they recognize that relationships take time and that they may have to work themselves into a group slowly (Asher, 1983; Furman, 1987).

Several clusters of traits likewise tend to characterize children who are unpopular with their peers (Asher & Dodge, 1986; Ausubel & Sullivan, 1970; Coie, Dodge, Terry & Wright, 1991; Denham, McKinley, Couchoud & Holt, 1990; Dodge, 1983; French, 1988; French & Waas, 1985). First, there are those who are social isolates because they are physically listless, lethargic, and apathetic. Second, there are the children who are so psychologically introverted—timid, over-dependent on adults, and withdrawn—that they do not have much contact with their peers. And third, there are the children who are overbearing, aggressive, and egocentric—those who are described by their peers and teachers as noisy,

Standards of Excellence: Physical Attractiveness

Among the most important traits influencing peer relationships and popularity are those having to do with physical attractiveness and body build. Children who meet their culture's standards enjoy a decided advantage in their peer relationships over youngsters who do not. *(Bob Daemmrich/The Image Works)*

attention-seeking, demanding, rebellious, and arrogant. Such children have often been labeled "hyperactive" and placed on amphetamines in order to "control" their behavior (see the boxed insert). Unpopular children require help from parents and teachers—at times from professionals—because evidence suggests that they continue to have the same problems even when placed in totally new situations with unfamiliar peers (Coie & Kupersmidt, 1983). Significantly, early peer rejection in the first two months of kindergarten forecasts less favorable school perceptions among youngsters, higher levels of school avoidance, and lower performance levels (Ladd, 1990). And rejected children are more likely to experience serious adjustment problems in later life (Asher & Dodge, 1986; Hymel, 1986;

Hymel, Rubin, Rowden & LeMare, 1990). It is hoped that these children can acquire more effective social skills through interventions (Asher, 1983; Coie & Krehsiel, 1984; Dishion, 1990; Ladd & Golter, 1988; Patterson, Kupersmidt & Griesler, 1990; Pettit, Dodge & Brown, 1988; Quay & Jarrett, 1984).

Social Maturity Children's social maturity increases rapidly during the early school years (French, 1984). A. Jackson Stenner and William G. Katzenmeyer (1976) found that in one school system 50 percent of the first-graders said they would rather play with younger children. This figure dropped to one-third among third-graders. Moreover, whereas one out of three first-graders said they would rather play alone, fewer than one in five third-graders expressed this preference. And although being with other children bothered one out of three first-graders, only one out of five third-graders reported this difficulty. In fact, some children go through school with few or no friends. For example, Norman E. Gronlund (1959) found that about 6 percent of third- through sixth-grade children in one school system were not selected by any classmate on a sociometric questionnaire. More recently, Steven R. Asher and his colleagues (1984) found that more than 10 percent of children from third through sixth grade reported feelings of loneliness and social dissatisfaction, and these feelings were significantly related to their sociometric status.

Self-Esteem

*A man cannot be comfortable
without his own approval.*—MARK TWAIN
What Is a Man? 1906

In interacting with peers and adults, the child is provided with clues to their appraisals of his or her desirability, worth, and status. Through the accepting and rejecting behaviors of others, children continually receive answers to the questions "Who am I?" "What kind of person am I?" and "How valued am I?" Central to much theory and research in social psychology is the notion that people discover themselves in the behavior of others toward them (Vander Zanden, 1987). The writings of social psychologists such as Charles Horton Cooley (1902, 1909) and George Herbert Mead (1934), and of neo-Freudian psychiatrists such as Harry Stack Sullivan (1947, 1953), are based on the view that our self-conceptions

Behavior Pills
for Hyperactive Children?

The average child is an almost non-existent myth. To be normal one must be peculiar in some way or other.—HEYWOOD BROUN

Sitting in the World

The incidence and treatment of "hyperactivity" in children remains a matter of concern and controversy. The use of drugs, primarily amphetamines, in the management of "problem" children is widespread. Current estimates place the number of U.S. school children who are receiving amphetamines for the control of "attention-deficit hyperactivity disorder," or ADHD (the designation employed by the American Psychiatric Association), at between 500,000 and 1.5 million.

Hyperactivity is a descriptive term that entails a judgment about a child's behavior. Since it involves a collection of vague and global symptoms, medical experts tend to disagree on its nature and the means for diagnosing it. Children who tend to be labeled as having ADHD are those who have short attention spans, exhibit sleep problems, throw temper tantrums, and have difficulty learning, sitting still, or responding to discipline. In sum, the hallmark of childhood hyperactivity is "trouble." The youngsters have trouble getting things done at home and school and have trouble getting along with peers and adults. The "trouble" frequently occurs in a child and in a context in which an obvious explanation is lacking: The youngster exhibits no marked intellectual deficits, thought disorders, emotional disturbances, or family problems (Henker & Whalen, 1989). In addition, hyperactives in late adolescence and early adulthood experience difficulties in many areas of social functioning and personal well-being, with the most frequent problems involving antisocial activity, conduct disorder, and substance abuse (Lambert, 1988; Thorley, 1984). Yet this relatively gloomy assessment must be balanced by the fact that approximately half of hyperactive children seem to function quite well as adults (Gittelman, Mannuzza, Shenker & Bonagura, 1985; Weiss & Hechtman, 1986).

Experts have advanced a variety of theories to explain the source of ADHD, including genetic defects, poor parenting, food additives, spicy foods, allergies, lead poisoning, fluorescent lights, insufficient oxygenation, and too much television. More recently, researchers at the National Institute of Mental Health have related ADHD to metabolic dysfunction in the brain (Kolata, 1990). They have used a new and sophisticated brain-imaging technique—positron emission tomography, or PET, scans—to measure glucose metabolic activity in the brain cells of individuals with the disorder. The scientists find not only that overall brain metabolism is 8 percent lower in hyperactive subjects than in a control group but that the largest differences are found in two regions of the brain known to be involved in regulating attention and motor control (the premotor cortex and the superior prefrontal cortex). Although the source of these metabolic differences is not known, the research seems to establish a link between brain chemistry and hyperactive behavior. This insight may help us to understand why amphetamines produce their calming effect on hyperactive youngsters (although, paradoxically, they have an opposite, stimulating effect on adults).

In many cases parents, teachers, and peers report a significant improvement in symptoms, classroom behavior, and academic performance as a result of administering amphetamines (commonly Ritalin) to hyperactive children (Whalen, Henker, Castro & Granger, 1987; Whalen, Henker & Dotemoto, 1981). Some researchers believe that the medication somehow allows the hyperactive child to attend to critical aspects of the learning situation and to filter out distractions (Ellis, Witt, Reynolds & Sprague, 1974; Henker & Whalen; 1989; Peloquin & Klorman, 1986; Swanson & Kinsbourne, 1976). However, not all children respond to drug therapy. Moreover, as with any medication, adverse side effects occasionally occur—insomnia, gastrointestinal distress, dizziness, weight loss, and retardation of growth.

Many professionals and members of the public fear that the widespread enthusiasm for administering amphetamines to "hyperactive" children has led to abuses and to the acceptance of drug therapy for children who may not benefit from it. It becomes frighteningly easy for parents and teachers to control behavioral "problems" and "difficulties" under the guise of giving children "medicine." The drugs then become "conformity pills" for rebellious youngsters. Some physicians have prescribed medication on the basis of teachers' and parents' reports that a child is doing poorly in school, without giving the child a thorough medical evaluation. While some children benefit from amphetamine treatment, the trend toward its indiscriminate use is cause for concern.

Self-Appraisals as Reflected Appraisals
How we come to perceive ourselves is powerfully influenced by other people's definitions of us—how they respond to us plays a part in how we respond to ourselves. Children who are respected and approved of for what they are have more self-esteem and self-acceptance than children who aren't. This self-confidence is reflected in their achievements. *(Alan Carey/The Image Works)*

emerge from social interaction with others and that our self-conceptions in turn influence and guide our behavior.

According to this social psychological tradition, individuals' self-appraisals tend to be "reflected appraisals." If children are accepted, approved, and respected for what they are, they will most likely acquire attitudes of self-esteem and self-acceptance. But if the significant people in their lives belittle, blame, and reject them, they are likely to evolve unfavorable self-attitudes. On the whole, social psychological research has supported the overall postulate that we hold the keys to one another's self-conceptions and identities (Berkowitz, 1988; Rosenberg, 1989; Vander Zanden, 1987). However, the reflected-appraisal

process often finds expression in the attitudes of groups (a general sense of how others view us) rather than necessarily in the attitudes of a specific, meaningful person (Andersen & Cole, 1990; DePaulo, Kenny, Hoover, Webb & Oliver, 1987; Felson, 1989).

But the fact is not simply that children can *discover* themselves only in the actions of others toward them. The sociologist J. Milton Yinger (1965; p. 149) observes:

> More than that, the self is *formed* out of the actions of others, which become part of the individual as a result of his having identified with these others and responded to himself in their terms. Retrospectively, one can ask "Who am I?" *But in practice, the answer has come before the question.* The answer has come from all the definitions of one's roles, values, and goals that others begin to furnish at the moment of birth. "You are a boy; you are my son; you are French"; "You are a good boy and fully part of this group" (with rewards confirming the words); or "You are a bad boy" (with significant others driving the point home by the sanctions they administer).

Note, however, that children are not simply passive beings who mirror other people's attitudes toward them. They *actively* shape their self-conceptions as they go about their daily activities and test their power and competence in a great many situations. Through their interactions with others and through the effects they produce on their material environment, they derive a sense of their energy, skill, and industry (Franks & Marolla, 1976).

Stanley Coopersmith (1967) has studied the kinds of parental attitudes and practices that are associated with the development of high levels of self-esteem in a sample consisting of eighty-five preadolescent boys. He found that three conditions were correlated with high self-esteem in children. First, the parents themselves had high levels of self-esteem and were very accepting toward their children (Coopersmith, 1967, pp. 178–179):

> The mothers of children with high self-esteem are more loving and have closer relationships with their children than do mothers of children with less self-esteem. . . . The child apparently perceives and appreciates the attention and approval expressed by his mother and tends to view her as favoring and supportive. He also appears to interpret her interest and concern as an indication of his significance; basking in these signs of his personal importance, he comes to regard himself favorably. This is success in its most personal expression—the concern, attention, and time of significant others.

Second, Coopersmith (1967; p. 238) found that

children with high self-esteem tended to have parents who enforced clearly defined *limits:*

> Imposition of limits serves to define . . . the point at which deviation from . . . [group norms] is likely to evoke positive action; enforcement of limits gives the child a sense that norms are real and significant, contributes to self-definition, and increases the likelihood that the child will believe that a sense of reality is attainable.

Consequently, such children are more likely to be independent and creative than those reared under open and permissive conditions.

Third, although parents of children with high self-esteem did set and enforce limits for their children's behavior, they showed *respect* for the children's rights and opinions. Thus, within "benign limits" the children were given considerable latitude. The parents supported their children's right to have their own points of view and to participate in family decision making.

These findings from the Coopersmith study suggest that competent, firm, accepting, and warm parenting tends to be associated with the development of high self-esteem. By providing well-defined limits, the parents structure their children's world so that the children have effective standards by which to gauge the appropriateness of their behavior. And by accepting their children, the parents convey a warm, approving reflection that allows the children to fashion positive self-conceptions. On the whole, other researchers have confirmed Coopersmith's finding that warm and accepting parenting tends to be associated with children who have high self-esteem (Felson & Zielinski, 1989; Gecas & Schwalbe, 1986; Loeb, Horst & Horton, 1980; Sears, 1970). So does "mattering," the feeling that we matter to others and that we make a difference in their lives (Rosenberg, 1985; Rosenberg & McCullough, 1981). Once again we encounter the benefits to be derived from authoritative parenting (see Chapter 10).

Conformity to the Peer Group

Trumpet in a herd of elephants;
crow in the company of cocks; bleat
in a flock of goats.
Malay Proverb

Peer influences operate in many ways. One of the most important is through the pressure that peer groups put on their members to conform to various standards of conduct. Although peer groups constrain the behavior of their members,

they also facilitate interaction. They define shared goals and clarify acceptable means for pursuing these goals. Social and behavioral scientists have employed two primary procedures in the laboratory for investigating social conformity.

The first procedure, developed by the social psychologist Muzafer Sherif (1936), involves the use of an optical illusion: the so-called *autokinetic effect.* If a small, fixed spot of light is briefly exposed in a darkened room, it appears to move in an erratic manner. Individuals—both children and adults—differ in their estimates of how far the spot "moves." Sherif found that when tested alone, each individual evolves a standard or norm by which he or she gauges the light's "movement."

Sherif brought together in peer groups individuals who had developed standards very *different* from one another in their solitary sessions. He exposed them collectively to the light and asked them to report aloud on their appraisal of its movement. Under these experimental conditions the group members quickly converged toward a common estimate of the light's movement. Moreover, when they were later brought back again for individual sessions, the group-evolved norms persisted. And the majority of subjects reported not only that their judgments were made before the others spoke but also that they were *not* influenced by the others.

A second procedure for studying group factors in conformity was developed by the social psychologist Solomon E. Asch (1952). In this research design seven to nine people are seated side by side. Unlike the Sherif procedure, in which a vague, *ambiguous* stimulus is employed, individuals in the Asch type of experiment are presented with an *unambiguous* situation. Two sets of cards with lines drawn on them are placed in the front of the room, and subjects are asked to match the lines in length (see Figure 12-3). Each subject gives his or her response aloud.

The catch is that except for one person, the so-called critical subject, all the members of the peer group are confederates of the experimenter. They have previously been briefed to provide unanimous incorrect answers on certain trials. Asch has found that although the correct answer is obvious, nearly one-third of all judgments by adult "critical" subjects contain errors identical with or in the direction of the rigged errors of the majority. Moreover, 74 percent of the adult subjects conform on at least one of the trials.

Studies reveal that children display different conformity responses to the two types of experiments. Where the highly *ambiguous* autoki-

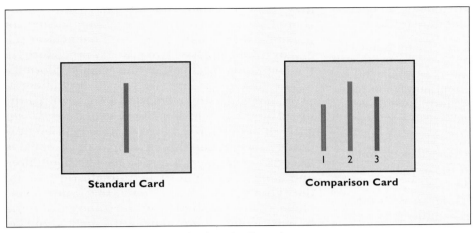

Figure 12-3   Cards in Asch-Type Conformity Experiments
Two sets of cards like these are placed at the front of the room, and subjects are asked to match the lines in length. One card has a single black line (the standard). The other card has three lines, one of which is the same length as the standard while the other two are obviously either longer or shorter. When answers are written anonymously, control subjects match the lines with almost complete accuracy. But under experimental conditions, where there is pressure toward group conformity, many "naïve" subjects, who are asked to match the lines publicly after confederates of the experimenter intentionally give incorrect answers, also give the incorrect answers.

netic effect is employed, conformity tends to *increase* with age over the elementary school years (Hamm & Hoving, 1969). But where the task is *unambiguous*, as in the Asch type of experiment, conformity *declines* with age (Allen & Newston, 1972; Berenda, 1950; Cohen, Bornstein & Sherman, 1973; Hoving, Hamm & Galvin, 1969). For example, in her classic Asch-type experiments conducted over three decades ago, Ruth W. Berenda (1950) found that although 93 percent of younger children (aged 7 to 10) can provide correct responses when alone under anonymous conditions, only 43 percent actually do so under the pressure of the peer group. On the other hand, while 94 percent of older children (aged 10 to 13) can provide the correct responses when alone under anonymous conditions, a higher proportion—54 percent—actually does so in the group setting.

Berenda also varied the Asch type of experiment by employing a two-person situation—a child and the child's teacher. When the teacher, functioning as Berenda's confederate, gave incorrect answers, only 14 percent of the younger children yielded to her influence. Even fewer of the older children—5 percent—gave the teacher's incorrect answers. This result suggests that the influence of the teacher was significantly weaker than the influence of the children's peers.

The research of Berenda points to the conclusion that no simple statement concerning peer conformity is valid. Much depends upon the age of the children, the kind of peers they are with, the nature and clarity of the task, and the structure of the social situation.

Racial Awareness and Prejudice

I have a dream that my four little children will one day live in a nation where they will not be judged by the color of their skin but by the content of their character.—MARTIN LUTHER KING, JR.
Speech, June 15, 1963

A key aspect of many children's peer experiences involves relations with members of different racial and ethnic groups. A considerable body of research indicates that children as young as 3 can correctly identify racial differences between blacks and whites. By the age of 5 the vast majority of children can make such identifications accurately (Branch & Newcombe, 1986; Goodman, 1952; Katz, 1976; Porter, 1971; Williams & Morland, 1976). Children's perceptions and concepts about racial differences follow a developmental sequence similar to that of their perceptions and concepts about other stimuli (Clark, Lotto & McCarthy, 1980). Their own social identities as members of particular ethnic groups evolve slowly with age, as they subjectively identify with a group and assimilate notions of ethnicity and belonging within their self-concepts (Rosenthal,

1987; Rotheram-Borus, 1990; Spencer and Mark-strom-Adams, 1990). Labeling oneself as a member of an ethnic group is one of the earliest expressions of a child's social identity and typically is acquired by 8 years of age (Aboud, 1987).

Phyllis A. Katz, M. Sohn, and S. R. Zalk (1975) find that during the preschool period white children attend less to differences among blacks than they do among whites. For instance, the presence of eyeglasses or a smile on black faces is a less important distinguishing feature than the same cue is for white faces. During middle childhood white children explore racial cues more and attend more closely to the vast individual differences that are to be found among both black and

Racial Awareness

The vast majority of children in our society can accurately identify a person's racial membership by the time they reach five years of age. (Patrick Reddy)

white people. However, as the children enter adolescence, they once more pay less attention to individual differences among blacks, suggesting that they have come to perceive and think about blacks in more stereotyped terms.

Prejudice studies give us little information about the specific interracial behavior that children should exhibit. Indeed, it is doubtful that children, especially younger grade-school children, show coherent, consistent **prejudice**—a system of negative conceptions, feelings, and action orientations regarding the members of a particular religious, racial, or nationality group. It is one thing to demonstrate that prejudice can develop in young children; it is quite another to say that prejudice is *characteristic* of young children (Katz, Sohn & Zalk, 1975; Westie, 1964). For instance, kindergartners and third-graders enrolled in an extraordinarily ethnically and racially diverse laboratory school located on the campus of the University of California at Los Angeles interacted and formed friendships independently of ethnic and racial memberships (Howes & Wu, 1990). At times, what adults perceive to be prejudice in children is instead a preference for other children who share similar subcultural practices and values and hence who provide a more comfortable "relational fit" (Steinberg & Hall, 1981). Moreover, some question exists as to whether skin color is the principal determinant of racial prejudice (Dent, 1978; Sorce, 1979). Hair and eye characteristics may play an equal or even more important role.

Much research shows that how people act in an interracial group situation bears little or no relation to how they feel or what they think (Prager, Longshore & Seeman, 1986; Vander Zanden, 1983, 1987; Wicker, 1969). The *social setting* in which individuals find themselves does much to determine their specific responses. Thus, in the United States today, a public show of blatantly racist and discriminatory behavior is commonly defined as counter to the nation's democratic ideals and as being "in poor taste." Yet simultaneously, many whites define an interracial neighborhood as unacceptable and "flee" from it to a virtually all-white suburb.

Interracial friendliness is promoted by policies that foster positive interracial contact at *early* ages in elementary schools and neighborhoods. For this reason desegregation should begin at the earliest possible grade, including preschool and kindergarten, to be most effective. Many racial and ethnic attitudes are formed early and adjusting to new environments and avoiding negative stereotypes is more difficult for older students than for younger ones. Indeed, the junior high school and middle school years may be the worst period in which to start desegregation (Hallinan & Williams, 1987, 1989; Hallinan & Teixeira, 1987; Patchen, 1982; Singleton & Asher, 1977). One of the most successful methods for reducing the hold of racism is grouping students into interracial learning teams, which, like sports teams, knit members together in common purpose that often leads to interracial friendships (Gaertner, Mann, Dovidio, Murrell & Pomare, 1990; Gaertner, Mann, Murrell & Dovidio, 1989; Perdue, Dovidio, Gurtman & Tyler, 1990).

The World of School

I tell you we don't educate our children in school; we stultify them and then send them out into the world half-baked. And why? Because we keep them utterly ignorant of real life. The common experience is something they never see or hear. All they know is pirates trooping up the beaches in chains, tyrants scribbling edicts, oracles condemning three virgins to be slaughtered to stop some plague. Action or language, it's all the same; great sticky honeyballs of phrases, every sentence looking as though it has been plopped and rolled in poppyseed and sesame.—GAIUS PETRONIUS

Roman satirist, first century A.D.

The nature and mission of schools have been a source of dispute through the ages. Contemporary Americans are no more in agreement about their schools than the citizens of Rome were 2,000 years ago. Controversy rages—about the content of school curricula, about teaching approaches (highly structured or informal), about busing to realize better racial mixes, about the amount and sources of school financing, about special programs for exceptional and disadvantaged youngsters, about the applications of academic freedom.

Developmental Functions of Schools

What the best and wisest parent wants for his own child, that must the community want for all its children.—JOHN DEWEY

We commonly think of **schools** as agencies that provide formal, conscious, and systematic training. Schools came into existence several thousand years ago to prepare a select few to govern the many and to occupy certain professions. Over the past century or so public schools have become the vehicle by which the entire population has been taught the basic skills of reading, writing, and arithmetic that an industrial-urban society requires. In fact, education has become a crucial investment in the economy and a major economic resource. Higher education has also become a major military resource. Throughout the world schools are increasingly seen as a branch of the state and as serving state

"But is showing you this toy and telling about it the whole story? Let's take a look at its sales record, as illustrated by this chart, which compares it with other toys in its price class."

(Drawing by Cheney; © 1990. The New Yorker Magazine, inc.)

purposes (Carnoy, 1984; Carnoy & Levin 1985; Ramirez & Boli, 1987).

Elementary schools serve many functions. First, they teach specific cognitive skills, primarily the three Rs. But they also inculcate, as they did in the past, more general skills, such as paying attention, sitting quietly, and participating in classroom activities (Murphy, Murphy & Newcomb, 1937, p. 652):

> [Children] are expected to conform to a group pattern imposed by an adult who is in charge of too many children to be constantly aware of each child as an individual. Flash cards are flashed at the group all at once. Stories are told and everybody must listen whether he will or not. Drawing paper and crayons are meted out whether you happen to feel like drawing at that moment or not. One child who found this shift quite beyond endurance remarked after his first day in school, "It's awful; all you do is mind all day long." And another day he added, "It really is awful. All you do is sit and sit and sit."

Indeed, some argue that the authoritarian structure of the school mirrors the bureaucratic hierarchy of the workplace (Apple, 1982; Apple & Weis, 1983; Bowles & Gintis, 1976). So schooling functions to prepare students for future work conditions. Even the school grading system of A, B, C, D, and E has its parallel in the system of wage and salary scales as a device for motivating individuals. And like their counterparts in industry, students often suffer boredom and alienation (Everhart, 1983).

Second, schools have come to share with the family the responsibility for transmitting a society's dominant cultural goals and values. The schools perform a similar function in other societies. Like the United States, both China and Russia stress patriotism, national history, obedience, diligence, personal cleanliness, physical fitness, the correct use of language, and so on in their schools. With respect to basic social norms, values, and beliefs, all education indoctrinates.

Third, to one degree or another, schools function as a "sorting and sifting agency" that selects young people for upward social mobility. In the United States, for instance, the continual expansion of technical, managerial, and professional jobs has allowed able and industrious students to ascend the social ladder through careers open to the "talents." Schools, especially colleges and universities, seek to transmit various technical competencies and to encourage the development of leadership and decision-making skills. Hence in many cases, education operates as a critical intervening variable in the transmission of status from one generation to the next. Families also influence the careers of their children by socializing them to high educational and occupational aspirations and by providing them with the support necessary for achieving these aspirations (Blau & Duncan, 1967; Sewell, 1981). Early schooling experiences seem to be particularly important. Although early academic success does not ensure later success, early academic failure strongly predicts later academic failure (Temple & Polk, 1986).

Fourth, schools attempt to overcome gross deficits or difficulties in individual children that interfere with their adequate social functioning and participation (see the boxed insert). Often, schools work in consultation with parents as well as with school psychologists and guidance personnel.

In addition, schools meet a variety of needs not directly educational. They serve a custodial function, providing a baby-sitting service that keeps children out from under the feet of adults and from under the wheels of automobiles. They function as a dating and marriage market. And compulsory education, coupled with child labor laws, serves to keep younger children out of the labor market and hence out of competition with adults for jobs in the society.

The Effectiveness of Schools

The principal goal of education is to create men [and women] who are capable of doing new things, not simply of repeating what other generations have done—men [and women] who are creative, inventive and discoverers.—JEAN PIAGET

Over the past decade there has been an outpouring of reports decrying the state of the U.S. educational system. In 1983 *A Nation at Risk,* a product of the National Commission on Excellence in Education, set an alarmist tone that pointed to a "rising tide of mediocrity" in the schools. Other reports, criticisms, and recommendations followed. Yet there is little evidence that matters are better today than they were ten years ago, despite society's demands for better trained and more skilled members. According to an analysis of national test results by the National Assessment of Educational Progress, fewer than 10 percent of the nation's high school seniors have the skills necessary to perform demanding jobs or do college work (Center for Education Statistics, Department of Education, 1990). The reports point to many of the same indicators, including poor achievement test scores; a long-term decrease in college entrance test scores;

Learning Disabilities

Educators have come to employ the term **learning disabilities** as an umbrella concept to refer to children and adolescents who encounter difficulty with school-related material despite the fact that they appear to have normal intelligence and lack a demonstrable physical, emotional, or social impairment (some prefer the term "differently abled"). In practice, the notion implies that a discrepancy exists between a student's estimated ability and his or her academic performance. Unlike those diagnosed as mentally retarded, the population of youngsters categorized as learning disabled is relatively unrestricted. In fact, as part of their efforts to secure adequate funding, school officials often reclassify pupils as learning disabled to fit a program that will provide financial assistance.

A variety of youngsters are designated as learning disabled. There are some whose eyes see correctly but whose brains improperly receive or process the informational input. Or instead of zeroing in on what is directly in front of their noses, they take a wide-angle view (Geiger & Lettvin, 1987). In either case, they may get letters mixed up, reading "saw" for "was" or "dog" for "god." Others have difficulty selecting the specific stimulus that is relevant to the task at hand from among a mass of sensory information. Still others may hear but fail to remember what they have heard by virtue of an auditory-memory problem. For instance, they may turn to the wrong page in the book or attempt the wrong assignment when they rely on oral instructions. However, whatever the source may be, learning disabled youngsters have problems in reading *(dyslexia)*, in writing *(dysgraphia)*, or in mathematics *(dyscalcula)*.

Such disabilities are often called "the invisible handicap." They do not end with childhood. There are an estimated 5 to 10 million adults in the United States with a variety of thought and behavior problems that confuse and frustrate them in the course of their everyday activities (Pennington, Van Orden, Smith, Green & Haith, 1990; Spreen,

1988). However, learning disabilities do not automatically lead to low achievement. Many accomplished scientists (Albert Einstein), political leaders (Woodrow Wilson and Nelson Rockefeller), authors (Hans Christian Andersen), artists (Leonardo da Vinci), sculptors (Auguste Rodin), actors (Tom Cruise), athletes (Bruce Jenner), and military figures (George Patton) are believed to have experienced learning disabilities (Schulman, 1986).

The placement of children in a category like "learning disabled" is a serious matter. It can blight their lives by stigmatizing them, reducing their opportunities, lowering their self-esteem, and alienating them from others. However, such labeling can open doors to services and experiences that can facilitate learning, a sense of self-worth, and social integration. Hence, teachers and the public must be aware of the possible harmful effects of labeling so that the labels are not used for obscure, covert, or hurtful purposes.

Over the past two decades there has been appreciable change in the policy and philosophy of educators toward those youngsters with mild or moderate learning disabilities. It has resulted in a shift away from segregated or separate classrooms toward **mainstreaming**—the integration of students with special needs within the regular programs of the school. The movement has received an impetus from federal legislation that has required that youngsters with special needs be educated in the "least restrictive environment" that is possible. While considerable hope has been placed in mainstreaming, educators and psychologists warn that the mere physical presence of children with special needs in regular classrooms does not guarantee academic or social success. It works only where school officials, teachers, parents, and students are committed to making it work through designing, implementing, and supporting appropriate restructuring of the educational enterprise (Madden & Slavin, 1983).

declines in both enrollments and achievement in science and mathematics; low levels of communication, writing, and thinking skills; the high cost incurred by business and the military for remedial and training programs; the substantial levels of functional illiteracy among the U.S. population; and the poor performance of U.S. students on international tests (see the boxed insert on page 348).

Educators, psychologists, and sociologists have examined what makes a school effective. Michael Rutter (1979*a*, 1983) led a University of London team in a three-year study of students entering twelve London inner-city secondary schools. These schools—only a scant distance apart and with students of similar social backgrounds and intellectual abilities—had quite different educational results. The most important factor seemed

Do Good Schools Make a Difference?
Considerable controversy has raged in academic circles regarding findings that suggest a school's physical facilities, including libraries and labs, contribute little to the academic achievement of students. According to one view, children's achievement is dependent on their family and community background and schools bear little influence. Other educators dispute this view, contending that a school's facilities set the "tone" for the educational program that is found there. (Frank Siteman/Monkmeyer)

to be the school "ethos" or "climate." The successful schools fostered expectations for order in the classrooms; they did not leave matters of student discipline to be worked out by individual teachers. So teachers found that it was easier for them to do a good job of teaching in some schools than in others. Moreover, the effective schools emphasized academic concerns: The teachers took considerable care in planning their lessons; high-achievement expectations permeated the classrooms; students spent a high proportion of their time on instruction and learning activities;

homework was considered important; and students were encouraged to use the library. Additionally, schools that fostered respect for students as responsible people and held high expectations for proper behavior achieved better academic results.

Other researchers have also concluded that successful schools foster expectations that order will prevail and that learning is a serious matter (Clark, Lotto & McCarthy, 1980; Lee & Bryk, 1989; Linney & Seidman, 1989). Much of the success of private and Catholic schools has derived from their ability to provide students with an orderly environment and strong academic demands (Coleman, Hoffer & Kilgore, 1982*a*; Coleman & Hoffer, 1987; Flanigan, 1991; Jensen, 1986; Putka, 1991). Academic achievement is similarly high in the public sector when the policies and resulting behavior are like those in the private sector (Coleman, Hoffer & Kilgore, 1982*b*; Coleman & Hoffer, 1987). Successful schools, then, possess "coherence"; things work together and have predictable relationships with one another.

Moreover, research demonstrates that good teachers make a difference (Brophy, 1986). Using a complicated and innovative methodology, Eigil Pedersen, Thérèse A. Faucher, and William W. Eaton (1978) were able to show a positive relationship between one first-grade teacher and the adult success of children from a disadvantaged urban neighborhood. Two-thirds of "Miss A's" pupils achieved the highest adult status; less than half of the former pupils of other first-grade teachers did. None of her pupils were in the lowest category, although more than a third of other teachers' students were.

"Miss A" enjoyed a reputation as an excellent teacher. She gave extra time to slow learners and invariably stayed after hours to help children. The researchers concluded that "Miss A," by helping to shape the academic self-concept and achievement of a pupil, laid an early foundation that yielded cumulative benefits in later life. Although not all schools may be effective, capable teachers apparently can make a difference. Such teachers seemingly tap children's spontaneous curiosity and desire to learn, a matter to which we now turn our attention.

Motivating Students

Most of us assume that behavior is functional and that people do certain things because the outcomes somehow meet their needs. This premise underlies the concept of motivation. **Motivation** involves those inner states and processes that prompt, direct, and sustain activity. Motivation influences the rate of student learning, the retention of information, and performance (Stipek & MacIver, 1989). Here we will examine a small portion of the topic that is most relevant to our consideration of the schooling process.

Intrinsic and Extrinsic Motivation Mark Twain once observed that work consists of whatever we are obligated to do, whereas play consists of whatever we are not obligated to do. Work is a means to an end; play is an end in itself. Many psychologists make a similar distinction between extrinsic motivation and intrinsic motivation. **Extrinsic motivation** entails activity that is undertaken for some purpose other than its own sake. Rewards such as school grades, honor rolls, wages, and promotions are extrinsic, because they are independent of the activity itself and because they are controlled by someone else. **Intrinsic motivation** involves activity that is undertaken for its own sake. Intrinsic rewards are those inherent to the activity itself and over which we have a high degree of self-control (Deci, 1980; Greene & Lepper, 1974; Notz, 1975).

As we have repeatedly noted in earlier chapters, children want to feel effective and self-determining in dealing with their environment. Unhappily, formal education often undermines children's spontaneous curiosity and desire to learn. Most psychologists agree that punishment and pain impede classroom learning. But over the

"How do you know I'm an underachiever? —Maybe you're just an overdemander!"

(Baloo © 1988 from The Wall Street Journal. Permission, Cartoon Features Syndicate.)

past two decades they have also become aware that even rewards can be the enemies of curiosity and exploration (Deci, 1975; Deci & Ryan, 1980, 1985; Deci, Schwartz, Sheinman & Ryan, 1981).

Research by Mark R. Lepper and David Greene suggests that parents and teachers can unwittingly undermine intrinsic motivations by providing youngsters with extrinsic rewards. They observed children in a school located on the campus of Stanford University and recorded which ones enjoyed drawing with felt-tipped pens of various bright colors. Then the felt pens were removed from the classrooms for two weeks. After this interval the children who had displayed interest in them were brought one by one to another room and asked to make drawings using felt pens. Before beginning their drawing, one-third of the children were shown a "good player award" (a card with a gold star and a red ribbon) that they would receive upon completing their project. Another third were not told about the reward until they had finished drawing. The other third neither expected nor received a reward (Greene & Lepper, 1974; Lepper & Greene, 1975; Lepper, Greene & Nisbett, 1973).

A week later the teachers once again set out felt pens on a number of classroom tables. It was found that the children who had previously expected to receive an award for their pictures spent only half as much time playing with the felt pens as they had done before the experimental session. By contrast, children who had not received an award or had been given an award unexpectedly showed about the same interest in the felt pens after the experimental session as they had before it. Lepper and Greene take this and evidence from other studies they have conducted as showing that lavish praise, gold stars, and other extrinsic rewards serve to undermine children's intrinsic interest in many activities. They suggest that parents and educators should use rewards only when necessary to draw children into activities that do not at first attract their interest. But even in these cases, extrinsic rewards should be phased out as quickly as possible.

Attributions of Causality Closely linked to the matter of intrinsic and extrinsic rewards is another matter—people's perceptions of the *factors* that produce given outcomes (Hamilton, Blumenfeld & Kushler, 1988). Consider the following experience. You have been watching a game involving your favorite football team. With five seconds left in the game and the score tied, a player on your team intercepts a pass and races for the goal line. As the player stumbles into the end zone, the gun sounds ending the game. Your team has won. Your friend, who preferred the other team, says, "Your guys were just *lucky!*" You indignantly respond, "Luck my eye! That was true *ability.*" "Naw," exclaims another friend. "Your guys were more psyched up. They put out more *effort.*" To which a fourth observer interjects, "Heck, it was an *easy* interception. No one was between him and the goal line!" Four differing explanations were set forth for the same event: luck, ability, effort, and the difficulty of the task (Weiner, 1972, 1979).

Youngsters also attribute their academic successes to these differing explanations. And it makes a considerable difference which of the explanations they employ. Educational psychologists find that when students attribute their successes to high ability, they are more likely to view future success as highly probable than if they attribute their success to other factors. By the same token, the attribution of an outcome to low ability makes future failure seem highly probable. The perception that one has failed because one has low ability is considerably more devastating than the perception that one has failed because of bad luck, lack of effort, or task difficulty.

It seems that both success and failure feed on themselves. Students with histories of performing better than their peers commonly attribute their superior performances to high ability, and so they anticipate future success. Should they encounter periodic episodes of failure, they attribute them to bad luck or lack of effect. But youngsters with histories of low attainment typically attribute their successes to good luck or high effort and their failures to poor ability. Consequently, high attainment leads to attributions that maintain a high self-concept of ability, high academic motivation, and continued high attainment. It is otherwise for those youngsters with low attainment (Boggiano, Main & Katz, 1988; Carr, Borkowski & Maxwell, 1991; Forsyth & McMillan, 1981; Skinner, Chapman & Bates, 1988).

Locus of Control The research on attributions of causality has been influenced by the concept of *locus of control.* In Chapter 11 we noted in our discussion of stress that locus of control refers to people's perception of who or what is responsible for the outcome of events and behaviors in their lives. A good many studies have shown a relationship between locus of control and academic achievement. It seems that locus of control plays a mediating role in determining whether students become involved in the pursuit of achieve-

ment. Externally controlled youngsters tend to follow the theory that no matter how hard they work, the outcome will be determined by luck or chance; they have little incentive to invest personal effort in their studies, to persist in attempts to find a solution to a problem, or to change their behavior to ensure success. In contrast, internally controlled youngsters believe that their behavior accounts for their academic successes or failures and that they can direct their efforts to succeed in academic tasks. Not surprisingly, pupils who have an internal sense of control generally show superior academic performance (Bar-Tal & Bar-Zohar, 1977; Boggiano, Main & Katz, 1988; Carr, Borkowski & Maxwell, 1991; Massari & Rosenblum, 1972). The impressive academic success of many Asian Americans seems related to the folk belief that "If I study hard, I can succeed, *and* education is the best way to succeed" (Sue & Okazaki, 1990). (See the boxed insert dealing with the academic achievement of Japanese, Taiwanese, and U.S. children.) Low educational attainment is often associated with socioeconomic disadvantage, a topic that bears closer scrutiny.

School Performance and Social Class

We must open the doors of opportunity. But we must also equip our people to walk through those doors.—
LYNDON B. JOHNSON
Address, December 10, 1964

Study after study has shown a close relationship between school performance and socioeconomic status (Boocock, 1972; Hodgkinson, 1986; Matras, 1975). This relationship is evident regardless of the measure employed (occupation of principal breadwinner, family income, or parents' education). Studies have shown that the higher the social class of children's families, (1) the greater will be the number of the formal grades the children will complete, the academic honors and awards they will receive, and the effective offices they will hold; (2) the greater will be their participation in extracurricular activities; (3) the higher will be their scores on various academic achievement tests; and (4) the lower will be their rates of failure, truancy, suspensions, and premature dropping out of school. Among the hypotheses that have been advanced to explain these facts are the middle-class bias of schools, subcultural differences, and educational self-fulfilling prophecies.

Middle-Class Bias Boyd McCandless (1970, p. 295) has observed that "schools succeed rela-

The Academic Achievement of Japanese, Taiwanese, and U.S. Children

School children in the United States lag behind children in Japan and Taiwan from the day they enter school (see Table 12-1). These findings suggest that improving the quality of U.S. education requires changes in U.S. homes as well as in U.S. schools. Cultural differences in family socialization seem to contribute to differences in school readiness. For instance, in soliciting their children's obediance, U.S. mothers assert their authority, something Japanese mothers avoid. Instead, Japanese mothers appeal to their children's feelings or to the consequences of disobedience. The Japanese strategy seems more effective in instilling the values and norms of adults and so better prepares children for school discipline. Having internalized their mothers' expectations, the Japanese youngsters are more likely than Americans to approach the classroom with "receptive diligence."

Additionally, Japanese culture has traditionally emphasized the "goodness" of the child to the point of sanctifying it. The child is treated as an autonomous learner with an inner potential that is not particularly responsive to external agents. But at the same time, Japanese culture instills discipline through notions of interpersonal harmony, knowing one's role, and role perfectionism. These polar views of children as autonomous and disciplined beings are reconciled in the cultural emphasis upon "effort" as responsible for individual accomplishment (Hamilton, Blumenfeld, Akoh & Miura, 1990; Stevenson, Azuma & Hakuta, 1986).

American mothers also have much lower expectations of their children's academic performance and are more satisfied with their children's education than are their Japanese or Taiwanese counterparts. And while the old adage depicts Americans as confirmed believers in hard work, U.S. mothers rate ability as a stronger factor than effort in their children's school success. In contrast, Japanese and Taiwanese mothers rate effort as more important than ability. Not surprisingly, U.S. mothers generally do not regard homework as having much value. Parents who think success depends more upon ability than effort are less likely to require their children to work hard at learning than are parents who value effort.

The lower achievement level of U.S. youngsters is also related to the way U.S. schools manage instruction. For one thing, the average school year is shorter in the United States—180 days versus 240 in Japan and Taiwan—and the school day is a half hour to two hours shorter. For another, U.S. children spend less than half as much time as the Taiwanese and less than two-thirds as much as the Japanese on academic activities. American youngsters are more likely to use classroom time staring into space, wandering around the room, asking irrelevant questions, and talking to peers (Stevenson et al., 1985; Stevenson, Lee & Stigler, 1986; Stigler, Lee & Stevenson, 1987; Uttal, Lummis & Stevenson, 1988).

Within the United States Asian-American young people also seem to enjoy disproportionate educational achievement. Although a scant 2.1 percent of the U.S. population is Asian, Asians represent about 12 percent of the students at Harvard, 20 percent at Stanford and the Massachusetts Institute of Technology, and 30 percent at the University of California at Berkeley. During the 1980s,

Table 12.1

Academic Achievement in the United States, Japan, and Taiwan					
	Mean Number of Questions Answered Correctly		Percent of Class Time Spent on Reading	Percent of Class Time Spent on Math	Percent of the Time Students Paid Attention in Class
	Math	Reading Comprehension			
First Grade					
United States	17.1	21.3	50.6	13.8	45.3
Japan	20.1	22.8	36.2	24.5	66.2
Taiwan	21.2	25.6	44.7	16.5	65.0
Fifth Grade					
United States	44.4	82.6	41.6	17.2	46.5
Japan	53.8	82.5	24.0	23.4	64.6
Taiwan	50.8	84.6	27.6	28.2	77.7

Source: Harold W. Stevenson, University of Michigan, 1984.

Are Japanese Schools Better Than American Schools?

Japanese schools have produced educational results that place their average 18-year-old on a par with the average American college graduate. On achievement tests, the 50th percentile Japanese student would score in the 98th percentile on an American examination. Japanese schools provide a more orderly, focused, and faster-paced education than do their American counterparts. However, at the college and university level Americans do a better job than do the Japanese. (left, Ethan Hoffman/Archive; right, Richard Hutchings/Photo Researchers)

Asian-American youngsters won about a quarter of the Westinghouse Science Talent Search scholarships (the nation's most prestigious high school science contest); in 1986, they were awarded all five top scholarships.

One explanation for the success of Asian-Americans lies in the Confucian ethic that still infuses China, Korea, Japan, and Vietnam. The Confucian legacy—an ethical code rather than a religion—centers on tightly knit families, discipline, and a high respect for all forms of learning. Children have the strong support and encouragement of their families throughout their schooling. In turn, children work hard to bring honor to their families. A survey in the San Francisco area found that Asian Americans are more likely than other ethnic groups to do homework, enroll in college preparatory courses, earn more high school credits, and take more courses in science, math, and foreign languages. They also received consistently

better grades than other students regardless of their parents' level of education or their families' social and economic status (Butterfield, 1986; Mordkowitz & Ginsburg, 1987; Oxnam, 1986).

Another explanation for Asian-American success is that members of these minorities experience restrictions to upward mobility in careers or jobs that are unrelated to education (for instance, entertainment, sports, and politics). Consequently, education assumes importance as a vehicle for moving vertically from one social status to another. One indication that Asian-American academic effort is propelled by the need to overcome discrimination is that their academic achievement tends to drop from one generation to the next. It seems that the more Americanized Asian-Americans become, the less they worry about being frozen out of sectors of the economy because of

(Continued)

their ethnic memberships (Dornbusch, Ritter, Leiderman, Roberts & Fraleigh, 1987; Ritter & Dornbusch, 1989; Sue & Okazaki, 1990).

Still another explanation is that the children are the offspring of a unique group of immigrants, drawn largely from the intellectual and professional elites of their native lands. Many middle-class and well-educated Chinese and Vietnamese fled to the United States when communist regimes came to power; there has also been a brain drain of engineers, physicians, and scientists from Taiwan, South Korea, India, and other Asian nations. Significantly, earlier generations of youngsters from the nation's older Chinatowns did not perform nearly as well as have recent arrivals.

Although many Asian-American youth enjoy remarkable academic success, they may be encountering discrimination. Asian-American leaders say their young people are not being evaluated on their merits when they apply to the nation's most prestigious universities. In 1989, the Chancellor of the University of California at Berkeley publicly apologized for "disadvantaging" Asians in the admissions process (Takagi, 1990). On the job, too, Asian-Americans complain that they soon "top out," reaching positions beyond which their employers fail to promote them (Asian-Americans made up 4.3 percent of professionals and technicians but just 1.4 percent of office managers in 1985) (McLeod, 1986; Schwartz, 1987).

tively well with upper- and middle-class youngsters. After all, schools are built for them, staffed by middle-class people, and modeled after middle-class people." Even when teachers are originally from a different social class, they still view their role as one of encouraging the development of a middle-class outlook on such matters as thrift, cleanliness, punctuality, respect for property and established authority, sexual morality, ambition, and neatness.

In some cases middle-class teachers, without necessarily being aware of their prejudice, find lower-class youngsters unacceptable—indeed, different and depressing. Their students tend to respond by taking the attitude "If you don't like me, I won't cooperate with you." The net result is that the children fail to acquire basic reading, writing, and math skills.

Subcultural Differences Children of different social classes are thought to bring somewhat different experiences and attitudes into the school situation (Entwisle & Alexander, 1990; Harrison, Wilson, Pine, Chan & Buriel, 1990; McLoyd, 1990; Tolson & Wilson, 1990). Middle-class parents generally make it clear to their children that they are *expected* to apply themselves to school tasks. And their children commonly enter school already exposed to and possessing a variety of skills that lower-class children often lack—for example, conceptions regarding books, crayons, pencils, drawing paper, numerals, and the alphabet.

Robert J. Havighurst, a distinguished educator who conducted a survey of Chicago schools, observes:

> These [ghetto] children come to school pitifully unready for the usual school experiences, even at the kindergarten level. Teachers remark that some don't even know their own names and have never held a pencil. Their speech is so different from that of the teachers and the primer that they almost have a new language to learn. They have had little practice in discriminating sounds, colors or shapes, part of the everyday experiences of the middle-class preschool child, whose family supplies educational toys and endless explanations. (Quoted by Star, 1965: 59)

Perhaps even more important, middle-class children are much more likely than disadvantaged youngsters to possess the conviction that they can affect their environments and their futures (Friend & Neale, 1972; Stephens & Delys, 1973). For instance, although many black youth express a high regard for education in *abstract* terms, they are less likely than white children to believe in the value of education in their *own* lives (Mickelson, 1990). Members of social groups that face a job ceiling know that they do, and this knowledge channels and shapes their children's academic behaviors (Dreeben & Gamoran, 1986; Ogbu, 1978). Moreover, youngsters from disadvantaged households are more likely to find themselves engulfed in recurrent school transfers—they fall behind time and again and find that they must start anew with each parental move (Graham, 1990). Finally, as pointed out by Havighurst, minority-group children who speak Spanish or black English are likely to find themselves handicapped in schools where standard English is employed (Bernstein, 1990; Gay & Tweney, 1975; Rossel & Ross, 1986; Tharp, 1989).

Educational Self-Fulfilling Prophecies. Another explanation for social class difference is that lower-class and minority children are frequently the victims of **educational self-fulfilling prophecies,** or *teacher expectation effects.* The children fail to learn because those who are charged with teaching them do not believe that they will learn, do not expect that they can learn, and do not act toward them in ways that help them to learn (Clark, 1965; Crano & Mellon, 1978; Dusek, 1985; Jussim, 1989; Tharp, 1989). For the most part, white teachers rate white students higher than either their black or their Hispanic counterparts (Jensen & Rosenfeld, 1974). Moreover, schools and school districts do not provide equal learning opportunities, particularly facilities, equipment, and teacher quality. Black and Hispanic students are disadvantaged by schools in very much the same ways that their communities are disadvantaged in their interactions with major societal institutions (Cummins, 1986; Dreeben & Gamoran, 1986). Many minority and lower-class youth respond by dropping out of school. The annual graduation rate is 82 percent for whites, 75 percent for blacks, and 55 percent for Hispanics (Kelly, 1991). Overall, youth from low-income families are three times as likely to drop out of high school as are youth from high-income families (Riche, 1986).

SUMMARY

1. Peer groups provide children with situations in which they are independent of adult controls, give them experience in egalitarian relationships, furnish them with status in a realm where their own interests reign supreme, and transmit informal knowledge.
2. Sex cleavage reaches its peak at about the fifth-grade level. Although same-sex friendships predominate during the elementary school years, children show a steady and progressive development of cross-sex interests as they advance toward puberty.
3. Elementary school children arrange themselves in hierarchies with regard to various standards, including physical attractiveness, body build, and behavioral characteristics.
4. Children's self-conceptions tend to emerge from the feedback that others provide regarding their desirability, worth, and status. But children are not simply passive beings who mirror other people's attitudes toward them. Through their interactions with others and through the effects they produce on their material environment, they derive a sense of their energy, skill, and industry.
5. Over the elementary school years conformity tends to increase with age in situations in which children are confronted with highly ambiguous tasks. But where the tasks are unambiguous, conformity tends to decline with age.
6. Children develop racial awareness between 3 and 5 years of age. However, whether children, especially younger school children, show coherent, consistent prejudice is doubtful.
7. Schools teach specific cognitive skills (the three Rs), general skills associated with effective participation in classroom settings, and the society's dominant cultural goals and values. They also function as a "mobility escalator" for able students to rise in status, and they attempt to overcome gross deficits in individual children that interfere with the children's effective social participation.
8. Although not all schools are effective, capable teachers can make a difference. Furthermore, effective schools differ from ineffective ones in important ways. Perhaps the most important element is the climate of the school. Successful schools foster expectations that order will prevail and that learning is a serious matter.
9. Motivation influences the rate of student learning, the retention of information, and performance. Ideally, motivation comes from within—instrinsic motivation. People's perceptions of the factors that produce given outcomes are also important: luck, ability, effort, and the difficulty of the task. In addition, attributions of causality are influenced by locus of control.

10. Overall, the higher the social class of children's families, the higher their academic achievement is likely to be. A number of hypotheses have been advanced to explain this fact, including the middle-class bias of schools, subcultural differences, and educational self-fulfilling prophecies.

KEY TERMS

Educational Self-fulfilling Prophecies Children fail to learn because those who are charged with teaching them do not believe that they will learn, do not expect that they can learn, and do not act toward them in ways that help them to learn.

Extrinsic Motivation Activity that is undertaken for some purpose other than its own sake.

Group Two or more people who share a feeling of unity and are bound together in relatively stable patterns of social interaction.

Intrinsic Motivation Activity that is undertaken for its own sake.

Learning Disability An umbrella concept referring to difficulty with school-related material despite the appearance of normal intelligence and lack of a demonstrable physical, emotional, or social impairment.

Mainstreaming The integration of students with special needs within the regular programs of the school.

Motivation Those inner states and processes that prompt, direct, and sustain activity.

Prejudice A system of negative conceptions, feelings, and action orientations regarding the members of a particular religious, racial, or nationality group.

School An agency that provides formal, conscious, and systematic training.

Sex Cleavage The tendency for elementary school boys to associate with boys and elementary school girls with girls.

Sociometry An objective method for assessing patterns of attraction, rejection, or indifference among group members. Individuals are asked to name three (or sometimes five) individuals in the group with whom they would most like (or least like) to interact in a given context.

Value A criterion that people use in deciding the relative merit and desirability of things (themselves, other people, objects, events, ideas, acts, and feelings).

Part Six

Adolescence

Chapter 13

ADOLESCENCE: DEVELOPMENTAL ACCELERATION AND GAINS

Puberty

The Development of Identities and Self-Concepts

Cognitive and Moral Development

*When I was a boy of about fourteen
or fifteen, it seemed to me that life was a
miserable thing and that I was the unhappiest
person around. Hardly anything ever went right.
If I liked a certain girl it would take me two weeks
to get up enough nerve to call her, and then I would
come down with a bad cold on the day we
were supposed to meet. Or if someone told me that
she liked me, I wouldn't believe it. . . . I made the
baseball team, which cheered me up a little, but I
struck out a lot, and that was humiliating. . . .
About half the time I didn't do my homework. . . .
Naturally I felt guilty about that. . . . As a
matter of fact I felt guilty about getting up late
for breakfast, and staying up late at night,
and swiping cigarettes, and doing a lot
of things.*—JAMES LINCOLN COLLIER

Strong cultural currents within American life glorify the period between childhood and adulthood. Some observers have called this "the cult of youth." Adolescence is frequently depicted as a carefree age of physical attractiveness, vitality, robust fun, love, enthusiasm, and activity. However, many adolescents, like the writer James Lincoln Collier quoted above, find it an extremely difficult period. And although many adult Americans glorify youth, they hold contrasting images of adolescents. Sometimes, they regard young people as "the enemy within," given to juvenile delinquency, political extremism, drug addiction, premarital pregnancies, and "disrespect" for authority. At other times, they stereotype adolescents as being less hypocritical, dishonest, materialistic, and cynical than their elders (Conger, 1977).

It is easy to become so locked into our own cultural perspective that we overlook the considerable diversity that societies throughout the world show in their approach to adolescence. Indeed, in much of the world adolescence is not a socially distinct period in the human life span. Although young people everywhere undergo puberty, children often assume many adult responsibilities by age 13 and even younger. Consequently, adolescence may be largely glossed over (Burbank, 1988).

In the United States adolescence appears to be an "invention" of the past hundred years (Demos & Demos, 1969; Kett, 1977; Lapsley, Enright & Serlin, 1985; Modell, 1989; Troen, 1985). As the nation changed from a rural to an urban society, the role of children shifted. They no longer had a significant economic function in the family once the workplace became separated from the home. In time, mandatory school attendance, child labor laws, and special legal procedures for "juveniles" served to establish adolescence as a well-defined social reality.

Puberty

During adolescence young people undergo changes in growth and development that are truly revolutionary. After a lifetime of inferiority they suddenly catch up with adults in physical size and strength. And accompanying these changes is the rapid development of the reproductive organs that signals sexual maturity. The term **puberty** is applied to this period of the life cycle when sexual and reproductive maturation becomes evident. Puberty is not a single event or set of events but a crucial phase in a long and complex process of maturation that begins prenatally (Petersen & Taylor, 1980). However, unlike infants and young children, older children experience the dramatic changes of puberty through a developed sense of consciousness and self-awareness. So not only do they respond to the biological changes, but their psychological states also have a bearing on those changes (Boxer, Tobin-Richards & Petersen, 1983).

Hormonal Changes in Puberty

The dramatic changes that occur in children at puberty are regulated, integrated, and orchestrated by the central nervous system and endocrine glands. The *pituitary gland,* a pea-sized structure located at the base of the brain, plays a particularly important role. It is called the "master gland" because it secretes hormones into the bloodstream that, in turn, stimulate other glands to produce their particular kind of hormone. At puberty the pituitary gland steps up the production of the growth hormones and triggers the manufacture of the two gonadotrophic hormones *(gonadotrophins):* the *follicle-stimulating hormone (FSH)* and the *luteinizing hormone (LH).* In females FSH and LH stimulate the ovaries to manufacture and secrete the feminizing hormones, estrogen and progesterone (see Chapter 3). In males LH is termed the *interstitial-cell-stimulating hormone (ICSH),* since it stimulates the interstitial cells of the testes to manufacture and secrete the masculinizing sex hormone, testosterone. Hence, puberty is a time when a system that was established prenatally becomes activated.

Biological Change and Cognitive Processes   In recent years researchers have taken a closer look at the influence biological changes have on cognitive processes during adolescence (Waber, Mann, Merola & Moylan, 1985). The brains of children from 3 to 11 years of age seem to use twice as much energy as do the brains of adults (see Chapter 6). From 11 to 14 years of age this metabolic activity gradually falls to the adult level. Deep sleep patterns also change. Children experience twice as much deep sleep as do adults (see Chapter 5). But again, from 11 to 14 years of age adolescents move into adult sleep patterns. Some researchers believe that the more metabolically active child's brain requires more deep sleep (Blakeslee, 1986). As we explained in Chapter 6, the mature brain seems to emerge as excessive or unused synapses are chipped away, possibly under the influence of hormonal changes (Greenough, Black & Wallace, 1987). Such alterations in the brain may be associated with a growing capacity for formal operational thought, which we will consider later in the chapter.

Biological Change and Social Relations Biological factors also have consequences for social relations during adolescence. Pubertal maturation, independent of changes in chronological age, is associated with increased emotional distance between youngsters and their parents (Steinberg, 1987a, 1988). In addition, researchers at the National Institute of Mental Health have turned up evidence in support of a long-suspected link between hormones and adolescent behavior. They find that higher sex steroid and lower adrenal androgen levels are associated with good adjustment. High levels of adrenal androgens appear to be related to feelings of sadness and confusion. And boys showing a profile of relatively low levels of testosterone and high levels of androstenedione (an adrenal androgen) are more likely than other boys to exhibit behavior problems, including rebelliousness, talking back to adults, and fighting with classmates. The links between hormone levels and behavior tend to be considerably stronger and more consistent for boys than for girls. This research suggests that the activating influences of hormones may be reflected in the emotions of adolescents because neural tissues are the targets for some puberty-related hormones (Susman et al., 1987). This research, still in its infancy, indicates the need for considering hormonal processes in the behavioral development of adolescents (Udry & Talbert, 1988; Udry, Talbert & Morris, 1986). But even though puberty has a biological foundation, its social and psychological significance is a major determinant of how it is experienced by adolescents (Brooks-Gunn & Warren, 1989; Stattin & Magnusson, 1990).

Sociobiological Theory We have seen that biological factors have consequences for teenagers' social relationships. Some developmental psychologists take the argument a step further and contend that pubertal timing itself is *an outcome of social experience.* Recently Jay Belsky, Laurence Steinberg, and Patricia Draper (1991) have advanced an exceedingly controversial theory that some young mothers are responding to a pattern in human evolution that induces individuals who grow up under stressful circumstances to bear children early and often. In so doing, they address a matter that has troubled a good many U.S. policy makers, namely the large numbers of inner-city young women who in their early teens become mothers. The theory draws upon notions derived from sociobiology (see Chapter 2). According to this view, the teenage mothers are implementing a reproductive strategy which, from an evolutionary perspective, makes good sense. Belsky and his associates argue that youngsters growing up in dangerous conditions are "primed" to boost the chances of having their genes survive into the next generation by initiating sex early and entering motherhood early. One element of the theory is that girls reared in homes where there is a good deal of emotional stress, and especially where the father is absent, typically enter puberty at an earlier age than do girls reared in households where care and nurturance are relatively more abundant and predictable. In sum, rather than being a biological given, puberty is said to be partially "set" by early experience. In this manner, human beings, like many other animals, *adjust* their life histories in response to environmental conditions that enhance reproductive fitness.

The sociobiological theory suggests that there are two grand strategies for reproductive success in human beings. In stressful conditions, evolution is said biologically to "prime" individuals to pursue a "quantity" as opposed to a "quality" reproductive strategy. In contrast, under less stressful childhood conditions, it makes "evolutionary sense" to postpone sexual activity, have fewer youngsters, and expend more time and energy on each child. People do not consciously or deliberately pursue one strategy or the other. Belsky and his associates (disclaiming notions that one strategy is more "morally correct" or "proper" than the other) say each plan is a biological response that has historically proven successful in evolutionary adaptation. Put another way, when a child learns in its first five to seven years that the world is an insecure and risky place, the biological response is to get into reproduction as soon as possible. Failure to do so raises the prospect that the child will not reproduce at all. So experience shapes development. In sum, the model hypothesizes that (1) young women who grow up under conditions of family stress (2) experience behavioral and psychological problems that (3) provoke earlier reproductive readiness. In support of their theory, Belsky and his associates cite cross-cultural evidence that girls reared in father-absent households have an earlier onset of puberty than do girls whose fathers are present in the household.

But many developmental psychologists have expressed skepticism regarding these sociobiological formulations (Goleman, 1991). For instance, Eleanor E. Maccoby (1991) favors a simpler explanation for the earlier pregnancies of girls from troubled homes: They receive less parental supervision. Other dissenters point out that girls tend to enter puberty at the same age as did their mothers by virtue of genetic factors. Those girls who develop sexually at earlier ages are more likely to date and marry early but are also more likely to make the "worst" marital choices and terminate their marriages with divorce (see Chapter 14). So the girls whose parents are divorced may simply have had mothers who also tended to have undergone puberty at an earlier age. Significantly, Belsky has recently hinted that this "genetic transmission model may provide a more parsimonious account" than does his sociobiological model (Moffitt, Caspi, Belsky & Silva, 1992). Sociologists also distance themselves from sociobiological formulations, contending that the more immediate cause of teenage sexuality and pregnancy is to be found in the lack of jobs and the presence of severe poverty in inner-city neighborhoods (Anderson, 1990; Massey, 1990; Sampson, 1987; Wilkie, 1991).

The Adolescent Growth Spurt

During the early adolescent years most children experience the **adolescent growth spurt,** a rapid increase in height and weight. Usually, this spurt occurs in girls two years earlier than in boys (see Figure 13-1). The average age at which the peak is reached varies somewhat depending on the people being studied. Among British and North American children it comes at about age 12 in girls and age 14 in boys. For a year or more the child's rate of growth approximately doubles. Consequently, children often grow at a rate they last experienced when they were 2 years old

(Tanner, 1970, 1972, 1973). The spurt usually lasts about two years, and during this time girls gain about 6 to 7 inches and boys about 8 to 9 inches in height. By age 17 in girls and age 18 in boys, the majority of young people have reached 98 percent of their final height.

James M. Tanner (1972, p. 5), an authority on adolescent growth, writes that practically all skeletal and muscular dimensions of the body take part in the spurt, although not to an equal degree:

> Most of the spurt in height is due to acceleration of trunk length rather than length of legs. There is a fairly regular order in which the dimensions accelerate; leg length as a rule reaches its peak first, followed by the body breadths, with shoulder width last. Thus a boy stops growing out of his trousers (at least in length) a year before he stops growing out of his jackets. The earliest structures to reach their adult status are the head, hands, and feet. At adolescence, children, particularly girls, sometimes complain of having large hands and feet. They can be reassured that by the time they are fully grown their hands and feet will be a little smaller in proportion to their arms and legs, and considerably smaller in proportion to their trunks.

Adolescent Growth Spurt
The rapid increase in height and weight that accompanies early adolescence tends to occur two years earlier in girls than in boys. *(Chris Sheridan/Monkmeyer)*

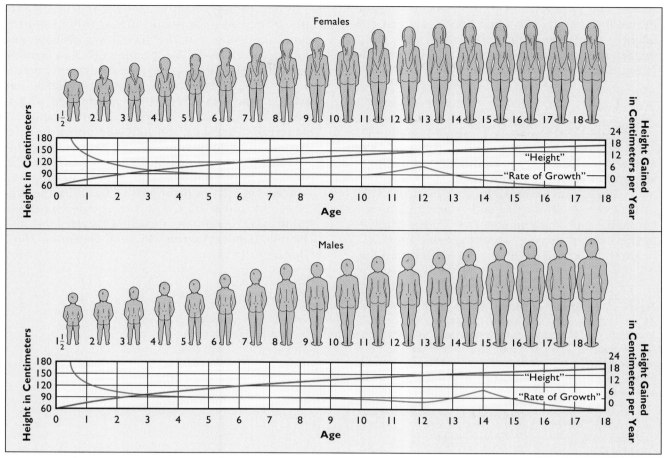

Figure 13-1   Growth from Infancy to Maturity

The figure depicts, for each sex, the changes in body form and the increases in height that occur between infancy and adulthood. In each case the height curve (black) is an average for children in North America and western Europe. Superimposed on the height curve is the curve for the rate of growth (color). This curve shows the increments of height that are gained from one age to the next. Note the sharp peak in the rate of growth that is associated with the adolescent growth spurt. As the graph illustrates, this peak is achieved two years earlier in girls than in boys. SOURCE: J. M. Tanner, "Growing Up," *Scientific American*, Vol. 229 (September 1973), pp. 36–37. Copyright © 1973 by Scientific American, Inc. All rights reserved.

Asynchrony is a term used to describe this dissimilarity in the growth rates of different parts of the body. As a result of asynchrony, many teenagers have a long-legged or coltish appearance. Asynchrony often results in clumsiness and misjudgments of distances, which may lead to various minor accidents, such as tripping on or knocking over furniture. It can produce an exaggerated sense of self-consciousness and awkwardness in adolescents.

The marked growth of muscle tissue during adolescence contributes to differences between and within the sexes in strength and motor performance (Chumlea, 1982). A muscle's strength— its force when it is contracted—is proportional to its cross-sectional area. Men typically have larger muscles than do women, which accounts for the greater strength of most males. Girls' performance on motor tasks involving speed, agility, and balance peaks at about 14 years of age. However, the performance of boys on similar tasks improves throughout adolescence.

At puberty the head shows a small acceleration in growth after remaining almost the same size for six to seven years. The heart grows more rapidly, almost doubling in weight. The abdominal viscera also increase in size. However, the lymphoid tissues (thymus, lymph nodes, and intestinal lymph masses) shrink. Most children steadily put on subcutaneous fat between 8 years of age and puberty, but the rate drops off when the adolescent growth spurt begins. Indeed, boys actually tend to lose fat at this time; girls simply experience a slowdown in fat accumulation (Chumlea, 1982; Tanner, 1969).

Maturation Among Girls

In addition to incorporating the adolescent growth spurt, puberty is characterized by the development of the reproductive system. The complete transition to reproductive maturity takes place over several years and is accompanied by extensive physical changes (see Figure 13-2). As in the case of the adolescent growth spurt, girls begin their sexual development earlier than boys.

When puberty begins in girls, the breasts increase in size as a result of the proliferation of glandular cells and the formation of fatty and connective tissue. The pigmented area around the nipple (the areola) becomes elevated, and the nipples begin to project forward. This change usually starts at about 10 years of age and is called the *bud stage* of breast development. (In some girls, perhaps one-half, the appearance of unpigmented pubic down—soft hair in the pubic region—precedes the bud stage.) Also early in puberty, hormonal action begins to produce an increase in fatty and supportive tissue in the buttocks and hip region. Another visible change in puberty is the growth of axillary (underarm) hair (Brooks-Gunn, Warren, Rosso & Gargiulo, 1987; Chumlea, 1982).

Figure 13-2 Effects of Six Hormones on Development at Puberty
At puberty the production of the pituitary gonadotrophins (the follicle-stimulating hormone and the luteinizing hormone) stimulates the manufacture and secretion of the sex hormones. The release of these hormones affects a wide range of body tissues and functions. SOURCE: From *Human Sexualities* by John H. Gragnon. Copyright © 1977 by Scott, Foresman and Company. Reprinted by permission.

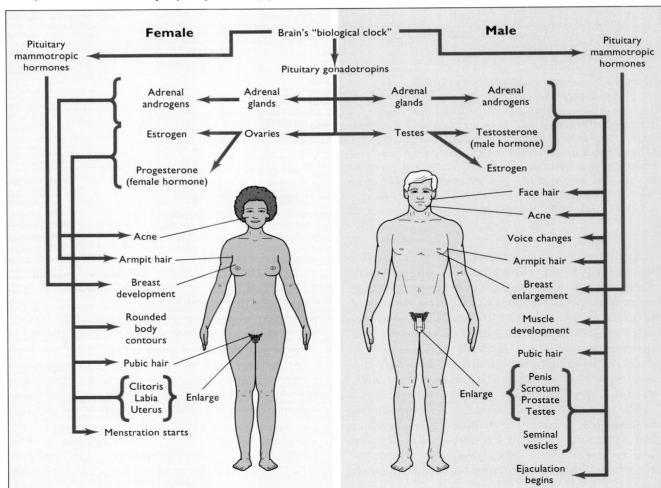

Maturation Among Young Women
The complex transition to reproductive maturity occurs over several years. As in the case of the adolescent growth spurt, women begin their sexual development earlier than men do. The photo, showing 13-year-old girls at a birthday party, reveals the variation in development among girls. *(Bruce Kliewe/Jeroboam)*

Menarche The uterus and vagina mature simultaneously with the development of the breasts. However, **menarche**—the first menstrual period—occurs relatively late in puberty, usually following the peak of the growth spurt (Brooks-Gunn, Warren, Rosso & Gargiulo, 1987; Faust, 1977; Tanner, 1973). Early menstrual periods tend to be irregular. Furthermore, *ovulation* (the release of a mature ovum) usually does not take place for twelve to eighteen months after the first menstruation; hence, the girl remains sterile during this time (Boxer, Tobin-Richards & Petersen, 1983).

The Earlier Onset of Menarche For over 100 years the average age of menarche in industrialized nations has shown a steady downward trend. This development has paralleled the decade-by-decade increase in the average stature of children in the Western world (see Chapter 6). However, at least half of what has often passed as an increase in children's size is merely the result of their growing up at an earlier age. Hence, most of the trend toward greater size in children seems to be due to more rapid maturation; only a minor part reflects a larger ultimate size (Tanner, 1972).

The earlier onset of menarche appears to be caused largely by nutritional improvement. James M. Tanner (1972) points out that among well-nourished Western populations the onset of menarche occurs at about 12 to 13 years of age. In contrast, the latest recorded menarcheal ages

are found among peoples with scarce food resources—in the highlands of New Guinea the average age of onset is 17, among the marginally nourished Bush people of the Kalahari 16.5, in the Kikuyu poverty areas of Kenya 15.9, and the Bantu poverty areas of South Africa 15.5 (Eveleth, 1986; Howell, 1979; Tanner, 1972; Worthman, 1986). Well-nourished girls of the African upper classes, however, have a median menarcheal age of 13.4.

Among European women the average age for menarche was between 14 and 15 years in 1840, whereas today it is between 12 and 13 (Bullough, 1981). A similar trend has occurred in the United States, where the average age has fallen by about a year and a half since 1905. But among middle-class girls, at least, the trend toward a decline in age at menarche seems to have ended; over the past thirty or so years it has stabilized at about 12.8 years of age. Although girls show considerable variation in age at their first menstrual period, early menarche tends to be associated with a stout physique and late menarche with a thin one (Faust, 1977; Zacharias, Rand & Wurtman, 1976). Menarche is also delayed by strenuous physical exercise, occurring at about 15 years of age among dancers and athletes in affluent countries (Wyshak & Frisch, 1982).

Rose E. Frisch (1978) advances the hypothesis that menarche requires a critical level of fat stored in the body. She reasons that pregnancy and lactation impose a great caloric drain. Consequently, if fat reserves are inadequate to meet this demand, a woman's body responds by limiting its reproductive ability. The improvement in children's nutrition has apparently contributed to an earlier onset of menarche because they reach the critical fat/lean ratio, or "metabolic level," sooner.

The Significance of Menarche Menarche is a pivotal event in an adolescent girl's experience (Greif & Ulman, 1982; Koff, Rierdan & Silverstone, 1978). Most girls are both happy and frightened by their first menstruation (Petersen, 1983). It is a symbol of a girl's developing sexual maturity and portends her full-fledged status as a woman. As such, menarche plays an important part in shaping a girl's image of her body and her sense of identity as a woman. Postmenarcheal girls report that they experience themselves as more womanly and that they give greater thought to their reproductive role.

In the above respects, menarche has positive connotations. But simultaneously, it is also portrayed within many Western nations as a hygienic crisis (Ruble & Brooks-Gunn, 1982). Menstruation is often associated with a variety of negative events, including physical discomfort, moodiness, and disruption of activities. And the adolescent girl is often led to believe that menstruation is somehow unclean and embarrassing, even shameful. Unhappily, such negative expectations of menstruation may prove to be self-fulfilling prophecies (Brooks-Gunn & Ruble, 1982). Thus, preparedness for menarche is important. Indeed, the better prepared a woman feels she was as a girl, the more positive she rates the experience of menarche and the less likely she is to encounter menstrual distress as an adult (Petersen, 1983).

Maturation Among Boys

The first sign of puberty in males begins at about 12 years of age with an acceleration in the growth of the testes and scrotum, followed by the appearance of fine, straight hair at the base of the penis. When boys are between 13 and 16 years of age, pubic hair multiplies, the testes and scrotum continue growing, the penis lengthens and thickens, and the voice begins to change as the larynx enlarges and the vocal folds double in length (resulting at times in the embarrassing cracking of the adolescent boy's voice). When a boy is about 14 years of age, the prostate gland is producing fluid that can be ejaculated during orgasm. However, mature sperm are not present in the ejaculatory fluid until about a year later, although there is a wide variation among individuals. Also at about 14 to 15 years of age, boys begin to have "wet dreams" or involuntary emissions of seminal fluid during sleep. For most contemporary males their first ejaculation elicits both very positive and slightly negative responses. Given greater openness about the matter today than in the past, the vast majority of boys have some preparation for the event (Gaddis & Brooks-Gunn, 1985).

Axillary and facial hair generally make their first appearance about two years after the beginning of pubic hair growth. The relationship is sufficiently variable, however, so that in some cases axillary hair appears first. The growth of facial hair begins with an increase in the length and pigmentation of the hair at the corners of the upper lip, which spreads to complete the mustache. Next, hair appears on the sides of the face in front of the ears and just below the lower lip, and finally it sprouts on the chin and lower cheeks. Facial hair is downy at first but becomes coarser by late adolescence (Brooks-Gunn, Warren, Russo & Gargiulo, 1987; Tanner, 1969, 1973).

Whereas girls develop fat deposits in the breasts and the hip region, boys acquire additional weight in the form of increased muscle mass. Furthermore, whereas the female pelvis undergoes enlargement at puberty, the most striking expansion in males takes place in the shoulders and rib cage (Chumlea, 1982).

Generally, men do not develop a hairy chest until late adolescence or the early twenties. The loss of head hair, causing indentation of the male hairline on each side of the upper forehead, is another postpubertal development.

Maturation Among Young Men
Puberty begins at about 12 years of age among males although individual boys show great variation in its onset. Girls usually enter puberty earlier than boys do. (Rick Kopstein/Monkmeyer)

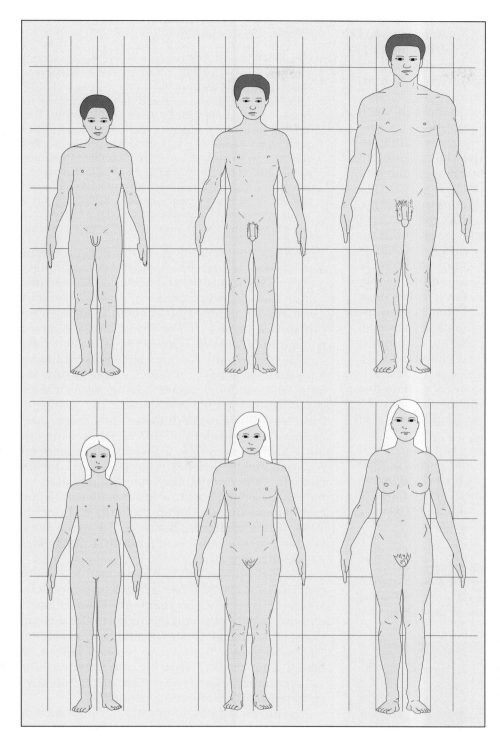

Figure 13-3   Variations in Adolescent Growth
All the girls in the lower row are the same chronological age: 12.75 years. All the boys in the upper row are also the same chronological age: 14.75 years. Some persons of the same sex have completed their growth and sexual matura-tion when the others are just beginning the process. SOURCE: J. M. Tanner, "Growing Up," *Scientific American,* Vol. 229 (September 1973), p. 38. Copyright © 1973 by Scien-tific American, Inc. All rights reserved.

The Impact of Early or Late Maturation

Children show enormous variation in growth and sexual maturation. As Figure 13-3 demon-strates, some children do not begin their growth spurt and the development of secondary sexual characteristics until other children have virtually completed these stages (Tanner, 1970, 1973). A study of 781 girls in a middle-class Boston suburb revealed that the age at menarche ranged from 9.1 to 17.7 (Zacharias, Rand & Wartman, 1976). Thus, one cannot appreciate the facts of physical growth and development without taking account of individual differences.

Young people in the United States move in chronological lockstep through elementary and secondary school. Consequently, fairly standardized criteria are applied to children of the same age with respect to their physical, social, and intellectual development. But because children mature at varying rates, they differ in their ability to meet these standards. Individual differences become most apparent at adolescence. Whether adolescents mature early or late has important consequences for them in their relationships with both adults and peers.

Because of different rates of maturation, some adolescents have an advantage in the "ideals" associated with height, strength, physical attractiveness, and athletic prowess (Martel & Biller, 1987; Stattin & Magnusson, 1990; Watkins & Montgomery, 1989). Hence, some young people receive more favorable feedback regarding their overall worth and desirability, which in turn influences self-image and behavior. For example, the value placed on manly appearance and athletic excellence means that early-maturing boys often enjoy the admiration of their peers. In contrast, late-maturing boys often receive negative feedback from their peers and hence may be more susceptible to feelings of inadequacy and insecurity.

Investigators at the University of California at Berkeley studied the physical and psychological characteristics of a large group of individuals over an extended period of time. On the basis of this work, Mary Cover Jones and Nancy Bayley

(1950, p. 146) reached the following conclusion regarding adolescent boys:

> Those who were physically accelerated are usually accepted and treated by adults and other children as more mature. They appear to have relatively little need to strive for status. From their ranks came the outstanding student-body leaders in senior high school. In contrast, the physically retarded boys exhibit many forms of relatively immature behaviors: this may be in part because others tend to treat them as the little boys they appear to be. Furthermore, a fair proportion of these boys give evidence of needing to counteract their physical disadvantage in some way—usually by greater activity in striving for attention, although in some cases by withdrawing.

The late-maturing boys in the Berkeley study also tended to exhibit feelings of inadequacy, negative self-concept, and feelings of rejection. These feelings were coupled with a rebellious quest for autonomy and freedom from restraint (Mussen & Jones, 1957). Results of a study of college students by Donald Weatherley (1964) largely confirm the findings of Jones and Bayley. Late-maturing boys of college age were less likely than their earlier-maturing peers to have resolved the conflicts attending the transition from childhood to adulthood. They were more inclined to seek attention and affection from others and readier to defy authority and assert unconventional behavior. More recent research also supports the finding that later maturation for boys is associated with a less positive self- and body-image (Boxer, Tobin-Richards & Petersen, 1983; Tobin-Richards, Boxer & Petersen, 1983). For boys, being "late" is apparently a psychological disadvantage.

A follow-up study of the early- and late-maturing males in the Berkeley sample was conducted when the men were 33 years old. Their behavior patterns were surprisingly similar to the descriptions recorded of them in adolescence (Jones, 1957). The early maturers were more poised, relaxed, cooperative, sociable, and conforming. Late maturers tended to be more eager, talkative, self-assertive, rebellious, and touchy.

In contrast, research on girls has produced diverse and contradictory results. Some findings show that late-maturing girls exhibit greater sociability, leadership, poise, cheerfulness, and expressiveness than early-maturing girls (Jones, 1949). Other research indicates that, as with boys, late physical maturation has adverse effects on the personality adjustment of girls (Weatherley, 1964). And still other research suggests that for girls being "on time" is associated with a more

Some Youth Are Favored by Early Maturation
Since athletic excellence is usually prized among American adolescents, those boys who mature early are at a decided advantage in winning the admiration of their peers. *(Jack Elness/Comstock)*

positive set of self-perceptions than being "off time—either early or late (Tobin-Richards, Boxer & Petersen, 1983).

These conflicting findings suggest that the situation for girls is more complicated than that for boys. Research by Margaret S. Faust (1960, p. 185) reveals that among sixth-grade girls early maturation tends to be a handicap. But when the late-maturing girls enter middle or junior high school, the picture shifts and they are at a disadvantage:

> The findings of the present research point out the complex nature of variables which interact in producing a girl's reputation during adolescence. . . . The discontinuity between rate of change in evaluations of prestige and rate of physical changes during adolescence means that, for girls, accelerated development is not a sustained asset throughout the adolescent period, as it is for boys. Accelerated development for girls is somewhat detrimental to prestige status before the junior high school years, while it places a girl in a very favorable social position throughout the junior high school years.

Psychologists also point to still another factor. Early-maturing girls are more likely to be stout and to develop a stocky physique. In contrast, late maturing girls are more likely to be thin and to acquire a slim, slight build that is more in keeping with the feminine ideal of many Western nations. Thus, over the long run (in contrast to the short run), late maturation in girls may be associated with factors other than maturation itself that function as assets in social adjustment (Brooks-Gunn & Petersen, 1983; Jones & Mussen, 1958).

Self-Image

The image that adolescents have of themselves is particularly susceptible to peer influences. Any difference from the peer group in growth and development tends to be a difficult experience for the adolescent. The difference is especially difficult to handle when it places the individual at a physical disadvantage or in a position of unfavorable contrast to peers. Adolescents are quick to reject or ridicule age-mates who deviate in some way from the physical norm. Indeed, few words have the capacity to cause as much pleasure—and as much pain—to adolescents as does the word "popularity." Consequently, many teenagers are preoccupied with their physical acceptability and adequacy (Eisert & Kahle, 1982; Lerner, Iwawaki, Chihara & Sorell, 1980; Rich-

ards, Boxer, Petersen & Albrecht, 1990). These concerns take place during a time when the nature and significance of friendship patterns are undergoing substantial developmental change (Gottman & Mettetal, 1987; Larson & Richards, 1991; O'Brien & Bierman, 1988; Wong & Csikszentmihalyi, 1991). The ability to establish close, intimate friendships becomes more integral to social and emotional adjustment and well-being during adolescence than during preadolescence (Buhrmester, 1990).

Puberty brings with it an intensification of gender-related expectations (Hill & Lynch, 1983; Galambos, Almeida & Petersen, 1990; Stattin & Magnusson, 1990). Adolescent girls often feel troubled about the development, size, and shape of their breasts (Brooks-Gunn & Warren, 1988; Gargiulo, Attie, Brooks-Gunn & Warren, 1987). And they express considerable concern about their facial features, including their skin and hair (Tobin-Richards, Boxer & Petersen, 1983). Teenage boys tend to worry about the size of their bodies and, in particular, the relative size of their penises. Boys are particularly anxious to develop athletic-related strengths and abilities. Concern and self-consciousness over their complexions are common among adolescents. The acne, blackheads, and pimples that frequently accompany puberty are a common source of anxiety and tension. Other frequently expressed concerns are irregular teeth, orthodontic braces, glasses, and the shape of their faces and noses.

A large proportion of adolescents want to change their weight; they feel that they are either "too thin" or "too heavy." Indeed, medical authorities classify at least 10 percent of North American elementary school children as obese and 30 to 35 percent of adolescents as overweight. About one-fourth of all boys show a large increase in fatty tissue during early adolescence; another 20 percent show a moderate increase (Stolz & Stolz, 1951). During the adolescent growth spurt, however, the rate of fat accumulation declines in both boys and girls. Whatever the source of obesity, the overweight adolescent is at a personal and social disadvantage. In fact, a stigma is associated with obesity in the United States (see the boxed insert). Given this state of affairs, particularly for women, it is hardly surprising that adolescent girls are extremely sensitive regarding their body configurations and that even moderate amounts of fat generate intensely negative feelings (Brooks-Gunn & Petersen, 1983; Desmond, Price, Gray & O'Connell, 1986; Mendelson & White, 1985).

Obesity

F ew of our characteristics are more readily apparent than our physical appearance. And our appearance has a major impact on our self-esteem. This principle seems to be especially true during adolescence. Developmental psychologists such as Erik Erikson stress that adolescents are consumed with such questions as What am I like? How good am I? and What will I become? Although being liked and accepted is important at any age, it may be particularly crucial during adolescence. Personal appearance plays a central part in one's relations with others. Consequently, social expectations of and reactions to body build are a preoccupation among many adolescents (Attie & Brooks-Gunn, 1989; Desmond, Price, Gray & O'Connell, 1986; Hendry & Gillies, 1978; Mendelson & White, 1985).

Obesity in children and adolescents often portends ill for their health. Obese children are at greater risk for high blood pressure, respiratory disease, diabetes, and orthopedic disorders. Thus, that childhood obesity is more common now than in the past is of considerable concern. The proportion of children age 6 to 11 who are obese has increased by 54 percent over the past fifteen years; the proportion of obese youth age 12 to 17 has increased 39 percent. Complicating matters, obesity has proven quite difficult to treat (Brody, 1987a; Carey, 1987).

Our understanding of obesity has undergone change in recent years (Bennett & Gurin, 1982; Brody, 1987a, 1987b). The major assumption long underlying the treatment of obesity was that overweight results from excess food consumption due to faulty eating habits. Yet several decades of research have shown that, on the whole, the obese eat no more than the lean. The proposition that obese people eat abnormally large amounts of food simply does not hold in many cases. Furthermore, studies of eating behavior—the number, timing, and composition of meals and snacks, the rate at which bites are taken, and the size of bites—reveal no consistent differences between the obese and the lean. And an accumulating body of research clearly indicates that overeating alone is not sufficient to cause most people to become or to remain obese.

These findings have led researchers to a closer examination of energy expenditure. Yet studies of activity levels in the obese have produced highly variable results. There are about an equal number of studies that show no differences in activity levels between the obese and the lean and studies that demonstrate lower activity levels in the obese. And among those researchers who do find differences between the two groups, some claim that obese people are less active because of their excess weight, rather than the other way around.

Various psychiatrists used to argue that obesity is a response to psychological disorders (for instance, women who are fearful of men subconsciously gain weight to create a protective shell and keep men at a distance). But this premise has found little support among researchers. Being fat in our society may be associated with self-disdain and rejection by others—and with feelings of being deprived, left out, and lonely—but these problems appear to be more the consequences of obesity than the causes of it.

People have long assumed that obesity tends to run in families. Folklore has placed the blame almost entirely on household gluttony and sloth. But

The Development of Identities and Self-Concepts

According to the neo-Freudian psychoanalyst Erik Erikson, the main task of adolescence is to build and confirm a reasonably stable identity. In the simplest terms, **identity** is composed of the answers an individual gives to the questions Who am I? and Who am I to be? Identity is a person's sense of placement within the world—the meaning that one attaches to oneself in the broader context of life.

In their everyday lives people interact with one another not so much on the basis of what they actually are as of what conceptions they have of themselves and of others. Accordingly, their identity leaves its signature on everything they do. Identities are not fixed, formed once and for all time. They undergo continual shaping and reshaping over the course of the human life span. So although adolescence poses identity tasks that seem to play an important part in a successful transition to adulthood, the process does not end with adolescence (Adams, Abraham & Markstrom, 1987; Kahn, Zimmerman, Csikszentmi-

researchers are finding that genetic factors seem to predispose many people to gain weight easily, particularly in a nation of plenty where there is little need for physical exertion (Brody, 1987*a*, 1987*b*). A study of 540 adopted children in Denmark found that the children tended to develop the body builds of their biological parents rather than the shapes of the parents who reared them (Price, Cadoret, Stunkard & Troughton, 1987). Other research shows that identical twins share the same level of obesity twice as often as do nonidentical twins. Much obesity, then, is a family affair, with the probability of obesity becoming greater as the proportion of family members who are obese increases (Price, Cadoret, Stunkard & Troughton, 1987; Rosenthal, 1990; Stunkard, Foch & Hrubec, 1986).

Environmental factors, such as urban living and sedentary lifestyles, influence whether family tendencies translate into actual weight gain. For instance, researchers find that children in the Northeast are two to three times as likely to be obese as those in the West. And in urban areas, youngsters are three times as likely to be obese as those in rural areas (Rosenthal, 1990). Obesity is also related to socioeconomic status. In developing nations obesity is rare among disadvantaged women but prevalent among advantaged women. In developed societies, by contrast, higher socioeconomic status is associated with a decrease in the prevalence of obesity among women. Significantly, obesity tends to be positively evaluated by people in developing societies and negatively evaluated by people in developed nations (Sobal & Stunkard, 1989).

Another recent explanation that has attracted considerable interest holds that fat babies and fat children are more likely to become overweight adults because they develop a permanent excess of fat cells. This excess provides them with a life-long storehouse of fat cells capable of being filled. When such individuals later become adults, the existing fat cells enlarge but are not thought to increase in number.

Still another popular theory postulates the existence of a metabolic regulator or "set-point" (Bennett & Gurin, 1982; Nisbett, 1972). According to this view, a control system is built into each of us—a kind of fat thermostat that dictates how much fat we should carry. Some of us have a high setting and tend to be obese; others of us have a low setting and tend to be lean. Consequently, the attempt by obese people to lose weight is in most cases bound to fail because it constitutes an attempt to overpower the body's internal controls. Likewise, the skinny person who seeks to gain weight by overeating is fighting a losing battle.

The confused state of our knowledge regarding obesity has led some obese people to challenge prevailing social stereotypes and prejudices. Like the physically handicapped, the obese wear their "problem" for all to see at all times. Yet unlike the physically handicapped, obese people are held responsible for their condition. They are the object of much concern, criticism, and overt discrimination. Negative attitudes seem to intensify during adolescence, particularly among females. But increasingly, obese people are "fighting back." They call for a revamping of prevailing cultural stereotypes that proclaim "large is ugly," and they insist that their needs and feelings be given at least as much consideration as are those of other people.

halyi & Getzels, 1985; Orlofsky & Frank, 1986; Shirk, 1987).

Erikson: The Crisis of Youth

Don't laugh at a youth for his affectations;
he is only trying on one face after another to find
a face of his own.—LOGAN PEARSALL SMITH
Afterthoughts, 1931

Erik Erikson's work has focused attention on the struggle of adolescents to develop and clarify their identity. As described in Chapter 2, Erikson divides the developmental sequence into eight psychosocial stages. Each stage poses a somewhat different issue—presents a necessary turning point or crucial period, when development must move in either a positive or negative direction. The focus of each psychosocial stage is upon a major task in ego development or self-development.

Erikson's fifth stage, which covers the period of adolescence, consists of the search for identity. He suggests (1968*b*, p. 165) that an optimal feeling of identity is experienced as a sense of well-being: "Its most obvious concomitants are a feel-

(Drawing by R. Chast; © 1991 The New Yorker Magazine, Inc.)

ing of being at home in one's body, a sense of 'knowing where one is going,' and an inner assuredness of anticipated recognition from those who count."

Erikson observes that the adolescent, like a trapeze artist, must release his or her safe hold on childhood and reach in midair for a firm grasp on adulthood. The search for identity becomes paticularly acute because the individual is undergoing rapid physical change while confronting many imminent adult tasks and decisions. The adolescent must often make an occupational choice or at least decide whether to continue formal schooling. Other aspects of the environment also provide testing grounds for the self-concept: broadening peer relationships, sexual contacts

and roles, moral and ideological commitments, and emancipation from adult authority.

Adolescents must synthesize a variety of new roles in order to come to terms with themselves and their environment. Erikson suggests that some societies, such as our own, allow a *moratorium*, or period of delay, during which adolescents can experiment with or "try on" various roles, ideologies, and commitments. It is a stage between childhood and adulthood when the individual can explore various dimensions of life without yet having to choose any. Adolescents may start or stop, abandon or postpone, implement or transform given courses of action.

As a result of "trying on" various roles and facing the complications of arriving at a stable sense of self, many adolescents are left with a blurred self-image. Erikson calls this difficulty **role confusion,** a state characterized by bewilderment about who one is, where one belongs, and where one is going. Erikson believes that a certain amount of role confusion is an almost inevitable, indeed even desirable, experience of adolescence. To "find" oneself too soon, he argues, is to run the risk of inadequately exploring alternative roles and foreclosing many of life's potentialities.

Since the identities of adolescents are diffuse, uncrystallized, and fluctuating, Erikson says, adolescents are often at sea with themselves and others. He believes (1968*b,* p. 132) that this ambiguity and lack of stable anchorage lead many adolescents to overcommit themselves to cliques, allegiances, loves, and social causes:

> To keep themselves together they temporarily overidentify with the heroes of cliques and crowds to the point of an apparently complete loss of individuality. Yet in this stage not even "falling in love" is entirely, or even primarily, a sexual matter. To a considerable extent adolescent love is an attempt to arrive at a definition of one's identity by projecting one's diffused self-image on another and by seeing it thus reflected and gradually clarified. This is why so much of young love is conversation. On the other hand, clarification can also be sought by destructive means. Young people can become remarkably clannish, intolerant, and cruel in their exclusion of others who are "different," in skin color or cultural background, in tastes and gifts, and often in entirely petty aspects of dress and gesture arbitrarily selected as the signs of an in-grouper or out-grouper.

According to Erikson, this clannishness explains the appeal that various extremist and totalitarian movements have for some adolescents.

In Erikson's view, every adolescent confronts a major danger: that he or she will fail to arrive at a consistent, coherent, and integrated identity. Consequently, adolescents may experience what Erikson terms **identity diffusion**—a lack of ability to commit oneself, even in late adolescence, to an occupational or ideological position and to assume a recognizable station in life. Another danger is that adolescents will fashion a **negative identity**—a debased self-image and social role (Erikson, 1964*a,* p. 97). Still another course taken by some adolescents is formation of a **deviant identity**—a lifestyle that is at odds with, or at least not supported by, the values and expectations of society. Some psychologists and psychiatrists deem identity crises to be precipitating factors in two eating disorders, anorexia ner-

vosa and bulimia (Bruch, 1982) (see the boxed insert).

Portrayal of "Storm and Stress"

Erikson's view of adolescence is in keeping with a long psychological tradition that has portrayed adolescence as a difficult period. The notion that adolescence is a distinct and turbulent developmental period received impetus in 1904 with the publication of G. Stanley Hall's monumental work, *Adolescence.* Hall, one of the major figures of early U.S. psychology, depicted adolescence as a stage of "storm and stress." According to Hall, adolescence is characterized by inevitable turmoil, maladjustment, tension, rebellion, dependency conflicts, and exaggerated peergroup conformity. This view was subsequently taken up and popularized by Anna Freud (1936) and other psychoanalysts (Blos, 1962). Indeed, Anna Freud (1958, p. 275) went so far as to assert: "The upholding of a steady equilibrium during the adolescent process is itself abnormal." Viewed from this perspective, the adolescent undergoes so many rapid changes that a restructuring of identity or self-concept is required if these changes are to be properly integrated into the individual's personality.

Any number of sociologists and anthropoligists have suggested that few people make the transition from childhood to adulthood more difficult than Western nations do (Dragastin & Elder, 1975; Elkind, 1979; Sebald, 1977). At adolescence boys and girls are expected to stop being children, yet they are not expected to be men and women. The definitions provided for them are quite inconsistent. They are told that they are no longer children, but they are still treated like dependents, economically supported by their parents, and frequently viewed by society as untrustworthy and irresponsible individuals. According to this view, conflicting expectations generate an identity crisis among U.S. and European youth.

Many non-Western societies make the period of adolescence considerably easier—or at least more definitive. They ease the shift in status by providing **puberty rites**—initiation ceremonies that socially symbolize the transition from childhood to adulthood (Brown, 1969; Gilmore, 1990; Herdt, 1981, 1982; Hollos & Leis, 1989; Perlez, 1990; Worthman, 1986). Adolescents are subjected to various thoroughly distasteful, painful, and humiliating experiences during such cere-

Anorexia Nervosa
and Bulimia

Anorexia nervosa is a disorder in which the individual willfully suppresses appetite, resulting in self-starvation. Once considered to be quite rare, the incidence of anorexia nervosa has increased dramatically over the past twenty-five years. It occurs primarily in adolescent or young adult females of the middle and upper-middle classes. The victims have a fierce desire to succeed in their project of self-starvation; have a morbid terror of having any fat on their bodies; and deny that they are thin or ill, insisting that they have never felt better even when they are so weak they can barely walk. Simultaneously, these people may long for food and even have secret binges of eating (often interrupted by self-induced vomiting).

One explanation for the recent epidemic in cases of anorexia nervosa is the emphasis that Western societies place on slimness. From a historical perspective, the preoccupation with weight and thinness, especially among affluent women in the Western world, reflects a relatively recent but growing cultural trend (Attie & Brooks-Gunn, 1987). The development of eating problems apparently represents one mode of accommodation that some girls make to pubertal change. As girls mature sexually, they experience a "fat spurt" (they accumulate large quantities of fat in subcutaneous tissues). Early maturers seem at greater risk for eating problems, partly due to the fact that they are likely to be heavier than their late-maturing peers (Attie & Brooks-Gunn, 1989; Brooks-Gunn, 1988). In some cases the refusal to eat is preceded by "normal" dieting, which may be prompted by casual comments that the young woman is "filling out" or "getting plump." Furthermore, the victim's overestimation of her body size seems to increase with the severity of the illness. According to this interpretation, the disorder entails self-induced starvation by women who desperately want to be beautiful but end up being grotesquely unattractive.

Another explanation of the disorder is that it is an attempt to avoid adulthood and adult responsibilities. The anorexic young woman invariably diets away her secondary sexual characteristics: her breasts diminish; her periods cease entirely (interestingly, menstruation ceases *prior* to pronounced weight reduction and hence cannot be attributed to starvation); and her body comes to resemble that of a prepubescent child. According to this view, such women are seeking a return to the remembered comfort and safety of childhood (Garner & Garfinkel, 1985; Kay, 1979).

Approximately two-thirds of anorexic victims recover or improve, with one-third remaining chronically ill or dying of the disorder. Most authorities now recognize that anorexia nervosa usually has multiple causes and that it requires a combination of various treatment strategies adjusted to the individual needs of the patient (Bemis, 1978; Garner & Garfinkel, 1985; Schwartz & Thompson, 1981).

A number of psychiatrists have suggested that a subgroup of male athletes—"obligatory runners"—resemble anorexic women (Yates, Leehey & Shisslak, 1983). These men devote their lives to running and are obsessed with the distance they run, their diets, their equipment, and their daily routines while ignoring illness and injury. Both anorexics and obligatory runners lead strict lives that assiduously avoid pleasure. Both groups are concerned about their health, feel uncomfortable with anger, are self-effacing and hard working, and tend to be high achievers from affluent families. And like anorexics, obligatory runners are exceedingly concerned about their weight and feel compelled to maintain a lean body mass.

A stepsister disorder of anorexia nervosa is *bulimia* (also termed the *binge-purge syndrome*). Bulimia is a disorder characterized by repeated episodes of binging, particularly on high-calorie foods like candy bars and ice cream. The binge is followed by an attempt to get rid of the food through self-induced vomiting, taking laxatives, or fasting.

Like anorexics, bulimics have an obsessive fear of becoming fat. However, bulimics are typically within normal weight range and have healthy, outgoing appearances, whereas anorexics are skeletally thin. Although young women are the primary victims of the binge-purge syndrome, young men in contact sports, especially wrestling, may likewise engage in similar behavior to squeeze into a lower weight class. The disorder can produce such long-term side effects as ulcers, hernias, dental problems (stomach acid destroys the teeth), and electrolyte imbalance (resulting in heart attacks). Like anorexia nervosa, bulimia calls for treatment. Some researchers believe that a hereditary form of depression may underlie some forms of both disorders, and indeed some patients respond to antidepressant medication (Hinz & Williamson, 1987; Wamboldt, Kaslow, Swift & Ritholz, 1987).

Puberty Rites for Women
Although puberty rites are more common for boys than for girls, some societies seclude their young women at menarche. For example, upon their first menstrual period, Balese women in Zaire live apart from the village in a special hut and observe certain rituals and taboos. *(Wrangham/Anthro-Photo)*

monies, but they are then pronounced grown up. Boys may be terrorized, ritualistically painted, and circumcised; girls may be secluded at menarche. But the tasks and tests are clearly defined, and young people know that if they accomplish the goals set for them, they will acquire adult status.

The Dahomeans of West Africa are a people who have puberty rites (Murdock, 1934, p. 579):

> A boy shortly before his twentieth year is circumcised in company with a group of youths of his own age. The specialist who performs the latter operation keeps the youths in his own house until they have recovered, when he shaves their heads and sends them home. . . . When a girl reaches puberty she is isolated from the opposite sex for five or seven days and receives visits and presents from her female relatives and friends. When she emerges from her chamber, her father gives her a white mantle and a new mat and sends her to the market on a ceremonial errand.

Hence, many societies of the world recognize puberty through special initiation ceremonies. By doing so, they are believed to provide an institutional means of easing the transition of their youth to adulthood. Even so, Western societies do provide a number of less obvious rites of passage. There is the Jewish Bar Mitzvah and Bat Mitzvah and the Christian confirmation. Securing a driver's license at age 16 or 17 and voting at age 18 also function in their own fashion as rites of passage. And graduation from high school and college—each affording a formal diploma and pomp—are special kinds of initiation ceremonies. But all these are rather mild versions of what youth must go through in many non-Western societies (Raphael, 1988).

The Self-Concept and Self-Esteem of Adolescents

In recent years researchers have increasingly come to the conclusion that adolescence in the United States is *not* the period of "storm and stress" that earlier psychologists and sociologists held it to be (Blyth & Traeger, 1983; Nottelmann, 1987; Prawat, Jones & Hampton, 1979; Savin-Williams & Demo, 1984; Simmons & Blyth, 1987). They do not deny that young people of Western nations undergo changes in self-image and self-concept during adolescence (Montemayor & Eisen, 1977; Rosenberg, 1986, 1989; Waterman, 1982; Waterman, Geary & Waterman, 1974) but suggest that the changes are not necessarily "stormy."

Adolescence: Not Necessarily Stormy nor Stressful The psychologist Albert Bandura (1964) believes that the stereotyped storm-and-stress portrait of adolescence most closely fits the behavior of "the deviant 10 percent of the adolescent population that appears repeatedly in psychiatric clinics, juvenile probation departments, and in the newspaper headlines." Bandura argues that the "stormy-decade myth" is due more to cultural expectations and the representations of teenagers in movies, literature, and the media than to actual fact.

Daniel Offer (1969; Offer, Ostrov & Howard, 1981) likewise finds little evidence of "turmoil" or "chaos" in his longitudinal study of a sample of sixty-one middle-class adolescent boys. Most were happy, responsible, and well-adjusted boys who respected their parents. Adolescent "disturbance" tended to be limited mostly to "bickering" with their parents. Like Bandura, Offer concludes that the portrayal of adolescence as a turbulent period comes from the work of such investigators as Erik Erikson who have spent their professional careers primarily studying disturbed adolescents. He concludes (Offer & Offer, 1975, p. 197): "Our data lead us to hypothesize that adolescence, as a stage in life, is not a uniquely stressful period." Offer's more recent study of some 6,000 adolescents in ten nations (Australia, Bangladesh, Hungary, Israel, Italy, Japan, Taiwan, Turkey, the United States, and West Germany) lends cross-cultural support to this conclusion (Offer, Ostrov, Howard & Atkinson, 1988).

Offer's conclusion finds support in a longitudinal study involving students in grades five through twelve undertaken by Jerome B. Dusek and John F. Flaherty (1981). The self-concepts of the adolescents developed in a continuous and stable way. Rather than experiencing dramatic change and turbulence, the adolescents gradually fashioned their self-concepts on the basis of their social circumstances and evolving cognitive competencies and skills. These findings are hardly surprising given the fact that the changes associated with adolescence typically extend over a period of time and allow adolescents ample opportunity to adjust to them. But when the changes occur simultaneously, the probability of disturbance is more likely (Coleman, 1978).

According to a longitudinal study of 2,213 young men conducted by the Institute for Social Research at the University of Michigan (Bachman, O'Malley & Johnston, 1978), adolescence may also be overrated as a time of major attitudinal change. Aspirations, self-concepts, and political attitudes (including those on racial issues) generally are well established by age 16. Though differences in these areas show up between individuals who achieve success in education (and later on the job) and those who do not, these differences are already largely established by the tenth grade. In other words, young people who enter high school with high aspirations and positive self-concepts are likely to retain these advantages at least five years beyond high school.

Hence, students in graduate and professional schools typically have high self-esteem that mirrors the positive self-images they possessed five years earlier. Similarly, the poor self-images of school dropouts are already established before these adolescents withdraw from school. Thus, individual differences are quite stable across time. Data from longitudinal studies first undertaken with youngsters between 1928 and 1931 by psychologists at the University of California at Berkeley and then followed by researchers for more than fifty years confirm these findings: Competent adolescents have more stable careers and marriages than less competent ones, and they experience less personality change over the adult years (Clausen, 1991).

On the whole, many researchers find that the overall self-esteem of most individuals increases with age across the adolescent years (McCarthy & Hoge, 1982; O'Malley & Bachman, 1983; Savin-Williams & Demo, 1984; Shirk, 1987). Of course, there are exceptions. Changes in social environment, including changing schools, in some cases interfere with those forces that otherwise bolster a child's self-esteem. Thus, the transition into a middle or junior high school can have a disturbing effect under certain circumstances, particularly for girls (Fenzel & Blyth, 1986; Hirsch & Rapkin, 1987; Nottelmann, 1987). Indeed, the self-esteem of adolescent girls is now the focus of considerable interest and controversy.

Carol Gilligan: Girls' Self-Esteem Is Lost on Way to Adolescence According to a recent survey of 3,000 youngsters commissioned by the American Association of University Women, women emerge from adolescence with a poorer self-image, relatively lower expectations for life, and considerably less confidence in themselves and their abilities than do men (Daley, 1991). During their elementary school years, most girls are confident, assertive, and feel positively about themselves. But by the time they reach high school, less than a third still feel this way. Boys also lose some measure of self-worth, but they end up far ahead of the girls. For instance, 67 percent of the elementary school boys said they "always" felt "happy the way I am." By high school, 46 percent of the boys still offered this response. With girls, the figure dropped from 60 percent to 29 percent. Black young women seemed an exception; far more black than white women were still self-confident in high school. Apparently, many black young women identify with the strong, competent black women in their lives who hold full-time jobs and run their households. In addition, black parents often instill in their youngsters the belief that there is nothing wrong with them, only with the way the world treats them.

Developmental psychologist Carol Gilligan, who assisted in the design of the survey, finds that adolescence is a time when girls begin to doubt themselves. As we will see in Chapter 15, Gilligan has argued that women hold a "justice perspective" on morality that leads them to be more concerned than men with human relationships and caring for others. Whereas men first define their identity as separate from others and then seek out intimate relationships, women reverse the process. They focus primarily on close relationships and then wrestle with how to care for themselves (Gilligan 1982a, 1982b).

During the 1980s Gilligan and her colleagues undertook a series of projects designed to connect her earlier research on adult women to that of girls. She found that 11-year-old girls typically maintain the self-confident attitudes evidenced during the elementary school years: They retain honesty about what they like and what hurts in relationships, their belief in their own authority in the world, and their assured outspokenness. However, by age 15 or 16, they increasingly say, "I don't know. I don't know. I don't know." In brief, Gilligan finds that during adolescence girls begin to doubt the authority of their own inner voices and feelings and their commitment to meaningful relationships. Whereas as 11-year-olds they assert themselves and still speak their minds, in adolescence they come to fear rejection and anger, and so they mute their voices and repress their autonomy. Western culture, Gilligan says, calls upon young women to buy into the image of the "perfect" or "nice" girl—one who avoids being mean and bossy and instead projects an air of calmness, quietude, and cooperation. Schools contribute to the problem by educating primarily for autonomy while negating the pursuit of rewarding relationships. More recently, Gilligan has turned her attention to developing programs that will assist young women in writing authentic and meaningful scripts for their own lives and in preventing them from "going underground" with their feelings (Prose, 1990).

A Time of Stress for Parents Although adolescence may not be unusually stressful for many youth, especially boys, it frequently is a time of storm and stress for their *parents*. Mothers and fathers report that adolescence is by far the most difficult stage of parenting. The reasons parents cite for their difficulties have to do primarily with issues of autonomy—"loss of control" over

youngsters, failure to adhere to parental advice, aggravation over youth pushing for "too much" freedom, and fear for adolescents' safety as they exercise increasing independence (Pasley & Gecas, 1984; Small, Cornelius & Eastman, 1983). Significantly, research on marital satisfaction shows that the least satisfying period of marriage is typically when children are in their teens. As discussed in Chapter 18, when youngsters leave home, the marital relationship often reasserts and restores itself (Rollins & Feldman, 1970; Umberson, 1989; Waite & Lillard, 1991; White & Edwards, 1990). Although earlier research on adolescence exaggerated the conflict that occurred between parents and their children, the stresses that mothers and fathers report in parenting teenagers suggests that we should be wary of now exaggerating the degree of harmony during adolescence (Gecas & Seff, 1990; Silverberg & Steinberg, 1990). Conflict is most frequently reported over issues of rule breaking and noncompliance with parental requests—for instance, such everyday family issues as school work, home chores, choice of activities and friends, failure to finish tasks, teasing siblings, and personal hygiene (Smetana, 1989).

However parents experience their youngsters' adolescent years, the manner in which they parent has substantial consequences for their children. Much of what we had to say in Chapter 12 regarding youngsters' self-esteem during later childhood also holds for adolescence. Overall, the greater the amount of parental support (such things as involvement, communication, physical affection, companionship, and sustained contact), the greater the amount of adolescent competence. Adolescent competence is related positively to self-esteem, cognitive development, moral behavior, internal locus of control, and academic achievement. And once more we find that authoritative parenting is associated with positive outcomes (Gecas & Seff, 1990; Hauser, Powers, Noam & Bowlds, 1987; Peterson & Rollins, 1987; Rollins and Thomas, 1979; Simons & Miller, 1987). Under these conditions, youngsters are most likely to identify with their parents, internalize their parents' values and expectations, and become receptive participants in their own socialization.

Conclusions Perhaps the most reasonable conclusion to be drawn from cross-cultural studies and from the variations encountered in our own society is that puberty and adolescence have different meanings for different people. There is not one adolescent experience but many experiences; hence, there are multiple roads to adulthood. Because of the diversity found among cultures, and even among individuals within the same culture, it is hardly surprising that the beliefs, feelings, and perceptions associated with puberty are not neatly preprogrammed in some rigidly fashioned mold. The boxed insert on pages 375–377 examining the ups and downs of teenagers' moods and days bears out this observation.

Cognitive and Moral Development

During adolescence young people gradually acquire several substantial new intellectual capacities. They begin to reflect about themselves; their parents, teachers, and peers; and the world they live in. They develop an increasing ability to think about hypothetical and future situations and events. In our society they also must evolve a set of standards regarding family, religion, school, drugs, and sexuality.

Period of Formal Operations

Thinking is not a heaven-born thing. . . . It is a gift men and women make for themselves. It is earned, and it is earned by effort. There is no effort, to my mind, that is comparable in its qualities, that is so taxing to the individual, as to think, to analyze fundamentally.
—SUPREME COURT JUSTICE LOUIS D. BRANDEIS

Jean Piaget called adolescence the **period of formal operations,** the final and highest stage in the development of intelligence from infancy to adulthood. This mode of thought has two major attributes. First, adolescents gain the ability to think about their own thinking—to deal efficiently with the complex problems involved in reasoning. Second, they acquire the ability to imagine many possibilities inherent in a situation—to generate mentally all possible outcomes of an event and thus to place less reliance upon real objects and events. In sum, adolescents gain the capacity to think in *logical* and *abstract* terms.

Formal operational thought so closely parallels scientific thinking that it is termed by some "scientific reasoning." It allows people to mentally restructure information and ideas so that they can make sense out of a new set of data. Through logical operations individuals can transfer the strategic attack skills they employ in a familiar problem area to an unfamiliar area and thus derive new answers and solutions. In so doing, they generate a higher level of analytical capability in

discerning relationships among various classes of events.

Formal operational thought is quite different from the concrete operational thought of the previous period (see Chapter 11). Piaget said that children in the period of concrete operations cannot transcend the immediate. They are limited to solving tangible problems of the present and have difficulty dealing with remote, future, or hypothetical matters. For instance, a 12-year-old will accept and think about the following problem: "All three-legged snakes are purple; I am hiding a three-legged snake; guess its color" (Kagan, 1972a, p. 92). In contrast, 7-year-old children are confused by the initial premise because it violates their notion of what is real. Consequently, they refuse to cooperate.

Likewise, if adolescents are presented with the problem: "There are three schools, Roosevelt, Kennedy, and Lincoln schools, and three girls, Mary, Sue, and Jane, who go to different schools. Mary goes to the Roosevelt school, Jane to the Kennedy school. Where does Sue go?" they

The Development of Formal Operational Thought
Formal operational thought allows people to generate a higher level of analytical capability allowing them to discern new relationships among various classes of events. It closely parallels the reasoning encountered in scientific thinking *(Charles Gupton/Stock, Boston)*

Charting the Ups and Downs of Teenagers' Moods and Days

A detailed portrait of the day-to-day world of U.S. teenagers has emerged from a study undertaken by University of Chicago social scientists Mihaly Csikszentmihalyi and Reed Larson (1984). They sought to describe what it is like to be an adolescent from the inside. So for a week they let seventy-five teenagers tell what they did, felt, and hoped for as they went about their daily rounds, from breakfast to school, from English class to lunch period, from the afternoons spent watching television to the wild parties on weekends. To do so, the researchers equipped the thirty-nine boys and thirty-six girls with small electronic pagers of the sort used by doctors. A transmitter activated the pagers at random moments during the week, signaling the teenagers to fill out a questionnaire reporting their thoughts, feelings, and activities at the time. The subjects were randomly selected at a 4,000-student Chicago area high school.

Among the findings of the research were the following:

❏ Drastic mood swings seem to be a normal feature of adolescent life and do not necessarily signal deeply rooted psychological difficulties. From their reports youth whose moods changed the most were as happy and as much in control of their lives as were their peers, and they seemed well-adjusted in other spheres of life.

❏ Youth who spent more time with their families and less time with their peers achieved better school grades, were less likely to be absent from school, and were rated by their teachers as being more intellectually involved.

❏ Many of the adolescents reported that conflict with their siblings generated as much difficulty as did generational tensions with their parents.

❏ Time spent at school and studying occupied about a quarter of the adolescents' waking time (about thirty-eight hours). Another quarter of their time was spent alone. The Chicago researchers concluded that solitude was an important aspect of a healthy adolescence.

❏ The teenagers spent the largest part of their waking time in leisure activities (forty-two hours): socializing (16 percent), watching television (7.2 percent), non-school reading (3.5 percent), sports and games (3.4 percent), and listening to music (1.4 percent).

❏ On average, the adolescents spent 19 percent of their waking hours with family members, 23 percent with classmates, and 29 percent with friends.

However, these broad findings hide the considerable diversity that existed among the youth. Three days in the life of Greg, a disaffected, rebellious youth, and in the life of Kathy, a very directed student and accomplished violinist, reflect these differences (see Figure 13-4). The substantial mood swings experienced by Greg and Kathy were not untypical. It usually took the teenagers about forty-five minutes to come down from extreme happiness or up from deep sadness, whereas it usually takes adults several hours. Unhappiness frequently arose from the drudgery of schoolwork, jobs, and chores. The young people seemed to get the most satisfaction from meeting challenges that were appropriate to their skills and that provided them with meaningful rewards. Those youth who were active in sports and hobbies, for instance, felt stimulated to move on to new levels of challenge and accomplishment. But many also fell into patterns of aimless drifting, television viewing, and searching for short-term pleasures. And some simply removed themselves from work and play, relying on crutches (like smoking pot) rather than developing skills that would help them in later life. Coming to terms with ups and downs seems to be one of the greatest challenges that teenagers confront. When Csikszentmihalyi and Larson (1984) repeated the study two years later with some of the adolescents, they found that many youth reported that their lives had become better. It was not so much that the reality of good and bad experiences had changed but that the young people had shifted their perspective in ways that allowed them to better view and cope with the world.

---

quickly respond "Lincoln." The 7-year-old may excitedly answer, "Sue goes to Roosevelt school, because my sister has a friend called Sue and that's the school she goes to" (Kagan, 1972*a*, p. 93).

Similarly, Bärbel Inhelder and Piaget (1958, p. 252) found that below 12 years of age most children cannot solve this verbal problem:

Edith is lighter than Suzanne.
Edith is darker than Lily.
Which is the darkest of the three?

Children under 12 often conclude that both Edith and Suzanne are light-complexioned and that Ed-

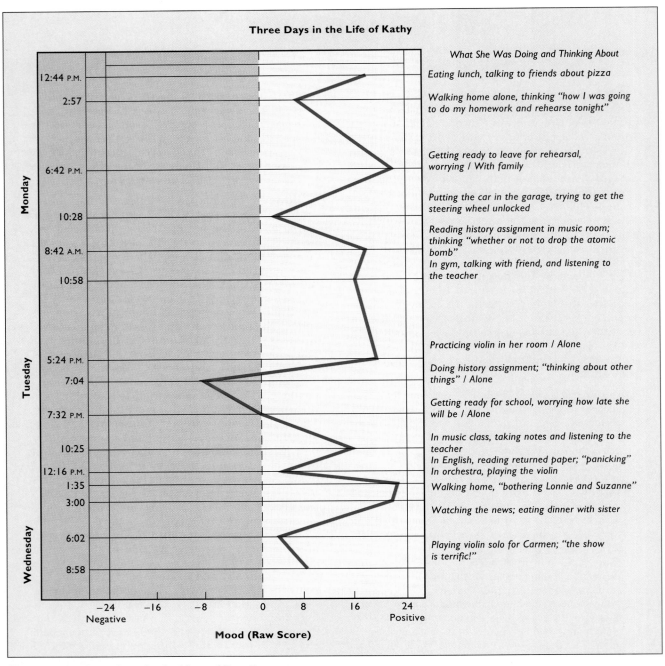

Figure 13-4   Three Days in the Lives of Two Teenagers
SOURCE: Adapted from Mihaly Csikszentmihalyi and Reed Larson, *Being Adolescent: Conflict and Growth in the Teen-Age Years.* Copyright © 1984 by BasicBooks, Inc. Reprinted by permission of BasicBooks, a division of Harper Collins Publishers, Inc.

ith and Lily are dark-complexioned. Accordingly, they say that Lily is the darkest, Suzanne is the lightest, and Edith falls in between. In contrast, children in the stage of formal operations can correctly reason that Suzanne is darker than Edith, that Edith is darker than Lily, and therefore that Suzanne is the darkest girl.

Piaget suggested that the transition from concrete operational to formal operational thought takes place as children become increasingly proficient in organizing and structuring input from their environment with concrete operational methods (see Chapter 11). In so doing, they come to recognize the inadequacies of concrete opera-

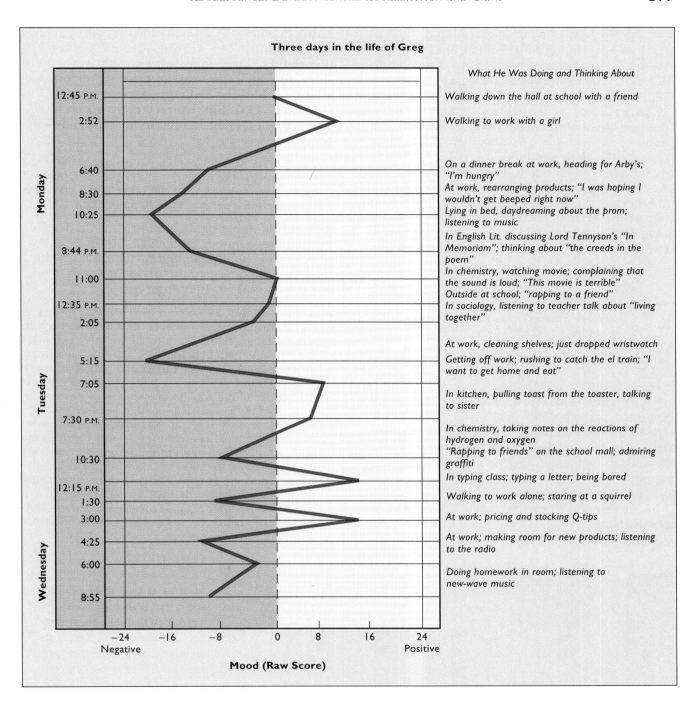

Three days in the life of Greg

What He Was Doing and Thinking About

Walking down the hall at school with a friend

Walking to work with a girl

On a dinner break at work, heading for Arby's; "I'm hungry"
At work, rearranging products; "I was hoping I wouldn't get beeped right now"
Lying in bed, daydreaming about the prom; listening to music
In English Lit. discussing Lord Tennyson's "In Memoriam"; thinking about "the creeds in the poem"
In chemistry, watching movie; complaining that the sound is loud; "This movie is terrible"
Outside at school; "rapping to a friend"
In sociology, listening to teacher talk about "living together"

At work, cleaning shelves; just dropped wristwatch
Getting off work; rushing to catch the el train; "I want to get home and eat"

In kitchen, pulling toast from the toaster, talking to sister

In chemistry, taking notes on the reactions of hydrogen and oxygen
"Rapping to friends" on the school mall; admiring graffiti
In typing class; typing a letter; being bored

Walking to work alone; staring at a squirrel

At work; pricing and stocking Q-tips

At work; making room for new products; listening to the radio

Doing homework in room; listening to new-wave music

Monday: 12:45 P.M., 2:52, 6:40, 8:30, 10:25, 8:44 P.M., 11:00
Tuesday: 12:35 P.M., 2:05, 5:15, 7:05, 7:30 P.M., 10:30
Wednesday: 12:15 P.M., 1:30, 3:00, 4:25, 6:00, 8:55

−24 −16 −8 0 8 16 24
Negative / Positive

Mood (Raw Score)

tional methods for solving problems in the real world—the gaps, uncertainties, and contradictions inherent in concrete operational processes.

Not all adolescents, or for that matter all adults, attain full formal operational thought. Therefore, they fail to acquire its associated abilities for logical and abstract thinking. This lack of ability is shown, for instance, by people who score below average on standard intelligence tests (Jackson, 1965; Neimark, 1974; Yudin, 1966). Indeed, as judged by Piaget's strict testing standards, less than 50 percent of U.S. adults reach the stage of formal operations (Martorano, 1977; Roberge & Flexer, 1979). Some evidence suggests that secondary schools may provide students with experiences in mathematics and science that expedite the development of formal operational thought. And some psychologists speculate that these experiences may be necessary to its development (Hobbs & Robinson, 1982; Lehman & Nisbett, 1990; Sharp, Cole & Lave, 1979).

Furthermore, cross-cultural studies fail to demonstrate the full development of formal operations in all societies (Ashton, 1975; Douglas & Wong, 1977). For example, rural villagers in Turkey never seem to reach the formal operational stage, yet urbanized educated Turks do reach it (Kohlberg & Gilligan, 1971). Overall, a growing body of research suggests that full formal operational thinking may not be the rule in adolescence (Dulit, 1972; Elkind, 1975; Galotti, 1989).

Adolescent Egocentricity

Every one believes in his youth that the world really began with him, and that all merely exists for his sake.—GOETHE
December 6, 1829

Piaget (1967) said that adolescence produces its own characteristic form of egocentrism, a view expanded by the psychologist David Elkind (1967, 1968*b*). As adolescents gain the ability to conceptualize their own thought, they also achieve the capacity to conceptualize the thought of others. But adolescents do not always make a clear distinction between the two.

In turning their new powers of thought introspectively, adolescents simultaneously assume that their thoughts and actions are equally interesting to others. They conclude that other people are as admiring or critical of them as they are themselves. They tend to view the world as a stage on which they are the principal actors and all the world is the audience. According to Elkind (1968*a*, p. 153), this characteristic accounts for the fact that teenagers tend to be extremely self-conscious:

> The [preoperational] child is egocentric in the sense that he is unable to take another person's point of view. The adolescent, on the other hand, takes the other person's point of view to an extreme degree.

As a result, adolescents tend to view themselves as somehow unique and even heroic—as destined for unusual fame and fortune. Elkind dubs this romantic imagery the *personal fable.*

Elkind (1967, p. 103) observes:

> A good deal of adolescent boorishness, loudness, and faddish dress is probably provoked, partially in any case, by a failure to differentiate between what the young person believes to be attractive and what others admire. It is for this reason that the young person frequently fails to understand why adults disapprove of the way he dresses and behaves. The same sort of egocentrism is often seen in behavior directed toward the opposite sex. The boy who stands in front of the mirror for 2 hours combing his hair is probably imagining the swooning reactions he will produce in the girls. Likewise, the girl applying her makeup is more likely than not imagining the admiring glances that will come her way. When these young people actually meet, each is more concerned with being the observed than with being the observer.

Adolescent Egocentricity
Adolescents tend to be self-conscious and preoccupied with the impression that they are projecting of themselves. Teenagers commonly take the other person's point of view to an extreme degree and believe that others are constantly admiring or criticizing them. *(Larry Nicholson/Photo Researchers)*

Elkind (1968*b*, p. 153) suggests that adolescent egocentrism helps explain the importance of the peer group to the teenager:

> The adolescent is so concerned with the reactions of others toward him, particularly his peers, that he is willing to do many things which are opposed to all of his previous training and to his own best interests. At the same time, this egocentric impression that he is always on stage may help to account for the many and varied adolescent attention-getting maneuvers.

By 15 to 16 years of age, this extreme egocentrism gradually declines, as the adolescent comes to realize that other people are primarily concerned with themselves and their own problems.

Other psychologists, such as Robert Selman (1980), also find that young adolescents become aware of their own self-awareness. They recognize that they can consciously monitor their own mental experience and control and manipulate their thought processes. However, only later in adolescence do they come to realize that some mental experiences that influence their actions are not accessible to conscious inspection. In brief, they become capable of distinguishing between conscious and nonconscious levels of experience. Hence, although they retain a conception of themselves as self-aware beings, they realize that their ability to control their own thoughts and emotions has limits. In so doing, they gain a more sophisticated notion of their mental self and what constitutes self-awareness (Broughton, 1978; Damon & Hart, 1982).

The Adolescent as a Moral Philosopher

The fundamental idea of good is thus, that it consists in preserving life, in favoring it, in wanting to bring it to its highest value, and evil consists in destroying life, doing it injury, hindering its development.—ALBERT SCHWEITZER

June 13, 1953

At no other period in life are people as likely to be as concerned with moral values and principles as they are during adolescence. A recurrent theme of American literature from *Huckleberry Fin* to *Catcher in the Rye* has been the innocent child who is brought at adolescence to a new awareness of adult reality, and who concludes that the adult world is hypocritical, corrupt, and decadent (Kohlberg & Gilligan, 1971). Adolescent idealism, coupled with adolescent egocentricity, frequently breeds "egocentric reformers": adolescents who assume that it is their solemn duty to reform their parents and the world in keeping with their own highly personalized standards (Hurlock, 1968).

Some two and a half millenia ago Aristotle came to somewhat similar conclusions about the young people of his time: Youths "have exalted notions, because they have not yet been humbled by life or learned its necessary limitations; moreover, their hopeful disposition makes them think themselves equal to great things—and that means exalted notions. . . . All their mistakes are in the direction of doing things excessively and vehemently. . . . They love too much, hate too much, and the same with everything else." Significantly, young people have played a major role in many social movements that have reshaped the contours of history. In Czarist Russia the schools were "hotbeds of radicalism." In China, students contributed to the downfall of the Manchu dynasty at the turn of the century and again to the political turmoil of 1919, the 1930s, and 1988–1989. And German students were largely supportive of different forms of right-wing nationalism from the mid-nineteenth century through support in student council elections for the Nazis in the 1930s (Lipset, 1989).

As discussed in Chapter 11, Kohlberg and his colleagues have found that in the course of moral development people tend to pass through an orderly sequence of six stages. These six stages of moral thought are divided into three major levels: the *preconventional,* the *conventional,* and the *postconventional.* Preconventional children are responsive to cultural labels of good and bad out of consideration for the kinds of consequences of their behavior—punishment, reward, or the exchange of favors. Persons at the conventional level view the rules and expectations of their family, group, or nation as valuable in their own right. Such people hold rather simplistic, absolutist conceptions of what is right and true. Individuals who pass to the postconventional level (and most people do not) come to define morality in terms of self-chosen principles that they view as having universal ethical validity and application (see Figure 13-5).

The impetus for moral development results from increasing cognitive sophistication of the sort described by Piaget. Consequently, postconventional morality becomes possible only with the onset of adolescence and the development of formal operational thought—the ability to think in logical and abstract terms. Thus, postconventional morality depends primarily on changes in the structure of thought, rather than on an increase in the individual's knowledge of cultural

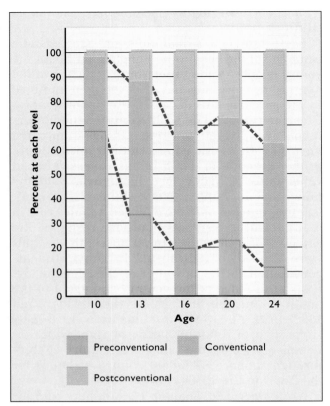

Figure 13-5 Age and Level of Moral Development
The subjects in this study were urban middle-class male Americans. All percentages are approximate and are extrapolated from charts in the references cited below. The sizes of the samples studied are not stated in the originals. SOURCE: Reprinted by permission of *Daedalus*, Journal of the American Academy of Arts and Sciences, *Twelve to Sixteen: Early Adolescence*, Vol. 100, no. 4, Fall 1971, Cambridge, MA; Lawrence Kohlberg, "Continuities in Childhood and Adult Moral Development Revisited," in L. Kohlberg (ed.), *Collected Papers on Moral Development and Moral Education.* Mimeographed.

values (de Vries & Walker, 1986). In other words, Kohlberg's stages tell us *how* an individual thinks, not *what* he or she thinks about given matters.

Kohlberg and his colleagues (Kramer, 1968) have come across some cases in which young people seemingly "retrogress" in moral development, especially after entering college. From a mixture of conventional (stage 4) and social contract (stage 5) thought at the end of high school, they appear to return to a stage 2 orientation, one distinguished by an extreme relativistic and instrumental outlook. (Refer to Table 11-1, which summarizes the characteristics of these and other stages.) Such individuals often deny the existence of any universal or divinely inspired set of moral

values or principles. Accordingly, they argue that one outlook cannot be said to be morally superior to another. One "retrogressor" observes (Kohlberg & Gilligan, 1971, p. 1074):

> I don't think anybody should be swayed by the dictates of society. It's probably very much up to the individual all the time and there's no general principle except when the views of society seem to conflict with your views and your opportunities at the moment and it seems that the views of society don't really have any basis as being right and in that case, most people, I think, would tend to say forget it and I'll do what I want.

However, retrogressors generally return to a stage 5 morality by age 25.

Elliot Turiel (1969, 1974, 1978) comes to a somewhat different conclusion about the moral relativism expressed by some young people during late adolescence and early adulthood. Although Turiel also finds that some of his subjects deny the validity of moral judgments, he notes that they simultaneously make moral statements regarding war, civil rights, and other issues.

Turiel takes this observation as clear evidence that these young people do not genuinely regress to a stage 2 type of morality. Rather, freed from their previously unquestioned, simplistic, and absolutist conventional thinking, they begin to consider an infinite number of possible alternatives. One set of beliefs appears no more inherently truthful to them than another. Yet they do not "opt out," since they view themselves as holding moral beliefs on particular issues.

Turiel concludes that the retrogressors are passing through a transitional phase between stage 4 and stage 5 morality. As they shift from one moral stage to another, the moral structure or outlook that characterized their thinking in the earlier period breaks apart or is otherwise "deformed," since it needs to be integrated into a new moral structure or outlook. The process is one of rejecting the logic of an existing stage and fashioning a new stage. In sum, Turiel views changes in moral reasoning as the result of disequilibrium and the need to construct a new equilibrium.

Development of Political Thinking

*If I do not acquire ideals when young,
when will I? Not when I am old.*—MAIMONIDES
(A Twelfth-Century Jewish Scholar)

The development of political thinking, like the development of moral values and judgments, depends to a considerable extent on an individual's level of cognitive development (Abraham, 1983; Moore, 1989; Torney-Purta, 1989; Turiel, 1989). The psychologist Joseph Adelson (1972, 1975, 1980) and his colleagues have interviewed large numbers of adolescents between 11 and 18 years of age. Their aim has been to discover how adolescents of different ages and circumstances think about political matters and organize their political philosophies.

Adelson (1972, p. 107) presents adolescents with the following premise:

> Imagine that a thousand people venture to an island in the Pacific to form a new society; once there they must compose a political order, devise a legal system, and in general confront the myriad problems of government.

Each subject is then asked a large number of hypothetical questions dealing with justice, crime, the citizen's rights and obligations, the functions of government, and so on.

Adelson (1975, pp. 64–65) summarizes his findings as follows:

> The earliest lesson we learned in our work, and the one we have relearned since, is that neither sex, nor race, nor level of intelligence, nor social class, nor national origin is as potent a factor in determining the course of political thought in adolescence as is the youngster's sheer maturation. From the end of grade school to the end of high school, we witness some truly extraordinary changes in how the child organizes his thinking about society and government.

Adelson finds that the most important change in political thought that occurs during adolescence is the achievement of increasing abstractness. This finding parallels that of Piaget, who described the hallmarks of formal operational thought in terms of the ability to engage in logical and abstract reasoning. Consider, for example, the answers given by 12- and 13-year-olds when they are asked, "What is the purpose of laws?" (Adelson, 1972, p. 108):

They do it, like in schools, so that people don't get hurt.
If we had no laws, people could go around killing people.
So people don't steal or kill.

Now consider the responses of subjects two or three years older (Adelson, 1972, p. 108):

To ensure safety and enforce the government.
To limit what people can do.
They are basically guidelines for people. I mean, like this is wrong and this is right and to help them understand.

An essential difference between the two sets of responses is that the younger adolescents limit their answers to concrete examples such as stealing and killing. Eleven-year-olds have trouble with abstract notions of justice, equality, or liberty. In contrast, older adolescents can usually move back and forth between the concrete and the abstract. In brief (Adelson, 1975, p. 68):

> The young adolescent can imagine a church but not the church, the teacher and the school but not education, the policeman and the judge and the jail but not the law, the public official but not the government.

Another difference between the political thinking of younger and older adolescents is that the former tend to view the political universe in rigid and unchangeable terms. Younger adolescents have difficulty dealing with historical causes. They fail to understand that actions taken at one time have implications for future decisions and events.

There is also a sharp decline in authoritarian responses as the child moves through adolescence. Pre-adolescents are arbitrary and even brutal in their views toward lawbreakers. They see issues in terms of good guys and bad guys, the strong against the weak, and rampant corruption versus repressive cures. They are attracted to one-person rule and favor coercive and even totalitarian modes of government. By late adolescence children generally have become more liberal, humane, and democratic in their political perspectives.

Adelson finds some national variations among young people of different political cultures. Germans tend to dislike confusion and to admire a strong leader. British adolescents stress the rights of the individual citizen and the responsibility the government has to provide an array of goods and services for its citizens. Americans emphasize social harmony, democratic practices, the protection of individual rights, and equality among citizens.

The Concept of Generations

It is mere childishness to expect men to believe as their fathers did; that is, if they have any minds of their own. The world is a whole generation older and wiser than when the father was of his son's age.—OLIVER WENDELL HOLMES
Over the Teacups, 1891

Each generation of young people is usually typified by a somewhat different image: the "roaring twenties," the "political radicalism" of the 1930s, the "wild kids" of the war years in the 1940s, the

Generations
The social orientations typical of generations differ because of the unique economic, political, or military events that occur during their formative years. The members of each generation share a somewhat different location in the social and historical process. Consider the contrast in social worlds of youth in the 1920s (left) and those involved in the civil rights demonstrations of the 1960s (right). *(left, Culver Pictures; right, Dan Budnik/Woodfin Camp & Associates)*

"silent generation" of the 1950s, the "involved generation" of the 1960s, the "Me generation" of the 1970s, and the "conservative, materialistic" generation of the 1980s. Sociologist Karl Mannheim (1893–1947) suggested that a **generation** is a historically conscious group of individuals who come of age at a certain point in time and experience in common certain decisive economic, social, political, or military events (see Chapter 1).

Also called an *age cohort* (Ryder, 1965) or an *age stratum* (Riley, Johnson & Foner, 1972), a generation is a social category similar to sex, social class, race, and religion. Individuals forming a generation share "a common location in the social and historical process" and thereby have a similar range of potential experience (Mannheim, 1952, p. 291). Because society is always changing, each new generation confronts an environment different from that faced by earlier generations. As a consequence of the unique events and circumstances of the era in which they enter adolescence and live out their lives (periods of economic depression or prosperity, social turmoil, and war), each generation tends to fashion a somewhat unique style of thought and life (Braungart & Braungart, 1986; Elder, 1974; Elder & Caspi, 1990; Riley, 1978, 1987; Roberts, 1986; Weil, 1987). Significantly, sociologists find that different cohorts recall different national and world events, and these memories come pri-

marily from adolescence and early adulthood (Schuman & Scott, 1989).

According to the *impressionable years hypothesis*, the socialization influences individuals experience when they are adolescents have a profound impact on their thinking throughout their lives. As a result of this process, members of each generation presumably come to resemble one another closely in their basic values, attitudes, and world views. Cohort replacement then becomes a major vehicle of social change—those generations with earlier socialization experiences die off as cohorts with more recent life experiences enter adulthood. The flow of new generations results in some loss to the cultural inventory, a reevaluation of some of its components, and the introduction of new elements (Krosnick & Alwin, 1989; Riley, Foner & Waring, 1988).

Mannheim (1952) observed that occasionally, at particular junctures in history, an emerging youth cohort develops an unusually sharp consciousness of itself as a distinct group with a distinctive ideology. An **ideology** is a set of shared definitions that offer interpretations and solutions to what is felt to be an unsatisfactory social condition. Something of this sort occurred among U.S. youth during the last half of the 1960s and the early years of the 1970s. Whether one thinks of the civil rights movement, the ghetto outbreaks, the antiwar protests, "flower children," or the women's movement, youth were at the center of the action. Events surrounding the challenge to racist institutions and to the war in Vietnam, as well as a growing disenchantment with the work-success ethic, contributed to the flowering of a youth counterculture. The "hang-loose" ideology of the period had a strong anti-Establishment, present-time, and self-expression ("do your own thing") orientation (Langman, 1971). Research has demonstrated the continuing impact of the 1960s on the "involved generation's" political participation, attitudes, and life-styles (Cross & Kleinhesselink, 1985; Fendrich & Lovoy, 1988; Fendrich & Turner, 1989; Whalen & Flacks, 1989). Even so, individuals' political attitudes and other orientations do not necessarily crystallize in the preadult years or even in early adulthood; these attitudes remain open to change throughout life (Brim & Kagan, 1980; Holsti & Rosenau, 1980; Jennings & Niemi, 1981).

Since 1970, young people in the United States have shifted away from the more radical political mood of the 1960s. But although radical political activism is gone, the new lifestyles have remained. In some respects young people have pressed forward in their search for a cultural rev-

olution while taking a step backward from political revolution. Compared with college classes in the 1960s, contemporary students desire more sexual freedom and privacy and put more emphasis on careers.

Although some sociologists such as Mannheim have sought explanations for generational differences in the differing historical circumstances to which differing cohorts of youth are exposed, others have advanced another explanation (Johnson, 1984). They find that adolescents tend to reject the conventional wisdom of their instructors when they perceive it as constituting a monolithic orthodoxy. It matters little whether the orthodoxy is radical or conservative, idealistic or materialistic. According to this view, a principal reason that contemporary college students have turned to self-advancement is that they are reacting against the left-wing idealism of their professors, many of whom participated in the social movements of the 1960s and early 1970s. Thus, whereas youth of the 1930s responded to the Great Depression by moving to the political left and embracing idealism, contemporary youth reacted to the prosperity of the 1980s by moving to

"The sixties are over, Ralph. The seventies and the eighties, for God's sake, are over. Give it a rest!"

(Drawing by Ziegler; © 1990 The New Yorker Magazine, Inc.)

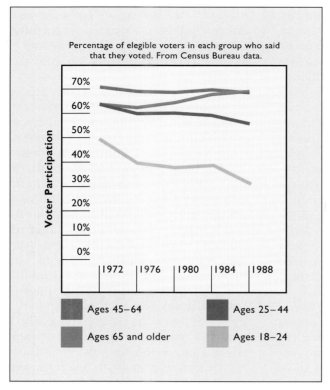

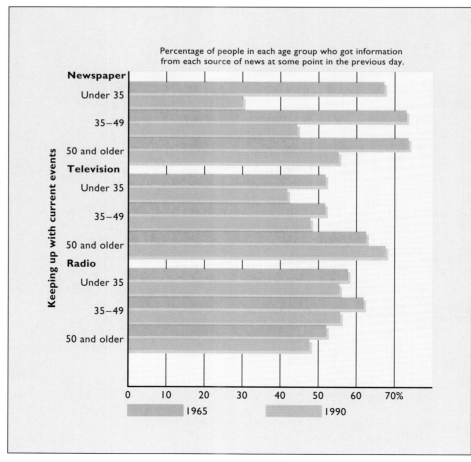

Figure 13-6   High Levels of Political Indifference Among Contemporary Young People

It seems that Americans under age 35 know less about what is going on in the nation and the world than any other generation in the past 50 years. From 1941 to 1975 young Americans were on a par with their elders in public knowledge and in following major news events closely. But since 1975, younger adults have been less attentive. From a Times Mirror Survey for the Times Mirror Center for the People and the Press. The most recent survey was conducted from January to March 1990; 3,678 people 18 or older were interviewed by phone. SOURCE: *New York Times,* June 28, 1990, p. All. Copyright © 1990 by The New York Times Company. Reprinted by permission.

the political right and embracing materialism. Proponents of this thesis take the political indifference of today's young people (see Figure 13-6) as evidence that they are "rebelling against rebellion." Each generation, then, rejected the dominant orthodoxy of the previous generation. Yet, as will be noted in the next chapter, it is easy to overemphasize the differences between generations.

Summary

1. During adolescence young people experience a very rapid increase in height and weight, which is referred to as the *adolescent growth spurt*. The spurt typically occurs in girls two years earlier than in boys.

2. Adolescence is also characterized by the development of the reproductive system. The complete transition to reproductive maturity takes place over several years and is accompanied by extensive physical changes.

3. Children of the same chronological age show enormous variations in growth and sexual maturation. Whether they mature early or late has important consequences for them in their relationships with both adults and peers. Because of different rates of maturation, some adolescents have an advantage in height, strength, physical attractiveness, and athletic prowess.

4. Any difference from the peer group in growth and development tends to be a difficult experience for the adolescent. The difference is especially difficult to handle when it places the individual at a physical disadvantage or in a position of unfavorable contrast to peers.

5. According to Erik Erikson, the main task of adolescence is to build and confirm a reasonably stable identity. He says that the adolescent, like a trapeze artist, must release his or her safe hold on childhood and reach in mid-air for a firm grasp on adulthood.

6. Erikson's view of adolescence is in keeping with a long psychological tradition that has portrayed it as a difficult and turbulent period. According to this perspective, adolescence is characterized by inevitable turmoil, maladjustment, tensions, rebellion, dependency conflicts, and exaggerated peer-group conformity.

7. In recent years researchers have increasingly come to the conclusion that adolescence in the United States is not the period of "storm and stress" that earlier psychologists and sociologists held it to be. Many young people of Western nations undergo changes in self-image and self-concept during adolescence. But these changes need not be a source of turmoil.

8. Developmental psychologist Carol Gilligan believes that girls' self-esteem is lost on the way to adolescence. It seems that women emerge from adolescence with a poorer self-image, relatively lower expectations for life, and considerably less confidence in themselves and their abilities than do men. Western culture, Gilligan says, calls upon young women to buy into the image of the "perfect" or "nice" girl—one who avoids being mean and bossy and instead projects an air of calmness, quietude, and cooperation.

9. Jean Piaget called adolescence the period of formal operations. Its hallmarks are logical and abstract reasoning. Neither all adolescents nor all adults, however, attain the stage or acquire its associated abilities for logical and abstract thought.

10. Adolescence produces its own form of egocentrism. In turning their new powers of thought upon themselves, adolescents assume that their thoughts and actions are equally interesting to others.

11. At no other period of life are individuals as likely to be concerned with moral values and principles as they are during adolescence. Some, but not all, adolescents attain Kohlberg's postconventional level of morality. In the process a number of young people go through a transitional phase of moral relativism.

12. During adolescence young people undergo major changes in the way they organize their thinking about society and government. Maturation appears to be the most potent source of these changes. As children move through adolescence, their political thinking becomes more abstract, less static, and less authoritarian.

13. As a consequence of the unique events and

circumstances of the era in which they enter adolescence, each generation tends to fashion a somewhat unique style of thought and life. At particular junctures in history an emerging youth cohort may develop an unusually sharp consciousness of itself as a distinct group with a distinctive ideology.

KEY TERMS

Adolescent Growth Spurt   A period that begins at about age 12 in girls and 14 in boys when they undergo a very rapid increase in height and weight.

Asynchrony   A dissimilarity in the growth rates of different body parts.

Deviant Identity   A lifestyle that is at odds with, or at least not supported by, the values and expectations of the larger society.

Generation   A historically conscious group of individuals who come of age at a certain time and experience in common certain decisive economic, social, political, or military events.

Identity   The answers given by an individual to the questions Who am I? and Who am I to be? Identity is a person's sense of placement within the world—the meaning that one attaches to oneself in the broader context of life.

Identity Diffusion   A lack of ability to commit oneself, even in late adolescence, to an occupational or ideological position and to assume a recognizable station in life.

Ideology   A set of shared definitions that offer interpretations and solutions to what is felt to be an unsatisfactory social condition.

Menarche   The first menstrual period.

Negative Identity   A debased self-image and social role.

Period of Formal Operations   In Piaget's theory the fourth and highest state in the development of cognition or intelligence from infancy to adulthood. During this period individuals gain the ability to think about their own thinking and to imagine many possibilities inherent in a situation.

Puberty   The period of the life cycle during which sexual and reproductive maturation takes place.

Puberty Rites   An initiation ceremony that socially symbolizes the transition from childhood to adulthood.

Role Confusion   A state characterized by bewilderment about who one is, where one belongs, and where one is going.

ADOLESCENCE: THRESHOLD OF ADULTHOOD

Chapter 14

ADOLESCENCE: THRESHOLD OF ADULTHOOD

Peers and Family

The Adolescent Peer Group ◆ Adolescents and Their Families

Dating, Love, and Sexuality

Dating ◆ Love ◆ Sexual Attitudes and Behavior

◆ New Codes of Sexual Morality ◆ Teenage Pregnancy

Vocational Choice

Some Special Issues

Drug Abuse ◆ Teenage Suicide ◆ Juvenile Delinquency ◆ High School Dropouts

◆

n the United States the social boundaries of adolescence are rather ill defined. By tradition the shift from elementary to junior high school signaled entry into adolescence. But with the advent of the middle school the transition became blurred. Nor is it entirely clear when a person leaves adolescence. Roughly speaking, adolescence is regarded as having ended when the individual assumes one or more adult roles, such as marriage, parenthood, full-time employment, or financial independence.

Many Western industrialized nations have put off entrance into adulthood for economic, educational, and other reasons. Today, college postpones full adult status for many socially and economically advantaged young people. Unemployment and underemployment produce a somewhat similar effect among less advantaged groups. At the same time, children are reaching puberty earlier than children did a century ago (see Chapters 6 and 13). Thus, physically mature people are told that they must wait ten and in some cases twenty years before they can assume the full rights and obligations of adulthood. Many young people are thereby placed in a kind of social no-man's-land.

The extension of adolescence and youth has posed two related problems for society and for young people. Society has the problem of providing the young with a bridge to adult roles through appropriate socialization and role allocation. Young people have the problem of achieving independence, deciding on future alternatives, and establishing a stable identity.

Peers and Family

The notion of a **generation gap** has been widely popularized by the mass media and humorists such as Erma Bombeck. The term implies the existence of mutual antagonism, misunderstanding, and separation between youth and adults. At its most benign level this term has been used to refer to the tendency of adults to view youth as spirited, rambunctious, and frolicking and for young people to view adults as well intentioned but dull, dated, and bumbling. In its more extreme usage it has alluded to the tendency of adults to consider young people "the enemy within" and for young people to renounce adults and the adult world, including major societal institutions (Sheleff, 1981). In sum, we gain an image of adolescence as a time when the world of peers and the world of parents are at war with each other. However, we derive a quite different picture from psychological and sociological research. Let us examine these matters more carefully.

The Adolescent Peer Group

We are coming to live in a society that is segregated not only by race and class, but also by age.—URIE BRONFENBRENNER
Two Worlds of Childhood, 1970

Western industrial societies have not only prolonged the period between childhood and adulthood, they also have tended to segregate young people. The organization of schools into grades based on age means that students of the same age spend a considerable amount of time together. In both academic and extracurricular activities the schools form little worlds of their own. This segregation reaches its most extreme expression in college communities. Middle-aged and older people also tend to create a kind of psychological segregation through the stereotypes they hold of adolescents. They frequently define adolescence as a unique period in life, one that is somehow set apart from—indeed, even at odds with—the integrated web of ongoing human activity.

The Notion of Youth Culture To the extent that young people are physically and psychologically segregated, they are encouraged to develop their own unique lifestyles (Bronfenbrenner, 1970). Some psychologists and sociologists say that Western societies, by prolonging the transition to adulthood and by segregating their youth, have given rise to a kind of institutionalized adolescence or **youth culture**—more or less standardized ways of thinking, feeling, and acting that are characteristic of a large body of young people. A parallel case may be arising among older people in our society, although for different reasons (see Chapter 20).

The most obvious features of the youth culture revolve around various peer-group trademarks: preferred recordings, dance steps, and entertainment idols; approved personal adornment and hair styles; and distinctive jargon and slang. These features separate teenagers from adults and identify adolescents who share related feelings. Such trademarks facilitate a **consciousness of oneness**—a sympathetic identification in which group members come to feel that their inner experiences and emotional reactions are similar.

Among the central ingredients in the youth culture are various ideas about the qualities and

A Distinctive Youth Culture?
Some psychologists and sociologists believe that the educational institution segregates young people within high schools and colleges and affords conditions conducive to a distinctive youth culture. *(Susan Lapides/Design Conceptions)*

achievements that reveal an individual's masculinity or femininity. For boys the critical signs of manhood are physical mastery, athletic skill, sexual prowess, risk taking, courage in the face of aggression, and willingness to defend one's honor at all costs. For girls the most admired qualities are physical attractiveness, personal vivaciousness, the ability to delicately manipulate various sorts of interpersonal relationships, and skill in exercising control over sexual encounters (Conger, 1977; Sebald, 1984, 1986).

The youth culture tends to have ambivalent attitudes toward academic achievement. Indeed, it harbors negative sentiments toward a person labeled a "brain"—one who devotes excessive energy to getting high grades. Simultaneously, intelligence is positively related to acceptance by peers, especially as it is shown in presenting a "cool" self-image in highly competitive situations. Overall, two qualities are essential for obtaining high status in the adolescent society: first, the ability to project an air of confidence in one's essential masculinity or femininity and, second, the ability to deliver a smooth performance in a variety of situations and settings. Part of presenting a "cool" self-image is the display of the appropriate status symbols and behaviors (Burlingame, 1970; Coleman, 1961; Sebald, 1984, 1986).

Although many young people share certain standardized ways of thinking, feeling, and acting that differentiate them from other age groups, the differences should not be overestimated or exaggerated. Some psychologists and sociologists believe that the term "culture" in the expression "youth culture" clouds our understanding of adolescence. It implies that there in fact exists a large gap or break between generations. Indeed, rather than being impressed by the differences between young people and adults in values and attitudes, some researchers have been struck by the similarities they find between the two groups (Elkin & Westley, 1955; Hill & Aldous, 1969; Sebald, 1986).

The Developmental Role and Course of Peer Groups Conformity to peer groups plays a prominent role in the lives of many teenagers (Brown, Clasen & Eicher, 1986; Clasen & Brown, 1985; Csikszentmihalyi & Larson, 1984; O'Brien & Bierman, 1988). Peer pressure is an important mechanism for transmitting group norms and maintaining loyalties among group members. Although peers serve as major socialization agents in adolescence, peer pressure varies in strength and direction across grades. The importance of clique membership seems to take on a growing significance for many sixth-, seventh-, and eighth-graders, but then group membership drops off as the individual aspects of social relationships take on greater importance (Brown, Eicher & Petrie, 1986; Burlingame, 1970; Crockett, Losoff & Petersen, 1984). In high school the overall picture of adolescent relationships shifts from tightly knit cliques to more diffuse, less structured networks of individuals with fewer overlapping friendships (Gavin & Furman, 1989; Shrum & Cheek, 1987).

Note, however, that at no time does an all-encompassing, monolithic peer group or culture exist for all adolescents. Teenagers differ in a great many ways. Many of these differences arise from differences in socioeconomic, racial, and ethnic backgrounds (Sebald, 1984). Furthermore, every high school typically has several "crowds"—cliques that are often mutually exclusive and even antagonistic to one another. Such distinctions as "brains," "hoods," "freaks," "jocks," "goodies," "swingers," "burn-outs," and the like are encountered in most high schools (Clasen & Brown, 1985). Additionally, a "cycle of popularity" seems to bring some teenagers together within relatively stable cliques (for instance, cheerleaders and athletes). Members of the leading crowd are often highly regarded and envied by their schoolmates (Coleman, 1961). In due course, however, many "outsiders" come to resent and dislike their "popular" counterparts who they define as "stuck up" (Eder, 1985). Even so, leading-crowd members tend to exhibit higher self-esteem than do "outsiders" (Brown & Lohr, 1987). In sum, our search for similarities among young people should not lead us to overlook the differences that also exist among them.

Adolescents and Their Families

When I was sixteen, I thought my father was a damn fool. When I became twenty-one, I was amazed to find how much he had learned in five years.—MARK TWAIN

As we noted earlier in the chapter, the media have made a good deal out of generational differences between young people and their parents. However, the notion of the generation gap vastly oversimplifies the relationship between young people and adults. It implies that attachment to one group precludes attachment to the other. Furthermore, it assumes that the discontinuity between generations is total and pervades every area of an individual's life. Neither of these premises is supported by research (Kandel, 1978; Sebald, 1984; Troll & Bengtson, 1982).

Notable shifts have occurred in the orientation of young people toward parents and peers over the past twenty-five years. In 1963, 1976, and 1982, identical questionnaires were administered to comparable samples of teenagers to determine whose advice they sought on major issues and concerns. In the 1960s girls were highly parent-oriented and boys highly peer-oriented. By the 1980s the patterns were more balanced. But whereas girls became more peer-oriented and less parent-oriented across the quarter century, boys became somewhat more parent-oriented than did their counterparts in 1976 (Sebald, 1986).

Overall, today's teenagers see their attitudes toward drugs, education, work, sex, and most other matters as closer to their parents' views

than teenagers did in the 1970s (Bachman, 1987; Cromer, 1984; Peterson, 1990; Steinberg, Elmen & Mounts, 1989). Three-fourths of the nation's young people (grades 7 through 12) report having no serious family problems and feeling close to their parents. Some fifteen years ago only half of the youth felt this way, and more than 40 percent said they would be happier living away from home.

Influence in Different Realms of Behavior Both the family and the peer group are anchors in the lives of most teenagers. However, the relative influence of the two groups varies with the issue involved. No behavior comes under the exclusive dominance of a particular generation, either peers or parents. When the issues pertain to finances, education, and career plans, adolescents overwhelmingly seek advice and counsel from adults, particularly parents. When issues involve the specifics of social life—including matters of dress, personal adornment, dating, drinking, musical tastes, and entertainment idols—they are more attuned to the opinions and standards of the peer group (Bachman, Johnston & O'Malley, 1987; Dornbusch, 1989; Krosnick & Judd, 1982; Lau, Quadrel & Hartman, 1990; Wils, 1986). Even the college activists of the 1960s and early 1970s were not rebelling against parental values so much as carrying these values to their logical conclusion in political expression (Bengston, 1970; Braungart, 1975; Braungart & Braungart, 1979; Cross & Kleinhesselink, 1985).

In many respects there is little in adolescent beliefs and values that fundamentally differs from the beliefs and values of the adult world. A great many of the values and interests of adolescents seem to be derived from and shared by a majority of their parents. Indeed, a substantial proportion of young people see no reason to differentiate between the value system of their parents and that of their friends (Troll & Bengston, 1982). So there is little foundation for the "hydraulic" view, which holds that the greater the influence of the one group, the less the influence of the other. Contrary to some psychoanalytic formulations, adolescents do not seem to develop autonomy and identity by severing their ties with parents. Rather, teenagers benefit in their development by remaining connected with parents and by using them as important resources in their lives (Steinberg & Silverberg, 1986; Youniss & Smollar, 1985). The boxed insert on page 334 dealing with girls' relationships pursues these matters further.

Overestimating the socializing influence that occurs among peer-group members is common. But much of the similarity found in the attitudes and behaviors of friends is the result of people purposely selecting as friends individuals who are already compatible with them. Not surprisingly, therefore, adolescents who share similar political orientations, values, and levels of educational aspiration are more likely to associate with one another and then to influence one another as a result of continued association (Cohen, 1983; Kandel, 1978).

There are, however, generational differences in the perception of intergenerational continuity in values, beliefs, and attitudes. Youth tend to overestimate the differences, whereas parents tend to underestimate them. Overall, young people see less intergenerational closeness, understanding, and communication than their parents perceive (Acock & Bengston, 1980; Demo, Small & Savin-Williams, 1987; Whitbeck & Gecas, 1988). Various explanations have been offered for these differences. According to one view, teens exaggerate intergenerational differences out of a developmental need for emancipation, whereas parents minimize the differences out of a developmental need for validation (Lerner, Karson, Meisels & Knapp, 1975). According to a second view, parents, after years of investing themselves in their offspring, have more at stake in maintaining the relationship than do children (Hagestad, 1981; Thompson, Clark & Gunn, 1985).

Different Kinds of Experience Afforded Parents and peers provide adolescents with different kinds of experience (Hunter, 1985; Montemayor, 1982). Time with parents centers around household activities like eating, shopping, performing

"I'm not either being sassy—I'm giving you *feedback!*"

(Baloo © 1989 from The Wall Street Journal. *Permission, Cartoon Features Syndicate.)*

chores, and viewing television. Peer time is spent "hanging out," playing games, joking, and conversing. The extent and intimacy of peer relationships increases dramatically between middle childhood and adolescence (Berndt, 1982; Buhrmester, 1990; Larson & Richards, 1991).

Overall, parent-child and peer relations fulfill fundamentally different functions for young people (Hunter & Youniss, 1982). Teenagers report that they look to interaction with friends to produce "good times" (Larson, 1983). They characterize these positive times as containing an element of "rowdiness": They act "crazy," "out of control," "loud," and even "obnoxious"—deviant behavior that they describe as "fun." Such activities provide a spirited, contagious mood, a group state in which they feel free to do virtually anything. In contrast, interactions within the family typically afford less opportunity for this kind of fluid, convivial interchange. Family interaction more closely parallels the goals of socialization dictated by the larger community. The functional constraints provided by the family and the excitement by friends both have their part to play in development.

Girls tend to find that their peer relationships with members of either sex afford them strong, rewarding friendships (Wright & Keple, 1981; Wong & Csikszentmihalyi, 1991). And they typically view their mothers as offering them more interpersonal rewards than their fathers do (except in those cases where they frequently argue with their mothers). Boys report few differences in the interpersonal rewards that they receive from their parents and peers. Even so, boys tend to regard their relationships with female friends as more rewarding to them than those with male friends.

Shift in the Family Power Equation We have seen that during adolescence the cohesion or emotional closeness between parent and child ideally becomes transformed from one of considerable dependency to a more balanced connectedness that permits the youngster to develop as a distinct individual capable of assuming adult status and roles. Another shift also occurs in family structure. Power of hierarchical relations undergo change (Cowan & Avants, 1988; Smetana, 1988). Across adolescence, parents typically make increasingly less use of unilateral power strategies and greater use of strategies that share power with their youngsters (Cowan, Drinkard & MacGavin, 1984; Feldman & Gehring, 1988; Youniss & Smollar, 1985).

It seems that between childhood and adolescence sons tend to acquire power at the expense

Girls: Relationships with Their Mothers and Girlfriends

Popular literature depicts the relationships between teenagers and their parents as a battlefield, with peer groups and parents polarized enemies. If the influence of parents is weak, the influence of peers must be strong; if adolescents experience poor relationships with their parents, they must be more deeply involved with their peers; and if teenagers attempt to achieve greater autonomy, they must necessarily develop closer ties with their peers. Viewed in this manner, adolescent friendships fill an interpersonal space that in earlier life was reserved for parents. In short, parental and peer relationships are in fundamental opposition.

Research by Martin Gold and Denise S. Yanof (1985) challenges these notions. They surveyed 134 Dearborn, Michigan, high school girls, asking them to rate the affection they shared with their mothers, how authoritarian they believed their mothers to be, and how appropriate they thought their mothers were as role models. The teenage girls also evaluated their relationship with a close girlfriend, assessing the degree of affection they shared, the extent of the friend's dominance in the relationship, and how much they wanted to be like their girlfriend.

Gold and Yanof (1985) found that girls who felt a good deal of affection for their mothers and who saw them as appropriate role models were also the ones who had the warmest and most rewarding relationships with friends. And girls who identified with a democratic mother reported more mutual influence in their friendships. In contrast, those girls who lacked intimacy at home were the ones

Mothers and Daughters

A warm, supportive relationship between mother and daughter affords a young woman a firm foundation and resource that frequently translates into more fulfilling relationships with other people. Rewarding ties at home seem to inspire more satisfactory relationships with peers. (Lester Sloan/Woodfin Camp & Associates)

least likely to develop satisfactory bonds with their peers. Although teenagers may move closer to peers when their relationship with their parents is

of their mothers, while the father-son relationship remains relatively unchanged (Steinberg, 1981). During early adolescence males become more assertive in their dealings with their parents, particularly with their mothers. Only during the later stage of puberty does the conflict subside, which largely results from the mother's having backed off. Hence, an important shift seems to occur in the two-parent family's interaction patterns. Prior to a son's puberty parents have about equal influence over family decisions, and the son occupies a subordinate position. But by late puberty the adolescent enjoys a position in the influence hierarchy above that of the mother and below that of the father.

In sum, for the most part the majority of young people and their parents do not find the generation gap to be the problem that the mass media and various social critics and clinical observers would have us think it to be (Grecas & Seff, 1990; Troll & Bengtson, 1982).

Dating, Love, and Sexuality

One of the most difficult adjustments, and perhaps the most critical, that adolescents must make revolves about their developing sexuality. Biological maturity coupled with social pressures require that adolescents come to terms with their

poor, the peer relationships are likely to be less affectionate, inspire less identification, and evince less mutuality than relationships between adolescents who enjoy good relationships with their parents.

Gold and Yanof (1985) suggest that Erik Erikson's epigenetic hypothesis regarding intimacy may offer a clue to these findings (see Chapter 2). Teenage girls who feel affection for their mothers, who believe that their mothers treat them democratically, and who identify with their mothers are likely to have had the opportunity to develop the interpersonal trust and personal autonomy that underlie the capacity for intimacy. So friendships formed to compensate for a lack of love at home do not make satisfactory substitutes.

Terri Apter (1990) has also studied adolescent daughters and their mothers. She selected sixty-five mother-daughter pairs in the United States and Great Britain, women from diverse ethnic and socioeconomic backgrounds. When she undertook her research, Apter had expected to find deep-seated intergenerational tensions and stress. She thought that the talk of daughters would center about having to free themselves from smothering, overprotective mothers and having to wage a struggle to be their "own persons." But instead, the daughters spoke much more about their "connections" with their mothers, dotting their conversations with "her view is," "she thinks I'm," and "the way she sees things." A good many of the teenagers said "the person they felt closest to, the person they felt most loved by, the person who offered them the greatest support" was their mother.

Apter found that mother-daughter quarrels are at root a conversational currency: while often filled with anger and frustration, they do not represent so much a quest for separation as they do the adolescent demand, "See me as I am, and love me for what I am." The countless arguments and endless bickering over school, chores, clothes, hours, and other matters were in fact "little puff balls" to get mothers to listen—"to get, this time, the right response, the correct effect." In contrast, daughters rarely had intense "fights" with their fathers, in part because fathers rarely supply the emotional meaning and stability that mothers do.

Apter makes a point that is rapidly gaining ascendancy among social and behavioral scientists, namely, we need models of adolescent development that make sense of the *continuity* in love and caring between youngsters and parents. She regards the continuing connectedness of parent and child as a sign of strength, not immaturity. Separation, Apter notes, can mean *individuation*—a process of becoming a distinct person with one's own values, needs, and dreams—and *divorce*—a process of severing ties and turning away in an effort to replace one person with another. Teenagers, she contends, typically gain a sense of self not by rejecting their parents but by striking a new balance with them. Nor for their part are mothers consumed with feelings of jealousy and competition with their daughters, begrudging them their youthfulness, beauty, and opportunities. Instead, although mothers and daughters may quarrel and argue, much warmth and love also binds them.

awakening sexual impulses. Consequently, sexual attraction and sexual considerations become dominant forces in their lives. Indeed, first sexual intercourse is a developmental milestone of major personal and social significance (Jessor, Costa, Jessor & Donovan, 1983). It is often viewed as a declaration of independence from parents, an affirmation of sexual identity, and a statement of capacity for interpersonal intimacy (Jessor & Jessor, 1975).

Youth vary a good deal in the age at which they first experience intercourse (involuntary sex accounts for a large proportion of all sexual exposure before the age of 14 among females). Early pubertal development applies a downward

pressure on the age of sexual debut. Sociologist J. Richard Udry and his colleagues report strong evidence for a hormonal basis of sexual motivation and behavior, particularly in adolescent males (Udry, 1988; Udry & Billy, 1987; Udry, Talbert & Morris, 1986). In addition, among both males and females, delinquent behavior, smoking, alcohol and drug use, and early onset of sexual intercourse tend to occur among the same teenagers (Ensminger, 1990; Miller & Moore, 1990). Young people who remain virgins longer than their peers are more likely to value academic achievement, enjoy close ties with their parents, report stricter moral standards, begin dating later, and exhibit more conventional behavior with respect to alcohol and drug use. However, virgins are decidedly not "maladjusted," socially marginal, or otherwise unsuccessful. They report no less satisfaction and no more stress than do nonvirgins, and they typically achieve greater educational success than nonvirgins (Eckenique, 1986; Jessor, Costa, Jessor & Donovan, 1983). In many cases teenagers, especially girls, select as their friends individuals whose sexual behavior is similar to their own (Billy, Rodgers & Udry, 1984; Billy & Udry, 1985).

Aspects of family life also affect adolescent sexual behavior. Generally speaking, the earlier the mother's first sexual experience and first birth, the earlier the daughter's sexual experience. And teenagers with older sexually active siblings are more likely to begin sexual intercourse at an earlier age. Living in poverty also tends to be associated with early sexual activity and early pregnancy. Unwed adolescent pregnancies are several times more likely among youth with poor academic skills and from economically disadvantaged families. Moreover, adolescents, especially daughters, from single-parent households typically begin sexual activity at younger ages than do their peers from two-parent families. A number of factors apparently contribute to the higher rates of sexual intercourse among adolescents in single-parent families (in Chapter 13 we discussed an explanation advanced by sociobiologists that is rooted in evolutionary adaptation). First, there is often less parental supervision in single-parent households. Second, single parents are themselves often dating, and their sexual behavior provides a role-model for their youngsters. And third, adolescents and parents who have experienced divorce tend to have more permissive attitudes about sexual activity outside of marriage (Flewelling & Bauman, 1990; Hogan, Hao & Parish, 1990; Hogan & Kitagawa, 1985; Miller & Bingham, 1989; Miller & Moore, 1990).

Dating

In the United States dating has been the principal vehicle for fostering and developing heterosexual relations. Over the past quarter century, however, dating has undergone rapid change. Traditionally, dating began with a young man inviting a young woman for an evening's public entertainment at his expense. The first invitation was often given during a nervous conversation on the telephone several days or even weeks in advance. Ideally, the man would call for the woman at the appointed hour in a car and return her by car.

Although the traditional pattern has not been entirely replaced, new patterns of dating were swept in on the wave of the various youth movements of the late 1960s and early 1970s. The term "dating" itself has become in many ways too stiff and formal to describe the "just hanging out" and "getting together" that takes place among contemporary youth (Gross, 1990; Knox, 1980; Zeman, 1990). A more relaxed style has come to govern the interaction between the sexes, including roving in packs through malls, informal get-togethers, group activities like "keggars," and spur-of-the-moment mutual decisions to go out for a pizza. Even so, by the 1980s there was some indication of a return to dating, but the term had been broadened to encompass both formal and casual arrangements. In some cases the two separate streams had come to coexist, the one reminiscent of the 1950s and the other characterized by a spirit of comradeship and more continuous interaction (Scanzoni & Scanzoni, 1981).

In whatever form dating occurs, it serves a variety of functions. Dating allows members of the opposite sex to meet and explore mutual compatibility. It occurs within a framework that permits either partner to end the relationship without losing face. Dating allows occasions for sexual exploration and discovery within mutually acceptable limits. It provides companionship—a friend for informal pair activities and sympathetic problem sharing. And dating is a means of status grading and achievement in which individuals who are seen with persons rated as "highly desirable" may raise their status and prestige within the peer group (Skipper & Nass, 1966).

Love

Americans, who make more of marrying for love than any other people, also break up more of their marriages . . . but the figure reflects not so much failure of love as the determination of people not to live without it.—MORTON HUNT
The National History of Love, 1967

In the United States everyone is expected to fall in love eventually. Pulp literature, women's magazines, "brides only" and traditional "male" publications, movies, television, and popular music reverberate with themes of romantic ecstasy. In sharp contrast to the U.S. arrangement, consider the words of the elders of an African tribe (Gluckman, 1955; p. 76). They were complaining to the 1883 Commission on Native Law and

Custom about the problems of "runaway" marriages and illegitimacy: "It is all this thing called love. We do not understand it at all. This thing called love has been introduced." The elders viewed romantic love as a disruptive force. In their culture marriage did not necessarily involve a feeling of attraction for the spouse-to-be; marriage was not the free choice of the couple marrying; and considerations other than love played the most important part in mate selection.

Clearly, different societies view romantic love quite differently (Cancian, 1987; Luhmann, 1986). At one extreme are societies that consider a strong love attraction as a laughable or tragic aberration. At the other are societies that define marriage without love as shameful. American society tends to insist on love; traditional Japan and China tend to regard it as irrelevant; ancient Greece in the period after Alexander, and ancient Rome during the Roman Empire, fell somewhere in the middle (Goode, 1959).

All of us are familiar with the concept of romantic love, yet social scientists have found it exceedingly difficult to define. If letters to "Dear Abby" and "Ann Landers" are any indication, a good many Americans—especially teenagers—are also uncertain about what love is supposed to feel like and how they can recognize the experience within themselves. Some social psychologists conclude that romantic love is simply an agitated state of physiological arousal that individuals come to *define* as love (Berscheid & Walster, 1974; Rubin, 1977). The stimuli producing the agitated state may be sexual arousal, gratitude, anxiety, guilt, loneliness, anger, confusion, or fear. What makes these diffuse physiological reactions love, they say, is that individuals *label* them as love.

Some researchers reject the notion that love and other states of physiological arousal are interchangeable except for the label we give them. For instance, Michael R. Liebowitz (1983) says that love has a unique chemical basis, perhaps associated with phenylthylamine (a compound related to the amphetamines). In romantic attraction certain brain centers are believed to release vast amounts of the substance, setting in motion a chain of neurochemical events that resemble an amphetamine high. Liebowitz claims that love and romance are among the most powerful activators of the brain's pleasure centers. And they may also contribute to a special transcendent feeling—a sense of being beyond time, space, and one's own body—that Liebowitz says parallels descriptions of psychedelic experiences. Intense romantic attractions may trigger neurochemical reactions that produce effects much like those produced by such psychedelic drugs as LSD, mescaline, and psilocybin. Just how we come to experience such changes in brain chemistry as feelings of love remains for Liebowitz an unanswered question.

Romantic love generally refers to an awestruck state of deep involvement with another person. The social psychologist Zick Rubin (1973) has found that persons who report that they love their boyfriends or girlfriends express a number of sentiments. From a seventy-item questionnaire given to University of Michigan students, Rubin identified three components as making up romantic love: (1) *attachment* (for example, "If I could never be with _____, I would feel miserable"), (2) *caring* (for example, "I would do almost anything for _____"), and (3) *intimacy* (for example, "I feel that I can confide in _____ about almost anything"). Rubin's work demonstrates that love, like any other attitude, can be measured.

Sexual Attitudes and Behavior

Although we commonly equate adolescent sexuality with heterosexual intercourse, sexual expression takes a good many different forms. Furthermore, sexuality begins early in life and merely takes on more adult forms during adolescence.

Development of Sexual Behavior Observations of male and female infants suggest that at least some of them are capable of sexual arousal and orgasm. Although we do not know what their subjective experiences are, their behavior so closely resembles that of sexually aroused adults that authorities have little doubt that the behavior is sexual in nature. Sexual arousal is easier to detect in boys than in girls because it finds visible expression in penile erections. However, even though erections may be observed among male newborns, they appear to be reflexive in origin. Just when and how this reflexive response becomes "eroticized" is as yet poorly understood (Katchadourian, 1984; Rosen & Hall, 1984).

Both male and female infants show interest in exploring their own bodies, initially in a random and indiscriminate fashion. Even at 4 months of age babies respond to genital stimulation in a manner that suggests that they are experiencing erotic pleasure. When children reach 2 and 3 years of age, they will investigate their playmates' genitals and, if permitted, those of adults as well.

But by this time strong social prohibitions come into effect, and children are socialized to restrain these behaviors.

Masturbation, erotic self-stimulation, is common among children. In many cases children experience their first orgasm through self-stimulation. It may occur through the fondling of the penis or the manual stimulation of the clitoris or by rubbing against a bedcover, mattress, toy, or other object. Boys often learn about masturbation from other boys, whereas girls learn to masturbate primarily through accidental discovery (Kinsey, Pomeroy & Martin, 1948; Kinsey, Pomeroy, Martin & Gebhard, 1953).

A good many children also engage in some form of sex play with other children prior to adolescence. The activity is usually sporadic and typically does not culminate in orgasm. On the basis of his research in the 1940s and early 1950s, Alfred C. Kinsey and his associates (1948, 1953) found that the peak age for sex play among girls was 9, when about 7 percent engaged in heterosexual play and 9 percent in homosexual play. The peak age for boys was 12, when 23 percent participated in heterosexual play and 30 percent in homosexual play. But Kinsey believed that his reported figures were too low and that about a fifth of all girls and the vast majority of all boys had engaged in sex play with other children before reaching puberty.

Adolescent Sexual Expression   Adolescent sexuality finds expression in a number of ways, including masturbation, nocturnal orgasm, heterosexual petting, heterosexual intercourse, and homosexual activity. Teenage masturbatory behavior is often accompanied by erotic fantasy. One study of 13- to 19-year olds found that 57 percent of the males and 46 percent of the females reported that they fantasized on most occasions while masturbating; about 20 percent of the males and 10 percent of the females rarely or never fantasized when masturbating (Sorensen, 1973). Many myths have attributed harmful effects to masturbation. However, the physiological harmlessness of the practice has now been so thoroughly documented by medical authorities that there is no need to labor the issue. But individuals may experience a good deal of guilt about the practice for a variety of social, religious, or moral reasons.

Adolescent boys commonly begin experiencing *nocturnal orgasms,* or "wet dreams," between ages 13 and 15. Erotic dreams that are accompanied by orgasm and ejaculation occur most commonly among men in their teens and twenties and less frequently later in life. Women also have erotic dreams that culminate in orgasm, but apparently they are less frequent among women than among men.

Petting refers to erotic caressing that may or may not lead to orgasm. If it eventuates in sexual intercourse, petting is more accurately termed "foreplay." Although usually applied to heterosexual encounters, homosexual relations may entail similar techniques. There are few current statistics on the incidence of petting among teenagers because the practice is exceedingly prevalent, and both public and scientific interests have moved beyond the issue (Katchadourian, 1984).

Adolescent Heterosexual Behavior   The past twenty-five years have seen substantial changes in U.S. attitudes toward teenage sexual activity. Greater openness and permissiveness prevail today with regard to premarital sex, homosexuality, extramarital sex, and a variety of specific sexual acts. And television, movies, and magazines bombard young people and adults alike with sexual stimuli on an unprecedented scale.

Yet one can easily overemphasize the changes that have occurred (Diepold & Young, 1979). Sociologist Ira L. Reiss (1972, p. 167) notes:

> One of our most prevalent myths is that in past centuries the typical form of courtship was that of two virgins meeting, falling in love, and doing little with each other sexually. They then married, learned about sex together in the marital bed, and remained faithful to each other until death separated them. I am certain that some couples did have exactly that type of experience. . . . But the key point is that I am sure it was never the common pattern for the majority of Americans. . . . We know . . . that in Massachusetts at a well-known church in the last part of the eighteenth century one in every three women who married confessed fornication to her minister. The major reason for making such a confession would be that the woman was pregnant and if she did not make that confession at her marriage, the baby could not be baptized.

Evidence also suggests that this century has witnessed *two* periods of very rapid change regarding sexual attitudes and behavior. The first period occurred around the time of World War I; the second, during the Vietnam War years.

Before 1915 approximately 75 percent of all first-time brides were virgins; by 1920 the figure had dropped to around 50 percent (Burgess & Wallin, 1953; Kinsey, Pomeroy, Martin & Gebhard, 1953; Terman, 1938). This decrease in virginity among women could be accounted for largely in terms of the increase in the proportion

"But, Dad, in your day sex was still in the future."

(Drawing by Wm. Hamilton; © 1991 The New Yorker Magazine, Inc.)

of women having premarital relations with their future husbands. During the same period the proportion of men in middle-class samples who were virgins at marriage declined from about 51 percent to around 33 percent (Burgess & Wallin, 1953; Terman, 1938). However, these figures understate the incidence of male premarital sexual experience because they are derived from samples of middle-class men. Men from lower- and working-class backgrounds appear to have had a considerably higher rate of premarital experience. One study placed the figure for men with only a grade school education at 98 percent, for those with a high school education at 85 percent, and for those with some college education at 68 percent (Kinsey, Pomeroy, Martin & Gebhard, 1953).

Research suggests that in the United States during the period 1920 to 1965, little overall change occurred in actual premarital sexual *behavior*. The proportion of women who had premarital sexual relations stabilized at about 50 percent and that of men at around 85 percent (Reiss, 1972, 1976). However, in the post-World War II period *attitudes* did change, becoming more permissive (Clayton, 1979; Reiss, 1976).

Dramatic changes in sexual behavior showed up again after 1965. A growing proportion of teen-

agers are sexually active and are beginning their sexual activity at earlier ages. As reflected in Table 14-1, national surveys show that half of the country's young people have had sexual inter-

World War II: Changing Sexual Attitudes

The dictates of World War II profoundly disrupted the lives of American youth. Men were drafted to serve in the military while many women were drawn into war industries. These changes contributed to a shift in sexual attitudes. However, premarital sexual behavior remained at similar levels to those of youth during the 1920s and 1930s. (Culver Pictures)

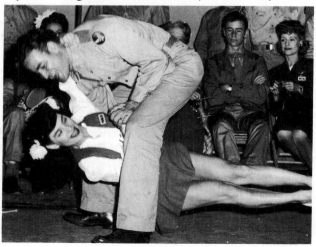

Table 14-1

Percent of Young People Sexually Active at Specific Ages		
Age	Women %	Men %
15	5.4	16.6
16	12.6	28.7
17	27.1	47.9
18	44.0	64.0
19	62.9	77.6
20	73.6	83.0

Source: *National Research Council, Risking the Future: Adolescent Sexuality, Pregnancy, and Childbearing,* © 1987 by the National Academy of Sciences.

course by the time they are 17 (National Research Council, 1987). More boys than girls have had sexual experience at every age level. By the time they reach age 20, 62.9 percent of women have had intercourse. In contrast, less than 20 percent of women in their mother's generation had engaged in sexual intercourse while in their teens (Kinsey, Pomeroy, Martin & Gebhard, 1953).

The shift in sexual attitudes and behavior has also been pronounced among college students (Bell & Coughey, 1980; Clayton & Bokemeier, 1980; Lueptow, 1984). The change largely reflects a narrowing of the gap between the sexual activity of males and females, rather than a marked increase in that of males. For instance, at the University of Georgia the percentage of men having premarital intercourse rose from 65.1 percent in 1965 to 77.4 percent in 1980; during this same period the percentage of the women having premarital intercourse rose from 28.7 percent to 63.5 percent (Robinson & Jedlicka, 1982). In most college communities an equalitarian premarital sexual standard appears to be replacing the traditional double standard. Furthermore, the decision among college women to have sexual intercourse appears to be less dependent on engagement to marry and more dependent on their feelings of affection for and emotional involvement with a male. However, college students today are more conservative in their sexual attitudes and behavior than were students of the 1960s and 1970s. They are less likely to engage in casual sex, and they apparently feel more guilt about their sexual behavior. These changes parallel the conservative shift in values in other realms of U.S. life. Moreover, sexual guilt seems to be associated with being more religious and taking a more conservative political stance (Elias, 1986*b*; Hellmich, 1986).

Adolescent Homosexual Behavior Research on homosexual behavior among adolescents is relatively limited. What evidence there is suggests that growing up gay is often a tortured journey toward self-acceptance. To be different is difficult at any age, and it is especially so during adolescence, when conformity is celebrated and minor eccentricities can mean ostracism. In middle schools and high schools youngsters call one another a great many names, but few labels are more mortifying than "faggot." For youth who are gay, the social pressures can be intense. Consequently, many young gays keep their feelings hidden from friends and family. Should they seek out school counselors or physicians for help, they are often simply advised to "go straight." Such sentiment leaves many young gays feeling alienated and lonely. And although heterosexual teenagers learn how to date and establish relationships, gay youth are often precluded from such opportunities. Instead, they learn that they must hide their true feelings (Kantrowitz, 1986*a*).

Note, however, that a few adolescent homosexual experiences do not necessarily mean a lifetime of homosexuality. Genital exhibition, demonstration of masturbation, group masturbation, and related activities apparently are not uncommon among group-oriented preteen boys (Katchadourian, 1984). This prepubescent homosexual play generally stops at puberty. However, even though homosexual behavior during prepuberty does not necessarily lead to adult homosexuality, adult homosexuals typically report that their homosexual orientation had already been established before they reached puberty (see Chapter 16). Usually, the transition from homosexual experiences to predominantly heterosexual relationships occurs easily because many teenage boys do not regard their sexual contact with other boys as "homosexual" in the adult sense (Rosen & Hall, 1984).

The Impact of the AIDS Epidemic Government statistics show that each year 2.5 million adolescents contract a sexually transmitted disease (Leary, 1990). Despite the publicity surrounding AIDS and other sexually transmitted diseases, only 48 percent of teenagers strongly believe that sexual activity carries the risk that one will acquire these diseases. Teenage girls are more concerned about venereal disease than are boys: 55 percent of teenage girls and 42 percent of teenage boys strongly agree that teenage sex carries the risk of disease (Schwartz, 1987). Moreover, a survey of 860 Massachusetts teens, ages 16 to 19, found that although 96 percent had heard of

AIDS, only 15 percent had changed their sexual behavior as a result (Findlay, 1987c). Evidence of this sort has led public-health experts to worry openly that sexually active teenagers will be the next AIDS "high-risk" group (Eckholm, 1990; Kantrowitz, 1987a). Yet there is an encouraging note: Although young people do not seem to be changing their levels of sexual activity, the incidence of condom use is currently two to three times higher than it was in the 1970s (Painter, 1990a, 1990b; Sonenstein, Pleck & Ku, 1989).

New Codes of Sexual Morality

Recent changes in patterns of sexual behavior among many young people do not amount to a breakdown in morality, as is sometimes charged. Rather, these changes mean that young people have modified the codes of moral behavior. If anything, the young appear to be more concerned today with the moral aspects of sexual behavior than previous generations were.

Many young people have come to judge the acceptability of sexual behavior in terms of a couple's emotional involvement. Sexual intercourse is defined as morally permissible as long as the couple are engaged or feel love or strong affection for each other (Reiss, 1976). Any sexual behavior, even "petting," is unacceptable if affection is absent.

Clearly, most young Americans do not regard the new morality as license for promiscuous thrill seeking (Lueptow, 1984; McKenry, Walters & Johnson, 1979; Miller & Moore, 1990; Robinson, Ziss, Ganza, Katz & Robinson, 1990). They appear to seek a sense of identity through an affectionate and emotionally involved form of physical intimacy. And in keeping with this focus, the new morality includes a desire for greater openness and honesty about sex. Although there seems to have been a movement since 1975 toward the older attitudes that prevailed before the so-called sexual revolution, there remains a tendency to hold both men and women to the *same* standards for behavior. Thus, there is a greater tendency among college students today than in 1975 to judge sexual intercourse with a great many partners as immoral regardless of the person's sex (Robinson & Jedlicka, 1982; Robinson, Ziss, Ganza, Katz & Robinson, 1991).

Although it may seem that young people are in rebellion against adult values, in truth the newer morality is an attempt to realize many traditional U.S. values: equalitarianism, honesty, openness, autonomy, free choice, love, happiness, and indi-

vidual well-being. This morality has been fostered by many of the same social sources that produced the equalitarian movements for black and women's rights. Today, many people of college age believe that they have as much right to choose their sexual life-style as their political or religious lifestyle or their marriage partners (Reiss, 1976). Indeed, the differences between generations may not be as great as they seem. On the whole, adults are also becoming more permissive in their sexual norms, with single adults in particular speaking up in favor of premarital intercourse (Hunt, 1974; Yankelovich, 1981).

Teenage Pregnancy

More than four out of ten young women in the United States become pregnant before they turn 20 (more than a million U.S. teenagers become pregnant each year). A decade or so ago, teenage pregnancy and childbearing were seen primarily as health problems. But many of the risks can be mitigated through proper health care, especially good prenatal care and nutrition (see Chapter 14). More recently, public concern has focused on teenage childbearing as one of the major sources of poverty in the United States (Furstenberg, 1991). Teen parents are less likely than other youth to graduate from high school and are more likely to suffer a variety of educational deficits. Consequently, early childbearers have difficulty obtaining the skills required by society and end up in low-paying, low-status jobs or dependent on welfare for support (71 percent of women under 30 who receive Aid to Families with Dependent Children had their first child as a teenager). The birth of a child increases a young person's income requirements, and the lack of a diploma is a significant liability in today's job market. Although many young mothers resume their education later in life, they typically do not catch up with women who postpone childbearing. But even though early childbearing contributes to long-term social disadvantage, it need not create lasting social devastation: A substantial majority of young mothers complete high school, find regular employment, and escape from public assistance (Adams, 1987; Furstenberg, Brooks-Gunn & Morgan, 1987; Kenney, 1987; National Research Council, 1987; Passell, 1991; Teti & Lamb, 1989; Upchurch & McCarthy, 1990).

Early childbearing also has implications for family life. Most teenagers who give birth are not married. Among young women 15 to 17 years of age, 81 percent of the births occurred out of

Teenage Pregnancy
The photo shows a 14-year-old mother-to-be and an 18-year-old father-to-be. Young couples often experience difficult financial circumstances. *From* Newsweek *Special Issue, Summer 1990; © 1990, Newsweek, Inc. All rights reserved. Reprinted by permission.*

wedlock between 1985 and 1989 (the comparable figures were 41 percent between 1965 and 1969 and 59 percent between 1975 and 1979). For women 18 or 19 years of age, the proportion of births occurring out of wedlock was 59 percent between 1985 and 1989 (compared to 20 percent in the late 1960s and 37 percent in the late 1970s) (Pear, 1991).

Of those teenagers who do marry, pregnancy is often a major reason (one-third of brides under age 18 are pregnant). Teen marriages are highly unstable. They are from two to three times more likely to break up than marriages occurring after age 20, and most adolescent mothers spend at least some portion of their lives as single parents (60 percent of brides aged 17 years or less divorce within six years; 20 percent divorce within the first year). The children of teen parents are also

affected. Inept parenting, child neglect, and child abuse are comparatively more common among teenage parents. Moreover, children of younger parents tend to score lower than the children of older parents on intelligence tests, and they typically do less well in school. In addition, children of younger parents are more prone to behavioral and adjustment disorders and are more likely to become teen parents themselves (Brooks-Gunn & Furstenberg, 1989; Elster, Lamb, Peters, Kahn & Tavare, 1987; Furstenberg, Brooks-Gunn & Chase-Lansdale, 1989; Furstenberg, Brooks-Gunn & Morgan, 1987).

The teenage pregnancy rate in the United States is more than twice as high as the rates in England, France, and Canada; almost three times as high as the rate in Sweden; and seven times as high as that in the Netherlands. This country's youth are exposed to mixed messages about contraception, and birth control services are not effectively delivered to the nation's teenagers (Brooks-Gunn & Furstenberg, 1989). Each year, one out of every ten teenage American women becomes pregnant, and eight out of ten of these pregnancies are unintended (some teenagers hope that having a baby will solve their problems, provide someone who will love them, and make them feel grown up). Only about 47 percent of teen pregnancies end in live birth; 40 percent are terminated by abortions, and 13 percent result in miscarriages.

Most teenagers do not consciously plan to become sexually active, and so they do not foresee their first sexual experience. As such, their first sexual experience often is not experienced as a decision but rather as something that "just happened" (Chilman, 1983; Harris and Associates, 1986). Moreover, most teenagers wait almost a year after becoming sexually active before they seek medically supervised contraceptive care. Indeed, almost half of first teen pregnancies occur within six months of an adolescent's first sexual encounter, and one-fifth in the first month. Adolescents frequently have a sense of invulnerability and fail to associate consequences with action. Only one-third of sexually active teenagers say they use birth control all the time; 19 percent "most of the time"; and 15 percent "sometimes." Asked why teenagers do not use birth control, 39 percent give answers that can be summed up as "not wanting to" ("feels better without it," "don't think about it," "want to get pregnant"). Twenty-five percent give answers involving lack of knowledge or access; 24 percent do not use contraception because of fear or embarrassment; 20 percent do not expect to need contraception or do not want to take the time; and 14 percent are not worried about pregnancy (some teenagers cite multiple reasons) (National Research Council, 1987). Significantly, as adolescents become more sexually experienced, they tend to become more consistent contraceptive users. In addition, teenagers who have high educational expectations and school success are more likely to use contraception effectively (Miller & Moore, 1990).

An examination of state-to-state differences in teenage pregnancies and births suggests that broad societal patterns seem to affect teen decisions about childbearing. States in which the status of women is higher have lower teen birth rates and higher abortion rates; politically liberal states have relatively low rates of pregnancy and birth; states with large fundamentalist religion populations have higher birth rates; and states with substantially higher dropout rates from school have higher pregnancy and birth rates and somewhat lower abortion rates. Other findings reveal that Western nations with the most liberal attitudes toward sex, the most extensive sex education programs, and the most easily accessible birth-control services have the *lowest* rates of teenage pregnancy, abortion, and childbearing (Kenney, 1987).

Vocational Choice

We cannot always build the future for our youth, but we can build our youth for the future.—FRANKLIN D. ROOSEVELT
Speech of September 20, 1940

A critical developmental task confronting adolescents involves making a variety of vocational decisions. In the United States, as in other Western societies, the jobs that people hold have significant implications for their lives. The positions they assume in the labor force influence their general life-style, important aspects of their self-concept, their children's life-chances, and most of their relationships with others in the community (Bock & Moore, 1986; Schulenberg, Vondracek & Crouter, 1984; Sewell, 1981; Stern & Eichorn, 1989). Additionally, jobs tie individuals into the wider social system and give them a sense of purpose in life.

One focus of the transition from childhood to adulthood is preparation for finding and keeping a job in the adult years. Given the importance of the job entry process, adolescents are surprisingly ill prepared for making vocational decisions. Most teenagers have only vague ideas about what they are able to do successfully, what

they would enjoy doing, what requirements are attached to given jobs, what the current job market is like, and what it will probably be like in the future (DeFleur & Menke, 1975). Of course, many teenagers work. Should young people seek and gain work during their teen years, their working can have far-reaching consequences for their relationships with their parents, for their schooling, for their acceptance and status among their peers, and for the standard of living and life-style they assume (the boxed insert on page 404 examines a number of these matters).

Some teens encounter special difficulties in entering the job market, especially women and those from racial and ethnic minorities. Sex differences surface early, mirroring those of the adult work world (Greenberger & Steinberg, 1983). Young men are more likely than young women to be employed as manual laborers, newspaper deliverers, and recreation aides, whereas young women are more likely to work as clerical workers, retail sales clerks, child care workers, health aides, and education aides. Sex segregation also occurs within industries. Among food service workers, young men more often work with things (they cook food, bus tables, and wash dishes), whereas young women more often work with people (they fill orders and serve as waitresses and hostesses). And among hucksters, young men are overrepresented in jobs that require selling "on the street," whereas young women predominate in "telephone sales."

For many U.S. teenagers a steady, decent-paying job is a distant hope (Coleman & Husen, 1985; Hamilton, 1990: Wilson, 1987). High rates of unemployment have traditionally been the lot of many young people, especially blacks in big-city ghettos. Two decades ago U.S. young people could find a job in manufacturing, construction, or sales and expect to make a career of it. But increasingly, young Americans without skills, and often those with them, cannot count on good wages and steady work. For example, whereas 44 percent of young men under age 20 worked in manufacturing jobs in 1973, the proportion had fallen to 22 percent by 1987 (Schwartz, 1988). And a recent study by the Economic Policy Institute reported that, from 1979 to 1988, the incomes of households whose principal earner was under 25 years of age fell 19 percent in terms of the food, clothing, or housing they could afford. Moreover, working men with only high school diplomas suffered a 7.4 percent erosion in the value of their wages in the same time span, while the wages of male college graduates rose 7 percent (Kilborn, 1990). With urban public school systems failing to

Should Teenagers Work?

Two out of three high school students currently work part-time during the school year, and 80 percent will hold part-time jobs at some point before they graduate. In contrast, in 1940 less than 5 percent of U.S. high school students had a part-time job. The virtues of work for teenagers has been espoused over the years by a number of blue-ribbon commissions (Carnegie Commission, 1980; National Commission on Youth, 1980). A job is thought to teach adolescents responsibility, to instill in them an appreciation for hard work, to bring them into closer contact with adults from whom they can learn, and to keep them out of trouble.

Yet an emerging body of research suggests that extensive part-time employment may take a considerable toll on adolescent development (Bachman, 1987; Cole, 1980; Greenberger & Steinberg, 1986; Steinberg & Dornbusch, 1991). Though working is often associated with greater personal responsibility, requiring high levels of punctuality, dependability, and self-reliance on the job, there is little evidence to support the notion that working enhances adolescents' concern for others or promotes overall social responsibility.

One common assumption is that work provides youth with on-the-job training of a technically useful kind. Yet it actually affords very little. In practice, younger teenagers are confined to doing odd jobs such as mowing lawns, shoveling snow, delivering newspapers, and baby-sitting, while older teenagers clerk in stores, wash dishes, flip hamburgers, bag groceries, and wait on tables at local cafes. Usually, the jobs involve repetitive op-

Part-Time Employment for Teenagers

The jobs that are open to teenagers typically involve repetitive operations that require few skills. Although it is commonly assumed that youth gain on-the-job training, they actually derive very little that is technically useful to them. But they do gain a "work orientation" and practical knowledge of how the business world operates. (Carrie Boretz)

erations that require little training or skills learned in other settings. So there is a high degree of discontinuity between adolescent and adult work.

About half of the more than 400,000 workers in McDonald's restaurants are under 20—and more than 60,000, or 13 percent, are blacks. Critics have

prepare many students for the more demanding jobs the economy is creating, black and Hispanic young people are at growing risk of missing early work experience and of finding steady, well-paying jobs in adulthood (Levine, 1990). Some evidence suggests that racism is a factor contributing to the high black unemployment level, since the unemployment rate of white high-school *dropouts* is about equal to that of black high-school *graduates*. Poor job location—living in central cities whereas many jobs are in the suburbs—is another factor.

Society pays a high price for the unemployment of its adolescents and young adults. Whereas full-time employment is associated with low arrest rates for crime, unemployment is associated with high arrest rates. Low-quality employment—poor pay and hours—is also asso-

ciated with high youth arrest rates (Allan & Steffensmeier, 1989). Sociologists find that many other inner-city problems—educational underachievement, drug and alcohol abuse, and welfare dependency—are an outgrowth of a more fundamental problem: no jobs (Anderson, 1990; Duncan & Rogers, 1988; Lichter, 1988; Sampson, 1987; Wilson, 1987).

Some Special Issues

*To me it seems that youth is, like spring,
an overpraised season . . . more remarkable,
as a general rule, for biting east winds, than
genial breezes.*—SAMUEL BUTLER

Although adolescence is often heralded in the United States as the "beautiful age," many ado-

long viewed McDonald's as representative of the "K-Mart economy" of low-wage, dead-end work. Yet employers like McDonald's function as de facto training programs by teaching young people the basics of *how* to work. Adolescents gain a "work orientation"—practical knowledge of how the business world operates and how to find and hold a job. And teenagers are exposed to a variety of new situations in which they must learn to deal with many different kinds of people. For some teenagers, just donning the uniform makes them feel important and part of a U.S. institution. In addition, jobs such as "bin man" may be quite demanding—a kind of fast-food economist who balances supply and demand in calculating how many sandwiches will be needed within a short time span. For workers who show initiative, McDonald's offers opportunities for advancement. Yet, despite all the success stories, statistics reveal that most McDonald's workers will never be promoted to manager. Nor should one overlook the fact that McDonald's hires many young people precisely because it can secure their services at relatively low wages (Marby, 1989).

But high school sophomores who work more than fifteen hours a week and seniors who work more than twenty hours also tend to fall behind in school and are at greater risk for dropping out. Indeed, teenagers' investment in long hours of work seems to be a major factor contributing to the decline in the quality of education in U.S. schools. Working students pressure teachers to cut back on their expectations and assignments. All the while, students use a variety of corner-cutting strategies, including taking less demanding courses and arranging their school schedules to meet the dictates of the workplace. And working teenagers are more likely to copy other students' homework, cheat, and skip school.

While taking time out for work hurts students academically, the money they earn seems to hurt them in other ways. The more hours students work, the more likely they are to use alcohol and drugs, in part because they have the money to buy such things. Moreover, the stress of performing dull and routine tasks makes the use of alcohol and drugs seem attractive. And too much discretionary income distorts adolescent priorities. A University of Michigan survey found that more than 80 percent of high school seniors spent all or nearly all their earnings on their own needs and activities (cars, stereos, clothes, records, alcohol, and drugs). In short, they consume what they earn, and they put very little money aside for expenses of the early adult years such as an education or a house. Many psychologists fear that "premature affluence" will lead to disillusionment in later years, when most income must go to paying the rent and food bills. Finally, the more teenagers work at boring, hateful tasks, the more cynical and jaded they become. From interviews with some 500 teenaged workers, psychologists Ellen Greenberger and Laurence Steinberg (1986) conclude that schoolwork and after-school activities like sports are more likely to build character than is work.

lescents have great difficulty with it. Even if adolescents do not perceive themselves as having "problems"—as in the past, many do not in the case of their marijuana use—adult society nonetheless defines various teenage behaviors as "deviant." Since adults control the channels of power, including legislative agencies, the court, the police, and the mass media, they are in a better position than adolescents to make their definitions and values the predominant ones in human affairs.

Drug Abuse

Nowadays, everyone talks about drugs, but the word itself is imprecise. If we consider a drug to be a chemical, then everything that we ingest is technically a drug. To avoid this difficulty, a *drug* is usually arbitrarily defined as a chemical that produces some extraordinary effect beyond the life-sustaining functions associated with food and drink. For instance, a drug may heal, put to sleep, relax, elate, inebriate, produce a mystical experience, or whatever.

Our society assigns different statuses to different types of drugs. Through the Federal Drug Administration, the Bureau of Narcotics, and other agencies, the government takes formal positions on whether a given drug is "good" or "bad," and if "bad," how bad. Sociologists note that some drugs, like caffeine and alcohol, enjoy official approval. Caffeine is a mild stimulant that finds institutional approval through the coffee break and coffee shop. Likewise, the consumption of alcohol, a central nervous system depressant, has become so prevalent in recreational and business settings that nonusers of the drug are often regarded as somewhat peculiar. And at least until a few years ago, the same held true for the use of nicotine (smoking), a drug usually categorized as a stimulant (though the smoking ritual itself is experienced by many people as relaxing).

Whether or not they are culturally sanctioned, drugs can be abused. **Drug abuse** refers to the excessive or compulsive use of chemical agents to an extent that interferes with people's health, their social or vocational functioning, or the functioning of the rest of society. Among adolescents, as among their elders, alcohol is the most frequently abused drug in the United States. According to surveys conducted by the Institute of Social Research at the University of Michigan, drinking remained relatively stable among college students during the 1980s (Barringer, 1991). In 1989, some 76 percent of college students reported they had had a drink in the previous month, compared to 82 percent in 1980; the proportion of heavy drinkers—students who had drunk five or more drinks in a row some time in the previous two weeks—was virtually unchanged, declining from 44 percent in 1980 to 42 percent in 1989 (Carmody, 1990). College and university officials agree that binge drinking is a major problem on most of the nation's campuses. It also has far-ranging consequences. For instance, nearly two-thirds of those who commit campus crimes admit using alcohol and nearly half say their crime—a sex offense, other violence, vandalism—was alcohol-related (Burgett, 1990).

Another drug frequently used by adolescents is marijuana. The effects of marijuana differ from user to user. Most commonly, it produces a relatively mild and light-headed form of inebriation. Some users also report an increase in the intensity of sense impressions; for instance, colors may appear brighter and music may sound richer and more resonant. In 1982 the National Academy of Sciences summarized the available scientific evidence about the health effects of marijuana. Although it found no conclusive evidence that the drug has long-term, permanent effects, it nonetheless said that marijuana's short-term effects justify "serious national concern." It concluded that marijuana temporarily impairs motor coordination; hampers short-term memory, oral communication, and learning; and may trigger temporary confusion and delirium. Thus, daily use can be expected to harm the adolescent user's academic performance. Chronic use may lead to impaired lung function, decreased sperm counts, interference with ovulation, diminished immune response, and possibly lung cancer.

According to federal health officials, as the nation entered the 1990s, more than a quarter of a million young people, mostly boys, used steroids to build muscles and enhance athletic performance. The nonmedical use of anabolic steroids is illegal. More than half of the users had started usage by age 16, and 85 percent, by age 17. Medical authorities say adolescents whose bodies are still developing are at special risk for adverse effects in using steroids, including stunted growth, mood changes, long-term dependence on steroids, acne, fluid retention, breast development in males, masculinization in females, high blood pressure, and reversible sterility in males. Teenagers are particularly vulnerable to steroid use because of strong concerns about appearance, peer approval, and "being large and strong enough to make the team" in competitive sports (*New York Times,* September 8, 1990, p. 31).

Each year, for nearly two decades, the University of Michigan's Institute for Social Research has surveyed U.S. high school seniors on their drug use. Illegal drug use—marijuana, cocaine, crack, and related drugs—has been on the decline, dropping to 48 percent in 1990, down from a high of 66 percent in 1981 (see Figure 14-1). Antidrug messages have made the use of illegal drugs increasingly "unfashionable" while providing information about the risks of drug abuse (Bachman, Johnston & O'Malley, 1990). All the while, alcohol use has remained at a fairly steady two-thirds level. Forty-one percent of the 1990 high school seniors reported heavy drinking in the two weeks prior to the survey, and 12 percent said they smoked daily.

Many psychologists say that coping with the presence of drugs in their social environment is now a developmental task that adolescents must reckon with, just as they must reckon with separation from parents, career development, and sexuality (Bentler, 1987; Collins, 1983a; Kovach & Glickman, 1986; Newcomb & Bentler, 1988). One longitudinal study that followed a group of San Francisco Bay area children from nursery school through late adolescence is particularly insightful (Block & Block, 1980; Block, Block & Keyes, 1988; Shedler & Block, 1990). The youngsters were assessed on wide-ranging batteries of psychological measures at ages 3, 4, 5, 7, 11, 14, and 18. The researchers found that casual drug experimentation among youth often is associated with good social and personal adjustment and does not in-

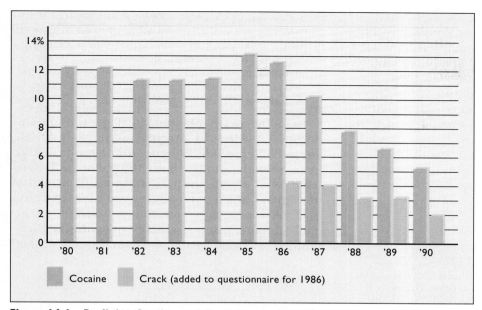

Figure 14-1   Declining Cocaine and Crack Use in High Schools
The figure shows the percentage of high school seniors saying that they had used cocaine or crack in the 12 months prior to their year of graduation. Cocaine is a white crystaline powder, derived from the coca plant, and is typically sniffed. Crack is a smokable form of cocaine made by boiling the drug in water. In its smokable form, the drug gets to the brain more rapidly and has a stronger impact. The survey is conducted by the Institute for Social Research at the University of Michigan. SOURCE: New York Times, January 25, 1991, p. A10. Copyright © 1991 by The New York Times Company. Reprinted by permission.

variably lead to addiction. Given the prevalence and availability of marijuana in the peer culture, it may not be surprising that psychologically healthy, sociable, and reasonably inquisitive young people would have been tempted to try marijuana. But the findings also show that adolescents who use drugs frequently tend to be maladjusted, showing a distinct personality syndrome marked by interpersonal alienation, poor impulse control, and significant emotional distress. For these youngsters, experimentation with drugs is highly destructive and easily leads to pathological functioning.

Other researchers confirm that heavy and abusive use of drugs during adolescence is associated with increased loneliness, social isolation, disorganized and suicidal thought processes, and unusual beliefs—aspects that significantly interfere with problem solving and social and emotional adjustment. And heavy drug use impairs competence in the crucial maturational and developmental tasks of adolescence and adulthood by generating premature involvement in work, sexuality, and family roles (Newcomb & Bentler, 1988, 1989). Also of interest, researchers find that many school programs designed to combat drug

use may actually lead to increased use among curious teenagers (Bard, 1975; Kerr, 1986; Pereira, 1989; Stuart, 1974). In addition, teens see many of their peers using drugs without any apparent harmful effects, creating a climate of disbelief in antidrug campaigns (Elias, 1986a; Martz, 1990).

A variety of factors have contributed to the illicit use of drugs by young people. One overriding circumstance has been the very important part that the recreational use of illegal drugs has played in many adolescent peer groups over the past twenty years. Generally speaking, adolescents who use illegal drugs move in peer groups in which drugs are not only approved but also have an important part in day-to-day interactions (Brook, Whiteman & Gordon, 1983; Hays, Widaman, DiMatteo & Stacy, 1987; Kandel & Adler, 1982; Marcos, Bahr & Johnson, 1986). Another contributor in the use of illegal drugs by young people is that they view their parents as users of psychoactive drugs—such as tranquilizers, barbiturates, and stimulants (Kandel, 1974, 1990; Simons & Robertson, 1989; Smart & Fejer, 1972). The contribution that parental drug behavior makes to children's illegal use of drugs is certainly not intended by the parents; more than 80 percent of adolescents report that their family has a rule against illicit drugs. Nonetheless, children in the United States are reared in a pill-oriented, happiness-seeking society. Many see their parents using psychoactive drugs, and, as a consequence, the children begin taking mood-changing drugs themselves. In this context drug use by adolescents is a juvenile manifestation of adult behavior. It is more accurate to view drug abuse not simply as a teenage problem but as a societywide problem (Barnes, Farrel & Cairns, 1986; Collins 1983*a).*

Teenage Suicide

To die—to sleep—No more; and by a sleep to say we end The heartache, and the thousand natural shocks That flesh is heir to. 'Tis a consummation Devoutly to be wish'd. To die—to sleep.—WILLIAM SHAKESPEARE

Hamlet, Act III, Scene 1

Suicide ranks today as the second or third leading cause of death among adolescents in virtually every industrialized nation of the world. In the United States the teenage suicide rate has tripled over the past thirty years. Suicide currently accounts for more than five thousand deaths—or nearly 20 percent of all deaths each year—among Americans between the ages of 15 and 24 (Strother, 1986). Unreported suicides would push the figures much higher. Since a stigma is often attached to suicide in Western countries, medical personnel frequently report a suicidal death as an accident or as a death from natural causes.

Government statistics reveal that about 10 percent of adolescent boys and 20 percent of adolescent girls have attempted suicide (Leary, 1990). Although more females attempt suicide, completed suicides are higher among males (see Figure 14-2). Males typically use active methods—shooting or hanging—while females commonly use passive methods—taking poisons or drugs (Farberow & Shneidman, 1961; Strother, 1986). Note that individuals differ in the seriousness of their suicidal attempts. Erwin Stengel (1964, p. 71), a psychiatrist, observes:

It is generally believed that most if not all people who commit suicidal acts are clearly determined to die. The study of attempted suicides does not bear this out. Many suicidal attempts and quite a few suicides are carried out in the mood "I don't care whether I live or die," rather than with a clear and unambiguous determination to end life. A person who denies, after what seems an obvious suicidal attempt, that he *really* wanted to kill himself, may be

telling the truth. Most people, in committing a suicidal act, are just as muddled as they are whenever they do anything of importance under emotional stress. Carefully planned suicidal acts are as rare as carefully planned acts of homicide. Many are carried out on sudden impulse, although suicidal thoughts were usually present before.

In many cases psychological depression underlies suicide and suicidal attempts (McCall, 1991; Pfeffer, 1986; Robertson & Simons, 1989). Depression is usually characterized by prolonged feelings of gloom, despair, and futility, profound pessimism, and a tendency toward excessive guilt and self-reproach. Other common symptoms include fatigue, insomnia, poor concentration, irritability, anxiety, reduced sexual interest, and

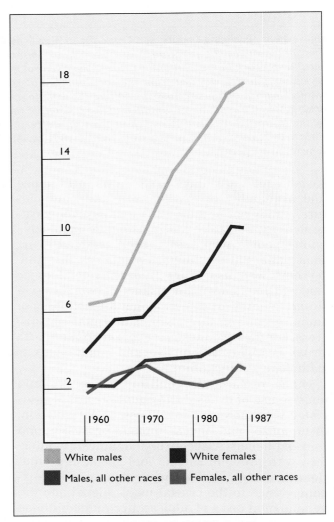

Figure 14-2   Suicide Rate per 100,000 Youth, Ages 15–19
SOURCE: Newsweek Special Issue, Summer 1990, p. 15. U.S. Department of Health and Human Services.

Suicide Warning Signals Among Adolescents

Teachers and other school personnel are often in a unique position to notice behavior changes that may indicate that an adolescent is at high risk for suicide. Such changes include the following:

❑ A dramatic decline in the quality of schoolwork.
❑ Social behavior changes, including excessive use of drugs or alcohol.
❑ Changes in daily behavior and living patterns, including extreme fatigue, boredom, decreased appetite, preoccupation, or inability to concentrate.
❑ Open signs of mental illness, including hallucinations or delusions.
❑ Giving away prized possessions.
❑ Any type of serious sleep disturbance—nightmares, difficulty in falling asleep, or early morning awakening.
❑ A preoccupation with thoughts and signs of death, which may be expressed in statements such as these:

"Oh, I don't care. I won't be around anyway to find out what happens!"; "I would like to sleep forever and never wake up!"; "Sometimes I would just like to take a gun and blow off my head . . . but I'm only joking!"; or "How many aspirin does it take to kill yourself?"

We should trust in our own judgment and our own subjective feelings in assessing a potentially suicidal person. If we believe that someone is in danger of suicide, we should act on our belief. We would be well advised not to let others mislead us into ignoring suicidal signals.

The troubled adolescent should be put in touch with an appropriate agency or specialist. One program that has come into existence in recent years is the *crisis hot line*. Hot lines are staffed by volunteers who have been screened and trained to respond in an appropriate fashion. Their job is to listen, to buy time, and to refer callers to counselors.

overall loss of interest and boredom. At times, depression appears in the guise of other disorders—for instance, vague pains, headaches, or recurrent nausea. The rate of depression for adolescent girls is twice that of boys, with a prime factor being the preoccupation many teenage girls have with their appearance. The U.S. Office of Education has named depression as a major cause of students' dropping out of college.

Medical authorities do not agree on what causes depression. Some trace their patients' feelings of helplessness and despair to emotionally difficult life circumstances and stresses (Seligman, 1975). Others believe that both depression and suicide are rooted in the malfunction of the chemistry of the brain, particularly in the levels of serotonin (Brown, Ebert & Goyer, 1982; Gold, Goodwin & Chrousos, 1988; Stanley, Virgilio & Gershon, 1982). Still others attribute depression to some combination of biochemical factors and psychological feelings of worthlessness (Beck, 1967, 1976; Willner, 1985). Increasing evidence suggests that all three views may be correct. Apparently, depression is not a single illness but an illness of various kinds, just as there are different kinds of pneumonia (Holden, 1986; Scarf, 1977). Although the symptoms may be similar, the causes of depression may differ among different individuals.

After studying the life histories of fifty adolescents who attempted suicide, Jerry Jacobs (1971) concluded that they typically became increasingly cut off from sympathetic, warm, and secure contacts and ties with others. In the course of this progressive isolation they tended to pass through the following phases (1971, p. 64):

1. A long-standing history of problems (from childhood to the onset of adolescence).
2. A period of "escalation of problems" (since the onset of adolescence and in excess of those "normally" associated with adolescence).
3. The progressive failure of available adaptive techniques for coping with old and increasing new problems which leads the adolescent to a progressive social isolation from meaningful social relationships.
4. The final phase, characterized by the chain reaction dissolution of any remaining meaningful social relationships in the weeks and days preceding the suicide attempt.

See the boxed insert above for a discussion of suicide warning signals among adolescents.

Researchers find that risk factors for suicide among young people include a family history of alcohol and drug abuse; family breakdown; an absence of biological parents; parental unemployment; a history of behavioral problems, delinquency, and school truancy; and symptoms of depression (Cohen-Sandler, Berman & King, 1982; Garfinkel, Froese & Hood, 1982; Robertson & Simons, 1989; Shafii, Carrigan, Whittinghill & Derrick, 1985). Estimates suggest that drug-using teenagers are at least three times more likely to attempt suicide than are drug-free adolescents. Impulsivity seems to be a major element in many teenage suicides (Newcomb & Bentler, 1988, 1989). Breakup of a relationship is the number-one traumatic event triggering suicide for both sexes. Perhaps factors involving shame, guilt, and humiliation are especially difficult for immature egos to handle (Holden, 1986). Even so, completed suicide does not occur on the spur of the moment or as the impulsive act of an otherwise healthy teenager; emotional disorders are often present (Pfeffer, 1986; Shafii, Carrigan, Whittinghill & Derrick, 1985). New research is also focusing on "suicide clusters," in which young people apparently follow the examples of peers in their school who take their own lives (Head, 1984; Strother, 1986).

Treatment of adolescents with suicidal tendencies usually involves psychotherapy. The therapist seeks to help the teenager come to terms with his or her problems and acquire more effective techniques for coping with life and stressful circumstances. The therapist also attempts to foster self-understanding, a sense of inner strength, self-confidence, and a positive self-image. In more severe cases the patient may also be placed on antidepressant medication. Dramatic progress has been made in recent years in the treatment of depression with such medications as Elavil, Tofranil, and Prozac (Shuchman & Wilkes, 1990).

Juvenile Delinquency

Youthful "deviance" has been a common problem reported by societies throughout human history. The United States is no exception. Young men aged 15 to 29 are responsible for a significant proportion of the nation's crime (seven-eighths of all people arrested in the 1980s were men, and one-third of them were 18 to 24 years old). Men of this age group are also involved disproportionately with the criminal justice system. For instance, in California, young men between the ages of 20 and 29 represent 45 percent of those in prison, on parole, or on probation, although they constitute only 8 percent of the

state's overall population. A particularly troubling statistic is the rise in murder rates. After dipping between 1980 and 1985, the nation's murder rates have again mounted, fueled in large measure by growing numbers of adolescent and young adult males dealing in cocaine, carrying assault weapons, and taking a more casual attitude about human life (Kelley, 1990; Minerbrook, 1990; Wolff, 1990). Between 1984 and 1988 alone, there was a tenfold increase in juvenile arrests for dealing in hard drugs (Meddis, 1989). Homicide now is the leading killer of black males aged 15 to 24 and the second leading cause for whites after auto accidents. Each day more than 100,000 U.S. juveniles are held in custody in juvenile institutions and adult prisons (Diesenhouse, 1990).

In recent years youth 18 years of age and under have accounted for about 20 percent of all violent-crime arrests in the United States, 44 percent of all serious property arrests, and 39 percent of overall serious-crime arrests. Chronic youthful offenders commit many more crimes than do chronic adult offenders—an average of thirty-six per year for juveniles and twelve a year for adults. Childhood antisocial behavior—juvenile delinquency, conduct disorder, and violent temper tantrums—is linked to a wide variety of troublesome adult behaviors, including criminal careers, general deviance, economic dependency, educational failure, employment instability, and marital discord (Sampson & Laub, 1990; Wolfgang, Thornberry & Figlio, 1987). Even so, many juvenile delinquents later become law-abiding citizens. Apparently, they change not from fear of being arrested but because they realize that what was "fun" as a teenager is no longer appropriate behavior for an adult (Shannon, 1982; Steffensmeier, Allan, Harer & Streifel, 1989).

According to statistics of the Justice Department, teenagers are twice as likely as adults to be the victims of crime. A recent survey found that youth 12 to 19 years of age were the victims of about 1.8 million violent crimes and 3.7 million thefts a year. About one-third of all violent crimes against younger teenagers and 83 percent of the thefts occur at school. Older teenagers are victims of 14 percent of violent crimes and 42 percent of the thefts at school (*New York Times*, December 28, 1986, p. 13). In addition, between 500,000 and 1 million teenagers run away from home each year. Surveys of homeless youth in shelters reveal that more than 60 percent of them report being physically or sexually abused by parents or other family members (Barden, 1990). Typically the runaways then must live on the street, a world filled with drug addicts, muggers, pimps, prostitutes, and pushers.

High School Dropouts

Estimates place the dropout rate among high-school students in the United States at about 23 percent. However, the proportion is higher among the poor and minorities (24 percent for blacks and 44 percent for Hispanics). And in some big-city school systems like Chicago and St. Louis, 52 percent of the young people do not graduate from high school. Many later regret leaving school (Boyer, 1987a, 1987b; National Center for Education Statistics, 1983).

Because of the technological orientation and requirements of contemporary society, young people who do not complete high school or who fail to acquire basic reading, writing, and mathematical skills find themselves at a serious disadvantage in the job market. Whereas in 1950, 34 percent of all jobs were open to workers without a high school diploma, by 1970 only 9 percent were open, and today the rate is even lower. Consequently, there are fewer jobs for high school dropouts. Many dropouts spend their time visiting and loafing, and some engage in a wide range of problem behaviors, including the use of hard drugs, drinking, smoking, physical aggression, theft, and drug dealing (Anderson, 1990; Biddle, Bank & Anderson, 1981; Williams, 1989). Those who fail to move into stable employment by age 20 find it increasingly difficult to make the transition to an adult life of gainful employment (Finn, 1987; Osterman, 1980).

School difficulties, both educational and social, are prominent in the history of most dropouts. Lucius Cervantes (1965) has made a comparative study of high school graduates and dropouts. He found that dropouts tended to share a number of characteristics: Many had failed at least one grade; by seventh grade they were two years behind their classmates in reading and arithmetic; their attendance record was poor; often they were "underachievers"; they had changed schools frequently; many had behavior problems or were troubled emotionally; and they tended to resent authority. Usually, students who are most vulnerable to early school termination can be identified by the seventh grade. Boys and girls who are at high risk for dropping out reveal high

levels of aggressive behavior and low levels of academic performance. And they are more likely to come from families in which they have to make decisions on their own and in which their parents evidence little interest in their education. Overall, research reveals that academic difficulties become cumulative, showing a gradual rise over the elementary school years and reaching a high point in the ninth and tenth grades (Cairns, Cairns & Neckerman, 1989; Fitzsimmons, Cheever, Leonard & Macunovich, 1969; Rumberger, Ghatak, Poulos, Ritter & Dornbusch, 1990; Velez, 1989). Some 24 percent of high school dropouts leave school in their sophomore year; 47 percent in their junior year; and 29 percent in their senior year (National Center for Education Statistics, 1983).

Not surprisingly, students who have difficulties with academic work and who view their assignments as incomprehensible and not germane typically find school frustrating and disheartening. Moreover, many adolescents fail to see any "payoff" associated with school attendance and continued effort. Many young people, especially those in the nation's big-city ghettos, regard the school experience as irrelevant to their personal, social, and vocational needs.

For the most part, school authorities, police officials, and the public have argued that young people should be retained in school at least until they complete high school. The idea is that school will keep adolescents out of mischief while simultaneously providing them with the skills necessary for gainful employment. Research over the past quarter century, however, is questioning this line of reasoning (Bachman, O'Malley & Johnston, 1978; Elliott, 1966; Finn, 1987; Kelly, 1971; Toby, 1989). Although it is indisputable that high school dropouts have a higher delinquency rate and poorer self-image than students who stay in school, their having dropped out does not appear to aggravate these difficulties (Rosenberg, Schooler & Schoenbach, 1989).

Indeed, these adolescents' scores on self-esteem tests improve somewhat after they drop out (Bachman, O'Malley & Johnston, 1978). And sociological evidence suggests that dropouts commit fewer offenses after leaving school than in a comparable period before they dropped out (Elliot, 1966; Toby, 1987). Seemingly, the boy or girl who drops out is no longer involved in unequal competition at school and escapes the frustration of continual failure. Simply because young people are in a building that looks and smells like a school does not mean they are receiving an education. They may be learning little, except how to survive as internal dropouts instead of external ones. In sum, dropping out of school is more likely to reflect an adolescent's problems than to be a cause of them.

Summary

1. Western industrial nations have prolonged the transition from childhood to adulthood and segregated the young from the rest of society and its activities. This segregation has given rise to a kind of institutionalized adolescence or youth culture.
2. The most obvious features of the youth culture revolve about various peer-group trademarks: preferred recordings, dance steps, and entertainment idols; approved personal adornment; and distinctive jargon and slang. It is also embodied in conceptions of qualities and performances that are thought to reveal an individual's masculinity or femininity.
3. The notion of the generation gap oversimplifies the relationship between youth and adults. Both the family and the peer group are anchors in the lives of most teenagers.
4. One of the most difficult adjustments, and perhaps the most critical, that adolescents must make revolves about their developing sexuality. In the United States, dating has been the principal vehicle for fostering and developing heterosexual relations. Over the past twenty years dating has undergone rapid change.
5. In the United States notions concerning romantic love play an important part in our spouse selection and in our conceptions of married life. However, societies throughout the world view romantic love quite differently.
6. In the twentieth century there have been two periods of very rapid change in sexual attitudes and behavior. The first period occurred around the time of World War I; the second, during the Vietnam War years.
7. Recent changes in patterns of sexual behavior among many young people do not amount to a breakdown in morality. Rather, they mean that the young have modified the codes of moral behavior. Many adolescents have come to judge the acceptability of sexual behavior in terms of the degree of a couple's emotional involvement.
8. A critical developmental task confronting adolescents is that of deciding on a vocation. Yet adolescents usually have only vague ideas about the working world. And those who do work typically get less out of the experience than proponents of youth job programs have hoped.
9. Many young people have great difficulty with adolescence. Among the problems some of them face are those associated with drug abuse, suicide, delinquency, disinterest in and dropping out of school, and high levels of unemployment.

Key Terms

Consciousness of Oneness A sympathetic identification in which group members come to feel that their inner experiences and emotional reactions are similar.

Drug Abuse The excessive or compulsive use of chemical agents to an extent that interferes with people's health, their social or vocational functioning, or the functioning of the rest of society.

Generation Gap The existence of mutual antagonism, misunderstanding, and separation between young people and adults.

Youth Culture More or less standardized ways of thinking, feeling, and acting that are characteristic of a large body of young people.

Part Seven

Early Adulthood

Chapter 15

EARLY ADULTHOOD: PERSPECTIVES AND DEVELOPMENT

Developmental Perspectives

Demographic Aspects of Adulthood ♦ Conceptions of Age Periods ♦ Age Norms and the Social Clock ♦ Age-Grade Systems ♦ Life Events

The Search for Periods in Adult Development

Erikson: Psychosocial Stages ♦ Levinson: Phases in Adult Male Development ♦ Phases in Adult Female Development ♦ The Stage Approach Controversy

Physical Changes and Health

Physical Performance ♦ Physical Health ♦ Mental Health

Cognitive Development

Post-Formal Operations? ♦ Thought and Information Processing ♦ Moral Reasoning

♦

When we truly comprehend and enter into the rhythm of life, we shall be able to bring together the daring of youth with the discipline of age in a way that does justice to both.—J. S. BIXLER

Two Blessings of Joseph

The term "adulthood" generally lacks the concreteness of "infancy," "childhood," and "adolescence." Even in the scientific literature it has functioned as a kind of catchall category for everything that happens to individuals after they "grow up." Sigmund Freud, for instance, viewed adult life as merely a ripple on the surface of an already set personality structure; Jean Piaget assumed that no additional cognitive changes occur after adolescence; and Lawrence Kohlberg saw moral development as reaching a lifetime plateau after early adulthood.

Following the earlier lead of psychologists like Erik Erikson (1963, 1968a), Charlotte Bühler (Bühler & Massarik, 1968), Carl G. Jung (1933), Sidney L. Pressey (Pressey & Kuhlen, 1957), and others, the scientific community has come to recognize that adulthood is not a single monolithic stage—an undifferentiated phase of life between adolescence and old age (Neugarten & Neugarten, 1987). Scientists increasingly see the individual as undergoing change across the entire life span. The notion that adulthood is a state of *being*—a sort of mopping-up operation—is being replaced by a view of adulthood as a process of *becoming* (Baltes & Willis, 1977; Eichorn, Clausen, Haan, Honzik & Mussen, 1982; Lerner & Busch-Rossnagel, 1981). Thus, adulthood is coming to be seen not as a plodding passage across a plateau but as an adventure that involves negotiating ups and downs and changing direction to surmount obstacles.

Developmental Perspectives

In the United States the beginning of adulthood is most often defined as the point at which a person leaves school, takes a full-time job, or gets married. However, becoming an adult is a rather different matter for different segments of the society. And adulthood itself has different meanings for different age groups within the population. Since adulthood is not one experience but many experiences, people's conceptions of adulthood frequently differ.

Demographic Aspects of Adulthood

People's feelings, attitudes, and beliefs about adulthood are influenced by the relative proportion of individuals who are adults. In the United States major population changes are under way that will have important social consequences. By 1990, the typical American was 32.5 years of age (up from 30 years in 1980 and 27.9 years in 1970). The baby-boom generation—those born between 1946 and 1961—represents a huge "age lump" passing through the population—a sort of demographic tidal wave. This age cohort—more than 79 million Americans—was responsible for the 70 percent jump in the number of school-age children between 1950 and 1970. The bumper crop of baby-boomers were 32 to 47 years old in 1993 and constituted about a third of the U.S. population.

In the 1950s the baby-boomers made the United States a child-oriented society of new schools, suburbs, and station wagons. The baby-boomers born before 1955 provided the nation with Davy Crockett and rock 'n' roll, went to Woodstock and Vietnam, and fueled the student, civil rights, and peace movements of the 1960s and early 1970s. Later, as the baby-boomers made their way into middle age, the contemplation—even celebration—of the middle years found expression in popular culture. It is hardly a coincidence that two family sitcoms, "The Cosby Show" and "Family Ties," dominated the TV ratings in the 1980s. By contrast, "The Mary Tyler Moore Show" of the 1970s, focusing on single life and work, played to what was then a younger audience.

The baby-boomers have brought about a rapid expansion of the nation's labor force. In the early 1970s there were about 52 million Americans between 20 and 39 years of age (25.8 percent of the population). By 1980 the number had risen to 72.4 million (32 percent of the population) (see Figure 15-1). As the boomers have moved into their middle years, they have become more productive (often having acquired additional skills), and they earn more money and save more money—all of which will likely give a competitive life to the United States in world economic arenas in the 1990s (Jones, 1990). Other economic consequences also have followed. When the boomers were in their twenties, they wanted small rental apartments and pint-sized condominiums. But as they have entered their forties, they have preferred single-family residences and three-bedroom city apartments (Vander Zanden, 1990).

Many of the schools built to accommodate the boomers in the 1960s are now closed or half empty, and colleges are scrambling to keep enrollments up. The college-age population (individuals aged 18 to 24) peaked in 1981 at 30 million Americans. By 1995, only 24 million Ameri-

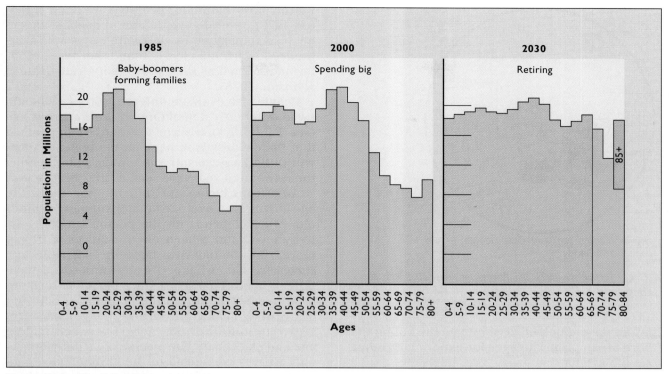

Figure 15-1   The Baby-Boom Generation
Baby-boomers should be a formidable force in U.S. life well into the twenty-first century. SOURCE: *Fortune,* © 1987 Time, Inc. All rights reserved. Based on data from the Census Bureau.

cans will be 18 to 24 years old, a 22 percent decline from 1981. Colleges are turning to adult education in hopes of maintaining enrollments. The armed forces will also experience recruiting difficulties as the young adult population declines. To maintain current annual requirements, the military will have to recruit 55 percent of all qualified and available 18-year-olds in 1995. They now recruit about 42 percent. Along with colleges and the armed forces, businesses that rely on young, low-wage workers, such as the food service and tourism industries, will feel the impact of labor shortages. Already fast-food chains are recruiting older Americans to staff the grills and cash registers (Vander Zanden, 1990).

As we noted in our discussion of generations in Chapter 13, each new generation of Americans enters adulthood with its own unique experiences and hence its own expectations for family life, work, and material well-being. Today's young adults were born in the late 1960s and early 1970s. They grew up during a period when adults were redefining the rules of work, marriage, family, and material success. As they now come of age they are bringing a more materialistic version of the American Dream to their lives. Although marriage and family remain important to young people who graduated from high

school in 1986, they are more likely than their earlier baby-boom counterparts to see money as the most important reason to work. And their life goals are relatively less family-oriented (Crimmins, Easterlin & Saito, 1991). We will have more to say on these matters in this and the following chapter.

Conceptions of Age Periods

Historical evidence suggests that age distinctions were more blurred and chronological age played a less important role in the organization of U.S. society prior to 1850 than they do today (Chudacoff, 1989). It seems that age consciousness has grown over the past 140 years in response to developments in education, psychology, and medicine. The public school system imposed strict age grading in the classroom. Psychological theories of development afforded a rationale for age legislation regarding child labor, school attendance, and pension benefits. And in medicine, pediatrics emerged as a specialty whereas old age became identified as a period of senescene and senility. Popular culture, as expressed in fiction, song lyrics, birthday celebrations, and advice columns of popular magazines,

"Senior citizens are very OLD people — like Mommy and Daddy."

("Family Circus" © 1991 Bill Keane, Inc. Reprinted with special permission of King Features Syndicate.)

picked up and helped disseminate the notion that there are appropriate ages for experiencing various life events.

For the most part, Americans perceive adults of all ages in a favorable fashion. Nevertheless, older adults are viewed less favorably and as less desirable to be around than younger adults. Such attitudes are influenced by a variety of factors. Adults who have had more formal education and more experience with a range of older adults have more positive attitudes toward older people than is true of the population generally. Adults who encounter burdens or conflicts associated with the elderly have more negative attitudes toward them (Knox, 1977).

College students, for instance, tend to evaluate older people more negatively than they do younger people. They see young people as more adaptable, more capable of pursuing goals, and more active than older people (O'Connell & Rotter, 1979). Overall, age, in and of itself, seems to be less important in determining people's attitudes toward the elderly than other types of information such as their personality traits (Kite & Johnson, 1988).

People also evaluate different stages of the life cycle differently depending on their current age (see Table 15-1). It surprises many young people that their elders look back on the teenage years with little enthusiasm. And among older people, the retirement years are seen as the "best years."

Americans have some difficulty specifying the age at which an average man or woman becomes old. Much depends on the person's health, activity level, and related circumstances. Furthermore, the boundaries between adjacent age stages are somewhat permeable. Americans have little difficulty characterizing a person as a young or an elderly adult. But the boundaries between adjacent age categories are vague. For instance, regarding the transition period between middle age and elderliness, the placing of an individual is only weakly connected to the chronological age of the person being judged (Kogan, 1979). Even so, older adults hold more elaborate conceptions about development (its richness and differentiation) throughout the adult years than do younger adults (Heckhausen, Dixon & Baltes, 1989).

A person's gender likewise makes a difference. Women are viewed as aging more quickly than men do. But this tendency to assign women to older categories than comparably aged men becomes less pronounced when categorizing the elderly. And women are less inclined than men to employ a "double standard of aging" (Kogan, 1979; O'Connell & Rotter, 1979).

According to surveys of adult Americans, two-thirds perceive themselves as being younger than they actually are, though those under 30 years of

Table 15-1

What Are the Best Years?

The table shows the responses of people in different age groups to the question: People feel differently about what years are the best time of a person's life. Which of these do you think are the best time of life?

By Age:	Childhood	Teenage Years	The Twenties	The Thirties	The Forties	The Fifties	Retirement Years
18–29 years	22%	29%	42%	9%	4%	1%	3%
30–44 years	22%	21%	28%	31%	13%	4%	5%
45–59 years	17%	16%	24%	22%	20%	13%	8%
69 years and over	14%	14%	19%	20%	16%	11%	31%

Note: Multiple responses per respondent. Don't know/no answer (not shown) ranged from 4–8%.
Source: Survey by the Roper Organization (Roper Report 84-4), March 17-24, 1984, in Public Opinion, *February/March 1985, p. 33. Reprinted with permission of the Roper Organization, Inc., and American Enterprise Institute for Public Policy Research.*

age often perceive themselves as being older than they actually are (Montepare & Lachman, 1989; Nemy, 1982). It seems that younger people desire to be grown up and to disassociate themselves from potential social stigmas and disadvantages attached to being "too young." Once individuals reach middle age, however, they think of themselves as from 5 to 15 years younger. Indeed, people frequently say that they feel between 30 and 35 years old, regardless of their actual age. The thirties seem to have eternal appeal.

Overall, men say they feel about six years younger and women seven years younger than in fact they are. The peak period for feeling younger is the decade between 40 and 49 years of age. The feeling then trails off during the fifties, tapering off more rapidly for women than for men. Like those under 30, those over 60 perceive themselves as being older than they are, but to a lesser degree. These findings have proven of interest to those concerned with marketing products. They help to explain the failure of "special food for seniors" and the even more dismal failure of a shampoo aimed at "hair over forty." Indeed, in overall terms, adults expect their gains greatly to outnumber their losses throughout most of adulthood (Heckhausen, Dixon & Baltes, 1989). In addition, consistent with the notion that "You're only as old as you feel," self-conceptions of age seem to be better predictors of aging people's mental and physical functioning than is their chronological age (Montepare & Lachman, 1989).

Age Norms and the Social Clock

We commonly associate adulthood with **aging**— biological and social change across the life span. **Biological aging** refers to changes in the structure and functioning of the human organism through time. **Social aging** refers to changes in an individual's assumption and relinquishment of roles through time. People pass through a socially regulated cycle from birth to death just as surely as they pass through the biological cycle. So the life course of individuals is punctuated by transition points—the relinquishment of familiar roles and the assumption of new ones.

Age, as reckoned by society, is a set of behavioral expectations associated with given points in the life span. Much social behavior is prescribed for us in terms of dos and don'ts. Conformity with these expectations generally has favorable results; violation, unpleasant ones. Such dos and don'ts are termed **social norms**—standards of behavior that mem-

bers of a group share and to which they are expected to conform. Social norms are enforced by positive and negative sanctions.

Social norms define what is appropriate for people to be and to do at various ages—what are termed **age norms.** A societal "Big Ben" (the age norms) tends to define the "best age" for a man or woman to marry, to finish school, to settle on a career, to hold a top job, to become a grandparent, and to be ready to retire. Individuals tend to set their personal "watches" (their internalized age norms) by society's Big Ben (Kimmel, 1980). Age norms are most obvious when they are embodied in *formal* rules or explicit policies about a role. Examples are compulsory school attendance laws, the minimum voting age in election laws, the age at which youth may purchase alcoholic beverages, and the age at which individuals become eligible for Social Security benefits.

Age norms may also represent *informal* expectations about the kinds of roles appropriate for people

Age Stereotypes Do Not Necessarily Fit People's Self-Perceptions
Surveys reveal that the vast majority of adult Americans see themselves as being younger than they actually are. So they often do not feel inhibited when engaging in behaviors that run counter to age-related stereotypes. *(Rocky Weldon/Jeroboam)*

of various ages. At times, such expectations are only vague notions about who is "too old," "too young," or "the right age" for certain activities. The appeal "Act your age!" pervades a great many aspects of life. Variations on this theme are often heard in such remarks as, "She's too young to wear that style of clothing" and "That's a strange thing for a man of his age to say."

Age grading at the social level, the arranging of people in social layers that are based on periods in the life cycle, creates a **social clock**—a set of internalized concepts that regulate our progression through the age-related milestones of the adult years. The social clock sets the standards that individuals use in assessing their conformity to age-appropriate expectations. Adult men and women readily tell an interviewer what they believe to be the best age to marry, to have children, to become grandparents, to be settled in one's career, to have reached the top, and to retire (see Table 15-2). Likewise, people describe what personality characteristics ought to be salient in particular age periods; for example, they think it appropriate to be impulsive in adolescence but not in middle age.

And they readily report whether they themselves are "early," "late," or "on time" with regard to family and occupational events. Such an internal sense of social timing can act as a "prod" to speed up accomplishment of a goal or as a "brake" to slow down passage through age-related roles.

Any period of transition or crisis in life can initiate a life review process and an assessment of where one stands with respect to age-related milestones (Bourque & Back, 1977). Exposure to death has the power to do this at all ages, even when one is not of an age when one's own death is imminent. Serious illness—one's own or that of another—may also have such an impact.

Although the members of a society tend to share similar expectations about their life cycle, some variations do occur. Social class is one important factor. The lower the social class, the more rapid the pacing of the social clock tends to be. The higher the social class, the later the individual generally leaves school, acquires his or her first job, gets married, begins parenthood, secures his or her top job, and begins grandparenthood (Neugarten, 1968a). And new gener-

Table 15-2

Notions of the "Right Time"

Two surveys asked Americans 20 years apart (late 1950s and late 1970s) what's the right age for various major events and achievements of adult life. A dramatic decline occurred in the consensus among middle-class, middle-aged people.

Activity/Event	Appropriate Age Range	Late 1950s Study (% Who Agree) Men	Late 1950s Study (% Who Agree) Women	Late 1970s Study (% Who Agree) Men	Late 1970s Study (% Who Agree) Women
Best age for a man to marry	20–25	80%	90%	42%	42%
Best age for a woman to marry	19–24	85	90	44	36
When most people should become grandparents	45–50	84	79	64	57
Best age for most people to finish school and go to work	20–22	86	82	36	38
When most men should be settled on a career	24–26	74	64	24	26
When most men hold their top jobs	45–50	71	58	38	31
When most people should be ready to retire	60–65	83	86	66	41
When a man has the most responsibilities	35–50	79	75	49	50
When a man accomplishes most	40–50	82	71	46	41
The prime of life for a man	35–50	86	80	59	66
When a woman has the most responsibilities	25–40	93	91	59	53
When a woman accomplishes most	30–45	94	92	57	48

Source: Adapted from "Age Norms and Age Constraints Twenty Years Later," P. Passuth, D. Maines, and B. L. Neugarten. Paper presented at the Midwest Sociological Society meeting, Chicago, April 1984, as appeared in Psychology Today, *May 1987.*

Have You Set an Inner "Social Clock"?
Do you have notions concerning the "best age" to graduate from college, settle on a career, marry, have children, and hold a "good job"? If so, are you "on time"? If you are "off time," how do you feel about it? Have your feelings affected your behavior? *(Spencer Grant/Monkmeyer)*

ations may reset the social clock. For instance, young women currently prefer earlier ages for educational and occupational events and later ages for family events than did earlier generations (Ryff, 1985).

Bernice L. Neugarten (1987) believes that the distinctions between life periods are blurring in U.S. life. She notes the appearance of the "young-old" category: retirees and their spouses who are healthy and vigorous, relatively well-off financially, and well integrated within community life. A young-old person may be 55 or 85. The line between middle age and old age is no longer clear. What was once considered old now characterizes a minority of elderly people—the "old-old," a particularly vulnerable group who often are in need of special support and care. Neugarten observes that increasingly we have

conflicting images rather than firm stereotypes of age: the 18-year-old who is married and supporting a family, but also the 18-year-old college student who still lives at home; and the 70-year-old in a wheelchair, but also the 70-year-old on the tennis court. A more fluid life cycle affords new freedoms for many people. But even though some timetables may be losing their significance, others are becoming more compelling. Young adults may feel themselves failures if they have not "made it" in a corporation or law office by the time they are 35. And a young woman may delay marriage in the interests of a career but then hurry to catch up with parenthood even though she may expect to live to 85.

Age-Grade Systems

In a number of African societies, age norms are embodied in an age-grade system (Foner & Kertzer, 1978). Members of each grade are alike in chronological age or life stage and have certain roles that are age-specific. For instance, the Latuka of Sudan distinguish among five age grades: children, youths, rulers of the village, retired elders, and the very old. In such societies the individuals of each age grade are viewed as a corporate body and move as a unit from one age grade to another. For example, among the African Tiriki uninitiated boys may not engage in sexual intercourse, they must eat with other children and with women, and they are permitted to play in the women's section of the hut. After initiation they may engage in sexual intercourse, are expected to eat with other men, and are forbidden to enter the women's section of the hut.

Furthermore, age grades differ in the access they afford their members to highly rewarded economic and political roles. In Western societies, in contrast, people's chronological age is but a partial clue to their social locations. Class and ethnic factors cut across lines of age stratification and provide additional sources of identity.

On the surface, societies with age-grade systems seem to provide an orderly method for role allocation and reallocation. But in practice, the transition process is often less than orderly. Conflicts frequently arise between age grades, essentially a version of the time-honored struggle between the "ins" and the "outs." The desire of people to gain access to or hold on to various privileges and rewards fuels social discord and individual grievances. The rules governing transition may not be clear. Even when they seem to be unambiguous, the rules are always open to different interpretations and to "bending" in one or another group's favor. The continuing debate in the United States over Social Security funding and benefits reflects this type of tugging between the young and the elderly.

All societies are faced with the fact that aging is inevitable and continuous. Hence, they all must make provision for the perpetual flow of one cohort after another by fitting each age group into an appropriate array of social roles. Societies with age-grade systems attempt to achieve the transition by establishing points in the life course for entering roles and leaving them. Another solution, more closely approximated in Western societies, is to allow "natural" forces to operate: Younger people assume adult roles when they are ready to do so, while older people give up roles when they are ready to do so or when they become ill or die.

In the United States no collective rituals mark the passage from one age grade to another. High school and college graduation ceremonies are an exception, but even here not all individuals in a cohort graduate from either high school or college. And there is some flexibility in the operation of the age system in that gifted children skip grades in elementary school and bright youths are allowed to enter college after only two or three years of high school. At the older age levels, too, flexibility often operates—within some companies and some occupations—with regard to retirement (for instance, one can retire from the military after 20 years of service). Nevertheless, age norms serve as a counterpart of the age-grade system in broadly defining what is appropriate for people to be and to do at various ages.

Life Events

People locate themselves across the life span in terms of social timetables. They also do so in terms of **life events**—turning points at which individuals change direction in the course of their lives. Some life events are related to social clocks, including entering school, graduating from school, and starting to work. But others may take place under circumstances that are largely independent of age, including losing a limb in an automobile accident, being raped, winning a lottery, undergoing a "born again" conversion, or living at the time Pearl Harbor was attacked. The boxed insert discusses being raped as a life event. We often employ major events as reference points or time markers in our lives, speaking of

Life Events

Leaving home for college is a major life event that individuals often use as a "bench mark" in their lives. *(Dratch/The Image Works)*

"the time I left home for school," "the day I had my heart attack," and "when I started going with Chris." Such life events define transitions.

Life events may be examined in a great many ways (Brim, 1980; Elder, 1986; Headey & Wearing, 1989; Hultsch & Plemmons, 1979; Robins & Block, 1988). For instance, some are associated with internal growth or aging factors like puberty or old age. Others, including wars, national economic crises, and revolutions, are the consequences of living in society. And still others derive from events in the physical world such as fires, storms, tidal waves, earthquakes, or avalanches. And there are those events that have a strong inner or psychological component, including a profound religious experience, the realization that one has reached the zenith of one's career, or the decision to leave one's spouse. Any of these events we may view as good or bad, a gain or a loss, controllable or uncontrollable, and stressful or unstressful.

Rape as a Stressful Life Event

Rape is commonly defined as sexual relations obtained through physical force, threats, or intimidation (Bourque, 1989). About one in four women report that a man they were dating persisted in attempting to force sex on them despite their crying, pleading, screaming, or resistance (Celis, 1991; Goleman, 1989; Ward, Chapman, Cohn, White & Williams, 1991). In many respects, each rape and coping experience is unique (Kelly, 1988; Roberts, 1989). Yet there are common ingredients in what is typically perceived as a stressful life event. For instance, researchers find that victims show a significant increase in health-related problems in the year following the rape (Kilpatrick, Resick & Veronen, 1981; King & Webb, 1981). Moreover, the vast majority of rape victims blame themselves (Frazier, 1990). Controversy rages, however, as to whether self-blame is a healthy or unhealthy response.

According to one view, self-blame can be a highly adaptive strategy in the aftermath of a rape. Victims who blame themselves may cope successfully so long as they direct the blame at specific, controllable behaviors that they define to be "foolish" or "careless." The women can feel that if they change these behaviors they can avoid being raped in the future. In contrast, assigning blame to one's own personality or character is maladaptive because it does not provide women with the same sense of control (Janoff-Bulman, 1979; Janoff-Bulman & Lang-Gunn, 1988). According to another view, blaming oneself for negative events such as rape is associated with increased depression and malfunctioning. Most research supports the second view (Becker, Skinner, Abel, Howell & Bruce, 1982; Frazier, 1990; Katz & Burt, 1988; Meyer & Taylor, 1986; Rose, 1986).

Societal attention to the problems that surround rape is a recent phenomenon. It seems that behavior in which some people are victimized is accorded public concern only when the victims have enough power to demand attention. The current concern with rape has paralleled the emergence of the women's movement (Cann, Calhoun, Selby & King, 1981; Estrich, 1987). Yet rape myths abound in U.S. life. Psychologist Martha R. Burt (1980) found that over half of her representative sample of Minnesota residents agreed with such statements as "In the majority of rapes, the victim was promiscuous or had a bad reputation," and "A woman who goes to the home or apartment of a man on a first date implies she is willing to have sex." And studies of college males reveal that from 35 to 44 percent say they would personally rape a woman if they could be assured of not being caught and punished (Malamuth, 1981, 1983; Check & Malamuth, 1983). Such attitudes form part of a larger and interrelated ideology that includes acceptance of traditional sex-role stereotyping, interpersonal violence (particularly when directed against women), the sexual harassment on the job of women by male bosses and coworkers, and the view that sexual relationships are adversary relationships (Baron & Straus, 1989). The threat of rape affects women whether or not they are its actual victims (Gordon & Riger, 1989), limiting their freedom, keeping them off the streets at night, and at time imprisoning them in their homes. Women who carry the highest burden of fear are those with the fewest resources—the elderly, ethnic minorities, and those with low incomes.

Date rape is also a serious social problem. A recent three-year study of 6,200 male and female students on thirty-two campuses found that 15 percent of all women reported experiences that met legal definitions of forcible rape. More than half of the incidents were date rapes. Some 73 percent of the women forced into sex avoided using the term "rape" to describe their experiences, and only 5 percent reported the incident to authorities. Since acquaintance rape is such a paralyzing event, so outside the realm of normal events, women are left without a way of understanding it. Instead, they feel shame and guilt and attempt to bury the experience (Celis, 1991; Leo, 1987; Lewin, 1991). Rape is a stressful life event that may have unique meanings because of the extent to which other people blame victims of rape (Coates, Wortman & Abbey, 1979). Many campuses and rape crisis centers now sponsor speeches and programs directed at preventing date rape.

Often in thinking about a life event, we ask ourselves three questions: "Will it happen to me?"; "If so, when will it occur?"; and "If it happens, will others also experience it or will I be the only one?" The first question concerns the probability of an event's taking place, for instance, getting married or experiencing a serious football injury. If we believe that the probability of an event's occurring is low, we are unlikely to attend to or anticipate it in advance (for instance, most of us are more likely to give thought to and prepare for marriage than we are for a serious football injury). The second question involves an event's correlation with chronological age, for example, the death of one's spouse or the suffering of a heart attack. Age-relatedness matters because it influences whether or not we are caught unexpectedly by the event. The third question concerns the social distribution of an event, whether everyone will experience it or just one or a few persons. This question is important because it will largely determine whether people will organize social support systems to assist us in buffering the change.

The Search for Periods in Adult Development

Any number of psychologists have undertaken the search for what they view as the regular, sequential periods and transitions in the life cycle (see Chapter 2). Like childhood, they conceive of adult development as a succession of stages. They depict adulthood as a sort of stairway made up of a series of discrete, step-like levels. One of the most popular versions of the stage approach is contained in Gail Sheehy's best-selling book *Passages* (1976). She views each stage as posing problems that must be resolved before the individual can successfully advance to the next stage. By passing from one stage to the next—*passages*—each person acquires new strengths and evolves an *authentic identity*. Such an identity has many of the qualities that Abraham Maslow associates with the self-actualized person (see Chapter 2).

Other psychologists have taken exception to the stage approach. Some believe that an individual's identity is fairly well established during the formative years and does not fundamentally change much in adulthood. According to this view, people may change jobs, addresses, even faces, but the personality persists, much in the manner of adult height and weight, with only minor changes. Let us examine these matters more carefully.

Erikson: Psychosocial Stages

One of the most influential stage approaches has been that pioneered by Erik Erikson. Recall from our discussion in Chapter 2 that Erikson

Young Adulthood: Intimacy Versus Isolation
According to Erik Erikson, the major developmental task confronting young adults has to do with developing the capacity to reach out and establish close and intimate relationships with others. *(Paula M. Lerner/The Picture Cube)*

identified eight lifespan stages, three of which apply to adulthood: early adulthood, which involves intimacy versus isolation; middle adulthood, which involves generativity versus stagnation; and old age, which involves integrity versus despair.

The principal developmental task confronting young adults in the stage of intimacy versus isolation is one of reaching out and making contact with other people. They must cultivate the ability to enter and establish close and intimate relationships with others. Should they fail to accomplish this task, they confront the danger of leading shallow lives devoid of meaningful bonds.

In middle adulthood the task of generativity requires individuals to reach out beyond their own immediate concerns and assist younger people to realize their potentials. During this stage they assume responsibility for the generation that is to follow them. Should they instead become preoccupied with themselves, they confront stagnation and emptiness.

As individuals approach their later years, Erikson contends, they must finally come to terms with themselves and with the meaning of their lives. They take stock of themselves, looking back and reminiscing about what they have accomplished through the years. In doing so, they can experience a positive sense of achievement or a negative feeling of despair regarding their worth.

Erikson says that each stage of life confronts individuals with a unique crisis with which they must grapple. When successfully mastered, the crisis serves as a turning point that allows each person to reach a higher level of development and potential. Should the individual fail to come to terms with the critical developmental task of a stage, the rest of his or her development is impaired. The person has difficulty coming to terms with reality and finding happiness in life. (For example, unresolved identity issues carrying over from adolescence may persist into young adulthood, contributing to students temporarily dropping out of college—see the boxed insert on page 428).

The psychiatrist George E. Vaillant and his associates (Vaillant & Milofsky, 1980) found support for Erikson's formulations when they followed up a group of 392 white lower-class youth and 94 highly educated men who were first studied in the 1940s. They concluded, as Erikson contends, that the postchildhood stages of an individual's life cycle must be passed through sequentially. Failure to master one of Erikson's stages typically precluded mastery of later stages. However, the age at which the men mastered a given stage varied enormously. In fact, one man in six was still struggling in his forties with adolescent-type issues. When the researchers examined subsequent employment patterns, those men who typically showed the greatest childhood maturity were five times more likely to have ended up being well paid for their adult work than those men showing the least maturity. Furthermore, the most emotionally mature boys were sixteen times less likely to have experienced significant unemployment by the time they had reached their mid-forties.

Levinson: Phases in Adult Male Development

Whoever, in middle age, attempts to realize the wishes and hopes of his early youth, invariably deceives himself. Each ten years of a man's life has its own fortunes, its own hopes, its own desires.—GOETHE

Elective Affinities, 1809

A number of Yale researchers, led by psychologist Daniel J. Levinson (Levinson, Darrow, Klein, Levinson & McKee, 1978), have also approached adulthood from a stage perspective. They have constructed a descriptive framework for defining phases in the lifespan development of adult males. On the basis of their study of forty men in their mid-thirties to mid-forties (who represented blue- and white-collar workers in industry, business executives, academic biologists, and novelists), the Yale psychologists designate six periods ranging from the late teens or early twenties to the late forties. (They also speculate on the stages that may follow after the late forties, but these stages are not reviewed in this text because they are tentative and not grounded in the research.)

(Drawing by Crawford; © 1991 The New Yorker Magazine, Inc.)

Levinson and his associates say that the overriding task throughout adulthood is the creation of a structure for life. A man must periodically restructure his life by creating a new structure or reappraising an old one. He must formulate goals, work out means to achieve them, modify long-held assumptions, memories, and perceptions regarding himself and the world, and then initiate the appropriate goal-seeking behaviors. Transition periods tend to loom within two or three years of, and on either side of, the symbolically significant birthdays—20, 30, 40, 50, and 60.

The Yale researchers portray the man and his environment as interacting in such a manner as to move him developmentally through a series of new levels of life organization. The approach focuses on the underlying set of developmental tasks confronting men rather than on the timing of major life events. The levels, which are depicted in Figure 15-2, may be summarized as follows:

❑ *Leaving the Family.* The process begins in the individual's late teens or early twenties, when he leaves the family. This phase is a period of transition between his adolescent life, which was centered in the family, and his entry into the adult world. Young men may choose a transitional institution, such as the military or college, to start them on their way, or they may work while continuing to live at home. During this period a roughly equal balance exists between "being in" the family and "moving out." Getting across the boundary of the family represents the major developmental task. He must become less financially dependent, enter new roles and living arrangements, and achieve greater autonomy and self-responsibility. The period lasts about three to five years.

❑ *Getting into the Adult World.* This period begins with the shift in the center of gravity of a man's life away from his family of origin. Through adult friendships, sexual relationships, and work experiences, he arrives at an initial definition of himself as an adult. This definition allows him to fashion a temporary life structure that links him to the wider society. During this period men explore and tentatively begin committing themselves to adult

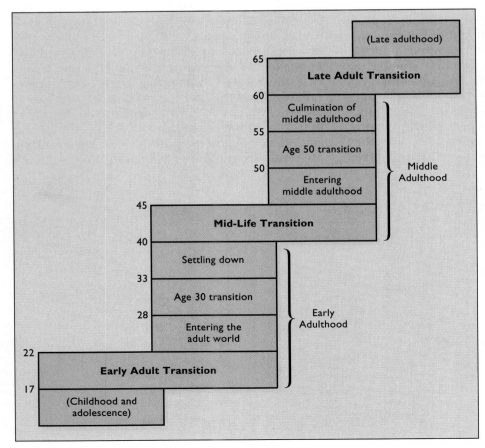

Figure 15-2 Periods in Adult Male Development
Daniel J. Levinson conceives of adult male development as characterized by a succession of periods. Each period requires the restructuring of critical aspects of a man's assumptions regarding himself and the world. SOURCE: *The Season of Man's Life* by Daniel J. Levinson. Copyright © 1978 by Daniel J. Levinson. Reprinted by permission of Alfred A. Knopf, Inc.

roles, responsibilities, and relationships that reflect their evolving set of priorities. A man may lay the groundwork for a career; he may develop one career and then discard it; or he may drift aimlessly, precipitating a crisis at about age 30, when the pressures become strong to achieve more order and stability within his life.

❏ *Settling Down.* This period usually begins in the early thirties. The man establishes his niche in society, digs in, builds a nest, and makes and pursues more long-range plans and goals. By this time he has often evolved a *dream,* a vision of his own future. In succeeding years a major shift in life direction may occur when a man revives the dream and experiences a sense of betrayal, disillusionment, or compromise with respect to it. Careers, such as those of professional athletes, may interfere with the satisfaction of the developmental tasks associated with this phase (see the boxed insert on pages 430–431).

❏ *Becoming One's Own Man.* This period tends to occur in the middle to late thirties and represents the high point of early adulthood and the beginning of what lies beyond. A man frequently feels that no matter what he has accomplished so far, he is not sufficiently independent. He may long to get out from under the authority of those over him. He commonly believes that his superiors control too much and delegate too little; he impatiently awaits the time when he will be able to make his own decisions and get the enterprise "really going." If a man has a mentor—a teacher, experienced coworker, boss, or the like—he will often give him up now. At this time, men want to be affirmed by society in the roles that they most value. They will try for a crucial promotion or some other form of recognition.

❏ *The Mid-Life Transition.* This period is a time of developmental transition, a turning point or boundary region between two periods of greater stability. It usually emerges during a man's early forties and occurs whether the man succeeds or fails in achieving his goals. A man may do extremely well, yet find his success hollow or bittersweet. If he fails, he experiences a sense of failure for not being able to "make it." Commonly, he has a sense of disparity between "what I've got now" and "what it is I really want," which leads to an interval of soul-searching.

❏ *Restabilization.* At around age 45 there seems to be a three- to four-year period when the mid-life transition comes to an end and a new life structure begins to take shape, providing a basis for living in middle adulthood. It is not the last developmental period, but it is the last one that the Yale researchers have studied so far. It is a time both of challenge to achieve further growth and of a threat to the self. Men like Sigmund Freud, Carl G. Jung, Eugene O'Neill, Frank Lloyd Wright, Francisco Goya, and Mohandas Gandhi went through a profound mid-life crisis and made tremendous creative gains through it. Other men such as Dylan Thomas, F. Scott Fitzgerald, and Sinclair Lewis were unable to manage the crisis and were destroyed. Whether the sequence of stages depicted by Levinson holds for men who are less well educated and not of the upper-middle class remains to be determined.

The Yale researchers plan to continue their study into the years beyond the forties. And they have undertaken explorations into the adult development of women. Their research lays to rest the popular myth that by the end of adolescence people have their lives more or less together and enter into a relatively stable, integrated life pattern that continues indefinitely until old age.

Phases in Adult Female Development

Although there is a growing interest in adult development, studies dealing with phases in adult female development have lagged behind those of men (Mercer, Nichols & Doyle, 1989; Moen, 1991; Reinke, Ellicott, Harris & Hancock, 1985). Such research is clearly called for. For example, although Erik Erikson (1963) says the formation of identity in adolescence is followed by the capacity for intimacy in early adulthood, many women describe the opposite progression, with the sense of identity developing more strongly in mid-life (Baruch & Barnett, 1983; Kahn, Zimmerman, Csikszentmihalyi & Getzels, 1985). Indeed, a longer life span, coupled with women's increasing educational attainments and participation in the labor force, has made obsolete much of previous research and theory. Growing numbers of women enter or reenter the labor force, change jobs, undertake new careers, or return to school. Of equal significance are the growing numbers of women who rear their children first in two-parent, then in one-parent, and then again in two-parent households. Numerous combinations of career, marriage, and children occur with respect to both timing and commitment, and each pattern has different ramifica-

Temporarily Dropping Out of College

Each year, countless students drop out of or take time off from college. Parents and college officials typically resign themselves to acts they often attribute to youthful "immaturity" and "impetuousness." More benignly, "taking time out" is seen as a way for young people "to find themselves." And this optimism may be well placed since many returning leave takers report that their leaves were beneficial.

Students give a variety of reasons for dropping out of college: They feel they are wasting time; they lack a sense of direction; their courses seem unrelated to the real world; they are disillusioned with the college experience; and/or they feel apathetic or depressed. Occasionally, a time-out speaks directly to the issue of career choice: The potential doctor may manage a field experience as a hospital technician, and the foreign language student may spend a year in Italy. Yet most leaves seem deliberately unrelated to any conceivable career a student might envision. Some leave takers set up housekeeping in a remote rural community, hitchhike across Europe, or find work on a Great Lakes ore boat. Even so, leaves with little apparent connection to potential careers may contribute to a renewed sense of purpose (Ochberg, 1986).

Some leave takers report that the very act of dropping out contributes to their sense of autonomy. They defy their parents' expectations in leaving, and they determine for themselves when they will return. In Erik Erikson's terms, they seem to be fashioning a sense of personal identity. Should these youth remain in a college environment, they may feel that they are still in a halfway station and question whether they can really take care of themselves. At college they may simply surround themselves with a dense net of social support that restricts a testing of their own resources. Moreover, young adults often wonder whether their values and preferences are truly their own or simply mirror images of the undigested influence of parents and peers. By dropping out of school, young adults disrupt the expected schedule of education and career that they feel others are attempting to impose upon them. And by setting up residence far from home, they escape the history of their previous social encounters and explore new ways. In sum, they may welcome an opportunity to become "their own person."

Leave takers often read their experiences while out of school as confirmation of their self-reliance and of their readiness to take on the challenges of the larger world. So equipped, they may return to college with renewed dedication. Of course, not all leaves end with young people ready to embark upon the challenges of young adulthood. Leave takers may not wish to bring the experimental, tentative period of moratorium to a conclusion. Or leave takers may return to school still at sea, inwardly continuing to view their choices as provisional. In sum, young people make and unmake their choices. When they "unmake" a choice, they may go home, and when they choose again, they leave (Barringer, 1990; Ochberg, 1986; Schnaiberg & Goldenberg, 1989).

---

tions. Some variations in life arrangements also include returning to the parental home for a period.

New Social Definitions Until relatively recently, a woman's life was seen primarily in terms of her reproductive role—bearing and rearing children, menopause, and "the empty nest" being the major events of the women's adult years. Indeed, people commonly equated the female life cycle with the family life cycle. Not surprisingly, the major psychosocial transitions in the lives of contemporary U.S. women now between the ages of 50 and 65 were more likely to be associated with phases of the family cycle than with chronological age (Baruch & Brooks-Gunn, 1984; Harris, Ellicott & Holmes, 1986; Moen, 1991;

Stewart & Healy, 1989). But today, with 90 percent of all women working for pay at some point in their lives, employment outside the home is playing an increasingly important role in the self-esteem and identity of women (McLaughlin et al., 1988; Mercer, Nichols & Doyle, 1989). Although the participation of white and nonwhite women in the labor force has increased from 1890 to the present, proportionately more nonwhite women have been employed outside their own homes than white women (Matthews & Rodin, 1989). Figure 15-3 provides data on the employment of American women.

Family and Work An accumulating body of evidence suggests that women progress through the same developmental periods as did the men in Levinson's study and at roughly the same ages. But even though the timing of the periods and the nature of the developmental tasks are similar, the ways women approach these tasks and the outcomes they achieve are different. In large measure these differences derive from the greater complexity of women's visions for their future and the difficulties they encounter in carrying them out. Unlike men, most women do not report dreams in which careers stand out as the primary component; women are more likely to view a career as insurance against not marrying or a bad marriage and difficult economic circumstances. Instead, the dreams of most women contain an image in which they are immersed in a world centered in relationships with others, particularly husbands, children, and colleagues (Brown, 1987; Roberts & Newton, 1987).

Work and family have traditionally been separate spheres of living for most men. But for most women they have not. Even today, single mothers or married women tend to work only in the interest of the family and only after all the other needs of its members have been addressed. Further-

more, the more successful a man is, the more likely it is that he will marry and have a family. But for women it is the other way around. Hence, whereas 51 percent of women executives at top corporations are single, only 4 percent of their male counterparts are single; in addition, whereas 61 percent of the women are childless, only 3 percent of the men have no children (Fraker, 1984). Clearly, the choice between work and family is more immediate and the cost more apparent for women (L. B. Rubin, 1980). Consequently, women have a particularly difficult time finding a balance between their career and their family.

Given these differences in the worlds of men and women, the age-30 transition period tends to be one in which many women reverse the priorities they established when they were in their twenties. Women typically reappraise the relative importance of family and career. Women who had emphasized marriage and motherhood in their twenties tend to develop more individualistic work-oriented goals for their thirties; women who had focused on their careers become more concerned with marriage and family. Some

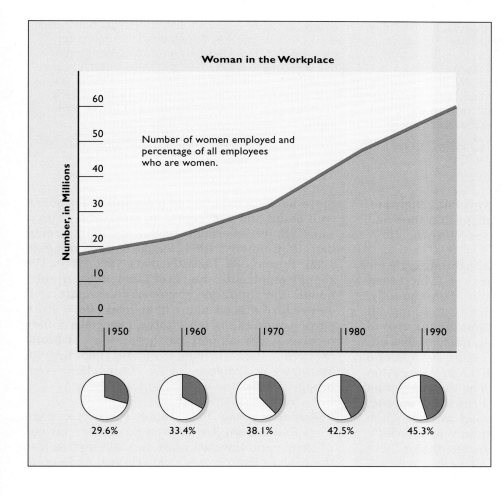

Woman in the Workplace

Number of women employed and percentage of all employees who are women.

Figure 15-3 Women in the U.S. Work Force
The figure provides data on the number of women who were employed and the percentage of all employees who were women between 1950 and 1990. SOURCE: *New York Times,* October 11, 1991, p. A11. Copyright © 1991 by The New York Times Company. Reprinted by permission.

The Losing Game:
The Dilemma Confronting Star Athletes

Many young people harbor fantasies of celebrity status as football, baseball, basketball, or hockey stars. Yet the dream may be better than the reality. In due course, elite athletes must make the transition from a pampered and protected life as a professional player to the real world (Anderson, 1991; Lipsyte, 1986; Newman, 1991). Many had fame thrust upon them when their peers were primarily worried about acne and dating.

Although all professional athletes differ in their playing experiences and transitional problems, each must let go of a passion that consumed his life for perhaps two or three decades. Each must crawl out of the protective cocoon afforded by a team and quite literally drop from hero to zero in a relatively short time span. "While you're playing," says David Meggyesy, a former pro linebacker, "you think, 'Hey, I'll just ride this pony and deal with it all later'" (quoted by Lipsyte, 1986, p. 61). Unhappily, the pony ride averages only three and a half seasons for the average pro football player. "Later" means an end to the camaraderie of the team experience. "Later" also means getting another job.

The jobs offered to former professional athletes invariably trade on their earlier fame. Yet bar-hopping public relations for a beer company or golf with prospective clients of a stockbroker do not teach the skills required in business. Ex-players are often resented by coworkers who feel they have not paid their dues. And having been told what to do during their athletic careers, many of them have little initiative and are afraid to show how little they actually know. In many cases they were slipped in the back doors of college, segregated from mainstream college life, insulated from academic expectations, wrung dry of their athletic-commercial usefulness, and then slung out the back door even less suited for societal employment than they were when they entered college (Will, 1986). Some cannot maintain a checkbook, make travel arrangements, or take care of their own laundry.

However, not all athletes are doomed to failure once they end their professional careers. The roster of men attaining success after football includes Secretary of Housing and Urban Development (HUD) Jack Kemp, once a quarterback for the Buffalo Bills; U.S. Senator Bill Bradley, once a pro basketball star; Willie Davis, a hall-of-fame lineman who is a West Coast beer and wine distributor; and a number of television personalities, including Alex Karras, a former Detroit Lion, Merlin Olsen, who played for the Los Angeles Rams, and O.J. Simpson, once a Buffalo Bill. Unfortunately, the story ends on a less promising note for most other ex-players. Says Shari Theismann, former wife of Joe Theismann, a star Washington Redskins quarterback, "We put them [athletic superstars] beyond what they can stand, their image of themselves is so overblown they can't get back to where they want to go" (quoted by Lipsyte, 1986, p. 65).

women, however, rather than reversing their priorities, simply add the component that they had neglected earlier in their lives (Brown, 1987; Roberts & Newton, 1987).

As we will see in later chapters, the struggle for greater equality between the sexes has increased women's roles and workloads. Consequently, some women encounter difficulty fulfilling all their work and family obligations, giving rise to role conflict and role overload. *Role conflict* ensues when they experience pressures within one role that are incompatible with the pressures that arise within another role, such as the conflicting demands made upon them as a parent, spouse, and paid worker. *Role overload* occurs when women have too many role demands and too little time to fulfill them. Women who encounter these types of role strains—and not all women do—are more likely to experience a diminished sense of well-being and a decrease in work and marital satisfaction (Coverman, 1989; Kopelman, Greenhaus & Connolly, 1983; Pleck, Staines & Lang, 1980; Rosenfield, 1989; Tiedje et al., 1990). We should emphasize, however, that most women handle their multiple responsibilities quite well and realize a good many beneficial effects from participation in the labor force, especially if they receive social support on the job and at home (Baruch & Barnett, 1986; Hoffman, 1989; Repetti, Matthews & Waldron, 1989; Thoits, 1986; Verbrugge, 1986).

Reentering the Paid Labor Force Levinson finds that toward age 40 men reconsider various of their commitments and often attempt to free themselves from a previously central male men-

A Wrenching Transition: Retirement from Professional Sports
Professional athletes are symbols of adoration and envy among many Americans. But after 20 or so years as elite athletes, their careers are over. Some describe it as a kind of "social death." Willie Davis (left), a Football Hall of Fame player on Vince Lombardi's Green Bay Packer teams of the 1960s, has made a successful transition as a West Coast beer and wine distributor. But many other professional baseball, basketball, and football players discover they are not equipped to deal with the realities of life as ordinary citizens. Travis Williams (right), known as "Road Runner" during his glory years, along with Davis on Lombardi's championship teams, never got the handle on life. He died at age 45, penniless and homeless, from heart, liver, and kidney problems compounded by years of alcoholism. According to those who know him, Williams thought that he would play football forever. *(left, Jim Caccavo/Picture Group; right, Jo McNally, Contra Costa Times)*

tor—the BOOM phenomenon (Becoming One's Own Man). But women may not enter the world of work (or reenter it) until they are in their late thirties, and few women have mentors, either male or female (Barnett & Baruch, 1983). Moreover, women confront an additional problem: Although men can act as mentors, attempts at cross-gender mentoring are vulnerable to disruption by sexual attractions (Roberts & Newton, 1987). Furthermore, despite current legal and social trends, there is still considerable job discrimination against women, particularly older middle-aged women.

Not uncommonly, contemporary women in their forties and fifties stopped their schooling or work at the time of marriage or the birth of their first child and remained in the home during the early child-raising years. However, when they now attempt to resume their paid labor roles, they find that jobs are scarcer in the fields—traditional "women's jobs" such as teaching and social work—in which they were trained years ago. In other fields, such as nursing, knowledge acquired earlier is likely to be dated and inadequate (Mogul, 1979). Even so, a national survey reveals that working women at mid-life are healthier, have higher self-esteem, and suffer less anxiety than do homemakers (Coleman & Antonucci, 1983). Apparently, work acts as a stabilizing force for women during critical junctures of the life cycle.

Stocktaking Psychiatrist Kathleen M. Mogul (1979) also finds that the "stocktaking" that occurs in men in their forties may occur earlier among women. Childless women in their thirties

"You're the chef? Well, my compliments anyway."

(Drawing by Weber; © 1990 The New Yorker Magazine, Inc.)

often have a "last chance" feeling with regard to motherhood. On the other hand, those who became mothers earlier experience a decrease in their absorption in and in the burdens of child care. And the large number of middle-aged women who have children and simultaneously work outside the home also begin to reflect upon their coming life pattern.

Differing Adult Experiences Psychologists such as Georgia Sassen (1980), Carol Gilligan (1982*a*, 1982*b;* Gilligan, Ward & Taylor, 1989), and Lawrence D. Cohn (1991) likewise stress that the adult experience may be somewhat different for women than for men. As we noted in Chapter 13, Gilligan questions the traditional psychological assumption that boys and girls both struggle to define a distinct identity for themselves during adolescence. Instead, she contends that girls must struggle to resist the loss of psychological strengths and positive conceptions of themselves that they had possessed in childhood. Put another way, the development of women is not a steady progression but the recovery in adulthood of confidence, assertiveness, and a positive sense of self that Western society compromises during adolescence.

Part of the difficulty, Gilligan says, is that women hold a moral perspective of care and responsibility. Women often find it difficult to commit themselves to competitive success because they are oriented toward the achievement of cooperation, mutuality, and consensus. Many women focus on preserving rather than negating relationships. It was otherwise for the men interviewed by Levinson, for whom "friendship was largely noticeable by its absence" and work typically fostered distance between self and others. Indeed, life in contemporary bureaucracies and corporations frequently rewards those who relate to others not as persons but as objects to be manipulated to get ahead. Significantly, the ten most popular sports for men are mostly competitive activities such as softball, basketball, billiards, and pool, while women's top ten tend to be noncompetitive such as aerobics, running, hiking, and calisthenics (fishing ranks first and swimming second with men while swimming ranks first and bicycling second with women) (*The Gallup Report,* February 1989).

Yet it is easy to overstate the differences between men and women (Archer & Waterman, 1988; Cohn, 1991; Epstein, 1988). Indeed, men and women are more similar than different, and most of their apparent differences are culturally and socially produced. The physical and symbolic segregation of men and women in different social spheres feeds dichotomous thinking about gender and creates self-fulfilling prophecies that provide the foundations for social arrangements that keep men and women in separate and unequal roles.

Higher Incidence of Depression Women are more than twice as likely as men to suffer major depression. Approximately one in every four women and one in every eight men suffers a serious clinical depression at some time in their lives. Although depression rates before puberty are about the same for boys and girls, at around age 12 girls begin to have higher rates (Goleman, 1990). Worry about their physical attractiveness is one reason that adolescence is more stressful for girls than for boys. Body image constitutes a large part of how girls think of themselves.

The disproportionate rate of depression among women seems to be related to cultural traditions that diminish feminine worth and induce passive, dependent personality patterns and negative thinking. Maggie Scarf (1980) interviewed more than 150 depressed women and observed others in treatment at a psychiatric clinic. She concludes, as does Carol Gilligan, that emotional attachments tend to mean much more to women than to men. She finds that a woman's depression tends to mirror the life-span stage in which the woman finds herself. In the teens and early twenties depression is typically associated with separating from parents. Later, in the twenties, the need for intimacy and commitment becomes intermingled with career issues and occupies center stage. The biggest increase in depression comes in the early thirties, a time when many women conclude that their lives are not measuring up to what they had expected and when they may feel trapped in a relationship. In the forties depression is often linked to feelings of inadequacy and a lack of fulfillment—a sense that they have not been able to achieve more and that time is running out for them. These feelings may persist into the fifties and become intensified by a loss in physical attractiveness. Finally, depression in the sixties and seventies is often tied to widowhood and loneliness.

The Stage Approach Controversy

Not all psychologists and sociologists are happy with stage approaches to adult develop-

ment. They believe that these approaches oversimplify adult life (Rosenfeld & Stark, 1987). First, as pointed out earlier in the chapter, they note that the timing of many life events is becoming less regular; age is losing many of its customary meanings, and the trends are toward a more fluid life cycle and an age-irrelevant society. In the United States it is no longer unusual to encounter the 28-year-old mayor, the 30-year-old college president, the 35-year-old grandmother, the 50-year-old retiree, the 65-year-old new father, and the 70-year-old student (Neugarten, 1979; Neugarten & Neugarten, 1987). Indeed, vast structural changes in the U.S. educational and occupational systems have led to a widespread destandardization of the youthful years: The life stage "youth" is no longer a short period of transition, and the events (and their sequencing) are not as highly predictable as they were a few decades ago (Buchman, 1989).

Second, Bernice L. Neugarten (1979, p. 891) points out that the psychological themes reported by adults of all ages are recurrent ones that do not typically follow in a single, fixed order:

> [The themes of adulthood] do not in truth emerge at only given movements in life, each to be resolved and then put behind as if they were beads on a chain. Identity is made and remade; issues of intimacy and freedom and commitment to significant others, the pressures of time, the reformulation of life goals, stocktaking and reconciliation and acceptance of one's successes and failures—all of these preoccupy the young as well as the old. It is a truism, even though it sometimes goes unmentioned, that the psychological preoccupations of adults are recurrent. They appear and reappear in new forms over long periods of time. This being so, it is something of a distortion to describe adulthood as a series of discrete and neatly bounded stages, as if adult life were a staircase.

Indeed, chance events play a large part in shaping adult lives. Careers and marriages often result from the happenstance of meeting the right—or wrong—person at the right—or wrong —time. But even though the events may be random, their consequences are not (Cooney & Hogan, 1991; Rosenfeld & Stark, 1987).

Third, Neugarten points out that many inner changes occur slowly across the life span and not in a stagelike fashion. For example, her research reveals that middle-aged people commonly view the world as rewarding the bold; hence, they are willing to undertake more risky ventures. However, as they age, people increasingly come to see themselves as making their peace with the world and its demands. And the research of David

Gutmann (1969, 1977) suggests that after their children are grown, men and women move in opposite directions, with men becoming less assertive and aggressive and women becoming more so, and thus patterns of a later-life "unisex" emerge (see Chapter 17).

Fourth, most of the people studied by Levinson and other researchers were born before and during the Great Depression of the 1930s. Moreover, the subjects of the investigations were predominantly male, white, and upper-middle class. What held for these people may not hold for today's 40-year-olds who were born in the more optimistic years following World War II. The image we gain of men in mid-life from the Levinson research may strike future developmental psychologists as simply "burned out" at a young age, rather than as reflecting an invariant developmental process that all men pass through in their forties (Rosenfeld & Stark, 1987). As we noted in our discussion of generations in Chapter 13, coming of age at a certain point in time and experiencing certain decisive economic, social, political, or military events has a profound impact on people's lives. For instance sociologist Glen H. Elder, Jr., finds that the same historical events, such as the Great Depression of the 1930s and World War II, can have quite different consequences depending on the age and sex of those experiencing these events. The Depression experience for boys born between 1920 and 1921 was ultimately beneficial, whereas it was detrimental for boys born between 1928 and 1929. The older boys, who were adolescents during much of the 1930s, were able to assist their financially strapped families by getting jobs or doing house chores during the economically difficult years, whereas the younger boys were unable to do so. And during World War II, most of the older boys entered military service, gaining a wide range of experience and many educational and vocational benefits that afforded opportunities for upward social mobility. By contrast, the home-front experiences of the boys born between 1928 and 1929 consisted of continued dependence on their families during the stressful war years (Elder, 1974, 1985, 1986; Elder & Clipp, 1988; Elder, van Nguyen & Caspi, 1985).

A true stage theory typically has four characteristics (Kohlberg, 1973). First, a stage theory implies that qualitative differences in structure take place at given points in development. Second, the stage-related structures form an invariant sequence or order. Third, the various ingredients making up a distinct structure appear as an integrated cluster of responses. And fourth, higher stages displace or reintegrate the structures found at lower stages. Yet Neugarten (1977) cautions that these characteristics of a true stage theory are not often applicable to adulthood, where it is frequently difficult to perceive qualitative changes, where there is no firmly fixed biological timetable, and where major life events take place in a less invariant order than in childhood.

Any number of psychologists and sociologists also question whether the completion of one phase in the course of life necessarily entails some sort of "life crisis" such as those postulated by Erikson. They reject the notion that one must resolve certain developmental tasks in one stage before going on to the next (Atchley, 1975; Brim, 1976; Rosenfeld & Stark, 1987). These sociologists and psychologists point out that critical transitions—"passages" or "turning points"—need not be characterized by stress and turmoil. We actively welcome and embrace some new roles. Consider, for instance, the thrill associated with one's first "real" job (Bush & Simmons, 1981).

For his part, Levinson acknowledges that a life-cycle theory does not mean that adults—any more than children—march in lockstep through a series of stages. He recognizes that the pace and degree of change in a person's life are influenced by personality and environmental factors (war, a death in the family, poor health, or a sudden windfall). Hence, Levinson does not deny that very wide variations occur among people in any one life period.

Yet Levinson disagrees with those who claim that development during adulthood lacks order simply because people differ in so many respects (Rosenfeld & Stark, 1987). He defines his task as one of finding basic principles by which people's lives unfold over time. He uses the analogy of fingerprints. If we have a theory of fingerprints, we have a basis for order, in that we can identify individuals because we know the basic principles around which fingerprints vary. Likewise, a theory of adult development provides basic principles by which we can identify the orderly changes that occur in people's lives as well as individual variations from these broad tendencies.

Physical Changes and Health

Our physical organism changes across the life span. But in and of themselves such changes may be less important than what people *make* of them. As we pointed out in Chapter 1, cultural stereotypes and social attitudes have a profound effect on our perceptions of biological change and our experience of it. Whereas the physical changes associated with puberty are comparatively easy to identify, later changes (with the possible exception of menopause) are less easy to pinpoint as marking stages in adulthood.

Physical Performance

To most individuals, getting older means losing a measure of their physical attractiveness, vigor, and strength. Yet although physical changes take place throughout adulthood, for the most part they have only minimal implications for an individual's daily life in early adulthood. The period from 18 to about 30 represents peak years for speed and agility. Most Olympic athletes fall between these ages. However, in some events, such as women's gymnastics, women of 18 are deemed "old." For long-distance running and most categories of baseball, the peak age of performance is about 28 years of age, whereas top tennis players reach their highest levels of performance at age 24. Golfers, in contrast, peak at about 31 years of age. In swimming events, men typically peak at 18 or 19 years of age, and women at 16 or 17 years of age (Schulz & Curnow, 1988). Studies confirm that maximum physical strength is highest in the twenties, after which it declines (Rikli & Busch, 1986; Welford, 1977). Some research suggests that hand grip strength in the thirties is 95 percent of what it was in the twenties, falling to 91 percent in the forties, 87 percent in the fifties, and 79 percent in the sixties. Back strength also diminishes to about 97 percent in the forties, 93 percent in the fifties, and 85 percent in the sixties. But such averages mask the considerable variation found among individuals. Complex sensorimotor coordination also begins slowing in the thirties.

One area in which individuals in early and middle adulthood are most likely to note changes is in their vision. Between 30 and 45 years, individuals tend to experience some loss in the power and elasticity of the lens. Through early and middle adulthood individuals who are nearsighted tend to become more nearsighted and those who are farsighted tend to become more farsighted. Aging also produces deterioration in the human auditory and vocal systems, but these changes are of little consequence for those in early and middle adulthood.

Physical Health

Adult health is a function of a wide variety of factors, including heredity, nutrition, exercise, previous illness, and the demands and constraints of the social environment. For the most part, the vast majority of young adults enjoy good health. Infectious diseases—particularly upper respiratory infections and sexually transmitted infections—are among the most common illnesses. Motor vehicle accidents tend to take a higher toll in death and disfigurement among young people than among other age groups.

The excessive consumption of alcohol is also a serious health problem for some young adults. As noted in Chapter 14, a recent survey of U.S. college students found that 76 percent drank alcoholic beverages and 42 percent were heavy drinkers (Carmody, 1990). Figure 15-4 provides data on the explanations college students give for their drinking. A 1987 Gallup poll found that 65 percent of Americans say they use alcoholic beverages. Of those who drink, 38 percent said they had a drink within twenty-four hours of being interviewed (*New York Times,* August 23, 1987, p. 12). Polls show that the number of families touched by problems related to drinking increased to 24 percent in 1987 from 12 percent in 1974 (*New York Times,* April 26, 1987, p. 13).

The primary effect of alcohol—and a major reason that people enjoy drinking—is that it produces a gradual dulling of the reactions of the brain and nervous system. Contrary to popular opinion, alcohol is *not* a stimulant but a tranquilizer or relaxant. However, the loss of inhibition that it fosters may lead to aggressiveness or the illusion of greater creativity. And many people find that a few drinks make them feel unusually alert and witty, even if those around them do not share their perspective. Medical scientists have confirmed the observation of Shakespeare (through the Porter in *Macbeth*) that alcohol "provokes the desire [for sex] but takes away from the performance" (it decreases a man's ability to maintain an erection). Heavy drinking invariably produces problems at work, with one's family, and with the law. It is also implicated in over half of all automobile accidents. Heavy drinkers are at risk for cardiomyopathy (a condition in which the heart's muscular tissues become weak and damaged), chronic gastritis, cirrhosis of the liver, and liver, mouth, and esophagus cancers. Mounting evidence suggests that alcoholism is a disease rather than a social phenomenon; some evidence suggests that severe alcoholics metabolize alcohol differently than nonalcoholics do (Brody, 1987*c*).

Smoking poses another health hazard. Tobacco contains three dangerous chemicals: tar, nicotine, and carbon monoxide. Smokers are fourteen times more likely to die from cancer of

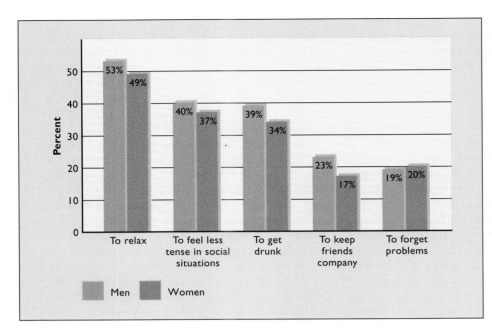

Figure 15-4   Explanations First-Year Students Provide for Drinking
Students could secure more than one reason. The survey was based on the responses of 1,669 first-year college students at 14 Massachusetts colleges and universities. SOURCE: Wechsler and McGadden for AAA Foundation for Traffic Safety. *USA Today,* March 14, 1991, p. D1. Copyright © 1991, *USA Today.* Reprinted with permission.

the lung, throat, or mouth than are nonsmokers; four times more likely to die from cancer of the esophagus; and twice as likely to die from leukemia and a heart attack. Smoking is a chief cause of emphysema and bronchitis and increases the risk of high blood pressure. A study of the smoking habits of all adults who lived and died in Erie, Pennsylvania, between 1972 and 1974 found that men who smoke cigarettes throughout their lives die nearly eighteen years earlier than men who never start. Smokers hurt not only themselves but their nonsmoking work associates and family members. Numerous national health agencies have documented that nonsmokers are placed at increased risk for developing disease as the result of exposure to environmental tobacco smoke (Altman, 1990). The Federal Centers for Disease Control estimated that 29 percent of Americans smoked in 1990, down from a high of 42 percent in 1967.

Data collected by the Department of Health and Human Services reveal that compared with nonsmokers, adult smokers are more likely to be risk takers and to have extroverted, defiant, and impulsive personalities. Among men, blue-collar workers are the heaviest smokers; whereas among women, white-collar workers smoke more. Working women are less likely to smoke than are full-time homemakers.

Young adults frequently smoke because their friends do. Among teenagers smoking tends to be regarded as a symbol of swaggering maturity while serving to hide outward signs of shyness or awkwardness in social situations. Compared with

nonsmoking peers, teenagers who smoke are more outgoing and rebellious toward authority. College-bound youth are less likely to smoke than are other youth. Girls who smoke are more social and less athletic than are nonsmokers; they read less, get lower grades, and are more likely to hate school than do their nonsmoking peers (Brody, 1984*a*).

For the young adult concerned with physical health, exercise affords both physical and psychological benefits. (See the boxed insert on leisure among Americans.) During exercise we breathe more deeply to get more oxygen into our lungs, and our hearts beat harder to pump blood to the muscles. Strong lungs and an efficient, resilient heart place one at a health advantage. Furthermore, people who exercise on a regular basis report that they sleep better, feel more alert, and are better able to concentrate than nonexercisers. According to the Federal Centers for Disease Control in Atlanta, sedentary living, not an elevated level of cholesterol in the blood, is the most important factor in deaths from heart attacks in the United States. Coronary heart disease accounts for about 27 percent of the 2.1 million deaths each year among Americans. Studies typically show that sedentary people are about twice as likely to die from a heart attack as are people who are physically active. By sedentary, researchers mean individuals who either do no purposeful physical activity or who exercise irregularly (less than three times a week or less than 20 minutes at a time or both) (Brody, 1990). As shown in Figure 15-5, even moderate exercise during the week can substantially drop a person's risk of early death.

Research done at The Johns Hopkins Hospital in Baltimore reveals that a family history of early heart disease is a strong indicator of risk (Findlay, 1983): 42 percent of individuals under age 50 from at-risk families have significant high blood pressure compared with 20 percent of the general population; 28 percent have seriously high blood levels of cholesterol compared with 5 to 10 percent of the general population; and 25 percent show evidence of "silent" coronary artery disease, double the rate of the general population. Other researchers at Harvard find that individuals at risk for early heart disease improperly metabolize cholesterol, which builds up in the walls of arteries, leading to severe clogging and ultimately to a heart attack (Bishop, 1983; Monmaney, 1987). By identifying and treating people with cholesterol abnormalities early, scientists hope to cut the incidence of heart disease among susceptible individuals (see Chapter 17).

Mental Health

The National Institute of Mental Health has sponsored a broad-based survey of more than 11,500 people 18 years old and over living in the metropolitan areas of New Haven, Baltimore, and St. Louis, supplemented by studies of more than 6,000 other Americans in Los Angeles and North Carolina (Nelson, 1983*a*). This research shows that Americans 25 to 45 years old report that they have experienced a much higher incidence of psychiatric disorders at some point in their lives than do elderly people. One partial explanation seems to be that older people sometimes overlook the mental difficulties that they had earlier in life.

Although depression has generally been believed to be the most common mental ailment of adult Americans, the NIMH study reveals that alcohol abuse and dependence is the most common disorder, affecting 13.6 percent of the population. Men report problems of alcohol abuse about five

Figure 15-5   Exercise and Longevity: Even a Little Affords Health Gain
A study, carried out by the Institute for Aerobics Research and the Cooper Clinic in Dallas, followed more than 13,000 men and women for an average of eight years to determine how physical fitness relates to death rates. Heart and respiratory fitness were measured by performance on a treadmill test. Men and women were each grouped into five categories from least to most fit. Although all those in the study were deemed healthy, the least fit group had death rates more than three times that of the most fit group. The data were adjusted statistically in an attempt to ascertain that the drop in mortality was associated with fitness and not smoking, cholesterol level, blood pressure, blood sugar levels, and family history of coronary heart disease. SOURCE: Journal of the American Medical Association. Philip J. Hilts, Exercise and longevity: A little goes a long way. *New York Times,* November 3, 1989, pp. 1, 10. Figure p. 10. Copyright © 1989 by The New York Times Company. Reprinted by permission.

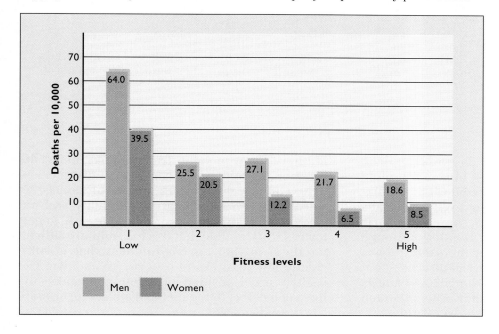

Spending Leisure Time

The ultimate egalitarian resource may well be time: Each one of us gets twenty-four hours of it a day, neither a second more nor less. How we spend out time is a trade-off. We must allot time between work and leisure, future-oriented (investment) and present-oriented (consumption) activities, family and friends, and so on. In turn, we must apportion time among specific activities. Consider leisure, an activity we choose for its own sake. Leisure is not simply "free time"—the portion of the day left over after we fulfill our work, family, household, and other obligations. Unemployed persons and prisoners have a good deal of "free time," but most of them do not experience it as "leisure time." It is the quality rather than the form of an activity that makes it leisure—the element of choice and the meaning the experience has for us. Virtually any activity can be leisure, depending on how we view it (Kelly, 1981, 1987).

The leisure activities of Americans often have the characteristics of work. A good many Americans think that playtime should be used "productively." About seven out of ten Americans say that hardly any of their free time is "wasted." And some six of ten say leisure time is best spent focused on certain goals (Brozan, 1982a). These notions are reflected in the recent concern with physical fitness. Health-conscious Americans chart their weekly progress in jogging or on muscle-building machines much as they monitor sales and profits at the office. Travel agents package bite-size, three-day getaways for those who do not believe they can afford a whole week off from work. And golf, tennis, racketball, and aerobics are seen as opportunities to make contacts and secure clients.

Americans feel that they have less free time nowadays than they once did. Thirty-two percent of Americans between 18 and 64 years of age report they always feel rushed to do the things they have to do, up from 28 percent in 1975 and 25 percent in 1965. Yet data from the Americans' Use of

Must Leisure Time Be Used Productively?
If leisure is an activity people choose for its own sake, can the physical fitness preoccupation of many Americans be viewed as "leisure"? *(John Blaustein/Woodfin Camp & Associates)*

Time Project reveals that Americans have more free time today than ever before. Men have forty hours of free time a week; women have 39 hours. There are a number of reasons for the increase in free time. For one thing, the work week is shorter today than it was a quarter century ago. For another, women do less housework than their counterparts did several decades ago. In addition, Americans are spending more of their lives unmarried, and the unmarried have more free time than do the married (Robinson, 1989, 1990a). Many people feel more time-pressured now because "passive" forms of leisure, such as television, consume a bigger bite out of the average week (television viewing now takes up to fifteen hours a week, up from fewer than eleven hours in 1965) (Cutler, 1990). As shown in Table 15-3, television viewing is by far the most prevalent leisure-time activity of Americans (Robinson, 1990c).

---

times more frequently than do women. Drug abuse and dependence is the next most often cited problem, affecting 5.6 percent of the population. About one-sixth of the surveyed Americans said that they had suffered from some psychiatric disorder in the previous six months. Although men and women report about the same rate of disorders, they differ in the types of disorders that they report. Men suffer most from alcohol abuse, phobias, and drug abuse, in that order. Women

are most likely to suffer from phobias, major depression, and obsessive-compulsive disorders.

Psychological disorders and disturbances result from both individual vulnerability and environmental stresses. Some people are genetically so susceptible that it is exceedingly difficult for them to find an environment that is sufficiently low in stress to prevent breakdown. Hereditary predisposition most commonly takes the form of a defect in the metabolism of one or more

Table 15-3

How Americans Spend Their Leisure Time

| | (Hours per week men and women aged 18 to 64 spend in leisure activities, by type of activity, 1965, 1975, and 1985) | | | | | | | | |
| | Total | | | Men | | | Women* | | |
	1985	1975	1965	1985	1975	1965	1985	1975	1965
Total	40.1	38.3	34.5	41.1	38.6	34.4	39.6	38.3	34.4
TV	15.1	15.2	10.5	15.7	16.2	11.7	14.5	14.1	9.3
Visiting	4.9	5.5	6.6	5.0	5.1	5.8	4.8	5.7	7.5
Talking	4.3	2.2	2.6	3.5	1.9	1.6	5.1	2.7	3.6
Traveling	3.1	2.6	2.7	3.4	2.8	3.0	3.0	2.4	2.4
Reading	2.8	3.1	3.7	2.7	3.0	4.2	2.9	3.3	3.3
Sports/outdoors	2.2	1.5	0.9	2.9	2.3	1.4	1.5	0.8	0.5
Hobbies	2.2	2.3	2.1	1.9	1.6	1.4	2.6	3.0	2.8
Adult education	1.9	1.6	1.3	2.2	2.1	1.6	1.6	1.3	0.9
Thinking/relaxing	1.0	1.1	0.5	1.2	1.0	0.2	0.9	1.2	0.6
Religion	0.8	1.0	0.9	0.6	0.8	0.7	1.0	1.3	1.0
Cultural events	0.8	0.5	1.1	0.8	0.3	1.3	0.8	0.6	0.9
Clubs/organizations	0.7	1.2	1.0	0.8	0.9	0.8	0.6	1.5	1.2
Radio/recording & listening	0.3	0.5	0.6	0.4	0.6	0.7	0.3	0.4	0.4

* Women have one hour less leisure time a week than men, but they spend more time than men talking, enjoying hobbies, and going to church.

Note: figures may not total due to rounding.

Source: Americans' Use of Time Project, University of Maryland; Blayne Cutler, Where does the free time go? American Demographics, 12 (November):38.

Changes in the economy have affected leisure activity and spending patterns. More than half of all adult women now work full-time outside the home. Most return home to assume domestic chores and care of children (Pleck, 1985). All the while, conflicts in schedules make it increasingly difficult for family members to participate in leisure activities together. Accompanying these changes is a substantial increase in spending for leisure products, more than doubling between 1975 and 1985 to $181.1 billion. Yet determining the size of leisure business is difficult, in part because it is embedded in many industries that are considered utilitarian. For instance, the big shift in the multibillion-dollar clothing industry has been toward "casual" clothes, mirroring the growth of leisure activities. In many ways how Americans handle their "free time" runs counter to the sense of "pure enjoyment" that constitutes genuine leisure.

neurotransmitters. At the other end of the continuum are those people who are so resilient and resistant to stress that few, if any, environments would trigger severe disturbance. For example, some political prisoners, despite years of torture and solitary confinement, manage to retain their sanity. In sum, people differ greatly in their vulnerability to mental disorder and disturbance (Allred & Smith, 1989; Rhodewalt & Zone, 1989; Wiebe, 1991; Zubin & Spring, 1977).

One of the most disheartening disorders that usually appears in late adolescence and early adulthood is schizophrenia (see Chapter 3). The National Institute of Mental Health estimates that about 2 million Americans—about 1 percent of the population—suffer from the disorder. On the average, about one-fourth of sufferers fully recover from their first attack, the majority remain chronically ill and require long-term treatment, and another one-fifth do poorly, regardless of treatment. Statistical data lend support to the hypothesis that schizophrenia is a brain disease. The vast majority of studies report statistically significant differences in brain variables between people with schizophrenia and people who are not psychiatrically impaired (Birchwood, Hallet & Preston, 1989; Goleman, 1990; Helmchen & Henn, 1987; Johnson, 1989).

Overall, two elements stand out in any consideration of mental health. First, from a social perspective, mental health involves the ability of people to function effectively in their social roles and to carry out the requirements associated with group living. Second, from a psychological perspective, mental health entails a subjective sense of well-being—happiness, contentment, and satisfaction. Yet adequate social functioning and a sense of psychological well-being are not so much a state of being as a process. Mental health requires that people continually change and adapt to life's fortunes. In brief, mental health is commonly taken to indicate that people have found a comfortable fit between themselves and the world—that they "have gotten it all together." The box on pages 442–444 takes a closer look at the part stress plays in our lives.

Cognitive Development

The events of adult life pose new challenges and require that we continually refine our reasoning capabilities and problem-solving techniques. Be it the realm of interpersonal relationships, work, parenting, or household management, we confront new circumstances, uncertainties, and difficulties that call for decision making and resourceful thought. Consequently, we must learn to identify problems, analyze them by breaking them down into their relevant components, and devise coping strategies.

Post-Formal Operations?

For Jean Piaget the stage of formal operations constituted the last stage in cognitive development. Recall from our discussion in Chapter 13 that Piaget depicted adolescence as opening a new horizon in thought. During this period adolescents gain the abililty to think about their own mental processes. Moreover, they achieve the ability to imagine multiple possibilities in a situa-

tion and to generate mentally numerous hypothetical outcomes. In brief, adolescence opens to teenagers the prospect of thinking in logical and abstract terms.

Any number of psychologists have speculated about whether a fifth, and qualitatively higher, level of thought may follow formal operations (Kramer, 1983; Riegel, 1973, 1975b, 1976). Common to the various formulations is the notion that post-formal operational thought is characterized by three features. First, adults come to realize that knowledge is not absolute but relativistic. They recognize that there are no such things as facts, pure and simple, but deem facts to be constructed realities—attributes we impute to experience and construe by the activities of the mind.

Second, adults come to accept the contradictions contained in life and the existence of mutually incompatible systems of knowledge. This understanding is fostered by the adult's expanding social world. In the larger community the adult is confronted by differing viewpoints and incompatible roles. And he or she is constantly required to select a course of action from among a multitude of possibilities.

And third, because they recognize that contradiction is inherent in life, adults must find some encompassing whole by which to organize their experience. In other words, adults must integrate or synthesize contradiction within an overriding system, interpreting it as part of a larger totality.

Here, then, is a working model of post-formal operational thought. Future research will be needed to determine the appropriateness of models that set forth a fifth stage in cognitive development.

Or perhaps future research will show that a Piagetian model has limited usefulness. Piagetian models have been losing much of their appeal during the 1980s. Critics are increasingly challenging the assumptions underlying the perspective. For instance, evidence suggests that younger and older adults may merely differ in their cognitive competencies: Younger adults seem to place greater reliance on rational and formal modes of thinking; older adults seem to develop a greater measure of subjectivity in their reasoning, and they place greater reliance on intuition and the social context in which they find themselves (Datan, Rodeheaver & Hughes, 1987; Labouvie-Vief, 1986; Labouvie-Vief, DeVoe & Bulka, 1989). In any event, most psychologists now acknowledge that cognitive development is a lifelong process, a viewpoint that has only gained widespread acceptance within the past fifteen years (Baltes, 1987; Howe & Brainerd, 1988; Schooler & Schaie, 1987).

Thought and Information Processing

Adult thought is a complex process. We would be little more than glorified cameras and projectors if information handling were limited to storage and retrieval. But **thinking**—rational thought—entails changing and reorganizing information in order to create new information. Indeed, it is this feature of human mental performance that we commonly label *intelligence* (see Chapter 9).

The psychologist Robert J. Sternberg (1979, 1981, 1986a) has studied how we think by examining what is involved in information processing. He views **information processing** as the step-by-step mental operations that we use in tackling intellectual tasks. He examines what happens to information from the time we perceive it until the time we act on it. The various stages or components of this process are highlighted by an analogy problem: *Washington* is to *one* as *Lincoln* is to (a) five, (b) ten, (c) fifteen, (d) fifty.

In approaching this problem, we first *encode* the items, identifying each one and retrieving from our long-term memory store any information that may be relevant to its solution. For instance, we may encode for "Washington" such attributes as "president," "depicted on paper currency," and "Revolutionary War leader." Encodings for "Lincoln" may include "president," "depicted on paper currency," and "Civil War leader." Encoding is a critical operation. In this example our failure to encode either individual as having his portrait on paper currency will preclude our solving the problem.

Next, we must *infer* the relationship between the first two terms of the analogy: "Washington" and "one." We may infer that "one" makes reference to Washington's having been the first president or to his being portrayed on the one-dollar bill. Should we make the first linkage and fail to make the second, we will again by stymied in solving the problem.

Then, we must examine the second half of the analogy, which concerns "Lincoln." We must *map* the higher-order relationship that links "Washington" to "Lincoln." On all three dimensions the men share similarities: both were presidents, both are depicted on currency, and both

were war leaders. Should we fail to make the connection that both Washington and Lincoln are portrayed on currency, we will not find the correct answer.

In the next step we must *apply* the relation that we infer between the first two items ("Washington" and "one") and the third item ("Lincoln") to each of the four alternative answers. Of course, Washington appears on the one-dollar bill and Lincoln on the five-dollar bill. Here we may fail to recognize the relationship because we make a faulty application (we may mistakenly recall Lincoln as appearing on the fifty-dollar bill).

We then attempt to *justify* our answer. We check our answer for errors of omission or commission. We may recall that Lincoln was the sixteenth president, but if we are uncertain, we may select "fifteen," figuring we are somewhat amiss in our recollection. Finally, we *respond* with the answer that we conclude is most appropriate.

Sternberg finds that the best problem solvers are not necessarily those who are quickest at executing each of the above steps. In fact, the best problem solvers spend more time on "encoding" than do poor problem solvers. Good problem solvers take care to put in place the relevant information that they may need later for solving the problem. Consequently, they have the information that they require in later stages. Thus, expert physicists spend more time encoding a physics problem than beginners do, and they are repaid by an increased likelihood of finding the correct solution.

Moral Reasoning

In Chapter 11 we discussed Lawrence Kohlberg's approach to moral development. He identifies six stages in the development of moral reasoning and groups them in three levels: preconventional (stages 1 and 2), conventional (stages 3 and 4), and postconventional (stages 5 and 6). Of particular significance, Kohlberg's cognitive-developmental theory stresses the universal and invariant character of the sequence, which he contends derives from the inherent structuring of thought in the stages described by Piaget. We pointed out that the existence of Kohlberg's sixth stage—a stage characterized by noble ideals of brotherhood and the community good—is debatable.

For more than a decade Carol Gilligan (1982a, 1982b) has conducted thoughtful and systematic

Stress

We all experience demands in the course of our daily lives that place physical and emotional pressure on us. We commonly term these experiences *stress*. According to Hans Selye (1956), our body responds to stress in several stages. The first stage is the *alarm reaction*. The nervous system is activated; digestion slows; heartbeat, blood pressure, and breathing rate increase; and the level of blood sugar rises. In brief, the body pulsates with energy. Then, the stage of *resistance* sets in. The body mobilizes its resources to overcome the stress. During this phase the heart and breathing rates often return to normal. But the appearance of normality is superficial, since the pituitary hormone ACTH remains at high levels. Finally, if some measure of equilibrium is not restored, a stage of *exhaustion* is reached. The body's capacity to handle stress becomes progressively undermined, physiological functioning is impaired, and eventually the organism dies.

By virtue of having been linked to various disorders, including heart disease, high blood pressure, ulcers, asthma, and migraine headaches, stress has acquired a bad name (see Chapter 21). Yet stress is a factor in everyone's life. Indeed, without some stress we would find life quite drab, boring, and stagnant. Therefore, psychologists are increasingly coming to the conclusion that stress in and of itself is not necessarily bad. Much depends on how we react to the various stresses in our lives. Even so, most of us experience some events as more stressful than others (see Table 15-4).

More often than not, stress resides neither in the individual nor in the situation alone but in how the person defines a particular event (Folkman & Lazarus, 1980; Lazarus, 1966). Not surprisingly, some individuals seem to be more stress-resistant than others by virtue of the attitudes they bring to their lives, and, consequently, they enjoy better health (Allred & Smith, 1989; Rhodewalt & Zone, 1989; Wiebe, 1991). Psychologists Suzanne C. Kobasa, S. R. Maddi, and S. Kahn (1982) find that hardiness is associated with an openness to change, a feeling of involvement in what one is doing, and a sense of control over events. Take the matter of a person's attitude toward change.

"I suppose one could say that stress is an inescapable part of the human condition."

(Drawing by Lorenz; © 1991 The New Yorker Magazine, Inc.)

research involving Kohlberg's framework. She finds that as individuals move through their young adult years, men and women take a somewhat different approach to the moral dilemmas employed by Kohlberg in his research (see Chapter 11). Indeed, women tend to score lower than men on Kohlberg's scale of moral development. Gilligan contends that the lower scores result from bias in Kohlberg's approach.

According to Gilligan, men and women have

Table 15-4

Stress Ratings of Various Life Events

Thomas H. Holmes and Richard H. Rahe developed a forty-three item Social Readjustment Rating Scale to measure the amount of change required by life events. Each of these events is given a numerical rating in "life-change units" on a scale from 1 to 100. The highest score is 100 points, which is assigned to the death of a spouse. A risk score is then computed by adding a person's life-change units for a given time period.

Events	Scale of Impact	Events	Scale of Impact
Death of spouse	100	Son or daughter leaving home	29
Divorce	73	Trouble with in-laws	29
Marital separation	65	Outstanding personal achievement	28
Jail term	63	Spouse begins or stops work	26
Death of close family member	63	Begin or end school	26
Personal injury or illness	53	Change in living conditions	25
Marriage	50	Revision of personal habits	24
Fired at work	47	Trouble with boss	23
Marital reconciliation	45	Change in work hours or conditions	20
Retirement	45	Change in residence	20
Change in health of family member	44	Change in schools	20
Pregnancy	40	Change in recreation	19
Sex difficulties	39	Change in church activities	19
Gain in new family member	39	Change in social activities	18
Business readjustment	39	Taking out a mortgage or loan for a lesser purchase	17
Change in financial state	38	Change in sleeping habits	16
Death of close friend	37	Change in number of family get-togethers	15
Change to different line of work	36	Change in eating habits	15
Change in number of arguments with spouse	35	Vacation	13
Taking out a mortgage or loan for a major purchase	31	Christmas	12
Foreclosure of mortgage or loan	30	Violations of the law	11
Change in responsibilities at work	29		

Source: Reprinted with permission from Journal of Psychosomatic Research, *Vol. 11, Thomas H. Holmes and Richard H. Rahe, "The Social Readjustment Rating Scale," 1967, pp. 213-218, Pergamon Press Ltd., Oxford, England.*

Should a man lose his job, for example, he can view it either as a catastrophe or as an opportunity to begin a new career more to his liking. Likewise, stress-resistant individuals get involved in life rather than hanging back on its fringes: They immerse themselves in meaningful activity. Furthermore, psychologically hardy people believe that they can actively influence many of the events that take place within their lives and that they have an impact on their surroundings.

(continued)

different moral domains. Men define moral problems in terms of right and rules—the "justice approach." In contrast, women perceive morality as an obligation to exercise care and to avoid hurt—the "responsibility approach." Men deem autonomy and competition to be central to life. Hence, they depict mortality as a system of rules for taming aggression and adjudicating rights. Women consider relationships to be central to life. Thus, they portray morality as protecting the

Since we are social beings, the quality of our lives depends in large measure on our interpersonal relationships. One strength of the human condition is our propensity for giving and receiving support from one another under stressful circumstances. *Social support* consists of the exchange of resources among people based on their interpersonal ties. Group and community supports affect how we rspond to stress through their health-sustaining and stress-buffering functions. Those of us with strong support systems appear better able to cope with major life changes and daily hassles. As we will see in Chapter 21, people with strong social ties live longer and have better health than those without such ties (Berkman and Breslow, 1983; House, Landis & Umberson, 1988). Studies over a range of illnesses, from depression to arthritis to heart disease, reveal that the presence of social support helps people fend off illness, and the absence of such support makes poor health more likely (Cohen & Williamson, 1991; Reis, Wheeler, Kernis, Spiegel, & Nezlek, 1985; Rook, 1987; Wallston, Alagna, DeVellis & DeVellis, 1984).

Social support cushions stress in a number of ways (Cohen & Wills, 1985; Litwak & Messeri, 1989; Seeman, Seeman & Sayles, 1985; Wellman & Wortley, 1990). First, friends, relatives, and co-workers may let us know that they value us. Our self-esteem is strengthened when we feel accepted by others despite our faults and difficulties. Second, other people often provide us with informational support. They help us to define and understand our problems and find solutions to them. Third, we typically find social companionship supportive. Engaging in leisure-time and recreational activities with others helps us to meet our social needs while simultaneously distracting us from our worries and troubles. Finally, other people may give us instrumental support—financial aid, material resources, and needed services—that reduces stress by helping us resolve and cope with our problems. In Chapter 21 we will discuss additional factors that affect a person's reaction to stress.

Severe and Persistent Stress

Stress is an inescapable aspect of modern life. Indeed, without some stress in our lives we would find little stimulation in the course of our everyday activities. However, stress that is severe and continuous undermines physical and mental health. Fifteen years of almost uninterrupted shelling and bombing have taken a heavy toll on residents of Beirut, Lebanon. Despite the presence of Syrian troops, car bombs and terrorist acts are commonplace among Lebanon's warring fractions. *(AP/Wide World Photos)*

integrity of relationships and maintaining human bonding. In sum, whereas men view development as a means of separating from others and achieving independence and autonomy, women view it as a means of integrating oneself within the larger human enterprise.

The two ethics provide a somewhat different basis for finding one's identity and integrating the

self. Gilligan calls upon developmental psychologists to recognize that the feminine moral construction is as credible and mature as its masculine counterpart. The full response to Gilligan's call is as yet not in. And not all researchers have supported her contention that men and women differ in their orientation for moral reasoning (Walker, 1984, 1986; Walker, DeVries & Trevethan, 1987). Others have found only limited support for Gilligan's assertion that women are more attuned to issues of care in moral conflicts and men more attuned to issues of justice (Ford & Lowery, 1986). Still others stress that the realm of care is not an exclusively female realm nor justice an exclusively male realm (Archer & Waterman, 1988; Baumrind, 1986; Boldizar, Wilson & Deemer, 1989; Deaux, 1985; Ford & Lowery, 1986).

Given the "political" quality of many of the features that characterize Kohlberg's stages, it is not surprising that researchers should also have looked for evidence of a linkage between moral reasoning and political attitudes. Overall, individuals with liberal leanings are more likely to reason at the postconventional level, while conservatives are more likely to reason at the conventional level. This finding has led a number of psychologists to investigate the possibility that individual differences in adult moral reasoning reflect differences in their political ideologies (Emler, Renwick & Malone, 1983). They find that right-wing and politically moderate individuals increase their principled-reasoning scores if they are given the task of responding in a manner that they believe characterizes left-wingers. Such results suggest that variations in adult moral reasoning are more a product of political position than of developmental status. In other words, people seem to have some ability to differentiate among moral reasons and to use them in their own interests. In practice, people often draw upon ideological "scripts" of the political left or right and use these "moral reasons" to advance their political cause (de Vries & Walker, 1986; Sparks & Durkin, 1987).

SUMMARY

1. People's feelings, attitudes, and beliefs about adulthood are influenced by the relative proportion of individuals who are adults. At the present time the post–World War II baby-boom generation has brought about a rapid expansion in the nation's labor force. The surplus of well-educated individuals may result in keen competition for an array of managerial and professional positions.

2. For the most part, people in the United States perceive adults of all ages in a favorable fashion. Nevertheless, older adults are viewed less favorably and as less desirable to be around than younger adults. People also evaluate different points in the life cycle differently depending upon their current age. A person's gender likewise makes a difference. Women are viewed as aging faster than men.

3. The life course of individuals is punctuated by transition points—the relinquishment of familiar roles and the assumption of new ones. Societies commonly prescribe sets of behavioral expectations for various periods in the life span. Age norms are most obvious when they are embodied in formal rules or explicit policies about a role, such as are found in compulsory school attendance laws, the minimum voting age, and the retirement age specified by employers. Age norms may also represent informal expectations about the kinds of roles appropriate for people of various ages (notions about who is "too old," "too young," or "the right age" for certain activities).

4. Age grading at the societal level (the arranging of people in social layers that are based upon periods in the life cycle) creates the social clock phenomenon—the internalized standards that individuals use in assessing their conformity to age-appropriate expectations. Such an internal sense of social timing can act as a "prod" to speed up accomplishment of a goal or as a "brake" to slow down passage through age-related roles.

5. People also locate themselves across the life span in terms of life events. Some life events are related to social clocks, while others take place under circumstances that are largely independent of age. In thinking about a life event, we often ask ourselves three questions: "Will it happen to me?"; "If so, when will it occur?"; and "If it happens, will others also experience it or will I be the only one?"

6. A number of Yale researchers, led by Daniel J. Levinson, have attempted to identify developmental stages in adulthood. They have constructed a descriptive framework that defines six stages in adult male development up to the late forties. Levinson and his associates say that the overriding task throughout adulthood is the creation of a structure for life. A man must periodically restructure his

life by creating a new structure or reappraising an old one. Consequently, he must at intervals modify his long-held assumptions about himself and the world.

7. Although there is a growing interest in adult development, the phases in adult female development remain largely unexplored. Until relatively recently, people commonly viewed a woman's life primarily in terms of her reproductive role. But today, with 90 percent of all women working for pay at some point in their lives, employment outside the home plays an increasingly important role in the self-esteem and identity of women. Overall, there has been a decrease in the importance of marital status in determining the sorts of activities and roles a woman adopts.

8. Some researchers believe that a stage approach may oversimplify adult life. First, the timing of life events is becoming less regular, and the trends are toward a more fluid life cycle. Second, the psychological themes reported by adults of all ages are recurrent ones that appear and reappear in new forms and do not typically follow in a single, fixed order. And finally, many inner changes occur slowly across the life span and not in a stagelike fashion.

9. Levinson acknowledges that a life-cycle theory does not mean that adults march in lockstep through a series of stages. Yet he disagrees with those who claim that development during adulthood lacks order simply because people differ. He defines his task as one of finding basic principles by which people's lives unfold over time.

10. Our physical organism changes across the life span. Although physical changes take place throughout adulthood, for the most part they have only minimal implications for an individual's daily life in early adulthood. From eighteen to about thirty are the peak years for speed and agility.

11. Adult health is a function of a wide variety of factors, including heredity, nutrition, exercise, previous illness, and the demands and constraints of the social environment. Alcohol and smoking are major health hazards. Exercise affords both physical and psychological benefits. Mental health requires that people continually change and adapt to life's fortunes. It is commonly taken to indicate that people have found a comfortable "fit" between themselves and the world.

12. Some psychologists postulate the existence of a post-formal operational stage in cognitive development. However, future research will be needed to determine the appropriateness of such models. Or perhaps future research will show that a Piagetian model has limited usefulness. In any event, adult thought is a complex process. Robert J. Sternberg depicts it as involving information processing, the step-by-step mental operations that we use in tackling intellectual tasks.

13. Carol Gilligan concludes that men and women have different moral domains. Men define moral problems in terms of rights and rules—the "justice approach." In contrast, women perceive morality as an obligation to exercise care and to avoid hurt—the "responsibility approach." Gilligan calls for developmental psychologists to recognize that both domains are equally valid.

KEY TERMS

Age Norm A social expectation that specifies what constitutes appropriate and inappropriate behavior for people at various periods in the life span.

Aging Biological and social change across the life span.

Biological Aging Changes in the structure and functioning of the human organism through time.

Information Processing The step-by-step mental operations that we use in tackling intellectual tasks.

Life Event A turning point at which individuals change some direction in the course of their lives.

Social Aging Changes in an individual's assumption and relinquishment of roles through time.

Social Clock A set of internalized concepts that regulate our progression through the age-related milestones of the adult years.

Social Norm A standard of behavior that members of a group share and to which they are expected to conform. Social norms are enforced by positive and negative sanctions.

Thinking A process by which we change and reorganize information in order to create new information.

EARLY ADULTHOOD: LOVE AND WORK

Chapter 16

EARLY ADULTHOOD: LOVE AND WORK

Options in Lifestyles

Singles ◆ **Living Together** ◆ **Young Adults Living at Home** ◆

Homosexual and Lesbian Couples ◆ **Marriage**

The Family Life Cycle and Parenthood

Stages in the Family Life Cycle ◆ **Pregnancy** ◆ **Transition to Parenthood** ◆

Employed Mothers ◆ **Single-Parent Mothers** ◆ **Single-Parent Fathers**

Work

The Significance of Work ◆ **Status Attainment: The Socioeconomic Life Cycle**

◆

To love and to work.—SIGMUND FREUD
When asked for the capacities
that are characteristic of a mature person

*One can live magnificently
in this world, if one knows how to work and
how to love.*—COUNT LEO TOLSTOY, 1856

As Freud and Tolstoy suggest in the above quotations, love and work provide the central themes of adult life. Both love and work place us in a complex web of relationships with others. Indeed, our humanness arises out of our relationships with other people. Of equal significance, our humanness must also be sustained through such relationships, and fairly steadily so. We cannot be human all by ourselves. Adulthood, like other periods of human life, can only be understood within the social context in which it occurs.

Central to any lifestyle are the bonds we forge with other people (Fischer, Sollie, Sorell & Green, 1989). We must become linked with other people in relatively stable sets of expectations—what sociologists term **social relationships.** Two common types of bonds are *expressive ties* and *instrumental ties.*

An **expressive tie** is a social link formed when we invest ourselves in and commit ourselves to another person. Many of our needs can only be satisfied in this fashion. Through association with people who are meaningful to us, we realize a sense of security, love, acceptance, companionship, and personal worth.

Social interactions that rest on expressive ties are termed **primary relationships.** We view these relationships—with friends, family, and lovers—as ends in themselves, valuable in their own right. Such relationships tend to be personal, intimate, and cohesive.

An **instrumental tie** is a social link that is formed when we cooperate with another person to achieve a limited goal. At times, this relationship may mean working with our enemies, as in the old political saying, "Politics makes strange bedfellows." More commonly, it merely means that we find ourselves integrated in complex networks of diverse people—for instance, the division of labor extending from the farmers who grow wheat to the grocers who sell bread.

Social interactions that rest on instrumental ties are called **secondary relationships.** We view such relationships as means to ends rather than as ends in their own right. Examples are our relationship with the cashier at the supermarket, the clerk in the registrar's office, or a gas station attendant. Secondary relationships are everyday touch-and-go contacts in which individuals need have little or no knowledge of one another.

Options in Lifestyles

People in modern complex societies typically enjoy some options in selecting and changing their lifestyles. A **lifestyle**—the overall pattern of living whereby we attempt to meet our biological, social, and emotional needs—provides the context in which we come to terms with many of the issues discussed in the previous chapter. More particularly, lifestyle affords the framework by which we work out the issues of intimacy versus isolation that Erik Erikson described. Intimacy involves our ability to experience a trusting, supportive, and tender relationship with another person. It implies a capacity for mutual empathy and for both giving and receiving pleasure within an intimate context. Comfort and companionship are among the ultimate rewards to be found in a close relationship.

A striking aspect of U.S. society over the past thirty-five years has been the rapid expansion in lifestyles. Much of the turmoil of the late 1960s revolved around the range of choices in living arrangements that people should be allowed to make. From the various liberation movements (black, Chicano, American Indian, women, gay, and youth) there has come a broader acceptance of pluralistic standards for judging behavior. Greater latitude is permitted individuals in tailoring a lifestyle that is less constrained by standards of what a "respectable" person should be like.

Singles

Census data reveal that single status among both men and women under 35 years of age has sharply increased in recent years. This increase has resulted in part from the tendency of young people to postpone marriage. Figure 16-1 provides information on the incidence of men and women living alone in the United States. Many men and women have simply postponed marriage; however, the changes in data suggest that a growing proportion of Americans will never marry at all. Even so, the population remaining single today is smaller than it was at the turn of the century, when fully 42 percent of all U.S. adult men and 33 percent of adult women were never married (Kain, 1984).

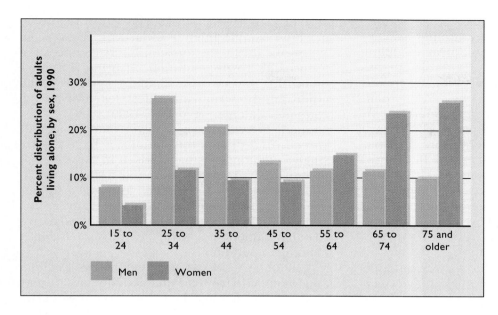

Figure 16-1   Living Alone
Adult men are more likely than women to live alone, but women live longer than do men. SOURCE: Bureau of the Census, *Current Population Reports,* Series P-20, No. 450.

More than two-thirds of adult singles live with someone else: a friend, relative, or "spouse equivalent." However, increasing numbers of singles are living alone. Some 23.6 million Americans now live by themselves, a 91 percent jump for women since 1970, and a 156 percent increase for men over the same period. And the singles population is far from being a monolothic group, with the divorced (11.5 million), widowed (12.7 million), and never-married (45.7 million) comprising distinct groups of those aged 15 and older.

A variety of factors have fueled the increase in nonfamily households: the deferral of marriage among young adults, a high rate of divorce, and the ability of the elderly to maintain their own homes alone. Singlehood is also a reclaimable state. A person may be single, then choose to marry or cohabit, and perhaps later divorce and become single again.

Since colonial days and until perhaps a decade or so ago, a stigma was attached to the terms "spinster" and "bachelor," and the single state

Single Living
Over the past fifteen or so years there has been a sharp increase in the proportion of younger adults who are not married. This has resulted from the tendency of young people to postpone marriage and from the rise in divorce rates. *(Hazel Hankin/Stock, Boston)*

was actively discouraged. Older single women were ridiculed, often despised, treated as life's failures, and stereotyped as sour, prim, meddling busybodies and pathetic misfits. (Poll surveys in 1957 showed that 80 percent of Americans believed that a woman had to be "sick," "neurotic," or "immoral" to remain unmarried. By 1978 the proportion had dropped to 25 percent [Yankelovich, 1981].) Bachelors were likewise mocked and treated with disapproval. In colonial times single men found themselves virtually in the class of suspected criminals; people believed that they required continual surveillance lest they fall into wayward habits. Many colonies had a weekly "bachelor tax" as an incentive for men to enter the married state.

Over the past generation, the notion that individuals must marry if they are to achieve maximum happiness and well-being has been increasingly questioned (Blakeslee, 1991). Many Americans no longer view "singlehood" as a residual category for the unchosen and lonely. For instance, a Detroit area survey of 916 families found that only a fourth of the young men and women said it would bother them a great deal if they did not marry; another quarter said it would not bother them at all (*New York Times*, December 23, 1982). Furthermore, 40 percent of the mothers in the survey said they would be both-

"I love you, but, hey, I'm flexible."

(Drawing by Cline; © 1990 The New Yorker Magazine, Inc.)

ered if a child never married; only 10 percent said it would trouble them a good deal. Even so, in Western culture, the nuclear family composed of a husband, a wife, and their offspring continues to be the measure or standard against which other family forms and lifestyles are judged (Ganong, Coleman & Mapes, 1990).

Single individuals (both never-married and divorced) find that as their numbers have grown, singles communities have arisen in most metropolitan areas. They can move into a singles apartment complex, go to a singles bar, take a singles trip, join a singles consciousness-raising group, and so on. If they choose, they can lead an active sex life without acquiring an unwanted mate, child, or reputation.

Although singleness may offer greater freedom and independence than married life does, it may also be accompanied by greater loneliness. The impersonal nature of singles bars has led them to be labeled "meat racks," "body works," and other nicknames that signify a sexual marketplace. Still, many singles remain wary about marriage and look to their work and other interests for the primary fulfillment of their life satisfactions.

Living Together

The number of adults who are sharing living quarters with an unrelated adult of the opposite sex has increased substantially over the past thirty years, to more than 2.5 million in 1990. It is easier for unmarried couples to live together today because of more permissive codes of morality. Even twenty-five years ago cohabitation was looked upon by many as morally wrong. Now university officials, landlords, and other agents of the establishment tend to ignore the matter, in marked contrast to their attitude twenty-five years ago. In the less sexually permissive days of 1968, a Barnard College sophomore named Linda LeClair became a national celebrity after the public revelation that she was living off campus with a former Columbia University student. Columbia officials made the front pages all over the nation when they decreed that she should be punished by being denied use of the college's snack bar and cafeteria and prohibited from attending any social event in the dormitories.

Following the campus turbulence and the peace and student-power movements of the late 1960s and early 1970s, this picture changed radically. Surveys at major universities showed that by the mid-1970s about a fourth to a third of the students either were currently living with or had lived with someone of the opposite sex (Henze & Hudson, 1974; Macklin, 1974; Peterman, Ridley & Anderson, 1974). However, the trend is now reversing. On college campuses such as Ohio State University, many students have come to view cohabitation as a restrictive and demanding lifestyle (Pentella, 1983). Students today are more likely to say that they prefer their "freedom" and do not want to be "tied down." Simultaneously, there has been a shift toward more conservative values and stronger religious conviction among the students.

Cohabitation seems most attractive to young adults. Adults under age 30 are nearly twice as likely as all adults to be cohabiting. However, 45 percent of people aged 30 to 34 have lived with an unmarried partner at some time in their lives. In the late 1960s and early 1970s, some 11 percent of adults lived together before their first marriage, but the share had risen to 44 percent by the early 1980s. The high proportion of married couples who live together prior to marriage suggests that premarital cohabitation may become institutionalized as a new step between dating and marriage (Gwartney-Gibbs, 1986). Cohabiting between marriages is even more prevalent: 58 percent of recently remarried couples have (Otten, 1988).

Although the media have at times labeled cohabiters "unmarried marrieds" and their relationships "trial marriages," the couples usually do not see themselves in this category. College students typically view cohabitation as part of the courtship process rather than as a long-term alternative to marriage. A study of students in the Boston area showed cohabiting couples to be no less likely to marry, and no more likely to break up, than noncohabiting couples who were "going together" (Risman, Hill, Rubin & Peplau, 1981). Nor does research support the notion that cohabitation before marriage is associated with later marital success (it seems that the "kinds of people" who choose to flout convention by cohabiting are the same "kinds of people" who flout traditional conventions regarding marital behavior, have a lower commitment to marriage as an institution, and are more likely to disregard the stigma of divorce) (Glenn, 1990).

In many cases living together as an alternative to marriage is not radically different from marriage. For instance, the partners easily fall into traditional gender roles and engage in many of the same activities that married couples do (Cole, 1977; Macklin, 1974; Newcomb, 1979). Moreover, unmarried couples typically encounter many of the same sorts of problems found among married couples (Gross, 1977). And, perhaps surprisingly, for the population as a whole the incidence of interpersonal violence is higher among cohabiting than among married couples (Yllo & Straus, 1981). The differences between living together and being married tend to be more subtle than the similarities. Commonly, however, the unmarried couples view themselves as less securely anchored, so that they feel more tentative about their capacity to endure difficult periods.

Breaking up is not as easy for an unmarried couple as popular belief has it. The emotional trauma may be every bit as severe as among married couples undergoing divorce. And in some cases there are legal complications associated with apartment leases and with property that was jointly secured and owned. Overall, the dissolution of cohabitation resembles divorce in that the partners in each case experience similar processes of disengagement and adjustment (Cole, 1977).

Young Adults Living at Home

In recent decades norms have dictated that U.S. youth leave home and make their own way in the world. But lately, adult children have been making their way back to the parental home in increasing numbers. Today's young adults are remaining home longer than has any generation since the early 1940s. A Census Bureau survey found that among 25- to 34-year-olds, 32 percent of single men and 20 percent of single women were living with their parents in 1990 (Gross, 1991). More than half of those from 18 to 24 years of age are living with their parents, compared with 42 percent in 1960 (Barringer, 1991).

A good many factors have contributed to this trend: postponed careers, high divorce rates, high housing costs, high levels of youth unemployment, expectations for a high standard of living, more liberal sexual attitudes, high rates of unmarried births, and damaged lives resulting from drug abuse. Youths are more likely to live at home in families with two biological parents than are youths from stepfamily or single-parent homes (Aquilino, 1990; Goldscheider & Goldscheider, 1989; Mitchell, Wister & Burch, 1989). Anita Tarjan, a 24-year-old teacher who lives with her parents, says (Lindsey, 1984, p. 10):

I want to strike out on my own, be independent, take care of my own affairs and have privacy. But unfortunately I can't afford to. You get out of college believing you're going to have this terrific job, and then when you finally do get a job, your salary just doesn't meet your expectations. You can't survive and there you are, living at home again, just like a teenager.

The goal of raising independent children was grounded historically in the expanding employment opportunities that prevailed in the United States for much of the twentieth century (Kohn, 1959, 1963; Parsons, 1943; Parsons & Bales, 1955; Schnaiberg & Goldenberg, 1975). Yet it is easy to overlook the prevalence of extended family arrangements during the nineteenth century. For instance, in U.S. and English textile communities, different generations often resided in the same household, providing a good deal of assistance to one another (Hareven, 1982, 1987; Ruggles, 1987). Constricted employment and opportunity structures for young people may now again lead to greater and more prolonged reliance by young adults on their parents (Schnaiberg & Goldenberg, 1989).

Living with parents has proven highly successful for some and disastrous for others, with many gradations in between (Aquilino & Supple, 1991). Those who find themselves pleased with the arrangement say that it affords them the benefits historically available in extended family living. There is a sense of warmness, closeness, and emotional support at a time of widespread personal alienation. Young couples find built-in baby-sitting advantages, and grandparents have an opportunity to know and enjoy their grandchildren. One 27-year-old student who returned home to live with his parents and who is now a sophomore at Ohio State University told the author:

> I'm really getting to know my parents all over again. And I am finding that they are quite different than I thought they were. I have gained new respect for them. You know, they're really awfully nice people.

But there are also disadvantages in returning to the parental home to live. Perhaps the most common complaint voiced by members of both generations concerns the loss of privacy. Couples report that they feel uncomfortable fighting in front of family members. Young adults, especially the unmarried, complain that parents cramp their sex lives or their stereo playing, treat them like children, and reduce their independence. Parents often grumble that their peace and quiet is disturbed, the phone rings at odd hours, they lie awake at night worrying and listening for the adult child to return home, meals are rarely eaten together because of conflicting schedules, and too much of the burden of baby-sitting falls on them. Then, too, higher expenses may compel parents to relinquish long-awaited vacations, and a need for space means they must postpone a move to a smaller, cheaper home.

Usually, the happiest refilled nests are those with ample space and open, trusting communication. Those that are most difficult are associated with grown children who lack resilience and maturity and who have drug problems. Under these circumstances parents may treat the 25-year-old like a 15-year-old, and the 25-year-old behaves like one. Family therapists express concern that those who stay at home do not have opportunities to fully develop their sense of individuality. Staying at home tends to aggravate tendencies toward excessive protectiveness in parents and toward a lack of self-confidence in youth. Many financially dependent young people receive a conflicting message from their parents: "You are grown up now but I don't feel you can really make it on your own." The tensions that result lead some families to seek professional help.

Homosexual and Lesbian Couples

Homosexuality is assuredly no advantage but it is nothing to be ashamed of, no vice, [no] degradation, it cannot be classified as an illness. . . . Many highly respectable individuals of ancient and modern times have been homosexuals, several of the greatest men among them (Plato, Michelangelo, Leonardo da Vinci, etc.). It is a great injustice to persecute homosexuality as a crime, and cruelty too.—SIGMUND FREUD

Letter to the mother of a homosexual, April 9, 1935

Heterosexuality involves a preference for an individual of the *opposite* sex as a sexual partner. **Homosexuality** involves a preference for an individual of the *same* sex as a sexual partner. Most of the general public assumes that there are two kinds of people, heterosexuals and homosexuals. In reality, however, a more accurate view is that heterosexuality and homosexuality are poles on a continuum. Individuals show various degrees of preference, including **bisexuality,** in which both opposite- and same-sex partners are about equally preferred. Since there are so many gradations in sexual behavior and preferences, some authorities take the position that there are heterosexual or homosexual *practices* but not heterosexual or homosexual *individuals* (Bell, Weinberg & Hammersmith, 1981; Bermant & Davidson, 1974; Ellis & Ames, 1987; Greenberg,

PORTION OF THE BAS-RELIEF "THE REPUBLIC," BY DALOU.

**Acceptance of Homosexual Relationships
by the Ancient Greeks**

**Societies vary considerably in the sexual activities of which
they approve and disapprove. In ancient Greece, sexual pleasure was seen as a valuable goal, and the naked male body
symbolized the ideal of both physical and emotional love.
Homosexual relationships were common among men of all
ages. Indeed, since the Greeks regarded homosexual feelings
as "natural," they made no attempt to explain why one man
should be sexually attracted to another.** *(North Wind Picture
Archives)*

1988). In sum, "homosexuality" and "heterosexuality" are terms that describe behavior. A gay
man or a lesbian may or may not elect to engage
in homosexual behavior.

The commonness of homosexual relations is
borne out by Alfred Kinsey's data (Kinsey,
Pomeroy, Martin & Gebhard, 1953), which indicate that by age 40 about 37 percent of males and
13 percent of females have reached homosexual
orgasm at least once in their lives. Of all the
people who have had homosexual experience,
however, those who never had a heterosexual
partner constitute only a very small proportion.
Kinsey found that among single males 20 to 35
years old, those who had exclusively homosexual
experience ranged in various samples from 3 to
16 percent, and among females that age, from 1 to
3 percent. However, surveys by the National Research Council in 1970 and 1988 suggest that the
number of U.S. men who have had at least one

homosexual experience is lower than the estimates compiled by Kinsey. It finds that roughly
20 percent of U.S. adult men have had one or
more homosexual experiences and some 3 to
4 percent have such contacts with some frequency. However, researchers with the National
Research Council caution that their figures may
be too low: They point out that many men have
been reluctant to admit same-gender sexual experiences given the history of discrimination and
oppression gays have encountered (Fay, Turner,
Klassen & Gagnon, 1989).

In the Western world individuals practicing
homosexual behavior have experienced a history
of oppression by a culture that has long regarded
the behavior as sinful and sick. Indeed, until 1973
the American Psychiatric Association included
homosexuality in its manual of pathological behaviors. And the subject of the pathology of homosexuality continues to be hotly debated by
psychiatrists, clinical psychologists, and others.
(For a discussion of theories dealing with the
sources of homosexuality, see the boxed insert on
pages 456–457.) Since 1977, the Gallup poll has
surveyed Americans, asking, "Do you think homosexual relations between consenting adults
should or should not be legal?" In 1977, 1982, and
1985, the public was closely split, with no clear
majority either way. But in 1986 and 1987, with
the growing linkage of AIDS and homosexuality,
public opinion turned negative, 54 to 33 percent.
In 1989, 47 percent of U.S. adults said that homosexual relations between consenting adults
should be legal, and 36 percent said they should
not. And 71 percent said gays should have equal
job opportunities, compared with 59 percent two
years earlier (Kagay, 1989).

Gays and lesbians are a varied group (Bell &
Weinberg, 1978; Bell, Weinberg & Hammersmith,
1981; Hooker, 1969; Kurdek & Schmitt, 1986).
They reflect all occupational fields, political out-
looks, religious affiliations, and racial and ethnic
groups. In some cases they "pass" for heterosexuals, are married, have children, and in most respects seem indistinguishable from the larger
population. Some seek transitory encounters
(Bell, Weinberg & Hammersmith, 1981; Humphreys, 1970). Others establish relatively durable
relationships involving mutual affection (Harry &
Lovely, 1979). And still others enter homosexual
unions repeatedly, each time hoping they have
found an ideal lover. "One-night stands" are
much less common among lesbians than among
gay men; lesbians tend to form more lasting ties
than gays, and they are less often detected and

Theories Regarding Homosexuality

The current state of scientific knowledge makes it difficult to arrive at firm conclusions regarding the causes or sources of homosexuality, but there is no shortage of theories. Indeed, some gays deeply resent the search for the "causes" of homosexuality, contending the search implies that heterosexuality is normative behavior whereas homosexuality is deviant behavior (Gelman, 1992).

Over 30 years ago, the psychoanalyst Irving Bieber (1962) advanced the hypothesis that the family is the architect of homosexuality. Bieber argued that gays tend to come from homes in which fathers are ineffective, coldly detached, and often rejecting toward their sons; mothers tend to be the dominant adult in the family, excessively intimate with their sons, overly binding and protective, and jealous of any interest that their sons show in other females. Consequently, the sons fail to identify with a male figure and simultaneously develop a fear and hatred of the female figure. Bieber concluded, therefore, that homosexuality is derailed heterosexuality. Little is known about the background family relationships of lesbians, but some psychiatrists believe that as children, they were deprived of maternal love. A related approach, derived from learning theory, explains homosexual behavior as being rooted in the expectation of punishment from the opposite sex or as being a learned aversion to the opposite sex.

Bieber's theory, although popular among many practicing psychoanalysts and psychiatrists, has not found support among researchers (Friedman, 1988; Lewes, 1988; Roberts, Green, Williams & Goodman, 1987; Robinson, Skeen, Hobson & Herrman, 1982). Michael Schofield (1965), for instance, undertook a careful study of a sample of gay men living in England. He could find no support for the hypothesis that ineffective fathers and dominant mothers provide the basis for homosexual behavior. Similarly, in the United States researchers at the Kinsey Institute have concluded that male homosexuality has little to do with overbearing mothers and distant fathers (Bell, Weinberg & Hammersmith, 1981). Indeed, if there is a connection between a boy's early experiences with his father and homosexuality, the neuroanatomist Simon LeVay believes "nature" comes first: "My point would be that gays are extremely different when they're young and as a *result* they can develop hostile relationships with their fathers. It's just a big mistake to think it's the other way around

and the relationships are causative" (quoted by Gelman, 1992, p. 49).

Another theory favored by many practicing psychiatrists has emphasized the predisposing effect of certain temperaments and physical characteristics (Green, 1974, 1987; Roberts, 1987). In this view, for example, a relatively timid, unaggressive boy or a boy with physical limitations, such as poor coordination, may find it difficult to associate successfully with friends of the same sex. As a result, he may compensate by seeking the companionship of girls, becoming involved in their activities and internalizing feminine gender roles. However, scales of masculinity and femininity have not been successful in detecting individuals who practice homosexual behavior (Singer, 1970). Indeed, personality tests given to college students who had rated themselves as homosexual, bisexual, or heterosexual revealed no significant differences on any measure of masculinity or femininity (Storms, 1980).

Researchers at the Kinsey Institute nevertheless do find that "gender nonconformity" is the single most important factor in predicting the eventual sexual preference of homosexual men. As boys, they often show less interest in sports and enjoy solitary activities like drawing, reading, and music more than boys who develop heterosexual preferences do. And recently, Richard Green (1987) has reported that three-fourths of forty-four extremely feminine boys followed from early childhood to adolescence or young adulthood matured as homosexuals or bisexuals, as against only one bisexual among a comparison group of more typically masculine boys. Even so, one-fourth of the heterosexual men in a San Francisco Bay area sample said that their behavior was not particularly gender conforming when they were youngsters (and half of the gay men in the survey had typical masculine interests and activities in their childhood). For lesbians "gender nonconformity" was found to be the second most important predictive factor, surpassed by homosexual involvement in adolescence. Yet only a third of the heterosexual women in a California sample described themselves as "highly feminine" in their childhood. Since "gender nonconformity" emerged early in childhood, the researchers concluded that it reflects an already-established, underlying homosexual orientation and is not a cause of it. Homosexual feelings almost always precede a person's homosexual activity by several years. In fact, an individual's sexual preference is usually established by the teens (Bell, Weinberg & Hammersmith, 1981).

Biological theories of homosexuality likewise abound. Frantz J. Kallmann (1952, 1953) advanced a hereditary interpretation based on a study of eighty-five male homosexuals and their twin brothers. Of the eighty-five, forty were identical twins, and Kallmann managed to locate their twin brothers in thirty-seven cases. In every instance the identical-twin brother was homosexually inclined, and in twenty-eight cases he was exclusively homosexual. Among the forty-five nonidentical twins Kallmann traced twenty-six of the twin brothers, and only three were homosexual. More recently, psychologist Michael Baily and psychiatrist Richard Pillard (1991) found in their survey of gay men (recruited through newspaper advertisements) that 52 percent of the identical twin brothers of 56 gay men were also gay. In contrast, only 22 percent of the fraternal twin brothers of 54 gay men were also gay. Psychiatrists at a Boston medical center have also found evidence that male homosexuality seems to "clump" in families (Pillard & Weinrich, 1986). They questioned fifty heterosexual and fifty-one predominately gay men about their sex lives and then contacted and interviewed the men's unmarried siblings who were at least 20 years old. The researchers found that 4 percent of the heterosexuals had brothers who were gay. In contrast, about 22 percent of the gay men had gay or bisexual brothers. Sisters of the gay men were not more likely to be bisexuals or lesbians than sisters of the heterosexual men. The Boston researchers caution, however, that their study does not show whether heredity or upbringing is more important in the origins of homosexuality.

A recent study by Simon LeVay (1991), a neurobiologist at the Salk Institute in La Jolla, California, also raises, but does not answer, the question of whether male homosexuality has a biological basis. In forty-one autopsies, he has detected structural differences in the brains of gay and heterosexual men. According to LeVay, one segment of the hypothalamus in gay men is a quarter to a half the size of the same region in heterosexual men. In studies of male rats and monkeys, researchers have also found that injury to this portion of the brain causes males to lose interest in females although they continue to exhibit sexual vigor through such activities as masturbation. LeVay does not know whether the brain differences arise during the development of the brain (predisposing the men to homosexual behavior) or whether a man's homosexual preferences fashion the contours of certain neural pathways later in life (a consequence of homosexual behavior). If the report is confirmed by other researchers, it could have important implications for a good many scientific, political, and social issues (Angier, 1991a, 1991b).

A few researchers have reported male hormonal differences between gay men and heterosexual men (Evans, 1972; Kolodny, Jacobs, Masters, Toro & Daughaday, 1972; Loraine, Ismail, Adamopolous & Dove, 1970; Newmark, Rose, Todd, Birk & Naftolin, 1979). Other researchers find no differences between adults engaging in predominantly heterosexual and homosexual behaviors (Tourney & Hatfield, 1973), and another study reports that testosterone levels in a group of exclusively gay men were significantly higher than those in a control group of heterosexual men (Brodie, 1974). Furthermore, low levels of certain male hormones have been found among men under stress, including army recruits during early basic training and Green Berets before combat missions in Vietnam (Rose, et al., 1969). Moreover, administering male hormones to gay men increases the sex drive but does not alter sexual preference. Some physiological research suggests that in a number of cases gay men may have been affected by hormonal disturbances that their mothers experienced during pregnancy (Ehrhardt & Meyer-Bahlburg, 1981; Money, 1987; Yalom, Green & Fisk, 1973).

Other researchers look to complex combinations of genetic, hormonal, neurological, and environmental factors that operate prior to birth as largely determining what a person's sexual orientation will be. However, they believe the orientation itself typically awaits the onset of puberty to be activated and may not entirely stabilize until early adulthood. The involvement of learning, by and large, is thought only to alter how, when, and where the orientation is expressed (Ellis & Ames, 1987). All in all, given the multiplicity of theories, the best course at present seems to be to keep an open mind on these matters and await further research.

harassed (Bell & Weinberg, 1978; Kinsey, Pomeroy, Martin & Gebhard, 1953; Mileski & Black, 1972).

A study by researchers at the Kinsey Institute for Sex Research at Indiana University (Bell & Weinberg, 1978, p. 216) concludes that

> homosexual adults who have come to terms with their homosexuality, who do not regret their sexual orientation, and who can function effectively sexually and socially, are no more distressed psychologically than are heterosexual men and women.

The researchers had examined the social and psychological adjustment of a sample of nearly a thousand gays and lesbians living in the San Francisco Bay area. On the whole, they found that adults practicing homosexual behavior resemble adults practicing heterosexual behavior in their reports about their physical health and their feelings of happiness or unhappiness.

In contrast to heterosexual and lesbian couples, gay couples tolerate outside sexual relations quite well (Blumstein & Schwartz, 1983; Kurdek & Schmitt, 1986). About 90 percent of gays with established partners have sexual relations with other men. Fidelity is typically not defined by sexual behavior but rather by each person's emotional commitment to the other. For most couples the passion of the sexual encounter dwindles rapidly after two or three years and outside sexual activity increases. Gay couples are more likely to break up over money issues and other incompatibilities than over the issue of sexual faithfulness. Household duties tend to be sorted out according to an individual's skills and preferences and seldom on the basis of stereotyped roles of "husband" and "wife."

In recent years there has occurred a marked decrease in casual sex among individuals practicing homosexual and heterosexual behavior (Salholz, 1990). Part of the reason can be traced to new fear of such diseases as acquired immune deficiency syndrome (AIDS) and herpes. But it also reflects a trend toward greater conservatism after the sexual revolution of the 1960s and 1970s. In particular, the AIDS epidemic has created anxiety and caution within gay communities throughout the United States because many victims of the lethal disease have been gay (lesbians have a low incidence of any kind of venereal disease and are not among the high-risk groups for AIDS). The AIDS organism (the HIV virus) is generally thought to be an infectious agent that is spread by bodily secretions, particularly semen and blood. It results in the collapse of the body's immune system, rendering the victim susceptible to cancers and various infections.

By virtue of the hostility of the larger community, individuals practicing homosexual behavior have often had to live double lives, "gay" at home and "straight" on the job. But shifts in public attitudes and gay rights laws have prompted many to live openly, particularly in large cities like San Francisco, Los Angeles, and New York. Furthermore, gay organizations and political caucuses have been vigorously championing gay rights measures. (Adam, 1987; Herek, 1990; Salholz, 1990).

Marriage

A lifestyle that apparently exists in all societies is **marriage**—a socially sanctioned union between a woman and a man with the expectation that they will play the roles of wife and husband. After studying extensive cross-cultural data, the anthropologist George P. Murdock (1949) concluded that reproduction, sexual relations, economic cooperation, and the socialization of offspring are functions of families throughout the world. We now recognize that Murdock overstated the matter, since there are a number of societies—for instance, Israeli kibbutz communities—in which the family does not encompass all four of these activities (Gough, 1960; Spiro, 1954). What Murdock describes are commonly encountered tendencies in family functioning in most cultures.

Societies differ in how they structure marriage relationships. Four patterns are found: *monogamy,* one husband and one wife; *polygyny,* one husband and two or more wives; *polyandry,* two or more husbands and one wife; and *group marriage,* two or more husbands and two or more wives. Although monogamy exists in all societies, Murdock discovered that other forms may be not only allowed but preferred. Of 238 societies in his sample, only about one-fifth were strictly monogamous.

Polygyny has been widely practiced throughout the world. The Old Testament reports that both King David and King Solomon had several wives. In his cross-cultural sample of 238 societies, Murdock found that 193 of them permitted husbands to take several wives. In one-third of these polygynous societies, however, less than one-fifth of the married men had more than one wife. Usually, only the rich men in a society can afford to support more than one family.

In contrast with polygyny, polyandry is rare among the world's societies. And in practice, polyandry has not usually allowed freedom of mate selection for women; it has often meant simply that younger brothers have sexual access to the wife of an older brother. Thus, where a father is unable to afford wives for each of his sons, he may secure a wife for only his oldest son. W. H. R. Rivers (1906, p. 515) gives this account of polyandrous practices among the Todas, a non-Hindu tribe of India:

> The Todas have a completely organized and definite system of polyandry. When a woman marries a man, it is understood that she becomes the wife of his brothers at the same time. When a boy is married to a girl, not only are his brothers usually regarded as also the husbands of the girl, but any brother born later will similarly be regarded as sharing his older brother's right. . . . The brothers live together, and my informants seemed to regard it as a ridiculous idea that there should even be disputes or jealousies

Fraternal Polyandry

Ethnic Tibetans along the Tibet-Nepal border in central Asia practice polyandry. A number of brothers jointly take a wife. Although the eldest brother is typically the dominant figure in the household, all the brothers share the work and participate as sexual partners with the wife. Here a 12-year-old bride stands with three of her five husbands-to-be. The grooms, ages 19, 17, and 7, are brothers. Two other brothers, ages 14 and 21, are off on a trading trip. The cultural ideal calls on the wife to show all the brothers equal affection and sexual favor, but deviations from the ideal occur, especially when there are considerable differences in age. (Thomas L. Kelly)

of the kind that might be expected in such a household. . . . Instead of adultery being regarded as immoral . . . according to the Toda idea, immorality attaches rather to the man who grudges his wife to another.

Anthropologists disagree on whether group marriage genuinely exists in any society as a normatively encouraged lifestyle. There is some evidence that it may take place among the Marquesans of the South Pacific, the Chukchee of Siberia, the Kaingang of Brazil, and the Todas of India. On occasion, as among the Todas, polyandry slides into group marriage when a number of brothers share more than one wife.

As in the past, monogamy remains the dominant lifestyle in the United States. Of Americans aged 35 or older, over 90 percent have been married at least once. But about four in ten marriages end in divorce. If current divorce rates continue, about 32 percent of the couples married in 1952 will divorce. The figure stands at 45 percent for those married in 1967. And population experts predict that fully half of all recently married couples could eventually divorce. If a marriage lasts 10 years, about 30.0 percent of the couples will eventually divorce; if it lasts 25 years, 7.8 percent will eventually divorce; and if it lasts 30 years, only 3.8 percent will eventually divorce (Tooley, 1989). In most cases—four out of five—divorced people remarry (an estimated 44 percent of all current marriages are remarriages). In turn, about 45 percent of those who divorce and remarry divorce a second time. Hence, rather than having recourse to polygyny, polyandry, or group marriage, many Americans have maintained a monogamous arrangement through *serial monogamy*—a pattern of marriage, divorce, and remarriage.

In sum, Americans have not given up on marriage. Public opinion surveys show that Americans depend very heavily on their marriages for their psychological well-being (Glenn & Weaver, 1981). Indeed, history reveals marriage to be a very resilient institutional arrangement. Not surprisingly, marriage is the most prevalent American life-style (see Figure 16-2). Increasing numbers of Americans have simply come to define marriage as something that can be ended and reentered. Hence, many Americans no longer view it as a permanent institution. Moreover, marriages differ. Marriage encompasses a wide range of interaction patterns, each of which entails a somewhat different lifestyle. We will return to this topic in Chapter 18.

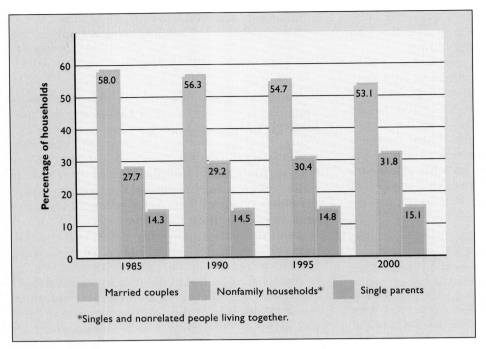

Figure 16-2 Household Compositions
The Census Bureau expects nonfamily households—singles and unmarried or unrelated couples living together—to grow to almost one-third of the total by the year 2000. Fairly high divorce rates are cited as one factor. In addition, young adults continue to put off marriage. And an increasingly elderly population, with more women outliving their husbands, is also contributing to the growth in singles households. SOURCE: Copyright 1987, *USA Today.* Reprinted with permission. Based on data from the Census Bureau. Original art by J. L. Albert, *USA Today.*

The Family Life Cycle and Parenthood

We hear a good deal nowadays about the "demise of the American family." Yet as discussed in the boxed insert on page 462, for most Americans the family remains a central and vital institution. Over the course of their lives most Americans find themselves members of two family groups. First, a person belongs to a nuclear family that typically consists of oneself and one's father, mother, and siblings. This group is termed the *family of orientation.* Second, since over 90 percent of Americans marry at least once, the vast majority of the population are members of a nuclear family consisting of oneself and one's spouse and often children. This group is termed the *family of procreation.*

Various psychologists and sociologists have sought to find a framework for describing the changes that occur across a person's life span that are related to these shifts in family patterns. One tool that they have devised is the concept of the **family life cycle**—the sequential changes and realignments that occur in the structure and relationships of family life between the time of marriage and the death of one or both spouses (Deutscher, 1964; Glick, 1989; Hill, 1986; Nock, 1979; Rapoport, Rapoport & Strelitz, 1976). The family life cycle model views families, like individuals, as undergoing development that is characterized by identifiable phases or stages.

Stages in the Family Life Cycle

In the United States families have traditionally had a fairly predictable natural history. Major changes in expectations and requirements are imposed upon a husband and wife as their children are born and grow up. The sociologist Reuben Hill (1964) describes the major milestones in a nine-stage cycle:

1. Establishment—newly married, childless.
2. New parents—until first infant 3 years old.

3. Preschool family—oldest child 3 to 6 years old, possibly younger siblings.
4. School-age family—oldest child 6 to 12 years old, possibly younger siblings.
5. Family with adolescent—oldest child 13 to 19 years old, possibly younger siblings.
6. Family with young adult—oldest child 20 years or more, until first child leaves home.
7. Family as launching center—from departure of first child to departure of last child.
8. Postparental family—after children have left home, until father retires.
9. Aging family—after retirement of father.

As viewed by Hill and other sociologists, the family begins with the simple husband-wife pair and becomes increasingly complex as members are added, creating new roles and multiplying the number of interpersonal relations. The family then stabilizes for a brief period, after which it begins shrinking as each of the adult children is launched. Finally, the family returns once again to the husband-wife pair and then terminates with the death of a spouse.

However, in the contemporary United States some individuals do not form families, and many families do not pass through these stages (between 1980 and 1990, the "traditional" family declined from 31 percent to 26 percent of all households) (Aldous, 1990; Glick, 1989). Since the family life cycle revolves around the reproductive process, the approach is not particularly helpful in understanding childless couples. Nor does the family life cycle approach apply to single-parent families, divorced couples, and stepfamilies (Hill, 1986). Critics such as Glenn H. Elder, Jr. (1974, 1983) also contend that the family life cycle approach does not adequately consider the developmental processes of individual family members. Many behaviors do not occur at the usual ages or in the typical sequence assumed by the family life cycle model. At times decisive economic, social, political, or military events intervene to alter the normal course of events. In addition, it is important whether parents are in their early twenties or their late thirties during the childbearing stage of the cycle. And a retarded or handicapped child may stay with the family long after the normatively established "launching" period. But despite its shortcomings, the family life cycle model provides a clear picture of family change, particularly for those families that remain intact and in which children are present.

Each modification in the role content of one family member has implications for all other members, since they are bound together in a network of complementary roles—a set of mutually contingent relationships. Consequently, each stage in the family life cycle requires new adaptations and adjustments. Of particular importance are the events surrounding parenthood. Accordingly, let us examine more closely the significance of parenthood for young adults.

Pregnancy

Within the life cycle of a couple, particularly a woman, the first pregnancy is an event of unparalleled importance (Gloger-Tippelt, 1983; Grossman, Eichler & Winickoff, 1980; Michaels & Goldberg, 1988; Rindfuss, Morgan & Swicegood, 1988; Ruble et al., 1990; Valentine, 1982). The first pregnancy signals that a couple is entering into the family cycle, bringing about new role requirements. As such, the first pregnancy functions as a major marker or transition and confronts a couple with new developmental tasks (Belsky, Lang & Huston, 1987; Duvall, 1977).

Pregnancy requires a woman to marshal her resources and adjust to a good many changes. Unfortunately, in many cases a woman's earliest experiences of pregnancy may be somewhat negative; she may encounter morning sickness, vomiting, and fatigue (see Chapter 4). Pregnancy may also compel a woman to reflect on her long-term life plans, particularly as they relate to mar-

"We've been married 17 years, Howard. When are we going to develop some *momentum?*"

(Baloo © 1990 from The Wall Street Journal. *Permission, Cartoon Features Syndicate.)*

Is the U.S. Family Disintegrating or Merely Changing?

Some 90 percent of U.S. men and women consider marriage the best way to live (Walsh, 1986). So worry about the future of the family is hardly surprising given the directions in which family life has been moving in recent decades. However, opinion differs as to the significance and meaning of the changes (Aldous, 1990; Berger & Berger, 1983; Glick, 1989). There are those who say that the family is a durable feature of the human experience, a resilient institution rooted in our social and animal nature. But since the institutional structure of society is always changing, the family must change to reflect this fact (Scanzoni, Polonko, Teachman & Thompson, 1989; Spanier, 1989; Sweet & Bumpass, 1987; Waldrop, 1988). Others contend that the family is in crisis (Popenoe, 1988; Will, 1991). They point out that divorce rates have soared; birth rates have fallen; the proportion of unwed mothers has increased; single-parent households have proliferated; mothers of young children have entered the labor force in large numbers; and the elderly are placing growing reliance on the government rather than the family for financial support (Carlson, 1988; Fuchs, 1983; Gilder, 1987).

The notion that family life is disintegrating implies that at an earlier time in history the family was a more stable and harmonious institution than currently. Yet historians have never located a golden age of the family (Cherlin, 1983; Degler, 1980; Flandrin, 1979). Their research reveals that the marriages of seventeenth-century England and New England were based on family and property needs, not on choice and affection. Loveless marriages, the tyranny of husbands, and the beating and abuse of children were commonplace (Shorter, 1975). Additionally, families were riddled by desertion and death to an unimaginable degree. In fact, because of fewer deaths, disruptions of marriages up through the completion of child rearing have been *declining* in the United States since 1900 (Uhlenberg, 1980).

The idea that families should consist of a bread-

Reports of the Death of the American Family Are Greatly Exaggerated
Throughout human history the family has been subject to a wide variety of pressures. It has proven itself an adaptive, resilient institution. Although new challenges confront today's families, it seems that people continue to prefer and vitally need the kinds of relationships that a healthy family life can provide. *(Michal Heron/Woodfin Camp & Associates)*

winner husband, a homemaker wife, and their dependent children is a relatively recent one. The rural, preindustrial family was a largely self-sufficient unit, meeting most of its consuming needs. Husbands, wives, children, and lodgers were all expected to participate in gainful work. Later, with the onset of industrialization, more and more family members sought work for wages in factories and workshops. This trend led Karl Marx and his coworker Friedrich Engels to deplore the employment of cheap female and child workers to run factory machines, compelling able-bodied men to accept "children's work at children's wages." Throughout the Western world the nascent labor movement pressed for the establishment of a "living wage," an income sufficient for a male breadwinner to support a wife and children in modest comfort.

riage and a career. And pregnancy may cause her to reconsider her sense of identity. Many women seek out information on birth and motherhood that assists them in testing and constructing new self-definitions (Deutsch, Ruble, Fleming, Brooks-Gunn & Stangor, 1988). The woman's partner faces many of these same concerns. He

may have to reappraise his conception of age, responsibility, and autonomy. Similarly, pregnancy frequently contributes to changes in the couple's sexual behavior. Since few events equal pregnancy in suddenness or significance, many couples experience the initial phase of pregnancy as somewhat disruptive (Gloger-Tippelt, 1983).

Americans began sorting jobs into male and female categories during the nineteenth century. The domestic sphere was defined as the "special place" of women. If women were in the labor force outside the home, it was expected that they would stop working after marriage or make a lifetime commitment of secular celibacy as nurses and school teachers. The restriction of large numbers of married women to domestic activities took place only after industrialization was well established (Carlson, 1986; Cherlin, 1983).

Contrary to popular myth, family life prior to the 1950s was hardly orderly (Coontz, 1988; Mintz & Kellogg, 1988; Spanier, 1989). Family members expected young adults to postpone leaving home or to put off marriage to assist the family in meeting an unexpected economic crisis or a parental death. At the turn of the century young people married relatively late because they were often obligated to help support their parents and siblings. The economic prosperity of the post-World War II years contributed to a sharp drop in the average age at which marriage occurred. Today's young adults, however, are reversing the trend and marrying at later ages (Cherlin, 1983). The view that family life should meet emotional needs—accompanied by the transformation of the family into a highly private institution—did not spread beyond the middle class until this century. The development of affectionate and private bonds within a small nuclear family were accelerated in the early 1900s with the decline in the boarding and lodging of nonfamily members, the growing tendency for unmarried adults to leave home, and the fall in fertility (Laslett, 1973).

All in all, reports of the death of the U.S. family are greatly exaggerated. A recent public opinion poll by Louis Harris and Associates (1987), designed to assess the quality of family life, found the following:

❏ Members in 89 percent of the households said they were satisfied with the relationship with their spouse or the person they live with. Among those with children, 93 percent reported satisfaction with the quality of the relationship.

❏ Eighty-six percent were pleased with how family members rally behind one another in crisis.

❏ Eighty-six percent reported they were satisfied with the way the interests of each family member are respected.

❏ Eighty-five percent said the pleasures in family life outweigh the troubles.

The pollsters found that parents, by a margin of two to one, expressed a preference for having both the father and mother work instead of having the woman stay home to raise the children. Although showing that 79 percent of families are in relatively good shape, the poll revealed that 21 percent—primarily single-parent, minority, female-headed households—are in difficulty. One of the most poignant statistics from the survey came in response to the question "Do you want your lifestyle to be that of your children?" Overall, three-quarters of Americans said yes. But 77 percent of the dissatisfied category indicated otherwise.

Overall, family life, although often presenting challenges and frustrations, is something that most people vitally need, particularly when many other spheres of life are becoming "depersonalized." Many of us believe, as does developmental psychologist Urie Bronfenbrenner (1977a, p. 47), that "the relationships in families are the juice of life, the longings and frustrations and intense loyalties. We get our strength from those relationships, we enjoy them, even the painful ones. Of course, we also get some of our problems from them, but the power to survive those problems comes from the family, too." In sum, although we may think that the grindstones of social change are pulverizing family organization, for most Americans the family remains a vital, adaptive, resilient human institution.

On the broader social level, relatives, friends, and acquaintances commonly offer judgments on numerous matters, including whether the woman stands in a proper social relationship with the father-to-be. An employed woman may have to confront changed relationships in the work setting as her employer and colleagues reappraise their ties with her. If she should withdraw from the paid work force in preparation for childbirth, the mother-to-be may find that her domestic situation also alters: the more egalitarian values and role patterns of dual-career couples tend to give way to the stereotyped role patterns found in traditional nuclear families.

Pregnancy: A Time of Developmental Change
Pregnancy functions as a major marker or transition in the life of a woman. It confronts her with new developmental tasks, including coming to terms with her pregnancy, taking better physical care of herself, and redefining her relationships with other people who are important to her. It also sets the stage for changes in the lives of others who are closely tied in a woman's network of relationships. (*J. Howard/Stock, Boston*)

Researchers have identified four major developmental tasks confronting a pregnant woman. First, she must come to accept her pregnancy. She must define herself as a parent-to-be and incorporate into her life frame an impending sense of parenthood. This process requires developing an emotional attachment to her unborn child. Women typically become progressively preoccupied with the fetus and, especially around the time that they begin to detect clear movements of the child in the uterus, ascribe personal characteristics to it.

Second, as a woman's pregnancy progresses, she must come to differentiate herself from the fetus and establish a distinct sense of self. She may accomplish this task by reflecting on a name for the infant and imagining what the baby will look like and how it will behave. This process is expedited when her increasing size brings about alterations in her clothing and she assumes a "pregnancy identity."

Third, a pregnant woman typically reflects on and reevaluates her relationship with her own mother (Fischer, 1981). This process often entails the woman's reconciliation with her mother and the working through of numerous feelings, memories, and identifications.

Fourth, a woman must come to terms with the issue of dependency. Her pregnancy and impending motherhood often arouse anxiety concerning her loss of certain freedoms and her reliance on others for some measure of support, maintenance, and help. Such concerns are frequently centered on her relationship with her husband or partner.

The accomplishment of these developmental tasks is often expedited by childbirth-training classes (Doering, Entwisle & Quinlan, 1980). Such classes teach women what to expect during pregnancy and labor. They have an opportunity to verbalize their concerns. And the knowledge and techniques they gain from the classes afford them a measure of "active control" and self-help. Finally, when husbands or partners also participate in the training classes, mothers-to-be find additional social support and assistance. Both preparation in pregnancy and a husband's presence are positively associated with the quality of a woman's birth experience (Norr, Block, Charles, Meyering & Meyers, 1977). Indeed, much that happens before birth influences what transpires between parent and child after birth (Harriman, 1986; Heinicke, Diskin, Ramsey-Klee & Given, 1983).

Transition to Parenthood

Psychologists and sociologists who view the family as an integrated system of roles and statuses have often depicted the onset of parenthood as a "crisis" because it involves a shift from a two-person to a three-person system (Dyer, 1963; LeMasters, 1957; Robenstein, 1989). The three-person system is thought to be inherently more stressful than the two-person system. Sociologist

Alice S. Rossi (1968, p. 35) also finds other reasons that the transition to parenthood may pose a crisis:

> The birth of a child is not followed by any gradual taking on of responsibility, as in the case of a professional work role. It is as if the woman shifted from a graduate student to a full professor with little intervening apprenticeship experience of slowly increasing responsibility. The new mother starts out immediately on twenty-four-hour duty, with responsibility for a fragile and mysterious infant totally dependent on her care.

But many researchers have questioned these conclusions (Hobbs, 1965, 1968; Hobbs & Cole, 1976). Their research suggests that relatively few couples view the onset of parenthood as especially stressful. They point out that any role change is likely to involve transitional difficulties and that it seems an exaggeration to term the experience a "crisis" (Lamb, 1978; McLaughlin & Micklin, 1983; Ruble, Fleming, Hackel & Stangor, 1988).

A continuing study of more than two-hundred-fifty families by Jay Belsky and his colleagues is providing a rich array of insights about the transition to parenthood (Belsky, 1985; Belsky, Lang & Huston, 1987; Belskey, Lang & Rovine, 1985; Belskey & Rovine, 1990; Belsky, Spanier & Rovine, 1983; Hawkins & Belsky, 1989). This research shows that having children does not turn good marriages into bad ones or bad marriages into good ones. Yet overall, couples seem to give up a measure of romantic intimacy as they invest themselves in a child. After the birth of a baby, couples typically experience a modest decline in the overall quality of their marital life. Husbands and wives show one another less affection, and they share fewer leisure activities. The decline in marital satisfaction tends to be greater for wives than for husbands. But on the positive side, there is an increase in a couple's sense of partnership and mutual caretaking. And with the addition of a second child, fathers often become more involved in the work of the home, taking on more household tasks and significantly increasing their interaction with the firstborn youngster (Stewart, 1990). Couples who are most likely to report marital problems in early parenthood are those who held the most unrealistic expectations of parenthood, in which the lives of one or both partners is complicated by problems at work, and in which one spouse (usually the wife) has to assume a heavily disproportionate share of the division of household chores.

Although having a baby may not save a marriage, a study by researchers associated with the Rand Corporation found that a first baby may have a stabilizing effect on marriages (Waite, Haggstrom, & Kanouse, 1985). The researchers followed 5,540 new parents and 5,284 nonparents for three years; the couples were matched on such factors as age and years married. The study showed that by the time their children were two years of age, the parents had a divorce rate under 8 percent. The nonparents had a rate of more than 20 percent. But why should babies make a marriage more stable? The Rand researchers speculate that people who decide to have children may be happier together to begin with, that children are a deterrent to divorce because they add complexity and expense to a breakup, and that parents acquire a bond with their partners through their children. (Parents may initially experience a short period termed the *postpartum blues,* which is discussed in the boxed insert.)

Overall, contemporary parents seem to have a less romantic and more realistic view of the probable effects of children on their lives than did earlier generations of parents. This recognition seems to prepare them for coping with the changes that parenthood brings. They have to juggle a whole new set of questions about their work roles, demands on their time, communication patterns, privacy, and the companionship as-

"Hey, here's somebody who looks just like a young you!"

(Drawing by Wm Hamilton; © 1989 The New Yorker Magazine, Inc.)

Postpartum Blues

About two or three days after delivery, some new mothers experience what is commonly termed the *postpartum blues*. The symptoms include irritability, waves of sadness, frequent crying spells, difficulty in sleeping, diminished appetite, and feelings of helplessness and hopelessness. Generally, the episode is mild and lasts only a short time—several days to two weeks (Fleming, Ruble, Flett & Shaul, 1988). Similar symptoms often appear in women who adopt a child, and some new fathers also report that they feel "down in the dumps." One study reported that 89 percent of new mothers experienced some symptoms that have been traditionally associated with the postpartum blues and 62 percent of the fathers had similar symptoms (Collins, 1981*b*).

Various explanations have been advanced for the postpartum blues. Some authorities believe that hormonal changes associated with childbirth and metabolic readjustment to a nonpregnant state can influence a woman's psychological state. Following childbirth, marked changes occur in the levels of various hormones, and changes may occur in thyroid and adrenal hormones. All these changes can contribute to depressive reactions.

Other explanations of a more psychological nature emphasize the adjustments required of a woman in her new role as a mother (Hopkins, Marcus & Campbell, 1984). Many women experience a loss of independence—a sense of being tied down and trapped by the new infant. Other women may feel guilty about the anger they develop when their infants cry and cannot be comforted. And some women also feel overwhelmed by the responsibility of caring for, rearing, and shaping the behavior of another human being. More particularly, women with temperamentally difficult youngsters may find that child care severely taxes their emotional and psychological resources, contributing to depression. Although mothers can do little to alter their infants' basic temperament, they can more successfully cope with the stress by developing a network of supportive people (Cutrona, 1984; Cutrona & Troutman, 1986).

Psychoanalytic theorists say that the precipitating factor in postpartum blues is the unconscious conflict a woman experiences when she assumes the mothering role. The conflict is derived from a woman's ambivalent identification with her own mother. According to this view, deep-seated, repressed childhood feelings of attraction (love) and repulsion (aggressive and destructive impulses) toward her mother are activated when a woman becomes a mother in her own right. Since she identifies with her mother as a woman, the new mother develops a love-hate conflict with respect to herself. The result is psychological depression.

In a small number of cases the birth of a child may act as a catalyst that triggers severe mental illness among women who are predisposed to schizophrenic or manic-depressive psychoses. Psychiatrists generally make no distinction between a psychosis that appears during the postpartum period and a psychotic episode at other periods of life, except for the fact that the precipitating event is the birth of a child. In more devastating forms of mental illness, a woman may attempt suicide and require hospitalization.

---

pects of their relationship. But on the whole, they report enormous satisfaction in parenthood.

Employed Mothers

If a woman's adult efforts are concentrated exclusively on her children, she is more likely to stifle than broaden her children's perspective and preparation for adult life.—ALICE S. ROSSI
The Woman in America

One aspect of motherhood that some women experience as stressful is the balancing of motherhood and career. Despite "the sexual revolution," employed women still bear the brunt of being the primary parent and the primary person responsible for keeping house (Hochschild, 1989; Hoffman, 1986; Menaghan & Parcel, 1990; Scarr, Phillips & McCartney, 1989). Economist Sylvia Ann Newlett notes (quoted by Castro, 1991, p. 10):

In the U.S. we have confused equal rights with identical treatment, ignoring the realities of family life. After all, only women can bear children. And in this country, women must still carry most of the burden of raising them. We think that we are being fair to everyone by stressing identical opportunities, but in fact we are punishing women and children.

Over the past several decades more and more mothers with young children have found employment outside the home. By 1990, 66 percent of children between the ages of 6 and 17 had mothers in the labor force, and some 53 percent of all mothers with preschool children were employed outside the home. The decrease in the time required for homemaking chores and in the number of children in the family have substantially changed the role of the full-time mother. All the while, rising educational levels for women have increased both their ability and motivation to obtain employment outside the home. Moreover, a great many families find it essential that the woman find income-generating employment. Indeed, most divorced, single, and widowed mothers must work to avoid poverty. Moreover, in two-parent families a second income is often required to maintain an acceptable standard of living. And present living arrangements and the growing prevalence of working mothers have increased the full-time homemaker's isolation from other adults (Hoffman, 1989; Menaghan & Parcel, 1990; Scarr, Phillips & McCartney, 1989). As with men, a place in the workplace allows women to participate in the larger society. Significantly, in its original formulation, the family life cycle approach made no reference at all to the mother's participation in the paid labor force. Newer versions of the scheme have recognized that the career woman and the mother are increasingly one and the same person (Mattessich & Hill, 1987; Waite, 1980). (See the discussion of the phases in adult female development in Chapter 15.)

Serious concern is frequently voiced about the future of U.S. children as more and more mothers enter the work force (see Chapters 8 and 10). Many people fear that the working mother represents a loss to children in terms of supervision, love, and cognitive enrichment. Much of the earlier research of maternal employment and juvenile delinquency was based on this assumption: Mothers were working, children were unsupervised, and thus, they became delinquents. But the matter is not that simple. In a classic study of lower-class boys Sheldon and Eleanor Glueck (1957) found that sons of regularly employed mothers were no more likely to be delinquent than sons of nonemployed mothers. However, inadequate supervision does appear to be associated with delinquency, whatever the mother's employment status (Hoffman, 1974).

Flora F. Cherry and Ethel L. Eaton (1977) studied 200 lower-income families in order to determine possible harmful outcomes due to maternal employment during a child's first three years of life. When the children were 7 and 8 years old, they were all compared with respect to physical growth and weight, IQ and reading, arithmetic, and spelling achievement. Cherry and Eaton found that those whose mothers had worked were no different in physical and cognitive development from those whose mothers had not worked. Most researchers have arrived at essentially the same conclusion (Farel, 1980; Hoffman, 1989; Phillips, McCartney & Scarr, 1987; Scarr, 1984; Schachter, 1981).

Increasingly, psychologists and sociologists are no longer asking whether it is good or bad that mothers work outside the home. Instead, they are finding that the central question is whether the mother, regardless of employment, is satisfied in her situation (Hock & DeMeis, 1990; Hoffman, 1989; MacEwen & Barling, 1991; Scarr, 1984; Stuckey, McGhee & Bell, 1982; Sweeney, 1982). Researchers conclude that the working mother who obtains personal satisfaction from employment, who does not feel excessive guilt, and who has adequate household arrangements is likely to perform as well as or better than the nonemployed mother. Mothers who are *not* working and would like to, and working mothers whose lives are beset by harassment and strain, are the ones whose children are most likely to show maladjustment and behavioral problems. Time spent with one's children is not so predictive of young children's development as is the attitudes and behaviors their parents take toward them (Easterbrooks & Goldberg, 1984; Greenberger & Goldberg, 1989). In sum, an important ingredient linking the mother's employment status to the effects on her child is the woman's "morale." Hence, much depends on the family's socioeconomic circumstances, the father's role, the attitudes of other family members, and the availability of support systems ranging from child-care facilities to helpful friends and relatives (Menaghan & Parcel, 1991; Moorehouse, 1991; Rogers, Parcel & Menaghan, 1991).

The working mother also provides a somewhat different role model for her children from that of the nonemployed mother. Consequently, maternal employment tends to be associated with less traditional gender role concepts, more approval of working mothers, and a higher evaluation of female competence (Gold & Andres, 1978*a*, 1978*b*, Hoffman, 1989; Shreve, 1984; Stephan & Corder, 1986). An additional finding is that employed mothers seem to emphasize independence training more than do nonemployed mothers (Hoffman, 1989; Weinraub, Jaeger & Hoffman, 1988).

Among dual-earner couples with children, parents frequently work different shifts. By virtue of the rapid growth in evening, night, and weekend work, many dual-income marriages come to resemble single-parent families (McEnroe, 1991). Although split-shift parenting reduces the time in the evening or night that both parents can be with the children, it maximizes the time that at least

Three Sociological Approaches to Poverty

"The poor you have always with you," says St. John's Gospel. Sociologists seem to agree. They have advanced three theories to explain poverty: the culture of poverty thesis, the situational thesis, and the structural thesis.

The Culture of Poverty Thesis According to the culture of poverty thesis, economically disadvantaged people in industrial nations lack effective participation and integration within the larger society (Lewis, 1959, 1961, 1966). Their clustering in large inner-city ghettos contributes to a sense of marginality, helplessness, dependence, and inferiority. Consequently, they evolve ways of thinking, feeling, and acting that set them apart from their more affluent counterparts: (1) a sense of passivity and resignation because of enduring poverty; (2) a present-time orientation because of the pressures of day-to-day survival; (3) a sense of fatalism and powerlessness deriving from a lack of political resources; (4) low aspirations because of an absence of economic opportunity; (5) feelings of inferiority because of the larger society's contempt; and (6) the creation of female-headed families because of the inability of poor men to be adequate breadwinners. These patterns become self-perpetuating as the ethos associated with the culture of poverty are transmitted to successive generations through socialization.

Although the culture of poverty thesis enjoys widespread acceptance among the public, it is roundly criticized by many social scientists who consider it a variation of "blaming the victim" arguments (Demos, 1990; Duncan, Hill & Hoffman, 1988; Liebow, 1967; Sanders, 1990; Wilson, 1987). They portray the disadvantaged as very much immersed in U.S. life and not as carriers of an independent culture of poverty. The critics say that the so-called pathological consequences of poverty will disappear when the poor are provided with decent jobs and other social resources (Ellwood, 1988; Riemer, 1988).

The Situational Thesis Another view sees poverty as largely *situational*. Research undertaken by the Institute for Social Research at the University of Michigan (Duncan, 1984; Duncan, Hill & Hoffman, 1988) depicts the poverty population as a kind of pool with people flowing in and out. Its findings are based on a 1968 survey of 5,000 U.S. families who were then followed for a decade thereafter. The study casts doubt on the culture of poverty thesis that being poor at one time means being poor always. Over the ten-year period, only 2.6 percent of the sample were classified as persistently poor (individuals who failed to meet the government's income standard for escaping poverty in eight or more of the ten years). About 25 percent of the families re-

---

one parent can be present. However, by the same token, shift work has a modest but generally negative effect on marital quality and satisfaction (Hertz & Charlton, 1989; White & Keith, 1990).

Single-Parent Mothers

Over the past thirty years single-parent families have increased seven times more rapidly than have traditional two-parent, or nuclear, families. Currently 20 percent of all U.S. youngsters live in single-parent households. Some 42 percent of contemporary white children and 86.7 percent of contemporary black children will live in a single-parent household sometime in their youth. Eighty-five percent of single-parent white children and 94 percent of black children live with their mothers (Lewin, 1990). Of the children

in single-parent households, 38.6 percent are living with a divorced parent, and 30.6 percent are living with a parent who has never married (others reside with a parent who is married but separated or are offspring of a widowed parent) (Barringer, 1991).

Single-parent homes are produced by divorce, desertion, marital separation, death, or unmarried parenthood. Now that many states have begun permitting unmarried persons to adopt children, a small number also result from adoption. In single-parent families the responsibilities fall upon one adult rather than two. Single parents must allocate their time to cover both their own and their children's physical, social, and psychological needs. The matter is complicated by the fact that schools and workplaces have inflexible hours, and these hours do not coincide. Single mothers frequently suffer from a lack of free

ceived welfare at one time or another over the decade, but many received it for only short periods. Often they slipped into poverty after experiencing an adverse event such as divorce or illness. For these families welfare benefits serve as a sort of "safety net" or "insurance protection," something they briefly avail themselves of but then dispose of as soon as possible. The Michigan researchers conclude that there is "little evidence that individual attitudes and behavior patterns affect individual economic progress." Instead, people "are the victims of their past, their environment, luck, and chance."

Even so, 70 percent of the women who were under age 25 when they first received welfare stayed on welfare for at least five years, and more than one-third remained on the rolls for at least a decade. For older and divorced women, welfare tends to be a benign source of assistance. But youthful mothers who have babies out of wedlock do not get married as often as their peers, do not remarry as quickly, and do not get into the paid labor force with the same degree of success. Although the Michigan data reveal that the majority of people who have *ever* been on welfare have been on the rolls for less than five years, a majority of the people on the rolls *at any point in time* are in the midst of long spells of welfare dependence (Pear, 1986).

The Structural Thesis Still another view depicts poverty as a *structural* feature of capitalist societies. Cycles of economic expansion and retraction—boom or bust—contribute to sharp fluctuations in employment. Minorities are particularly vulnerable because historically they have been the last hired and the first fired. Complicating matters, structuralists point to the emergence in recent decades of a "new industrial order" that is characterized by a significant shift from manufacturing to service-sector employment. Well-paying jobs in manufacturing traditionally provided a major avenue of job security and occupational advancement for the nation's minorities and disadvantaged. But the decline of manufacturing jobs has meant that the cities no longer function as opportunity ladders for these groups. In brief, structuralists say that the problem of poverty is fundamentally a problem of lack of income-producing employment (Kasarda, 1989; Baca-Zinn, 1989; Marks, 1991).

Adherents of the culture of poverty and structural positions see a "second nation" emerging within black America that is outside the economic mainstream and becoming a permanent underclass of have-nots. The situational approach disputes this notion.

time, spiraling child-care costs, loneliness, and the unrelenting pressures of attempting to fill the needs posed by both home and work.

Being a single parent calls for a somewhat different kind of parenting. Many single parents report that they establish a closer tie with their children, since another adult is not present. Frequently, single parents find themselves making "the speech," as one mother termed it, explaining (McCoy, 1982, p. 21):

> I sat down with my three children and said, "Look. Things are going to have to be different. We're all in this together and we're going to have to be partners. I'm earning a living for us now. I'm doing it all. I need your help, if this household is going to work."

Women heading single-parent families typically experience greater stress than women in two-parent families (Fassinger, 1989; McLanahan, 1983). Lower incomes and lower levels of social

support lead to chronic strain. Disruptions due to substantial income changes, residential relocations, and household composition changes are also more likely. Not surprisingly, female heads report much lower self-esteem, a lower sense of effectiveness, and less optimism about the future than their counterparts in two-parent settings. However, recently divorced, separated, and widowed women are more likely to experience major life-event disruptions than women who have been single for three or more years. And while many women do not choose single parenting, most are proud of their ability to survive under adverse circumstances (Richards, 1989).

Not uncommonly, single mothers find themselves in difficult economic circumstances. Nearly half of families headed by single mothers live below the poverty level, and many are dependent on government agencies for assistance (see Figure 16-3). There is a critical difference be-

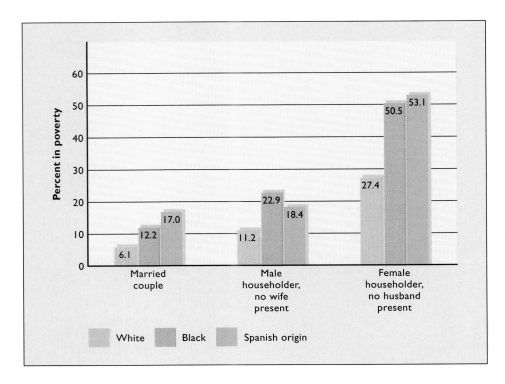

Figure 16-3 Poverty Rates of Families, 1987
Poverty continues to be a major problem among female-headed families, particularly among those headed by blacks or women of Hispanic origin. SOURCE: Copyright 1987, *USA Today.* Based on data from *The American Woman, 1987–1988, A Report in Depth.* Original art by J. L. Albert, *USA Today.*

tween the married poor with children and the single-parent poor: On average, the married poor move out of poverty; the single-parent poor do not (Weiss, 1984). The National Advisory Council of Economic Opportunity describes what it labels "the feminization of poverty" as "the most compelling social fact" of recent years (Mann, 1983). Lack of job training, loss of skill during the childbearing years, and discriminatory hiring and promotion patterns often mean that single mothers work for low wages. As economist Sylvia Ann Hewlett points out, our society ignores "the fact that individuals who are nurturing children cannot compete on equal footing with those who are not" (quoted by Castro, 1991, p. 10). The boxed insert on pages 468–469 discusses three theories that sociologists have advanced to explain poverty.

In addition, a social stigma often attaches to the single mother as a result of her unwed or divorced status, and she is further discriminated against as a female head of household. In her dealings with people in the world about her, she must contend with being stereotyped as financially irresponsible, sexually "fair game," and psychologically "disabled." In many respects a single father is in a better position than a single mother, since he is frequently viewed as a heroic figure who is doing something extraordinary.

According to the Census Bureau, child support still appears to be a 50-50 proposition. About 59 percent of women raising children without the children's father have been awarded child support, but only 51.3 percent of these receive full payment (24.9 percent receive partial payments and 23.9 percent do not receive any payments) (Dunn, 1990). In the United States, divorce often removes all a man's fathering functions save for one, the monetary obligation. And as men start seeing their children less, they often start paying less. Among never-married mothers, only 6 percent get any financial help from their children's father (Fletcher, 1989; Jencks, 1982). It is hardly surprising, then, that 74 percent of never-married mothers aged 15 to 24 live in poverty. And children living with divorced single-parent mothers typically experience a dramatic decline in their standard of living compared with their pre-divorce, two-parent household (Hoffman & Duncan, 1988).

Many families headed by women survive these hardships with few ill effects. Some even blossom as a result of the spirit of cooperation that is required to make the households work. But a disturbing number of children and parents are saddled with problems (Fine, Donnelly & Voydanoff, 1986; Richards, 1989). Children living in single-parent families are much more likely to be enrolled below the grade that is modal for their age and to be experiencing school difficulties than are children living with both parents (Bianchi, 1984; Milne, Myers, Rosenthal &

Ginsburg, 1986). Some studies also show that juvenile-delinquency rates are twice as high for children from single-parent households as they are for children from two-parent households. Lack of parental supervision and chronic social and psychological strains are often complicated by the problems associated with poverty (Mann, 1983; Richards, 1989).

Social isolation can create a sense of vulnerability for single mothers. Yet most women report having a partner, boyfriend, friends, or relatives who provide them with assistance on a fairly regular basis (Parish, Hao & Hogan, 1991; Richards, 1989). In about 50 percent of all single-parent families, the parent remarries within five years. This change results in a "blended" or "reconstituted" family, which can produce complicated kinship networks (see Chapter 18). Where both partners have been previously married, each has to deal with the former spouse of the current partner as well as with his or her own former spouse. Adding to the difficulties are stepparent-stepchildren relationships—one's own children's reactions to the current spouse, one's own reactions to the current spouse's children, and the children's reactions to one another.

Single-Parent Fathers

What was portrayed in the hit movie *Kramer vs. Kramer* is becoming a way of life for increasing numbers of U.S. men: rearing children alone. Because of prenatal medical attention and advances in medical technology, the number of men who become single parents as a result of their wives' death has declined. But overall the number of single fathers has grown, as more men are awarded custody of children in divorce proceedings and as a growing number of women leave their families in search of new lifestyles and working opportunities. Indeed, twenty years ago a father was awarded custody of his children only if he could demonstrate in court that the mother was "unfit" for parenthood.

Although the expectations attached to the father role in a two-parent family are fairly explicit, they are not so explicit for a father in the single-parent family. The vast majority of single fathers previously performed their parental responsibilities in partnership with their children's mothers. But in single fatherhood there is no role clarity about what they are to do and how they are to do it. Indeed, single fathers who care for their children may be seen as less manly because they are doing something that is traditionally thought

to be part of a woman's role. One single father observes, "I'm a male mother in a society in which only women are supposed to mother!" Another father notes, "When I help out at my son's school, I am listed as 'room mother'" (Jacob, 1987).

A number of studies have shown that even though single fathers are confronted with some unique adjustment requirements, most of them are successful in raising their children (Greif, 1985; Risman, 1986). But juggling work and child care commonly poses difficulties for single fathers, especially those with preschool youngsters. One widower with small children notes (Thornton, 1982, p. 620):

> You have to worry about the kids all the time. You get accustomed to doing everything alone—refereeing battles or playing Solomon over the telephone. You have to make sure that keys are always available. Schools and doctors have to have your phone number at work. You must keep easy-to-prepare food at the house in case you can't get home in time to fix meals. You cancel your social plans quite often, too.

Compared with single mothers, however, fathers often have more money and greater job flexibility, allowing them somewhat greater leeway in adjusting to their children's daily needs (Meredith, 1985). Overall, the single father is neither the extraordinary human being nor bumbling "Mr. Mom" depicted in many popular stereotypes (Greif, 1985; Risman, 1986; Robinson, 1988).

Many fathers try at first to have someone come into their homes and care for the children while they are at work. The vast majority, however, soon find this to be an unsatisfactory arrangement. Fathers generally report that their children are inadequately supervised and cared for by hired baby-sitters. Furthermore, the arrangement tends to be unstable, with a high turnover rate among the caretakers. Consequently, fathers tend to gravitate toward nurseries and child-care centers, where they feel that the staff has a professional commitment to children (Mendes, 1976).

Once the children begin attending elementary school, fathers usually allow them to stay alone after school. Simultaneously, a good many fathers try to structure after-school activities on some weekdays by having their children join scout organizations or athletic teams or take gymnastic, music, or dancing lessons. At times, fathers undertake to supervise their children's activities by telephone.

Instead of hiring domestic help, most single fathers themselves assume the responsibility for cleaning, cooking, shopping, and generally managing the household. However, they are more inclined than two-parent families to assign their children various household chores and to integrate the children into the management of the home. Some fathers eliminate the irksome problem of ironing by purchasing nothing but wash-and-wear clothing.

Generally, single fathers seem better prepared for the physical aspects of parenting—shopping, cooking, cleaning, taking the child to the doctor, and the like—than for dealing with their children's emotional needs. Men who adeptly juggle work schedules to stay home and nurse a sick child report that they fall apart in the face of a healthy temper tantrum. They view their children's strong displays of emotion as "irrational," especially when they cannot trace those emotions to some specific event in the children's lives. In sum, a good many single fathers admit that they have had to learn to deal with their children's emotional needs and to develop their own nurturing skills (Dullea, 1978).

Single fathers with daughters often report that they are concerned and even troubled about their daughters' sexuality. Many, especially men over 40, find it difficult to discuss sexual matters with their daughters; they believe that this discussion is a task for women. Single fathers also tend to express more anxiety over the sexual behavior of their daughters than of their sons. And many are concerned about the absence of adult female role models within the home. Overall, however, single fathers feel that they are successful in rearing their daughters.

Perhaps the biggest difficulty that fathers have in making the transition to single parenthood is losing their wife's companionship. Their greatest stress is associated with becoming single rather than becoming a single parent (Smith & Smith, 1981). Consequently, dating is often an important part of the man's lifestyle. When studying a sample of twenty single fathers in the Greensboro, North Carolina, area, Dennis K. Orthner, T. Brown, and D. Ferguson (1976) found that most of the fathers considered themselves to be "dating around" rather than seeing one woman exclusively. The men appeared to be in no hurry to marry again. Indeed, half were uncertain if they wanted to remarry and were committed to remaining single for the present.

Overall, single-parent fathers, like single-parent mothers, find that one of their greatest difficulties is balancing the demands of work and parenthood. So let us examine the role that work plays in the lives of adults.

Work

Originality and the feeling of one's own dignity are achieved only through work and struggle.—FYODOR DOSTOEVSKY
Diary of a Writer, 1873

The central portion of the adult life span for both men and women is spent at work. However, today's men are spending less of their lives working than they did during the 1950s and 1960s. It seems that the current generation of fathers are less willing to place work above family. Indeed, many contemporary men say they missed out on a relationship with their own fathers and want things to be different for their youngsters (McEnroe, 1991). In contrast, time spent by women in the paid labor force has increased steadily since the turn of the century. Women currently spend about ten fewer years in the work force than men do, compared with twenty-six fewer years in 1900. The work experience of Americans has also undergone a significant change over the past 150 years. Although more than 70 percent of the labor force worked on the farm in 1820, by 1910 only 31 percent were engaged in agriculture. Today, employment in the service industries is approaching 70 percent, the same number that were involved in farming a century and a half ago.

For many American young people (58 percent) the transistion to adult occupational roles is postponed by college. Most youth view a college education primarily as a bargaining chip for use in the job market rather than as a vehicle for broadening their intellectual horizons. In recent years, however, the number of students enrolling in college right after graduating from high school has been dropping. In 1970 the percentage of college freshmen who went directly from high school to college was 65 percent. Today, the figure stands at 54 percent, with about 21 percent waiting one to three years before enrolling in college; another 25 percent wait four years or more.

One of the most significant developments in higher education in recent years is that U.S. colleges are opening up to "nontraditional" students, those over 25 who for one reason or another have put off getting a degree. Over the past decade the number of people 25 and over enrolled in colleges and universities grew by over 70 percent. Part-timers now account for nearly half of all college students. The older students are more likely to come from working-class backgrounds, and they strive for the kind of education that people from more affluent backgrounds take for granted. Although their high school grades are often lower than those of younger students, "nontraditionals'" college grades tend to be higher (Boyer, 1987a; Rowe, 1986).

Sociologists Elizabeth Cooksey and Ronald Rindfuss tracked the careers of 12,000 men and women in their late twenties between 1979 and 1985. They grouped activities into four categories: work, school, unemployment, and "other" (for instance, homemakers, labor force dropouts, the severely disabled, and those in jail). The sociologists found a high degree of variety in the paths the young adults followed. Some alternated between work and school; others went to school and worked simultaneously; many experienced spells of unemployment; still others combined work and homemaker roles; and then there were those who worked, assumed homemaker roles, and in time returned to school. Fewer than two-thirds of the white men, a little over half of the black men, and about one-third of the white and black women worked all six years (Otto, 1990).

The Significance of Work

People work for a great many reasons. "Self-interest" in its broadest sense, including the interests of one's family and friends, is an underlying motivation of work in all societies. However, self-interest is not simply the accumulation of wealth. For instance, among the Maori, a Polynesian people of the Pacific, a desire for approval, a

The Social Significance of Work
Work is a social link integrating people within a network of human relationships. Through their work people meet many needs in addition to that for money. *(Charles Harbutt/Archive)*

sense of duty, a wish to conform to custom, a feeling of emulation, and a pleasure in craftsmanship also contribute to economic activity (Hsu, 1943).

Even in the United States, few activities seriously compete with work in providing basic life satisfaction (Csikszentmihalyi & LeFevre, 1989; Menaghan & Parcel, 1990; Weiss, 1990). In a study conducted over thirty years ago (Morse & Weiss, 1955), and since replicated several times (Kaplan & Tausky, 1972; Opinion Roundup, 1980), a representative sample of U.S. men were asked whether they would continue working if they inherited enough money to live comfortably. About 80 percent said they would. The reasons are not difficult to discover. Work, in addition to its economic functions, structures time, provides a context in which to relate to other people, offers an escape from boredom, and sustains a sense of worth. Perhaps not surprisingly, then, only one in four million-dollar lottery winners quits working after hitting the jackpot.

As sociologist Harry Levinson (1964, p. 20) observes, work has quite a few social meanings:

> When a man works he has a contributing place in society. He earns the right to be the partner of other men. . . . The fact that someone will pay for his work is an indication that what he does is needed by others, and therefore that he himself is a necessary part of the social fabric. He matters—as a man. . . .
>
> A man's work . . . is a major social device for his identification as an adult. Much of who he is, to himself and others, is interwoven with how he earns his livelihood.

"You're doing a great job as corporate psychiatrist, but would you please keep your hands off the workaholics?"

(Arnie Levin © 1990.)

Much the same assessment can be made regarding the meaning that work has for women. Although paid work is becoming an economic necessity for an increasing number of women, one of the central themes of the women's movement has been the symbolic meaning of a paid job. For many contemporary women exclusive commitment to the unpaid work of homemaker and mother implies being cut off from the full possibilities of self-fulfillment. A paid job is seen as a badge of membership in the larger society. It has increasingly come to be defined as the "price of admission" to independence and as a symbol of self-worth (Yankelovich, 1978, 1981).

Our work is an important socializing experience that influences who and what we are (Lorence & Mortimer, 1985; MOW International Research Team, 1987; Perlmutter, Kaplan & Nyquist, 1990; Schwalbe, 1985). Consider individuals who have a college education. Sociologist Melvin L. Kohn and C. Schooler (1983) have found that college-educated people are more likely to acquire jobs that require independent judgment and lead to higher rankings in the class system. By virtue of the intellectual demands of their work, the college-educated evolve an intellectual prowess that carries over to their nonoccupational lives. They even seek out intellectually demanding activities in their leisure pursuits. Typically, people who engage in self-directed work come to value self-direction more highly, to be more open to new ideas, and to be less authoritarian in their relationships with others. They develop self-conceptions consistent with these values, and, as parents, they pass these characteristics on to their children (Luster, Rhoades & Haas, 1989; Miller, Slomczynski & Kohn, 1985). Kohn and his colleagues similarly find that men who are more advantageously located in the class structure of Japan and Poland are more likely to value self-direction for their children, to be intellectually flexible, and to be self-directed in their orientations than are less advantageously located men (Kohn, Naoi, Schoenbach, Schooler & Slomczynski, 1990).

The willingness and capacity of adults to work may have its roots in childhood (Vaillant & Vaillant, 1981). Among 456 white men from working-class families who were tested and interviewed at periodic intervals over a thirty-five-year period, those who had been industrious as youngsters turned out to be the best-adjusted adults. They also had the most successful work lives and the warmest and most satisfying personal relationships. Industriousness proved more predictive of mental health in adulthood than

having a strong family background. Indeed, in some cases boys who showed early industriousness went on to reap its promise despite having very weak home environments as children.

In the United States it is a blunt and ruthlessly public fact that to do nothing is to be nothing and to do little is to be little. Work is commonly viewed as the measure of the individual. To be out of work is to be out of the day-to-day operations of society. Thus, to be unemployed, especially in the case of a man, is to be a social outcast whose very membership in U.S. society is suspended.

Anthropologist Elliot Liebow (1967, pp. 57–58, 63), in a study of black "streetcorner men" living in a Washington, D.C., ghetto, found that the inability to gain steady, remunerative, and meaningful employment undermines an individual's sense of self-respect and self-worth:

> For his part, the streetcorner man puts no lower value on the job than does the larger society around him. . . . In a real sense, every pay day, he counts in dollars and cents the value placed on the job by society at large. . . . Neither the streetcorner man who performs the jobs nor the society which requires him to perform them assesses the job as one "worth doing and worth doing well." Both employee and employer are contemptuous of the job. The employee shows his contempt by his reluctance to accept it or keep it, the employer by paying less than is required to support a family. Nor does the low-wage job offer prestige, respect, interesting work, opportunity for learning or advancement, or any other compensation. . . his job fails him. The job and the man are even. The job fails the man and the man fails the job.

Liebow concluded that much of the behavior of the streetcorner man is directed toward attempting to achieve the goals and values of the larger society, and when he fails to do so, he tries to conceal this failure as best he can from himself and others.

Status Attainment: The Socioeconomic Life Cycle

Sociologists Peter Blau and Otis Dudley Duncan (1967, 1972) have developed a technique for studying the course of an individual's occupational status attainment over the life cycle. Termed the **socioeconomic life cycle,** it entails a sequence of stages that begins with birth into a family with a specific social status and proceeds through childhood, socialization, schooling, job seeking, occupational achievement, marriage, and the formation and functioning of a new family unit. The outcomes of each stage are seen as affecting *subsequent stages* in the cycle. Blau and Duncan based their formulations on data collected by the Census Bureau in 1962 from a single cross-sectional sample of the U.S. adult male population. In order to capture the specific contributions of each stage, the researchers analyzed the the data by means of a statistical procedure called **path analysis** (1972, p. 163):

> We think of the individual's life cycle as a sequence in time that can be described, however partially and crudely, by a set of classificatory or quantitative measurements taken at successive stages. . . . Given this scheme, the questions we are continually raising in one form or another are: how and to what degree do the circumstances of birth condition [determine] subsequent status? And how does status attained . . . at one stage of the life cycle affect the prospects for a subsequent stage?

Blau and Duncan (1972) concluded that the social status of a man's parents typically has little *direct* impact on his occupational attainment. Instead, the primary influence of parental status is *indirect,* through its effect on a man's level of schooling. (One of the virtues of path analysis is its ability to sort out direct from indirect effects.) Overall, education (years of schooling completed) was the factor that had the greatest impact on a man's occupational attainment, both early and late. Formal education seems to be equally important in other advanced industrial societies (Chen & Uttal, 1988; Featherman & Hauser, 1978; Krymkowski, 1991; Stevenson, 1988).

Studies by sociologist Christopher Jencks (1979; Jencks, Crouse & Mueser, 1983; Mayer & Jencks, 1989) largely confirm these findings. The portrait drawn by Jencks is that of a class-ridden society, in which being born into the "right" family assumes considerable importance. According to Jencks, by seventh grade a man's academic test scores shape his own expectations and those of others toward him (none of Jenck's surveys include women, a serious drawback). Of particular importance in "getting ahead in America" is educational attainment; but what counts most is finishing college and getting credentials, rather than what one learns while in college.

Like other sociologists, Jencks finds that the factors making for success are interrelated: If a man comes from the right family background, he is more likely to finish college, to have high academic test scores, and to have the personality characteristics associated with success. But Jencks also recognizes that much depends on a variety of intangible factors, which in an early study (1972, p. 227) he labeled "luck"—countless unpredictable accidents such as

> chance acquaintances who steer you to one line of work rather than another, the range of jobs that happen to be available in a particular community when you are job hunting, . . . whether bad weather destroys your strawberry crop, [and] whether the new super highway has an exit near your restaurant.

Much of the work on educational and occupational attainment has been undertaken by sociologists. However, psychologists suggest that an additional ingredient can be profitably added to the picture: the ability to delay gratification. They point out that life repeatedly confronts us with the necessity of choosing between pleasures and rewards available in the present and the prospect of achieving greater rewards and pleasure in the future by being willing to wait or work for them. Examples include staying in a boring school environment to receive a degree later on or postponing present consumption in order to invest money in a college education. Youngsters who display the ability to defer gratification seem to possess a variety of traits that increases their chances for success, for instance, a tolerance for stress, rationality, attentiveness, planfulness, and cognitive resourcefulness (Funder & Block, 1989; Mischel, Shoda & Peake, 1988). In sum, a number of intervening or mediating variables contribute to status attainment, including family socioeconomic status, educational attainment, and the ability to defer gratification.

SUMMARY

1. Love and work provide the central themes of adult life. Both place us in a complex web of relationships with others. Relationships derive from two types of bonds: expressive ties and instrumental ties. Relationships that rest on expressive ties are termed primary relationships; those that rest on instrumental ties are termed secondary relationships.

2. Individuals in modern complex societies generally enjoy some options in selecting and

changing their lifestyles. A striking aspect of U.S. society over the past twenty-five years has been the rapid expansion in lifestyles. Greater latitude is permitted individuals in tailoring a lifestyle that is less constrained by standards of what a "respectable" person should be like.

3. Census data revel that single status among both men and women under 35 years of age has sharply increased in recent years. This increase has resulted in part from the tendency of young people to postpone marriage. More than two-thirds of adult singles live with someone else: a friend, a relative, or a "spouse equivalent."

4. The number of couples who are not married but live together has increased substantially over the past decade, and those who follow this lifestyle do so more openly than they used to. The backgrounds of cohabiting and non-cohabiting college students are surprisingly similar. Cohabitation is not restricted to the younger generation. It is becoming increasingly prevalent among the middle-aged and elderly who are divorced or widowed.

5. Norms have dictated that U.S. youth leave home and make their own way in the world. But lately, adult children have been making their way back to the parental home in increasing numbers. Family therapists express concern that those who stay at home or return home do not have opportunities to fully develop their sense of individuality. The practices aggravate tendencies toward excessive protectiveness in parents and aggravate tendencies toward a lack of self-confidence in youth.

6. Homosexuals are a varied group. The current state of scientific knowledge does not allow us to arrive at firm conclusions regarding the causes or sources of homosexuality, though there is no shortage of theories.

7. Marriage is a lifestyle found in all societies. It remains the dominant lifestyle in the United States. Since about four in ten marriages end in divorce, many Americans have managed to maintain a monogamous arrangement through serial monogamy.

8. Families, like individuals, undergo development. In the United States most families have traditionally had a fairly predictable natural history. Major changes in expectations and requirements are imposed on a husband and wife as their children are born and grow up.

9. Within the life cycle of a couple, particularly a woman, the first pregnancy is an event of un-

paralleled importance. It signals that a couple is entering the family cycle, bringing about new role requirements. As such, the first pregnancy functions as a major marker or transition and confronts a couple with new developmental tasks.

10. Psychologists and sociologists who view the family as an integrated system of roles and statuses have often depicted the onset of parenthood as a "crisis" because it involves a shift from a two-person to a three-person system. But many researchers have questioned this conclusion. Their research suggests that relatively few couples view the onset of parenthood as especially stressful.

11. One aspect of motherhood that appears particularly stressful is the balancing of motherhood and career. Many people fear that the working mother represents a loss to children in terms of supervision, love, and cognitive enrichment. But researchers are finding that the working mother who obtains personal satisfaction from employment, who does not feel excessive guilt, and who has adequate household arrangements is likely to perform as well as or better than the nonworking mother.

12. Single-parent mothers frequently suffer from a lack of free time, spiraling child-care costs, loneliness, and the unrelenting pressures of attempting to fill the needs posed by both home and work. Not uncommonly, they find themselves in difficult economic circumstances. Nearly one-half live below the poverty level.

13. Increasing numbers of men are becoming single-parent fathers. Studies show that even though single fathers are confronted with some unique adjustment requirements, most of them are successful in raising their children. Like single-parent mothers, single-parent fathers find that one of their greatest difficulties is balancing the demands of work and parenthood.

14. Work plays an important part in the lives of adults, not only because of the money it brings in but also because work is tied to people's self-definitions.

15. Sociological studies suggest that parental status serves to influence the adolescent's aspirations, which then contribute to the individual's educational attainment, which in turn influences the person's first occupational placement and, through it, later occupational attainment.

KEY TERMS

Bisexuality　An equal preference for individuals of the same and opposite sex as sexual partners.

Expressive Tie　A social link formed when we invest ourselves in and commit ourselves to another person.

Family Life Cycle　The sequential changes and realignments that occur in the structure and relationships of a family between the time of marriage and the death of one or both spouses.

Heterosexuality　A preference for an individual of the opposite sex as a sexual partner.

Homosexuality　A preference for an individual of the same sex as a sexual partner.

Instrumental Tie　A social link formed when we cooperate with another person to achieve a limited goal.

Lifestyle　The overall pattern of living whereby an individual attempts to meet his or her biological, social, and emotional needs.

Marriage　A socially sanctioned union between a woman and a man with the expectation that they will play the roles of wife and husband.

Path Analysis　A statistical procedure employed for determining how status attained at one stage of the life cycle affects the prospects for a subsequent stage.

Primary Relationship　A social interaction that rests on an expressive tie between people. In primary relationships people experience warmth and closeness.

Secondary Relationship　A social interaction that rests on an instrumental tie between people. Secondary relationships are everyday, touch-and-go contacts in which individuals need to have little or no knowledge of one another.

Social Relationship　An association in which two people become linked together by a relatively stable set of mutual expectations.

Socioeconomic Life Cycle　The sequence of stages that individuals experience over the life span in the course of status attainment.

Part Eight

Middle Adulthood

Chapter 17

MIDDLE ADULTHOOD: CONTINUITY AND CHANGE

Physical Changes and Health

Vision and Hearing ◆ Menopause and Female Mid-Life Change

◆ Male Mid-Life Change ◆ Sexuality ◆ Health

Personality Across the Adult Years

Psychosocial Tasks of Middle Adulthood ◆ Psychological Conceptions

of Personality ◆ Personality Continuity and Discontinuity

◆ Dynamic Properties of Growth

◆ Continuity and Discontinuity in Gender Characteristics

Adaptation Across the Adult Years

Maturity and Self-Concept ◆ Life Satisfaction

◆

Middle-aged Americans are often deemed to be the power brokers, the decision makers, and the "establishment" of our society. The middle years tend to be a time of peak earnings and well-being. Yet precisely which years of life comprise the middle years is a rather nebulous matter. Does middle age begin at 40, 45, or 50? And does middle age end at 60, 65, or 70? If we think of middle age as roughly the years between 45 and 64, middle-aged Americans comprise about a fifth of the population. They were born shortly before or during the Great Depression of the 1930s and lived out their youth during World War II and the Korean War. They entered the job market and made their way in the labor force during the economic golden years of the 1950s and early 1960s. Now they are experiencing the physical changes of middle life and, for many, the psychological pressures associated with the shift from the "smokestack" industrial age to the age of computers.

But significantly, having learned to cope with the many contingencies of childhood, adolescence, and young adulthood, middle-aged individuals have a substantial repertoire of strategies for dealing with life (Goleman, 1990; Maloney, 1982). Joining the large number of Americans who already are in their fifties and sixties are the baby-boomers (see Chapter 15). The oldest baby-boomers will turn 50 in 1996. During the 1990s, the number of people aged 45 and older will grow by 18 million, compared with no net increase for those under 45.

Physical Changes and Health

In the fashion of aging machines, a human body that has been functioning for a number of decades tends to work less efficiently than it did when it was "new." At age 50 or 60, the kidneys, lungs, heart, and other organs are less efficient than they were at 20. Yet across middle adulthood the physical changes that occur are for the most part not precipitous. They are so gradual as to present not a steep slope but a long plateau (Troll, 1975). After adolescence most integrated body functions decline at the rate of about 1 percent a year. But even in later adulthood at age 75 the heart's efficiency is about 70 percent of what it was at 30 years of age, the lungs' efficiency is 60 percent, the liver's efficiency is 90 percent, and the kidneys' efficiency is about 60 percent.

Overall, middle-aged individuals report that they are not appreciably different from what they were in their early thirties. They mention that their hair has grayed, they have more wrinkles, they are paunchier, they have "lost a step," they tire more easily, and they rebound less quickly. Even so, except for those in poor health, they find that on the whole they carry on in much the manner that they did in their younger years. The best preventive of disabling loss of strength and vitality is an active life and exercise.

Vision and Hearing

During middle adulthood the eye loses its ability to "zoom" in the manner that it did in youth. Accordingly, most people in their forties find that they need glasses, especially to see near objects. (If this problem is not corrected, people find they can read printed material only by holding it farther and farther away from their eyes, until eventually they cannot see to read even at arm's length.) Adaptation to darkness and recovery from glare also take longer, making night driving somewhat more taxing. Distance acuity, contrast sensitivity, visual search, and pattern recognition are also diminished (Kosnik, Winslow, Kline, Rasinski & Sekuler, 1988; Madden, 1990).

A number of disorders that affect sight become more common with age. In *glaucoma* pressure builds up inside the eye because the normal drainage of fluid does not occur properly. The disorder has no symptoms in the early stages and can be detected only by an eye examination. If the disease is detected early, it can be treated, but failure to receive treatment eventually leads to blindness. Another condition, the *cataract*, typically occurs much later in life but in some instances appears among individuals in their late fifties and early sixties. The most common cause is the deterioration and clouding of the lens, contributing to a progressive loss of vision. The condition can usually be remedied by surgical removal of the affected lens. The resulting vision impairment can then be corrected by eyeglasses, a contact lens, or a plastic lens placed in the eye at the time of the operation.

Changes in hearing usually begin about age 30. Typically, the ability to hear high-pitched notes declines, but the magnitude of the change varies appreciably among individuals. At age 50 about one in every three men and one in every four women have difficulty understanding a whisper. However, only about 5 percent of the population at 50 can be deemed to have substantial hearing problems (at age 75, some 27 percent have hearing difficulties). People who have jobs associated with high noise levels—miners, truck drivers, air-hammer operators, and so on—are particularly at risk. Also, some individuals in their sixties report that they "take in" information more slowly than they did earlier in life.

Menopause and Female Mid-Life Change

One of the more notable changes that takes place among women in middle age is **menopause**—the end of menstrual activity. It is one of the most readily identifiable signs of the climacteric. The **climacteric** is characterized by changes in the ovaries and in the various biological processes associated with these changes. Probably the most significant change is the profound drop in the production of the female hormones (particularly estrogen) by the ovaries. The average age at which there is a complete cessation of menses is around 47 to 52 years in Western countries. In less than 4 percent of all cases menopause occurs before age 40; and in less than 2 percent, after age 55—but only rarely does it occur later than age 58 (Bongaarts, 1982; Greene, 1984). Younger women also undergo an early menopause should they have their ovaries surgically removed.

The stoppage of menstruation typically takes two to four years, with an intermittent missing of periods and the extension of the intervals between periods. Symptoms that have been commonly attributed to menopause include hot flashes (feelings of extreme heat), hot flushes (the flushing of the skin), episodes of profuse sweating, fatigue, dizziness, headaches, insomnia, nervousness, and depression. In fourteen large surveys of normal menopausal women, hot flashes were reported by 61 to 75 percent of the women. The hot flashes may have occurred rarely or often and over a few days or a few years. Sweating seems less prevalent; it was reported by about 31 to 58 percent of the women (Greene, 1984).

During the 1960s estrogen-replacement therapy (ERT) became one of the hottest fads in the medical management of menopause, especially in the treatment of hot flashes. By 1975 some 27 million estrogen prescriptions were being written annually. However, about this time evidence was uncovered connecting ERT with increased risks of cancer of the uterus (Shapiro, 1985). As a result, there was a marked drop in ERT. More recently, scientists have found that women who take estrogen tend to live longer than other postmenopausal women. For instance, those on estrogen for at least 15 years had death rates 40 percent below nonusers. It seems that estrogen reduces mortality primarily through improving cardiovascular health and osteoporosis (helping prevent heart disease, strokes, and broken bones). In *osteoporosis* the bone tissue thins as a result of a dimished supply of estrogen, rendering women vulnerable to fracture of the hips, forearms, and spinal vertebrae. However, uncertainty still persists as to whether estrogen increases a woman's risk for breast and uterine cancer. Consequently estrogen therapy is not recommended for women with a family history of breast or uterine cancer. Clearly women face a dilemma with respect to estrogen therapy, and each case must be judged on its own merits (Kolata, 1990, 1991*a*, 1991*b*).

There are still many "old wives' tales" that contribute to the anxiety some women feel about menopause. Indeed, the research of Bernice L. Neugarten, V. Wood, R. J. Kraines, and B. Loomis (1963) suggests that often the most upsetting thing about menopause is the anticipation of it. Although psychoanalytic literature stresses the adverse psychological impact of being no longer able to bear children, less than 5 percent of all menopausal women report that they feel distressed by this fact (Healy, 1985). Many women are relieved that they no longer have to worry about becoming pregnant, and some report an improvement in their sex lives. And when menopause occurs on time during mid-life, it is not likely to be a source of psychological distress (Lennon, 1982).

Women are more likely to feel upset if they view menopause as signaling the end of their attractiveness, usefulness, and sexuality. Such feelings may be heightened by our youth-oriented culture, which tends to devalue older people. Evidence suggests that the climacteric typically does not cause problems that were not already present in a women's life. Women with preexisting or long-standing difficulties may be more susceptible to problems and react more adversely in the climacteric than less vulnerable women (Greene, 1984). Fortunately, at least two-thirds of postmenopausal women believe that they "feel better after menopause than they have for years" and that "after the change of life, a woman feels freer to do things for herself" (Neugarten, Wood, Kraines & Loomis, 1963). Many women express satisfaction that their children are grown and have left home, opening all sorts of new possibilities for them (Goleman, 1990). Clearly, in and of itself menopause should not be viewed as some sort of "illness" (Greene, 1984; McCrea, 1983).

Coming to Terms with Middle Age
In a society that stresses youthfulness and physical attractiveness, the transition to middle age may pose difficulties for some individuals. This is especially true for those people whose definition of self resides in youthful vigor and "good looks." *(Credit to come)*

Another significant marker of mid-life for women occurs in the workplace as they move back into the labor force or shift to full-time work schedules in tandem with declining parental obligations (Long & Porter, 1984). Family life-cycle transitions are particularly important in women's lives, given the preeminence of their family roles and responsibilities (see Chapters 15 and 16). Women who were in their middle adult years during the 1970s confronted substantial change in the social roles and options available to them. The oldest cohort (those over age 54 in 1970) came to adulthood during the Great Depression of the 1930s, a time when social norms discouraged women's employment but often required it for family financial reasons. The youngest cohort (those 35 to 44 in 1970) began their adulthood in the 1950s, when the prevailing norms dictated that women assume domestic roles. Women in the middle cohort (those 45 to 54 in 1970) may have participated in the labor force as their patriotic duty during World War II, but most returned to domesticity in the postwar years (Moen, 1991).

Given the rapid changes in gender roles during the 1970s, women in the different age cohorts faced different motivations and impediments to entry into the work force. Although marriage and motherhood continued to affect women's employment, the influence of those forces was eroding. During the ten-year decade from 1970 to 1980, few women spent their entire middle years fully engaged in the labor force, just as few remained totally outside the labor force. In brief, the vast majority of women moved intermittently into and out of income-generating employment.

Women continued to be wives, mothers, and workers—but in varying amounts and in varying sequences. Marriage, children, and poor health reduced the likelihood that a woman would enter the labor force, but higher levels of education promoted such involvement. Viewed in historical perspective, the 1970s were a transitional period in women's labor-force involvement. Consequently, women who move into midlife in the 1990s and beyond will most likely reenter employment earlier and spend more years in the work force over their life course. Given a stronger attachment to the labor force, contemporary women may be better prepared, both economically and psychologically, for the family transitions they will encounter (Moen, 1991).

Male Mid-Life Change

Men do not undergo menopause. However, in middle age they are likely to experience enlargement of the prostate gland. About 10 percent of men aged 40 already have recognizable enlargement of the prostate, and by age 60 the condition is virtually universal. The exact reasons for the enlargement are unclear, but hormonal changes associated with aging are thought to be implicated in the process. The *prostate* is a walnut-sized gland that surrounds the *urethra*—the tube that emerges from the bladder and carries urine to the outside world via the penis. As the prostate enlarges, it may impinge on the urethra, which may contribute to a decreased force in the urinary stream, a difficulty in beginning urination, and an increased urge to urinate, particularly at night. Although the condition is not dangerous itself, it can hamper the release of urine and contribute to bladder and kidney disorders and infections.

Should serious obstruction to the outflow of urine occur, the tissue causing the enlargement of the prostate can be removed. The most common procedure is a *transurethral resection* (TUR). It is accomplished by passing a thin tube up the penis to the prostate. In the tip of the tube is an electrical cutting device guided by a miniature telescope. Only rarely does a patient become impotent after the operation.

A more serious problem is cancer of the prostate. It occurs in fewer than one man in 10,000 from ages 40 to 50, but its occurrence is five times greater for men in their sixties. A major risk is that the cancer, if not discovered and treated early, will metastasize and spread to the bones. Fortunately, most cancers of the prostate, particularly in older men, grow at a slow pace. By age 80 the majority of men have prostate cancer. Even so, most outlive it and die from something else.

Cultural stereotypes have frequently depicted men in their forties and fifties as suddenly undergoing severe psychological disturbance—in popular terms, "flipping out." They leave their wives for women young enough to be their daughters, quit their jobs to become beachcombers, or begin drinking to excess. Their difficulties are commonly attributed to a "male menopause." Medical authorities are quick to point out, however, that what has never been—menses—cannot cease to be. Furthermore, in healthy males there is no decrease in the production of the male sex hormones (primarily testosterone) with age or only a gradual decline (Tsitouras, Martin & Harman, 1982; Vermeulen, Rubens & Verdonck, 1976).

The question of what part hormonal changes play in the mid-life crisis that some men experience is a matter of lively and sometimes angry medical conterversy. Psychologists and sociologists, however, mostly look for nonbiological explanations, especially for changes in a man's life circumstances that produce a crisis in his self-concept. The middle years call for readjustments and reassessments, some of which may be unpleasant. Most commonly, troubling events are spread over one or two decades. When they coincidentally cluster, they create conditions for some men that can be devastating (Teltsch, 1989).

The psychologist David J. Levinson (1986) and his associates at Yale University (Levinson, Darrow, Klein, Levinson & McKee, 1978), as part of their research into the stages of male adult development described in Chapter 15, conclude that men often experience a turning point in their lives during the ten years between 35 and 45. More recently, Levinson has concluded that men's inner struggles occur with renewed intensity in the mid-fifties (Goleman, 1989). The Yale researchers believe that a man cannot go through his middle adult years unchanged, since he must face changing circumstances during this time of life. He encounters the first indisputable signs of aging and reaches a point at which he is compelled to reassess the fantasies and illusions he has held about himself. The realization that the career elevator is not going up any longer and may indeed be about to descend can add to a man's frustrations and stresses. Hence, if a man has not done what he had hoped with his life, he now becomes keenly aware that he does not have much more time or many more chances to do it. And even when he has reached his goals—say, a high executive position or a full professorship—he often finds that what he has achieved is less rewarding than he had anticipated. A man may ask himself, "If I am making so much money and doing so well, how come I don't feel better and my life seems so empty?" On the other hand, a blue-collar worker of more modest means may ask, "How much longer am I going to have to put up with this dull job?" Even so, research shows that for most people aspirations gradually come to match attainments without severe upset and turmoil (Bridgman, 1984; Mortimer & Simmons, 1978). And as we noted in Chapter 15, given psychological changes do not occur at any exact ages; the timing depends more on the benchmarks of work, family, and life events than on precise chronological age (Goleman, 1989).

In their fifties, both men and women confront the fact that there are time limits to their lives. A powerful reminder is the symbolic meaning attached to the number 50. In terms of the life span, age 50 is roughly two-thirds of the way through life. But because 50 marks a half century, the 50th birthday carries a strong symbolic connotation that many men and women see as marking their entry into the "last half of life." While people at age 50 do not see themselves as "old"—indeed, many find it somewhat strange and not quite believable that they are no longer young—a reversal nonetheless occurs in their sense of time. They begin counting the number of birthdays left to them rather than how many they have reached. So the fifties become a time for more introspective reflection and stock taking (Goleman, 1989; Karp, 1988).

Some men reach mid-life and begin to look at what they have missed along the way in their marital and family relationships. In many cases they find that they have reached the highest rung they will achieve on the corporate ladder and feel "topped out." But at the very time when their interest in family and marriage may be increasing, their wives may be moving out of the family role for personal fulfillment in the job market. Many women had put their own careers on hold in order to rear children. So at a time when many men are developing an exit mentality, calculating how many work years are left, their wives are calculating how many years are left for them to make a mark in the world of work. Husbands and wives, then, may have opposite attitudes toward their careers (Goleman, 1989; Karp, 1988). The husband's ego may also have to adapt to competition from his wife in the breadwinner role. And the woman's excitement and involvement in her own career at a time when her husband may be ambivalent about his may be an additional source of isolation for a man. The middle years, then, are a "crisis point" for some marriages.

The reality of death also presses on a man in his middle years in a host of new ways: through the aging or dying of parents, the death of friends, and the obvious signs of his decreasing vigor and his own aging (gray hair, balding, a tendency to gain weight, and so on). The Yale researchers also find that men's concerns about sexuality are a major problem area, including fears about the possibility of waning virility and worries about declining physical attractiveness. Whereas during their first three decades men tend to view life as a steady ascent, they find at mid-life that they have reached a leveling-off, the end of youth. Alan Ginsburg's description of his middle age captures this dilemma: "Everything is already known, and everything has stopped happening. Everything has been encountered: sex, love, friendship, drugs, even fame, even the boundary dimensions of the self" (quoted by Brim, 1976, p. 172).

Researchers have followed a sample of unusually accomplished, self-reliant, and healthy Harvard University first-year students (drawn mostly from the classes of 1942 to 1944) until their late forties. Despite inner turmoil, the men judged to have had the best outcomes in their late forties regarded the period from 35 to 49 as the happiest in their lives and the seemingly calmer period from 21 to 35 as the least happy. But the men least well adapted at mid-life longed for the relative calm of young adulthood and regarded the storms of mid-life as unusually painful (Rosenfeld & Stark, 1987).

The responses men make to middle age are varied. Some seem to move calmly through it;

others have a stormy passage. Middle age may be a time of new personality growth—a period when a man may move toward a new kind of intimacy in his marriage, greater fulfillment in his work, and a more realistic and satisfying relationship with his children. But for other men it may be a time of developmental defeat, leading to such problems as depression, alcoholism, obesity, and a chronic sense of futility and failure (Farrell & Rosenberg, 1981).

Sexuality

Americans have well-established stereotypes regarding the sexual lives of various age groups (Bulcroft & O'Conner-Roden, 1986; Cameron, 1970). They think of young adults as the most sexually active—as desiring, attempting, and achieving the most sex. They view the middle-aged as the most sexually knowledgeable and skilled. They consider the old as asexual or sexless, and they regard a display of erotic interest by old people as unnatural and undignified. (For example, what our youth-oriented society considers virility in a 20-year-old male is viewed as lechery in a 65-year-old; it makes him a "dirty old man.")

Despite such stereotypes, the research of William H. Masters and Virginia E. Johnson (1966) reveals that sexual effectiveness need not disappear as human beings age. Like their other activities, people's sexual performance may not be characterized by the same physical energy in the later years of life as in the earlier years. But Masters and Johnson find that many healthy men and women do function sexually into their eighties. Although time takes its toll, it need not eliminate sexual desire nor bar its fulfillment.

Sexual arousal in human beings is the product of a complex interaction of affective, cognitive, and physiological processes (Cohen, Rosen & Goldstein, 1985; Marx, 1988; Morokoff, 1985). But what happens in far too many cases is that older people come to accept social definitions of their sexlessness; they become victims of the myth. Believing that they will lose their sexual effectiveness becomes a *self-fulfilling prophecy,* and some older people do lose it even though their bodies have not lost the capacity to perform. The belief that they are sexless may be reinforced in some men when they are unable to attain or maintain an erection during a number of sexual attempts (an occurrence that is not uncommon among men of any age group and may be associated with overindulgence in alcohol). Indeed, fear of failure is not uncommon among older men. Often, a wife is unaware of her husband's fears and mistakes his caution for disinterest.

Changes nonetheless do occur with age. Men find that it takes longer for them to achieve an erection once they pass into their fifties. The erection of older men, particularly those over 60, is generally not as firm or full as when they were younger; maximum erection is achieved only just before orgasm. With advancing age comes a reduction in the production of sperm and seminal fluid, in the number of orgasmic contractions, and in the force of the ejaculation. And the frequency of sexual activity typically declines with advancing age. The Baltimore Longitudinal Study on Aging found that the sexual activity of healthy participants declined progressively with age from a mean of forty-three events per year in men 60 to 64 years to 21 events in men 75 to 79. Overall, the general level of sexual activity of the individuals when they were between 20 and 39 years of age correlated highly with the frequency of their sexual activity in later life (Tsitouras, Martin & Harman, 1982). Hence, if men have maintained elevated levels of sexual activity from their earlier years, and if acute or chronic ill health does not intervene, they are able to continue some form of active sexual expression into advanced age. However, if aging males are not stimulated over long periods of time, their responsiveness may be permanently lost (Masters & Johnson, 1966).

Physicians find that many medical problems manifest themselves sexually. Medical problems that affect male sexual performance include diabetes, which occurs in about 10 percent of men over age 50, and Peyronie's disease, a scarring of the tissue inside the shaft of the penis, more common with men who have diabetes or high blood pressure. Psychological depression is also associated with a decrease in sexual desire. In recent years physicians have become aware of the sexual side effects of medications for heart disease, high blood pressure, and coronary artery disease. Blocking agents used to control high blood pressure, for instance, reduce the flow of blood into the pelvic area. In a younger person, it may not matter much, but among older men the result is often impotence.

Masters and Johnson also find no reason that menopause or advancing age should interfere with the sexual capacity, performance, or drive of women. Basically, older women respond as they did when they were younger, and they continue to be capable of sexual activity and orgasm. Older women tend to lubricate more slowly than they did earlier in life. And the walls of the vagina become thinner, which means that the tissues can be easily irritated and torn with forceful sexual activity. Male gentleness and the use of

artificial vaginal lubricants can do much to minimize this difficulty. Like aging men, older women also typically have fewer orgasmic contractions (younger women average between five and ten contractions, whereas older women average between three and five contractions).

According to the Kinsey (Kinsey, Martin & Gebhard, 1953) research and the National Fertility Study (Westoff, 1974), married couples in their teens have intercourse nearly three times a week, on the average. The frequency drops to about twice a week at age 30, one and a half times a week at age 40, once a week by age 50, and once about every twelve days by age 60. However, these average figures conceal considerable variation among couples.

The incidence of sexual problems among adults has only recently been the subject of scientific investigation. The University of Pittsburgh's Department of Psychiatry studied 100 middle-class couples who described themselves as happily married. Almost half of the women and one-third of the men reported problems with sex (the average age of the women was 35; that of the men, 37). Nonetheless, 90 percent said that they would marry the same person if they had their lives to live over.

Difficulty in becoming aroused was the most frequently reported factor in women's sexual dissatisfaction (nearly half of the women had this difficulty, and 46 percent had difficulty reaching an orgasm). Many of these women said that they could not relax during sex and complained of too little foreplay and too little tenderness after intercourse. The most frequent problem mentioned by the men was premature ejaculation (36 percent); 16 percent had difficulty getting or maintaining an erection.

The American male is often stereotyped in the popular media as preoccupied with sex. Yet a Louis Harris and Associates survey (1979) of men between the ages of 18 and 49 revealed that slightly less than half (49 percent) described sex as being "very important" for their own personal happiness. And from a list of factors commonly linked to adult happiness, 17 percent of the men reported that sex is among the least important. When the men were asked to select the three values in life most important to them personally, the following were the most frequently cited: family life, 56 percent; health, 35 percent; peace of mind, 32 percent; love, 25 percent; money, 25 percent; friends, 20 percent; work, 19 percent; religion, 16 percent; respect from others, 10 percent; education, 9 percent; sex, 8 percent.

It also appears that American men are becoming more aware of their own sensitivity and humanness. Within the privacy of their own minds, they are increasingly coming to recognize—and even approve—the presence of such feelings as tenderness, dependence, weakness, and pain. But a good many of them, especially older men, are not yet able to talk freely about these traditionally "unmasculine" emotions. If men are becoming more aware of their own sensitivity and humanness, over the past two decades women have become more aware of their own sexuality. A growing number of women are tired of the traditional pattern of sexual relations, which focused on male erection, male penetration, and male orgasm. Women are increasingly admitting to themselves what they like sexually and are asking their partners for it. In large measure, this shift in attitudes has been associated with the women's movement.

Health

As people grow older, the incidence of various health problems increases (see Table 17-1). Overall, about 35 million Americans—1 in 7—have disabilities ranging from arthritis, diabetes, and emphysema to mental disorders (Kleinhuizen, 1991). However, as we emphasized in

Chapter 15, people can maximize their chances for leading healthy and long lives by altering their lifestyles to include a variety of health-conscious practices such as regular exercise. The experience of 10,000 devout Mormons residing in California is illuminating. The individuals observe lifestyle habits recommended by the Church of Jesus Christ of Latter Day Saints which include abstaining from tobacco, alcohol, caffeine, and drugs, eating meat sparingly, consuming plenty of herbs, fruits and grains, securing ample sleep, and engaging in regular physical activity. Middle-aged Mormon men have only 34 percent the cancer death rate found among middle-aged non-Mormon white men and only 14 percent of the cardiovascular-disease death rate (a 25-year-old Mormon man has a life expectancy of 85 years, whereas the average American white male of the same age can expect to reach age 74). Middle-aged Mormon women have 55 percent the cancer mortality rate found among middle-aged non-Mormon white women and 34 percent of the cardiovascular-disease death rate (a 25-year-old Mormon woman has a life expectancy of 86 years, six more than their white female counterparts). Studies of other nonsmoking, health-conscious religious groups such as the Seventh Day Adventists also show low rates of mortality from cancer

Table 17-1

Chronic Health Conditions Among Americans					
	Total	Under 18	18 to 44	45 to 64	65 +
Chronic sinusitis	139.7	61.4	157.5	188.0	173.0
Arthritis	129.9	2.3	53.3	257.1	485.7
High blood pressure	121.5	2.3	64.7	257.8	373.0
Deformity/orthopedic impairment	111.6	28.8	131.4	150.9	161.1
Hay fever or allergic rhinitis	93.0	63.4	114.6	99.4	71.4
Hearing impairment	90.8	17.0	48.7	147.6	315.2
Heart disease	84.1	23.3	39.8	135.9	295.8
Chronic bronchitis	49.4	54.3	39.0	56.1	64.8
Hemorrhoids	45.8	1.3	53.8	78.2	64.5
Asthma	41.2	49.9	38.7	34.8	41.4
Migraine headache	38.3	14.2	55.5	45.4	18.4
Dermatitis	37.5	34.9	42.5	36.1	27.2
Visual impairment	34.7	9.1	29.2	47.7	90.7
Varicose veins	31.7	—	26.6	56.8	80.2
Tinnitus	26.4	1.1	16.0	49.2	83.9
Diabetes	25.8	2.2	9.2	54.6	92.4

Note: The table shows the most commonly reported chronic conditions among the general population per 1,000 persons by age.

Source: National Center for Health Statistics, *Current Estimates from the National Health Interview Survey,* 1988, Series 10, No. 173, American Demographics, 12 (April 1990), p. 34.

	No tobacco	Low-fat diet	High-fiber diet	Avoid alcohol	Avoid salted, pickled food	Diet high in vegetables and fruits	Exercise, weight control
Cancer							
Lung	√√√	√	√			√	
Breast		√√√	√			√√	√
Colon		√√√	√√√			√√√	√
Liver				√√√	√	√√	
Heart attack	√√√	√√√				√√	√√
Stroke	√				√√√	√√	√√
Adult diabetes		√√√	√			√√	√√

√√√ Highly effective √√ Moderately effective √ Somewhat effective

Figure 17-1 Minimizing the Perils of Major Disease by Following Health-Promoting Habits
When the health habits of large groups of people are matched with respect to chronic ailments, people who adhere to healthful practices are less likely to be afflicted with cancer, heart attacks, stroke, and diabetes. SOURCE: Jane E. Brody, Personal health, *New York Times*, January 31, 1991, p. 9. Copyright © 1991 by the New York Times Company. Reprinted by permission.

and heart disease (Nazario, 1989). Of course, health-promoting habits afford no guarantees but merely weight the odds in a person's favor (see Figure 17-1) (Brody, 1991; Jeffery, 1989; Seeman, 1989).

Cardiovascular (heart and blood vessel) disease accounts for almost half of all deaths in the United States. Most of these deaths are due to coronary artery disease and hypertension (high blood pressure), which are caused by *atherosclerosis,* a thickening of the internal lining of the blood vessels that is thought to be associated with fatty substances (including cholesterol) in the blood. Approximately one-third of the deaths of people between the ages of 35 and 64 years result from heart disease. The American Heart Association reports that heart disease afflicts nearly 43 million Americans, including 37 million with high blood pressure. Close to one million die of heart disorders or strokes each year (representing nearly half of all deaths in the United States, or almost twice the number of cancer deaths and more than ten times the number of accident-related deaths). Of the 1.5 million people who suffer heart attacks, nearly two-thirds survive and must be treated with drugs or surgery.

Some individuals are more at risk for heart disease than others are. More young men than young women suffer from cardiovascular disease, although the risk for women increases after menopause (women over 60 are nearly as susceptible to the disorder as are men). Death from the disorder in the 35 to 45 age group is five times more common among smokers than among nonsmokers. Male diabetics are twice as susceptible as other men, and female diabetics are five times as susceptible as other women. People who are overweight and who have sedentary jobs are also more at risk for heart disease (see Chapter 15). Moreover, half of all coronary deaths before age 55 occur in just 5 percent of American families, suggesting that genetic risk factors such as high cholesterol levels with high blood pressure may be implicated. And as discussed in the boxed insert on page 491, "Type A" patterns of behavior have been implicated in cardiovascular disorders.

The cardiovascular disease death rate in the United States has dropped about 40 percent since the early 1960s. Among individuals aged 25 to 44 heart disease has declined from first to third place as a cause of death, but for people 45 and over, it remains the leading cause. The decline in overall cardiovascular mortality has meant that both men and women have gained more than two years in life expectancy over the past decade.

"Wellness clinics, stress-management checkups, hypertension screenings, lab tests, crisis after crisis. Fibre foods, fish-oil capsules, unsaturated spreads, plaque. Say what they may, McCormack, we did it our way."

(Drawing by Booth; © 1988 The New Yorker Magazine, Inc.)

Many factors are associated with the decline in death from cardiovascular disease. More people are smoking less, eating more sensibly, and jogging more (the boxed insert on page 492 examines why many people do not succeed in eliminating unhealthy practices). Medical services have also improved. And new drugs that control high blood pressure and cardiac arrest have revolutionized the treatment of cardiovascular disease. When patients do not respond to drugs, *coronary bypass surgery* may be employed (surgeons take veins, usually from the leg, and create detours around blocked arteries). A new, cheaper, and simpler technique is called *coronary angioplasty*—a thin tube tipped by a tiny balloon is threaded into a blocked artery and is then inflated, dispersing the blockage and allowing the blood to flow freely. By using a somewhat similar procedure, physicians can inject a clot-dissolving enzyme called *streptokinase* into a blocked artery and liquefy a blood clot, stopping early the damage that results from a heart attack.

Medical researchers are nearly unanimous in concluding that countless lives could be saved each year if everyone in the United States with a high level of blood cholesterol would reduce their cholesterol to normal. A recent thirty-two-year study found that for people under age 50 each 10-milligram decrease in cholesterol level was associated with about a 5 percent decrease in the death rate from all causes and a 9 percent drop in death from heart disease (Findlay, 1987a). Cholesterol is found in animal products (eggs, meat, and milk; an egg contains about 250 milligrams of cholesterol) but not in grains, beans, vegetables, or vegetable oils (see Table 17-2). Another study supported by the National Heart, Lung and Blood Institute followed 3,806 men, aged 35 to 59, for ten years (Boffey, 1984). All the men had unusually high cholesterol levels for their age group. During the study they ate a moderately low cholesterol diet, and half of them took a cholesterol-lowering drug, cholestyramine. The restricted diet lowered the level of cholesterol 3.5

Stress and Heart Disease

Stress plays an important part in heart disease. Psychologists have recognized a behavior pattern, termed *Type A*, that characterizes people having a higher incidence of cardiovascular problems. Type As are described as hard-driving, competitive, and ambitious, preoccupied with a sense of time urgency, impatient, and easily angered when things go "wrong" (Friedman & Booth-Kewley, 1988; Friedman & Rosenman, 1974; Matthews, 1982, 1988; Siegman & Dembroski, 1989) (see Table 17-3). A non-coronary-prone pattern known as *Type B* is defined by the relative absence of these traits. Apparently, Type A behavior poses as significant a risk for heart disease as do smoking, high cholesterol level, and high blood pressure (Dembroski, 1981). Type A people are about twice as likely to die of heart disease as are their Type B counterparts.

Some psychologists have suggested that the Type A pattern arises from reactions to uncontrollable stress. Just how Type A behavior affects the cardiovascular system is poorly understood. But Type As seem to overrespond physiologically under stress. Their blood pressure rises sharply, and other changes simultaneously occur in their circulatory systems. In some individuals the blood vessels actually become more resistant to change under stress than they normally do, requiring the heart to pump very hard against considerable resistance (much like trying to drive a car at high speed with the brakes on). In any event, an intense state of cardiovascular readiness for long periods may produce permanent damage (Brody, 1983*b*).

Seemingly Type A behavior appears rather early in life (Elias, 1983; MacEvoy, Lambert, Karlberg, Klackenberg-Larsson & Klackenberg, 1988; Weidner, Sexton, Matarazzo, Pereira & Friend, 1988). Confronted with a task and a deadline, 12-year-old Type A children reveal much higher blood-pressure and heart-rate increases than their Type B playmates do. Similar differences are found even in 3-year-olds. When working simple arithmetic problems, Type A elementary school youngsters set higher standards for their behavior and expend greater effort in excelling than do Type Bs. Like their Type A elders, youthful Type As show aggression and greater impatience sooner, but they are also rewarded by being more successful in competitive tasks. Yet even though Type A children exist, not all of them grow up to be Type A adults (Steinberg, 1986). This discussion suggests that preventive medical care and psychological interventions might wisely be instituted early for some Type A individuals.

Table 17-3

Type A Behavior Characteristics

Concentrating on more than one activity at a time
Measuring one's own and others' success in terms of numbers
Challenging and competing with others even in noncompetitive situations
Exhibiting explosive and accelerated speech patterns
Believing that if one wants something done right, one has to do it oneself
Becoming excessively irritated when forced to wait in line or when driving behind a car traveling slowly
Developing impatience when watching others do things that one thinks one can do better or more rapidly
Hurrying others who are speaking
Having difficulty sitting and doing nothing
Gesticulating when talking
Engaging in finger tapping or knee jiggling
Making a fetish about promptness
Locking up a good deal of free-floating hostility
Failing to notice the interesting and beautiful aspects in the world

percent among all participants. But the levels were reduced as much as 25 percent for those who took cholestyramine. And there was an overall 19 percent lower rate of fatal and nonfatal heart attacks for those who lowered their cholesterol levels an average of 8 percent. For those who reduced their cholesterol by 25 percent, the heart-attack rate fell 50 percent (for every 1 percent reduction in cholesterol, there was a 2 percent fall in rate of coronary heart disease).

Although heart disease is by far the greatest killer of Americans, cancer is the disease people typically fear the most. *Cancer* is not a single disease. It is the name applied to a group of dis-

Why Do We Have Difficulty Changing Unhealthy Habits?

Why is it so difficult for even the most intelligent and motivated of us to unlearn bad health habits and cultivate good ones? For instance, why do people say they care about good nutrition but in practice do very little about it? Or why do people agree that exercise is good for them but do so little of it? Or why do people worry about automobile accidents yet not fasten their seat belts? According to psychologist Albert Bandura, the answer to these questions involves *self-efficacy*—your perception that you are capable of accomplishing a task. In other words, if you believe in your ability to reach some goal, you are more likely to reach it. When you have a strong sense of efficacy and are beset by difficulties, you exert greater effort to overcome and master the challenges. In contrast, should you entertain doubts about your capabilities, you are more likely to slacken your efforts (*University of California, Berkeley Wellness Letter,* May 1987).

Many factors influence your sense of efficacy, including your past performance. If you tried to lose weight and you previously succeeded in accomplishing your goal, you are likely to be bolstered by your earlier success. Vicarious experience also helps. If someone you admire has successfully shed pounds, you may gain confi-

Weight-Loss Programs
Here a dieting woman wears a surgical face mask to prevent her from nibbling food while she is preparing it.
(Arnold J. Kaplan/The Picture Cube)

Table 17-2

Some Foods with High Cholesterol Levels	
Food	Cholesterol in Milligrams
One egg yolk	250
Beef liver (4 oz.)	500
Shrimp (4 oz.)	170
Kidneys (3 oz.)	315–650
Butter (1 tbsp.)	35
Beef, chicken, veal, pork, lamb (4 oz.)	110–120
Fish (4 oz. salmon, halibut, tuna)	30–65
Lobster (3 oz.)	75
Big Mac	86
Cheese (1 oz.)	18–31

Source: U.S. Department of Agriculture, 1983.

eases in which body cells multiply and spread uncontrollably. Except in blood cancers like leukemia, the unchecked spread of cells develops into a *malignant* tumor, which keeps growing and invades neighboring tissues. Noncancerous tumors are termed *benign*. Although benign tumors may enlarge, the cells do not multiply and spread uncontrollably. In malignant tumors the cells *metastasize,* or spread, and form secondary growths in other parts of the body. Contrary to general impressions, cancer does not become increasingly common among very old people. The peak increase in cancer incidence and mortality occurs between the ages of 45 and 65, after which the risk of cancer levels off. Whereas cancer accounts for 30 percent of the deaths among people from the ages of 65 to 69, it is the cause of death in

dence in your own ability. And the encouragement of others likewise helps. But should your friend or spouse doubt your ability to lose weight, this attitude may undermine your self-confidence. Additionally, should you fear failure, you increase your chances for succumbing to obstacles and failing.

How can you determine your self-efficacy and, if necessary, go about improving it? First, closely examine what you are attempting to accomplish, be it losing weight, taking up an exercise program, or quitting smoking. Then, list the various tasks that are involved in achieving your goal and honestly estimate your chances of sticking to each task. To improve your chances, recruit your family and/or friends as a support network, join a support group such as Weight Watchers, and set goals along the way (for instance, "I will lose one pound this week!").

You must genuinely want to change unhealthy habits if you are to succeed. Sole reliance on group support, peer pressure, external rewards, or a nagging spouse usually backfires in the long run. People often relapse after leaving a support group. Alcoholics Anonymous is unique because it is not a transitory group and people make a life-long commitment to its goals. Similarly, if you undertake behavioral change merely to please someone else, you are not likely to persist in the change. For instance, 400 patients suffering from high blood pressure were studied by researchers at Johns Hopkins University. In one group, members attended explanatory sessions with a health counselor; in another group, members attended voluntary group meetings; and in still another group, a counselor made a home visit with a family member who had influence with the patient. In the short run, the home visits proved most effective. But in the long run, five years later, members of this group had the poorest record of complying with the blood-pressure-control regimen. When the patients themselves are bypassed, the chances for long-term failure are increased because there is no underlying change in the patient's belief system. As for the nagging spouse, this approach often galvanizes resistance to change.

In order to succeed, people have to come to terms with themselves and recognize the severity of their problem. And they must believe that they can do something about it. For most people good health by itself may be only one aspect of their motivation. In addition, they may be concerned about their health because they would like to be more attractive, more effective, more competitive, or less dependent. So for a person to maximize coming to terms with unhealthy practices, health needs should be linked with values that are already important to that person (Brody, 1987*d;* Seeman, 1989).

---

only 12 percent of those over age 80 (Brody, 1984*b).*

Although a diagnosis of cancer is cause for considerable concern, it should not be regarded as an automatic death sentence. The data on cancer hardly justify a fatalistic outlook. Cancer therapy has made considerable strides in recent decades. Surgery remains the most common method of treating cancers that form solid tumors, such as breast, colon, and rectal cancers. Radiation is also a common treatment. It takes advantage of the fact that many types of cancer cells are more sensitive than normal cells are to the destructive effects of radiation. Finally, more than sixty drugs have been found effective against cancer. Drug therapy—known as *chemotherapy*—may be employed as the primary therapy or as an adjunct to surgery and radiation. Unfortunately, radiation and chemotherapies commonly produce side effects, including nausea, vomiting, diarrhea, temporary hair loss, increased susceptibility to infection, fatigue, and depression.

Much can be done to prevent cancer. Many medical scientists believe that up to 80 percent of all cancers result in part from contamination of the environment by chemicals called *carcinogens.* Exactly how these substances cause cells to become malignant is as yet poorly understood. Among substances that have been identified as carcinogens are asbestos, coal tar pitch, benzene, vinyl chloride, and nuclear radiation. The American Cancer Society estimates that 75,000 lives a year could be saved in the United States by getting 15 million of the nation's 33 million smokers to stop.

A variety of behaviors and practices have been found to heighten a person's chances of contracting some forms of cancer. For instance, it seems that among societies where a large proportion of dietary calories come from foods containing fat, breast cancer is a leading killer of women. Consequently, breast cancer is prevalent among northern Europeans and North Americans but relatively rare among Asians. Significantly, Japanese-American women become more susceptible to breast cancer the longer they have lived in the United States and the more they have adopted U.S. culture. Likewise, rates of colon cancer are highest in countries like ours, where fat consumption is high and fiber consumption is low (Brody, 1991; Cohen, 1987). Indeed, eating more fruit, vegetables, and grains may lower a person's risk for cancer of the colon and rectum by as much as 40 percent (Sperling, 1990). In addition, an estimated 600,000 new cases of skin cancer are detected each year in the United States, the vast majority attributable to overexposure to the sun (Blumenthal, 1990).

Personality Across the Adult Years

We must always change, renew, rejuvenate ourselves; otherwise we harden.—JOHANN WOLFGANG VON GOETHE

Traditionally, developmental psychologists have focused their attention on changes that occur during infancy, childhood, and adolescence. But in recent years a life-span perspective of development has emerged that views adulthood as a period of continuing change. Individuals must constantly adapt to new life situations and make a variety of role transitions. This adaptation involves the performance of new tasks, the relinquishing of others, and the redefinition of basic assumptions, attitudes, and behaviors. And in the process of this ongoing adaptation, people are required to reorient and reorganize their personalities.

Psychosocial Tasks of Middle Adulthood

As pointed out in Chapter 2 and again in Chapter 15, Erik Erikson (1963) deems the central task of middle age to be resolving the issue of generativity versus stagnation. He stresses that humans are both learning and instructing beings. Whereas personality development in the earlier phases of the life cycle centers on learning, in later phases instruction is the focal point. Erikson's notion of *generativity* captures this concern. It entails the expansion of one's own being to encompass a commitment to younger people, assisting them in making their way in life. Rather than indulge oneself, the developing person

brings his or her special talents and gifts to bear on the "ultimate concerns" of advancing the overall interests of humankind. To do otherwise is to become self-centered and to turn inward, resulting in a type of psychological invalidism.

The psychologist Robert C. Peck (1968) follows in Erikson's footsteps. However, he takes a closer look at middle life and suggests that it is useful to identify more precisely the tasks confronting individuals during it. The four aspects he defines include valuing wisdom versus valuing physical powers, socializing versus sexualizing in human relationships, cathectic flexibility versus cathectic impoverishment, and mental flexibility versus mental rigidity.

Valuing Wisdom Versus Valuing Physical Powers As individuals pass into middle age, they experience a decline in their physical strength. Even more importantly, in a culture that emphasizes looking youthful, people lose much of their 1ge in physical attractiveness. But they also enjoy new advantages. The sheer experience of longer living brings with it an increase in accumulated knowledge and greater judgmental powers. Rather than relying primarily on their "hands" and physical capabilities, they must now come to employ their "heads" with greater frequency in coping with life.

Socializing Versus Sexualizing in Human Relationships Allied to middle-life physical decline, although in some ways separate from it, is the sexual climacteric. In their interpersonal lives individuals must now cultivate greater understanding and compassion. They must come to value others as personalities in their own right rather than chiefly as sex objects.

Cathectic Flexibility Versus Cathectic Impoverishment This task concerns the ability to become emotionally flexible. In doing so, people find the capacity to shift emotional investments from one person to another and from one activity to another. At this time of life many middle-aged individuals confront the death of their parents and the departure of their children from the home. Hence, they must widen their circle of acquaintances to embrace new people in the community. And they must try on and cultivate new roles to replace those that they are relinquishing.

Mental Flexibility Versus Mental Rigidity As they grow older, people too often become "set in their ways." And they become "close-minded," unreceptive to new ideas. Since many of them have reached their peak in status and power, they are tempted to forgo the search for novel solutions to problems. But what worked in the past may not work in the future. Hence, they must strive for mental flexibility and, on an ongoing basis, cultivate new perspectives as provisional guidelines to tackling problems.

The formulations of Erikson and Peck provide a more positive image of middle age than those portraying midlife as a time of turmoil and crisis as people reevaluate their lives. For their part, adult Americans also see middle age as a time during which people deepen their relationships and intensify their acts of caring. A recent survey of 1,200 men and women commissioned by the American Board of Family Practice (a professional organization for physicians) found that 84 percent of Americans agree that "at middle age a person becomes more compassionate to the needs of others," and 89 percent view middle age as a time of becoming closer to friends and family. A variety of studies confirm that people in their fifties become more altruistic and community-oriented than they were at age 25. A striving for symbolic immortality by furthering a worthy cause or group seems to arise from an awakened confrontation with one's own mortality. In general, those individuals who have consolidated their marriages and careers have a secure base from which to reach out to assist others (Goleman, 1990).

Psychological Conceptions of Personality

Although personality development has long been a major interest of many psychologists, they have not been able to arrive at a mutually accepted definition of personality. Underlying most of their approaches, however, is the notion that each individual has a relatively unique and enduring set of psychological tendencies and reveals them in the course of interacting with the environment.

Trait Models of Personality Until relatively recently, most psychologists believed that personality patterns are established during childhood and adolescence and then remain relatively stable over the rest of the life span. This view largely derived from Sigmund Freud's psychoanalysic theory. As described in Chapter 2, Freud traced the roots of behavior to personality components formed in infancy and childhood—needs, defenses, identifications, and so on. He deemed any changes that occur in adulthood as simply vari-

ations on established themes, for he believed that an individual's character structure is relatively fixed by late childhood.

Likewise, clinical psychologists and personality theorists have typically assumed that an individual gradually forms certain characteristics that become progressively resistent to change with the passage of time. These patterns are usually regarded as reflections of inner traits, cognitive structures, dispositions, habits, or needs. Indeed, almost all forms of personality assessment assume that the individual has stable traits (stylistic consistencies in behavior) that the investigator is attempting to describe (Buss, 1989; Church & Katigbak, 1989; Goldberg, 1990; Wolfe & Kasmer, 1988).

Similarly, whenever a person's life is reviewed, whether in an autobiography, a biography, a psychohistory, or a clinical report, an implicit assumption is usually made: Not only is the subject's life uniquely different from that of other people, but it has a certain coherence. Indeed, a biography would be unimaginable if the events in the subject's life course were portrayed in a purely haphazard, unordered fashion (Csikszentmihalyi & Beattie, 1979). Moreover, each of us typically looks at our own life as a unit. We view ourselves as having a measure of consistency, and we anticipate and adapt to many events without appreciably changing our picture of the entirety of our lives. We evolve "scripts"—images of ourselves—that organize aspects of our lives and behavior in an orderly fashion and give us a sense of continuity. So we see ourselves as essentially stable even though we assume somewhat different guises in response to changing life circumstances (Bourque & Back, 1977; Fisseni, 1985; Lerner and Busch-Rossnagel, 1981; Tomkins, 1986).

Situational Models of Personality The trait approach to personality views a person's behavior in terms of recurring patterns. In contrast, proponents of situational models view a person's behavior as the outcome of the characteristics of the situation in which the person is momentarily located. The cognitive learning theorist Walter Mischel (1968, 1969, 1977, 1985) provides a forthright statement of the situational position. Mischel says that behavioral consistency is in the eye of the beholder and hence is more illusory than real. Indeed, he wonders if it makes sense to speak of "personality" at all. Mischel concludes that we are motivated to believe that the world around us is orderly and patterned because only in this manner can we take aspects of our daily lives for granted and view them as predictable. Consequently, we perceive our own behavior and that of other people as having continuity. Even so, Mischel admits that a fair degree of consistency exists in people's performance on certain intellectual and cognitive tasks. However, he notes that correlations between personality test scores and behavior seem to reach a maximum of about .30, not a particularly high figure (see Chapter 9). People's behavior across situations is highly consistent only when the situations in which the behavior is tested are quite similar. When circumstances vary, little similarity is apparent.

Interactionist Models of Personality In recent years psychologists have come to recognize the inadequacies of both the trait and situational models. Instead, they have come to favor an interactionist approach to personality. Pointing out that the question "Which is more important, the trait or the situation?" is meaningless, they claim that behavior is always a joint product of the person and the situation (see Chapter 3). Moreover, people seek out congenial environments—selecting settings, activities, and associates that provide a comfortable context and fit—and thereby reinforce their preexisting bents (Caspi & Herbener, 1990; Snyder & Ickes, 1985). And through their actions individuals create as well as select environments (Rausch, 1977): By fashioning their own circumstances, they produce some measure of stability in their behavior (Bandura, 1982; Datan, Rodeheaver & Hughes, 1987; Epstein, 1979; Kenrick, McCreath, Govern, King & Bordin, 1990).

Psychologists have employed a variety of approaches for specifying the form of interaction that transpires between a person and a situation. One approach is to distinguish between those people for whom a given trait can be used to predict behavior across situations and those people for whom that trait cannot be used. For example, individuals who report that their behavior is consistent across situations with respect to friendliness and conscientiousness do indeed exhibit these traits in their behavior. In contrast, individuals who report that their behavior is inconsistent across situations with respect to these qualities reveal little consistency in their behavior with regard to them (Bem & Allen, 1974). Moreover, people vary in their consistency on different traits (Funder & Colvin, 1991; Underwood & Moore, 1981; Zuckerman et al., 1988). Hence, if we are asked to characterize a friend, we typically do not run through a rigid set of traits that we use to inventory all people. Instead, we

select a small number of traits that strike us as particularly pertinent and discard as irrelevant the ten thousand or so other traits. Usually, the traits that we select are those that we find hold for the person across a variety of situations.

Personality Continuity and Discontinuity

Psychologists have long been interested in the degree to which our personalities remain the same across the life span. Yet the evidence that they have produced is contradictory (Epstein, 1979, 1980). Some studies suggest that personality remains largely the same; others, that it

Personality Change and Stability
Our personalities are complex and multifaceted. Some of the components change markedly over time, while others show considerable continuity. This photo is of a retired teacher, 80 years of age; the portrait in the background shows her as a young adult. *(Lynn McLaren/Photo Researchers)*

changes over time. Such conflicting results suggest that personality is complex and multifaceted, not one but many things. As a consequence, some components may show considerable stability and others considerable change (Finn, 1986; Stevens & Truss, 1985). On the whole, the greatest consistency appears in various intellectual and cognitive dimensions, such as IQ, cognitive style, and self-concept. The least consistency is found in the realm of interpersonal behavior and attitudes (Burns & Seligman, 1989; E. L. Kelly, 1955; Mischel, 1969).

Psychologist E. Lowell Kelly (1955; Kelly & Conley, 1987) has investigated personality constancy and change from a longitudinal perspective. As part of a marriage study, Kelly administered a battery of psychological tests to nearly three hundred engaged college students between 1935 and 1938. In 1954 he was able to locate and readminister the tests to 86 percent of the people in the initial sample. Of the thirty-eight personality variables that Kelly measured, twenty showed no significant change over the two decades. In the case of the other eighteen variables, change had occurred, but for the most part it was not substantial. Values and vocational interests tended to be most stable; self-ratings were moderately consistent; attitudes (toward marriage, religion, entertaining, gardening, and the like) were least consistent. Kelly (1955, p. 681) concluded:

> Our findings indicate that significant changes in the human personality may continue to occur during the years of adulthood. Such changes, while neither so large nor sudden as to threaten the continuity of the self percept or impair one's day-to-day interpersonal relations, are potentially of sufficient magnitude to offer a basis of fact for those who dare to hope for continued psychological growth during the adult years.

Diana S. Woodruff and James E. Birren (1972), like Kelly, were able to follow up on a sample of college students who had completed a self-descriptive personality inventory (the California Test of Personality) in 1944. In 1969, twenty-five years later, longitudinal comparisons revealed that the men and women described themselves in virtually the same terms they had used in 1944. In addition to describing themselves, the follow-up subjects were asked to answer the California Personality Test as they thought they had answered it in 1944 (Woodruff & Birren, 1972, p. 257):

> In the retrospection condition, adults projected a relatively negative picture of themselves as adolescents. In retrospect they thought that their adoles-

"*Another thing I remember about the 1960 release is that back then you identified with the slaves.*"

(Drawing by D. Reilly; © 1991 The New Yorker Magazine, Inc.)

cent level of adjustment was much lower than it actually had been. Adults seemed to subjectively experience a discontinuity between their adolescent and adult personality which did not exist objectively.

Researchers have also followed up on the sample of Berkeley and Oakland youth who were first studied in the 1930s when they were in their early teens (see Chapter 1). The individuals were again assessed when they were in their late teens, mid-thirties, and mid-forties (Block, 1980). On the vast majority of the ninety personality scales, researchers found statistically significant correlations between the earliest and later scores. Even so, despite strong evidence of continuity, individuals differed in the consistency they exhibited in their personalities over time.

The picture gained from the research undertaken by psychologists at the Gerontology Research Center in Baltimore is not too different. Paul T. Costa, Jr., and Robert R. McCrae (1980, 1988; Costa et al., 1986) find considerable continuity in a person's personality across the adult years. They have tracked individuals' scores over time on standardized self-report personality scales. On such personality dimensions as warmth, impulsiveness, gregariousness, assertiveness, anxiety, and disposition to depression, high correlations exist in the ordering of persons from one decade to another. An assertive 19-year-old is typically an assertive 40-year-old and later an assertive 80-year-old. Likewise, "neurotics" are likely to be "complainers" throughout life (they may complain about their love life in early adulthood while decrying their poor health in late adulthood). Although people may "mellow" with age or become less impulsive by the time they are in their sixties, the relation of individuals to one another regarding a given trait remains much the same (when tested, most persons drop the same few standard points).

In sum, for many facets of our personality there is strong evidence of continuity across the adult years (Caspi, Elder & Bem, 1987; Conley, 1985; Costa, McCrae & Arenberg, 1980; Moss & Susman, 1980). This element of stability makes us adaptive; we know what we are like and hence can make more intelligent choices regarding our living arrangements, careers, spouses, and friends. If our personality continually changed in an erratic fashion, mapping our future and making wise decisions would be severely impaired.

Dynamic Properties of Growth

Although our personality possesses an underlying coherence across time, we are dynamic organisms capable of growth (Brim & Kagan, 1980; Helson & Moane, 1987). We are active, vigorous beings, not simple carriers of stable motives and traits. Because the world in which we live is constantly changing, we must continually undertake to cope with and master our environment. Likewise, as we move through different phases in life, we undergo physical alterations in our bodies that are often mirrored in our circumstances and roles. Life-cycle transitions, then, are a major source of change (Datan, Rodheaver & Hughes, 1987; Elder, 1985; Moen, 1991). Consequently, the human experience reflects a tension between continuity and change.

This conclusion is supported by studies undertaken in Kansas City by Bernice L. Neugarten and K. Weinstein (1964). In particular, the research sheds light on personality change over the life span. The first set of studies was based on cross-sectional data from more than 700 men and women aged 40 to 70 from all socioeconomic levels. The second set of data came from a group of nearly 300 people aged 50 to 90 who were interviewed at regular intervals over a six-year period. Analyzing this research, Neugarten (1964, pp.

189–190) identified a number of fairly consistent age-related differences in personality:

> Forty-year-olds seem to see the environment as one that rewards boldness and risk-taking and to see themselves possessing energy congruent with the opportunities presented in the outer world. Sixty-year-olds seem to see the environment as complex and dangerous, no longer to be reformed in line with one's wishes, and to see the self as conforming and accommodating to outer-world demands. This change . . . [involves] movement from active to passive mastery. . . . Older men seem to be more receptive than younger men of their affiliative, nurturant, and sensual promptings; older women, more receptive than younger women of their aggressive and egocentric impulses. Men appear to cope with the environment in increasingly abstract and cognitive terms; women, in increasingly affective and expressive terms. . . . Older people seem to move toward more eccentric, self-preoccupied positions and to attend increasingly to the control and the satisfaction of personal needs.

Researchers associated with the Baltimore Longitudinal Study (Douglas & Arenberg, 1978) also found age-related differences and changes that occurred across time. Participants were male volunteers who ranged in age from 17 to 98 years, were in relatively good health, and were employed in (or retired from) professional or managerial positions. A seven-year follow-up revealed that the pace of activity of men in their twenties had increased, while that of those over 50 had declined. Likewise, the "masculinity" scores of the men in the survey (as measured by highly "masculine" interests and restraint in displaying emotion) had declined. Over the period of the study a decline also occurred among men of all ages in scores associated with thoughtfulness (introspective and meditative behavior), personal relations (trustfulness, tolerance, and cooperativeness), and friendliness (agreeable and nonbelligerent tendencies). But these latter changes appeared to reflect cultural changes associated with the times, rather than maturational factors. Women, too, show changes in personality that are attuned to the requirements of adult development. For instance, there seems to be a gender role specialization among many women in their late twenties and then a decrease in their later years that is accompanied by increases in confidence, dominance, and coping skills (Helson & Moane, 1987).

Not surprisingly, various investigators have uncovered major discontinuities in some facets of personality across the life span. As Neugarten

The Sandwich Generation
Middle age often brings with it responsibilities for one's own children, grandchildren, and aging parents. The tasks fall disproportionally upon women who, in the American gender division of labor, are the persons assigned primary responsibility for family care-taking. *(David Schaefer/Jeroboam)*

(1968*b*, 1969, 1983; Neugarten & Neugarten, 1987) notes, the psychological realities confronting the individual shift with time. Middle age, for instance, often brings with it responsibilities for aging parents and for one's own minor children. With these obligations comes the awareness of oneself as the bridge between the generations—the so-called sandwich generation (Lang & Brody, 1983). As a perceptive woman observed in Neugarten's study (1968*b*, p. 98):

> It is as if there are two mirrors before me, each held at a partial angle. I see part of myself in my mother who is growing old, and part of her in me. In the other mirror, I see part of myself in my daughter. I have had some dramatic insights, just from looking in those mirrors. . . . It is a set of revelations that I suppose can only come when you are in the middle of three generations.

In a sense, individuals in their forties and fifties are catching up with their own parents; therefore, they may experience increased identification

with them and a greater awareness of their own approaching senescence (Stein, Holzman, Karasu, & Charles, 1978). Some of the issues of middle age are related to increased stocktaking, in which individuals come to restructure their time perspective in terms of time-left-to-live rather than time-since-birth.

Old age confronts the individual with still other issues (Neugarten, 1969, p. 122):

> Some are issues that relate to renunciation—adaptation to losses of work, friends, spouse, the yielding up of a sense of competency and authority . . . reconciliation with members of one's family, one's achievements, and one's failures . . . the resolution of grief over the death of others, but also over the approaching death of self . . . the need to maintain a sense of integrity in terms of what one has been, rather than what one is . . . the concern with "legacy" . . . how to leave traces of oneself . . . the psychology of survivorship.

Thus, as Neugarten points out, one's concerns and preoccupations alter and shift across the life cycle.

Continuity and Discontinuity in Gender Characteristics

In the long years liker must they grow; The man be more of woman, she of man.—ALFRED, LORD TENNYSON
The Princess

As mentioned earlier, some research has suggested that men and women move in *opposite* directions across the life span with respect to assertiveness and aggressiveness, so that patterns of a later-life "unisex" tend to emerge (Helson & Moane, 1987; Zube, 1982). David Gutmann (1969) pursued this possibility by comparing the male subjects in Neugarten's Kansas City study with men in a number of other cultures: the subsistence, village-dwelling, lowland and highland Maya of Mexico; the migratory Navajo herdsmen of the high desert plateau of northeastern Arizona; and the village-dwelling Galilean Druze herdsmen and farmers of Israel. Gutmann found that the younger men (aged 35 to 54) in all four cultures relied on and relished their own internal energy and creative capabilities. They tended to be competitive, aggressive, and independent. On the other hand, the older men (aged 55 and over) tended to be more passive and self-centered. They relied on supplicative and accommodative techniques for influencing others. Gutmann concluded that this

Age-Related Differences and Changes in Personality?
David Gutmann finds that men aged 55 and over tend to move from active to passive techniques in dealing with the demands of their surroundings. In contrast, women seem to move in the opposite direction—from passivity to active mastery. *(Hazel Hankin/Stock, Boston)*

change from active to passive mastery seems to be more age- than culture-related. Other researchers similarly report that, on the whole, older men are more reflective, sensual, and mellow than are younger men (Zube, 1982).

Gutmann (1977) has continued to study personality and aging in a wide range of cultures. In subsequent research he reports that his earlier finding has been confirmed—that around age 55, men begin to use passive instead of active techniques in dealing with the demands of their environment. Women, however, appear to move in the opposite direction, from passive to active mastery. They tend to become more forceful, domineering, managerial, and independent. He concludes (1977, p. 312):

> In effect, "masculine" and "feminine" qualities are distributed not only by sex but by life period. Men are not forever "masculine"; rather, they can be defined as the sex that shows "masculine" traits before the so-called "feminine" pattern. The reverse is true for women.

Gutmann suggests a tentative explanation for these sex differences. He believes that the requirements of parenthood place different demands on the sexes in early adulthood. If women are to succeed in their roles as the primary caretakers of children (given traditional patterns in the division of labor), they need to cultivate the tender, affiliative elements in their personalities while suppressing the aggressive components. By

the same token, if men are to succeed in their traditional role as economic providers, they need to highlight and free the aggressive aspects of their personalities and constrain the more tender, affiliative aspects. But as their children grow up, both parents can afford to express the full potential of their personalities. Men can recapture the "femininity" that was previously repressed in the interests of economic competition, ambition, and accomplishment; women can recapture the "masculinity" that was repressed in order to provide emotional security for their offspring.

Guttmann's approach to gender behaviors—a functional, role-based theory—is admittedly controversial. S. Shirley Feldman and Sharon C. Nash (1979) find some support for the theory among a sample of white, upper-middle-class, married Americans. As predicted by Gutmann, grandparents showed heightened interest in babies. Indeed, grandfathers showed greater responsiveness to babies than did men at any other point in the life cycle. But contrary to Gutmann's expectations, the men's masculinity scores did not significantly change in the later stages of life. Although the men gave evidence of a higher incidence of typically "feminine" traits in their later years, they did not do so at the expense of their well-established masculinity. Likewise, women showed an increase in their masculinity scores without a decline in their femininity.

In recent years many psychologists have moved away from the traditional assumption that masculinity and femininity are inversely related characteristics of personality and behavior, the former appropriate to men and the latter to women. *Androgyny*—the incorporation of both male-typed and female-typed characteristics within a single personality—provides an alternative perspective. As was pointed out in Chapter 9, individuals differ in their gender role attitudes and behaviors along a continuum of gender roles. Androgynous individuals do not restrict their behavior to that embodied in cultural stereotypes of masculinity and femininity. The findings of Gutmann and other researchers seem to suggest that in later life people tend toward androgyny. Androgynous responses are thought to be associated with increased flexibility and adaptability and hence with successful aging (Sinnott, 1977, 1982).

Other research suggests that the conceptions individuals have of their own and other people's gender roles fluctuate in accordance with specific life situations. Social definitions "call forth" certain types of attitudes and behaviors. Accordingly, sexist social arrangements can be expected to elicit highly sex-typed behaviors, whereas more equalitarian arrangements will result in a higher incidence of androgynous behaviors (Abrahams, Feldman & Nash, 1978).

Adaptation Across the Adult Years

Perhaps no theme has been more recurrent throughout this text than that life is a process of unending adaptation. Not only do we age in our biological structure and functioning, but also the life course from birth to death is punctuated by transition points in which we relinquish familiar roles and assume new ones. To complicate matters further, the world itself alters because of wars, economic crises, shifts in governments and governmental policies, shortages of natural resources, epidemics, and the like. Consequently the stage on which we enact our roles is in constant flux. The other actors, the script (culture), and the audience likewise change over time. All these changes require that we continuously assess and reassess our behavior as we cope with life's new fortunes and evolve new patterns of adjustment. These dynamic qualities are captured by dialectical psychology, the subject of the boxed insert on pages 502–503.

Maturity and Self-Concept

Most personality theorists emphasize the importance to individuals of maturity as they move through life. **Maturity** is the capacity of individuals to undergo continual change in order to adapt successfully and cope flexibly with the demands and responsibilities of life. Maturity is not some sort of plateau or final state but a lifetime process of becoming. It is a never-ending search for a meaningful and comfortable fit between ourselves and the world—a struggle to "get it all together." Gordon W. Allport (1961, p. 307) identifies six criteria that psychologists commonly employ for assessing individual personalities:

The mature personality will (1) have a widely extended sense of self; (2) be able to relate himself warmly to others in both intimate and nonintimate contacts; (3) possess a fundamental emotional security and accept himself; (4) perceive, think, and act with zest in accordance with outer reality; (5) be capable of self-objectification, of insight and humor; (6) live in harmony with a unifying philosophy of life.

Underlying many of these elements of the mature personality is a positive self-concept. **Self-concept** is the view we have of ourselves through time as "the real me" or "I myself as I really am." The self-concept in part derives from our social interaction because it is based on the feedback that other people provide us. But it also derives from the effectiveness we impute to ourselves as we confront and adapt to life's circumstances and events.

Self-concept is more independent and stable than are **self-images**—mental pictures we have of ourselves that are relatively temporary and subject to change as we move from one social situation to another. For the most part, a succession of self-images serves to *edit* rather than supplant the self-concept (Turner, 1968).

Self-concept has considerable impact on behavior (McCrae & Costa, 1988; Pelham & Swamm, 1989). Consider the "born losers"—people whose lives are stalked by failure and misfortune. Frequently, they appear to be on the verge of success, only to find that adversity mysteriously snatches triumph from their grasp. Psychiatrists and clinical psychologists have many clients of this sort, individuals who seem bent on making themselves miserable by setting up situations in which they will eventually fail. Seemingly, born losers acquire a conception of themselves as "failures" and then undertake to be "true to self" by failing. They bring about failure in order to maintain a consistent conception of themselves and the

Adult Maturity

Maturity is a lifelong process of finding a meaningful and comfortable fit between ourselves and the world—a process of coming to terms with ourselves. *(Joe McNally/Wheeler Pictures)*

Dialectical Psychology

By acting on the external world and changing it, he [the individual] at the same time changes his own nature.—KARL MARX
Das Kapital

Over the past years psychologist Klaus F. Riegel (1925–1977), among others, pioneered a dialectical approach to human development (Bidell, 1988). **Dialectical psychology,** as it has come to be called, seeks to understand the changing individual in the changing world. Among those who have contributed to this tradition are Georg Hegel, Karl Marx, and Friedrich Engels (Lawler, 1975). Dialectical psychology focuses on "becoming"—the notion of constant change.

Viewed from the dialectical perspective, human life is characterized by contradictions and conflict. All change is said to be the product of a constant conflict between opposites, arising from the contradiction inherent in all things and all processes. Development proceeds through the resolution of existing contradictions and the eventual emergence of new contradictions. The outcome of the clash between opposing forces in a person's life is not a compromise (an averaging out of the differences among them) but an entirely new product, one born of struggle. Individuals make their own history—they evolve or develop—as they confront and master the requirements of life. Thus, people forge their own personalities as they actively and relentlessly pursue their various ends.

Riegel (1975a, 1975b, 1976) thinks of human development as moving simultaneously along at least four dimensions: (1) inner biological, (2) individual psychological, (3) cultural sociological, and (4) outer physical. Development occurs when these dimensions get out of balance. For instance, an inner biological crisis may arise from an incapacitating illness. Because of it the individual may be unable to meet the requirements of the individual psychological dimension, such as the requirements of the child-parent or husband-wife relationship. Or a crisis in the cultural sociological dimension (as represented in various social groups such as families, social classes, business organizations, communities, or nations) may arise as the result of change in the outer physical dimension by virtue of an earthquake, flood, or some climatic change.

Since changes along the various dimensions are not always synchronized, conflict develops between them and produces a crisis. A **crisis** is a highly demanding situation in which individuals must adjust their behavior to new circumstances (Lieberman, 1975, p. 139):

> Crises are events that elicit in the person subjective experiences of control and loss. Generally, most of those events considered crises are of two major types: events associated with a break in previous attachments to persons, places, or things; and situations that *disrupt the customary modes of behavior* of the people concerned, which alter both their circumstances and their plans and impose a need for strenuous psychological work. They present the individual with the opportunity and obligation to abandon many assumptions and to replace them with others, thereby constituting a challenge.

The loss of a job, marriage, the birth of a child, departure of children, divorce, serious illness, death of a parent, moving, and retirement are events across the adult life span that require major adjustment.

Thus, as viewed from the perspective of dialectical psychology, crises are not necessarily negative happenings. Rather, by forcing constructive confrontations, they are the vehicles through which contradiction gives impetus to change within individuals and society (Riegel, 1975b, p. 51):

> The changing events within individuals interact with and influence the changing events in the outer world of which they are a part. Conversely, the changing events in the outer world are influencing the changing events within the individual.

Development, then, lies neither in the individual alone nor in the social group alone but in the *dynamic interactions* of both. Individuals are involved in a reciprocal relationship with the world. Consequently, by acting to change the world, they change it in ways that in turn ultimately act back upon themselves and bring about new changes in themselves.

Dialectical psychologists believe, for instance, that Piaget's conceptions of cognitive development do not go far enough (Riegel, 1976, pp. 696–697):

> A dialectical interpretation of human development, in contrast to Piaget's theory of cognitive development, does not emphasize the plateaus at which equilibrium or balance is achieved. Development is rather seen as consisting in continuing changes along several dimensions of progressions at the same time. Critical changes occur whenever two sequences are in conflict, that is, when coordination fails and synchrony breaks down. These contradictory conditions are the basis for developmental progressions. Stable plateaus of balance, stability, and equilibrium occur when a developmental or historical task is completed. *But developmental and historical tasks are never completed.* At the very moment when completion seems to be achieved, new questions and doubts arise in the individual and in society. The organism, the individual, society, and even outer nature are never at rest. . . . There is no preestablished harmony. [Italics added]

In sum, whereas Piaget views development as reaching periodic levels of balance and harmony, dialectical psychologists believe that a developmental plateau lasts only a short time. They say that new discrepancies continually arise that produce new contradictions and conflict—and with them, change. Dialectical psychology highlights the disharmonious aspects of development. It draws our attention to the part that conflict and crisis play in compelling change.

world (Aronson & Carlsmith, 1962; Baumeister & Scher, 1988).

Some individuals use the ploy of self-defeat just at the moment when they have gained a triumph. For instance, a business executive who is awarded a prestigious position in a company may begin a flamboyant affair with the company's receptionist and lose his job as a result. Others play an intricate gamesmanship that entails accepting blame or a loss of one sort so that they can avoid the risk of a setback that seems even more threatening. For example, people who say they missed an important job interview because they lost track of the time may be more prepared to accept the appearance of momentary incompetence than the risk of failing in the interview (Goleman, 1987e).

Taking a group of female college students as subjects, Jeanne Marecek and David R. Mettee (1972) explored the relationship between low self-esteem subscales of the California Psychological Inventory, a personality test, to distinguish between women who had low self-esteem and women who had high self-esteem. They also found out which women in both groups were certain and convinced of their self-appraisals and which ones were uncertain and unconvinced. (That is, the researchers determined the validity of the women's self-esteem appraisals.) The subjects were next given a task in which they earned points by matching geometric figures on a display board. At the halfway point (after ten of the twenty trials), the subjects were casually informed that they were doing quite well. But half were told that their success was entirely a matter of luck, while the other half were told that their achievement came from skill. Then, the subjects completed the trials.

Following the break, Marecek and Mettee (1972) found that (1) all high self-esteem groups showed improvement in the trials, (2) low self-esteem subjects who had been uncertain of their

MOUTH-OFF AT THE O.K. CORRAL

(Drawing by Frascino; © 1991 The New Yorker Magazine, Inc.)

low self-appraisal improved as much as the high-esteem subjects did, (3) low self-esteem subjects who had been certain of their low self-appraisal and who had been told that their first-half success was due to *luck* improved more than any other group, and (4) low self-esteem subjects who had been certain of their low self-appraisal and who had been told that their first-half success was due to their *own skill* failed to show any improvement.

These results demonstrate that not all people with low self-esteem undertake to avoid success; rather, it is only those who harbor a chronic and consistently low self-concept who avoid success. Even they are capable of achieving a successful outcome *provided* they believe that their success

Finding Happiness in Life

Psychologists find that sad people and happy people each bring to the world a somewhat different cognitive template through which they view their experiences. How they structure their experiences in turn influences how they appraise their satisfaction with life. *(Michael O'Brien/Archive)*

is *not self-produced*. But when individuals with chronic low self-esteem believe that success is the product of their own efforts, they experience inner pressure to behave in a self-consistent manner, and hence, they fail. Such individuals find themselves locked into patterns of self-imposed failure. This is one way the self-concept plays a key role in fashioning behavior.

Mounting evidence suggests that sad people and happy people are each biased in their basic perceptions of themselves and the world (Burns & Seligman, 1989; Carver & Ganellen, 1983; Kanfer & Zeiss, 1983). Each brings to the world a somewhat different cognitive template or filter through which they view their experiences. And the way they structure their experiences determines their mood and behavior. Hence, if we see things as negative, we are likely to feel and act depressed. If we see things as positive, we are likely to feel and act happy. For instance, depressed people are more likely to recall tasks that they fail on, whereas nondepressed people are more likely to recall tasks that they succeed on (Beck, 1976). Such perceptions tend to reinforce and even intensify people's feelings about their self-worth and their adequacy in the larger world.

Life Satisfaction

Most people, including most researchers and professional therapists, seem to agree that life satisfaction is a major component in any overall conception of "adjustment" and "mental health." Research reveals, however, that the objective conditions of people's lives are not closely related to their evaluations of their happiness. For instance, during the period 1957 to 1972, often viewed as the "golden age of American prosperity," most indicators of economic growth and social improvement were moving rapidly upward in the United States. However, during this same period the proportion of the population who described themselves as "very happy" steadily declined. And this decline was limited almost entirely to the more affluent part of the population under the age of 50 (Campbell, 1981; Campbell, Converse & Rodgers, 1976). By the same token, the Japanese do not seem much happier than the citizens of India, and the people of Latin American countries are in some respects happier than those of European nations (Diener, 1984).

Those realms that are closest and most immediate to people's personal lives are those that most influence their sense of well-being. Self-esteem is especially important. People who think well of themselves tend to be happy people (Campbell, 1981; Pelham & Swamm, 1989; Ryff, 1989). Good health also plays a central part in life satisfaction (Chatters, 1988; Flanagan, 1978; Quinn, 1983; Sears, 1977). Income is important, but it is not so much the absolute level of goods and services that a person can afford that makes the difference. Education, status, and power usually vary with income, and these ingredients in their own right contribute to many people's sense of well-being and allow them to feel they have control of their lives. Income seems to come into play only as a particularly influential factor among those living in poverty (poorer people also report poorer health, less satisfying marriages and families, and less pleasurable social lives, in addition to greater financial insecurity) (Black, 1985; Diener, 1984). Significantly, lottery winners are no happier than the average person (Brickman, Coates & Janoff-Bulman, 1978). Marriage and family satisfaction are also good predictors of happiness (Coombs, 1991; Diener, 1984; Emmons, Larson, Levine & Diener, 1983; Glenn, 1990; Wood, Rhodes & Whelan, 1989). Divorced and separated people report considerably less happiness than do those who have never married, those who are widowed, and those who are married (Black, 1985; Campbell, 1981; Kurdek, 1991). Finally, people seem to report greater happiness as they move across the life span, with older adults reporting greater happiness than younger adults (see Figure 17-2). As people age, they become increasingly comfortable with themselves and their lives (Gove, Ortega & Style, 1989).

As part of a larger longitudinal study—the Oakland Growth Study, begun in 1932 with a sample of school children—forty-six men and forty-five women were asked when they were 38 years old to estimate the average satisfaction of each year of their past (Runyan, 1979). They were also asked to identify the events and experiences that determined their ratings. In the first decade following high school, men said that high points were associated with family life (a new marriage and/or children—48 percent), occupational success (20 percent), and a new job or environment (18 percent). Women most frequently attributed high points to family life (a new marriage and/or children—80 percent) and a new job or environment (9 percent).

In the second decade after high school, men attributed high points to occupational success (39 percent), general enjoyment (18 percent), and family life (a new marriage and/or children —16 percent). The reasons most often cited by women were family life (a new marriage and/or children—41 percent) and general enjoyment (14 percent). During this same period men most frequently attributed their low points to occupational stress (41 percent), physical or emotional health problems (23 percent), and problems in marriage or child rearing (15 percent); women, to the death or absence of loved ones (40 percent) and physical or emotional health problems (25 percent).

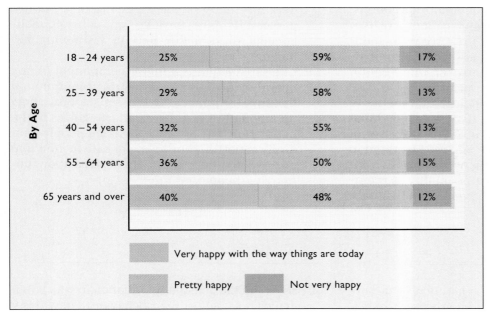

Figure 17-2 Growing Old Gracefully and Contentedly
The data show responses by different age groups to the question: Taken altogether, how would you say things are these days—would you say that you are very happy, pretty happy, or not too happy? SOURCE: Surveys by the National Opinion Research Center, General Social Surveys, 1982, 1983, and 1984 combined. *Public Opinion* (February/March 1985), p. 33. Reprinted with permission of American Enterprise Institute for Public Policy Research.

SUMMARY

1. In the fashion of aging machines, a human body that has been functioning for a number of decades tends to work less efficiently than it did when it was "new." At age 50 or 60 the kidneys, lungs, heart, and other organs are less efficient than they were at twenty. Even so, middle-aged individuals typically report that they are not appreciably different from what they were in their early thirties.

2. During middle adulthood the eye loses its ability to "zoom" in a manner that it did in youth. Accordingly, most people in their forties find that they need glasses, especially to see near objects. Changes in hearing usually begin about age 30. Typically, a fall-off takes place in the ability to hear high-pitched notes.

3. The average age at which women complete menopause is around 47 to 52. There are still many "old wives' tales" that contribute to the anxiety some women feel about menopause. Very often however, the most upsetting thing about menopause is its anticipation.

4. Some men experience a mid-life crisis. To explain it, psychologists and sociologists look mostly for changes in a man's life circumstances that produce a crisis in his self-concept.

5. Sexual effectiveness need not disappear as humans age. Healthy men and women often function sexually into their eighties. Although time takes it toll, it need not eliminate sexual desire nor bar its fulfillment.

6. As people grow older, they are more likely to suffer from a number of health problems. Cardiovascular disease and cancer are two problems. Over the past thirty-five years medical science has made great strides in combating these illnesses. However, prevention remains the number-one priority.

7. Underlying most psychological approaches to personality is the notion that each individual has a relatively unique and enduring set of psychological tendencies and reveals them in the course of interacting with the environment. Trait models view personality as recurring patterns in the behavior of individuals. Situational models see a person's behavior as the outcome of the characteristics of the situation in which the person is momentarily located. Interactionist models see personality as a joint product of the person and the situation.

8. Research has provided contradictory data regarding personality continuity over the life span. On the whole, the greatest consistency appears in various intellectual and cognitive dimensions, such as IQ cognitive style, and self-concept. The least consistency is found in the realm of interpersonal behavior and interpersonal attitudes.

9. Some research suggests that men and women move in opposite directions across the life span with respect to assertiveness and aggressiveness, so that patterns of a later-life "unisex" tend to emerge. David Gutmann finds support for this hypothesis in his study of personality and aging in a wide range of cultures. However, in recent years many psychologists have moved away from the traditional assumption that masculinity and femininity are inversely related characteristics of personality and behavior, the former appropriate to men and the latter to women. Androgyny—the incorporation of both male-typed and female-typed characteristics within a single personality—provides an alternative perspective.

10. Maturity is not some sort of plateau or end state but a life-long process of becoming. Underlying many of the elements of a mature personality is a positive self-concept. Self-concept plays a key part in fashioning behavior.

11. Life satisfaction is a major component in any overall conception of adjustment and mental health. Differences in life satisfaction show up among the various social categories in the population. For instance, married people generally report higher levels of satisfaction and positive feelings about their lives than unmarried people.

KEY TERMS

Climacteric   The gradual degeneration of the ovaries and the various biological processes associated with it.

Crisis   A highly demanding situation in which individuals must adjust their behavior to new sets of circumstances.

Dialectical Psychology   A theoretical approach that seeks to understand the changing individual in a changing world. It stresses the contradictions and conflicts that characterize human life and hence give to it the quality of ceaseless flux and change.

Maturity   The capacity of individuals to undergo continual change in order to adapt successfully and cope flexibly with the demands and responsibilities of life.

Menopause   The cessation in women of menstrual activity, one of the most readily identifiable signs of the climacteric. In popular usage menopause refers to a wide array of biological and psycholog-ical symptoms that are commonly associated with the climacteric and the ending of a woman's reproductive ability.

Self-Concept   The view we have of ourselves through time as "the real me" or "I myself as I really am."

Self-Image   The mental picture we have of ourselves that is relatively temporary and subject to change as we move from one social situation to another.

Chapter 18

MIDDLE ADULTHOOD: LOVE AND WORK

The Psychosocial Domain

Social Behavior ◆ Couples ◆ Extramarital Sexual Relations ◆

Divorce ◆ Remarriage ◆ Stepfamilies ◆ The Empty Nest:

Postparental Life ◆ Care for Elderly Parents

The Workplace

Job Satisfaction ◆ Mid-Life Career Change ◆

The Impact of Unemployment ◆ Gender Roles: Persistence

and Change ◆ Dual-Earner Couples

◆

As in other phases of life, in middle adulthood change and adaptation are central features. Human development over the life span remains a process of becoming something different while staying in some respects the same. Some of the changing aspects of middle age are associated with the family life cycle (see Chapter 16). Parents enter the "empty nest" period of life. But simultaneously, many of them find that they have to assume increasing responsibility for their own elderly parents. Changes also take place in the workplace. Job obsolescence because of technology and international competition confronts many blue-collar workers. And those in white-collar and professional positions may be reaching the upper limits of ladder-type careers and realize that they now must settle for lateral occupational shifts. In this chapter we will consider the changing psychosocial context of middle adulthood.

The Psychosocial Domain

Within our social relationships we meet most of our psychological needs and realize various social satisfactions. From them we derive companionship, a sense of worth, acceptance, and a general feeling of well-being. We appreciate this aspect of group life when we leave home to attend college, get married, or take a job. We feel "homesick"—nostalgic for a meaningful group from which we have suddenly been severed. Through our association with others we achieve a certain psychological fusion of our various individualities. The wholeness that results expresses a sense of social affiliation encompassing mutual sympathy and identification. In sum, we live our lives embedded in a social network consisting of our family, friends, and acquaintances. We may think of this network as a *social convoy* by which we travel the years between birth and death in the company of other people (Kahn & Antonucci, 1980).

Social Behavior

Individuals seem to maintain a relatively stable pattern in their social behavior throughout much of their adult lives. However, making and keeping new friends in later years often becomes more difficult because the pool of likely candidates diminishes (Zube, 1982). And as people pass middle age, they are more likely to report that others occasionally annoy or irritate them (Lowenthal, Thurner & Chiriboga, 1975).

Women are more likely to enjoy intimate friendships than men are. Indeed, whereas men often have many acquaintances, they frequently have few or no "friends." For instance, elderly men report more friendships than elderly women do, yet they are less likely to confide in their friends (Hess, 1979). And when the social contacts of elderly men are examined more closely, they are often seen to be restricted to their wives, their children, and their children's families. Moreover, women tend to maintain family contacts and emotionally invest themselves in the family to a greater degree than men do.

Women's friendships often take up where their marriages leave off. A woman's best friends typically compensate her for the deficits of intimacy she encounters within her marriage. And shared experiences of child rearing promote a moral and social dialogue among women that gives their friendships depth and intimacy. In sum, women's networks of interpersonal ties work to satisfy their emotional needs and add coherence to lives pulled in multiple directions by the fragmenting demands of modern life (Oliker, 1989).

Overall, women are socialized to be more sensitive and "tuned in" to people than men are (Zube, 1982). In contrast, the roles traditionally held out to men by Western societies have consisted of activities that entail aloof and nonintimate connections. Male relationships are often limited to formalized settings involving teenage gangs, school, college, work, sports, and the military. And men's conversations tend to center on impersonal topics, such as sports, politics, and automobiles.

Numerous social constraints limit the development of closeness among men (Pogrebin, 1986; Tognoli, 1980). Fear of homosexuality is a primary factor keeping men emotionally apart. Males typically maintain three times greater distance from a man perceived to be a homosexual than females do from a woman perceived to be a lesbian (Morin & Garfinkle, 1978). Competition likewise tends to impair closeness. Though in some instances competitive team sports superficially promote male bonding, the need to project and maintain a macho image stifles intimacy and self-disclosure. Men have also tended to disenfranchise themselves from the house, the primary center of security, warmth, and nurturance. They are more likely to construe the house as a "physical structure." In contrast, women tend to define the house more in terms of a "personalized place" affording "relationships with others." Hence, men commonly socialize outside the home. The boxed insert on page 512 dealing with friendship examines these matters more closely.

Couples

The vast majority of adult Americans have a profound wish to be part of a couple. Most people want to establish a close tie with another person and make the relationship work. This finding underlies a study of U.S. couples undertaken by sociologists Philip Blumstein and Pepper Schwartz (1983). They investigated the experiences of four types of couples: married, cohabiting, homosexual male, and lesbian. Detailed questionnaires were widely distributed in New York, Seattle, and San Francisco. This procedure provided 12,000 completed questionnaires from which Blumstein and Schwartz selected 300 couples for in-depth interviews. Eighteen months later they sent half the couples a follow-up questionnaire to determine if they were still together. As with most volunteer surveys, the sample was biased, composed overwhelmingly of white, affluent, well-educated couples.

The study revealed U.S. couples to be more conventional than the researchers had initially expected. Take work: Although 60 percent of the wives worked outside the home, only 30 percent of the men and 39 percent of the women believed that both spouses should work. Even when the wives had full-time jobs, they did most of the housework. Only 22 percent of the men as opposed to 59 percent of the women contributed eleven or more hours a week to household chores. Husbands so objected to doing housework that the more they did of it, the more unhappy they were, the more they argued with their wives, and the greater were the chances the couple would divorce. But if a man did not contribute what a woman felt to be his fair share of the housework, the relationship was not usually imperiled. Much the same pattern held for cohabiting couples.

Men, both straight and homosexual, placed a considerable premium on power and dominance. Heterosexual men could take pleasure in their partner's success only if it was not superior to their own. Homosexual males likewise tended to be competitive about career successes. In contrast, lesbians did not feel themselves particularly threatened by their partner's achievements, perhaps because women are not socialized to link self-esteem with success in the workplace.

Most married couples pooled their money. In some cases, however, wives did not place their earnings in the couple's joint bank account, in effect saying to their husbands, "Your money is ours, but my money is mine." Regardless of how much the wife earned, married couples measured their financial success by the husband's income. In contrast, cohabiters and gay couples appraised their economic status individually rather than as a unit.

Typically, one partner in a marriage expressed a desire for "private time." Early in marriage husbands were more likely than wives to complain that they needed more time on their own. But in long-standing marriages, it was the wives who more often complained that their husbands were too demanding, preferring more time to themselves. Women with retired husbands who "hung around" the house were especially troubled by the constant presence of their partner.

For all four types of couples both the quantity and quality of sex assumed importance. Heterosexual cohabiters engaged in sex more often than did married couples, whereas sexual activity was least frequent among lesbian couples. Most married couples had sexual relations at least once a week. Even after ten years of marriage, about two-thirds of the couples engaged in sex at least this often. Nearly three-quarters of the heterosexual couples reported that they performed oral sex at least some of the time. Although women were often ambivalent about oral sex, heterosexual men who performed and received oral sex tended to be happier than did those who did not. Women placed a premium upon their partner's ability to be tender and expressive—a major difference between men and women, both heterosexual and homosexual, is that women tend to link sex and love whereas men often do not.

All couples benefited when one or both members served as the "caretaker" of the relationship. Women were more likely than were men to function as emotional caretakers, although 39 percent of the men said that they focused more on their relationship than they did on work. In about a fourth of the marriages, both partners said they were relationship-centered. Other researchers find that it is particularly helpful to marital adjustment if the partners enjoy a capacity to take another person's perspective and if they confide in their spouses (Fitzpatrick, 1988; Lee, 1988; Long & Andrews, 1990).

Sociologists Jeanette Lauer and Robert Lauer (1985) have looked into the question of what makes successful marriages. They surveyed 300 happily married couples, asking them why their

Friendships

"A friend," said Ralph Waldo Emerson, "may well be reckoned the masterpiece of nature." So it is not surprising that most Americans feel they do not have enough friends or they think the friendships they have are not close enough. One difficulty seems to be that we have unrealistic notions about friendships, expecting them to be perfect. Another difficulty is in defining just who a friend is. We use "friend" as an inclusive category that includes people ranging from acquaintances or "bit players" in our lives to "soul mates" (Pogrebin, 1986).

Most Americans have only one or two really close friends; the maximum tends to be about five. Many sociologists and social psychologists say that rewards, costs, and alternatives underlie our friendships. Since friendship typically involves nonobligatory interaction, we usually get together with people we like. The expectation is that from the acts of friendship will flow a reward—perhaps some desired expression of recognition, gratitude, love, sense of security, or material benefit. Unless our hopes remain unfulfilled, the rewards we give one another in the course of interaction maintain mutual attraction and continuing association. Viewed in this fashion, friendship is reduced to a kind of cost-benefit analysis in which we implicitly calculate returns on investments. We may be willing to go through periods of drought and famine in long-standing friendships in the expectation that the friend will reciprocate our good will in the future. But generally, if the rewards are too few, the costs too high, and the alternatives too many—if there is someone else to take a person's place—a friendship ends. And for the most part, friendships do not end with a bang but just peter out (Slade, 1986).

Friendships also serve as vehicles for self-affirmation. By treating us in ways that help us believe what we want to believe about ourselves, friends validate our identities (Rubin, 1985). Of course, one problem is that over time what we want to believe about ourselves may change. And so across the life span we may seek out different sorts of friends. For instance, when we are new parents, we often want friends who will talk to us about children and discipline and who will share child-rearing experiences.

Significantly, the quality of men's and women's friendships differ profoundly (Oliker, 1989; Rubin, 1985). Nearly four out of five men report having "friendly relations" with other men, but only one in five says he has a close male friend—someone he sees often and feels he can count on. Indeed, 84 percent of men report they dare not fully disclose themselves to other men (Stains, 1986). Interestingly, both men and women turn to women for intimacy and understanding. Men's relationships with men tend to be competitive or activity-oriented rather than intimate. They get together for fishing trips, at the golf course, or over drinks at a neighborhood bar. When men achieve closeness with one another, they do so by sharing adventures or risks. Whereas men tend to engage in activities that validate their masculine gender identities, women often get together specifically to make self-disclosures, to unburden themselves, and to seek emotional support from one another. Whereas men share experiences, women share details of their lives (Pogrebin, 1986).

One arena for friendship is the workplace. Friends can make work easier and even bad jobs tolerable. But many men have difficulty making friends on the job. They see people at work as the competition. Competitive individualism and corporate competitiveness make trust seem like weakness. Men fear that if they open themselves up to others, the information will be used against them.

marriages survived. The most frequently cited reason was having a positive attitude toward one's spouse. The partners often said that "my spouse is my best friend" and "I like my spouse as a person." A second key to a lasting marriage was a belief that marriage is a long-term commitment and a sacred institution. In one way or another, many partners said that sometimes marriage demands that you grit your teeth and remain on track despite the difficulties. Overall, many couples do not think marriage is more fun than it used to be or somehow that it has taken a more ideal form than in the past. But the alternatives to marriage look less promising to many couples today than they did a decade or so ago.

Extramarital Sexual Relations

Traditionally, Western society has strongly disapproved of extramarital sexual relations (often termed adultery). Mainly, this opposition has been the result of two beliefs: first, that marriage provides a sexual outlet and therefore the married person is not sexually deprived; and second, that extramarital involvement threatens the mar-

Men's and Women's Friendships Differ
Men's friendships typically revolve about activities, often of a competitive sort. Women's friendships tend to focus on intimacy, understanding, and self-disclosure. And whereas women are likely to view the home as a personal place centered in relationships with other people, men are more likely to see it as a physical structure and to seek relationships outside the home. *(left, Alan Carey/The Image Works; right, Inge Morath/Magnum)*

In brief, men do not seem to feel particularly secure with one another. They fear getting put down, being embarrassed, or appearing unmanly. Complicating matters are homophobia concerns: Heterosexual men fear that any close relationships with other men will be seen as homosexual (Evans, 1986; Pogrebin, 1986; Stains, 1986).

However, changes may be occurring in how men, especially younger men, view friendship with other men. The demands of masculinity testing may be less rigorous than in earlier eras. The women's movement seems to have had the effect of allowing men to be more open with each other.

riage relationship and therefore imperils the family institution. These beliefs find expression in religious taboos that brand extramarital sexual activity sinful. And until relatively recently, the psychiatric literature portrayed extramarital sexual relations as "sick" behavior deriving from an immature, self-centered, and neurotic personality.

Extramarital sex has been a topic that sells "adult" paperbacks, but few careful and objective studies have dealt with it. Alfred Kinsey (Kinsey, Pomeroy, Martin & Gebhard, 1953) found that approximately 50 percent of U.S. males had had

an extramarital sexual relationship by the age of 40; among women, approximately 26 percent reported such a relationship by the same age. Although we lack good studies on extramarital relations, research suggests that the incidence of marital infidelity has risen in the nearly four decades since Kinsey undertook his research. Current estimates indicate that 30 to 50 percent of all married women have had extramarital affairs. And younger women, freed by greater economic opportunities and the sexual revolution of the 1960s and 1970s, are as likely as their male peers to enter extramarital relationships (T. Hall, 1987).

For instance, for people under 25, roughly 25 percent of both men and women have engaged in extramarital sex (Blumstein & Schwartz, 1983). However, most surveys were undertaken before heterosexuals became concerned about AIDS. Although Americans do not seem to be giving up affairs entirely, they are reacting to the AIDS threat by becoming more cautious and by avoiding one-night stands (T. Hall, 1987; Schmidt, 1990).

In their study of U.S. couples, Blumstein and Schwartz (1983) found that husbands were more likely than wives to engage in and repeat extramarital relationships. But the transgressions of the husbands did not necessarily indicate dissatisfaction with either their wife or the marital relationship as a whole. In contrast, women often strayed just once and then out of curiousity. However, when a women did become involved in an extramarital relationship, it was more likely to blossom into a full-fledged love affair. For both husbands and wives, extramarital liaisons signaled a reduced faith in the future of their marriage.

Sex does not seem to be the major lure for extramarital affairs. Loneliness, emotional excitement, and proof that one is not getting old tend to be more frequently cited reasons (Elias, 1986b). Additionally, many people report that they seek a new partner because they crave companionship and someone to make them feel special (Hall, 1987).

Divorce

Many Americans follow a path leading from marriage to divorce, remarriage, and widowhood (Wilson, 1991). Although U.S. divorce rates had been on an upswing in recent decades, they seem to have stabilized in the 1980s. Even so, should current rates persist, Census Bureau experts predict that six out of ten U.S. women now in their thirties will go through at least one divorce. For the 70 percent who remarry, 52 percent will experience a second divorce. The projection for women in their twenties is an eventual 50 percent divorce rate; for those in their forties, a 46 percent rate; and for those in their fifties, a 24 percent rate (Census Bureau projections refer only to women because women's responses to census surveys have been found to be more accurate than men's). Apparently, women currently in their thirties are a somewhat unique group. They were the ones who pioneered new ways during the turbulent Vietnam War era. They had been

brought up on traditions that were already beginning to erode: They had been reared with expectations that they should go out and find a man, settle down, and raise a family. Instead, they became the generation that were trendsetters, entering the work force in extraordinary numbers and shaping new social standards. These changes had vast consequences for husband-wife relationships.

Young people now in their twenties are heirs to the new traditions and so may escape some of the stresses experienced by the baby-boom generation. In fact, the overall divorce rate now seems to be slowing and even turning downward. Whereas a decade or so ago many Americans were willing to take a chance on divorce, in recent years they have become more conservative and more realistic in their marital expectations. More and more couples are finding it better to make up than break up (Hall, 1991; Kantrowitz, 1987b; Scott, 1990). Significantly, there have been noteworthy fluctuations in the divorce rate in the United States throughout the past century. A low point of 1.3 divorces per 1,000 population occurred in 1933 at the depth of the Great Depression; the rate rose sharply after World War II to a peak of 4.3 in 1946. Thereafter, the rate declined slowly, reaching a low of 2.1 in 1958. It then moved upward peaking at 5.3 in 1979 and again in 1981 (Glick & Lin, 1986).

Although divorce has become relatively more common, it is hardly a routine experience. In many cases divorce exacts a greater emotional and physical toll than almost any other life stress, including the death of a spouse (Brody, 1983f; Kaslow & Schwartz, 1987; Kitson & Morgan, 1990). Compared with married, never-married, and widowed adults, the divorced have higher rates of psychological difficulties, accidental death, and death from cardiovascular disease, cancer, pneumonia, and cirrhosis of the liver. For instance, relative to married women, the suicide rate is one and a half times as great for single women, twice as great for widowed women, and nearly three and a half times as great for separated or divorced women. Study after study documents that individuals who are divorced or separated are overrepresented among psychiatric patients, whereas individuals who are married and living with their spouses are underrepresented (Bloom, Asher & White, 1978; Stack, 1990). The boxed insert on page 515 examines the uncoupling process by which relationships typically end.

Divorced men and women confront new problems in maintaining a household, and many must

Uncoupling: A Look at How Relationships End

By virtue of her experience with separation and divorce after twenty years of marriage, sociologist Diane Vaughan (1986) became interested in the process by which two people who have been living together drift apart. After researching the matter and undertaking 103 interviews with couples whose relationships were unraveling or had unraveled, she concludes that leaving follows a predictable pattern, proceeding in distinct phases. Whether a couple is married or cohabiting, heterosexual or gay, the dynamics of the process she calls "uncoupling" are the same.

The person who wants out of the relationship—the "initiator"—begins a psychological distancing before the partner realizes that something is wrong. All the while, the parties "cooperate" to keep the troubled nature of the relationship secret. Rather than confronting their differences, they opt for indirect strategies. Initiators typically seek out a confidant as a "transitional person" to talk to, perhaps a friend, lover, counselor, minister, or sister. They search for sympathetic ears to reassure themselves that their feelings are justified. They also throw themselves with new vigor into outside activities and cultivate new interests, creating a "separate world" away from the partner. Like children by the wading pool, initiators test the water to see what their lives would be like without the relationship. They may go on a vacation alone, go to movies about people who have changed their lives, or read alternative-lifestyle magazines.

As the distancing process progresses, the partner begins to realize that something is amiss and is likely to feel more and more threatened. By then, the initiator has already taken substantial strides in disengaging from the relationship. A confrontation is likely to take place, usually provoked by the initiator, who takes some action that lets the partner know something is seriously wrong. At this time, the couple are likely to acknowledge to one another that the relationship is in trouble. The partner often experiences feelings of shock, hurt, and betrayal. But the initiator, too, has suffered pain, only earlier in the process. The partner often wants to "fix" things, and an effort is made—some-times feeble, sometimes with sincerity—to save the relationship. Occasionally, a partner turns an initiator around. However, some initiators agree to try, but they really expect or want to fail; the initiator may violate some "rule" that humiliates the partner, so that the partner in turn throws him or her out. Finally, uncoupling is achieved when the parties have created a world for themselves that does not involve the other person. Even so, some partners never completely succeed in uncoupling. To some degree, they continue to hang on to their identity with their ex-partner.

Vaughan (1986) says the uncoupling process is not inevitable. People can take charge of a relationship and alter it should they become aware early enough of what is happening and take measures to save it. She cautions that the process is not some sort of conveyor belt that people are obligated to ride until the end. Vaughan believes that ongoing communication, confrontation, and negotiation are essential to a successful relationship. Each partner needs to pay attention not only to what the other person says but also to what he or she does. The fact that a person says "I love you" or gives you a hug and kiss each evening does not necessarily mean all is well. Such expressions may simply serve as habitual rituals that are manifestations of a "cover-up." More important indicators are whether one feels excluded from the other person's life, whether one has a sense that the other person is slipping away, and whether the partner is complaining about oneself in public. The more social support there is for the relationship—among friends and relatives—the longer it takes to uncouple. Typically, people who cohabit or are in a gay relationship lack such support, so their bonds generally come apart more quickly.

In many respects the process of uncoupling is a reversal of what occurs when people couple (Kersten, 1990). In coupling you connect with another person and evolve a shared identity, you start going to places together, you merge your belongings, and you create a network of shared friends. As you uncouple, you begin moving into two quite separate worlds again.

also provide child care. As discussed in Chapter 10, the households of divorced mothers and fathers are considerably more disorganized than are those of intact families. The first two or three years after divorce are particularly stressful. Divorced parents do not communicate as well with their children, are less affectionate, and are more inconsistent discipliners than are parents in intact families. Divorced mothers of teenage sons face an especially difficult time. But very young children also greatly complicate the lives of divorced men and women. The trauma of divorce tends to be the greatest for women who are older, who are married longer, who have two or more children, whose husband initiated the divorce, and who still have positive feelings for their husbands or want to punish them (Goode, 1956; Weitzman, 1985).

The so-called **displaced homemaker**— women in mid- and late life—are often particularly devastated by divorce (Lewin, 1990; Uhlenberg, Cooney & Boyd, 1990). As pointed out in Chapter 10, in many cases they are women who dedicated their lives to managing a home and raising children and who then find themselves jettisoned after years of marriage. Current rates suggest that about one woman in eight will have her first marriage end in divorce after she reaches age 40. Many of the women find themselves ill equipped to deal with the financial consequences of divorce. Often, they have not worked outside their homes since before they were married some forty or more years earlier. They frequently find themselves cut off from their ex-husband's private pension plans and from medical insurance (at age 64 they become eligible for Medicare in their own right). For women of their age cohort, marriage was thought to be forever; hence, divorce is viewed by them as the ultimate failure. They tend to engage in a good deal of self-recrimination and a nagging, haunting quest for reasons and explanations.

When a couple who are in their forties or fifties divorce, the woman usually anticipates the breakup much sooner than the man does (Hagestad & Smyer, 1983). Wives typically recognize that their marriage is not working ten years or more before the actual divorce. In contrast, men usually come to realize that their marriage is crumbling fewer than three years before the divorce. Apparently, women monitor their marriages more closely than men do. Consequently, more women than men report that the worst part of the divorce is the period before the divorce decree. Women start the process of mourning earlier and make earlier attempts to get their lives back in order, such as securing a job. Generally, women receive more support from their children than men do, at times leading to bitterness among fathers, as illustrated in the case history below (Jacobs, 1983, p. 1297).

> Case 3. Mr. C, a forty-five-year-old divorcing father of a twelve-year-old boy and a fourteen-year-old girl, came to [psychiatric] treatment anxious and depressed, complaining that his wife was turning his children against him. . . . Mr. C reported that his children's complaints were very similar to his wife's accusations that she was not getting enough money

and that he was not providing enough economic security. He would respond to his children by saying, "This is none of your business. How dare you take her side? Stay out of it." He reported that simultaneously he had fantasies of fleeing to the Caribbean and living as a beach-comber for the rest of his life.

Divorce has changed considerably over the past thirty years. In 1970 California became the first state to abandon the "fault" concept of divorce, and by 1984 only South Dakota did not have a "no-fault" measure. Most states previously required long separations to demonstrate that a divorce was warranted. And judges were called on to determine which partner caused the rift and to specify a reason such as "mental cruelty" or "adultery." Under "no-fault" arrangements grounds for divorce usually include mutual consent, incompatibility, living apart for a specified period, or irretrievable breakdown of the marriage. As discussed in Chapter 10, the laws have been designed by their framers to treat women and men equally. But in practice, they have created hardship for many divorced women and their children. But even though divorce is a disruptive experience—often frightening, frustrating, and depressing—it can simultaneously be exciting and liberating (Bursik, 1991; Spanier & Thompson, 1984). Young divorced people, particularly women, often experience a greater sense of personal competence and independence once they have adjusted to their divorce (Yarrow, 1987).

Remarriage

Most divorced people eventually remarry. About five of every six divorced men and three of every four divorced women marry again. In fact, nearly half of all recent marriages are remarriages for one or both partners. And some of these remarriages are third and fourth marriages. This social pattern is known as "conjugal succession" or "serial marriage." Although lifelong marriage still remains an ideal, in practice marriage has become for most Americans a conditional contract (Bumpass, Sweet & Martin, 1990; Martin & Bumpass, 1989). The net result is that only about four of ten adult Americans are currently married to their first spouses; the others are either single, cohabiting, or remarried.

Men are more likely to remarry than women for a number of reasons. For one thing, men typically marry younger women, and thus they have a larger pool of potential partners from which to

"This next one goes out to all those who have ever been in love, then become engaged, gotten married, participated in the tragic deterioration of a relationship, suffered the pains and agonies of a bitter divorce, subjected themselves to the fruitless search for a new partner, and ultimately resigned themselves to remaining single in a world full of irresponsible jerks, noncommittal weirdos, and neurotic misfits."

(Drawing by Cheney; © 1991 The New Yorker Magazine, Inc.)

choose. Moreover, men are more likely to marry someone who was not previously married. And men often marry women with less education than themselves. For all these reasons, the likelihood that a woman will remarry declines with age and with increasing levels of education.

A survey of 1,100 middle-aged singles in the East, mostly upper-middle-income people, highlights some of these findings (Brooks, 1983). Marvin Berkowitz, an associate professor of market research at Fairfield University, observed:

> Most men say they want a woman at least five to ten years younger while most women say their ideal mate is their own age. By chasing younger women, men through the ages have rejuvenated themselves. Women rarely have this option. Rejection isn't comfortable for anyone. But if the woman isn't aggressive or hasn't retained fabulous looks or hasn't a marvelous personality, she can expect a few blows to her self-esteem. Men tend to think they are attractive no matter how they look, how they dress or how old they are. (Quoted by Brooks, 1983, p. 23)

Whereas 40 percent of the men indicated they would be content with a woman with a high school education, only 11 percent of the women said they would find acceptable a mate who had not gone to college. The women also were look-ing for someone who could be a good provider and could give them additional social status. Only 25 percent of the men and about 30 percent of the women said that religion was an important consideration for them. Sixty percent of the singles indicated that they were not satisfied with their "intimate relationships."

Should divorced individuals remarry, they are more likely to divorce again than individuals in first marriages are. Current projections are that 61 percent of men and 54 percent of women in their thirties who remarry will experience a second divorce. Furthermore, in recent years there has been an upward trend in second divorces, indicating that those who divorce once may have fewer of the personality traits or social skills that make a marriage work (Brody, Neubaum & Forehand, 1988; Martin & Bumpass, 1989). And having undergone a divorce, they may feel less threatened by the experience.

Some research suggests that remarriage itself does not necessarily contribute to the newly remarried person's sense of well-being (Brody, Neubaum & Forehand, 1988; Spanier & Furstenberg, 1982). But individuals who report the quality of the new marriage to be good also report a renewed feeling of well-being (Coleman &

Battered Women

The expression "coming out of the closet" is an apt one when applied to battered women. Abused wives have been as reluctant to reveal their plight as gay persons have been to reveal their sexual preferences. Indeed, some evidence suggests that battered women may spend more energy attempting to hide their situation than in finding a way to escape it. Until relatively recently, most women attempted to keep the indignities that they experienced at the hands of their husbands locked inside the family home. But abuse and beating are not limited to married couples. Some 50 percent of such incidents involve persons no longer married or never legally married (Brody, Neubaum & Forehand, 1988; O'Reilly, 1983). At least one-third of those who date have experienced physical aggression at some point in their dating history (Lloyd, 1991; Stets & Henderson, 1991; Sugarman & Hotaling, 1989).

Estimates of battered women vary widely. It is difficult to obtain valid information about family behavior, particularly when the behavior is seen as socially unacceptable. The best estimates suggest that 1.6 million wives are beaten each year. And at least one in ten married women have experienced marital rape (Gelles & Cornell, 1985; Straus & Gelles, 1986, 1989). The nation's police spend about one-third of their time responding to domestic violence calls (40 percent of all police injuries and 20 percent of all police deaths on duty are the result of being caught in episodes of family violence). According to FBI statistics, nearly 20 percent of all murders are committed by family members, and about one-third of all female homicide victims are killed by their husbands or boyfriends (Emery, 1989).

Both men and women engage in violence (sociologist Murray Straus, an expert on family violence, estimates that 282,000 men are beaten by their wives each year). Since men are usually stronger than women, they typically can do more damage than their female partners can (Levinson, 1989). Apparently men find it easier to control the weaker members of the family by force (Walker, 1989, 1990). It is usually simpler to control than to negotiate because negotiation requires skills. Moreover, within U.S. society there is a widespread acceptance of coercion and violence as appropriate means to achieve ends and to deal with problems and conflicts (Gelles & Straus, 1988; Walker, 1990). At times, sexual abuse accompanies the battering of women (perhaps in one-third of the episodes). Although alcohol abuse is found in many cases of wife abuse, many psychologists say that drinking is not so much a cause as an expression of the tensions underlying the relationship (Goodstein & Page, 1981).

Women put up with battering for a variety of reasons (Gelles, 1985; Strube, 1988; Strube & Barbour, 1983). First, on the whole, the less severe and less frequent the violence, the more likely a wife is to remain with her husband. Of the women in one sample, 42 percent of those who had been struck once during their marriage had sought outside assistance. This figure contrasts with 100 percent of those who had been hit at least once a month and 83 percent of those assaulted at least once a week. Women who are abused at least once a week are less likely than those abused once a month to seek outside help because they are more terrorized by their violent husbands and fear provoking even more lethal reactions from them (Gelles, 1979, 1980).

Second, the more a wife was struck as a child by her parents and witnessed violence in her childhood home, the more likely she is to remain with her abusive husband. Presumably, experience with violence as a victim and observer teaches a

Ganong, 1990). Apparently, men have a harder time living alone than women do (Brody, 1985*f*; Bumpass, Sweet & Martin, 1990). If men do not remarry, their rates of car accidents, drug abuse, alcoholism, and emotional problems tend to rise, especially five to six years after their divorce.

Stepfamilies

Remarriage often results in stepfamilies. Since 60 percent of remarried persons are parents, their new partner's become stepparents. Almost one-fifth of all married couples with children have at least one stepchild under age 18 living with them. A little more than a third of children born today will live in a stepfamily before they are 18. So remarriage means having to accommodate "strangers in the home" (Beer, 1989).

Stepparents are probably the most overlooked group of parents in the United States. Professionals have by and large studied intact, original families or single-parent families. And for their part, a good number of stepparents feel stigmatized. Images of wicked stepmothers, cruel stepbrothers and stepsisters, and victimized step-person to tolerate the use of violence. In sum, exposure to violence provides a "role model" for violence. Many of the women's lives seem structured around the men's violent episodes, just as their parental family was preoccupied with the father's violence (Hilberman, 1980; Kalmuss, 1984). Moreover, many women become "entrapped" in abusive relationships, a process whereby they escalate their commitment to a previously chosen but failing course of action in order to justify or "make good" on their prior investments. Put another way, the women come to believe that they have "too much invested to quit" (Herbert, Silver & Ellard, 1991; Strube, 1988).

Third, the fewer the resources a wife has and the less power she enjoys in the marriage, the more likely she is to stay with her violent husband. The more resources a woman has is in the form of education or job skills—the better able she is to support herself and her children—the less willing she is to acquiesce in violence and the more likely she is to reach out for assistance. Not surprisingly, unemployment among battered women is high.

Fourth, society has been biased in the emphasis placed on the wife and mother roles as opposed to the husband and father roles. Traditional values have held that marriage and motherhood are the most important roles for women. Moreover, the burden of family harmony has been placed on the woman, the implication being that she has failed should her marriage disintegrate. Women who hold very deep views about religious morals and believe in the sanctity of the family in particular have considerable difficulty leaving. Such social definitions lead many women to tolerate abuse.

Note that simply calling the police or seeking assistance from a social agency does not guarantee that a woman will receive meaningful help (Fer-

raro, 1989; Ford, 1983). Most legal organizations and agencies are unprepared to provide beaten women with assistance. Unless a victim dies, the chances that the court will deal in a serious manner with the offender are slight. Much official acceptance exists regarding domestic violence, encompassed in the belief that such matters are a "private affair." Additionally, many women fear exposing their circumstances to public attention lest the myth of a peaceful family life be exploded. And many women point to the futility of entering official complaints with the law: Their husbands are seldom detained by the police. Consequently, the men are free to return and inflict even more suffering on the women. However, researchers find that arrest of offenders is the most effective means for preventing new incidents of wife battery (Berk & Newton, 1985).

Researchers suggest that other factors may also be involved (Hilberman, 1980; Truninger, 1971). For one thing, many abused women have negative self-concepts, which inhibit them from seeking outside help. Then too, many abused women believe that their partners will reform. And in practical terms, it is frequently difficult for unskilled women with children to get work.

All this evidence points to the need for an overhaul of the legal system from police policy to court proceedings. Social service agencies need to be restructured so that the battered wife can find meaningful help. Remedial laws need to be enacted. And more refuges should be established to shelter abused women and their children during crises. Perhaps of even greater importance, a cultural revolution of attitudes and values is required to eradicate the abuse of women.

---

children, found in such tales as *Cinderella, Snow White* and *Hansel and Gretel,* still abound. Nor do present-day depictions of blended families like television's *Brady Bunch* help matters because they are so simple-minded as to becloud the realities of stepfamily life.

Most stepparents are stepfathers (nine out of ten stepchildren live with their biological mothers and stepfathers). Stepfamilies consisting of biological mothers and stepfathers have lower incomes than the average for all married couples with children. And 35 percent of stepfathers have some college education, compared with 44 per-

cent for all fathers (Otten, 1990). Overall, research suggests that relationships between children and stepparents are better in mother-stepfather families than in father-stepmother families (Brand, Clingempeel & Bowen-Woodward, 1988; Guisinger, Cowan & Schuldberg, 1989; Santrock & Sitterle, 1987). In fact, John Santrock, R. Warshak, C. Lindbergh, and L. Meadows (1982) found that boys 6 to 11 years of age who lived in stepfather families showed more maturity and confidence in a variety of situations than boys in single-parent or intact families. However, girls from stepfather families tended to

Stepfamilies
A growing number of American households are composed of stepfamilies. Since half of all remarried persons are parents, their new partners become stepparents. In this family, two children are the man's and two are the woman's. On the basis of the research currently available, it seems fair to conclude that children may turn out well or poorly in either a stepfamily or a natural family. *(Ann Chwatsky/Leo de Wys)*

be more anxious. Apparently, boys benefit from the introduction of a man into a single-parent household, whereas girls may find that their mothers do not give them as much attention as they once did (Ganong & Coleman, 1984; Robinson, 1984).

Despite the fact that stepchildren on the whole seem to do as well with their stepfathers as other children do with their natural fathers, stepfathers see themselves as less adequate than do biological fathers. In some cases stepfathers feel they have failed their own offspring of a previous marriage (with whom they no longer live) and project that concern onto their new parent-child relationships. They are also more likely to reflect on their roles and responsibilities and, consequently, to be more self-conscious and self-critical. In contrast, natural fathers are more likely to take their fatherhood for granted (Bohannan & Erickson, 1978).

Family counselors generally agree that stepparents need to tread cautiously. One stepfather puts it this way: "It has to be approached the same way that porcupines make love—very carefully." A stepfather, after all, is moving into an already functioning ingroup. The mother and children share a common history. He has a quite different personal history. Accordingly, the new family has two subgroups: husband and wife compose one group; mother and children the other. Moreover, 25 percent of preschool-age stepchildren gain a half sibling in the first 18 months following remarriage (58 percent if their

mother is under age 25), and one-sixth of children 10 to 13 years of age gain a half sibling (Coleman & Ganong, 1990).

Children typically approach a parent's remarriage with apprehension rather than joy. Remarriage shatters their fantasy that the mother and father will get together again someday. And the new spouse may seem to threaten the special bond that often forms between a child and a single parent. Moreover, after having dealt with divorce or separation and single parenthood, children are again confronted with new upheaval and adjustment. Matters are complicated because people often expect instant love in the new arrangement. Many women assume, "I love my new husband, so I will love his children and they will love me, and we all will find happiness overnight." Such notions invite disappointment because relationships take time to develop (Hetherington, Stanley-Hagan & Anderson, 1989; Nelson & Nelson, 1982).

The process of creating a new stepfamily is stressful, and family members cannot always avoid conflict. Complicated scenarios like the following arise that would not occur in traditional families (Fishman, 1983, p. 365):

My ex-husband has money and he bought our son Ricky a car. That's great! But when my stepson David needs transportation, he is not permitted to borrow Ricky's car because my ex is adamant about not wanting to support someone else's child. Ricky would love to share the car with his stepbrother, but he can't risk angering his father. Besides, David is sensitive about being the "poor" brother and would not drive it anyway. It just burned us up [her and her current husband]. So we scraped together some money we could ill afford and bought an old junker for David. Of course, we fixed it up so it runs safely, and now we've put that problem behind us.

Most stepparents attempt to recreate an intact-family setting because it is the only model they have. However, they cannot do so because of the complicating relationships that a stepfamily entails (Beer, 1989; Hetherington, Stanley-Hagan & Anderson, 1989; Kurdek & Fine, 1991; Mills, 1984; Pill, 1990). The more complex the social system of the remarriage (for instance, stepsiblings, stepgrandparents, and in-laws from a previous marriage), the greater the likelihood of difficulties. One woman in a stepfamily with seven children tells of this experience (Collins, 1983b, p. 21):

Our first-grader had a hard time explaining to his teacher whether he had two sisters or four, since two of them weren't living in our home. The teacher said, "Justin seems unusually confused about his family situation," and we told her, "He's absolutely right to be confused. That's how it is."

Consequently, each stepfamily presents its own set of problems and requires its own unique solutions.

Five matters of everyday living are common sources of friction for stepfamilies (Bohannan & Erickson, 1978; Visher & Visher, 1979; White & Booth, 1985):

❑ **Food** Differences in food preferences are quite salient, especially to the stepchildren.

❑ **Division of labor** To resolve the problem of who is going to do which chores, many families find they must put up charts on the wall allocating duties. This practice seems to work.

❑ **Personal territory** Changes in living arrangements pose problems of "turf." The stepparent finds that areas of the house are already designated for particular uses, and intrusions are deeply resented. This matter is more easily handled by moving to a new house.

❑ **Financial matters** Since the stepfather often is making child-support payments to another household, there may be financial strains when that money is needed to support the present family. Where monies come from and for whom and how funds should be used are matters that must be dealt with.

❑ **Discipline** Perhaps the touchiest point of all is discipline. Children used to one pattern of discipline have to make adjustments to an-

other. Most professionals agree that the parenting styles of both adults must yield to change and compromise so that the children are presented with a united front. Children must not have the opportunity to pit one parent against the other. In natural families parenting techniques can evolve gradually as the parents and their children move through the family life cycle. But in blended families there is no time for such evolution. Whatever is decided must be fast and firm, and such decisions are best worked out prior to taking the marriage vows (Einstein, 1979).

Given these tensions, it is hardly surprising that stepparents report significantly less satisfaction with their family life than do married couples with biological children. Research shows that 17 percent of remarriages that involve stepchildren on both sides wind up in divorce within three years, compared with 6 percent of first-time marriages and 10 percent of remarriages without stepchildren (White & Booth, 1985). Moreover, one divorce and remarriage does not end the family transitions for a good many youngsters. About half of those whose parents divorce will experience a second divorce (Brody, Neubaum & Forehand, 1988).

With stepfamilies there is yet another dimension—the absent natural parent, whose existence can pose loyalty problems for the children. They wonder, "If I love my stepfather (stepmother), will I betray my 'real' Dad (Mom)?" In most cases children are happier when they can maintain an easy relationship with the absent parent. Not uncommonly, however, ex-husbands resent having lost control of raising their children and fail to maintain strong relationships or make child-support payments.

On the basis of the research currently available, we can reasonably conclude that children may turn out well or poorly in either a stepfamily or a natural family. Clearly, the stepfamily is required to adjust to many types of challenges not encountered by most natural families. To succeed, the stepfamily must loosen the boundaries existing in the two previous biological families and structure a new social unit (Paernow, 1984; Pasley & Ihinger-Tallman, 1989; Whiteside, 1989). As old arrangements unfreeze, members must evolve enough mutual empathy to support a shared awareness so that the new family can act to meet its members' needs. Most workable solutions leave some of the "old" ways of doing things intact while fashioning new ones that set the stepfamily apart from the previous family. Moreover, the opportunities for personal growth and satisfaction are considerable. As Aristotle once observed, "Those who educate children well are more to be honored than those who produce them." Although some strains are associated with stepfamilies, so is a good deal of positive adaptation (Furstenberg & Spanier, 1984).

The Empty Nest: Postparental Life

The term **empty nest** is applied to that period of life when children have grown up and left home. Although both men and women experience the transition, it has been viewed as especially stressful for women. Women lose a major component of the feminine role, that of mother—a central ingredient in many women's lives and identities. Clinical psychologists and psychiatrists have emphasized the emotional difficulties that women face when their children leave home, dubbing the problems the **empty nest syndrome** (Bart, 1972; Curlee, 1969). Full-page advertisements in the *American Journal of Psychiatry* and the *Journal of the American Medical Association* herald the need and value of antidepressant medications in combating the syndrome. Likewise, the horrors of the empty nest have been a journalistic staple for years, with editors portraying the middle-aged woman as sitting alone at home, unneeded, unwanted, neglected, and miserable.

The description undoubtedly does fit some individuals. Difficulty is often most apparent among couples who have used their children's presence to disguise the emptiness of their own relationship. Similarly, a parent who has found his or her meaning in life primarily in the children often experiences a profound sense of loss when the children are no longer around. One mother who had been completely wrapped up in a selfless nurturing of her four children told the author a few months after the last child had left home for college, "I feel such a hole in my life, such a void. It is like I'm a rock inside. Just a vast, solid emptiness. Really, I have nothing to look forward to. It is all downhill from here on!"

Overall, however, the findings of research do not support the view that most couples experience difficulty with the empty nest period (Campbell, 1981; Harkins, 1978; Menaghan, 1983). Based on a representative sample of 2,164 Americans, Angus Campbell (1975, p. 39) observes:

> Couples settled back in the "empty nest" reported feelings of companionship and mutual understanding even higher than they felt as newlyweds. Raising a family seems to be one of those tasks, like losing weight or waxing the car, that is less fun to be doing than to have done.

Similarly, the sociologist Norval Glenn (1975), analyzing data from six national surveys, found that middle-aged wives whose children had left home experienced greater general happiness and enjoyment of life, as well as greater marital happiness, than did middle-aged wives with children still living at home. For men, the differences were less, but fathers whose children were no longer at home were also somewhat happier than were fathers with children still at home. A more recent national sample originally interviewed in 1980 and again in 1983 and 1988 found that emptying the nest is associated with a significant improvement in marital happiness and often in life satisfaction as well (White & Edwards, 1990).

Couples often report that they view the empty nest period "as a time of new freedom." One 42-year-old woman whose two children were off at college and who had returned to Ohio State University to secure her degree in accounting told the author:

> Sure, I experienced a throb or two when Ida [her youngest child] left home. But, you know, I had expected it to be a lot worse. I really like the freedom I have now. I can do the things I want to do when I want to do them and I don't have to worry about getting home to make dinner or to do household chores. I'm now back in school, and I love it.

A neighbor voiced to the author a concern that is often heard today among middle-class parents:

> Jennie and I finally have got the kids off. And it feels great. We have more time for traveling, entertaining, and hobbies. What scares the h— out of me, though, is that they'll land back on our doorstep. Bee is having trouble in her marriage and I just pray she doesn't expect to come back home. Jean is in her last year at college and hasn't gotten a job yet. I told her not to major in English but you know kids! Hank, though—thank God for Hank. He's off, married, got two kids, and is already an office manager at Arthur Andersen [a Big Eight accounting firm].

Often, both parents and children can adjust to the empty nest on a gradual basis. Children may live at home for a period after securing their first job. Or they may go off to college and return home for vacations. One 45-year-old mother voiced this observation recently to the author while we both were waiting in a checkout line at a supermarket:

> Pete [her only son] left home last year for college. But we still get to see him. He was home for Thanks-

giving and in three weeks he'll be back again for Christmas break. I used to worry what would happen to me when he went off to college. But I started preparing myself in his junior year about the time he was taking the SAT tests. I got a part-time job and took a closer look at my life and where I was going. And during the summer break between his junior and senior years in high school I encouraged Pete to go off with his friend on a five-week trip. It gave Pete and me a chance to try out what it would be like.

In sum, most parents seem to accommodate themselves to the empty nest period quite well.

Care for Elderly Parents

Psychologists term middle-aged adults the **sandwich generation.** The middle generation find themselves with responsibilities for their own teenage children on the one side and for their elderly parents on the other. At the very time that they are launching their own children and looking forward to more time for themselves, middle-aged individuals often encounter new demands from their parents. In some cases a couple at mid-life find that they no sooner reach the empty nest stage of the family life cycle than the nest is refilled either with an elderly parent or a grown son or daughter who returns home after a divorce or the loss of a job (see Chapter 16). According to a 1988 U.S. House of Representatives report, the average U.S. woman will spend 17 years raising children and 18 years helping aged parents. And because many U.S. couples delayed childbirth during the 1980s, more couples will find themselves "sandwiched" between child care and elder care (Beck, 1990; Rossi & Rossi, 1990).

At times, aging parents require increased time, emotional energy, and financial aid from their adult children. In 1980, more than 95 percent of 40-year-olds had at least one surviving parent; among 50-year-olds, the proportion was 80 percent (Buglass, 1989). Despite the profound changes in the roles of family members, it is the grown children who still bear the primary responsibility for their aged parents. The sense of obligation is strong even when the emotional ties between the parent and child were previously weak (Baruch & Barnett, 1983; Cicirelli, 1981, 1983; Fischer, 1986). In 80 percent of the cases any care an elderly person will require will be provided by their families. This assistance may be supplemented by help with income and health care costs through Social Security, Medicare, and Medicaid programs. Public opinion polls show that about 72 percent of Americans say that chil-

dren should care for their elderly parents (Baumann, 1991; Koretz, 1990). Despite the fact that the vast majority of adult children provide help to their parents, Americans continue to echo the myth that "nowadays, adult children do not take as much care of their parents as they did in past generations."

Responsibility for the elderly falls most commonly on daughters and daughters-in-law. These women have traditionally been regarded as the guardians of aging parents—the "kin keepers" of our society (Brody, 1990; Finley, 1989; Gelman, 1990; Lang & Brody, 1983). Sons tend to transfer parent care responsibilities to their wives. Daughters are three times more likely to provide parent care than are sons (Dwyer & Coward, 1991). Yet 61 percent of middle-aged women also work (although the average caregiver is 45 years old, female, and married, 35 percent of caregivers

From "Mommy Track" to "Daughter Track"

Although many women on the "Mommy Track" believe they will be able to get back to their careers when they have raised their youngsters, they find they are on an even longer "Daughter Track" with their parents or their husband's parents aging and becoming frail. *(Caroline Pallat)*

to the elderly are themselves older than 65 years of age, and 10 percent are older than 75). Not surprisingly, "women in the middle" are subjected to role-overload stresses similar to those experienced by younger women in relation to work, child care, and other household responsibilities. Their difficulties are often compounded by their own age-related circumstances, such as lower energy levels, the onset of chronic ailments, and family losses (Brody, 1990; Brody, Johnsen, Fulcomer & Lang, 1983; Schulz, Visinainer, & Williamson, 1990). And large numbers of these middle-aged women will end up caring for their husbands in the years ahead because women typically marry older men (Day, 1986). (These facts in part explain the appeal that religion has for many middle-aged and elderly women; see the boxed insert on page 525.) According to the American Association of Retired Persons, about 14 percent of contemporary caregivers to the elderly have switched from full- to part-time jobs, and 12 percent have left the work force (Beck, 1990). One 60-year-old woman, whose 90-year-old father shares her home along with her husband and 30-year-old daughter, who moved back home to save money, says (Langway, 1982, p. 61):

> At a time of my life I should have less to do, I have greater demands put on me. I have my own getting older to cope with. Sometimes I get angry, not at him [her father], but at what age brings with it. Whenever he gets ill, I panic: now what? Still I couldn't live with myself if I resorted to a nursing home.

Although being employed substantially reduces the hours of assistance that sons provide their elderly parents, it does not have a significant impact on that provided by daughters (Fischer, 1986; Stoller, 1983). Despite the changing roles of women, when it comes to the elderly, the old maxim still seems to hold: "A son's a son till he takes a wife, but a daughter's a daughter for the rest of her life." Thus, adult daughters and daughters-in-law often face complex time allocation pressures. They must juggle competing role demands of employed worker, homemaker, wife, mother, grandmother, and caregiving daughter.

The motivations, expectations, and aspirations of the middle-aged and the elderly differ to some extent because of their different life periods and cohort memberships (see Chapter 13). At times, these differences may be a source of intergenerational strain (Scharlach, 1987). However, resentment and hostility are usually less where the financial independence of the generations enables them to maintain separate residences. Both the elderly and their adult offspring seem to prefer intimacy "at a distance" and opt for residing independently as long as possible. Consequently, the elderly parents who need to call on children for assistance are apt to be frail, greatly disabled, gravely ill, or failing mentally. When middle-aged adults express reluctance to take on primary care for an ailing parent, they are not necessarily being "hardhearted." Rather, their reluctance is often born of the realization that the situation may be more emotionally stressful than they can handle. The person recognizes that his or her own marriage or emotional health may be endangered by taking on caretaking responsibilities (Miller & McFall, 1991). Simultaneously, this realization may produce strong feelings of guilt (Dressel & Clark, 1990; Hess & Waring, 1978). Most children would rather make sacrifices to care for their parents than place them in a nursing home (Brody, 1990; Hansson et al., 1990; Hull, 1985).

Evidence suggests that adult children are more likely to provide helping behavior to a parent when they feel a greater sense of filial responsibility and when they live near each other (Cicirelli, 1983). It is reinforced by a feeling of attachment, the type of affectional or emotional bond that arises between children and their parents (Walker, Pratt, Shin & Jones, 1990) (see Chapter 8). Indeed, 83 percent or more U.S. women perceive their relationships with their mothers as either quite or extremely close (Adams, 1968; Russell, 1990). Many women experience the mother-daughter relationship as a source of considerable psychological gratification and support (Baruch & Barnett, 1983; Boyd, 1989; Fischer, 1986; Walker & Pratt, 1991).

The Workplace

Today, new currents are at play in the workplace. These currents involve new technologies, new industries, new markets, job migration, and population shifts. Old jobs in manufacturing, mining, and on the farm are disappearing. The smokestack belt extending through the Midwest from Pennsylvania to eastern Iowa has been particularly hard-hit by these developments. Some have applied the label "Second Industrial Revolution" to the vast changes being brought about by computers and other electronic innovations. In some respects old terms like "blue-collar," "white-collar," and "service economy" no longer define the realities of the workplace with precision.

Religion

Religion involves how people deal with the ultimate problems of life. It focuses on aspects of experience that transcend the mundane events of everyday existence and center on some kind of "beyond" or "otherness." Religion is one of the principal means by which human beings come to terms with the ultimate questions of the meaning and purpose of life. As such, religion provides interpretations for the most complex problems such as suffering, death, injustice, evil, and uncertainty.

Polls show that about 95 percent of Americans say they believe in God, compared with 98 percent in India, 88 percent in Italy, 76 percent in Great Britain, 72 percent in France, and 63 percent in Scandinavia (Gallup, 1985; Opinion Roundup, 1983, 1985). Some 55 percent of Americans say that religion is "very important" in their lives, and 81 percent consider themselves to be religious. Of interest, 58 percent of American adults claim to have experienced ESP, 27 percent say that they have talked with one or more dead friends, and 6 percent indicate that they have undergone profound mystical encounters very much like that experienced by Saint Paul on the road to Damascus (Hadden & Swann, 1981).

Religion is a significant coping resource for many people, helping them to deal with the "breaking points" of life (Maton, 1989; Taylor & Chatters, 1991). Humanity is confronted with more or less recurrent crises and haunting preplexities—the holocausts of nature, flood, epidemic, drought, famine, war, accident, sickness, vast and sudden social change, personal defeat and humiliation, conflict and dissension, injustice, the nature and meaning of life, the mystery of death, and the enigma of the hereafter. At "breaking points" beyond ordinary, daily experience, religion provides "answers" and offers the prospect of hope. For such reasons, evangelistic messages on radio and television have a large audience. The programs typically appeal to the poor and less educated segments of society, individuals who often have a good many problems and feel a sense of helplessness in dealing with them. Television evangelism attracts an audience of over 20 million viewers. Two-thirds to three-quarters of them are 50 years of age or over, roughly two-thirds of whom are women (Clymer, 1987; Hadden & Swann, 1981; Lord, 1987). Sociologists also find evidence that religion exerts a strong positive effect on the health of many elderly individuals (Idler & Kasel, 1992).

Religion plays an important role in consecrating important life events. Birth, maturity, marriage, and death—universal aspects of the human life cycle—are celebrated and explained by most religions. The beliefs and rituals surrounding these events additionally afford support for basic societal values. Festivities, marriage and funeral ceremonies, church services, and public gatherings symbolize the reality of the group and people's relation to the larger community.

Job Satisfaction

Without work all life goes rotten. But when work is soulless, life stifles and dies.—ALBERT CAMUS

In the above quotation, Albert Camus captures the importance of work in giving meaning and satisfaction to our lives. Significantly, Americans have been entering the labor force in ever-increasing numbers since the 1960s, so that today about 67 percent of the working-age population holds jobs or seeks them (Uchitelle, 1990). Yet work that is not fulfilling can erode and undermine much of our humanness. Some psychologists and sociologists have employed the concept of alienation for describing many of our troubles and have sought solutions to these problems in programs designed to decrease alienation. As commonly used, **alienation** implies a pervasive sense of powerlessness, meaninglessness, normlessness, isolation, and self-estrangement (Erikson, 1986; Kanungo, 1979; Seeman, 1959). At times, alienation may find expression in "job burnout" (see the boxed insert on page 527).

Many of the major ideas regarding alienation have come from the writings of Karl Marx and Erich Fromm. Marx (1844/1960, p. 500) believed that in capitalist societies individuals lose control of their labor and become commodities, objects used by others.

> Labor . . . is external to the worker, i.e., it does not belong to his essential being; . . . in his work, therefore, he does not affirm himself but denies himself. . . . His labor is . . . merely a *means* to satisfy needs external to it. . . . It belongs to another; it is the loss of self.

Erich Fromm (1947, pp. 69–70, 72) likewise argued that individuals become alienated from work when they can no longer experience themselves as creators of their own acts:

> The principle of evaluation is the same on both the personality and the commodity market: on the one, personalities are offered for sale; on the other commodities. . . . We find that only in exceptional cases is success predominantly the result of skill and of certain other human qualities like honesty, decency, and integrity. . . . Success depends largely on how well a person sells himself on the market, how well he gets his personality across, how nice a "package" he is; whether he is "cheerful," "sound," "aggressive," "reliable," "ambitious." . . . Since modern man experiences himself both as the seller and as the commodity to be sold on the market, his self-esteem depends on conditions beyond his control. If he is "successful," he is valuable; if he is not, he is worthless.

Despite theoretical formulations about alienation, pollsters find that most Americans are satisfied with their jobs. A 1987 poll found that nearly two-thirds of all workers like their work "a great deal." And four out of five Americans say they usually or always enjoy going to work. If people call their work a "career," they like it even more: Four-fifths of people who call their work a "career" like it a great deal, compared with about a third who say their work is just a "job" (Giese, 1987). When asked to choose whether they enjoy work or their free time more, over 60 percent of employed Americans say they enjoy both equally or that they cannot choose between the two (Robinson, 1989). Of interest, in most other nations the average worker receives longer vacations and more holidays than does the average U.S. worker (in France, for instance, the law guarantees every employee five weeks off a year). Additionally, polls show that more than two-thirds of all U.S. workers are satisfied with the forty-hour work week. Fewer than one worker in ten would choose to have more leisure and less income; about one in every four U.S. workers would actually prefer longer hours and more pay (Church, 1987).

Whatever the satisfactions Americans receive from their work, for the great majority it is also an economic necessity. Beginning in the early 1970s the typical worker's real hourly income—pay discounted for inflationary price increases—began to slide. For instance, the average real earnings of men between the ages of 20 and 40 in 1987 were lower or just barely above the earnings of men in that age range in 1974 (in 1987 men 30 to 35 had average earnings $2,300 a year less than the comparable age group in 1974) (Otten, 1990). Deep changes in the economy and foreign competition

have wiped out many high-paying factory jobs. In 1990 a thirty-four-member Commission on the Skills of the American Work Force concluded that many Americans—clerks, secretaries, machinists, drivers, farm workers, and other non-college-educated "front line" workers—"will see their dreams slip away" unless our society invests far more in improving their skills in school and on the job (Brock & Marshall, 1990). Significantly, the U.S. standard of living has grown more slowly over the past eighteen years than that in Japan, Germany, Italy, Canada, Britain, and France.

All this is not to say that people do not show considerable differences in their reactions to work requirements (Bokemeier & Lacy, 1987). What one person finds a challenge another may view as an unendurable pressure. Even assessments of monotony vary widely. Indeed, almost any job will seem boring to some people (Stagner, 1975).

Overall, studies reveal that job satisfaction is associated with the opportunity to exercise discretion, accept challenges, and make decisions (Gruenberg, 1980; Mottaz, 1985; MOW International Research Team, 1987; Schwalbe, 1985; Stroud, 1990). In terms of psychological effects, the problem that confronts most people in occupational life today is not so much that they are employees rather than employers but that they cannot gain a sense of self-actualization in their work. People appear to thrive on occupational challenges. Hence, the most potent factors in job satisfaction are those that relate to workers' self-respect, their chance to perform well, their opportunities for achievement and growth, and the chance to contribute something personal and quite unique.

Work affects an individual's personal and family life in many ways (Small & Riley, 1990). For instance, jobs that permit occupational self-direction—initiative, thought, and independent judgment in work—foster people's intellectual flexibility. Individuals with such jobs become more open approaching and weighing evidence on current social and economic issues. The effects of occupational self-direction also generalize to other nonwork settings. Individuals who enjoy opportunities for self-direction in their work are more likely to become more self-confident, less authoritarian, less conformist in their ideas, and less fatalistic in their nonwork lives than other individuals are. In turn, these traits lead, in time, to more responsible jobs that allow even greater latitude for occupational self-direction.

In sum, the job affects the person and the person affects the job in a reciprocal relationship

Job Burnout

Work that once was fulfilling and satisfying may over time become unfulfilling and unsatisfying. Psychologists term this condition **job burnout.** Its symptoms include a sense of boredom, apathy, reduced efficiency, fatigue, frustration, and even despondency (Brody, 1982; Pines & Aronson, 1988). The psychologist Christina Maslach says that burnout typically occurs in three phases (Bishop, 1980). First, the individual experiences emotional exhaustion, a feeling of being drained, used up, and having nothing more to give. Second, the person becomes increasingly cynical, callous, and insensitive toward the people encountered in the work setting. Finally, the individual concludes that his or her career has been unsuccessful and that all job effort is fruitless.

Victims of burnout are often highly efficient, competent, and energetic people. They tend to be idealistic and dedicated individuals with unrealistically high expectations of making the world a better place in which to live. Indeed, "in order to burn out, a person needs to have been on fire at one time" (Pines & Aronson, 1988, p. 11). For instance, nurses seem particularly vulnerable to burnout, a fact that may account for the shortage of nurses. Nursing commonly attracts committed and compassionate individuals who later may find themselves unprepared for the frustrations of their jobs, the constant pressures, the erratic hours, and the constraints on rewarding interactions with patients. Others who are especially prone to burnout are divorce and criminal lawyers, police officers, teachers, and staffers in mental hospitals and hospices. At times, the realities confronting workers in the helping professions crush their humanism and render them severely disillusioned. Still

other victims are ambitious people who are blocked in climbing the corporate ladder and people who are driven by relentless creative impulses.

A case in point is Gail R., a 38-year-old social worker for a mental health center (Bishop, 1980, p. 32). Ten years earlier she had returned to college to earn a master's degree in psychology:

> Since then, things have soured. Federal funds for her clinic have been reduced. She's swamped with cases . . . who call her at home. She says she tries to help, but they won't listen. She has no chance to get a supervisory job, but she can't quit because her divorce five years ago left her with two children to support.
>
> Her supervisor doesn't care, she says, because he's much more interested in interagency politics. Gail's childhood asthma has resumed, as have her allergies. And she alternately starves and gorges herself, just as she did as a fat teenager.

Self-insight and self-awareness are probably the best defenses against burnout. But people living on the treadmill of work are unlikely to stop long enough to analyze their circumstances. An important step in avoiding burnout is to develop nonwork interests and supports for self-esteem. And individuals must learn to say "no," to set realistic standards for their performance, and to savor the small blessings of life. Cultivating family and friendship ties can also make a big difference. Some individuals find it helpful to set aside a "decompression period" at least once a week in which they afford themselves an opportunity to relax and leisurely pursue their hobbies and personal interests. But if one feels incapable of remedying the situation by oneself, professional assistance should be sought (Farber, 1983; Freudenberger & Richelson, 1981; Pines & Aronson, 1988).

---

across adult life (Kohn, Naoi, Schoenbach, Schooler & Slomczynski, 1990; Kohn & Schooler, 1982; Miller, Slomczynski & Kohn, 1985).

Research on work satisfaction has consistently shown that older people are more satisfied with their jobs than younger people (Janson & Martin, 1982; Kalleberg & Loscocco, 1983; MOW International Research Team, 1987; Wright & Hamilton, 1978). Two major hypotheses have been advanced as explanations for this tendency. According to one interpretation, the "now" generation of workers subscribes to a set of leisure-oriented values that are different from those of the past. Proponents of this view cite as key features of the "new values" a willingness to question authority, a weakening of materialist standards, and a de-

mand that work be fulfilling and enriching. These values contradict those of an industrial order founded on deference to authority and responsiveness to such traditional rewards as income and promotion.

Data from various public opinion surveys since 1955 suggest that some measure of slippage has occurred from one generation to the next in the satisfaction that individuals derive from their work (Eisenberger, 1989; Glenn & Weaver, 1982). Even so, a 1982 Gallup survey revealed that 84 percent of Americans take a great deal of pride in their work (only 36 percent of Europeans and 37 percent of Japanese had this response). Although polls show that Americans *believe* that people currently take less pride in their work than they did a decade ago, it seems premature to conclude that the U.S. work ethic has fallen by the wayside (Wright & Hamilton, 1978; Yankelovich, 1982).

A second interpretation of age differences in job satisfaction looks to life-cycles effects (Quinn, Staines & McCullough, 1974; Wright & Hamilton, 1978). Proponents of this hypothesis say that older workers are more satisfied with their jobs because on the whole they have better jobs than younger workers do. In the usual career pattern a person begins at or near the bottom and, where possible, moves up. Young people typically begin their careers when they have relatively few pressing responsibilities. Usually, they are unmarried or without children or both. They require little more than a start—a job that is "good enough" for the immediate present, supplies sufficient money to meet short-term needs, and affords some opportunity for advancement. There are many jobs that, although not providing much meaning or enrichment and requiring little skill, are good enough—satisfactory, if not satisfying. But as the needs of workers change (as they marry, have children, and grow old), they also accumulate the experience, skills, and seniority that allow them to find positions that are progressively more satisfying. Using data gathered by the University of Michigan's Survey Research Center (based on national surveys of the economically active U.S. labor force), sociologists find age differences in the rewards that workers look for from their jobs and in certain of their work values (Kalleberg & Loscocco, 1983; Wright & Hamilton, 1978). For instance, young workers attach considerably greater importance to their promotion and advancement chances than older workers. But young workers attach less importance than older workers to job security, fringe benefits, and convenient hours. These differing concerns can be explained by life-cycle effects. What is typically required at the beginning of a career is not so much a secure job and the certainty of retirement provisions but a chance to move up. In sum, today's younger workers hold many of the same values as did their elders at a comparable point in the latter's career cycle.

Mid-Life Career Change

Most of us start off our careers with the assumption that we will spend our lives in one line of work. This perspective is most characteristic of professionals such as physicians, lawyers, accountants, engineers, and college professors.

Such individuals spend their late adolescence and early adulthood acquiring special skills and credentials. They—and their family, friends, and associates, as well—assume that they will spend their remaining years successfully pursuing a career that constitutes a lifetime commitment. Their work is expected to produce a considerable sense of fulfillment and, with few exceptions, unfold in an orderly progression of steps from an entry position to eventual retirement. Each step—for instance, assistant professor, associate professor, and professor for academics, and staff, senior, manager, and partner for accountants—is thought to bring new levels of satisfaction and well-being.

But according to the psychologist Seymour B. Sarason (1977), this view is excessively optimistic and for many people quite unrealistic. He tracked the careers of 2,300 individuals listed in *Who's Who*. Roughly 40 percent of them had experienced a career shift. And nearly 10 percent of the shifts represented a substantial movement from one area to another, such as from medicine to business or vice versa. A recent survey shows that over half of the Americans polled had switched careers at least once, and 43 percent said a future switch is somewhat or very likely (Giese, 1987).

Both men and women switch careers for a variety of reasons. Some find that their career has not provided the fulfillment that they had expected or that it no longer challenges them. One professor who left academic life at age 43 for a career in marketing told the author:

> I just got fed up with teaching. It no longer turned me on. I would wake up in the morning and dread the day ahead. When driving over to the university I would develop waves of nausea. I began thinking to myself, "This is no way to spend the rest of my life." I had always been interested in marketing and I had done consulting for a number of years before I left the university. It took me about five years before I got the business really rolling but now I'm doing pretty well. I like being my own boss and I like making money—big money. I never could do that as a prof.

Others leave one career for another because they feel bored, because they would like to give a new direction to their lives, or because they have been having difficulty with their supervisor or employer. At mid-life many people take stock of themselves and reassess where they are going and what they are doing with their lives (see Chapter 15). Some look to formal education to provide them with new skills. Others may build on contacts, interests, skills, or hobbies that they have acquired. They reach a point at which they find themselves disenchanted with their existing work situation and decide that rather than remain alienated in a one-career trap, they had better strike out in a new direction (Clopton, 1973; Levinson, Darrow, Klein, Levinson & McKee, 1978). So they change their career—a "repotting" so to speak—to stimulate interests they can pursue into old age.

The Impact of Unemployment

Most people find unemployment a painful experience. Unemployment may result from the inability to find a first job, layoffs, recession, dismissal because of poor job performance, or even leaving a job voluntarily. Sociologists find that unemployment has adverse effects on physical and mental health (Kessler, House & Turner, 1987). Based on data for the 1970s, M. Harvey Brenner (1973, 1975, 1976) of Johns Hopkins University has calculated that a rise of 1 percentage point in the national rate of unemployment, when sustained over a six-year period, is associated with a 4.1 percent increase in suicide, a 5.7 percent increase in homicide, and a 4.3 percent increase in first-time male admissions to state mental institutions. More recent research confirms these findings (Hamilton, Broman, Hoffman & Renner, 1990; Perrucci, Perrucci, Targ & Targ,

1988). The worst psychological effects of job loss, however, can be minimized if opportunities exist for reemployment (Kessler, Turner & House, 1989). Unemployment also increases the financial and role strains of parents, intensifies conflict between parents and their children, and undermines the school achievement and health of children (Flanagan, 1990; Lempers, Clark-Lempers & Simons, 1989; McLoyd, 1989).

George Clem, a 31-year-old unemployed manufacturing worker in Jackson, Michigan, observes (Nelson, 1983b, p. 8):

> I've lost everything I ever had—it's all gone. I've lost my job. I've lost my home. I thought I had my future assured, but now I know I have no future.

A woman in the same community says:

> Emotionally, you begin to feel worthless. Rationally, you know you're not worthless but the rational and the emotional don't always meet.

Studies of workers reveal that their reactions to unemployment typically pass through several stages (Kaufman, 1982). Initially, they undergo a sequence of shock, relief, and relaxation. In many cases they have anticipated that they were about to lose their jobs. Hence, when the dismissal comes, they may feel a sense of relief that at last the suspense has ended. On the whole, they remain confident and hopeful that they will find a

"Well, it's official. This household is definitely in a recession."

(Drawing by Ziegler; © 1990 The New Yorker Magazine, Inc.)

new job when they are ready. During this time they maintain normal relationships with their family and friends. The first stage lasts for about a month or two.

The second stage centers on a concerted effort to find a new job. If workers have been upset or angry about losing their jobs, the feeling tends to evaporate as they marshal their resources and concentrate their energy on finding a new job. This stage may last for up to four months. But if another job is not found during this time, individuals move into the third stage, which lasts about six weeks. Their self-esteem begins to crumble, and they experience high levels of self-doubt and anxiety. Those nearing retirement age find their fortunes particularly bleak (Love & Torrence, 1989).

The fourth stage finds unemployed workers drifting into a state of resignation and withdrawal. They become exceedingly discouraged and convinced that they are not going to find work. They either stop looking for work or search for it only halfheartedly and intermittently. Some come through the stage and look back on it as a "cleansing" experience. They may make a conscious decision to change careers or to settle for some other line of work. And they may look for other sources of self-esteem, including their family, friends, and hobbies.

However, individuals who undergo long-term unemployment often find that their family life deteriorates. Unemployment benefits end, and most Americans lose their health insurance when they lose their jobs. Financial pressures mount. People are unable to keep up their mortgage payments, or they fall behind in the rent. They see their cars and furniture repossessed. It is little wonder that they feel that they are losing control of their lives. Child abuse, violence, family quarreling, alcoholism, and other evidences of maladjustment mount. The divorce rate soars among the long-term unemployed. Many men feel emasculated when confronted by an involuntary change of roles in the family, and they lash out with destructive reactions.

When the husband is unemployed and the wife becomes the principal breadwinner, the stress may become intense. (Conger et al., 1990; Robertson, Elder, Skinner & Conger, 1991; Voydanoff, 1990). One unemployed assembly-line worker admits that he is ashamed to be financially dependent on his wife (Hymowitz, 1982; p. 1): "You better believe I feel badly about her being out there on her feet all those hours. It's supposed to be the other way around. I don't like taking her money." Some days, he says, he feels

"so disgusted" that he drinks until he is "in pretty high spirits." He adds, "I can't continue to stay around here like this." Appalachia has been especially hard hit. Jobs in the region's mining and logging industries have given way to automation, leaving a growing number of unemployed and broken-spirited men. As men's jobs disappear, women enter the workplace, and men grow dependent on their wives' salaries, many women report that their husbands become depressed and turn hostile (Kilborn, 1991).

Gender Roles: Persistance and Change

Among all the achievements of the past century, . . . it may be doubted whether any is so profoundly significant and in the long run so beneficial as the emancipation of women.—DAG HAMMARSKJÖLD

In the past most women provided unpaid child-rearing and domestic services. Although most men in our society have always belonged to the wage sector of the economy, until very recently the vast majority of women were left out of the wage economy altogether. Since household labor and child care take place outside of trade and the marketplace, they often have not been considered "real work"—a reflection of a sexist value system. In a society where money determines worth, women's domestic labor has at times been belittled because it does not yield a monetary return.

But the past two or so decades have brought considerable economic and social change in the status of women. At the turn of the century less than 20 percent of U.S. women worked outside the home (Silk, 1987). By 1960 the figure had risen to 35 percent. Today, the figure is 55 percent (the percentage of men is 76 percent). Women hold 44 percent of all available jobs, and, since 1980, they have taken 80 percent of the new jobs created in the economy (Hacker, 1986). Less than 11 percent of women today are the stereotyped "housewife"—a married woman, not in the labor force, with children at home. Of interest, a 1986 Gallup poll found that 71 percent of the at-home mothers said they would like to work. And some 75 percent of working mothers said they would work even if they did not need the money (Kantrowitz, 1986b).

The expansion of the female work force can be traced to many factors: the increasing availability of new contraceptive methods and legal abortions; a growing preference for smaller families; economic pressures that have made two family paychecks increasingly attractive; a rising divorce rate, which has contributed to a substantial rise in the number of households headed by women; an increasing number of female college graduates who desire careers; expansion of the service-oriented economy, which has been accompanied by an increased demand for white-collar workers; changing attitudes toward careers for women outside the home; and legislation that has broken down discriminatory barriers and increased employment opportunities for women.

Despite these changes, many of the current figures on the employment of women bear a striking resemblance to those of previous decades. There was little substantial change in the gender segregation of occupations between 1990 and 1900. Since then gender segregation has shown only a modest decline (DiPrete & Grusky, 1990; Glass, 1990; Goldin, 1990; Jacobs, 1989; Parcel & Mueller, 1989; Reskin & Boos, 1990). Much of the increase in female employment has been achieved through the displacement of men by women in some low-paying categories and through the rapid expansion of the "pink-collar" occupations. In the United States women still fill more than 90 percent of all secretarial, bookkeeping, and receptionist positions. Moreover, many jobs in the service industries involve an extension of the work that women do as homemakers—teaching children, nursing the sick, and preparing food.

Women also earn less than men do (a woman working full-time in 1991 earned about 72 cents for each dollar earned by her male counterpart; see Table 18-1). Underlying this gap is the occupational segregation discussed above. Earnings in traditional "female" jobs and professions

Table 18-1

The Pay Gap Between Men and Women, 1990		
Men	Annual Salary After Graduation (Discrepancy in Pay Scales) School*	Women
$77,539	MIT 32.5%	$58,500
67,397	Virginia 24.1%	54,306
62,785	UCLA 22.8%	51,147
65,009	Columbia 18.6%	54,817
46,521	Rochester 15.2%	40,367
61,400	**Average 12.1%**	54,749
80,412	Stanford 7.3%	74,925
57,393	Dartmouth 5.0%	54,643
54,058	Michigan 4.6%	51,702
54,322	Berkeley 2.6%	52,934
53,762	Cornell −1.2%	54,433
	Industry	
$50,441	Info Systems 29.5%	$38,950
58,434	Management 13.6%	51,445
72,704	Consulting 9.0%	66,731
53,134	Marketing 6.5%	49,902
56,664	Finance 3.3%	54,840

* The five largest and smallest gaps among the top 20
Source: Monica Roman, Women, beware: An MBA doesn't mean equal pay, *Business Week*, October 29, 1990, p. 57.

are considerably lower than those in comparable male- dominated occupations. Over a decade ago, sociologists David L. Featherman and Robert M. Hauser (1978) calculated that discrimination accounts for 84 percent of the earnings gap between men and women. More recently, economist Barbara R. Bergmann (1987) has calculated that discrimination accounts for about half of the wage gap; differences in experience, training, and related factors account for the other half. In sum,

Figure 18-1   The Income of Women and Men
The income of women lags behind that of men across the life span. The gap widens in the postthirties age period. SOURCE: Copyright 1987 *USA Today*. Reprinted with permission. Based on data from *The American Woman, 1987-1988: A Report in Depth*. Original art by Sam Ward, *USA Today*.

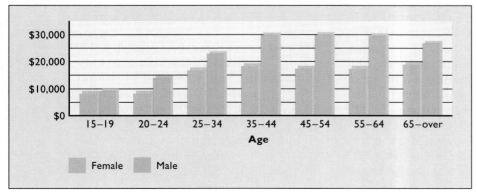

Changing Gender Patterns?
Despite recent changes, many of the current figures on the employment of women are quite similar to those of previous decades. Although the proportion of women in the labor force has greatly increased, there has been little substantial change in the sex labeling or sex segregation of occupations since 1900. Women predominantly work at low-paying jobs in office settings. Even so, we should not overlook the social significance of the breakdown in traditional occupational patterns that has taken place in recent years, including the employment of women as police officers. *(left, Joe Nettis/Photo Researchers; right, Joel Gordon)*

the earnings of contemporary women still seem to be determined by the Old Testament rule, as stated in Leviticus 27:3–4: "A male between 20 and 60 years old shall be valued at 50 silver shekels. . . . If it is a female, she shall be valued at 30 shekels" (see Figure 18-1).

One of the most significant trends in recent years has been the movement of women into fields that traditionally have been closed to them. Four of every ten law degrees now go to women, and nearly one in every three new physicians is a woman. And over the past 15 years the percentage of Ph.D. scientists who are women doubled from 10 percent to 20 percent. Yet one can easily overestimate the magnitude of the gains that women have made. For instance, of the sixty U.S. scientists elected to the highly coveted National Academy of Sciences in 1991, only six were women (Angier, 1991). And in the business world, there appears to be a "glass ceiling" for women in senior management positions at the $75,000 to $125,000 salary level. When *Fortune* magazine sifted through the lists of highest paid officers and directors of the 799 public companies on its list of the 1,000 largest industrial and service companies, it found 4,012 names of whom only 19 were women (less than ½ of 1%). Equally telling, *Fortune* expects few women to move into the biggest corporate suites in the near future. Of 9,293 names of division heads and assistant vice presi-

dents in 255 major companies, only 5 percent were women (Fierman, 1990). Hispanic and black women are particularly absent from the management pipeline (Alexander, 1990).

Various explanations are advanced for the failure of women to reach senior-level management positions. Ann Carol Brown, a consultant to a number of the nation's largest corporations, says that the biggest hurdle is the matter of male comfort, since competence does not seem to be an issue:

> Men I talk to would like to see more women in senior management. But they don't recognize the subtle barriers that stand in the way. At senior management levels, competence is assumed. What you're looking for is someone who fits, someone who gets along, someone you trust. Now that's subtle stuff. How does a group of men feel that a woman is going to fit? I think it's very hard. (Quoted by Fraker, 1984, p. 40)

Says Jayne E. Benish, a vice president at Honeywell Inc. who has spent twenty-five years climbing the high-tech firm's corporate ladder: "I feel today like I played by all the rules. I did everything they asked me to do. I didn't always do it quietly. But I did it. And when the time came, I didn't get there. That's the real world. The good ol' boys are still running it, unfortunately" (Rebello, 1990, p. A1).

A common concern of women, especially in law, accounting, and investment banking is that men receive the best assignments. Consequently, women have fewer opportunities to shine and win advancement. Furthermore, women do not receive the same types of constructive feedback and criticism that men receive from their male colleagues and superiors. Male supervisors often fail to confront female workers because they believe women "can't handle it" (they think the women will break down and cry). Women point to the persistence of discriminatory stereotypes in the workplace: If they are too feminine, they are seen as softies and pushovers; too masculine, they are shrill and abrasive.

It is also difficult for women to rise in an organization without depending on the sponsorship and protection of a male superior. Yet the danger confronting women in this type of situation is that the man may attempt to exploit the friendship and trust to initiate a sexual affair. A sexual affair with a mentor typically hurts a woman's career, causing her to lose credibility within the organization and to be resented by her peers (Deutsch, 1991; Sandroff, 1988). To combat these patterns, women across the United States have been organizing female career networks to broaden their business contacts, facilitate their promotions, and provide themselves with emotional support.

Sexual harassment remains a common workplace hazard for women (Lublin, 1991). The Equal Employment Opportunity Commission defines sexual harassment as "unwelcome" sexual attention, whether verbal or phsyical, that affects an employees' job conditions or creates a "hostile" working environment (Adler, 1991). Examples of sexual harassment include unsolicited and unwelcome flirtations, advances, or propositions; graphic or degrading comments about an employee's appearance, dress, or anatomy; the display of sexually suggestive objects or pictures; ill-received sexual jokes and offensive gestures; sexual or intrusive questions about an employee's personal life; explicit descriptions of a male's "own" sexual experiences; abuse of familiarities such as "honey," "baby," and "dear"; unnecessary, unwanted physical contact such as touching, hugging, pinching, patting, or kissing; whistling and catcalls; and leering. We lack precise statistics on the actual incidence of sexual harassment. However, a 1991 *New York Times/CBS News* poll found four of ten women indicating that they had encountered some form of what they regarded as sexual harassment at work and five of ten men said that at some point while on the job they had said or done something that could have been construed by a female colleague as harassment (Kolbert, 1991).

Given our family and work arrangements, the economic advancement of women is also complicated by the social organization of child care (Van Velsor & O'Rand, 1984). A number of economists note that women who have children encounter a substantial career disadvantage (Fuchs, 1986; Hewlett, 1986a, 1986b; Thurow, 1981). The years between ages 25 and 35 constitute the decade in the life span that is especially critical in the development of a career. During this period lawyers and accountants become partners in the top firms, business managers make it onto the "fast track," college professors secure tenure at good universities, and blue-collar workers find positions that generate high earnings and seniority. But it is also the decade when women are most likely to leave the labor force to have children. When they do, the present system for achieving promotions and acquiring critical skills extracts an enormous lifetime price. Even when new mothers return to work within a few months, men often assume that they are no longer free to take on time-consuming tasks, and the women are passed over for promotion (Fraker, 1984). When economist David E. Bloom (1986) compared women managers with similar educational backgrounds, he found that those with children made about 20 percent less than those who remained childless. Additionally, responsibility for children often affects the choice of a job; women accept lower wages in exchange for shorter or more flexible hours, a location near home, and limited travel.

In sum, the career patterns of women are quite different from those of men. And given our contemporary family and work arrangements, the economic advancement of women is complicated by the social organization of child care. The bitterest complaints often come from women who have reached age 40 and find themselves childless, having put their careers first. They note that 90 percent of male executives 40 and under are fathers but only 35 percent of their female counterparts have children. As they enter their forties, many career women find that "the clock has run out" and "they cannot control infertility" (Wallis, 1989). These factors give a decidedly different cast to the life cycle of women (Desai & Waite, 1991).

Other gender gaps also exist. Take health. Heart disease kills men and women in roughly equal number. Yet medical researchers studying health problems, including heart disease, typically use only male subjects—whether humans or rodents. For instance, in 1988, research on 22,071 male doctors found that aspirin reduces the risk of heart attacks (Ames, 1990). But does aspirin benefit women? Physicians simply do not know (for example, estrogen levels are known to influence the incidence and severity of heart disease). Nor are physicians certain whether high blood pressure may be less lethal to women than to men and whether treatments that work for men may be ineffective or even harmful for women (Rosenthal, 1991). Yet such information would seem important (Altman, 1991). Consider that a woman entering a hospital with a heart attack is 43.8 percent more likely to die before leaving than is a man admitted with the same condition. Significantly, by the time women with heart disease are referred to surgeons for coronary bypass surgery, they are much sicker than men who receive the same operation (10 times as many men as women undergo exercise stress tests and radioactive heart scans before they are sent to surgery) (Bishop, 1990; Winslow, 1991). Many women's organizations argue that inequity does not stop with heart disease. They say that women also get short shift because such areas as breast cancer, contraception, and depression are not adequately studied (Hamilton, 1990; Raymond, 1991; Rodin & Ickovics, 1990; Wallis, 1991).

Dual-Earner Couples

Of the 45.1 million married couples drawing paychecks in the United States in 1990, 29.4 million, or 65 percent, were dual-earner pairs (Connelly, 1990). The figure continues to grow as more women take jobs outside the home. The stress associated with our society's transition from the one-income to the two-income household has fallen primarily on women (Biernat & Wortman, 1991; Chassin, Zeiss, Cooper & Reaven, 1985; Gappa, O'Barr & St. John-Parsons, 1980; Schwartz, 1981). Most household responsibilities continue to be shouldered by women (two-thirds of dual-earning couples have children at home). Married women who are employed outside the home typically give precedence to their families in balancing their work and family identities; married men have the discretion of building identities with both work and family roles without trading one off against the other (Bielby & Bielby, 1989). According to sociologist Arlie Hochschild (1989), working women do 75 percent of the housework—and only 18 percent of hus-

bands share housework equally (61 percent of the men do little or no housework). In effect, Hochschild says women work two full jobs in a 24-hour day, coming home to "the second shift." Other researchers also find that no matter how equal men and women are in their careers, or how deeply they believe in sexual equality, couples typically revert to traditional gender roles (Cooper, Chassin, Braver, Zeiss & Khavari, 1986; Gappa, O'Barr & St. John-Parsons, 1980). When women are expected to assume an unequal portion of the household division of labor, they may be less effective on the job than they otherwise would be and they may not realize their true career potential or advancement. Or they may fall victim to the superwoman syndrome, attempting to excel both on the job and in the home.

If a spouse has to give up something in a dual-career arrangement, it is almost always the wife who makes the sacrifice. For instance, if a husband is offered a better position elsewhere in the country, the wife typically makes the move regardless of the effect that the transfer has on her career. Rarely does the reverse pattern occur, although today's young career women are less likely to "follow the leader" (Stern, 1991). In sum, the burden of meshing the differing career cycles of the husband and wife typically falls on the wife.

". . . And as part of your community service, you're to help your wife with the cooking and cleaning around the house."

(Robert Sims © 1991 from The Wall Street Journal. Permission, Cartoon Features Syndicate.)

In dual-earner families the man tends to have a larger voice in major household decisions than the woman does. Most families entail junior-senior relationships, with the wife usually secondary in most respects (Cooper, Chassin, Braver, Zeiss & Khavari, 1986; Gappa, O'Barr & John-Parsons, 1980). For example, the husband commonly decides where the family should live. Furthermore, some wives fear that should they assume responsibility for their own finances, their husbands will feel that their masculinity is threatened. But should they relinquish control of their income to the husband, they often feel some measure of resentment and bitterness. Consequently, many couples maintain separate accounts or pool only a portion of their salaries. One 38-year-old teacher who earns one-third her banker husband's salary finds that keeping completely separate accounts "makes me feel more equal than I am. I see where my money goes. I see clothes on the kids and music lessons" (Moore, 1981, p. 94).

For middle-aged men, accommodating a wife's new career can often be a confusing and bruising experience. These men are of a generation that typically viewed marriage as a one-provider, one-homemaker effort. Historically, the professional achievements of many married men were "propped up" by the roles that their wives played in creating complementary entertainment, home, and psychological environments that facilitated their husbands' careers (Fowlkes, 1980). When their wives undertake a career outside the home, they may feel isolated and conclude that their wives value their careers more highly than they do their marriages. For those who manage to overcome their doubts and fears, their wives' new careers often add new dimensions of excitement and vibrancy to their relationships. Furthermore, family income also swells. Says one man whose wife embarked on an airline career at age 46, "I felt deflated. She could get along without me. But in a way it was a relief. After all, I had been the only one bringing in the outside world" (Bralove, 1981, p. 1).

Scheduling time together presents a frequent source of tension for dual-earner pairs (Moore, 1984). Some couples with children attempt to stagger their working hours (one out of six two-earner couples with children have no overlap in their work hours). Scheduling time with one another often becomes a highly charged emotional issue because scheduling often masks problems of commitment, lack of intimacy, and divergent goals. Arguments about work schedules typically have more to do with "how much does he/she care" than with the amount of time the couple actually spend together. Guilt about working so hard and long or anger for having to wait around for the spouse can poison mates' feelings for each other. Hence, couples need to identify their problems and find ways to structure time for being together.

Another source of tension concerns income differences. On average, women earn only 60 percent as much as do men. However, in nearly one-fifth of dual-income couples, the wife brings home more money than the husband (Crispell, 1989). Under these circumstances couples run a higher risk of mutual psychological and physical abuse, marital conflict, and sexual difficulty. Apparently, patterns of sexist thinking lead many of the husbands to experience a loss in self-esteem. But even if the risks run high in these marriages, they are not insuperable (Rubenstein, 1982). Couples can come to terms with old expectations and new realities and learn what works best for them. Women are growing more confident of their knowledge and their right to a voice in money matters, and men are learning to share family responsibility and power. The dynamics of decision making in the family are currently undergoing change in the United States. In the process dual-earner couples are evolving new patterns and traditions for family life (Coltrane, 1989; Cooper, Chassin, Braver, Zeiss & Khavari, 1986; Guelzow, Bird & Koball, 1991; Schnittger & Bird, 1990). Work outside the home, while creating new sources of conflict for many couples, affords new sources of personal fulfillment as well (Blumstein & Schwartz, 1983). In addition, workplace parental-leave policies and other institutional arrangements that can provide relief to dual-earner couples are moving to the front burner as political issues.

SUMMARY

1. Individuals seem to maintain a relatively stable pattern in their social behavior throughout much of their adult lives. But making and keeping new friends in later years often becomes more difficult because the pool of likely candidates diminishes. Women are

more likely to enjoy intimate friendships than men are.

2. Most adult Americans have a profound wish to be part of a couple. Despite recent changes, U.S. couples remain quite conventional. Women still do most of the household chores. Men, both straight and homosexual, place a considerable premium on power and dominance. All couples benefit when one or both members serve as the "caretaker" of the relationship.

3. Traditionally, Western society has strongly disapproved of extramarital sexual relations. Husbands are more likely than wives to engage in and repeat extramarital liaisons.

4. Although divorce is becoming more common, it is hardly a routine experience. In many cases divorce exacts a greater emotional and physical toll than almost any other life stress, including the death of a spouse. Compared with married, never-married, and widowed adults, the divorced have higher rates of psychological difficulties, accidental death, and death from cardiovascular disease, cancer, pneumonia, and cirrhosis of the liver. The trauma of divorce tends to be greatest for women who are older, who are married longer, who have two or more children, whose husband initiated the divorce, and who still have positive feelings for their husbands or want to punish them.

5. Most divorced people eventually remarry. About five of every six divorced men and about three of every four divorced women marry again. Men typically marry younger women; thus, they have a larger pool of potential partners from which to choose.

6. Half of remarried persons are parents, and, for better or worse, their new partners become stepparents. A good number of stepparents feel stigmatized. Most stepparents are stepfathers. Boys particularly seem to benefit when their mothers remarry.

7. Middle-aged adults constitute a sandwich generation. They find themselves with responsibilities for their own teenage children on the one side and for their elderly parents on the other side. In 80 percent of the cases any care an elderly person will require will be provided by their families. The responsibility for the elderly falls most commonly on daughters and daughters-in-law.

8. Job satisfaction is associated with the opportunity to exercise discretion, accept challenges, and make decisions. People appear to thrive on occupational challenges.

9. The past two decades have brought considerable economic and social change in the status of women. Despite such changes, however, many of the current figures on the employment of women in American industry bear a striking resemblance to those of previous decades.

10. The stress associated with our society's transition from the one-income to the two-income household has fallen primarily on women. Most household responsibilities continue to be shouldered by women. If a spouse has to give up something in a dual-career arrangement, it is almost always the wife who makes the sacrifice.

KEY TERMS

Alienation A pervasive sense of powerlessness, meaninglessness, normlessness, isolation, and self-estrangement.

Displaced Homemaker A woman who dedicates her life to managing a home and raising children and then finds herself widowed or divorced.

Empty Nest That period in life when children have grown up and left home.

Empty Nest Syndrome The emotional difficulties that individuals, particularly women, face when their children leave home.

Job Burnout A condition that results when work that once was fulfilling and satisfying becomes, over time, unfulfilling and unsatisfying.

Religion The manner in which people deal with the ultimate problems of life.

Sandwich Generation Middle-aged adults who find themselves with responsibilities for their own teenage children on the one side and for their elderly parents on the other.

Part Nine

Later Adulthood

Chapter 19

LATER ADULTHOOD: PHYSICAL AND COGNITIVE DEVELOPMENT

Aging: Myth and Reality

The Elderly: Who Are They? ◆ Women Live Longer Than Men ◆ Myths ◆ Health

Biological Aging

Physical Changes ◆ Biological Theories of Aging

Cognitive Functioning

The Varied Course of Different Abilities ◆ Overestimating the Effects of Aging

◆ Memory and Aging ◆ Learning and Aging ◆ Alzheimer's Disease

◆

539

*Each of us stands alone
at the heart of the Earth
Pierced through by a ray of sunlight:
And suddenly it's evening.*—SALVATORE QUASIMODO

Many of us have a half-conscious and irrational fear that one day we will find ourselves old. It is as if we will suddenly fall off a cliff—as if what we will become in old age has little to do with what we are now (Horn & Meer, 1987; Neugarten, 1971; Neugarten & Neugarten, 1987). But at no point in life do people stop being themselves and suddenly turn into "old people." Aging does not destroy the continuity of what we have been, what we are, and what we will be.

Unlike some cultures, Japan for instance, in which aging is viewed positively, in our culture it is seen ambivalently—even negatively. The older the elderly become, especially as they reach quite advanced age, the more likely they are to be unfavorably stereotyped. Yet our stereotypes of the elderly contain contradictory properties. Older adults are often depicted as frail, slow, critical, miserly, grouchy, tired, and dependent; they are also portrayed as emphasizing deep and meaningful friendships, enjoying hobbies, being family oriented, valuing companionship, and exuding serenity (Braithwaite, 1986; Hummert, 1990; Kite, Deaux & Miele, 1991; Kite & Johnson, 1988). Moreover, although our society may negatively stereotype elderly people as a whole, we have quite different attitudes toward different kinds of older adults: Americans view elderly people in "sage," "John Wayne conservative," "grandparent," and "liberal matriarch/patriarch" roles quite favorably, whereas they view those in "reclusive," "nosy neighbor," "shrew/curmudgeon," and "vagrant" roles unfavorably (Schmidt & Boland, 1986). On rating scales, older people are judged less likely to possess masculine characteristics, but ratings of feminine traits are relatively unaffected by age (Kite, Deaux & Miele, 1991). And although the elderly are thought to perform more poorly than the young on many tasks, younger adults are more likely to give the elderly credit for their good performances than to blame them for their poor performances (Lachman & McArthur, 1986).

Aging: Myth and Reality

Ignorance, superstition, and prejudice have surrounded aging for generations. Although myths of one sort or another have clouded the issue, scientific evidence can help to dispel some of the mystery and confusion. The field of study that deals with aging and the special problems of the elderly is termed **gerontology**. **Geriatrics** is that branch of medicine that is concerned with the diseases, debilities, and care of elderly persons.

The Elderly: Who Are They?

A grandmother becomes palsied. Her grown child gives her a wooden bowl that trembling hands cannot break. The old woman dies, and the bowl is discarded. But the granddaughter retrieves it; the bowl, she knows, will be needed again.—A YIDDISH FOLK ANECDOTE

The time at which old age begins is ill defined. It varies according to period, place, and social rank. In preindustrial societies life expectancy tends to be relatively short and the onset of old age early (Amoss & Harrell, 1981). One researcher reported, for instance, that the Arawak of Guyana (South America) seldom lived more than fifty years and that between the thirtieth and fortieth years in the case of men, and even earlier in the case of women, "the body, except the stomach, shrinks, and fat disappears, [and] the skin hangs in hideous folds" (Im Thurn, 1883). Life expectancy for the Andaman Islanders of the Bay of Bengal rarely exceeded sixty years (Portman, 1895), and the Arunta women of Australia were regarded as fortunate to reach 50 (Spencer & Gillen, 1927). In addition, the Creek of North America were considered lucky if they lived to see gray hair on the heads of their children (Adair, 1775).

In contrast, there are several regions of the world in which some of the inhabitants are reported to live to be 140 or 150 years old. One of these is Vilcabamba in southern Ecuador. Baptismal records, which date back several centuries, have been cited to show that some villagers living ten years ago were born before the U.S. Civil War. However, researchers have discounted these claims (Mazess & Forman, 1979). They find that individuals begin exaggerating their age at about 70 years (for instance, one man who had said he was 122 in 1971 claimed to be 134 when again interviewed in 1974). Furthermore, since many living and deceased villagers have identical names, baptismal records are an unreliable indicator of a person's birth date. Careful investigation has shown that the average age of the reputed centenarians in Vilcabamba is 86 years, with a range of from 75 to 96 years.

Elderly Abkhasians
Abkhasians of advanced age remain active and enjoy a prominent, prestigious, and authoritative role in their society. *(Eve Arnold/Magnum)*

Likewise, any number of scientists are skeptical of reports that mountain villagers in the Soviet Caucasus enjoy exceedingly long life spans (W. Sullivan, 1982). Because older people are so revered there, they are given to overstating their ages. In 1982 Soviet scientists interviewed 115 villagers who claimed to be over 90. Using techniques that connected the life histories of these people with datable events such as blizzards and battles, the researchers concluded that only about 38 percent of them were really over 90, and none were over 110. Other research also suggests that superlongevity is no more prevalent in the Soviet Union than in the United States *(University of California, Berkeley, Wellness Letter,* May 1987). In 1985 over 32,000 people residing in the United States were 100 years of age or older (about 90 percent of them were under 105).

Throughout the world the number of elderly people is growing at an unprecedented rate. According to the Federal Centers for Disease Control, the average life expectancy of Americans reached 75 years and 5 months in 1990 (white men born in 1990 could expect to live 72 years, 7 months; black men had a life expectancy of 66 years; white women born in 1990 had a life expectancy of 79 years, 4 months; black women could expect to live 74 years, 6 months). The Japanese live about 4.1 years longer but surpass the average Hungarian by nearly 10 years. Overall, the United States ranks near the middle of thirty-three countries in life expectancies (see

Table 19-1). Yet for the question "When does old age begin?" probably the simplest and safest rule is to consider individuals "old" whenever they become so regarded and treated by their contemporaries (Golant, 1984; Simmons, 1960).

Indeed, although our society is getting older, the old are getting younger. The activities and attitudes of a 70-year-old today closely approximate those of a 50-year-old two or so decades ago (Horn & Meer, 1987). The number and proportion of elderly people in the United States is growing (see Figure 19-1). In 1860 one person in thirty-seven was 65 or older. In 1960 the ratio was one in twelve; at the present time it is one in nine. An even more substantial rise will occur between 2010 and 2030, when the post–World War II baby-boom generation passes 65. At that time the proportion will be nearly one in five.

Those 85 and over are projected to be the fastest-growing part of the population, jumping to more than 5 percent of the total population in 2050 from slightly more than 1 percent in 1990. Among some of the likely effects of these population changes are (1) increased societal and governmental attention to the aged, especially regarding problems of health and income; (2) an increased dependency ratio in the nation—today, 75 percent of the adult population is in the labor force compared with a projected figure of less than 60 percent in 2020; (3) increased demand by the aged for various resources: Social Security, welfare, medical facilities and services, recrea-

Table 19-1

Life Expectancies in Thirty-Three Nations			
Australia	76.3	Italy	75.5
Austria	75.1	Japan	79.1
Belgium	74.3	Luxembourg	74.1
Britain	75.3	Malta	74.8
Bulgaria	71.5	The Netherlands	76.5
Canada	76.5	New Zealand	74.2
Czechoslovakia	71.0	Norway	76.3
Denmark	74.9	Poland	71.0
East Germany	73.2	Portugal	74.1
West Germany	75.8	Rumania	69.9
Finland	74.8	Soviet Union	69.8
France	75.9	Spain	76.6
Greece	76.5	Sweden	77.1
Hungary	69.7	Switzerland	77.6
Iceland	77.4	United States	75.0
Ireland	73.5	Yugoslavia	71.0
Israel	75.2		

Source: Federal Centers for Disease Control, April 1990, as quoted in *New York Times*, U.S. Life Expectancy Ranked in Middle of List of 33 Lands, April 1990, p. 8.

tional centers, and so on; and (4) the emergence of older people as a political force and social movement (Uhlenberg, 1987). Since some 30 percent of the annual federal budget is going to the elderly—a figure expected to rise to about 60 percent over the next several decades—there is a growing concern over the so-called graying of the budget. Although people have long accepted that there is no politics of age in the United States, uneasiness that age divisiveness may appear is increasing. The boxed insert on pages 544–545 takes a close look at such generational tensions.

Figure 19-1   Americans Age 65 and Over
From 6.8 percent of the population in 1940, older Americans may grow to 13.1 percent of the population by the year 2000 and to 21.1 percent by 2030. SOURCE: U.S. Department of Commerce.

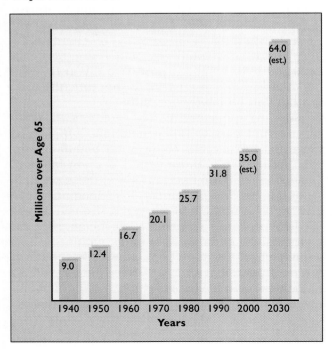

Women Live Longer Than Men

The gap between the life expectancy rates of men and women has been increasing since 1920. Boys born in 1990 can expect to live 76.1 years and girls to age 83.4 (see Table 19-2). Because of the greater longevity of women, there are currently in the United States three women for every two men over the age of 65. And in the over 85 bracket, the margin increases to more than two to one (centenarians are also more likely to be women than men, with from 31 to 43 men per 100 women). Although at birth there are about 105 males for every 100 females, the male death rate is consistently higher, so that by their early twenties, females start outnumbering men. Health statistics typically reveal that women have higher rates of acute illnesses and of most nonfatal chronic conditions than do men. But men have higher rates of the leading fatal conditions, which parallel their higher mortality. However, some researchers point to evidence suggesting that men may also evidence an equal, or even a higher, incidence of acute illnesses than do women when such factors as health-reporting behaviors, environmentally acquired risks, and various psychosocial aspects of illness are taken into account (Verbrugge, 1989).

Table 19-2

Projected Life Expectancy of Americans, 1990				
If you are now . . .	Your life expectancy at birth was . . .		Your life expectancy today is . . .	
	Men	Women	Men	Women
25	72.7	80.6	76.2	83.1
45	70.4	77.9	77.3	82.8
65	64.1	71.9	80.6	84.9
85	54.0	61.4	90.5	91.9

Source: Office of the Actuary, Social Security Administration; found in Sharon Begley, The Search for the Foundation of Youth, *Newsweek,* March 5, 1991, p. 46.

Genetic differences may play a part in granting women greater longevity than that enjoyed by men (Epstein, 1983). Women seem to be more durable organisms because of an inherent sex-linked resistance to some types of life-threatening disease. Apparently, a woman's hormones give her a more efficient immune system. The different effects of the female hormone estrogen and the male hormone testosterone point to estrogen as a means of protection against cardiovascular disease. Premenopausal women have a substantially lower risk of heart disease than men of comparable ages do.

Lifestyle differences also contribute to gender differences in life expectancies. A major factor is the higher incidence of smoking among men (Holden, 1983). A retrospective study of the smoking habits of 4,394 people who died in Erie County, Pennsylvania, between 1972 and 1974 revealed that men who never smoked and were not killed by violence lived as long as women. But the study appears to overstate the impact of smoking. Another study examined 17,000 Seventh Day Adventists (nonsmoking vegetarians) and found that women outlived men by three years. Most medical experts believe that smoking accounts for about half of the difference in longevity between men and women (Enstrom, 1984). Hence, the rising incidence of smoking among teenaged girls may mean that women will lose some of their statistical advantage.

Myths

It is not old age that is at fault but our attitude toward it.—CICERO (106–43 B.C.)

The facts of aging are befogged by a great many myths that have little to do with the actual process of growing old:

❏ **Myth:** Much of the elderly population lives in hospitals, nursing homes, homes for the aged, and other such institutions.

❏ **Fact:** Only 12 persons out of 1,000 in the 65-to-74 age group live in nursing homes. The figure rises to 59 for the 75-to-84 range, and 237 above age 85. Overall, only one in five Americans over 65 will ever be relegated to a nursing home.

❏ **Myth:** Many of the elderly are incapacitated and spend much of their time in bed because of illness.

❏ **Fact:** In the United States about 3 percent of the elderly who live at home are bedridden and about 9 percent are housebound (Census Bureau, 1986a). An additional 5 percent are seriously incapacitated, and another 11 to 16 percent are restricted in mobility. By contrast, one-half to three-fifths function without any limitation (even 37 percent of those 85 and over report no incapacitating limitation on their activity). Furthermore, people over 65 years of age experience 14.5 days of bed disability per year compared with 6.9 days for individuals of all ages. And whereas 34.8 out of every 100 persons of all ages are injured each year, only 21.4 of the elderly experience injuries (Turner, 1982).

❏ **Myth:** Most people over 65 find themselves in serious financial straits.

❏ **Fact:** As a group Americans older than 65 are in better financial shape than they were three decades ago (Hurd, 1989; DeParle, 1991; Longino & Crown, 1991). Since 1970 income levels of the elderly have climbed relative to the rest of the population because Social Security benefits rose 46 percent, after adjustment for inflation, while the buying power of people earning wages and salaries fell 7 percent. In contrast, the rate of poverty among the nation's children has worsened. Moreover, the elderly pay a smaller share of their income to taxes. And nearly three-quarters of elderly householders

Generational Tensions: How Should We Allocate Resources?

The consequences of the growing proportion of elderly in our society will affect every American and every U.S. institution. Over the past five decades a variety of social policies have been put in place that have allowed the elderly both to disengage from economically productive activities and to experience an improved standard of living. In 1935 Congress set up the Social Security program and since then has significantly expanded its benefits; Medicare provides the old with national health insurance, while the Supplemental Security Income program provides them with a guaranteed minimum income; and the Older Americans Act supports an array of services specifically intended for older persons. Government spending on the elderly has risen steadily. In fiscal 1965 (the year Medicare was enacted), spending on the elderly accounted for 16 percent of federal outlays. In 1990, the federal government spent an estimated $354 billion, or 29 percent, on the elderly (Samuelson, 1990). Significantly, the nation's bill for Medicare is growing almost twice as rapidly as is Social Security (in 1990, Medicare outlays totaled $110 billion, or 9 percent of all federal spending; military spending accounted for 24 percent of the federal budget) (Pear, 1991).

Currently, most programs for the elderly seem on sound financial footing. For instance, contributions to Social Security exceed outlays. As the baby-boom generation moves into its peak earning years and the number of retired people remains relatively small, the funds should keep swelling. Even so, the Social Security system is headed for difficulty. In 1965 the number of births dropped below 4 million a year, inaugurating the baby-bust generation. Today, 3.3 workers toil to support a single beneficiary. By 2010, when the first wave of

boomers nears 65, the figure will fall to 2.9 workers. And after 2030 the support ratio withers to 1.9 workers per beneficiary (Smith, 1987*b*). All the while, medical advances since 1960 have added five years to the average American's life expectancy and retirement. By the year 2008, on the basis of current trends, the system is projected to pay out more than it takes in. Moreover, no society in the history of the world has experienced a situation in which over 20 percent of its population was 65 years of age and over (Uhlenberg, 1987). Not surprisingly, many Americans—especially those aged eighteen to 30—have lost confidence in the Social Security system.

There are those who argue that Social Security, as currently constructed, is a mechanism for redistributing income from the younger to the older generation. For example, the elderly who retired in the early years of Social Security had to pay the program's taxes for only a few years before retiring, and the initial taxes were low. The maximum annual Social Security tax, including both employer and employee shares, was $189 in 1958 and still was only $348 in 1965. However, today's younger workers must pay Social Security taxes of several thousand dollars a year for their entire working careers. Some economists estimate that, adjusted for inflation and investment potential, payroll taxes paid by a middle-income 25-year-old will exceed benefits by nearly $40,000. In contrast, today's 70-year-old retiree who had the same inflation-adjusted salary at age 25 would receive $20,000 more in benefits than he or she had paid in taxes.

One answer to the problems of the Social Security system has been later retirement. Legislation already passed raises the age for drawing full

own their own home, half of them without a mortgage. However, these figures disguise the fact that some 25 percent of Americans over age 65 remain below or just over the government's designated poverty line.

Although 68 percent of the public assume that money is a major difficulty for people over 65, only 17 percent of the elderly report that "not having enough money to live on" is a serious problem. Significantly, a higher proportion of people aged 18 to 64—18 percent—report this difficulty (Harris, 1981; Neugarten, 1982*b*). Moreover, elderly Americans tend to be more satisfied with their financial circum-

stances than are other Americans (see Figure 19-2).

Today, 92 percent of Americans over 65 receive Social Security benefits (compared with 60 percent in 1965). Social Security provides 38 percent of the total income of older Americans. It is followed by earnings from employment, 23 percent; income from assets, 19 percent; money from private pensions, 7 percent; government pensions, 7 percent; local public assistance, 2 percent; and other sources, 4 percent (Gottschalk, 1983).

Despite some gains in the financial status of

Social Security benefits to 66 beginning in 2009 and to 67 in 2027. But Americans may have to redefine the privileged status "old" even more. The members of cohorts reaching age 65 now and in the future, compared with those in earlier cohorts, are better educated, more skilled, and healthier, and so they have much to contribute to societal welfare (Uhlenberg, 1987; Eckholm, 1990). Another proposal is to raise payroll taxes. Some estimates project that in order to cover all the benefits promised to today's younger workers, Social Security payroll tax rates would have to be raised to at least 33 percent (perhaps even 40 percent), compared with 14 percent today. Given this state of affairs, some contend that the Social Security system should be financed from a national trust fund. It would be made up of government revenues and based on a percentage of the gross national product (Hess, 1985).

Many people do not realize that Social Security was never intended to provide for all their needs when they retired or became disabled. Pension planners typically view Social Security as one leg of a three-legged stool, with private pensions and savings providing the other two kinds of support. Critics of the system contend that most people could do much better if they were able to put their Social Security contributions into a private pension plan. But this argument fails to consider the disability and survivor's benefits that workers or their families may begin drawing at an early age. Moreover, economists say that we cannot make Social Security voluntary. Low-cost people would get out because they could get better investment returns and benefits elsewhere. The high-cost people would stay in, and the system would collapse.

Given these issues, the question of how the na-

"I decided to buy now and let my kids pay for it."

(Bo Brown © 1991 from The Wall Street Journal. Permission, Cartoon Features Syndicate.)

tion should allocate its resources among generations is making its way into political discourse. Some contend that the generation currently in power is passing the bill for its needs and upkeep to its successors. Growing numbers of Americans are expressing concern that our nation is mortgaging our children's and our children's children's futures. For instance, the national debt more than doubled during the Reagan administration. Since 1973 yearly earnings for workers younger than 35 have declined 15 percent, adjusting for inflation. Younger families are finding it increasingly difficult to purchase their own homes. And the percentage of children who live below the poverty line has increased 50 percent since 1980. Overall, then, the nation is confronting some difficult choices (Ferraro, 1990; Lamm, 1990; Pampel, Williamson & Stryker, 1990; Stone, 1991).

the elderly, about 13 percent of the elderly live in poverty. Older women are its most likely victims. Many are women without families and without friends (two out of ten elderly women who live alone exist in poverty); a vast number of them are minority women (three out of ten elderly blacks fall below the federal poverty level).

❑ **Myth:** People's lives and interests change radically in later life.
❑ **Fact:** A study among undergraduates at the University of Wisconsin, Madison, revealed that the favorite activities of these young people are such things as horseback riding, sailing, and basketball. But when asked to list the leisure activities they most often actually pursued, the students listed napping, walking, eating, and conversation, in that order. A similar survey among Madison area elderly showed that their most common leisure activities were napping, walking, eating, and conversation—the same ordering of activities indicated by the college students (Harper, 1978).
❑ **Myth:** Most elderly people are "prisoners of fear" who are "under house arrest" by virtue of their fear of crime.

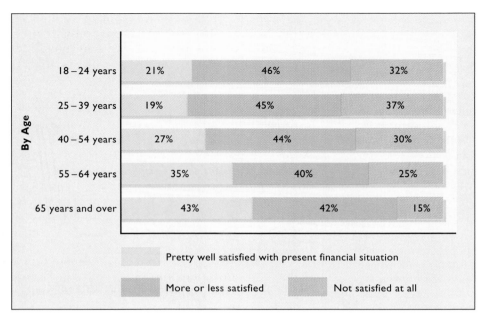

By Age

18 – 24 years	21%	46%	32%
25 – 39 years	19%	45%	37%
40 – 54 years	27%	44%	30%
55 – 64 years	35%	40%	25%
65 years and over	43%	42%	15%

Pretty well satisfied with present financial situation

More or less satisfied   Not satisfied at all

Figure 19-2   How Americans View Their Finances
The results of a survey asking people of different age groups the question: We are interested in how people are getting along financially these days. So far as you and your family are concerned, would you say that you are pretty well satisfied with your present financial situation, more or less satisfied, or not satisfied at all? SOURCE: Surveys by the National Opinion Research Center, General Social Surveys, 1982, 1983, and 1984 combined. *Public Opinion* (February/March 1985), p. 34. Reprinted with permission of the American Enterprise Institute for Public Policy Research.

❏ **Fact:**   Although 74 percent of the public view fear of crime as a major concern of people over 65, only 25 percent of the elderly agree (Harris, 1981). Meanwhile, crimes against the elderly are half as likely to occur as against younger people, and the violent crime rate against the elderly has declined 50 percent since 1973. Overall, those 65 and older have the lowest victimization rates of any age group (Fattah & Sacco, 1989).

Clashing Stereotypes of Older Americans
The American public is increasingly being pulled between conflicting images of the elderly. On the one hand older people are depicted as lonely and socially isolated. On the other, they are portrayed as enjoying a life of affluence and leisure at the expense of hardworking younger generations. *(left, Gilles Peress/Magnum; right Costa Manos/Magnum)*

Additional myths will be considered in the course of this chapter. Although the problems cited above are often folklore as far as the majority of the elderly are concerned, they are realities for some segments of the older population, especially for those who are poor and black. But by and large there is a great gap between the actual experiences of most older people and the problems attributed to them by others. Most of the elderly are resilient and very much alive and not a hopeless, inert mass teetering on the edge of senility and death. Generalizations that depict the elderly as an economically and socially deprived group may actually do them a disservice by tagging them with unfavorable societal definitions and reflected appraisals. And such stereotypes allow younger people to separate themselves comfortably from older ones and to relegate the elderly to inferior status.

Health

Since I came to the White House, I got two hearing aids, a colon operation, skin cancer, a prostate operation and I was shot. The damn thing is, I've never felt better in my life.—RONALD REAGAN, *on turning 76*

Although 47 percent of the general public attribute "poor health" to the elderly, only 21 percent of those 65 and over consider poor health to be a serious problem for them (Harris, 1981). Indeed, the incidence of self-reported acute illnesses (upper respiratory infections, injuries, digestive disorders, and the like) is lower among the elderly than among other segments of the population. However, the incidence of chronic diseases (heart conditions, arthritis, diabetes, varicose veins, and so on) rises steadily with advancing years. Under age 15 there are about four chronic diseases to every ten children, while at age 65 there are about forty chronic diseases to every ten adults (many of the adults have multiple disorders). This is a tenfold increase in the incidence of chronic diseases. Despite the higher incidence of chronic health problems among the elderly, most older individuals do not consider themselves to be seriously handicapped in pursuing their ordinary activities. Fully 56 percent of people over age 65 who are not in institutions rate their health as good to excellent compared with 74 percent of the total population (see Figure 19-3).

Most of the conditions that create chronic dis-

Figure 19-3 Rating of Health by Age
Data presented here show the survey responses to the question: Would you say your own health, in general, is excellent, good, fair, or poor? Note: In response to another question from the combined 1980, 1983, and 1984 NORC General Social Surveys, 45% of those 65 and over said they had not been hospitalized during the last five years, 20% had been hospitalized both in the prior four years and in the last year. SOURCE: Surveys by the National Opinion Research Center, General Social Surveys, 1980, 1982, and 1984. *Public Opinion* (February/March 1985), p. 35. Reprinted with permission of the American Enterprise Institute for Public Policy Research.

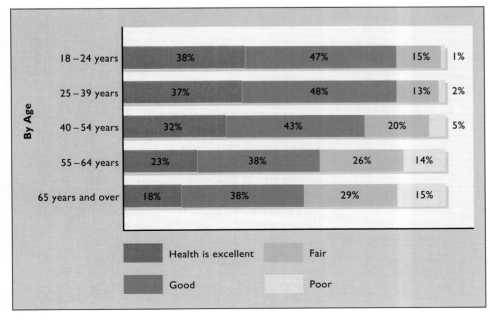

ease increase with advanced age. The fact that larger numbers of Americans are living to be 85 or over means that the nation has a growing population of people with chronic disease disability (Lewin, 1991). Since women live on average seven years longer than men do, women spend a larger percentage of their lives with more chronic infirmities and disabilities. Whereas men between 65 and 69 spend an average of 71 percent of their remaining years in good health, their female counterparts can expect to live only 54 percent of the rest of their lives in good health. For those over 85, men can expect to enjoy func-

Elderly Pet Owners Go to the Doctor Less

Psychologist Judith M. Siegel finds that elderly pet owners visit their doctors less often than do those who lack pets, and dog owners have the fewest visits of all. Dogs—more than other pets—provide their owners with companionship and an object of attachment. More particularly, pets seem to help their owners in times of stress. Pet ownership is a way of life for 49 percent of those aged 50 to 54, and for nearly one-third of adults aged 70 or older. (Kent Reno/Jeroboam)

tional health for 51 percent of their remaining years and women for 36 percent (Katz, 1983).

The Baltimore Longitudinal Study, which began in 1958, has contributed much to our understanding of the health of older Americans (Fialka, 1982; Fozard, Metter & Brant, 1990; Hallfrisch, Muller, Drinkwater, Tobin & Andres, 1990; Hallfrisch, Tobin, Muller & Andres, 1988; Knudson, 1980). The study's focus was a group of 950 volunteers ranging in age from the early twenties through the late eighties. Every two years the individuals undergo two and a half days of exhaustive physical tests. The study's findings that many people over 65 tend to be "overweight" has caused researchers to reexamine traditional weight tables that equate healthy with thin. Furthermore, since 60 percent of those over age 60 have high blood-sugar levels in glucose-tolerance tests, medical authorities are questioning many diagnoses of diabetes in older people. Perhaps a slowing down in insulin production is a normal occurrence. As a result of this research the American Diabetes Association and the World Health Organization have narrowed the statistical range used to diagnose the disease. Observes Dr. Reubin Andres, one of the researchers with the project, "Think of it, several million people 'cured' by the stroke of a pen."

Proper exercise appropriately and carefully pursued throughout life—even into the eighties and beyond—can significantly deter the deterioration of bodily functions that traditionally accompany aging. Disuse is thought to account for about half the functional decline that typically occurs between ages 30 and 70. Among the demonstrated benefits of exercise are increased work capacity, improved heart and respiratory function, lower blood pressure, increased muscle strength, denser bones, greater flexibility, quicker reaction times, clearer thinking, and reduced susceptibility to depression. Although exercise by the elderly is not without risk, recent studies show that age-associated declines can be delayed by fitness-promoting exercise (Brody, 1990; Clarkson-Smith & Hartley, 1989; Hart, 1986; Shephard & Montelpare, 1988).

Good nutrition is another factor contributing to health in old age that can be controlled. Although energy requirements decrease with advancing age, elderly people do not require fewer nutrients than younger adults. Indeed, they may require more. Recent research suggests that substantial changes occur in the metabolism of vitamins and minerals with aging and that the recommended dietary allowances derived from younger popula-

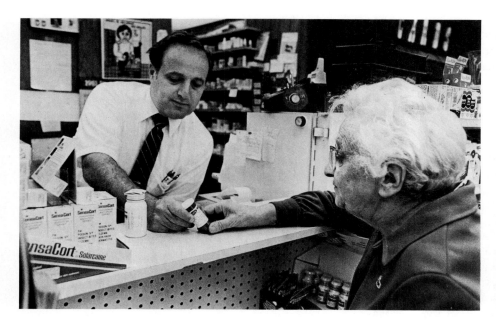

Overmedication
Some of the health problems experienced by older Americans result from the side effects of their medications. When some medications are taken in combination with one another, they can produce severe reactions. Indeed, some authorities believe that elderly Americans are overmedicated. *(Bryce Flynn/Picture Group)*

tions may be misleading and of little use to elderly persons. Complicating matters, the intake levels for various nutrients differ for older persons living in institutions and those living in the community (Schneider, Vining, Hadley & Farnham, 1986).

Elderly women may require calcium supplements to forestall broken hips and fractured wrists in later life (Horsman, Jones, Francis & Nordin, 1983; Mitchell & Lyles, 1990; Schneider, Vining, Hadley & Farnham, 1986). From 150,000 to 200,000 women fracture their hips every year in the United States because of **osteoporosis**—a condition associated with a slow, insidious loss of calcium, producing porous bones. Calcium supplements seem to slow or stop bone loss, but by themselves they do not increase bone mass. However, in some cases an increase in bone mass can occur when fluoride is taken in conjunction with the calcium supplements. The therapy should be supervised by a physician since overdoses of fluoride can be highly toxic. Similarly, estrogen therapy may be useful in treating the condition. But estrogen therapy has little or no effect if not started in the decade following menopause. Although there is no absolute cure for osteoporosis, if treatment is begun early enough, its progress can be slowed and later fractures prevented. Women who remain physically active, have good leg and arm muscles, and exercise into the seventh and eighth decade seem to have less of a problem, while women who lead a sedentary life are more likely to develop the problem.

Brief blackouts are also a major hazard among the elderly that can result in broken hips, bleeding inside the skull, and other injuries. Medical researchers find that many elderly people have a 20-point drop in their blood pressure when they stand up. Eating also lowers the blood pressure in the elderly for an hour after meals. When the two factors coincide, an elderly person may experience a fainting spell (Lipsitz, 1983).

Some of the health problems experienced by older Americans are the product of side effects associated with medication. Currently, there are more than 7,000 prescription drugs and over 100,000 over-the-counter medications available in the United States. Elderly persons do not absorb drugs as readily from the intestinal tract, their livers are less efficient in metabolizing medications, and their kidneys are 50 percent less efficient than those of a younger person in excreting chemicals. Hence, a person over age 60 is two to seven times more likely to suffer adverse side effects than a younger patient.

Although older people need higher doses of some medications, they need lower doses of others. For instance, the aging brain and nervous system are unusually sensitive to antianxiety drugs such as Valium and Librium, so that confusion and lethargy can result from taking these medications (for instance, the plasma half-life of Valium increases substantially with aging—rising from fifty-five hours in 50-year-old persons to as long as ninety hours in 80-year-olds). Sedatives such as phenobarbital often have a paradoxical

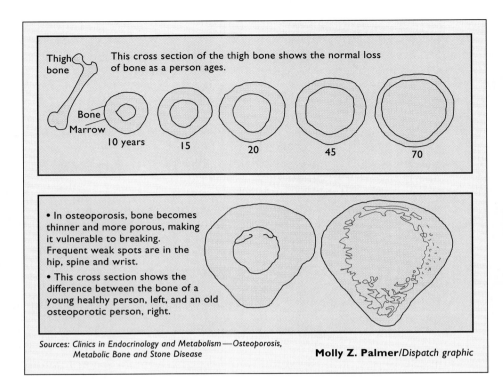

Thigh bone

This cross section of the thigh bone shows the normal loss of bone as a person ages.

Bone Marrow

10 years   15   20   45   70

• In osteoporosis, bone becomes thinner and more porous, making it vulnerable to breaking. Frequent weak spots are in the hip, spine and wrist.

• This cross section shows the difference between the bone of a young healthy person, left, and an old osteoporotic person, right.

Sources: Clinics in Endocrinology and Metabolism—Osteoporosis, Metabolic Bone and Stone Disease

Molly Z. Palmer/Dispatch graphic

Figure 19-4 Osteoporosis: Bone Loss
Osteoporosis is associated with a loss of calcium. Some evidence suggests that poor nutrition, even at a young age, may contribute to bone loss later in life. SOURCE: Graphic by Molly Z. Palmer, *The Columbus Dispatch,* November 19, 1991. Reprinted with permission from *The Columbus, Ohio, Dispatch.*

effect on the elderly, inducing excitement and agitation rather than sleep.

These facts are quite dismaying when we realize that people over 65 take more than 25 percent of all prescription drugs. Indeed, the average *healthy* elderly person takes at least eleven different prescription medicines in the course of a year. When taken in combination, the medications can produce severe secondary reactions (Gilman, 1984). At times, problems arise because the elderly have different doctors treating them for different conditions. Hence, each doctor may prescribe several potent medications, unaware of the other medications that have been prescribed.

Biological Aging
To me old age is always fifteen years older than I am.—BERNARD BARUCH

Biological aging refers to changes that occur in the structure and functioning of the human organism through time. It is sometimes termed **senescence.** Aging is a continuous process that begins at conception and ceases at death. As human beings advance from infancy through young adulthood, biological change typically enables them to make a more efficient and effective adaptation of the environment. Beyond this pe-

riod, however, biological change generally leads to impairment in the ability to adapt to the environment; and ultimately, it jeopardizes survival. Improvements in the conditions of life and advances in medicine, however, have allowed more people to reach old age and have facilitated successful aging (Begley, 1990; Rowe & Kahn, 1987).

Physical Changes

Some of the most obvious changes associated with aging are related to an individual's physical characteristics. The hair grows thinner, turns gray, and becomes somewhat courser. The skin changes texture, loses its elasticity and moistness, and gathers spot pigmentation. Some of the subcutaneous fat and muscle bulk built up during earlier adulthood begins to decrease; this decrease, coupled with the loss of the elasticity of the skin, produces skin folds and wrinkling. A slight loss in stature accompanies these changes because of alterations in the discs between the spinal vertebrae. The spine also bows, producing a stooping posture.

Collagen, a substance that constitutes a very high percentage of the total protein in the body, appears to be implicated in the aging process. It is a basic structural component of connective tissue. Loose connective tissue resembles packing material. It supports and holds in place blood vessels, nerves, and internal organs while simultaneously permitting them some freedom of movement. It also holds muscle cells together and binds skin to underlying tissue. Over time, collagen fibers become thicker and less elastic. In early life these changes are fundamental to development. But once set in motion, the process apparently is not halted, contributing to a loss of elasticity in the skin, hardening of the arteries, and stiffening of the joints. Thus over time, collagen speeds the destruction of the organism that it helped to build.

Some sensory abilities also decline with age. As discussed in earlier chapters, visual efficiency decreases after age 40. Some visual loss in later life may also be associated with a loss in both the quantity and quality of the neurons in the brain's visual cortex (Devaney & Johnson, 1980). Studies also reveal a marked loss of hearing among older people, especially in the higher frequencies. Long-term exposure to noise in urban and industrial environments appears to be a contributing factor. Hearing loss can often be partially remedied by a properly prescribed hearing aid. The apparatus contains a tiny microphone that collects sounds and turns them into electrical signals, an amplifier that increases the strength of the signals, and an earphone that transforms the signals into louder sounds. Overall, more than one in five adults aged 65 to 74 has a hearing problem, and almost 10 percent of people in this age group have some trouble seeing. These difficulties become more prevalent with advanced age: 48 percent of adults aged 85 and older have a hearing problem, and 27 percent have trouble seeing (National Center for Health Statistics, 1986).

Older people frequently report impairment in their ability to enjoy food (Murphy & Withee, 1986; Spitzer, 1988; Weiffenbach, Tylenda & Baum, 1990). This problem is related to a decline in the taste buds per papilla (the small nipplelike protuberances on the surface of the tongue). Young adults average 245 taste buds per papilla, but persons 70 to 85 years old average only 88 (Bartoshuk, Rifkin, Marks & Bars, 1986; Shock, 1962). However, olfactory sensitivity (smell—the ability to distinguish oranges from lemons or chocolate from cheese) also declines among the elderly and helps to explain why many elderly people complain about their food. More than half of those 65 to 80 years old evidence major olfactory impairment; after 80 years of age more than three-quarters do (Doty et al., 1984). Touch sensitivity also decreases, but older people differ considerably in this respect (Kenshalo, 1986; Thornbury & Mistretta, 1981).

Sensitivity to temperature changes decreases among the elderly (Kenshalo, 1986). Young adults can detect a temperature drop of only 1 degree Fahrenheit in the surrounding air. Elderly individuals may fail to notice a drop of up to 9 degrees Fahrenheit. Consequently, older people tend to be susceptible to **hypothermia**—a condition in which body temperature falls more than 4 degrees Fahrenheit and persists for a number of hours. It can be life threatening, especially because the aging body becomes less able to maintain an even temperature in winter weather. Early symptoms of hypothermia include drowsiness and mental confusion. A loss of consciousness follows.

Aging is likewise accompanied by various physiological changes. One of the most obvious is a decline in the individual's capacity for physical work and exercise. According to the physiologist Nathan W. Shock (1962), the maximum oxygen intake declines 60 percent and the maximum ventilatory volume declines 57 percent during exercise between 30 and 70 years of age. Since oxygen is needed to combine with nutrients for the release of chemical building blocks and energy, the older person generally has less staying power and lower reserves. Furthermore, the heart pumps only about 65 percent as much blood at age 75 as at age 30. (The brain receives 80 percent as much blood, but the kidneys only 42 percent as much.) However, the nerve fibers that connect directly with the muscles show little decline with age—the speed of nerve impulses along single fibers in elderly people is only 10 to 15 percent less than in young people. Even so, psychomotor performance is slower and less consistent in the elderly (Kallman, Plato & Tobin, 1990; Stelmach, Amrhein & Goggin, 1988).

Sleep patterns also change across the life span (see Chapter 5). For instance, the sleep of healthy men and women between the ages of 50 and 60 years is characterized by more frequent and prolonged awakenings and shorter sleep stages than is that of people between 20 and 30 years. Older men display greater age-related sleep changes than older women do (Reynolds et al., 1991; Webb, 1982). Overall, elderly individuals distribute their sleep somewhat differently across the twenty-four-hour cycle. It is quite normal for them to take several catnaps of 15 to 60 minutes several times during the daytime hours (Aber & Webb, 1986; Morin & Gramling, 1989; Zepelin & McDonald, 1987).

Biological Theories of Aging

Many theories seek to explain the biological processes of aging, but so far none has been widely accepted by researchers (Birren & Bengtson, 1988; Eckholm, 1986; Shock, 1977). Indeed, the process of aging may be too complex for any one-factor explanation. Here are a number of the more prominent theories:

❏ **Genetic preprogramming.** Some scientists think that deterioration and death are "written" into the fertilized egg by the hereditary language of genes much as gray hair and menopause are "written" in. About thirty years ago, scientists discovered that normal human cells growing in tissue culture are not immortal but eventually degenerate and die after many generations of reproduction. This finding led some scientists to speculate that certain types of cells have built-in "time clocks" that count off the amount of life already lived (a biochemical mechanism within the cells counts the number of divisions or replications and allows only so many more). Consequently, once the propagation of the species is ensured and an additional eighteen or so years provided for the rearing of offspring, nature is

ready for the organism to die and make way for newcomers. In brief, the genes "selfishly" produce disposable bodies because this process is the most economical way of perpetuating the genes themselves (Comfort, 1976; Hayflick, 1980; Johnson, 1988; Lockshin & Zakeri, 1990).

❏ **Mean time to failure.** Engineers contend that every machine has a built-in obsolescence and that its lifetime is limited by the wear and tear on the parts. In the same way, aging is viewed as a product of the gradual deterioration of the various organs needed for life (Hayflick, 1980). Most significantly, DNA repair capacity declines with age while DNA damage accumulates (Pitot, 1989; Warner & Price, 1989).

❏ **Aging effects of hormones.** Hormones can promote or inhibit aging depending on the conditions. Reducing the secretion of some hormones (for instance pituitary hormones) in rodents depresses their body metabolism and delays the aging of their tissues. Caloric restrictions likewise seem to slow aging processes. However, a reduction in the secretion of many hormones also occurs with age in rodents and humans. Increasing these hormones (for instance, growth hormone) enhances metabolism and stimulates organ functioning (Angier, 1990; Everitt & Meites, 1989).

❏ **Accumulation of copying errors.** According to this theory, human life eventually ends because body cells develop errors in copying. The prints taken from prints are thought to deteriorate in accuracy with the number of recopying events (Busse, 1969; Comfort, 1976; Lumpkin, McClung, Pereira-Smith & Smith, 1986).

❏ **Error in DNA.** Another line of evidence suggests that alterations (mutations) occur in the DNA molecules of the cells—that is, errors creep into the chemical blueprint—that impair cell function and division (Busse, 1969; Comfort, 1976; Wareham, Lyon, Glenister & Williams, 1987).

❏ **Autoimmune mechanisms.** Some scientists believe that aging has a marked impact on the capabilities of the immunity system. They are convinced that the body's natural defenses against infection begin to attack normal cells because the information is blurring or because the normal cells are changing in ways that make them appear "foreign" (Comfort, 1976; Miller, 1989; Schmeck, 1982; Walford, 1969).

❏ **Accumulation of metabolic wastes.** Biologists have suggested that organisms age because their cells are slowly poisoned or hampered in functioning by waste products of

"Guess what, Grampa? You're the only big people I know who likes to get up early!"

("Dennis the Menace" ® used by permission of Hank Ketcham and © by North American Syndicate.)

metabolism. Such waste products accumulate, leading to progressive organic malfunctioning (Carpenter, 1965; Chown, 1972). For instance, researchers have found significant changes with age in the amounts and kinds of metals in certain organs, including the lens of the eye. Additionally, molecules that are the normal by-products of cells' use of oxygen—called "free radicals"—react with virtually every other molecule they encounter, wreaking havoc on vital cellular machinery.

❑ **Stochastic processes.** "Stochastic" implies that the probability of a random happening increases with the number of events. Radiation, for instance, may alter a chromosome through a random "hit," which either kills a cell or produces a mutation in it (Busse, 1969; Comfort, 1970). The chances for such an event obviously increase the longer one lives.

❑ **Longevity assurance theory.** The theories outlined above focus on cell-destroying mechanisms. In sharp contrast to these approaches, George Sacher offers what he terms a "positive" theory of aging because he portrays evolution as having prolonged life among some species. Thus, instead of asking why organisms age and die, he asks why they live as long as they do. Sacher observes that the life spans of mammals vary enormously, from about two years for some shrews to more than sixty years for great whales, elephants, and human beings. He says that in long-living species natural selection has favored genes that repair cells while weeding out genes that impair cell functioning. Individuals who are the bearers of cell repair genes are more likely to survive and thus pass on their favorable genes to their offspring. In support of this explanation Sacher notes that when researchers exposed cells from seven species to ultraviolet light, the amount of DNA repair that occurred was in direct proportion to the lifetime of the species. Because animals with large brains produce small litters, evolution has favored them with longevity genes that lengthen the life span and make up for the losses in reproductive potential (Lewin, 1981).

Many of the explanations of biological aging overlap. Furthermore, the processes that they depict may coincide to produce similar outcomes. Although the effects of aging are often confounded with the effects of disease, aging is not the same thing as disease (Rowe & Kahn, 1987; Weg, 1973). However, some scientists view aging itself as a pathological condition and, hence,

Human Life Span, Despite Medical Advances, Seems to Have an Upper Limit

Many demographers and gerontologists believe that human beings have taken life about as far as it can go. Barring an unexpected breakthrough in basic science that could forestall aging processes, the era of rapid extension in human longevity seems to have come to an end, particularly in devloped nations. So few deaths now take place before age 50, that their total elimination would add only 3.5 years of life expectancy at birth. Even wiping out cancer and heart disease would not boost life expectancy for most people much beyond age 85. What is more likely is that progress in science will boost the proportion of elderly people who live close to the limits of life expectancy. The photo is Rembrandt's Portrait of An Old Man. (Scala/Art Resource)

merely a special kind of disease (Rosenfeld, 1976).

Cognitive Functioning

There is a wicked inclination in most people to suppose an old man decayed in his intellect. If a young or middle-aged man, when leaving a company, does not recollect where he laid his hat, it is nothing; but if the same inattention is discovered in an old man, people will shrug their shoulders and say "His memory is going."—SAMUEL JOHNSON

Longfellow on Old Age

But why, you ask me, should this tale be told
Of men grown old, or who are growing old?
Ah, Nothing is too late
Till the tired heart shall cease to palpitate;
Cato learned Greek at eighty; Sophocles
Wrote his grand *Oedipus,* and Simonides
Bore off the prize of verse from his compeers,
When each had numbered more than four score
  years,
And Theophrastus, at four score and ten,
Had just begun his *Characters of Men.*
Chaucer, at Woodstock with the nightingales,
At sixty wrote the *Canterbury Tales;*
Goethe at Weimar, toiling to the last,
Completed *Faust* when eighty years were past.

These are indeed exceptions; but they show
How far the gulf-stream of our youth may flow
Into the artic regions of our lives
When little else than life itself survives.
Shall we then sit us idly down and say
The night hath come; it is no longer day?
The night hath not yet come; we are not quite
Cut off from labor by the failing light;
Some work remains for us to do and dare;
Even the oldest tree some fruit may bear;
And as the evening twilight fades away
The sky is filled with stars, invisible by day.
                    —HENRY WADSWORTH LONGFELLOW
                         Morituri Salutamus, 1875

We commonly think that cognitive functioning declines in advanced adulthood and old age (though the poet Henry Wadsworth Longfellow, for one, made an eloquent plea for recognition of the creative potential of the elderly; see the boxed insert above).

On the whole, psychological literature supports the view that a decline in intellectual ability often does accompany aging (Hertzog & Schaie, 1988). However, there is less decline—and in many cases little or no decline—for people who enjoy favorable lifestyles and good health (Field, Schaie & Leino, 1988; Manton, Siegler & Woodbury, 1986; Perlmutter & Nyquist, 1990; Over, 1989; Schaie, 1988; Simonton, 1988). Indeed, a growing body of research suggests that disease, including depression, metabolic disorders, hardening of the arteries, chronic liver and kidney failure, amnesia, or Alzheimer's disease—not age in itself—underlies much of the decline and loss of cognitive and intellectual functioning among the elderly. Researchers looking at the physiology of aging brains are surprised at their flexibility and resilience. For instance, contrary to what constituted established scientific opinion only a few years ago, investigators find that both old and young rats are capable of growing new brain connections after experimenters damage a particular region (Kolata, 1990). Overall, although there is some decline in cognitive functioning for some people in their seventies and more in people in their eighties, many people seem not to be affected. Let us take a closer look at some of these issues.

Intellectual Functioning Among the Elderly

Although some aspects of cognitive functioning diminish after age sixty, the decline is often of little consequence and greatly exaggerated. *(Fushira/Monkmeyer)*

The Varied Course of Different Abilities

As discussed in Chapter 9, intelligence is not a unitary concept in the same sense that a chemical compound is a single entity. People do not have intelligence as such but, rather, intelligences. Thus, different abilities may follow quite different courses as a person grows older (Cornelius &

Caspi, 1987; Denny, 1985; Denny & Palmer, 1981). Many traditional measures of intelligence deal with those abilities that are useful in academic environments. For instance, tests that measure *verbal* abilities tend to show little or no decline after the age of 60 or 65, whereas those that measure *performance* do seem to show a decline (Bluem, Fosshage & Jarvik, 1972; Doppelt & Wallace, 1955; Eisdorfer & Wilkie, 1973; Schaie, 1989). Verbal scores usually come from tests in which people are asked to do something verbally, such as define a series of words, solve arithmetic story problems, or determine similarities between two objects. Performance scores are commonly based on people's ability to do something physically, such as assemble a puzzle or fill in symbols to correspond to numbers.

Some psychologists distinguish between **fluid intelligence**—the ability to make original adaptations in novel situations—and **crystallized intelligence**—the ability to reuse earlier adaptations on later occasions (Cattell, 1943, 1971). Fluid intelligence (Horn, 1976) is generally tested by measuring an individual's facility in reasoning, often by means of figures and non-word materials (letter series, matrices, mazes, block designs, and picture arrangements). Crystallized intelligence is commonly measured by testing an individual's awareness of concepts and terms in vocabulary and general-information tests (science, mathematics, social studies, English literature, and many other areas).

Presumably, fluid intelligence is "culture-free" and based on the physiological structure of the organism, while crystallized intelligence is acquired in the course of social experience. It is the scores on tests of crystallized intelligence, rather than those on tests of fluid intelligence, that are most influenced by formal education. Often, crystallized intelligence shows an increase with age (or, at least, does not decline), while fluid intelligence shows a drop with age in later life (Cockburn & Smith, 1991; Hayslip & Sterns, 1979; Horn & Cattell, 1967; Horn & Donaldson, 1977).

Critics of traditional intelligence testing suggest that aspects of adult functioning, such as social or professional competence and the ability to deal with one's environment, should also be considered (Meer, 1986; Sternberg, 1984). Many psychologists are developing new measures of adult intelligence and revising our notions of adult intelligence. For example, psychologist Gisela Labouvie-Vief (1985, 1986; Adams, Labouvie-Vief, Hobart & Dorosz, 1990) is investigating how people approach everyday problems in logic. She notes that researchers usually find that

the elderly do poorly on measures of formal reasoning ability. But Labouvie-Vief contends that this poor performance results from differences in the way younger adults and older adults approach tasks. Older adults tend to personalize the tasks, to consider alternative ways to answer a question, and to examine affective and psychological components associated with a problem solution. She says that reasoning by intuition rather than by principles of formal logic is not an inferior mode of problem solving—merely a different one. In other research (cited in Meer, 1986) Labouvie-Vief has found that when older people are asked to give summaries of fables they have read, they excel at recalling the metaphoric meaning of a passage. In contrast, college students try to remember the text as precisely as they can. Other researchers also find that the lower performance of older people stems from the fact that they may view some things as unimportant and hence selectively ignore what younger people may attempt to capture (Bandura, 1989; Meer, 1986).

Cognitive functioning depends to some extent on the elderly's use of their abilities. For instance, people can perform such complex cognitive tasks as playing chess or the cello well into old age at the same time as they are losing many simpler abilities. Many elderly persons find that what they have been doing they can keep on doing. Pianist Artur Rubinstein, entertainer Bob Hope, guitarist Andrés Segovia, artist Pablo Picasso, playwright George Bernard Shaw, philosopher Bertrand Russell, and West German politician Konrad Adenauer are examples of people who continued to excel at the same high standards of performance well into advanced age (Bales, 1985). Moreover, cognitive-training techniques can in many cases reverse declines (Baltes, Sowarka & Kliegl, 1989; Lerner, 1990; Willis & Nesselroade, 1990). K. Warner Schaie and Sherry L. Willis (1986) found, in a long-term study of a sample of older adults, that individualized training resulted in an improvement in spatial orientation and deductive reasoning for two-thirds of those they studied. Nearly 40 percent of those whose abilities had declined returned to a level they had evidenced fourteen years earlier. In brief, much of our fate is in our own hands, with "use it or lose it" as an underlying principle. Although the elderly may slow down in their performance of many tasks (Bashore, Osman & Heffley, 1989; Cerella, 1988; Hertzog, 1989)—and although slower reflexes may be a disadvantage in driving a car—for many activities speed is relatively unimportant (Meer, 1986).

In sum, from a review of the research, these conclusions seem to be the most reasonable: A decline in intellectual ability tends to occur with aging, particularly in very late life. Some aspects of intelligence, mainly those that are measured by tests of performance and fluid ability, appear to be more affected by aging than others. But older people can learn to compensate. They can still learn what they need to, although it may take them a little longer. Other aspects of intelligence, notably crystallized ability, may increase, at least until rather advanced age. There are also considerable differences among people, some faring poorly and others quite well. One of the major factors in maintaining or improving mental capabilities is using them. Too often the expectation of decline becomes a self-fulfilling prophecy. Those who expect to do well in old age seem to remain involved in the world about them and thus do not become ineffective before their time.

Overestimating the Effects of Aging

What happens in psychological aging is complex and only poorly understood. What is becoming clear, however, is that psychologists have taken too negative a view of the impact that aging has upon intellectual functioning. One reason is that researchers have relied too heavily on cross-sectional studies. As described in Chapter 1, cross-sectional studies employ the snapshot approach; they test individuals of *different* ages and compare their performance. Longitudinal studies, in contrast, are more like case histories; they retest the *same* individuals over a period of years.

Psychologists such as Baltes and Schaie (1974, 1976) have pointed out that cross-sectional studies of adult aging do not allow for *generational* differences in performance on intelligence tests. Because of increasing educational opportunities and other social changes, successive generations of Americans perform at progressively higher levels. Hence, the measured intelligence (IQ) of the population is increasing. When individuals who were 50 years old in 1963 are compared with those who were 50 in 1956, the former make higher scores. But since the people who were 50 years old in 1963 were 43 in 1956, a cross-sectional study undertaken in 1956 would falsely suggest that they were "brighter" than those who were 50 in 1956. This result would lead to the false conclusion that intelligence declines with age. When you compare people from different generations—80-year-olds with 40-year-olds, for instance—you are comparing people from different environments. Thus, cross-sectional studies tend to confuse generational differences with differences in chronological age.

Other factors have also contributed to an overestimation of the decline in intellectual functioning that occurs with aging. Research suggests that a marked intellectual decline, called the **death-drop** (also, the *terminal decline phenomenon*), occurs just a short time before a person dies (Johansson & Berg, 1989; Riegel & Riegel, 1972; Siegler, McCarty & Logue, 1982). Since relatively more people in an older age group can be expected to die within any given span of time, the average scores of older age groups are depressed relatively more as a result of the death-drop effect than the average scores for younger age groups.

Whereas the cross-sectional method tends to magnify or overestimate the decline in intelligence with age, the longitudinal method tends to minimize or underestimate it. One reason is that some people drop out of the study over time. Generally, it is the more able, healthy, and intelligent subjects who remain available. Those who perform poorly on intelligence tests tend to be less available for longitudinal retesting. Consequently the researchers are left with an increasingly biased sample as the subjects are retested at each later period (Botwinick, 1977; Siegler & Botwinick, 1979).

Memory and Aging

Memory is one aspect of cognitive functioning that frequently is affected by aging. Elderly people often volunteer the opinion that difficulty in remembering individuals' names is the first sign of cognitive aging they notice. Apparently, recalling names becomes a harder task as people age. But by the same token, the pool of names they know also becomes larger, and so the recall of a particular name also becomes longer. In other words, older people may not remember as well, not so much because their memories are not as good as they once were, but because older people have more things stored in their memory and searching therefore takes longer.

Although the memory for names seems to decline regularly over a lifetime, vocabulary memory remains stable and may even increase slightly (Bales, 1985). Moreover, a progressive loss of memory does not *necessarily* accompany advancing age (Arbuckle, Gold & Andres, 1986; Craik, Byrd & Swanson, 1987; Denney, Miller, Dew & Levav, 1991). Instead, some memory loss is found in an increasing proportion of older people with each advance in chronological age. Thus, a part of the elderly population retains a sound memory regardless of age. Nor are all aspects of memory equally affected by aging (Hultsch, Hertzog & Dixon, 1990; Smith, Park, Cherry & Berkovsky, 1990); for instance, age-related decreases are more severe for recall tasks than for recognition tasks (Inman & Parkinson, 1983) (see Chapter 9).

Phases in Information Processing   When information is remembered, three things occur: (1) **encoding,** the process by which information is put into the memory system; (2) **storage,** the process by which information is retained in memory until it is needed; and (3) **retrieval,** the process by which information is regathered from memory when it is required. These components are assumed to operate sequentially. Incoming signals are transformed into a "state" where they can be stored, termed a **trace.** A trace is a set of information; it is the residue of an event that remains in memory after the event has vanished. When encoded, the trace is said to be placed in storage. Finally, depending on environmental requirements, the individual actively searches for the stored material.

Information processing has been likened to a filing system (Vander Zanden & Pace, 1984). Suppose you are a secretary and have the task of filing a company's correspondence. You have a letter from a customer criticizing a major product of your firm. Under what category are you going to file the letter? If the contents of the letter involve a defect in a product, will you decide to create a new category—"product defects"—or will you file the letter under the customer's name? The procedure you employ for categorizing the letter must be used consistently for categorizing all other correspondence you receive. You cannot file this letter under "product defects" and the next letter like it under the customer's name.

Encoding involves perceiving information, abstracting from it one or more characteristics needed for classification, and creating corresponding memory traces for it. As in the case of the filing system, the way in which you encode information has an enormous impact on your ability to retrieve it. If you "file" an item of experience haphazardly, you will have difficulty recalling it. But encoding is not simply a passive process whereby you mechanically register environmental events on some sort of trace. Rather, in information processing you tend to abstract general ideas from material. Hence, you are likely to have

a good retention of the meaning or gist of prose material but poor memory for the specific words.

Memory Failure   Memory failure may occur at any phase in information processing. For instance, difficulty may occur in the encoding phase. Returning to the example of the office filing system, you may receive a letter from a customer and accidentally place the letter with trash and discard it. In this case the letter is never encoded because it is not placed in the filing cabinet. It is unavailable since it was never stored. This difficulty is more likely to be experienced by older than by younger people. Older individuals are not as effective as younger ones are in carrying out the elaborate encoding of information that is essential to long-term retention. For instance, the elderly tend to organize new knowledge less well and less completely than they did when they were younger (Hess & Slaughter, 1990; Mitchell & Perlmutter, 1986; Puglisi, Park, Smith & Dudley, 1988). Thus, overall, older adults process information less effectively than younger adults (Cohen & Faulkner, 1983; Petros, Zehr & Chabot, 1983; Strayer, Wickens & Braune, 1987).

Memory failure may also stem from storage problems (Foos, 1989). For instance, when filing, you may place the letter in the filing cabinet but by mistake put it in the wrong folder. The letter is available but it is not accessible because it was improperly stored. Apparently, the elderly encounter this problem more frequently than younger adults. But other factors are also involved. Some psychologists have suggested a **decay theory**—forgetting is due to deterioration in the memory traces in the brain (Broadbent, 1963; Posner, 1967). The process is believed to resemble the gradual fading of a photograph over time or the progressive obliteration of the inscription of a tombstone. Others have advanced an **interference theory**—retrieval of a cue becomes less effective as more and newer items come to be classed or categorized in terms of it (Gerard, Zacks, Hasher & Radvansky, 1991; Tulving & Pearlstone, 1966). For example, as you file more and more letters in the cabinet, more items compete for attention. Thus, your ability to find a letter is impaired by all the other folders and letters.

Faulty retrieval of knowledge is a third major cause of memory loss. Older persons may suffer breakdown in the mechanisms and strategies by which stored information is recalled (Burke & Light, 1981; Howard, Heisey & Shaw, 1986; Shaw & Craik, 1989). Fergus I. M. Craik (1977) suggests that the elderly may experience a higher incidence of *cue overload*—a state of being overwhelmed or engulfed by excessive stimuli. Accordingly, they may fail to process retrieval information effectively. (For instance, they may not sharpen the retrieval cue sufficiently until it comes to specify adequately the desired event in memory. Analogously, you may file the letter under the customer's name but later lack the proper cue to activate the category under which you filed it.) Some researchers suggest that the elderly may be subject to greater inertia or failure of a "selector mechanism" to differentiate between appropriate and inappropriate sets of responses (Coyne, Allen & Wickens, 1986; Hoyer, Rebok & Sved, 1979). Also, retrieval time becomes longer with advancing age (Anders & Fozard, 1972; Madden, 1985; Puglisi, 1986).

Overall, older adults have more difficulty with memory than younger adults. This fact has practical implications. Older people are more likely to be plagued by doubts as to whether or not they carried out particular activities—"Did I mail that letter this morning?"; "Did I close the window earlier this evening?" (Kausler & Hakami, 1983). And they are more likely to have difficulty remembering where they placed an item or where buildings are geographically located (Pezdek, 1983).

Learning and Aging

Psychologists are finding that the distinctions they once made between learning and memory are becoming blurred. Learning parallels the encoding process whereby individuals put into memory material that is presented to them. Indeed, the psychologist Endel Tulvig (1968) says that learning constitutes an improvement in retention. Hence, he contends, the study of learning is the study of memory.

Clearly, all processes of memory have consequences for learning. If people do not learn (encode) well, they have little to recall. And conversely, if their memory is poor, they show few signs of having learned much. Not surprisingly, therefore, psychologists find that younger adults do better than older adults on various learning tasks (Arenberg & Robertson-Tchabo, 1977). This fact has given rise to the old adage "You can't teach an old dog new tricks." But this adage is clearly false. Both older dogs and human beings can and do learn. They would be incapable of adapting to their environment and coping with new circumstances if they did not.

Research suggests that both younger and older individuals benefit when they are given more time to inspect a task (Arenberg & Robertson-Tchabo, 1977; Labouvie-Vief & Schell, 1982). Allowing people ample time gives them more opportunity to rehearse a response and establish a linkage between events. It increases the probability that information will be encoded in a fashion that facilitates later search and recall. Older adults benefit even more than younger ones when more time is made available for them to learn something.

Older people often give the impression that they have learned less than younger people have because they tend to be more reluctant to venture a response. At times, the elderly do not provide learned responses, especially at a rapid pace, although they can be induced to do so under appropriate incentive conditions. And when tested in a laboratory setting, older adults seem to be less motivated to learn arbitrary materials that appear to be irrelevant and useless to them. Complicating matters, today's young adults are better educated than their older counterparts. Furthermore, another hidden bias is that many elderly individuals take medications that can diminish mental function. All these factors suggest that we should exercise caution when appraising the learning potential of the elderly lest we prematurely conclude that they are incapable of learning new things.

Alzheimer's Disease

My wife refused to believe I was her husband.
Every day we went through the same routine:
I would tell her we had been married for thirty years,
that we had four children. She listened, but she still
thought she lived in her hometown with her parents.
Every night when I got into bed she'd say, "Who are
you?"—HUSBAND OF AN ALZHEIMER'S PATIENT

Until recently, many physicians and members of the lay public accepted the view that senility is the penalty people pay for living longer than the biblical three score and ten years. *Senility* is typically characterized by progressive mental deterioration, memory loss, and disorientation regarding time and place. Irritability and other personality changes usually accompany the intellectual decline.

In persons over 65 about 20 to 25 percent of all senility results from **multiinfarcts** (better known as "little strokes"), each of which destroys a small area of brain tissue. Another 50 percent is due to **Alzheimer's disease**—a progressive, degenerative disorder that involves deterioration of brain cells. Autopsies of victims show microscopic changes in brain structure, especially in the cerebral cortex. Some of the nerve cells look like infinitesimal bits of braided yarn. Apparently, the clumps of degenerating nerve cells disrupt the passage of electrochemical signals across the brain and nervous system. One hallmark of the disease seems to be a breakdown of the system that produces the neurotransmitter acetylcholine.

Alzheimer's disease affects some 4 million Americans. Although an estimated 3 percent of the elderly between 65 and 74 years of age suffer from the disease, the figure rises to 18.7 percent for those aged 75 to 84 and mushrooms to 47.2 percent for those 85 and older (Leary, 1989). The National Institutes of Health estimate that 60 percent of nursing-home patients over age 65 suffer from the disease. It is also the fourth leading cause of death in the United States.

Unfortunately, as yet there is no cure for Alzheimer's disease. But new scientific findings offer hope in the midst of despair. Pharmaceutical companies are testing more than 100 compounds that may relieve or delay the symptoms of the disease. The disorder has a devastating impact not only on its victims but on their relatives as well. Many family members complain bitterly about the lack of skilled nursing facilities for Alzheimer patients; the failure of government insurance programs to pay for needed care during the prolonged period of deterioration; the absence of counselors and programs to assist families in coping with the demands of patients; and the ignorant, indifferent, and even callous attitudes of many physicians (Clipp & George, 1990; Holden, 1987; Kolata, 1991b). Not surprisingly, family members caring for Alzheimer's disease patients are at especially high risk for depressive disorders (Moritz, Kasl & Berkman, 1989; Pruchno, Kleban, Michaels & Dempsey, 1990; Williamson & Schulz, 1990). Families find their loved one progressively regressing, eventually unable to perform the simplest tasks. (See the boxed insert on page 560 for a discussion of a number of ways that can prove helpful in caring for Alzheimer victims.) One woman, Marion Roach (1983, p. 22), tells of her experiences with her 54-year-old mother who suffers from the disease:

In the autumn of 1979, my mother killed the cats. We had seven; one morning, she grabbed four, took them to the vet and had them put to sleep. She said she didn't want to feed them anymore. . . . Day by day, she became more disoriented. She would seem surprised at her surroundings, as if she had just appeared there. She stopped cooking, and had difficulty remembering the simplest things. . . . Until she recently began to take sedation, she would hallucinate that the television or the toaster was in flames. She repeats the same few questions and stories over and over again, unable to remember that she has just done so a few moments before.

Another woman, Jean Freeman, reports that her husband, a victim of Alzheimer's disease, is like a child again. He follows her about the house babbling and needs to be bathed and dressed. But whereas a child learns and progresses, her husband regresses. After thirty-four years of marriage she is disturbed that her husband "doesn't remember anything that was part of our life. It's like he is gone, but still here" (Fedak, 1982, p. C–1).

The disease typically proceeds through a number of phases (Schneck, Reisberg & Ferris, 1982; Teri, Hughes & Larson, 1990). At first, in the "forgetfulness phase," individuals forget where things are placed and have difficulty recalling events of the recent past. Later, in the "confusional phase," difficulties in cognitive functioning worsen and can no longer be overlooked. Finally, in the "dementia phase," individuals become severely disoriented. They are likely to confuse a spouse or a close friend with another person. Behavior problems surface: Victims may wander off, roam the house at night, engage in bizarre actions, hallucinate, and exhibit "rage reactions" of verbal and even physical abuse. In time, they become incontinent and unable to feed or otherwise care for themselves. Victims show a marked decrease in life expectancy in comparison with age-matched men and women. Patients usually die of infections, often from pneumonia. The course of the illness varies enormously with different individuals—from under three years to over twenty years before death ensues.

Alzheimer's researchers resemble the blind men studying the elephant: Each grabs onto a different part of the disease and comes to a different conclusion as to its causes. One hypothesis relates Alzheimer's disease to a puzzling infectious agent known as a "slow virus." Such brain disorders as kuru and Creutzfeldt-Jakob disease are caused by slow viruses and are accompanied by distinctive brain lesions or plaques that bear a close resemblance to those that characterize Alzheimer's disease. Kuru, a disease occurring in

Caring for a Family Member with Alzheimer's Disease

Alzheimer's disease has been described as "a funeral that has no end." It takes a heavy toll not only on the victim but on the victim's family as well. Caring for a person with the disease is an exceedingly taxing and frustrating experience. To do so requires considerable stamina, fortitude, patience, and love. Below are listed a number of guidelines offered by experts (Brody, 1983d, 1983e; Cook & Miller, 1985; Evans, 1987):

❑ Provide the patient with an uncluttered and well-organized environment and with consistent routines. In the early stages of the disease, employ memory aids including labels and word pictures on appliances and doors, especially in the bathroom.
❑ Provide the patient with clothing that has elasticized waistbands instead of buttons and zippers and slip-on shoes instead of shoes with laces.
❑ Remove knicknacks that can be easily knocked over and furniture that might be tripped over.
❑ Install grab bars where needed in the bathroom, strong railings on staircases, and night-lights in poorly lit but frequently traveled areas.

❑ Have the patient wear an identification bracelet with his or her name, address, and phone number and the words "memory impaired" inscribed on it.
❑ Provide instructions in a soft, calm voice, using short sentences and simple words.
❑ Allow the patient to perform tasks within his or her capabilities, such as watering the plants or folding the laundry. Keep the tasks simple and focused on one step at a time.
❑ Find satisfaction in what one can with the patient, but do not hold excessive expectations.
❑ Recognize that family members of Alzheimer patients often feel despair, resentment, guilt, and sadness.
❑ Avoid angry outbursts, but acknowledge to oneself the right to feel anger toward the patient.
❑ Do not assume that the patient does irritating things because he or she is vindictive or mean.
❑ Learn as much as you can about the disease.
❑ Get in touch with the Alzheimer's Disease and Related Disorders Association (ADRDA), an organization that has assisted many families immeasurably in dealing with the burden of the disease.

New Guinea and once believed to be of hereditary origin, is a slow-acting virus infection transmitted from person to person by ritual cannibalism. Creutzfeldt-Jakob disease may simply be a form of pre-senile dementia that strikes at an earlier age than Alzheimer's disease. Researchers find that the brains of patients suffering from "slow virus" diseases have a huge deficit in a key enzyme, choline acetyltransferase (a substance used in the manufacture of material employed by the brain to transmit nerve signals from cell to cell). Another hypothesis implicates increased levels of a toxic brain chemical—beta amyloid protein—that results from some biochemical blunder as the source of Alzheimer's disease (Marx, 1991). Still another hypothesis postulates the existence of a defect in the immune system of Alzheimer victims. And finally, since Alzheimer's disease tends to run in families, a genetic predisposition is thought by some to underlie the disorder. Additional evidence of the importance of genetic or chromosomal factors is found in studies of Down's syndrome showing that many adults with the syndrome eventually succumb to

Alzheimer's lesions (Katzman, 1986; Kolata, 1991a; Schmeck, 1987b). It may also be true that different cases of Alzheimer's disease may spring from different causes and that it is a group of closely associated disorders rather than a single illness (Stipp, 1990).

Senility is one of the most serious conditions that a physician can diagnose in a patient. The prognosis is grim, and the effectiveness of current treatments is uncertain. Consequently, it is incumbent upon professionals who treat the elderly to do a full battery of tests to make certain a treatable cause for a patient's symptoms has not been overlooked. Often, underlying physical diseases that may make an elderly person *seem* senile go unnoticed and untreated. Such individuals are simply dumped into the wastebasket category of "senile" by families and physicians who have accepted the conventional wisdom that senility is an inevitable part of the aging process. Among common problems often mistakenly diagnosed as senility are tumors; vitamin deficiencies (especially B_{12} or folic acid); anemia; depression; such metabolic disorders as hyperthyroidism and chronic liver or kidney failure; and toxic reactions to prescription or over-the-counter drugs (including tranquilizers, anticoagulants, and heart and high-blood-pressure medications).

Many of these conditions can be reversed if they are identified and treated early in the course of the illness.

SUMMARY

1. At no point in life do people stop being themselves and suddenly turn into "old people," with all the stereotypes and myths that the term implies. Aging does not destroy the continuity between what we have been, what we are, and what we will be.
2. The gap between the life expectancy rates of men and women has been increasing since 1920. On the average, women live seven years longer than men. Women seem to be more durable organisms because of an inherent sex-linked resistance to some types of life-threatening disease. Lifestyle differences also contribute to gender differences in life expectancies. A major factor is the higher incidence of smoking among men.
3. The facts of aging are befogged by a great many myths that have little to do with the actual process of growing old. Included among these myths are those that portray a large proportion of the elderly as institutionalized, incapacitated, in serious financial straits, and living in fear of crime.
4. Despite the higher incidence of chronic health problems among the elderly, most older individuals do not consider themselves to be seriously handicapped in pursuing their ordinary activities. Most of the conditions that create chronic disease increase with advanced age. Some of the health problems experienced by older Americans are the product of side effects associated with medication.
5. Some of the most obvious changes associated with aging are related to an individual's physical characteristics. The hair grows thinner, the skin changes texture, some of the bulk built up during earlier adulthood begins to decrease, and some individuals experience a slight loss in stature. The sensory abilities also decline with age. Aging is likewise accompanied by various physiological changes.

One of the most obvious is a decline in the individual's capacity for physical work and exercise. Sleep patterns also change.
6. Many theories seek to explain the biological process of aging by focusing on cell-destroying mechanisms. Many of the mechanisms overlap. Although the effects of aging are often confounded with the effects of disease, aging is not the same thing as disease.
7. A decline in adult intelligence becomes clearly evident after age 60. Small declines may even begin to occur by 53 years of age. However, different abilities follow quite different courses as a person grows older. Those aspects of intelligence that are measured by tests of performance and fluid ability appear to be more affected by aging than others.
8. Psychologists have traditionally taken too negative a view of the impact that aging has on intellectual functioning. One reason is that researchers have relied too heavily upon cross-sectional studies.
9. Memory is one aspect of cognitive functioning that in many cases is affected by aging. But to assume that a progressive loss of memory *necessarily* accompanies advancing age is incorrect. Memory loss among the elderly has many causes, some of them related to the acquisition of new knowledge, others to the retention of knowledge, and still others to the retrieval of knowledge.
10. Senility is typically characterized by progressive mental deterioration, memory loss, and disorientation regarding time and place. In persons over 65 about 20 to 25 percent of all senility results from multiinfarcts. Another 50 percent is due to Alzheimer's disease—a progressive, degenerative disorder that involves deterioration of brain cells. The disorder has a devastating impact not only on its victims but on their relatives as well.

KEY TERMS

Alzheimer's Disease A progressive, degenerative disorder that involves deterioration of brain cells.

Collagen A substance that constitutes a very high percentage of the total protein of the body and that appears to be implicated in the aging process. It is a basic component of connective tissue.

Crystallized Intelligence   The ability to reuse earlier adaptations on later occasions.

Death Drop   A marked drop in intelligence that may occur just a short time before a person dies.

Decay Theory   The view that forgetting is due to deterioration in the memory traces in the brain.

Encoding   The process by which information is put into the memory system.

Fluid Intelligence   The ability to make original adaptations in novel situations.

Geriatrics   The branch of medicine that is concerned with the diseases, debilities, and care of elderly persons.

Gerontology   The field of study that deals with aging and the special problems of the elderly.

Hypothermia   A condition in which body temperature falls more than 4 degrees Fahrenheit and persists for a number of hours. It can be life threatening.

Interference Theory   The view that retrieval of a cue becomes less effective as more and newer items come to be classed or categorized in terms of it.

Multiinfarct   A "little stroke," or the rupture of blood vessels in the brain.

Osteoporosis   A condition associated with excessive loss of bone mass, making the bones susceptible to fracture.

Retrieval   The process by which information is regathered from memory when it is needed.

Senescence   Changes that occur in the structure and functioning of the organism through time.

Storage   The process by which information is retained in memory until it is needed.

Trace   A set of information; it is the residue of an event that remains in memory after the event has vanished.

LATER ADULTHOOD: PSYCHOSOCIAL DEVELOPMENT

Chapter 20

LATER ADULTHOOD: PSYCHOSOCIAL DEVELOPMENT

The Psychosocial Domain

Psychosocial Tasks of Later Adulthood ◆ **Personality and Patterns of Aging**

◆ **Self-Concept and Life Satisfaction**

Theories of Adjustment to Aging

Disengagement Theory ◆ **Activity Theory** ◆ **Role Exit Theory**

◆ **Social Exchange Theory**

Psychosocial Aspects of Aging

Retirement ◆ **Marital Relations** ◆ **Kin and Friendship Ties** ◆ **Grandparents**

◆ **Institutional Care** ◆ **The Impact of Personal Control and Choice**

◆

Grow old along with me! The best is yet to be,
The last of life, for which the first was made.
—ROBERT BROWNING
Rabbi Ben Ezra

The specter of old age holds terrors for a good many Americans. With our culture's focus on youthfulness, aging is seen as something of a tragedy. Yet growing old is not necessarily the scourge that it once was. Continuing advances in medicine allow more and more people to reach later life with fewer ailments. And the quality of the life enjoyed by most of the elderly has improved in recent decades. Thus, Americans not only are living longer but also are staying active longer. Given present trends in mortality, a larger segment of the population will live to advanced ages and then succumb over a narrow age range in their mid-eighties. Even now, the sight of vigorous people in their eighth and ninth decades is no longer particularly unusual. On the whole, people find that adapting to aging is simply a continuation of the lifelong process of coping with life (Langway, 1982; Rowe & Kahn, 1987).

Contrary to the stereotyped thinking of many younger people, most elderly people cope quite well. Indeed, nationwide surveys reveal that nearly two-thirds of Americans over age 65 are quite pleased with the way things are going in their lives. In contrast, only about half of Americans between 18 and 49 say that they are very satisfied with their lives. People in their middle years, 50 to 64, also tend to be more satisfied with their lives than are younger Americans, but they are less sanguine about it than are the elderly. Significantly, older people express less concern with matters of money and retirement, less feelings of loneliness and depression, and less fear of disease and death than do their younger counterparts. And although older people acknowledge that they are not having as much fun in life as they once did, they do not seem particularly troubled about it. On the down side, however, the older the elderly become, the less satisfied they become with their health (Roark, 1989). This portrait—one which depicts life as generally improving with age—contradicts many notions Americans have in which they think of old age as a time of desolation and desperation.

The Psychosocial Domain

A recurrent theme of this book has been that psychosocial development occurs across the entire life span. According to Erik Erikson (1959, 1963), the elderly confront the task of coming to terms with the issue of integrity versus despair (see Chapter 2). In this stage individuals recognize that they are reaching the end of life. Provided they have successfully navigated the previous stages of development, they are capable of facing their later years with optimism and enthusiasm. They can take satisfaction in having led an active, full, and complete life. This recognition produces contentment and compensates for decreased potency and performance. They find a new unification in their personality, producing a sense of integrity.

But it is otherwise for those who appraise their life as having been wasted. They experience a sense of despair. They realize that time is running out and that it is too late to make up for past mistakes. They view their lives with a feeling of disappointment, loss, and purposelessness. Consequently, they approach death with regret and fear.

Psychosocial Tasks of Later Adulthood

The riders in a race do not stop short when they reach the goal. There is a little finishing canter before coming to a standstill. There is time to hear the kind voice of friends and to say to one's self: "The work is done." But just as one says that, the answer comes: "The race is over, but the work is never done while the power to work remains." The canter that brings you to a standstill need not be only coming to rest. It cannot be, while you still live. For to live is to function. That is all there is in living.—OLIVER WENDELL HOLMES

In a radio address broadcast on his ninetieth birthday, 1931

The psychologist Robert C. Peck (1968) provides a somewhat related but more focused view of personality development during the later years than Erikson does. He says that old age confronts men and women with three issues, or tasks, which we will examine here.

Ego Differentiation Versus Work Role Preoccupation The central issue here is posed by retirement from the work force. Men and women must redefine their worth in terms other than their work roles. They confront this question: "Am I a worthwhile person only insofar as I can do a full-time job; or can I be worthwhile in other, different ways—as a performer of several other roles and also because of the kind of person I am?" (Peck, 1968, p. 90). The ability to see themselves as having multiple dimensions allows individuals to pursue new avenues for finding a sense of satisfaction and worthwhileness.

Body Transcendence Versus Body Preoccupation As people age, they may encounter chronic illness and a substantial decline in their physical capabilities. For those men and women who equate pleasure and comfort with physical well-being, this decrease in health and strength may constitute the gravest of insults. They can either become preoccupied with their bodily health or find new sources of happiness and comfort in life. Many elderly persons suffer considerable pain and physical unease and yet manage to enjoy life greatly. They do not succumb to their physical aches, pains, and disabilities but find human relationships and creative mental activities to be sources of fulfillment. One 76-year-old widow with severe arthritis, Rose Baron, says: "I tell myself, yesterday is a canceled check. Tomorrow is a promissory note—you don't know if you'll be able to cash it. Today counts—make the best of today" (Agrest, 1982, p. 59). A retired accountant, she reviews the books of her son's limousine business once a week, plays a weekly canasta game, exchanges letters with her grandson, and writes poetry.

Ego Transcendence Versus Ego Preoccupation
Younger individuals typically define death as a distant possibility, but this privilege is not accorded the elderly. They must come to terms with their own mortality. But their adaptation need not be one of passive resignation. Rather, the elderly can come to see themselves as living on after death through their children, their work, their contributions to culture, and their friendships. Thus, they perceive themselves as transcending a mere earthly presence.

Common to the approaches taken to psychosocial development by Erikson, Peck, and many other psychologists is the notion that life is never static and seldom allows a prolonged respite (Datan, Rodeheaver & Hughes, 1987; Haan, Millsap & Hartka, 1986; Levinson, Darrow, Klein, Levinson & McKee, 1978; Shneidman, 1989). Follow-up research on Terman's gifted men and women (see Chapter 1) documents the importance to good mental health and psychological well-being of establishing and maintaining appropriate goals and commitment throughout adulthood, including late adulthood (Holahan, 1988). Both the individual and the environment constantly change, necessitating new adaptations and new life structures.

Personality and Patterns of Aging

Most of us go about our daily lives "typing" or "pigeonholing" people on the basis of a number of traits that seem particularly prominent in their behavior. They reveal these traits in the course of interacting with others and with the environment (see Chapter 17). On the basis of this observation, a number of psychologists, including Bernice L. Neugarten, R. J. Havighurst, and S. Tobin (1968), have attempted to identify major personality patterns that have relevance for the aging process. They followed several hundred persons aged 50 to 80 in the Kansas City area for over a six-year period. From their study they identified four major personality types: integrated, armored-defended, passive-dependent, and disintegrated.

The *integrated* elderly are well-functioning individuals who reveal a complex inner life, intact cognitive abilities, and competent egos. They are flexible, mellow, and mature. However, they differ from one another in their activity levels. The *reorganizers* are capable people who place a premium on staying young, remaining active, and refusing to "grow old." As they lose one role in life, they find another, continually reorganizing their patterns of activity. The *focused* display medium levels of activity. They are selective in what they choose to do and center their energy on one or two role areas. The *disengaged* also show integrated personalities and high life satisfaction. But they are self-directed people who pursue their own interests in a calm, withdrawn, and contented fashion, with little need for complex patterns and networks of social interaction.

The *armored-defended* elderly are striving, ambitious, achievement-oriented individuals, with high defenses against anxiety and with the need to retain tight control over events. Here, too, there are differences. The *holders-on* view aging as a threat and relentlessly cling as long as possible to the patterns of middle age. They take the approach "I'll work until I drop dead." They are successful in their adaptation as long as they can continue their old patterns. The *constricted* elderly structure their world to ward off what they regard as an imminent collapse of their rigid defenses. They tend to be preoccupied with "taking care of themselves," but in doing so, they close themselves off from people and experience.

A third group of personalities are *passive-dependent* types. The *succorance-seeking* have strong dependency needs and elicit responsiveness from others. They appear to do well as long as they have one or two people on whom they can lean and who meet their emotional needs. The *apathetic* type are "rocking chair" people who have disengaged from life. They seem to "survive" but with medium to low levels of life satisfaction.

Finally, there are those elderly who show a *disintegrated* pattern of aging. They reveal gross defects in psychological functions and an overall deterioration in their thought processes. Both their activity levels and life satisfaction levels are low.

Neugarten and her associates (1968) conclude that personality is an important dimension influencing how people adapt to the aging process. It has major consequences for predicting their relationships with other people, their level of activity, and their satisfaction with life. These patterns do not so much represent a break with those developed during earlier years as a continuation and an accentuation of them.

Self-Concept and Life Satisfaction

The Indian Summer of Life should be a little sunny and a little sad, like the season, and infinite in wealth and depth of tone.—HENRY BROOKS ADAMS
The Education of Henry Adams

As noted above, most older people do not experience sudden and dramatic transformations in personality (Neugarten & Neugarten, 1987). For instance, longitudinal research reveals that people who are happy, emotionally stable, and of high ego strength as young adults are likely to be contented and well-adjusted during their later years (Goleman, 1990; Mussen, Honzik & Eichorn, 1982). Nor does individual self-concept necessarily become more negative. Indeed, older people in general—those 55 years of age and over—appear to view themselves quite positively—at least as positively as younger people do (Gove, Ortega & Style, 1989; Riley & Foner, 1968; Ryff, 1991).

Older people, however, are hardly a homogeneous group. Those who are relatively affluent appear to have a more favorable self-concept than those who are less affluent (Caspi & Elder, 1986; Harris, 1981). Likewise, those who live in private residences tend to have a more positive self-concept than those who live in institutions (Riley & Foner, 1968).

Moreover, many older people are pleasantly surprised with their later years (Horn & Meer, 1987; Roark, 1989). Many of the problems that they had anticipated fail to materialize (see Figure 20-1). For every person who feels that life after 65 is worse than he or she thought it would be, there are three who say that it is better than they had expected. And there are as many people under 65 who feel that their lives have fallen short of their expectations as there are people over 65 who express this opinion (Harris, 1981). Moreover, older people who are married tend to

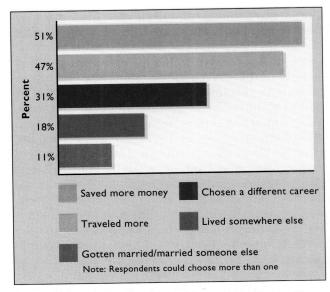

Figure 20-1 What the Elderly Would Have Changed in Their Lives
SOURCE: *USA Today*, August 14, 1990, p. D1. Marriott Seniors' attitudes survey of 1,004 adults age 65 and over. Copyright © 1990, *USA Today*. Reprinted with permission.

view their marriage relationships favorably—indeed, as having improved and increased in satisfaction in their later years (Lipman, 1961; Stinnett, Carter & Montgomery, 1972). Overall, a thirteen-nation international survey on human values and well-being over the adult life span found that in most cases people over 50 years of age indicated more contentment, satisfaction, and stability in their lives than did younger adults (Butt & Beiser, 1987).

Not only do four in five older people look back on their past with satisfaction, but three in four feel that their present life is as interesting as it ever was. Although nearly half of the elderly feel that life could be happier for them, a slightly higher proportion of those under 65 feel the same way (Harris, 1981). Overall, the best predictors of life satisfaction among the elderly are financial adequacy and good health (Beck, 1982; Larson, 1978; Markides & Martin, 1979).

As we noted earlier in the chapter, one's personality also seems to make a difference. At five-year intervals, researchers have followed some 173 men who graduated from Harvard University in the early 1940s (Goleman, 1990). The project provides insights as to which factors matter, for better or worse, in later life. The investigators view emotional health among the elderly as the "clear ability to play and work and to love," and to achieve satisfaction with life. An ability to handle life's blows without passivity, blame, or bitterness proved especially important. Such men could acknowledge the clouds in their lives, but they could also see the silver lining. Men who in college were rated by a psychiatrist as being good practical organizers of course work, rather than as having a theoretical, speculative, or scholarly bent, were among those making the best emotional adjustment in their later years. So were those who as college sophomores had been related as "steady, stable, dependable, thorough, sincere, and trustworthy." These two traits—pragmatism and dependability—seemed to matter more than did such traits as spontaneity and the ability to make friends easily (traits that seemed important for psychological adjustment during the college years).

Many factors of early life, even a relatively bleak childhood (such as being poor, orphaned, or a child of divorce), had little effect on well-being at age 65 for the Harvard men. However, severe psychological depression earlier in life was associated with persistent problems. One factor surprised researchers: Being close to one's siblings while in college was strongly linked to later emotional health. In contrast, at age 47, the quality of one's relationships with brothers and sisters seemed unimportant whereas having a good marriage and an enjoyable job were strongly related with emotional health and life satisfaction. Indeed, being close at college age with a brother or sister emerged as an intriguing sleeper variable, more strongly predicting emotional well-being in late adulthood than having had a good marriage and successful career or coming from an emotionally close home life as a child. Perhaps those who had had good relationships with their siblings had laid the seeds for good relationships late in life (also see Cicirelli, 1989). As other researchers have also found, the Harvard project (known as the Grant study after the W. T. Grant Foundation, which initially supported it) revealed that people are extraordinarily adaptable and that over a half-century most people retain the capacity to recover from adversity and get on with their lives.

Theories of Adjustment to Aging

As this book has said repeatedly, human beings are above all social creatures, and they need social settings to develop and express their humanness. Accordingly, psychologists and sociologists have advanced a number of theories that describe changes in the elderly in terms of the changes in their social environment.

Disengagement Theory

In the early 1960s Elaine Cumming and William E. Henry (1961) formulated the **disengagement theory of aging,** which views aging as a progressive process of physical, psychological, and social withdrawal from the wider world. On the physical level people slow down their activity and conserve their energy. On the psychological level they withdraw their concern from the wider world to focus on those aspects of life that immediately touch them. Simultaneously, they shift attention from the outer world to the inner world of their own feelings and thoughts. And on the social level a mutual withdrawal is initiated, which results in decreased interaction between the aging and other members of the society.

According to Cumming and Henry (1961), the process is one of double withdrawal. The individual disengages from society, and society from the individual. Accordingly, they view disengagement as a gradual and mutually satisfying process by which society and the individual prepare *in advance* for the ultimate "disengagement" of incurable, incapacitating disease and death. They speak of the elderly as "wanting" to disengage and as doing it by reducing the number of roles they play, severing many relationships, and weakening the intensity of the relationships that remain. Consequently, the elderly can face death peacefully, knowing that their social ties are minimal, that they have said all their goodbyes, and that nothing more remains for them to do.

For its part, society encourages disengagement because it can gradually transfer the functions previously performed by the aged to the young. In this manner, society minimizes the problems and disruption that otherwise might be associated with the increasing incompetence or inevitable death of the aged.

The disengagement theory has been widely attacked and widely defended. Scores of articles have presented evidence on one side or the other. Generally, cross-sectional studies have been used by both sides; and as discussed in the previous section, these studies tend to confuse generational differences with age differences. On the whole, however, the weight of the evidence seems to be generally against the major tenets of the theory, at least in the unqualified form stated above (Douglas & Arenberg, 1978; Maddox, 1969;

Differing Responses to Aging
Bernice L. Neugarten and her associates have identified a number of personality patterns that influence how people respond to the aging process. "Reorganizers" search for settings that permit them to remain integrated by carrying on an active life; the "disengaged" seek integration through more solitary activities. *(left, Joel Gordon; right, Harvey Stein)*

Palmore, 1975). Indeed, at least for those under 75, aging seems to be accompanied by stability and by continuity in levels of participation in such voluntary associations as religious, civic, service, patriotic, and fraternal or sororal organizations (Cutler, 1977). And one survey—using a sample of those 65 and older residing in a midwestern community of 35,000—found no evidence of a sharp drop in such affiliations, not even for those 80 or over. However, the very elderly were less likely to hold multiple memberships and to be active participants in groups (Babchuck, Peters, Hoyt & Kaiser, 1979). In sum, the disengagement theory exaggerates the isolation and separation of the elderly from significant aspects of their preretirement lives (Mindel & Vaughan, 1978).

Activity Theory

Sociologists Robert J. Havighurst, Bernice L. Neugarten, and Sheldon S. Tobin (1968, p. 161), among others, have proposed the **activity theory of aging** as an alternative to the disengagement theory:

Except for the inevitable changes in biology and in health, older people are the same as middle-aged people, with essentially the same psychological and social needs. In this view, the decreased social interaction that characterizes old age results from the withdrawal by society from the aging person; and the decrease in interaction proceeds against the desires of most aging men and women. The older person who ages optimally is the person who stays active and who manages to resist the shrinkage of his social world. He maintains the activities of middle age as long as possible and then finds substitutes for those activities he is forced to relinquish.

On the whole, activity theorists agree with disengagement theorists that disengagement tends to increase sometime after 60 or 65. They also find, however, that as an elderly person's level of activity declines, so also do feelings of satisfaction, contentment, and happiness (Havighurst, 1973; Neugarten, 1964). Some research confirms this conclusion (Graney, 1975; Maddox, 1963; Palmore, 1975). Hence, activity theorists deny a basic premise of disengagement theory, namely, that disengagement represents a desirable or optimum course.

Activity theorists find that the majority of healthy older persons maintain fairly stable levels of activity (Bowling & Browne, 1991; Longino & Kart, 1982; Moen, Dempster-McClain & Williams, 1989; Palmore, 1975; Shanas et al., 1968). Of interest, in recent presidential elections one-third of Americans who voted were age 55 or older. Seven out of ten of those age 55 to 74 voted—the highest rate of participation of any age group. Even those age 75 or over were almost as likely to vote as the electorate in general.

The amount of engagement or disengagement that does occur among the elderly appears to be more a function of past life patterns, socioeconomic status, and health than of any inherent or inevitable aging process (Magaziner, Cadigan, Hebel & Parry, 1988; Morgan, 1988; Ward, 1979). However, an abundance of social activities is not necessarily associated with a more positive life adjustment among older people. High levels of responding has both positive and negative aspects (Fredrickson & Carstensen, 1990; Reich, Zautra & Hill, 1987; Rook, 1984). Moreover, although some elderly persons find happiness in a crowd, others seek contentment in a more solitary existence with equally positive results.

Consequently, any number of researchers emphasize that is not such social activities and roles that determine successful aging but rather the person's inner, subjective experience of personal adjustment (Chappell & Badger, 1989; Costa, McRae & Norris, 1981; Liang, Dvorkin, Kahana & Mazian, 1980). Morale, a sense of well-being and life satisfaction are apparently a measure of the quality—the deeper meaning—of the life experience (Conner, Powers & Bultena, 1979).

Role Exit Theory

> *We start by growing old in other people's eyes, then slowly we come to share their judgment.*—MALCOLM COWLEY
> The View from 80

Sociologist Zena Smith Blau (1973) has formulated the **role exit theory of aging.** According to Blau, retirement and widowhood terminate the participation of the elderly in the principal institutional structures of society—the job and the family. Accordingly, the opportunities open to the elderly for remaining socially useful are severely undermined. Blau regards the loss of occupational and marital statuses as particularly devastating, since these positions are *master* statuses or *core* roles—anchoring points for adult identity.

Sociologist Irving Rosow (1974) takes a somewhat similar position. He argues that in the United States people are not effectively socialized to old age. The social norms that define the behavioral expectations for old age are weak, limited, and ambiguous. Furthermore, the elderly have little motivation to conform to an essentially "roleless role"—a socially devalued status. Thus, even if there were adequate norms for guiding behavior in older age, Rosow concludes that few people would want to conform to a role that excludes them from equal opportunities for social participation and rewards. Hence, role loss is said to be a stressful experience for the elderly (Elwell & Maltbie-Crannell, 1981; Hansson, 1986).

Critics contend, however, that role exit theorists exaggerate the social losses felt by most older persons (Gove, Ortega & Style, 1989; Palmore, 1976). The Duke Longitudal Studies and other research dealing with life satisfaction indicate that most older people perceive little or no overall social loss (Shanas et al., 1968). Many indicate that the loss of their work and parental roles is offset by the increased freedom and opportunity to do things that they had always wanted to do but had no time for.

Social Exchange Theory

Sociologists such as James J. Dowd (1975, 1980, 1984) have applied the **social exchange theory of aging.** According to this theory, people enter into social relationships because they derive *rewards* from doing so—economic sustenance, recognition, a sense of security, love, social approval, gratitude, and the like. In the process of seeking such rewards, however, they also incur *costs*—they have negative, unpleasant experiences (effort, fatigue, embarrassment, and so on) or they are forced to abandon positive, pleasant experiences in order to pursue the rewarding activity. *Profit* is total reward minus total cost. In interaction, people are viewed as engaging in a sort of mental bookkeeping that involves a ledger of rewards, costs, and profits. A relationship tends to persist only as long as both parties receive profit from it.

As applied to old age, social exchange theory suggests that the elderly find themselves in a situation of increasing vulnerability because of the deterioration in their bargaining position. In industrial societies the skills they once had become increasingly outmoded through technological change, and the skills they still have can often be provided more efficiently and with less cost by others. Furthermore, as long as older workers remain on the job, they block the upward career paths of younger workers. As a consequence of the declining power available to the elderly, older workers exchange their position in the labor force for the promise of Social Security and Medicare; that is, they "retire." However, as their numbers and political resources grow, the elderly may mount social movements in the years ahead to extract from society a more favorable distribution for themselves of benefits and privileges (Dowd, 1980).

Social exchange formulations underlie **modernization theory,** the notion that the status of the aged tends to be high in traditional societies and lower in urbanized, industrialized societies (Cowgill, 1974, 1986; Cowgill & Holmes, 1972). The theory assumes that the position of the aged in preindustrial, traditional societies is high because the aged tend to accumulate knowledge and control through their years of experience. Modernization theorists believe that industrialization, however, undermines the importance of traditional knowledge and control. Some evidence supports the contentions of modernization theorists (Bengston, Dowd, Smith & Inkeles, 1975; Gilleard & Gurkan, 1987; Kertzer & Schaie, 1989).

However, exceptions can be found to the modernization theorists' assumption that the aged are assigned low status in modern industrial societies. Japan is one exception, for the Japanese values of filial piety and ancestor worship have mediated the impact of economic factors on the treatment of the elderly (Martin, 1989; Palmore, 1975; Palmore & Maeda, 1985). Moreover, historical evidence from nineteenth-century England reveals that the effects of industrialization differed dramatically by industry and region, so that under some conditions the position of old people actually improved with greater mechanization of an industry. For instance, the invention of the sewing machine increased the output of seamstresses who did piecework at home (Quadagno, 1982). Although social exchange theory and modernization theory are helpful in drawing attention to elements of exchange that influence the position of the elderly in a society, we need to employ the theories with care and recognize that they fall short of providing a complete explanation (Foner, 1984; Ishii-Kuntz & Lee, 1987).

Psychosocial Aspects of Aging

Unless we are old already, the next "old people" will be us.—ALEX COMFORT
A Good Old Age, 1976

The social world of later adulthood differs in some respects from that of early and middle adulthood. Changes in physical vigor and health and in cognitive functioning have social consequences. And shifts in work and marital roles profoundly affect the lives of elderly people

through the behavioral expectations and activities that they allow. Hence, the "social life space" of aging adults provides the context in which elderly men and women, like their younger counterparts, define reality, formulate their self-images, and generate their interaction with other individuals.

Retirement

Retirement is a relatively recent notion. In 1900 the average American male had a life expectancy of 46.3 years and, on average, spent only 3 percent of his lifetime in retirement. In 1986, with a life expectancy of 70 years, a man could expect to be retired for about 10 percent of his life. In point of fact, however, Americans now spend an even greater proportion of their lives in retirement by virtue of the exodus of older adults from the labor force at younger ages (see Figure 20-2). The proportion of males aged 65 and over who were gainfully employed dropped from 68 percent in 1890, to 48 percent in 1947, to only 16 percent today. Of equal social significance, employed men aged 55 to 64 declined from 89 percent in 1947 to 69 percent currently, a drop of 20 percentage points. The Bureau of Labor Statistics estimates that by the year 2000 only one in four men 60 years of age and over will be working (Lewin, 1990).

Three-fourths of men and more than four-fifths of women retiring on Social Security currently leave their jobs before they are 65, and in companies with high early-retirement pension benefits, the retirement age drops below 60. In government, nearly two out of three civil servants retire before age 62. If they retire at age 60 or 62, many of today's workers can expect to have fifteen to thirty years of life remaining. So retirement appears to be a factor of mounting significance in the lives of U.S. men. And it is taking on added significance in the lives of women, as more and more women enter the labor force (about 8 percent of women over 65 hold jobs or are seeking work, down from 9.5 percent in 1971).

Involuntary Retirement In 1978 Congress passed legislation banning compulsory retirement for most workers before age 70 and in 1986 passed legislation largely abolishing mandatory retirement at any age. Many Americans view the practice of compelling workers to retire as a curtailment of basic rights. Prior to 1978 about half of the nation's employers had policies requiring employees to step down at 65. Business organizations like the U.S. Chamber of Commerce opposed bans on forced retirement; they argued that it would severely disrupt companies' personnel and pension planning and would keep younger people from advancing. For the most part, however, these fears have not been realized. Despite the changes in the law, there has not been an increase in the labor force participation of older Americans. People have increasingly wanted and chosen to retire at earlier ages, so the new laws have affected only a small minority of workers (Dentzer, 1990). Nevertheless, high unemployment in many industries (especially in mining and manufacturing), coupled with the prospect of an extended layoff or a difficult search for a new job, has led many older workers to opt for early retirement. And in other cases some older workers have been crowded out of their jobs or have been given special incentives for leaving to make room for younger workers (women have generally not worked enough years

to be eligible for the generous pension inducements offered by many firms) (Gohmann, 1990; Uchitelle, 1991). Contemporary employers, although often pleased with the work habits of older employees, still harbor many negative attitudes toward older workers that are rooted in concerns about higher health insurance costs and older employees' ability to use new technology such as computers. A 1990 survey undertaken for the Commonwealth Fund, a New York philanthropic organization, suggests that there are nearly 2 million nonworking Americans 50 to 64 years old who are ready and able to work but who are not currently in the labor force (about 66 percent said they would work full-time, 60 percent said they would work standing up most of the day, and 54 percent said they would accept weekend or evening hours) (Solomon & Funchsberg, 1990).

In a recent survey the National Center for Health Statistics asked both working and retired persons aged 55 to 74 about their ability and de-

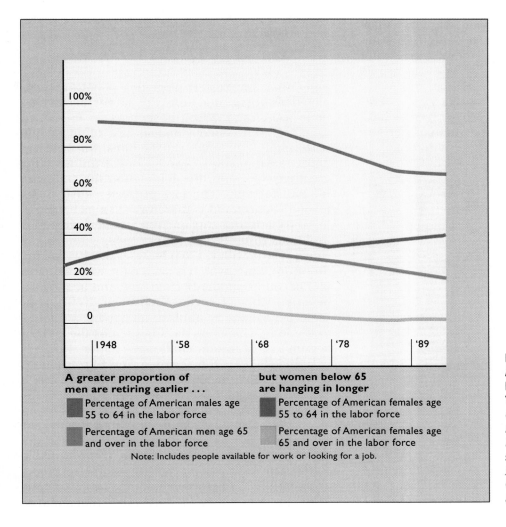

A greater proportion of men are retiring earlier . . .

■ Percentage of American males age 55 to 64 in the labor force

■ Percentage of American men age 65 and over in the labor force

but women below 65 are hanging in longer

■ Percentage of American females age 55 to 64 in the labor force

■ Percentage of American females age 65 and over in the labor force

Note: Includes people available for work or looking for a job.

Figure 20-2 Elderly Americans, Particularly Men, Have Shown an Increased Willingness to Retire Early
Over the past five decades, the nation's older workers have been retiring at an earlier age.
SOURCE: *U.S. News & World Report*, May 14, 1990, p. 49. Copyright © 1990, U.S. News & World Report.

sire to work. People were asked if they had any difficulty performing ten work-related activities, such as walking up steps, bending over or kneeling, and carrying 10 or 25 pounds. Six out of ten respondents indicated that they had no difficulty with any of the activities. Two-thirds of the respondents who had retired for reasons other than health said they could hold a job. But only 12 percent of them expressed a desire to go back to work.

The figures cast doubt on whether changes in retirement laws will affect the age at which Americans actually retire (Myers, 1991). Seemingly, businesses looking to elderly workers to make up for labor shortages may have to offer rather substantial financial inducements to lure some of them out of retirement (many people value their free time and independence more than they do the buying power or other benefits of a job) (Robinson, 1991; Teltsch, 1991). Surveys undertaken by the American Association of Retired Persons show that from a quarter to a half of older workers and retirees would delay retirement if they could work fewer hours. Such findings seem to suggest that it does not make sense to operate on a system where people go from working all the time to one where they do not work at all (Lewin, 1990).

Retirement: Negative and Positive Views Traditionally, retirement has been portrayed as having profoundly negative consequences for the

Early Retirement
Although federal legislation virtually bars mandatory retirement, increasing numbers of Americans are choosing to retire earlier than age 65. When their financial circumstances are adequate and secure, they may elect to retire in their late fifties or early sixties. Although it was once thought that retirement has negative consequences, new research suggests that most people view their retirement quite positively. (Jane Schreibman/Photo Researchers)

individual. In Western societies people are depicted as integrated into the larger society by their work roles. Work is seen as an important aspect of self-concept and as providing people with many personal satisfactions, meaningful peer relationships, and opportunities for creativity—in sum, the foundation for enduring life satisfactions. The loss of these satisfactions through retirement is therefore seen as being inherently demoralizing and the precursor of major problems in older age (Back, 1969; Cumming & Henry, 1961; Miller, 1965; Mowsesian, 1987). Furthermore, time, which is scarce for working people, becomes suddenly excessive and acquires a negative value. Hence, much of postretirement life is believed to be aimless, and giving structure to the long, shapeless days is seen as the retired person's most urgent challenge (Butler, 1975).

In recent years the negative view of retirement has been challenged (Matthews & Brown, 1987; Palmore, Burchett, Fillenbaum, George & Wallman, 1985; Parnes et al., 1985). Probably no more than a third of Americans find retirement stressful, either as a transition or as a life stage (Bosse, Aldwin, Levenson & Workman-Daniels, 1991). There is reason to believe, for instance, that attitudes toward work and retirement have been changing in the United States. Indeed, over

"Since Frank retired two years ago, he's been on the alert for some long-dormant artistic talent to develop."

(Drawing by Booth; © 1990 The New Yorker Magazine, Inc.)

three decades ago, Robert Dubin (1956) found that for three out of four male industrial workers, work was *not* a central life interest. Furthermore, only one worker in ten saw his important primary social relationships as located in the workplace. Moreover, recent research suggests that it is money that is most missed in retirement and that when people are assured an adequate income, they will retire early (Atchley, 1971; Beck, 1982; Shanas, 1972). One longitudinal survey of 5,000 men found that most men who retire for reasons other than poor health are "very happy" in retirement and would, if they had to do it over again, retire at the same age. Only about 13 percent of whites and 17 percent of blacks said they would choose to retire later if they could choose again (Parnes, 1981). Other studies have similarly found that when individuals are healthy and their incomes are adequate, they typically express satisfaction with retirement (Atchley, 1976; Herzog, House & Morgan, 1991; Horn & Meer, 1987; Parnes et al., 1985). Significantly, more and more retirees are also going back to college. The Census Bureau reported in 1989 that some 320,000 Americans age 50 and over were enrolled in college courses, including more than 65,000 at the graduate and professional levels (Beck, 1991).

Social scientists are increasingly coming to recognize that preretirement lifestyle and planning play an important part in retirement satisfaction (Bosse, Aldwin, Levenson & Workman-Daniels, 1991; Ekerdt, Vinick & Bosse, 1989; McPherson & Guppy, 1979). Positive anticipation of retirement and concrete and realistic planning

for this stage in life are related to adjustment in retirement. On the whole, voluntary retirees are more likely to have positive attitudes and higher satisfaction in retirement than nonvoluntary retirees. However, other factors, not always controllable, also influence retirement satisfaction. For instance, those with better health and higher socioeconomic status seem to make a better adjustment to retirement.

Marital Relations

Americans generally believe that marriages that do not terminate in divorce begin with passionate love and evolve into cooler but closer companionship. However, researchers portray a somewhat different picture. Both marital satisfaction and adjustment begin declining quite early in marriage. The speed and intensity of this decline varies from one study to another. In the middle and later stages of the family life cycle, the evidence is less clear (Spanier, Lewis & Cole, 1975). Some investigators find a continual decline (Depner & Ingersoll-Dayton, 1985; Paris & Luckey, 1966; Swensen & Trahaug, 1985). Usually, however, they report a U-shaped curve, with a decline in satisfaction during the early years, a leveling off during the middle years, and an increase in satisfaction during the later years (Ade-Ridder & Brubaker, 1983; Anderson, Russell & Schumm, 1983; Glenn, 1989, 1990; Rollins & Feldman, 1970).

Satisfaction with Marriage Among the Elderly
Most elderly couples report greater happiness and satisfaction with marriage than at any time since the newlywed phase. Many say their marriage improved during late adulthood. The couple shown here are celebrating their fiftieth wedding anniversary. *(Robert V. Eckert, Jr./EKM—Nepenthe)*

While the quality of marriage varies from couple to couple, most elderly husbands and wives report greater happiness and satisfaction with marriage during their later years than at any other time except for the newlywed phase. Many say that companionship, respect, and the sharing of common interests improve during later adulthood (Powers & Bultena, 1976; Stinnett, Carter & Montgomery, 1972). One study found that about 90 percent of older couples felt that their relationships were harmonious "most of the time." Less than 10 percent indicated that they had negative feelings about their marriages more than once or twice a month (Rollins & Feldman, 1970). Of interest, researchers are finding that couples who originally bore no particular resemblance to each other when first married come to resemble each other after twenty-five or so years of marriage. The resemblance is often subtle; however, the happier the couple, the greater the resemblance tends to be (Goleman, 1987c).

A number of factors appear to contribute to the improvement of marriage in the later years. For one thing, children are launched. Parenthood requires a heavy commitment and is often the source of role overload and strain (Rollins & Cannon, 1974; Schumm & Bugaighis, 1986). Children also interfere with the amount of communication that takes place between spouses and with the time that they have available for companionable activities (Fitzpatrick, 1988; Miller, 1976; Thornton, 1977). And children often create new sources of conflict while intensifying existing sources (Urdy, 1971). Furthermore, in later life problems with such issues as in-laws, money, and sex have often been resolved or the stresses associated with them dissipated. And as pointed out in Chapter 17, older adults tend to be more androgynous in their roles than younger adults are.

However, retirement may create new strains for a couple. One retiree points out (Brody, 1981, p. 13):

> A husband and wife may each have a dream of what retirement would be, but those dreams don't necessarily mesh. They've got to sit down, and talk—outline their activities, restructure their time and define their territories. I discovered that my wife was very afraid that after I retired she'd have to wait on me hand and foot and would lose all her freedom.

Some women report that they feel "smothered" having their husbands about the house so much of the time. Men may attempt to increase their involvement in household tasks and be seen by their wives as intruders. Even so, some wives welcome the participation of their husbands, as it

(© 1990 Scott A. Masear, Eugene, Oregon)

leads to a decrease in their own responsibilities. Furthermore, the loss of privacy and independence is often offset by opportunities for nurture and companionship. And wives mention the "time available to do what you want" and the greater flexibility afforded in life schedules as advantages of retirement. Yet perhaps the most important factors influencing a wife's satisfaction with her husband's retirement are her own and her husband's good health and adequate finances (Brubaker, 1990; Hill & Dorfman, 1982; Keating & Cole, 1980; Lee & Shehan, 1989).

Study after study documents another interesting fact: Marriage seems to protect people from premature death. Married individuals are healthier than unmarried individuals, and death rates are consistently higher among single and socially isolated people (even after adjustments are made for age, initial health status, smoking, physical activity, and obesity). Significantly, although popular folklore depicts marriage as a blessed state for women and a burdensome trap for men, it is men rather than women who researchers find receive marriage's greatest mental and physical benefits. Overall, it seems that the married experience less emotional and physical pathology than the unmarried because they have continuous companionship with a spouse who provides interpersonal closeness, nurturing, emotional gratification, and support in dealing with life's hassles and stress. Indeed, married men and women are typically happier and less stressed than are the unmarried (Coombs, 1991; Kitson & Morgan, 1990; Wilson & Schoenborn, 1989; Zick & Smith, 1991). In addition, married men in a dozen countries earn more than do their single colleagues, with the average pay edge ranging from 3 percent in Poland to 31 percent in the United States (in the United States, the gap starts out at 28.8 percent at age 30, widens to 30.3 percent at age 40, and rises to 32.5 percent by age 50) (Schoeni, 1990).

Kin and Friendship Ties

The notion that most aged people are lonely and isolated from their families and other meaningful social ties is false (Adams & Blieszner, 1989; Jones & Vaughan, 1990; Thomas, 1988; van Willigen, 1989). A Harris poll (1981) shows that although 65 percent of the public assume that most of the elderly are frequently lonely, only 13 percent of people 65 and over view loneliness as a serious problem for them. Furthermore, about four of every five of the elderly have living children. Of this group reputable surveys show that 85 percent live within an hour's travel of at least

one child, 55 percent see their children every day or so, and another 26 percent see them about every week. Moreover, the elderly are often involved in exchanges of mutual aid with their grown children as both providers and receivers. Many times, the elderly parent helps the adult child by performing child care and other home-related roles, whereas the adult child helps the parent with heavy housework, shopping, bureaucratic mediation, and transportation. And as discussed in Chapter 18, in 80 percent of the cases any care elderly people will require will be provided by their families. In fact, as shown in Figure 20-3, older Americans are less likely than their adult children to believe that when elderly parents can no longer take care of themselves, the best solution is for them to move in with their children. (See the boxed insert on pages 578–579 on home care for the elderly.) In sum, the elderly are not so isolated from kin and friendship networks as is commonly believed (Aldous, 1987; Powers & Bultena, 1976; Quinn, 1983).

A majority of elderly men—75 percent—live with their spouses. But because there are far more widows than there are widowers, only 37 percent of elderly women still reside with their husbands. Thirty percent of noninstitutionalized individuals 65 and over live alone, 16 percent of

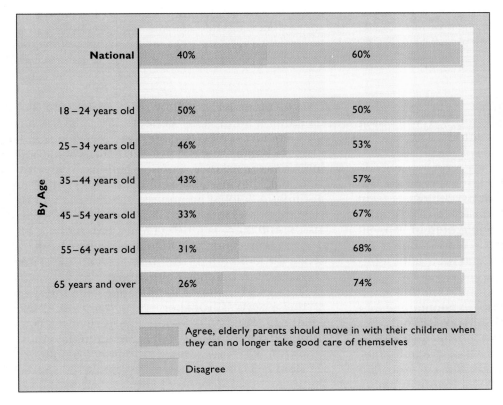

Figure 20-3 Elderly Parents: Family Ties

This graph depicts different age groups' responses to the question: I would like to ask you to tell me whether you agree or disagree with a number of statements that are sometimes made about marriage and families. . . . When elderly parents can no longer take good care of themselves, it is the best solution to have them move in with their children. Note: Sample size = 1,230. SOURCE: *Public Opinion* (December/January 1986), p. 34. Reprinted with permission of American Enterprise Institute for Public Policy Research.

Home Care
for the Elderly

Family members often feel reluctant and ill prepared to take on responsibility for aged parents, even when they have a value commitment to the desirability of home-based health care. In formulating plans and a course of action, middle-aged sons and daughters would be well advised to keep in mind that elderly people are not infants. They should be thoroughly involved in planning their own future. Far too often parents are kept in ignorance of decisions and misled as to why a particular decision was reached.

Healthy or sick, the great majority of the elderly live at home on their own. In providing for the elderly, geriatric specialists recommend that where possible "permanent" solutions—such as a move to a nursing home or other custodial care—be avoided because they usually involve severe changes (Stevenson, 1979). Often, a more satisfactory approach is to take the problem apart and examine it in manageable pieces, carefully going through the daily activities of the elderly parent to determine which areas are being adequately dealt with and which areas pose difficulty. A parent may simply need handrails around the bathtub and toilet, not admission to an institution.

Although temporary solutions may demand time and ingenuity, they are worth it in terms of the self-respect and quality of life they afford the elderly person. Included may be a variety of measures: better lighting on stairways and halls; as-sistance with strenuous activities, heavy cleaning, and clothes care; transportation to and from grocery stores, drug stores, church, and bank; and simplified stoves and other appliances for those with failing eyesight. In sum, a good rule of thumb is to avoid trying to find the perfect solution and instead initiate a process of constantly updating temporary solutions (Stevenson, 1979).

Most psychologists, psychiatrists, and other health care professionals agree that, where possible, the elderly should be cared for in home settings. Most contend that the present nursing-home system hurts rather than helps many of the people it serves. Although some elderly individuals are so incapacitated as to require care in a special residential facility, others are there because they have nowhere else to go.

One of the most promising alternatives to a nursing home is an adult day-care center that offers part-time supervision for infirm and disabled individuals so that their relatives have a chance to work and carry on their usual daily routines. In 1970 there were about 12 such centers in the United States, but by 1987 their number had grown to at least 1,200. The centers typically provide medical treatment, rehabilitation and counseling services, and custodial care. But governmental support for such programs is still limited, and they are continually under attack by budget trimmers.

The kinds of services available at home are also

the men and 40 percent of the women. By 1980 only 15 percent of the elderly lived with their children, down from 30 percent in 1950.

The elderly value their privacy and independence (Cherlin & Furstenberg, 1986; Cicirelli, 1981). Those with adult children prefer to live near but not with them, what psychologists term "intimate distance." And contrary to the popular view that grandmothers are delighted to baby-sit for their grandchildren, many older women resent the frequent imposition that their adult children make on their time and energy.

Overall, friends are more important and satisfying to older people in terms of companionship than relationships with their offspring are (Beckman, 1981; Larson, Mannell & Zuzanek, 1986). In fact, some research suggests that greater loneliness exists among the single elderly who live with relatives than among those who live alone.

Hence, an elderly widow who lives with her daughter's family may be quite lonely if she has little contact with associates her own age. Children no longer seem to provide a form of old-age happiness insurance. Public opinion surveys reveal that having children contributes little or nothing to "global happiness" among the elderly (Glenn & McLanahan, 1981; Lee & Ellithorpe, 1982). And there is little evidence that individuals derive important psychological rewards or a sense of emotional well-being from the later stages of parenthood (Keith, 1983).

Siblings often play a significant role in the lives of the elderly (Brubaker, 1990; Cicirelli, 1989; Goetting, 1986; Gold, 1989). They provide a continuity in family history that is uncommon to most other family relationships—the only fragment of the family of origin that may remain. A shared family history frequently affords a foundation for

expanding rapidly. In most localities visiting nurses are available. Some communities also afford meals-on-wheels (programs that deliver hot meals to the homebound elderly) and home-care programs (including physician and therapist visits, home health aides, homemakers, volunteer companions who make home visits, and volunteer phone networks that daily telephone elderly persons living alone). John Pagano, a 72-year-old resident of Manhattan who suffered from a severe respiratory illness and who was the beneficiary of such programs, noted: "I want to be on my own. I like to watch television when I want, sleep as late as I want, eat what I want. They've made my life bearable" (Waldholz, 1983, p. 1). Physicians who monitored his health said that because of his vulnerability to infection he was better off at home than he would have been in a nursing home.

Depending on the state, home-care assistance may be available under the following programs: Medicare, Medicaid, the Older Americans Act, and Title 20 of Social Security. Home care offers a great many psychological and medical benefits. Individuals typically recover more rapidly in a home than in a hospital environment. They eat better, sleep better, and feel better when in familiar surroundings. They take more responsibility for their own care at home and are less prone to become dependent on others. And the family is often less disrupted, since frequent trips to the hospital or nursing home are not necessary.

For adult children who must engage in the long-distance care of the elderly, stress can become a way of life. The stress inheres not only in working out the logistics of medical and hospital arrangements at a distance but also in coping with the minutiae of caretaking that follows a hospital stay. One woman who lives in Manhattan and is managing the care of her elderly father in upstate New York reports that she had to make arrangements for at least forty-five people in a six-month period. On one occasion she left $200 with her father (Collins, 1984*a*, p. 17):

> When I came back next week it was all gone, and I knew he hadn't spent it. I'm sure it was the nurse, but how can you prove it? After a while you get to depending on the caretakers so much, that even if they are stealing, you don't want to confront them on it, because you're so tired of training new people. There are times when I feel totally helpless.

In coming to terms with their problems, both adult children and elderly parents must recognize that there is no one solution that is right. Each party has to appraise what he or she can and cannot do. No remedy is perfect. Ideally, each party should be able to deal openly and honestly with the other in arriving at ongoing adjustments and readjustments.

---

interaction that supplies companionship and a support network as well as a validation for an older person's reminiscences of family events. As they advance into old age, many siblings report that they think more often about one another and find their acceptance, companionship, and closeness deepens. The most frequent contact occurs among siblings in relatively close physical proximity. The sister-sister relationship tends to be the most potent sibling relationship, followed by the sister-brother and brother-brother relationship.

As in other aspects of human affairs, individuals differ enormously in what they view as adequate or inadequate contact with other people (Chappell & Badger, 1989; Essex & Nam, 1987). Indeed, research reveals that lifelong isolates tend to have average or better morale in old age, and to be no more prone to mental illness, than anyone else (Lowenthal, 1964). Furthermore, it is not a certain absolute degree of isolation that produces feelings of loneliness in old age but, rather, the fact of *becoming* socially more isolated than one had previously been (Gubrium, 1974).

Loneliness is not simply a matter of being alone (Busse & Pfeiffer, 1969, p. 188):

> Solitude need not be experienced as loneliness, while loneliness can be felt in the presence of other people. For instance, persons residing in nursing homes often complain of loneliness, even though they are surrounded by people and, at a superficial level, are interacting with them. Loneliness is the awareness of an absence of meaningful integration with other individuals or groups of individuals, a consciousness of being excluded from the system of opportunities and rewards in which other people participate.

In sum, the quality of a relationship is more important than is the mere frequency of contact.

Overall, the maintenance of even one meaningful, stable relationship is more closely associated with good mental health and high morale among the eldery than is a high level of social interaction. A confidant serves as a buffer against gradual losses in interaction and against the losses associated with widowhood and retirement (Connidis & Davies, 1990; Depner & Ingersoll-Dayton, 1988; Kendig, Coles, Pittelkow & Wilson, 1988; Krause, 1986). Moreover, being able to give to and for others seems to be very rewarding for older people and seems to reinforce their own sense of well-being and independence (Roberto & Scott, 1986).

Grandparents

Child psychologists emphasize that both children and their grandparents are better off when they spend a good deal of time in each other's company (Kornhaber & Woodward, 1981). Yet at the turn of the century surviving grandparents were in short supply. Children born in 1900 had one chance in four of having four grandparents alive, and one chance in fifty of having all survive until they reached age 15. Now, with the increase in adult life expectancies, more youngsters have living grandparents. By and large, too, grandparents are healthier, more active, and better educated than they used to be, and many have more money and leisure time (Cherlin & Furstenberg, 1986). Today, 94 percent of older people with children are grandparents; 46 percent are great-grandparents. So almost half of all persons 65 and over in the United States who have living children are members of four-generation families. The likelihood of being a great-grandparent increases with age, so that among persons 80 and over almost three-fourths are great-gandparents. In fact, one-fourth of those aged 66 are already great-grandparents (great-grandparents are now more common than grandparents were at the turn of the century).

Traditionally, the media have portrayed grandmothers as jolly, white-haired, bespectacled older women who lavish goodies and attention on their grandchildren. But grandmothers are also depicted as meddlesome intruders in family life who must be politely tolerated. And grandfathers are often seen as "male grandmothers." In fact, when college students are asked to list their images of the roles of grandfather and grandmother, they make few distinctions between them (Hess & Markson, 1980). Many youth report that they are closer to their maternal grandparents than to

their paternal grandparents, but this difference seems to be a product of having greater access to the former than to the latter in their childhood (Matthews & Sprey, 1985). For their part, grandmothers tend to report greater satisfaction with grandparenting than do grandfathers (Thomas, 1986).

Despite stereotyped portrayals of what grandparents are like, research suggests that grandparents vary in the ways they approach their role. Much depends on the age and health of the grandparents, their race and ethnic background, and geographic distance. In some cases, by virtue of death, divorce, or other family disruption, the grandparents are obligated to take on a larger role in the lives of their grandchildren. Indeed, they may assume primary caretaking responsibility for a grandchild while the mother works. Grandparents tend to be more involved with grandchildren when the children's mothers are divorced or unmarried (Denham & Smith, 1989; Hetherington, 1989; Presser, 1989). And countless grandparents have stepped into the breach to rescue their grandchildren when families falter from drugs, abuse, and crime (Creighton, 1991). So although some grandparents may be emotionally or geographically remote, others are very closely involved with their grandchildren. Two sociological observers comment: "Grandparents in America are like volunteer firefighters: they are required to be on the scene when needed but

Being a Grandparent

Regardless of culture, grandparents can be an important developmental resource for their grandchildren. And they can reap important psychological satisfactions. Here a Inuit grandmother acquaints her grandchild with hand-made sealskin boots that are a part of Inuit culture. *(John Eastcott/Yva Momatiuk/The Image Works)*

"Mom, you shoulda been in the living room! Grampa told Dad to *sit down and be quiet!*"

("Dennis the Menace" ® used by permission of Hank Ketcham and © by North American Syndicate.)

otherwise keep their assistance in reserve" (Cherlin & Furstenberg, 1986, p. 183). The most common relationship nowadays is the companionate style, where the grandparent and grandchild are essentially good pals. Grandparents may play, joke, and watch television with their grandchildren, but today, they are less inclined to discipline them. Overall, grandparents of yesteryear do not seem to have been more involved in their grandchildren's lives than they are today, despite stereotyped images of gramps down at the fishin' hole with Junior. But by the same token, grandparents also want freedom and fulfillment—to spend their leisure time as they please and have close but not constant association with their children and grandchildren (Cherlin & Furstenberg, 1986; Neugarten & Weinstein, 1964; Smolowe, 1990).

Although the grandparenting role has different meanings for different people, there nonetheless do appear a number of recurring themes. First, for many individuals it is a source of *biological renewal and/or continuity*. Being a grandparent evokes a sense of renewal and the extension of self and family into the future. Second, the role is often a source of *emotional self-fulfillment*. It generates feelings of companionship and satisfaction

between an adult and a child that were often absent in the earlier parent-child relationship. Grandchildren provide many grandparents with pleasure and pride.

Arthur Kornhaber and Kenneth L. Woodward (1981) conducted lengthy interviews with 300 grandchildren and as many grandparents. They concluded that the bond between grandparents and grandchildren is second in emotional power and influence only to the parent-child relationship. But only 5 percent of the grandchildren said they had close, regular contact with at least one grandparent. Nearly 80 percent reported that they saw their grandparents only intermittently. The reason was less one of geographical distance than one of the grandparents' having chosen to remain emotionally distant.

For those grandchildren and grandparents who are close, the relationship provides mutual rewards. The children derive unadulterated doses of tender, loving care. They may also acquire a storyteller, family historian, mentor, wizard, confidant, and role model for the grandchild's own old age. And the grandparents feel loved and needed at a time when society may be affording them less meaningful roles. Moreover, the relationship can serve to buffer the frequently tense relationship between the child and the parents. Kornhaber and Woodward conclude that grandparents are to families what elders are to society.

Institutional Care

In the United States there are 1.4 million elderly people in some 22,000 nursing homes—5 percent of all those 65 and over. The figure is expected to reach 2 million by the year 2000, 2.8 million by 2020, and 4.4 million by 2040. (Table 20-2 shows the characteristics of nursing-home residents.) Like people, each caregiving environment has a unique personality, and some social climates are friendlier, more oriented toward independence, and better organized than others (Timko & Moos, 1991). Certainly many facilities are doing their best to provide the elderly with decent care. Even so, nursing homes are hardly "homes." Frequently, they are institutions where the majority of residents share a small bedroom with others, eat mass-prepared, high-carbohydrate meals in a large, linoleum-floored dining hall, and watch television in a common recreation room. In 1990, more than a third of the nation's skilled-care nursing homes failed to meet federal standards for clean food, and nearly a

Selecting a Nursing Home

Americans have an enormous fear of growing old, becoming infirm, losing their minds, and being placed in a nursing home. And for their part, the vast majority of adult children typically postpone the arrangement as long as they can. When they do place an elderly parent, it is usually at the point of desperation (Corbin & Strauss, 1988; Newman, Struyk, Wright & Rice, 1990). Adult children find the decision to be an exceedingly excruciating one, and they commonly experience high levels of ambivalence, shame, and guilt. One 49-year-old East Coast public relations woman tells of her anguish after her 80-year-old mother had suffered a number of small strokes (Moore, 1983, p. 30):

> When it was clear that she couldn't go on living alone, we hired round-the-clock nurses at $400 a week. But first one didn't show up; then my mother didn't like another. Each time it was something else.
>
> So we brought her to our house for a while, but it was extremely hard on me and the rest of the family. We talked about a nursing home. And though she didn't want to go, it became apparent that it was the only way.
>
> She started in a minimum-care facility. But she became more and more confused, so they decided to switch her to their skilled-care facility—a decision in which I had no choice. . . . It's very sad. She keeps asking: "When can I get out of here and get on with my life?"

Clearly, the prospect of nursing-home care can be a traumatic one for both the aging parents and their adult children. Should a nursing home be required, the planning should be shared, where possible, with the person involved. A number of nursing homes should be visited before a decision is made. A list of licensed nursing homes can generally be secured from the local Social Security office or county nursing service. Since nursing homes can choose their patients, they often give preference to those who demand the least attention and care. Many good nursing homes have a waiting list.

There are a number of things to look for in a home.

THE FACILITY

- ❏ Is the nursing home licensed by a governmental agency?
- ❏ What arrangements exist for the transfer of a patient to a hospital, should it be required?
- ❏ Are the rooms clean, relatively odor-free, and comfortable?
- ❏ What are the visiting hours? Who is welcome?
- ❏ Does each room have a window, and does the room open to a corridor?

SAFETY

- ❏ Is the building fire-resistant? Does it have a sprinkler system? Are emergency exit routes clearly posted?
- ❏ Are there ramps for wheelchairs and handicapped persons?
- ❏ Are the hallways well lighted?
- ❏ Are the floor coverings nonskid and safe?
- ❏ Are there grab bars in appropriate settings, including bathrooms?

quarter did not administer drugs properly. The elderly poor, especially blacks, are often placed in public facilities—frequently state mental hospitals—that generally provide an inferior form of care (Kart & Beckham, 1976; Sullivan, 1984). In some cases nursing homes are warehouses for the elderly and dying—catacombs for the not-quite-living (Bumsted, 1986). Bedsores and other

Table 20-2

Residents of Nursing Homes	
White	92%
Elderly	90+
Predominantly women	73
Widows or widowers	62
No immediate family or friends regularly visiting	50
Partially disoriented	30
Chronic brain changes	25
Previous stroke victim	15

Source: "Nursing Homes," *Mayo Clinic Health Letter* (Rochester, Minn: Mayo Clinic, 1987).

STAFF

❑ Are a physician and a registered nurse on call at all times?

❑ What provision is made for patient dental care?

❑ Are the staff patient with questions, and are they happy to have visitors inspect the facility?

❑ Is there a physical therapy program staffed by a certified therapist?

❑ Are most of the patients out of bed, dressed, and groomed? (Be suspicious if you see many patients physically restrained in their beds or chairs or if they appear to be overtranquilized.)

❑ Are staff members on the floor actually assisting residents?

ACTIVITIES

❑ Does the facility offer a recreation program?

❑ Are the grounds well maintained, and are patients encouraged to get outdoors when weather permits?

❑ How are patients kept busy? Are patients allowed to idle without care or interest?

❑ Are activities scheduled outside the facility and in the community?

FOOD

❑ Are the meals adequate and appetizing? Are they served at the proper temperature?

❑ Does a dietician prepare the menu?

❑ Is the menu posted, and does it accurately describe the meal?

❑ Does someone notice if a resident is not eating?

❑ What provision is made for patients who have difficulty feeding themselves?

❑ What arrangements are made for patients requiring special diets?

ATMOSPHERE

❑ Are patients accorded privacy in receiving phone calls, visits, and in dressing?

❑ Can residents send and receive mail unopened?

❑ Are patients allowed to have personal belongings, including items of furniture?

❑ May residents have plants?

❑ Is there an outdoor area where residents can sit?

❑ Do residents of the home recommend it? What do they have to say about it?

❑ Are patients permitted to wear their own clothing?

❑ Are the patients well groomed?

❑ What arrangements are made so that a patient can follow his or her religious practices?

❑ Are patients treated with warmth and dignity?

COST

❑ Is the facility approved for Medicare/Medicaid reimbursement?

❑ Will the patient's own insurance policy cover any of the expenses?

❑ Is the cost quoted inclusive, or are there extra charges for laundry, medicines, and special nursing procedures?

❑ Are advance payments required? Are the payments refunded should the patient leave the home?

infections are far too common, partly because staff procedures are inadequate and because the level of hygiene is primitive (Garibaldi, Brodine & Matsumiya, 1981). Frail and disabled elderly are often pushed into passive roles (Landsberger, 1985; Shield, 1988). Indeed, some patients are tethered to their beds or wheelchairs or given powerful tranquilizing drugs on the premise that "a quiet patient is a good patient" (Kolata, 1991). And researchers find that thousands of nursing-home patients face an increased risk of dying sooner than they otherwise would because the staff fails to diagnose and adequately treat depression (Parmelee, Katz & Lawton, 1989; Winslow, 1991). Most nursing homes in the United States are owned by private proprietors and operated for profit (chain-operated nursing homes constituted 41 percent of the homes in

1985, up from 28 percent of the total in 1977). In European countries, in contrast, long-term institutional care is usually under government sponsorship, with local public control operating in accordance with national guidelines (Kane & Kane, 1978; Landsberger, 1985).

Inadequate staffing is a major problem in many nursing homes (Timko & Moos, 1990). Nonsupervisory personnel—aides, orderlies, janitors, and kitchen help—are often drawn from the urban lower class. The jobs themselves are viewed as unattractive and low paying. In some cases the people who work in nursing homes have what the sociologist Erving Goffman (1963) terms "spoiled identities," meaning that they are former mental patients, persons with criminal records, alcoholics, and drifters who need temporary employment. Such personnel may not develop a strong commitment to their jobs or to the nursing home and under these circumstances abuse the patients (Stannard, 1973). (The boxed insert on page 582 provides a number of suggestions about what to look for when you are selecting a nursing home.)

As the nursing-home industry has evolved in the United States, nursing homes have become a place of last resort for a variety of problems. They are used by terminally ill patients who require intensive nursing care, by recuperating individuals who need briefer convalescence, and by less ill but infirm aged who lack the social and financial resources necessary to manage in the community. Consequently, nursing-home residents differ greatly in degree of physical impairment and mental disorientation. Indeed, about 15 to 40 percent of the elderly in nursing facilities could be more appropriately cared for in private homes (Campion, Bang & May, 1983; Edelman & Hughes, 1990; Noelker & Bass, 1989; Roberts, Wasik, Casto & Ramey, 1991).

Government regulations have cast nursing homes in the role of miniature hospitals (Winslow, 1990). The quality of life they afford is largely determined by bureaucratic requirements regarding Medicare and Medicaid and by state regulations mandating standards for licensing. The resulting organization emphasizes the meeting of medical needs but often at the expense of fostering psychological and economic dependency among the elderly. Hence, the hospital model has imposed a medical solution on a variety of *social* problems. Residents are defined as "patients," and their day-to-day activities are controlled by physicians and nurses.

Yet many problems of the nursing-home elderly are more social than medical. Indeed, some residents could be maintained independently in the community if our societal bias toward institutionalizing the old did not exist. Large numbers of the elderly could be cared for more appropriately, as well as more economically, in their homes— with the help of visiting nurses and "meals-on-wheels" services. A further alternative is sheltered housing—a type of protected communities arranged in apartment complexes or detached cottages—that provides such supportive services as centrally prepared meals, recreational options, and health care. By 1991, nearly 250,000 Americans—average age of 82—lived in 700 continuing-care retirement communities (Garland, 1991; Lewin, 1991). And for those living with relatives, day-care centers afford harried family members a chance to work or catch up on tasks (in 1990 there were more than 2,100 day-care centers for the elderly in the United States, up from about 12 in 1970) (Beck, 1990; Weissert et al., 1990).

The Impact of Personal Control and Choice

Once in a nursing home, the elderly typically become physically, emotionally, and economically dependent on the facility for the rest of their lives (Campion, Bang & May, 1983; Shield, 1988). Research documents that staff practices all too often foster and promote patient dependency (Barton, Baltes & Orzech, 1980; Caporael, 1981; Wacker, 1985). Indeed, some of the characteristics frequently encountered among the institutionalized aged, including depression, feelings of helplessness, and accelerated decline, are partly attributable to the loss of control over their lives (Rodin, 1986; Schulz & Hanusa, 1980; Smith et al., 1988). The elderly are deprived of the opportunity to make decisions and choices for themselves. Under these circumstances they come to see themselves as powerless—as passive objects manipulated and buffeted by the environment.

As psychologists since Alfred Adler have noted, a sense of control over one's fate is essential to mental health. Indeed, the greater a person's need to feel in control, the greater the likelihood is that the individual will become depressed in the face of frustrating, inescapable events (Goleman, 1986b). A lost sense of mastery may explain, for instance, why elderly people are often adversely affected when they are forced to relocate. One study examined the impact upon elderly people of being involuntarily moved from their homes in a deteriorating neighborhood to federally subsidized housing. Despite the better housing, the group experienced more hospitalizations, admissions to nursing homes, and a higher incidence of stroke and heart ailments than did a group of elderly who did not move. There is also evidence of stronger effects of uncontrollable stress on the immune system of elderly people than on that of younger people (Rodin, 1986).

The important contribution that a sense of responsibility, usefulness, and purpose makes to successful aging is highlighted by the research of the social psychologists Ellen J. Langer and Judith Rodin (1976). They investigated the impact that feelings of control and personal choice had among residents of a high-quality nursing home in Connecticut. Forty-seven residents on one floor of the home heard a talk by the nursing-home administrator in which he stressed the responsibility that the residents had in caring for themselves and in shaping the home's policies and programs. At the conclusion of his talk he presented each resident with a plant "to keep and take care of as you'd like." He also informed them that a movie would be shown on two nights and that "you should decide which night you'd like to go, if you choose to see it at all."

Forty-five residents on another floor of the four-story building were also given a talk by the administrator. This time, however, he emphasized the responsibility that the staff felt for the residents. He gave them plants with the comment, "The nurses will water and care for them for you." Finally, he told them that they would be seeing a movie the following week and would be notified later about the day "you're scheduled to see it."

The residents were individually interviewed by a trained researcher one week before and again three weeks after the administrator's talk. To prevent bias, the researcher was not told the purpose or the nature of the experiment. The questions she asked the residents dealt with how much control they felt they had over their lives and how happy and active they believed themselves to be. She also rated each resident on an eight-point scale for alertness.

On the same two occasions a questionnaire was also filled out by each member of the nursing staff. The nurses were asked to evaluate each resident in terms of his or her overall activity, happiness, alertness, sociability, and dependence. As in the case of the interviewer, the nurses were not aware of the nature and purpose of the study.

According to the various ratings made before the administrator's talks, the two groups of residents were quite similar in their feelings of control, alertness, and satisfaction. Three weeks after the talks, however, the differences were marked.

Despite the high-quality care given them, 71 percent of those in the second group (the group in which the staff retained control and took primary responsibility) were rated as having become more debilitated—and this over a mere three-week period. In contrast, 93 percent of those in the first group (the group in which the residents were encouraged to make their own decisions and were given decisions to make) showed overall improvement. Langer and Rodin (1976, p. 197) conclude that their findings support the view that "some of the negative consequences of aging may be retarded, reversed, or possibly prevented by returning to the aged the right to make decisions and a feeling of competence."

In a follow-up study two years later, Rodin and Langer (1977) found that the group of residents who had been given responsibilities during the experimental period were healthier than comparable residents who had been treated in the conventional manner. The two treatment groups also showed different death rates. By the time of the follow-up twice as many members of the conventional-treatment group, compared with the responsibility-induced group, had died.

SUMMARY

1. Psychosocial development occurs across the entire life span. According to Erik Erikson, the elderly confront the task of coming to terms with the issue of ego integrity versus despair. The psychologist Robert C. Peck provides a somewhat related but more focused view of personality development during the later years. He says that old age confronts men and women with three issues, or tasks: ego differentiation versus work role preoccupation; body transcendence versus body preoccupation; and ego transcendence versus ego preoccupation.

2. Bernice L. Neugarten and her associates have identified four major personality types or patterns of aging. The integrated elderly are well-functioning persons who reveal a complex inner life, intact cognitive abilities, and competent egos. The armored-defended elderly are striving, ambitious, achievement-oriented individuals, with high defenses against anxiety and with the need to retain tight control over events. Passive-dependent elderly have strong dependency needs. The disintegrated elderly reveal gross defects in psychological functions and an overall deterioration of thought processes.

3. Most older people do not experience sudden and dramatic transformations in personality or self-concept. Moreover, for every older person who feels that life is now worse than he or she thought it would be, there are three who say life is currently better than they had expected.

4. Sociologists have advanced many theories that describe changes in the elderly in terms

of changes in their social environment. These theories include disengagement theory, activity theory, role exit theory, social exchange theory, and modernization theory.

5. Traditionally, the scientific literature has portrayed retirement as having profoundly negative consequences for individuals. But more recently, this view has been challenged. Attitudes toward work and retirement have been changing in the United States. Research suggests it is money that is most missed in retirement; when people are assured an adequate income, they will retire early.

6. The quality of marriage varies from couple to couple, but most elderly husbands and wives report greater happiness and satisfaction with their marriage during their later years than at any other time except for the newlywed phase. Many say that companionship, respect, and the sharing of common interests improves during later adulthood.

7. The notion that most aged people are lonely and isolated from their families and other meaningful social ties is false. Yet overall, friends are more important and satisfying to older people in terms of companionship than are relationships with their offspring and extended family.

8. Child psychologists emphasize that both children and their grandparents are better off when they spend a good deal of time in each other's company. But for many U.S. youngsters grandparents are becoming a vanishing breed. One survey shows that only 5 percent of the grandchildren said they had close, regular contact with at least one grandparent.

9. In the United States 5 percent of all people who are 65 and older live in nursing homes. Inadequate staffing and care are major problems for the eldelry in institutional settings.

10. Once in a nursing home, the elderly typically become physically, emotionally, and economically dependent on the facility for the rest of their lives. Staff practices all too often foster and promote patient dependency. Studies show, however, that the elderly should not be deprived of the opportunity to make decisions and choices for themselves.

KEY TERMS

Activity Theory of Aging The view that except for inevitable changes in biology and in health, older people are the same as middle-aged people, with essentially the same psychological and social needs. According to activity theory, successful aging requires sustained social interaction with others.

Disengagement Theory of Aging The notion that aging is a progressive process of physical, psychological, and social withdrawal from the wider world. The theory assumes that aging involves a mutual withdrawal that results in decreased interaction between the elderly and other members of the society.

Modernization Theory The notion that the status of the aged tends to be higher in traditional societies and lower in urbanized, industrialized societies.

Role Exit Theory of Aging The view that retirement and widowhood terminate the participation of the elderly in the principal institutional structures of society—the job and the family. The loss of these roles is regarded as devastating to the self-identity of older people.

Social Exchange Theory of Aging The idea that people in their interactions are engaged in a sort of mental bookkeeping that involves a ledger of rewards, costs, and profits. As applied to the elderly, the theory suggests that they find themselves in a situation of increasing vulnerability because of deterioration in their bargaining position.

Chapter 21

DEATH

Chapter 21

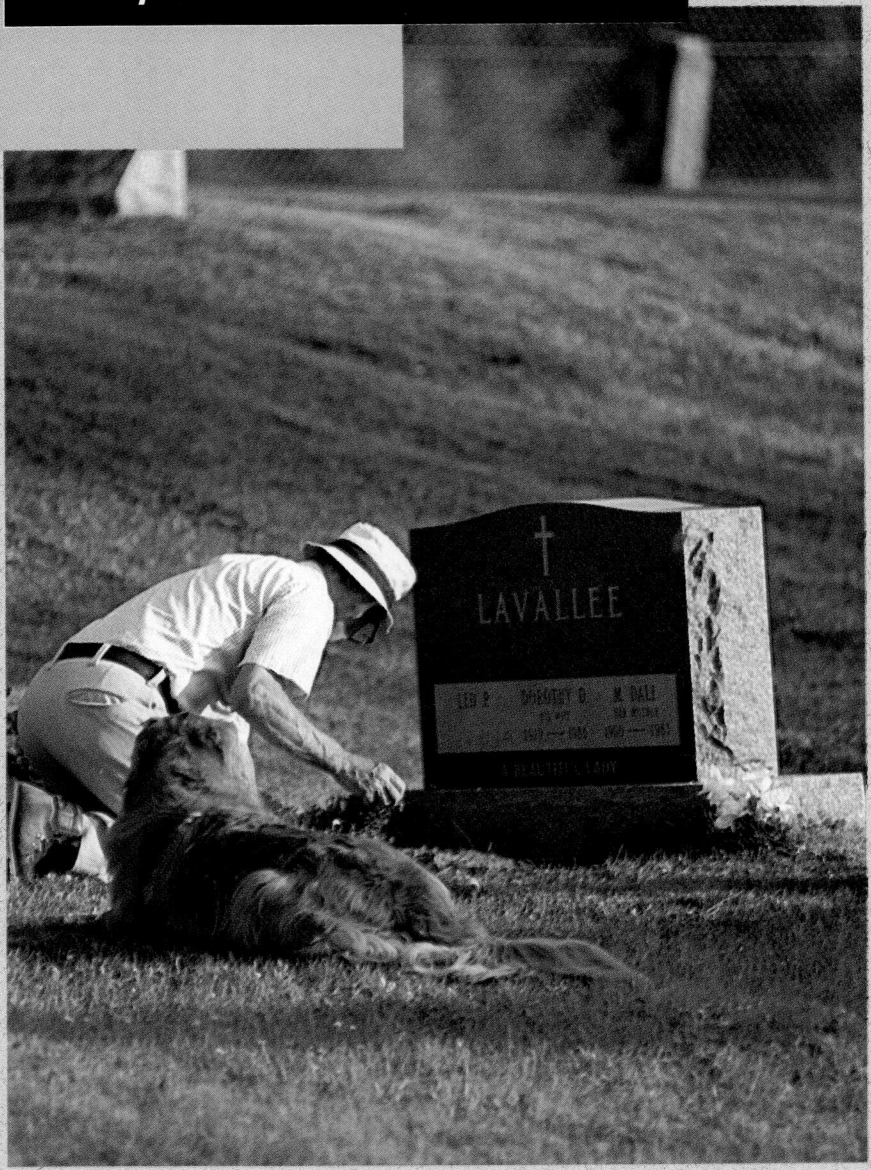

DEATH

The Dying Process

Defining Death ◆ Confronting Death ◆ Dying

The Quest for "Healthy Dying"

The Right-to-Die Movement ◆ Near-Death Experiences ◆ The Hospice Movement

Bereavement

Adjusting to the Death of a Loved One ◆ Widows and Widowers

◆

Until very recently, death has been a taboo subject in Western society, something to be kept out of sight and out of mind. Even medical schools avoided the topic of dying and death, and physicians did their best to ignore it in dealing with dying patients and their families. Indeed, some social scientists claim that the United States is a "death-denying culture." Americans stress youth, beauty, and physical fitness. Less than 25 percent have wills, and many are made uncomfortable by discussions of death. And Americans commonly isolate their terminally ill in hospitals or nursing homes.

During the past thirty years these patterns have been reversed (Feifel, 1990). With considerable truth it can be said that Western society has "rediscovered" death. An outpouring of scholarly works in sociology and psychology, television documentaries, paperback books, and feature articles in newspapers and weekly magazines have drawn attention to various aspects of the topic. The field of **thanatology**—the study of death—has grown. Simultaneously, controversy has swirled in the mass media about such matters as "the right to die," "clinical death," the death penalty, and life after death.

The Dying Process

Human societies have always given death their most elaborate and reverent attention (Ariès, 1978; 1981; Huntington & Metcalf, 1979; Kamerman, 1988; Williams, 1990). Some of the world's most gigantic constructions, its most splendid works of art, and its most elaborate rituals have been associated with death. More than 500,000 years ago, ceremonial rituals for burying the dead were being employed by Peking Man. And we still are awed by the Egyptian pyramids (witness our fascination with King Tut), the huge European burial mound of Silbury Hill, the towering Pyramid Tomb of the High Priest in the Central American Yucatan forest, the beehive tombs at Mycenae, and the burial remains of the megalithic inhabitants of northwestern Europe. The great monotheistic religions—Judaism, Christianity, and Islam—put an end to the practice of equipping the elite dead with wives, concubines, slaves, jewels, armor, and other luxuries in hopes of guaranteeing their enjoyment and comfort in the next world. However, Christianity did nothing to impede the elaboration of rituals surrounding the act of dying, mourning rituals, funeral rites, and rituals to appease and assist the souls of the departed.

Defining Death

The earliest biblical sources, as well as English common law, considered a person's ability to breathe independently to be the prime index of life. This view coincided with the physiological state of the organism. In the past, absence of spontaneous breath or heartbeat resulted in the prompt death of the brain. Conversely, destruction of the brain produced prompt cessation of respiration and circulation.

Over the past thirty-five years technological advances have rendered these traditional definitions of death obsolete. In 1962 Johns Hopkins University physicians developed a coordinated method of resuscitation by artificial ventilation, heart compression (CPR), and electric shock (defibrillation) by which many victims of cardiac arrest can be saved. Another advance has been the invention of the mechanical respirator, which sustains breathing when the brain is no longer sending out the proper signals to the lungs. Still another technological innovation has been the use of an artificial pacemaker to induce regular heartbeat after failure of the heart's own electrical conduction system. And dialysis machines prolong the lives of patients suffering kidney failure.

These life-extending technologies have compelled courts and legislatures to grapple with new definitions of death. The need for accepting brain death as one standard has now been acknowledged in most states and endorsed by the American Medical Association, the American Bar Association, and in 1981 by the President's Commission for the Study of Ethical Problems in Medicine. A series of landmark court decisions have upheld the validity of the brain-death criterion. Such cases have often involved organ transplantation (such as cornea, kidney, or heart) and have included cases of alleged murder in which organs were removed from the victims for transplantation purposes with the permission of the family. In their trials defendants have alleged that death resulted not from their violent attacks on the victims but from the removal of the organs. But the courts have invariably affirmed the pretransplantation death of the victims on the basis of brain-death criteria.

Confronting Death

In one manner or another, everyone must adapt to the fact of dying and death. Indeed, a realistic acceptance of death may well be the hallmark of emotional maturity. People differ

Confronting Death

Research shows that only a relatively small proportion of the elderly express profound fear of death. The uncertainty of the experience may be a source of concern to them, but on the whole they show less fear of death than do younger people. *(Robert Houser/Comstock)*

death as the dissolution of bodily life and the doorway to a new life, a passing into another world. Those with Western religious convictions often express the belief that in death they will be reunited with loved ones who have died. For such individuals death is seen as a transition to a better state of being. Seldom are there direct expressions that death will entail punishment. There are also people who look with resignation on death as "the end"—the cessation of being (Jeffers & Verwoerdt, 1969).

Researchers tend to agree that only a relatively small proportion of the elderly—perhaps 10 percent or less—express fear of death (Jeffers & Verwoerdt, 1969; Roark, 1989; Swenson, 1961). This is not to say that the problem of such fear does not exist for older people. As one of the elderly subjects in the Duke study put it (Jeffers & Verwoerdt, 1969, p. 170):

> No, I'm not afraid to die—it seems to me to be a perfectly normal process. But you never know how you will feel when it comes to a showdown. I might get panicky.

Generally, however, younger people show greater fear of death than those 65 and over (Riley, 1983).

Physicians who care for the elderly report that patients frequently tell them, "I am not so much afraid of death as I am of dying." A good many Americans fear painful, lonely, debilitating illness. The tormenting pain of cancer or the progressive onset of senility are paramount concerns. Of interest, over a century ago the Canadian physician Sir William Osler, in a study of

considerably, however, in the degree to which they are consciously aware of death (Marshall, 1980; Riley, 1983). Some individuals, for instance, erect formidable defenses to shield themselves from facing the necessity that they too must die. Duke University researchers studied a sample of 140 elderly persons between 60 and 94 years of age who lived in noninstitutional settings. This study found that 5 percent of the elderly denied that they ever thought about death, 25 percent indicated that they thought about it less than once a week, 20 percent said that it came to mind about once a week, and 49 percent reported that they were reminded of death in one fashion or another at least once a day (Jeffers & Verwoerdt, 1969).

Death is a highly personal matter, and its meaning tends to vary from individual to individual. The Duke University researchers found that the elderly are no exception. Some visualize

"Welcome aboard. You are now exempt from federal, state, and local taxes."

(Drawing by Bernard Schoenbaum; © 1990 The New Yorker Magazine, Inc.)

some 500 deaths, found that only 18 percent of the dying suffered physical pain and only 2 percent felt any great anxiety. Osler concluded: "We speak of death as the king of terrors, and yet how rarely the act of dying appears to be painful" (quoted by Ferris, 1991, p. 44).

Psychologist Robert N. Butler (1963, 1971) suggests that the elderly tend to take stock of their lives, to reflect and reminisce about it—a process he calls the **life review.** Often, the review proceeds silently without obvious manifestations and provides a positive force in personality reorganization. In some cases, however, it finds pathological expression in intense guilt, self-deprecation, despair, and depression. Reviewing one's life may be a response to crises of various types: for instance, retirement, the death of one's spouse, or one's own imminent death. In Butler's opinion, the life review is an important element in an individual's overall adjustment to death, a continuation of personality development right to the very end of life. In some cases the process can be expedited by having people write autobiographical accounts of their lives. They often give new meaning to people's present lives by helping them understand the past more fully (Birren, 1987). To the extent that the elderly are able to achieve a sense of lifetime integrity, competence, and continuity, the life-review process contributes to successful aging through increased self-understanding, personal meaning, self-esteem, and life satisfaction (Coleman, 1986; Lieberman & Tobin, 1983; Wong & Watt, 1991).

Various investigators report that systematic psychological changes occur before death, even several months ahead of the event, what is sometimes called "death-drop." These changes do not appear to be a simple result of physical illness. Individuals who become seriously ill and recover apparently do not exhibit similar changes. Morton Lieberman and Annie S. Coplan (1970) report, for instance, that individuals whom they later found to be a year or less away from death showed poorer cognitive performance, lower introspective orientation, and a less aggressive and more docile self-image on personality tests than did those who were three or more years away from death. A number of researchers also report a decline in measured intelligence and the complexity of information processessing for those who die within a year as compared with those who die a number of years later (Riegel & Riegel, 1972; Siegler, McCarthy & Logue, 1982; Suedfeld & Piedrahita, 1984; White & Cunningham, 1988). Psychomotor performance tests, depression scales, and self-health ratings likewise have pre-

dictive value and can alert the physician to trouble ahead (Botwinick, West & Storandt, 1978). Duke University researchers, however, have generally found less evidence of a death drop than that reported by other investigators (Palmore & Cleveland, 1976). Furthermore, a critical loss in intellectual functioning is less useful for predicting further survival for people beyond 80 years of age than for the young-old (Steuer, LaRue, Blum & Jarvik, 1981).

Dying

Sociologists observe that modern societies attempt to control death by turning over its management to large, bureaucratic organizations (De Vries, 1981; Lofland, 1978; Riley, 1983). Only a few generations ago, most people in the United States died at home. The family assumed the responsibility for laying out the corpse and otherwise preparing for the funeral. Today, the nursing home or hospital typically cares for the terminally ill and manages the crisis of dying. A mortuary establishment—euphemistically called a "home"—prepares the body and makes the funeral arrangements or undertakes the cremation (cremation is now used in about 17 percent of deaths, compared with 11 percent ten years ago). In this manner, the average person's exposure to death is minimized. The dying and the dead are segregated from others and placed with specialists for whom contact with death has become a routine and impersonal matter (Ariès, 1981; Glaser & Strauss, 1965; Kamerman, 1988). But as death becomes an increasingly foreign experience for many people, there is less opportunity for passing along the lessons of how to cope adequately with it. Neither the person who is dying nor the family and friends have the understanding necessary for dealing with the death experience in an effective manner. These trends concern many thanatologists, who point out that people are often ill equipped to do the "grief work" so essential to coming to terms with the death of a loved one. And they point out that funerals, memorial services, and other forms of grieving rites give continuity to both family and community life.

In recent years Elisabeth Kübler-Ross (1969, 1981) has contributed a good deal to the movement to restore dignity and humanity to death and to reinstate the process of dying to the full course of human life. She notes that when medical personnel and the family know that a patient is dying and attempt to hide the fact, they create a

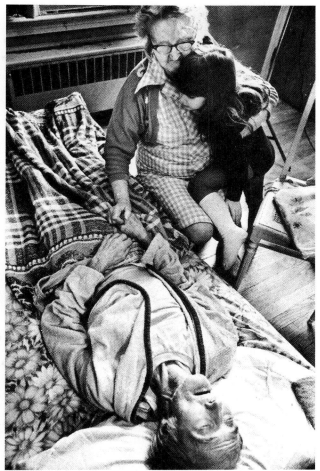

Dying at Home
For the most part people want to die at home among loved ones and surroundings that are familiar and comforting. Eighty-one-year-old Frank Tugen died at home and had the support of family members until the very end. (Mark and Dan Jury)

barrier that prevents everyone from preparing for death. Furthermore, the dying patient generally sees through the make-believe. Kübler-Ross finds that it is better for all parties if their genuine emotions are respected and allowed expression. In this fashion, dying can afford a new opportunity for personal growth. Indeed, surveys reveal that four out of five individuals would want to be told if they had an incurable disease. And today, physicians are sharing with patients and family members information as to the likely medical outcome of an illness.

Thanatologists are finding that dying, like living, is a process. While there are different styles of dying—in much the fashion that there are different styles of living—there are a number of common elements to the death experience.

Kübler-Ross (1969) has observed that dying persons typically pass through five stages. But not everyone goes through all the stages. Moreover, there can be some slipping back and forth between stages, and in some cases several stages may occur at the same time.

The first stage is one of *denial.* Individuals resist acknowledging the reality of impending death. In effect, they say "No!" to it.

Anger is the next stage. Dying people ask the question, "Why me?" They may look at the persons around them and feel envy, jealousy, and rage over their health and vigor. During this phase a dying person often makes life difficult for others, criticizing friends, family, and medical personnel with little justification.

Bargaining is the middle stage of the process. Dying individuals often begin to bargain with God, fate, or the illness itself, hoping to arrange a temporary truce. For instance, a person may say, "Just let me live long enough to attend my son's marriage," or "Allow me to get my business in order." In turn, the patient promises to be "good" or to do something constructive during his or her remaining time alive.

The "bargain" generally is successful for only a short period, since the advance of the illness itself invalidates the "agreement." This change produces a new stage, that of *depression.* Dying people begin to mourn their own approaching death, the loss of all the people and things they have found meaningful, and the plans and dreams never to be fulfilled—they experience what Kübler-Ross terms "preparatory grief."

The last stage is one of *acceptance.* The dying have by this time mourned their impending loss, and they begin to contemplate the coming of the end with a degree of quiet expectation. In most cases they are tired and quite weak. They no longer struggle against death but make their peace with it (Kübler-Ross, 1969, p. 113):

> Acceptance should not be mistaken for a happy stage. It is almost void of feelings. It is as if the pain had gone, the struggle is over, and there comes a time for "the final rest before the long journey," as one patient phrased it.

Psychologist Robert Kastenbaum (1975, p. 43) points out that although Kübler-Ross's theory has merit, it neglects certain aspects of the death process. One of the most important is the nature of the disease itself, which greatly affects pain, mobility, the length of the terminal period, and the like:

> Within the realm of cancer alone, for example, the person with head or neck cancer looks and feels

different from the person with leukemia. The person with emphysema, subject to terrifying attacks in which each breath of air requires a struggle, experiences his situation differently from the person with advanced renal failure, or with a cardiovascular trajectory [condition]. Although Kübler-Ross's theory directs welcome attention to the universal psychosocial aspects of terminal illness, we also lose much sensitivity if the disease process itself is not fully respected.

Other factors that must be considered are differences in sex, ethnic-group membership, personality, developmental level, and the death environment (a private home or a hospital). Kastenbaum believes that Kübler-Ross's stages are very narrow and subjective interpretations of the dying experience. He claims that her stages are cast with an exaggerated salience and are isolated from the total context of the individual's previous life and current circumstances. And he is concerned lest this stage approach encourage an attitude in which, for instance, medical personnel or the family are able to say, "He is just going through the anger stage," when there may be concrete, realistic factors that are arousing the patient's ire (Kastenbaum & Costa, 1977).

The Quest for "Healthy Dying"

Over the past fifteen years public and professional awareness of the dying person's experience has increased dramatically. "Death with dignity!" has become a major rallying cry. The death awareness movement asserts that a basic human right is the power to control one's own dying process. It points out that in the United States some 80 percent of those who die spend part of their final year in a nursing home or hospital, often in pain and alone. So allowing someone to die naturally often involves a team of professionals who must make a conscious decision whether to continue medical treatment (some professionals draw a distinction between ordinary and extraordinary treatment, contending that ordinary measures such as nutrition and hydration should be continued, whereas extraordinary treatment such as dialysis with a kidney machine or artificial maintenance of blood circulation may be halted if the case is hopeless). Death-with-dignity advocates insist that "aggressive" medical care—the norm that life must be maintained at all costs—prevents people from dying quickly and naturally. In a number of states they have secured the passage of laws that provide for the drawing up of *living wills*—legal documents that give an individual the right to refuse "heroic measures" to prolong his or her life in the event of terminal illness. Recent developments, including the considerable sales of a do-it-yourself suicide manual (Derek Humphry's 1991 book, *Final Exit*) and widespread fascination with a suicide machine invented by a Michigan doctor (Dr. Jack Kevorkian), suggest that some Americans want still more control at the end of life (Rosenthal, 1991; Shapiro, 1991). Let us consider, then, the right-to-die movement.

The Right-to-Die Movement

Among some segments of the U.S. population, the quest for "healthy dying" has become a consumer demand (see the boxed insert dealing with living wills). Public opinion surveys show that eight of ten Americans believe patients should be allowed to die under some circumstances, and about half say some incurably ill people have the moral right to commit suicide. Only 15 percent say that doctors and nurses should always do everything possible to save a patient's life. Fifty-nine percent would want their doctors to stop administering life-sustaining treatment if they had a terminal illness and were encountering a great deal of physical pain. Significantly, a third of adult Americans can imagine themselves taking the life of a loved one who was suffering terribly from a terminal illness. Only four in ten adults would like to live to be 100 years old, and half emphatically tell pollsters that they do *not* want to live that long (Times Mirror Center for the People and the Press, 1990). Much criticism is currently leveled at how modern technology is applied to the terminally ill. According to this view, too much is done for too long a period at too high a cost, all at the expense of basic human considerations and sensitivities. The terminally ill, it is charged, become the property of health care institutions, which override individual autonomy and personhood. Indeed, modern medicine has come to be seen by some as the enemy rather than the friend of the terminally ill.

The medical profession responds to these criticisms by pointing out that physicians have a problem in deciding what medical measures they should undertake. At times, patients and their families are so distraught and frightened that they will not or cannot say what they want done. Furthermore, physicians have often withheld antibiotics from terminally ill and senile patients who develop respiratory infections. In one study researchers at George Washington University Medical Center in Washington, D.C., examined "do not resuscitate" (DNR) orders at thirteen American hospitals (the orders—signed by patients or relatives—say doctors should not try to revive a terminally ill patient when death is imminent or inevitable). They found that 39 percent of patients who died in intensive care had DNR orders and 94 percent of patients who had DNR orders died in the hospital *(Journal of the American Medical Association,* January 17, 1986). In another study researchers checked the treatment or nontreatment provided for 190 patients in nine Seattle convalescent homes (Altman, 1979). Most of the patients were over 60 years old and had developed fevers indicative of an infection. Presumably, the fevers could have been treated with a simple course of antibiotics, and 109 of the patients were so treated. However, the other 81 did not receive antibiotic therapy, and 48 of them subsequently died from the infection (many of the patients were terminally ill with cancer). The researchers concluded that in most of these 81 cases nontreatment was a deliberate decision on the part of the nurses and physicians. They also noted that it is the nurses who shoulder much of the responsibility for making such decisions—they may decide not to call the physician after the onset of fever, or they may influence the physicians to opt for nontreatment. Significantly, the American Hospital Association estimates that fully 70 percent of the 6,000 deaths occurring in the United States every day are somehow timed or negotiated by patients, families, and doctors who arrive at a private consensus not to do all that they can do and instead allow a dying patient to die (Malcolm, 1990).

A taboo has long operated to silence medical personnel who have sped up the death of an incurably ill patient or helped such individuals commit suicide. When pressed on the issue, the medical profession typically concedes that throughout history some physicians have helped their patients end their own lives. In recent years, a number of physicians have publicly confided that they have sped up the death of an incurably ill patient or helped such individuals commit suicide. They have injected overdoses of narcotics or written prescriptions for drugs potent enough to end their patients' suffering (Altman, 1991*a,* 1991*b,* 1991*c).* In addition, when *Nursing Life* magazine surveyed nurses on ethical dilemmas, 8 percent admitted to giving overdoses of narcotics to dying patients intentionally (Maloney, 1983).

Some of the most painful decisions physicians confront concern newborns. With today's neonatal technology about half the infants born weighing 750 grams (1 pound 10 ounces) can be saved. However, there is a high risk that they will experience serious physical or mental handicaps. Another dilemma concerns infants with Down's syndrome, a form of severe mental retardation (see Chapter 3). Some 25 percent of such babies have a life-threatening complication, such as a blockage of the intestinal tract or a heart defect, that requires surgical correction. A somewhat similar issue is posed by newborns with *meningomyelocele,* a condition in which the spinal cord is deformed and protrudes outside the body. If untreated by surgery, infants develop a spinal infection and die; if treated, they often suffer paralysis and incontinence. All these cases entail decisions as to whether severely handicapped infants should be treated so that they can survive.

The American Medical Association said in 1986 that doctors could ethically withhold "all means of life-prolonging medical treatment," including food and water, from patients in irreversible comas even if death were not imminent. The withholding of such therapy should occur only when a patient's coma "is beyond doubt irreversible and there are adequate safeguards to confirm the accuracy of the diagnosis." Although the opinion of the 271,000-member association did not make such an action mandatory for doctors, it did open the way for them to withdraw life-prolonging treatment with less fear of being taken to court and to use the opinion as a defense if they are challenged. While technological developments continue to outpace the nation's legal framework, the overall trend seems to be toward basing decisions less on strictly legalistic interpretations regarding specific treatments and more on balancing benefits on a case-by-case basis (Malcolm, 1986). The debate on these issues has spread to the treatment of patients with acquired immune deficiency syndrome, a matter discussed in the boxed insert (on page 600).

Probably most controversial of all is the issue of **euthanasia,** or "mercy killing." As noted earlier in the chapter, surveys reveal a substantial turnaround in recent years in public opinion approving of euthanasia (Louis Harris and Associates, 1987). However, most religious groups maintain their traditional opposition to the practice. For example, the Roman Catholic Church has periodically reaffirmed its condemnation of euthanasia, although stating that individuals in certain circumstances have the right to renounce

Stress as a Cause of Illness and Death

Because of the reduction in deaths from birth defects and from infectious and contagious diseases, life expectancy at birth in the United States has increased from forty-five years in 1900 to over seventy-five years today. With this advance in age has come an increase in the relative incidence of deaths attributed to diseases suspected of being related in one fashion or another to stress—diseases of the heart, cerebrovascular diseases (chiefly stroke), and cancer.

Virtually every ill that befalls the body—from the common cold to diabetes to heart disease and cancer—can be influenced, positively or negatively, by stress (in Chapter 15 we examined the relationship between stress and heart disease). Animal and human studies show that stress reactions can depress the immune system, setting the stage for a variety of ills (Felten & Olschowka, 1987; Jemmott & Locke, 1984; Laudenslager, 1988; O'Leary, 1990). Researchers in Pittsburgh and Britain have found that high levels of psychological stress can nearly double a person's chances of catching a cold by lowering the individual's resistance to viral infection (Brody, 1991). In another study examining the relationship between stress and illness, Richard H. Rahe (1968) asked 2,500 officers and enlisted men aboard three U.S. Navy cruisers to report their life changes and histories for the previous six months. He then followed the men's health over the next six months through their shipboard medical records. In the first month at sea those men who were judged to be in a high-risk category by virtue of the stressful events they had experienced in the preceding six months had nearly 90 percent more first illnesses than those men who were in a low-risk category.

Other research also points to a relationship between situational factors associated with stress and the onset and course of disease. For instance, otherwise healthy men show a significant decline in lymphocyte (disease-fighting cells) functions within a month or two of the death of their wives from breast cancer (Schleifer, Keller, McKegney & Stein, 1980). Similarly, herpes patients who are depressed suffer significantly more recurrences of the disease, and these depressed people also have much lower immune-cell function than optimistic people (Elias, 1985a). And West Point cadets who have high motivation and overachieving fathers but do poor academic work are more likely than other cadets to develop clinical symptoms of infectious mononucleosis (Kasl, Evans & Neiderman, 1979). Additionally, stress may play a role in the onset and course of cancers in animals and humans (Laudenslager, Ryan, Drugan, Hyson & Maier, 1983; Levy, 1982; Sklar & Anisman, 1981).

Moreover, circumstances of extreme stress, such as that experienced by torture victims, can contribute to long-term mental and neurologic symptoms, including impaired memory, anxiety, depression, sleep disturbances, and sexual dysfunction. In many cases torture victims reveal irreversible brain damage associated with cerebral atrophy (Jensen et al., 1982; Rasmussen & Lunde, 1980).

Not all individuals, however, develop chronic diseases or psychiatric disorders after exposure to stressful conditions (Cohen & Williamson, 1991; Dohrenwend & Dohrenwend, 1974; Rabkin & Struening, 1976). The psychiatrist Richard W. Hudgens (1974, p. 119) notes:

> We should remember that most people do not become severely disabled psychiatrically when terrible things happen to them, and that those who do become disabled regain their equilibrium in a reasonably short time.

Thus, conditions other than stress also need to

extraordinary and burdensome life-support systems.

A number of converging concerns and attitudes have prompted the right-to-die movement. For one thing, Americans tend to favor a quick transition between life and death. But this belief that "the less dying, the better" has come up against an altered biomedical technology, in which people are increasingly approaching death through a "lingering trajectory." Many people also have a profound fear of being held captive in a state between life and death—as "vegetables" sustained entirely by life-support equipment. Coupled with these concerns is a pervasive nonacceptance and intolerance of pain—the growing expectation that one should be without pain and discomfort in the ordinary course of life. Increasing numbers of Americans have become dependent on aspirin and other analgesics for the control of even relatively minor discomfort.

The "healthy dying" quest has led some thanatologists to expound on the "good," "accept-

Religious Healing

Many societies assign responsibility for the treatment of illness to faith healers and shamans, individuals who work with supernatural power. Modern medicine is taking a closer and more sympathetic look at folk healers such as the !Kung shaman in South Africa who places his arms around a patient in a healing trance (left). Although folk medicine has generated much skepticism, people who believe they are victims of an evil spirit not only think they are ill but are ill. So they often respond to the supernatural entreaties of traditional healers. Faith healing is not uncommon in the United States (right). (left, Irven DeVore/Anthro-Photo; right, James R. Rolland/Stock, Boston)

be considered when studying illness (Cohen & Williamson, 1991; DeLongis, Folkman & Lazarus, 1988; Kamarck & Jennings, 1991). For this reason, the purely biological model of disease based on the notion "one germ, one disease, and one therapy" is recognized as much too simplistic (Krantz, Grunberg & Baum, 1985; Miller, 1983). A more complex and holistic model is winning acceptance, one that draws attention to the interactions among biological, social, and psychological factors that produce illness (see Figure 21-1). Apparently, conditions are optimal for illness when there is (1) a preexisting biological susceptibility to a given disorder, such as diabetes, (2) the presence of a disease agent, (3) a stress that an individual perceives to be a stress, and (4) an inability to cope with or adapt to the stressful conditions (Hinkle, 1974; Jemmott & Locke, 1984; Rabkin & Struening, 1976).

able," or "self-actualized" death (Kastenbaum, 1979). According to this view, it is not sufficient that death be reasonably free of pain and trauma. Instead, it is argued, individuals suffering a terminal illness should be able to select the particular style of exit that they believe to be consistent with their total lifestyle—for example, a romantic death, a brave death, or a death that integrates and confirms the person's unique identity. More than a decade has passed since the *New York Times* startled many of its readers with the story of Jo Roman, a 62-year-old artist with terminal cancer, who took her own life with an overdose of Seconal after gathering intimates around her for a "last day." With her family and friends she completed a "life-sculpture" that consisted of a coffinlike pine box containing photograph albums, scrapbooks, paintings, and other cherished items, and drank champagne toasts in a rite of farewell (Johnston, 1979).

A number of physicians have cautioned that the current preoccupation with the issues of pa-

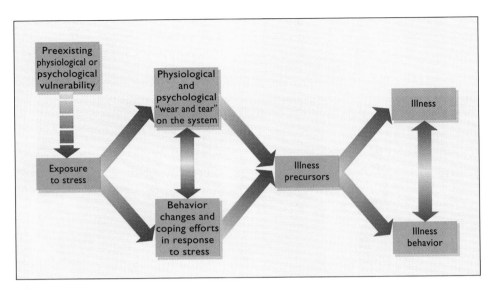

Figure 21-1   The Relationship Between Stress and Illness

As viewed in this model, exposure to stress can produce not only changes in a person's physical and psychological condition but also changes in behavior as the person tries to cope with the stress. These changes influence one another, as the two-way arrow shows. Both types of changes can produce precursors (early signs and symptoms) of illness: The outcome may be that the person not only becomes ill but also acts ill (for instance, stays home in bed, and so avoids the sources of stress). The two-way arrow indicates that illness and illness behavior can likewise influence each other. SOURCE: Shelley E. Taylor, *Health Psychology*, McGraw-Hill, 1991, p. 191. Reprinted with permission of McGraw-Hill, Inc.

tient autonomy and death with dignity can lead doctors and patients to make clinically inappropriate decisions. They warn of the perils of taking patients at their word. Depressed patients are particularly likely to tell doctors that they do not wish to live any longer and to ask that they be allowed to die. David L. Jackson and Stuart Youngner (1979) have described several cases they encountered in the intensive-care unit at University Hospital of Cleveland. In one case an 80-year-old man with chronic lung disease said he did not want to be kept alive by a respirator. However, he later changed his mind. The case, they said (1979, p. 407), shows that

> one must be cautious not to act precipitously on the side of the patient's ambivalence with which one agrees, while piously claiming to be following the principle of patient autonomy.

A 56-year-old woman with cancer urged her doctors to do all they could to help her because she wanted to live long enough to see the birth of her first grandchild. When her condition worsened and she lost consciousness, her family requested that treatment be terminated. But the attending physicians refused, and the woman recovered sufficiently to go home and share the

birth of her granddaughter, as well as Thanksgiving, Christmas, and New Year's Day.

Jackson and Youngner (1979, pp. 407–408) conclude:

> Our purpose is not to refute the importance of patient autonomy or discredit the more complex concept of death with dignity. Rather, we . . . [attempt] to provide a specific clinical perspective that may help clarify the difficult and often conflicting factors underlying the decisions made daily at the bedsides of critically ill patients. . . . We must continue to emphasize our professional responsibility for thorough clinical investigation and the exercise of sound judgment. Living up to this responsibility can only enhance the true autonomy and dignity of our patients.

In 1983 a presidential commission proposed that decisions on whether to continue life-sustaining medical treatment be generally left to mentally competent patients. Family members would be permitted to make similar decisions for mentally incompetent patients. But the commission said that the ending of a patient's life intentionally could not be sanctioned on moral grounds. Even so, doctors would be allowed to administer a pain-relieving drug that hastens death provided that the sole reason for giving the drug is to relieve the pain (Schmeck, 1983*b).* In a related development an increasing number of states have enacted "living will" laws that afford protection against dehumanized dying and confer immunity upon physicians and hospital personnel who comply with a patient's wishes.

Near-Death Experiences

The theme of "a beautiful death" has been linked by some with belief in a life hereafter. The "life-after-life" movement claims scientific evidence of a spiritual existence beyond death. In some cases persons pronounced clinically dead but then resuscitated by medical measures have provided stories of having left their bodies and undergone otherworldly experiences. The experiences are commonly precipitated by a medical illness, a traumatic accident, a surgical operation, childbirth, or drug ingestion. An estimated 20 to 40 percent of people who survive a brush with death report a near-death experience (Irwin, 1985; Ring, 1984).

The "typical" report runs along the following lines (Greyson & Stevenson, 1980; Irwin, 1985; Osis & Haraldsson, 1977; Ring, 1984): The dying individuals watch, as spectators from a few yards above their bodies, the resuscitation efforts being made to save them. Then, about a third report passing through a tunnel and entering some unearthly realm. Half say they see guides or the spirits of departed relatives, a religious figure, or a "being of light." At some point many individuals find themselves approaching a sort of border, seemingly representing the divide between earthly and next-worldly life. But they cannot cross the divide. They find they must go back to earth, for the time of their death has not yet arrived. They resist turning back, for they are overwhelmed by intense feelings of joy and peace. In some manner they are then reunited with their physical body and they live. In many cases a near-death experience serves as a catalyst for spiritual awakening and development in the months and years following the episode. Many individuals develop firmer beliefs in God and an afterlife, become less materialistic and more spiritual, feel a greater concern for other people, and spend more time searching for the meaning of life (Ring, 1984).

Skeptics such as the psychologist Ronald K. Siegel (1981) suggest that the visions reported by dying people are virtually identical to the descriptions given by individuals experiencing hallu-cinations. For example, persons who undergo drug-induced hallucinations often report hearing voices and seeing bright lights and tunnel imagery. The episodes, Siegel says, derive from intense arousal of the central nervous system and disorganization of the brain's normal information-processing procedures. A gradual loss of oxygen by the nerve cells of the brain may induce such mental states. A related interpretation holds that at death various forces combine to sever the connections between consciousness and somatic processes while the brain remains active. Dying people, aware that they are dying, may turn their thoughts to the possibility of reuniting with loved ones and the broader meaning of life. And experiences of intense joy, profound insight, and love may be produced by endorphins (molecules that act as both neurotransmitters and hormones) that were designed in the course of evolution to blot out overwhelming pain (Irwin, 1985).

Another skeptic, the psychologist Robert Kastenbaum (1977), suggests that the current fascination with "life after life" is simply another "mind trip." He cites cases of heart-attack victims who, when pronounced clinically dead and then resuscitated, have no recollection of an out-of-body experience. And he tells of people in respiratory failure (choking on a bone or undergoing an acute episode of emphysema) who later report feeling as though they had been in direct hand-to-hand combat with death. Kastenbaum (1977, p. 33) expresses concern lest death be "romanticized" and cautions:

> Death seems to be less demanding, perhaps more friendly, than life. . . . I do not believe the frustrated adolescent, the unemployed worker, the grieving widow or the ailing old person needs to be offered the invitation to suicide on quite so glittering a silver platter.

Hence, considerable controversy surrounds what is actually involved in various near-death experiences (Greyson & Flynn, 1984).

The Hospice Movement

In medieval times a hospice was a place where sick and weary travelers could seek comfort and care before continuing on their journey. The **hospice** of today likewise provides comfort and care, but with the knowledge that the recipients are nearing the end of their life's journey—that they are dying. The approach is modeled after the system in operation since 1967 at St. Christopher's Hospice in England. It entails a variety of

AIDS: A Plague Mentality?

AIDS (acquired immune deficiency syndrome) has become an obsession among many Americans, leading to a plague mentality in some quarters. Parents have withdrawn their youngsters from school upon learning that a classmate has AIDS; they have even evicted from the community families whose children are infected by the AIDS virus. Adults with AIDS have been denied jobs, housing, schooling, dental care, health services, and insurance; those with jobs are often harassed and threatened by coworkers. The stigma of AIDS has taken on an irrational life of its own—even people who know that the disease is not spread casually engage in discriminatory acts (Barringer, 1991; Hilts, 1990). Nor does a clean bill of health necessarily place a person beyond suspicion: An insurance company refused a policy to a Colorado man who voluntarily provided the results of an AIDS test that came out negative; the company said the fact that he got tested at all made him too great a risk (Silverman, 1987). A 1987 Gallup poll found that 52 percent of American adults favor testing all Americans for AIDS; the respondents overwhelmingly favored testing immigrants seeking permanent residence, by 90 percent; members of the armed force, by 83 percent; couples applying for marriage licenses, by 80 percent; and visitors from foreign countries, by 66 percent (*New York Times*, July 13, 1987, p. 11).

AIDS has been likened to the Black Death—the plague that killed a quarter to half of Europe's population in a three-year span from 1347 to 1350. But AIDS would have to kill 60 to 120 million Americans in a three-year period to have a similar impact. And unlike the many plagues of old, AIDS does not spread through casual contact: It cannot be contracted from doorknobs, drinking glasses, toilet seats, or social kissing. But since it is a disease that can be transmitted in the course of sexual encounters, fear of contracting AIDS has had the social effect of compelling many Americans to alter their sexual practices (a 1991 survey found that half of American adults who are single and under 45 years of age say they have changed their sexual behavior because of fear of getting AIDS) (Kagay, 1991).

According to the Federal Centers for Disease Control, between 1981 and 1990, 100,777 Americans died from complications caused by AIDS. The disease is the second leading cause of death in men aged 25 to 44, surpassing heart disease, cancer, suicide, and homicide. Only accidental injuries, including auto accidents, cause more deaths among men in this age group. By mid-1991, the Centers for Disease Control reported 179,136 Americans had been diagnosed with AIDS since 1981; another 500,000 to 1 million Americans are believed to carry the AIDS virus. Although early predictions regarding the spread of AIDS were on the gloomy side, a growing number of experts (including those with the World Health Organization) now believe that the steep rise in new AIDS cases in the United States during the 1980s will level off by the mid-1990s because of a decline in infection rates and better treatment at early stages of the disease (Altman, 1991; Brookmeyer, 1991; Kolata, 1991). However, AIDS cases in Africa and Asia are expected to continue their rise beyond the year 2000 (it is currently killing up to a third of the adult population in some areas of Africa) (Chase, 1991).

During the 1980s, most AIDS cases in the United States fell into three categories: homosexual men, intravenous drug users, and hemophiliacs. About 40 percent of the nation's diagnosed AIDS cases are black and Hispanic, although these minorities make up less than a fifth of the population. Nearly half of the minority victims are heterosexuals, chiefly intravenous drug users or their sex partners. The inequality is even more striking among babies: Black babies are 25 times more likely to get the disease than are white babies (Kolata, 1991; Levine, 1987b; Pearl, 1990). Even at present levels, AIDS cases threaten to swamp the nation's health care system with immense costs and a sizable caseload of slowly dying patients (overall, federal authorities estimate that about 40 percent of all AIDS patients will eventually be without means or insurance and will thus depend on Medicaid to pay physicians and hospitals) (Chase, 1987; Edmondson, 1990).

Scientists have learned a good deal about how the AIDS virus infects cells. But efforts to devise a vaccine or a treatment have been complicated by the fact that AIDS is caused by dozens of strains of the virus, and each virus mutates frequently. Urban problems of poverty, housing, homelessness,

programs designed to afford an alternative to conventional hospital care for the terminally ill, especially cancer patients.

The hospice takes a positive attitude toward dying. It does not discontinue such medical treatments as chemotherapy and radiation when they are conducive to the comfort of the patient. But the emphasis falls on "comfort-care" rather than on attempts to prolong life. Comfort-care involves an aggressive treatment of symptoms, both phys-

Mysterious and Incurable Diseases Often Foster a Plague Mentality
During the terrible Black Death that swept Europe in the fourteenth century, thousands of Jews were massacred in countless communities because gentiles blamed them for the disease. The painting depicts Jews being burned to death. *(The Granger Collection)*

drug abuse, and racism make prevention and treatment even more difficult (Perrow & Guillen, 1990). At present, education is the nation's lone "vaccine." Consequently, a panel of scientists assembled by the prestigious Institute of Medicine of the National Academy of Sciences has recommended a massive national educational campaign centering on two precepts. First, random sex of any sort is dangerous (when a person engages in a sexual act, the person is not just sexually connected with that partner; he or she is sexually connected to everybody that partner has had sexual relations with in the past ten years). Second, all sex outside monogamous relationships with well-known partners should be accompanied by the use of a condom. Significantly, the panel of distinguished scientists rejected ideas for a massive national quarantine program or mandatory blood testing to detect the AIDS virus. The panel argued that those in high-risk groups were not likely to comply with quarantine or mandatory screening programs and that it would be neither ethical nor

in keeping with American civil liberties to compel them to do so. Indeed, the number of exposed people in some cities is already so high that a quarantine would be impractical (Church, 1986; Hilts, 1991; Musto, 1987).

Some Americans worry that the nation is losing perspective in its concern with AIDS. In 1988 the federal government spent $800 million for AIDS education, testing, and research. Yet in the same year federal spending on schizophrenia came to about $30 million, less than 4 percent of the $800 million for AIDS. Schizophrenia afflicts some 1.5 million Americans, a large number of whom are still young and perhaps 10 percent of whom will commit suicide. Although few deny that AIDS is a horrible disease that deserves a high ranking on the list of national concerns, there are those who contend that the suffering and needs of other Americans should not be overlooked in the nation's preoccupation with AIDS (Freundlich, 1990; Smith, 1987a).

ical and emotional, through the use of counseling, antidepressive medications, and high-dose morphine preparations (designed to free patients from the severe and recurrent pain that frequently accompanies terminal cancer).

Most hospice programs are centered about care of the dying person at home. Mary A. Cooke, hospice director at Manhattan's Cabrini Medical Center, says:

Hospice

A hospice provides comfort and care for terminally ill patients. Here a granddaughter spends time with her grandfather in a hospice setting. *(Joel Gordon)*

They don't want to be institutionalized; they want to be at home. Our emphasis is on helping the family take care of the patient. (Quoted in Freudenheim, 1983, p. 8)

Visiting physicians, nurses, social workers, and volunteers provide emotional and spiritual assistance as well as medical care. In a developing trend a number of hospitals and nursing homes have established hospicelike care units. Some hospices have facilities where patients may be admitted for short periods of treatment. Here, visiting hours are maintained round the clock, rigid rules are avoided, and personal effects and pets are permitted. But the hospice is not so much a place as it is a program or a mode of care. It seeks to give dying patients greater independence and control over their lives rather than surrendering themselves to the care of impersonal bureaucratic organizations. Consequently, the services can be quite personal. One hospice had a client whose one wish was to walk again, and so the hospice arranged for a physical therapist who helped the man regain his ability to walk. Another client wanted to make a last trip to Hawaii, and the hospice set it up (Walters, 1991). In sum, the hospice movement undertakes to restore dignity to death.

Advocates of the hospice approach say that it is difficult for physicians and nurses taking care of patients in hospital settings to accept the inevitability of death. Hospitals are geared to curing illness and prolonging life. An incurable case is an embarrassment, evidence of medical failure. Consequently, hospice proponents say, an alternative-care arrangement is required that accepts the inevitability of death and provides for the needs of the dying and their families. Hospice programs hope to make dying less emotionally traumatic for both patient and loved ones. Indeed, much effort is directed toward helping family members face the problems that surround terminal illness. And a bereavement follow-up service maintains contact with the family in the period following the loved one's death. Most major health insurance plans, including Medicare, now cover virtually the entire cost of treatment in hospices that meet standards set by the U.S. Department of Health and Human Services (Walters, 1991).

Bereavement

When a person is born, all his dear ones rejoice. When he dies they all weep. It should not be so. When a person is born, there is as yet no reason for rejoicing over him, because one knows not what kind of a person he will be by reason of his conduct, whether righteous or wicked, good or evil. When he dies there is cause for rejoicing if he departs with a good name and departs this life in peace.—The Talmud

We know for certain that there is life after death—for the relatives and friends who survive. As they go on with their lives, they must come to terms with the death of the loved one. Many types of adjustment must be made. First, there is psychological coping, often termed "grief work" (mourning, talking about, and acknowledging the loss). Second, there are numerous procedural details that must be attended to, including funeral arrangements and legal routines (dealing with attorneys, settling the estate, filing for Social Security benefits, and the like). Third, there is the social void produced by the death of a family member, which requires the revamping of life patterns and family roles (for instance, housekeeping, marketing, securing a livelihood).

Adjusting to the Death of a Loved One

It is sweet to mingle tears with tears; griefs, where they wound in solitude, wound more deeply.—SENECA

Agamemnon, first century A.D.

Bereavement is a state in which a person has been deprived of a relative or friend by death. **Grief** involves keen mental anguish and sorrow over the death of a loved one. **Mourning** refers to the socially established manner of displaying signs of sorrow over a person's death (for instance, wailing, wearing black, hanging flags at half-mast, and the like).

In *Macbeth* Shakespeare proclaims: "Give sorrow words. The grief that does not speak, whispers the o'erfraught heart and bids it break." And a Turkish proverb declares, "He that conceals his grief finds no remedy for it." Many contemporary clinicians and psychologists agree with these statements. In the process of ventilating anguished feelings, sympathetic assistance is all-important. Rather than uttering platitudes ("She lived a full life"), psychologists suggest that well-meaning individuals offer emotional support and a ready ear. Bereavement is less an intellectual process than one of coming to terms with one's feelings. A social worker who found herself "on the fringe of madness" when her husband died of a heart attack eight years earlier, leaving her with three young children, asserts: "Being strong and bucking up is a lot of baloney. You don't feel like bucking up. It is a real process that you must be allowed to go through" (Gelman, 1983, p. 120). People who receive the support and comfort of family and friends typically have a lower incidence of mental and physical disorders following bereavement. But there are exceptions. The expression of grief following the death of a loved one may be an important component in the recovery of most people. But for those whose grief encompasses an intense yearning and a high degree of dependency on the deceased person, recovery tends to be more problematic (Parkes & Weiss, 1983).

Unfortunately, cultural expectations, social values, and community practices at times interfere with necessary "grief work." Dying is left to medical technology and commonly takes place in a facility outside the home. Funerals are abbreviated and simplified, and mourning is thought of as a form of mental pathology (the cultural ideal is the self-contained widow who displays a "stiff upper lip"). Yet thanatologists say that expressions of grief and mourning rituals are therapeutic for survivors. Such traditions as the Irish *wake* and the Jewish *shivah* assist the bereaved in coming to terms with the loss and in reconstructing new life patterns through family and friends. For those with a religious commitment church organizations may provide significant support systems (Wuthnow, Christiano & Kuzlowski, 1980).

Bereavement and grief often have a considerably greater impact than is evident in the immediate short-term period following the death of a loved one. The survivor experiences a height-

Bereavement Ceremonies

Throughout the world societies have evolved funerals and other rituals to assist their members in coming to grips with the death of a loved one. The ceremonies highlight the finality of death. Here mourners in Ghana express their grief in such a ritual. *(Hector R. Acebes/Photo Researchers)*

ened vulnerability to physical illness and mental illness, even to death, especially if the bereavement is sudden and unexpected. On the whole, bereaved people show a more-than-average incidence of illness, accidents, mortality, unemployment, and other indices of a damaged life (Fenwick & Barresi, 1981; Greenblatt, 1978; Kastenbaum & Costa, 1977; Osterweis, Solomon & Green, 1984; Stroebe & Stroebe, 1983). Overall, however, the effects on psychological states, especially depression, seem considerably more serious than the effects on physical health (Murrell & Himmelfarb, 1989; Murrell, Himmelfarb & Phifer, 1988; Norris & Murrell, 1990; Perkins & Harris, 1990). Even one year after death, some 20 to 26 percent of bereaved persons are still depressed (Norris & Murrell, 1990; Zisook & Schucter, 1986). In addition, significant clinical depression at the time of a spouse's death substantially increases the risk for psychological complications during the bereavement process, and survivors of spouses who committed suicide are at even greater risk (Gilewski, Farberow, Gallagher & Thompson, 1991).

Phyliss Silverman (1983, p. 65), an authority on bereavement, has this to say about grief:

> It isn't a problem or an illness that can be solved or cured. That's why it is really inappropriate for someone to say: "You can get over this. You can recover." In fact, people can't recover in the sense of going back to the way things were. You must make changes in your life in order to go on. The death and the bereavement wizen you, weather you and make you look at life differently.

Violent and premature deaths often result in the most severe grief reactions. Suicide is one of the most difficult types of death for survivors to handle. They may have difficulty acknowledging the truth of the suicide. And even when they do, guilt and shame often impair normal mourning. They frequently feel that they are somehow to blame—for not seeing the signs and for not fulfilling the stated or unstated needs of the person who died. They also must bear the thought that the dead person did not believe they were worth living for. And guilt may be intensified if survivors experience a sense of relief after an ordeal of mental illness or of suicide threats and attempts (*The Harvard Medical School Mental Health Letter,* April 1987).

The loss of a child is also frequently associated with depression, anger, guilt, and despair; recovery can take a very long time. Parents must come to recognize the limits of their protective powers. Women who find their primary satisfactions in the mother role may feel useless without someone to care for. Guilt can be especially intense after a death from Sudden Infant Death Syndrome (see Chapter 5). And in some cases parents of children who die from cancer may find their grief intensifies during the second year. Parents who feel they did all they could do to care for a child during the final illness seem to make a more speedy recovery. Some evidence suggests that parents who chose hospital care rather than home care are more depressed, socially withdrawn, and uncomfortable afterward (*The Harvard Medical School Mental Health Letter,* March 1987).

In adult bereavement the individual typically passes through a number of phases (Greenblatt, 1978; Malinak, Hoyt & Patterson, 1979). The first phase is characterized by shock, numbness, denial, and disbelief. The most intense feelings of shock and numbness usually last several days, although the process of struggling with denial and disbelief may persist many days and even months.

The second phase entails pining, yearning, and depression. It usually reaches its peak within five to fourteen days but can continue longer. Weeping, hopeless feelings, a sense of unreality, feelings of emptiness, distance from people, lack of vigor and interest, and preoccupation with the image of the deceased are quite common during this stage. Other symptoms may include anger, irritability, fear, sleeplessness, episodes of impaired recall or concentration, lack of appetite, and weight loss. Not uncommonly, the bereaved may idealize the dead person, maintaining an element of "reverence" despite a recognition of the deceased's human faults and failings. In fact, survivors of a bad marriage may become hopelessly stuck in grief. They mourn not only for the marriage that was but also for the marriage that might have been and was not. In cases of pathological grief following the death of a spouse, three factors are typically present: an unexpected death, ambivalence regarding the marriage, and overdependence on the spouse (Parkes & Weiss, 1983). Recovery from grief seems to be quicker and more complete when a marriage was happy.

The third phase of bereavement involves emancipation from the loved one and an adjustment to the new circumstances. In this period the individual mobilizes his or her resources, attempts to become reconnected with people and activities, and seeks to establish a new equilibrium that will permit some element of satisfaction and comfort. Some people may complete the psychological and emotional work of this stage in about six to eight weeks, others in a matter of months; but for still others the process may continue for years.

The fourth phase is characterized by identity reconstruction. The person crystallizes new relationships and assumes new roles without the loved one. At this stage approximately half of the survivors report realizing some benefit or experiencing some growth from bereavement. These gains include an increased sense of self-reliance and strength, a greater caring for friends and loved ones, and a more general quickening to life and deepening appreciation of existence.

Yet people display considerable variation in how they handle the death of a loved one, their specific symptoms of grief, and the intensity and duration of the symptoms (Johnson, Lund & Dimond, 1986; Joyce, 1984; Osterweis, Solomon & Green, 1984; Zisook, Devaul & Click, 1982). The reactions cannot be neatly plotted in a series of well-defined stages, nor is the progression from the time of death to the resolution of bereavement necessarily a straight line. And although shock, anger, and depression are common reactions to loss, not everyone experiences them, no matter how deeply they cared about the person they lost. For instance, a man who lost his wife six months earlier may say he is ready to remarry, and a young mother may laugh with friends only days after the loss of her child. Between a quarter and two-thirds of those who experience the loss of a loved one do not evidence great distress. Indeed, the absence of extreme distress can be a sign of psychological strength and resilience (Goleman, 1989). New interests and strong social networks seem to promote adjustment (Goldberg, Comstock & Harlow, 1988; Krause, 1986; Norris & Murrell, 1990).

However, some aspects of "grief work" do not end for a significant proportion of bereaved individuals. They still feel themselves strongly affected by the deceased person, say they are upset on the yearly anniversary of the person's death, and experience an emotional void in their lives. Their sense of loss may overshadow other experiences, changing the way in which they interpret even positive events (the events remind them of their loss and their inability to share the experiences with the loved one) (Zautra, Reich & Guarnaccia, 1990). At unguarded moments people may stumble into "little ambushes" of grief. One widower tells of being out driving and spotting a woman with a hairstyle similar to his wife's:

I said to myself, "There's Nola." Then I laughed out loud and told myself, "How silly of me. Nola is dead."

Then my next thought was, "I must go home and tell Nola how silly I just was." It all happened in a fraction of a second. (Quoted in Gelman, 1983, p. 120)

In sum, we are increasingly coming to realize that there is not a universal prescription for how best to grieve, and that people handle grief in a great many different ways (Goleman, 1989).

Widows and Widowers

Two are better than one, because they have a good reward for their toil. For if they fall, one will lift up his fellow; but woe to him who is alone when he falls and has not another to lift him up. Again, if two lie together, they are warm; but how can one be warm alone?—ECCLESIASTES, 4:9–11

Three out of four American men 65 years old and older are married and living with their wives. This compares with one out of three women in the same age group who are married and living with their husbands. Among those over the age of 75, two-thirds of the men are living with a spouse, while less than one-fifth of the women are. Hence, women 65 and older are much more likely to be widowed than married. This situation results from the fact that the life expectancy of women tends to be seven or more years longer than that of men and from the tradition that has ordained that women marry men older than themselves (of interest, women married to men younger than themselves tend to live longer than would otherwise be expected, whereas women married to older men tend to die sooner than would be expected) (Klinger-Vartabedian & Wispe, 1989). Consequently, remarriage tends to be a male prerogative: After age 65 men remarry at a rate eight times that of women (Horn & Meer, 1987).

Of the more than 800,000 people widowed each year, some 20 to 26 percent still suffer serious depression a year or more later. Alcohol, drug, and cigarette use rise. Health problems in survivors tend to be worse among those already in poor physical or mental health, those who are alcohol or drug abusers, and those lacking a social support network. Survivors with strong social support or who remarry seem to suffer fewer health problems.

The death of a spouse seems particularly stressful for men (Osterweis, Solomon & Green, 1984). The death rate of widowers is seven times as high as among married men of comparable age. Widowers die four times as often from suicide, three times as often from motor vehicle ac-

Should You Have a Living Will?

Planning for one's death does not top most people's list of fun activities. However, a 1990 ruling on the "right to die" by the U.S. Supreme Court has caused many people to think about it. The case involved Nancy Cruzan, a 32-year-old Missouri woman who had been unconscious since a 1983 automobile accident. Her physicians afforded no hope that she would ever recover, and so her parents asked the hospital to disconnect her life-support systems (doctors had said that Ms. Cruzan could live another 30 years in her unconscious condition). Even though her parents asserted that their daughter had expressed a desire not to be kept alive after a serious injury if she could not function normally, the hospital refused the request (Schultz, 1990).

The nation's highest court said for the first time that the Constitution protects an individual's decision to refuse artificial life support. But, upholding a lower court's rejection of the parents' request, a majority of the justices said that states may require a high standard of proof of a patient's wishes (Ms. Cruzan died in December 1990, twelve days after a Missouri probate court permitted her family to stop nourishment). The Supreme Court held that when a permanently unconscious person has left no clear instructions, a state is free to carry out its interest in "the protection and preservation of human life" by denying a family's request to terminate treatment (Greenhouse, 1990).

Karen Ann Quinlan's case was the most celebrated right-to-die case before Cruzan's. In 1975, after she had been comatose for seven months, Quinlan's father asked the New Jersey Supreme Court to have her respirator turned off. The court agreed, and the U.S. Supreme Court declined to consider the case further. After the ruling, Ms. Quinlan, removed from the life-support system, lived nine more years breathing on her own. Until the Cruzan decision, a consensus had been building in medical and legal circles that patients have a major say in dictating their course of treatment. Patients and their relatives had regularly invoked the principle in deciding that extraordinary techniques not be used.

The Cruzan decision seems to hedge a person's right to refuse medical treatment (Angell, 1990). By emphasizing the need for "clear and convincing" proof of a patient's wishes, the Cruzan ruling has encouraged greater use of *living wills*—documents that you sign, date, and have witnessed which state in advance your wishes regarding life-sustaining technology and treatment when you are dying. The importance of a living will is that it allows you to state clearly and in advance your preference for treatment in the event you can no longer make your wishes known. And it removes much of the burden from family members and health-care providers faced with making difficult treatment decisions. Most states and the District of Columbia have living-will legislation, but the provisions differ from state to state (Hill & Shirley, 1990).

Although many people have drawn up living wills, there is no guarantee that doctors or other health-care workers will honor them (Miles, Singer & Siegler, 1989). Physicians often say that the instructions are unclear and that they are hesitant to withhold life-prolonging treatment on the strength of a piece of paper. Most living wills simply indicate that the bearer does not want heroic measures taken in the case of terminal illness, but they do not speak to specific circumstances and hence are subject to interpretation. So some legal and medical experts suggest that you also need another document, a health care proxy, in which you designate a surrogate who has legal authority to make medical decisions in the event you are incapacitated and unable to offer an opinion. The living will and health care proxy can be combined in a variety of ways. The Federal Patient Self-Determination Act, which took effect in 1990, requires hospitals and nursing homes to advise patients in writing of their right to refuse treatment (Rosenthal, 1991).

Many physicians complain that they are not

---

cidents, and six times as often from heart disease. But note that over half of all men between 46 and 65 who are widowed remarry, and substantial numbers remarry beyond the age of 65 (there are nine bridegrooms to every bride over the age of 65). Since healthy widowers presumably remarry relatively rapidly, the statistics showing higher mortality among the widowed may apply primarily to the less healthy widowers (Cleveland & Gianturco, 1976; Greenberg, 1981b).

One problem confronted by widowers is that men are not supposed to feel emotion and pain and say, "I need help." By virtue of this cultural dictate, men traditionally have had difficulty expressing emotion. Furthermore, many have trouble cooking and caring for themselves. They

Is There a Right to Die?
The daughter of Joseph and Joyce Cruzan of Missouri (pictured above) was one of 10,000 Americans in comalike conditions, unable to communicate and with no chance of recovering. The notion that the critically ill have a constitutional right to die has infuriated activists in the right-to-life movement. In recent years they have expanded their anti-abortion stance to include opposition to right-to-die policies. *(API/Wide World Photos)*

lawyers and do not know whether the documents they are provided are correctly executed, whether the patient has changed his or her mind, and whether the statement is understood in the same way as medical personnel do (for instance, the definition of "terminally ill"). These physicians say that life-and-death questions are best left to their practical judgment and that it is their job to "know when to try and when to quit." So some doctors caution, "No living will or advance directive entirely takes the place of dealing with a doctor you know and trust" (Alper, 1991, A10; also see Winslow, 1991).

develop poor eating habits, which, together with other poor health practices—as well as feelings of loneliness and emptiness—often leads to heavy drinking, sleeplessness, and chronic ailments. Overall, U.S. men seem to have a more difficult time living alone than do women, and they are far less likely to receive help from others (Coombs, 1991; Hyman, 1983).

Our knowledge regarding widows is substantially greater than that about widowers, largely owing to research by sociologist Helena Znaniecki Lopata (1973, 1981). The women studied by Lopata lived in metropolitan Chicago and were interviewed by the National Opinion Research Center. Lopata was able to distinguish three categories of widows on the basis of the extent of their involvement in different types of social relationships.

At one extreme were women—primarily better educated and belonging to the middle class—who were strongly involved in the role of wife when their husbands were still alive. They built many other roles on the husband's presence as a person, a father, and a partner in leisure-time activities. There was a strong tendency for these women to idealize the late husband, often to the point of sanctification (also see Futterman, Gallagher, Thompson, Lovett & Gilewski, 1990). At the other extreme were women—primarily lower- or working-class and living in black or ethnic neighborhoods—who belonged to sex-segregated worlds and were immersed in kin, neighboring, or friendship relationships with other women. Between these two extremes were women who led multidimensional lives in which the husband was involved in only part of the total set of relations. The adjustments confronting the women tended to vary with the degree to which their social relationships revolved about or were integrated with those of their husbands.

The main conclusion that Lopata drew from her data was that the higher the women's education and socioeconomic class, the more disor-

ganized her self-identity and life became with her husband's death—but by the same token, the more resources she had to form a new lifestyle once her "grief work" was accomplished. Other research has suggested that the negative long-term consequences of widowhood seem to derive from socioeconomic deprivation rather than from widowhood itself (Balkwell, 1981; Bound, Duncan, Laren & Oleinick, 1991; Burkhauser, Holden & Feaster, 1988; Norris & Murrell, 1990).

Of considerable interest, Lopata found that about half of the widows lived entirely alone, and most of these women said they much preferred to do so. Only 10 percent had moved in with their married children. One reason this figure was so low is that the widows cherished their independence, which they did not wish to jeopardize by giving up their own homes and moving into an unfamiliar network of relations. Furthermore, the widows anticipated problems in their role as mothers of grown-up children. They said that if they could not criticize or speak up, they would feel inhibited, but that if they did speak up, their children would become upset. They regarded their relationships with grandchildren as presenting similar problems.

SUMMARY

1. Until very recently, death has been a taboo topic in Western society. During the past twenty-five years, however, this pattern has been reversed. Indeed, considerable controversy swirls about such matters as the right to die, clinical death, the death penalty, and life after death.

2. The earliest biblical sources, as well as English common law, considered a person's ability to breathe independently the prime index of life. Over the past twenty-five years technological advances have rendered this traditional definition of death obsolete. Such advances have included methods to resuscitate victims of cardiac arrest, mechanical respirators, and artificial heart pacemakers. A growing acceptance in medical and legal circles of the need for an additional criterion of death has resulted in a legal definition that includes the absence of spontaneous brain function.

3. A realistic acceptance of death may well be the hallmark of emotional maturity. People differ considerably, however, in the degree to which they are consciously aware of and think about death. Furthermore, death is a highly personal

matter, and its meaning tends to vary from individual to individual. Researchers agree that only a relatively small proportion of the elderly express a fear of death.

4. Elisabeth Kübler-Ross identifies five stages through which dying persons typically pass: denial, anger, bargaining, depression, and acceptance.

5. Over the past fifteen years public and professional awareness of the dying person's experience has increased dramatically. "Death with dignity!" has become a major rallying cry. The death awareness movement asserts that a basic human right is the power to control one's own dying process. Much criticism is currently leveled at the way modern technology is applied to the terminally ill. According to this view, too much is done for too long a period at too high a cost, all at the expense of basic human considerations and sensitivities.

6. In some cases persons pronounced clinically dead but then resuscitated by medical measures have provided stories of having left their bodies and undergone otherworldly experiences. Some individuals have interpreted such

experiences as scientific evidence of a spiritual existence beyond death. Skeptics rejoin that the visions reported by dying people are hallucinations associated with the intense arousal of the central nervous system and the disorganization of normal brain functioning.

7. The hospice approach entails a variety of programs that are designed to afford an alternative to conventional hospital care for the terminally ill, especially cancer patients. The emphasis of the movement falls on "comfort-care" rather than on attempts to prolong life. Comfort-care involves an aggressive treatment of symptoms, both physical and emotional, through the use of counseling, antidepressive medications, and high-dose morphine preparations. Most hospice programs are centered about care of the dying person at home.

8. Bereavement and grief have a considerably greater impact than is evident in the immediate short-term period following the death of a loved one. The survivor experiences a heightened vulnerability to physical and mental illness, even to death. In adult bereavement the individual typically passes through a number of phases. The first phase is characterized by shock, numbness, denial, and disbelief. The second phase entails pining, yearning, and depression. The third phase involves emancipation from the loved one and an adjustment to the new circumstances. The fourth phase is characterized by identity reconstruction.

9. Women 65 and over are much more likely to be widowed than married. The difficulty women have in adjusting to widowhood tends to vary with the degree to which their social relationships revolved about or were integrated with those of their husbands.

KEY TERMS

Bereavement A state in which a person has been deprived of a relative or friend by death.

Euthanasia Mercy killing; putting to death painlessly an individual suffering from an incurable and painful disease.

Grief Keen mental anguish and sorrow over the death of a loved one.

Hospice A program or mode of care that seeks to make dying less painful and emotionally traumatic for both patient and loved one.

Life Review A process in which the elderly take stock of their lives, reflecting and reminiscing about them.

Mourning The socially established manner of displaying signs of sorrow over a person's death (for instance, wailing, wearing black, hanging flags at half-mast, and the like).

Thanatology The study of death.

APPENDIX A:
GENETICS AND
HEREDITY

n response to the diverse needs of instructors, we have placed detailed biological information about genetics and heredity in this Appendix. While some professors maintain that this material is crucial to students in the introductory human development course, others feel that it is only necessary for reference. We hope that the Appendix format solves this problem and meets the needs of all current and future users of the Fifth Edition. The following material can be used to supplement the text's existing coverage of the biological foundations of human development (which can be found in Chapter 3). It provides students with important information about the study of genetics and heredity—from its fascinating historical origins to current day issues and problems.

Genetics and Heredity

Chromosomes ◆ Genes ◆ Dominance ◆ Mendel's Principles

Determination of Sex ◆ Linked Characteristics ◆ Chromosomal Abnormalities

Incomplete Dominance ◆ Penetrance and the Norm of Reaction

◆

Genetics and Heredity

All of us begin life as a single fertilized cell. Fertilization is the major event determining our biological inheritance. The zygote contains all the hereditary material that bridges the generations. Precisely blue-printed in this original cell are the 200 billion or so cells that we possess nine months later at birth. The scientific study of biological inheritance is termed **genetics.**

Chromosomes

Around the turn of the twentieth century the study of cellular tissue with microscopes led to the discovery of chromosomes. **Chromosomes** are long, threadlike bodies that contain the hereditary materials found in the nuclei of all cells. Chromosomes are normally invisible under ordinary light microscopes. During cell division, however, they coil into thicker bodies and can be seen more easily, particularly if a cell is killed and stained with dyes.

Upon fertilization the twenty-three chromosomes of the ovum are combined with the twenty-three chromosomes of the sperm, bringing the total number of chromosomes to forty-six, or twenty-three pairs (see Figure 1). In the formation of most of the cells of the body (somatic cells), a cell division termed *mitosis* occurs. Each single chromosome splits lengthwise to form a new pair.

Through this process a cell divides into two daughter cells identical to the original one (see Chapter 4).

In reproduction a new individual arises from the fusion of two cells, an ovum and a sperm; therefore, the distribution of the chromosomes cannot occur in the usual manner. Meiosis solves this problem. **Meiosis** involves two cell divisions, during which the chromosome number is halved.

Suppose, for example, that a gamete had one pair of chromosomes. When a sperm and an ovum fused at the time of fertilization, the resulting zygote would have two pairs of chromosomes—a double dose. In the next generation the already doubled number would double again, making four pairs. Since the number would double in each generation, cells would soon contain an astronomical amount of hereditary material. Even the addition of one chromosome to the standard forty-six can lead to disaster, a topic considered later in the chapter.

So that disaster does not occur and so that the constant number or chromosomes is maintained, the total number of chromosomes is reduced by half when gametes are formed. As a consequence, each gamete receives only one chromosome from each pair in every parental cell. This is half the usual number, allowing each parent to contribute half the total number of chromosomes. Thus, upon fertilization the full number of chromosomes (and pairs) is restored (see Figure 2).

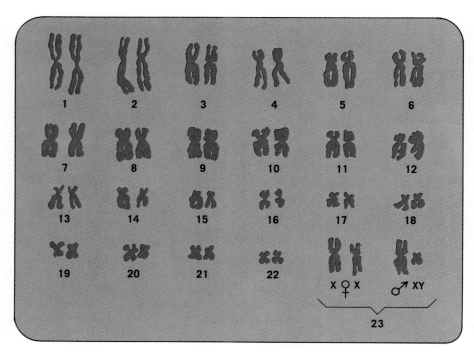

Figure 1:
Human Chromosomes
Every cell-nucleus contains twenty-three types of chromosomes—two of each type. Each parent provides one member of the pair. Chromosomes differ in size and shape. For convenience in talking about them, scientists arrange the twenty-three pairs in descending order by size, and number them accordingly. The members of each chromosome pair look alike, with the exception of the twenty-third pair in males. As the drawing shows, the twenty-third chromosome is the sex-determining chromosome. An XX combination of chromosomes in this pair produces a female; an XY combination, a male.

Genes

So far this chapter has spoken of chromosomes as if they were the ultimate hereditary units. But actually, each chromosome contains a number of smaller units that divide it into regions called **genes.** If a chromosome is like a book in a library, then a gene is like a page in the book. In turn, genes are made up of numerous molecules called **deoxyribonucleic acid,** or **DNA.** DNA is the active substance of genes and thus governs the heredity of all life. It stores inherited information that serves as a "recipe" or "blueprint" telling cells how to manufacture vital protein substances (including enzymes, hormones, antibodies, and structural proteins). This code of life is carried in a large molecule shaped like a double helix or twisted rope ladder (see Figure 3). The human *genome*—a person's genetic map locating the "homes" of all the genes on their appropriate chromosomes—has approximately 100,000 genes and 3 billion genetic subunits.

The discoveries of Gregor Johann Mendel (1822-1884), and Austrian monk, laid the foundations for our modern understanding of genes and for the science of genetics. By crossing varieties of peas in his small monastery garden, Mendel was able to formulate the cardinal principles of heredity. He published his results in 1866, but for various reasons his work was largely ignored until 1900. In that year three researchers, working independently in the Netherlands, Austria, and Germany, reported their own experiments, in which they reached conclusions similar to those of Mendel. To their credit, each acknowledged that in searching the literature, he had found that Mendel had discovered the principles of hereditary thirty-four years before.

Central to Mendelian theory is the notion that independent units (which Mendel called *factors*) determine inherited characteristics. As noted earlier, today we call these units genes. Mendel's conclusion regarding hereditary factors was based on his observation that characteristics commonly appear in two alternative forms. He noted, for instance, that his pea plants were characterized by either red *or* white flowers, tall *or* dwarf stems, green *or* yellow pods, smooth *or* wrinkled seeds, and so on.

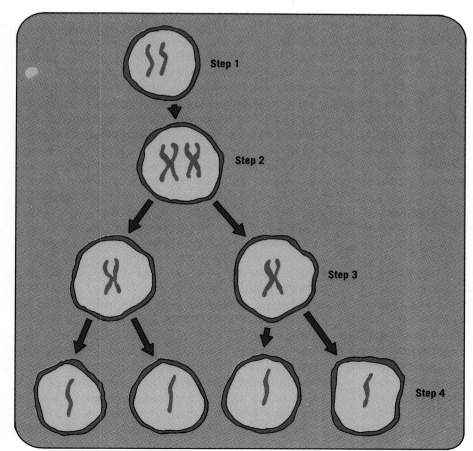

Figure 2:   Meiosis

This simplified diagram illustrates how gametes (ova and sperm) are formed through meiosis. In step 1 each chromosome teams up with its partner. During step 2 the first meiotic division occurs; both chromosomes of each pair are duplicated. (For simplicity, the figure portrays only one pair, although human beings normally have twenty-three pairs.) Each original chromosome and its exact copy, termed a chromatic, are joined at the center. Step 3 involves a second meiotic division. Each of the two original chromosomes and its copy become a part of an intermediary cell. In step 4 each chromatid—the original and its copy—segregates into a separate ovum or sperm gamete. Thus, the intermediate cells undergo cell division without chromosome duplication. This process produces four gametes.

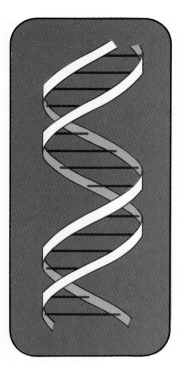

Figure 3:   A Model of the DNA Molecule
The double-chained structure of a DNA molecule is coiled in a helix. During cell division the two chains pull apart, or "unzip." Each half is now free to assemble a new complementary half.

Mendel reasoned that the genes that control a single hereditary characteristic must exist in pairs. Advances in microbiology and genetics have confirmed Mendel's hunch. Genes occur in pairs, one on a maternal chromosome and the other on the *homologous,* or corresponding paternal chromosome. The two genes in a pair are said to occupy a certain *locus,* or position, on each of the homologous chromosomes. For instance, scientists have recently been able to produce an image of the gene that directs production of hemoglobin, the substance that carries oxygen in the blood. This discovery has allowed them to detect certain debilitating and sometimes fatal forms of anemia, caused by an inadequate supply of hemoglobin. With a normal gene the image shows a row of fuzzy-looking black bands. But if one or more bands is missing, part or all of the genetic instruction is missing, a condition associated with two types of anemia (alpha-thalassemia and beta-delta-thalassemia).

We apply the term **allele** to each member of a pair of genes. An allele is a gene at a given locus on a chromosome. Alleles are different forms of the same gene. There can be only two different alleles per person for any characteristic, one from

each parent (one on the maternal chromosome and one on the paternal chromosome).

Dominance

Mendel demonstrated that in a cross between pea varieties, one allele—the **dominant character** —completely masks or hides the other allele—the **recessive character.** Mendel used letters of the alphabet as symbols for genes. A capital letter (for example, *A*) signified the dominant allele and a lowercase letter (in this instance, *a*) the recessive allele. Say that we wanted to talk about the alleles responsible for the color of a plant's flowers. We could use *A* as a symbol for red (the dominant allele) and *a* for white (the recessive allele). Then, we would refer to a purebred red-flowered pea as *AA,* since this pea is characterized by a pair of two dominant alleles—one allele from each parental unit. And we would call a purebred white-flowered pea *aa,* since the pea is characterized by a pair of two recessive alleles.

In one of his experiments Mendel transferred the pollen of purebred red-flowered peas (*AA*) to plants of white-flowered peas (*aa*). This cross resulted in first-generation offspring that were all red-flowered, since the red-flowered allele is dominant. The offspring secured one allele from each parent, resulting in an *Aa* pair of alleles. In this manner Mendel demonstrated the distinction between the **genotype,** the genetic makeup of an organism, and the **phenotype,** the observable characteristics of the organism. (Among human beings the phenotype includes physical, physiological, and behavioral traits.)

A genotype that contains two red-flowered genes, or two white-flowered genes, is termed **homozygous,** or "pure" for that trait. A genotype that contains one red-flowered gene and one white-flowered gene is termed **heterozygous,** or "hybrid." Recessive genes produce their effect on the phenotype only when they are homozygous. A dominant gene produces its effect on the phenotype whether it is homozygous or heterozygous.

Human beings also possess dominant and recessive genes, some of which are listed in Table 1. Albinos (people who have milky white skin and colorless hair) are a case in point. Albinism is a relatively rare condition caused by a recessive gene that results in the failure of melanin (a dark pigment) to form in the body. Both parents of an albino are generally normal in phenotype, but in genotype they are heterozygous (*Aa*). Accordingly,

Table 1

Some Dominant and Recessive Human Genetic Characteristics	
Dominant	Recessive
Skin pigmentation	Albinism
Curly hair	Straight hair
Brown eyes	Blue or hazel eyes
Near- or farsightedness	Normal vision
Glaucoma	Normal
Normal color vision	Color blindness
Normal hearing	Congenital deafness
Free earlobes	Attached earlobes
Normal metabolism	Phenylketonuria
Polydactylism (extra fingers and toes)	Normal number of digits
Dark hair	Light or red hair
Hereditary cataract	Normal vision
Long eyelashes	Short eyelashes
Broad lips	Thin lips
Ichthyosis (scaly skin)	Normal skin
Achondroplasia (dwarfism)	Normal
Huntington's chorea	Normal

both parents carry the albino gene *a*. The genetic combination that can occur in their offspring are *AA, Aa,* and *aa.* Only the *aa* genotype leads to albinism.

Mendel's Principles

Mendel demonstrated that the characteristic that is hidden or masked in the first generation (the recessive allele) is not lost, since it reappears among some members of the second hybrid generation. He reasoned that characteristics do not blend with or contaminate one another but preserve their original integrity as they pass unchanged in succeeding generations from child to grandchild. This proposition is termed the **principle of segregation.**

For example, when Mendel crossed the red-flowered, first-generation hybrid plants with each other, about three-fourths had red flowers (*AA* or *Aa*) and one-fourth had white flowers (*aa*). Of the red-flowered plants, about two-thirds were hybrids (*Aa*) and one-third were purebreds (*AA*). All the white-flowered plants, however, were purebreds (*aa*) (see Figure 4).

The principle of segregation is highlighted among human beings in cases of genetic disease. Dominant, single-gene defects can be transmitted by one affected parent. For each of the more than one thousand such disorders so far identified, each pregnancy entails a 50 percent risk of trans-

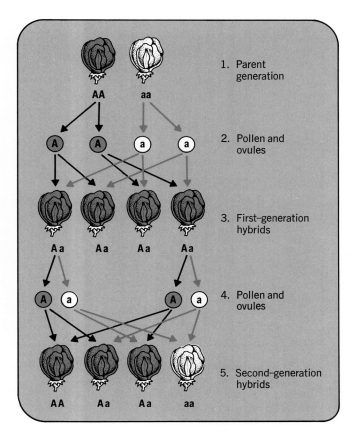

Figure 4: Mendelian Principle of Segregation
In step 1 a purebred red-flowered pea plant and a purebred white-flowered pea plant are crossed by transferring pollen from the flower of one plant to that of the other. As step 2 shows, the pollen and ovule grains (gametes) contain one allele for flower color—red (shown here in color) being the dominant allele and white the recessive allele. In step 3 all offspring of the first generation of hybrids have one dominant and one recessive allele, but the dominant trait masks the recessive trait. In step 4 self-fertilization of the first generation hybrids produces all combinations of alleles. (For the sake of simplicity the gametes for only two of the four first-generation hybrids are shown here.) In step 5, the second generation, three-fourths of the flowers are red, one-fourth white.

mitting the defect if one parent is affected, and a 75 percent risk if both parents carry the gene (see Figure 5).

Huntington's chorea is one of the better-known genetic disorders. It is caused by a single *autosomal* (non-sex-linked) dominant gene. Scientists have recently found the approximate location of the genetic defect that is associated with the disorder. Such a location is called a *marker,* a distinctive DNA segment on a particular chromosome. The disorder results in the degeneration of the

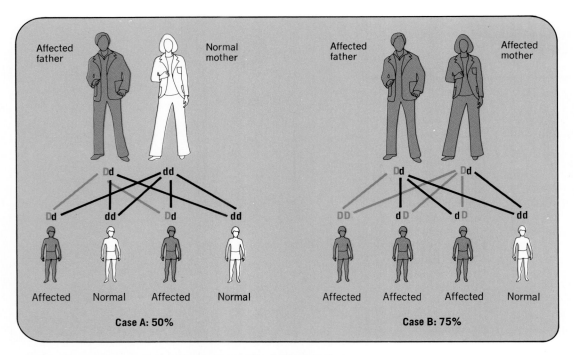

Figure 5:   The Transmission of Dominant, Single-Gene Defects
Case A: One affected parent has a single faulty gene (D), *which dominates its normal counterpart. Each child's chance of inheriting either the* D *or* d *allele from the affected parent is 50 percent. Case B: Both affected parents have a single faulty gene* (D), *which dominates its normal counterpart. Each child's chance of inheriting a* D *allele from one of the parents is 75 percent.*

nervous system, mental deterioration, and the uncontrolled twitching of the limbs. It generally appears when patients are in their thirties and forties (see Figure 6). There is no known cure, and the disease is fatal. Woody Guthrie, a talented folk singer, was a victim of Huntington's chorea.

Defects caused by recessive genes will occur in the next generation only if the recessive gene is received from each parent. If both parents are carriers of the gene, there is a 25 percent chance in each pregnancy of producing an affected child (see Figure 7). Today, there are more than eight hundred recognized recessive, single-gene disorders, and the list grows yearly as others are identified. *Tay-Sachs disease,* associated with an enzyme defect, is one. It is a degenerative neurological disorder that leads to death, and it occurs primarily in the children of Ashkenazic Jews whose parents came from eastern Europe. It is estimated that one in thirty Jews with Ashkenazic ancestry carries the gene for the disease.

In the course of his pea experiments Mendel also found that the distribution of one genetic trait is not affected by the distribution of another genetic trait. He observed, for instance, that the shape of a pod of a pea plant is independent of the color of

its flower and the length of its stem. This observation led Mendel to formulate his second principle: the **principle of independent assortment.** It states that every characteristic is inherited independently of every other characteristic. Thus, the genetic composition of an organism is an expression of statistical probability that is based on the laws of chance.* In other words, the combination of traits (the phenotype) that characterizes an organism is a function of the random recombining of given gene pairs.

Determination of Sex

Of the forty-six chromosomes (totaling twenty-three pairs) that each human being normally possesses, twenty-two pairs are similar in size and shape in both men and women. These pairs are termed **autosomes.** The twenty-third pair, the **sex chromosomes,** are similar in females but dissimilar in males. Women have two X chro-

---

* The law of probability states that the chance of two or more independent events occurring together is the product of the chances of their separate occurrences.

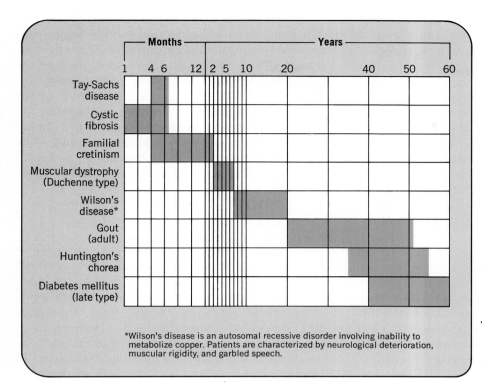

Figure 6:   Eight Genetic Diseases: Age Range at Onset

In many disorders a genetic disease shows up during the first year of life. But in others the symptoms do not become apparent until much later. Huntington's chorea is an example of a late-onset disorder.

*Wilson's disease is an autosomal recessive disorder involving inability to metabolize copper. Patients are characterized by neurological deterioration, muscular rigidity, and garbled speech.

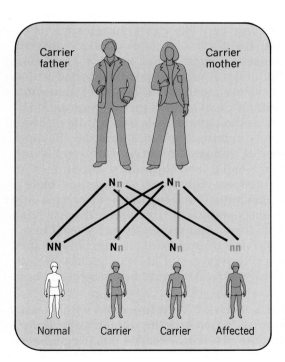

Figure 7:   Transmission of Recessive, Single-Gene Defects

Both parents, usually themselves unaffected by the faulty gene, carry a normal gene (N) that dominates its faulty recessive counterpart (n). The odds for each child are (1) a 25 percent chance of being NN, normal: inheriting two Ns and accordingly being free of the faulty recessive gene; (2) a 50 percent chance of being Nn and therefore a carrier like both parents; and (3) a 25 percent risk of being nn, affected: inheriting a "double dose" of n genes, which may cause a serious genetic disease.

mosomes (XX); men, an X and a Y chromosome (XY). The Y chromosome is somewhat smaller and has considerably fewer genes than the X chromosome.

Among human beings the sex of the offspring is determined by the male. Since women are XX, all their ova carry the X chromosome. But since males are XY, some of their sperm contain X chromosomes and some Y chromosomes. If a sperm with an X chromosome fertilizes the ovum, the offspring will be a female; if a sperm with a Y chromosome, a male. In sum, mothers give one of their X chromosomes to each child, but fathers give a Y chromosome to their sons and an X chromosome to their daughters.

Linked Characteristics

We now know that Mendel's principle of independent assortment applies only to genes that are transmitted in different "linkage groups." In other words, genes are inherited independently only if they are on different chromosomes. If they are linked so that they appear on the same chromosome, the genes tend to be inherited together.

Fortunately, as George and Muriel Beadle point out (1966, p. 68), Mendel did not encounter the effects of linked genes in his experiments.

> Knowing nothing about chromosomes or genes, let alone the phenomenon of linkage, Mendel might well have decided that his hypothesis was wrong—and very possibly he would have quit. He was spared this fate because, out of all the possible traits in peas which he might have picked for study, he happened to choose seven traits *each of which is controlled from a different chromosome.* (The probability of anyone's making such a happy choice, in random picks, is only about 1 in 163!) . . . Because of Mendel's good luck in this matter, linkage did not confuse his results; and each trait *did* segregate independently.

A good example of linked genes is seen in sex-linked traits. The X chromosome, for instance, contains many genes that are not directly related to the sexual traits of the individual. Hemophilia, a hereditary defect that interferes with the normal clotting of blood, is a sex-linked characteristic carried by the X chromosome. There are about one hundred fifty other know sex-linked disorders, including red-green color blindness, a type of muscular dystrophy, certain forms of night blindness, Hunter's disease (a severe form of mental retardation), and juvenile glaucoma (hardening of the eyeballs).

The vast majority of sex-linked genetic defects occur in men, since men have only one X chromo-

some (see Figure 8). In women the harmful action of a gene on one X chromosome is usually suppressed by a dominant gene on the other chromosome.* Thus, although they are themselves unaffected by a sex-linked disorder, women can be carriers of it. A man is affected if he receives from his mother an X chromosome bearing the genetic defect. A man cannot receive the abnormal gene from his father. Males transmit an X chromosome only to their daughters, never to their sons, who always receive a father's Y chromosome.

Chromosomal Abnormalities

The normal number of chromosomes in human beings is forty-six, or twenty-three pairs. A number of disorders are associated with the presence of too few or too many chromosomes. For example, *Down's syndrome* (no longer referred to as Mongolism, because of the unfortunate racial connotations of the term) is a disorder that occurs in 1 out of every 600 live births. Down's syndrome is caused by an extra chromosome, which gives the infant a total of forty-seven chromosomes rather than the normal forty-six. (Three chromosomes of type 21 occur in the individual's cells, a condition called *trisomy 21*.) The extra chromosome is responsible for such characteristics as upward-slanted eyes, a short squat nose, a protruding underlip, underdeveloped genitals, broad stubby hands, deep tongue tissue, a short neck, neuromotor disabilities, and serious mental retardation.

Although the children affected by this disorder vary widely in temperament, many are affectionate, cheerful, and good-natured. They readily imitate other people, and they show a fondness for music. Children with Down's syndrome have a higher incidence of congenital disorders and greater susceptibility to infectious disease than normal children. Consequently, most used to die before the age of ten. With the development of antibiotics, however, the life expectancy of children with Down's syndrome has increased about fourfold.

The risk of giving birth to a child with Down's syndrome increases with the woman's age. Before age thirty the risk is 1 in every 1,000 pregnancies; at age forty it is 1 in 100; and at age forty-five it is 1 in 45. This drastic increase in the incidence of

---

* A woman can inherit such a disorder only if the X chromosome she receives from her mother and the X chromosome she receives from her father both bear a gene for a given disease. This event rarely happens.

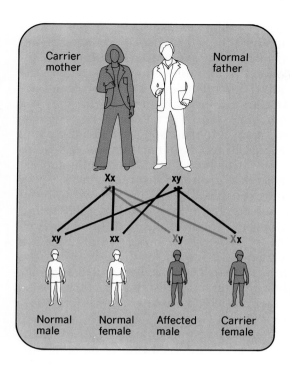

Figure 8:   Transmission of Sex-linked Genetic Defects

In most sex-linked genetic disorders the female sex chromosome of an unaffected mother (a woman who does not herself show the disorder) carries one faulty chromosome (X) and one normal chromosome (x). The father carries a normal x and y chromosome. The statistical odds for each male child are (1) a 50 percent risk of inheriting the faulty X chromosome and hence the disorder and (2) a 50 percent chance of inheriting normal x and y chromosomes. For each female child the statistical odds are (1) a 50 percent risk of inheriting one faulty X chromosome and hence becoming a carrier like her mother and (2) a 50 percent chance of inheriting no faulty gene.

Down's syndrome with advancing maternal age suggests that an environmental factor that has not yet been identified may contribute to the chromosomal defect.

A number of other disorders are linked to sex chromosome abnormalities. Normal men have an X and a Y chromosome (XY). Normal women have two X chromosomes (XX). But in *Klinefelter's syndrome,* males have two X chromosomes and one Y chromosome (XXY). Such individuals possess undeveloped testes and commonly develop into tall, thin men with enlarged breasts. They are sterile and may show some mental impairment (Pennington, Bender, Puck, Salbenblatt, & Robinson, 1982; Rubin, Reinisch, & Haskett, 1981).

In *Turner's syndrome,* women, instead of having two X chromosomes, have only one (XO). These women are usually short in stature, with "webbed" necks, broad chests, and low-set ears. Although they have female sex organs, at puberty they fail to develop secondary sexual characteristics (they do not have ovaries and hence are deficient in female hormones). In some cases they are also mentally impaired, and they evidence immature, inadequate social relationships (McCauley, Kay, Ito, & Treder, 1987).

In the past twenty years another sex chromosome abnormality, XYY, has attracted considerable attention. Early studies suggested that such men tend to be superaggressive and violent because of the extra Y, or male, chromosome. More recent research reveals that XYY men are no more likely to commit violent crimes than XY men. (Pages 73–77 and Figure 3–4 discuss how some of these conditions can be detected in the unborn child by new testing procedures.)

Incomplete Dominance

In the case of some traits one gene is not completely dominant over the other. This phenomenon is called **incomplete dominance.** The resulting phenotype represents a blending of the phenotypes of parents. It is not produced by a blending or dilution of the genotype; genes are still inherited as discrete units. Rather, each allele affects the other's action in producing a given outcome. An example is *sickle-cell anemia.* The disease usually strikes people of African heritage, although a similar gene is found among some populations in Greece, southern Turkey, Yemen, India, and Burma.

In sickle-cell anemia the red cells of persons take on a sickle or crescent shape rather than the normal circular form. The sickle cells tend to be sticky. They clamp onto one another and, like a logjam in a river, clog the blood vessels of the circulatory system. The clogging impedes the circulation of oxygen and carbon dioxide to and from the tissues. Tissue damage, severe pain, and often death result. The spleen also destroys blood cells more rapidly than the body can replace them. This factor underlies the anemia.

Sickle-cell anemia occurs in persons who carry homozygous genes (*SS*) for the trait. Under these conditions both of the sickle-cell genes direct the body to manufacture the abnormal blood molecule. People who are heterozygous with respect to the sickle-cell trait have one sickle-cell allele (*S*) and one normal hemoglobin allele (*A*). The sickle-cell allele and the normal hemoglobin allele each direct the production of its particular type of blood. Neither functions as a dominant or a recessive gene. This condition provides a person with a roughly equal mixture of the two types of blood cells. Accordingly, the sickle cell and the normal hemoglobin alleles are said to behave in a *codominant* fashion (and therefore, each allele is designated by a capital letter).

Individuals with the single sickle-cell allele (the heterozygous condition—*AS*) have difficulty only if they go to high altitudes, where the oxygen in the air is thin. However, they seem to be protected against malaria in regions where the disease is prevalent. The sickle-cell gene apparently produces conditions that are unfavorable to the growth of the malarial parasite in the blood. Hence, the single sickle-cell allele has adaptive value in malaria-infected localities. Thus, sickle-cell anemia may be the price a population must pay for the ability of a substantial proportion of its members to be protected against malaria.

Penetrance and the Norm of Reaction

So far we have discussed dominant genes and homozygous recessive genes as if they were always apparent in the person who has them. This is not quite true, since the expression of many genes depends upon their interaction with other genes and with the environment. **Penetrance** refers to the ability of a gene to manifest itself in the person who carries it. Penetrance is measured in terms of the percentage of people who carry a gene in proper combination with other factors to permit its expression in their phenotype. All Mendel's experiments were characterized by 100 percent penetration. If a dominant gene is expressed in only 80 percent of the individuals known to carry it, the penetrance of the gene is said to be 80 percent.

Consider *bipolar disorder (formally called manic-depressive illness)*. Some geneticists believe that a genotype for bipolar disorder may not always result in the illness because of reduced penetrance (Kolata, 1986). Victims of the illness fluctuate between two extreme emotional states. In the manic phase victims become expansive and extravagant, are often unable to sleep or eat, and may talk incessantly. The depressive phase plunges them into sorrow, hopelessness, and boundless guilt, feelings that sometimes lead to suicide. Scientists have found that manic-depressive illness is a group of disorders, rather than simply one, and that there are at least two different genetic defects that may produce similar symptoms. Children of individuals with bipolar disorder have a 50 percent chance of inheriting it. However, only 63 percent of those carrying the gene show signs of the disorder, which suggests that other genetic or environmental factors also play a role in its expression (Hostetler, 1987; Schmeck, 1987a).

Some geneticists employ the concept **norm of reaction** to designate the range of possible outcomes that genetic influences have in different environmental settings. A genotype may result in a variety of phenotypes, depending upon environmental conditions. The norm of reaction refers to the limits—the upper and lower boundaries—within which environmental factors interact with the genotype to determine the eventual outcome (the phenotype). The norm of reaction has particular relevance for the understanding of human behavior. Note, though, that there are no genes for behavior, as such. A gene does not turn on and magically blossom into a behavior. A genotype influences human behavior through the effects it has upon the hormones, enzymes, neurotransmitters, and neurons that mediate the path between the genes and the psychosocial aspects of behavior that we term personality. A gene, then, can give a nudge in one direction or another, but it does not directly control behavior.

Bibliography

Aber, R, & Webb, W. B. 1986. Effects of a limited nap on night sleep in older subjects. *Psychology and Aging, 1,* 300–302.

Aboud, F. 1987. The development of ethnic self-identification and attitudes. In J. Phinney & M. Rotheram (Eds.), *Children's ethnic socialization: Pluralism and development.* Newbury Park, Calif.: Sage.

Abraham, K. G. 1983. Political thinking in the elementary years: An empirical study. *Elementary School Journal, 84,* 221–231.

Abrahams, B., Feldman, S. S., & Nash, S. C. 1978. Sex role self-concept and sex role attitudes: Enduring personality characteristics or adaptations to changing life situations? *Developmental Psychology, 14,* 393–400.

Abramov, I., Gordon, J., Hendrickson, A., Hainline, L., Dobson, V., & LaBossiere, E. 1982. The retina of the newborn human infant. *Science, 217,* 265–267.

Abramovich, R., Corter, C., Pepler, D. J., & Stanhope, L. 1986. Sibling and peer interactions: A final followup and a comparison. *Child Development, 57,* 217–229.

Abravanel, E., & Sigafoos, A. D. 1984. Exploring the presence of limitation during early infancy. *Child Development, 55,* 381–392.

Achenbach, T. M., Phares, V., Howell, C. T., Rauh, V. A., & Nurcombe, B. 1990. Seven-year outcome of the Vermont intervention program for low-birthweight infants. *Child Development, 61,* 1672–1681.

Acock, A., & Bengtson, V. 1980. Socialization and attribution processes: Actual versus perceived similarity among parents and youth. *Journal of Marriage and the Family, 42,* 501–514.

Acock, A. C., & Kiecolt, K. J. 1989. Is it family structure or socioeconomic status? Family structure during adolescence and adult adjustment. *Social Forces, 68,* 553–571.

Acredolo, L., & Goodwyn, S. 1988. Symbolic gesturing in normal infants. *Child Development, 59,* 450–466.

Acredolo, L. P., & Hake, J. K. 1982. Infant perception. In B. B. Wolman (Ed.), *Handbook of developmental psychology.* Englewood Cliffs, N.J.: Prentice-Hall.

Adair, J. 1975. *The history of the American Indians.* London: E. D. Dilly.

Adams, B. 1968. *Kinship in an urban setting.* Chicago: Markham.

Adam, B. D. 1987. *The rise of a gay and lesbian movement.* Boston: Twayne.

Adams, C., Labouvie-Vief, G., Hobart, C. J., & Dorosz, M. 1990. Adult age group differences in story recall style. *Journal of Gerontology, 45,* P17–27.

Adams, G. C. 1987. The dynamics of welfare recipiency among adolescent mothers. Memorandum of March 17, Human Resources and Community Development Division, Congressional Budget Office, Washington, D.C.

Adams, G. R., Abraham, K. G., & Markstrom, C. A. 1987. The relations among identity development, self-consciousness, and self-focusing during middle and late adolescence. *Developmental Psychology, 23,* 292–297.

Adams, G. R., & Crane, P. 1980. An assessment of parents' and teachers' expectations of pre-school children's social preference for attractive and unattractive children and adults. *Child Development, 51,* 224–231.

Adams, J. A. 1984. Learning of movement sequences. *Psychological Bulletin, 96,* 3–28.

Adams, J. A. 1987. Historical review and appraisal of research on the learning, retention, and transfer of human motor skills. *Psychological Bulletin, 101,* 41–74.

Adams, R. G., & Blieszner, R. (Eds.). 1989. *Older adult friendship: Structure and process.* Newbury Park, Calif.: Sage.

Adelson, J. 1972. The political imagination of the young adolescent. In J. Kagan & R. Coles (Eds.). *Twelve to sixteen.* New York: Norton.

Adelson, J. 1975. The development of ideology in adolescence. In S. E. Dragastin & G. H. Elder, Jr. (Eds.), *Adolescence in the life cycle: Psychological change and social context.* New York: Wiley.

Adelson, J. 1980. Children and other political naifs. *Psychology Today, 14* (November), pp. 56–70.

Ade-Ridder, L., & Brubaker, T. H. 1983. The quality of long-term marriages. In T. H. Brubaker (Ed.), *Family relationships in later life.* Beverly Hills, Calif.: Sage.

Adler, J. 1987. Cause for concern—and optimism. *Newsweek* (March 16), pp. 63–66.

Adler, S. J. 1991. Suits over sexual harassment prove difficult due to issue of definition. *Wall Street Journal* (October 9), pp. B1, B4.

Agrest, S. 1982. "This is mine and I'm the boss." *Newsweek* (November 1), p. 59.

Ahrens, R. 1954. Beitrag zur entwicklung des physiognomieund mimikerkennens. *Zeitschrift für Experimentelle und Angewandte Psychologie, 2,* 412–454, 599–633.

Ainsworth, M. D. S. 1967. *Infancy in Uganda: Infant care and the growth of attachment.* Baltimore: Johns Hopkins University Press.

Ainsworth, M. D. S. 1983. Patterns of infant-mother attachment as related to maternal care. In D. Magnusson & V. Allen (Eds.), *Human development: An interactional perspective.* New York: Academic Press.

Ainsworth, M. D. S. 1989. Attachments beyond infancy. *American Psychologist, 44,* 709–716.

Ainsworth, M. D. S., & Bell, S. M. 1970. Attachment, exploration, and separation: Illustrated by the behavior of one-year-olds in a strange situation. *Child Development, 41,* 49–67.

Ainsworth, M. D. S., & Bell, S. M. 1974. Mother-infant interaction and the development of competence. In K. Connolly & J. Bruner (Eds.), *The growth of competence.* New York: Academic Press.

Ainsworth, M. D. S., & Bell, S. M. 1977. Infant crying and maternal responsiveness: A rejoinder to Gewirtz and Boyd. *Child Development, 48,* 1208–1216.

Ainsworth, M. D. S., Bell, S. M., & Stayton, D. J. 1974. Infant-mother attachment and social development. In M. P. M. Richards (Ed.), *The integration of a child into a social world.* Cambridge: Cambridge University Press.

Ainsworth, M. D. S., Blehar, M. C., Waters, E., & Wall, S. 1979. *Patterns of attachment: A psychological study of the strange situation.* New York: Halsted.

Ainsworth, M. D. S., & Wittig, B. A. 1969. Attachment and the exploratory behavior of one-year-olds in a strange situation. In B. M. Foss (Ed.), *Determinants of infant behavior* (Vol. 4). London: Methuen.

Albin, R. 1979. Children and divorce. *APA Monitor, 10,* 4.

Aldous, J. 1987. New views on the family life of the elderly and the near-elderly. *Journal of Marriage and the Family, 49,* 227–234.

Aldous, J. 1990. Family development and the life course: Two perspectives on family change. *Journal of Marriage and the Family, 52,* 571–583.

Aleksandrowicz, M. K., & Aleksandrowicz, D. R. 1974. Obstetrical pain-relieving drugs as predictors of infant behavior variability. *Child Development, 45,* 935–945.

Alexander, K. L. 1990. Both racism and sexism block the path to management for minority women. *Wall Street Journal* (July 25), p. B1.

Allan, E. A., & Steffensmeier, D. J. 1989. Youth, underemployment, and property crime: Differential effects of job availability and job quallity on juvenile and young adult arrest rates. *American Sociological Review, 54,* 107–123.

Allen, V. L. & Newtson, D. 1972. Development of conformity and independence. *Journal of Personality and Social Psychology, 22,* 18–30.

Alley, T. R. 1983. Growth-produced changes in body shape and size as determinants of perceived age and adult caretaking. *Child Development, 54,* 241–248.

Allman, W. F. 1991. The clues in the idle chatter. *U. S. News & World Report* (August 19), pp. 61–62.

Allport, G. W. 1961. *Pattern and growth in personality.* New York: Holt, Rinehart and Winston.

Allport, G. W. 1962. Prejudice: Is it societal or personal? *Journal of Social Issues, 18,* 120–134.

Allred, K. D., & Smith, T. W. 1989. The hardy personality: Cognitive and physiological responses to evaluative threat. *Journal of Personality and Social Psychology, 56,* 257–266.

Alper, P. R. 1991. A living will is a bloodless document. *Wall Street Journal* (January 11), p. A10.

Altman, L. K. 1979. Study of dying disputes idea that doctors prolong life at any cost. *New York Times* (June 3), p. 50.

Altman, L. K. 1986. Childhood death: Respiratory ailments are now no. 1 cause. *New York Times* (April 8), pp. 17, 20.

Altman, L. K. 1990a. The evidence mounts on passive smoking. *New York Times* (May 29), pp. B5, B7.

Altman, L. K. 1990b. Infant mortality rates in nation decline to a record low in 1989. *New York Times* (August 31), p. A12.

Altman, L. K. 1990c. Pregnancy problems, hormone linked. *New York Times* (November 13), p. B7.

Altman, L. K. 1991a. Doctor says he agonized but gave drug for suicide. *New York Times* (March 7), pp. A1, A16.

Altman, L. K. 1991b. Jury declines to indict a doctor who said he aided in a suicide. *New York Times* (July 27), pp. 1, 7.

Altman, L. K. 1991c. More physicians broach forbidden subject of euthanasia. *New York Times* (March 12), p. B6.

Altman, L. K. 1991d. Study of women seeks to establish effect of aspirin on heart attacks. *New York Times* (July 29), p. A8.

Altman, L. K. 1991e. W.H.O. says 40 million will be infected with AIDS virus by 2000. *New York Times* (June 18), p. B8.

Altshuler, J. L., & Ruble, D. N. 1989. Developmental changes in children's awareness of strategies for coping with uncontrollable stress. *Child Development, 60,* 1337–1349.

Amabile, T. M. 1983. *The social psychology of creativity.* New York: Springer.

Ambert, A. M. 1984. Longitudinal changes in children's behavior toward custodial parents. *Journal of Marriage and the Family, 46,* 463–467.

American Academy of Pediatrics. 1990. News release and statement provided by Dr. Victor Strasburger of the University of New Mexico School of Medicine, April 16.

American Psychological Association. 1982. *Ethical principles in the conduct of research with human participants.* Washington, D.C.: American Psychological Association.

Ames, K. 1990. Our bodies, their selves. *Newsweek* (December 17), p. 60.

Ames, K. 1991. And donor makes three. *Newsweek* (September 30), pp. 60–61.

Amoss, P. T., & Harrell, S. (Eds.), 1981. *Other ways of growing old: Anthropological perspectives.* Stanford: Stanford University Press.

Anastasi, A. 1958. Heredity, environment, and the question "how?" *Psychological Review, 65,* 197–208.

Anastasi, A. 1988. *Psychological testing* (6th ed.). New York: MacMillan.

Anders, T. R., & Fozard, J. L. 1972. Effects of age upon retrieval from short-term memory. *Developmental Psychology, 6,* 214–217.

Andersen, S. M., & Cole, S. W. 1990. "Do I know you?": The role of significant others in general social perception. *Journal of Personality and Social Psychology, 59,* 384–399.

Anderson, A. 1982. How the mind heals. *Psychology Today, 16* (December), pp. 51–56.

Anderson, D. 1991. Travis Williams thought football was forever. *New York Times* (March 5), p. B10.

Anderson, E. 1990. *Streetwise: Race, class, and change in an urban community.* Chicago: University of Chicago Press.

Anderson, K. E., Lytton, H., & Romney, D. M. 1986. Mothers' interactions with normal and conduct-disordered boys: Who affects whom? *Developmental Psychology, 22,* 604–609.

Anderson, S. A., Russell, C. S., & Schumm, W. R. 1983. Perceived marital quality and family lifecycle categories: A further analysis. *Journal of Marriage and the Family, 45,* 127–139.

Angell, M. 1990. The right to die in dignity. *Newsweek* (July 23), p. 9.

Angier, N. 1990a. Hard work found not to harm pregnancy. *New York Times* (October 1), p. B7.

Angier, N. 1990b. Human growth hormone reverses effects of aging. *New York Times* (July 5), p. A1, A12.

Angier, N. 1990c. Seasons sway human birth rates. *New York Times* (October 2), p. B8.

Angier, N. 1991a. The biology of what it means to be gay. *New York Times* (September 1), pp. E1, E4.

Angier, N. 1991b. Older women at no greater risk in bearing children with defects. *New York Times* (March 29), p. 9.

Angier, N. 1991c. Women join the ranks of science but remain invisible at the top. *New York Times* (May 21), pp. B5, B8.

Angier, N. 1991d. Zone of brain linked to men's sexual orientation. *New York Times* (August 31), pp. A1, A18.

Angoff, W. H. 1988. The nature-nurture debate, aptitudes, and group differences. *American Psychologist, 43,* 713–720.

Anisfeld, M. 1979. Interpreting "imitative" responses in early infancy. *Science, 205,* 214–215.

Ansbacher, H. L., & Ansbacher, R. R. 1956. *The individual psychology of Alfred Adler.* New York: Basic Books.

Antell, S. E., Caron, A. J., & Myers, R. S. 1985. Perception of relational invariants by newborns. *Developmental Psychology, 21,* 942–948.

Apgar, V. 1953. Proposal for a new method of evaluation of the newborn infant. *Anesthesia and Analgesia, 32,* 260–267.

Apple, D. 1956. The social structure of grandparenthood. *American Anthropoligist, 58,* 656–663.

Apple, M. W. 1982. *Education and power.* London: Routledge and Kegan Paul.

Apple, M. W., & Weis, L. 1983. *Ideology and practice in schooling.* Philadelphia: Temple University Press.

Applebome, P. 1991. Although urban blight worsens, most people don't feel its impact. *New York Times* (January 28), pp. A1, A12.

Apter, T. 1990. *Altered loves: Mothers and daughters during adolescence.* New York: St. Martin's Press.

Aquilino, W. S. 1990. The likelihood of parent-adult child coresidence: Effects of family structure and parental characteristics. *Journal of Marriage and the Family, 52,* 405–419.

Aquilino, W. S., & Supple, K. R. 1991. Parent-child relations and parent's satisfaction with living arrangements when adult children live at home. *Journal of Marriage and the Family, 53,* 13–27.

Arbuckle, T. Y., Gold, D., & Andres, D. 1986. Cognitive functioning of older people in relation to social and personality variables. *Journal of Psychology and Aging, 1,* 55–62.

Archer, S. L., & Waterman, A. S. 1988. Psychological individualism: Gender differences or gender neutrality? *Human Development, 31,* 65–91.

Arenberg, D., & Robertson-Tchabo, E. A. 1977. Learning and aging. In J. E. Birren & K. W. Schale (Eds.), *Handbook of the psychology of aging.* New York: Van Nostrand Reinhold.

Ariès, P. 1962. *Centuries of childhood* (R. Baldick, Trans.). New York: Random House.

Ariès, P. 1978. *Western attitudes toward death: From the Middle Ages to the present.* Baltimore: Johns Hopkins University Press.

Ariès, P. 1981. *The hour of our death.* New York: Knopf.

Aronson, E., & Carlsmith, J. M. 1962. Performance expectancy as a determinant of actual performance. *Journal of Abnormal and Social Psychology, 65,* 178–182.

Asch, S. E. 1952. *Social psychology.* Englewood Cliffs, N.J.: Prentice-Hall.

Asher, S. R. 1983. Social competence and peer status: Recent advances and future directions. *Child Development, 54,* 1427–1434.

Asher, S. R., & Dodge, K. A. 1986. Identifying children who are rejected by their peers. *Developmental Psychology, 22,* 444–449.

Asher, S. R., Hymel, S., & Renshaw, P. D. 1984. Loneliness in children. *Child Development, 55,* 1456–1564.

Ashton, P. T. 1975. Cross-cultural Piagetian research: An experimental perspective. *Harvard Educational Review, 45,* 475–506.

Ashton, R. 1976. Infant state and stimulation. *Developmental Psychology, 12,* 569–570.

Atchley, R. C. 1971. Retirement and work orientation. *The Gerontologist, 2,* 29–32.

Atchley, R. C. 1975. The life course, age-grading, and age-linked demands for decision making. In N. Datan & L. Ginsberg (Eds.), *Life span developmental psychology: Normative life crises.* New York: Academic Press.

Atchley, R. C. 1976. *The sociology of retirement.* Cambridge, Mass: Schenkman.

Attie, I, & Brooks-Gunn, J. 1987. Weight-related concerns in women: A response to or a cause of stress? In R. C. Barnett, L. Biener & G. K. Baruch (Eds.), *Gender and stress.* New York: Free Press.

Attie, I, & Brooks-Gunn, J. 1989. Development of eating problems in adolescent girls: A longitudinal study. *Developmental Psychology, 25,* 70–79.

Ausubel, D. P., & Sullivan, E. V. 1970. *Theory and problems of child development* (2nd ed.). New York: Grune & Stratton.

Azmitia, M. 1988. Peer interaction and problem solving: When are two heads better than one? *Child Development, 59,* 87–96.

Babchuk, N., Peters, G. R., Hoyt, D. R., & Kaiser, M. A. 1979. The voluntary associations of the aged. *Journal of Gerontology, 34,* 579–587.

Baca-Zinn, M. 1989. Family, race, and poverty in the eighties. *Signs, 14,* 856–874.

Bachman, J. G. 1987. An eye on the future. *Psychology Today, 21* (July), pp. 6–8.

Bachman, J. G., Johnston, L. D., & O'Malley, P. M. 1987. *Monitoring the future. Questionnaire responses from the nation's high school seniors, 1986.* Ann Arbor: University of Michigan Institute for Social Research.

Bachman, J. G., Johnston, L. D., & O'Malley, P. M. 1990. Explaining the recent decline in cocaine use among young adults: Further evidence that perceived risks and disapproval lead to reduced drug use. *Journal of Health and Social Behavior, 31,* 173–184.

Bachman, J. G., O'Malley, P., & Johnston, J. 1978. *Youth in transition.* Vol. 6: *Adolescence to adulthood—changes and stability in the lives of young men.* Ann Arbor: Institute for Social Research, University of Michigan.

Back, K. W. 1969. The ambiguity of retirement. In E. W. Busse & E. Pfeiffer (Eds.),

Behavior and adaptation in late life. Boston: Little, Brown.

Bacon, K. H. 1990. Child deaths from AIDS seen soaring. *Wall Street Journal* (September 26), p. B4.

Bailey, M., & Pillard, R. 1991. Are some people born gay? *New York Times* (December 17), p. A15.

Baillargeon, R., & Graber, M. 1988. Evidence of location memory in 8-month-old infants in a nonsearch AB task. *Developmental Psychology, 24,* 502–511.

Bailyn, L. 1959. Mass media and children. *Psychological Monographs, 73,* 1–48.

Bakan, D. 1972. Adolescence in America: From idea to social fact. In J. Kagan & R. Coles (Eds.), *Twelve to sixteen: Early adolescence.* New York: Norton.

Bakeman, R., & Adamson, L. B. 1984. Coordinating attention to people and objects in mother-infant and peer-infant interaction. *Child Development, 55,* 1278–1289.

Bakeman, R., Adamson, L. B., Konner, M., & Barr, R. G. 1990. !Kung infancy: The social context of object exploration. *Child Development, 61,* 794–809.

Bakeman, R., Brown, J. V. 1977. Behavioral dialogues: An approach to the assessment of mother-infant interaction. *Child Development, 48,* 195–203.

Bakeman, R., Brownlee, J. R. 1980. The strategic use of parallel play: A sequential analysis. *Child Development, 51,* 873–878.

Baker, L. A., & Daniels, D. 1990. Nonshared environmental influences and personality differences in adult twins. *Journal of Personality and Social Psychology, 58,* 103–110.

Baldwin, D. A., & Markman, E. M. 1989. Establishing word-object relations: A first step. *Child Development, 60,* 381–398.

Baldwin, D. V., & Skinner, M. L. 1989. Structural model for antisocial behavior: Generalization to single-mother families. *Developmental Psychology, 25,* 45–50.

Bales, J. 1984. Freedom, support boost creativity. *APA Monitor* (November), p. 28.

Bales, J. 1985. Impact of aging varies with skill. *APA Monitor* (December), p. 28.

Balkwell, C. 1981. Transition to widowhood: A review of the literature. *Family Relations, 30,* 117–127.

Baltes, P. B. 1979. Life-span developmental psychology: Some converging observation of history and theory. In P. B. Baltes & O. G. Brim, Jr. (Eds.), *Life-span development and behavior* (Vol. 2). New York: Academic Press.

Baltes, P. B. 1987. Theoretical propositions of life-span development psychology: On the dynamics of growth and decline. *Developmental Psychology, 23,* 611–626.

Baltes, P. B., Featherman, D. L., and Lerner, R. M. (Eds.). 1988. *Life-span development and behavior* (Vol 8.), Hillsdale, N.J.: Erlbaum.

Baltes, P. B., & Nesselroade, J. R. 1984. Paradigm lost and paradigm regained. *American Sociological Review, 49,* 841–847.

Baltes, P. B., & Schaie, K. W. 1974. The myth of the twilight years. *Psychology Today, 7* (March), pp. 35–38f.

Baltes, P. B., & Schaie, K. W. 1976. On the

plasticity of intelligence in adulthood and old age. *American Psychologist, 31,* 720–725.

Baltes, P. B., Sowarka, D., & Kliegl, R. 1989. Cognitive training research on fluid intelligence in old age: What can older adults achieve by themselves? *Psychology and Aging, 4,* 217–221.

Baltes, P. B., & Willis, S. L. 1977. Toward psychological theories of aging and development. In J. E. Birren & K. W. Schale (Eds.), *Handbook on the psychology of aging.* New York: Van Nostrand.

Band, E. B., & Weisz, J. R. How to feel better when it feels bad: Children's perspectives on coping with everyday stress. *Developmental Psychology, 24,* 247–253.

Bandura, A. 1964. The stormy decade: Fact or fiction? *Psychology in the Schools, 1,* 224–231.

Bandura, A. 1971a. *Psychological modeling: Conflicting theories.* Chicago: Aldine-Atherton.

Bandura, A. 1973. *Aggression: A social lerning analysis.* Englewood Cliffs, N.J.: Prentice-Hall.

Bandura, A. 1977. *Social learning theory.* Englewood Cliffs, N.J.: Prentice-Hall.

Bandura, A. 1982. The psychology of chance encounters and life paths. *American Psychologist, 37,* 747–755.

Bandura, A. 1986. *Social foundations of thought and action: A social cognitive theory.* Englewood Cliffs, N.J.: Prentice-Hall.

Bandura, A. 1989a. Human agency in social cognitive theory. *American Psychologist, 44,* 1175–1184.

Bandura, A. 1989b. Regulation of cognitive processes through perceived self-efficacy. *Developmental Psychology, 25,* 729–735.

Bandura, A., & Cervone, D. 1983. Self-evaluative and self-efficacy mechanisms governing the motivational effects of goal systems. *Journal of Personality and Social Psychology, 45,* 1017–1028.

Bandura, A., Grusec, J. E., & Menlove, F. L. 1967. Vicarious extinction of avoidance behavior. *Journal of Personality and Social Psychology, 5,* 16–23.

Bandura, A., Ross, D., & Ross, S. 1961. Transmission of aggression through imitation of aggressive models. *Journal of Abnormal and Social Psychology, 63,* 575–582.

Bandura, A., Ross, D., & Ross, S. 1963. Imitation of film-mediated aggressive models. *Journal of Abnormal and Social Psychology, 66,* 3–11.

Bane, M. J. 1976. *Here to stay: American families in the twentieth century.* New York: Basic Books.

Bane, M. J., & Ellwood, D. T. 1989. One fifth of the nation's children: Why are they poor? *Science, 245,* 1047–1053.

Barclay, C. R., & Newell, K. M. 1980. Children's processing of information in motor skill acquisition. *Journal of Experimental Child Psychology, 30,* 98–108.

Bard, B. 1975. The failure of our school drug abuse program. *Phi Delta Kappan, 57,* 251–255.

Barden, J. C. 1990a. Poverty rate is up sharply for very young, study says. *New York Times* (April 16), p. A7.

Barden, J. C. 1990b. Toll of troubled families: Flood of homeless youth. *New York Times* (February 5), pp. A1, B7.

Bardouille-Crema, A., Black, K. N., & Feldhusen, J. 1986. Performance on Piagetian tasks of black children of differing socioeconomic levels. *Developmental Psychology, 22,* 841–844.

Barenboim, C. 1977. Developmental changes in the interpersonal cognitive system from middle childhood to adolescence. *Child Development, 48,* 1467–1474.

Barenboim, C. 1981. The development of person perception in childhood and adolescence: From behavioral comparisons to psychological constructs to psychological comparisons. *Child Development, 52,* 129–144.

Barnes, G. M., Farrell, M. P., & Cairns, A. 1986. Parental socialization factors and adolescent drinking behaviors. *Journal of Marriage and the Family, 48,* 27–36.

Barnes, K. E. 1971. Preschool play norms: A replication. *Developmental Psychology, 5,* 99–103.

Barnett, A. B., Weiss, I. P., Sotillo, M. V., Ohlrich, E. S., Shkurovich, M., & Cravioto, J. 1978. Abnormal auditory evoked potentials in early infancy malnutrition. *Science, 201* (August 4), pp. 450–451.

Barnett, M. A. 1987. Empathy and related responses in children. In N. Eisenberg & J. Strayer (Eds.), *Empathy and its development.* New York: Cambridge University Press.

Barnett, R. C., & Baruch, G. K. 1983. *Lifeprints: New patterns of love and work for today's women.* New York: New American Library.

Baron, L., & Straus, M. A. 1989. *Four theories of rape in American society.* New Haven, Conn.: Yale University Press.

Barr, H. M., Streissguth, A. P., Darby, B. L., & Sampson, P. D. 1990. Prenatal exposure to alcohol, caffeine, tobacco, and aspirin: Effects on fine and gross motor performance in 4-year-old children. *Developmental Psychology, 26,* 339–348.

Barrera, M. E., & Maurer, D. 1981a. Discrimination of strangers by the three-month-old. *Child Development, 52,* 558–563.

Barrera, M. E., & Maurer, D. 1981b. Recognition of mother's photographed face by the three-month-old infant. *Child Development, 52,* 714–716.

Barrett, D. E., Radke-Yarrow, M., & Klein, R. E. 1982. Chronic malnutrition and child behavior. *Developmental Psychology, 18,* 541–556.

Barringer, F. 1989. Study on marriage patterns revised, omitting impact of women's careers. *New York Times* (November 11), p.

Barringer, F. 1990. What is youth coming to? *New York Times* (August 19), p. 1E.

Barringer, F. 1991a. Changes in U.S. households: Single parents amid solitude. *New York Times* (June 7), pp. A1, A12.

Barringer, F. 1991b. The sting of AIDS, the scorn of strangers. *New York Times* (February 9), pp. 1, 10.

Barringer, F. 1991c. With teens and alcohol, it's just say when. *New York Times* (June 23), pp. E1, E4.

Barron, F. 1969. *Creative person and creative process.* New York: Holt, Rinehart and Winston.

Bart, P. B. 1972. Depression in middle-age women. In V. Gornick & B. K. Moran (Eds.), *Women in sexist society.* New York: The New American Library.

Bar-Tal, D., & Bar-Zohar, Y. 1977. The relationship between perception of locus of control and academic achievement. *Contemporary Educational Psychology, 2,* 181–199.

Barth, R. P., & Berry, M. 1988. *Adoption and disruption: Rates, risks, and responses.* Hawthorne, NY: Aldine de Gruyter.

Barton, E. M., Balters, M. M., & Orzech, M. J. 1980. Etiology of dependence in older nursing home residents during morning care: The role of staff behavior. *Journal of Personality and Social Psychology, 38,* 423–431.

Bartoshuk, L. M., Rifkin, B., Marks, L. E., & Bars, P. 1986. Taste and aging. *Journal of Gerontology, 41,* 51–57.

Bartsch, K., Wellman, H. 1989. Young children's attribution of action to beliefs and desires. *Child Development, 60,* 946–964.

Baruch, G., & Barnett, R. C. 1983. Adult daughters' relationships with their mothers. *Journal of Marriage and the Family, 45,* 601–606.

Baruch, G., & Brooks-Gunn, J. (Eds.). 1984. *Women in midlife: Women in context.* New York: Plenum.

Baruch, G. K., & Barnett, R. 1986. Role quality, multiple role involvement, and psychological well-being in midlife women. *Journal of Personality and Social Psychology, 51,* 578–585.

Baruch, G. K., & Barnett, R. C. 1986. Consequences of fathers' participation in family work: Parents' role strain and well-being. *Journal of Personality and Social Psychology, 51,* 983–992.

Bashore, T. R., Osman, A., & Heffley, E. F., III. 1989. Mental slowing in elderly persons. A cognitive psychophysiological analysis. *Psychology and Aging, 4,* 235–244.

Baskett, L. M. 1985. Sibling status effects: Adult expectations. *Developmental Psychology, 21,* 441–445.

Bass, M., Kravath, R. E., & Glass, L. 1986. Death-scene investigation in sudden infant death. *New England Journal of Medicine, 315,* 100–105.

Bates, E., Bretherton, I., & Snyder, L. 1988. *From first words to grammar: Individual differences and dissociable mechanisms.* New York: Cambridge University Press.

Bates, E., O'Connell, B., & Shore, C. 1987. Language and communication in infancy. In J. Osofsky (Ed.), *Handbook of infant development* (2nd ed.). New York: Wiley.

Bates, E., & Snyder, L. 1987. The cognitive hypothesis in language development. In I. Uzgiris & J. McV. Hunt (Eds.), *Research with scales of psychological development in infancy.* Champaign-Urbana: University of Illinois Press.

Bates, E., Thal, D., Whitesell, K., Fenson, L., & Oakes, L. 1989. Integrating language and gesture in infancy. *Developmental Psychology, 25,* 1004–1019.

Batson, C. D. 1990. How social an animal? The human capacity for caring. *American Psychologist, 45,* 336–346.

Batson, C. D., Dyck, J. L., Brandt, J. R., Batson, J. G., Powell, A. L., McMaster, M. R., & Griffitt, C. 1988. Five studies testing two new egotistic alternatives to the empathy-altruism hypothesis. *Journal of Personality and Social Psychology, 55,* 52–77.

Bauer, P. J., & Mandler, J. M. 1989. One thing follows another: Effects of temporal structure on 1- to 2-year-olds' recall of events. *Developmental Psychology, 25,* 197–206.

Baumann, M. 1991. Caring for parents. *USA Today* (January 8), p. D1.

Baumeister, R. F., & Scher, S. J. 1988. Self-defeating behavior patterns among normal individuals: Review and analysis of common self-destructive tendencies. *Psychological Bulletin, 104,* 3–22.

Baumrind, D. 1966. Effects of authoritative parental control on child behavior. *Child Development, 37,* 887–907.

Baumrind, D. 1971a. Current patterns of parental authority. *Developmental Psychology Monographs, 4,* 1–103.

Baumrind, D. 1972. Socialization and instrumental competence in young children. In W. W. Hartup (Ed.), *The young child* (Vol. 2). Washington, D.C.: National Association for the Education of Young Children.

Baumrind, D. 1986. Sex differences in moral reasoning. *Child Development, 57,* 511–521.

Baumrind, D. 1989. The permanence of change and the impermanence of stability. *Human Development, 32,* 187–195.

Bayley, N. 1935. The development of motor abilities during the first three years. *Monographs of the Society for Research in Child Development, 1.*

Bayley, N. 1956. Individual patterns of development. *Child Development, 27,* 45–74.

Bayley, N. 1965. Research in child development: A longitudinal perspective. *Merrill-Palmer Quarterly, 11,* 184–190.

Beaconsfield, P., Birdwood, G., & Beaconsfield, R. 1980. The placenta. *Scientific American, 243* (August), pp. 95–102.

Beadle, G., & Beadle, M. 1966. *The language of life.* Garden City, N.Y.: Doubleday.

Beal, C. R., & Belgrad, S. L. 1990. The development of message evaluation skills in young children. *Child Development, 61,* 705–712.

Beck, A. T. 1967. *Depression: Clinical, experimental, and theoretical aspects.* New York: Harper & Row.

Beck, A. T. 1976. *Cognitive therapy and the emotional disorders.* New York: International Universities Press.

Beck, M. 1990a. Aging: Trading places. *Newsweek* (July 16), pp. 48–54.

Beck, M. 1990b. A home away from home. *Newsweek* (July 2), pp. 56–58.

Beck, M. 1991. School days for seniors. *Newsweek* (November 11), pp. 60–64.

Beck, S. H. 1982. Adjustment to and satisfaction with retirement. *Journal of Gerontology, 37,* 616–624.

Becker, J. Skinner, L., Abel, G., Howell, J., & Bruce, K. 1982. The effects of sexual assault on rape and attempted rape victims.

Victimology: An International Journal, 7, 106–113.

Becker, M. T. 1976. *A learning analysis of the development of peer-oriented behavior in nine-month-old infants.* Paper presented at the 56th Annual Meeting of the Western Psychological Association, Los Angeles (April).

Becker, W. C. 1964. Consequences of different kinds of parental discipline. In M. L. Hoffman & L. W. Hoffman (Eds.), *Review of child development research.* New York: Russell Sage Foundation.

Beckman, L. J. 1981. Effects of social interaction and children's relative inputs on older women's psychological well-being. *Journal of Personality and Social Psychology, 41,* 1075–1086.

Beer, W. R. 1989. *Strangers in the house: The world of stepsiblings and half-siblings.* New Brunswick, N.J.: Transaction.

Begley, S. 1990. The search for the fountain of youth. *Newsweek* (March 5), pp. 44–48.

Begley, S. 1991. Do you hear what I hear? *Newsweek Special Issue* (Summer), pp. 12–14.

Behrend, D. A. 1990. The development of verb concepts. Children's use of verbs to label familiar and novel events. *Child Development, 61,* 681–696.

Behrens, M. L. 1954. Child rearing and the character structure of the mother. *Child Development, 20,* 225–238.

Beilin, H. 1989a. Commentary. *Human Development, 32,* 358–362.

Beilin, H. 1989b. Piagetian theory. In R. Vasta (Ed.), Six developmental theories: Revised formulations and current issues. *Annals of Child Development, 6,* 85–131.

Beilin, H. 1990. Piaget's theory: Alive and more vigorous than ever. *Human Development, 33,* 362–365.

Belkin, L. 1985. Counseling and support following miscarriage. *New York Times* (June 6), p. 20.

Bell, A. P., and Weinberg, M. S. 1978. *Homosexualities: A study of diversity among men and women.* New York: Simon & Schuster.

Bell, A. P., Weinberg, M. S., & Hammersmith, S. K. 1981. *Sexual preference: Its development in men and women.* Bloomington: Indiana University Press.

Bell, R. Q. 1953. Convergence: An accelerated longitudinal approach. *Child Development, 24,* 145–152.

Bell, R. Q. 1954. An experimental test of the accelerated longitudinal approach. *Child Development, 25,* 281–286.

Bell, R. Q. 1968. A reinterpretation of effects in studies of socialization. *Psychological Review, 75,* 81–95.

Bell, R. R., & Coughey, K. 1980. Premarital sexual experience among college females, 1958, 1968, 1978. *Family Relations, 29,* 353–357.

Bell, R. W., & Bell, N. J. 1989. (Eds.). *Sociobiology and the social sciences.* Lubbock, Texas: Texas Tech University Press.

Bell, S. M. 1970. The development of the concept of object as related to infant-mother attachment. *Child Development, 41,* 291–311.

Bell, S. M., & Ainsworth, M. D. S. 1972. Infant crying and maternal responsiveness. *Child Development, 43,* 1171–1190.

Belsky, J. 1981. Early human experience. A family perspective. *Developmental Psychology, 17,* 3–23.

Belsky, J. 1984a. The determinants of parenting: A process model. *Child Development, 55,* 83–96.

Belsky, J. 1984b. Two waves of day care research: Developmental effects and conditions of quality. In R. Ainslie (Ed.). *The child and the day care setting.* New York: Praeger.

Belsky, J. 1985. Exploring individual differences in marital change across the transition to parenthood: The role of violated expectations. *Journal of Marriage and the Family, 47,* 1037–1044.

Belsky, J. 1988. The "effects" of infant day care reconsidered. *Early Childhood Research Quarterly, 3,* 235–272.

Belsky, J. 1990. Parental and nonparental child care and children's socioemotional development: A decade in review. *Journal of Marriage and the Family, 52,* 885–903.

Belsky, J., & Isabella, R. 1988. Maternal, infant, and social contextual determinants of attachment security. In J. Belsky & T. Nezworski (Eds.), *Clinical implications of attachment.* Hillsdale, N.J.: Erlbaum.

Belsky, J., Lang, M., & Huston, T. L. 1987. Sex typing and division of labor as determinants of marital change across the transition to parenthood. *Journal of Personality and Social Psychology, 50,* 517–522.

Belsky, J., Lang, M. E., & Rovine, M. 1985. Stability and change in marriage across the transition to parenthood: A second study. *Journal of Marriage and the Family, 47,* 855–865.

Belsky, J., & Rovine, M. 1987. Temperament and attachment security in the strange situation: An empirical rapproachement. *Child Development, 58,* 787–795.

Belsky, J., & Rovine, M. J. 1988. Nonmaternal care in the first year of life and the security of infant-parent attachment. *Child Development, 59,* 157–167.

Belsky, J., & Rovine, M. 1990. Patterns of marital change across the transition to parenthood: Pregnancy to three years postpartum. *Journal of Marriage and the Family, 52,* 5–19.

Belsky, J., Spanier, G. B., & Rovine, M. 1983. Stability and change in marriage across the transition to parenthood. *Journal of Marriage and the Family, 45,* 567–577.

Belsky, J., & Steinberg, L. D. 1978. The effects of day care: A critical review. *Child Development, 49,* 929–949.

Belsky, J., Steinberg, L., & Draper, P. 1991. Childhood experience, interpersonal development, and reproductive strategy: An evolutionary theory of socialization. *Child Development, 62,* 647–670.

Belsky, J., Youngblade, L., Rovine, M., & Volling, B. 1991. Patterns of marital change and parent-child interaction. *Journal of Marriage and the Family, 53,* 487–498.

Bem, D., & Allen, A. 1974. On predicting some of the people some of the time: The search for cross-situational consistencies in behavior. *Psychological Review, 81,* 506–520.

Bem, S. 1981. Gender schema theory: A cognitive account of sex typing. *Psychological Bulletin, 88,* 354–364.

Bem, S. L. 1989. Genital knowledge and gender constancy in preschool children. *Child Development, 60,* 649–662.

Bemis, K. M. 1978. Current approaches to the etiology and treatment of anorexia nervosa. *Psychological Bulletin, 85,* 593–617.

Benedek, E. P., & Benedek, R. S. 1979. Joint custody: Solution or illusion? *American Journal of Psychiatry, 136,* 1540–1544.

Benedict, H. 1976. *Language comprehension in 10 sixteen-month-old infants.* Unpublished doctoral dissertation, Yale University.

Bengtson, V. L. 1970. The generation gap: A review and typology of social-psychological perspectives. *Youth and Society, 2,* 7–32.

Bengtson, V. L., Dowd, J. J., Smith, D. H., & Inkeles, A. 1975. Modernization, modernity, and perceptions of aging: A cross-cultural study. *Journal of Gerontology, 30,* 688–695.

Bengston, V. L., & Starr, J. M. 1975. Contrast and consensus: A generational analysis of youth in the 1970s. In R. J. Havighurst & P. H. Dreyer (Eds.), *Youth: The seventy-fourth yearbook of the National Society for the Study of Education.* Chicago: University of Chicago Press.

Bennet, A. 1987. Losing ground? Surveyed firms report fewer women directors. *Wall Street Journal* (July 17), p. 17.

Bennett, N. G., Bloom, D. E., & Craig, P. H. 1986. *Black and white marriage patterns: Why so different?* Unpublished manuscript.

Bennett, N. G., Bloom, D. E., & Craig, P. H. 1989. The divergence of black and white marriage patterns. *American Journal of Sociology, 95,* 692–722.

Bennett, W., & Gurin, J. 1982. *The dieter's dilemma.* New York: Basic Books.

Bennett, W. J. 1986. *First lessons: A report on elementary education in America.* Washington, D.C.: Government Printing Office.

Benson, J. B., & Uzgiris, I. C. 1985. Effect of self-initiated locomotion on infant search activity. *Developmental Psychology, 21,* 923–931.

Benson, L. 1968. *Fatherhood: A sociological perspective.* New York: Random House.

Bentler, P. M. 1987. Drug use and personality in adolescence and young adulthood: Structural models with nonnormal variables. *Child Development, 58,* 65–79.

Berenda, R. W. 1950. *The influence of the group on the judgments of children.* New York: King's Crown Press.

Bergeman, C. S., Plomin, R., McClearn, G. E., Pedersen, N. L., & Friberg, L. T. 1988. Genotype-environment interaction in personality development: Identical twins reared apart. *Psychology and Aging, 3,* 399–406.

Berger, R., & Berger, P. L. 1983. *The War over the family.* Garden City, N.Y.: Anchor Books.

Berger, J. 1989. All in the game. *New York*

Times Special Section on Education (August 6), pp. 23–24.

Bergmann, B. R. 1987. *The economic emergence of women.* New York: Basic Books.

Berk, R. A., & Newton, P. J. 1985. Does arrest really deter wife battery? An effort to replicate the findings of the Minneapolis spouse abuse experiment. *American Sociological Review, 50,* 253–262.

Berkman, L. F., & Breslow, L. 1983. *Health and ways of living: The Alameda County study.* New York: Oxford University Press.

Berkowitz, L. (Ed.). 1988. *Advances in experimental social psychology.* Vol. 21: *Social psychological studies of the self: Perspectives and programs.* San Diego, Calif.: Academic Press.

Berman, P. W. 1980. Are women more responsive than men to the young? A review of developmental and situational variables. *Psychological Bulletin, 88,* 668–695.

Bermant, G., & Davidson, J. M. 1974. *Biological bases of sexual behavior.* New York: Harper & Row.

Berndt, T. J. 1871*a.* Age changes and changes over time in prosocial intentions and behavior between friends. *Developmental Psychology, 17,* 408–416.

Berndt, T. J. 1981*b.* Effects of friendship on prosocial intentions and behavior. *Child Development, 52,* 636–643.

Berndt, T. J. 1982. The features and effects of friendship in early adolescence. *Child Development, 53,* 1447–1460.

Berndt, T. J., & Ladd, G. W. (Eds.). 1989. *Peer relationships in child development.* New York: Wiley.

Berndt, T. J., & Walster, E. 1974. A little bit about love. In E. L. Huston (Ed.), *Foundations of interpersonal attraction.* New York: Academic Press.

Bernstein, A., & Warner, G. 1984. *Women treating women.* New York: International Universities Press.

Bernstein, I. L. 1990. Salt preference and development. *Developmental Psychology, 26,* 552–554.

Bernstein, R. 1990. In U.S. schools a war of words. *New York Times Magazine* (October 14), pp. 34, 48+.

Berscheid, E., & Walster, E. 1974. A little bit about love. In Huston, E. L. (Ed.), *Foundations of interpersonal attraction.* New York: Academic Press.

Besharov, D. J. (Ed.). 1988. *Protecting children from abuse and neglect: Policy and practice.* Springfield, Ill.: Charles C. Thomas.

Besharov, D. J., Quin, A., & Zinsmeister, K. 1987. A portrait in black and white: Out-of-wedlock births. *Public Opinion, 10* (May/June), 43–45.

Best, C. T. (Ed.). 1985. *Hemispheric function and collaboration in the child.* Orlando, Fla.: Academic Press.

Bettes, B. A. 1988. Maternal depression and motherese: Temporal and intonational features. *Child Development, 59,* 1089–1096.

Bianchi, S. M. 1984. Children's progress through school: A research note. *Sociology of Education, 57,* 184–192.

Bianchi, S. M., & Seltzer, J. A. 1986. Life with-out father. *American Demographics, 8* (December), 43–47.

Biddle, B. J., Bank, B. J., & Anderson, D. S. 1981. The structure of idleness. *Sociology of Education, 54,* 106–119.

Bidell, T. 1988. Vygotsky, Piaget and the dialectic of development. *Human Development, 31,* 329–348.

Bieber, I. 1962. *Homosexuality: A psychoanalytic study of male homosexuals.* New York: Basic Books.

Bielby, W. T., & Bielby, D. D. 1989. Family ties: Balancing commitments to work and family in dual earner households. *American Sociological Review, 54,* 776–789.

Biernat, M., & Wortman, C. B. 1991. Sharing of home responsibilities between professional employed women and their husbands. *Journal of Personality and Social Psychology, 60,* 844–860.

Bigler, R. S., & Liben, L. S. 1990. The role of attitudes and interventions in gender-schematic processing. *Child Development, 61,* 1440–1452.

Bijou, S. W., & Baer, D. M. 1965. A social learning model of attachment. Socialization—the development of behavior to social stimuli. In *Child development II.* New York: Appleton-Century-Crofts.

Bilgé, B., & Kaufman, G. 1983. Children of divorce and one-parent families: Cross-cultural perspectives. *Family Relations, 32,* 59–71.

Biller, H. B. 1971. *Father, child, and sex roles.* Lexington, Mass.: Heath Lexington Books.

Biller, H. B. 1974. *The father-infant relationship: Some naturalistic observations.* Unpublished manuscript, University of Rhode Island.

Biller, H. B. 1976. The father and personality development: Paternal deprivation and sex-role development. In M. E. Lamb (Ed.), *The role of the father in child development.* New York: Wiley.

Biller, H. B. 1982. Fatherhood: Implications for child and adult development. In B. B. Wolman (Ed.), *Handbook of developmental psychology.* Englewood Cliffs, N.J.: Prentice-Hall.

Billy, J. O. G., Rodgers, J. L., & Udry, J. R. 1984. Adolescent sexual behavior and friendship choice. *Social Forces, 62,* 653–678.

Billy, J. O. G., & Udry, J. R. 1985. Patterns of adolescent friendship and effects of sexual behavior. *Social Psychology Quarterly, 48,* 27–41.

Birch, L. L., Birch, D., Marlin, D. W., & Kramer, L. 1982. *Appetite, 3,* 125–134.

Birchwood, M. J., Hallett, S. E., & Preston, M. C. 1989. *Schizophrenia: An integrated approach to research and treatment.* New York: New York University Press.

Bird, G. W., Bird, G. A., & Scruggs, M. 1984. Determinants of family task sharing: A study of husbands and wives. *Journal of Marriage and the Family, 46,* 345–355.

Birnholz, J. C., & Benacerraf, B. R. 1983. The development of human fetal hearing. *Science, 222,* 516–518.

Birns, B., & Hay, D. F. (Eds.). 1988. *The different faces of motherhood.* New York: Plenum.

Birns, G., Blank, M., & Bridger, W. H. 1966. The effectiveness of various soothing techniques on human neonates. *Psychosomatic Medicine, 28,* 316–322.

Birren, J. E. 1987. The best of all stories. *Psychology Today, 21* (May), pp. 91–92.

Birren, J. E., & Bengtson, V. L. (Eds.). 1988. *Emergent theories of aging.* New York: Springer.

Bischof, L. J. 1976. *Adult psychology* (2nd ed.). New York: Harper & Row.

Bishop, J. E. 1980. The personal and business costs of "job burnout." *Wall Street Journal* (November 11), pp. 25, 32.

Bishop, J. E. 1983. New gene probes may permit early predictions of disease. *Wall Street Journal* (December 23), p. 11.

Bishop, J. E. 1986. Researchers close in on some genetic bases of antisocial behavior. *Wall Street Journal* (February 12), pp. 1, 20.

Bishop, J. E. 1990. Study finds doctors tend to postpone heart surgery for women, raising risk. *Wall Street Journal* (April 16), p. B4.

Bisping, R., Steingrueber, H. J., Oltmann, M., & Wenk, C. 1990. Adults' tolerance of cries: An experimental investigation of acoustic features. *Child Development, 61,* pp. 1218–1229.

Bjorklund, D. F. 1987. A note on neonatal imitation. *Developmental Review, 7,* pp. 86–92.

Black, G. S. 1985. The life quality index. *Public Opinion, 8* (June/July), pp. 52–54.

Blackman, A. 1991. Making babies. *Time* (September 30), pp. 56–63.

Blackwood, B. M. 1935. *Both sides of Buka passage.* New York: Oxford University Press.

Blake, J. 1989. *Family size and achievement.* Berkeley: University of California Press.

Blakeslee, S. 1986. Rapid changes seen in young brain. *New York Times* (June 24), pp. 17, 20.

Blakeslee, S. 1987. Genetic discoveries raise painful questions. *New York Times* (April 21), pp. 19, 23.

Blakeslee, S. 1989. Crib death: Suspicion turns to the brain. *New York Times* (February 14), pp. 17, 19.

Blakeslee, S. 1991*a.* Bachelorhood after 40: It may be a state of mind. *New York Times* (August 28), pp. B1, B6.

Blakeslee, S. 1991*b.* Brain yields new clues on its organization for language. *New York Times* (September 10), pp. B5, B6.

Blakeslee, S. 1991*c.* Research on birth defects turns to flaws in sperm. *New York Times* (January 1), pp. 1, 16.

Blanchard R. W., & Biller, H. B. 1971. Father availability and academic performance among third-grade boys. *Developmental Psychology, 4,* 301–305.

Blasi, A. 1980. Bridging moral cognition and moral action: A critical review of the literature. *Psychology Bulletin, 88,* 1–45.

Blass, E. M. 1990. Suckling: Determinants, changes, mechanisms, and lasting impressions. *Developmental Psychology, 26,* 520–533.

Blass, E. M., Fillion, T. J., Rochat, P., Hoffmeyer, L. B., & Metzger, M. A. 1989. Sensorimotor and motivational determinants of hand-mouth coordination in 1–3 day-old human infants. *Developmental Psychology, 25,* 963–975.

Blau, P. M., & Duncan, O. D. 1967. *The American occupational structure.* New York: Wiley.

Blau, P. M., & Duncan, O. D. 1972. *The American occupational structure* (2nd ed.). New York: Wiley.

Blau, Z. S. 1973. *Old age in a changing society.* New York: New Viewpoints.

Bleichfield, B., & Moely, B. E. 1984. Psychophysiological responses to an infant cry. *Developmental Psychology, 20,* 1082–1091.

Block, J. 1980. From infancy to adulthood: A clarification. *Child Development, 51,* 622–623.

Block, J. H. 1974. Conceptions of sex role: Some cross-cultural and longitudinal perspectives. In R. F. Winch & B. B. Spanier (Eds.), *Selected studies in marriage and the family* (4th ed.). New York: Holt, Rinehart and Winston.

Block, J. H., & Block, J. 1980. The role of ego-control and ego-resiliency in the organization of behavior. In W. A. Collins (Ed.), *Minnesota symposia on child psychology.* Vol. 13. Hillsale, N.J.: Erlbaum.

Block, J. H., Block, J., & Gjerde, P. F. 1986. The personality of children prior to divorce: A prospective study. *Child Development, 57,* 827–840.

Block, J., Block, J. H., & Keyes, S. 1988. Longitudinally foretelling drug usage in adolescence: Early childhood personality and environmental precursors. *Child Development, 59,* 336–355.

Bloom, B. L., Asher, S. J., & White, S. W. 1978. Marital disruption as a stressor: A review and analysis. *Psychological Bulletin, 85,* 867–894.

Bloom, B. S. 1969. Letter to the editor. *Harvard Educational Review, 39,* 419–421.

Bloom, D. E. 1986. Women and work. *American Demographics, 8* (September), 25–30.

Bloom, L. 1970. *Language development: Form and function in emerging grammar.* Cambridge, Mass.: MIT Press.

Bloom, L. 1973. *One word at a time.* The Hague: Mouton.

Blos, P. 1962. *On adolescence: A psychoanalytic interpretation.* New York: Free Press of Glencoe.

Blount, B. G. 1975. Studies in child language, *American Anthropologist, 77,* 580–600.

Blum, J. E., Fosshage, J. L., & Jarvik, L. F. 1972. Intellectual changes and sex differences in octogenarians: A twenty-year longitudinal study of aging. *Developmental Psychology, 7,* 178–187.

Blumenthal, D. 1990. Covering up in the season to take it off. *New York Times* (April 28), p. 16.

Blumer, H. 1969. *Symbolic interactionism: Perspective and method.* Englewood Cliffs, N.J.: Prentice-Hall.

Blumstein, P., & Schwartz, P. 1983. *American couples.* New York: Morrow.

Bluth, D. A., & Traeger, C. M. 1983. The self-concept and self-esteem of early adolescents. *Theory Into Practice, 22,* 91–97.

Bock, R. D., & Moore, E. G. J. 1986. *Advantage and disadvantage: A profile of American youth.* Hillsdale, N.J.: Erlbaum.

Boffey, P. M. 1984. Study reports prove cholesterol can cut heart diseases' risk. *New York Times* (January 13), pp. 1, 11.

Boffey, P. M. 1985. Alzheimer's disease: Families are better. *New York Times* (May 7), pp. 15, 18.

Boggiano, A. K., Main, D. S., & Katz, P. A. 1988. Children's preference for challenge: The role of perceived competence and control. *Journal of Personality and Social Psychology, 54,* 134–141.

Bohannan, P., & Erickson, R. 1978. Stepping in. *Psychology Today, 11* (January), pp. 53+.

Bokemeier, J. L., & Lacy, W. B. 1987. Job values, rewards, and work conditions as factors in job satisfaction among men and women. *Sociological Quarterly, 28,* 189–204.

Boldizar, J. P., Perry, D. G., & Perry, L. C. 1989. Outcome values and aggression. *Child Development, 60,* 571–579.

Boldizar, J. P., Wilson, K. L., & Deemer, D. K. 1989. Gender, life experiences, and moral judgment development: A process-oriented approach. *Journal of Personality and Social Psychology, 57,* 229–238.

Bolton, F., Jr., Morris, L. A., & MacEachron, A. 1989. *Males at risk: The other side of child sexual abuse.* Newbury Park, Calif.: Sage.

Bongaarts, J. 1982. Malnutrition and fertility. *Science, 215,* 1273–1274.

Boocock, S. S. 1972. *An introduction to the sociology of learning.* Boston: Houghton Mifflin.

Boonsong, S. 1968. The development of concentration of mass, weight, and volume in Thai children. Unpublished master's thesis, College of Education, Bankok, Thailand.

Booth, C. L., Mitchell, S. K., Bernard, K. E., & Spieker, S. J. 1989. Development of maternal social skills in multiproblem families: Effects on the mother-child relationship. *Developmental Psychology, 25,* 403–412.

Borke, H. 1975. Piaget's mountains revisited: Change in the egocentric landscape. *Developmental Psychology, 11,* 240–243.

Bornstein, M. H. 1976. Infants' recognition memory for hue. *Developmental Psychology, 12,* 185–191.

Bornstein, M. H. 1989*a*. Information processing (habituation) in infancy and stability in cognitive development. *Human Development, 32,* 129–136.

Bornstein, M. H. 1989*b*. Sensitive periods in development: Structural characteristics and causal interpretations. *Psychological Bulletin, 105,* 179–197.

Bornstein, M. H., Kessen, W., & Weiskopf, S. 1976. Color vision and hue categorization in young human infants. *Journal of Experimental Psychology: Human Perception and Performance, 2,* 115–129.

Bornstein, M. H., & Marks, L. E. 1982. Color revisionism. *Psychology Today, 16* (January), pp. 64–73.

Bornstein, M. H., & Sigman, M. D. 1986. Continuity in mental development from infancy. *Child Development, 57,* 251–274.

Boskin, N. J. 1986. *Too many promises: The uncertain future of Social Security.* New York: Dow-Jones-Irwin.

Bosse, R., Aldwin, C. M., Levenson, M. R., & Workman-Daniels, K. 1991. How stressful is retirement? Findings from the normative aging study. *Journal of Gerontology, 46,* pp. 9–14.

Botvin, G. J., & Murray, F. B. 1975. The efficacy of peer modeling and social conflicts in the acquisition of conservation. *Child Development, 46,* 796–799.

Botwinick, J. 1977. Intellectual abilities. In J. E. Birren & K. W. Schaie (Eds.), *Handbook of the psychology of aging.* New York: Van Nostrand.

Botwinick, J. 1978. *Aging and behavior: A comprehensive integration of research findings* (2nd ed.). New York: Springer.

Botwinick, J., West, R., & Storandt, M. 1978. Predicting death from behavioral test performance. *Journal of Gerontology, 33,* 755–762.

Bouchard, T. J., Jr., Lykken, D. T., McGue, M., Segal, N.L., & Tellegen, A. 1990. Sources of human psychological differences: The Minnesota study of twins reared apart. *Science, 250,* 223–228.

Bound, J., Duncan, G. J., Laren, D. S., & Oleinick, L. 1991. Poverty dynamics in widowhood. *Journal of Gerontology, 46,* S115–124.

Bourque, L. B. 1989. *Defining rape.* Durham, N.C.: Duke University Press.

Bourque, L. B., & Back, K. W. 1977. Life graphs and life events. *Journal of Gerontology, 32,* 669–674.

Bouton, K. 1982. Fighting male infertility. *New York Times Magazine* (June 13), pp. 84+.

Bower, T. G. R. 1971. The object in the world of the infant. *Scientific American, 225* (October), pp. 30–38.

Bower, T. G. R. 1974. *Development in infancy.* San Francisco: Freeman.

Bower, T. G. R. 1975. Infant perception of the third dimension and object concept development. In L. B. Cohen & P. Salapatek (Eds.), *Infant perception: From sensation to cognition* (Vol. 2). New York: Academic Press.

Bower, T. G. R. 1976. Repetitive processes in child development. *Scientific American, 235* (November), pp. 38–47.

Bower, T. G. R. 1977. *A primer of infant development.* San Francisco: Freeman.

Bowerman, C., & Irish, D. 1962. Some relationships of stepchildren to their parents. *Journal of Marriage and the Family, 36,* 498–514.

Bowers, W. A., Jr., Brackbill, Y., Conway, E., & Steinschneider, A. 1970. The effects of obstetrical medication on fetus and infant. *Monographs of the Society for Research in Child Development, 35* (Whole No. 137).

Bowlby, J. 1969. *Attachment.* New York: Basic Books.

Bowlby, J. 1988. *A secure base: Clinical applications of attachment theory.* London: Routledge.

Bowles, S., & Gintis, H. 1976. *Schooling in capitalist America: Educational reform and the contradictions of economic life.* New York: Basic Books.

Bowling, A., & Browne, P. D. 1991. Social networks, health, and emotional well-being among the oldest old in London. *Journal of Gerontology, 46,* S20–32.

Boxer, A. M., Tobin-Richards, M., & Petersen, A. C. 1983. Puberty: Physical change and its significance in early adolescence. *Theory Into Practice, 22,* 85–90.

Boyd, C. J. 1989. Mothers and daughters: A discussion of theory and research. *Journal of Marriage and the Family, 51,* 291–301.

Boyer, E. L. 1987a. *College—the undergraduate experience in America.* New York: Harper & Row.

Boyer, E. L. 1987b. Early schooling and the nation's future. *Educational Leadership* (March), pp. 4–6.

Boyes, M. C., & Walker, L. J. 1988. Implications of cultural diversity for the universality claims of Kohlberg's theory of moral reasoning. *Human Development, 31,* 44–59.

Brachfield-Child, S. 1986. Parents as teachers: Comparisons of mothers' and fathers' instructional interactions with infants. *Infant Behavior and Development, 9,* 127–131.

Brackbill, Y. 1979. Obstetrical medication and infant behavior. In J. D. Osofsky (Ed.), *Handbook of infant development.* New York: Wiley.

Brackbill, Y., & Nichols, P. L. 1982. A test of the confluence model of intellectual development. *Developmental Psychology, 18,* 192–198.

Braddock, J. H., II. 1985. School desegregation and black assimilation. *Journal of Social Issues, 41,* 9–22.

Braddock, J. H. II, Crain, R. L., & McPartland. 1984. A long-term view of school desegregation: Some recent studies of graduates as adults. *Phi Delta Kappan, 66,* 259–264.

Bradley, R. H., & Caldwell, B. M. 1984a. 174 Children: A study of the relationship between home environment and cognitive development during the first 5 years. In A. W. Gottfried (Ed.), *Home environment and early cognitive development.* Orlando, Fla.: Academic Press.

Bradley, R. H., & Caldwell, B. M. 1984b. The relation of infants' home environments to achievement test performance in first grade: A follow-up study. *Child Development, 55,* 803–809.

Bradley, R. H., Caldwell, B. M., & Rock, S. L. 1988. Home environment and school performance: A ten-year follow-up and examination of three models of environmental action. *Child Development, 59,* 852–867.

Bradsher, K. 1990. For the man under 30, where is the woman? *New York Times* (January 17), pp. 14, 20.

Braine, M. D. S. 1963. The ontogeny of English phrase structure: The first phase. *Language, 39,* 1–14.

Brainerd, D. J. 1978. The stage question in cognitive-developmental theory. *Behavioral and Brain Sciences, 1,* 173–213.

Brainerd, C. J. 1979. Concept learning and development. In H. J. Klausmeir (Ed.). *Cognitive development from an information processing and a Piagetian view: Results of a longitudinal study.* Cambridge, Mass: Ballinger.

Braithwaite, V. A. 1986. Old age stereotypes: Reconciling contradictions. *Journal of Gerontology, 41,* 353–360.

Brake, S. C., Fifer, W. P., Alfasi, G., & Fleischman, A. 1988. The first nutritive sucking responses of premature newborns. *Infant Behavior and Development, 11,* 1–19.

Bralove, M. 1981. For middle-aged man, a wife's new career upsets old balances. *Wall Street Journal* (November 9), pp. 1, 24.

Branch, C. W., & Newcombe, N. 1986. Racial attitude development among young black children as a function of parental attitudes; A longitudinal and cross-sectional study. *Child Development, 57,* 712–721.

Brand, E., Clingempeel, W. E., & Bowen-Woodward, K. 1988. Family relationships and children's psychological adjustment in stepmother and stepfather families. In E. M. Hethrington & J. D. Arasteh (Eds.), *Impact of divorce, single-parenting, and stepparenting on children.* Hillsdale, N.J.: Erlbaum.

Brandwein, R. A., Brown, C. A. & Fox, E. M. 1974. Women and children last: The social situation of divorced mothers and their families. *Journal of Marriage and the Family, 36,* 498–514.

Braungart, R. G. 1975. Youth and social movements. In S. E. Dragastin & G. H. Elder, Jr. (Eds.), *Adolescence in the life cycle: Psychological change and social context.* New York: Wiley.

Braungart, R. G., & Braungart, M. M. 1979. Reference group, social judgment, and student politics. *Adolescence, 14,* 135–157.

Braungart, R. G., & Braungart, M. M. 1986. Life-course and generational politics. *Annual Review of Sociology, 12,* 205–231.

Brazelton, T. B. 1962. Observations of the neonate. *Journal of Child Psychiatry, 1,* 38–58.

Brazelton, T. B. 1978. Introduction. In A. J. Sameroff (Ed.), Organization and stability of newborn behavior: A commentary on the Brazelton Neonatal Behavior Assessment Scale. *Monographs of the Society for Research in Child Development, 43* (177), 1–13.

Brazelton, T. B. 1990a. Saving the bathwater. *Child Development, 61,* 1661–1671.

Brazelton, T. B. 1990b. Why is America failing its children? *New York Times Magazine* (September 9), pp. 41–50+.

Brazelton, T. B., Robey, J. S., & Collier, G. A. 1969. Infant development in the Zinacanteco Indians of Southern Mexico. *Pediatrics, 44,* 274–293.

Bremner, J. G. 1988. *Infancy.* Oxford, England: Basil Blackwell.

Brendt, T. J., & Perry, T. B. 1986. Children's perceptions of friendships as supportive relationships. *Developmental Psychology, 22,* 640–648.

Brenner, M. H. 1973. *Mental illness and the economy.* Cambridge, Mass.: Harvard University Press.

Brenner, M. H. 1975. Trends in alcohol consumption and associated illnesses: Some effects of economic changes. *American Journal of Public Health, 65,* 1279–1292.

Brenner, M. H. 1976. Estimating the social

costs of national economic policy: Implications for mental and physical health and criminal aggression (Paper No. 5). *Report to the Congressional Research Service of the Library of Congress and Joint Committee of Congress.* Washington, D.C.: Government Printing Office.

Brenton, M. 1977. What can be done about child abuse? *Today's Education, 66,* 51–53.

Bretherton, I., Fritz, J., Zahn-Waxler, C., & Ridgeway, D. 1986. Learning to talk about emotions: A functionalist perspective. *Child Development, 57,* 529–548.

Bretherton, I., & Waters, E. 1985. Growing points of attachment theory and research. *Monographs of the Society for Research in Child Development, 209* (50).

Breu, G. 1990. For a family facing incurable Huntington's disease, finding out is better than the dread of suspicion. *People* (November 5).

Brickman, P., Coates, D., & Janoff-Bulman, R. 1978. Lottery winners and accident victims: Is happiness relative? *Journal of Personality and Social Psychoogy, 36,* 917–927.

Bridgman, M. 1984. Midlifers accept situations and look ahead. *Columbus* (Ohio) *Dispatch* (December 28), p. C1.

Bridges, L. J., Connell, J. P., & Belsky, J. 1988. Similarities and differences in infant-mother and infant-father interaction in the strange situation: A component process analysis. *Developmental Psychology, 24,* 92–100.

Brim, O. G., Jr. 1976. Male mid-life crisis: A comparative analysis. In B. Hess (Ed.), *Growing old in America.* New Brunswick, N.J.: Transaction, Inc.

Brim, O. G., Jr. 1980. Types of life events. *Journal of Social Issues, 36,* 148–157.

Brim, O. G., Jr., & Kagan, J. (Eds.). 1980. *Constancy and change in human development.* Cambridge, Mass.: Harvard University Press.

Bristol, M., Gallagher, J. J., & Schopler, E. 1988. Mothers and fathers of young developmentally disabled and nondisabled boys: Adaptation and spousal support. *Developmental Psychology, 24,* 441–451.

Broadbent, D. E. 1963. Flow of information within the organism. *Journal of Verbal Learning and Verbal Behavior, 2,* 34–39.

Brock, B., & Marshall, R. 1990. *America's choice: High skills or low wages!* New York: Commission on the Skills of the American Work Force.

Brockman, L. M., & Ricciuti, H. N. 1971. Severe protein-calorie malnutrition and cognitive development in infancy and early childhood. *Developmental Psychology, 4,* 312–319.

Broderick, C. B., & Row, G. P. 1968. A scale of preadolescent heterosexual development. *Journal of Marriage and the Family, 30,* 97–101.

Brodie, H. K. 1974. Plasma testosterone levels in heterosexual and homosexual men. *American Journal of Psychiatry, 131,* 82–83.

Brody, E. M. 1990. *Women in the middle: Their parent-care years.* New York: Springer.

Brody, E. M., Johnsen, P. T., Fulcomer, M. C.,

& Lang, A. M. 1983. Women's changing roles and help to elderly patients. *Journal of Gerontology, 38,* 597–607.

Brody, G. H., Neubaum, E., & Forehand, R. 1988. Serial marriage: A heuristic analysis of an emerging family form. *Psychological Bulletin, 103,* 211–222.

Brody, J. E. 1981. Planning to prevent retirement "shock." *New York Times* (May 27), p. 13.

Brody, J. E. 1982. Examining the causes, symptoms and treatment of burnout. *New York Times* (October 6), p. 19.

Brody, J. E. 1983*b.* Heart attacks: Turmoil beneath the calm. *New York Times* (June 21), pp. 17, 19.

Brody, J. E. 1983*d.* A disease afflicting the mind. *New York Times* (November 23), p. 16.

Brody, J. E. 1983*e.* Guidance in the care of patients with Alzheimer's disease. *New York Times* (November 30), p. 17.

Brody, J. E. 1983*f.* Divorce's stress extracts long-term health toll. *New York Times* (December 13), pp. 17 +.

Brody, J. E. 1983*g.* Emotional deprivation seen as devastating form of child abuse. *New York Times* (December 20), pp. 21–22.

Brody, J. E. 1984*a.* The growing militancy of the nation's nonsmokers. *New York Times* (January 15), p. 6E.

Brody, J. E. 1984*b.* Hope grows for vigorous old age. *New York Times* (October 2), pp. 19, 20.

Brody, J. E. 1984*c.* Seeking to prevent teenage suicide. *New York Times* (March 7), pp. 15, 17.

Brody, J. E. 1986*a.* Aging: Studies point toward ways to slow it. *New York Times* (June 10), pp. 15, 18.

Brody, J. E. 1986*b.* Effects of alcohol during pregnancy. *New York Times* (January 15), p. 16.

Brody, J. E. 1987*a.* Parents and childhood obesity. *New York Times* (May 27), p. 14.

Brody, J. E. 1987*b.* Research lifts blame from many of the obese. *New York Times* (March 24), p. 19.

Brody, J. E. 1987*c.* Role of heredity in alcoholism. *New York Times* (August 19), p. 14.

Brody, J. E. 1987*d.* Why many efforts fail to change unhealthy habits. *New York Times* (April 28), p. 19.

Brody, J. E. 1990*a.* Personal health. *New York Times* (October 11), p. B7.

Brody, J. E. 1990*b.* Strength training for the elderly: Discovering an exhilarating road back from muscle atrophy. *New York Times* (August 30), p. B8.

Brody, J. E. 1991*a.* To avoid catching a cold, don't worry about it. *New York Times* (August 29), p. A13.

Brody, J. E., 1991*b.* Foods figuring in cancer fight. *Columbus Dispatch* (March 3), p. 7C.

Brody, J. E. 1991*c.* Personal health: In pursuit of the best possible odds of preventing or minimizing the perils of major diseases. *New York Times* (January 31), p. B9.

Brody, J. E. 1991*d.* A quality of life determined by a baby's size. *New York Times* (October 1), pp. A1, A13.

Broman, S. H., Nichols, P. L., & Kennedy, W. A. 1975. *Preschool IQ: Prenatal and early developmental correlates.* Hillsdale, N.J.: Erlbaum.

Bronfenbrenner, U. 1970. *Two worlds of childhood: U.S. and U.S.S.R.* New York: Russell Sage Foundation.

Bronfenbrenner, U. 1977*a.* Nobody home: The erosion of the American family. *Psychology Today, 10* (May), pp. 40–47.

Bronfenbrenner, U. 1977*b.* Toward an experimental ecology of human development. *American Psychologist, 32,* 513–531.

Bronfenbrenner, U. 1979. *The ecology of human development: Experiments by nature and design.* Cambridge, Mass.: Harvard University Press.

Bronfenbrenner, U. 1986*a.* Alienation and the four worlds of childhood. *Phi Delta Kappan, 67* (February), 430–436.

Bronfenbrenner, U. 1986*b.* Ecology of the family as a context for human development research perspectives. *Developmental Psychology, 22,* 723–742.

Bronfenbrenner, U., & Crouter, A. C. 1983. The evolution of environmental models in developmental research. In P. H. Mussen (Ed.), *Handbook of child psychology* (4th ed., Vol. 1). New York: Wiley.

Bronson, G. 1977*a.* Long exposure to waste anesthetic gas is peril to workers, U.S. Safety unit says. *Wall Street Journal* (March 1), p. 10.

Bronson, G. 1977*b.* Mean sperm counts in American men may have dropped. *Wall Street Journal* (October 12), p. 16.

Bronson, G. W. 1972. Infants' reactions to unfamiliar persons and novel objects. *Monographs of the Society for Research in Child Development, 37* (3).

Bronson, G. W. 1974. The postnatal growth of visual capacity. *Child Development, 45,* 873–890.

Bronson, W. 1974. Mother-toddler interaction: A perspective on studying the development of competence. *Merrill-Palmer Quarterly, 20,* 275–301.

Bronson, W. C. 1985. Growth in the organization of behavior over the second year of life. *Developmental Psychology, 21,* 108–117.

Brook, J. S., Whiteman, M., & Gordon, A. S. 1983. Stages of drug use in adolescence: Personality, peer, and family correlates. *Developmental Psychology, 19,* 269–277.

Brookhart, J., & Hock, E. 1976. The effects of experimental context and experiential background on infants' behavior toward their mothers and a stranger. *Child Development, 47,* 333–340.

Brookmeyer, R. 1991. Reconstruction and future trends of the AIDS epidemic in the United States. *Science, 253,* 37–42.

Brooks, A. 1983. Older singles found to value tradition. *New York Times* (June 5), p. 23.

Brooks, A. 1986. When studies mislead. *New York Times* (December 29), p. 17.

Brooks-Gunn, J. 1988. Antecedents and consequences of variations in girls' maturational timing. *Journal of Adolescent Health Care, 9,* 1–9.

Brooks-Gunn, J., & Furstenberg, F. F., Jr. 1989. Adolescent sexual behavior. *American Psychologist, 44,* 249–257.

Brooks-Gunn, J., & Petersen, A. C. (Eds.).

1983. *Girls at puberty: Biological and psychosocial perspectives.* New York: Plenum.

Brooks-Gunn, J., & Ruble, D. N. 1982. The development of menstrual-related beliefs and behaviors during early adolescence. *Child Development, 53,* 1567–1577.

Brooks-Gunn, J., & Warren, M. P. 1988. The psychological significance of secondary sexual characteristics in nine- to eleven-year-old girls. *Child Development, 59,* 1061–1069.

Brooks-Gunn, J., & Warren, M. P. 1989. Biological and social contributions to negative affect in young adolescent girls. *Child Development, 60,* 40–55.

Brooks-Gunn, J., Warren, M. P., Rosso, J., & Gargiulo, J. 1987. Validity of self-report measures of girls' pubertal status. *Child Development, 58,* 829–841.

Brophy, J. 1986. Teacher influences on student achievement. *American Psychologist, 41,* 1069–1077.

Brotten, D. 1986. A randomized clinical trial of early hospital discharge and home follow-up of very-low-birth-weight infants. *New England Journal of Medicine, 315,* 934–939.

Broughton, J. 1978. Development of concepts of self, mind, reality, and knowledge. *New Directions for Child Development, 1,* 75–100.

Brown, A. L. 1975. The development of memory: Knowing, knowing about knowing, and knowing how to know. In H. W. Reese (Ed.), *Advances in child development* (Vol 10). New York: Academic Press.

Brown, A. L. 1982. Learning and development: The problems of compatibility, access and induction. *Human Development, 25,* 89–115.

Brown, B. B., Clasen, D. R., & Eicher, S. A. 1986. Perceptions of peer pressure, peer conformity dispositions, and self-reported behavior among adolescents. *Developmental Psychology, 22,* 521–530.

Brown, B. B., Eicher, S. A., & Petrie, S. 1986. The importance of peer group ("crowd") affiliation in adolescence. *Journal of Adolescence, 9,* 73–96.

Brown, B. B., & Lohr, M. J. 1987. Peer-group affiliation and adolescent self-esteem. *Journal of Personality and Social Psychology, 52,* 47–55.

Brown, G. L., Ebert, M. H., & Goyer, P. F. 1982. Aggression, suicide, and serotonin: Relationships to CSF amine metabolites. *American Journal of Psychiatry, 139,* 741–746.

Brown, J. K. 1969. Female initiation rites: A review of the current literature. In D. Rogers (Ed.), *Issues in adolescent psychology.* New York: Appleton-Century-Crofts.

Brown, J. V., Bakeman, R., Snyder, P. A., Fredrickson, W. T., Morgan, S. T., & Hepler, R. 1975. Interactions of black inner city mothers with their newborn infants. *Child Development, 46,* 677–686.

Brown, P. L. 1987. Studying seasons of a woman's life. *New York Times* (September 14), p. 23.

Brown, R. 1973. *A first language.* Cambridge, Mass.: Harvard University Press.

Brown, R., & Herrnstein, R. J. 1975. *Psychology.* Boston: Little, Brown.

Brown, R. E. 1966. Organ weight in malnutrition with special reference to brain weight. *Developmental Medicine and Child Neurology, 8,* 512–522.

Brown, T. 1988. Ships in the night: Piaget and American cognitive science. *Human Development, 31,* 60–64.

Brownell, C. A. 1986. Convergent developments: Cognitive-developmental correlates of growth in infant/toddler peer skills. *Child Development, 57,* 275–286.

Brownell, C. A. 1988. Combinatorial skills: Converging developments over the second year. *Child Development, 59,* 675–685.

Brownell, C. A. 1990. Peer social skills in toddlers: Competencies and constraints illustrated by same-age and mixed-age interaction. *Child Development, 61,* 838–848.

Brownell, C. A., & Carriger, M. S. 1990. Changes in cooperation and self-other differentiation during the second year. *Child Development, 61,* 1164–1174.

Brownlee, J. 1990. The assurances of genes. *U.S. News & World Report* (July 23), pp. 57–60.

Brozan, N. 1982a. Family is focus of leisure time, study finds. *New York Times* (December 15), p. 19.

Brozan, N. 1982b. Infertility: Couples' reactions. *New York Times* (July 26), p. 20.

Brozan, N. 1983a. Hot flashes are topic for research and group therapy. *New York Times* (January 12), p. 13.

Brozan, N. 1983b. New look at fears of children. *New York Times* (May 2), p. 20.

Brozan, N. 1986. Care of infirm relatives: A new potent issue for women. *New York Times* (November 13), p. 17.

Brubaker, T. H. 1990. Families in later life: A burgeoning research area. *Journal of Marriage and the Family, 52,* 959–981.

Bruch, H. 1982. Anorexia nervosa: Therapy and theory. *American Journal of Psychiatry, 139,* 1531–1538.

Bruckner, D. J. R. 1985. Children's nuclear-war fears in dispute. *New York Times* (June 23), p. 24E.

Bruner, J. 1972. Nature and uses of immaturity. *American Psychologist, 27,* 687–708.

Bruner, J. 1983. *Child's talk: Learning to use language.* New York: Norton.

Bruner, J. 1990. Culture and human development: A new look. *Human Development, 33,* 344–355.

Bruner, J. 1991. *Acts of meaning.* Cambridge, Mass.: Harvard University Press.

Bruner, J. S. 1970. A conversation with Jerome Bruner. *Psychology Today, 4* (December), pp. 51–74.

Bruner, J. S. 1979. Learning how to do things with words. In D. Aaronson & R. W. Rieber (Eds.), *Psycholinguistic research: Implications and applications.* Hillsdale, N.J.: Erlbaum.

Bruner, J. S., Goodnow, J. J., & Austin, G. A. 1956. *A study of thinking.* New York: Wiley.

Bruner, J. S., & Koslowski, B. 1972. Visually pre-adapted constituents of manipulatory action. *Perception, 1,* 3–14.

Bruner, J. S., Oliver, R. R., & Greenfield, P. M. 1966. *Studies in cognitive growth.* New York: Wiley.

Bryant, B. K., & Crockenberg, S. B. 1980. Correlates and dimensions of prosocial behavior. A study of female siblings with their mothers. *Child Development, 51,* 529–544.

Buchman, M. 1989. *The script of life in modern society: Entry into adulthood in a changing world.* Chicago: University of Chicago Press.

Buckley, J. 1987. What you need to know. *U.S. News & World Report* (July 20), pp. 58–59.

Buckley, N., Siegel, L. S., & Ness, S. 1979. Egocentrism, empathy, and altruistic behavior in young children. *Developmental Psychology, 15,* 329–330.

Bugental, D. B., Blue, J., & Cruzcosa, M. 1989. Perceived control over caregiving outcomes: Implicatons for child abuse. *Developmental Psychology, 25,* 532–539.

Bugental, D. B., Blue, J., & Lewis, J. 1990. Caregiver beliefs and dysphoric affect directed to difficult children. *Developmental Psychology, 26,* 631–638.

Bugental, D. B., & Shennum, W. A. 1984. "Difficult" children as elicitors and targets of adult communication patterns: An attributional-behavioral transactional analysis. *Monographs of the Society for Research in Child Development, 49* (No. 205).

Buglass, K. 1989. The business of eldercare. *American Demographics, II* (September), pp. 32–39.

Bühler, C., & Massarik, F. 1968. *The course of human life: A study of goals in the humanistic perspective.* New York: Springer.

Buhrmester, D. 1990. Intimacy of friendship, interpersonal competence, and adjustment during preadolescence and adolescence. *Child Development, 61,* 1101–1111.

Buhrmester, D., & Furman, W. 1990. Perceptions of sibling relationships during middle childhood and adolescence. *Child Development, 61,* 1387–1398.

Buka, S. L., & Lipsitt, L. P. 1991. Newborn sucking behavior and its relation to grasping. *Infant Behavior and Development, 14,* 59–67.

Bukowski, W. M., & Newcomb, A. F. 1985. Variability in peer groups perceptions: Support for the "controversial" sociometric classification group. *Developmental Psychology, 21,* 1032–1038.

Bucroft, K., & O'Connor-Roden, M. 1986. Never too late. *Psychology Today, 20* (June), pp. 66–69.

Bullock, M., & Lutkenhaus, P. 1988. The development of volitional behavior in the toddler years. *Child Development, 59,* 664–674.

Bullough, V. L. 1981. Age at menarche: A misunderstanding. *Science, 213,* 365–366.

Bumpass, L., Sweet, J., & Martin, T. C. 1990. Changing patterns of remarriage. *Journal of Marriage and the Family, 52,* 747–756.

Bumsted, B. 1986. Elderly care: "Thousands warehoused." *USA Today* (May 22), p. 1A.

Burbank, Y. K. 1988. *Aboriginal adolescence: Maidenhood in an aboriginal community.* New Brunswick, N.J.: Rutgers University Press.

Burchinal, L. G. 1964. Characteristics of adolescents from unbroken, broken, and reconstitued families. *Journal of Marriage and the Family, 26,* 44–51.

Burchinal, M., Lee, M., & Ramey, C. 1989. Type of day-care and preschool intellectual development in disadvantaged children. *Child Development, 60,* 128–137.

Burgess, E., & Wallin, P. 1953. *Engagement and marriage.* Philadelphia: Lippincott.

Burgett, C. 1990. Alcohol abuse plays large role in crime. *USA Today* (December 5), p. 8A.

Burke, D. M., & Light, L. L. 1981. Memory and aging: The role of retrieval processes. *Psychological Bulletin, 90,* 513–546.

Burkhauser, R. V., Holden, K. C., & Feaster, D. 1988. Incidence, timing, and events associated with poverty: A dynamic view of poverty in retirement. *Journal of Gerontology, 43,* S46–52.

Burlingame, W. V. 1970. The youth culture. In E. D. Evans (Ed.), *Adolescents: Readings in behavior and development.* Hinsdale, Ill: Dryden Press.

Burns, M. O., & Seligman, M. E. P. 1989. Explanatory style across the life span: Evidence for stability over 52 years. *Journal of Personality and Social Psychology, 56,* 471–477.

Bursik, K. 1991. Adaptation to divorce and ego development in adult women. *Journal of Personality and Social Psychology, 60,* 300–306.

Burt, M. R. 1980. Cultural myths and supports for rape. *Journal of Personality and Social Psychology, 38,* 217–230.

Burton, R. V. 1976. Honesty and dishonesty. In T. Lickona (Ed.), *Moral development and behavior: Theory, research, and social issues.* New York: Holt, Rinehart and Winston.

Bush, D. M., & Simmons, R. G. 1981. Socialization processes over the life course. In M. Rosenberg & R. H. Turner (Eds.), *Social psychology: Sociological perspectives.* New York: Basic Books.

Bushnell, E. W. 1985. The decline of visually guided reaching during infancy. *Infant Behavior and Development, 8,* 139–155.

Buss, A. H. 1989. Personality as traits. *American Psychologist, 44,* 1378–1388.

Busse, E. W. 1969. Theories of aging. In E. W. Busse & E. Pfeiffer (Eds.), *Behavior and adaptation in late life.* Boston: Little, Brown.

Busse, E. W., & Pfeiffer, E. 1969. Functional psychiatric disorders in old age. In E. W. Busse & E. Pfeiffer (Eds.), *Behavior and adaptation in late life.* Boston: Little, Brown.

Bussey, K., & Bandura, A. 1984. Influence of gender constancy and social power on sex-linked modeling. *Journal of Personality and Social Psychology, 47,* 1292–1302.

Butler, R. N. 1963. The life review: An interpretation of reminiscence in the aged. *Psychiatry, 26,* 65–76.

Butler, R. N. 1971. The life review. *Psychology Today, 5* (December), pp. 49–51f.

Butler, R. N. 1975. *Why survive?* New York: Harper & Row.

Butt, D. S., & Beiser, M. 1987. Successful aging: A theme for international psychology. *Psychology and Aging, 2,* 87–94.

Butterfield, F. 1986. Why Asians are going to the head of the class. *New York Times* (August 3), pp. 18–23.

Bybee, R. W. 1979. Violence toward youth: A

new perspective. *Journal of Social Issues, 35*, 1–14.

Byrne, D., Ervin, C. H., & Lamberth, J. 1970. Continuity between the experimental study of attraction and real-life computer dating. *Journal of Personality and Social Psychology, 16*, 157–165.

Byrne, J. M., & Horowitz, F. D. 1981. Rocking as a soothing intervention: The influence of direction and type of movement. *Infant Behavior and Development, 4*, 207–218.

Cahill, S. E. 1990. Childhood and public life: Reaffirming biographical divisions. *Social Problems, 37*, 390–402.

Cairns, R. B. 1991. Multiple metaphors for a singular idea. *Developmental Psychology, 27*, 23–26.

Cairns, R. B., Cairns, B. D., & Neckerman, H. J. 1989. Early school dropout: Configurations and determinants. *Child Development, 60*, 1437–1452.

Caldera, Y. M., Huston, A. C., & O'Brien, M. 1989. Social interactions and play patterns of parents and toddlers with feminine, masculine, and neutral toys. *Child Development, 60*, 70–76.

Cameron, P. 1970. The generation gap: Beliefs about sexuality and self-reported sexuality. *Developmental Psychology, 3*, 272.

Campbell, A. 1975. The American way of mating: Marriage si, children only maybe. *Psychology Today, 8*(May), pp. 37–43.

Campbell, A. 1981. *The sense of well-being in America: Recent patterns and trends.* New York: McGraw-Hill.

Campbell, A., Converse, P. E., & Rodgers, W. L. 1976. *The quality of American life: Perceptions, evaluations, and satisfactions.* New York: Russell Sage Foundation.

Campion, E. W., Bang, A., & May, M. I. 1983. Why acute-care hospitals must undertake long-term care. *New England Journal of Medicine, 308*, 71–75.

Campos, J., Barrett, K. C., Lamb, M. E., Goldsmith, H., & Stenberg, C. 1983. Socioemotional development. In M. M. Haith & J. J. Campos (Eds.), *Infancy and developmental psychobiology.* Vol. 2. of P. H. Mussen, *Handbook of child psychology.* New York: Wiley.

Campos, J. J., Campos, R. G., & Barrett, K. C. 1989. Emergent themes in the study of emotional development and emotion regulation. *Developmental Psychology, 25*, 394–402.

Campos, J. J., & Stenberg, C. R. 1978. Perception, appraisal, and emotion: The onset of social referencing. In M. E. Lamb & L. R. Sherrod (Eds.), *Infant social cognition.* Hillsdale, N.J.: Erbaum.

Campos, R. G. 1989. Soothing pain-elicited distress in infants with swaddling and pacifiers. *Child Development, 60*, 781–792.

Camras, L. A., Ribordy, S., Hill, J., Martino, S., Sachs, V., Spaccarelli, S., & Stefani, R. 1990. Maternal facial behavior and the recognition and production of emotional expression by maltreated and nonmaltreated children. *Developmental Psychology, 26*, 304–312.

Camras, L. A., Ribordy, S., Hill, J., Martino, S., Spaccarelli, S., & Stefani, R. 1988. Rec-

ognition and posing of emotional expressions by abused children and their mothers. *Developmental Psychology, 24*, 776–781.

Cancian, F. M. 1987. *Love in America: Gender and self-development.* New York: Cambridge University Press.

Cann, A., Calhoun, L. G., Selby, J. W., & King, H. E. 1981. Rape: A contemporary overview and analysis. *Journal of Social Issues, 37*, 1–4.

Cann, A., & Newbern, S. R. 1984. Sex stereotype effects in children's picture recognition. *Child Development, 55*, 1085–1090.

Cantor, D. S., Fischel, J. E., & Kaye, H. 1983. Neonatal conditionability: A new paradigm for exploring the use of interoceptive cues. *Infant Behavior and Development, 6*, 403–413.

Caplan, F., & Caplan, T. 1973. *The power of play.* Garden City, N.Y.: Anchor Books.

Caplan, P. J. 1989. *Don't blame mother: Mending the mother-daughter relationship.* New York: Harper & Row.

Caporael, L. R. 1981. The paralanguage of caregiving: Baby talk to the institutionalized aged. *Journal of Personality and Social Psychology, 40*, 876–884.

Caputo, D. V., & Mandell, W. 1970. Consequences of low birth weight. *Developmental Psychology, 3*, 363–383.

Carey, J. 1984. Loving—and mourning—your baby. *USA Today* (April 10), p. 4D.

Carey, J. 1987. Battling the bulge at an early age. *U.S. News & World Report* (March 2), pp. 66–67.

Carey, J. 1990. The genetic age. *Business Week* (May 28), pp. 68–83.

Carlsmith, L. 1964. Effect of early father-absence on scholastic aptitude. *Harvard Educational Review, 34*, 3–21.

Carlson, A. C. 1986. What happened to the "family wage"? *The Public Interest, 83*, 3–17.

Carlson, A. C. 1988. *Family questions: Reflections on the American social crisis.* New Brunswick, N.J.: Transaction.

Carlson, V., Cicchetti, D., Barnett, D., & Braunwald, K. 1989. Disorganized/disoriented attachment relationships in maltreated infants. *Developmental Psychology, 25*, 525–531.

Carmody, D. 1990. College drinking: Changes in attitude and habit. *New York Times* (March 7), p. B7.

Carnegie Commission. 1980. *Giving youth a better chance.* San Francisco: Jossey-Bass.

Carnegie Forum on Education and the Economy. 1986. *A nation prepared: Teachers for the 21st century.* New York: Carnegie Corporation.

Caron, A. J., Caron, R. F., Caldwell, R. C., & Weiss, S. J. 1973. Infant perception of the structural properties of the face. *Developmental Psychology, 9*, 385–399.

Caron, A. J., Caron, R. F., & MacLean, D. J. 1988. Infant discrimination of naturalistic emotional expressions: The role of face and voice. *Child Development, 59*, 604–616.

Carnoy, M. 1984. *The state and political theory.* Princeton, N.J.: Princeton University Press.

Carnoy, M., & Levin, H. M. 1985. *Schooling and work in the democratic state.* Stanford, Calif.: Stanford University Press.

Carpenter, D. G. 1965. Diffusion theory of aging. *Journal of Gerontology, 20*, 191–195.

Carpenter, E. 1965. Comments. *Current Anthropology, 6*, 55.

Carr, M., Borkowski, J. G., & Maxell, S. E. 1991. Motivational components of underachievement. *Developmental Psychology, 27*, 108–118.

Carroll, J. J., & Steward, M. S. 1984. The role of cognitive development in children's understandings of their own feelings. *Child Development, 55*, 1486–492.

Carter, D. B., & Levy, G. D. 1988. Cognitive aspects of early sex-role development: The influence of gender schemas on preschooler's memories and preferences for sex-typed toys and activities. *Child Development, 59*, 782–792.

Carver, C. S., & Ganellen, R. J. 1983. Depression and components of self-punitiveness. *Journal of Abnormal Psychology, 92*, 330–337.

Carver, C. S., Ganellen, R. J., Froming, W. J., & Chambers, W. 1983. Modeling an analysis in terms of category accessibility. *Journal of Experimental Social Psychology, 19*, 403–421.

Case, R. 1985. *Intellectual development. Birth to adulthood.* Orlando, Fla.: Academic Press.

Caspi, A., & Elder, G. H., Jr. 1986. Life satisfaction in old age: Linking social psychology and history. *Psychology and Aging, 1*, 18–26.

Caspi, A., Elder, G. H., & Bem, D. J. 1987. Moving against the world: Life-course patterns of explosive children. *Developmental Psychology, 23*, 308–313.

Caspi, A., Elder, G. H., Jr., & Bem, D. J. 1988. Moving away from the world: Life-course patterns of shy children. *Developmental Psychology, 24*, 824–831.

Caspi, A., & Herbener, E. S. 1990. Continuity and change: Assortative marriage and the consistency of personality in adulthood. *Journal of Personality and Social Psychology, 58*, 250–258.

Cassidy, J. 1988. Child-mother attachment and the self in six-year-olds. *Child Development, 59*, 121–134.

Castro, J. 1991. Watching a generation waste away. *Time* (August 26), pp. 10–12.

Catherwood, D., Crassini, B., & Freiberg, K. 1989. Infant response to stimuli of similar hue and dissimilar shape: Tracing the origins of the categorization of objects by hue. *Child Development, 60*, 752–762.

Cattell, R. B. 1943. The measurement of adult intelligence. *Psychological Bulletin, 40*, 153–193.

Cattell, R. B. 1971. *Abilities: Their structure, growth, and action.* Boston: Houghton Mifflin.

Cavan, R. S. 1964. Structural variations and mobility. In H. T. Christensen (Ed.), *Handbook of marriage and the family.* Chicago: Rand McNally.

Cavior, N., & Dokecki, P. R. 1973. Physical attractiveness, perceived attitude similarity, and academic achievement as contributors to interpersonal attraction among adolescents. *Developmental Psychology, 9*, 44–54.

Cavior, N., & Lombardi, D. A. 1973. Developmental aspects of judgment of physical attractiveness in children. *Developmental Psychology, 8,* 67–71.

Celis, W., III. 1991. Growing talk of date rape separates sex from assault. *New York Times* (January 2), pp. A1, B7.

Census Bureau. 1983. *America in transition: An aging society.* P–23, No. 128. Washington, D.C.: Government Printing Office.

Census Bureau, 1986a. *Disability, functional limitation, and health insurance coverage: 1984/85* (Household Economic Studies, Current Populations Reports, Series P–70, No. 8). Washington, D.C.: Government Printing Office.

Census Bureau. 1986b. Earnings in 1983 of married-couple families, by characteristics of husbands and wives. *Current population reports* (Series P–60, No. 153). Washington, D.C.: Bureau of the Census.

Center for Education Statistics. 1990. *America's challenge: Accelerating academic achievement.* Washington, D.C.: Department of Education.

Cerella, J. 1985. Information processing rates in the elderly. *Psychological Bulletin, 98,* 67–83.

Cernoch, J. M., & Porter, R. H. 1985. Recognition of maternal axillary odors by infants. *Child Development, 56,* 1593–1598.

Cervantes, L. 1965. *The dropout: Causes and cures.* Ann Arbor: University of Michigan Press.

Chan, K. S. 1978. Locus of control and achievement motivation—critical factors in educational psychology. *Psychology in the Schools, 15,* 104–110.

Chance, P., & Fischman, J. 1987. The magic of childhood. *Psychology Today, 21* (May), pp. 48–58.

Chapman, M. 1988. Contextuality and directionality of cognitive development. *Human Development, 31,* 92–106.

Chapman, M., & Lindenberger, U. 1988. Functions, operations, and decalage in the development of transitivity. *Developmental Psychology, 24,* 542–551.

Chapman, M., Zahn-Waxler, C., Cooperman, G., & Iannotti, R. 1987. Empathy and responsibility in the motivation of children's helping. *Developmental Psychology, 23,* 140–145.

Chappell, N. L., & Badger, M. 1989. Social isolation and well-being. *Journal of Gerontology, 44,* S169–176.

Charlesworth, R., & Hartup, W. W. 1967. Positive social reinforcement in the nursery school peer group. *Child Development, 38,* 993–1002.

Chase, M. 1987. AIDS costs. *Wall Street Journal* (May 18), pp. 1, 12.

Chase, M. 1991. New cases of AIDS in U.S. and Europe to taper off in '95, says health group. *Wall Street Journal* (June 18), p. B5.

Chasnoff, I. J. 1985. Cocaine use in pregnancy. *New England Journal of Medicine, 313,* 666–669.

Chassin, L., Zeiss, A., Cooper, K., & Reaven, J. 1985. Role perceptions, self-role congruence and marital satisfaction in dual-worker couples with preschool children. *Social Psychology Quarterly, 48,* 301–311.

Chatters, L. M. 1988. Subjective well-being evaluations among older black Americans. *Psychology and Aging, 3,* 184–190.

Chatters, L. M., Taylor, R. J., & Neighbors, H. W. 1989. Size of informal helper network mobilized during a serious personal problem among black Americans. *Journal of Marriage and the Family, 51,* 667–676.

Chechile, R. A., Richman, C. L., Topinka, C., & Ehrensbeck, K. 1981. A developmental study of the storage and retrieval of information. *Child Development, 52,* 251–259.

Check, J. V. P., & Malamuth, N. M. 1983. Sex role stereotyping and reactions to depictions of stranger versus acquaintance rape. *Journal of Personality and Social Psychology, 45,* 344–356.

Chedd, G. 1981. Who shall be born? *Science 81, 2* (January), pp. 32–41.

Chehrazi, S. 1986. Female psychology: A review. *Journal of the American Psychoanalytic Association, 34,* 141–162.

Chen, C., & Uttal, D. H. 1988. Cultural values, parents' beliefs, and children's achievement in the United States and China. *Human Development, 31,* 351–358.

Cherlin, A. 1983. Changing family and household: Contemporary lessons from historical research. *Annual Review of Sociology, 9,* 51–66.

Cherlin, A. J., & Furstenberg, F. F., Jr. 1986. *The new American grandparent: A place in the family, a life apart.* New York: Basic Books.

Cherlin, A. J., Furstenberg, F. F., Jr., Chase-Lansdale, P. L., Kiernan, K. E., Robins, P. K., Morrison, D. R., & Teitler, J. O. 1991. Longitudinal studies of effects of divorce on children in Great Britain and the United States. *Science, 252,* 1386–1389.

Cherry, F. F., & Eaton, E. L. 1977. Physical and cognitive development in children of low-income mothers working in the child's early years. *Child Development, 48,* 158–166.

Chilamn, C. S. 1983. *Adolescent sexuality in a changing American society: Social and psychological perspectives for the human services professions* (2nd ed.). New York: Wiley.

Chira, S. 1990a. Crack babies turn 5, and schools brace. *New York Times* (May 25), pp. A1, A11.

Chira, S. 1990b. Preschool aid for the poor: How big a head start? *New York Times* (February 14), pp. B1, B8.

Chira, S. 1991. Poverty's toll on health is plague of U.S. schools. *New York Times* (October 5), pp. 1, 8.

Chodorow, N. J. 1989. *Feminism and psychoanalytic theory.* New Haven: Yale University Press.

Chomsky, N. 1957. *Syntactic structures.* The Hague: Mouton.

Chomsky, N. 1965. *Aspects of a theory of syntax.* Cambridge, Mass.: MIT Press.

Chomsky, N. 1968. *Language and mind.* New York: Harcourt Brace Jovanovich.

Chomsky, N. 1975. *Reflections on language.* New York: Pantheon Books.

Chomsky, N. 1980. *Rules and representations.* New York: Columbia University Press.

Chown, S. M. (Ed.) 1972. *Human aging.* Baltimore: Penguin Books.

Chudecoff, H. P. 1989. *How old are you? Age consciousness in American culture.* Princeton, N.J.: Princeton University Press.

Chugani, H. T., & Phelps, M. E. 1986. Maturational changes in cerebral functions in infants determined by FDG positron emission tomography. *Science, 231,* 840–843.

Chumlea, W. C. 1982. Physical growth in adolescence. In B. B. Wolman (Ed.), *Handbook of developmental psychology.* Englewood Cliffs, N.J.: Prentice-Hall.

Church, A. T., & Katigbak, M. S. 1989. Internal, external, and self-report structure of personality in a non-Western culture: An investigation of cross-language and cross-cultural generalizability. *Journal of Personality and Social Psychology, 57,* 857–872.

Church, G. J. 1986. Call to battle. *Time* (November 10), pp. 18–20.

Church, G. J. 1987. The work ethic lives! *Time* (September 17), pp. 40–42.

Cicirelli, V. G. 1973. Effects of sibling structure and interaction on children's categorization style. *Developmental Psychology, 9,* 132–139.

Cicirelli, V. G. 1978. The relationship of sibling structure to intellectual abilities and achievement. *Review of Educational Research, 48,* 365–379.

Cicirelli, V. G. 1980. A comparison of college women's feelings toward their siblings and parents. *Journal of Marriage and the Family, 42,* 111–118.

Cicirelli, V. G. 1981. *Helping elderly parents: The role of adult children.* Boston: Auburn House.

Cicirelli V. G. 1983. Adult children's attachment and helping behavior to elderly parents: A path model. *Journal of Marriage and the Family, 45,* 815–825.

Cicirelli, V. G. 1989. Feelings of attachment to siblings and well-being in later life. *Psychology and Aging, 4,* 211–216.

Clancy, P. 1986a. For women in 30s, 6 of 10 marriages fail. *USA Today* (April 4), pp. 1, 2.

Clancy, P. 1986b. 23% of kids live with single parent. *USA Today* (December 10), p. 3A.

Clark, D. L., Lotto, L. S., & McCarthy, M. M. 1980. Factors associated with success in urban elementary schools. *Phi Delta Kappan, 61,* 467–470.

Clark, E. V., Gelman, S. A., & Lane, N. M. 1985. Compound nouns and category structure in young children. *Child Development, 56,* 84–94.

Clark, J. E., & Watkins, D. L. 1984. Static balance in young children. *Child Development, 55,* 854–857.

Clark, K. B. 1965. *Dark ghetto.* New York: Harper & Row.

Clarke-Stewart, K. A. 1989. Infant day care: Maligned or malignant? *American Psychologist, 44,* 266–273.

Clarke-Stewart, K. A., & Hevey, C. M. 1981. Longitudinal relations in repeated observations of mother-child interaction from 1 to 2½ years. *Developmental Psychology, 17,* 127–145.

Clarkson-Smith, L., & Hartley, A. A. 1989. Relationships between physical exercise and cognitive abilities in older adults. *Psychology and Aging, 4,* 183–189.

Clary, E. G., & Miller, J. 1986. Socialization and situational influences on sustained altruism. *Child Development, 57,* 1358–1369.

Clasen, D. R., & Brown, B. B. 1985. The multidimensionality of peer pressure in adolescence. *Journal of Youth and Adolescence, 14,* 451–468.

Clausen, J. A. 1966. Family structure, socialization and personality. In L. W. Hoffman & M. L. Hoffman (Eds), *Review of child development research* (Vol. 2). New York: Russell Sage Foundation.

Clausen, J. S. 1991. Adolescent competence and the shaping of the life course. *American Journal of Sociology, 96,* 805–842.

Clayton, R. R. 1979. *The family, marriage, and social change* (2nd ed.). Lexington, Mass.: Heath.

Clayton, R. R., & Bokemeier, J. L. 1980. Premarital sex in the seventies. *Journal of Marriage and the Family, 42,* 759–775.

Cleveland, W. P., & Gianturco, D. T. 1976. Remarriage probability after widowhood: A retrospective method. *Journal of Gerontology, 31,* 99–103.

Clifton, R. K., Morrongiello, B. A., Kulig, J. W., & Dowd, J. M. 1981. Newborns' orientations toward sound: Possible implications for cortical development. *Child Development, 52,* 833–838.

Clingempeel, W. G., & Reppucci, N. D. 1982. Joint custody after divorce: Major issues and goals for research. *Psychological Bulletin, 91,* 102–127.

Clipp, E. C., & George, L. K. 1990. Caregiver needs and patterns of social support. *Journal of Gerontology, 45,* S102–111.

Clopton, W. 1973. Personality and career change. *Industrial Gerontology, 17,* 9–17.

Clymer, A. 1987. Survey finds many skeptics among evangelists' viewers. *New York Times* (March 31), pp. 1, 14.

Coates, D., Wortman, C., & Abbey, A. 1979. Reactions to victims. In I. H. Frieze, D. Bartal & J. S. Carroll (Eds.), *New approaches to social problems.* San Francisco: Jossey-Bass.

Cockburn, J., & Smith, P. T. 1991. The relative influence of intelligence and age on everyday memory. *Journal of Gerontology, 46,* P31–36.

Cohen, A. S., Rosen, R. C., & Goldstein, L. 1985. EEG hemispheric asymmetry during sexual arousal: Psychophysiological patterns in responsive, unresponsive, and dysfunctional men. *Journal of Abnormal Psychology, 94,* 580–590.

Cohen, G., & Faulkner, D. 1983. Age differences in performance on two information-processing tasks. *Journal of Gerontology, 38,* 447–454.

Cohen, J. 1983. Peer influence on college aspirations with initial aspirations controlled. *American Sociological Review, 48,* 728–734.

Cohen, J., & Tronick, E. Z. 1987. Mother-infant face-to-face interaction: The sequence of dyadic states at 3, 6, and 9 months. *Developmental Psychology, 23,* 68–77.

Cohen, L. A. 1987. Diet and cancer. *Scientific American, 257* (November), pp. 42–48.

Cohen, L. B., DeLoache, J. S., & Strauss, M. S. 1979. Infant visual perception. In J. D. Osofsky (Ed.), *Handbook of infant development.* New York: Wiley.

Cohen, L. B., & Gelber, E. R. 1975. Infant visual memory. In L. B. Cohen & P. Sal-
apetek (Eds.), *Infant perception: From sensation to cognition* (Vol.1). New York: Academic Press.

Cohen, L. D. 1991. Sex differences in the course of personality development: A meta-analysis. *Psychological Bulletin, 109,* 252–266.

Cohen, L. E., & Land, K. C. 1987. Age structure and crime. *American Sociological Review, 52,* 170–183.

Cohen, M. E., Hoffman, H. S., Kelley, N. E., & Anday, E. K. 1988. A failure to observe habituation in the human neonate. *Infant Behavior and Development, 11,* 297–304.

Cohen, R., Bornstein, R., & Sherman, R. C. 1973. Conformity behavior of children as a function of group makeup and task ambiguity. *Developmental Psychology, 9,* 124–131.

Cohen, S., & Williamson, G. M. 1991. Stress and infectious disease in humans. *Psychological Bulletin, 109,* 5–24.

Cohen, S., & Wills, T. A. 1985. Stress, social support, and the buffering hypothesis. *Psychological Bulletin, 98,* 310–357.

Cohen, S. E., & Beckwith, L. 1977. Caregiving behaviors and early cognitive development as related to ordinal position in preterm infants. *Child Development, 48,* 152–157.

Cohn-Sandler, R., Berman, A. L., & King, R. A. 1982. Life stress and symptomatology: Determinants of suicidal behavior in children. *Journal of the American Academy of Child Psychiatry, 21,* 178–186.

Coie, J. D., Dodge, K. A., Terry, R., & Wright, V. 1991. The role of aggression in peer relations: An analysis of aggression episodes in boys' play groups. *Child Development, 62,* 812–826.

Coie, J. D., & Krehsiel, G. 1984. Effects of academic tutoring on the social status of low-achieving, socially rejected children. *Child Development, 55,* 1465–1478.

Cole, J. D., & Kupersmidt, J. B. 1983. A behavioral analysis of emerging social status in boys' groups. *Child Development, 54,* 1400–1416.

Colby, A., & Kohlberg, L. 1987. *The measurement of moral judgment.* (Vols. I, II). New York: Cambridge University Press.

Colby, A., Kohlberg, L., Gibbs, J., & Lieberman, M. 1983. A longitudinal study of moral judgment. *Monographs of the Society for Research in Child Development, 48* (200).

Colby, K. M., & Stoller, R. J. 1988. *Cognitive science and psychoanalysis.* Hillsdale, N.J.: Erlbaum.

Cole, C. L. 1977. Cohabitation in social context. In R. W. Libby & R. N. Whitehurst (Eds.), *Marriage and alternatives.* Glenview, Ill.: Scott, Foresman.

Cole, D. 1987. It might have been: Mourning the unborn. *Psychology Today, 21* (July), pp. 64–65.

Cole, M., Gay, J., Glick, J., & Sharp, D. 1971. *The cultural context of learning and thinking.* New York: Basic Books.

Cole, P. M. 1985. Display rules and the socialization of effective displays. In G. Zivin (Ed.), *The Development of Expressive Behavior: Biology-Environment Interactions.* New York: Academic Press.
Cole, P. M. 1986. Children's spontaneous control of facial expression. *Child Development, 57,* 1309–1321.

Cole, R. A. 1979. Navigating the slippery stream of speech. *Psychology Today, 12* (April), pp. 77–87.

Cole, S. 1980. Send our children to work? *Psychology Today, 14* (July), pp. 44–68.

Coleman, J. 1961. *The adolescent society.* New York: Free Press.

Coleman, J. 1978. Current contradictions in adolescent theory. *Journal of Youth and Adolescence, 7,* 1–11.

Coleman, J., Hoffer, T., & Kilgore, S. 1982a. *High school achievement: Public catholic and other private schools compared.* New York: Basic Books.

Coleman, J., Hoffer, T., & Kilgore, S. 1982b. Cognitive outcomes in public and private schools. *Sociology of Education, 55,* 65–76.

Coleman, J. S., & Hoffer, T. 1987. *Public and private high schools: The impact on communities.* New York: Basic Books.

Coleman, J. S., & Husen, T. 1985. *Becoming adult in a changing society.* Paris, France: Centre for Educational Research and Innovation.

Coleman, L. M., & Antonucci, T. C. 1983. Impact of work on women at midlife. *Developmental Psychology, 19,* 290–294.

Coleman, M., & Ganong, L. H. 1990. Remarriage and stepfamily research in the 1980s: Increased interest in an old family form. *Journal of Marriage and the Family, 52,* 925–940.

Coleman, P. G. 1986. *Aging and reminiscence processes: Social and clinical implications.* New York: Wiley.

Coles, R. 1990. *The spiritual life of children.* Boston: Houghton Mifflin.

Collins, G. 1981a. The childhood "industry": Conflicting advice. *New York Times* (March 16), p. 17.

Collins, G. 1981b. Fathers get postpartum blues, too. *New York Times* (April 6), p. 19.

Collins, G. 1983a. U.S. social tolerance of drugs found on rise. *New York Times* (March 27), pp. 1, 9.

Collins, G. 1983b. Stepfamilies share their joys and woes. *New York Times* (October 24), p. 21.

Collins, G. 1984a. Care for far-off elderly: Sources of help. *New York Times* (January 5), pp. 15, 17.

Collins, G. 1984b. New studies on 'girl toys' and 'boy toys.' *New York Times* (February 13), p. 17.

Collins, G. 1986. Studying the behavior of bully and victim. *New York Times* (May 12), p. 13.

Collins, J. A., Wrixon, W., Janes, L. B., & Wilson, E. H. 1983. Treatment-independent pregnancy among infertile couples. *New England Journal of Medicine, 309,* 1201–1209.

Colombo, J. 1982. The critical period concept: Research, methodology, and theoretical issues. *Psychological Bulletin, 91,* 260–275.

Colombo, J., Moss, M., & Horowitz, F. D. 1989. Neonatal state profiles: Reliability and short-term prediction of neurobehavioral status. *Child Development, 60,* 1102–1110.

Coltrane, S. 1989. Household labor and the routine production of gender. *Social Problems, 36,* 473–490.

Columbus Dispatch. 1990*a*. More babies have low birth weight. (March 9), p. 4A.

Columbus Dispatch. 1990*b*. Racial differences affect low-birth-weight babies. (June 5), p. 9A.

Columbus Ohio Dispatch. 1991. Profit motive is factor in repeating Caesarean sections, study says. (January 3), p. 5A.

Comfort, A. 1970. Biological theories of aging. *Human Development, 13,* 127–139.

Comfort, A. 1976. *A good age.* New York: Crown.

Commons, M. L., Richards, F. A., & Kuhn, D. 1982. Systematic and metasystematic reasoning: A case for levels of reasoning beyond Piaget's stage of formal operations. *Child Development, 53,* 1058–1069.

Compas, B. E. 1987. Coping with stress during childhood and adolescence. *Psychological Bulletin, 101,* 393–403.

Condon, W. S., & Sander, L. W. 1974*a*. Neonate movement is synchronized with adult speech: Interactional participation and language acquisition. *Science, 183,* 99–101.

Condon, W. S., & Sander, L. W. 1974*b*. Synchrony demonstrated between movements of the neonate and adult speech. *Child Development, 45,* 456–462.

Condry, J. 1989. *The psychology of television.* Hillsdale, N.J.: Erlbaum.

Condry, J. C., & Ross, D. F. 1985. Sex and aggression: The influence of gender label on the perception of aggression in children. *Child Development, 56,* 225–233.

Conger, J. J. 1977. *Adolescence and youth* (2nd ed.). New York: Harper & Row.

Conger, R. D., Burgess, R. L., & Barrett, C. 1979. Child abuse related to life change and perceptions of illness: Some preliminary findings. *Family Coordinator, 28,* 73–78.

Conger, R. D., Elder, G. H., Jr., Lorenz, F. O., Conger, K. J., Simons, R. L., Whitbeck, L. B., Huck, S., & Melby, J. N. 1990. Linking economic hardship to marital quality and instability. *Journal of Marriage and the Family, 52,* 643–656.

Conger, R. D., McCarty, J. A., Yang, R. K., Lahey, B. B., & Kropp, J. P. 1984. Perception of child, child-rearing values, and emotional distress as mediating links between environmental stressors and observed maternal behavior. *Child Development, 55,* 2234–2247.

Conley, J. J. 1985. Longitudinal stability in personality. *Journal of Personality and Social Psychology, 49,* 1266–1282.

Connelly, J. 1990. How dual-income couples cope. *Fortune* (September 24), pp. 129–136.

Conner, K. A., Powers, E. A., & Bultena, G. L. 1979. Social interaction and life satisfaction: An empirical assessment of late-life patterns. *Journal of Gerontology, 34,* 116–121.

Connidis, I. A., & Davies, L. 1990. Confidants and companions in later life: The place of family and friends. *Journal of Gerontology, 45,* S141–149.

Cook, S. W. 1984. The 1954 Social Science Statement and school desegregation. *American Psychologist, 39,* 819–832.

Cook, S. W. 1985. Experimenting on social issues: The case of school desegregation. *American Psychologist, 40,* 452–460.

Cook, T. H., & Miller, N. E. 1985. The challenge of Alzheimer's disease. *American Psychologist, 40,* 1245–1250.

Cooke, R. A. 1982. The ethics and regulation of research involving children. In B. B. Wolman (Ed.), *Handbook of developmental psychology.* Englewood Cliffs, N.J.: Prentice-Hall.

Cooley, C. H. 1902. *Human nature and the social order.* New York: Scribner.

Cooley, C. H. 1909. *Social Organization.* New York: Scribner.

Cooney, T. M., & Hogan, D. P. 1991. Marriage in an institutionalized life course: First marriage among American men in the twentieth century. *Journal of Marriage and the Family, 53,* 178–190.

Cooney, T. M., & Uhlenberg, P. 1990. The role of divorce in men's relations with their adult children after mid-life. *Journal of Marriage and the Family, 52,* 677–688.

Coontz, S. 1988. *The social origins of private life: A history of American families, 1600–1900.* New York: Verso.

Coombs, R. H. 1991. Marital status and personal well-being: A literature review. *Family Relations, 40,* 97–102.

Cooper, J. E., Holman, J., & Braithwaite, V. A. 1983. Self-esteem and family cohesion: The child's perspective and adjustment. *Journal of Marriage and the Family, 45,* 153–159.

Cooper, K., Chassin, L., Braver, S., Zeiss, A., & Khavari, K. A. 1986. Correlates of mood and marital satisfaction among dual-worker and single-worker couples. *Social Psychology Quarterly, 49,* 322–329.

Cooper, R. P., & Aslin, R. N. 1990. Preference for infant-directed speech in the first month after birth. *Child Development, 61,* 1584–1595.

Coopersmith, S. 1967. *Antecedents of self-esteem.* San Francisco: Freeman.

Corballis, M. C. 1983. *Human laterality.* New York: Academic Press.

Corbin, J. M., & Strauss, A. 1988. *Unending work and care: Managing chronic illness at home.* San Francisco: Jossey-Bass.

Coren, S., & Halpern, D. F. 1991. Left-handedness: A marker for decreased survival fitness. *Psychological Bulletin, 109,* 90–106.

Coren, S., Porac, C., & Duncan, P. 1981. Lateral preference behaviors in preschool children and young adults. *Child Development, 52,* 443–450.

Cornelius, S. W., & Caspi, A. 1987. Everyday problem solving in adulthood and old age. *Psychology and Aging, 2,* 144–153.

Costa, P. T., Jr., & McCrae, R. R. 1980. Still stable after all these years: Personality as a key to some issues in adulthood and old age. In P. B. Baltes & O. G. Brim, Jr. (Eds.), *Life-span development and behavior* (Vol. 3). New York: Academic Press.

Costa, P. T., Jr., & McCrae, R. R. 1988. Personality in adulthood: A six-year longitudinal study of self-reports and spouse ratings on the NEO personality inventory. *Journal of Personality and Social Psychology, 54,* 853–863.

Costa, P. T., Jr., McCrae, R. R., & Arenberg, D. 1980. Enduring dispositions in adult males. *Journal of Personality and Social Psychology, 38,* 793–800.

Costa, P. T., Jr., McCrae, R. R., & Norris, A. H. 1981. Personal adjustment to aging: Longitudinal prediction from neuroticism and extraversion. *Journal of Gerontology, 36,* 78–85.

Costa, P. T., Jr., McCrae, R. R., Zonderman, A. B., Barbano, H. E., Lebowitz, B., & Larson, D. M. 1986. Cross-sectional studies of personality in a national sample. *Psychology and Aging, 1,* 144–149.

Cortese, A. J. 1990. *Ethnic ethics: The restructuring of moral theory.* Albany: State University of New York Press.

Coverman, S. 1989. Role overload, role conflict, and stress: Addressing consequences of multiple role demands. *Social Forces, 67,* 965–982.

Cowen, G., & Avants, S. K. 1988. Children's influence strategies: Structure, sex differences, and bilateral mother-child influence. *Child Development, 59,* 1303–1313.

Cowen, G., Drinkard, J., & MacGavin, L. 1984. The effects of target, age and gender on use of power strategies. *Journal of Personality and Social Psychology, 47,*1391–1398.

Cowart, B. J. 1981. Development of taste perception in humans: Sensitivity and preference throughout the life span. *Psychological Bulletin, 90,* 43–73.

Cowgill, D. O. 1974. Aging and modernization: A revision of the theory. In J. F. Gubrium (Ed.), *Late life.* Springfield, Ill: Thomas.

Cowgill, D. O. 1986. *Aging around the world.* Belmont, Calif.: Wadsworth.

Cowgill, D. O., & Holmes, L. D. (Eds.). 1972. *Aging and modernization.* New York: Appleton-Century-Crofts.

Cowley, G. 1990. Made to order babies. *Newsweek Special Issue* (Winter/Spring), pp. 94–100.

Cox, B. D., Ornstein, P. A., Naus, M. J., Maxfield, D., & Zimler, J. 1989. Children's concurrent use of rehearsal and organizational strategies. *Developmental Psychology, 25,* pp. 619–627.

Cox, M. J., Owen, M. T., Lewis, J. M., & Henderson, V. 1989. Marriage, adult adjustment, and early parenting. *Child Development, 60,* 1015–1024.

Coyne, A. C., Allen, P. A., & Wickens, D. D. 1986. Influence of adult age on primary and secondary memory search. *Psychology and Aging, 1,* 187–194.

Craik, F. I. M. 1977. Age differences in human memory. In J. E. Birren & K. W. Schaie (Eds.), *Handbook of the psychology of aging.* New York: Van Nostrand.

Craik, F. I. M., Byrd, M., & Swanson, J. M. 1987. Patterns of memory loss in three elderly samples. *Psychology and Aging, 2,* 79–86.

Craik, F. I. M., & Lockhart, R. S. 1972. Levels of processing: A framework for memory research. *Journal of Verbal Learning and Verbal Behavior, 11,* 671–684.

Crain, R. L., & Mahard, R. T. 1983. The effect of research methodology on desegregation-achievement studies. *American Journal of Sociology, 88,* 839–854.

Crandall, V. C., Katkovsky, W., & Crandall, V. J. 1965. Children's beliefs in their own control of reinforcement in intellectual-academic situations. *Child Development, 36,* 91–109.

Crano, W. D., & Aronoff, J. 1978. A cross-cultural study of expressive and instrumental role complementarity in the family. *American Sociological Review, 43,* 463–471.

Crano, W. D., & Mellon, P. M. 1978. Causal influence of teachers' expectancies on children's academic performance: A cross-lagged panel analysis. *Journal of Educational Psychology, 70,* 39–49.

Cratty, B. J. 1970. *Perceptual and motor development in infants and children.* New York: Macmillan.

Crawford, C. B., & Anderson, J. L. 1989. Sociobiology: An environmental discipline? *American Psychologist, 44,* 1449–1459.

Creighton, L. L. 1990. The new orphanages. *U.S. News & World Report* (October 8), pp. 37–41.

Creighton, L. L. 1991. Silent saviors. *U.S. News & World Report* (December 16), pp. 80–89.

Crimmis, E. M., Easterlin, R. A., & Saito, Y. 1991. What young adults want. *American Demographics, 13* (July), pp. 24–33.

Crispell, D. 1989. More bacon. *American Demographics, 11* (December), pp. 9–10.

Crnic, K. A., & Greenberg, M. T. 1990. Minor parenting stresses with young children. *Child Development, 61,* 1628–1637.

Crockenberg, S., & Litman, C. 1990. Autonomy as competence in 2-year-olds: Maternal correlates of child defiance, compliance, and self-assertion. *Developmental Psychology, 26,* 961–971.

Crockenberg, S., & McCluskey, K. 1986. Change in maternal behavior during the baby's first year of life. *Child Development, 57,* 746–753.

Crockenberg, S. B., & Smith, P. 1982. Antecedents of mother-infant interaction and infant irritability in the first three months of life. *Infant Behavior and Development, 5,* 105–119.

Crockett, L. Losoff, M., & Petersen, A. 1984. Perceptions of the peer group and friendship in early adolescence. *Journal of Early Adolescence, 4,* 155–181.

Cromer, J. 1984. *The mood of American youth.* Washington, D.C.: National Association of Secondary School Principals.

Cronbach, L. J., & Snow, R. E. 1977. *Aptitudes and instructional methods: A handbook for research on interactions.* New York: Irvington.

Crook, C. K. 1978. Taste perception in the newborn infant. *Infant Behavior and Development, 1,* 52–69.

Crook, C. K., & Lipsitt, L. P. 1976. Neonatal nutritive sucking: Effects of taste stimulation upon sucking rhythm and heart rate. *Child Development, 47,* 518–522.

Cross, H. J., & Kleinhesselink, R. R. 1985. The impact of the 1960s on adolescence. *Journal of Early Adolescence, 5,* 517–531.

Cross, K. P. 1976. *Accent on learning.* San Francisco: Jossey-Bass.

Crouter, A. C., Perry-Jenkins, M., Huston, T. L., & Hale, S. M. 1987. Processes underlying father involvement in dual-earner and single-earner families. *Developmental Psychology, 23,* 431–440.

Crowell, J. A., & Feldman, S. S. 1988. Mothers' internal models of relationships and

children's behavioral and developmental status: A study of mother-child interaction. *Child Development, 59,* 1273–1285.

Cruikshank, R. M. 1941. The development of visual size constancy in early infancy. *Journal of Genetic Psychology, 58,* 327–351.

Csikszentmihalyi, M., & Beattie, O. A. 1979. Life themes: A theoretical and empirical exploration of their origins and effects. *Journal of Humanistic Psychology, 19,* 45–63.

Csikszentmihalyi, M., & Larson, R. 1984. *Being adolescent: Conflict and growth in the teenage years.* New York: Basic Books.

Csikszentmihalyi, M., & LeFevre, J. 1989. Optimal experience in work and leisure. *Journal of Personality and Social Psychology, 56,* 815–822.

Culbertson, J. L., Krous, H. F., & Bendell, R. D. (Eds.). 1988. *Sudden infant death syndrome: medical aspects and psychological management.* Baltimore, MD: Johns Hopkins University Press.

Culp, R. E., Appelbaum, M. I., Osofsky, J.D., & Levy, J. A. 1988. Adolescent and older mothers: Comparison between prenatal maternal variables and newborn interaction measures. *Infant Behavior and Development, 11,* 353–362.

Cumming, E., & Henry, W. E. 1961. *Growing old.* New York: Basic Books.

Cummings, E. M., Iannotti, R. J., & Zahn-Waxler, C. 1985. Influence of conflict between adults on the emotions and aggression of young children. *Developmental Psychology, 21,* 495–507.

Cummings, E. M., Iannotti, R. J., & Zahn-Waxler, C. 1989. Aggression between peers in early childhood: Individual continuity and develpmental change. *Child Development, 60,* 887–895.

Cummings, J. S., Pellegrini, D. S., Notarius, C. I., & Cummings, E. M. 1989. Children's responses to angry adult behavior as a function of marital distress and history of interparent hostility. *Child Development, 60,* 1035–1043.

Cummins, J. 1986. Empowering minority students: A framework for intervention. *Harvard Educational Review, 56,* 18–36.

Curlee, J. 1969. Alcoholism and the empty-nest. *Bulletin of the Menninger Clinic, 33,* 165–171.

Curtiss, S. 1977. *Genie: A psycholinguistic study of a modern day "wild child."* New York: Academic Press.

Cutler, B. 1989. The Swedish example. *American Demographics, 10,* 70.

Cutler, B. 1990. Where does the free time go? *American Demographics, 12* (November), pp. 36–39.

Cutler, S. J. 1977. Aging and voluntary association participation. *Journal of Gerontology, 32,* 470–479.

Cutrona, C. E. 1984. Social support and stress in the transition to parenthood. *Journal of Abnormal Psychology, 93,* 378–390.

Cutrona, C. E., & Troutman, B. R. 1986. Social support, infant temperament, and parenting self-efficacy. *Child Development, 57,* 1507–1518.

Cuvo, A. J. 1975. Developmental differences in rehearsal and free recall. *Journal of Experimental Child Psychology, 19,* 265–278.

Daehler, M. W., & Bukatko, D. 1985. *Cognitive development.* New York: Knopf.

Dale, P. S. 1976. *Language development: Structure and functions* (2nd ed.). New York: Holt, Rinehart and Winston.

Daley, S. 1991. Girls' self-esteem is lost on way to adolescence, new study finds. *New York Times* (January 9), pp. B1, B6.

Damico, S. B., & Sparks, C. 1986. Cross-group contact opportunities: Impact on interpersonal relationships in desegregated middle schools. *Sociology of Education, 59,* 113–123.

Damon, W. 1977. *The social world of the child.* San Francisco: Jossey-Bass.

Damon, W., & Hart, D. 1982. The development of self-understanding from infancy through adolescence. *Child Development, 53,* 841–864.

Daniels, D. 1986. Differential experiences of siblings in the same family as predictors of adolescent sibling personality differences. *Journal of Personality and Social Psychology, 51,* 339–346.

Daniels, D., Dunn, J., Furstenberg, F. F., Jr., & Plomin, R. 1985. Environmental differences within the family and adjustment differences within pairs of adolescent siblings. *Child Development, 56,* 764–774.

Daniels, D., & Plomin, R. 1985. Origins of individual differences in infant shyness. *Developmental Psychology, 21,* 118–121.

Dannemiller, J. L. 1989. A test of color constancy in 9- and 20-week-old human infants following simulated illuminant changes. *Developmental Psychology, 25,* 171–184.

Danner, F. W., & Day, M. C. 1987. Eliciting formal operations. *Child Development, 48,* 1600–1606.

Darnton, N. 1991a. The end of innocence. *Newsweek Special Issue* (Summer), pp. 62–64.

Darnton, N. 1991b. The pain of the last taboo. *Newsweek* (October 7), pp. 70–72.

Dasen, P. R. (Ed.). 1977. *Piagetian psychology: Cross-cultural contributions.* New York: Gardner Press.

Datan, N., Rodeheaver, D., & Hughes, F. 1987. Adult development and aging. *Annual Review of Psychology, 38,* 153–180.

Davids, A., Holden, R. H., & Gray, G. B. 1963. Maternal anxiety during pregnancy and adequacy of mother and child adjustments 8 months following childbirth. *Child Development, 34,* 993–1002.

Davies, M., & Kandel, D. B. 1981. Paternal and peer influences on adolescents' educational plans: Some further evidence. *American Journal of Sociology, 87,* 363–387.

Davis, B. 1986. Survival odds are improving for even smallest "preemies." *Wall Street Journal* (April 25), p. 19.

Davis, C. 1938. The self-selection of diet experiment: Its significance for feeding in the home. *Ohio State Medical Journal, 34,* 862–868.

Davis, K. 1949. *Human society.* New York: Macmillan.

Davison, M. L., King, P. M., Kitchener, K. S., & Parker, C. A. 1980. The stage sequence concept in cognitive and social development. *Developmental Psychology, 16,* 121–131.

Dawson, D. A. 1991. Family structure and

children's health and well-being: Data from the 1988 National Health Interview Survey on Child Health. *Journal of Marriage and the Family, 53*, pp. 573–584.

Day, A. T. 1986. *Who cares? Demographic trends challenge family care for the elderly.* Washington, D.C.: Population Reference Bureau.

Dean, A. L., Malik, M. M., Richards, W., & Stringer, S. A. 1986. Effects of parental maltreatment on children's conceptions of interpersonal relationships. *Developmental Psychology, 22*, 617–626.

Deaux, K. 1985. Sex and gender. *Annual Review of Psychology, 36*, 49–81.

Deaux, K. & Major, B. 1987. Putting gender into context: An interactive model of gender-related behavior. *Psychological Review, 94*, pp. 369–389.

DeCasper, A. J., & Carstens, A. A. 1981. Contingencies of stimulation: Effects on learning and emotion in neonates. *Infant Behavior and Development, 4*, 19–35.

DeCasper, A. J., & Fifer, W. P. 1980. Of human bonding: Newborns prefer their mothers' voices. *Science, 208*, 1174–1176.

DeCherney, A. H., & Berkowitz, G. S. 1982. Female fecundity and age. *New England Journal of Medicine, 306*, 424–426.

Decker, H. S. 1990. *Freud, Dora and Vienna 1990.* New York: The Free Press.

Deci, E. L. 1975. *Intrinsic motivation.* New York: Plenum.

Deci. E. L. 1980. *The psychology of self-determination.* Lexington, Mass: D. C. Heath.

Deci, E. L. & Ryan, R. M. 1980. The empirical exploration of intrinsic motivational processes. In L. Berkowitz (Ed.), *Advances in experimental social psychology.* Vol. 13. New York: Academic Press.

Deci, E. L. & Ryan, R. M. 1985. *Intrinsic motivation and self-determination in human behavior.* New York: Plenum Press.

Deci, E. L., Schwartz, A. J., Sheinman, L., & Ryan, R. M. 1981. An instrument to assess adults' orientations toward control versus autonomy with children: Reflections on intrinsic motivation and perceived competence. *Journal of Educational Psychology, 73*, 642–650.

DeCourcy Hinds, M. 1990. Addiction to crack can kill parental instinct. *New York Times* (March 17), pp. 1, 8.

DeFleur, L. B., & Menke, B. A. 1975. Learning about the labor force: Occupational knowledge among high school males. *Sociology of Education, 48*, 324–345.

Degler, C. 1980. *At odds: Women and the family in America from the Revolution to the present.* New York: Oxford University Press.

Degler, C. N. 1991. *In search of human nature: The decline and revival of Darwinism in American social thought.* New York: Oxford University Press.

De Lacoste-Utamsing, C., & Holloway, R. L. 1982. Sexual dimorphism in the human corpus callosum. *Science, 216*, 1431–1432.

deLemos, M. M. 1969. The development of conservation in Aboriginal children. *International Journal of Psychology, 4*, 255–269.

DeLongis, A., Folkman, S., & Lazarus, R. S. 1988. The impact of daily stress on health and mood: Psychological and social re-

sources as mediators. *Journal of Personality and Social Psychology, 54*, 486–495.

Deluty, R. H. 1985. Consistency of assertive, aggressive and submissive behavior for children. *Journal of Personality and Social Psychology, 49*, 1054–1065.

deMause, L. 1974. The evolution of childhood. In L. deMause (Ed.), *The history of childhood.* New York: Harper & Row.

Dembroski, T. M. 1981. The type A coronary-prone behavior pattern: A review. *Circulation, 63*, 1199–1215.

Demo, D. H. & Acock, A. C. 1988. The impact of divorce on children. *Journal of Marriage and the Family, 50*, 619–648.

Demo, D. H., Small, S. A., & Savin-Williams, R. C. 1987. Family relations and the self-esteem of adolescents and their parents. *Journal of Marriage and the Family, 49*, 705–716.

Demos, J. 1986. *Past, present and personal: The family and the life course in historical perspective.* New York: Oxford University Press.

Demos, J., & Demos, V. 1969. Adolescence in historical perspective. *Journal of Marriage and the Family, 31*, 632–638.

Demos, V. 1986. Crying in early infancy: An illustration of the motivational function of affect. In T. B. Brazelton & M. Yogman (Eds.), *Affect and early infancy.* New York: Ablex.

Demos, V. 1990. Black family studies in the Journal of Marriage and the Family and the issue of distortion: A trend analysis. *Journal of Marriage and the Family, 52*, 603–612.

Demtrious, A. (Ed.). 1988. *The Neo-Piagetian theories of cognitive development: Toward an integration.* Amsterdam: North-Holland.

Denham, S. A., McKinley, M., KCouchoud, E. A., & Holt, R. 1990. Emotional and behavioral predictors of preschool peer ratings. *Child Development, 61*, 1145–1152.

Denham, S. A., Renwick, S. M., & Holt, R. W. 1991. Working and playing together: Prediction of preschool social-emotional competence from mother-child interaction. *Child Development, 62*, 242–249.

Denham, T. E. & Smith, C. L. 1989. The influence of grandparents on grandchildren: A review of the literature and resources. *Family Relations, 38*, 345–350.

Denney, N. W., Miller, B. V., Dew, J. R., & Levav, A. L. 1991. An adult developmental study of contextual memory. *Journal of Gerontology, 46*, P44–50.

Denney, N. W., & Palmer, A. M. 1981. Adult age differences on traditional and practical problem-solving measures. *Journal of Gerontology, 36*, 323–328.

Dennis, W. 1973. *Children of the crèche.* New York: Appleton-Century-Crofts.

Dennis, W., & Dennis, M. G. 1940. The effect of cradling practices upon the onset of walking in Hopi children. *Journal of Genetic Psychology, 56*, 77–86.

Denny, N. W. 1985. A review of life span research with the twenty questions task: A study of problem-solving ability. *International Journal of Aging and Development, 21*, 161–173.

Dent, E. M. 1978. The salience of prowhite/anti-black bias. *Child Development, 49*, 1280–1283.

Dentzer, S. 1990. Do the elderly want to work? *U.S. News & World Report* (May 14), pp. 48–50.

DeParle, J. 1991a. Child poverty twice as likely after family split, study says. *New York Times* (March 2), p. 8.

DeParle, J. 1991b. Suffering in the cities persists as U.S. fights other battles. *New York Times* (January 27):1, 15.

DeParle, J., & Applebome, P. 1991. Ideas to aid poor abound but consensus is wanting. *New York Times* (January 29), pp. A1, A12.

DePaulo, B. M., Kenny, D. A., Hoover, C. W., Webb, W., & Oliver, P. V. 1987. Accuracy of person perception: Do people know what kinds of impressions they convey? *Journal of Personality and Social Psychology, 52*, 303–315.

Depner, C. E., & Ingersoll-Dayton, B. 1985. Conjugal social support: Patterns in later life. *Journal of Gerontology, 40*, 761–766.

Depner, C. E., & Ingersoll-Dayton, B. 1988. Supportive relationships in later life. *Psychology and Aging, 3*:348–357.

Depue, R. A., & Monroe, S. M. 1978. Learned helplessness in the perspective of the depressive disorders: Conceptual and definitional issues. *Journal of Abnormal Psychology, 87*, 3–20.

Desai, S., & Waite, L. J. 1991. Women's employment during pregnancy and after the first birth: Occupational characteristics and work commitment. *American Sociological Review, 56*, 551–566.

Desmond, S. M., Price, J. H., Gray, N., & O'Connell, J. K. 1986. The etiology of adolescents' perceptions of their weight. *Journal of Youth and Adolescence, 15*, 461–474.

Despert, J. L. 1953. *Children of divorce.* Garden City, N.Y.: Doubleday.

Deur, J. L., & Parke, R. D. 1970. Effects of inconsistent punishment on aggression in children. *Developmental Psychology, 2*, 403–411.

Deutsch, C. H. 1991. The boss who plays now pays. *New York Times* (June 13), pp. C1, C17.

Deutsch, F. M., Ruble, D. N., Fleming, A., Brooks-Gunn, J., & Stangor, C. 1988. Information-seeking and maternal self-definition during the transition to motherhood. *Journal of Personality and Social Psychology, 55*, 420–431.

Deutscher, I. 1964. The quality of postparental life: Definitions of the situation. *Journal of Marriage and the Family, 26*, 52–59.

Devaney, K. O., & Johnson, H.A. 1980. Neuron loss in the aging visual cortex of man. *Journal of Gerontology, 35*, 836–841.

Devereux, E. C., Shouval, R., Bronfenbrenner, U., Rodgers, R. R., KavVenaki, S., Kiely, E., & Karson, E. 1974. Socialization practices of parents, teachers, and peers in Israel: The kibbutz versus the city. *Child Development, 45*, 269–281.

DeVito, J. A. 1970. *The psychology of speech and language.* New York: Random House.

De Vos, G. 1967. *Japan's invisible race: Caste in culture and personality.* Berkeley, Calif.: University of California Press.

de Vries, B., & Walker, L. J. 1986. Moral reasoning and attitudes toward capital punishment. *Developmental Psychology, 22*, 509–513.

De Vries, R. G. 1981. Birth and death: Social construction at the poles of existence. *Social Forces, 59*, 1074–1093.

Diamond, M. C. 1988. *Enriching heredity: The impact of the environment on the anatomy of the brain.* New York: Free Press.

Dick-Read, G. 1944. *Childbirth without fear: The principles and practice of natural childbirth.* New York: Harper & Row.

Dickstein, S., & Parke, R. D. 1988. Social referencing in infancy: A glance at fathers and marriage. *Child Development, 59*, 506–511.

Diener, C. I., & Dweck, C. S. 1980. An analysis of learned helplessness: II. The processing of success. *Journal of Personality and Social Psychology, 39*, 940–952.

Diener, E. 1984. Subjective well-being. *Psychological Bulletin, 95*, 542–575.

Diepold, J., Jr., & Young, R. D. 1979. Empirical studies of adolescent sexual behavior: A critical review. *Adolescence, 14*, 45–64.

Diesenhouse, S. 1990. A rising tide of violence leaves more youths in jail. *New York Times* (July 8), p. E4.

DiPietro, J.A., Larson, S. K., & Porges, S. W. 1987. Behavioral and heart rate pattern differences between breast-fed and bottle-fed neonates. *Developmental Psychology, 23*, 467–474.

DiPrete, T. A., & Grusky, D. B. 1990. Structure and trend in the process of stratification for American men and women. *American Journal of Sociology, 96*, 107–143.

Dirks, J., & Gibson, E. 1977. Infants' perception of similarity between live people and their photographs. *Child Development, 48*, 124–130.

Dishion, T. J. 1990. The family ecology of boys' peer relations in middle childhood. *Child Development, 61*, 874–892.

Dix, T., Ruble, D. N., Grusec, J. E., & Nixon, S. 1986. Social cognition in parents: Inferential and affective reactions to children of three age levels. *Child Development, 57*, 879–894.

Dix, T., Ruble, D. N., & Zambarano, R. J. 1989. Mothers' implicit theories of discipline: Child effects, parent effects, and the attribution process. *Child Development, 60*, 1373–1391.

Dixon, J. A., & Moore, C. F. 1990. The development of perspective taking: Understanding differences in information and weighting. *Child Development, 61*, 1502–1513.

Dobzhansky, T. 1962. *Mankind evolving.* New Haven: Yale University Press.

Dodge, K. A. 1983. Behavioral antecedents of peer social status. *Child Development, 54*, 1386–1399.

Dodge, K. A. 1989. Coordinating responses to aversive stimuli: Introduction to a special section on the development of emotion regulation. *Developmental Psychology, 25*, 339–342.

Dodge, K. A., Bates, J. E., & Pettit, G. S. 1990. Mechanisms in the cycle of violence. *Science, 250*, 1678–1683.

Dodge, K. A., Coie, J. D., Pettit, G. S., & Price, J. M. 1990. Peer status and aggression in boys' groups: Developmental and contextual analyses. *Child Development, 61*, 1289–1309.

Dodge, K. A., & Frame, C. L. 1982. Social cognitive biases and deficits in aggressive boys. *Child Development, 53*, 620–635.

Dodge, K. A., Price, J. M., Coie, J. D., & Christopoulos, C. 1990. On the development of aggressive dyadic relationships in boys' peer groups. *Human Development, 33*, 260–270.

Dodge, K. A., & Somberg, D. R. 1987. Hostile attributional biases among aggressive boys are exacerbated under conditions of threats to the self. *Child Development, 58*, 213–224.

Doering, S. G., Entwisle, D. R. & Quinlan, D. 1980. Modeling the quality of women's birth experience. *Journal of Health and Social Behavior, 21*, 12–21.

Dohrenwend, B. S., & Dohrenwend, B. P. (Eds.). 1974. *Stressful life events: Their nature and effects.* New York: Wiley.

Donate-Bartfield, E., & Passman, R. H. 1985. Attentiveness of mothers and fathers to their baby's cries. *Infant Behavior and Development, 8*, 385–393.

Donovan, W. L., & Leavitt, L. A. 1989. Maternal self-efficacy and infant attachment: Integrating physiology, perceptions, and behavior. *Child Development, 60*, 460–472.

Doppelt, J. E., & Wallace, W. L. 1955. Standardization of the Wechsler Adult Intelligence Scale for older persons. *Journal of Abnormal and Social Psychology, 51*, 312–330.

Dornbusch, S. 1989. The sociology of adolescence. *Annual Review of Sociology, 15*, 233–259.

Dornbusch, S. M., Carlsmith, J. M., Bushwall, S. J., Ritter, P. L., Leiderman, H., Hastorf, A. H., & Gross, R. T. 1985. Single parents, extended households, and the control of adolescents. *Child Development, 56*, 326–341.

Dornbusch, S. M., Ritter, P. L., Leiderman, P. H., Roberts, D. F., & Fraleigh, M. J. 1987. The relations of parenting style to adolescent school performance. *Child Development, 55*, 1244–1257.

Doty, R. L., Shaman, P., Applebaum, S. L., Giberson, R., Siksorski, L., & Rosenberg, L. 1984. Smell identification ability: Changes with age. *Science, 226*, 1441–1443.

Douglas, J. D., & Wong, A. C. 1977. Formal operations: Age and sex differences in Chinese and American children. *Child Development, 48*, 689–692.

Douglas, J. W. B., Ross, J. M., & Simpson, H. R. 1968. *All our future.* London: Peter Davies.

Douglas, K., & Arenberg, D. 1978. Age changes, cohort differences, and cultural changes on the Guilford-Zimmerman Temperament Survey. *Journal of Gerontology, 33*, 737–747.

Dowd, J. J. 1975. Aging as exchange: A preface to theory. *Journal of Gerontology, 30*, 584–594.

Dowd, J. J. 1980. Exchange rates and old people. *Journal of Gerontology, 35*, 596–602.

Dowd, J. J. 1984. Beneficence and the aged. *Journal of Gerontology, 39*, 102–108.

Dowd, J. J. 1990. Ever since Durkheim: The socialization of human development. *Human Development, 33*, 138–159.

Dowd, J. M., & Tronick, E. Z. 1986.Temporal coordination of arm movements in early infancy: Do infants move in synchrony with adult speech? *Child Development, 57*, 762–776.

Doyle, A., Connolly, J., & Rivest, Louis-Paul. 1980. The effect of playmate familiarity on social interactions of young children. *Child Development, 51*, 217–223.

Drabman, R. S., & Thomas, M. H. 1974. Does media violence increase children's toleration of real-life aggression? *Developmental Psychology, 10*, 418–421.

Dragastin, S. E., & Elder, G. H., Jr. 1975. *Adolescence in the life cycle.* New York: Wiley.

Dreeben, R., & Gamoran, A. 1986. Race, instruction, and learning. *American Sociological Review, 51*, 660–669.

Dressel, P. L., & Clark, A. 1990. A critical look at family care. *Journal of Marriage and the Family, 52*, 769–782.

Duberman, L. 1973. Step kin relationships. *Journal of Marriage and the Family, 35*, 283–292.

Dubin, R. 1956. Industrial workers' worlds. *Social Problems, 3*, 131–142.

DuBois, D. L., & Hirsch, B. J. 1990. School and neighborhood friendship patterns of blacks and whites in early adolescence. *Child Development, 61*, 524–536.

Dubow, E. F., & Tisak, J. 1980. The relation between stressful life events and adjustment in elementary school children: The role of social support and social problem-solving skills. *Child Development, 60*, 1412–1423.

Dudley, J. R. 1991. Increasing our understanding of divorced fathers who have infrequent contact with their children. *Family Relations, 40*, 279–285.

Duffy, F. H., Als, H., & McAnulty, G. B. 1990. Behavioral and electrophysiological evidence for gestational age effects in healthy preterm and full term infants studied two weeks after expected due date. *Child Development, 61*, 1271–1286.

Dugan, T. F., & Coles, R. (Eds.). 1989. *The child in our times: Studies in the development of resiliency.* New York: Brunner/Mazel.

Dulit, E. 1972. Adolescent thinking à la Piaget: The formal stage. *Journal of Youth and Adolescence, 1*, 281–301.

Dullea, G. 1978. Divorced fathers: Who are happiest? *New York Times* (February 4), p. 20.

Dullea, G. 1984. Parents, children and food. *New York Times* (January 16), p. 20.

Duncan, G. J. 1984. *Years of poverty, years of plenty.* Ann Arbor, Mich.: Institute for Social Research, University of Michigan.

Duncan, G. J., Hill, M. S., & Hoffman, S. D. 1988. Welfare dependence within and across generations. *Science, 239*, 467–471.

Duncan, G. J., & Rogers, W. L. 1988. Longitudinal aspects of childhood poverty. *Journal of Marriage and the Family, 50*, 1007–1022.

Dunn, J. 1983. Sibling relationships in early

childhood. *Child Development, 54,* 787–811.

Dunn, J. 1988. *The beginnings of social understanding.* Cambridge, Mass.: Harvard University Press.

Dunn, J., & Plomin, R. 1990. *Separate lives: Why siblings are so different.* New York: Basic Books.

Dunn, W. 1990. More single moms living in poverty. *USA Today* (August 2), P. 6A.

Durrett, M. E., Richards, P., Otaki, M., Pennebaker, J. W., & Nyquist, L. 1986. Mother's involvement with infant and her perception of spousal support, Japan and America. *Journal of Marriage and the Family, 48,* 187–194.

Dusek, J. B. (Ed.). 1985. *Teacher expectancies.* Hillsdale, N.J.: Erlbaum.

Dusek, J. B., & Flaherty, J. F. 1981. The development of the self-concept during the adolescent years. *Monographs of the Society for Research in Child Development, 46* (191).

Duvall, E. M. 1977. *Family development* (5th ed.). Philadelphia: Lippincott.

Dweck, C. S. 1975. The role of expectations and attributions in the alleviation of learned helplessness. *Journal of Personality and Social Psychology, 31,* 674–685.

Dwyer, J. W., & Coward, R. T. 1991. A multivariate comparison of the involvement of adult sons versus daughters in care of impaired parents. *Journal of Gerontology, 46,* S259–269.

Dyer, E. D. 1963. Parenthood as crisis: A restudy. *Marriage and Family Living, 25,* 196–201.

Eagly, A. H. 1987. *Sex differences in social behavior: A social-role interpretation.* Hillsdale, N.J.: Erlbaum.

Easterbrooks, M. A., & Goldberg, W. A. 1984. Toddler development in the family: Impact of father involvement and parenting characteristics. *Child Development, 55,* 740–752.

Eccles, J., Adler, T. F., Futterman, R., Goff, S. B., Kaczala, C. M., Meece, J. L., & Midgley, C. 1983. Expectations, values, and academic behaviors. In J. T. Spence (Ed.), *Achievement and achievement motivation.* San Francisco: W. H. Freeman.

Eccles, J., Adler, T. F., & Kaczala, C. M. 1982. Socialization of achievement attitudes and beliefs: Parental influences. *Child Development, 53,* 310–321.

Eccles, J. S., & Jacobs, J. E. 1986. Social forces shape math attitudes and performance. *Signs, 11,* 367–389.

Echenique, J. 1986. Early dating may lead to early sex. *USA Today* (November 12), p. 1D.

Eckerman, C. O., Davis, C. C., & Didow, S. M. 1989. Toddlers' emerging ways of achieving social coordinations with a peer. *Child Development, 60,* 440–453.

Eckerman, C. O., & Didow, S. M. 1988. Lessons drawn from observing young peers together. *Acta Paediatrica Scandinavica, 77,* 55–70.

Eckerman, C. O., & Stein, M. R. 1990. How imitation begets imitation and toddlers' generation of games. *Developmental Psychology, 26,* 370–378.

Eckerman, C. O., Whatley, J. L., & Kutz, S. L. 1975. Growth of social play with peers during the second year of life. *Developmental Psychology, 11,* 42–49.

Eckholm, E. 1985. Experts predict vaccinations by 1990 for virtually every child on earth. *New York Times* (October 20), p. 12.

Eckholm, E. 1986. Aging: Studies point toward ways to slow it. *New York Times* (June 10), pp. 15, 18.

Eckholm, E. 1990a. An aging nation grapples with caring for the frail. *New York Times* (March 27), pp. A1, A10.

Eckholm, E. 1990b. Cut down as they grow up: AIDS stalks gay teen-agers. *New York Times* (December 13), pp. A1, A14.

Edelman, P., & Hughes, S. 1990. The impact of community care on provision of informal care to homebound elderly persons. *Journal of Gerontology, 45,* S74–84.

Edelson, M. 1988. *Psychoanalysis: A theory in crisis.* Chicago: University of Chicago Press.

Eder, D. 1985. The cycle of popularity: Interpersonal relations among female adolescents. *Sociology of Education, 58,* 154–165.

Eder, D., & Hallinan, M. T. 1978. Sex differences in children's friendships. *American Sociological Review, 43,* 237–250.

Eder, R. A. 1989. The emergent personologist: The structure and content of 3 1/2-, 5 1/2-, and 7 1/2-year-olds' concepts of themselves and other persons. *Child Development, 60,* 1218–1228.

Eder, R. A. 1990. Uncovering young children's psychological selves: Individual and developmental differences. *Child Development, 61,* 849–863.

Edmonds, M. H. 1976. New directions theories of language acquisition. *Harvard Educational Review, 46,* 175–198.

Edmondson, B. 1990. AIDS and aging. *American Demographics,* 12 (March), pp. 28–31, 34.

Edwards, C. P., & Whiting, B. B. 1988. *Children of different worlds.* Cambridge, Mass.: Harvard University Press.

Edwards, J. N. 1991. New conceptions: Biosocial innovations and the family. *Journal of Marriage and the Family, 53,* 349–360.

Egan, K. 1980. On Piaget and education. *Harvard Educational Review, 50,* 263–269.

Egeland, B., & Brunquell, D. 1979. An at-risk approach to the study of child abuse: Some preliminary findings. *Journal of the American Academy of Child Psychiatry, 18,* 219–235.

Egeland, B., & Farber, E. 1984. Infant-mother attachment: Factors related to its development and changes over time. *Child Development, 55,* 753–771.

Egeland, B., & Jacobvitz, D. 1984. Intergenerational continuity of parental abuse: Causes and consequences. Paper presented at the Conference on Biosocial Perspectives in Abuse and Neglect, York, Maine.

Egeland, B., Jacobvitz, D., & Sroufe, L. A. 1988. Breaking the cycle of abuse. *Child Development, 59,* 1080–1088.

Egeland, B., & Sroufe, L. A. 1981a. Attachment and early maltreatment. *Child Development, 52,* 44–52.

Egeland, B., & Sroufe, L. A. 1981b. Develop-

mental sequelae of maltreatment in infancy. In R. Rizley & D. Cicchetti (Eds.), *Developmental perspectives on child maltreatment: New directions for child development.* San Francisco: Jossey-Bass.

Ehrhardt, A. A., & Meyer-Bahlburg, H. F. L. 1981. Effects of prenatal sex hormones on gender-related behavior. *Science, 211,* 1312–1318.

Eibl-Eibesfeldt, I. 1989. *Human ethology.* New York: Aldine de Gruyter.

Eichenwald, H. F., & Fry, P. C. 1969. Nutrition and learning. *Science, 163,* 644–648.

Eichorn, D. H., Clausen, J. A., Haan, N., Honzik, M. P., & Mussen, P. H. (Eds.). 1982. *Present and past in middle life.* New York: Academic Press.

Eimas, P. D. 1985. The perception of speech in early infancy. *Scientific American, 252* (January), pp. 46–52.

Einstein, A. 1949. Autobiography. In P. Schilpp. Ed. *Albert Einstein: Philosopher-Scientist.* Evanston, Ill.: Library of Living Philosophers.

Einstein, E. 1979. Stepfamily lives. *Human Behavior, 8* (April), 63–68.

Eisdorfer, C., & Wilkie, E. 1973. Intellectual changes with advancing age. In L. F. Jarvik, C. Eisdorfer, & J. E. Blum (Eds.), *Intellectual functioning in adults.* New York: Springer.

Eisenberg, N. 1986. *Altruistic emotion, cognition and behavior.* Hillsdale, NJ: Erlbaum.

Eisenberg, N., Lennon, R., & Roth, K. 1983. Prosocial development: A longitudinal study. *Developmental Psychology, 19,* 846–855.

Eisenberg, N., & Miller, P. A. 1987. The relation of empathy to prosocial and related behaviors. *Psychological Bulletin, 101,* 91–119.

Eisenberg, N., Wolchik, S. A., Hernandez, R., & Pasternack, J. F. 1985. Parental socialization of young children's play: A short-term longitudinal study. *Child Development, 56,* 1506–1513.

Eisenberger, R. 1989. *Blue Monday: A loss of the work ethic in America.* New York: Paragon House.

Eisert, D. C., & Kahle, L. R. 1982. Self-evaluation and social comparison of physical and role change during adolescence: A longitudinal analysis. *Child Development, 53,* 98–104.

Ekerdt, D. J., Vinick, B. H., & Bosse, R. 1989. Orderly endings: Do men know when they will retire? *Journal of Gerontology, 44,* S28–35.

Ekman, P. 1972. Universal in cultural differences in facial expressions of emotion. In J. K. Cole (Ed.), *Nebraska symposium on motivation* (Vol. 19). Lincoln: University of Nebraska Press.

Ekman, P. 1980. *The face of man: Expressions of universal emotions in a New Guinea village.* New York: Garland STPM Press.

Elder, G. 1983. Families, kin, and the life course. In R. Parke (Ed.), *The family.* Chicago: University of Chicago Press.

Elder, G. H., Jr. 1974. *Children of the great depression.* Chicago: University of Chicago Press.

Elder, G. H., Jr. 1985. Perspectives on the life course. In G. H. Elder, Jr. (Ed), *Life course dynamics: Trajectories and transitions, 1968-1980.* Ithaca, N.Y.: Cornell University Press.

Elder, G. H., Jr. 1986. Military times and turning points in men's lives. *Developmental Psychology, 22,* 233–245.

Elder, G. H., Jr., & Caspi, A. 1990. Studying lives in a changing society: Personological explorations. In A. I. Rabin, R. A. Zucker, & S. Frank (Eds.), *Studying persons and lives.* New York: Springer.

Elder, G. H., Jr., & Clipp, E. 1988. Wartime losses and social bonding: Influences across 40 years in men's lives. *Psychiatry, 51,* 177–198.

Elder, G. H., Jr., van Nguyen, T., & Caspi, A. 1985. Linking family hardship to children's lives. *Child Development, 56,* 361–375.

Elfant, A. B. 1985. Nurturing the beleagured child. *Contemporary Psychology, 30,* 789–790.

Elias, M. 1983. Do aggressive type A kids risk heart attacks as adults? *USA Today* (December 23), p. 1.

Elias, M. 1984. A happy marriage makes bright tots. *USA Today* (June 5), p. D1.

Elias, M. 1985a. Be upbeat and beat illness, stress. *USA Today* (August 26), p. D1.

Elias, M. 1985b. Casual sex on campus declines. *USA Today* (January 10), p. D1.

Elias, M. 1986a. Drug scare tactics don't impress kids. *USA Today* (October 20), p. D1.

Elias, M. 1986b. Sex isn't the main lure for extra-marital affairs. *USA Today* (April 17), p. D1.

Elias, M. 1987. Divorce is easier on well-off kids. *USA Today* (March 16), p. D1.

Elias, M. 1989. Inborn traits outweigh environment. *USA Today* (August 9), pp. 1D, 2D.

Elias, M. 1991. Helping baby sleep soundly. *USA Today* (April 15), p. D1.

Elias, M., & Clabby, J. 1986. *Teach your child to decide.* New York: Doubleday.

Elkin, F., & Westley, W. A. 1955. The myth of adolescent peer culture. *American Sociological Review, 20,* 680–684.

Elkind, D. 1961. Children's discovery of the conservation of mass, weight, and volume: Piaget replication study II. *Journal of Genetic Psychology, 98,* 219–227.

Elkind, D. 1967. Egocentrism in adolescence. *Child Development, 38,* 1025–1034.

Elkind, D. 1968a. Cognitive development in adolescence. In J. F. Adams (Ed.), *Understanding adolescence.* Boston: Allyn & Bacon.

Elkind, D. 1968b. Giant in the nursery—Jean Piaget. *New York Times Magazine* (May 26), pp. 25ff.

Elkind, D. 1970. Erik Erikson's eight ages of man. *New York Times Magazine* (April 5), pp. 25ff.

Elkind, D. 1974. *A sympathetic understanding of the child from birth to sixteen.* Boston: Allyn & Bacon.

Eklind, D. 1975. Recent research on cognitive development in adolescence. In S. E. Dragastin & G. H. Elder, Jr. (Eds.), *Adolescence in the life cycle.* New York: Wiley.

Elkind, D. 1979. Growing up faster. *Psychology Today, 12* (February), pp. 38–45.

Elkind, D. 1981. *The hurried child.* Reading, Mass.: Addison-Wesley.

Elkind, D. 1986. *The miseducation of children: Superkids at risk.* New York: Knopf.

Elkind, D. 1987. Superkids and super problems. *Psychology Today, 21* (May) pp. 60–61.

Elkington, J. 1985. *The poisoned womb.* New York: Viking Penguin.

Elliott, D. S. 1966. Delinquency, school attendance, and dropout. *Social Problems, 13,* 307–314.

Ellis, L., & Ames, M. A. 1987. Neurohormonal functioning and sexual orientation: A theory of homosexuality-heterosexuality. *Psychological Bulletin, 101,* 233–258.

Ellis, M. J., Witt, P. A., Reynolds, R., & Sprague, R. L. 1974. Methylphenidate and the activity of hyperactives in the informal setting. *Child Development, 45,* 217–220.

Ellwood, D. T. 1988. *Poor support: Poverty in the American family.* New York: Basic Books.

Elster, A. B., Lamb, M., Peters, L., Kahn, J., & Tavare, J. 1987. Judicial involvement and conduct problems of fathers of infants born to adolescent mothers. *Pediatrics, 79,* 230–234.

Elwell, F., & Maltbie-Crannell, A. D. 1981. The impact of role loss upon coping resources and life satisfaction of the elderly. *Journal of Gerontology, 36,* 223–232.

Emde, R. N., Kligman, D. H., Reich, J. H., & Wade, T. 1978. Emotional expression in infancy: 1. Initial students of social signaling and an emergent model. In M. Lewis & L. Rosenblum (Eds.), *The development of affect.* New York: Plenum.

Emery, R. 1982. Interparental conflict and the children of discord. *Psychological Bulletin, 92,* 310–330.

Emery, R. E. 1989. Family violence. *American Psychologist, 44,* 321–328.

Emler, N., Renwick, S., & Malone, B. 1983. The relationship between moral reasoning and political orientation. *Journal of Personality and Social Psychology, 45,* 1073–1080.

Emmons, R. A., Larsen, R. J., Levine, S., & Diener, E. 1983. *Factors predicting satisfaction judgments.* Paper presented at the meeting of the Midwestern Psychological Association, Chicago (May).

Engen, T., Lipsitt, L. P., & Kaye, H. 1963. Olfactory responses and adaptation in the human neonate. *Journal of Physiology and Psychology, 56,* 73–77.

Engen, T., Lipsitt, L. P., & Peck, M. B. 1974. Ability of newborn infants to discriminate sapid substances. *Developmental Psychology, 10,* 741–744.

Ensminger, M. E. 1990. Sexual activity and problem behaviors among black, urban adolescents. *Child Development, 61,* 2032–2046.

Enstrom, J. E. 1984. Smoking and longevity studies. *Science, 225,* 878.

Entwisle, D. R., & Alexander, K. L. 1990. Beginning school math competence: Minority and majority comparisons. *Child Development, 61,* 454–471.

Epstein, A. S., & Radin, N. 1975. Motivational components related to father behavior and cognitive functioning in preschoolers. *Child Development, 46,* 831–839.

Epstein, C. F. 1988. *Deceptive distinctions: Sex, gender, and the social order.* New Haven, Conn.: Yale University Press.

Epstein, J. L. 1985. After the bus arrives: Resegregation in desegregated schools. *Journal of Social Issues, 41,* 23–44.

Epstein, L. H., & Wing, R. R. 1987. Behavioral treatment of childhood obesity. *Psychological Bulletin, 101,* 331–342.

Epstein, S. 1979. The stability of behavior: I. On predicting most of the people much of the time. *Journal of Personality and Social Psychology, 37,* 1097–1126.

Epstein, S. 1980. The stability of behavior: II. Implications for psychological research. *American Psychologist, 35,* 790–806.

Epstein, S. H. 1983. Why do women live longer than men? *Science 83, 4* (October), pp. 30–31.

Erikson, E. H. 1980. On the generational cycle. *International Journal of Psychoanalysis, 61,* 213–223.

Erikson, E. H. 1959. Identity and the life cycle. *Monograph, Psychological Issues* (Vol. 1). New York: International Universities Press.

Erikson, E. H. 1963. *Childhood and society.* New York: Norton.

Erikson, E. H. 1964a. *Insight and responsibility.* New York: Norton.

Erikson, E. H. 1964b. Inner and outer space: Reflections on womanhood. *Daedalus, 93,* 582–606.

Erikson, E. H. 1968a. Life cycle. In D. L. Sills (Ed.), *International encyclopedia of the social sciences* (Vol. 9). New York: Free Press and Macmillan.

Erikson, E. H. 1968b. *Identity: Youth and crisis.* New York: Norton.

Erikson, E. H. 1987. *A way of looking at things: Selected papers from 1930 to 1980.* New York: Norton.

Erikson, K. 1986. On work and alienation. *American Sociological Review, 51,* 1–8.

Ernst, C., & Angst, A. 1983. *Birth order.* New York: Springer-Verlag.

Eron, L. D. 1982. Parent-child interaction, television violence, and aggression of children. *American Psychologist, 37,* 197–211.

Essex, M. J., & Nam, S. 1987. Marital status and loneliness among older women: The differential importance of close family and friends. *Journal of Marriage and the Family, 49,* 93–106.

Estrich, S. 1987. *Real rape.* Cambridge, Mass.: Harvard University Press.

Evans, O. 1986. Are men more open with men? *New York Times* (February 3), p. 20.

Evans, O. 1987. Talking with the elderly. *New York Times* (April 27), p.19.

Evans, R. B. 1972. Physical and biochemical characteristics of homosexual men. *Journal of Consulting and Clinical Psychology, 39,* 140–147.

Eveleth, P. B. 1986. Timing of menarche: Secular trend and population differences. In J. B. Lancaster & B. A. Hamburg (Eds.), *School-age pregnancy and parenthood: Biosocial dimensions.* Hawthorne, N.Y.: Aldine de Gruyter.

Everhart, R. B. 1983. *Reading, writing and resistance: Adolescence and labor in a junior high school.* Boston: Routledge and Kegan Paul.

Everitt, A., & Meites, J. 1989. Aging and anti-aging effects of hormones. *Journal of Gerontology, 44,* B139–147.

Everson, R. B. 1986. Detection of smoking-related covalent DNA adducts in human placenta. *Science, 231,* 54–57.

Eversteine, D. S., & Everstine, L. 1989. *Sexual trauma in children and adolescents: Dynamics and treatment.* New York: Brunner/Mazel.

Exter, T. 1987. How to figure your chances of getting married. *American Demographics, 9* (June), 50–52.

Exter, T. G. 1987. Where the money is. *American Demographics, 9* (March), 26–32.

Fabes, R. A., Eisenberg, N., McCormick, S. E., & Wilson, M. S. 1988. Preschoolers' attributions of the situational determinants of others' naturally occurring emotions. *Developmental Psychology, 24,* 376–385.

Fabes, R. A., Eisenberg, N., & Miller, P. A. 1990. Maternal correlates of children's vicarious emotional responsiveness. *Developmental Psychology, 26,* 639–648.

Fabes, R. A., Fultz, J., Eisenberg, N., May-Plumlee, T., & Christopher, F. S. 1989. Effects of rewards on children's prosocial motivation: A socialization study. *Developmental Psychology, 25,* 509–515.

Fabricius, W. V., Schwanenflugel, P. J., Kyllonen, P. C., Barclay, C. R., & Denton, S. M. 1989. Developing theories of the mind: Children's and adults' concepts of mental activities. *Child Development, 60,* 1278–1290.

Fabricius, W. V., & Wellman, H. M. 1983. Children's understanding of retrieval cue utilization. *Developmental Psychology, 19,* 15–21.

Fagot, B. I. 1985. Beyond the reinforcement principle: Another step toward understanding sex role development. *Developmental Psychology, 21,* 1097–1104.

Fagot, B. I., & Hagan, R. 1991. Observations of parent reactions to sex-stereotyped behaviors: Age and sex effects. *Child Development, 62,* 617–682.

Fagot, B. I., Hagan, R., Leinbach, M. D., & Kronsberg, S. 1985. Differential reactions to assertive and communicative acts of toddler boys and girls. *Child Development, 56,* 1499–1505.

Fagot, B. I., & Leinbach, M. D. 1989. The young child's gender schema: Environmental input, internal organization. *Child Development, 60,* 663–672.

Fagot, B. I., Leinbach, M. D., & Hagan, R. 1986. Gender labeling and the adoption of sex-typed behavior. *Developmental Psychology, 22,* 440–443.

Fantz, R. L. 1963. Pattern vision in newborn infants. *Science, 140,* 296–297.

Fantz, R. L. 1966. Pattern discrimination and selective attention as determinants of perceptual development from birth. In A. H. Kidd & J. F. Rivoire (Eds.), *Perceptual development in children.* New York: International Universities Press.

Fantz, R. L. 1970. Visual perception and experience in infancy: Issues and ap-

proaches. In B. Lindsly & F. Young (Eds.), *Early experience and visual information processing in perceptual and reading disorder.* Washington, D.C.: National Academy of Sciences.

Fantz, R. L., Fagan, J. F., & Miranda, S. B. 1975. Early visual selectivity. In L. B. Cohen & P. Salapatek (Eds.), *Infant perception: From sensation to cognition* (Vol. 1). New York: Academic Press.

Fantz, R. L., & Miranda, S. B. 1975. Newborn infant attention to form of contour. *Child Development, 46,* 224–228.

Farber, B. A. (Ed.). 1983. *Stress and burnout in the human service professions.* Elmsford, N.Y.: Pergamon Press.

Farberow, N. L., & Shneidman, S. E. 1961. *The cry for help.* New York: McGraw-Hill.

Farel, A. M. 1980. Effects of preferred maternal roles, maternal employment, and sociodemographic status on school adjustment and competence. *Child Development, 51,* 1179–1186.

Farley, C. J. 1991. Robert Coles looks at God through children's eyes. *USA Today* (December 4), p. 4D.

Farrell, M. P., & Rosenberg, S. D. 1981. *Men at midlife.* Boston: Auburn House.

Fassinger, P. A. 1989. Becoming the breadwinner: Single mothers' reactions to changes in their paid work lives. *Family Relations, 38,* 404–411.

Fattah, E. A., & Sacco, V. L. F. 1989. *Crime and victimization of the elderly.* New York: Springer-Verlag.

Faust, M. S. 1960. Developmental maturity as a determinant in prestige of adolescent girls. *Child Development, 31,* 173–186.

Faust, M. S. 1977. Somatic development of adolescent girls. *Monographs of the Society for Research in Child Development, 42* (No. 1).

Fay, R. E., Turner, C. F., Klassen, A. D., & Gagnon, J. H. 1989. Prevalence and patterns of same-gender sexual contact among men. *Science, 243,* 338–348.

Featherman, D. L., & Hauser, R. M. 1978a. *Opportunity and change.* New York: Academic Press.

Featherman, D. L., & Hauser, R. M. 1978b. Sexual inequalities and socioeconomic achievement in the U.S., 1962–1973. *American Sociological Review, 41,* 462–483.

Fedak, L. 1981. Child rearing the "expert" way. *Columbus* (Ohio) *Dispatch* (April 10), p. C1.

Fedak, L. 1982. Trapped in a diminishing world. *Columbus Dispatch* (February 17), p. C1.

Feifel, H. 1990. Psychology and death: Meaningful rediscovery. *American Psychologist, 45,* 537–543.

Fein, G. 1981. Pretend play in childhood: An integrative review. *Child Development, 52,* 1095–1118.

Feingold, A. 1988. Cognitive gender differences are disappearing. *American Psychologist, 43,* 95–103.

Feistritzer, E. 1987. Children at risk, and more of them. *Wall Street Journal* (July 7), p. 24.

Feldman, S. S., & Gehring, T. M. 1988. Changing perceptions of family cohesion and power across adolescence. *Child Development, 59,* 1034–1045.

Feldman, S. S., & Nash, S. C. 1979. Sex differences in responsiveness to babies among mature adults. *Developmental Psychology, 15,* 430–436.

Felson, R. B. 1989. Parents and the reflected appraisal process: A longitudinal analysis. *Journal of Personality and Social Psychology, 56:*965–971.

Felson, R. B., & Zielinski, M. A. 1989. Children's self-esteem and parental support. *Journal of Marriage and the Family, 51,* 727–735.

Felten, D. Y., & Olschowka, J. A. 1987. Noradrenergic sympathetic innervation of the spleen: II. Tyrosine hydroxylase (TH)-positive nerve terminals from synaptic-like contacts on lymphocytes in the splenic white pulp. *Journal of Neuroscience Research, 18,* 137.

Fendrich, J. M., & Lovoy, K. L. 1988. Back to the future: Adult political behavior of former student activists. *American Sociological Review, 53,* 780–784.

Fendrich, J. M., & Turner, R. W. 1989. The transition from student to adult politics. *Social Forces, 67,* 1049–1057.

Fenson, L., Kagan, J., Kearsley, R. B., & Zelazo, P. R. 1976. The developmental progression of manipulative play in the first two years. *Child Development, 47,* 232–236.

Fenwick, R., & Barresi, C. M. 1981. Health consequences of marital-status change among the elderly: A comparison of cross-sectional and longitudinal analyses. *Journal of Health and Social Behavior, 22,* 106–116.

Fenzel, L. M., & Blyth, D. A. 1986. Individual adjustment to school transitions: An exploration of the role of supportive peer relations. *Journal of Early Adolescence, 6,* 315–329.

Fernald, A. 1985. Four-month-old infants prefer to listen to motherese. *Infant Behavior and Development, 8,* 181–195.

Fernald, A. 1990. Intonation and communicative intent in mothers' speech to infants: Is the melody the message? *Child Development, 60,* 1497–1510.

Ferrar, P. J. 1984. Expand IRAs to Social Security. *Wall Street Journal* (December 7), p. 24.

Ferraro, J. J. 1989. Policing woman battering. *Social Problems, 36,* 61–74.

Ferraro, K. F. 1990. Group benefit orientation toward older adults at work? A comparison of cohort analytic methods. *Journal of Gerontology, 45,* S220–227.

Ferreira, A. J. 1969. *Prenatal environment.* Springfield, Ill.: Thomas.

Ferreiro, B. W. 1990. Presumption of joint custody: A family policy dilemma. *Family Relations, 39,* 420–426.

Ferris, T. 1991. A cosmological event. *New York Times Magazine* (December 15), pp. 44+.

Feshbach, S. 1970. Aggression. In P. H. Mussen (Ed.), *Carmichael's manual of child psychology* (3rd ed., Vol. 2). New York: Wiley.

Feuerstein, R. 1979. *The dynamic assessment of retarded performers.* Baltimore: University Park Press.

Feuerstein, R. 1980. *Instrumental enrichment.* Baltimore: University Park Press.

Fialka, J. J. 1982. Long-term federal study on aging debunks some old medical ideas. *Wall Street Journal* (March 30), p. 29.

Field, D. 1981. Can preschool children really learn to conserve? *Child Development, 52,* 326–334.

Field, D., Schaie, K. W., & Leino, E. V. 1988. Continuity in intellectual functioning: The role of self-reported health. *Psychology and Aging, 3,* 385–392.

Field, T. 1991. Quality infant day-care and grade school behavior and performance. *Child Development, 62,* 863–870.

Field, T., Healy, B., Goldstein, S., Perry, S., Bendell, D., Schanberg, S., Zimmerman, E. A., & Kuhn, K. 1988. Infants of depressed mothers show "depressed" behavior even with nondepressed adults. *Child Development, 59,* 1569–1579.

Field, T. M., Woodson, R., Greenberg, R., & Cohen, D. 1982. Discrimination and imitation of facial expressions by neonates. *Child Development, 218,* 179–181.

Fields, C. M. 1981. Minors found able to decide on taking part in research. *The Chronicle of Higher Education* (September 9), p. 7.

Fierman, J. 1990. Why women still don't hit the top. *Fortune* (July 30), pp. 40–62.

Fincham, F. D., Hokoda, A., & Sanders, R., Jr. 1989. Learned helplessness, test anxiety, and academic achievement: A longitudinal analysis. *Child Development, 60,* 138–145.

Findlay, S. 1983. Study finds family link to heart ills. *USA Today* (December 6), p. 1.

Findlay, S. 1984. Mate abuse hits sexes equally hard. *USA Today* (November 2), p. 1D.

Findlay, S. 1985a. At-home births: No extra risks. *USA Today* (March 15), p. D1.

Findlay, S. 1985b. Drugs during pregnancy: At what risk? *USA Today* (April 24), p. D1.

Findlay, S. 1987a. Evidence in: Watch your cholesterol. *USA Today* (April 24), p. A1.

Findlay, S. 1987b. "No exercise" a suspect in heart disease. *USA Today* (July 10), p. 1A.

Findlay, S. 1987c. When it comes to AIDS, many teens are ignorant. *USA Today* (May 5), p. D1.

Fine, G. A. 1981. Friends, impression management, and preadolescent behavior. In G. Stone & H. Farberman (Eds.), *Social psychology through symbolic interaction.* New York: Wiley.

Fine, G. A. 1987. *With the boys: Little League baseball and preadolescent culture.* Chicago: University of Chicago Press.

Fine, M. A., Donnelly, B. W., & Voydanoff, P. 1986. Adjustment and satisfaction of parents. *Journal of Family Issues, 7,* 391–404.

Finkelhor, D. 1979. *Sexually victimized children.* New York: Free Press.

Finley, N. J. 1989. Theories of family labor as applied to gender differences in caregiving for elderly parents. *Journal of Marriage and the Family, 51,* 79–86.

Finn, C. E., Jr. 1987. The high school dropout problem. *The Public Interest, 87* (Spring), 3–22.

Finn, S. E. 1986. Stability of personality self-ratings over 30 years: Evidence for an age/cohort interaction. *Journal of Personality and Social Psychology, 50,* 813–818.

Fischer, J. L., Sollie, D. L., Sorell, G. T., &

Green S. K. 1989. Marital status and career stage influences on social networks of young adults. *Journal of Marriage and the Family, 51,* 521–534.

Fischer, K. W., & Silvern, L. 1985. Stages and individual differences in cognitive development. *Annual Review of Psychology, 36,* 613–648.

Fischer, L. R. 1981. Transitions in the mother-daughter relationship. *Journal of Marriage and the Family, 43,* 613–622.

Fischer, L. R. 1986. *Linked lives: Adult daughters and their mothers.* New York: Harper & Row.

Fisher, C. B., Ferdinandsen, K., & Bornstein, M. H. 1981. The role of symmetry in infant form discrimination. *Child Development, 52,* 457–462.

Fishman, B. 1983. The economic behavior of step-families. *Family Relations, 32,* 359–366.

Fisichelli, V., & Karelitz, S. 1963. The cry latencies of normal infants and those with brain damage. *Journal of Pediatrics, 62,* 724–734.

Fiske, E. B. 1987. Integration lags at public schools. *New York Times* (July 26), pp. 1, 15.

Fisseni, H. J. 1985. Perceived unchangeability of life and some biographical correlates. In J. M. A. Munnichs, P. Mussen, E. Olbrich, & P. G. Coleman (Eds.), *Life-span and change in a gerontological perspective.* New York: Academic Press.

Fitts, P. M., & Posner, M. I. 1967. *Human performance.* Belmont, Calif.: Wadsworth.

Fitzpatrick, M. A. 1988. *Between husbands and wives: Communication in marriage.* Newbury Park, Calif.: Sage.

Fitzsimmons, S. J., Cheever, J., Leonard, E., & Macunovich, D. 1969. School failures: Now and tomorrow. *Developmental Psychology, 1,* 134–146.

Flanagan, C. A. 1990. Change in family work status: Effects on parent-adolescent decision making. *Child Development, 61,* 163–177.

Flanagan, J. C. 1978. A research approach to improving our quality of life. *American Psychologist, 33,* 138–147.

Flandrin, J. F. 1979. *Families in former times: Kinship, household, and sexuality.* New York: Cambridge University Press.

Flanigan, P. M. 1991. A school system that works. *Wall Street Journal* (February 12), p. A12.

Flaste, R. 1977. Survey finds that most children are happy at home but fear world. *New York Times* (March 2), p. A12.

Flaste, R. 1991. Sidelined by loneliness. *New York Times: The Good Health Magazine* (April 28), pp. 14+.

Flavell, J. H. 1963. *The developmental psychology of Jean Piaget.* Princeton, N.J.: Van Nostrand.

Flavell, J. H. 1978. Developmental stage: Explanans or explanandum? *Behavioral and Brain Sciences, 1,* 187.

Flavell, J. H. 1982. On cognitive development. *Child Development, 53,* 1–10.

Flavell, J. H. 1985. *Cognitive development.* Englewood Cliffs, N.J.: Prentice-Hall.

Flavell, J. H. 1986. Really and truly. *Psychology Today, 20* (January), pp. 38–44.

Flavell, J. H., Flavell, E. R., Green, F. L., &

Moses, L. J. 1990. Young children's understanding of fact beliefs versus value beliefs. *Child Development, 61,* 915–928.

Flavell, J. H., & Wohlwill, J. F. 1969. Formal and functional aspects of cognitive development. In D. Elkind & J. H. Flavell (Eds.), *Studies in cognitive development: Essays in honor of Jean Piaget.* New York: Oxford University Press.

Fleishman, J. A. 1984. Personality characteristics and coping patterns. *Journal of Health and Social Behavior, 25,* 229–244.

Fleming, A. S., Flett, G. L., Ruble, D. N., & Shaul, D. L. 1988. Postpartum adjustment in first-time mothers: Relations between mood, maternal attitudes, and mother-infant interactions. *Developmental Psychology, 24,* 71–81.

Fleming, A. S., Ruble, D. N., Flett, G. L., & Shaul, D. L. 1988. Postpartum adjustment in first-time mothers: Relations between mood, maternal attitudes, and mother-infant interactions. *Developmental Psychology, 24,* 71–81.

Fleming, P., Baum, A., & Singer, J. E. 1984. Toward an integrative approach to the study of stress. *Journal of Personality and Social Psychology, 46,* 939–949.

Fletcher, C. N. 1989. A comparison of incomes and expenditures of male-headed households paying child support and female-headed households receiving child support. *Family Relations, 38,* 412–417.

Fletcher, J. C., & Evans, M. I. 1983. Maternal bonding in early fetal ultrasound examinations. *New England Journal of Medicine, 308,* 392–393.

Flewelling, R. L. & Bauman, K. E. 1990. Family structure as a predictor of initial substance use and sexual intercourse in early adolescence. *Journal of Marriage and the Family, 52,* 171–181.

Floyd, N. M., & Levin, E. 1987. An expert finds that bullies and their victims are linked in a strange, unconscious courtship. *People* (April 13), pp. 143–146.

Fogel, A., & Thelen, E. 1987. Development of early expressive and communicative action: Reinterpreting the evidence from a dynamic systems perspective. *Developmental Psychology, 23,* 747–761.

Folkman, S., & Lazarus, R. S. 1980. An analysis of coping in a middle-aged community sample. *Journal of Health and Social Behavior, 21,* 219–239.

Folkman, S., & Lazarus, R. S. 1985. If it changes it must be a process: Study of emotion and coping during three stages of a college examination. *Journal of Personality and Social Psychology, 48,* 150–170.

Foner, A., & Kertzer, D. 1978. Transitions over the life course: Lessons from age-set societies. *American Journal of Sociology, 83,* 1081–1104.

Foner, N. 1984. *Ages in conflict: A cross-cultural perspective on inequality between old and young.* New York: Columbia University Press.

Foos, P. W. 1989. Adult age differences in working memory. *Psychology and Aging, 4,* 269–275.

Ford, D. A. 1983. Wife battery and criminal justice: A study of victim decision making. *Family Relations, 32,* 463–476.

Ford, M. R., & Lowery, C. R. 1986. Gender differences in moral reasoning: A comparison of the use of justice and care orientations. *Journal of Personality and Social Psychology, 50,* 777–783.

Formanek, R. 1983. How children's fears are changing. *U.S. News & World Report* (August 22), pp. 43–44.

Forsyth, D. R., & McMillan, J. H. 1981. Attributions, affects, and expectations. *Journal of Educational Psychology, 73,* 393–403.

Fortes, M. 1949. *The web of kinship among the Tallensi.* Fair Lawn, N.J.: Oxford University Press.

Forward, S. 1989. *Toxic parents: Overcoming their hurtful legacy and reclaiming your life.* New York: Bantam Books.

Forys, S., & McCune-Nicolich, L. 1984. Shared pretend: Sociodramatic play at 3 years of age. In I. Bretherton (Ed.), *Symbolic play: The development of social understanding.* New York: Academic Press.

Fowlkes, M. R. 1980. *Behind every successful man: Wives of medicine and academe.* New York: Columbia University Press.

Fox, N. A. 1989. Psychophysiological correlates of emotional reactivity during the first year of life. *Developmental Psychology, 25,* 364–372.

Fozard, J. L., Metter, E. J., & Brant, L. J. 1990. Next steps in describing aging and disease in longitudinal studies. *Journal of Gerontology, 45,* P 116–127.

Fraiberg, S. H. 1959. *The magic years.* New York: Scribner.

Fraiberg, S. H. 1977. *Every child's birthright.* New York: Basic Books.

Fraker, S. 1984. Why women aren't getting to the top. *Fortune* (April 16), pp. 40–45.

Frankel, M. S. 1978. Social, legal, and political responses to ethical issues in the use of children as experimental subjects. *Journal of Social Issues, 34,* 101–113.

Franks, D. R., & Marolla, J. 1976. Efficacious action and social approval as interacting dimensions of self-esteem: A tentative formulation through construct validation. *Sociometry, 39,* 324–341.

Franz, C. E., McClelland, D. C., & Weinberger, J. 1991. Childhood antecedents of conventional social accomplishment in midlife adults: A 36-year prospective study. *Journal of Personality and Social Psychology, 60,* 586–595.

Frazier, P. A. 1990. Victim attributions and post-rape trauma. *Journal of Personality and Social Psychology, 59,* 298–304.

Fredrickson, B. L. & Carstensen, L. L. 1990. Choosing social partners: How old age and anticipated endings make people more selective. *Psychology and Aging, 5,* 335–347.

Freinkel, N. 1985. Care of the pregnant woman with insulin-dependent diabetes mellitus. *New England Journal of Medicine, 313,* 96–101.

French, D. C. 1984. Children's knowledge of the social functions of younger, older, and same-age peers. *Child Development, 55,* 1429–1433.

French, D. C. 1988. Heterogeneity of peer-rejected boys: Aggressive and nonaggressive subtypes. *Child Development, 59,* 976–985.

French, D. C., & Waas, G. A. 1985. Behavior problems of peer-neglected and peer-rejected elementary-age children. *Child Development, 56,* 246–252.

Freud, A. 1936. *The ego and the mechanisms of defense.* New York: International Universities Press.

Freud, A. 1958. Adolescence. *Psychoanalytic Study of the Child, 16,* 225–278.

Freud, S. 1930/1961. *Civilization and its discontents.* London: Hogarth.

Freud, S. 1940. An outline of psychoanalysis. In J. Strachey (Ed. and Trans.), *The standard edition of the complete psychological works of Sigmund Freud.* London: Hogarth.

Freudenberger, H. J., and Richelson, G. 1981. *Burn-out.* New York: Bantam.

Freudenheim, M. 1983. Hospices for the dying show dramatic growth. *New York Times* (December 24), p. 8.

Freund, L. S. 1990. Maternal regulation of children's problem-solving behavior and its impact on children's performance. *Child Development, 61,* 113–126.

Freundlich, N. 1990. No, spending more on AIDS isn't unfair. *Business Week* (September 17), p. 97.

Fried, P. A., Watkinson, B., & Dillon, R. 1987. Neonatal neurological status in a low-risk population after exposure to cigarettes, marijuana, and alcohol. *Developmental and Behavioral Pediatrics, 8,* 318–326.

Friedman, H. S. & Booth-Kewley, S. 1988. Validity of the Type A construct: A reprise. *Psychological Bulletin, 104,* 381–383.

Friedman, M., & Rosenman, R. 1974. *Type A behavior and your heart.* New York: Knopf.

Friedman, R. C. 1988. *Male homosexuality: A contemporary psychoanalytic perspective.* New Haven, Conn.: Yale University Press.

Friedrich, L. K., & Stein, A. H. 1973. Aggressive and prosocial television programs and the natural behavior of preschool children. *Monographs of the Society for Research in Child Development, 38* (No. 151).

Friedrich-Cofer, L., & Huston, A. C. 1986. Television violence and aggression: The debate continues. *Psychological Bulletin, 100,* 364–371.

Friend, R. M., & Neale, J. M. 1972. Children's perceptions of success and failure. *Developmental Psychology, 7,* 124–128.

Friend, T. 1990. Doctor's age key in decision on Caesareans. *USA Today* (August 29), p. D1.

Friend, T. 1990. Infant mortality could soar. *USA Today* (March 1), p. 1A.

Friend, T. 1991. Sperm may carry cocaine to egg. *USA Today* (October 9), p. 1.

Frisch, R. E. 1978. Menarche and fatness. *Science, 200* (June 30), 1509–1513.

Frodi, A., & Lamb, M. 1978. Sex differences in responsiveness to infants: A developmental study of psychophysiological and behavioral responses. *Child Development, 49,* 1182–1188.

Frodi, A., Lamb, M., Leavitt, L. A., Donovan, W. L., Neff, C., & Sherry, D. 1978. Fathers' and mothers' responses to the faces and cries of normal and premature infants. *Developmental Psychology, 14,* 490–498.

Frodi, A., & Senchak, M. 1990. Verbal and behavioral responsiveness to the cries of atypical infants. *Child Development, 61,* 76–84.

Froming, W. J., Allen, L., & Jensen, R. 1985. Altruism, role-taking, and self-awareness. *Child Development, 56,* 1223–1228.

Fromm, E. 1947. *Man for himself.* New York: Holt, Rinehart and Winston.

Fry, D. P. 1988. Intercommunity differences in aggression among Zapotec children. *Child Development, 59,* 1008–1019.

Frye, D., Braisby, N., Lowe, J., Maroudes, C., & Nicholls, J. 1989. Young children's understanding of counting and cardinality. *Child Development, 60,* 1158–1171.

Fuchs, D., & Thelen, M. H. 1988. Children's expected interpersonal consequences of communicating their affective state and reported likelihood of expression. *Child Development, 59,* 1314–1322.

Fuchs, V. R. 1983. *How we live: An economic perspective on Americans from birth to death.* Cambridge, Mass.: Harvard University Press.

Fuchs, V. R. 1986. Sex differences in economic well-being. *Science, 232,* 459–464.

Fuchs, V. R. 1990. Economics applies to child care too. *Wall Street Journal* (April 2), p. A12.

Funder, D. C., & Block, J. 1989. The role of ego-control, ego-resiliency, and IQ in delay of gratification in adolescence. *Journal of Personality and Social Psychology, 57,* 1041–1050.

Funder, D. C., & Colvin, C. R. 1991. Explorations in behavioral consistency: Properties of persons, situations, and behaviors. *Journal of Personality and Social Psychology, 60,* 773–794.

Fuqua, R. W., Bartsch, T. W., & Phye, G. D. 1975. An investigation of the relationship between cognitive tempo and creativity in preschoolage children. *Child Development, 46,* 779–782.

Furman, W. 1987. Acquaintanceship in middle childhood. *Developmental Psychology, 23,* 563–570.

Furman, W., & Bierman, K. L. 1983. Developmental changes in young children's conceptions of friendship. *Child Development, 54,* 549–556.

Furman, W., & Bierman, K. L. 1984. Children's conceptions of friendship: A multimethod study of developmental changes. *Developmental Psychology, 20,* 925–931.

Furman, W., & Buhrmester, D. 1985. Children's perceptions of the personal relationships in their social networks. *Developmental Psychology, 21,* 1016–1024.

Furstenberg, F., Brooks-Gunn, J., & Morgan, S. P. 1986. *Adolescent mothers in later life.* New York: Commonwealth Fund.

Furstenberg, F. F., Jr. 1991. As the pendulum swings: Teenage childbearing and social concern. *Family Relations, 40,* 127–138.

Furstenberg, F. F., Jr., Brooks-Gunn, J., & Chase-Lansdale, L. 1989. Teenaged pregnancy and childbearing. *American Psychologist, 44,* 313–320.

Furstenberg, F. F., Jr., Brooks-Gunn, J., & Morgan, S. P. 1987. *Adolescent mothers in later life.* New York: Cambridge University Press.

Furstenberg, F. F., Jr., & Cherlin, A. J. 1991.

Divided families. Cambridge, Mass.: Harvard University Press.

Furstenberg, F. F., Jr., & Spanier, G. B. 1984. *Recycling the family: Remarriage after divorce.* Beverly Hills: Sage.

Futterman, A., Gallagher, D., Thompson, L. W., Lovett, S., & Gilewski, M. 1990. Retrospective assessment of marital adjustment and depression during the first 2 years of spousal bereavement. *Psychology and Aging, 5,* 277–283.

Gabennesch, H. 1990. The perception of social conventionality by children and adults. *Child Development, 61,* 2047–2059.

Gaddis, A., & Brooks-Gunn, J. 1985. The male experience of pubertal change. *Journal of Youth and Adolescence, 14,* 61–69.

Gaertner, S. L., Mann, J. A., Dovidio, J. F., Murrell, A. J., & Pomare, M. 1990. How does cooperation reduce intergroup bias? *Journal of Personality and Social Psychology, 59,* 692–704.

Gaertner, S. L., Mann, J. A., Murrell, A. J., & Dovidio, J. F. 1989. Reducing intergroup bias: The benefits of recategorization. *Journal of Personality and Social Psychology, 57,* 239–249.

Galambos, N. L., Almeida, D. M., & Peterson, A. C. 1990. Masculinity, femininity, and sex role attitudes in early adolescence: Exploring gender intensification. *Child Development, 61,* 1905–1914.

Galbraith, R. C. 1982. Sibling spacing and intellectual development: A closer look at the confluence models. *Developmental Psychology, 18,* 151–173.

Galda, L., & Pellegrini, A. D. (Eds.). 1985. *Play, language and stories: The development of children's literate behavior.* Norwood, N.J.: Ablex.

Gallup, G., Jr. 1985. *Religion in America.* Princeton, N.J.: The Gallup Report.

Galotti, K. M. 1989. Approaches to studying formal and everyday reasoning. *Psychological Bulletin, 105,* 331–351.

Gandour, M. J. 1989. Activity level as a dimension of temperament in toddlers: Its relevance for the organismic specificity hypothesis. *Child Development, 60,* 1092–1098.

Ganong, L. H., & Coleman, M. 1984. The effects of remarriage on children: A review of the empirical literature. *Family Relations, 33,* 389–406.

Ganong, L. H., Coleman, M., & Mapes, D. 1990. A meta-analytic review of family structure stereotypes. *Journal of Marriage and the Family, 52,* 287–297.

Gappa, J. M., O'Barr, J. F., & St. John-Parsons, D. 1980. The dual-career couple and academe: Can both prosper? *Anthropology Newsletter, 21,* 16+.

Garbarino, J., & Crouter, A. 1978. Defining the community context for parent-child relations: The correlates of child maltreatment. *Child Development, 49,* 604–616.

Garbarino, J., & Sherman, D. 1980. High-risk neighborhoods and high-risk families: The human ecology of child maltreatment. *Child Development, 51,* 188–198.

Garber, J. 1984. Classification of childhood psychopathology: A developmental perspective. *Child Development, 55,* 30–48.

Garber, J., & Seligman, M. E. P. 1980. *Human helplessness: Theory and applications.* New York: Academic Press.

Garcia, J. 1972. IQ: The conspiracy. *Psychology Today 6* (September), pp. 40–43ff.

Gardner, H. 1979. Getting acquainted with Jean Piaget. *New York Times* (January 3), pp. C1, C9.

Gardner, H. 1983. *Frames of mind: The theory of multiple intelligences.* New York: Basic Books.

Gardner, H. 1985. *The mind's new science: A history of the cognitive revolution.* New York: Basic Books.

Gardner, L. 1972. Deprivation dwarfism. *Scientific American, 227* (July), pp. 76–82.

Gardner, M. 1987. The child-care quandary—attitudes are shifting. *Christian Science Monitor* (May 14), p. 27.

Garfinkel, B. D., Froese, A., & Hood, J. 1982. Suicide attempts in children and adolescents. *American Journal of Psychiatry, 139,* 1257–1261.

Gargiulo, J., Attie, I., Brooks-Gunn, J., & Warren, M. P. 1987. Dating in middle schools girls: Effects of social context, maturation, and grade. *Developmental Psychology, 23,* 730–737.

Garibaldi, R. A., Brodine, S., & Matsumiya, S. 1981. Infections among patients in nursing homes. *New England Journal of Medicine, 305,* 731–735.

Garland, S. 1991. Before you settle on a retirement community. *Business Week* (May 20), pp. 150–151.

Garmezy, N. 1983. Stressors of childhood. In N. Garmezy & M. Rutter (Eds.), *Stress, coping and development in children.* New York: McGraw-Hill.

Garmezy, N. 1985. Stress-resistant children: The search for protective factors. In J. E. Stevenson (Ed.), *Recent research in developmental psychopathology. Journal of Child Psychology and Psychiatry. Book Supplement 4.* Elmsford, N.Y.: Pergamon Press.

Garner, D. M., & Garfinkel, P. E. (Eds.). 1985. *Handbook of psychotherapy for anorexia nervosa and bulimia.* New York: Guilford Press.

Garvey, C., & Hogan, R. 1973. Social speech and social interaction: Egocentrism revisited. *Child Development, 44,* 562–568.

Gaudia, G. 1972. Race, social class, and age of achievement of conservation on Piaget's tasks. *Developmental Psychology, 6,* 158–165.

Gavin, L. A., & Furman, W. 1989. Age differences in adolescents' perceptions of their peer groups. *Developmental Psychology, 25,* 827–834.

Gay, J., & Tweney, R. D. 1975. Comprehension and production of standard and black English by lower-class black children. *Developmental Psychology, 12,* 262–268.

Geber, M. 1958. The psycho-motor development of African children in the first year, and the influence of maternal behavior. *Journal of Social Psychology, 47,* 185–195.

Geber, M., & Dean, R. F. 1957a. Gesell tests on African children. *Pediatrics, 20,* 1055–1065.

Geber, M., & Dean, R. E. 1957b. The state of development of newborn African children. *Lancet, 1,* 1216–1219.

Gecas, V., & Seff, M. A. 1990. Families and adolescents: A review of the 1980s. *Journal of Marriage and the Family, 52,* 941–958.

Gecas, V., & Schwalbe, M. L. 1986. Parental behavior and adolescent self-esteem. *Journal of Marriage and the Family, 48,* 37–46.

Geen, R. G., & Thomas S. L. 1986. The immediate effects of media violence on behavior. *Journal of Social Issues, 42,* 7–28.

Geiger, G., & Lettvin, J. Y. 1987. Peripheral vision in persons with dyslexia. *New England Journal of Medicine, 316,* 1238–1243.

Gelfand, D. M., Hartmann, D. P., Cromer, C. C., Smith, C. L., & Page, B. C. 1975. The effects of instructional prompts and praise on children's donation rates. *Child Development, 46,* 980–983.

Gelles, R. J. 1979. *Family violence.* Beverly Hills: Sage.

Gelles, R. J. 1980. Violence in the family: A review of research in the seventies. *Journal of Marriage and the Family, 42,* 873–885.

Gelles, R. J. 1985. Family violence. *Annual Review of Sociology, 11,* 347–367.

Gelles, R. J., & Conte, J. R. 1990. Domestic violence and sexual abuse of children: A review of research in the eighties. *Journal of Marriage and the Family, 52,* 1045–1058.

Gelles, R. J., & Cornell, C. P. 1985. *Intimate violence in families.* Beverly Hills: Sage.

Gelles, R. J., & Straus, M. A. 1979. Violence in the American family. *Journal of Social Issues, 35,* 15–39.

Gelles, R. J. & Straus, M. A. 1988. *Intimate violence.* New York: Simon & Schuster.

Gelman, D. 1983. A great emptiness. *Newsweek* (November 7), pp. 120–126.

Gelman, D. 1990. Fixing the 'between.' *Newsweek* (July 2): 42–43.

Gelman, D. 1992. Born or bred? *Newsweek* (February 24), pp. 46–53.

Gelman, R., & Baillargeon, R. 1983. A review of some Piagetian concepts. In J. H. Flavell & E. M. Markman (Eds.), *Handbook of child psychology.* Vol. 3, *Cognitive development* (4th Ed.). New York: Wiley.

Gelman, R., & Gallistel, C. R. 1978. *The child's understanding of number.* Cambridge, Mass.: Harvard University Press.

Gelman, R., & Meck, E. 1986. The notion of principle: The case of counting. In J. Hiebert (Ed.), *Conceptual and procedural knowledge: The case of mathematics.* Hillsdale, N.J.: Erlbaum.

Gelman, R., Meck, E., & Merkin, S. 1986. Young children's numerical competence. *Cognitive Development, 1,* 1–29.

Gelman, S. A., & Ebeling, K. S. 1989. Children's use of nonegocentric standards in judgments of functional size. *Child Development, 60,* 920–932.

Gelman, S. A., & Kremer, K. E. 1991. Understanding natural cause: Children's explanations of how objects and their properties originate. *Child Development, 62,* 396–414.

Gerall, A. A. 1973. Influence of perinatal androgen on reproductive capacity. In J. Zubin & J. Money (Eds.), *Contemporary sexual behavior: Critical issues in the 1970s.* Baltimore: Johns Hopkins University Press.

Gerard, H. B. 1983. School desegregation. *American Psychologist, 38,* 869–877.

Gerard, L., Zacks, R. T., Hasher, L., & Radvansky, G. A. 1991. Age deficits in retrieval: The fan effect. *Journal of Gerontology, 46,* P131–136.

Gesell, A. 1928. *Infancy and human growth.* New York: Macmillan.

Gesell, A., & Ames, L. B. 1947. The development of handedness. *Journal of Genetic Psychology, 70,* 155–175.

Gerwitz, J. L. 1972. *Attachment and dependency.* Washington, D.C.: Winston.

Getzels, J. W., & Csikszentmihalyi, M. 1976. *The creative vision.* New York: Wiley.

Gibbons, A. 1991. The brain as "sexual organ." *Science, 253,* 957–959.

Gibbons, A. 1991. Deja vu all over again: Chimp-language wars. *Science, 251,* 1561–1562.

Gibbs, J. C., & Schnell, S. V. 1985. Moral development "versus" socialization. *American Psychologist, 40,* 1071–1080.

Gibson, E. J. 1969. *Principles of perceptual learning and development.* New York: Appleton-Century-Crofts.

Gibson, E. J. 1982. The concept of affordances in development: The renascence of functionalism. In W. A. Collins (Ed.), *The concept of development: Minnesota symposia on child psychology.* Vol. 15. Hillsdale, N.J.: Erlbaum.

Gibson, E. J., & Walk, R. D. 1960. The "visual cliff." *Scientific American, 202* (April), pp. 64–71.

Gibson, J. J. 1979. *The ecological approach to perception.* Boston: Houghton-Mifflin.

Giese, W. 1987. 4 of 5 of us say we enjoy going to work. *USA Today* (June 15), pp. 1, 2.

Gilewski, M. J., Farberow, N. L., Gallagher, D. E., & Thompson, L. W. 1991. Interaction of depression and bereavement on mental health in the elderly. *Psychology and Aging, 6,* 67–75.

Gilder, G. 1987. The collapse of the American family. *The Public Interest, 89,* 20–25.

Gilleard, C. J., & Gurkan, A. A. 1987. Socioeconomic development and the status of elderly men in Turkey: A test of modernization theory. *Journal of Gerontology, 42,* 353–357.

Gilligan, C. 1982. Why should a woman be more like a man? *Psychology Today, 16* (June), pp. 68–77.

Gilligan, C. 1982a. *In a different voice: Psychological theory and women's development.* Cambridge, Mass.: Harvard University Press.

Gilligan, C., Ward, J. V., & Taylor, J. M. Eds. 1989. *Mapping the moral domain.* Cambridge, Mass.: Harvard University Press.

Gilligan, C. F. 1963. *Responses to temptation: An analysis of motives.* Unpublished doctoral dissertation, Harvard University.

Gilman, A. D. 1984. Grandma junkies. *Health* (January), pp. 52–55.

Gilmore, D. D. 1990. *Manhood in the making: Cultural concepts of masculinity.* New Haven, Conn.: Yale University Press.

Gittelman, R., Mannuzza, S., Shenker, R., & Bonagura, N. 1985. Hyperactive boys almost grown up: I. Psychiatric status. *Archives of General Psychiatry, 42,* 937–947.

Giulian, G. G., Gilbert, E. F., & Moss, R. L. 1987. Elevated fetal hemoglobin levels in sudden infant death syndrome. *New England Journal of Medicine, 316,* 1122–1126.

Gjerde, P. F. 1988. Parental concordance on child rearings and the interactive emphases of parents: Sex-differentiated relationships during the preschool years. *Developmental Psychology, 24,* 700–706.

Glaser, B. G., & Strauss, A. L. 1965. Temporal aspects of dying as a nonscheduled status passage. *American Journal of Sociology, 71,* 48–59.

Glass, D.C., Neulinger, J., & Brim, O. G., Jr. 1974. Birth order, verbal intelligence, and educational aspiration. *Child Development, 45,* 807–811.

Glass, J. 1990. The impact of occupational segregation on working conditions. *Social Forces, 68,* 779–796.

Glenn, N. D. 1975. Psychological well-being in the post-parental stage: Some evidence from national surveys. *Journal of Marriage and the Family, 37,* 105–110.

Glenn, N. D. 1989. Duration of marriage, family composition, and marital happiness. *National Journal of Sociology, 3:3–24.*

Glenn, N. D. 1990. Quantitative research on marital quality in the 1980s: A critical review. *Journal of Marriage and the Family, 52,* 818–831.

Glenn, N. D., & McLanahan, S. 1981. The effects of offspring on the psychological well-being of older adults. *Journal of Marriage and the Family, 43,* 409–421.

Glenn, N. D., & Weaver, C. N. 1981. The contribution of marital happiness to global happiness. *Journal of Marriage and the Family, 43,* 161–168.

Glenn, N. D., & Weaver, C. N. 1982. Enjoyment of work by full-time workers in the U.S., 1955 and 1980. *Public Opinion Quarterly, 46,* 459–470.

Glick, P. C. 1984. How American families are changing. *American Demographics, 6* (January), 21–25.

Glick, P. C. 1988. Fifty years of family demography: A record of social change. *Journal of Marriage and the Family, 50,* 861–873.

Glick, P. C. 1989. The family life cycle and social change. *Family Relations, 38,* 123–129.

Glick, P. C., & Lin, S. L. 1986. Recent changes in divorce and remarriage. *Journal of Marriage and the Family, 48,* 737–747.

Gloger-Tippelt, G. 1983. A process model of the pregnancy course. *Human Development, 26,* 134–148.

Gluckman, M. 1955. *Custom and conflict in Africa.* Oxford: Blackwell.

Glueck, S., & Glueck, E. 1957. Working mothers and delinquency. *Mental Hygiene, 41,* 327–352.

Goetting, A. 1986. The developmental tasks of siblingship over the life cycle. *Journal of Marriage and the Family, 48,* 703–714.

Goetz, T. E., & Dweck, C. S. 1980. Learned helplessness in social situations. *Journal of Personality and Social Psychology, 39,* 246–255.

Goffman, E. 1963. *Stigma.* Englewood Cliffs, N.J.: Prentice-Hall.

Gohmann, S. F. 1990. Retirement differences among the respondents to the retirement history survey. *Journal of Gerontology, 45,* S120–127.

Golant, S. M. 1984. *A place to grow old: The meaning of environment in old age.* New York: Columbia University Press.

Gold, D., & Andres, D. 1978a. Comparisons of adolescent children with employed and nonemployed mothers. *Merrill-Palmer Quarterly, 24,* 243–254.

Gold, D., & Andres, D. 1978b. Developmental comparisons between ten-year-old children with employed and nonemployed mothers. *Child Development, 49,* 75–84.

Gold, D. T. 1989. Generational solidarity: Conceptual antecedents and consequences. *American Behavioral Scientist, 33,* 19–32.

Gold, D. T., Woodbury, M. A., & George L. K. 1990. Relationship classification using grade of membership analysis: A typology of sibling relationships in later life. *Journal of Gerontology, 45,* S43–S51.

Gold, M., & Yanof, D. 1985. Mothers, daughters, and girlfriends. *Journal of Personality and Social Psychology, 49,* 654–659.

Gold, P. W., Goodwin, F. K., & Chrousos, G. P. 1988. Clinical and biochemical manifestations of depression. *New England Journal of Medicine, 319,* 348–353.

Goldberg, E. L., Comstock, G. W., & Harlow, S. D. 1988. Emotional problems and widowhood. *Journal of Gerontology, 43,* S206–208.

Goldberg, L. R. 1990. An alternative "description of personality": The big-five factor structure. *Journal of Personality and Social Psychology, 59,* 1216–1229.

Goldberg, W. A., & Easterbrooks, M. A. 1984. Role of marital quality in toddler development. *Developmental Psychology, 20,* 504–514.

Goldfarb, W. 1945. Psychological privation in infancy and subsequent adjustment. *American Journal of Orthopsychiatry, 15,* 247–255.

Golfarb, W. 1947. Variations in adolescent adjustment of institutionally reared children. *American Journal of Orthopsychiatry, 17,* 449–457.

Goldfarb, W. 1949. Rorschach test differences between family-reared, institution-reared, and schizophrenic children. *American Journal of Orthopsychiatry, 19,* 624–633.

Goldfield, E. C. 1989. Transition from rocking and crawling: Postural constraints on infant movement. *Developmental Psychology, 25,* 913–919.

Goldin, C. 1990. *Understanding the gender gap: An economic history of American women.* New York: Oxford University Press.

Goldin-Meadow, S., & Feldman, H. 1977. The development of languagelike communication without a language model. *Science, 197,* 401–403.

Goldin-Meadow, S., & Mylander, C. 1983. Gestural communication in deaf children: Noneffect of parental input on language development. *Science, 221,* 372–373.

Goldin-Meadow, S., & Mylander, C. 1984. Gestural communication in deaf children. *Monographs of the Society for Research in Child Development 49* (No. 207).

Goldscheider, F. K. & Goldscheider, C. 1989. Family structure and conflict: Nest-leaving expectations of young adults and their parents. *Journal of Marriage and the Family, 51,* 87–97.

Goldsmith, H. H. & Campos, J. J. 1990. The structure of temperamental fear and pleasure in infants: A psychometric perspective. *Child Development, 61,* 1944–1964.

Goldstein, J., Freud, A., & Solnit, A. J. 1973. *Beyond the best interests of the child.* New York: Macmillan.

Goldstein, K. M., Caputo, D. V., & Taub, H. B. 1976. The effects of prenatal and perinatal complications on development at one year of age. *Child Development, 47,* 613–621.

Goleman, D. 1981. Forgetfulness of things past. *Psychology Today, 15* (October), pp. 17–20.

Goleman, D. 1985. Spacing of siblings strongly linked to success in life. *New York Times* (May 28), pp. 17, 18.

Goleman, D. 1986a. Child development theory stresses small moments. *New York Times* (October 21), pp. 19, 21.

Goleman, D. 1986b. Feeling of control viewed as central in mental health. *New York Times* (October 7), pp. 19, 23.

Goleman, D. 1986c. Major personality study finds that traits are mostly inherited. *New York Times* (December 2), pp. 17, 18.

Goleman, D. 1986d. Parental influence: New subtleties found. *New York Times* (July 29), pp. 17, 18.

Goleman, D. 1987a. The bully: New research depicts a paranoid, lifelong loser. *New York Times* (April 7), pp. 19, 23.

Goleman, D. 1987b. For each sibling, there appears to be a different family. *New York Times* (July 28), pp. 13, 15.

Goleman, D. 1987c. Long-married couples do look alike, study finds. *New York Times* (August 11), pp. 19, 23.

Goleman, D. 1987d. Motivations of surrogate mothers. *New York Times* (January 20), pp. 15, 16.

Goleman, D. 1987e. New research illuminates self-defeating behavior. *New York Times* (September 1), pp. 13, 17.

Goleman, D. 1988. An emerging theory on blacks' I.Q. scores. *New York Times Education Section* (April 10), pp. 22–24EDUC.

Goleman, D. 1989a. Brain's design emerges as a key to emotions. *New York Times* (August 15), pp. 15, 19.

Goleman, D. 1989b. For many, turmoil of aging erupts in the 50's, studies find. *New York Times* (February 7), pp. 17, 21.

Goleman, D. 1989c. New studies find many myths about mourning. *New York Times* (August 8), p. 17.

Goleman, D. 1989d. When the rapist is not a stranger. *New York Times* (August 29), pp. 13, 21.

Goleman, D. 1990a. Brain structure differences linked to schizophrenia in study of twins. *New York Times* (March 22), p. B7.

Goleman, D. 1990b. Child's skills at play crucial to success, new studies find. *New York Times* (October 2), pp. B1, B6.

Goleman, D. 1990c. Men at 65: New findings on well-being. *New York Times* (January 16), pp. 19, 23.

Goleman, D. 1990d. In midlife, not just crisis but care and comfort, too. *New York Times* (February 6), pp. B1, B8.

Goleman, D. 1990e. As a therapist, Freud fell short, scholars find. *New York Times* (March 6), pp. B5, B9.

Goleman, D. 1990f. Why girls are prone to depression. *New York Times* (May 10) p. B7.

Goleman, D. 1991. Theory links early puberty to childhood stress. *New York Times* (July 30), pp. B5, B6.

Goode, E. E. 1990. How infants see the world. *U.S. News & World Report* (August 20), pp. 51–52.

Goode, E. E. 1991. Where emotions come from. *U.S. News & World Report* (June 24), pp. 54–62.

Goode, W. J. 1956. *Women in divorce.* New York: Free Press.

Goode, W. J. 1959. The theoretical impor-

Goodhart, D. E. 1985. Some psychological effects associated with positive and negative thinking about stressful event outcomes: Was Pollyanna right? *Journal of Personality and Social Psychology, 48,* 216–232.

Goodman, M. E. 1952. *Race awareness in young children.* Reading, Mass.: Addison-Wesley.

Goodnow, J. J. 1988. Parents' ideas, actions, and feelings: Models and methods from developmental and social psychology. *Child Development, 59,* pp. 286–320.

Goodnow, J. J. 1990. Using sociology to extend psychological accounts of cognitive development. *Human Development, 33,* pp. 81–107.

Goodstein, R. K., & Page, A.W. 1981. Battered wife syndrome: Overview of dynamics and treatment. *American Journal of Psychiatry, 138,* 1036–1044.

Goodwin, R. S., & Michel, G. F. 1981. Head orientation position during birth and in infant neonatal period, and hand preference at nineteen weeks. *Child Development, 52,* 819–826.

Gopnik, A., & Graf, P. 1988. Knowing how you know: Young children's ability to identify and remember the sources of their beliefs. *Child Development, 59,* 1366–1371.

Gordon, M. T., & Riger, S. 1989. *The female fear.* New York: Free Press.

Gorman, C. 1991. Beware of the pillow. *Time* (July 8), p. 48.

Gorman, C. 1991. Incest comes out of the dark. *Time* (October 7), pp. 46–47.

Gottfried, A. W., & Rose, S. A. 1980. Tactile recognition memory in infants. *Child Development, 51,* 69–74.

Gottfried, A. W., Wallace-Lande, P., Sherman-Brown, S., King, J., & Coen, C. 1981. Physical and social environment of newborn infants in special care units. *Science, 214* (November 6), 673–675.

Gottlieb, G. 1991. Experiential canalization of behavioral development: Theory. *Developmental Psychology, 27,* 4–13.

Gottman, J. M. 1983. How children become

friends. *Monographs of the Society for Research in Child Development, 48* (201).

Gottman, J. M., & Katz, L.F. 1989. Effects of marital discord on young children's peer interaction and health. *Developmental Psychology, 25,* 373–381.

Gottman, J. M., & Mettetal, G. 1987. Speculations about social and affective development: Friendship and acquaintanceship through adolescence. In J.M. Gottman & J. G. Parker (Eds.), *Conversations of friends: Speculations on affective development.* New York: Cambridge University Press.

Gottschalk, E. C., Jr. 1983. The aging made gains in the 1970s, outpacing rest of the population. *Wall Street Journal* (February 17), pp. 1, 16.

Gough, E. K. 1960. Is the family universal? The Nayar case. In N. W. Bell & E. F.Vogel (Eds.), *A modern introduction to the family.* New York: Free Press.

Gould, C. G. 1983. Out of the mouths of beasts. *Science 83, 4* (April), pp. 69–72.

Gould, J. B., Davey, B., & Stafford, R. S. 1989. Socioeconomic differences in rates of Caesarean section. *New England Journal of Medicine, 321,* 233–239.

Gould, J. L., & Marler, P. 1987. Learning by instinct. *Scientific American, 256* (January), pp. 74–85.

Gove, W. R., Oretega, S. T., & Style, C. B. 1989. The maturational and role perspectives on aging and self through the adult years: An empirical evaluation. *American Journal of Sociology, 94,* 1117–1145.

Graham, E. 1990. Lost in the shuffle. *Wall Street Journal* (November 14), pp. A1, A9.

Graney, M. J. 1975. Happiness and social participation in aging. *Journal of Gerontology, 30,* 701–706.

Gratch, G., and Schatz, J. A. 1988. Evaluating Piaget's infancy books as works-in-progress. *Human Development, 31,* 82–91.

Gray, W. M., & Hudson, L. M. 1984. Formal operations and the imaginary audience. *Developmental Psychology, 20,* 619–627.

Graziano, W. G., Moore, J. S., & Collins, J. E., II. 1988. Social cognition as segmentation of the stream of behavior. *Developmental Psychology, 24,* 568–573.

Grecas, V., & Seff, M. A. 1990. Families and adolescents: A review of the 1980s. *Journal of Marriage and the Family, 52,* 941–958.

Greco, C., & Daehler, M. W. 1985. Immediate and long-term retention of basic-level categories in 24-month-olds. *Infant Behavior and Development, 8,* 459–474.

Green, J. A., Jones, L. E., & Gustafson, G. E. 1987. Perception of cries by parents and nonparents: Relation to cry acoustics. *Developmental Psychology, 23,* 370–382.

Green, R. 1974. *Sexual identity: Conflict in children and adults.* New York: Basic Books.

Green, R. 1987. *The "sissy boy syndrome" and the development of homosexuality.* New Haven: Yale University Press.

Greenberg, D. F. 1988. *The construction of homosexuality.* Chicago: University of Chicago Press.

Greenberg, D. J., Hillman, D., & Grice, D. 1973. Infant and stranger variables related to stranger anxiety in the first year of life. *Developmental Psychology, 9,* 207–212.

Greenberg, J. 1981*a*. Unstable emotions of children tied to poor diet. *New York Times* (August 18), pp. 15, 17

Greenberg, J. 1981*b*. Study finds widowers die more quickly than widows. *New York Times* (July 3), pp. 1, 7.

Greenberg, M. 1986. *The birth of a father.* New York: Avon.

Greenberger, E., & Goldberg, W. A. 1989. Work, parenting, and the socialization of children. *Developmental Psychology, 25,* 22–35.

Greenberger, E., & Steinberg, L. 1983. Sex differences in early labor force experience: Harbinger of things to come. *Social Forces, 62,* 467–486.

Greenberger, E., & Steinberg, L. 1986. *When teenagers work: The psychological and social costs of adolescent employment.* New York: Basic Books.

Greenblatt, M. 1978. The grieving spouse. *American Journal of Psychiatry, 135,* 43–47.

Greene, D., & Lepper, M. R. 1974. How to turn play into work. *Psychology Today, 8* (September), pp. 49–54.

Greene, J. G. 1984. *The social and psychological origins of the climacteric syndrome.* Brookfield, Vt.: Gower.

Greenfield, P. M. 1966. On culture and conservation. In J. Bruner, R. R. Olver, & P. M. Greenfield (Eds.), *Studies in cognitive growth.* New York: Wiley.

Greenfield, P. M., & Bruner, J. S. 1971. Work with the Wolof. *Psychology Today, 2* (July), pp. 40–43ff.

Greenfield, P. M., & Smith, J. H. 1976. *The structure of communication in early language development.* New York: Academic Press.

Greenhouse, L. 1990. Justices find a right to die, but the majority see need for clear proof of intent. *New York Times* (June 26), pp. A1, A12.

Greenhouse, S. 1986. Passing the buck from one generation to the next. *New York Times* (August 17), p. 5E.

Greeno, J., Riley, M., & Gelman, R. 1984. Conceptual competence and children's counting. *Cognitive Psychology, 16,* 94–143.

Greeno, J. G. 1989. A perspective on thinking. *American Psychologist, 44,* 134–141.

Greenough, W. T., Black, J. E., & Wallace, C. S. 1987. Experience and brain development. *Child Development, 58,* 539–559.

Greenspan, S., & Greenspan, N. T. 1985. *First feelings.* New York: Viking Press.

Greer, W. R. 1986. The changing women's marriage market. *New York Times* (February 22), p. 16.

Greif, E. B., & Ulman, K. J. 1982. The psychological impact of menarche on early adolescent females: A review of the literature. *Child Development, 53,* 1413–1430.

Greif, G. L. 1985. *Single fathers.* Lexington, Mass.: Lexington Books.

Gretarsson, S. J., & Gelfand, D. M. 1988. Mother's attributions regarding their children's social behavior and personality characteristics. *Developmental Psychology, 24,* 264–269.

Greyson, B., & Flynn, C. P. (Eds.). 1984. *The*

near-death experience. Springfield, Ill.: Thomas.

Greyson, B., & Stevenson, I. 1980. The phenomenology of near-death experiences. *American Journal of Psychiatry, 137,* 1193–1196.

Gronlund, N. E. 1959. *Sociometry in the classroom.* New York: Harper & Row.

Gross, A. 1977. Marriage counseling for unwed couples. *New York Times Magazine* (April 24), pp. 52ff.

Gross, D. 1990. Roses are red, violets blue . . . *New York Times* (February 14), p. A19.

Gross, J. 1986. Rise in cocaine abuse is posing threat to infants. *New York Times* (February 3), p. 13.

Gross, J. 1991. More young single men clinging to apron strings. *New York Times* (June 16), pp. 1, 10.

Grossman, F. K., Eichler, L. S., & Winickoff, S. S. 1980. *Pregnancy, birth and parenthood.* San Francisco: Jossey-Bass.

Grossman, F. K., Pollack, W. S., & Golding, E. 1988. Fathers and children: Predicting the quality and quantity of fathering. *Developmental Psychology, 24,* 82–91.

Grossman, K., Thane, K., & Grossmann, K. E. 1981. Maternal tactual contact of the newborn after various postpartum conditions of mother-infant contact. *Developmental Psychology, 17,* 158–169.

Grotevant, H. D. 1978. Sibling constellations and sex typing of interests in adolescence. *Child Development, 49,* 540–542.

Gruenberg, B. 1980. The happy worker: An analysis of educational and occupational differences in determinants of job satisfaction. *American Journal of Sociology, 86,* 247–271.

Grusec, J. E. 1991. Socializing concern for others in the home. *Developmental Psychology, 27,* 338–342.

Grusec, J. E., & Kuczynski, L. 1981. Direction of effect in socialization: A comparison of the parent's versus the child's behavior as determinants of disciplinary techniques. *Developmental Psychology, 16,* 1–9.

Grusec, J. E., Kuczysnki, L., Rushton, J. P., & Simutis, Z. M. 1979. Learning resistance to temptation through observation. *Developmental Psychology, 15,* 233–240.

Grusec, J. E., & Skubiski, S. L. 1970. Model nurturance, demand characteristics of the modeling experiment, and altruism. *Journal of Personality and Social Psychology, 14,* 352–359.

Grych, J. H., & Fincham, F. D. 1990. Marital conflict and children's adjustment: A cognitive-contextual framework. *Psychological Bulletin, 108,* 267–290.

Gubrium, J. F. 1974. Marital desolation and the evaluation of everyday life in old age. *Journal of Marriage and the Family, 36,* 107–113.

Guelzow, M. G., Bird, G. W., & Koball, E. H. 1991. An exploratory path analysis of the stress process for dual-career men and women. *Journal of Marriage and the Family, 53,* 151–164.

Guidubaldi, J., & Perry, J. D. 1985. Divorce and mental health sequelae for children: A two-year follow-up of a nationwide sample. *Journal of the American Academy of Child Psychiatry, 24,* 531–537.

Guilford, J. P. 1967. *The nature of human intelligence.* New York: McGraw-Hill.

Guillemin, R. 1982. Growth hormone-releasing factor from a human pancreatic tumor that caused acromegaly. *Science, 218,* 583–587.

Guillen, M. A. 1984. The I and the beholder. *Psychology Today, 18* (April), pp. 68–69.

Guisinger, S., Cowen, P. A., & Schuldberg, D. 1989. Changing parent and spouse relations in the first years of remarriage of divorced fathers. *Journal of Marriage and the Family, 51,* 445–456.

Gupta, P. D., & Bryant, P. E. 1989. Young children's causal inferences. *Child Development, 60,* 1138–1146.

Gustafson, G. E. 1984. Effects of the ability to locomote on infants' social and exploratory behaviors: An experimental study. *Developmental Psychology, 20,* 397–405.

Gustafson, G. E., & Green, J. A. 1989. On the importance of fundamental frequency and other acoustic features in cry perception and infant development. *Child Development, 60,* 772–780.

Gutmann, D. 1969. *The country of old men: Cross-cultural studies in the psychology of later life.* (Occasional Papers in Gerontology No. 5). Ann Arbor: Institute of Gerontology, University of Michigan-Wayne State.

Gutmann, D. 1977. The cross-cultural perspective. In J. E. Birren & K. W. Schaie (Eds.), *Handbook of the psychology of aging.* New York: Van Nostrand.

Guttmacher, A. F. 1973. *Pregnancy, birth and family planning.* New York: American Library.

Gwartney-Gibbs, P. A. 1986. The institutionalization of premarital cohabitation: Estimates from marriage license applications, 1970 and 1980. *Journal of Marriage and the Family, 48,* 423–434.

Haake, R. J., & Somerville, S. C. 1985. Development of logical search skills in infancy. *Developmental Psychology, 21,* 176–186.

Haaf, R. 1974. Complexity and facial resemblance as determinants of response to facelike stimuli by 5- and 10-week-old infants. *Journal of Experimental Child Psychology, 18,* 480–487.

Haan, N., Millsap, R., & Hartka, E. 1986. As time goes by: Change and stability in personality over fifty years. *Psychology and Aging, 1,* 220–232.

Hacker, A. 1986. Women at work. *The New York Review of Books* (August 14), pp. 26–32.

Hadden, J. K., & Swann, C. E. 1981. *Prime time preachers: The rising power of televangelism.* Reading, Mass.: Addison-Wesley.

Hagestad, G., & Smyer, M. 1983. Divorce at middle-age. In S. Weissman, R. Cohen, & B. Cohen (Eds.), *Dissolving personal relationships.* New York: Academic Press.

Hagestad, G. O. 1981. Problems and promises in the social psychology of intergenerational relations. In R. W. Fogel, E. Hartfield, S. B. Kiesler, & E. Shanas (Eds.), *Aging stability and change in the family.* New York: Academic Press.

Hahn, W. K. 1987. Cerebral lateralization of function: From infancy through childhood. *Psychological Bulletin, 101,* 376–392.

Haith, M. H., & Campos, J. J. 1977. Human infancy. In M. R. Rosenzweig & L. W. Porter (Eds.), *Annual review of psychology* (Vol. 28). Palo Alto, Calif.: Annual Reviews Inc.

Haith, M. M. 1980. *Rules that babies look by: The organization of newborn visual activity.* Hillsdale, N.J.: Erlbaum.

Haith, M. M., Bergman, T., & Moore, M. J. 1977. Eye contact and face scanning in early infancy. *Science, 198,* 853–854.

Haith, M. M., & Goodman, G. S. 1982. Eye-movement control in newborns in darkness and in unstructured light. *Child Development, 53,* 974–977.

Hale, E. 1986. Many accept suicide for the terminally ill. *USA Today* (May 16), p. D1.

Hale, S. 1990. A global developmental trend in cognitive processing speed. *Child Development, 61,* 653–663.

Halford, G. S. 1989. Reflections on 25 years of Piagetian cognitive developmental psychology, 1963–1988. *Human Development, 32,* 325–357.

Halford, G. S. 1990. Is children's reasoning logical or analogical? *Human Development, 33,* 356–361.

Hall, G. S. 1891. Notes on the study of infants. *The Pedagogical Seminary, 1,* 127–138.

Hall, G. S. 1904. *Adolescence* (Vols. 1 and 2). New York: Appleton-Century-Crofts.

Hall, H. 1987. Carry on: A cure for chronic crying. *Psychology Today, 21* (January), p. 10.

Hall, T. 1987. Infidelity and women: Shifting patterns. *New York Times* (June 1), p. 20.

Hall, T. 1991. Breaking up is becoming harder to do. *New York Times* (March 14), pp. B1, B4.

Hall, W. M., & Cairns, R. B. 1984. Aggressive behavior in children: An outcome of modeling or social reciprocity? *Developmental Psychology, 20,* 739–745.

Hallfrisch, J., Muller, D., Drinkwater, D., Tobin, J., & Andres, R. 1990. Continuing diet trends in men: The Baltimore Longitudinal Study of Aging. *Journal of Gerontology, 45,* M186–191.

Hallfrisch, J., Tobin, J. D., Muller, D. C., & Andres, R. 1988. Fiber intake, age, and other coronary risk factors in men of the Baltimore Longitudinal Study. *Journal of Gerontology, 43,* M64–68.

Hallinan, M. T., & Teixeira, R. B. 1987. Opportunities and constraints: Black-white differences in the formation of interracial friendships. *Child Development, 58,* 1358–1371.

Hallinan, M. T., & Williams, R. A. 1987. The stability of students' interracial friendships. *American Sociological Review, 52,* 653–664.

Hallinan, M. T., & Williams, R. A. 1989. Interracial friendship choices in secondary schools. *American Sociological Review, 54,* 67–78.

Hallinan, M. T., & Williams, R. A. 1990. Students' characteristics and the peer-influence process. *Sociology of Education, 63,* 122–132.

Halverson, H. M. 1931. An experimental

study of prehension in infants by means of systematic cinema records. *Genetic Psychology Monographs, 10,* 107–286.

Hamachek, D. E. 1977. Humanistic psychology: Theoretical-philosophical framework and implications for teaching. In D. J. Treffinger, J. K. Davis, & R. E. Ripple (Eds.), *Handbook on teaching educational psychology.* New York: Academic Press.

Hamilton, J. O. 1987. "No smoking" sweeps America. *Business Week* (July 27), pp. 40–46.

Hamilton, J. O. 1990. When medical research is for men only. *Business Week* (July 16), p. 33.

Hamilton, S. F. 1990. *Apprenticeship for adulthood: Preparing youth for the future.* New York: Free Press.

Hamilton, V. L., Blumenfeld, P. C., Akoh, H., & Miura, K. 1990. Credit and blame among American and Japanese children: Normative, cultural, and individual differences. *Journal of Personality and Social Psychology, 59,* 442–451.

Hamilton, V. L., Blumenfeld, P. C., & Kushler, R. H. 1988. A question of standards: Attributions of blame and credit for classroom acts. *Journal of Personality and Social Psychology, 54,* 34–48.

Hamilton, V. L., Broman, C. L., Hoffman, W. S., & Renner, D. S. 1990. Hard times and vulnerable people: Initial effects of plant closing on autoworkers' mental health. *Journal of Health and Social Behavior, 31,* 123–140.

Hamm, N. H., & Hoving, K. L. 1969. Conformity of children in an ambiguous perceptual situation. *Child Development, 40,* 773–783.

Haney, D. Q. 1985. Creativity is fragile and easily stifled. *Columbus* (Ohio) *Dispatch* (February 3), p. C–1.

Hansson, R. O. 1986. Relational competence, relationships, and adjustment in old age. *Journal of Personality and Social Psychology, 50,* 1050–1058.

Hansson, R. O., Nelson, R. E., Carver, M. D., NeeSmith, D. H., Dowling, E. M., Fletcher, W. L., & Suhr, P. 1990. Adult children with frail elderly parents: When to intervene? *Family Relations, 39,* 153–158.

Hareven, T. K. 1982. *Family time and industrial time.* New York: Cambridge University Press.

Hareven, T. K. 1987. Historical analysis of the family. In M. E. Sussman & S. K. Steinmetz (Eds.), *Handbook of marriage and the family.* New York: Plenum.

Harkins, E. B. 1978. Effects of empty nest transition on self-report of psychological and physical well-being. *Journal of Marriage and the Family, 40,* 549–556.

Harkness, S., Edwards, C. P., & Super, C. M. 1981. Social roles and moral reasoning: A case study in a rural African community. *Developmental Psychology, 17,* 595–603.

Harkness, S., & Super, C. M. 1985. The cultural context of gender segregation in children's peer groups. *Child Development, 56,* 219–224.

Harlow, H. F. 1971. *Learning to love.* San Francisco: Albion.

Harper, P. A., & Wiener, G. 1965. Sequelae of low birthweight. *Annual Review of Medicine, 16,* 405–420.

Harper, T. 1978. It's not true about people 65 or over. *Green bay* (Wis.) *Press-Gazette* (November 15), p. D1.

Harriman, L. C. 1986. Marital adjustment as related to personal and marital changes accompanying parenthood. *Family Relations, 34,* 233–239.

Harris, H. 1989. The Philip Morris Companies Inc. Family Survey II: Child Care. New York: Louis Harris and Associates, Inc.

Harris, K. M., & Morgan, S. P. 1991. Fathers, sons, and daughters: Differential paternal involvement in parenting. *Journal of Marriage and the Family, 53,* 531–544.

Harris, L. 1981. *Aging in the eighties: America in transition.* Washington, D.C.: National Council on Aging.

Harris, Louis, and Associates. 1979. The Playboy report on American men. *Playboy, 26* (March), pp. 91 + .

Harris, Louis, and Associates. 1986. *American teens speak: Sex, myths, TV, and birth control.* New York: Louis Harris and Associates.

Harris, M. B. 1970. Reciprocity and generosity: Some determinants of sharing in children. *Child Development, 41,* 313–326.

Harris, M. B. 1971. Models, norms, and sharing. *Psychological Reports, 29,* 147–153.

Harris, P. L. 1985. What children know about the situations that provoke emotion. In M. Lewis & C. Sasrni (Eds.), *The socialization of emotions.* New York: Plenum.

Harris, R. L., Ellicott, A. M., & Holmes, D. S. 1986. The timing of psychosocial transitions and changes in women's lives: An examination of women aged 45 to 60. *Journal of Personality and Social Psychology, 51,* 409–416.

Harrison, A. O., Wilson, M. N., Pine, C. J., Chan, S. Q., & Buriel, R. 1990. Family ecologies of ethnic minority children. *Child Development, 61,* 347–362.

Harry, J., & Lovely, R. 1979. Gay marriages and communities of sexual orientation. *Alternative Lifestyles, 2,* 177–200.

Hart, B. A. 1986. Fractionated myotatic reflex times in women by activity level and age. *Journal of Gerontology, 41,* 361–367.

Hart, C. H., Ladd, G. W., & Burleson, B. R. 1990. Children's expectations of the outcomes of social strategies: Relations with sociometric status and maternal disciplinary styles. *Child Development, 61,* 127–137.

Hart, S. N. 1991. From property to person status. *American Psychologist, 46,* 53–59.

Hart, S. N., & Brassard, M. R. 1987. A major threat to children's mental health. *American Psychologist, 42,* 160–165.

Harter, S., & Buddin, B. J. 1987. Children's understanding of the simultaneity of two emotions: A five-stage developmental acquisition sequence. *Developmental Psychology, 23,* 388–399.

Hartshorne, H., & May, M. A. 1928. *Studies in the nature of character.* Vol. 1: *Studies in deceit.* New York: Macmillan.

Hartshorne, H., May, M. A., & Maller, J. B. 1929. *Studies in the nature of character.* Vol. 2: *Studies in self-control.* New York: Macmillan.

Hartshorne, H., May, M. A., & Shuttleworth, F. K. 1930. *Studies in the nature of char-*

acter. Vol. 3: *Studies in the organization of character.* New York: Macmillan.

Hartup, W. W. 1970. Peer interaction and social organization. In P. H. Mussen (Ed.), *Carmichael's manual of child psychology* (3rd ed., Vol. 2). New York: Wiley.

Hartup, W. W. 1983. Peer relations. In P. H. Mussen (Series Ed.) & E. M. Hetherington (Vol. Ed.), *Handbook of child psychology* (Vol. 3). New York: Wiley.

Hartup, W. W. 1989. Social relationships and their developmental significance. *American Psychologist, 44,* 120–126.

Hartup, W. W., Laursen, B., Stewart, M. I., & Eastenson, A. 1988. Conflict and the friendship relations of young children. *Child Development, 59,* 1590–1600.

Harvey, C. D., & Bahr, H. M. 1974. Widowhood, morale, and affiliation. *Journal of Marriage and the Family, 36,* 97–106.

Haskett, G. J. 1971. Modification of peer preferences of first-grade children. *Developmental Psychology, 4,* 429–433.

Haskins, R. 1989. Beyond metaphor: The efficacy of early childhood education. *American Psychologist, 44,* 274–282.

Hattie, J., & Rogers, H. J. 1986. Factor models for assessing the relation between creativity and intelligence. *Journal of Educational Psychology, 78,* 482–485

Haugaard, J. J., & Reppucci, N. D. 1988. *The sexual abuse of children: A comprehensive guide to current knowledge and intervention strategies.* San Francisco: Jossey-Bass.

Hauser, S. T., Powers, S. I., Noam, G., & Bowlds, M. K. 1987. Family interiors of adolescent ego development trajectories. *Family Perspective, 21,* 263–282.

Havighurst, R. J. 1973. Social roles, work, leisure, and education. In C. Eisdorfer & M. P. Lawton (Eds.), *The psychology of adult development and aging.* Washington, D.C.: American Psychology Association.

Havighurst, R. J., Neugarten, B. L., & Tobin, S. S. 1968. Disengagement and patterns of aging. In B. L. Neugarten (Ed.), *Middle age and aging.* Chicago: University of Chicago Press.

Haviland, J. M., & Lelwica, M. 1987. The induced affect response: 10-week-old infants' responses to three emotion expressions. *Developmental Psychology, 23,* 97–104.

Hawkins, A. J., & Belsky, J. 1989. The role of father involvement in personality change in men across the transition to parenthood. *Family Relations, 38,* 378–384.

Hay, D. F., Murray, P., Cecire, S., & Nash, A. 1985. Social learning of social behavior in early life. *Child Development, 56,* 43–57.

Hayden-Thomson, L., Rubin, K. H., & Hymel, S. 1987. Sex preferences in sociometric choices. *Developmental Psychology, 23,* 558–562.

Hayflick, L. 1980. The cell biology of aging. *Scientific American, 242* (January), pp. 58–65.

Hayne, H., Rovee-Collier, C., & Perris, E. E. 1987. Categorization and memory retrieval by three-month-olds. *Child Development, 58,* 750–767.

Haynes, H., White, B. L., & Held, R. 1965. Visual accommodation in human infants. *Science, 148,* 528–530.

Hays, R. D., Widaman, K. F., DiMatteo, M. R., & Stacy, A. W. 1987. Structural-equation models of current drug use. Are appropriate models so simple(x)? *Journal of Personality and Social Psychology, 52,* 134–144.

Hayslip, B., & Sterns, H. L. 1979. Age differences in relationships between crystallized and fluid intelligences and problem solving. *Journal of Gerontology, 34,* 404–414.

Hazen, N. L., & Black, B. 1989. Preschool peer communication skills: The role of social status and interaction context. *Child Development, 60,* 867–876.

Head, J. 1984. Death cluster areas studied. *USA Today* (March 16), p. 3A.

Headey, B., & Wearing, A. 1989. Personality, life events, and subjective well-being: Toward a dynamic equilibrium model. *Journal of Personality and Social Psychology, 57,* 731–739.

Healy, M. 1985. Menopause doesn't harm health. *USA Today* (August 27), p. D–1.

Heckhausen, J., Dixon, R. A., & Baltes, P. B. 1989. Gains and losses in development throughout adulthood as perceived by different adult age groups. *Developmental Psychology, 25,* 109–121.

Heer, D. M. 1985. Effects of sibling number on child outcome. *Annual Review of Sociology, 11,* 27–47.

Heimann, M. 1989. Neonatal imitation, gaze aversion, and mother-infant interaction. *Infant Behavior and Infant Development, 12,* 495–505.

Heinicke, C. M., Diskin, S. D., Ramsey-Klee, D. M., & Given, K. 1983. Pre-birth parent characteristics and family development in the first year of life. *Child Development, 54,* 194–208.

Heinonen, O. P., Slone, D., Monson, R. R., Hook, E. B., & Shapiro, S. 1977. Cardiovascular birth defects and antenatal exposure to female sex hormones. *New England Journal of Medicine, 296,* 67–70.

Heinonen, O. P., Slone, D., & Shapiro, S. 1977. *Birth defects and drugs in pregnancy.* Littleton, Mass.: Publishing Sciences Group.

Heinstein, M. I. 1963. Behavioral correlates of breast-bottle regimens under varying parent-child relationships. *Monographs of the Society for Research in Child Development, 28* (4).

Helfer, R. E., & Kempe, C. H. 1977. *The battered child.* Chicago: University of Chicago Press.

Heller, S. 1987. Scholars spar over marriage-prospects study. *Chronicle of Higher Education* (January 28), p. 12.

Hellmich, N. 1986. The new campus attitude on sex. *USA Today* (February 5), p. D–1.

Hellmich, N. 1991. Picky preschoolers still eat enough. *USA Today* (January 24), D1.

Helmchen, H., & Henn, F. A. 1987. *Biological perspectives of schizophrenia.* New York: Wiley.

Helson, R., & Moane, G. 1987. Personality change in women from college to midlife. *Journal of Personality and Social Psychology, 53,* 176–186.

Helwig, C. C., Tisak, M. S., & Turiel, E. 1990. Children's social reasoning in context: Reply to Gabennesch. *Child Development, 61,* 2068–2078.

Hendry, L. B., & Gillies, P. 1978. Body type, body esteem, school, and leisure: A study of overweight, average, and underweight adolescents. *Journal of Youth and Adolescence, 7,* 181–195.

Henig, R. M. 1981. The child savers. *New York Times Magazine* (March 22), pp. 34–44.

Henig, R. M. 1982. Saving babies before birth. *New York Times Magazine* (February 28), pp. 18–48.

Henker, B., & Whalen, C. K. 1989. Hyperactivity and attention deficits. *American Psychologist, 44,* 216–223.

Henze, L. F., & Hudson, J. W. 1974. Personal and family characteristics of cohabiting college students. *Journal of Marriage and the Family, 36,* 722–726.

Herbert, T. B., Silver, R. C., & Ellard, J. H. 1991. Coping with an abusive relationship: I. How and why do women stay? *Journal of Marriage and the Family, 53,* 311–325.

Herdt, G. H. 1981. *Guardian of the flutes: Idioms of masculinity.* New York: McGraw-Hill.

Herdt, G. H. (Ed.). 1982. *Rituals of manhood.* Berkeley: University of California Press.

Herek, G. M. 1990. Gay people and government security clearances. *American Psychologist, 45,* 1035–1042.

Herman, J., & Hirschman, L. 1981. Families at risk for father-daughter incest. *American Journal of Psychiatry, 138,* 967–970.

Herodotus. 1964. *The histories* (A. de Selincourt, Trans.). London: Penguin Books.

Herrenkohl, R. C., & Herrenkohl, E. C. 1981. Some antecedents and developmental consequences of child maltreatment. *New Directions for Child Development, 11,* 57–76.

Hershenson, M. 1964. Visual discrimination in the human newborn. *Journal of Comparative and Physiological Psychology, 58,* 270–278.

Hershenson, M. 1967. Development of the perception of form. *Psychological Bulletin, 67,* 328–336.

Hershenson, M., Kessen, W., & Munsinger, H. 1967. Ocular orientation in the human newborn infant: A close look at some positive and negative results. In W. Wathen-Dunn (Ed.), *Models for the perception of speech and visual form.* Cambridge, Mass.: MIT Press.

Hertz, R., & Charlton, J. 1989. Making family under a shiftwork schedule: Air force security guards and their wives. *Social Problems, 36,* 491–507.

Hertzog, C. 1989. Influences of cognitive slowing on age differences in intelligence. *Developmental Psychology, 25,* 636–651.

Hertzog, C., & Schaie, K. W. 1988. Stability and change in adult intelligence: 2. Simultaneous analysis of longitudinal means and covariance structures. *Psychology and Aging, 2,* 122–130.

Herzog, A. R., House, J. S., & Morgan, J. N. 1991. Relation of work and retirement to health and well-being in older age. *Psychology and Aging, 6,* 202–211.

Hess, B. B. 1979. Sex roles, friendship, and the life course. *Research on Aging, 1,* 494–515.

Hess, B. B. 1985. Aging policies and old

women: The hidden agenda. In A. S. Rossi (Ed.), *Gender and the life course.* New York: Aldine.

Hess, B. B., & Markson, E. W. 1980. *Aging and old age: An introduction to social gerontology.* New York: Macmillan.

Hess, B. B., & Waring, J. M. 1978. Parent and child in later life: Rethinking the relationship. In R. M. Lerner & G. B. Spanier (Eds.), *Child influences on marital and family interaction.* New York: Academic Press.

Hess, R., & Camara, K. 1979. Post-divorce family relationships as mediating factors in the consequences of divorce for children. *Journal of Social Issues, 35,* 79–96.

Hess, T. M., & Higgins, J. N. 1983. Context utilization in young and old adults. *Journal of Gerontology, 38,* 65–71.

Hess, T. M., & Slaughter, S. J. 1990. Schematic knowledge influences on memory for scene information in young and older adults. *Developmental Psychology, 26,* 855–865.

Hetherington, E. M. 1979. Divorce. *American Psychologist, 34,* 851–858.

Hetherington, E. M. 1989. Coping with family transitions: Winners, losers, and survivors. *Child Development, 60,* 1–14.

Hetherington, E. M., Cox, M., & Cox, R. 1976. Divorced fathers. *Family Coordinator, 25,* 417–427.

Hetherington, E. M., Cox, M., & Cox, R. 1977. Divorced fathers. *Psychology Today, 10* (April), pp. 42–46.

Hetherington, E. M., Stanley-Hagan, M., & Anderson, E. R. 1989. Marital transitions: A child's perspective. *American Psychologist, 44,* 303–312.

Hewlett, S. A.1986a. Family isn't getting the support it deserves. *USA Today* (May 2), p. 9A.

Hewlett, S. A. 1986b. *A lesser life: The myth of women's liberation in America.* New York: Morrow.

Hey, R. P. 1986a. Liberals, conservatives unite to reform child-support system. *Christian Science Monitor* (December 1), pp. 3, 6.

Hey, R. P. 1986b. Studies hint at better ways to head off child abuse. *Christian Science Monitor* (November 13), pp. 3, 6.

Higgins, B. S. 1990. Couple infertility: From the perspective of the close-relationship model. *Family Relations, 39,* 81–86.

Hilberman, E. 1980. Overview: The "wife-beater's wife" reconsidered. *American Journal of Psychiatry, 137,* 1336–1347.

Hill, E. A., & Dorfman, L. T. 1982. Reaction of housewives to the retirement of their husbands. *Family Relations, 31,* 195–200.

Hill, J. P., & Kochendorfer, R. A. 1969. Knowledge of peer success and risk of detection as determinants of cheating. *Developmental Psychology, 1,* 231–238.

Hill, J. P., & Lynch, M. E. 1983. The intensification of gender-related role expectations during early adolescence. In J. Brooks-Gunn & A. C. Petersen (Eds.), *Girls at puberty: Biological and psychosocial perspectives.* New York: Plenum.

Hill, R. 1964. Methodological issues in family development research. *Family Process, 3,* 186–206.

Hill, R. 1986. Life cycle stages for types of single parent families: Of family development theory. *Family Relations, 35,* 19–29.

Hill, R., & Aldous, J., Jr. 1969. Socialization for marriage and parenthood. In D. Goslin (Ed.), *Handbook of socialization theory and research.* Chicago: Rand McNally.

Hill, T. P., & Shirley, D. 1990. Living wills: Now more than ever. *USA Today* (June 27), p. 10A.

Hilts, P. J. 1990. AIDS bias grows faster than disease, study says. *New York Times* (June 17), p. 14.

Hilts, P. J. 1991a. U.S. abandons idea of carrying out household survey on cases of AIDS. *New York Times* (January 11), p. A10.

Hilts, P. J. 1991b. A brain unit seen as index for recalling memories. *New York Times* (September 24), pp. B5, B9.

Hilts, P. J. 1991c. Study finds a decline in breast-feeding. *New York Times* (October 3), p. A8.

Hinds, M. D. 1981b. The child victim of incest. *New York Times* (June 15), p. 22.

Hinds, M. D. 1982. Countries acting on baby formula. *New York Times* (May 2), p. 10.

Hines, M. 1982. Prenatal gonadal hormones and sex differences in human behavior. *Psychology Bulletin, 92,* 56–80.

Hines, M., & Shipley, C. 1984. Prenatal exposure to diethylstillbestrol (DES) and the development of sexually dimorphic cognitive abilities and cerebral lateralization. *Developmental Psychology, 20,* 81–94.

Hinkle, L. E., Jr. 1974. The effect of exposure to culture change, social change, and changes in interpersonal relationships on health. In B. S. Dohrenwend & B. P. Dohrenwend (Eds.), *Stressful life events: Their nature and effects.* New York: Wiley.

Hinz, L. D., & Williamson, D. A. 1987. Bulimia and depression: A review of the affective variant hypothesis. *Psychological Bulletin, 102,* 150–158.

Hiroto, D. S. 1974. Locus of control and learned helplessness. *Journal of Experimental Psychology, 102,* 187–193.

Hirsch, B. J., & Rapkin, B. D. 1987. The transition to junior high school: A longitudinal study of self-esteem, psychological symptomatology, school life, and social support. *Child Development, 58,* 1235–1243.

Hirshberg, L. M., & Svejda, M. 1990. When infants look to their parents: 1. Infants' social referencing of mothers compared to fathers. *Child Development, 61,* 1175–1186.

Hobbs, D. F., Jr. 1965. Parenthood as crisis: A third study. *Journal of Marriage and the Family, 27,* 367–382.

Hobbs, D. F., Jr. 1968. Transition to parenthood. A replication and an extension. *Journal of Marriage and the Family, 30,* 413–417.

Hobbs, D. F., Jr., and Cole, S. P. 1976. Transition to parenthood: A decade replication. *Journal of Marriage and the Family, 38,* 723–731.

Hobbs, N., and Robinson, S. 1982. Adolescent development and public policy. *American Psychologist, 37,* 212–223.

Hochschild, A. 1989. *The second shift: Working parents and the revolution at home.* New York: Viking.

Hock, E., & DeMeis, D. K. 1990. Depression in mothers of infants: The role of maternal employment. *Developmental Psychology, 26,* 285–291.

Hodges, W. F., Tierney, C. W., & Buchsbaum, E. K. 1984. The cumulative effect of stress on preschool children of divorced and intact families. *Journal of Marriage and the Family, 46,* 611–617.

Hodgkinson, H. L. 1986. Reform? Higher education? Don't be absurd! *Phi Delta Kappan, 68* (December), 271–274.

Hoff-Ginsberg, E. 1986. Function and structure in maternal speech: The relation to the child's development of syntax. *Developmental Psychology, 22,* 155–163.

Hoff-Ginsberg, E., & Shatz, M. 1982. Linguistic input and the child's acquisition of language. *Psychological Bulletin, 92,* 3–26.

Hoffman, C., & Hurst, N. 1990. Gender sterotypes: Perception or rationalization? *Journal of Personality and Social Psychology, 58,* 197–208.

Hoffman, J. 1990. Pregnant, addicted and guilty? *New York Times Magazine* (August 19), pp. 33–37+.

Hoffman, L. W. 1974. Effects of maternal employment on the child—a review of the research. *Developmental Psychology, 10,* 204–228.

Hoffman, L. W. 1986. Work, family and the child. In M. S. Pallak & R. O. Perloff (Eds.), *Psychology and work: Productivity, change, and employment.* Washington, D.C. American Psychological Association.

Hoffman, L. W. 1989. Effects of maternal employment in the two-parent family. *American Psychologist, 44,* 283–292.

Hoffman, M. L. 1971. Father absence and conscience development. *Developmental Psychology, 4,* 400–406.

Hoffman, M. L. 1984. Interaction of affect and cognition in empathy: In C. E. Ezard, J. Kagan, & R. B. Zajonc (Eds.), *Emotions, cognition, and behavior.* Cambridge, Mass.: Cambridge University Press.

Hoffman, S. D., & Duncan, G. J. 1988. What are the economic consequences of divorce? *Demography, 25,* 641–645.

Hoffman-Plotkin, D., & Twentyman, C. T. 1984. A multimodal assessment of behavioral and cognitive deficits in abused and neglected preschoolers. *Child Development, 55,* 794–802.

Hogan, D. P., Hao, L., & Parish, W. L. 1990. Race, kin networks, and assistance of mother-headed families. *Social Forces, 68,* 797–812.

Hogan, D. P., & Kitagawa, E. 1985. The impact of social status, family structure, and neighborhood on the fertility of black adolescents. *American Journal of Sociology, 90,* 825–836.

Holahan, C. K. 1988. Relation of life goals at age 70 to activity participation and health and psychological well-being among Terman's gifted men and women. *Psychology and Aging, 3,* 286–291.

Holden, C. 1983. Can smoking explain ultimate gender gap? *Science, 221,* 1 034.

Holden, C. 1986. Youth suicide. *Science, 233,* 839–841.

Holden, C. 1987. OTA cites financial disaster of Alzheimer's. *Science, 236,* 253.

Holden, C. 1991. Is "gender gap" narrowing? *Science, 253,* 959–960.

Holden, G. W., & West, M. J. 1989. Proximate regulation by mothers: A demonstration of how differing styles affect young children's behavior. *Child Development, 60,* 64–69.

Hollenbeck, A. R., Gewirtz, J. L., Sebris, S. L., & Scanlon, J. W. 1984. Labor and delivery medication influences parent-infant interaction in the first post-partum month. *Infant Behavior and Development, 7,* 201–209.

Hollos, M., & Leis, P. E. 1989. *Becoming Nigerian in Ijo society.* New Brunswick, N.J.: Rutgers University Press.

Holmes, D. L., Nagy, J. N., & Slaymaker, F. 1982. Early influences of prematurity, illness, and prolonged hospitalization on infant behavior. *Developmental Psychology, 18,* 744–750.

Holstein, C. B. 1976. Irreversible, stepwise sequence in the development of moral judgment: A longitudinal study of males and females. *Child Development, 47,* 51–61.

Holsti, O. R., & Rosenau, J. N. 1980. Does where you stand depend on when you were born? The impact of generation on post-Vietnam foreign policy beliefs. *Public Opinion Quarterly, 44,* 1–22.

Holtzman, N. A. 1986. Effect of age at loss of dietary control on intellectual performance and behavior of children with phenylketonuria. *New England Journal of Medicine, 314,* 593–598.

Hooker, E. 1969. *Final report of the Task Force on Homosexuality.* Bethseda, Md.: National Institute of Mental Health.

Hopkins, J., Marcus, M., & Campbell, S. B. 1984. Postpartum depression: A critical review. *Psychological Bulletin, 95,* 498–515.

Horn, J. 1983. The Texas Adoption Project: Adopted children and their intellectual resemblance to biological and adoptive parents. *Child Development, 54,* 268–275.

Horn, J. 1985. Bias? Indeed! *Child Development, 56,* 779–780.

Horn, J. C., & Meer, J. 1987. The vintage years. *Psychology Today, 21* (May) pp. 76–84+.

Horn, J. L. 1976. Human abilities. A review of research and theory in the early 1970s. *Annual Review of Psychology, 27,* 437–485.

Horn, J. L., and Cattell, R. B. 1967. Age differences in fluid and crystallized intelligence. *Acta Psychologica, 26,* 107–129.

Horn, J. L., & Donaldson, G. 1977. Faith is not enough. *American Psychologist. 32,* 369–373.

Horowitz, F. D., Ashton, J., Culp, R., Gaddis, E., Levin, S., & Reichmann, B. 1977. The effects of obstetrical medication on the behavior of Israeli newborn infants and some comparisons with Uruguayan and American infants. *Child Development, 48,* 1607–1623.

Horsman, A., Jones, M., Francis, R., & Nordin, C. 1983. The effect of estrogen dose on postmenopausal bone loss. *New England Journal of Medicine, 309,* 1405–1407.

Hostetler, A. J. 1987. Scientists warn role of biology miscast in wake of Amish study. *APA Monitor* (May), pp. 16–17.

House, J. S., Landis, K. R., & Umberson, D. 1988. Social relationships and health. *Science, 241,* 540–545.

Householder, J., Hatcher, R., Burns, W., & Chasnoff, I. 1982. Infants born to narcotic-addicted mothers. *Psychological Bulletin, 92,* 453–468.

Hoving, K. L., Hamm, N., & Galvin, P. 1969. Social influence as a function of stimulus ambiguity at three age levels. *Developmental Psychology, 1,* 631–636.

Howard, D. V., Heisey, J. G., & Shaw, P. J. 1986. Aging and priming of newly learned associations. *Child Development, 22,* 78–85.

Howell, N. 1979. *The demography of the Dobe! Kung.* New York: Academic Press.

Howes, C. 1985. Sharing fantasy: Social pretend play in toddlers. *Child Development, 56,* 1253–1258.

Howes, C. 1990. Can the age of entry into child care and the quality of child care predict adjustment in kindergarten? *Developmental Psychology, 26,* 292–303.

Howes, C., Rodning, C., Galluzzo, D., & Myers, L. 1988. Attachment and child care: Relations with mother and caregiver. *Early Childhood Research Quarterly, 3,* 403–416.

Howes, C., & Stewart, P. 1987. Child's play with adults, toys, and peers: An examination of family and child care influences. *Developmental Psychology, 23,* 423–430.

Howes, C., Unger, O., & Seidner, L. B. 1989. Social pretend play in toddlers: Parallels with social play and with solitary pretend. *Child Development, 60,* 77–84.

Howes, C., & Wu, F. 1990. Peer interactions and friendships in an ethnically diverse school setting. *Child Development, 61,* 537–541.

Howe, M. L., & Brainerd, C. J. (Eds.). *Cognitive development in adulthood: Progress in cognitive development research.* New York: Springer-Verlag.

Howes, P., & Markman, H. J. 1989. Marital quality and child functioning: A longitudinal investigation. *Child Development, 60,* 1044–1051.

Hoyer, W. J., Rebok, G. W., & Sved, S. M. 1979. Effects of varying irrelevant information on adult age differences in problem solving. *Journal of Gerontology, 34,* 553–560.

Hronsky, S. L., & Emory, E. K. 1987. Neurobehavioral effects of caffeine on the neonate. *Infant Behavior and Development, 10,* 61–80.

Hsu, F. L. K. 1943. Incentives to work in primitive communities. *American Sociological Review, 8,* 638–642.

Hudgens, R. W. 1974. Personal catastrophe and depression. In B. S. Dohrenwend & B. P. Dohrenwend (Eds.), *Stressful life events: Their nature and effects.* New York: Wiley.

Huesmann, L. R. 1986. Psychological processes promoting the relation between exposure to media violence and aggressive behavior by the viewer. *Journal of Social Issues, 42,* 125–140.

Huesmann, L. R., Eron, L. D., & Yarmel, P. W. 1987. Intellectual functioning and aggression. *Journal of Personality and Social Psychology, 52,* 232–240.

Hull, J. B. 1985. Women find parents need them just when careers are resuming. *Wall Street Journal* (September 9), p. 21.

Hultsch, D. F., Hertzog, C., & Dixon, R. A. 1990. Ability correlates of memory performance in adulthood and aging. *Psychology and Aging, 5,* 356–368.

Hultsch, D. F., Masson, M. E. J., & Small, B. J. 1991. Adult age differences in direct and indirect tests of memory. *Journal of Gerontology, 46,* P22–30.

Hultsch, D. F., & Plemmons, J. K. 1979. Life events and life span development. In P. B. Baltes & O. G. Brim, Jr. (Eds.), *Life-span development and behavior* (Vol. 2). New York: Academic Press.

Hummel, R. F., Leavy, W. F., Rampolla, M., & Chorost, S. 1987. *AIDS: Impact on public policy.* New York: Plenum.

Hummert, M. L. 1990. Multiple stereotypes of elderly and young adults: A comparison of structure and evaluations. *Psychology and Aging, 51,* 182–193.

Humphrey, T. 1978. Function of the nervous system during prenatal life. In U. Stave (Ed.), *Perinatal physiology.* Hillside, N.J.: Erlbaum.

Humphreys, L. 1970. *Tearoom trade. Impersonal sex in public places.* Chicago: Aldine.

Humphry, D. 1991. *Final exit.* Eugene, OR: The Hemlock Society.

Hunt, E. 1983. On the nature of intelligence. *Science, 219,* 141–146.

Hunt, J. C., & Rudden, M. 1986. Gender differences in the psychology of parenting: Psychoanalytic and feminist perspectives. *Journal of the American Academy of Psychoanalysis, 14,* 213–225.

Hunt, J. McV. 1969. Has compensatory education failed? Has it been attempted? *Harvard Educational Review, 39,* 278–300.

Hunt, M. 1974. *Sexual behavior in the 1970s.* Chicago: Playboy Press.

Hunter, F. T. 1985. Adolescents' perception of discussions with parents and friends. *Developmental Psychology, 21,* 433–440.

Hunter, F. T., McCarthy, M. E., MacTurk, R. H., & Vietze, P. M. 1987. Infants' social-constructive-interactions with mothers and fathers. *Developmental Psychology, 23,* 249–254.

Hunter, F. T., & Youniss, J. 1982. Changes in functions of three relations during adolescence. *Developmental Psychology, 18,* 806–811.

Huntington, R., & Metcalf, P. 1979. *Celebrations of death.* New York: Cambridge University Press.

Hurd, M. D. 1989. The economic status of the elderly. *Science, 244,* 659–664.

Hurlock, E. B. 1968. The adolescent reformer. *Adolescence, 3,* 273–306.

Huston, A. C., Watkins, B. A., & Kunkel, D. 1989. Public policy and children's television. *American Psychologist, 44,* 424–433.

Huston, A. C., Wright, J. C., Rice, M. L., Kerkman, D., & St. Peters, M. 1990. Development of television viewing patterns in early childhood: A longitudinal investigation. *Developmental Psychology, 26,* 409–420.

Hutchings, D. E. (Ed.). 1989. *Prenatal abuse*

of licit and illicit drugs. New York: New York Academy of Sciences.

Huttenlocher, J., Haight, W., Bryk, A., Seltzer, M., & Lyons, T. 1991. Early vocabulary growth: Relation to language input and gender. *Developmental Psychology, 27,* 236–248.

Hyde, D. M. 1959. *An investigation of Piaget's theories of the development of number.* Unpublished doctoral dissertation, University of London.

Hyde, J. S. 1981. How large are cognitive gender differences? *American Psychologist, 36,* 892–901.

Hyde, J. S. 1984. How large are gender differences in aggression? A developmental meta-analysis. *Developmental Psychology, 20.* 722–736.

Hyde, J. S., Fennema, E., & Lamon, S. J. 1990. Gender differences in mathematics performance: A meta-analysis. *Psychological Bulletin, 107,* 139–155.

Hyde, J. S., & Linn, M. C. 1988. Gender differences in verbal ability: A meta-analysis. *Psychologial Bulletin, 104,* 53–69.

Hyde, J. S., & Rosenberg, B. G. 1976. *Half the human experience.* Lexington, Mass.: Heath.

Hyman, H. H. 1983. *The time of widowhood.* Durham, N.C.: Duke University Press.

Hymel, S. 1986. Interpretations of peer behavior: Affective bias in childhood and adolescence. *Child Development, 57,* 431–445.

Hymel, S., Rubin, K. H., Rowden, L., & LeMare, L. 1990. Children's peer relationships: Longitudinal prediction of internalizing and externalizing problems from middle to late childhood. *Child Development, 61,* 2002–2021.

Hymowitz, C. 1982. Wives of jobless men support some families—but at heavy cost. *Wall Street Journal* (December 8), pp. 1, 14.

Hyson, M. C., & Izard, C. E. 1985. Continuities and changes in emotion expressions during brief separation at 13 and 18 months. *Developmental Psychology, 21,* 1165–1170.

Iannotti, R. J. 1985. Naturalistic and structured assessment of prosocial behavior in preschool children: The influence of empathy and perspective taking. *Developmental Psychology, 21,* 46–55.

Ickes, W., & Turner, M. 1983. On the social advantages of having an older, opposite-sex sibling. *Journal of Personality and Social Psychology, 45,* 210–222.

Idler, E. L., & Kasl, S. V. 1992. Religion, disability, depression, and the timing of death. *American Journal of Sociology, 97,* 1052–1079.

Imperato-McGinley, J., Peterson, R. E., Gautier, T., & Sturla, E. 1981. The impact of androgens on the evolution of male gender identity. In S. J. Kogan & E. S. E. Hafez (Eds.), *Pediatric andrology.* The Hague: Martinus Nijhoff.

Im Thurn, E. F. 1883. *Among the Indians of Guiana.* London: Kegan Paul, Trench & Trubner.

Ingalls, Z. 1983. Although drinking is widespread, student abuse of alcohol is not

rising, new study finds. *The Chronicle of Higher Education* (January 19), p. 9.

Inhelder, B., & Piaget, J. 1958. *The growth of logical thinking from childhood to adolescence.* New York: Basic Books.

Inman, V. W., & Parkinson, S. R. 1983. Differences in Brown-Peterson recall as a function of age and retention interval. *Journal of Gerontology, 38,* 58–64.

Intons-Peterson, M. J. 1988. *Gender concepts of Swedish and American youth.* Hillside, N.J.: Erlbaum.

Irwin, H. J. 1985. *Flight of mind: A psychological study of the out-of-body experience.* Metuchen, N.J.: Scarecrow Press.

Isabella, R. A., Belsky, J., & von Eye, A. 1989. Origins of infant-mother attachment: An examination of interactional synchrony during the infant's first year. *Developmental Psychology, 25,* 12–21.

Ishii-Kuntz, M., & Lee, G. R. 1987. Status of the elderly: An extension of the theory. *Journal of Marriage and the Family, 49,* 413–420.

Istvan, J. 1986. Stress, anxiety, and birth outcomes: A critical review of the evidence. *Psychological Bulletin, 100,* 331–148.

Izard, C. E. 1977. *Human emotions.* New York: Plenum.

Izard, C. E. 1980. The young infant's ability to produce discrete emotion expression. *Developmental Psychology, 16,* 132–140.

Izard, C. E., & Haynes, O. M. 1986. A commentary on emotion expression in early development: An alternative to Zivin's framework. *Merrill-Palmer Quarterly, 32,* 313–319.

Izard, C. E., Hembree, E., Dougherty, L., & Spizziri, C. 1983. Changes in two-to-nineteen month old infants' facial expression following acute pain. *Developmental Psychology, 19,* 418–426.

Izard, C. E., Hembree, E. A., & Huebner, R. R. 1987. Infants' emotion expressions to acute pain: Developmental change and stability of individual differences. *Developmental Psychology, 23,* 105–113.

Izard, C. E., & Malatesta, C. Z. 1987. Perspectives on emotional development: 1. Differential emotions theory of early emotional development. In J. D. Osofsky (Ed.), *Handbook of infant development* (2nd ed.). New York: Wiley.

Jablonski, E. M. 1974. Free recall in children. *Psychological Bulletin, 81,* 522–539.

Jacklin, C. N. 1989. Female and male: Issues of gender. *American Psychologist, 44,* 127–133.

Jacklin, C. N., & Maccoby, E. E. 1978. Social behavior at thirty-three months in same-sex and mixed sex-dyads. *Child Development, 49,* 557–569.

Jackson, D. L., & Youngner, S. 1979. Patient autonomy and "death with dignity." *New England Journal of Medicine, 301,* 404–408.

Jackson, R. M. 1989. The reproduction of parenting. *American Sociological Review, 54,* 215–232.

Jackson, S. 1965. The growth of logical thinking in normal and subnormal children. *British Journal of Educational Psychology, 35,* 255–258.

Jacob, B. 1987. Single fathers are demanding respect. *USA Today* (September 1), p. 5D.

Jacobs, B. S., & Moss, H. A. 1976. Birth order and sex of sibling as determinants of mother-infant interaction. *Child Development, 47,* 315–322.

Jacobs, J. 1971. *Adolescent suicide.* New York: Wiley.

Jacobs, J. A. 1989. Long-term trends in occupational segregation by sex. *American Journal of Sociology, 95,* 160–173.

Jacobs, J. W. 1983. Treatment of divorcing fathers. *American Journal of Psychiatry, 140,* 1294–1299.

Jacobson, J. L., Jacobson, S. W., Fein, G. C., Schwartz, P. M., & Dowler, J. K. 1984. Prenatal exposure to an environmental toxin: A test of the multiple effects model. *Developmental Psychology, 20,* 523–532.

Jacobson, S. W. 1979. Matching behavior in the young infant. *Child Development, 50,* 425–430.

Jacobson, S. W., Fein, G. G., Jacobson, J. L, Schwartz, P. M., & Dowler, J. L. 1984. Neonatal correlates of prenatal exposure to smoking, caffeine, and alcohol. *Infant Behavior and Development, 7,* 253–265.

James, W. 1890. *The principles of psychology* (Vol. 1). New York: Dover, 1950.

Janoff-Bulman, R. 1979. Characterological versus behavioral self-blame: Inquiries into depression and rape. *Journal of Personality and Social Psychology, 37,* 1798–1809.

Janoff-Bulman, R., & Lang-Gunn, L. 1988. Coping with disease, crime, and accidents: The role of self-blame attributions. In L. Y. Abramson (Ed.), *Social cognition and clinical psychology: A synthesis.* New York: Guilford Press.

Jaynes, G. D., & Williams, R. M., Jr. (Eds.). 1989. *A common destiny: Blacks and American society.* Washington, D.C.: National Academy Press.

Janson, P., & Martin, J. K. 1982. Job satisfaction and age: A test of two views. *Social Forces, 60,* 1089–1102.

Jeffers, F. C., & Verwoerdt, A. 1969. How the old face death. In E. W. Busse & E. Pfeiffer (Eds.), *Behavior and adaptation in late life.* Boston: Little, Brown.

Jeffery, R. W. 1989. Risk behaviors and health: Contrasting individual and population perspectives. *American Psychologist, 44,* 1194–1202.

Jelliffe, D. B., & Jelliffe, F. F. P. 1979. *Nutrition and growth* (Vol. 2). New York: Plenum.

Jemmott, J. B. III, & Locke, S. E. 1984. Psychosocial factors, immunologic mediation and human susceptibility to infectious diseases: How much do we know? *Psychological Bulletin, 95,* 78–108.

Jencks, C. 1972. *Inequality: A reassessment of the effect of family and schooling in America.* New York: Basic Books.

Jencks, C. 1979. *Who gets ahead? The determinants of economic success in America.* New York: Basic Books.

Jencks, C. 1982. Divorced mothers, unite! *Psychology Today, 16* (November), pp. 73–75.

Jencks, C., Crouse, J., & Mueser, P. 1983. The Wisconsin model of status attainment: A national replication with improved measures of ability and aspiration. *Sociology of Education, 56,* 3–19.

Jenness, D. 1922. The life of the Copper Eskimos. *Report of the Canadian Arctic expedition, 1913-1918* (Vol. 12).

Jennings, M. K., & Niemi, R. G. 1981. *Generations and politics: A panel study of young adults and their parents.* Princeton, N.J.: Princeton University Press.

Jensen, A. R. 1969. How much can we boost IQ and scholastic achievement? *Harvard Educational Review, 39,* 1–123.

Jensen, A. R. 1972. The heritability of intelligence. *Saturday Evening Post* (Summer), p. 149.

Jensen, A. R. 1973a. Race, intelligence and genetics: The differences are real. *Psychology Today, 7* (December), pp. 80–86.

Jensen, A. R. 1973b. *Educability and group differences.* New York: Harper & Row.

Jensen, A. R. 1977. Did Sir Cyril Burt fake his research on heritability of intelligence? Part II. *Phi Delta Kappan, 56,* 471, 492.

Jensen, A. R. 1980. *Bias in mental testing.* New York: Free Press.

Jensen, A. R. 1984. Political ideologies and educational research. *Phi Delta Kappan, 65* (March), 460–462.

Jensen, A. R., & Rosenfeld, L. B. 1974. Influence of mode of presentation, ethnicity, and social class on teachers' evaluations of students. *Journal of Educational Psychology, 66,* 540–547.

Jensen, G. F. 1986. Explaining differences in academic behavior between public-school and Catholic-school students. A quantitative case study. *Sociology of Education, 59,* 32–41.

Jensen, K. 1932. Differential reactions to taste and temperature stimuli in newborn infants. *Genetic Psychological Monographs, 12,* 363–479.

Jensen, T. S., Genefke, I. K., Hyldebrandt, N., and others. 1982. Cerebral atrophy in young torture victims. *New England Journal of Medicine, 307,* 1341.

Jersild, A. T., & Holmes, F. B. 1935a. Children's fears. *Child Development Monographs* (No. 20).

Jersild, A. T., & Holmes, F. B. 1935b. Methods of overcoming children's fears. *Journal of Psychology, 1,* 75–104.

Jersild, A. T., Telford, C. W., & Sawrey, J. M. 1975. *Child psychology* (7th ed.). Englewood Cliffs, N.J.: Prentice-Hall.

Jessor, R., Costa, F., Jessor, L., & Donovan, J. E. 1983. Time of first intercourse: A prospective study. *Journal of Personality and Social Psychology, 44,* 608–626.

Jessor, S., & Jessor, R. 1975. Transition from virginity to nonvirginity among youth: A social-psychological study over time. *Developmental Psychology, 11,* 473–484.

Johansson, B., & Berg, S. 1989. The robustness of the terminal decline phenomenon: Longitudinal data from the Digit-Span Memory Test. *Journal of Gerontology, 44,* P 184–186.

Johnson, C. N. 1990. If you had my brain, where would I be? Children's understanding of the brain and identity. *Child Development, 61,* 962–972.

Johnson, D. 1987. Fear of AIDS stirs new attacks on homosexuals. *New York Times* (April 24), p. 8.

Johnson, D. L. 1989. Schizophrenia as a brain disease. *American Psychologist, 44,* 553–555.

Johnson, J. 1986. '90s home: Make room for step-families. *USA Today* (March 6), p. 1A.

Johnson, J., Ludtke, M., & Riley, M. 1990. Shameful bequests to the next generation. *Time* (October 8), pp. 42–46.

Johnson, M. M. 1975. Fathers, mothers, and sex typing. *Sociological Inquiry, 45,* 15–26.

Johnson, P. 1984. The loss of ideals of youth. *New York Times Magazine* (March 25), pp. 90–98.

Johnson, R. J., Lund, D. A., & Dimond, M. F. 1986. Stress, self-esteem and coping during bereavement among the elderly. *Social Psychology Quarterly, 49,* 273–279.

Johnson, T. E. 1988. Genetic specification of life span: Processes, problems, and potentials. *Journal of Gerontology, 43,* B87–92.

John-Steiner, V. 1986. *Notebooks of the mind: Explorations of thinking.* Albuquerque: University of New Mexico Press.

Johnston, J. R., Kline, M., & Tschann, J. M. 1989. Ongoing postdivorce conflict in families contesting custody: Do joint custody and frequent access help? *American Journal of Orthopsychiatry, 59,* 576–592.

Johnston, L. 1979. Artist ends her life after ritual citing "self-termination" right. *New York Times* (June 17), pp. 1, 10.

Jones, C. P., & Adamson, L. B. 1987. Language use in mother-child and mother-child-sibling interactions. *Child Development, 58,* 356–366.

Jones, D. C., & Vaughan, K. 1990. Close friendships among senior adults. *Psychology and Aging, 5,* 451–457.

Jones, H. E. 1949. Adolescence in our society. *The family in a democratic society: Anniversary papers of the Community Service Society of New York.* New York: Columbia University Press.

Jones, L. V. 1984. White-black achievement differences: The narrowing gap. *American Psychologist, 39,* 1207–1213.

Jones, M. C. 1957. The later careers of boys who were early- or late-maturing. *Child Development, 28,* 113–128.

Jones, M. C., & Bayley, N. 1950. Physical maturing among boys as related to behavior. *Journal of Educational Psychology, 41,* 129–148.

Jones, M. C., & Mussen, P. H. 1958. Self-conceptions, motivations and interpersonal attitudes of early- and late-maturing girls. *Child Development, 29,* 491–501.

Jones, S. S. 1985. On the motivational bases for attachment behavior. *Developmental Psychology, 21,* 848–857.

Jones, S. S., Smith, L. B., & Landau, B. 1991. Object properties and knowledge in early lexical learning. *Child Development, 62,* 499–516.

Jones, T. L. 1990. In demographics, advantage goes to U.S. *Investor's Daily* (February 22), pp. 1+.

Joseph, N. 1981. Campus couples and violence. *New York Times* (June 23), p. 22.

Jouriles, E. N., Pfiffner, L. J., & O'Leary, S. G. 1988. Marital conflict, parenting, and toddler conduct problems. *Journal of Abnormal Child Psychology, 16,* 197–206.

Joyce, C. 1984. A time for grieving. *Psychology Today, 18* (November), pp. 42–46.

Jung, C. G. 1933. *Modern man in search of a soul.* New York: Harcourt, Brace & World.

Jussim, L. 1989. Teacher expectations: Self-fulfilling prophecies, perceptual biases, and accuracy. *Journal of Personality and Social Psychology, 57,* 469–480.

Juster, F. T., & Stafford, F. P. (Eds.). 1985. *Time, goods, and well-being.* Ann Arbor, Mich.: ISR Publishing Division.

Kagan, J. 1965. Reflection-impulsivity and reading ability in primary-grade children. *Child Development, 36,* 609–628.

Kagan, J. 1966. Reflection-impulsivity: The generality and dynamics of conceptual tempo. *Journal of Abnormal Psychology, 71,* 17–24.

Kagan, J. 1970. The determinants of attention in the infant. *American Scientist, 58,* 298–306.

Kagan, J. 1972a. A conception of early adolescence. In J. Kagan & R. Coles (Eds.), *Twelve to sixteen: early adolescence.* New York: Norton.

Kagan, J. 1972b. Do infants think? *Scientific American, 226* (March), pp. 74–82.

Kagan, J. 1973. Do the first two years matter? *Saturday Review of Education, 1* (3), 41–43.

Kagan, J. 1981. *The second year: The emergence of self-awareness.* Cambridge, Mass.: Harvard University Press.

Kagan, J. 1983. Stress and coping in early development. In N. Garmezy & M. Rutter (Eds.), *Stress, coping, and development.* New York: McGraw-Hill.

Kagan, J. 1984a. The idea of emotion in human development. In C. E. Izard, J. Kagan, & R. Zajonc (Eds.), *Emotions, cognition, and behavior.* New York: Cambridge University Press.

Kagan, J. 1984b. *The nature of the child.* New York: Basic Books.

Kagan, J. 1989. Temperamental contributions to social behavior. *American Psychologist, 44,* 668–674.

Kagan, J., Kearsley, R. B. & Zelazo, P. R. 1978. *Infancy: Its place in human development.* Cambridge, Mass.: Harvard University Press.

Kagan, J., & Klein, R. E. 1973. Cross-cultural perspectives on early development. *American Psychologist, 28,* 947–961.

Kagan, J., Klein, R. E., Haith, M. M., & Morrison, F. J. 1973. Memory and meaning in two cultures. *Child Development, 44,* 221–223.

Kagan, J., & Moss, H. A. 1962. *Birth to maturity.* New York: Wiley.

Kagan, J., Pearson, L., & Welch, L. 1966. Conceptual impulsivity and inductive reasoning. *Child Development, 37,* 583–594.

Kagan, J., Reznick, J. S., Clarke, C., Snidman, N., & Garcia-Coll, C. 1984. Behavioral inhibitions to the unfamiliar. *Child Development, 55,* 2212–2225.

Kagan, J., Reznick, J. S., & Gibbons, J. 1989. Inhibited and uninhibited types of children. *Child Development, 60,* 838–845.

Kagan, J., Reznick, J. S., Snidman, N., Gibbons, J., and Johnson, M. O. 1988. Childhood derivatives of inhibition and lack of inhibition to the unfamiliar. *Child Development, 59,* 1580–1589.

Kagay, M. R. 1989. Homosexuals gain more acceptance. *New York Times* (October 25), p. 13.

Kagay, M. R. 1991. Fear of AIDS has altered behavior, poll shows. *New York Times* (June 18), pp. B5, B8.

Kahn, R. L., & Antonucci, T. C. 1980. Convoys over the life course. In P. B. Baltes & O. G. Brim, Jr. (Eds.), *Life-span development and behavior.* New York: Academic Press.

Kahn, S., Zimmerman, G., Csikszentmihalyi, M., & Getzels, J. W. 1985. Relations between identity in young adulthood and intimacy at midlife. *Journal of Personality and Social Psychology, 49,* 1316–1322.

Kail, R., & Nippold, M. A. 1984. Unconstrained retrieval from semantic memory. *Child Development, 55,* 944–951.

Kain, E. L. 1984. Surprising singles. *American Demographics, 6* (August), 16–19+.

Kaitz, M., Meschulach-Sarfaty, O., Auerbach, J., & Eidelman, A. 1988. A reexamination of newborns' ability to imitate facial expressions. *Developmental Psychology, 24,* 3–7.

Kaler, S. R., & Kopp, C. B. 1990. Compliance and comprehension in very young toddlers. *Child Development, 61,* 1997–2003.

Kalish, H. I. 1981. *From behavioral science to behavior modification.* New York: McGraw-Hill.

Kalleberg, A. L., & Loscocco, K. A. 1983. Aging, values, and rewards: Explaining age differences in job satisfaction. *American Sociological Review, 48,* 78–90.

Kallman, D. A., Plato, C. C., & Tobin, J. D. 1990. The role of muscle loss in the age-related decline of grip strength: Cross-sectional and longitudinal perspectives. *Journal of Gerontology, 45,* M82–88.

Kallmann, F. J. 1952. Twin sibships and the study of male homosexuality. *American Journal of Human Genetics, 4,* 136–146.

Kallmann, F. J. 1953. *Heredity in health and mental disorder.* New York: Norton.

Kalmuss, D. S. 1984. The intergenerational transmission of marital aggression. *Journal of Marriage and the Family, 46,* 11–19.

Kaltenbach, K., Weinraub, M., & Fullard W. 1980. Infant wariness toward strangers reconsidered: Infants' and mothers' reactions to unfamiliar persons. *Child Development, 51,* 1197–1202.

Kalter, H., & Warkany, J. 1983a. Congenital malformations. I. *New England Journal of Medicine, 308,* 424–431.

Kalter, H., & Warkany, J. 1983b. Cogenital malformations. II. *New England Journal of Medicine, 308,* 491–497.

Kamarck, T. & Jennings, J. R. 1991. Biobehavioral factors in sudden cardiac death. *Psychological Bulletin, 109,* 42–75.

Kamerman, J. B. 1988. *Death in the midst of life: Social and cultural influences on death, grief, and mourning.* Englewood Cliffs, NJ: Prentice-Hall.

Kamin, L. J. 1969. Predictability, surprise, attention and conditioning. In B. A. Campbell & R. M. Church (Eds.), *Punishment and aversive behavior.* New York: Appleton-Century-Crofts.

Kamin, L. J. 1974. *The science and politics of IQ.* Hillsdale, N.J.: Erlbaum.

Kamin, L. J. 1975. Is IQ heritable? *Contemporary Psychology, 20,* 545–547.

Kamin, L. J. 1977. Burt's IQ data. *Science, 195,* 246–248.

Kamin, L. J. 1981. Commentary. In S. Scarr (Ed.), *IQ: Race, social class, and individual differences.* Hillsdale, N.J.: Erlbaum.

Kandel, D. B. 1974. Inter- and intragenerational influences on adolescent marijuana use. *Journal of Social Issues, 30,* 107–135.

Kandel, D. B. 1978. Homophily, selection, and socialization in adolescent friendships. *American Journal of Sociology, 84,* 427–436.

Kandel, D. B. 1990. Parenting styles, drug use, and children's adjustment in families of young adults. *Journal of Marriage and the Family, 52,* 183–196.

Kandel, D. B., & Adler, I. 1982. Socialization into marijuana use among French adolescents: A cross-cultural comparison with the United States. *Journal of Health and Social Behavior, 23,* 295–309.

Kane, R. L., & Kane, R. A. 1978. Care of the aged: Old problems in need of new solutions. *Science, 200* (May 26), 913–919.

Kanfer, R., & Zeiss, A. M. 1983. Depression, interpersonal standard setting, and judgments of self-efficacy. *Journal of Abnormal Psychology, 92,* 319–329.

Kantrowitz, B. 1986a. Growing up gay. *Newsweek* (January 13), pp. 50–52.

Kantrowitz, B. 1986b. A mother's choice. *Newsweek* (March 31), pp. 46–51.

Kantrowitz, B. 1987a. Kids and contraceptives. *Newsweek* (February 16), pp. 54–65.

Kantrowitz, B. 1987b. Portrait of divorce in America. *Newsweek* (February 2), p. 78.

Kantrowitz, B. 1987c. Who keeps "Baby M"? *Newsweek* (January 19), pp. 44–49.

Kantrowitz, B. 1990. The crack children. *Newsweek* (February 12), pp. 62–63.

Kanungo, R. N. 1979. The concepts of alienation and involvement revisited. *Psychological Bulletin, 86,* 119–138.

Kaplan, B. J. 1972. Malnutrition and mental deficiency. *Psychological Bulletin, 78,* 321–334.

Kaplan, H., & Dove, H. 1987. Infant development among the Ache of eastern Paraguay. *Developmental Psychology, 23,* 190–198.

Kaplan, H. R., & Tausky, C. 1972. Work and the welfare Cadillac. *Social Problems, 19,* 469–483.

Karp, D. A. 1988. A decade of reminders: Changing age consciousness between fifty and sixty years old. *Gerontologist, 28,* 727–738.

Kart, C. S., & Beckham, B. L. 1976. Black-white differentials in the institutionalization of the elderly: A temporal analysis. *Social Forces. 54,* 901–910.

Kasarda, J. 1989. Urban industrial transition and the underclass. *Annuals, AAPSS* (January), pp. 26–47.

Kasl, S. V., Evans, A. S., & Neiderman, J. C. 1979. Psychosocial risk factors in the development of infectious mononucleosis. *Psychosomatic Medicine, 41,* 445–467.

Kaslow, F. W., & Schwartz, L. L. 1987. *The dynamics of divorce: A life-cycle perspective.* New York: Brunner/Mazel.

Kastenbaum, R. 1975. Is death a life crisis? On the confrontation with death in theory and practice. In N. Datan & L. H. Ginsburg (Eds.), *Lifespan developmental psychology: Normative life crisis.* New York: Academic Press.

Kastenbaum, R. 1977. Temptations from the ever after. *Human Behavior, 6* (September), 28–33.

Kastenbaum, R. 1979. "Healthy dying": A paradoxical quest continues. *Journal of Social Issues, 35,* 185–206.

Kastenbaum, R., & Costa, P. T., Jr. 1977. Psychological perspectives on death. In M. R. Rosenzweig & L. W. Porter (Eds.), *Annual review of psychology* (Vol. 28). Palo Alto, Calif.: Annual Reviews, Inc.

Kasun, J. R. 1978. A reply to zero population growth. *Society, 15* (May-June), pp. 9+.

Katchadourian, H. A. 1985. *Fundamentals of sexuality* (4th ed.). New York: Holt, Rinehart and Winston.

Katz, P. A. 1976. The acquisition of racial attitudes in children. In P. A. Katz, (Ed.), *Towards the elimination of racism.* New York: Pergamon Press.

Katz, P. A., Sohn, M., & Zalk, S. R. 1975. Perceptual concomitants of racial attitudes in urban grade-school children. *Developmental Psychology, 11,* 135–144.

Katz, S. 1983. Active life expectancy. *New England Journal of Medicine, 309,* 1218–1223.

Katz, S., & Burt, M. 1988. Self-blame: Help or hindrance in recovery from rape? In A. Burgess (Ed.), *Rape and sexual assault.* New York: Garland.

Katzman, R. 1986. Medical progress: Alzheimer's disease. *New England Journal of Medicine, 314,* 964–973.

Kaufman, H. G. 1982. *Professionals in search of work: Coping with the stress of job loss and underemployment.* New York: Wiley.

Kaufman, J., & Cicchetti, D. 1989. Effects of maltreatment on school-age children's socioemotional development: Assessments in a day-camp setting. *Developmental Psychology, 25,* 516–524.

Kaufman, J., & Zigler, E. 1987. Do abused children become abusive parents? *American Journal of Orthopsychiatry, 57,* 186–192.

Kazdin, A. E. 1988a. Childhood depression. In E. J. Mash & L. Terdal (Eds.), *Behavioral assessment of childhood disorders* (2nd ed.). New York: Guilford.

Kazdin, A. E. 1988b. *Child psychotherapy: Developing and identifying effective treatments.* New York: Pergamon.

Kazdin, A. E. 1989. Developmental psychopathology: Current research, issues, and directions. *American Psychologist, 44,* 180–187.

Kaufman, S. R. 1987. *The ageless self: Sources of meaning in late life.* Madison, Wis.: University of Wisconsin Press.

Kausler, D. H., & Hakami, M. K. 1983. Memory for activities: Adult age differences and intentionality. *Developmental Psychology, 19,* 889–894.

Kaye, E. 1979. On starving oneself to death. *Family Health* (September), pp. 38–43.

Kaye, K., & Wells, A. J. 1980. Mothers' jiggling and the burst-pause pattern in neonatal feeding. *Infant Behavior and Development, 3,* 29–46.

Keasey, C. B. 1975. Implicators of cognitive development for moral reasoning. In DePalma, D. J., and Foley, J. M. (Eds.), *Moral Development: Current Theory and Research*. Hillsdale, N.J.: Erlbaum.

Keating, N. C., & Cole, P. 1980. What do I do with him 24 hours a day? Changes in the housewife role afer retirement. *Gerontologist, 20,* 84–89.

Keefer, C. H., Tronick, E., Dixon, S., & Brazelton, T. B. 1982. Special differences in motor performance between Gusii and American newborns and a modification of the neonatal behavioral assessment scale. *Child Development, 53,* 754–759.

Keegan, P. 1989. Playing favorites. *New York Times Special Section on Education* (August 6), pp. EDUC 26–27.

Keith, P. M. 1983. A comparison of the resources of parents and childless men and women in very old age. *Family Relations, 32,* 403–409.

Keller, A., Ford, L. H., Jr., & Meacham, J. A. 1978. Dimensions of self-concept in preschool children. *Developmental Psychology, 14,* 483–489.

Keller, C. 1980. Epidemiologic characteristics of preterm births. In S. L. Friedman & M. Sigman (Eds.), *Preterm birth and psychological development*. New York: Academic Press.

Keller, W. D., Hildebrandt, K. A., & Richards, M. E. 1985. Effects of extended father-infant contact during the newborn period. *Infant Behavior and Development. 8,* 337–350.

Kelly, D. 1991. Minorities still playing academic catch-up. *USA Today* (February 20), p. 7D.

Kelly, D. H. 1971. Social failure, academic self-evaluation, and school avoidance and deviant behavior. *Youth and Society, 2,* 489–503.

Kelly, E. L. 1955. Consistency of the adult personality. *American Psychologist, 10,* 659–681.

Kelly, E. L. & Conley, J. J. 1987. *Journal of Personality and Social Psychology, 52,* 27–40.

Kelly, G. A. 1955. *The psychology of personal constructs*. New York: Norton.

Kelley, J. 1990. More male teens means more killings. *USA Today* (July 31), p. 6A.

Kelly, J. R. 1987. *Freedom to be: A new sociology of leisure*. New York: Macmillan.

Kelly, L. 1988. *Surviving sexual violence*. Minneapolis: University of Minnesota Press.

Kempe, R. S., & Kempe, C. H. 1978. *Child abuse*. Cambridge, Mass.: Harvard University Press.

Kendall, P. C., Howard, B., & Epps, J. 1988. The anxious child: Cognitive-behavioral treatment strategies. *Behavior Modification, 10,* 281–310.

Kendig, H. L., Coles, R., Pittelkow, Y., & Wilson, S. 1988. Confidants and family structure in old age. *Journal of Gerontology, 43,* S31–40.

Kendrick, C., & Dunn, J. 1980. Caring for a second baby: Effects on interaction between mother and firstborn. *Developmental Psychology, 16,* 303–311.

Keniston, K. 1970. Youth: A "new" stage in life. *American Scholar* (Autumn), pp. 586–595.

Kennell, J. H., Voos, D. K., & Klaus, M. H. 1979. Parent-infant bonding. In J. D. Osofsky (Ed.), *Handbook of infant development*. New York: Wiley.

Kenney, A. M. 1987. Teen pregnancy: An issue for the schools. *Phi Delta Kappan, 63* (June), 728–736.

Kenrick, D. T., McCreath, H. E., Govern, J., King, R., & Bordin, J. 1990. Person-environment intersections: Everyday settings and common trait dimensions. *Journal of Personality and Social Psychology, 58,* 685–698.

Kenshalo, D. R., Sr. 1986. Somesthetic sensitivity in young and elderly humans. *Journal of Gerontology, 41,* 732–742.

Kerr, P. 1986. Experts say some antidrug efforts by schools harm more than help. *New York Times* (September 17), pp. 1, 49.

Kershner, J. R., & Ledger, G. 1985. Effect of sex, intelligence, and style of thinking on creativity: A comparison of gifted and average IQ children. *Journal of Personality and Social Psychology, 48,* 1033–1040.

Kersten, K. K. 1990. The process of marital disaffection: Interventions at various stages. *Family Relations, 39,* 257–265.

Kertzer, D. I., & Schaie, K. W. (Eds.). 1989. *Age structure in comparative perspective*. Hillsdale, N.J.: Lawrence Erlbaum Associates.

Kessen, W. 1963. Research in the psychological development of infants: An overview. *Merrill-Palmer Quarterly, 9,* 83–94.

Kessen, W. 1965. *The child*. New York: Wiley.

Kessler, R. C., House, J. S., & Turner, J. B. 1987. Unemployment and health in a community sample. *Journal of Health and Social Behavior, 28,* 51–59.

Kessler, R. C., Turner, J. B., & House, J. S. 1989. Unemployment, reemployment, and emotional functioning in a community sample. *American Sociological Review, 54,* 648–657.

Kett, J. F. 1977. *Rites of passage: Adolescence in America, 1970 to the present*. New York: Basic Books.

Kidwell, J. S. 1981. Number of siblings, sibling spacing, sex, and birth order: Their effects on perceived parent-adolescent relationship. *Journal of Marriage and the Family, 43,* 315–332.

Kidwell, S. J. 1982. The neglected birth order: Middleborns. *Journal of Marriage and the Family, 44,* 225–235.

Kihlstrom, J. F., Cantor, N., Albright, J. S., Chew, B. R., Klein, S. B., & Niedenthal, P. M. 1988. Information processing and the study of the self. In L. Berkowitz (Ed.), *Advances in experimental social psychology* (Vol. 21). Orlando, Fla.: Academic Press.

Kilborn, P. T. 1990. Youths lacking special skills find jobs leading nowhere. *New York Times* (November 27), pp. A1, A11.

Kilborn, P. T. 1991. In Appalachia, from homemaker to wage earner. *New York Times* (July 7), pp. 1, 10.

Kilbride, J. E., Robbins, M. C., & Kilbride, P. L. 1970. The comparative motor development of Baganda, American white, and American black infants. *American Anthropologist, 62,* 1422–1428.

Kilpatrick, D. G., Resick, P., & Vernonen, L. 1981. Effects of rape experience: A longi

tudinal study. *Journal of Social Issues, 37,* 105–122.

Kimball, M. M., & Dale, P. S. 1972. The relationship between color naming and color recognition abilities of preschoolers. *Child Development, 43,* 972–980.

Kimble, G. A. 1984. Psychology's two cultures. *American Psychologist, 39,* 833–839.

Kimmel, D. C. 1980. *Adulthood and aging: An interdisciplinary, developmental view* (2nd ed.). New York: Wiley.

Kimmel, D. C., Price, K. F., & Walker, J. W. 1978. Retirement choice and retirement satisfaction. *Journal of Gerontology, 33,* 575–585.

Kinard, E. M., & Reinherz, H. 1986. Effects of marital disruption on children's school aptitude and achievement. *Journal of Marriage and the Family, 48* (May), 285–293.

Kinder, M. 1991. *Playing with power in movies, television, and video games: From Muppet Babies to Teenage Mutant Ninja Turtles*. Berkeley: University of California Press.

King, H. E., & Webb, C. 1981. Rape crisis centers. *Journal of Social Issues, 37,* 93–104.

King, N. J., Hamilton, D. I., & Ollendick, T. H. 1988. *Children's phobias: A behavioural perspective*. Chichester, England: Wiley.

Kinsey, A. C., Pomeroy, W. B., & Martin, C. E. 1948. *Sexual behavior in the human male*. Philadelphia: Saunders.

Kinsey, A. C., Pomeroy, W. B., Martin, C. E., & Gebhard, P. H. 1953. *Sexual behavior in the human female*. Philadelphia: Saunders.

Kipnis, D. 1987. Psychology and behavioral technology. *American Psychologist, 42,* 30–36.

Kirkpatrick, S. W., & Sanders, D. M. 1978. Body image stereotypes: A developmental comparison. *Journal of Genetic Psychology, 132,* 87–95.

Kisilevsky, B. S., & Muir, D. W. 1991. Human fetal and subsequent newborn responses to sound and vibration. *Infant Behavior and Development, 14,* 1–26.

Kitcher, P. 1987. Precis of vaulting ambition: Sociobiology and the quest for human nature. *Behavioral and Brain Sciences, 10,* 61–100.

Kite, M. E., Deaux, K., & Miele, M. 1991. Stereotypes of young and old: Does age outweigh gender? *Psychology and Aging, 6,* 19–27.

Kite, M. E., & Johnson, B. T. 1988. Attitudes toward older and younger adults: A metaanalysis. *Psychology and Aging, 3,* 233–244.

Kitson, G. C., & Morgan, L. A. 1990. The multiple consequences of divorce: A decade review. *Journal of Marriage and the Family, 52,* 913–924.

Klaus, M. H., & Kennell, J. H. 1976. *Maternalinfant bonding: The impact of early separation or loss on family development*. St. Louis: Mosby.

Klein, H. A., & Cordell, A. S. 1987. The adolescent as mother: Early risk identification. *Journal of Youth and Adolescence, 16,* 47–58.

Klein, P. S. 1984. Behavior of Israeli mothers

toward infants in relation to infants' perceived temperament. *Child Development, 55,* 1212–1218.

Kleinhuizen, J. 1991. Poor, elderly have more disabilities. *USA Today* (March 14), p. D1.

Klemesrud, J. 1981. Voice of authority still male. *New York Times* (February 2), p. 16.

Klimes-Dougan, B., & Kistner, J. 1990. Physically abused preschoolers' responses to peers' distress. *Developmental Psychology, 26,* 599–602.

Kline, M., Johnston, J. R., & Tschann, J. M. 1991. The long shadow of marital conflict: A model of children's postdivorce adjustment. *Journal of Marriage and the Family, 53,* 297–309.'

Kline, M., Tschann, J. M., Johnston, J. R., & Wallerstein, J. S. 1989. Children's adjustment in joint and sole physical custody families. *Developmental Psychology, 25,* 430–438.

Klinger-Vartabedian, L., & Wispe, L. 1989. Age differences in marriage and female longevity. *Journal of Marriage and the Family, 51,* 195–202.

Klinnert, M. D., Emde, R. N., Butterfield, P., & Campos, J. J. 1986. Social referencing. *Developmental Psychology, 22,* 427–432.

Kluckhohn, C. 1960. *Mirror for man.* Greenwich, Conn.: Fawcett.

Knox, A. B. 1977. *Adult development and learning.* San Francisco: Jossey-Bass.

Knox, D. 1980. Trends in marriage and the family—the 1980's. *Family Relations, 29,* 145–150.

Knudson, M. 1980. Baltimore study shows age not calendar matters. *Columbus Dispatch* (July 14), p. B3.

Kobasa, S. C., Maddi, S. R., & Kahn, S. 1982. Hardiness and health: A prospective study. *Journal of Personality and Social Psychology, 42,* 168–177.

Koch, H. L. 1956. Sissiness and tomboyishness in relation to sibling characteristics. *Journal of Genetic Psychology, 88,* 231–244.

Kochanska, G., Kuczynski, L., Radke-Yarrow, M., & Welsch, J. 1987. Resolutions of control episodes between well and affectively ill mothers and their young children. *Journal of Abnormal Child Psychology, 15,* 441–456.

Koepke, J. E., & Barnes, P. 1982. Amount of sucking when a sucking object is readily available to human newborns. *Child Development, 53,* 978–983.

Koepke, J. E., Hamm, M., Legerstee, M., & Russell, M. 1983. Neonatal imitation: Two failures to replicate. *Infant Behavior and Development, 6,* 113–116.

Koestner, R., Franz, C., & Weinberger, J. 1990. The family origins of empathic concern: A 26-year longitudinal study. *Journal of Personality and Social Psychology, 58,* 709–717.

Koff, E., Rierdan, J., & Silverstone, E. 1978. Changes in representation of body image as a function of menarcheal status. *Developmental Psychology, 14,* 635–642.

Kogan, N. 1979. A study of age categorization. *Journal of Gerontology, 34,* 358–367.

Kohen-Raz, R. 1968. Mental and motor development of kibbutz, institutionalized, and home-reared infants in Israel. *Child Development, 39,* 489–504.

Kohlberg, L. 1963. The development of children's orientations toward a moral order. I: Sequence in the development of human thought. *Vita Humana, 6,* 11–33.

Kohlberg, L. 1966. A cognitive-developmental analysis of children's sex-role concepts and attitudes. In E. E. Maccoby (Ed.), *The development of sex differences.* Stanford, Calif.: Stanford University Press.

Kohlberg, L. 1969. Stage and sequence: The cognitive-developmental approach to socialization. In D. A. Goslin (Ed.), *Handbook of socialization theory and research.* Chicago: Rand McNally.

Kohlberg, L. 1973. Continuities in childhood and adult moral development revisited. In P. B. Baltes, & K. W. Schaie (Eds.), *Lifespan developmental psychology: Personality and socialization.* New York: Academic Press.

Kohlberg, L. 1976. Moral stages and moralization. In T. Lickona (Ed.), *Moral development and behavior: Theory, research, and social issues.* New York: Holt, Rinehart and Winston.

Kohlberg, L. 1978. Revisions in the theory and practice of moral development. *New Directions for Child Development, 2,* 83–87.

Kohlberg, L. 1980. High school democracy and educating for a just society. In R. L. Mosher (Ed.), *Moral education.* New York: Praeger.

Kohlberg, L. 1981a. *Essays on moral development.* Vol. 1, *The philosophy of moral development.* San Francisco: Harper & Row.

Kohlberg, L. 1981b. *The philosophy of moral development.* New York: Harper & Row.

Kohlberg, L. 1984. *Essays on moral development.* Vol 2, *The psychology of moral development.* San Francisco: Harper & Row.

Kohlberg, L., & Gilligan, C. F. 1971. The adolescent as philosopher: The discovery of the self in a postconventional world. *Daedalus, 100,* 1051–1086.

Kohlberg, L., & Ullian, D. Z. 1974. Stages in the development of psychosexual concepts and attitudes. In R. C. Friedman, R. N. Richart, R. L. Vande Wiele (Eds.), *Sex differences in behavior.* New York: Wiley.

Kohn, A. 1987. Whatever happened to human potential? *Psychology Today, 21* (May), pp. 99–100.

Kohn, M. L. 1959. Social class and parental values. *American Journal of Sociology, 64,* 337–351.

Kohn, M. L. 1963. Social class and parent-child relationships. *American Journal of Sociology, 68,* 471–480.

Kohn, M. L. 1977. *Class and conformity: A study in values* (2nd ed.). Chicago: University of Chicago Press.

Kohn, M. L., Naoi, A., Schoenbach, C., Schooler, C., & Slomczynski, K. M. 1990. Position in the class structure and psychological functioning in the United States, Japan, and Poland. *American Journal of Sociology, 95,* 964–1008.

Kohn, M. L. & Schooler, C. 1982. Job conditions and personality: A longitudinal assessment of their reciprocal effects. *American Journal of Sociology, 87,* 1257–1286.

Kohn, M. L. & Schooler, C. 1983. *Work and personality: An inquiry into the impact of social stratification.* Norwood, N.J.: Ablex.

Kolata, G. 1983. Math genius may have hormonal basis. *Science,* 222:1312.

Kalata, G. 1984. Studying learning in the womb. *Science, 225,* 302–303.

Kolata, G. 1986. Manic-depression: Is it inherited? *Science, 232,* 575–576.

Kolata, G. 1989a. Gender gap in aptitude tests is narrowing, experts find. *New York Times* (July 1), pp. 1, 8.

Kolata, G. 1989b. Mind blowing? *New York Times Special Section on Education* (August 6), pp. EDUC 25–26.

Kolata, G. 1989. In cities, poor families are dying of crack. *New York Times* (August 11), pp. 1, 10.

Kolata, G. 1990a. Cancer risk in estrogen is slight, study asserts. *New York Times* (November 28), p. A11.

Kolata, G. 1990b. Hyperactivity is linked to brain abnormality. *New York Times* (November 15), pp. A1, A16.

Kolata, G. 1990c. Program helped underweight babies, study shows. *New York Times* (June 13), p. A10.

Kolata, G. 1991a. The aging brain: The mind is resilient, it's the body that fails. *New York Times* (April 16), pp. B5, B8.

Kolata, G. 1991b. Alzheimer's disease: Dangers and trials of denial. *New York Times* (February 28), p. B7.

Kolata, G. 1991c. Alzheimer's researchers close in on causes. *New York Times* (February 26), pp. B5, B9.

Kolata, G. 1991d. Estrogen after menopause cuts heart attack risk, study finds. *New York Times* (September 12), pp. A1, A13.

Kolata, G. 1991e. Experts debate whether AIDS epidemic has at last crested in U.S. *New York Times* (June 18), pp. B5, B8.

Kolata, G. 1991f. Nursing homes are criticized on how they tie and drug some patients. *New York Times* (January 23), p. A13.

Kolata, G. 1991g. Parents of tiny infants find care choices are not theirs. *New York Times* (September 30), pp. A1, A11.

Kolata, G. 1991h. Women face dilemma over estrogen therapy. *New York Times* (September 17), p. B8.

Kolata, G. B. 1975. Behavioral development: Effects of environment. *Science, 189,* 207–209.

Kolata, G. B. 1979. Scientists attack report that obstetrical medications endanger children. *Science, 204,* 391–392.

Kolodny, R. C., Jacobs, L. S., Masters, W. H., Toro, G., & Daughaday, W. H. 1972. Plasma gonadotrophins and prolactin in male homosexuals. *Lancet, 2,* 18–20.

Konner, M. 1976. Maternal care, infant behavior and development among the !Kung. In R. B. Lee & I. DeVore (Eds.), *Kalahari hunter-gatherers.* Cambridge, Mass.: Harvard University Press.

Konner, M. 1977. Infancy among the Kalahari Desert San. In P. H. Leiderman, S. R. Tulkin, & A. Rosenfeld (Eds.), *Culture and infancy.* New York: Academic Press.

Konner, M. 1990. *Why the reckless survive and other secrets of human nature.* New York: Viking.

Kopelman, R. E., Greenhaus, J. H., & Connolly, T. F. 1983. A model of work, family, and interrole conflict: A construct validation study. *Organizational Behavior and Human Performance, 32,* 198–215.

Kopp, C. 1982. Antecedents of self-regulation: A develpmental perspective. *Developmental Psychology, 18,* 199–214.

Kopp, C. B. 1989. Regulation of distress and negative emotions: A developmental view. *Developmental Psychology, 25,* 343–354.

Koretz, G. 1990. Does wealth inspire attention to elderly parents? *Business Week* (August 20), p. 18.

Korner, A. F. 1979. Conceptual issues in infancy research. In J. D. Osofsky (Ed.), *Handbook of infant development.* New York: Wiley.

Korner, A. F., Brown, B. W., Jr., Reade, E. P., Stevenson, D. K., Fernbach, S. A., & Thom, V. A. 1988. State behavior of preterm infants as a function of development, individual and sex differences. *Infant Behavior and Development, 11,* 111–124.

Korner, A. F., & Thoman, E. B. 1972. The relative efficacy of contact and vestibular-proprioceptive stimulation in soothing neonates. *Child Development, 43,* 443–453.

Kornhaber, A., & Woodward, K. L. 1981. *Grandparents/grandchild: The vital connection.* New York: Anchor Press.

Kosnik, W., Winslow, L., Kline, D., Rasinski, K., & Sekuler, R. 1988. Visual changes in daily life throughout adulthood. *Journal of Gerontology, 43,* P63–P70.

Kovach, J. A., & Glickman, N. W. 1986. Levels and psychosocial correlates of adolescent drug use. *Journal of Youth and Adolescence, 15,* 61–77.

Kovacs, M. 1989. Affective disorders in children and adolescents. *American Psychologist, 44,* 209–215.

Kowaz, A. M., & Marcia, J. E. 1991. Development and validation of a measure of Eriksonian industry. *Journal of Personality and Social Psychology, 60,* 390–397.

Kramer, D. A. 1983. Post-formal operations? A need for further conceptualization. *Human Development, 26,* 91–105.

Kramer, R. B. 1968. *Changes in moral judgment response pattern during late adolescence and young adulthood: Retrogression in a developmental sequence.* Unpublished doctoral dissertation, University of Chicago.

Krantz, D. S., Grunberg, N. E. & Baum, A. 1985. Health psychology. *Annual Review of Psychology, 36,* 349–383.

Krantz, M. 1982. Sociometric awareness, social participation, and perceived popularity in preschool children. *Child Development, 53,* 376–379.

Krause, N. 1986. Social support, stress, and well-being among older adults. *Journal of Gerontology, 41,* 512–519.

Krause, N., Jay, G., & Liang, J. 1991. Financial strain and psychological well-being among the American and Japanese elderly. *Psychology and Aging, 6,* 170–181.

Kreutzer, M. A., Leonard, C., & Flavell, J. H. 1975. An interview study of children's knowledge about memory. *Monographs of the Society for Research in Child Development, 40* (Serial No. 159).

Krogman, W. M. 1972. *Child growth.* Ann Arbor: University of Michigan Press.

Kropp, J. P. & Haynes, O. M. 1987. Abusive and nonabusive mothers' ability to iden-

tify general and specific emotion signals of infants. *Child Development, 58,* 187–190.

Krosnick, J. A., & Alwin, D. F. 1989. Aging and susceptibility to attitude change. *Journal of Personality and Social Psychology, 57,* 416–425.

Krosnick, J. A., & Judd, C. M. 1982. Transitions in social influence at adolescence: Who induces cigarette smoking? *Developmental Psychology, 18,* 359–368.

Krymkowksi, D. H. 1991. The process of status attainment among men in Poland, the U.S., and West Germany. *American Sociological Review, 56,* 46–59.

Kübler-Ross, E. 1969. *On death and dying.* New York: Macmillan.

Kübler-Ross, E. 1981. *Living with dying.* New York: Macmillan.

Kuchuk, A., Vibbert, M., & Bornstein, M.H. 1986. The perception of smiling and its experiential correlates in three-month-old infants. *Child Development, 57,* 1054–1061.

Kuczynski, L., & Kochanska, G. 1990. Development of children's noncompliance strategies from toddlerhood to age 5. *Developmental Psychology, 26,* 398–408.

Kuczynski, L., Kochanska, G., Radke-Yarrow, M., & Girnius-Brown, O. 1987. A developmental interpretation of young children's noncompliance. *Developmental Psychology, 23,* 799–806.

Kuhn, D. 1974. Inducing development experimentally: Comments on a research paradigm. *Developmental Psychology, 10,* 590–600.

Kurdek, L. A. 1991. The relations between reported well-being and divorce history, availability of a proximate adult, and gender. *Journal of Marriage and the Family, 53,* 71–78.

Kurdek, L. A., & Fine, M. A. 1991. Cognitive correlates of satisfaction for mothers and stepfathers in stepfather families. *Journal of Marriage and the Family, 53,* 565–572.

Kurdek, L. A., & Schmitt, J. P. 1986. Relationship quality of gay men in closed or open relationships. *Journal of Homosexuality, 12,* 85–99.

Kurtines, W. M. 1986. Moral behavior as rule governed behavior: Person and situation effects on moral decision making. *Journal of Personality and Social Psychology, 50,* 784–791.

Kutner, L. 1989. Baby's cute little ways may be true indications of temperament later in life. *New York Times* (November 2), p. 18.

Kutner, L. 1990a. It isn't ususual when the father-to-be wakes up feeling sick. *New York Times* (February 8), p. B8.

Kutner, L. 1990b. When taking risks is an appropriate way to learn and when it is something to be feared. *New York Times* (September 27), p. B5.

Labouvie-Vief, G. 1985. Intelligence and cognition. In J. E. Birrie & K. W. Schaie (Eds.), *Handbook of the psychology of aging.* New York: Van Nostrand Reinhold.

Labouvie-Vief, G. 1986. Modes of knowledge and the organization of development. In M. L. Commons, L. Kohlberg, F. A. Richards, & J. Sinnot (Eds.), *Beyond formal*

operations. Vol 3 Of *models and methods in the study of adult and adolescent thought.* New York: Praeger.

Labouvie-Vief, G., DeVoe, M., & Bulka, D. 1989. Speaking about feelings: Conceptions of emotion across the life span. *Psychology and Aging, 4,*425–437.

Labouvie-Vief, G., & Schell, D. A. 1982. Learning and memory in later life. In B. B. Wolman (Ed.), *Handbook of developmental psychology.* Englewood Cliffs, N.J.: Prentice-Hall.

Lachman, M. E., & McArthur, L. Z. 1986. Adulthood age differences in causal attributions for cognitive, physical, and social performance. *Psychology and Aging, 1,* 127–132.

Ladd, G. W. 1990. Having friends, keeping friends, making friends, and being liked by peers in the classroom: Predictors of children's early school adjustment? *Child Development, 61,* 1081–1100.

Ladd, G. W., & Emerson, E. S. 1984. Shared knowledge in children's friendships. *Developmental Psychology, 20,* 932–940.

Ladd, G. W., & Golter, B. S. 1988. Parents' management of preschooler's peer relations: Is it related to children's social competence? *Developmental Psychology, 24,* 109–117.

LaFreniere, P., Strayer, F. F., & Gauthier, R. 1984. The emergence of same-sex affiliative preferences among preschool peers. *Child Development, 55,* 1958–1965.

Lagercrantz, H., & Slotkin, T. A. 1986. *Scientific American, 254* (April), pp. 100–107.

Lamaze, F. 1958. *Painless childbirth: Psychoprophylactic method.* London: Burke.

Lamb, M. 1982. Second thoughts on first touch. *Psychology Today, 16* (April), pp. 9–11.

Lamb, M. E. 1975. Fathers: Forgotten contributors to child development. *Human Development, 18,* 245–266.

Lamb, M. E. 1976. The role of the father: An overview. In M. E. Lamb (Ed.), *The role of the father in child development.* New York: Wiley.

Lamb, M. E. 1977a. Father-infant and mother-infant interaction in the first year of life. *Child Development, 48,* 167–181.

Lamb, M. E. 1978. Influence of the child on marital quality and family interaction during the prenatal, perinatal, and infancy periods. In R. M. Lerner & G. B. Spanier (Eds.), *Child influences on marital and family interaction: A life-span perspective.* New York: Academic Press.

Lamb, M. E. (Ed.). 1981. *The role of the father in child development.* New York: Wiley.

Lamb, M. E., & Bornstein, M. H. 1987. *Development in infancy: An introduction* (2nd ed.). New York: Random House.

Lamb, M. E., Frodi, A. M., Hwang, C., Frodi, M., & Steinberg, J. 1982. Mother- and father-infant interaction involving play and holding in traditional and nontraditional Swedish families. *Developmental Psychology, 18,* 215–221.

Lamb, M. E., Gaensbauer, T. J., Malkin, C. M., & Schultz, L. A. 1985. The effects of child maltreatment on security of infant-adult attachment. *Infant Behavior and Development, 8,* 35–45.

Lamb, M. E., Hopps, K., & Elster, A. B. 1987. Strange situation behavior of infants with adolescent mothers. *Infant Behavior and Development, 10,* 39–48.

Lamb, M. E., Hwang, C., Bookstein, F. L., Broberg, A., Hult, G., & Frodi, M. 1988. Determinants of social competence in Swedish preschoolers. *Developmental Psychology, 24,* 58–70.

Lamb, M. E., & Sagi, A. (Eds.). 1983. *Fatherhood and family policy.* Hillsdale, N.J.: Erlbaum.

Lamb, M. E., & Sherrod, L. R. 1981. *Infant social cognition: Empirical and theoretical considerations.* Hillsdale, N.J.: Erlbaum.

Lamb, M. E., Thompson, R. A., Gardner, W., & Charnov, E. L. (Eds.). 1985. *Infant-mother attachment: The origins and developmental significance of individual differences in strange situation behavior.* Hillsdale, N.J.: Erlbaum.

Lambert, N. M. 1988. Adolescent outcomes for hyperactive children. *American Psychologist, 43,* 786–799.

Lamm, R. D. 1990. Again, age beats youth. *New York Times* (December 2), p. 19E.

Landsberger, B. H. 1985. *Long-term care for the elderly: A comparative view of layers of care.* New York: St. Martin's Press.

Landry, S. H., Chapieski, M. L., Richardson, M. A., Palmer, J. P., & Hall, S. 1990. The social competence of children born prematurely: Effects of medical complications and parent behaviors. *Child Development, 61,* 1605–1615.

Lang, A. M., & Brody, E. M. 1983. Characteristics of middle-aged daughters and help to their elderly mothers. *Journal of Marriage and the Family, 45,*193–202.

Lang, O. 1946. *Chinese family and society.* New Haven: Yale University Press.

Langer, E. J., & Rodin, J. 1976. The effects of choice and enhanced personal responsibility for the aged: A field experiment in an institutional setting. *Journal of Personality and Social Psychology, 34,* 191–198.

Langlois, J. H., & Downs, A. C. 1979. Peer relations as a function of physical attractiveness: The eye of the beholder or behavioral reality? *Child Development, 50,* 409–418.

Langlois, J. H., & Downs, A. C. 1980. Mothers, fathers, and peers as socialization agents of sex-typed play behaviors in young children. *Child Development, 51,* 1237–1247.

Langlois, J. H., Ritter, J. M., Roggman, L. A., & Vaughn, L. S. 1991. Facial diversity and infant preferences for attractive faces. *Developmental Psychology, 27,* 79–84.

Langlois, J. H., & Stephan, C. 1977. The effects of physical attractiveness and ethnicity on children's behavioral attributions and peer preferences. *Child Development, 48,* 1694–1698.

Langman, L. 1971. Dionysus—child of tomorrow. *Youth and Society, 3,* 84–87.

Langmeier, J., & Matějček, Z. 1974. *Psychological deprivation in childhood.* New York: Halsted Press.

Langway, L. 1982. Growing old, feeling young. *Newsweek* (November 1), pp. 56–65.

Langway, L. 1983. Bringing up superbaby. *Newsweek* (March 28), pp. 62–68.

Lapsley, D. K., Enright, R. D., & Serlin, R. C. 1985. Toward a theoretical perspective on the legislation of adolescence. *Journal of Early Adolescence, 5,* 441–466.

Lapsley, D. K., Milstead, M., Quintana, S. M., Flannery, D., & Buss, R. R. 1986. Adolescent egocentrism and formal operations. *Developmental Psychology, 22,* 800–807.

Larson, R. 1978. Thirty years of research on the subjective well-being of older Americans. *Journal of Gerontology, 33,* 109–125.

Larson, R., Mannell, R., & Zuzanek, J. 1986. Daily well-being of older adults with friends and family. *Psychology and Aging, 2,* 117–126.

Larson, R., & Richards, M. H. 1991. Daily companionship in late childhood and early adolescence: Changing developmental contexts. *Child Development, 62,* 284–300.

Larson, R. W. 1983. Adolescents' daily experience with family and friends: Contrasting opportunity systems. *Journal of Marriage and the Family, 45,* 739–750.

Lasky, R. E. 1977. The effect of visual feedback of the hand on the reaching and retrieval behavior of young infants. *Child Development, 48,* 112–117.

Lasky, R. E., Klein, R. E., Yarbrough, C., Engle, P. L., Lechtig, A., & Martorell, R. 1981. The relationship between physical growth and infant behavior development in rural Guatemala. *Child Development, 52,* 219–226.

Laslett, B. 1973. The family as a public and private institution: An historical perspective. *Journal of Marriage and the Family, 35,* 480–492.

Latané, B., & Darley, J. M. 1968. Group inhibition of bystander intervention in emergencies. *Journal of Personality and Social Psychology, 10,* 215–221.

Latané, B. & Darley, J. M. 1970. *The unresponsive bystander.* New York: Appleton-Century-Crofts.

Lau, R. R., Quadrel, M. J., & Hartman, K. A. 1990. Development and change of young adults' preventive health beliefs and behavior: Influence from parents and peers. *Journal of Health and Social Behavior, 31,* 240–259.

Laudenslager, M. L. 1988. The psychobiology of loss: Lessons from humans and nonhuman primates. *Journal of Social Issues, 44,* 19–36.

Laudenslager, M. L., Ryan, S. M., Drugan, R. C., Hyson, R. L., & Maier, S. F. 1983. Coping and immunosuppression: Inescapable but not escapable shock suppresses lymphocyte proliferation. *Science, 221,* 568–570.

Lauer, J. C., & Lauer, R. H. 1985. Marriages made to last. *Psychology Today, 19* (June), pp. 22–26.

Lavoie, J. C., & Looft, W. R. 1973. Parental antecedents of resistance-to-temptation behavior in adolescent males. *Merrill-Palmer Quarterly, 19,* 107–116.

Lawler, J. 1975. Dialectical philosophy and developmental psychology: Hegel and Piaget on contradition. *Human Development, 18,* 1–17.

Lawson, C. 1985. A conference on menopause. *New York Times* (July 8), p. 17.

Lawson, C. 1989. Girls still apply makeup, boys fight wars. *New York Times* (June 15), pp. 15, 19.

Lazar, I., & Darlington, R. 1982. Lasting effects of early education: A report from the Consortium for Longitudinal Studies. *Monographs of the Society for Research in Child Development, 47* (No. 195).

Lazarus, R. S. 1966. *Psychological stress and the coping process.* New York: McGraw-Hill.

Lazarus, R. S., & DeLongis, A. 1983. Pschological stress and coping in aging. *American Psychologist, 38,* 245–254.

Lazarus, R. S., DeLongis, A., Folkman, S., & Gruen, R. 1985. Stress and adaptational outcomes. *American Psychologist, 40,* 770–779.

Leary, W. E. 1989. Study finds Alzheimer's disease afflicts more than was estimated. *New York Times* (November 10), p. 1, 14.

Leary, W. E. 1990. Gloomy report on teenagers' health. *New York Times* (June 9), p. 8.

Leboyer, F. 1975. *Birth without violence.* New York: Knopf.

Lecuyer, R. 1989. Habituation and attention, novelty and cognition: Where is the continuity? *Human Development, 32,* 148–157.

Lee, G. R. 1988. Marital intimacy among older persons: The spouse as confidant. *Journal of Family Issues, 9,* 273–284.

Lee, G. R., & Ellithorpe, E. 1982. Intergenerational exchange and subjective well-being among the elderly. *Journal of Marriage and the Family. 44,* 217–224.

Lee, G. R., & Shehan, C. L. 1989. Retirement and marital satisfaction. *Journal of Gerontology, 44,* S226–230.

Lee, L. C. 1975. Toward a cognitive theory of interpersonal development: Importance of peers. In M. Lewis & L. A. Rosenblum (Eds.), *Friendship and peer relations.* New York: Wiley.

Lee, V. E., Brooks-Gunn, J., & Schnur, E. 1988. Does Head Start work? A 1-year follow-up comparison of disadvantaged children attending Head Start, no preschool, and other preschool programs. *Developmental Psychology, 24,* 210–222.

Lee, V. E., Brooks-Gunn, J., Schnur, E., & Liaw, F. 1990. Are Head Start effects sustained? A longitudinal follow-up comparison of disadvantaged children attending Head Start, no preschool, and other preschool programs. *Child Development, 61,* 495–507.

Lee, V. E., & Bryk, A. S. 1989. A multilevel model of the social distribution of high school achievement. *Socology of Education, 62,* 172–192.

Lef, T. 1984. A longitudinal study of moral judgment development in Taiwan. Paper presented at the Sixth International Symposium on Asian Studies, Hong Kong, 1984.

Lefcourt, H. M., Miller, R. S., Ware, E. E., & Sherk, D. 1981. Locus of control as a modifier of the relationship between stressors and moods. *Journal of Personality and Social Psychology, 41,* 357–369.

Legerstee, M., Corter, C., & Kienapple, K. 1990. Hand, arm, and facial actions of young infants to a social and nonsocial stimulus. *Child Development, 61,* 774–784.

Lehman, D. R. & Nisbett, R. E. 1990. A longitudinal study of the effects of undergraduate training on reasoning. *Developmental Psychology, 26,* 952–960.

Leishman, K. 1987. Heterosexuals and AIDS. *Atlantic Monthly* (February), pp. 39–58.

Lemann, N. 1991. Four generation in the projects. *New York Time Magazine* (January 13), pp. 16–23 +.

LeMasters, E. E. 1957. Parenthood as crisis. *Marriage and Family Living, 19,* 352–355.

Lempers, J. D., Clark-Lempers, D., & Simons, R. L. 1989. Economic hardship, parenting, and distress in adolescence. *Child Development, 60,* 25–39.

Lenneberg, E. H. 1967. *Biological foundations of language.* New York: Wiley.

Lenneberg, E. H. 1969. On explaining language. *Science, 164,* 635–643.

Lennon, M. C. 1982. The psychological consequences of menopause. The importance of timing of a life stage event. *Journal of Health and Social Behavior, 23,* 353–366.

Leo, J. 1987. Exploring the traits of twins. *Time* (January 12), p. 63.

Leo, J. 1987. When the date turns into rape. *Time* (March 23), p. 77.

Leonard, E. A. 1991. Good night, sleep tight. *Newsweek Special Issue* (Summer), pp. 42–43.

Lepper, M. R., & Greene, D. 1975. Turning play into work: Effects of adult surveillance and extrinsic rewards on children's intrinsic motivation. *Journal of Personality and Social Psychology, 31,* 479–486.

Lepper, M. R., Greene, D., & Nisbett, R. E. 1973. Undermining children's intrinsic interest with extrinsic reward. *Journal of Personality and Social Psychology, 28,* 129–137.

Lerner, J. V., & Galambos, N. L. 1985. Maternal role satisfaction, mother-child interaction, and child temperament: A process model. *Developmental Psychology, 21,* 1157–1164.

Lerner, J. V., Hertzog, C., Hooker, K. A., Hassibi, M., & Thomas, A. 1988. A longitudinal study of negative emotional states and adjustment from early childhood through adolescence. *Child Development, 59,* 356–366.

Lerner, R. M. 1976. *Concepts and theories of human development.* Reading, Mass.: Addison-Wesley.

Lerner, R. M. 1978. Nature, nurture, and dynamic interactionism. *Human development, 21,* 1–20.

Lerner, R. M. (Ed.). 1983. *Developmental psychology: Historical and philosophical perspectives.* Hillsdale, N.J.: Erlbaum.

Lerner, R. M. 1990. Plasticity, person-context relations, and cognitive training in aged years: A developmental contextual perspective. *Developmental Psychology, 26,* 911–915.

Lerner, R. M. 1991. Changing organism-context relations as the basic process of development: A developmental contextual perspective. *Developmental Psychology, 27,* 27–32.

Lerner, R. M., & Busch-Rossnagel, N. A. 1981. *Individuals as producers of their development.* New York: Academic Press.

Lerner, R. M., Iwaki, S., Chihara, T., & Sorell, G. T. 1980. Self-concept, self-esteem, and body attitudes among Japanese male and female adolescents. *Child Development, 51,* 847–855.

Lerner, R. M., Karson, M., Meisels, M., & Knapp, J. R. 1975. Actual and perceived attitudes of late adolescents and their parents: The phenomenon of the generation gaps. *Journal of Genetic Psychology, 126,* 195–207.

Lerner, R. M., & Lerner, J. V. 1977. Effects of age, sex, and physical attractiveness on child-peer relations, academic performance, and elementary school adjustment. *Developmental Psychology, 13,* 585–590.

Lessing, E. E., Zagorin, S. W., & Nelson, D. 1970. WISC subtest and IQ score correlates of father absence. *Journal of Genetic Psychology, 117,* 181–195.

Lester, B. M., Als, H., & Brazelton, T. B. 1982. Regional obstetric anesthesia and newborn behavior: A reanalysis toward synergistic effects. *Child Development, 53,* 687–692.

Lester, B. M., & Boukydis, C. F. Z. (Eds.). 1985. *Infant crying.* New York: Plenum.

Lester, B. M., Corwin, M. J., Sepkoski, C., Seifer, R., Peucker, M., McLaughlin, S., & Golub, H. L. 1991. Neurobehavioral syndromes in Cocaine-exposed newborn infants. *Child Development, 62,* 694–705.

Lester, B. M., & Dreher, M. 1989. Effects of marijuana use during pregnancy on newborn cry. *Child Development, 60,* 765–771.

Lester, B. M., Hoffman, J., & Brazelton, T. B. 1985. The rhythmic structure of mother-infant interaction in term and preterm infants. *Child Development, 56,* 15–27.

Lester, B. M., Kotelchuck, M., Spelke, E., Sellers, M. J., & Klein, R. E. 1974. Separation protest in Guatemalan infants: Cross-cultural and cognitive findings. *Developmental Psychology, 10,* 79–85.

Leung, E. H. L., & Rheingold, H. L. 1981. Development of pointing as a social gesture. *Developmental Psychology, 17,* 215–220.

LeVay, S. 1991. A difference in hypothalamic structure between heterosexual and homosexual men. *Science, 253,* 1034–1037.

Leventhal, G. S. 1970. Influence of brothers and sisters on sex-role behavior. *Journal of Personality and Social Psychology, 16,* 452–465.

Lever, J. 1978. Sex differences in the complexity of children's play and games. *American Sociological Review, 43,* 471–483.

Levine, A. 1987a. Mystics on main street. *U.S. News & World Report* (February 9), pp. 67–69.

Levine, A. 1987b. The uneven odds. *U.S. News & World Report* (August 17), pp. 31–33.

Levine, L. E. 1983. Mine: Self-definition in 2-year-old boys. *Developmental Psychology, 19,* 544–549.

Levine, R. 1990. Despite a rich decade, fewer New York teen-agers have their first job. *New York Times* (April 1), p. 20.

LeVine, R. A. 1970. Cross-cultural study in child psychology. In P. H. Mussen (Ed.), *Carmichael's manual of child psychology* (3rd ed.). New York: Wiley.

LeVine, R. A., Miller, P. M., & Maxwell, M. (Eds.). *Parental behavior in diverse societies.* San Francisco: Jossey-Bass.

Levinson, D. 1989. *Family violence in cross-cultural perspective.* Newbury Park, Calif.: Sage Publications.

Levinson, D. J. 1986. A conception of adult development. *American Psychologist, 41,* 3–13.

Levinson, D. J., Darrow, C. M., Klein, E. B., Levinson, M. H., & McKee, B. 1978. *The seasons of a man's life.* New York: Knopf.

Levinson, H. 1964. Money aside, why spend life working? *National Observer* (March 9), p. 20.

Levitsky, D. A. 1979. *Malnutrition, environment, and behavior.* Ithaca, N.Y.: Cornell University Press.

Levy, D. M. 1943. *Maternal overprotection.* New York: Columbia University Press.

Levy, G. D., & Carter, D. B. 1989. Gender schema, gender constancy, and gender-role knowledge: The roles of cognitive factors in preschooler's gender-role stereotype attributions. *Developmental Psychology, 25,* 444–449.

Levy, S. M. (Ed.). 1982. *Biological mediators of behavior and disease: Neoplasia.* New York: Elsevier Biomedical.

Levy, Y., Schlesinger, I. M., & Braine, M. D. S. (Eds.). 1988. *Categories and processes in language acquisition.* Hillsdale, N.J.: Erlbaum.

Levy-Shiff, R. 1982. The effects of father absence on young children in mother-headed families. *Child Development, 53,* 1400–1405.

Levy-Shiff, R., & Israelashvili, R. 1988. Antecedents of fathering: Some further exploration. *Developmental Psychology, 24,* 434–440.

Lewes, K. 1988. *The psychoanalytic theory of male homosexuality.* New York: Simon & Schuster.

Lewin, R. 1981. Is longevity a positive selection? *Science, 211,* 373.

Lewin, T. 1990a. Black children living with one parent put at 55 percent. *New York Times* (July 15), p. 11.

Lewin, T. 1990b. Drug use during pregnancy: New issue before the courts. *New York Times* (February 5), pp. A1, A12.

Lewin, T. 1990c. Plight of displaced homemakers is growing as many face poverty. *New York Times* (June 2), p. 13.

Lewin, T. 1990d. A question is raised about amniocentesis. *New York Times* (May 29), p. B8.

Lewin, T. 1990e. Too much retirement time? A move is afoot to change it. *New York Times* (April 22), pp. 1, 36.

Lewin, T. 1991a. Communities and their residents age gracefully. *New York Times* (July 21), pp. 1, 10.

Lewin, T. 1991b. As elderly population grows, so does the need for doctors. *New York Times* (May 31), pp. A1, A9.

Lewin, T. 1991c. Women found to be frequent victims of assaults by intimates. *New York Times* (January 17), p. A12.

Lewis, J. S. 1985. Fathers-to-be show signs of pregnancy. *New York Times* (April 3), p. 13.

Lewis, M. 1977. The busy, purposeful world of a baby. *Psychology Today, 10* (February), pp. 53–56.

Lewis, M. 1988. The socialization of emotions. In K. S. Friedman & J. Campos, (Eds.), *National Institutes of Child Health and Development workshop on the socialization of emotion.* Bethesda, MD.

Lewis, M., & Brooks-Gunn, J. 1979. *Social cognition and the acquisition of self.* New York: Plenum.

Lewis, M., & Michalson, L. 1983. *Children's emotions and moods.* New York: Plenum.

Lewis, M., & Saarni, C. (Eds.). 1985. *The socialization of emotions.* New York: Plenum.

Lewis, M., Stanger, C., & Sullivan, M. W. 1989. Deception in 3-year-olds. *Developmental Psychology, 25,* 439–443.

Lewis, M., & Starr, M. D. 1979. Developmental continuity. In J. D. Osofsky (Ed.), *Handbook of infant development.* New York: Wiley.

Lewis, M., Sullivan, M. W., Stanger, C., & Weiss, M. 1989. Self development and self-conscious emotions. *Child Development, 60,* 146–156.

Lewis, M., Young, G., Brooks, J., & Michalson, L. 1975. The beginning of friendship. In M. Lewis & L. A. Rosenblum (Eds.), *Friendship and peer relations.* New York: Wiley.

Lewis, M. M. 1936/1951. *Infant speech: A study of the beginnings of language.* London: Routledge & Kegan Paul.

Lewis, O. 1959. *Five families: Mexican case studies in the culture of poverty.* New York: Basic Books.

Lewis, O. 1961. *The children of Sanchez.* New York: Random House.

Lewis, O. 1966. *LaVida: A Puerto Rican family in the culture of poverty: San Juan and New York.* New York: Random House.

Lewis, T. L., Maurer, D., & Kay, D. 1978. Newborns' central vision: Whole or hole? *Journal of Experimental Child Psychology. 26,* 193–203.

Lewontin, R. C., Rose, S., & Kamin, L. J. 1984. *Not in our genes.* New York: Pantheon Books.

Liang, J., Dvorkin, L., Kahana, E., & Mazian, F. 1980. Social integration and morale: A reexamination. *Journal of Gerontology, 35,* 746–757.

Lichter, D. T. 1988. Racial differences in underemployment in American cities. *American Journal of Sociology, 93,* 771–792.

Lickona, T. 1976. Research on Piaget's theory of moral development. In T. Lickona (Ed.), *Moral development and behavior: Theory, research, and social issues.* New York: Holt, Rinehart and Winston.

Lieberman, M. A. 1975. Adaptive processes in late life. In N. Datan & L. H. Ginsberg (Eds.), *Life-span developmental psychology: Normative life crisis.* New York: Academic Press.

Lieberman, M. A., & Coplan, A. S. 1970. Distance from death as a variable in the study of aging. *Developmental Psychology, 2,* 71–84.

Lieberman, M. A., & Tobin, S. S. 1983. *The experience of old age: Stress, coping and survival.* New York: Basic Books.

Liebert, R. M., & Sprafkin, J. 1988. *The early window: Effects of television on children and youth* (3rd ed.). Oxford, England: Pergamon Press.

Liebow, E. 1967. *Tally's corner: A study of negro streetcorner men.* Boston: Little, Brown.

Liebowitz, M. R. 1983. *The chemistry of love.* Boston: Little, Brown.

Liederman, J., & Kinsbourne, M. 1980. The mechanism of neonatal rightward turning bias: A sensory or motor asymmetry? *Infant Behavior and Development, 3,* 223–238.

Limber, J. 1977. Language in child and chimp? *American Psychologist, 32,* 280–295.

Lind, S., Schoenbaum, S. C., Monson, R. R., Rosner, R., Stubblefield, P. C., & Ryan, K. J. 1983. The association of marijuana use with the outcome of pregnancy. *American Journal of Public Health, 73,* 1161–1164.

Lindsey, R. 1984. A new generation finds it hard to leave the nest. *New York Times* (January 25), p. 10.

Lindsey, R. 1987. Colleges accused of bias to stem Asians' gain. *New York Times* (January 19), p. 8.

Linn, S., Reznick, J. S., Kagan, J., & Hans, S. 1982. Salience of visual patterns in the human infant. *Developmental Psychology, 18,* 651–657.

Linney, J. A., & Seidman, E. 1989. The future of schooling. *American Psychologist, 44,* 336–340.

Linton, R. 1936. *The study of man.* New York: Appleton-Century-Crofts.

Lipinski, A. M. 1982. Nuclear war: The topic boggles a child's mind. *Columbus Dispatch* (July 16), p. C1.

Lipman, A. 1961. Role conceptions and morale of couples in retirement. *Journal of Gerontology, 16,* 267–271.

Lipset, S. M. 1989. Why youth revolt. *New York Times* (May 24), p. 27.

Lipsitt, L. P., & Levy, N. 1959. Electrotactual threshold in the neonate. *Child Development, 30,* 547–554.

Lipsyte, R. 1986. The athlete's losing game. *New York Times Magazine* (November 30), pp. 58–66.

Litwak, E., & Messeri, P. 1989. Organizational theory, social supports, and mortality rates: A theoretical convergence. *American Sociological Review, 54,* 49–66.

Livesley, W. J., & Bromley, D. B. 1973. *Person perception in childhood and adolescence.* New York: Wiley.

Lloyd, S. A. 1991. The darkside of courtship: Violence and sexual exploitation. *Family Relations, 40,* 14–20.

Lockshin, R. A., & Zakeri, Z. F. 1990. Programmed cell death: New thoughts and relevance to aging. *Journal of Gerontology, 45,* B135–140.

Loeb, R. C., Horst, L., & Horton, P. J. 1980. Family interaction patterns associated with self-esteem in preadolescent girls and boys. *Merrill-Palmer Quarterly, 26,* 205–217.

Loehlin, J. C. 1989. Partitioning environmental and genetic contributions to behavioral development. *American Psychologist, 44,* 1285–1292.

Loehlin, J. C., Horn, J. M., & Willerman, L. 1989. Modeling IQ change: Evidence from the Texas Adoption Project. *Child Development, 60,* 993–1004.

Loehlin, J. C., Lindzey, G., & Spuhler, J. N. 1975. *Race differences in intelligence.* San Francisco: Freeman.

Loehlin, J. C., Willerman, L., & Horn, J. M. 1988. Human behavior genetics. *Annual Review of Psychology, 39,* 101–133.

Lofland, L. 1978. *The craft of dying.* Beverly Hills: Sage.

Long, J., & Porter, K. L. 1984. Multiple roles of midlife women: A case for new directions in theory, research, and policy. In G. Baruch and J. Brooks-Gunn (Eds.), *Women in midlife.* New York: Plenum Press.

Long, E. C. J., & Andres, D. W. 1990. Perspective taking as a predictor of marital adjustment. *Journal of Personality and Social Psychology, 59,* 126–131.

Longino, C. F., Jr., & Crown, W. H. 1991. Older Americans: Rich or poor? *American Demographics, 13* (August), 48–52.

Longino, C. F., Jr., & Kart, C. S. 1982. Explicating activity theory: A formal replication. *Journal of Gerontology, 37,* 713–722.

Longshore, D., & Prager, J. 1985. The impact of school desegregation: A situational analysis. *Annual Review of Sociology, 11,* 75–91.

Lopata, H. Z. 1973. *Widowhood in an American city.* Cambridge, Mass.: Schenkman.

Lopata, H. Z. 1981. Widowhood and husband satisfaction. *Journal of Marriage and the Family, 43,* 439–450.

Loraine, J. A., Ismail, A. A. A., Adamopolous, D. A., & Dove, G. A. 1970. Endocrine function in male and female homosexuals. *British Medical Journal, 4,* 406–409.

Lord, L. J. 1987. An unholy war in the TV pulpits. *U.S. News & World Report* (April 6), pp. 58–65.

Lorence, J., & Mortimer, J. T. 1985. Job involvement through the life course: A panel study of three age groups. *American Sociological Review, 50,* 618–638.

Lorenz, K. Z. 1935. Imprinting. In R. C. Birney & R. C. Teevan (Eds.), *Instinct.* London: Van Nostrand, 1961.

Loughlin, K. A., & Daehler, M. W. 1973. The effects of distraction and added perceptual cues on the delayed reaction of very young children. *Child Development, 44,* 384–388.

Louv, R. 1991. *Childhood's future.* Boston: Houghton Mifflin.

Love, D. O., & Torrence, W. D. 1989. The impact of worker age on unemployment and earnings after plant closings. *Journal of Gerontology, 44,* S190–195.

Lovenheim, B. 1990. *Beating the marriage odds: When you are smart, single and over 35.* New York: Morrow.

Lovett, S. B., & Flavell, J. H. 1990. Understanding and remembering: Children's knowledge about the differential effects of strategy and task variables on comprehension and memorization. *Child Development, 61,* 1842–1858.

Lowenthal, M. F. 1964. Social isolation and mental illness in old age. *American Sociological Review, 29,* 54–70.

Lowenthal, M. F., & Haven, C. 1968. Interaction and adaptation: Intimacy as a critical variable. *American Sociological Review, 33,* 20–30.

Lowenthal, M. F., Thurner, M., & Chiriboga, D. 1975. *Four stages of life.* San Francisco: Jossey-Bass.

Lozoff, B. 1989. Nutrition and behavior. *American Psychologist, 44,* 231–236.

Lublin, J. 1991. Thomas battle spotlights harassment. *Wall Street Journal* (October 9), pp. B1, B4.

Ludemann, P. M., & Nelson, C. A. 1988. Categorical representation of facial expressions by 7-month-old infants. *Developmental Psychology, 24,* 492–501.

Luepnitz, D. A. 1982. *Child custody: A study of families after divorce.* Lexington, Mass.: Lexington Books.

Leuptow, L. B. 1984. *Adolescent sex roles and social change.* New York: Columbia University Press.

Luhmann, N. 1986. *Love as passion: The codification of intimacy.* Cambridge, Mass.: Harvard University Press.

Lumpkin, C. K., Jr., McClung, J. K., Pereira-Smith, O. M., & Smith, J. R. 1986. Existence of high abundance antiproliferative mRNA's in senescent human diploid fibroblasts. *Science, 232,* 393–395.

Lundstrom, M. 1990. Orphanges: Time to bring them back? *USA Today* (July 27), p. 6A.

Luster, T., Rhoades, K., & Haas, B. 1989. The relation between parental values and parenting behavior: A test of the Kohn hypothesis. *Journal of Marriage and the Family, 51,* 139–147.

Lynn, D. B. 1974. *The father: His role in child development.* Monterey, Calif.: Brooks/Cole.

Lynn, D. B. 1976. Fathers and sex-role development. *Family Coordinator, 25,* 400–409.

Lyons, R. D. 1983*a*. Health officials report herpes surge in newborns. *New York Times* (December 9), p. 8.

Lyons, R. D. 1983*b*. Sex in America: Conservative attitudes prevail. *New York Times* (October 4), pp. 17, 19.

Lytton, H. 1979. Disciplinary encounters between young boys and their mothers and fathers: Is there a contingency system? *Developmental Psychology, 15,* 256–268.

Lytton, H. 1980. *Parent-child interaction: The socialization process observed in twin and single families.* New York: Plenum.

Lytton, H., & Romney, D. M. 1991. Parents' differential socialization of boys and girls: A meta-analysis. *Psychological Bulletin, 109,* 267–296.

McCall, P. L. 1991. Adolescent and elderly white male suicide trends: Evidence of changing well-being? *Journal of Gerontology, 46,* S43-S51.

McCall, R. B. 1974. Exploratory manipulation and play in the human infant. *Monographs of the Society for Research in Child Development, 39* (2).

McCall, R. B. 1987. Roundtable: What is temperament? *Child Development, 58,* 524–526.

McCall, R. B., & Cool, S. J. 1976. Perceptual development. *Science, 193,* 478–479.

McCandless, B. R. 1970. *Adolescents: Behavior and development.* New York: Holt, Rinehart and Winston.

McCarthy, J. D., & Hoge, D. R. 1982. Analysis of age effects in longitudinal studies of adolescent self-esteem. *Developmental Psychology, 18,* 372–379.

McClelland, D. C. 1973. Testing for competence rather than for "intelligence." *American Psychologist, 28,* 1–14.

McClelland, D. C., Constantian, C. A., Regalado, D., and Stone, C. 1978. Making it to maturity. *Psychology Today, 12* (June), pp. 42+.

Maccoby, E. 1980. *Social development: Psychological growth and the parent-child relationship.* New York: Harcourt Brace Jovanovich.

Maccoby, E. E. 1961. The taking of adult roles in middle childhood. *Journal of Abnormal and Social Psychology, 63,* 493–503.

Maccoby, E. E. 1983. Social-emotional development and responses to stressors. In N. Garmezy & M. Rutter (Eds.), *Stress, coping, and development in children.* New York: McGraw-Hill.

Maccoby, E. E. 1988. Gender as a social category. *Developmental Psychology, 24,* 755–765.

Maccoby, E. E. 1990. Gender and relationships: A developmental account. *American Psychologist, 45,* 513–520.

Maccoby, E. E. 1991. Different reproductive strategies in males and females. *Child Development, 62,* 676–681.

Maccoby, E. E., Depner, C. E., & Mnookin, R. H. 1990. Coparenting in the second year after divorce. *Journal of Marriage and the Family, 52,* 141–155.

Maccoby, E. E., & Feldman, S. S. 1972. Mother-attachment and stranger-reactions in the third year of life. *Monographs of the Society for Research in Child Development, 37* (No. 1).

Maccoby, E. E., & Jacklin, C. N. 1974. *The Psychology of sex differences.* Stanford, Calif.: Stanford University Press.

Maccoby, E. E., & Jacklin, C. N. 1980. Sex differences in aggression: A rejoinder and reprise. *Child Development, 51,* 964–980.

Maccoby, E. E., & Jacklin, C. N. 1987. Gender segregation in childhood. In H. W. Reese (Ed.), *Advances in child development and behavior:* Vol. 20. New York: Academic Press.

Maccoby, E. E., & Maccoby, N. 1954. The interview: A tool of social science. In G. Lindzey (Ed.), *Handbook of social psychology.* Reading, Mass.: Addison-Wesley.

Maccoby, E. E., & Martin, J. A. 1983. Socialization in the context of the family: Parent-child interaction. In E. M. Hetherington (Ed.), *Handbook of child psychology.* Vol. 4: *Socialization, personality, and social development.* New York: Wiley.

Maccoby, E. E., & Masters, J. C. 1970. Attachment and dependency. In P. H. Mussen (Ed.), *Carmichael's manual of child psychology* (3rd ed.). New York: Wiley.

McCormick, C. M., & Maurer, D. M. 1988. Unimanual hand preferences in 6-month-olds: Consistency and relation to familial-handedness. *Infant Behavior & Development, 11,* 21–29.

McCoy, E. 1982. Children of single parents. *New York Times* (May 6), pp. 19, 21.

McCoy, E. 1988. Children through the ages. In K. Finsterbusch (Ed.), *Sociology 88/89.* Guilford, Conn.: Dushkin.

McCrea, F. B. 1983. The politics of menopause: The "discovery" of a deficiency disease. *Social Problems, 31,* 111–123.

McCrae, R. R., & Costa, P. T., Jr. 1988. Age, personality, and the spontaneous self-concept. *Journal of Gerontology, 43,* S177–S185.

MacDonald, K. B. 1988. *Social and personality development: An evolutionary synthesis.* New York: Plenum.

McDonald, R. L. 1968. The role of emotional factors in obstetric complications: A review. *Psychosomatic Medicine, 30,* 222–237.

McEnroe, J. 1991. Split-shift parenting. *American Demographics, 13* (February), 50–52.

MacEvoy, B., Lambert, W. W., Karlberg, P., Klackenberg-Larsson, I., & Klackenberg, G. 1988. Early affective antecedents of adult Type A behavior. *Journal of Personality and Social Psychology, 54,* 108–116.

McEwan, K. L., Costello, C. G., & Taylor, P. J. 1987. Adjustment to infertility. *Journal of Abnormal Psychology, 96,* 108–116.

MacEwen, K. E., & Barling, J. 1991. Effects of maternal employment experiences on children's behavior via mood, cognitive difficulties, and parenting behavior. *Journal of Marriage and the Family, 53,* 635–644.

McGilly, K., & Siegler, R. S. 1989. How children choose among serial recall strategies. *Child Development, 60,* 172–182.

McGilly, K., & Siegler, R. S. 1990. The influence of encoding and strategic knowledge on children's choices among serial recall strategies. *Developmental Psychology, 26,* 931–941.

McGloshen, T. H., & O'Bryant, S. L. 1988. The psychological well-being of older, recent widows. *Psychology of Women Quarterly, 12,* 99–116.

McGovern, M. A. 1990. Sensitivity and reciprocity in the play of adolescent mothers and young fathers with their infants. *Family Relations, 39,* 427–431.

McGraw, M. B. 1935. *Growth: A study of Johnny and Jimmy.* New York: Appleton-Century.

McGuire, K. D., & Weisz, J. R. 1982. Social cognition and behavior correlates of preadolescent chumship. *53,* 1478–1484.

McGurk, H., Turnure, C., & Creighton, S. J. 1977. Auditory-visual coordination in neonates. *Child Development, 48,* 138–143.

McKay, J., Sinisterra, L., McKay, A., Gomez, H., & Lloreda, P. 1978. Improving cognitive ability in chronically deprived children. *Science, 200* (April 21), 270–278.

McKenry, P. C., Walters, L. H., & Johnson, C. 1979. Adolescent pregnancy: A review of the literature. *Family Coordinator, 28,* 17–28.

McKenzie, B., & Over, R. 1983. Young infants fail to imitate facial and manual gestures. *Infant Behavior and Development, 6,* 85–96.

McKenzie, B. E., Tootell, H. E., & Day, R. H. 1980. Development of visual size constancy during the first year of human infancy. *Developmental Psychology, 16,* 63–174.

MacKinnon, C. E. 1989. An observational investigation of sibling interactions in married and divorced families. *Developmental Psychology, 25,* 36–44.

MacKinnon, D. W. 1975. IPAR's contribution to the conceptualization and study of creativity. In I. A. Taylor & J. W. Getzels (Eds.), *Perspectives in creativity*. Chicago: Aldine.

Mackintosh, E. 1982. Mysteries. *Science 82, 3* (October), p. 108.

Mackintosh, N.J. 1983. *Conditioning and associative learning*. Oxford Psychology Series, No. 3. Oxford: Clarendon Press.

Macklin, E. D. 1974. Going very steady. *Psychology Today, 8* (November), pp. 53–59.

McLanahan, S., & Booth, K. 1989. Mother-only families: Problems, prospects, and politics. *Journal of Marriage and the Family, 51*, 557–580.

McLanahan, S. S. 1983. Family structure and stress: A longitudinal comparison of two-parent and female-headed families. *Journal of Marriage and the Family, 45*, 347–357.

McLaughlin, S. D., Melber, B. D., Billy, J. G., Zimmerle, D. M., Winges, L. D., & Johnson, T. R. 1988. *The changing lives of American women*. Chapel Hill, N.C.: University of North Carolina Press.

McLaughlin, S. D., & Micklin, M. 1983. The timing of the first birth and changes in personal efficacy. *Journal of Marriage and the Family, 45*, 47–55.

McLeod, B. 1986. The Oriental express. *Psychology Today, 20* (July), 48–52.

McLoyd, V. C. 1989. Socialization and development in a changing economy: The effects of paternal job and income loss on children. *American Psychologist, 44*, 293–302.

McLoyd, V. C. 1990. The impact of economic hardship on black families and children: Psychological distress, parenting, and socioeconomic development. *Child Development, 61*, 311–346.

MacLusky, N. J., & Naftolin, F. 1981. Sexual differentiation of the central nervous system. *Science, 211*, 1294–1303.

McMauley, E., Kay, T., Ito, J., & Treder, R. 1987. The Turner syndrome: Cognitive deficits, affective discrimination, and behavior problems. *Child Development, 58*, 464–473.

McPherson, B., & Guppy, N. 1979. Preretirement life-style and the degree of planning for retirement. *Journal of Gerontology, 34*, 254–263.

MacTurk, R. H., McCarthy, M. E., Vietze, P. M., & Yarrow, L. J. 1987. *Developmental Psychology, 23*, 199–203.

Mactutus, C. F., & Fechter, L. D. 1984. Prenatal exposure to carbon monoxide: Learning and memory deficits. *Science, 223*, 409–411.

Madden, D. J. 1985. Adult age differences in memory-driven selective attention. *Developmental Psychology, 21*, 655–665.

Madden, D. J. 1990. Adult age differences in the time course of visual attention. *Journal of Gerontology, 45*, P9–P16.

Madden, N. A., & Slavin, R., F. 1983. Mainstreaming students with mild handicaps: Academic and social outcomes. *Review of Educational Research, 53*, 519–569.

Maddox, G. L. 1963. Activity and morale: A longitudinal study of selected elderly subjects. *Social Forces, 42*, 195–204.

Maddox, G. L. 1969. Disengagement theory: A critical evaluation. *The Gerontologist, 4*, 80–83.

Maddox, G. L., & Wiley, J. 1976. Scope, concepts and methods in the study of aging. In R. H. Binstock & E. Shanas (Eds.), *Handbook of aging and the social sciences*. New York: Van Nostrand.

Magaziner, J., Cadigan, D. A., Hebel, J. R., & Parry, R. E. 1988. Health and living arrangements among older women: Does living alone increase the risk of illness. *Journal of Gerontology, 43*, M127–133.

Makarenko, A. S. 1967. *The collective family: A handbook for Russian parents*. New York: Doubleday.

Makin, J., W., & Porter, R. H. 1989. Attractiveness of lactating females' breast odors to neonates. *Child Development, 60*, 803–810.

Malamuth, N. M. 1981. Rape proclivity among males. *Journal of Social Issues, 37*, 138–157.

Malamuth, N. M. 1983. Factors associated with rape predictors of laboratory aggression against women. *Journal of Personality and Social Psychology, 45*, 432–442.

Malatesta, C. Z., Culver, C., Tesman, J. R., & Shepard, B. 1989. The development of emotion expression during the first two years of life. *Monographs of the Society for Research in Child Development, 54* (Serial No. 219).

Malatesta, C. Z., Grigoryev, P., Lamb, C., Albin, M., & Culver, C. 1986. Emotion socialization and expressive development in preterm and full-term infants. *Child Development, 57*, 316–330.

Malcolm, A. H. 1986. Reassessing care of dying. *New York Times* (March 17), pp. 1, 13.

Malcolm, A. H. 1990. Giving death a hand: Rending issue. *New York Times* (June 9), 6A.

Malinak, D. P., Hoyt, M. F., & Patterson, V. 1979. Adults' reactions to the death of a parent: A preliminary study. *American Journal of Psychiatry, 136*, 1152–1156.

Malinowski, B. 1964. Parenthood—the basis of social structure. In R. Coser (Ed.), *The family: Its structure and functions*. New York: St. Martin's Press.

Maloney, L. D. 1982. Middle age. *U.S. News & World Report* (October 25), pp. 67–68.

Maloney, L. D. 1983. A new understanding of death. *U.S. News & World Report* (July 11), pp. 62–65.

Mann, J. 1983. One-parent family: The troubles and the joys. *Newsweek* (November 28), pp. 57–62.

Mannheim, K. 1952. The problem of generations. In K. Mannheim (Ed.), *Essays on the sociology of knowledge*. London: Routledge and Kegan Paul.

Manton, K. G., Siegler, I. C., & Woodbury. 1986. Patterns of intellectual development in later life. *Journal of Gerontology, 41*, 486–499.

Maracek, J., & Mettee, D. R. 1972. Avoidance of continued success as a function of self-esteem, level of esteem certainty, and responsibility for success. *Journal of Personality and Social Psychology, 22*, 98–107.

Maratsos, M. P. 1973. Nonegocentric communication abilities in preschool children. *Child Development, 44*, 697–700.

Marby, M. 1989. Inside the golden arches. *Newsweek* (December 18), pp. 46–47.

Marcos, A. C., Bahr, S. J., & Johnson, R. E. 1986. Test of a bonding/association theory of adolescent drug use. *Social Forces, 65*, 135–161.

Markides, K. S., & Martin, H. W. 1979. A causal model of life satisfaction among the elderly. *Journal of Gerontology, 34*, 86–93.

Markman, E. M. 1987. How children constrain the possible meanings of words. In U. Neisser (Ed.), *Concepts and conceptual development: Ecological and intellectual factors in categorization*. Cambridge: Cambridge University Press.

Markman, E. M., & Hutchinson, J. W. 1984. Children's sensitivity to constraints on word meaning: Taxonomic vs. thematic relations. *Cognitive Psychology, 16*, 1–27.

Marks, C. 1991. The urban underclass. *Annual Review of Sociology, 17*, 445–466.

Markus, H. 1977. Self-schemata and processing information about the self. *Journal of Personality and Social Psychology, 35*, 63–78.

Marotz-Baden, R., Adams, G. R., Bueche, N., Munro, B., & Munro, G. 1979. Family form or family process? Reconsidering the deficit family model approach. *Family Coordinator, 28*, 5–14.

Marshall, V. W. 1980. *Last chapters: A sociology of aging and dying*. Belmont, Calif.: Wadsworth.

Martel, L. F., & Biller, H. B. 1987. *Stature and stigma: The biopsychosocial development of short males*. Lexington, Mass.: Lexington Books.

Martin, C. L. 1989. Children's use of gender-related information in making social judgments. *Developmental Psychology, 25*, 80–88.

Martin, C. L., & Halverson, C. F., Jr. 1981. A schematic processing model of sex typing and stereotyping in children. *Child Development, 52*, 1119–1134.

Martin, C. L., & Little, J. K. 1990. The relation of gender understanding to children's sex-typed preferences and gender stereotypes. *Child Development, 61*, 1427–1439.

Martin, C. L., Wood, C. H., & Little, J. K. 1990. The development of gender stereotype components. *Child Development, 61*, 1891–1904.

Martin, J. A. 1981. A longitudinal study of the consequences of early mother-infant interaction. *Monographs of the Society for Research in Child Development, 46* (190).

Martin, L. G. 1989. *The graying of Japan*. Washington, D.C.: Population Reference Bureau.

Martin, M. J., & Walters, J. 1982. Familial correlates of selected types of child abuse and neglect. *Journal of Marriage and the Family, 44*, 267–276.

Martin, T. C., & Bumpass, L. L. 1989. Recent trends in marital disruption. *Demography, 26*, 37–51.

Martorano, S. C. 1977. A developmental analysis of performance on Piaget's formal operations tasks. *Developmental Psychology, 13*, 666–672.

Martz, L. 1990. A dirty drug secret: Hyping instant addiction doesn't help. *Newsweek* (February 19), pp. 74–77.

Maruyama, G., Miller, N., & Holtz, R. 1986. The relation between popularity and achievement: A longitudinal test of the lateral transmission of value hypothesis. *Journal of Personality and Social Psychology, 51,* 730–741.

Marx, J. 1991. Alzheimer's research moves to mice. *Science, 253,* 266–267.

Marx, J. L. 1982. Autoimmunity in left-handers. *Science, 217,* 141–144.

Marx, J. L. 1984. The riddle of development. *Science* (December 21), 1406–1408.

Marx, J. L. 1988. Sexual responses are—almost—all in the brain. *Science, 241,* 903–904.

Marx, K. 1844. Estranged labour—economic and philosophic manuscripts of 1844. In C. W. Mills (Ed.), *Images of man.* New York: Braziller, 1960.

Maslow, A. H. 1955. Deficiency motivation and growth motivation. In M. R. Jones (Ed.), *Nebraska Symposium on Motivation.* Lincoln: University of Nebraska Press.

Maslow, A. H. 1967. Self-actualization and beyond. In J. F. T. Bugental (Ed.), *Challenges of humanistic psychology.* New York: McGraw-Hill.

Maslow, A. H. 1968. *Toward a psychology of being* (2nd ed.). New York: Van Nostrand.

Maslow, A. H. 1970. *Motivation and personality* (2nd ed.). New York: Harper & Row.

Massari, D. J., & Rosenblum, D. C. 1972. Locus of control, interpersona trust and academic achievement. *Psychological Reports, 31,* 355–360.

Massey, D. S. 1990. American apartheid: Segregation and the making of the underclass. *American Journal of Sociology, 96,* 329–357.

Masters, J. C. 1979. Interpreting "imitative" responses in early infancy. *Science, 205,* 215.

Masters, J. C., & Carlson, C. R. 1984. Children's and adults' understanding of the causes and consequences of emotional states. In C. Izard, J. Kagan, & R. Zajonc (Eds.), *Emotions, cognition and behavior.* New York: Cambridge University Press.

Masters, J. C., & Furman, W. 1981. Popularity, individual friendship selection, and specific peer interaction among children. *Developmental Psychology, 17,* 344–350.

Masters, W. H., & Johnson, V. E. 1966. *Human sexual response.* Boston: Little, Brown.

Matarazzo, J. D. 1990. Psychological assessment versus psychological testing: Validation from Binet to the school, clinic, and courtroom. *American Psychologist, 45,* 999–1017.

Mathew, A., & Cook, M. 1990. The control of reaching movements by young infants. *Child Development, 61,* 1238–1257.

Maton, K. I. 1989. The stress-buffering role of spiritual support: Cross-sectional and prospective investigations. *Journal of the Scientific Study of Religion, 28,* 310–323.

Matras, J. 1975. *Social inequality, stratification, and mobility.* Englewood Cliffs, N.J.: Prentice-Hall.

Matsueda, R. L., & Heimer, K. 1987. Race, family structure, and delinquency. *American Sociological Review, 52,* 826–840.

Mattessich, P. & Hill, R. L. 1987. Life cycle and family development. In M. B. Sussman & S. K. Steinmetz (Eds.), *Handbook of marriage and the family.* New York: Plenum.

Matthews, A. M., & Brown, K. H. 1987. Retirement as a critical life event. *Research on Aging, 9,* 548–571.

Matthews, K. A. 1982. Psychological perspectives on the Type A behavior pattern. *Psychological Bulletin, 91,* 293–323.

Matthews, K. A. 1988. Coronary heart disease and Type A behaviors: Update on and alternative to the Booth-Kewley and Friedman (1987) quantitative review. *Psychological Bulletin, 104,* 373–380.

Matthews, K. A., & Rodin, J. 1989. Women's changing work roles. *American Psychologist, 44,* 1389–1393.

Matthews, S. H., & Sprey, J. 1985. Adolescents' relationships with grandparents. An empirical contribution to conceptual clarification. *Journal of Gerontology, 40,* 621–626.

Maurer, D. M., & Maurer, C. E. 1976. Newborn babies see better than you think. *Psychology Today, 10* (October), pp. 85–88.

Maurer, D. M., & Salapatek, P. 1976. Developmental changes in the scanning of faces by young infants. *Child Development, 47,* 523–527.

Mayer, S. E., & Jencks, C. 1989. Growing up in poor neighborhoods: How much does it matter? *Science, 243,* 1441–1145.

Mazess, R. B., & Forman, S. H. 1979. Longevity and age exaggeration in Vilcabamba, Ecuador. *Journal of Gerontology, 34,* 94–98.

Mead, G. H. 1934. *Mind, self, and other.* Chicago: University of Chicago Press.

Mead, M. 1935. *Sex and temperament in three primitive societies.* New York: Morrow.

Mead, M. 1949. *Male and female.* New York: Morrow.

Mead, M., & MacGregor, F. C. 1951. *Growth and culture: A photographic study of Balinese childhood.* New York: Putnam.

Mead, M., & Newton, N. 1967. Fatherhood. In S. A. Richardson & A. F. Guttmacher (Eds.), *Childbearing—its social and psychological aspects.* Baltimore: Williams and Wilkins.

Mechanic, D., & Hansell, S. 1989. Divorce, family conflict, and adolescents' well-being. *Journal of Health and Social Behavior, 30,* 105–116.

Medawar, P. B. 1977. Unnatural science. *New York Review of Books, 24* (February 3), pp. 13–18.

Meddis, S. 1989. Drug arrest rate higher for blacks. *USA Today* (December 20), p. 1A.

Meer, J. 1986. The reason of age. *Psychology Today, 20* (June), pp. 60–64.

Meier, B. 1987. Companies wrestle with threats to workers' reproductive health. *Wall Street Journal* (February 5), p. 21.

Melton, G. B., & Limber, S. 1989. Psychologists' involvement in cases of child maltreatment: Limits of role and expertise. *American Psychologist, 44,* 1225–1233.

Meltzoff, A. N. 1988a. Imitation of televised models by infants. *Child Development, 59,* 1221–1229.

Meltzoff, A. N. 1988b. Infant imitation and memory: Nine-month-olds in immediate and deferred tests. *Child Development, 59,* 217–225.

Meltzoff, A. N. 1988c. Infant imitation after a 1-week delay: Long-term memory for novel acts and multiple stimuli. *Developmental Psychology, 24,* 470–476.

Meltzoff, A. N., & Moore, M. K. 1977. Imitation of facial and manual gestures by human neonates. *Science, 198,* 75–78.

Meltzoff, A. N., & Moore, M. K. 1979. Interpreting "imitative" responses in early infancy. *Science, 205,* 217–219.

Meltzoff, A. N., & Moore, M. K. 1983. Methodological issues in studies of imitation: Comments on McKenzie & Over and Koepke et al. *Infant Behavior and Development, 6,* 103–108.

Metlzoff, A. N., & Moore, M. K. 1989. Imitation in newborn infants: Exploring the range of gestures imitated and the underlying mechanisms. *Developmental Psychology, 25,* 954–962.

Menaghan, E. G. 1983. Marital stress and family transitions: A panel analysis. *Journal of Marriage and the Family, 45,* 371–386.

Menaghan, E. G., & Parcel, T. L. 1990. Parental employment and family life: Research in the 1980s. *Journal of Marriage and the Family, 52,* 1079–1098.

Menaghan, E. G., & Parcel, T. L. 1991. Determining children's home environments: The impact of maternal characteristics and current occupational and family conditions. *Journal of Marriage and the Family, 53,* 417–431.

Mendelson, B. K., & White, D. R. 1985. Development of self-body-esteem in overweight youngsters. *Developmental Psychology, 21,* 90–96.

Mendes, H. A. 1976. Single fathers. *Family Coordinator, 25,* 439–444.

Menken, J., Trussell, J., & Larsen, U. 1986. Age and infertility. *Science, 233,* 1389–1394.

Mercer, R. T., Nichols, E. G., & Doyle, G. C. 1989. *Transitions in a woman's life: Major life events in developmental context.* New York: Springer.

Meredith, D. 1985. Dad and the kids. *Psychology Today, 19* (June), pp. 62–67.

Meredith, H. V. 1973. Somatological development. In B. B. Wolman (Ed.), *Handbook of general psychology.* Englewood Cliffs, N.J.: Prentice-Hall.

Merton, R. K. 1968. *Social theory and social structure* (enlarged ed.). New York: Free Press.

Mervis, C. B. 1985. On the existence of prelinguistic categories: A case study. *Infant Behavior and Development, 8,* 293–300.

Messer, D. J., McCarthy, M. E., McQuiston, S., MacTurk, R. H., Yarrow, L. J., & Vietze, P. M. 1986. Relation between mastery behavior in infancy and competence in early childhood. *Child Psychology, 22,* 366–372.

Meyer, C., & Taylor, S. 1986. Adjustment to rape. *Journal of Personality and Social Psychology, 50,* 1226–1234.

Michaels, G. Y., & Goldberg, W. A. (Eds.). 1988. *The transition to parenthood: Cur-*

rent theory and research. New York: Cambridge University Press.

Mickelson, R. A. 1990. The attitude-achievement paradox among black adolescents. *Sociology of Education, 63,* 44–61.

Midlarsky, E., Bryan, J. H., & Brickman, P. 1973. Aversive approval: Interactive effects of modeling and reinforcement on altruistic behavior. *Child Development, 44,* 321–328.

Midlarsky, E., & Hannah, M. E. 1985. Competence, reticence, and helping by children and adolescents. *Developmental Psychology, 21,* 534–541.

Miles, S. H., Singer, P. A., & Siegler, M. 1989. Conflicts between patients' wishes to forego treatment and the policies of health care facilities. *New England Journal of Medicine, 321,* 48–50.

Mileski, M., & Black, D. 1972. The social organization of homosexuality. *Urban Life and Culture, 1,* 187–199.

Milgram, S. 1974. *Obedience to authority.* New York: Harper & Row.

Miller, B., & McFall, S. 1991. The effect of caregiver's burden on change in frail older persons' use of formal helpers. *Journal of Health and Social Behavior, 32,* 165–179.

Miller, B. C. 1976. A multivariate developmental model of marital satisfaction. *Journal of Marriage and the Family, 38,* 643–657.

Miller, B. C., & Bingham, C. R. 1989. Family configuration in relation to the sexual behavior of female adolescents. *Journal of Marriage and the Family, 51,* 499–506.

Miller, B. C., & Moore, K. A. 1990. Adolescent sexual behavior, pregnancy, and parenting: Research through the 1980s. *Journal of Marriage and the Family, 52,* 1025–1044.

Miller, B. C., & Sollie, D. L. 1980. Normal stresses during the transition to parenthood. *Family Relations, 29,* 459–465.

Miller, E. 1981. Elevated maternal hemoglobin A in early pregnancy and major congenital anomalies in infants of diabetic mothers. *New England Journal of Medicine, 304,* 1331–1334.

Miller, J., Slomczynski, K. M., & Kohn, M. L. 1985. Continuity of learning-generalization: The effect of jobs on men's intellective process in the United States and Poland. *American Journal of Sociology, 91,* 593–615.

Miller, J. G., & Bersoff, D. M. 1988. When do American children and adults reason in social conventional terms? *Developmental Psychology, 24,* 366–375.

Miller, M. W. 1985. Study says birth defects more frequent in areas polluted by technology firms. *Wall Street Journal* (January 17), p. 6.

Miller, M. W. 1986. Effects of alcohol on the generation and migration of cerebral cortical neurons. *Science, 233,* 1308–1311.

Miller, N., & Brewer, M. B. (Eds.). 1984. *Groups in contact: The psychology of desegregation.* Orlando, Fla.: Academic Press.

Miller, N., & Maruyama, G. 1976. Ordinal position and peer popularity. *Journal of Personality and Social Psychology, 33,* 123–131.

Miller, N. E. 1983. Behavioral medicine: Symbiosis between laboratory and clinic. *Annual Review of Psychology, 34,* 1–31.

Miller, P., Danaher, D., & Forbes, D. 1986. Sex-related strategies for coping with interpersonal conflict in children aged five and seven. *Developmental Psychology, 22,* 543–548.

Miller, P. H., & Aloise, P. A. 1989. Young children's understanding of the psychological causes of behavior: A review. *Child Development, 60,* 257–285.

Miller, R. A. 1989. The cell biology of aging: Immunological models. *Journal of Gerontology, 44,* B4–8.

Miller, S. A. 1986. Certainty and necessity in the understanding of Piagetian concepts. *Developmental Psychology, 22,* 3–18.

Miller, S. A. 1988. Parents' beliefs about children's cognitive development. *Child Development, 59,* 259–285.

Miller, S. J. 1965. The social dilemma of the aging leisure participant. In A. M. Rose & W. A. Peterson (Eds.), *Older people and their social world.* Philadelphia: Davis.

Miller-Jones, D. 1989. Culture and testing. *American Psychologist, 44,* 360–366.

Mills, D. M. 1984. A model for stepfamily development. *Family Relations, 33,* 365–372.

Milne, A. M., Myers, D. E., Rosenthal, A. S., & Ginsburg, A. 1986. Single parents, working mothers, and the educational achievement of school children. *Sociology of Education, 59,* 125–139.

Milne, L. 1924. *The home of an eastern clan.* Oxford: Clarendon Press.

Mindel, C. H., & Vaughan, C. E. 1978. A multidimensional approach to religiosity and disengagement. *Journal of Gerontology, 33,* 103–108.

Minerbrook, S. 1990. Crack dealers' rotten lives. *U.S. News & World Report* (November 12), pp. 36–38.

Mintz, S., & Kellogg, S. 1988. *Domestic revolutions: A social history of American family life.* New York: Free Press.

Mirowsky, J., & Ross, C. E. 1990. Control or defense? Depression and the sense of control over good and bad outcomes. *Journal of Health and Social Behavior, 31,* 71–86.

Mischel, W. 1968. *Personality and assessment.* New York: Wiley.

Mischel, W. 1969. Continuity and change in personality. *American Psychologist, 24,* 1012–1018.

Mischel, W. 1970. Sex-typing and socialization. In P. H. Mussen (Ed.), *Carmichael's manual of child psychology* (3rd ed.), Vol. 2. New York: Wiley.

Mischel, W. 1971. *Introduction to personality.* New York: Holt, Rinehart and Winston.

Mischel, W. 1973. Toward a cognitive social learning reconceptualization of personality. *Psychological Review, 80,* 252–283.

Mischel, W. 1977. On the future of personality measurement. *American Psychologist, 32,* 246–254.

Mischel, W. 1985. Diagnosticity of situations. Paper presented at the October meeting of the Society for Experimental Social Psychology, Evanston, Ill.

Mischel, W., & Mischel, H. N. 1976. A cognitive social learning approach to moral-

ity and self-regulation. In T. Lickona (Ed.), *Moral development and behavior: Theory, research, and social issues.* New York: Holt, Rinehart and Winston.

Mischel, W., Shoda, Y., & Peake, P. K. 1988. The nature of adolescent competencies predicted by preschool delay of gratification. *Journal of Personality and Social Psychology, 54,* 687–696.

Mitchell, B. A., Wister, A. V., & Burch, T. K. 1989. The family environment and leaving the parental home. *Journal of Marriage and the Family, 51,* 605–613.

Mitchell, D. B., & Perlmutter, M. 1986. Semantic activation and episodic memory: Age similarities and differences. *Developmental Psychology, 22,* 86–94.

Mitchell, D. R., & Lyles, K. W. 1990. Glucocorticoid-induced osteoporosis: Mechanisms for bone loss: Evaluation of strategies for prevention. *Journal of Gerontology, 45,* M153–158.

Mitchell, J. E., Baker, L. A., & Jacklin, C. N. 1989. Masculinity and femininity in twin children: Genetic and environmental factors. *Child Development, 60,* 1475–1485.

Mittenhal, S. 1986. Kindergarten: Starting older and wiser. *New York Times* (November 20), pp. 19, 20.

Modell, J. 1989. *Into one's own: From youth to adulthood in the United States, 1920-1975.* Berkeley, Calif.: University of California Press.

Moen, P. 1991. Transitions in mid-life: Women's work and family roles in the 1970s. *Journal of Marriage and the Family, 53,* 135–150.

Moen, P., Dempster-McClain, D., & Williams, R. M., Jr. 1989. Social integration and longevity: An event history and analysis of women's role and resilience. *American Sociological Review, 54,* 635–647.

Moffitt, T. E., Caspi, A., Belsky, J., & Silva, P. A. Childhood experience and the onset of menarche: A test of a sociobiological model. *Child Development, 63,* 47–58.

Mogul, K. M. 1979. Women in midlife: Decisions, rewards, and conflicts related to work and careers. *American Journal of Psychiatry, 136,* 1139–1143.

Molotsky, I. 1986. Surgeon General, citing risks, urges smoke-free workplace. *New York Times* (December 17), p. 14.

Money, J. 1987. Sin, sickness, or status? Homosexual gender identity and psychoneuroendocrinology. *American Psychologist, 42,* 384–399.

Money, J., & Ehrhardt, A. 1972. *Man and woman; boy and girl.* Baltimore: Johns Hopkins University Press.

Money, J., & Tucker, P. 1975. *Sexual signatures: On being a man or a woman.* Boston: Little, Brown.

Monmaney, T. 1987. One for the heart. *Newsweek* (June 29), pp. 56–57.

Montagu, A. 1964. *Life before birth.* New York: New American Library.

Montagu, A. 1981. *Growing young.* New York: McGraw-Hill.

Montemayor, R. 1982. The relationship between parent-adolescent conflict and the amount of time adolescents spend alone and with parents and peers. *Child Development, 53,* 1512–1519.

Montemayor, R., & Eisen, M. 1977. The development of self-conceptions from childhood to adolescence. *Developmental Psychology, 13,* 314–319.

Montepare, J. M., & Lachman, M. E. 1989. "You're only as old as you feel": Self-perceptions of age, fears of aging, and life satisfaction from adolescence to old age. *Psychology and Aging, 4,* 73–78.

Moore, C., Bryant, D., & Furrow, D. 1989. Mental terms and the development of certainty. *Child Development, 60,* 167–171.

Moore, D. 1981. The perils of a two-income family. *New York Times Magazine* (September 27), pp. 91–96.

Moore, D. 1983. America's neglected elderly. *New York Times Magazine* (January 30), pp. 30–35.

Moore, D. 1984. It's either me or your job! *Working Woman* (April), pp. 108–111.

Moore, E. G. J. 1986. Family socialization and the IQ test performance of traditionally and transracially adopted black children. *Developmental Psychology, 22,* 317–326.

Moore, S. W. 1989. The need for a unified theory of political learning: Lessons from a longitudinal project. *Human Development, 32,* 5–13.

Moorehouse, M. J. 1991. Linking maternal employment patterns to mother-child activities and children's school competence. *Developmental Psychology, 27,* 295–303.

Moran, J. D. III, Milgram, R. M., Sawyers, J. K., & Fu, V. R. 1983. Original thinking in pre-school children. *Child Development, 54,* 921–926.

Mordkowitz, E. R., & Ginsburg, H. P. 1987. Early academic socialization of successful Asian-American college students. *Quarterly Newsletter of the Laboratory on Comparative Human Cognition, 9,* 85–91.

Morgan, D. L. 1988. Age differences in social network participation. *Journal of Gerontology, 43,* S129–137.

Morgan, G. A., & Ricciuti, H. N. 1969. Infants' responses to strangers during the first year. In B. M. Foss (Ed.), *Determinants of infant behavior* (Vol. 4). New York: Wiley.

Morgan, W. G. 1973. Situational specificity in altruistic behavior. *Representative Research in Social Psychology, 4,* 56–66.

Morin, C. M., & Gramling, S. E. 1989. Sleep patterns and aging: Comparison of older adults with and without insomnia complaints. *Psychology and Aging, 4,* 290–294.

Morin, S. F., & Garfinkle, E. M. 1978. Male homophobia. *Journal of Social Issues, 34,* 29–47.

Moritz, D. J., Kasl, S. V., & Berkman, L. F. 1989. The health impact of living with a cognitively impaired elderly spouse: Depressive symptoms and social functioning. *Journal of Gerontology, 44,* S17–27.

Morokoff, P. J. 1985. Effects of sex guilt, repression, sexual "arousability," and sexual experience on female sexual arousal during erotica and fantasy. *Journal of Personality and Social Psychology, 49,* 177–187.

Morrow, K. B., & Sorell, G. T. 1989. Factors affecting self-esteem, depression, and negative behaviors in sexually abused female adolescents. *Journal of Marriage and the Family, 51,* 677–686.

Morse, N. C., & Weiss, R. S. 1955. The function and meaning of work and the job. *American Sociological Review, 20,* 191–198.

Mortimer, J. T., & Simmons, R. G. 1978. Adult socialization. *Annual Review of Sociology, 4,* 421–454.

Morton, J., Johnson, M. H., & Maurer, D. 1990. On the reasons for newborns' responses to faces. *Infant Behavior and Development, 13,* 99–103.

Moses, L. J., & Flavell, J. H. 1990. Inferring false beliefs from actions and reactions. *Child Development, 61, 929–945.*

Moshman, D. 1977. Consolidation and stage formation in the emergence of formal operations. *Developmental Psychology, 13,* 95–100.

Moskowitz, B. A. 1978. The acquisition of language. *Scientific American, 239* (November), pp. 92–108.

Moss, H. A., & Susman, E. J. 1980. Constancy and change in personality development. In O. G. Brim, Jr., & J. Kagan (Eds.), *Constancy and change in human development.* Cambridge, Mass.: Harvard University Press.

Moss, M., Colombo, J., Mitchell, D. W., & Horwitz, F. D. 1988. Neonatal behavioral organization and visual processing at three months. *Child Development, 59,* 1211–1220.

Moss, R. J. 1987. The face of abuse. *Psychology Today, 21* (July), p. 20.

Mottaz, C. J. 1985. The relative importance of intrinsic and extrinsic rewards as determinants of work satisfaction. *The Sociological Quarterly, 26,* 365–385.

MOW International Research Team. 1987. *The meaning of working.* London: Academic Press.

Mowsesian, R. 1987. *Golden goals, rusted realities.* New York: New Horizon/Macmillan.

Moyles, E. W., & Wolins, M. 1971. Group care and intellectual development. *Developmental Psychology, 4,* 370–380.

Mueller, E., & Brenner, J. 1977. The origins of social skills and interaction among playgroup toddlers. *Child Development, 48,* 854–861.

Mueller, E. C., & Cooper, C. R. (Eds.). 1986. *Process and outcome in peer relationships.* Orlando, Fla.: Academic Press.

Mueller, E. & Lucas, T. 1975. A developmental analysis of peer interaction among toddlers. In M. Lewis & L. A. Rosenblum (Eds.), *Friendship and peer relations.* New York: Wiley.

Mueller, R. F. 1983. Evaluation of a protocol for post-mortem examination of stillbirths. *New England Journal of Medicine, 309,* 586–590.

Mueller, P. F., Campbell, H. E., Graham, W. E., Brittain, H., Fitzgerald, J. A., Hogan, N. A., Muller, V. H., & Ritterhouse, A. H. 1971. Perinatal factors and their relationship to mental retardation and other parameters of development. *American Journal of Obstetrics and Gynecology, 109,* 1205–1210.

Murdock, G. P. 1934. *Our primitive contemporaries.* New York: Macmillan.

Murdock, G. P. 1935. Comparative data on the division of labor by sex. *Social Forces, 15,* 551–553.

Murdock, G. P. 1949. *Social structure.* New York: Macmillan.

Murdock, G. P. 1957. Anthropology as a comparative science. *Behavioral Science, 2,* 249–254.

Murdock, G. P., Ford, C. S., Hudson, A. E., Kennedy, R., Simmons, L. W., & Whiting, J. W. M. 1971. *Outline of cultural materials.* New Haven: Human Relations Area Files.

Murphy, C., & Withee, J. 1986. Age-related differences in the pleasantness of chemosensory stimuli. *Psychology and Aging, 1,* 312–318.

Murphy, C. M. 1978. Pointing in the context of a shared activity. *Child Development, 49,* 371–380.

Murphy, G., Murphy, L. B., & Newcomb, T. 1937. *Experimental social psychology.* New York: Harper & Row.

Murphy, L. B. 1937. *Social behavior and child personality.* New York: Columbia University Press.

Murphy, M. D., Sanders, R. E., Gabriesheski, A. S., & Schmitt, F. A. 1981. Metamemory in the aged. *Journal of Gerontology, 36,* 185–193.

Murray, A. D., Dolby, R. M., Nation, R. L., & Thomas, D. B. 1981. Effects of epidural anesthesia on newborns and their mothers. *Child Development, 52,* 71–82.

Murrell, S. A. & Himmelfarb, S. 1989. Effects of attachment bereavement and pre-event conditions on subsequent depressive symptoms in older adults. *Psychology and Aging, 4,* 166–172.

Murrell, S. A., Himmelfarb, S., & Phifer, J. 1988. Effects of bereavement/loss and pre-event status on subsequent physical health in older adults. *International Journal of Aging and Human Development, 27,* 89–107.

Muson, H. 1979. Moral thinking: Can it be taught? *Psychology Today, 12* (February), pp. 48 +.

Mussen, P. H., Harris, S., Rutherford, R., & Keasey, C. B. 1970. Honesty and altruism among preadolescents. *Developmental Psychology, 3,* 169–194.

Mussen, P. H., Honzik, M. P., & Eichorn, D. H. 1982. Early adult antecedents of life satisfaction at age 70. *Journal of Gerontology, 37,* 316–322.

Mussen, P. H., & Jones, M. C. 1957. Self-conceptions, motivations, and interpersonal attitudes of late- and early-maturing boys. *Child Development, 28,* 243–256.

Musto, D. F. 1987. AIDS and panic: Enemies within. *Wall Street Journal* (April 26), p. 34.

Mydans, S. 1990. Science and the courts take a new look at motherhood. *New York Times* (November 4), p. 6E.

Myers, D. A. 1991. Work after cessation of career job. *Journal of Gerontology, 46,* S93–102.

Mynatt, C., & Sherman, S. J. 1975. Responsibility attribution in groups and individuals: A direct test of the diffusion of responsibility hypothesis. *Journal of Personality and Social Psychology, 32,* 1111–1118.

Nadel, S. F. 1951. *The foundations of social anthropology.* New York: Free Press.

Naeye, R. L. 1980. Sudden infant death. *Scientific American, 242* (April), pp. 56–62.

Namuth, T. 1991. The good, the bad and the difference. *Newsweek Special Issue* (Summer), pp. 48–50.

Nassi, A. J., & Abramowitz, S. I. 1979. Transition or transformation? Personal and political development of former Berkeley Free Speech Movement activists. *Journal of Youth and Adolescence, 8,* 21–35.

National Academy of Sciences. 1982. *Marijuana and health.* Washington, D.C.: National Academy Press.

National Center for Education Statistics. 1983. *High school and beyond.* Washington, D.C.: Government Printing Office.

National Center for Health Statistics. 1986. *Aging in the eighties, impaired senses for sound and light in persons age 65 and over* (Advance Data from Vital and Health Statistics, No. 125, DHHS Publ. No. PHs 86–1250). Washington, D.C.: Government Printing Office.

National Centers for Disease Control. 1984. Press release, March 22—on breast feeding.

The National Commission on Excellence in Education. 1983. *A nation at risk: The imperative for educational reform.* Washington, D.C.: Department of Education.

National Commission on Youth. 1980. *The transition of youth to adulthood: A bridge too long.* Boulder, Colo.: Westview Press.

National Research Council. 1987. *Risking the future: Adolescent sexuality, pregnancy, and childbearing.* Washington, D.C.: National Academy Press.

National Task Force on Education for Economic Growth. 1983. *Action for excellence: A comprehensive plan to improve our nation's schools.* Denver: Education Commission of the States.

Naus, M. J., Ornstein, P. A., & Kreshtool, K. 1977. Developmental differences in recall and recognition: The relationship between rehearsal and memory as test expectation changes. *Journal of Experimental Child Psychology, 23,* 252–265.

Nazario, S. L. 1989. Mormon rules aid long life, study discloses. *Wall Street Journal* (December 6), p. B4.

Nazario, S. L. 1990. Midwifery is staging revival as demand for prenatal care, low-tech births rises. *Wall Street Journal* (September 25), pp. B1, B5.

Needle, R. H., Su, S. S., & Doherty, W. J. 1990. Divorce, remarriage, and adolescent substance use: A prospective longitudinal study. *Journal of Marriage and the Family, 52,* 157–169.

Neimark, E. D. 1974. Intellectual development during adolescence. In F. Horowitz (Ed.), *Review of research in child development* (Vol.5). New York: Academic Press.

Neisser, U. 1967. *Cognitive psychology.* New York: Appleton-Century-Crofts.

Neisser, U. 1988. Five kinds of self-knowledge. *Philosophical Psychology, 1,* 35–39.

Nelson, B. 1982. Early memory: Why is it so elusive? *New York Times* (December 7), p. 17.

Nelson, B. 1983*a.* Age link is found for mental woes. *New York Times* (October 23), p. 24.

Nelson, B. 1983*b.* Despair among jobless is on rise, studies find. *New York Times* (April 2), p. 8.

Nelson, C. A., & Collins, P. F. 1991. Event-related potential and looking-time analysis of infants' responses to familiar and novel events: Implications for visual recognition memory. *Developmental Psychology, 27,* 50–58.

Nelson, C. A., & Dolgin, K. G. 1985. The generalized discrimination of facial expressions by seven-month-old infants. *Child Development, 56,* 58–61.

Nelson, J. 1987. Athletes paying price for fame. *Columbus* (Ohio) *Dispatch* (February 16), pp. 1–2C.

Nelson, K. 1972. The relation of form recognition to concept development. *Child Development, 43,* 67–74.

Nelson, K. 1973. Structure and strategy in learning to talk. *Monographs of the Society for Research in Child Development, 38* (No. 149).

Nelson, K. 1974. Concept, word, and sentence: Interrelations in acquisition and development. *Psychological Review, 81,* 267–285.

Nelson, K. 1981. Individual differences in language development: Implications for language development. *Developmental Psychology, 17,* 170–187.

Nelson, K. 1985. *Making sense: The acquisition of shared meaning.* Orlando, Fla.: Academic Press.

Nelson, K. 1988. Where do taxonomic categories come from? *Human Development, 31,* 3–10.

Nelson, K., & Lucariello, J. 1985. The development of meaning in first words. In M. D. Barrett (Ed.), *Children's single-word speech.* New York: Wiley.

Nelson, K., Rescorla, L., Gruendel, J., & Benedict, H. 1978. Early lexicons: What do they mean? *Child Development, 49,* 960–968.

Nelson, K. E. 1977. Facilitating children's syntax acquisition. *Developmental Psychology, 13,* 101–107.

Nelson, K. E., & Earl, N. 1973. Information search by preschool children: Induced use of categories and category hierarchies. *Child Development, 44,* 682–685.

Nelson, M., & Nelson, G. K. 1982. Problems of equity in the reconstituted family: A social exchange analysis. *Family Relations, 31,* 223–231.

Nelson, N. M., Enkin, M. W., Saigal, S., Bennett, K. J., Milner, R., & Sackett, D. L. 1980. A randomized clinical trial of the Leboyer approach to childbirth. *New England Journal of Medicine, 302,* 655–660.

Nemy, E. 1982. Most feel their age is unreal. *New York Times* (November 10), p. 19.

Neugarten, B. L. 1964. *Personality in middle and late life.* New York: Atherton Press.

Neugarten, B. L. 1968*a.* Adult personality: Toward a psychology of the life cycle. In E. Vinacke (Ed.), *Readings in general psychology.* New York: American Book.

Neugarten, B. L. 1968*b.* The awareness of middle age. In B. L. Neugarten (Ed.), *Middle age and aging.* Chicago: University of Chicago Press.

Neugarten, B. L. 1969. Continuities and dis-

continuities of psychological issues into adult life. *Human Development, 12,* 121–130.

Neugarten, B. L. 1971. Grow old along with me! The best is yet to be. *Psychology Today, 6* (December), pp. 45–48ff.

Neugarten, B. L. 1977. Personality and aging. In J. E. Birren & K. W. Schaie (Eds.), *Handbook of the psychology of aging.* New York: Van Nostrand.

Neugarten, B. L. 1979. Time, age, and the life cycle. *American Journal of Psychiatry, 136,* 887–894.

Neugarten, B. L. 1982*a.* The aging society. *National Forum, 42,*3.

Neugarten, B. L. 1982*b.* Age or need? *National Forum, 42,* 25–27.

Neugarten, B. L. 1983. *The study of aging and human development.* Paper presented at the Conference on Race, Class, Socialization and the Life Cycle, University of Chicago.

Neugarten, B. L., & Hagestad, G. O. 1976. Age and the life course. In R. H. Binstock & E. Shanas (Eds.), *Handbook of aging and the social sciences.* New York: Van Nostrand.

Neugarten, B. L., Havighurst, R. J., & Tobin, S. S. 1968. Personality and patterns of aging. In B. L. Neugarten (Ed.), *Middle age and aging.* Chicago: University of Chicago Press.

Neugarten, B. L., & Neugarten, D. A. 1987. The changing meanings of age. *Psychology Today, 21* (May), pp. 29–33.

Neugarten, B. L., & Weinstein, K. 1964. The changing American grandparent. *Journal of Marriage and the Family, 26,* 199–204.

Neugarten, B. L., Wood, V., Kraines, R. J., & Loomis, B. 1963. Women's attitudes toward the menopause. *Vita Humana, 6,* 140–151.

Newcomb, M. D., & Bentler, P. M. 1988. *Consequences of adolescent drug use: Impact on the lives of young adults.* Newbury Park, Calif.: Sage.

Newcomb, M. D., & Bentler, P. M. 1989. Substance use and abuse among children and teenagers. *American Psychologist, 44,* 242–248.

Newcomb, P. R. 1979. Cohabitation in America: An assessment of consequences. *Journal of Marriage and the Family, 41,* 597–603.

Newman, B. 1991. The last return. *Sports Illusrated* (March 11), pp. 38–41.

Newman, S. J., Struyk, R., Wright, P., & Rice, M. 1990. Overwhelming odds: Caregiving and the risk of institutionalization. *Journal of Gerontology, 45,* S173–183.

Newmark, S. R., Rose, L. I., Todd, R., Birk, L., & Naftolin, F. 1979. Gonadotropin, estradiol, and testosterone profiles in homosexual men. *American Journal of Psychiatry, 136,*767–771.

New York Times. 1982. New views on marriage. (December 23), p. 14.

New York Times. 1986. Teen-agers face more crime. (December 28), p. 13.

New York Times. 1990. Study cites steroid use by teen-agers. (September 8), p. 31.

New York Times. 1991*a.* Behavior varies in babies exposed to cocaine. (January 21), p. B6.

New York Times 1991*b*. Greater risk of cancer is reported in children of fathers who smoke. (January 24), p. 11A.

Nisan, M., & Kohlberg, L. 1982. Universality and variation in moral judgment: A longitudinal and cross-sectional study in Turkey. *Child Development, 53,* 865–876.

Nisbett, R. E. 1972. Hunger, obesity, & the ventromedial hypothalamus. *Psychological Review, 79,* 433–453.

Niswander, K. R. 1976. *Obstetrics.* Boston: Little, Brown.

Noble, K. B. 1986. End of forced retirement means a lot—to a few. *New York Times* (October 26), p. E5.

Nock, S. L. 1979. The family life cycle: Empirical or conceptual tool? *Journal of Marriage and the Family, 41,* 15–26.

Noelker, L. S. & Bass, D. M. 1989. Home care for elderly persons: Linkages between formal and informal caregivers. *Journal of Gerontology, 44,* S63–70.

Nolen-Hoeksema, S., Seligman, M. E. P., & Girgus, J. S. 1986. Learned helplessness in children: A longitudinal study of depression, achievement, and explanatory style. *Journal of Personality and Social Psychology, 51,* 435–442.

Nora, J. J., & Nora, A. H. 1973. Birth defects and oral contraceptives. *Lancet, 1,* 941–942.

Nora, J. J., & Nora, A. H. 1975. A syndrome of multiple congenital anomalies associated with teratogenic exposure. *Archives of Environmental Health, 30,* 17–21.

Nordheimer, J. 1987. To neighbors of shunned family, AIDS fear outweighs sympathy. *New York Times* (August 31), pp. 1, 14.

Norr, K. L., Block, C. R., Charles, A., Meyering, S., & Meyers, E. 1977. Explaining pain and enjoyment in childbirth. *Journal of Health and Social Behavior, 18,* 260–275.

Norris, F. H. & Murrell, S. A. 1990. Social support, life events, and stress as modifiers of adjustment to bereavement by older adults. *Psychology and Aging, 5,* 429–436.

Norton, A. J., & Moorman, J. E. 1987. Current trends in marriage and divorce among American women. *Journal of Marriage and the Family, 49,* 3–14.

Nottelmann, E. D. 1987. Competence and self-esteem during transition from childhood to adolescence. *Developmental Psychology, 23,* 441–450.

Notz, W. W. 1975. Work motivation and the negative effects of extrinsic rewards. *American Psychologist, 30,* 884–891.

Nucci, L. 1986. Synthesis of research on moral development. *Educational Leadership, 44,* 86–91.

Nugent, J. K. 1991. Cultural and psychological influences on the father's role in infant development. *Journal of Marriage and the Family, 53,* 475–485.

Nunner-Winkler, G., & Sodian, B. 1988. Children's understanding of moral emotions. *Child Development, 59,* 1323–1338.

Nye, F. I. 1957. Child adjustment in broken and in unhappy unbroken homes. *Marriage and Family Living, 19,* 356–361.

O'Brien, M., & Huston, A. C. 1985. Development of sex-typed play behavior in toddlers. *Developmental Psychology, 21,* 866–871.

O'Brien, S. F., & Bierman, K. L. 1988. Conceptions and perceived influence of peer groups: Interviews with preadolescents and adolescents. *Child Development, 59,* 1360–1365.

O'Bryant, S. L. 1988. Sibling support and older widows' well being. *Journal of Marriage and the Family, 50,* 173–183.

Ochberg, R. L. 1986. College dropouts: The developmental logic of psychosocial moratoria. *Journal of Youth and Adolescence, 15,* 287–302.

O'Connell, A. N., & Rotter, N. G. 1979. The influence of stimulus age and sex on person perception. *Journal of Gerontology, 34,* 220–228.

O'Connell, B., & Bretherton, I. 1984. Toddlers' play, alone and with mother. In I. Bretherton (Ed.), *Symbolic play: The development of understanding.* New York: Academic Press.

O'Connor, R. D. 1969. Modification of social withdrawal through symbolic modeling. *Journal of Applied Behavior Analysis, 2,* 15–22.

O'Discoll, P., & Newman, J. 1983. Federal hunger report due. *USA Today* (December 12), pp. 1, 2.

Offer, D. 1969. *The psychological world of the teenager: A study of normal adolescent boys.* New York: Basic Books.

Offer, D., & Offer, J. B. 1975. *From teenage to young manhood.* New York: Basic Books.

Offer, D., Ostrov, E., & Howard, K. I. 1981. *The adolescent: A psychological self-portrait.* New York: Basic Books.

Offer, D., Ostrov, E., Howard, K. I., & Atkinson, R. 1988. *The teenage world: Adolescents' self-image in ten countries.* New York: Plenum.

Ogbu, J. U. 1978. *Minority education and caste.* New York: Academic Press.

Ogbu, J. U. 1985. A cultural ecology of competence among inner-city blacks. In M. B. Spencer, G. K. Brookins, & W. R. Allen (Eds.), *Beginnings: The social and affective development of black children.* Hillsdale, N.J.: Erlbaum.

Ogbu, J. U. 1986. The consequences of the American caste system. In U. Neisser (Ed.), *The school achievement of minority children: New perspectives.* Hillsdale, N.J.: Erlbaum.

Okie, S. 1981. Parents inspire infant woes. *Columbus* (Ohio) *Dispatch* (January 11), p. E1.

O'Leary, A. 1990. Stress, emotion, and human immune function. *Psychological Bulletin, 108,* 363–382.

Oliker, S. J. 1989. *Best friends and marriage: Exchange among women.* Berkeley, Calif.: University of California Press.

Oller, D. K., & Eilers, R. E. 1988. The role of audition in infant babbling. *Child Development, 59,* 441–449.

Olson, S. L., Bates, J. E., & Bayles, K. 1984. Mother-infant interaction and the development of individual differences in children's cognitive competence. *Developmental Psychology, 20,* 166–179.

Olweus, D. 1978. *Aggression in the schools: Bullies and whipping boys.* Washington, D.C.: Hemisphere.

Olweus, D. 1979. Stability of aggressive reaction patterns in males: A review. *Psychological Bulletin, 86,* 852–875.

Olweus, D. 1980. Familial and temperamental determinants of aggressive behavior in adolescent boys: A causal analysis. *Developmental Psychology, 16,* 644–660.

O'Malley, P. M., & Bachman, J. G. 1983. Self-esteem: Change and stability between ages 13 and 23. *Developmental Psychology, 19,* 257–268.

Opinion Roundup. 1980. Work in the 70's. *Public Opinion, 3* (December/January), p.36.

Opinion Roundup. 1983. A look at the afterlife. *Public Opinion, 5* (January), p. 40.

Opinion Roundup. 1985. Religious belief in America. *Public Opinion, 8* (October/November), pp. 36–39.

Oppenheim, D., Sagi, A., & Lamb, M. E. 1988. Infant-adult attachments on the kibbutz and their relation to socioemotional development 4 years later. *Developmental Psychology, 24,* 427–433.

Oppenheimer, J. R. 1955. Analogy in science. *American Psychologist, 11,* 126–135.

O'Reilly, J. 1983. Wife beating: The silent crime. *Time* (September 5), pp. 23–26.

Orleans, M., Palisi, B. J., & Caddell, D. 1989. Marriage adjustment and satisfaction of stepfathers: Feelings and perceptions of decision making and stepchildren relations. *Family Relations, 38,* 371–377.

Orlofsky, J., & Frank, M. 1986. Personality structure as viewed through early memories and identity status in college men and women. *Journal of Personality and Social Psychology, 50,* 580–586.

Ornstein, P. A., Naus, M. J., & Liberty, C. 1975. Rehearsal and organizational processes in children's memory. *Child Development, 46,* 818–830.

Orthner, D. K., Brown, T., & Ferguson, D. 1976. Single-parent fatherhood: An emerging family life style. *Family Coordinator, 25,* 429–437.

Osis, K., & Haraldsson, E. 1977. *At the hour of death.* New York: Avon Books.

Osterman, P. 1980. *Getting started: The youth labor market.* Cambridge, Mass.: MIT Press.

Osterweis, M., Solomon, F., & Green, M. (Eds.). 1984. *Bereavement: Reactions, consequences, and care.* Washington, D.C.: National Academy Press.

Ostwald, P. F., & Peltzman, P. 1974. The cry of the human infant. *Scientific American, 230* (March), pp. 84–90.

Otten, A. 1988. People patterns. *Wall Street Journal* (June 14), p. 33.

Otten, A. L. 1990*a*. The '80s merger mania applies to families, too. *Wall Street Journal* (February 20), p. B1.

Otto, A. L. 1990*b*. Some young people take the great circle route. *Wall Street Journal* (November 29) p. B1.

Over, R. 1989. Age and scholarly impact. *Psychology and Aging, 4,* 222–225.

Overmier, J. B., & Seligman, M. E. P. 1967. Effects of inescapable shock upon subsequent escape and avoidance learning.

Journal of Comparative and Physiological Psychology, 63, 28–33.

Oviatt, S. L. 1980. The emerging ability to comprehend language: An experimental approach. *Child Development, 51,* 97–106.

Oxnam, R. B. 1986. Why Asians succeed here. *New York Times Magazine* (November 30), pp. 71–74 +.

Oyama, S. 1979. The concept of the sensitive period in developmental studies. *Merrill-Palmer Quarterly, 25,* 83–103.

Paernow, P. L. 1984. The stepfamily cycle: An experiential model of stepfamily development. *Family Relations, 33,* 355–363.

Pagel, M. D., Becker, J., & Coppel, D. B. 1985. Loss of control, self-blame, and depression: An investigation of spouse caregivers of Alzheimer's disease patients. *Journal of Abnormal Psychology, 94,* 169–182.

Paige, K. E., & Paige, J. M. 1973. The politics of birth practices: A strategic analysis. *American Sociological Review, 38,* 663–676.

Painter, K. 1987. Dads remain behind in child support. *USA Today* (August 21), p. A-1.

Painter, K. 1990*a.* More girls having sex as teens. *USA Today* (November 8), p. 1A.

Painter, K. 1990*b.* Sex habits of young women change little. *USA Today* (March 22), p. 1D.

Palca, J. 1991. Fetal brain signals time for birth. *Science, 253,* 1360.

Palkovitz, R. 1985. Fathers' birth attendance, early contact, and extended contact with their newborns: A critical review. *Child Development, 56,* 392–406.

Palmer, C. F. 1989. The discriminating nature of infants' exploratory actions. *Developmental Psychology, 25,* 885–893.

Palmore, E. 1975. *The honorable elders.* Durham, N.C.: Duke University Press.

Palmore, E. 1976. Review of Irving Roscow, *Socialization to Old Age. Social Forces, 55,* 215–216.

Palmore, E., & Cleveland, W. 1976. Aging, terminal decline, and terminal drop. *Journal of Gerontology, 31,* 76–81.

Palmore, E., & Maeda, D. 1985. *The honorable elders revisited: A revised cross-cultural analysis of aging in Japan.* Durham, N.C.: Duke University Press.

Palmore, E. B., Burchett, B. M., Fillenbaum, G. C., George, L. K., & Wallman, L. M. 1985. *Retirement: Causes and consequences.* New York: Springer.

Pampel, F. C., Williamson, J. B., & Stryker, R. 1990. Class context and pension response to demographic structure in advanced industrial democracies. *Social Problems, 37,* 535–550.

Parcel, ToL. & Mueller, C.W. 1989. Temporal change in occupational earnings attainment, 1970–1980. *American Sociological Review, 54,* 622–634.

Parekh, V. C., Pherwani, A., Udani, P. M., & Mukherjie, S. 1970. Brain weight and head circumference in fetus, infant and children of different nutritional and socio-economic groups. *Indian Pediatrics, 7,* 347–358.

Paris, B. L., & Luckey, E. B. 1966. A longitudinal study of marital satisfaction. *Sociology and Social Research, 50,* 212–223.

Paris, S. G. 1978. Memory organization during children's repeated recall. *Developmental Psychology, 14,* 99–106.

Parish, W. L., Hao, L., & Hogan, D. P. 1991. Family support networks, welfare, and work among young mothers. *Journal of Marriage & the Family, 53,* 203–215.

Park, K. A., & Waters, E. 1989. Security of attachment and preschool friendships. *Child Development, 60,* 1076–1081.

Parke, R. D. 1974. Rules, roles, and resistance to deviation: Recent advances in punishment, discipline, and self-control. In A. D. Pick (Ed.), *Minnesota Symposia on Child Psychology* (Vol. 8). Minneapolis: University of Minnesota Press.

Parke, R. D. 1979. Perspectives on father-infant interaction. In J. D. Osofsky (Ed.), *Handbook of infant development.* New York: Wiley.

Parke, R. D. 1981. *Fathers.* Cambridge, Mass.: Harvard University Press.

Parke, R. D., & Deur, J. L. 1972. Schedule of punishment and inhibiton of aggression in children. *Developmental Psychology, 7,* 266–269.

Parke, R. D., & Sawin, D. B. 1977. Fathering: It's a major role. *Psychology Today, 11,* pp. 109–112.

Parker, J. G., & Asher, S. R. 1987. Peer relations and later personal adjustment: Are low-accepted children at risk? *Psychological Bulletin, 102,* 357–389.

Parker, S. 1987. Mom's troubles affect the kids. *USA Today* (June 25), p. D-1.

Parkes, C. M., & Weiss, R. S. 1983. *Recovery from bereavement.* New York: Basic Books.

Parmelee, P. A., Katz, I. R., & Lawton, M. P. 1989. Depression among institutionalized aged: Assessment and prevalence estimation. *Journal of Gerontology, 44,* M22–29.

Parnes, H. S. 1981. *Work and retirement—a longitudinal study of men.* Cambridge, Mass.: MIT Press.

Parnes, H. S., Crowley, J. E., Haurin, R. J., Less, L. J., Morgan, W. R., Mott, F. L., & Nestel, G. 1985. *Retirement among American men.* Lexington, Mass.: Lexington Books.

Parpal, M., & Maccoby, E. E. 1985. Maternal responsiveness and subsequent child compliance. *Child Development, 56,* 1326–1334.

Parsons, T. 1943. The kinship of the contemporary United States. *American Anthropoligist, 45,* 22–38.

Parsons, T. 1955. Family structure and the socialization of the child. In T. Parsons & R. Bales (Eds.), *Family, socialization and interaction process.* New York: Free Press.

Parson, T., & Bales, R. F. 1955. *Family, socialization, and interaction process.* Glencoe, Ill.: The Free Press.

Parten, M. B. 1932. Social participation among preschool children. *Journal of Abnormal and Social Psychology, 27,* 243–269.

Parten, M. B., & Newhall, S. M. 1943. Social behavior of preschool children. In R. G. Barker, J. S. Kouin, & H. F. Wright (Eds.),

Child behavior and development. New York: McGraw-Hill.

Pasley, B. K., & Ihinger-Tallman, M. 1989. Boundary ambiguity in remarriage: Does ambiguity differentiate degree of marital adjustment and integration. *Family Relations, 38,* 46–52.

Pasley, K., & Gecas, V. 1984. Stresses and satisfactions of the parental role. *Personnel and Guidance Journal, 2,* 400–404.

Pasquali, L., & Callegari, A. I. 1978. Working mothers and daughters' sex-role identification in Brazil. *Child Development, 49,* 902–905.

Passell, P. 1991. When children have children. *New York Times* (September 4), p. C2.

Passman, R. H., & Blackwelder, D. E. 1981. Rewarding and punishing by mothers: The influence of progressive changes in the quality of their sons' apparent behavior. *Developmental Psychology, 17,* 614–619.

Patchen, M. 1982. *Black-white contact in schools: Its social and academic affects.* West Lafayette, Ind.: Purdue University Press.

Patterson, C. J., Kupersmidt, J. B., & Griesler, P. C. 1990. Children's perceptions of self and of relationships with others as a function of sociometric status. *Child Development, 61,* 1335–1349.

Patterson, G. R., Littman, R. A., & Bricker, W. 1967. Assertive behavior in children: A step toward a theory of aggression. *Monographs of the Society for Research in Child Development, 32* (5).

Pear, R. 1986. Poverty rate shows slight drop for '85, census bureau says. *New York Times* (August 27), pp. 1, 9.

Pear, R. 1991*a.* Bigger number of new mothers are unmarried. *New York Times* (December 4), p. A11.

Pear, R. 1991*b.* Medicare prognosis: Unwieldy growth fueled by more fees and beneficiaries. *New York Times* (March 10), p. 4E.

Pearl, D. 1982. *Television and behavior: 10 years of scientific research.* Washington, D.C.: Government Printing Office.

Pearl, D. 1990. AIDS spreads more rapidly among women. *Wall Street Journal* (November 30), pp. B1, B2.

Peck, R. C. 1968. Psychological developments in the second half of life. In B. L. Neugarten (Ed.), *Middle age and aging.* Chicago: University of Chicago Press.

Pedersen, E., Faucher, T. A., & Eaton, W. W. 1978. A new perspective on the effects of first-grade teachers on children's subsequent adult status. *Harvard Educational Review, 48,* 1–31.

Pedersen, F. A. (Ed.). 1980. *The father-infant relationship: Observational studies in the family setting.* New York: Praeger.

Pederson, D. R., Rock-Green, A., & Elder, J. L. 1981. The role of action in the development of pretend play in young children. *Developmental Psychology, 17,* 756–759.

Pelham, B. W., & Swamm, W. B., Jr. 1989. From self-conceptions to self-worth: On the sources and structure of global self-esteem. *Journal of Personality and Social Psychology, 57,* 672–680.

Peloquin, L. J., & Klorman, R. 1986. Effects of methylphenidate on normal children's mood, event-related potentials, and performance in memory scanning and vigilance. *Journal of Abnormal Psychology, 95,* 88–98.

Pennington, B. F., Bender, B., Puck, M., Salbenblatt, J., & Robinson, A. 1982. Learning disabilities in children with sex chromosome anomalies. *Child Development, 53,* 1182–1192.

Pennington, B. F., Van Orden, G. C., Smith, S. D., Green, P. A., & Haith, M. M. 1990. Phonological processing skills and deficits in adult dyslexics. *Child Development, 61,* 1753–1758.

Penk, W. E. 1969. Age changes and correlates of internal-external locus of control scale. *Psychological Reports, 25,* 857.

Pentella, C. 1983. More students say good night at the front door. *On Campus* (January), p.16.

Perdue, C. W., Dovidio, J. F., Gurtman, M. B., & Tyler, R. B. 1990. Us and them: Social categorization and the process of intergroup bias. *Journal of Personality and Social Psychology, 59,* 475–486.

Pereira, J. 1989. Even a school that is leading the drug war grades itself a failure. *Wall Street Journal* (November 10), pp. A1, A8.

Perinbanayagam, R. S. 1986. The meaning of uncertainty and the uncertainty of meaning. *Symbolic Interaction, 9,* 105–126.

Perkins, H. W. & Harris, L. B. 1990. Familial bereavement and health in adult life course perspective. *Journal of Marriage and the Family, 52,* 233–241.

Perlez, J. 1990. Puberty rite for girls is bitter issue across Africa. *New York Times* (January 15), p. 4.

Perlmutter, M., Kaplan, M., & Nyquist, L. 1990. Development of adaptive competence in adulthood. *Human Development, 33,* 185–197.

Perlmutter, M., & Myers, N. A. 1975. Young children's coding and storage of visual and verbal material. *Child Development, 46,* 215–219.

Perlmutter, M., & Myers, N. A. 1976. Recognition memory in preschool children. *Developmental Psychology, 12,* 271–272.

Perlmutter, M., & Nyquist, L. 1990. Relationships between self-reported physical and mental health and intelligence performance across adulthood. *Journal of Gerontology, 45,* P 145–155.

Perone, M., & Baron, A. 1982. Age-related effects of pacing on acquisition and performance of response sequences: An operant analysis. *Journal of Gerontology, 37,* 443–449.

Perris, E. E., & Clifton, R. K. 1988. Reaching in the dark toward sound as a measure of auditory localization in infants. *Infant behavior & Development, 11,* 473–491.

Perris, E. E., Myers, N. A., & Clifton, R. K. 1990. Long-term memory for a single infancy experience. *Child Development, 61,* 1796–1807.

Perrow, C., & Guillen, M. F. 1990. *The AIDS disaster: The failure of organizations in New York and the nation.* New Haven, Conn.: Yale University Press.

Perrucci, C. C., Perrucci, R., Targ, D. B., &

Targ, H. R. 1988. *Plant closings: International context and social costs.* Hawthorne, N.Y.: Aldine de Gruyter.

Perry, D. G., & Bussey, K. 1979. The social learning theory of sex differences: Imitation is alive and well. *Journal of Personality and Social Psychology, 37,* 1699–1712.

Perry, D. G., Perry, L. C., & Rasmussen, P. 1986. Cognitive social learning mediators of aggression. *Child Development, 57,* 700–711.

Perry, D. G., Perry, L. C., & Weiss, R. J. 1989. Sex differences in the consequences that children anticipate for aggression. *Developmental Psychology, 25,* 312–319.

Perry, D. G., Williard, J. C., & Perry, L. C. 1990. Peers' perceptions of the consequences that victimized children provide aggressors. *Child Development, 61,* 1310–1325.

Pesce, R. C., & Harding, C. G. 1986. Imaginary audience behavior and its relationship to operational thought and social experience. *Journal of Early Adolescence, 6,* 83–94.

Peterman, D. J., Ridley, C. A., & Anderson, S. M. 1974. A comparison of cohabiting and noncohabiting college students. *Journal of Marriage and the Family, 36,* 344–354.

Peters, R. D., & Bernfeld, G. A. 1983. Reflection-impulsivity and social reasoning. *Developmental Psychology, 19,* 78–81.

Peters, S. D., Wyatt, G. E., & Finkelhor, D. 1986. Prevalence. In D. Finkelhor (Ed.), *A sourcebook on child sexual abuse.* Beverly Hills, Calif.: Sage.

Petersen, A. C. 1983. Menarche: Meaning of measures and measures of meaning. In S. Golub (Ed.), *Menarche: The transition from girl to woman.* Lexington, Mass.: Heath.

Petersen, A. C., & Taylor, B. 1980. The biological approach to adolescence. In J. Adelson (Ed.), *Handbook of adolescent psychology.* New York: Wiley.

Peters-Martin, P., & Wachs, T. D. 1984. A longitudinal study of temperament and its correlates in the first 12 months. *Infant Behavior and Development, 7,* 285–298.

Peterson, G. W., & Rollins, B. C. 1987. Parent-child socialization: A review of research and applications of symbolic interaction concepts. In M. B. Sussman & S. K. Steinmetz (Eds.), *Handbook of marriage and the family.* New York: Plenum.

Peterson, K. S. 1990. Teens: Parents you're ok. *USA Today* (August 27), p. D1.

Peterson, K. S. 1991. A baby's death can haunt parents for years. *USA Today* (August 16), p. D1.

Peterson, R. R. 1989. *Women, work, and divorce.* Albany, N.Y.: State University of New York.

Petitto, L. A., & Marentette, P. F. 1991. Babbling in the manual mode: Evidence for the ontogeny of language. *Science, 251,* 1493–1496.

Petrig, B., Julesz, B., Kropfl, W., Baumgartner, G., & Anliker, M. 1981. Development of stereopsis and cortical binocularity in human infants: Electrophysiological evidence. *Science, 213,* 1402–1404.

Petros, T. V., Zehr, H. D., & Chabot, R. J.

1983. Adult age differences in accessing and retrieving information from long-term memory. *Journal of Gerontology, 38,* 589–592.

Pettit, G. S., Bakshi, A., Dodge, K. A., & Coie, J. D. 1990. The emergence of social dominance in young boys' play groups: Developmental differences and behavioral correlates. *Developmental Psychology, 26,* 1017–1025.

Pettit, G. S., & Bates, J. E. 1989. Family interaction patterns and children's behavior problems from infancy to 4 years. *Developmental Psychology, 25,* 413–420.

Pettit, G. S., Dodge, K. A., & Brown, M. M. 1988. Early family experience, social problem solving patterns, and children's social competence. *Child Development, 59,* 107–120.

Pezdek, K. 1983. Memory for items and their spatial locations by young and elderly adults. *Developmental Psychology, 19,* 895–900.

Pfeffer, C. 1986. *The suicidal child.* New York: Guilford Press.

Phares, E. J. 1976. *Locus of control in personality.* Morristown, N.J.: General Learning.

Phillips, D., McCartney, K., & Scarr, S. 1987. Childcare quality and children's social development. *Developmental Psychology, 23,* 537–543.

Phoenix, C. H., Goy, R. W., & Resko, J. A. 1969. Psychosexual differentiation as a function of androgenic stimulation. In M. Diamond (Ed.), *Reproduction and sexual behavior.* Bloomington: Indiana University Press.

Piaget, J. 1932. *The moral judgment of the child* (M. Gaban, Trans.). London: Kegan Paul, Trench, Trubner.

Piaget, J. 1952a. *The origins of intelligence in children* (M. Cook, Trans.). New York: International Universities Press.

Piaget, J. 1952b. *The child's conception of number.* New York: Humanities Press.

Piaget, J. 1954. *The construction of reality in the child.* New York: Basic Books.

Piaget, J. 1962. *Play, dreams and imitiation in childhood.* New York: Norton.

Piaget, J. 1963. *The origins of intelligence in children.* New York: Norton.

Piaget, J. 1965. *The child's conception of number.* New York: Norton. (Original work published in 1941.)

Piaget, J. 1967. *Six psychological studies.* New York: Random House.

Piaget, J. 1970. Conversations. *Psychology Today, 3* (May), pp. 25–32.

Piaget, J. 1972. Intellectual evolution from adolescence to adulthood. *Human Development, 15,* 1–12.

Piaget, J., & Inhelder, B. 1956. *The child's conception of space.* London: Routledge and Kegan Paul.

Pianta, R. C., Sroufe, L. A., & Egeland, B. 1989. Continuity and discontinuity in maternal sensitivity at 6, 24, and 42 months in a high-risk sample. *Child Development, 60,* 481–487.

Picariello, M. L., Greenberg, D. N., & Pillemer, D. B. 1990. Children's sex-related stereotyping of colors. *Child Development, 61,* 1455–1460.

Pick, H. L., Jr. 1989. Motor development: The

control of action. *Developmental Psychology, 25,* 867–870.

Pill, C. J. 1990. Stepfamilies: Redefining the family. *Family Relations, 39,* 186–193.

Pillard, R. C., & Weinrich, J. D. 1986. Evidence of familial nature of male homosexuality. *Archives of General Psychiatry, 43,* 808–912.

Pines, A., & Aronson, E. 1988. *Career burnout: Causes and cures.* New York: Free Press.

Pines, M. 1979*a.* Superkids. *Psychology Today, 12* (January), pp. 53–63.

Pines, M. 1979*b.* Good Samaritans at age two? *Psychology Today, 13* (June), pp. 66–77.

Pines, M. 1981. The civilizing of Genie. *Psychology Today, 15* (September), pp. 28–34.

Pines, M. 1982*a.* Baby, you're incredible. *Psychology Today, 16* (February), pp. 48–53.

Pines, M. 1983. Can a rock walk? *Psychology Today, 17* (November), pp. 46–54.

Pinker, S. 1984. *Language learnability and language development.* Cambridge, Mass.: Harvard University Press.

Pinker, S. 1991. Rules of language. *Science, 253,* 530–535.

Pinon, M. F., Huston, A. C., & Wright, J. C. 1989. Family ecology and child characteristics that predict young children's educational television viewing. *Child Development, 60,* 846–856.

Pipp, S., Fischer, K. W., & Jennings, S. 1987. Acquisition of self- and mother knowledge in infancy. *Developmental Psychology, 23,* 86–96.

Pitot, H. C. 1989. Aging and cancer: Some general thoughts. *Journal of Gerontology, 44,* 5–9.

Platt, B. S., & Stewart, R. J. C. 1971. Reversible and irreversible effects of protein-calorie deficiency on the central nervous system of animals and man. *World Review of Nutrition and Dietetics, 13,* 43–85.

Pleck, J. H. 1981. *The myth of masculinity.* Cambridge, Mass.: MIT Press.

Pleck, J. H. 1985. *Working wives working husbands.* Beverly Hills: Sage.

Pleck, J. H., Staines, G. L., & Lang, L. 1980. Conflicts between work and family life. *Monthly Labor Review, 103,* 29–32.

Plomin, R. 1983. Developmental behavioral genetics. *Child Development, 54,* 253–259.

Plomin, R. 1989. Environment and genes: Determinants of behavior. *American Psychologist, 44,* 105–111.

Plomin, R. 1990. *Nature and nurture: An introduction to human behavioral genetics.* Pacific Grove, Calif.: Brooks/Cole.

Plomin, R., & Daniels, D. 1987. Why are children in the same family so different from one another? *Behavioral and Brain Sciences, 10,* 1–16.

Plomin, R., DeFries, J. C., & Fulker, D. W. 1988. *Nature and nurture during infancy and early childhood.* New York: Cambridge University Press.

Plomin, R., & Foch, T. T. 1981. Sex differences and individual differences. *Child Development, 52,* 383–385.

Plomin, R., Lichtenstein, P., Pedersen, N. L., McClearn, G. E., and Nesselroade, J. R. 1990. Genetic influence on life events during the last half of the life span. *Psychology and Aging, 5,* 25–30.

Plomin, R., McClearn, G. E., Pedersen, N. L. Nesselroade, J. R., & Bergeman, C. S. 1988. Genetic influence on childhood environment perceived retrospectively from the last half of the life span. *Developmental Psychology, 24,* 738–745.

Plomin, R., & Rende, R. 1991. Human behavioral genetics. In M. Rosenzweig & L. W. Porter (Eds.), *Annual review of psychology* (Vol. 42).

Plumb, J. H. 1972. *Children.* London: Penguin Books.

Pogrebin, L. C. 1986. *Among friends: Who we like, why we like them and what we do about it.* New York: McGraw-Hill.

Popenoe, D. 1988. *Disturbing the nest: Family change and decline in modern societies.* New York: Aldine de Gruyter.

Popkin, B. M., Bilsborrow, R. E., & Akin, J. S. 1982. Breast-feeding patterns in low-income countries. *Science, 218,* 1088–1093.

Popkin, S. J. 1990. Welfare: Views from the bottom. *Social Problems, 37,* 64–79.

Porter, F. L., Porges, S. W., & Marshall, R. E. 1988. Newborn pain cries and vagal tone: Parallel changes in response to circumcision. *Child Development, 1988,* 495–505.

Porter, J. 1971. *Black child, white child: The development of racial attitudes.* Cambridge, Mass.: Harvard University Press.

Portman, M. V. 1895. Notes on the Andamanese. *Anthropological Institute of Great Britain and Ireland, 25,* 361–371.

Posner, M. I. 1967. Short-term memory systems in human memory. *Acta Psychologica, 27,* 267–284.

Postman, N. 1982. *The disappearance of childhood.* New York: Delacorte Press.

Power, F. C., Higgins, A., & Kohlberg, L. 1989. *Lawrence Kohlberg's approach to moral education.* New York: Columbia University Press.

Power, R. G. 1985. Mother- and father-infant play: A developmental analysis. *Child Development, 56,* 1514–1524.

Power, T. G., & Parke, R. D. 1983. Patterns of mother and father play with their 8-month-old infant: A multiple analyses approach. *Infant Behavior and Development, 6,* 453–459.

Powers, E. A., & Bultena, G. L. 1976. Sex differences in intimate friendships of old age. *Journal of Marriage and the Family, 38,* 739–747.

Prager, J., Longshore, D., & Seeman, M. (Eds.). 1986. *School desegregation research: New directions in situational analysis.* New York: Plenum.

Pratt, M. W., Kerig, P., Cowan, P. A., & Cowan, C. P. 1988. Mothers and fathers teaching 3-year-olds: Authoritative parenting and adult scaffolding of young children's learning. *Developmental Psychology, 24,* 832–839.

Prawat, R. S., Jones, H., & Hampton, J. 1979. Longitudinal study of attitude development in pre-, early, and later adolescent samples. *Journal of Educational Psychology, 71,* 363–369.

Presser, H. B. 1989. Some economic complexities of child care provided by grandmothers. *Journal of Marriage and the Family, 51,* 581–591.

Presser, H. B., & Cain, V. S. 1983. Shift work

among dual-earner couples with children. *Science, 219,* 876–879.

Pressey, S. L., & Kuhlen, R. G. 1957. *Psychological development through the life-span.* New York: Harper & Row.

Price, D. W. W., & Goodman, G. S. 1990. Visiting the Wizard: Children's memory for a recurring event. *Child Development, 61,* 664–680.

Price, R. A., Cadoret, R. J., Stunkard, A. J., & Troughton, E. 1987. Genetic contributions to human fatness: An adoption study. *American Journal of Psychiatry, 144,* 1003–1008.

Prince, J. R. 1968. The effect of Western education on science conceptualization in New Guinea. *British Journal of Educational Psychology, 38,* 64–74.

Prober, C. G. 1987. Low risk of herpes simplex virus infections in neonates exposed to the virus at the time of vaginal delivery to mothers with recurrent genital herpes simplex virus infections. *New England Journal of Medicine, 316,* 240–244.

Prose, F. 1990. Confident at 11, confused at 16. *New York Times Magazine* (January 7), pp. 22–25+.

Provenzo, E. G., Jr. 1991. *Video kids: Making sense of Nintendo.* Cambridge, Mass.: Harvard University Press.

Pruchno, R. A., Kleban, M. H., Michaels, J. E., & Dempsey, N. P. 1990. Mental and physical health of caregiving spouses: Development of a causal model. *Journal of Gerontology, 45,* P192–199.

Pruett, K. D. 1987. *The nurturing father.* New York: Warner Books.

Puglisi, J. T. 1986. Age-related slowing in memory search for three-dimensional objects. *Journal of Gerontology, 41,* 72–78.

Puglisi, J. T., Park, D. C., Smith, A. D., & Dudley, W. N. 1988. Age differences in encoding specificity. *Journal of Gerontology, 43,* P145–150.

Pulkkinen, L. 1982. Self-control and continuity from childhood to adolescence. In P. Baltes & O. G. Brim (Eds.), *Life-span development and behavior* (Vol. 4). New York: Academic Press.

Purvis, A. 1990. The sins of the fathers. *Time* (November 26), pp. 90–92.

Putallaz, M. 1983. Predicting children's sociometric status from their behavior. *Child Development, 54,* 1417–1426.

Putallaz, M. 1987. Maternal behavior and children's sociometric status. *Child Development, 58,* 324–340.

Putallaz, M., & Sheppard, B. H. 1990. Social status and children's orientations to limited resources. *Child Development, 61,* 2022–2027.

Putallaz, M., & Wasserman, A. 1989. Children's naturalistic entry behavior and sociometric status: A developmental perspective. *Developmental Psychology, 25,* 297–305.

Putka, G. 1991. Education reformers have new respect for Catholic schools. *Wall Street Journal* (March 28), pp. A1, A8.

Quadagno, D. M., Briscoe, R., & Quadagno, J. S. 1977. Effect of perinatal gonadal hormones on selected nonsexual behavior patterns: A critical assessment of the non-human and human literature. *Psychological Bulletin, 84,* 62–80.

Quadagno, J. E. 1982. *Aging in early industrial society.* New York: Academic Press.

Quay, L. C., & Jarrett, O. S. 1984. Predictors of social acceptance in preschool children. *Developmental Psychology, 20,* 793–796.

Quilter, R. E., Giambra, L. M., & Benson, P. E. 1983. Longitudinal age changes in vigilance over an eighteen year interval. *Journal of Gerontology, 38,* 51–54.

Quinn, R. P., Staines, G. L., & McCullough, M. R. 1974. *Job satisfaction: Is there a trend?* (Manpower Research Monograph No. 30, U.S. Department of Labor.) Washington, D.C.: Government Printing Office.

Quinn, W. H. 1983. Personal and family adjustment in later life. *Journal of Marriage and the Family, 45,* 57–73.

Quittner, A. L., Glueckauf, R. L., & Jackson, D. N. 1990. Chronic parenting stress: Moderating versus mediating effects of social support. *Journal of Personality and Social Psychology, 59,* 1266–1278.

Rabinowitz, J. C. 1984. Aging and recognition failure. *Journal of Gerontology, 39,* 65–71.

Rabkin, J. G., & Struening, E. L. 1976. Life events, stress, and illness. *Science, 194* (December 3), 1013–1020.

Radcliffe-Brown, A. R. 1940. On joking relationships. *Africa, 13,* 195–210.

Radke-Yarrow, M. 1989. Developmental and contextual analysis of continuity. *Human Development, 32,* 204–209.

Radke-Yarrow, M., & Zahn-Waxler, C. 1976. Dimensions and correlates of prosocial behavior in young children. *Child Development, 47,* 118–125.

Radke-Yarrow, M., Zahn-Waxler, C., & Chapman, M. 1983. Children's prosocial dispositions and behavior. In E. M. Hetherington (Ed.), *Handbook of child psychology.* Vol. 4, *Socialization, personality and social development.* New York: Wiley.

Rafferty, C. 1984. Study of gifted from childhood to old age. *New York Times* (April 23), p. 18.

Rahe, R. H. 1968. Life-change measurements as a predictor of illness. *Proceedings of the Royal Society of Medicine, 61,* 1124–1126.

Ramirez, F. O., & Boli, J. 1987. The political construction of mass schooling: European origins and worldwide institutionalization. *Sociology of Education, 60,* 2–17.

Ramsay, D. S. 1985. Fluctuations in unimanual hand preference in infants following the onset of duplicated syllable babbling. *Developmental Psychology, 21,* 318–324.

Raphael, R. 1988. *The men from the boys: Rites of passage in male America.* Lincoln, Neb.: University of Nebraska.

Rapoport, R., Rapoport, R. N., & Strelitz, Z. 1976. *Fathers, mothers, and society: Towards new alliances.* New York: Basic Books.

Raschke, H. J., & Raschke, V. J. 1979. Family conflict and children's self-concepts: A comparison of intact and single-parent families. *Journal of Marriage and the Family, 41,* 367–374.

Rasmussen, O. V., & Lunde, I. 1980. Evaluation of investigations of 200 torture victims. *Danish Medical Bulletin, 27,* 241–243.

Rausch, M. L. 1977. Paradox, levels, and junctures in person-situation systems. In D. Magnusson & N. S. Endler (Eds.), *Personality at the crossroads.* Hillsdale, N.J.: Erlbaum.

Raymond, C. 1989. New study reveals pitfalls in pushing children to succeed academically in preschool years. *Chronicle of Higher Education* (November 1), pp. A4–A6.

Raymond, C. 1991a. Cross-cultural study of sounds adults direct to infants shows that "baby talk" can be serious communication. *The Chronicle of Higher Education* (January 23), pp. A5, A7.

Raymond, C. 1991b. Pioneering research challenges accepted notions concerning the cognitive abilities of infants. *The Chronicle of Higher Education* (January 23), pp. A5–A7.

Raymond, C. 1991c. Recognition of the gender differences in mental illness and its treatment prompts a call for more health research on problems specific to women. *Chronicle of Higher Education* (June 12), pp. A5, A10.

Raymond, C. 1991d. Scholarship. *Chronicle of Higher Education* (September 25), p. A11.

Raymond, C. 1991e. Study of patient histories suggests Freud suppressed or distorted facts that contradicted his theories. *Chronicle of Higher Education* (May 29), pp. A4–A6.

Rebello, K. 1990. Women execs crash into "glass ceiling." *USA Today* (July 13), pp. 1B, 2B.

Rebenkoff, M. 1979. Study shows teen years are easiest for childbirth. *New York Times* (April 24), p. C5.

Redding, R. E., Morgan, G. A., & Harmon, R. J. 1988. Mastery motivation in infants and toddlers: Is it greatest when tasks are moderately challenging? *Infant Behavior and Development, 11,* 419–430.

Reed, E. S. 1982. An outline of a theory of action systems. *Journal of Motor Behavior, 14,* 98–134.

Reed, E. S. 1988. *James J. Gibson and the psychology of perception.* New Haven, Conn.: Yale University.

Reese, H. W., & Lipsitt, L. P. 1970. *Experimental child psychology.* New York: Academic Press.

Regev, E., Beit-Hallahmi, B., & Sharabany, R. 1980. Affective expression in kibbutz-communal, kibbutz-familial, and city-raised children in Israel. *Child Development, 51,* 232–237.

Reich, J. W., Zautra, A. J., & Hill, J. 1987. Activity, event transactions, and quality of life in older adults. *Psychology and Aging, 2,* 116–124.

Reinke, B. J., Ellicott, A. M., Harris, R. L., & Hancock, E. 1985. Timing of psychosocial changes in women's lives. *Human Development, 28,* 259–280.

Reis, H. T., Wheeler, L., Kernis, M. H., Spiegel, N., & Nezlek, J. 1985. On specificity in the impact of social participation on physical and psychological health. *Journal of Personality and Social Psychology, 48,* 456–471.

Reiss, I. L. 1972. Premarital sexuality: Past, present and future. In I. L. Reiss (Ed.), *Readings on the family system.* New York: Holt, Rinehart and Winston.

Reiss, I. L. 1976. *Family systems in America* (2nd ed.). Hinsdale, Ill.: Dryden Press.

Reissland, N. 1988. Neonatal imitation in the first hour of life: Observations in rural Nepal. *Developmental Psychology, 24,* 464–469.

Relman, A. S. 1982. *Marijuana and health.* Washington, D.C.: National Academy Press.

Repetti, R. L., Matthews, K. A., & Waldron, I. 1989. Employment and women's health. *American Psychologist, 44,* 1394–1401.

Reppucci, N. D. & Haugaard, J. J. 1989. Prevention of child sexual abuse: Myth or reality. *American Psychologist, 44,* 1266–1275.

Rescorla, L., 1976. *Concept formation in word learning.* Unpublished doctoral dissertation, Yale University.

Rescorla, R. A. 1987. A Pavlovian analysis of goal-directed behavior. *American Psychologist, 42,* 119–129.

Rescorla, R. A. 1988. Pavlovian conditioning: It's not what you think it is. *American Psychologist, 43,* 151–160.

Rescorla, R. A., & Holland, P. C. 1982. Behavioral studies of associative learning in animals. *Annual Review of Psychology, 33,* 265–308.

Rescorla, R. A., & Wagner, A. R. 1972. A theory of Pavlovian conditioning: Variations in the effectiveness of reinforcement and nonreinforcement. In A. H. Black, W. F. Prokasy (Eds.), *Classical Conditioning.* Vol. II, *Current Research and Theory.* New York: Appleton-Century-Crofts.

Reskin, B. F., & Boos, P. A. 1990. *Job queues, gender queues: Explaining women's inroads into male occupations.* Philadelphia: Temple University.

Reskin, B. F., & Hartmann, H. I. (Eds.). 1986. *Women's work, men's work: Sex segregation on the job.* Washington, D.C.: National Academy Press.

Resnick, L. B. 1986. The development of mathematical intuition. In M. Perlmutter (Ed.), *Perspectives on intellectual development: The Minnesota symposia on child psychology.* Vol. 19. Hillsdale, N.J.: Erlbaum.

Resnick, L. B. 1989. Developing mathematical knowledge. *American Psychologist, 44,* 162–169.

Rest, J. R. 1983. Morality. In P. H. Mussen (Ed.), *Handbook of child psychology* (4th Ed., Vol. 3). New York: Wiley.

Restak, R. 1975. Genetic counseling for defective parents: The danger of knowing too much. *Psychology Today 9* (September), pp. 21–23ff.

Retherford, R. D., & Sewell, W. H. 1991. Birth order and intelligence: Further tests of the confluence model. *American Sociological Review, 56,* 141–158.

Revicki, D. A., & Mitchell, J. P. 1990. Strain, social support, and mental health in rural elderly individuals. *Journal of Gerontology, 45,* S267–274.

Reynolds, C. F., III, Monk, T. H., Hoch, C. C., Jennings, J. R., Buysse, D. J., Houck, P. R., Jarrett, D. B., & Kupfer, D. J. 1991. Electroencephalographic sleep in the healthy "old old": A comparison with the "young old" in visually scored and automated measures. *Journal of Gerontology, 46,* M39–46.

Reznick, J. S., Kagan, J., Snidman, N., Gersten, M., Baak, K., & Rosenberg, A. 1986. Inhibited and uninhibited children: A follow-up study. *Child Development, 57,* 660–680.

Rheingold, H. L. 1961. The effect of environmental stimulation upon social and exploratory behavior in the human infant. In B. M. Foss (Ed.), *Determinants of infant behavior* (Vol. I). New York: Wiley.

Rheingold, H. L. 1968. Infancy. In D. Sills (Ed.), *International encyclopedia of the social sciences.* New York: Macmillan.

Rheingold, H. L. 1969a. The effect of a strange environment on the behavior of infants. In B. M. Foss (Ed.), *Determinants of infant behavior* (Vol. 4). New York: Wiley.

Rheingold, H. L. 1969b. The social and socializing infant. In D. A. Goslin (Ed.), *Handbook of socialization theory and research.* Chicago: Rand McNally.

Rheingold, H. L. 1982. Little children's participation in the work of adults, a nascent prosocial behavior. *Child Development, 53,* 114–125.

Rheingold, H. L. 1985. Development as the acquisition of familiarity. *Annual Review of Psychology, 36,* 105–130.

Rheingold, H. L., & Adams, J. L. 1980. The significance of speech to newborns. *Developmental Psychology, 16,* 397–403.

Rheingold, H. L., & Cook, K. V. 1975. The contents of boys' and girls' rooms as an index of parents' behavior. *Child Development, 46,* 459–463.

Rheingold, H. L., & Eckerman, C. O. 1973. Fear of the stranger: A critical examination. In H. W. Reese (Ed.), *Advances in child development and behavior* (Vol. 8). New York: Academic Press.

Rheingold, H. L., Hay, D. F., & West, M. J. 1976. Sharing in the second year of life. *Child Development, 47,* 1148–1158.

Rhodewalt, F., & Zone, J. B. 1989. Appraisal of life change, depression, and illness in hardy and nonhardy women. *Journal of Personality and Social Psychology, 56,* 81–88.

Rholes, W. S., & Ruble, D. N. 1986. Children's impressions of other persons. *Child Development, 57,* 872–878.

Ribble, M. A. 1943. *The rights of infants: Early psychological needs and their satisfaction.* New York: Columbia University Press.

Rice, M. L., Huston, A. C., Truglio, R., & Wright, J. 1990. Words from "Sesame Street": Learning vocabulary while viewing. *Developmental Psychology, 26,* 421–428.

Rice, M. L., & Woodsmall, L. 1988. Lessons from television: Children's word learning when viewing. *Child Development, 59,* 420–429.

Richards, L. N. 1989. The precarious survival and hard-won satisfactions of white single-parent families. *Family Relations, 38,* 396–403.

Richards, M. H., Boxer, A. M., Petersen, A. C., & Albrecht, R. 1990. Relation of weight to body image in pubertal girls and boys from two communities. *Developmental Psychology, 26,* 313–321.

Riche, M. F. 1986. The forking path. *American Demographics, 8* (February), 42–44.

Riegel, K. F. 1973. Dialectic operations: The final period of cognitive development. *Human Development, 16,* 346–370.

Riegel, K. F. 1975a. Adult life crises: A dialectic interpretation of development. In N. Datan & L. H. Ginsberg (Eds.), *Life-span developmental psychology: Normative life crisis.* New York: Academic Press.

Riegel, K. F. 1975b. Toward a dialectical theory of development. *Human Development, 18,* 50–64.

Riegel, K. F. 1976. The dialectics of human development. *American Psychologist, 31,* 689–700.

Riegel, K. F., & Riegel, R. M. 1972. Development, drop, and death. *Developmental Psychology, 6,* 306–319.

Riemer, D. R. 1988. *The prisoners of welfare: Liberating America's poor from unemployment and low wages.* New York: Praeger.

Rieser, J., Yonas, A., & Wikner, K. 1976. Radial localization of odors by human newborns. *Child Development, 47,* 856–859.

Rikli, R., & Busch, S. 1986. Motor performance of women as a function of age and physical activity level. *Journal of Gerontology, 41,* 645–649.

Riley, J. W., Jr. 1983. Dying and the meanings of death: Sociological inquiries. *Annual Review of Sociology, 9,* 191–216.

Riley, M. W. 1978. Aging, social change, and the power of ideas. *Daedalus, 107,* 39–52.

Riley, M. W. 1987. On the significance of age in sociology. *American Sociological Review, 52,* 1–14.

Riley, M. W. (Ed.). 1988a. *Social change and the life course.* Vol. 1, *Social structures and human lives.* Newbury Park, Calif.: Sage.

Riley, M. W. (Ed.). 1988b. *Social change and the life course.* Vol. 2, *Sociological lives.* Newbury Park, Calif.: Sage.

Riley, M. W., & Foner, A. 1968. *Aging and society: An inventory of research findings.* New York: Russell Sage Foundation.

Riley, M. W., Foner, A., & Waring, J. 1988. Sociology of age. In N. J. Smelser (Ed.), *Handbook of sociology.* Beverly Hills, Calif.: Sage.

Riley, M. W., Johnson, M., & Foner, A. 1972. *Aging and society: A sociology of age stratification* (Vol. 3). New York: Russell Sage Foundation.

Rindfuss, R. R., Morgan, S. P., & Swicegood, G. 1988. *First births in America: Changes in the timing of parenthood.* Berkeley, Calif.: University of California Press.

Ring, K. 1984. *Heading toward omega: In search of the meaning of the near-death experience.* New York: Morrow.

Risman, B. J. 1986. Can men "mother"? Life as a single father. *Family Relations, 35,* 95–102.

Risman, B. J., Hill, C. T., Rubin, Z., & Peplau, L. A. 1981. Living together in college: Implications for courtship. *Journal of Marriage and the Family, 43,* 77–83.

Ritter, P. L., & Dornbusch, S. M. 1989. Ethnic variation in family influences on academic achievement. Paper presented at the March American Educational Research Association Meeting, San Francisco.

Rivers, W. H. R. 1906. *The Todas.* New York: Macmillan.

Roach, M. 1983. Another name for madness. *New York Times Magazine* (January 16), pp. 22–31.

Roark, A. C. 1989. Most older people are happy, and getting happier. *Columbus Ohio Dispatch* (May 4), pp. 1, 2.

Roazen, P. 1990. *Encountering Freud: The politics and histories of psychoanalysis.* New Brunswick, N.J.: Transaction.

Roberge, J. J., & Flexer, B. K. 1979. Further examinations of formal operational reasoning abilities. *Child Development, 50,* 478–484.

Roberto, K. A., & Scott, J. P. 1986. Friendships of older men and women: Exchange patterns and satisfaction. *Psychology and Aging, 1,* 103–109.

Roberts, C. 1989. *Women and rape.* New York: New York University.

Roberts, C. W. 1986. Tracing formative influences on event recall: A test of Mannheim's sensitivity hypothesis. *Social Forces, 65,* 74–86.

Roberts, C. W., Green, R., Williams, K., & Goodman, M. 1987. Boyhood gender identity development: A statistical contrast of two family groups. *Developmental Psychology, 23,* 544–557.

Roberts, G. C., Block, J. H., & Block, J. 1984. Continuity and change in parents' child-rearing practices. *Child Development, 55,* 586–597.

Roberts, K. 1988. Retrieval of a basic-level category in prelinguistic infants. *Developmental Psychology, 24,* 21–27.

Roberts, M. 1987a. Class before birth. *Psychology Today, 21* (May), p. 41.

Roberts, M. 1987b. No language but a cry. *Psychology Today, 21* (June), pp. 57–58.

Roberts, P., & Newton, P. M. 1987. Levinsonian studies of women's adult development. *Psychology and Aging, 2,* 154–163.

Roberts, R. K. N., Wasik, B. H., Casto, G., & Ramey, C. T. 1991. Family support in the home: Programs, policy, and social change. *American Psychologist, 46,* 131–137.

Roberts, T. A. 1991. Gender and the influence of evaluations on self-assessments in achievement settings. *Psychological Bulletin, 109,* 297–308.

Robertson, E. B., Elder, G. H., Jr., Skinner, M. L., & Conger, R. D. 1991. The costs and benefits of social support in families. *Journal of Marriage and the Family, 53,* 403–416.

Robertson, J. F., & Simons, R. L. 1989. Family factors, self-esteem, and adolescent depression. *Journal of Marriage and the Family, 51,* 125–138.

Robins, C. J., & Block, P. 1988. Personal vulnerability, life events, and depressive symptoms: A test of a specific interactional model. *Journal of Personality and Social Psychology, 54,* 847–852.

Robins, L. N. & Rutter, M. (Eds.). 1990. *Straight and devious pathways from childhood to adulthood.* Cambridge: Cambridge University.

Robinson, B. 1988. *Teenage fathers.* Lexington, Mass.: Lexington Books.

Robinson, B. E. 1984. The contemporary American stepfather. *Family Relations, 33,* 381–388.

Robinson, B. E., Skeen, P., Hobson, C. F., & Herrman, M. 1982. Gay men's and women's perceptions of early family life and their relationships with parents. *Family Relations, 31,* 79–83.

Robinson, I., Ziss, K., Ganza, B., Katz, S., & Robinson, E. 1991. Twenty years of the sexual revolution, 1965–1985: An update. *Journal of Marriage and the Family, 53,* 216–220.

Robinson, I. E., & Jedlicka, D. 1982. Change in sexual attitudes and behavior of college students from 1965 to 1980: A research note. *Journal of Marriage and the Family, 44,* 237–240.

Robinson, J. P. 1989a. Time for work. *American Demographics,* 11 (April), p. 68.

Robinson, J. P. 1989b. Time's up. *American Demographics,* 11 (July), pp. 33–36.

Robinson, J. P. 1990a. I love my TV. *American Demographics,* 12 (September), pp. 24–27.

Robinson, J. P. 1990b. Thanks for reading this. *American Demographics,* 12 (May), pp. 6–7.

Robinson, J. P. 1990c. The time squeeze. *American Demographics,* 12 (February), pp. 30–33.

Robinson, J. P. 1991. Quitting time. *American Demographics,* 13 (May), pp. 34–36.

Rocha, R. E., & Rogers, R. W. 1976. Ares and Babbitt in the classroom: Effects of competition and reward on children's aggression. *Journal of Personality and Social Psychology, 33,* 588–593.

Rochat, P. 1989. Object manipulation and exploration in 2- to 5-month-old infants. *Developmental Psychology, 25,* 871–884.

Rochat, P., Blass, E. M., & Hoffmeyer, L. B. 1988. Oropharyngeal control of hand-mouth coordination in newborn infants. *Developmental Psychology, 24,* 459–463.

Roche, A. F. 1979. Secular trends in human growth, maturation, and development. *Monographs of the Society for Research in Child Development, 44* (Nos. 3–4).

Rodgers, J. L. 1984. Confluence effects: Not here, not now! *Developmental Psychology, 20,* 321–331.

Rodin, J. 1986. Aging and health: Effect of the sense of control. *Science, 233,* 1271–1276.

Rodin, J., & Ickovics, J. R. 1990. Women's health. *American Psychologist, 45,* 1018–1034.

Rodin, J., & Langer, E. J. 1977. Long-term effects of a control-relevant intervention with the institutionalized aged. *Journal of Personality and Social Psychology, 35,* 897–902.

Rodman, H., Pratto, D. J., & Nelson, R. S. 1985. Child care arrangements and children's functioning: A comparison of self-care and adult-care children. *Developmental Psychology, 21,* 413–418.

Roffwarg, H. P., Muzio, J. N., & Dement, W. C. 1966. Ontogenetic development of the human sleep-dream cycle. *Science, 152,* 604–619.

Rogers, C. R. 1970. *On becoming a person: A therapist's view of psychotherapy.* Boston: Houghton Mifflin—Sentry edition.

Rogers, C. R. 1977. Beyond education's watershed. *Educational Leadership, 34,* 623–631.

Rogers, S. J., Parcel, T. L., & Menaghan, E. G. 1991. The effects of maternal working conditions and mastery on child behavior problems: Studying the intergenerational transmission of social control. *Journal of Health and Social Behavior, 32,* 145–164.

Rohrbeck, C. A., & Twentyman, C. T. 1986. Multimodal assessment of impulsiveness in abusing, neglecting, and nonmaltreating mothers and their preschool children. *Journal of Consulting and Clinical Psychology, 54,* 231–236.

Rollins, B. C., & Cannon, K. L. 1974. Marital satisfaction over the family life cycle: A reevaluation. *Journal of Marriage and the Family, 36,* 271–282.

Rollins, B. C., & Feldman, H. 1970. Marital satisfaction over the family life cycle. *Journal of Marriage and the Family, 32,* 20–28.

Rollins, B. C., & Thomas, D. L. 1979. Parental support, power, and control techniques in the socialization of children. In W. R. Burr, R. Hill, F. I. Nye, and I. L. Reiss (Eds.), *Contemporary theories about the family* (Vol. 1). New York: Free Press.

Rook, K. S. 1984. The negative side of social interaction: Impact on psychological well-being. *Journal of Personality and Social Psychology, 46,* 1097–1108.

Rook, K. S. 1987. Social support versus companionship: Effects on life stress, loneliness, and evaluations by others. *Journal of Personality and Social Psychology, 52,* 1132–1147.

Roosa, M.W. 1984. Maternal age, social class, and the obstetric performance of teenagers. *Journal of Youth and Adolescence, 13,* 365–374.

Rosch, E. 1978. Principles of categorization. In E. Rosch & B. B. Lloyd (Eds.), *Cognition and categorization.* Hillsdale, N.J.: Erlbaum.

Rose, D. 1986. "Worse than death": Psychodynamics of rape victims and the need for psychotherapy. *American Journal of Psychiatry, 143,* 817–824.

Rose, R. M., Bourne, P. G., Poe, R. O., Mougey, E. H., Collins, D. R., & Mason, J. W. 1969. Androgen responses to stress. II. Excretion of testosterone, epitestosterone, androsterone, and etiocholanolone during basic combat training and under threat of attack. *Psychosomatic Medicine, 31,* 418–436.

Rose, S. A., Gottfried, A. W., & Bridger, W. H. 1979. Effects of haptic cues on visual recognition memory in full-term and preterm infants. *Infant Behavior and Development, 2,* 55–67.

Rose, S. A., Gottfried, A. W., Melloy-Carminar, P., & Bridger, W. H. 1982. Familiarity and novelty preferences in infant recognition memory. *Developmental Psychology, 18,* 704–713.

Rosen, R., & Hall, E. 1984. *Sexuality.* New York: Random House.

Rosenberg, M. 1985. Self-concept and psychological well-being in adolescence. In R. Leahy (Ed.), *The Development of the self.* New York: Academic Press.

Rosenberg, M. 1986. Self-concept from middle childhood through adolescence. In J. Suls & A. Greenwald (Eds.), *Psychological perspectives on the self* (Vol. 3). Hillsdale, N.J.: Erlbaum.

Rosenberg, M. 1989a. Self-concept research: A historical overview. *Social Forces, 68,* 34–44.

Rosenberg, M. 1989b. *Society and the adolescent self-image* (rev. ed.). Middletown, Conn.: Wesleyan University.

Rosenberg, M., & McCullough, C. B. 1981. Mattering: Inferred significance and mental health among adolescents. *Research in Community and Mental Health, 2,* 163–182.

Rosenberg, M., Schooler, C., & Schoenbach, C. 1989. Self-esteem and adolescent problems: Modeling reciprocal effects. *American Sociological Review, 54,* 1004–1018.

Rosenblatt, P. C., & Skoogberg, E. H. 1974. Birth order in cross-cultural perspective. *Developmental Psychology, 10,* 48–54.

Rosenfeld, A. 1976. *Prolongevity.* New York: Knopf.

Rosenfeld, A., & Stark, E. 1987. The prime of our lives. *Psychology Today, 21* (May), pp. 62–70.

Rosenfield, S. 1989. The effects of women's employment: Personal control and sex differences in mental health. *Journal of Health and Social Behavior, 30,* 77–91.

Rosenhan, D. 1972. Prosocial behavior in children. In W. W. Hartup (Ed.), *The young child* (Vol. 2). Washington, D.C.: National Association for the Education of Young Children.

Rosenhan, D., Moore, B. S., & Underwood, B. 1976. The social psychology of moral behavior. In T. Lickona (Ed.), *Moral development and behavior.* New York: Holt, Rinehart and Winston.

Rosenkoetter, L.I. 1973. Resistance to temptation: Inhibitory and disinhibitory effects of models. *Developmental Psychology, 8,* 80–84.

Rosenstein, K. D. & Oster, H. 1988. Differential facial responses to four basic tastes in newborns. *Child Development, 59,* 1555–1568.

Rosenthal, D. 1987. Ethnic identity development in adolescents. In J. Phinney & M. Rotheram (Eds.), *Children's ethnic socialization: Pluralism and development.* Newbury Park, Calif.: Sage.

Rosenthal, E. 1990. New insights on why some children are fat offer clues on weight loss. *New York Times* (June 4), p. 21.

Rosenthal, E. 1991a. Is high blood pressure less lethal to women? *New York Times* (September 4), p. B7.

Rosenthal, E. 1991b. Filling the gap where a living will won't do. *New York Times* (January 17), p. B7.

Rosenthal, E. 1991c. In matters of life and death, the dying take control. *New York Times* (August 18), pp. E1, E2.

Rosenthal, E. 1991d. As more tiny infants

live, choices and burden grow. *New York Times* (September 29), pp. 1, 16.

Rosenthal, E. 1991*e*. Technique for early prenatal test comes under question in studies. *New York Times* (July 10), p. B6.

Rosenthal, T. L, & Zimmerman, B. J. 1978. *Social learning and cognition.* New York: Academic Press.

Rosenzweig, M. R. 1984. Experience, memory, and the brain. *American Psychologist, 39,* 365–376.

Rosinski, R. R., Pellegrino, J. W., & Siegel, A. W. 1977. Developmental changes in the semantic processing of pictures and words. *Journal of Experimental Child Psychology, 23,* 282–291.

Rosow, I. 1974. *Socialization to old age.* Berkeley: University of California Press.

Ross, H. S. 1982. Establishment of social games among toddlers. *Developmental Psychology, 18,* 509–518.

Ross, H. S., & Lollis, S. P. 1987. Communication within infant social games. *Developmental Psychology, 23,* 241–248.

Ross, S. A. 1971. A test of the generality of the effects of deviant preschool models. *Development Psychology, 4,* 262–267.

Rossel, C., & Ross, J. M. 1986. *The social science evidence on bilingual education.* Boston: Boston University.

Rossi, A. S. 1968. Transition to parenthood. *Journal of Marriage and the Family, 30,* 26–39.

Rossi, A. S. 1977. A biosocial perspective on parenting. *Daedalus, 106,* 1–31.

Rossi, A., & Rossi, P. 1990. *Of human bonding: Parent-child relations across the life course.* New York: Aldine de Gruyter.

Rossi, S., & Wittrock, M. C. 1971. Developmental shifts in verbal recall between mental ages two and five. *Child Development, 42,* 333–338.

Rothbart, M. K. 1987. Roundtable: What is temperament? *Child Development, 58,* 505–529.

Rotheram-Borus, M. J. 1990. Adolescents' reference-group choices, self-esteem, and adjustment. *Journal of Personality and Social Psychology, 59,* 1075–1081.

Rotter, J. B. 1966. Generalized expectancies for internal versus external control of reinforcement. *Psychological Monographs, 80*: No. 1 (Whole No. 609).

Rowe, D. C., & Plomin, R. 1981. The importance of nonshared environmental influences in behavioral development. *Developmental Psychology, 17,* pp. 517–531.

Rowe, J. 1986. Continuing ed sheds its second-class image. *Christian Science Monitor* (October 24), pp. B1, B8.

Rowe, J. W., & Kahn, R. L. 1987. Human aging: Usual and successful. *Science, 237,* 143–149.

Rozin, P. 1990. Development in the food domain. *Developmental Psychology, 26,* 555–562.

Ruben, D. 1991. Sympathy symptoms. *Columbus Ohio Dispatch* (April 11), p. E1.

Rubenstein, C. 1982. Real men don't earn less than their wives. *Psychology Today, 16* (November), pp. 36–41.

Rubenstein, C. 1989. The baby bomb: Research reveals the astonishingly stressful social and emotional consequences of parenthood. *New York Times Magazine* (October 8), pp. 34–41.

Rubenstein, J., & Howes, C. 1976. The effects of peers on toddler interaction with mothers and toys. *Child Development, 47,* 597–605.

Rubin, J. 1986. Out of sight, out of mind? *Psychology Today, 20* (May), p. 14.

Rubin, J. Z., Provenzano, F. J., & Luria, Z. 1974. The eye of the beholder: Parents' views on sex of newborns. *American Journal of Orthopsychiatry, 43,* 720–731.

Rubin, K., Fein, G., & Vandenberg, B. 1983. Play. In E. M. Hetherington (Ed.), *Handbook of child psychology* (Vol. 4). New York: Wiley.

Rubin, K. H., Maioni, T. L., & Hornung, M. 1976. Free play behaviors in middle- and lower-class preschoolers: Parten and Piaget revisited. *Child Development, 47,* 414–419.

Rubin, L. B. 1980. Women of a certain age. *Society, 17* (March/April), pp. 68–76.

Rubin, L. B. 1985. *Just friends: The role of friendship in our lives.* New York: Harper & Row.

Rubin, R. T., Reinisch, J. M., & Haskett, R. F. 1981. Postnatal gonadal steroid effects on human behavior. *Science, 211* (March 20), 1318–1324.

Rubin, Z. 1973. *Liking and loving: An invitation to social psychology.* New York: Holt, Rinehart and Winston.

Rubin, Z. 1977. The love research. *Human Behavior, 6* (February), 56–59.

Rubin, Z. 1980. *Children's friendships.* Cambridge, Mass.: Harvard University Press.

Ruble, D. N., & Brooks-Gunn, J. 1982. The experience of menarche. *Child Development, 53,* 1557–1566.

Ruble, D. N., Brooks-Gunn, J., Fleming, A. S., Fitzmaurice, G., Stangor, C., & Deutsch, F. 1990. Transition to motherhood and the self: Measurement, stability, and change. *Journal of Personality and Social Psychology, 58,* 450–463.

Ruble, D. N., Fleming, A. S., Hackel, L. S., & Stangor, C. 1988. Changes in the marital relationship during the transition to first time motherhood: Effects of violated expectations concerning division of household labor. *Journal of Personality and Social Psychology, 55,* 78–87.

Ruggles, S. 1987. *Prolonged connections: The rise of the extended family in nineteenth century England and America.* Madison: University of Wisconsin.

Rugh, R., & Shettles, L. B. 1971. *From conception to birth: The drama of life's beginnings.* New York: Harper & Row.

Rule, B. G., & Ferguson, T. J. 1986. The effects of media violence on attitudes, emotions, and cognitions. *Journal of Social Issues, 42,* 29–50.

Rumberger, R. W., Ghatak, R., Poulos, G., Ritter, P. L., & Dornbusch, S. M. 1990. Family influences on dropout behavior in one California high school. *Sociology of Education, 63,* 283–299.

Runyan, W. M. 1979. Perceived determinants of highs and lows in life satisfaction. *Developmental Psychology, 15,* 331–333.

Rushton, J. P. 1976. Socialization and the altruistic behavior of children. *Psychological Bulletin, 83,* 898–913.

Russell, C. 1980. The elderly: Myths and facts. *American Demographics, 2,* 30–31.

Russell, C. 1990. This is close. *American Demographics, 12* (February), 9.

Russell, G. 1982. Shared-caregiving families: An Australian study. In M. E. Lamb (Ed.), *Nontraditional families: Parenting and child development.* Hillsdale, N. J.: Erlbaum.

Russell, J. A., & Ridgeway, D. 1983. Dimensions underlying children's emotion concepts. *Developmental Psychology, 19,* 795–804.

Rutter, D. R., & Kurkin, K. 1987. Turn-taking in mother-infant interaction: An examination of vocalizations and gaze. *Developmental Psychology, 23,* 54–61.

Rutter, M. 1974. *The qualities of mothering.* New York: Jason Aronson.

Rutter, M. 1979*a. Fifteen thousand hours: Secondary schools and their effects on children.* Cambridge, Mass.: Harvard University Press.

Rutter, M. 1979*b*. Maternal deprivation, 1972–1978: New findings, new concepts, new approaches. *Child Development, 50,* 283–305.

Rutter, M. 1980. Introduction. In M. Rutter (Ed.), *Scientific foundations of developmental psychiatry.* London: Heinemann.

Rutter, M. 1981. Stress, coping, and development: Some issues and some questions. *Journal of Child Psychology and Psychiatry, 22,* 323–356.

Rutter, M. 1983. School effects on pupil progress: Research findings and policy implications. *Child Development, 54,* 1–29.

Rutter, M. 1987. Psychosocial resilience and protective mechanisms. *American Journal of Orthopsychiatry, 57,* 316–331.

Rutter, M. 1990. Psychosocial resilience and protective mechanisms. In J. Rolf, A. S. Masten, D. Cicchetti, K. H. Nuechterlein, & S. Weintraub (Eds.), *Risk and protective factors in the development of psychopathology.* New York: Cambridge University.

Ryan, K. J. 1982. Hospital or home births. *The Harvard Medical School Health Letter, 8* (November), 3–4.

Ryder, N. 1965. The cohort as a concept in the study of social change. *American Sociological Review, 30,* 843–861.

Ryff, C. D. 1985. Subjective experience of life-span transition. In A. S. Rossi (Ed.), *Gender and the life course.* New York: Aldine de Gruyter.

Ryff, C. D. 1989. Happiness is everything, or is it? Explorations on the meaning of psychological well-being. *Journal of Personality and Social Psychology, 57,* 1069–1081.

Ryff, C. D. 1991. Possible selves in adulthood and old age: A tale of shifting horizons. *Psychology and Aging, 6,* 286–295.

Saarni, C. 1979. Children's understanding of display rules for expressive behavior. *Developmental Psychology, 15,* 424–429.

Sachs, J. 1987. Preschool boys' and girls' language use in pretend play. In S. U. Phillips, S. Steele, & C. Tanz (Eds.), *Language, gender and sex in comparative perspective.* Cambridge: Cambridge University.

Sage, G. H. 1971. *Introduction to motor behavior.* Reading, Mass.: Addison-Wesley.

Salapatek, P. 1975. Pattern perception in early infancy. In L. B. Cohen & P. Salapatek (Eds.), *Infant perception: From sensation to cognition.* New York: Academic Press.

Salapatek, P., & Kessen, W. 1966. Visual scanning of triangles by the human newborn. *Journal of Experimental Child Psychology, 3,* 155–167.

Salholz, E. 1986. Too late for Prince Charming? *Newsweek* (June 2), pp. 54–61.

Salholz, E. 1990. The future of gay America. *Newsweek* (March 12), pp. 20–25.

Saltz, R. 1973. Effects of part-time "mothering" on IQ and SQ of young institutionalized children. *Child Development, 44,* 166–170.

Sameroff, A. J. 1968. The components of sucking in the human newborn. *Journal of Experimental Child Psychology, 6,* 607–623.

Sameroff, A. J., & Cavanagh, P. J. 1979. Learning in infancy: A developmental perspective. In J. D. Osofsky (Ed.), *Handbook of infant development.* New York: Wiley.

Sampson, R. J. 1987. Urban black violence: The effect of male joblessness and family disruption. *American Journal of Sociology, 93,* 348–382.

Sampson, R. J., & Laub, J. H. 1990. Crime and deviance over the life course: The salience of adult social bonds. *American Sociological Review, 55,* 609–627.

Samuelson, R. J. 1990. Pampering the elderly. *Newsweek* (October 29), p. 61.

Sanders, J. M. 1990. Public transfers: Safety net or inducement into poverty? *Social Forces, 68,* 813–834.

Sanders-Phillips, K., Strauss, M. E., & Gutberlet, R. L. 1988. The effect of obstetric medication on newborn infant feeding behavior. *Infant Behavior and Development, 11,* 251–263.

Sandroff, R. 1988. Sexual harassment in the Fortune 500. *Working Woman* (December), pp. 69–82.

Sanger, D. E. 1987. Pregnancy transfers by A. T. & T. *New York Times* (January 14), p. 21.

Sanoff, A. P. 1990. Childhood's chronicler. *U.S. News & World Report* (December 3), pp. 66–69.

Santrock, J. W. 1972. Relation of type and onset of father absence to cognitive development. *Child Development, 43,* 455–469.

Santrock, J. W., & Sitterle, K. A. 1987. Parent-child relationships in stepmother families. In K. Pasley & M. Ihinger-Tallman (Eds.), *Remarriage and stepparenting: Current research and theory.* New York: Guilford.

Santrock, J. W., Smith, P. C., & Bourbeau, P. E. 1976. Effects of social comparison on aggression and regression in groups of young children. *Child Development, 47,* 831–837.

Santrock, J. W., Warshak, R., Lindbergh, C., & Meadows, L. 1982. Children's and parents' observed social behavior in stepfather families. *Child Development, 53,* 472–480.

Sapir, E. 1949. *Selected writings in language, culture, and personality.* Berkeley: University of California Press.

Sarason, S. B. 1977. *Work, aging, and social change: Professionals and the one life-one career imperative.* New York: Basic Books.

Sassen, G. 1980. Success anxiety in women: A constructivist interpretation of its source and significance. *Harvard Educational Review, 50,* 13–24.

Savin-Williams, R. C., & Demo, D. H. 1984. Developmental change and stability in adolescent self-concept. *Developmental Psychology, 20,* 1100–1110.

Sayers, Janet. 1991. *Mothers of psychoanalysis: Helene Deutsch, Karen Horney, Anna Freud, Melanie Klein.* New York: W. W. Norton.

Scafidi, F. A. 1986. Effects of tactile/kinesthetic stimulation on the clinical course and sleep/wake behavior of preterm neonates. *Infant Behavior and Development, 9,* 91–105.

Scafidi, F. A., Field, T. M., Schanberg, S. M., Bauer, C. R., Tucci, K., Roberts, J., Morrow, C., & Kuhn, C. M. 1990. Massage stimulates growth in preterm infants: A replication. *Infant Behavior and Development, 13,* 167–188.

Scanzoni, J., Polonko, K., Teachman, J., & Thompson, L. 1989. *The sexual bond: Rethinking families and close relationships.* Newbury Park, Calif.: Sage.

Scanzoni, L., & Scanzoni, J. 1981. *Men, women, and change* (2nd ed.). New York: McGraw-Hill.

Scarf, M. 1972a. He and she: The sex hormones and behavior. *New York Times Magazine* (May 7), pp. 30ff.

Scarf, M. 1977. From joy to depression. *New York Times Magazine* (April 24), pp. 31–36.

Scarf, M. 1980. *Unfinished business: Pressure points in the lives of women.* Garden City, N.Y.: Doubleday.

Scarf, M., & Grajek, S. 1982. Similarities and differences among siblings. In M. E. Lamb & B. Sutton-Smith (Eds.), *Sibling relationships.* Hillsdale, N.J.: Erlbaum.

Scarr, S. 1984. *Mother care/other care.* New York: Basic Books.

Scarr, S. 1985a. An author's frame of mind (review of *Frames of Mind* by H. Gardner). *New Ideas in Psychology, 3,* 95–100.

Scarr, S. 1985b. Constructing psychology. *American Psychologist, 40,* 499–512.

Scarr, S., & McCartney, K. 1983. How people make their own environments: A theory of genotype-environment effects. *Child Development, 54,* 424–435.

Scarr, S., Phillips, D., & McCartney, K. 1989. Working mothers and their families. *American Psychologist, 44,* 1402–1409.

Scarr, S., & Weinberg, R. A. 1976. IQ test performance of black children adopted by white families. *American Psychologist, 31,* 726–739.

Schachter, F. F. 1981. Toddlers with employed mothers. *Child Development, 52,* 958-964.

Schaefer, E. S. 1959. A circumplex model for maternal behavior. *Journal of Abnormal and Social Psychology, 59,* 226–235.

Schaffer, H. R. 1966. Activity level as a constitutional determinant of infantile reaction to deprivation. *Child Development, 37,* 595–602.

Schaffer, H. R. 1971. *The growth of sociability.* Baltimore: Penguin Books.

Schaffer, H. R., & Emerson, P. E. 1964. The development of social attachments in infancy. *Monographs of the Society for Research in Child Development, 29* (3).

Schaie, K. W. 1965. A general model for the study of development problems. *Psychological Bulletin, 64,* 92–107.

Schaie, K. W. 1988. Ageism in psychological research. *American Psychologist, 43,* 179–183.

Schaie, K. W. 1989. Perceptual speed in adulthood: Cross-sectional and longitudinal studies. *Psychology and Aging, 4,* 443–453.

Schaie, K. W., Campbell, R. T., & Rawlings, S. C. (Eds.). 1988. *Methodological issues in aging research.* New York: Springer.

Schaie, K. W., & Willis, S. L. 1986. Can decline in adult intellectual functioning be reversed? *Developmental Psychology, 22,* 223–232.

Schapiro, M. O., & Ahlburg, D. A. 1986. Why crime is down. *American Demographics, 8* (October), 56–58.

Scharlach, A. E. 1987. Relieving feelings of strain among women with elderly mothers. *Psychology and Aging, 2,* 9–13.

Schindler, P. J., Moely, B. E., & Frank, A. L. 1987. Time in day care and social participation of young children. *Developmental Psychology, 23,* 255–261.

Schleifer, S. J., Keller, S. E., McKegney, F. P., & Stein, M. 1980. Bereavement and lymphoctye function. In *New Research.* San Francisco: American Psychiatric Association.

Schmeck, H. M., Jr. 1976. Trend in growth of children lags. *New York Times* (June 10), p. 13C.

Schmeck, H. M., Jr. 1982. Mysterious thymus gland may hold the key to aging. *New York Times* (January 26), pp. 17, 18.

Schmeck, H. M., Jr. 1983b. U.S. panel calls for patients' right to end life. *New York Times* (March 22), pp. 1, 18.

Schmeck, H. M., Jr. 1986a. Fetal tests can now find many more genetic flaws? *New York Times* (March 11), pp. 21, 22.

Schmeck, H. M., Jr. 1986b. Ninety percent in poll support right to die. *New York Times* (December 2), p. 21.

Schmeck, H. M., Jr. 1987a. Burst of discoveries reveals genetic basis for many diseases. *New York Times* (March 31), pp. 17, 18.

Schmeck, H. M., Jr. 1987b. A form of Alzheimer's is linked to defective gene. *New York Times* (February 20), pp. 1, 11.

Schmidt, D. F., & Boland, S. M. 1986. Structure of perceptions of older adults: Evidence for multiple stereotypes. *Psychology and Aging, 1,* 255–260.

Schmidt, W. E. 1990a. Hard work can't stop hard times. *New York Times* (November 25), pp. 1, 30.

Schmidt, W. E. 1990b. Valentine in a survey: Fidelity is thriving. *New York Times* (February 12), p. B1.

Schnaiberg, A., & Goldenberg, S. 1975. Closing the circle: The impact of children on parental status. *Journal of Marriage and the Family, 37,* 937–953.

Schnaiberg, A., & Goldenberg, S. 1989. From empty nest to crowded nest: The dynamics of incompletely-launched young adults. *Social Problems, 36,* 251–269.

Schneck, M. K., Reisberg, B., & Ferris, S. H. 1982. An overview of current concepts of Alzheimer's disease. *American Journal of Psychiatry, 139,* 165–173.

Schneider, B. H., Rubin, K. H., & Ledingham, J. E. (Eds.). 1985. *Children's peer relationships. Issues in assessment and intervention.* New York: Springer-Verlag.

Schneider, E. L., & Brody, J. A. 1983. Aging, natural death, and the compression of morbidity: Another view. *New England Journal of Medicine, 309,* 854–855.

Schneider, E. L., Vining, E. M., Hadley, E. C., & Farnham, S. A. 1986. Recommended dietary allowances and the health of the elderly. *New England Journal of Medicine. 314,* 157–160.

Schneider, W. 1987. Homosexuals: Is AIDS changing attitudes? *Public Opinion, 10* (July/August), pp. 6–7+.

Schnittger, M. H., & Bird, G. W. 1990. Coping among dual-career men and women across the family life cycle. *Family Relations, 39,* 199–205.

Schoeni, R. 1990. News release, Population Studies Center, University of Michigan, Ann Arbor, Michigan, November 13.

Schofield, J. W. 1978. School desegregation and intergroup relations. In D. Dar Tal & L. Saxe (Eds.), *The social psychology of education.* New York: Halsted Press.

Schofield, J. W. 1982. *Black and white in school: Trust, tension, or tolerance?* New York: Praeger.

Schofield, M. 1965. *Sociological aspects of homosexuality: A comparative study of three types of homosexuals.* Boston: Little, Brown.

Schooler, C., & Schaie, K. W. (Eds.). 1987. *Cognitive functioning and social structure over the life course.* Norwood, N.J.: Ablex.

Schramm, W. T., Lyle, J., & Parker, E. B. 1961. *Television in the lives of our children.* Stanford, Calif: Stanford University Press.

Schulenberg, J. E., Vondracek, F. W., & Crouter, A. C. 1984. The influence of the family on vocational development. *Journal of Marriage and the Family, 46,* 129–143.

Schulman, S. 1986. Facing the invisible handicap. *Psychology Today, 20* (February), pp. 58–64.

Schultz, E. E. 1990. Ruling draws the worried to 'living wills.' *Wall Street Journal* (June 29), pp. C1, C8.

Schulz, R., & Curnow, C. 1988. Peak performance and age among superathletes: Track and field, swimming, baseball, tennis, and golf. *Journal of Gerontology, 43,* P113–P120.

Schulz, R., & Hanusa, B. H. 1980. Experimental social gerontology: A social psychological perspective. *Journal of Social Issues, 36,* 30–46.

Schulz, R., Visinainer, P., & Williamson, G. M. 1990. Psychiatric and physical morbidity effects of caregiving. *Journal of Gerontology, 45,* P181–191.

Schuman, H., & Scott, J. 1987. Problems in the use of survey questions to measure public opinion. *Science, 236,* 957–959.

Schuman, H., & Scott, J. 1989. Generations and collective memories. *American Sociological Review, 54,* 359–381.

Schumm, W. R., & Bugaighis, M. A. 1986. Marital quality over the marital career: Alternative explanations. *Journal of Marriage and the Family, 48,* 165–168.

Schwalbe, M. L. 1985. Autonomy in work and self-esteem. *The Sociological Quarterly, 26,* 519–535.

Schwartz, D. M., & Thompson, M. G. 1981. Do anorectics get well? *American Journal of Psychiatry, 138,* 319–323.

Schwartz, F. N. 1981. Reducing stress in two-career families—expert's advice. *U.S. News & World Report* (November 2), pp. 89–90.

Schwartz, G. M., Izard, C. E., & Ansul, S. E. 1985. The 5-month-old's ability to discriminate facial expressions of emotion. *Infant Behavior and Development, 8,* 65–77.

Schwartz, J. 1987. Teen attitudes. *American Demographics, 9* (August), 42–44.

Schwartz, J. 1987. A "superminority" tops out. *Newsweek* (May 11), pp. 48–49.

Schwartz, J. 1988. The forgotten market. *American Demographics, 10* (May), 12.

Schwartz, J. 1990. Is there life before bed? *American Demographics, 12* (March), 12.

Schwartz, J., & Crispell, D. 1991. Prenatal programs pay off. *American Demographics, 13* (February), 14–16.

Schweinhart, L.J., & Weikart, 1985. Evidence that good early childhood programs work. *Phi Delta Kappan, 66* (April), 545–553.

Scott, C. 1990. As baby boomers age, fewer couples untie the knot. *Wall Street Journal* (November 7), pp. B1, B5.

Scott, J. W. 1982. The mechanization of women's work. *Scientific American, 247,* pp. 167–187.

Searleman, A., Porac, C., & Coren, S. 1989. Relationship between birth order, birth stress, and lateral preferences: A critical review. *Psychological Bulletin, 105,* 397–408.

Sears, P. S., & Barbee, A. H. 1977. Career and life satisfaction among Terman's gifted women. In J. C. Stanley, W. C. George, & C. H. Solano (Eds.), *The gifted and the creative: Fifty-year perspective.* Baltimore: Johns Hopkins University Press.

Sears, R. R. 1963. Dependency motivation. In M. Jones (Ed.), *Nebraska Symposium on Motivation.* Lincoln: University of Nebraska Press.

Sears, R. R. 1970. Relation of early socialization experiences to self-concepts and gender role in middle childhood. *Child Development, 41,* 267–289.

Sears, R. R. 1972. Attachment, dependency, and frustration. In J. L. Gewirtz (Ed.), *Attachment and dependency.* Washington, D.C.: Winston.

Sears, R. R. 1977. Sources of life satisfactions of the Terman gifted men. *American Psychologist, 32,* 119–128.

Sears, R. R., Maccoby, E. E., & Levin, H. 1957. *Patterns of child rearing.* New York: Harper & Row.

Sears, R. R., Rau, L., & Alpert, R. 1965. *Identification and child rearing.* Stanford, Calif.: Stanford University Press.

Sebald, H. 1977. *Adolescence: A social psychological analysis* (2nd ed.). Englewood Cliffs, N.J.: Prentice-Hall.

Sebald, H. 1984. *Adolescence: A social psychological analysis.* Englewood Cliffs, N.J.: Prentice-Hall.

Sebald, H. 1986. Adolescents' shifting orientation toward parents and peers. *Journal of Marriage and the Family, 48,* 5–13.

Seeman, J. 1989. Toward a model of positive health. *American Psychologist, 44,* 1099–1109.

Seeman, M. 1959. On the meaning of alienation. *American Sociological Review, 24,* 783–791.

Seeman, M., Seeman, T., & Sayles, M. 1985. Social networks and health status: A longitudinal analysis. *Social Psychology Quarterly, 48,* 237–248.

Seitz, V. 1975. Integrated versus segregated school attendance and immediate recall for standard and nonstandard English. *Developmental Psychology, 11,* 217–223.

Seitz, V., Rosenbaum, L. K., & Apfel, N. H. 1985. Effects of family support intervention: A ten-year follow-up. *Child Development, 56,* 376–391.

Self, P. A., Horowitz, F. D., & Paden, L. Y. 1972. Olfaction in newborn infants. *Developmental Psychology, 7,* 349–363.

Seligman, M. E. P. 1973. Fall into helplessness. *Psychology Today, 7* (June), pp. 43–48.

Seligman, M. E. P. 1975. *Helplessness.* San Francisco: Freeman.

Seligman, M. E. P. 1978. Comment and integration. *Journal of Abnormal Psychology, 87,* 165–179.

Seligman, M. E. P. 1990. *Learned optimism.* New York: Knopf.

Seligman, M. E. P., & Maier, S. F. 1967. Failure to escape traumatic shock. *Journal of Experimental Psychology, 74,* 1–9.

Selman, R. L. 1980. *The youth of interpersonal understanding: Developmental and clinical analyses.* New York: Academic Press.

Selman, R. L., & Schultz, L. H. 1990. *Making a friend in youth.* Chicago: University of Chicago.

Seltzer, J. A. 1991. Legal custody arrangements and children's economic welfare. *American Journal of Sociology, 96,* 895–929.

Selye, H. 1956. *The stress of life.* New York: McGraw-Hill.

Serbin, L. A., & Sprafkin, C. 1986. The salience of gender and the process of sex typing in three- to seven-year-old children. *Child Development, 57,* 1188–1199.

Serbin, L. A., Sprafkin, C., Elman, M., & Doyle, A. 1984. The early development of sex differentiated patterns of social influence. *Canadian Journal of Social Science, 14,* 350–363.

Sewell, W. H. 1952. Infant training and the personality of the child. *American Journal of Sociology, 59,* 150–159.

Sewell, W. H. 1981. Notes on educational, occupational, and economic achievement in American society. *Phi Delta Kappan, 62,* 322–325.

Sewell, W. H., & Mussen, P. H. 1952. The effects of feeding, weaning, and scheduling procedures on childhood adjustment and the formation of oral symptoms.

Shafii, M., Carrigan, S., Whittinghill, J. R., & Derrick, A. 1985. Psychological autopsy of completed suicide in children and adolescents. *American Journal of Psychiatry, 142,* 1061–1064.

Shanas, E. 1972. Adjustment of retirement: Substitution or accommodation? In F. Carp (Ed.), *Retirement.* New York: Behavioral Publications.

Shanas, E., Townsend, P., Wedderburn, D., Fries, H., Milhoj, P., & Stehouwer, J. 1968. *Old people in three industrial societies.* New York: Atherton.

Shannon, L. 1982. *Assessing the relationship of adult criminal careers to juvenile careers.* Washington, D.C.: Government Printing Office.

Shapiro, J. 1991. A vote on legal euthanasia. *U.S. News & World Report* (September 30), pp. 32–34.

Shapiro, J. L. 1987. *When men are pregnant.* New York: Impact.

Shapiro, L. 1990. Guns and dolls. *Newsweek* (May 28), pp. 56–65.

Shapiro, S. 1985. Risk of localized and widespread endometrial cancer in relation to recent and discontinued use of conjugated estrogens. *New England Journal of Medicine, 313,* 269–272.

Sharp, D., Cole, M., & Lave, C. 1979. Education and cognitive development: The evidence from experimental research. *Monographs of the Society for Research in Child Development, 44* (178).

Sharpe, R., & Lundstrom, M. 1990. SIDS sometimes used to cover up child-abuse deaths. *USA Today* (December 17), p. 2D.

Shaw, R. J., & Craik, F. I. M. 1989. Age differences in predictions and performance on a cued recall task. *Psychology and Aging, 4,* 131–135.

Shedler, J., & Block, J. 1990. Adolescent drug use and psychological health: A longitudinal inquiry. *American Psychologist, 45,* 612–630.

Sheehy, G. 1976. *Passages.* New York: Dutton.

Sheldon, A. 1989. Conflict talk: Sociolinguistic challenges to self-assertion and how young girls meet them. Paper presented at the April biennial meeting of the Society for Research in Child Development, Kansas City.

Sheleff, L. 1981. *Generations apart: Adult hostility to youth.* New York: McGraw-Hill.

Shellenbarger, S. 1991. Work & family. *Wall Street Journal* (September 26), p. B1.

Shelton, J., & Hill, J. P. 1959. Effects on cheating of achievement anxiety and knowledge of peer performance. *Developmental Psychology, 1,* 449–455.

Shenon, P. 1983. What's new with dual-career couples. *New York Times* (March 6), p. F29.

Shephard, R. J., & Montelpare, W. 1988. Geriatric benefits of exercise as an adult. *Journal of Gerontology, 43,* M86–90.

Sherif, M. 1936. *The psychology of social norms.* New York: Harper & Row.

Sherman, J. 1978. *Sex-related cognitive differences.* Springfield, Ill.: Thomas.

Sherman, T. 1985. Categorization skills in infants. *Child Development, 56,* 1561–1573.

Shield, R. R. 1988. *Uneasy endings: Daily life in an American nursing home.* Ithaca, N.Y.: Cornell University.

Shirk, S. R. 1987. Self-doubt in late childhood and early adolescence. *Journal of Youth and Adolescence, 16,* 59–68.

Shneidman, E. 1989. The Indian summer of life: A preliminary study of septuagenarians. *American Psychologist, 44,* 684–694.

Shock, N. W. 1962. The physiology of aging. *Scientific American, 206* (January), pp. 100–110.

Shock, N. W. 1977. Biological theories of aging. In J. E. Birren & K. W. Schaie (Eds.), *Handbook of the psychology of aging.* New York: Van Nostrand.

Shore, C. 1986. Combinatorial play, conceptual development, and early multiword speech. *Developmental Psychology, 22,* 184–190.

Shore, C., O'Connell, B., & Bates, E. 1984. First sentences in language and symbolic play. *Developmental Psychology, 20,* 872–880.

Shorter, E. 1975. *The making of the modern family.* New York: Basic Books.

Shreve, A. 1984. The working mother as role model. *New York Times Magazine* (September 9), pp. 39–43+.

Shrum, W., & Cheek, N. H., Jr. 1987. Social structure during the school years. Onset of the degrouping process. *American Sociological Review, 52,* 218–223.

Shuchman, M. & Wilkes, M. S. 1990. Dramatic progress against depression. *New York Times Magazine, Part 2* (October 7), pp. 12, 30+.

Shulman, V. L., Restaino-Baumann, L. C., & Butler, L. (Eds.). 1985. *The future of Piagetian theory: The Neo-Piagetians.* New York: Plenum.

Shultz, T. R., & Kestenbaum, N. R. 1985. Causal reasoning in children. In G. Whitehead (Ed.), *Annals of child development* (Vol. 2). Greenwich, Conn.: JAI.

Shultz, T. R., & Wells, D. 1985. Judging the intentionality of action-outcomes. *Developmental Psychology, 21,* 83–89.

Shultz, T. R., Fisher, G. W., Pratt, C. C., & Rulf, S. 1986. Selection of causal rules. *Child Development, 57,* 143–152.

Shweder, R. A., Mahapatra, M., & Miller, J. G. 1987. Culture and moral development. In J. Stigler, R. A. Shweder, & G. Herdt (Eds.), *Cultural psychology: Essays on comparative human development.* New York: Cambridge University.

Siegal, M. 1987. Are sons and daughters treated more differently by fathers than mothers? *Developmental Review, 7,* 183–209.

Siegel, A. W., Kirasic, J. C., & Kilburg, R. R. 1973. Recognition memory in reflective and impulsive preschool children. *Child Development, 44,* 651–656.

Siegel, J. M. 1990. Stressful life events and use of physician services among the elderly: The moderating role of pet ownership. *Journal of Personality and Social Psychology, 58,* 1081–1086.

Siegel, R. K. 1981. Accounting for "afterlife" experiences. *Psychology Today, 15* (January), pp. 65–75.

Siegelman, M. 1973. Parent behavior correlates of personality traits related to creativity in sons and daughters. *Journal of Consulting and Clinical Psychology, 40,* 139–147.

Siegler, I. C., & Botwinick, J. 1979. A long-term longitudinal study of intellectual ability of older adults. The matter of selective subject attrition. *Journal of Gerontology, 34,* 242–245.

Siegler, I. C., McCarty, S. M., & Logue, P. E. 1982. Wechsler memory scale scores, selective attrition, and distance from death. *Journal of Gerontology, 37,* 176–181.

Siegler, R. S., & Jenkins, E. 1989. *How children discover new strategies.* Hillside, N.J.: Erlbaum.

Siegman, A. W., & Dembroski, T. M. (Eds.). 1989. *In search of coronary prone behavior: Beyond type A.* Hillside, N.J.: Erlbaum.

Sigman, M., Neumann, C., Carter, E., & Cattle, D. J. 1988. Home interactions and the development of Embu toddlers in Kenya. *Child Development, 59,* 1251–1261.

Sigman, M., Neumann, C., Jansen, A. A. J., & Bwibo, N. 1989. Cognitive abilities of Kenyan children in relation to nutrition, family characteristics, and education. *Child Development, 60,* 1463–1474.

Silk, L. 1987. Women gain, but at a cost. *New York Times* (February 6), p. 30.

Silverberg, S. B., & Steinberg, L. 1990. Psychological well-being of parents with early adolescent children. *Developmental Psychology, 26,* 658–666.

Silverman, M. 1987. Mandatory tests for AIDS? *U.S. News & World Report* (March 9), p. 62.

Silverman, P. 1983. Coping with grief—it can't be rushed. *U.S. News & World Report.* (November 14), pp. 65–68.

Siman, M. L. 1977. Application of a new model of peer group influence to naturally existing adolescent friendship groups. *Child Development, 48,* 270–274.

Simmons, L. W. 1945. *The role of the aged in primitive society.* New Haven: Yale University Press.

Simmons, L. W. 1960. Aging in preindustrial societies. In C. Tibbitts (Ed.), *Handbook of social gerontology.* Chicago: University of Chicago Press.

Simmons, R. G., & Blyth, D. A. 1987. *Moving into adolescence: The impact of pubertal change and school context.* New York: Aldine DeGruyter.

Simons, R. L., & Miller, M. G. 1987. Adolescent depression: Assessing the impact of negative cognitions and socio-environmental problems. *Social Work, 32,* 326–330.

Simons, R. L., & Robertson, J. F. 1989. The impact of parenting factors, deviant peers, and coping style upon adolescent drug use. *Family Relations, 38,* 273–281.

Simons, R. L., Whitbeck, L. B., Conger, R. D., & Chyi-In, W. 1991. Intergenerational transmission of harsh parenting. *Developmental Psychology, 27,* 159–171.

Simon, S. 1991. Joint custody loses favor for increasing children's feeling of being torn apart. *Wall Street Journal* (July 15), pp. B1, B2.

Simonton, D. K. 1984. *Genius, creativity, and leadership.* Cambridge, Mass.: Harvard University Press.

Simonton, D. K. 1988a. Age and outstanding achievement: What do we know after a century of research? *Psychological Bulletin, 104,* 251–267.

Simonton, D. K. 1988b. *Scientific genius: A psychology of science.* New York: Cambridge University.

Simpson, E. L. 1974. Moral development research: A case study of scientific cultural bias. *Human Development, 17,* 81–106.

Simpson, E. L. 1976. A holistic approach to moral development and behavior. In T. Lickona (Ed.), *Moral development and behavior: Theory, research, and social issues.* New York: Holt, Rinehart and Winston.

Singer, J. L., Singer, D. G., & Rapaczynski, W. S. 1984. Family patterns and television viewing as predictors of children's beliefs and aggression. *Journal of Communication, 34,* 73–89.

Singer, M. I. 1970. Comparisons of indicators of homosexuality on the MMPI. *Journal of Consulting and Clinical Psychology, 34,* 15–18.

Singh, S., Forrest, J. D., & Torres, A. 1990. *Prenatal care in the United States: A state and county inventory.* New York: The Alan Guttmacher Institute.

Singleton, L. C., & Asher, S. R. 1977. Peer preferences and social interaction among third-grade children in an integrated school district. *Journal of Educational Psychology, 69,* 330–336.

Sinnott, J. D. 1977. Sex-role inconstancy, biology, and successful aging. A dialectical model. *The Gerontolgist, 17,* 459–463.

Sinnott, J. D. 1982. Correlates of sex roles of older adults. *Journal of Gerontology, 37,* 587–594.

Siqueland, E. R. 1968. Reinforcement patterns and extinction in human newborns. *Journal of Experimental Child Psychology, 6,* 431–442.

Siwolop, S. 1987. The AIDS epidemic and business. *Business Week* (March 23), pp. 122–132.

Skeels, H. M. 1966. Adult status of children with contrasting early life experiences. *Monographs of the Society for Research in Child Development, 31* (3).

Skinner, B. F. 1957. *Verbal behavior.* New York: Appleton-Century-Crofts.

Skinner, E. A., Chapman, M., & Bates, P. B. 1988. Control, means-ends, and agency beliefs: A new conceptualization and its measurement during childhood. *Journal of Personality and Social Psychology, 54,* 117–133.

Skipper, J. K., & Nass, G. 1966. Dating behavior: A framework for analysis and an illustration. *Journal of Marriage and the Family, 28,* 412–420.

Sklar, L. S., & Anisman, H. 1981. Stress and cancer. *Psychological Bulletin, 89,* 369–406.

Slade, M. 1986. The ebb and flow of friends. *New York Times* (January 27), p. 15.

Slife, B. D., & Rychlak, J. F. 1982. Role of affective assessment in modeling aggressive behavior. *Journal of Personality and Social Psychology, 43,* 861–868.

Slobin, D. I. 1972. They learn the same way all around the world. *Psychology Today, 6* (July), pp. 71–82.

Sluckin, W., Herbert, M., & Sluckin. 1983. *Maternal bonding.* Oxford, England: Blackwell.

Small, S. A., Cornelius, S., & Eastman, G. 1983. Parenting adolescent children: A period of adult storm and stress? Paper presented at the annual meeting of the American Psychological Association, Anaheim, CA.

Small, S. A., & Riley, D. 1990. Toward a multidimensional assessment of work spillover into family life. *Journal of Marriage and the Family, 52,* 51–61.

Smart, M. S., & Smart, R. C. 1973. *Infants: Development and relationships.* New York: Macmillan.

Smart, R., & Fejer, D. 1972. Drug use among adolescents and their parents: Closing the generation gap in mood modification. *Journal of Abnormal Psychology, 79,* 153–160.

Smedslund, J. 1961. The acquisition of conservation of substance and weight in children. *Scandinavian Journal of Psychology, 2,* 71–84ff.

Smetana, J. G. 1984. Toddlers' social interactions regarding moral and conventional transgressions. *Child Development, 55,* 1767–1776.

Smetana, J. G. 1986. Preschool children's conceptions of sex-role transgressions. *Child Development, 57,* 862–871.

Smetana, J. G. 1988. Adolescents' and parents' conceptions of parental authority. *Child Development, 59,* 321–335.

Smetana, J. G. 1989. Adolescents' and parents' reasoning about actual family conflict. *Child Development, 60,* 1052–1067.

Smetana, J., G., Killen, M., & Turiel, E. 1991. Children's reasoning about interpersonal and moral conflicts. *Child Development, 62,* 629–644.

Smith, A. D., Park, D. C., Cherry, K., & Berkovsky, K. 1990. Age differences in memory for concrete and abstract pictures. *Journal of Gerontology, 45,* P205–209.

Smith, B. A., Fillion, T., J., & Blass, E. M. 1990. Orally mediated sources of calming in 1- to 3-day-old human infants. *Developmental Psychology, 26,* 731–737.

Smith, E. L. III, Bennett, M. J., Harwerth, R. S., & Crawford, M. L. J. 1978. Binocularity in kittens reared with optically induced squint. *Science, 204* (May 25), 875–877.

Smith, J. D., & Nelson, D. G. K. 1988. Is the more impulsive child a more holistic processor? A reconsideration. *Child Development, 59,* 719–727.

Smith, J. M. 1990. Mothers: Tired of taking the rap. *New York Times Magazine* (June 10), pp. 32–33+.

Smith, L. 1987a. Throwing money at AIDS. *Fortune* (August 31), pp. 64–67.

Smith, L. 1987b. The war between the generations. *Fortune* (July 20), pp. 78–82.

Smith, P. B., & Pederson, D. R. 1988. Maternal sensitivity and patterns of infant-mother attachment. *Child Development, 59,* 1097–1101.

Smith, P. K. 1978. A longitudinal study of social participation in preschool children: Solitary and parallel play reexamined. *Developmental Psychology, 14,* 517–523.

Smith, R. A. P., Woodward, N. J., Wallston, B. S., Wallston, K. A., Rye, P., & Zylstra, M. 1988. Health care implications of desire and expectancy for control in elderly adults. *Journal of Gerontology, 43,* P1–7.

Smith, R. M., & Smith, C. W. 1981. Child rearing and single-parent fathers. *Family Relations, 30,* 411–417.

Smith, T. E. 1990. Parental separation and the academic self-concepts of adolescents: An effort to solve the puzzle of separation effects. *Journal of Marriage and the Family, 52,* 107–118.

Smolowe, J. 1990. To grandma's house we go. *Time* (November 5), pp. 86–90.

Snarey, J., Kuehne, V. S., Son, L., Hauser, S., & Vaillant, G. 1987. The role of parenting in men's psychosocial development. *Developmental Psychology, 23,* 593–603.

Snarey, J. R. 1985. Cross-cultural universality of social-moral development: A critical review of Kohlbergian research. *Psychological Bulletin, 97,* 202–232.

Snarey, J. R. 1987. A question of morality. *Psychology Today, 21* (June), pp. 6–8.

Snider, M. 1991. "Safe" fetal surgery offers babies new hope. *USA Today* (February 13), p. 1A.

Snow, C. E. 1977. The development of conversation between mothers and babies. *Journal of Child Language, 4,* 1–22.

Snow, M. E., Jacklin, C. N., & Maccoby, E. E. 1981. Birth-order differences in peer sociability at thirty-three months. *Child Development, 52,* 589–595.

Snow, M. E., Jacklin, C. N., & Maccoby, E. E. 1983. Sex-of-child differences in father-child interaction at one year of age. *Child Development, 54,* 227–232.

Snyder, M., & Ickes, W. 1985. Personality and social behavior. In G. Lindzey & E. Aronson (Eds.), *Handbook of social psychology* (3rd ed.). Vol. 2. Reading, Mass.: Addison-Wesley.

Sobel, D. 1980. Siblings: Studies find rivalry, dependency revive in adulthood. *New York Times* (October 28), p. C1.

Sobel, J., & Stunkard, A. J. 1989. Socioeconomic status and obesity: A review of the literature. *Psychological Bulletin, 105,* 260–275.

Soeffing, M. 1975. Abused children are exceptional children. *Exceptional children, 42,* 126–133.

Sokolov, E. N. 1958/1963. *Perception and the conditioned reflex* (S. W. Waydenfeld, trans.). New York: Macmillan.

Sokolov, Y. N. 1969. The modeling properties of the nervous system. In M. Coles & I. Maltzman (Eds.), *A handbook of contemporary Soviet psychology.* New York: Basic Books.

Solimini, C. 1991. The career women's guide to fertility. *Working Woman* (January), pp. 90–95+.

Solomon, J., & Fuchsberg, G. 1990. Older Americans found ready, able to return to work. *Wall Street Journal* (January 26), p. A8.

Solnit, A. J., & Provence, S. 1979. Vulnerability and risk in early childhood. In J. D. Osofsky (Ed.), *Handbook of infant development.* New York: Wiley.

Sonenstein, F. K. L., Pleck, J. H., & Ku, L. C. 1989. Sexual activity, condom use, and AIDS awareness among adolescent males. *Family Planning Perspectives, 21,* 152–158.

Sontag, L. W. 1944. Differences in modifiability of fetal behavior and physiology. *Psychosomatic Medicine, 6,* 151–154.

Sontag, L. W. 1966. Implications of fetal behavior and environment for adult personalities. *Annals of the New York Academy of Science, 134,* 782–786.

Sontag, L. W., Reynolds, E. L., & Torbet, V. 1944. Status of infant at birth as related to basal metabolism of mothers in pregnancy. *American Journal of Obstetrics and Gynecology, 48,* 208–214.

Sophian, C., & Yengo, L. 1985. Infants' understanding of visible displacements. *Developmental Psychology, 21,* 932–941.

Sorce, J. F. 1979. The role of physiognomy in the development of racial awareness. *Journal of Genetic Psychology, 134,* 33–41.

Sorensen, R. C. 1973. *Adolescent sexuality in contemporary America.* New York: World Publishing.

Spanier, G. B. 1983. Married and unmarried cohabitation in the United States: 1980. *Journal of Marriage and the Family, 45,* 277–288.

Spanier, G. B. 1989. Bequeathing family continuity. *Journal of Marriage and the Family, 51,* 3–13.

Spanier, G. B., & Furstenberg, F. F., Jr. 1982. Remarriage after divorce: A longitudinal analysis of well-being. *Journal of Marriage and the Family, 44,* 709–720.

Spanier, G. B., Lewis, R. A., & Cole, C. L. 1975. Marital adjustment over the family life cycle: The issue of curvilinearity. *Journal of Marriage and the Family, 37,* 263–275.

Spanier, G. B., & Thompson, L. 1984. *Parting: The aftermath of separation and divorce.* Beverly Hills: Sage.

Sparks, P., & Durkin, K. 1987. Moral reasoning and political orientation: The context sensitivity of individual rights and democratic principles. *Journal of Personality and Social Psychology, 52,* 931–936.

Spearman, C. 1904. "General intelligence" objectively determined and measured. *American Journal of Psychology, 15,* 201–293.

Spearman, C. 1927. *The abilities of man.* New York: Macmillan.

Speer, J. R., & Flavell, J. H. 1979. Young children's knowledge of the relative difficulty of recognition and recall memory tasks. *Developmental Psychology, 15,* 214–217.

Spelke, E., Zelazo, P., Kagan, J., & Kotelchuck, M. 1973. Father interaction and separation protest. *Developmental Psychology, 9,* 83–90.

Spelke, E. S. 1988. Where perceiving ends and thinking begins: The apprehension of objects in infancy. In A. Yonas (Ed.), *Perceptual development in infancy: The Minnesota symposia on child psychology* (Vol. 20). Hillsdale, N.J.: Erlbaum.

Spelke, E. S., von Hofsten, C., & Kestenbaum, R. 1989. Object perception in infancy: Interaction of spatial and kinetic information for object boundaries. *Developmental Psychology, 25,* 185–196.

Spencer, B., & Gillen, F. J. 1927. *The Arunta* (Vol. 1). London: Macmillan.

Spencer, M. B., & Markstrom-Adams, C. 1990. Identity processes among racial and ethnic minority children in America. *Child Development, 61,* 290–310.

Sperling, D. 1990a. High-fiber diet may cut risk of cancer by 40%. *USA Today* (April 18), p. D1.

Sperling, D. 1990b. Summer cools off sperm. *USA Today* (July 5), p. 1A.

Spezzano, C. 1981. Prenatal psychology: Pregnant with questions. *Psychology Today, 15* (May), pp. 49–57.

Spilton, D., & Lee, L. C. 1977. Some determinants of effective communication in four-year-olds. *Child Development, 48,* 968–977.

Spinillo, A. G., & Bryant, P. 1991. Children's proportional judgments: The importance of "half." *Child Development, 62,* 427–440.

Spirduso, W. W. 1980. Physical fitness, aging, and psychomotor speed: A review. *Journal of Gerontology, 35,* 850–865.

Spiro, M. E. 1947. *Ifaluk: A South Sea culture.* Unpublished manuscripts, Coordinated Investigation of Micronesian Anthropology, Pacific Science Board, National Research Council, Washington, D.C.

Spiro, M. E. 1954. Is the family universal? *American Anthropologist, 56,* 839–846.

Spitz, R. A. 1945. Hospitalism: An inquiry into the genesis of psychiatric conditions in early childhood. *Psychoanalytic Study of the Child, 1,* 53–74.

Spitz, R. A. 1946. Hospitalism: A follow-up report. *Psychoanalytic Study of the Child, 2,* 113–117.

Spitz, R. A. 1957. *No and yes: On the genesis of human communication.* Madison, Conn.: International Universities Press.

Spitze, G., & Logan, J. 1990. Sons, daughters, and intergenerational social support. *Journal of Marriage and the Family, 52,* 420–430.

Spitzer, M. E. 1988. Taste acuity in institutionalized and noninstitutionalized elderly men. *Journal of Gerontology, 43,* P71–74.

Spreen, O. 1988. *Learning disabled children growing up: A follow-up into adulthood.* New York: Oxford University Press.

Sprunger, L. W., Boyce, W. T., & Gaines, J. A. 1985. Family-infant congruence: Routines and rhythmicity in family adaptations to a young infant. *Child Development, 56,* 564–572.

Sroufe, L. A. 1979. Socioemotional development. In J. Osofsky (Ed.), *Handbook of infant development.* New York: Wiley.

Sroufe, L. A. 1985. Attachment classification from the perspective of infant-caregiver relationships and infant temperament. *Child Development, 56,* 1–14.

Sroufe, L. A., Egeland, B., & Treutzer, T. 1990. The fate of early experience following developmental change: Longitudinal approaches to individual adaptation in childhood. *Child Development, 61,* 1363–1373.

Sroufe, L. A., & Jacobvitz, D. 1989. Diverging pathways, developmental transformations, multiple etiologies and the problem of continuity in development. *Human Development, 32,* 196–203.

Sroufe, L. A., & Rutter, M. 1984. The domain of developmental psychopathology. *Child Development, 55,* 17–29.

Stack, S. 1990. New micro-level data on the impact of divorce on suicide, 1959–1980: A test of two theories. *Journal of Marriage and the Family, 52,* 119–127.

Staddon, J. E. R. 1983. *Adaptive behavior and learning.* Cambridge: Cambridge University Press.

Staffieri, J. R. 1967. A study of social stereotype of body image in children. *Journal of Personality and Social Psychology, 7,* 101–104.

Staffieri, J. R. 1972. Body build and behavioral expectancies in young females. *Developmental Psychology, 6,* 125–127.

Stagner, R. 1975. Boredom on the assembly line: Age and personality variables. *Industrial Gerontology, 2,* 23–44.

Stains, L. 1986. Pals: Male friendships are not alive and well. *Columbus* (Ohio) *Dispatch* (November 11), p. 1B.

Stanhope, L., Bell, R. Q., & Parker-Cohen, N. Y. 1987. Temperament and helping behavior in preschool children. *Developmental Psychology, 23,* 347–353.

Stanley, M., Virgilio, J., & Gershon, S. 1982. Tritiated imipramine binding sites are decreased in the frontal cortex of suicides. *Science, 216,* 1337–1339.

Stannard, C. I. 1973. Old folks and dirty work: The social conditions for patient abuse in a nursing home. *Social Problems, 20,* 329–342.

Star, J. 1965. Chicago's troubled schools. *Look* (May 4), p. 59.

Stattin, H., & Magnusson, D. 1990. *Pubertal maturation in female development.* Hillsdale, N.J.: Erlbaum.

Staub, E. 1970. A child in distress: The influences of age and number of witnesses on children's attempts to help. *Journal of Personality and Social Psychology, 14,* 130–140.

Staub, E. 1971a. Helping a person in distress: The influence of implicit and explicit "rules" of conduct on children and adults. *Journal of Personality and Social Psychology, 17,* 137–144.

Staub, E. 1971b. The use of role playing and induction in children's learning of helping and sharing behavior. *Child Development, 42,* 805–816.

Staub, E. 1974. Helping a distressed person: Social, personality, and stimulus determinants. In L. Berkowitz (Ed.), *Advances in experimental social psychology* (Vol 7). New York: Academic Press.

Staub, E. 1975. To rear a prosocial child: Reasoning, learning by doing, and learning by teaching others. In D. J. DePalma & J. M. Foley (Eds.), *Moral development: Current theory and research.* Hillsdale, N.J.: Erlbaum.

Staub, E. 1978. *Positive social behavior and morality: Social and personal influences* (Vol 1). New York: Academic Press.

Staub, E., & Sherk, L. 1970. Need for approval, children's sharing behavior, and reciprocity in sharing. *Child Development, 41,* 243–253.

Stechler, G., & Halton, A. 1982. Prenatal influences on human development. In B. B. Wolman (Ed.), *Handbook of development psychology.* Englewood Cliffs, N.J.: Prentice-Hall.

Steele, B. G., & Pollock, C. B. 1968. A psychiatric study of parents who abuse infants and small children. In R. E. Helfer & C. H. Kempe (Eds.), *The battered child.* Chicago: University of Chicago Press.

Steelman, L. C. & Powell, B. 1989. Acquiring capital for college: The constraints of family configuration. *American Sociological Review, 54,* 844–855.

Steffe, L. P., & Cobb, P. 1988. *Construction of arithmetical meanings and strategies.* New York: Springer-Verlag.

Steffensmeier, D. J., Allan, E. A., Harer, M. D., & Streifel, C. 1989. Age and the distribution of crime. *American Journal of Sociology, 94,* 803–831.

Stein, A. H. 1967. Imitation of resistance to temptation. *Child Development, 38,* 157–169.

Stein, S. P., Holzman, S., Karasu, T. B., & Charles, E. S. 1978. Mid-adult development and psychopathology. *American Journal of Psychiatry, 135,* 676–681.

Steinberg, J. A., & Hall, V. C. 1981. Effects of social behavior on interracial acceptance. *Journal of Educational Psychology, 73,* 51–56.

Steinberg, L. 1986. Stability (and instability) of Type A behavior from childhood to young adulthood. *Developmental Psychology, 22,* 393–402.

Steinberg, L. 1987a. Impact of puberty on family relations: Effects of pubertal status and pubertal timing. *Developmental Psychology, 23,* 451–460.

Steinberg, L. 1987b. Single parents, stepparents, and the susceptibility of adolescents to antisocial peer pressure. *Child Development, 58,* 269–275.

Steinberg, L. 1988. Reciprocal relation between parent-child distance and pubertal maturation. *Developmental Psychology, 24,* 122–128.

Steinberg, L., & Dornbusch, S. M. 1991. Negative correlates of part-time employment during adolescence: Replication and elaboration. *Developmental Psychology, 27,* 304–313.

Steinberg, L., Elmen, J. D., & Mounts, N. S. 1989. Authoritative parenting, psychosocial maturity, and academic success among adolescents. *Child Development, 60,* 1424–1436.

Steinberg, L. D. 1981. Transformations in family relations at puberty. *Developmental Psychology, 17,* 833–840.

Steinberg, L. D., Catalano, R., & Dooley, D. 1981. Economic antecedents of child abuse and neglect. *Child Development, 52,* 975–985.

Steiner, J. E. 1979. Human facial expressions in response to taste and smell stimulation. In H. Reese & L. P. Lipsitt (Eds.), *Advances in child development and behavior* (Vol. 13). New York: Academic.

Steinmetz, S. K. 1977. *The cycle of violence.* New York: Praeger.

Stelmach, G. E., Amrhein, P. C., & Goggin, N. L. 1988. Age differences in bimanual coordination. *Journal of Gerontology, 43,* P18–23.

Stenberg, C., Campos, J. J., & Emde, R. N. 1983. The facial expression of anger in

seven-month-old infants. *Child Development, 54,* 178–184.

Stengel, E. 1964. *Suicide and attempted suicide.* Baltimore: Penguin Books.

Stenner, A. J., & Kalzenmeyer, W. G. 1976. Self-concept development in young children. *Phi Delta Kappan, 58,* 356–357.

Stephan, C. W., & Corder, J. 1985. The effects of dual-career families on adolescents' sex-role attitudes, work and family plans, and choices of important others. *Journal of Marriage and the Family, 47,* 921–929.

Stephan, C. W., & Langlois, J. H. 1984. Baby beautiful: Adult attributions of infant competence as a function of infant attractiveness. *Child Development, 55,* 576–585.

Stephens, M. W., & Delys, P. 1973. External control expectancies among disadvantaged children at preschool age. *Child Development, 44,* 670–674.

Stern, D., & Eichorn, D. (Eds.). 1989. *Adolescence and work: Influences of social structure, labor markets, and culture.* Hillsdale, N.J.: Erlbaum.

Stern, D. N. 1985. *The interpersonal world of the infant.* New York: Basic Books.

Stern, G. 1991. Young women insist on career equality, forcing the men in their lives to adjust. *Wall Street Journal* (September 16), pp. B1, B3.

Sternberg, R. J. 1979. The nature of mental abilities. *American Psychologist, 34,* 214–230.

Sternberg, R. J. 1981. Testing and cognitive psychology: *American Psychologist, 36,* 1181–1189.

Sternberg, R. J. 1982. Who's intelligent? *Psychology Today, 16* (April), pp. 30–39.

Sternberg, R. J. 1984. *Beyond IQ: A triarchic theory of human intelligence.* New York: Cambridge University Press.

Sternberg, R. J. 1986a. Inside intelligence. *American Scientist, 74* (March/April), pp. 137–143.

Sternberg, R. J. 1986b. *Intelligence applied.* San Diego: Harcourt Brace Jovanovich.

Sternberg, R. J. 1988. Mental self-government: A theory of intellectual styles and their development. *Human Development, 31,* 197–224.

Sternberg, R. J., & Downing, C. J. 1982. The development of higher-order reasoning in adolescence. *Child Development, 53,* 209–221.

Sternberg, R. J., & Okagaki, L. 1989. Continuity and discontinuity in intellectual development are not a matter of either-or. *Human Development, 32,* 158–166.

Stets, J. E., & Henderson, D. A. 1991. Contextual factors surrounding conflict resolution while dating: Results from a national study. *Family Relations, 40,* 29–36.

Steuer, J., LaRue, A., Blum, J. E., & Jarvik, L. F. 1981. "Critical loss" in the eighth and ninth decades. *Journal of Gerontology, 36,* 211–213.

Stevens, D. P., & Truss, C. V. 1985. Stability and change in adult personality over 12 and 20 years. *Developmental Psychology, 21,* 568–584.

Stevens, J. J., Jr. 1990. Social support, locus of control, and parenting in three low-income groups of mothers: Black teenagers,

black adults, and white adults. *Child Development, 59,* 635–642.

Stevenson, H. W. 1988. Special topic: Cross-cultural studies of parental influence on children's achievement. *Human Development, 31,* 349–350.

Stevenson, H. W., Azuma, H., & Hazkuta, K. (Eds.). 1986. *Child development and education in Japan.* New York: Freeman.

Stevenson, H. W., Lee, S., & Stigler, J. W. 1986. Mathematics achievement of Chinese, Japanese, and American children. *Science, 231,* 693–699.

Stevenson, H. W., Stigler, J. W., Lee, S., Lucker, G. W., Kitamura, S., & Hsu, C. 1985. Cognitive performance and academic achievement of Japanese, Chinese, and American children. *Child Development, 56,* 718–734.

Stevenson, J. S. 1979. Options often denied to aging parents. *Columbus* (Ohio) *Dispatch* (September 5), p. B3.

Stevenson, M. B., Leavitt, L. A., Thompson, R. H., & Roach, M. A. 1988. A social relations model analysis of parent and child play. *Developmental Psychology, 24,* 101–108.

Stevenson, M. R., & Black, K. N. 1988. Paternal absence and sex-role development: A meta-analysis. *Child Development, 59,* 793–814.

Stevenson, M. W., Ver Hoeve, J. N., Roach, M. A., & Leavitt, L. A. 1986. The beginning of conversation: Early patterns of mother-infant vocal responsiveness. *Infant Behavior and Development, 9,* 423–440.

Stewart, A. J., & Healy, J. M., Jr. 1989. Linking individual development and social changes. *American Psychologist, 44,* 30–42.

Stewart, R. B., Jr. 1990. *The second child: Family transitions and adjustments.* Newbury Park, Calif.: Sage.

Stigler, J. W., Lee, S., & Stevenson, H. W. 1987. Mathematics classrooms in Japan, Taiwan, and the United States. *Child Development, 58,* 1272–1285.

Stinnett, N., Carter, L. M., & Montgomery, J. E. 1972. Older persons' perceptions of their marriages. *Journal of Marriage and the Family, 34,* 665–670.

Stipek, D., & MacIver, D. 1989. Developmental change in children's assessment of intellectual competence. *Child Development, 60,* 521–538.

Stipek, D. J., Gralinski, J. H., & Kipp, C. B. 1990. Self-concept development in the toddler years. *Developmental Psychology, 6,* 972–977.

Stipp, D. 1990a. Alzheimer's is a group of disorders, not a single disease, researchers say. *Wall Street Journal* (September 13), p. B4.

Stipp, D. 1990. Genetic testing may mark some people as undersirable to employers, insurers. *Wall Street Journal* (July 9), pp. B1, B5.

Stocker, C., Dunn, J., & Plomin, R. 1989. Sibling relationships: Links with child temperament, maternal behavior, and family structure. *Child Development, 60,* 715–727.

Stoller, E. P. 1983. Parental caregiving by

adult children. *Journal of Marriage and the Family, 45,* 851–858.

Stoller, E. P., & Pugliesi, K. L. 1990. Other roles of caregivers: Competing responsibilities or supportive resources. *Journal of Gerontology, 44,* S231–238.

Stolz, H. R., & Stolz, L. M. 1951. *Somatic development of adolescent boys.* New York: Macmillan.

Stone, A. 1990. Number of foster kids is surging. *USA Today* (February 5), p. 1D.

Stone, A. 1991. Social Security no longer sacred. *USA Today* (January 3), p. A2.

Stone, C. A., & Day, M. C. 1978. Levels of availability of a formal operational strategy. *Child Development, 49,* 1054–1065.

Stone, L. 1977. *The family, sex and marriage in England, 1500–1800.* New York: Harper & Row.

Storms, M. D. 1980. Theories of sexual orientation. *Journal of Personality and Social Psychology, 38,* 783–792.

Story, M., & Brown, J. E. 1987. Do young children instinctively know what to eat? *New England Journal of Medicine, 316,* 103–106.

Stott, D. H. 1973. Follow-up study from birth of the effects of prenatal stresses. *Developmental Medicine and Child Neurology, 15,* 770–787.

Stott, D. H., & Latchford, S. A. 1976. Prenatal antecedents of child health, development and behavior: An epidemiological report of incidence and association. *Journal of the American Academy of Child Psychiatry, 15,* 161–191.

Straus, M. A., & Gelles, R. J. 1986. Societal change and change in family violence from 1975 to 1985 as revealed by two national surveys. *Journal of Marriage and the Family, 48,* 465–479.

Straus, M. A., & Gelles, R. J. (Eds.). 1989. *Physical violence in American families: Risk factors and adaptations to violence in 8,145 families.* New Brunswick, N.J.: Transaction Publications.

Straus, M. A., Gelles, R. J., & Steinmetz, S. K. 1980. *Behind closed doors: Violence in the American family.* Garden City, N.Y.: Doubleday.

Strayer, D. L., Wickens, C. D., & Braune, R. 1987. Adult age differences in the speed and capacity of information processing: 2. An electrophysiological approach. *Psychology and Aging, 2,* 99–110.

Strayer, J. 1986. Children's attributions regarding the situational determinants of emotion in self and others. *Developmental Psychology, 22,* 649–654.

Streissguth, A. P. 1984. Intrauterine alcohol and nicotine exposure: Attention and reaction time in 4-year-old children. *Developmental Psychology, 20,* 533–541.

Streissguth, A. P., Barr, H. M., Sampson, P. D., Darby, B. L., & Martin, D. C. 1989. IQ at age 4 in relation to maternal alcohol use and smoking during pregnancy. *Developmental Psychology, 25,* 3–11.

Stroebe, M. S., & Stroebe, W. 1983. Who suffers more? Sex differences in health risks of the widowed. *Psychological Bulletin, 93,* 279–301.

Strother, D. B. 1986. Suicide among the young. *Phi Delta Kappan, 67* (June), 756–759.

Stroud, M. 1990. More job control can lessen harmful work strains. *Investor's Daily* (April 17), p. 8.

Strube, M. J. 1988. The decision to leave an abusive relationship: Empirical evidence and theoretical issues. *Psychological Bulletin, 104,* 236–250.

Strube, M. J., & Barbour, L. S. 1983. The decision to leave an abusive relationship: Economic dependence and psychological commitment. *Journal of Marriage and the Family, 45,* 785–793.

Stuart, M. J., Gross, S. J., Elrad, H., & Graeber, J. E. 1982. Effects of acetyl-salicyclic-acid ingestion on maternal and neonatal hemostasis. *New England Journal of Medicine, 307,* 909–912.

Stuart, R. B. 1974. Teaching facts about drugs: Pushing or preventing. *Journal of Educational Psychology, 66,* 189–201.

Stuckey, M. F., McGhee, P. E., & Bell, N. J. 1982. Parent-child interaction: The influence of maternal employment. *Developmental Psychology, 18,* 635–644.

Stunkard, A. J., Foch, T. T., & Hrubec, Z. 1986. A twin study of human obesity. *Journal of the American Medical Association, 254,* 51–54.

Sue, S., & Okazaki, S. 1990. Asian-American educational achievements: A phenomenon in search of an explanation. *American Psychologist, 45,* 913–920.

Suedfeld, P., & Piedrahita, L. E. 1984. Intimations of mortality: Integrative simplification as a precursor of death. *Journal of Personality and Social Psychology, 47,* 848–852.

Sugarman, D. B., & Hotaling, G. T. 1989. Dating violence: Prevalence, context, and risk markers. In M. A. Pirog-Good & J. E. Stets (Eds.), *Violence in dating relationships: Emerging social issues.* New York: Praeger.

Sugarman, S. 1987. *Piaget's construction of the child's reality.* New York: Cambridge University.

Suggs, P. K. 1989. Predictors of association among older siblings: A black/white comparison. *American Behavioral Scientist, 33,* 70–80.

Sullivan, D. A., & Weitz, R. 1988. *Labor pains: Modern midwives and home birth.* New Haven, Conn.: Yale University.

Sullivan, H. S. 1947. *Conceptions of modern psychiatry.* Washington, D.C.: William A. White Psychiatric Foundation.

Sullivan, H. S. 1953. *The interpersonal theory of psychiatry.* New York: Norton.

Sullivan, M. W. 1982. Reactivation: Priming forgotten memories in human infants. *Child Development, 53,* 516–523.

Sullivan, R. 1984. Study reports bias in nursing homes. *New York Times* (January 28), p. 9.

Sullivan, W. 1982. Clues to longevity in the Soviet Union. *New York Times* (November 30), p. 17.

Super, C. M., Herrera, M. G., & Mora, J. O. 1990. Long-term effects of food supplementation and psychosocial intervention on the physical growth of Colombian infants at risk of malnutrition. *Child Development, 61,* 29–49.

Susman, E. J., Inoff-Germain, G., Nottelmann, E. D., Loriaux, D. L., Cutler, G. B.,

Jr., & Chrousos, G. P. 1987. Hormones, emotional dispositions, and aggressive attributes in young adolescents. *Child Development, 58,* 1114–1134.

Svejda, M. J., Campos, J. J., & Emde, R. N. 1980. Mother-infant "bonding": Failure to generalize. *Child Development, 51,* 775–779.

Swanson, J. M., & Kinsbourne, M. 1976. Stimulant-related state-dependent learning in hyperactive children. *Science, 192,* 1354–1357.

Swearingen, E. M., & Cohen, L. H. 1985. Life events and psychological distress: A prospective study of young adolescents. *Developmental Psychology, 21,* 1045–1054.

Sweeney, J. 1982. All moms spend about same time with kids. *Columbus (Ohio) Dispatch* (October 21), p. 11.

Sweet, J. A., & Bumpass, L. L. 1987. *Amerian families and households.* New York: Russell Sage Foundation.

Swensen, C. H., & Trahaug, G. 1985. Commitment and the long-term relationship. *Journal of Marriage and the Family, 47,* 939–945.

Swenson, W. M. 1961. Attitudes toward death in an aged population. *Journal of Gerontology, 16,* 49–52.

Symonds, P. M. 1939. *The psychology of parent-child relationships.* New York: Appleton-Century-Crofts.

Takagi, D. Y. 1990. From discrimination to affirmative action: Facts in the Asian American admissions controversy. *Social Problems, 37,* 578–591.

Tamis-LaMonda, C. S., & Bornstein, M. H. 1989. Habituation and maternal encouragement of attention in infancy as predictors of toddler language, play, and representational competence. *Child Development, 60,* 738–751.

Tan, G. C., Ray, M. P., & Cate, R. 1991. Migrant farm child abuse and neglect within an ecosystem framework. *Family Relations, 40,* 84–90.

Tanner, J. M. 1969. Growth and endocrinology of the adolescent. In L. I. Gardner (Ed.), *Endocrine and genetic diseases of childhood.* Philadelphia: Saunders.

Tanner, J. M. 1970. Physical growth. In P. H. Mussen (Ed.), *Carmichael's manual of child psychology* (3rd ed.). New York: Wiley.

Tanner, J. M. 1972. Sequence, tempo, and individual variation in growth and development of boys and girls aged twelve to sixteen. In J. Kagan & R. Coles (Eds.), *Twelve to sixteen: Early adolescence.* New York: Norton.

Tanner, J. M. 1973. Growing up. *Scientific American, 229* (September), pp. 34–43.

Tarquinio, N., Zelazo, P. R., Gryspeerdt, D. M., & Allen, K. M. 1991. Generalization of neonatal habituation. *Infant Behavior and Development, 14,* 69–81.

Task Force on Pediatric AIDS. 1989. Pediatric AIDS and human immunodeficiency virus infection. *American Psychologist, 44,* 258–264.

Taylor, C. W., & Barron, F. 1963. *Scientific*

creativity: Its recognition and development. New York: Wiley.

Taylor, M. 1988. Conceptual perspective taking: Children's ability to distinguish what they know from what they see. *Child Development, 59,* 703–718.

Taylor, M., & Gelman, S. A. 1989. Incorporating new words into the lexicon: Preliminary evidence for language hierarchies in two-year-old children. *Child Development, 60,* 625–636.

Taylor, R. J., & Chatters, L. M. 1991. Nonorganizational religious participation among elderly black adults. *Journal of Gerontology, 46,* S103–111.

Tellegen, A., Lykken, D. T., Bouchard, T. J., Wilcox, K. J., Segal N. L., & Rich, S. 1988. Personality similarity in twins reared apart and together. *Journal of Personality and Social Psychology, 54,* 1031–1039.

Teltsch, K. 1989. Is midlife a crisis or just a phase? A study begins. *New York Times* (December 18), pp. 15, 18.

Teltsch, K. 1991. New study of older workers finds they can become good investments. *New York Times* (May 21), p. A10.

Temple, M., & Polk, K. 1986. A dynamic analysis of educational attainment. *Sociology of Education, 59,* 79–84.

Templin, M. C. 1957. *Certain language skills in children.* Minneapolis: University of Minnesota.

Teri, L., Hughes, J. P., & Larson, E. B. 1990. Cognitive deterioration in Alzheimer's disease: Behavioral and health factors. *Journal of Gernotology, 45,* P58–63.

Terman, L. M. 1938. *Psychological factors in marital happiness.* New York: McGraw-Hill.

Terman, L. M., & Merrill, M. A. 1937. *Measuring intelligence.* Boston: Houghton Mifflin.

Termine, N. T., & Izard, C. E. 1988. Infants' responses to their mothers' expressions of joy and sadness. *Developmental Psychology, 24,* 223–229.

Tesch, S. A. 1983. Review of friendship development across the life span. *Human Development, 26,* 266–276.

Teti, D. M., & Ablard, K. E. 1989. Security of attachment and infant-sibling relationships: A laboratory study. *Child Development, 60,* 1519–1528.

Teti, D. M., & Lamb, M. E. 1989. Socioeconomic and marital outcomes of adolescent marriage, adolescent childbirth, and their co-occurrence. *Journal of Marriage and the Family, 51,* 203–212.

Tharp, R. G. 1989. Psychocultural variables and constants: Effects on teaching and learning in schools. *American Psychologist, 44,* 349–359.

Thatcher, R. W., Walker, R. A., & Giudice, S. 1987. Human cerebral hemispheres develop at different rates and ages. *Science, 236,* 1110–1113.

Thelen, E. 1981. Rhythmical behavior in infancy: An ethological perspective. *Developmental Psychology, 17,* 237–257.

Thelen, E. 1986. Treadmill-elicited stepping in seven-month-old infants. *Child Development, 57,* 1498–1506.

Thelen, E. 1989. The (re) discovery of motor development: Learning new things from an old field. *Developmental Psychology, 25,* 946–949.

Thelen, E., & Fogel, A. 1989. Toward an action-based theory of infant development. In J. Lockman & N. Hazen (Eds.), *Action in social context.* New York: Plenum.

Thoits, P. A. 1986. Multiple identities: Examining gender and marital status differences in distress. *American Sociological Review, 51,* 259–272.

Thoman, E. B., Korner, A. F., & Beason-Williams, L. 1977. Modification of responsiveness to maternal vocalization in the neonate. *Child Development 48,* 563–569.

Thomas, A., & Chess, S. 1984. Genesis and evolution of behavioral disorders: From infancy to early adult life. *American Journal of Psychiatry, 141,* 1–9.

Thomas, A., & Chess, S. 1987. Roundtable: What is temperament? *Child Development, 58,* 505–529.

Thomas, A., Chess, S., & Birch, H. G. 1970. The origin of personality. *Scientific American, 223* (August), pp. 102–109.

Thomas, A., Chess, S., Birch, H. G., Hertzig, M. E., & Korn, S. 1963. *Behavioral individuality in early childhood.* New York: New York University Press.

Thomas, J. L. 1986. Gender differences in satisfaction with grandparenting. *Psychology and Aging, 1,* 215–219.

Thomas, J. L. 1988. Predictors of satisfaction with children's help for younger and older elderly parents. *Journal of Gerontology, 43,* S9–14.

Thompson, L., Clark, K., & Gunn, W., Jr. 1985. Developmental stage and perceptions of intergenerational continuity. *Journal of Marriage and the Family, 47,* 913–920.

Thompson, R. A. 1987. Development of children's inferences of the emotions of others. *Developmental Psychology, 23,* 124–131.

Thompson, R. A. 1990. Vulnerability in research: A developmental perspective on research risk. *Child Development, 61,* 1–16.

Thompson, R. A., Connell, J. P., & Bridges, L. J. 1988. Temperament, emotion, and social interactive behavior in the strange situation: A component process analysis of attachment system functioning. *Child Development, 59,* 1102–1110.

Thorkildsen, T. A. 1989. Pluralism in children's reasoning about social justice. *Child Development, 60,* 965–972.

Thorley, G. 1984. Review of follow-up and follow-back studies of childhood hyperactivity. *Psychological Bulletin, 96,* 116–132.

Thornbury, J. M., & Mistretta, C. M. 1981. Tactile sensitivity as a function of age. *Journal of Gerontology, 36,* 34–39.

Thornton, A. 1977. Children and marital stability. *Journal of Marriage and the Family, 39,* 531–540.

Thornton, J. 1982. When fathers raise children alone. *U.S. News & World Report* (April 12), pp. 61–62.

Thurow, L. C. 1981. Why women are paid less than men. *New York Times* (March 8), p. E5.

Tiedje, L. B., Wortman, C. B., Downey, G., Emmons, C., Biernat, M., & Lang, E. 1990. Women with multiple roles: Role-compatibility perceptions, satisfaction,

and mental health. *Journal of Marriage and the Family, 52,* 63–72.

Tieger, T. 1980. On the biological basis of sex differences in aggression. *Child Development, 51,* 943–963.

Tietjen, A. M., & Walker, L. J. 1985. Moral reasoning and leadership among men in a Papua New Guinea society. *Developmental Psychology, 21,* 982–992.

Times Mirror Center for the People and the Press. 1990. Press release. June 12, 1990.

Timko, C., & Moos, R. H. 1990. Determinants of interpersonal support and self-direction in group residential facilities. *Journal of Gerontology, 45,* S184–192.

Timko, C., & Moos, R. H. 1991. A typology of social climates in group residential facilities for older people. *Journal of Gerontology, 46,* S160–169.

Tisak, M. S., & Turiel, E. 1988. Variation in seriousness of transgressions and children's moral and conventional concepts. *Developmental Psychology, 24,* 352–357.

Tobin-Richards, M., Boxer, A. M., & Petersen, A. C. 1983. The psychological significance of pubertal change: Sex differences in perceptions of self during early adolescence. In J. Brooks-Gunn & A. C. Petersen (Eds.), *Girls at puberty.* New York: Plenum.

Toby, J. 1987. Let students drop out—and back in. *Wall Street Journal* (August 5), p. 18.

Toby, J. 1989. Of dropouts and stay-ins: The Gershwin approach. *The Public Interest, 95,* 3–12.

Tognoli, J. 1980. Male friendship and intimacy across the life span. *Family Relations, 29,* 273–279.

Tolson, T. F. J., & Wilson, M. N. 1990. The impact of two- and three-generational black family structure on perceived family climate. *Child Development, 61,* 416–428.

Tomkins, S. S. 1986. Script theory. In J. Aronoff, R. A. Zucker, & A. I. Rabin (Eds.), *Structuring personality.* Orlando, Fla.: Academic Press.

Tooley, J. A. 1989. Matrimonial misses. *U.S. News & World Report* (February 27), p. 75.

Torney-Purta, J. 1989. Political cognition and its restructuring in young people. *Human Development, 32,* 14–23.

Tourney, G., & Hatfield, L. M. 1973. Androgen metabolism in schizophrenics, homosexuals, and normal controls. *Biological Psychiatry, 6,* 23–36.

Trevarthen, C. 1977. Descriptive analysis of infant communicative behavior. In H. R. Schaffer (Ed.), *Studies in mother-infant interaction.* London: Academic Press.

Trevarthen, C. 1988. Universal co-operative motives: How infants begin to know the language and culture of their parents. In G. Jahoda & I. M. Lewis (Eds.), *Acquiring culture: Cross cultural studies in child development.* London: Croom Helm.

Triandis, H. C., & Brislin, R. W. 1984. Cross-cultural psychology. *American Psychologist, 39,* 1006–1916.

Trickett, P. K., Aber, J. L., Carlson, V., & Cicchetti, D. 1991. Relationship of socioeconomic status to the etiology and developmental sequelae of physical child abuse. *Developmental Psychology, 27,* 148–158.

Trickett, P. K., & Susman, E. J. 1988. Parental perceptions of child-rearing practices in physically abusive and nonabusive families. *Developmental Psychology, 24,* 270–276.

Troen, S. K. 1985. Technological development and adolescence: The early twentieth century. *Journal of Early Adolescence, 5,* 429–440.

Troll, L. E. 1975. *Early and middle adulthood.* Monterey, Calif.: Brooks/Cole.

Troll, L. E., & Bengston, V. L. 1982. Intergenerational relations throughout the life span. In B. B. Wolman (Ed.), *Handbook of developmental psychology.* Englewood Cliffs, N.J.: Prentice-Hall.

Tronick, E. Z., & Cohn, J. F. 1989. Infant-mother face-to-face interaction: Age and gender differences in coordination and the occurrence of miscoordination. *Child Development, 60,* 85–92.

Trost, C. 1989. As drug babies grow older, schools strive to meet their needs. *Wall Street Journal* (December 27), pp. A1, A2.

Trost, C. 1990a. Census survey on child care increases concern about how much poor can pay. *Wall Street Journal* (August 15), p. A10.

Trost, C. 1990b. Increase in child-abuse cases is linked to rising cocaine problem, study says. *Wall Street Journal* (June 14), p. C9.

Trotter, R. J. 1987. You've come a long way, baby. *Psychology Today, 21* (May), pp. 34–45.

Troy, M., & Sroufe, L. A. 1987. Victimization among preschoolers: Role of attachment relationship history. *Journal of the American Academy of Child and Adolescent Psychiatry, 26,* 166–172.

Truninger, E. 1971. Marital violence: The legal solutions. *The Hastings Law Journal, 23,* 259–276.

Tschann, J. M., Johnston, J. R., Kline, M., & Wallerstein, J. 1989. Family process and children's functioning during divorce. *Journal of Marriage and the Family, 51,* 431–444.

Tsitouras, P. D., Martin, C. E., & Harman, S. M. 1982. Relationship of serum testosterone to sexual activity in healthy elderly men. *Journal of Gerontology, 37,* 288–293.

Tulving, E. 1968. Theoretical issues in free recall. In T. R. Dixon & D. L. Horton (Eds.), *Verbal behavior and general behavior theory.* Englewood Cliffs, N.J.: Prentice-Hall.

Tulving, E., & Pearlstone, Z. 1966. Availability versus accessibility of information in memory for words. *Journal of Verbal Learning and Verbal Behavior, 5,* 381–391.

Tuma, J. M. 1989. Mental health services for children. *American Psychologist, 44,* 188–199.

Turkheimer, E., & Gottesman, I. I. 1991. Individual differences and the canalization of human behavior. *Developmental Psychology, 27,* 18–22.

Turiel, E. 1969. Developmental process in the child's moral thinking. In P. H. Mussen, J. Langer, & M. Covington (Eds.), *Trends and issues in developmental psychology.* New York: Holt, Rinehart and Winston.

Turiel, E. 1974. Conflict and transition in adolescent moral development. *Child Development, 45,* 14–29.

Turiel, E. 1978. Conflict and transition in adolescent moral development, II: The resolution of disequilibrium through structural reorganization. *Child Development, 48,* 634–637.

Turiel, E. 1983. *The development of social knowledge: Morality and convention.* Cambridge: Cambridge University Press.

Turiel, E. 1989a. Commentary. *Human Development, 32,* 45–52.

Turiel, E. 1989b. Domain-specific social judgments and domain ambiguities. *Merrill-Palmer Quarterly, 35,* 89–114.

Turiel, E., Killen, M., & Helwig, C. C. 1987. Morality: Its structure, functions, and vagaries. In J. Kagan & S. Lamb (Eds.), *The emergence of moral concepts in young children.* Chicago: University of Chicago.

Turkle, S. 1987. Hero of the life cycle. *New York Times Book Review* (April 5), pp. 36–37.

Turner, B. F. 1982. Sex-related differences in aging. In B. B. Wolman (Ed.), *Handbook of develpmental psychology.* Englewood Cliffs, N.J.: Prentice-Hall.

Turner, R. H. 1962. Role-taking: Process versus conformity. In A. M. Rose (Ed.), *Human behavior and social processes.* Boston: Houghton Mifflin.

Turner, R. H. 1968. The self-conception in social interaction. In C. Gordon & K. J. Gergen (Eds.), *The self in social interaction.* New York: Wiley.

Tyler, L. E. 1983. *Thinking creatively.* San Francisco: Jossey-Bass.

Uchitelle, L. 1990. Unexpected shift in a labor rate. *New York Times* (July 16), p. C2.

Uchitelle, L. 1991. Why older men keep on working. *New York Times* (April 23), p. C2.

Udry, J. R. 1988. Biological predispositions and social control in adolescent sexual behavior. *American Sociological Review, 53,* 709–722.

Udry, J. R., & Billy, J. O. G. 1987. Initiation of coitus in early adolescence. *American Sociological Review, 52,* 841–855.

Udry, J. R., & Talbert, L. M. 1988. Sex hormone effects on personality at puberty. *Journal of Personality and Social Psychology, 54,* 291–295.

Udry, J. R., Talbert, L., & Morris, N. M. 1986. Biosocial foundations for adolescent female sexual behavior. *Demography, 23,* 217–227.

Uhlenberg, P. 1987. How old is "old age"? *The Public Interest, 88,* 67–78.

Uhlenberg, P., Cooney, T., & Boyd, R. 1990. Divorce for women after midlife. *Journal of Gerontology, 45,* S3–S11.

Uhlenberg, P. R. 1980. Death and the family. *Journal of Family History 5,* 313–320.

Umberson, D. 1989. Relationships with children: Explaining parents' psychological well-being. *Journal of Marriage and the Family, 51,* 999–1012.

U.S. Children's Bureau. 1924. *Infant care.* Care of Children Series No. 2. Bureau Publication No. 8 (revised).

Underwood, B., & Moore, B. S. 1981. Sources of behavioral consistency. *Journal of Per-*

sonality and Social Psychology, 40, 780–785.

Ungerer, J. A., Zelazo, P. R., Kearsley, R. B., & O'Leary, K. 1981. Developmental changes in the representation of objects in symbolic play from 18 to 34 months of age. *Child Development, 52,* 186–195.

Upchurch, D. M., & McCarthy, J. 1990. The timing of a first birth and high school completion. *American Sociological Review, 55,* 224–234.

Urdy, J. R. 1971. *The social context of marriage.* Philadelphia: Lippincott.

Uttal, D. H., Lummis, M., & Stevenson, H. W. 1988. Low and high mathematics achievement in Japanese, Chinese, and American elementary-school children. *Developmental Psychology, 24,* 335–342.

Vaillant, G. E., & Milofsky, E. 1980. Natural history of male psychological health. IX: Empirical evidence for Erikson's model of the life cycle. *American Journal of Psychiatry, 37,* 1348–1359.

Vaillant, G. E., & Valliant, C. O. 1981. Natural history of male psychological health. X: Work as a predictor of positive mental health. *American Journal of Psychiatry, 138,* 1433–1440.

Valentine, D. P. 1982. The experience of pregnancy: A developmental process. *Family Relations, 31,* 243–248.

Vandell, D., Henderson, V. K., & Wilson, K. S. 1988. A follow-up study of children in excellent, moderate and poor quality day care. *Child Development, 59,* 1286–1292.

Vandell, D., & Powers, C. 1983. Daycare quality and children's free play activities. *American Journal of Orthopsychiatry, 53,* 293–300.

Vandell, D. L., & Wilson, K. S. 1987. Infants' interactions with mother, sibling, and peer: Contrasts and relations between interaction systems. *Child Development, 58,* 176–186.

van Ijzendoorn, M. H. 1990. Developments in cross-cultural research on attachment: Some methodological notes. *Human Development, 33,* 3–9.

van Ijzendoorn, M. H., & Kroonenberg, P. M. 1988. Cross-cultural patterns of attachment: A meta-analysis of the strange situation. *Child Development, 59,* 147–156.

Vander Zanden, J. W. 1983. *American minority relations* (4th ed.). New York: Ronald Press.

Vander Zanden, J. W. 1987. *Social psychology* (4th ed.). New York: Random House.

Vander Zanden, J. W. 1990. *The Social experience* (2nd ed.). New York: McGraw-Hill.

Vander Zanden, J. W., & Pace, A. 1984. *Educational psychology* (2nd ed.). New York: Random House.

Van Veslor, E., & O'Rand, A. M. 1984. Family life cycle, work career patterns, and women's wages at midlife. *Journal of Marriage and the Family, 46,* 365–373.

van Willigen, J. 1989. *Gettin' some age on me: Social organization of older people in a rural American community.* Lexington: University Press of Kentucky.

Vaughan, D. 1986. *Uncoupling: Turning points in intimate relationships.* New York: Oxford University Press.

Vaughn, B. E., Block, J. H., & Block, J. 1988. Parental agreement on child rearing during early childhood and the psychological characteristics of adolescents. *Child Development, 59,* 1020–1033.

Vaughn, B. E., Lefever, G. B., Seifer, R., & Barglow, P. 1989. Attachment behavior, attachment security, and temperament during infancy. *Child Development, 60,* 728–737.

Velez, W. 1989. High school attrition among Hispanic and non-Hispanic white youths. *Sociology of Education, 62,* 119–133.

Verbrugge, L. M. 1986. Role burdens and physical health of women and men. *Women and Health, 11,* 47–77.

Verbrugge, L. M. 1989. The twain meet: Empirical explanations of sex differences in health and mortality. *Journal of Health and Social Behavior, 30,* 282–304.

Vermeulen, A., Rubens, R., & Verdonck, L. 1976. Testosterone secretion and metabolism in male senescence. *Journal of Clinical Endocrinology and Metabolism, 34,* 730–735.

Visher, E. B., & Visher, J. S. 1979. *Stepfamilies.* New York: Brunner/Mazel.

von Hofsten, C. 1982. Eye-hand coordination in the newborn. *Developmental Psychology, 18,* 450–461.

von Hofsten, C. 1989. Motor development as the development of systems: Comments on the special section. *Developmental Psychology, 25,* 950–953.

von Tetzchner, S., Siegel, L. S., & Smith, L. (Eds.). 1989. *The social and cognitive aspects of normal and atypical language development.* New York: Springer-Verlag.

Voydanoff, P. 1990. Economic distress and family relations: A review of the eighties. *Journal of Marriage and the Family: 52,* 1099–1115.

Vroegh, K. 1971. The relationship of birth order and sex of siblings to gender role identity. *Developmental Psychology, 4,* 407–411.

Vygotsky, L. S. 1962. *Thought and language.* Cambridge, Mass.: MIT Press.

Vygotsky, L. 1978. *Mind in society.* Cambridge, Mass.: Harvard University.

Waber, D. P., Mann, M. B., Merola, J., & Moylan, P. M. 1985. Physical maturation rate and cognitive performance in early adolescence: A longitudinal examination. *Developmental Psychology, 21,* 666–681.

Wacker, R. 1985. The good die younger. *Science, 85,* 6 (December), pp. 64–68.

Wahler, R. G. 1967. Child-care interactions in free field settings: Some experimental analyses. *Journal of Experimental Child Psychology, 5,* 278–293.

Wainryb, C. 1991. Understanding differences in moral judgments: The role of informational assumptions. *Child Development, 62,* 840–851.

Waite, L. J. 1980. Working wives and the family life cycle. *American Journal of Sociology, 86,* 272–294.

Waite, L. J., Haggstrom, G. W., & Kanouse, D. E. 1985. The consequences of parenthood for the marital stability of young adults. *American Sociological Review, 50,* 850–857.

Waite, L. J., & Lillard, L. A. 1991. Children and marital disruption. *American Journal of Sociology, 96,* 930–953.

Wald, M. S., Carlsmith, J. M., & Leiderman, P. H. 1988. *Protecting abused and neglected children.* Stanford, Calif.: Stanford University.

Walden, T. A., & Baxter, A. 1989. The effect of context and age on social referencing. *Child Development, 60,* 1511–1518

Walden, T. A., & Ogan, T. A. 1988. The development of social referencing. *Child Development, 59,* 1230–1240.

Waldholz, M. 1983. New programs seek to care for the aging in their own homes. *Wall Street Journal* (March 8), pp. 1, 22.

Waldrop, J. 1988. The fashionable family. *American Demographics, 10* (March), 22–26.

Walford, R. L. 1969. *The immunologic theory of aging.* Baltimore: Williams and Wilkins.

Walker, A. J., & Pratt, C. C. 1991. Daughters' help to mothers: Intergeneration aid versus caregiving. *Journal of Marriage and the Family, 53,* 3–12.

Walker, A. J., Pratt, C. C., Shin, H. Y., & Jones, L. L. 1990. Motives for parental caregiving and relationship quality. *Family Relations, 39,* 51–56.

Walker, A. J., & Thompson, L. 1983. Intimacy and intergenerational aid and contact among mothers and daughters. *Journal of Marriage and the Family, 45,* 841–849.

Walker, E., Downey, G., & Bergman, A. 1989. The effects of parental psychopathology and maltreatment on child behavior: A test of the diathesis-stress model. *Child Development, 60,* 15–24.

Walker, E., & Emory, E. 1985. Commentary: Interpretive bias and behavioral genetic research. *Child Development, 56,* 775–778.

Walker, L. D., & Gollin, E. S. 1977. Perspective role-taking in young children. *Journal of Experimental Child Psychology, 24,* 343–357.

Walker, L. E. A. 1989. Psychology and violence against women. *American Psychologist, 44,* 695–702.

Walker, L. E. A. 1990. *Terrifying love: Why battered women kill?* New York: Harper & Row.

Walker, L. J. 1982. The sequentiality of Kohlberg's stages of moral development. *Child Development, 53,* 1330–1336.

Walker, L. J. 1984. Sex differences in the development of moral reasoning: A critical review. *Child Development, 55,* 677–691.

Walker, L. J. 1986. Sex differences in the development of moral reasoning: A rejoinder to Baumrind. *Child Development, 57,* 522–526.

Walker, L. J. 1989. A longitudinal study of moral reasoning. *Child Development, 60,* 157–166.

Walker, L. J., de Vries, B., & Bichard, S. L. 1984. The hierarchical nature of stages of moral development. *Developmental Psychology, 20,* 960–966.

Walker, L. J., De Vries, B., & Trevethan, S. D. 1987. Moral stages and moral orientations in real-life and hypothetical dilemmas. *Child Development, 58,* 842–858.

Walker, L. J., & Taylor, J. H. 1991a. Stage transitions in moral reasoning: A longitudinal study of developmental processes. *Developmental Psychology, 27,* 330–337.

Walker, L. J., & Taylor, J. H. 1991b. Family interactions and the development of moral reasoning. *Child Development, 62,* 264–283.

Wallach, M. A., & Kogan, N. 1965. *Modes of thinking in young children: A study of the creativity-intelligence distinction.* New York: Holt, Rinehart and Winston.

Wallerstein, J., Corbin, S. B., & Lewis, J. M. 1988. Children of divorce: A ten-year study. In E. M. Hetherington & J. Arasteh (Eds.), *Impact of divorce, single-parenting, and stepparenting on children.* Hillsdale, N.J.: Erlbaum.

Wallerstein, J. S., & Blakeslee, S. 1989. *Second chances: Men, women, and children a decade after divorce.* New York: Ticknor and Fields.

Wallerstein, J. S., & Kelly, J. B. 1980. *Surviving the breakup: How children actually cope with divorce.* New York: Basic Books.

Wallis, C. 1989. Onward, women! *Time* (December 4), pp. 80–89.

Wallis, C. 1991. A puzzling plague: What is it about the American way of life that causes breast cancer? *Time* (January 14), pp. 48–52.

Wallston, B. S., Alagna, S. W., DeVellis, B. M., & DeVellis, R. F. 1984. Social support and health. *Health Psychology, 4,* 367–391.

Walsh, D. L. 1986. What women want. *American Demographics, 8* (June), 60.

Walters, J. 1991. Hospice care lets patients die in comfort of home. *USA Today* (March 11), p. 5D.

Walters, R. H., Leat, M., & Mezei, L. 1963. Inhibition and disinhibition of responses through empathetic learning. *Canadian Journal of Psychology, 17,* 235–243.

Wamboldt, F. S., Kaslow, N. J., Swift, W. J., & Ritholz, M. 1987. Short-term course of depressive symptoms in patients with eating disorders. *American Journal of Psychiatry, 144,* 362–364.

Ward, M. J., Vaughn, B. E., & Robb, M. D. 1988. Social-emotional adaptation and infant-mother attachment in siblings: Role of the mother in cross-sibling consistency. *Child Development, 59,* 643–651.

Ward, R. A. 1979. The meaning of voluntary association participation to older people. *Journal of Gerontology, 34,* 438–445.

Ward, S. 1987. Most want right to pull plug. *USA Today* (March 17), p. 1A.

Ward, S. K., Chapman, K., Cohn, E., White, S., & Williams, K. 1991. Acquaintance rape and the college social scene. *Family Relations, 40,* 65–71.

Wareham, K. A., Lyon, M. F., Glenister, P. H., & Williams, E. D. 1987. Age related reactivation of an X-linked gene. *Nature, 327,* 725–727.

Warner, H. R. & Price, A. R. 1989. Involvement of DNA repair in cancer and aging. *Journal of Gerontology, 44,* 45–54.

Warren-Leubecker, A., & Bohannon, J. N. III. 1984. Intonation patterns in child-directed speech: Mother-father differences. *Child Development, 55,* 1379–1385.

Wasik, B. H., Ramey, C. T., Bryant, D. M., & Sparling, J. J. 1990. A longitudinal study of two early intervention strategies: Project CARE. *Child Development, 61,* 1682–1696.

Wassarman, P. M. 1987. The biology and chemistry of fertilization. *Science, 235,* 553–560.

Waterman, A. S. 1982. Identity development from adolescence to adulthood: An extension of theory and a review of research. *Developmental Psychology, 18,* 341–358.

Waterman, A. S., Geary, P. S., & Waterman, C. K. 1974. Longitudinal study of changes in ego identity status from the freshman to the senior year at college. *Developmental Psychology, 10,* 387–392.

Waters, E., Matas, L., & Sroufe, L. A. 1975. Infants' reactions to an approaching stranger: Description, validation, and functional significance of wariness. *Child Development, 46,* 348–356.

Watkins, B. & Montgomery, A. B. 1989. Concepts of athletic excellence among children and adolescents. *Child Development, 60,* 1362–1372.

Watson, John B. 1928. *Psychological care of infant and child.* New York: Norton.

Watson, M. W., & Fischer, K. W. 1980. Development of social roles in elicited and spontaneous behavior during the preschool years. *Developmental Psychology, 16,* 483–494.

Waxman, S. R., & Kosowski, T. D. 1990. Nouns mark category relations: Toddlers' and preschoolers' word-learning biases. *Child Development, 61,* 1461–1473.

Weatherley, D. 1964. Self-perceived rate of physical maturation and personality in late adolescence. *Child Development, 35,* 1197–1210.

Webb, W. B. 1982. Sleep in older persons: Sleep structures of 50- to 60-year-old men and women. *Journal of Gerontology, 37,* 581–586.

Webster-Stratton, C. 1989. The relationship of marital support, conflict, and divorce to parent perceptions, behaviors, and childhood conduct problems. *Journal of Marriage and the Family, 51,* 417–430.

Wechsler, D. 1975. Intelligence defined and undefined. *American Psychologist, 30,* 135–139.

Weed, J. A. 1982. Divorce: Americans' style. *American Demographics, 4,* 13–17.

Weg, R. B. 1973. The changing physiology of aging. *The American Journal of Occupational Therapy, 27,* 213–217.

Weidner, G., Sexton, G., Matarazzo, J. D., Pereira, C., & Friend, R. 1988. Type A behavior in children, adolescents, and their parents. *Developmental Psychology, 24,* 118–121.

Weiffenbach, J. M., Tylenda, C. A., & Baum, B. J. 1990. Oral sensory changes in aging. *Journal of Gerontology, 45,* M121–125.

Weigel, C., Wertlieb, D., & Feldstein, M. 1989. Percepts of control, competence, and contingency as influences on the stress-behavior symptom relation in school-age children. *Journal of Personality and Social Psychology, 56,* 456–464.

Weil, F. D. 1987. Cohorts, regimes, and the legitimation of democracy: West Germany since 1945. *American Sociological Review, 52,* 308–324.

Weinberg, R. A. 1989. Intelligence and IQ: Landmark issues and great debates. *American Psychologist, 44,* 98–104.

Weiner, B. 1972. *Theories of motivation.* Chicago: Markham.

Weiner, B. 1979. A theory of motivation for some classroom experiences. *Journal of Educational Psychology, 71,* 3–25.

Weinraub, M., Brooks, J., & Lewis, M. 1977. The social network: A reconsideration of the concept of attachment. *Human Development, 20,* 31–47.

Weinraub, M., Clemens, L. P., Sockloff, A., Ethridge, T., Gracely, E., & Myers, B. 1984. The development of sex role stereotypes in the third year. *Child Development, 55,* 1493–1503.

Weinraub, M., Jaeger, E., & Hoffman. L. W. 1988. Predicting infant outcomes in families of employed and non-employed mothers. *Early Childhood Research Quarterly, 3,* 361–378.

Weisfeld, G. E. 1982. The nature-nurture issue and the integrating concept of function. In B. B. Wolman (Ed.), *Handbook of developmental psychology.* Englewood Cliffs, N.J.: Prentice-Hall.

Weisler, A., & McCall, R. B. 1976. Exploration and play. *American Psychologist, 31,* 492–508.

Weisman, A. D. 1984. *The coping capacity: On the nature of being mortal.* New York: Human Sciences Press.

Weisner, T. S., & Wilson-Mitchell, J. E. 1990. Nonconventional family life-styles and sex typing in six-year-olds. *Child Development, 61,* 1915–1933.

Weiss, G., & Hechtman, L. T. 1986. *Hyperactive children grown up.* New York: Guilford.

Weiss, M. J., Zelazo, P. R., & Swain, I. U. 1988. Newborn response to auditory stimulus discrepancy. *Child Development, 59,* 1530–1541.

Weiss, R. S. 1979. Growing up a little faster: The experience of growing up in a single-parent household. *Journal of Social Issues, 35,* 97–111.

Weiss, R. S. 1984. The impact of marital dissolution on income and consumption in single-parent households. *Journal of Marriage and the Family, 46,* 115–127.

Weiss, R. S. 1990. *Staying the course: The emotional and social lives of men who do well at work.* New York: Free Press.

Weissert, W. G., Elstin, J. M., Bolda, E. J., Zelman, W. N., Mutran, E., & Mangum, A. B. 1990. *Adult day care: Findings from a national survey.* Baltimore: Johns Hopkins University.

Weitzman, L. 1990. Women and children suffer most in divorce. *USA Today* (February 27), p. 9A.

Weitzman, L. J. 1985. *The divorce revolution: The unexpected consequences for women and children in America.* New York: Free Press.

Weitzman, N., Birns, B., & Friend, R. 1985. Traditional and nontraditional mothers' communication with their daughters and sons. *Child Development, 56,* 894–898.

Welford, A. T. 1977. Motor performance. In J. E. Birren & K. W. Schaie (Eds.), *Handbook of the psychology of aging.* New York: Van Nostrand.

Wellborn, S. N. 1987. How genes shape personality. *U.S. News & World Report* (April 13), pp. 58–62.

Wellman, B., & Wortley, S. 1990. Different strokes from different folks: Community ties and social support. *American Journal of Sociology, 96,* 558–588.

Wellman, H. M. 1977. The early development of intentional memory behavior. *Human Development, 20,* 86–101.

Wellman, H. M. 1985a. A child's theory of mind: Development of conceptions of cognition. In S. R. Yussen (Ed.), *The growth of reflection.* New York: Academic Press.

Wellman, H. M. 1985b. The origins of metacognition. In D. L. Forrest-Pressley, G. E. McKinnon, & T. G. Waller (Eds.), *Cognition, metacogniton, and performance.* New York: Academic Press.

Wellman, H. M., Collins, J., & Glieberman, J. 1981. Understanding the combination of memory variables: Developing conceptions of memory limitations. *Child Development, 52,* 1313–1317.

Wellman, H. M., Ritter, K., & Flavell, J. H. 1975. Deliberate memory behavior in the delayed reactions of very young children. *Developmental Psychology, 11,* 780–787.

Wells, A. S. 1991. Asking what schools have done, or can do to help desegregation. *New York Times* (January 16), p. B7.

Welsch, M. C., Pennington, B. F., Ozonoff, S., Rouse, B., & McCabe, E. R. B. 1990. Neuropsychology of early-treated phenylketonuria: Specific executive function deficits. *Child Development, 61,* 1697–1713.

Wenckstern, S., Weizmann, F., & Leenaars, A. A. 1984. Temperament and tempo of play in eight-month-old infants. *Child Development, 55,* 1195–1199.

Werner, E. E. 1990. Protective factors and individual resilience. In S. J. Meisel & J. Shonkoff (Eds.), *Handbook of early childhood intervention.* New York: Cambridge University.

Werner, E. E., & Smith, R. S. 1982. *Vulnerable but invincible: A longitudinal study of resilient children and youth.* New York: McGraw-Hill.

Werner, H. 1948. *Comparative psychology of mental development.* New York: International Universities Press.

Wertsch, J. V. 1985. *Vygotsky and the social formation of mind.* Cambridge, Mass.: Harvard University Press.

Westie, F. R. 1964. Race and ethnic relations. In R. E. L. Faris (Ed.), *Handbook of modern sociology.* Chicago: Rand McNally.

Westoff, C. F. 1974. Coital frequency and contraception. *Family Planning Perspectives, 6,* 136–141.

Wetherford, M. J. 1973. Developmental changes in infant visual preferences for novelty and familiarity. *Child Development, 44,* 416–424.

Wexler, K., & Culicover, P. W. 1981. *Formal principles of language acquisition.* Cambridge, Mass.: MIT Press.

Whalen, C. K., Henker, B., Castro, J., & Granger, D. 1987. Peer perceptions of hyperactivity and medication effects. *Child Development, 58,* 816–828.

Whalen, C. K., Henker, B., & Dotemoto, S. 1981. Teacher response to the Methylphenidate (Titalin) versus placebo status of hyperactive boys in the classroom. *Child Development, 52,* 1005–1014.

Whalen, J., & Flacks, R. 1989. *Beyond the*

barricades: The sixties generation grows up. Philadelphia: Temple University.

Whitbeck, L. B., & Gecas, V. 1988. Value attribution and transmission between parents and children. Journal of Marriage and the Family, 50, 829–840.

White, B. L. 1969. Child development research: An edifice without a foundation. Merrill-Palmer Quarterly, 15, 49–79.

White, B. L. 1973. Discussions and conclusions. In B. L. White & J. C. Watts (Eds.), Experience and environment. Englewood Cliffs, N.J.: Prentice-Hall.

White, B. L. 1975. The first three years of life. Englewood Cliffs, N.J.: Prentice-Hall.

White, B. L., & Watts, J. C. (Eds.). 1973. Experience and environment. Englewood Cliffs, N.J.: Prentice-Hall.

White, L., & Edwards, J. N. 1990. Emptying the nest and parental well-being: An analysis of national panel data. American Sociological Review, 55, 235–242.

White, L., & Keith, B. 1990. The effect of shift work on the quality and stability of marital relations. Journal of Marriage and the Family, 52, 453–462.

White, L. A. 1949. The science of culture: A study of man and civilization. New York: Farrar, Straus.

White, L. K., & Booth, A. 1985. The quality and stability of remarriages: The role of stepchildren. American Sociological Review, 50, 689–698.

White, N., & Cunningham, W. R. 1988. Is terminal drop pervasive or specific? Journal of Gerontology, 43, P141–144.

White, P. A. 1988. Causal processing: Origins and development. Psychological Bulletin, 104, 36–52.

White, S. H. 1975. Commentary. In L. B. Miller & J. L. Dyer (Eds.), Four preschool programs: Their dimensions and effects. Monographs of the Society for Research in Child Development, 40 (5–6), 168–170.

Whitehead, M. I., Townsend, P. T., & Pryse-Davies, J. 1981. Effects of estrogens and progestins on the biochemistry and morphology of the postmenopausal endometrium. New England Journal of Medicine, 305, 1599–1605.

White House Conference on Children. 1970. Profiles of children. Washington, D.C.: Government Printing Office.

Whitehurst, G. J. 1982. Language development. In B. B. Wolman (Ed.), Handbook of developmental psychology. Englewood Cliffs, N.J.: Prentice-Hall.

Whitehurst, G. J., & Valdez-Menchaca, M. C. 1988. What is the role of reinforcement in early language acquisition? Child Development, 59, 430–440.

Whitesell, N. R. & Harter, S. 1989. Children's reports of conflict between simultaneous opposite-valence emotions. Child Development, 60, 673–682.

Whiteside, M. F. 1989. Family rituals as a key to kinship connections in remarried families. Family Relations, 38, 34–39.

Whiting, B. B., & Edwards, C. P. 1988. Children of different worlds: The formation of social behavior. Cambridge, Mass.: Harvard University.

Whitman, D. 1987. The numbers game: When more is less. U.S. News & World Report (April 27), pp. 39–40.

Whorf, B. L. 1956. Language, thought, and reality. Cambridge, Mass.: MIT Press.

Wicker, A. W. 1969. Attitudes versus actions: The relationship of verbal and overt behavioral responses to attitude objects. Journal of Social Issues, 25, 41–78.

Wideman, M. V., & Singer, J. E. 1984. The role of psychological mechanisms in preparation for childbirth. American Psychologist, 39, 1357–1371.

Widom, C. S. 1989a. The cycle of violence. Science, 244, 160–166.

Widom, C. S. 1989b. Does violence beget violence? A critical examination of the literature. Psychological Bulletin, 106, 3–28.

Wiebe, D. J. 1991. Hardiness and stress moderation: A test of proposed mechanisms. Journal of Personality and Social Psychology, 60, 89–99.

Wiener, G. 1968. Scholastic achievement at age 12–13 of prematurely born infants. Journal of Special Education, 2, 237–250.

Wiener, G., Rider, R. V. Oppel, W. C., Fischer, L. K., & Harper, P. A. 1965. Correlates of low birth weight: Psychological status at six to seven years of age. Pediatrics, 35, 434–444.

Wilkie, J. R. 1991. The decline in men's labor force participation and income and the changing structure of family economic support. Journal of Marriage and the Family, 53, 111–122.

Wilks, J. 1986. The relative importance of parents and friends in adolescent decision-making. Journal of Youth and Adolescence, 15, 323–334.

Will, G. 1986. Our schools for scandal. Newsweek (September 15), p. 84.

Will, G. 1991. Old-fashioned families, not government, would be best cure for childhood poverty. Columbus Ohio Dispatch (September 26), p. 5A.

Willems, E. P., & Alexander, J. L. 1982. The naturalistic perspective in research. In B. B. Wolman (Ed.), Handbook of developmental psychology. Englewood Cliffs, N.J.: Prentice-Hall.

Williams, J. E., & Morland, J. K. 1976. Race, color, and the young child. Chapel Hill: University of North Carolina Press.

Williams, R. 1990. A Protestant legacy: Attitudes to death and illness among older Aberdonians. New York: Oxford University.

Williams, T. 1989. The cocaine kids: The inside story of a teenage drug ring. Reading, Mass.: Addison-Wesley.

Williamson, G. M. & Schulz, R. 1990. Relationship orientation, quality of prior relationship, and distress among caregivers of Alzheimer's patients. Psychology and Aging, 4, 502–509.

Willinger, M. 1989. SIDS: A challenge. Journal of NIH Research, 1, 73–80.

Willis, S, L., & Nesselroade, C. S. 1990. Long-term effects of fluid ability training in old-old age. Developmental Psychology, 26, 905–910.

Willits, F. K., & Crider, D. M. 1988. Health rating and life satisfaction in the later middle years. Journal of Gerontology, 43, S172–176.

Willner, P. 1985. Depression: A psychobiological synthesis. New York: Wiley.

Wilson, B. F. 1991. The marry-go-round.

American Demographics, 13 (October), 52–54.

Wilson, B. F., & Schoenborn, C. 1989. A healthy marriage. American Demographics, 11 (November), 40–43.

Wilson, C. 1987. Gay bashing: Brutal AIDS backlash. USA Today (March 12), p. D1.

Wilson, E. O. 1975. Sociobiology: A new synthesis. Cambridge, Mass.: Harvard University Press.

Wilson, E. O. 1984. Biophilia. Cambridge, Mass.: Harvard University Press.

Wilson, K. L., & Boldizar, J. P. 1990. Gender, segregation in higher education: Effects of aspirations, mathematics achievement, and income. Sociology of Education, 63, 62–74.

Wilson, R. S. 1985. Risk and resilience in early mental development. Developmental Psychology, 21, 795–805.

Wilson, W. J. 1987. The truly disadvantaged: The inner city, the underclass, and public policy. Chicago: University of Chicago.

Wingert, P., & Kantrowitz, B. 1990. The day care generation. Newsweek Special Issue (Winter/Spring), pp. 86–92.

Winick, M., Brasel, J., & Valasco, E. G. 1973. Effects of prenatal nutrition upon pregnancy risk. Clinical Obstetrics and Gynecology, 16, 184–198.

Winick, M., Rosso, P., & Waterlow, J. 1970. Cellular growth of cerebrum, cerebellum, and brain stem in normal and marasmic children. Experimental Neurology, 26, 393–400.

Winn, M. 1983. Children without childhood. New York: Pantheon Books.

Winn, M. 1991. Nintendo and the challenges of life. New York Times Book Review (December 22), p. 2.

Winslow, R. 1990. Study is good news for people waiting to have children. Wall Street Journal (March 8), p. B4.

Winslow, R. 1991a. Doctors and nurses are said to ignore some living wills. Wall Street Journal (March 28), p. B7.

Winslow, R. 1991b. Study cites failure to spot depression in nursing homes. Wall Street Journal (February 27), p. B3.

Winslow, R. 1991c. Third world birthing practice is safer, less costly than U.S. way, study finds. Wall Street Journal (May 1), p. B4.

Winslow, R. 1991d. Women face treatment gap in heart disease. Wall Street Journal (July 25), pp. B1, B4.

Winslow, R. K. 1990. Nursing homes get more sick patients due to U.S. policy. Wall Street Journal (January 4), p. B3.

Witkin, H. A., & Goodenough, D. R. 1981. Cognitive styles: Essence and origins. New York: International Universities Press.

Wohlwill, J. F. 1973. The concept of experience: S or R? Human Development, 16, 90–107.

Wolfe, R. N., & Kasmer, J. A. 1988. Type versus trait: Extraversion, impulsivity, sociability, and preferences for cooperative and competitive activities. Journal of Personality and Social Psychology, 54, 864–871.

Wolff, C. 1990. Guns offer New York teenagers a commonplace, deadly allure. New York Times (November 5), pp. A1, C12.

Wolff, P. H. 1966. The causes, controls, and

organization of behavior in the neonate. *Psychological Issues, 5* (Whole No. 17).

Wolff, P. H. 1987. *The development of behavioral states and the expression of emotions in early infancy.* Chicago: University of Chicago.

Wolfgang, M. E., Thornberry, T. P., & Figlio, R. M. 1987. *From boy to man, from delinquency to crime.* Chicago: University of Chicago.

Wong, M. M., & Csikszentmihalyi, M. 1991. Affiliation motivation and daily experience: Some issues on gender differences. *Journal of Personality and Social Psychology, 60,* 154–164.

Wong, P. T. P., & Watt, L. M. 1991. What types of reminiscence are associated with successful aging? *Psychology and Aging, 6,* 272–279.

Wood, W., Rhodes, N., & Whelan, M. 1989. Sex differences in positive well-being: A consideration of emotional style and marital status. *Psychological Bulletin, 106,* 249–264.

Woodruff, D. S., & Birren, J. E. 1972. Age changes and cohort differences in personality. *Developmental Psychology, 6,* 252–259.

Woodson, R., Drinkwin, J., & Hamilton, C. 1985. Effects of nonnutritive sucking on state and activity: Term-preterm comparisons. *Infant Behavior and Development, 8,* 435–441.

Woodward, K. L. 1987. Rules for making love and babies. *Newsweek* (March 23), pp. 42–43.

Woolley, J. D., & Wellman, H. M. 1990. Young children's understanding of realities, nonrealities, and appearances. *Child Development, 61,* 946–961.

Worthman, C. M. 1986. Developmental dysynchrony as normative experience: Kikuyu adolescents. In J. B. Lancaster & B. A. Hamberg (Eds.), *School-age pregnancy and parenthood: Biosocial dimensions.* Hawthorne, N.Y.: Aldine De Gruyter.

Wright, H. 1967. *Recording and analyzing child behavior.* New York: Harper & Row.

Wright, H., & Barker, R. 1950. *Methods in psychological ecology.* Lawrence: University of Kansas, Department of Psychology.

Wright, J. D., & Hamilton, R. F. 1978. Work satisfaction and age: Some evidence of the "job change" hypothesis. *Social Forces, 56,* 1140–1158.

Wright, P. H., & Keple, T. W. 1981. Friends and parents of a sample of high school juniors: An exploratory study of relationship intensity and interpersonal rewards. *Journal of Marriage and the Family, 43,* 550–570.

Wuthnow, R., Christiano, K., & Kuzlowski, J. 1980. Religion and bereavement: A conceptual framework. *Journal of the Scientific Study of Religion, 18,* 408–422.

Wyshak, G., & Frisch, R. E. 1982. Evidence for a secular trend in age of menarche. *New England Journal of Medicine, 306,* 1033–1035.

Yalom, N., Green, R., & Fisk, N. 1973. Prenatal exposure to female hormones: Effect on psychosexual development in boys. *Archives of General Psychiatry, 28,* 554–561.

Yamada, J. E. 1991. *Laura: A case for the modularity of language.* Cambridge, Mass.: MIT Press.

Yang, R. K., Zweig, A. R., Douthitt, T. C., & Federman, E. J. 1976. Successive relationships between maternal attitudes during pregnancy, analgesic medication during labor and delivery, and newborn behavior. *Developmental Psychology, 12,* 8–14.

Yaniv, I., & Shatz, M. 1990. Heuristics of reasoning and analogy in children's visual perspective taking. *Child Develpment, 61,* 1491–1501.

Yankelovich, D. 1978. The new psychological contracts at work. *Psychology Today, 11* (May), pp. 46–50.

Yankelovich, D. 1981. New rules in American life. *Psychology Today, 15* (April), pp. 35–91.

Yankelovich, D. 1982. The work ethic is underemployed. *Psychology Today, 16* (May), pp. 5–8.

Yarrow, A. L. 1987. Divorce at a young age: The troubled 20's. *New York Times* (January 12), p. 19.

Yarrow, L. J., MacTurk, R. H., Vietze, P. M., McCarthy, M. E., Klein, R. P., & McQuiston, S. 1984. Developmental course of parental stimulation and its relationship to mastery motivation during infancy. *Developmental Psychology, 20,* 492–503.

Yarrow, M. R., Scott, P. M., & Waxler, C. Z. 1973. Learning concern for others. *Developmental Psychology, 8,* 240–260.

Yates, A., Leehey, K., & Shisslak, C. M. 1983. Running—an analogue of anorexia? *New England Journal of Medicine, 308,* 251–255.

Yates, D. J., & Bremner, J. G. 1988. Conditions for Piagetian Stage IV search errors in a task using transparent occluders. *Infant Behavior and Development, 11,* 411–417.

Yinger, J. M. 1965. *Toward a field theory of behavior.* New York: McGraw-Hill.

Yllo, K., & Straus, M. A. 1981. Interpersonal violence among married and cohabiting couples. *Family Relations, 30,* 339–347.

Yogman, M. W., & Zeisel, S. H. 1983. Diet and sleep patterns in newborn infants. *New England Journal of Medicine, 309,* 1147–1149.

Yonas, A., Granrud, C. E., & Pettersen, L. 1985. Infants' sensitivity to relative size information at distance. *Developmental Psychology, 21,* 161–167.

Young, K. T. 1990. American conceptions of infant development from 1955 to 1984: What the experts are telling parents. *Child Development, 61,* 17–28.

Younger, B., & Gotlieb, S. 1988. Development of categorization skills: Changes in the nature or structure of infant form categories? *Developmental Psychology, 24,* 611–619.

Younger, B. A. 1985. The segregation of items into categories by ten-month-old infants. *Child Development, 56,* 1574–1583.

Youniss, J. 1980. *Parents and peers in social development.* Chicago: University of Chicago Press.

Youniss, J., & Smollar, J. 1985. *Adolescent relations with mothers, fathers, and friends.* Chicago: University of Chicago Press.

Yudin, L. W. 1966. Formal thought in adolescence as a function of intelligence. *Child Development, 37,* 697–708.

Yudkin, M. 1984. When kids think the unthinkable. *Psychology Today, 18* (April), pp. 18–25.

Zacharias, L., Rand, W. M., & Wurtman, R. J. 1976. A prospective study of sexual development and growth in American girls: The statistics of menarche. *Obsterical and Gynecological Survey, 31,* 325–337.

Zachry, W. 1978. Ordinality and interdependence of representation and language development in infancy. *Child Development, 49,* 681–687.

Zahn-Waxler, C. 1990. The ABCs of morality: Affect, behavior, and cognition. *Contemporary Psychology, 35,* 25–26.

Zahn-Waxler, C., Radke-Yarrow, M., & Brady-Smith, J. 1977. Perspective-taking and prosocial behavior. *Developmental Psychology, 13,* 87–88.

Zahn-Waxler, C., Radke-Yarrow, M., & King, R. A. 1979. Child rearing and children's prosocial initiations toward victims of distress. *Child Development, 50,* 319–330.

Zajonc, R. B. 1975. Dumber by the dozen. *Psychology Today, 8* (January), pp. 37–43.

Zajonc, R. B. 1976. Family configuration and intelligence. *Science, 192,* 227–236.

Zajonc, R. B. 1983. Validating the confluence model. *Psychological Bulletin, 93,* 457–480.

Zajonc, R. B. 1986. Mining new gold from old research. *Psychology Today, 20* (February), pp. 47–51.

Zajonc, R. B., Markus, G. B., Berbaum, M. L. Bargh, J. A., & Moreland, R. L. 1991. One justified criticism plus three flawed analyses equals two unwarranted conclusions: A reply to Retherford and Sewell. *American Sociological Review, 56,* 159–165.

Zarbatany, L., Hartmann, D. P., & Rankin, D. B. 1990. The psychological functions of preadolescent peer activities. *Child Development, 61,* 1067–1080.

Zarling, C. L., Hirsch, B. J., & Landry, S. 1988. Maternal social networks and mother-infant interactions in full-term and very low birthweight, preterm infants. *Child Development, 59,* 178–185.

Zautra, A. J., Reich, J. W., & Guarnaccia, C. A. 1990. Some everyday life consequences of disability and bereavement for older adults. *Journal of Personality and Social Psychology, 59,* 550–561.

Zelnick, M., & Kantner, J. F. 1972. Sexuality, contraception and pregnancy among young unwed females in the United States. In *Demographic and social aspects of population growth* (Vol. 1). Washington, D.C.: Government Printing Office.

Zelniker, T., & Jeffrey, W. E. 1976. Reflective and impulsive children: Strategies of information processes underlying differences in problem solving. *Monographs of the Society for Research in Child Development, 41* (168).

Zeman, N. 1990. The new rules of courtship.

Newsweek Special Issue (Summer), pp. 24–27.

Zeplin, H., & McDonald, C. S. 1987. Age differences in autonomic variables during sleep. *Journal of Gerontology, 42,* 142–146.

Zeskind, P. S., & Iacino, R. 1984. Effects of maternal visitation to preterm infants in the neonatal intensive care unit. *Child Development, 55,* 1887–1893.

Zeskind, P. S., & Lester, B. M. 1978. Acoustic features and auditory perceptions of cries of newborns with prenatal and perinatal complications. *Child Development, 49,* 580–589.

Zeskind, P. S., & Lester, B. M. 1981. Analysis of cry features in newborns with differential fetal growth. *Child Development, 52,* 207–212.

Zeskind, P. S., & Marshall, T. R. 1988. The relation between variations in pitch and maternal perceptions of infant crying. *Child Development, 59,* 193–196.

Zeskind, P. S., & Ramey, C. T. 1981. Preventing intellectual and interactional sequelae of fetal malnutrition: A longitudinal, transactional, and synergistic approach to development. *Child Development, 52,* 213–218.

Zick, C. D., & Smith, K. R. 1991. Marital transitions, poverty, and gender differences in mortality. *Journal of Marriage and the Family, 53,* 327–336.

Zigler, E. F. 1987. Formal schooling for four-year-olds? No. *American Psychologist, 42,* 254–260.

Zimmerman, B. J. 1978. A social learning explanation for age-related changes in children's conceptual behavior. *Contemporary Educational Psychology, 3,* 11–19.

Zimmerman, B. J., & Rosenthal, T. L. 1974. Conserving and retaining equalities and inequalities through observation and correction. *Developmental Psychology, 10,* 260–268.

Zimmerman, D. 1983. Where are you Captain Kangaroo? *USA Today* (December 22), p. 1D.

Zisook, S., Devaul, R. A., & Click, M. A., Jr. 1982. Measuring symptoms of grief and bereavement. *American Journal of Psychiatry, 139,* 1590–1593.

Zisook, S., & Schuchter, S. 1986. The first four years of widowhood. *Psychiatric Annals, 16,* 288–294.

Zube, M. 1982. Changing behavior and outlook of aging men and women: Implications for marriage in the middle and later years. *Family Relations, 31,* 147–156.

Zubin, J., & Spring, B. 1977. Vulnerability—a new view of schizophrenia. *Journal of Abnormal Psychology, 86,* 103–126.

Zuckerman, M., Koestner, R., DeBoy, T., Garcia, T., Maresca, B. C., & Sartoris, J. M. 1988. To predict some of the people some of the time: A reexamination of the moderator variable approach to personality theory. *Journal of Personality and Social Psychology, 54,* 1006–1019.

Zur-Szpiro, S., & Longfellow, C. 1982. Fathers' support to mothers and children. In D. Belle (Ed.), *Lives in stress: Women and depression.* Beverly Hills: Sage.

Key Term Index

Name Index

Subject Index